METALWORKING HANDBOOK

PRINCIPLES AND PROCEDURES

JEANNETTE T. ADAMS

ARCO PUBLISHING COMPANY INC.

219 Park Avenue South, New York, N.Y. 10003

ACKNOWLEDGMENTS

The author desires to acknowledge with thanks the assistance of the following national organizations and branches of the government that have cooperated in the production of this book.

Aluminum Company of America, American Brass Co., American Steel & Wire Co., Armstrong Manufacturing Co., Black & Decker Mfg. Co., Brown & Sharpe Mfg. Co., Carborundum Co., Carpenter Steel Co., Cincinnati Bickford Tool Co., Cincinnati Milling Machine Co., Cincinnati Planer Co., Cincinnati Shaper Co., Clayton & Lambert Mfg. Co., Cleveland Twist Drill Co., Copper & Brass Research Association, Delta Manufacturing Division, Rockwell Manufacturing Co., Desmond–Stephan Mfg. Co., Eugene Dietzen Co., General Motors Corp., Geometric Tool Co., Division Greenfield Tap and Die Corp., Giddings & Lewis Machine Tool Co., Henry Disston & Sons, Imperial Brass Mfg. Co., Industrial Diamond Tool Co., Ingersoll-Rand Co., International Business Machines, Kester Solder Co., L. S. Starrett Co., Niagara Machine & Tool Works, Nicholson File Co., Norton Co., Parker-Kalon Corp., Pratt & Whitney Division, Niles-Bement-Pond Co., Precision Truing Co., Rockwell Mfg. Corp., Ross Mfg. Co., South Bend Lathe Works, Standard Tool Co., Stanley Electric Tools (Division of the Stanley Works), Stanley Tool Co., Taft-Pierce Co., University of the State of New York (Bureau of Vocational Curriculum Development), U.S. Navy Training Publications Center, Bureau of Navy Personnel, U.S. Steel Corp., Warner & Swasey, William Sellers & Co.

The author is indebted to the many teachers and supervisors who have expressed an interest in this book and who have offered valuable opinions, comments, and suggestions.

Published by Arco Publishing Company, Inc.
219 Park Avenue South, New York, N.Y. 10003

Library of Congress Catalog Card Number 75-23577
ISBN 0-668-03857-8

Printed in the United States of America

Table of Contents

Preface

The *purpose* of this book is to assist the worker in becoming familiar with the fundamentals of metalworking; to provide reference material that may be of the broadest use, both to *beginner* and *apprentice* alike; as an *expert* in the machine or school shop; or as a *home mechanic.*

Craftsmanship in metalworking is a combination of knowledge of how to use tools and skill with the hands. Unfortunately, there is no magic shortcut to craftsmanship. No book could possibly give you all the tricks of the trade or the skill of the old master craftsman. These must be learned from practice at the bench and at the machine, through the sense of touch, familiarity with the tools themselves, and through endless trials and errors that teach the better ways of doing every single thing. On the other hand, books can supply the all-important source of knowledge for the mastery of basic principles—and later for broadening skills, the techniques and procedures upon which master craftsmanship is built.

The *Metalworking Handbook . . . Principles and Procedures* . . . explains the specific purposes, correct use, and proper care of metalworking hand- and power-driven tools for cutting, shaping, and drilling metals.

Several chapters deal with metals and plastics; measuring tools; metalworking hand tools; sheet metalworking machines, working with metal, soldering; riveting; sheet metal fasteners; metal spinning; metalworking power tools; layout and benchwork, machine tool controls; tools and die making; and lubrication and coolants. Other chapters cover the fundamental principles and operations of various types of metalworking machines.

The numerous illustrations and diagrams throughout this book should prove unusually helpful in comprehending the text. The many tables throughout the book should be of value even after the text becomes familiar.

The workers in metals and materials worthy of the most exacting skill may well enjoy a constant and enduring pride and satisfaction in their life's work. Their work is an occupation that has steadily and rapidly increased in value to industry, to the community, and to the nation today, and is sure to play an even more important role in the future.

The *Metalworking Handbook . . . Principles and Procedures* . . . has been produced with the conviction that it will be a welcome and valued aid to the many thousands who have desired a book of this type on the subject.

J. T. A.

Chapter 1

Metals and Plastics

To choose the metals and plastics best suited for fabrication or repair, you must have a knowledge of the physical and mechanical properties of materials and know the methods of identifying materials that are not clearly marked. For instance, stainless steel and copper-nickel are quite similar in appearance, but completely different in their mechanical properties, and cannot be used interchangeably. A thermosetting plastic may look like a thermoplastic, but the former is heat resistant, whereas the latter is highly flammable.

Properties of Materials

The physical properties of a metal or a plastic determine its behavior under stress, heat, and exposure to chemically active substances. In practical application, behavior of a material under these conditions determines its mechanical properties, indentation, and rusting. The mechanical properties of a material, therefore, are important considerations in selecting material for a specific job. The following information concerns metals. Plastics are discussed later in this chapter.

Stress is the amount of internal force with which a material resists a change in shape. *Strain* is the deformation or change in shape that is caused by an applied load.

Strength is the property of a material which enables it to resist strain when stress is applied. The maximum stress applied to rupture the material is called *ultimate* strength. Under tension stress (pulling apart) it is called *tensile* strength; under compression stress, it is called *compressive* strength. *Tensile strength* (Fig. 1), which is the commonly used strength term for metal, is measured in pounds of tension force necessary to cause failure of a one-square-inch cross section of the material. In engineering construction, each part is designed so that the working stress of the material is much less than the breaking stress. The ratio of ultimate strength of a part to its working stress is called the factor of safety. A factor of safety less than 4 to 1 is uncommon; in many cases it may be as great as 15 or 20 to 1.

Figure 1. Tensile strength.

Plasticity is the ability of a material to withstand extensive permanent deformation without breaking or rupturing. Note the use of the word *permanent* here. The term *plastic deformation* is used to indicate a *permanent* change of shape. Modeling clay is an example of a highly plastic material, since it can be deformed extensively and permanently without rupturing.

Ductility (Fig. 2) is the ability of a material to permanently deform without rupture under tensile loads. *Malleability* (Fig. 3) is the ability of a material to permanently deform without rupture under compression loads.

Figure 2. Ductility.

Figure 3. Malleability.

The properties known as ductility and malleability are special cases of plasticity. *Ductility* is the property that makes it possible for a material to be drawn out into a thin wire; in other words, it is the property that enables the material to withstand extensive permanent deformation from *tension. Malleability* is the property that makes it possible for a material to be stamped, hammered, or rolled into thin sheets. In other words, a malleable material is one that can withstand extensive permanent deformation from *compression.*

Most metals that exhibit one of these properties also exhibit the other. However, this is not always true. *For example,* lead is very malleable (it can be permanently deformed in compression without breaking), but it is not ductile (it cannot be permanently deformed in tension to any great extent).

Brittleness (Fig. 4) is the tendency of a material to break suddenly with little or no prior deformation. Hard materials often are brittle, although a metal may be hard and still not be brittle. An example of a brittle material is hard cast iron. On the other hand, tungsten tool steel is hard but not brittle.

Figure 4. Brittleness.

Toughness is the quality that enables a material to withstand shock, to endure stresses, and to be deformed without breaking. A tough material is not easily separated or cut and can be bent first in one direction and then in the opposite direction without fracturing.

Hardness (Fig. 5) of metal is generally defined as its ability to resist indentation, abrasion or wear, and cutting. Hardness of metals is usually associated with strength.

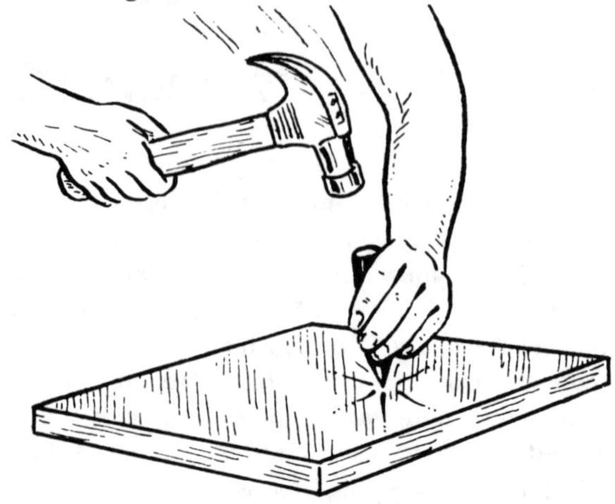

Figure 5. Hardness.

Fatigue is the action which takes place in a metal after a repetition of stress. When a sample is broken in a tensile machine, a definite load is required to cause that fracture. However, the same material will fail under a much smaller load if that load is applied and removed many times. In this way, a shaft may break after months of use even though the weight of the load has not been changed. The pieces of such a part will not show any sign of deformation. The mating areas of the section that fractured last will usually be quite coarse-grained, while the mating areas of other sections of the break will show signs of having rubbed together for quite some time.

Corrosion resistance is the ability of a material to withstand surface attack by the atmosphere, fluids, moisture, and acids. Some metals are highly resistant to practically all types of corrosive agents, others to some types of corrosive agents, and still others to only very few types of corrosive substances. Some metals, however, can be made less susceptible to corrosive agents by coating or by alloying with other metals that are corrosion resistant.

Heat resistance is the property of metal which retains strength or hardness at high temperatures. This is particularly true of some types of alloy steels. A metal that retains its strength or hardness at elevated temperatures is called heat resistant. Tungsten steel (which, even when red-hot, can be used to cut other metals) and chromium molybdenum steel (which is used for piping and valves in high temperature, high pressure steam systems) are examples of heat-resistant metals.

Although *weldability* and *machinability* are not strictly properties, in the sense of the other properties discussed, they are important practical considerations in the fabrication or repair of any metal part. *Weldability* refers to the relative ease with which a metal may be welded. *Machinability* is the term used to describe the ease with which a metal may be turned, planed, milled, or otherwise shaped in the shop. Some metals are not easily machined because they are too hard. Some soft metals are not easily machined because they are too tough. Both weldability and machinability are really based upon the *combination* of other properties of the material, rather than being properties in themselves.

There are no hard and fast rules that can be used in determining the machining characteristics of a metal. Many factors, such as the composition of the metal, the manufacturing process, and heat treatment, can have considerable effect on the machinability of a metal. *For example,* an increase of one of the elements in the composition can increase or decrease machining characteristics; differences in temperatures and rates of cooling used in heat treatment can change the metal from hard to soft, or vice versa. Hot or cold working or casting in the manufacturing process can change the machinability characteristics by changing the internal structure of the metal.

Metals

Metals are divided into two general types—ferrous and nonferrous. *Ferrous metals* are those whose major element is iron. *Iron* is the basis for all steels. *Nonferrous* metals are those whose major element is *not* iron, but they may contain a small amount of iron as an impurity.

Ferrous Metals

Iron ore, the basis of all ferrous metals, is converted to metal (pig iron) in a blast furnace. Alloying elements can later be added to the pig iron to obtain a wide variety of metals with different characteristics. The characteristics of metal can be further changed and improved by heat treatment and by hot or cold working.

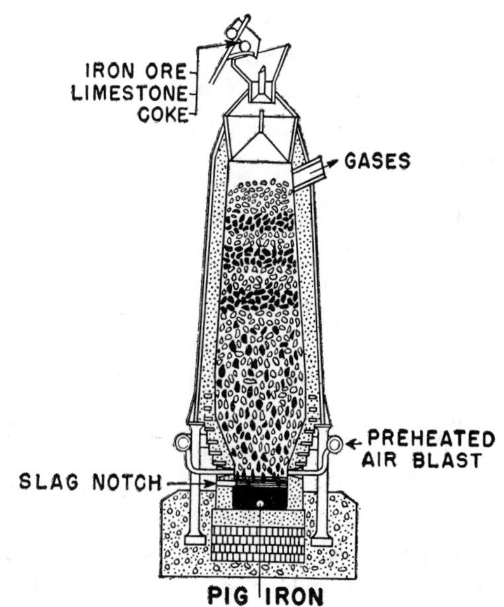

Figure 6. Blast furnace.

Irons

The product of the blast furnace (Fig. 6) is called *pig iron.* In early smelting practice, the arrangement of the sand molds into which the molten crude iron was drawn resembled groups of nursing pigs, hence the name.

Pig iron, which is composed of approximately 93 per cent iron, 3 to 5 per cent carbon, and varying amounts of impurities, is seldom used directly as an industrial manufacturing material. It is used as the basic ingredient in making cast iron, wrought iron, and steel.

Cast Iron. Cast iron is produced by resmelting a charge of pig iron and scrap iron in a furnace and removing some of the impurities from the molten metal by using various fluxing agents. There are many grades of cast iron as to strength and hardness. The quality depends upon the extent of refining, the amount of scrap iron used, and the method of casting and cooling the molten metal when it is drawn from the furnace. The higher the proportion of scrap iron, the lower the grade of cast iron. Cast iron has some degree of corrosion resistance and great compressive strength, but at best the metal is brittle and has a comparatively low tensile strength, and accordingly has very limited use in marine service.

Wrought Iron. Wrought iron is a highly refined pure iron which has uniformly distributed particles of slag in its composition. Wrought iron is considerably softer than cast iron and has a fibrous internal structure, created by the rolling and squeezing given to it when it is being made. Like cast iron, wrought iron is fairly resistant to corrosion and fatigue. Because of these characteristics, wrought iron is used extensively for low pressure pipe, rivets, and nails.

Plain Steels

Pig iron is converted into *steel* by a process which separates and removes impurities from the molten iron by use of various catalytic agents and extremely high temperatures. During the refining process, practically all of the carbon originally present in the pig iron is burned out. In the final stages, where high carbon alloys are desired, measured amounts of carbon are added to the relatively pure liquid iron to produce carbon steel of a desired grade. The amount of carbon added controls the mechanical properties of the finished steel to a large extent, as will be pointed out in the following paragraphs. After the steel has been drawn from the furnace and allowed to solidify, it may be sent either to the stockpile, or to shaping mills for rolling and forming into plates, billets, bars, or structural shapes.

Plain steels that have small additions of sulfur (and sometimes phosphorus) are called *free cutting steels*. These steels have good machining characteristics and are used in applications similar to carbon steels. Addition of sulfur are phosphorus results in limiting its ability to be formed hot.

LOW CARBON STEEL. Low carbon steel (0.05 to 0.030 per cent), usually referred to as *mild steel*, can be easily cut and bent and does not have great tensile strength, as compared with other steels.

MEDIUM CARBON STEEL. Medium carbon steel (0.30 to 0.60 per cent carbon) is considerably stronger than mild carbon steel. Heat treated machinery parts are made of this steel.

HIGH CARBON STEEL. High carbon steel (0.60 to 1.25 per cent) is used for many machine parts, hand tools, and cutting tools, and is usually referred to as *carbon tool steel*. Cutting tools of high carbon steel should not be used where the cutting temperature would exceed 400 degrees.

Alloy Steels

The steels previously discussed are true alloys of iron and carbon. When other elements are added to iron during the refining process, the resulting metal is called *alloy steel*. There are many types, classes, and grades of alloy steel. A few of the more common alloy steels and the effects of certain alloying elements upon the mechanical properties of steel are discussed briefly below.

Corrosion resistant steel (commonly called *stainless steel*) is an alloy which contains relatively large amounts of chromium and nickel. Corrosion resistant steel resists corrosion, attack by acid, and scaling. It is classified by the Society of Automotive Engineers as either a chromium alloy or a chromium nickel alloy.

NICKEL STEEL. Nickel steel, which usually contains 3 to 5 per cent nickel, has superior strength and toughness and is often used for armor plate.

VANADIUM STEEL. Vanadium steel (usually containing from 0.15 to 0.25 per cent vanadium) is used for crankshafts, axles, gears, and other machine parts where high strength and fatigue resistance is desired.

CARBON-MOLYBDENUM STEEL. Molybdenum, in combination with chromium and nickel, is added to steel to produce a tough carbon-molybdenum steel (CMo) suitable for steam fittings, valve bodies, and boiler plates. It is also used in place of the more expensive tungsten for the cheaper grades of high speed steel cutting tools.

HIGH SPEED STEEL (HS). High speed steel has the quality of red-hardness. Cutting tools made from the various types of HS steel can be used up to, and after, the time the point has become a dull red, or to a temperature of approximately 1100 degrees. There are several different types of HS steels, some of which are listed in this chapter.

TUNGSTEN BASE STEELS. Tungsten base steels are one of the most common types used. Though the percentages may vary with different grades, one common type is the T1. It is composed of 18 per cent tungsten, 4 per cent chromium, and 1 per cent vanadium.

MOLYBDENUM BASE STEELS. Molybdenum base steels are similar to tungsten base steels, except that some of the tungsten is replaced with molybdenum. One of the common types is the M2; it is composed of 5 per cent molybdenum, 6 per cent tungsten, 4 per cent chromium, and 2 per cent vanadium.

Nonferrous Metals

Copper, nickel, lead, zinc, tin, and aluminum are included among the nonferrous metals. These metals, and the many combinations in the form of alloys such as brass, bronze, copper-nickel, and so on, are used in large amounts in construction and maintenance.

COPPER. Copper is a metal which lends itself to a variety of uses. It comes in the form of wire, rod, bar, sheet plate, and pipe. Copper is used also in copper alloys such as brass and bronze. As a conductor of both heat and electricity, it ranks next to silver. It also offers a high resistance to salt water corrosion. The green tarnish which sometimes forms on its surface has a detrimental effect upon the metal and is easily cleaned off.

Copper becomes hard when worked, but can be softened easily by heating to a cherry red and then cooling. Its strength increases rapidly with temperatures above 400°F.

Pure copper is normally used in molded or shaped forms where machining is not required. Copper for normal use generally is alloyed with an element which provides good machinability characteristics.

NICKEL. Nickel is a hard, malleable, and ductile metal. It is resistant to corrosion and therefore is often used as a coating on other metals. Combined with other metals in an alloy, it makes a tough strong alloy.

LEAD. Lead weighs about 700 pounds per cubic foot. It is available in pig and sheet form. Sheet lead is used to line sinks or protect bench tops where a great deal of acid is used. The surface of lead is grayish in color, but when it is scratched or scraped, it becomes very white. Because of its softness, a lead block is often used as a backing material when punching holes with a hollow punch, or for bumping or hammering sheet metal forms. When lead is alloyed with tin in various proportions to form soft solders, you have one of the most commonly used alloys of nonferrous metals.

ZINC. Zinc is a comparatively soft, yet somewhat brittle metal. Its tensile strength is slightly greater than that of aluminum. In the manufacture of brass, zinc is used as an alloying metal, copper being the base metal. Because of its resistance to corrosion, zinc is used as a protective coating for less corrosion resistant metals, principally iron and steel. There are three methods of applying a zinc coating: (1) Electroplating in a zinc-acid solution; (2) hot dipping, where the metal is dipped into a bath of molten zinc; (3) sherardizing, where zinc is reduced to a gaseous state and deposited on the base metal.

TIN. Tin is seldom used except as an alloying ingredient. Alloyed with lead, it makes a soft solder, and alloyed with copper, it produces bronze. Lead and tin both resist corrosion very well, but tin has the added advantage of being nonpoisonous. Many food containers are fabricated from sheet material which has been coated with tin.

ALUMINUM. Aluminum is being used more and more in construction because of its light weight, easy workability, good appearance, and other desirable properties. Pure aluminum is soft and not very strong. When alloying elements such as magnesium, copper, nickel, and silicon are added, a much stronger metal is produced. Aluminum alloys can be strain hardened, solution heat treated, and age hardened, either artificially or naturally.

TRUE BRASS. True brass is an alloy of copper and zinc. Complex brasses are those containing additional agents, such as aluminum, lead, iron, manganese, or phosphorus.

Brass is classified as leaded and unleaded, meaning that small amounts of lead may or may not be used in the copper-zinc mixture. The addition of lead improves the machinability of brass.

BRONZE. Bronze made of 84 per cent copper and 16 per cent tin was the best metal available before steel making techniques were developed. Although bronze was originally an alloy of copper and tin, many complex bronze alloys containing three or more elements have been developed. There is no distinct line between brass and bronze. In fact, commercial bronze (used for hinges and other hardware) is really a low brass containing 90 to 95 per cent copper and 5 to 10 per cent zinc.

COPPER-NICKEL ALLOY. Copper-nickel alloy has come into its own in recent years, because of its high resistance to the corrosive effect of salt water. It is used in piping and tubing. In sheet form, you may use it to construct small storage tanks and hot-water reservoirs. Copper-nickel alloy may contain either 70 per cent copper and 30 per cent nickel or 90 per cent copper and 10 per cent nickel. This alloy must be worked cold, although it has the general working characteristics of copper. Copper-nickel is best joined by the silver soldering process.

NICKEL-COPPER ALLOYS. Nickel-copper alloys are stronger and harder than either nickel or copper. They have a high resistance to corrosion and are strong enough to be substituted for steel where corrosion resistance is of primary importance. Probably the best known nickel-copper alloy is "Monel" metal. Monel contains 64 to 68 per cent nickel, about 30 per cent copper, and small percentages of iron, manganese, silicon, and cobalt. It is actually a natural alloy, because the combination of nickel and copper exists in the ore when mined and is retained in the refining process.

K-MONEL. "K-Monel" is essentially the same as "Monel," except that it contains about 3 per cent aluminum, and is harder and stronger than other grades of Monel. K-Monel stock is very difficult to machine, but its machinability can be improved considerably by annealing the metal immediately before machining.

Designations and Markings

Knowledge of the standard designations of metals and the systems of marking metals is necessary so that you can select the proper material for a specific job. The standard designations discussed in this chapter are index numbers that are used to indicate the composition of the various metals. The two major systems used for iron and steel are those of the Society of Automotive Engineers (SAE) and the American Iron and Steel Institute (AISI). The Aluminum Association method is used for aluminum. Other nonferrous metals are designated by the percentage and types of elements in their composition.

FERROUS METAL DESIGNATIONS. You should be familiar with the system of steel classification used by SAE and AISI. These systems are in common use and utilize a four- or five-digit number to indicate the composition of the steel. The one major difference between the two systems is that the AISI system uses a letter before the number to show the process used in the making of the steel. The letters used are as follows: B—Acid Bessemer carbon steel; C—Basic open-hearth or basic electric furnace carbon steel; and E—Electric furnace alloy steel.

Example

SAE		10	20
AISI	C	10	20
	↑	↑	↑
	Basic Open-Hearth Carbon Steel	Plain Carbon Steel	Carbon Content

The first digit indicates the type of steel: 1 stands for carbon steel; 2 is nickel steel; 3 is nickel-chromium steel; 4 is molybdenum steel; 5 is chromium steel; 6 is chromium-vanadium steel; 8 is "National Emergency" steel; and 9 is silicon-manganese steel. (The group identified as "National Emergency" steel, number 8 in the SAE/AISI systems, includes various low alloy nickel-chromium-molybdenum steels developed during World War II. Much of the alloy content of these steels can be derived from scrap alloy, thus conserving the supply of alloy materials. These steels are retained in most steel classifications today.)

The second digit in the SAE/AISI number indicates the series within the group indicated by the first digit. The term *series* in this connection usually refers to the percentage of the chief alloying element. Sometimes the second digit gives the actual percentage of the chief alloying element. In other cases, however, the second digit may be used to indicate the relative *position* of the series in the group, without reference to the actual percentage. The last two or three digits indicate the average carbon content of the steel. In order to make the various steels fit into this classification it is sometimes necessary to vary the system slightly. These variations are easily understood if you understand the system. (See the following examples.)

(1) SAE 1035. The first digit is 1, so this is a carbon steel. The second digit, 0, indicates that there is no other important alloying element, therefore, this is a *plain* carbon steel. The next two digits, 35, indicate that the *average* percentage of carbon in steels of this series is 0.35 per cent. The actual carbon percentage in this series ranges from 0.32 to 0.38.

(2) SAE 1146. This is a carbon steel (first digit) with an average manganese content of 1.00 per cent (second digit) and an average carbon content of 0.46 per cent. The 1100 series of steels are known as free cutting steels.

(3) SAE 4017. The first digit, 4, indicates that this is a molybdenum steel. The second digit, 0, indicates that there is no other equally important alloying element; therefore, this is a plain molybdenum steel. The last two digits, 17, indicate that the average carbon content is 0.17 per cent.

Other series within the molybdenum steel group are indicated by the second digit. If the second digit is 1, the steel is chromium-molybdenum steel. If the second digit is 3, the steel is a nickel-chromium-molybdenum steel. If the second digit is 6, the steel is a nickel-molybdenum steel. In such cases, the second digit does not indicate the actual percentage of the alloying elements other than molybdenum.

(4) SAE 51100. This number indicates a chromium steel (first digit) with approximately 1.0 per cent chromium (second digit) and an average carbon content of 1.00 per cent (last three digits). The actual chromium content of SAE 51100 steels may vary from 0.5 to 1.10.

(5) SAE 52100. This number indicates a chromium steel (first digit) of a higher alloy series (second

digit) than the SAE 51100 steel previously described. *Note* that in this case the second digit, 2, merely identifies the series but does *not* indicate the percentage of chromium. A 52100 steel would actually have from 1.30 to 1.60 per cent chromium with an average carbon content of 1.00 per cent (last three digits).

There used to be a 7000 series SAE steel, but under a new system it is no longer used. The current commonly used tool steels have been classified by the American Iron and Steel Institute into seven major groups and each commonly accepted group or subgroup has been assigned an alphabetical letter. Methods of quenching, applications, special characteristics, and steels for particular industries were considered in the following type classification of tool steels.

Group	Symbol and type
Water hardening	W
Shock resisting	S
Cold work	O—Oil hardening A—Medium alloy D—High carbon—high chromium
Hot work	H—(H 1 to H 19 incl. chromium base, H 20 to H 39 incl. tungsten base, H40 to H59 incl. molybdenum base)
High speed	T—Tungsten base M—Molybdenum base
Special purpose	L—Low alloy F—Carbon tungsten
Mold steels	P

Nonferrous Metal Designations. Nonferrous metals are generally grouped according to the alloying elements. Examples of these groups are brass, bronze, copper-nickel, and nickel-copper. Specific designations of an alloy are described by the amounts and chemical symbols of the alloying elements. *For example,* a copper-nickel alloy might be described as copper-nickel, 70 Cu-30 Ni. The 70 Cu represents the percentage of copper, and the 30 Ni represents the percentage of nickel.

Common alloying elements and their chemical symbols are as follows.

Aluminum — — — Al
Carbon — — — C
Chromium — — — Cr
Cobalt — — — Co
Copper — — — Cu
Iron — — — Fe
Lead — — — Pb
Manganese — — — Mn
Molybdenum — — — Mo
Nickel — — — Ni
Phosphorus — — — P
Silicon — — — Si
Sulphur — — — S
Tin — — — Sn
Titanium — — — Ti
Tungsten — — — W
Vanadium — — — V
Zinc — — — Zn

In addition to the type of designations previously described, a trade name (such as Monel or Inconel) is sometimes used to designate certain alloys.

The Aluminum Association uses a four-digit designation system similar to the SAE/AISI system described for steels. The numerals assigned with their meaning for the first digits of this system are as follows.

Aluminum (99.00 per cent minimum and greater)	1xxx
Major Alloying Element	
Copper	2xxx
Manganese	3xxx
Silicon	4xxx
Magnesium	5xxx
Magnesium and Silicon	6xxx
Zinc	7xxx
Other element	8xxx

The first digit indicates the major alloying element, and the second digit indicates alloy modifications or impurity limits. The last two digits identify the particular alloy or indicate the aluminum purity.

In the 1xxx group for 99.00 per cent minimum aluminum, the last two digits indicate the minimum aluminum percentage to the right of the decimal point. The second digit indicates modifications in impurity limits. If the second digit in the designation is zero, it indicates that there is no special control on individual impurities. If it is 1 through 9, it indicates some special control of one or more individual impurities. As an example, 1030 indicates a 99.30 per cent minimum aluminum without special control on individual impurities, and 1130, 1230, 1330, and so on indicate the same purity with special control of one or more individual impurities.

Designations having the numbers 2 through 8 are aluminum alloys. In the 2xxx through 8xxx alloy groups, the second digit in the designation indicates alloy modification. The last two of the four digits in the designation have no special significance but serve only to identify the different alloys in the group.

In addition to the four digit alloy designation, a letter or letter/number is included as a temper designation. The temper designation follows the four digit alloy number and is separated from it by a dash. *For example,* 2024-T6 is an aluminum-copper alloy, solution heat treated, then artificially aged. T6 is the temper designation. The aluminum alloy temper designations and their meanings are as follows.

- F — As fabricated
- O — Annealed and recrystallized (wrought only)
- H — Strain hardened (wrought only)
  - H1, plus one or more digits, strain hardened only
  - H2, plus one or more digits, strain hardened then partially annealed
  - H3, plus one or more digits, strain hardened then stabilized
- W — Solution heat treated—unstable temper
- T — Treated to produce stable tempers other than F, O, or H
  - T2 Annealed (cast only)
  - T3 Solution heat treated, then cold worked
  - T4 Solution heat treated and naturally aged to a substantially stable condition
  - T5 Artificially aged only
  - T6 Solution heat treated, then artificially aged
  - T7 Solution heat treated, then stabilized
  - T8 Solution heat treated, cold worked, then artificially aged
  - T9 Solution heat treated, artificially aged, then cold worked
  - T10 Artificially aged, then cold worked

Note that while some temper designations apply only to wrought products and others only to cast products, most apply to both. A second digit may appear to the right of the mechanical treatment, indicating the degree of hardening: 2 is 1/4 hard, 4 is 1/2 hard, 6 is 3/4 hard, and 8 is full hard. *For example,* the alloy 5456-H32 is an aluminum/magnesium alloy, strain hardened, then stabilized, and is 1/4 hard.

Standard Marking of Metals. The metal markings described in this section include the color symbols used for nonferrous metals.

Continuous Identification Marking

The purpose of the continuous identification marking system is to provide a means for positive identification of metal products even after some portions have been used. In the continuous identification marking system, the markings appear at intervals of not more than three feet. Therefore, if you cut off a piece of bar stock, the remaining portion will still carry the proper identification. Some metals such as small tubing, coils of wire, and small bar stock cannot be marked readily by this method. On these items, tags with the required marking information are fastened to the metal.

The continuous identification marking is actually *printed* on the metals with a heavy ink that is almost like a paint.

The manufacturer is required to make these markings on materials before delivery. Figure 7 shows the normal spacing and layout.

For metal products, the continuous identification marking must include (1) the producer's name or registered trademark, and (2) the commercial designation of the material. The producer's name or trademark shown is that of the producer who performs the final processing or finishing operation before the material is marketed. The commercial designation includes (1) a material designation such as an SAE number, an AISI number, or an ASTM (American Society of Testing Materials) specification and (2) a *physical condition* and quality designation, that is, the designation of temper or other physical condition approved by a nationally recognized technical society or industrial association such as the American Iron and Steel Institute. Some

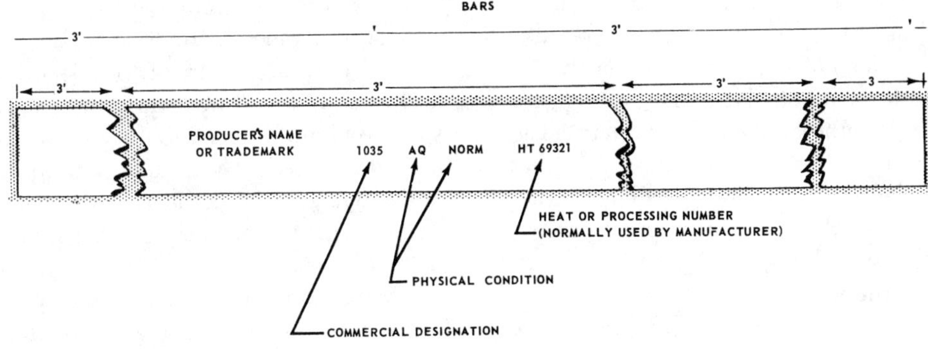

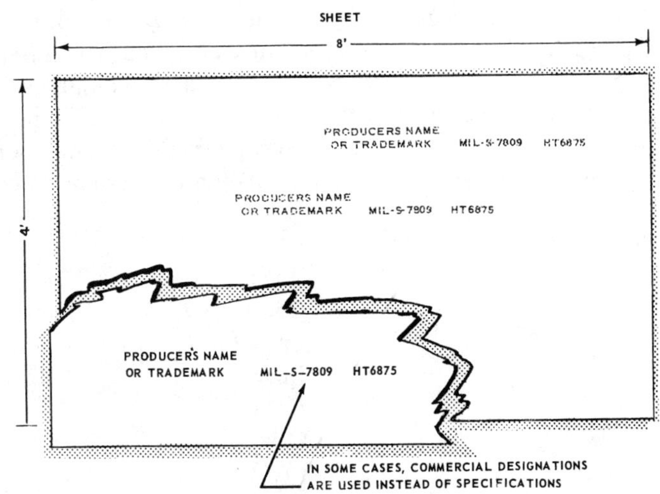

Figure 7. Continuous identification marking.

of the physical condition and quality designations for various metal products are as follows.

CR – cold rolled
CD – cold drawn
HR – hot rolled
AQ – aircraft quality
CQ – commercial quality
1/4H – quarter hard
1/2H – half hard
H – hard
HTQ – high tensile quality
AR – as rolled
HT – heat treated
G – ground

Color Marking

For some years, a system of color symbols with a related color code has been used for the identification of nonferrous metals. Although the color marking system is being replaced by continuous identification marking, you should still be familiar with the nonferrous color system. Some of the nonferrous stock that you obtain is likely to be marked with color symbols, since the material marked and coded under the color system may not be entirely used up for several years.

COLOR SYMBOLS. The term *color symbol* refers to the color marking actually painted on the nonferrous metal. A symbol is a design composed of one, two, or three colors and painted on a conspicuous area of the piece. When the symbol consists of more than one color, the colored areas are adjacent to each other.

There are two types of color symbols. *Spot* symbols that are applied to each end of solid stock that is at least 3/4 inch in diameter (for round stock) or at least 3/4 inch in the smallest dimension (for other shapes) are also used to mark ingots or other bulky pieces. *Peripheral* symbols are used primarily for tubular stock and for solid stock that is too small for the spot symbols. Peripheral symbols are painted in bands around each piece, approximately 6 inches from each end. Pieces that are too small for either spot or peripheral marking may be bundled and tagged. In such cases, the spot symbol should be clearly marked on the tag.

The color symbols, both spot and peripheral, are shown in Fig. 8. *Note* that the colors are referred to as *primary, secondary,* and *stripe.* The primary and secondary colors (when used) form the major part or parts of the design. When both primary and secondary colors are used, they cover areas of the same size and shape. The area of the stripe color in any symbol is always noticeably less than the area of the primary or the secondary color. The terms *primary* and *secondary* do not refer to any physical values of the colors; they merely indicate the relative alphabetical position of the first letters of the names of the colors.

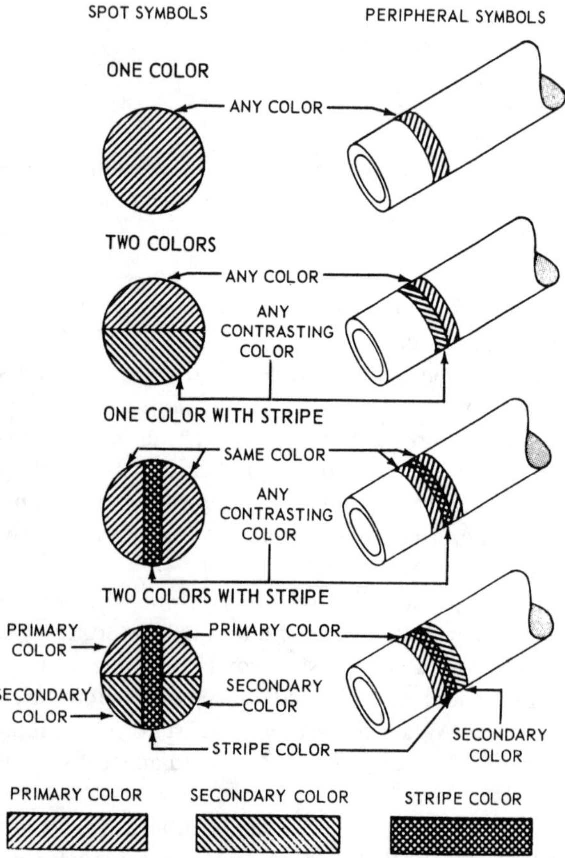

Figure 8. Metal color symbols.

The purpose of applying the color symbol at each end of the piece is to ensure the presence of one symbol even after part of the piece has been cut off and used. *Do not* forget this purpose. If for some reason the identifying symbol is cut off from both ends, *be sure* to renew the color symbol while you still know what the material is. Otherwise someone will be left with the problem of identifying an unmarked piece of metal.

COLOR CODE. The color code used for the identification of nonferrous metals is related to, but is *not* the same as, the color symbols just described. The color symbols are actual colors painted on the metal. The color code is a method describing these symbols in numbers. To have a numerical color code, each color must be given a number. There are 13 colors used in the color symbols, so the numbers used in the color code are 1 through 13. The colors are arranged alphabetically and then assigned a number. The color numbers are as follows.

Color	Number Code
Black	1
Blue	2
Bronze	3
Brown	4
Dark Blue	5
Green	6
Lead	7
Orange	8
Purple	9
Red	10
Tan	11
White	12
Yellow	13

The color with the lowest number in any color symbol (that is, the color name that occurs first in this alphabetical arrangement) is always referred to as the *primary* color. In a color code number, the first digit identifies the primary color. The other major color, therefore, becomes the *secondary* color and is expressed after the primary color. When a stripe is used, its color number is always expressed last.

Here are a few examples. A two-color symbol composed of red and green would be called a *green-red* symbol, and its color code would be 6-10. If a blue stripe is added, the color code would be 6-10-2. Suppose the color symbol is yellow divided into two equal areas by a green stripe—the yellow must be considered as being both a primary color and a secondary color, and is therefore written twice. You would then call this a *yellow-yellow-green* symbol with a color code of 13-13-6.

Identification of Metals

The various base metals, such as iron, copper, lead, zinc, and aluminum have certain identifying characteristics—surface appearance and weight—by which persons who work with or handle these materials readily distinguish them from one another. There are a number of related alloys which resemble each other and their base metal so closely that they defy accurate identification by simple means.

There are other means of identification of metals. It should be noted that these methods by no means provide positive identification and should not be used in critical situations where a specific metal is desired. Some of the methods that will be discussed in this section are magnet tests, chip tests, file tests, acid reaction tests, and spark tests. In Table 1 you will find information related to surface appearance magnetic reaction, lathe chip test, and file test. The acid test and the spark test are discussed in more detail later in this chapter. When performing these tests it is advisable to have a known sample of the desired material and make a comparison. When using these tests you will need good lighting, a strong permanent magnet, and access to a lathe. A word of caution when performing these tests: *Do not* be satisfied with the results of only one test. Use as many tests as possible so that you can increase the chances of making an accurate identification.

TABLE 1

IDENTIFICATION OF METALS

Metal	Surface Appearance or markings	Reaction to a Magnet	Lathe Chip test	Color of freshly filed surface
White cast iron	Dull gray	Strong	Short, crumbly chips	Silvery white
Gray cast iron	Dull gray	Strong	Short, crumbly chips	Light silvery gray
Aluminum	Light gray to white dull or brilliant	None	Easily cut, smooth long chips	White
Brass	Yellow to green or brown	None	Smooth long chips slightly brittle	Reddish yellow to yellowish white
Bronze	Red to brown	None	Short crumbly chips	Reddish yellow to yellowish white
Copper	Smooth; red brown to green (oxides)	None	Smooth long pliable chips	Bright copper color
Copper-nickel	Smooth; gray to yellow or yellowish green	None	Smooth, continuous chips	Bright silvery white
Lead	White to gray; smooth, velvety	None	Cut by knife, any shape chip	White
Nickel	Dark gray; smooth; sometimes green (oxides)	Medium	Cuts easily, smooth continuous chip	Bright silvery white
Nickel-copper	Dark gray, smooth	Very slight	Continuous chip; tough to cut	Light gray
Plain carbon steel	Dark gray; may be rusty	Strong	Varies depending upon carbon content	Bright silvery gray
Stainless steel (18-8) (25-20) "Note 1 below"	Dark gray; dull to brilliant; usually clean	None (faint if severely cold worked)	Varies depending upon heat treatment	Bright silvery gray
Zinc	Whitish blue, may be mottled	None	Easily cut; long stringy chips	White

1. Stainless steels that have less than 26 percent alloying elements react to magnet.

Spark Test

Spark testing is the identification of a metal by observing the color, size, and the shape of the spark stream given off when the metal is held against a grinding wheel. This method of identification is adequate for most shop purposes. Where the exact composition of a metal must be known, a chemical analysis must be made. Identification of metals by the spark test method requires considerable experience. To gain this experience, you will need to practice by comparing the spark stream of unknown specimens with that of sample specimens of known composition. It is the practice in many shops to maintain specimens of known composition for comparison with unknown samples.

Proper lighting conditions are essential for good spark testing practice. The test should be performed in an area where there is enough light, but harsh or glaring light should be avoided. In many shops you may find that a spark test cabinet has been erected. Generally, these cabinets consist of a box mounted on the top of a workbench and have a dark painted interior. Inside the cabinet a bench grinder is mounted. Test specimens of known composition are contained in shelves at the end of the cabinet. Where possible, the testing area should be in such a location that heavy drafts of air are eliminated. Air drafts can change the tail of the spark stream and may result in improper identification of the sample.

Speed and pressure are factors that need to be considered when making the spark test. The faster the speed of the wheel, the larger and longer the spark stream will be. Generally speaking, a suitable grinding wheel for spark testing is an 8-inch wheel turning 3600 revolutions per minte (r.p.m.). This provides a surface speed at 7537 feet per minute. The pressure of the piece against the wheel has similar effects. The more pressure applied to the test piece, the larger and longer the spark stream. The test piece should be held lightly but firmly against the wheel with just enough pressure applied to prevent the piece from bouncing. Remember that the same amount of pressure must be applied to the test specimen as is applied to the sample being tested.

The grain size of the grinding wheel should be from 30 to 60 grain. It is very important to remember that the wheel must be clean at all times. A wheel loaded with particles of metal will give off a spark stream of the type of metal in the wheel, mixed with the spark stream of the metal being tested. This will result in serious confusion as to the true nature of the metal. The wheel must be dressed before spark testing and before each new test of a different metal.

The spark test is made by holding a sample of the material against a grinding wheel. The sparks given off, or the lack of sparks, assist in identifying the metal. The length of the spark stream, its color, and the type of sparks are the features for which you should look. The definitions of the various terms used in spark testing are shown in Fig. 9.

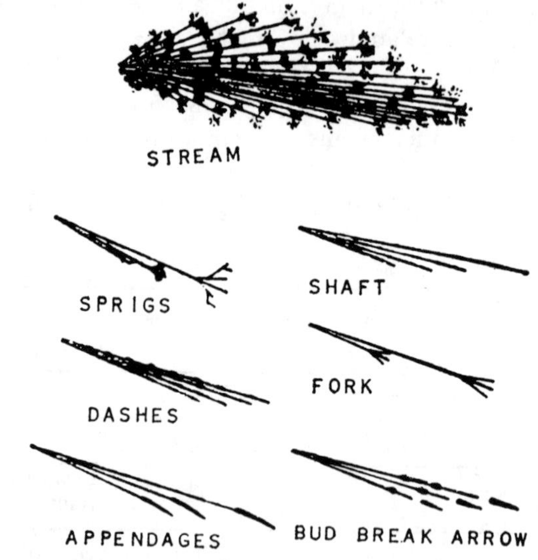

Figure 9. Meaning of the terms used in spark testing.

The greater the amount of carbon present in a steel, the greater the intensity of bursting that will take place in the spark stream. To understand the cause of the bursts, remember that while the spark is glowing and in contact with the oxygen of the air, the carbon present in the particle is burned to carbon dioxide (CO_2). As the solid carbon combines with oxygen to form CO_2 in the gaseous state, the increase in volume builds up a pressure that is relieved by an explosion of the particle. An examination of the small steel particles under a microscope when they are cold reveals a hollow sphere with one end completely blown away.

Steels having the same carbon content but differing alloying elements are not always easily identified because alloying elements affect the carrier lines, the bursts, or the forms of characteristic bursts in the spark picture. The effect of the alloying element may retard or accelerate the carbon spark, or make the carrier line lighter or darker in color. Molybdenum, *for example,* appears as a detached, orange-colored spearhead on the end of the carrier line. Nickel seems to suppress the effect of the carbon burst. But the nickel spark can be identified by tiny blocks of brilliant white light. Silicon suppresses the carbon burst even more than nickel. When silicon is present, the carrier line usually ends abruptly in a white flash of light.

To make the spark test, hold the piece of metal on the wheel in such a manner as to throw the spark stream about 12 inches at a right angle to your line of vision. You will need to spend a little time to discover at just what pressure you must hold the sample to get a stream of this length without reducing the speed of the grinder. It is important that you do not press too hard because the pressure will increase the temperature of the spark stream and the burst. It will also give the appearance of a higher carbon content than that of the metal actually being tested. After practicing to get the feel of correct pressure on the wheel until you are sure you have it, select a couple of samples of metal with widely varying characteristics, *for example,* low-carbon steel and high-carbon steel. Hold first one and then the other against the wheel, always being careful to strike the same portion of the wheel with each piece. With the eyes focused at a point about one-third of the distance from the tail end of the stream of sparks, watching only those sparks which cross the line of vision, you will find that after a little while you will form a mental image of the individual spark. After you can fix the spark image in mind, you are ready to examine the whole spark picture.

Note that the spark stream is long (about 70 inches normally) and that the volume is moderately large in low-carbon steel, while in high-carbon steel the stream is shorter (about 55 inches) and large in volume. The few sparklers which may occur at any place in low-carbon steel are forked, while in high-carbon steel the sparklers are small and repeating and some of the shafts may be forked. Both will produce a white spark stream.

White cast iron (Fig. 10) produces a spark stream approximately 20 inches in length. The volume of sparks is small with many small and repeating sparklers. The color of the spark stream close to the wheel is red, while the outer end of the stream is straw-colored.

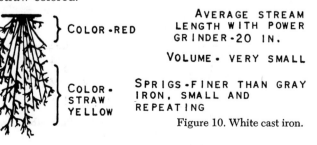

Figure 10. White cast iron.

Gray cast iron (Fig. 11) produces a stream of sparks about 25 inches in length. It is small in volume, with fewer sparklers than white cast iron. The sparklers are small and repeating. Part of the stream near the grinding wheel is red, and the outer end of the stream is straw-colored.

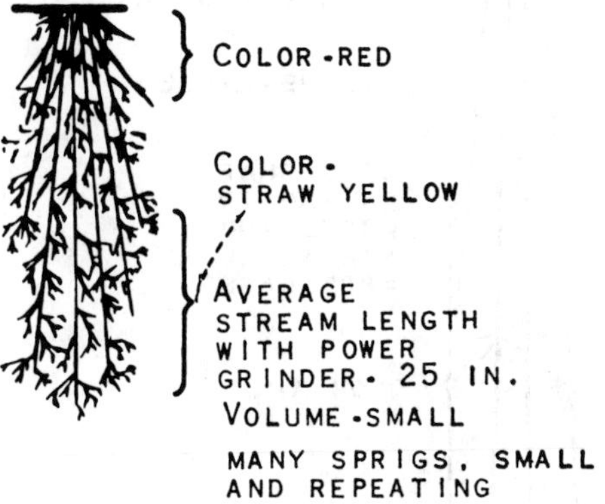

Figure 11. Gray cast iron.

The *malleable iron* spark test (Fig. 12) will produce a spark stream about 30 inches in length. It is of moderate volume, with many small, repeating sparklers toward the end of the stream. The entire stream is straw-colored.

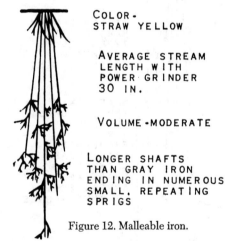

Figure 12. Malleable iron.

The *wrought iron* spark test (Fig. 13) produces a spark stream about 65 inches in length. The stream is of a large volume with few sparklers. The sparklers show up toward the end of the stream and are forked. The stream next to the grinding wheel is straw-colored, while the outer end of the stream is a bright red.

Stainless steel (Fig. 14) produces a spark stream approximately 50 inches in length, of moderate volume, with few sparklers. The sparklers are forked. The stream next to the wheel is straw-colored, while at the end it is white.

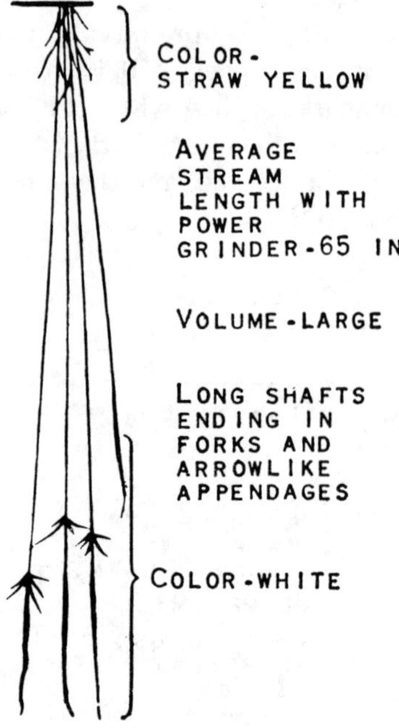

Figure 13. Wrought iron.

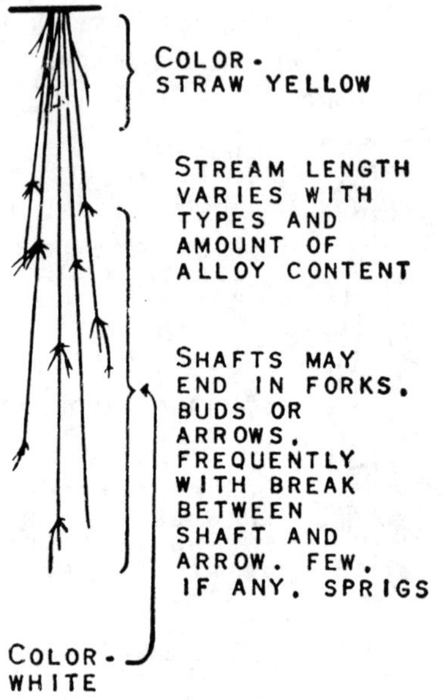

Figure 14. Alloy steel. (Spark shown is for stainless steel.)

Nickel (Fig. 15) produces a spark stream only about 10 inches in length. It is small in volume and orange in color. The sparks form wavy streaks with no sparklers.

Monel metal (Fig. 15) forms a spark stream almost identical to that of nickel, and must be identified by other means. Copper, brass, bronze, and lead form no sparks on the grinding wheel, but they are easily identified by other means, such as color, appearance, and chip tests.

Figure 15. Nickel.

(*See* Fig. 16 for low-carbon steel sparks. *See also* Fig. 17 for high-carbon steel sparks.)

You will find the spark tests easy and convenient to make. They require no special equipment and are adaptable to most any situation.

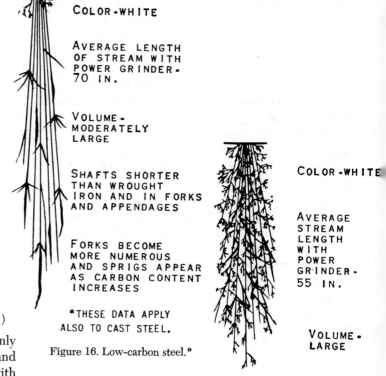

Figure 16. Low-carbon steel.*

Figure 17. High-carbon steel.

Acid Test

The *nitric acid test* is the most common test for metal, and it is used only in noncritical situations. For rapid identification of metal, the nitric acid test is one of the easiest tests to use and requires no special training in chemistry to perform. It is most helpful in distinguishing among stainless steel, Monel, copper-nickel, and carbon steels. The following safety precautions must be observed when using or handling acids of any type.

1. Never open more than one container of acid at one time.

2. In mixing, always pour acid slowly into water. *Never* pour water into acid because an explosion is likely to occur.

3. If any acid is spilled, dilute with plenty of water to weaken it so that it can safely be swabbed up and disposed of.

4. If an acid is spilled on the skin, wash immediately with large quantities of water. Then wash with a solution of borax and water.

5. Wear *clear-lens* safety goggles to ensure the detection of the reaction of metal to an acid test which may be evidenced by a color change, the formation of a deposit, or the development of a spot.

6. Conduct tests in a well ventilated area.

To perform the nitric acid test, place one or two drops of concentrated (full strength) nitric acid on a metal surface that has been cleaned by grinding or filing. Observe the resulting reaction (if any) for about two minutes. Then add three or four drops of water, one drop at a time, and continue observing the reaction. If there is no reaction at all, the test material may be one of the stainless steels. A reaction that results in a brown-colored liquid indicates a plain carbon steel. A reaction producing a brown to black color indicates a gray cast iron or one of the alloy steels containing as its principal element either chromium, molybdenum, or vanadium. Nickel steel reacts to the nitric acid test by the formation of a brown to greenish-black liquid, while a steel containing tungsten reacts slowly to form a brown-colored liquid with a yellow sediment.

When nonferrous metals and alloys are subject to the nitric acid test, instead of the brown-black colors that usually appear when ferrous metals are tested, various shades of green and blue appear as the material dissolves. Except with nickel and Monel, the reaction is vigorous. The reaction of nitric acid on nickel proceeds slowly, developing a pale green color. On Monel, the reaction takes place at about the same rate as on ferrous metals, but the characteristic color of the liquid is greenish-blue. Brass reacts vigorously, with the test material changing to a green color. Tin bronze, aluminum bronze, and copper all react vigorously in the nitric acid test with the liquid changing to a blue-green color. Aluminum and magnesium alloys, lead, lead-silver, and lead-tin alloys are soluble in nitric acid, but the blue or green color is lacking.

Heat Treatment

Heat treatment is the operation, or combination of operations, including heating and cooling of a metal in its solid state to develop or enhance a particular desirable mechanical property, such as hardness, toughness, machinability, or uniformity of strength. The theory of heat treatment is based upon the effect that the rate of heating, degree of heat, and the rate of cooling have on the molecular structure of a metal.

There are several forms of heat treating. The forms commonly used for ferrous metals are annealing, normalizing, hardening, tempering, and case-hardening.

ANNEALING. The chief purposes of *annealing* are (1) to relieve internal strains, and (2) to make a metal soft enough for machining. The process is accomplished by heating the metal to a high temperature, holding it at this temperature until the grain structure has been refined, and then allowing it to cool slowly. Both the temperature of the operation and the rate of cooling depend upon the metal being treated, and the purpose for which it is to be used.

Besides rendering metal more workable, annealing can also be used to alter other physical properties, such as magnetism and electrical conductivity. Annealing is often used for softening nonferrous alloys and pure metals after they have been hardened by cold work. Some of these alloys require annealing operations which are different from those for steel.

For ferrous metals, the annealing method most commonly used, if a controlled atmosphere furnace is not available, is to place the metal in a cast iron box, and to cover it with sand or fire clay. Packing this material around the metal prevents oxidation. The box is then placed in the furnace, heated to the proper temperature, held there for a sufficient period, and then allowed to cool slowly in the sealed furnace.

For annealing the more common metals, proceed as follows.

CAST IRON. Heat slowly to between 1400° and

1800°F, depending on composition. Hold at the specific temperature for 30 minutes, and then allow the metal to cool slowly in the furnace or annealing box.

STAINLESS STEEL (AUSTENITIC). For full annealing, heat to between 1850°F and 2050°F. Cool rapidly. For partial annealing, heat to between 1600° and 1700°F.

COPPER. Heat to 925°F. Quench in water. A temperature as low as 500°F will relieve most of the stresses and strains.

ZINC. Heat to 400°F. Cool in open, still air.

ALUMINUM. Heat to 750°F. Cool in open air. This reduces hardness and strength but increases electrical conductivity.

NICKEL-COPPER ALLOYS (INCLUDING MONEL). Heat to between 1400° and 1450°F. Cool by quenching in water or oil.

NICKEL-MOLYBDENUM-IRON AND NICKEL-MOLYBDENUM-CHROMIUM ALLOYS (STELLITE). Heat to between 2100° and 2150°F. Hold at this temperature a suitable time, depending on thickness. Follow by rapid cooling in a quenching medium.

BRASS. Annealing to relieve stress may be accomplished at a temperature as low as 600°F. Fuller anneals may be accomplished with increased temperatures. Larger grain size and loss of strength will result from too high temperatures. Do not anneal at temperatures exceeding 1300°F. Brass should be slowly cooled to room temperature. Either wrap the part with asbestos cloth, or bury in slaked lime or other heat-retarding material.

BRONZE. Heat to 1400°F. Cool in open furnace to 500°F, or place in a pan to avoid uneven cooling caused by draft.

NORMALIZING. *Normalizing,* a process similar to annealing, is done for a different purpose. Normalizing relieves stresses and strains caused by welding, forging work, and uneven cooling of castings. The metal is heated from 50° to 100° above its critical temperature. (*See* section on hardening.) Then allow the metal to cool evenly in air.

HARDENING. Cutting tools, chisels, twist drills, and many other pieces of equipment and tools must be hardened to enable them to retain their cutting edges. Surfaces of roller bearings, parallel blocks, and armor plate must be hardened to prevent wear or penetration. Metals and alloys can be hardened in several ways. A brief general description of one method of hardening follows.

Each steel has a critical temperature at which there will occur a marked change in the grain structure and physical properties. This critical temperature varies according to the carbon content of the steel. To be hardened, steel must be heated to a little more than this critical temperature—to ensure that every point in it will have reached critical temperature, and to allow for some slight loss of heat when the metal is transferred from the furnace to the cooling medium. It is then cooled rapidly by being quenched in oil, fresh water, or brine. Quenching firmly fixes the structural changes which occurred under heating, thus causing the metal to remain hard.

If allowed to cool too slowly, the metal will lose its hardness. On the other hand, to prevent too rapid quenching (which would result in warping and cracking), it is sometimes necessary to use oil instead of fresh water or salt water for high carbon and alloy steels. Salt water, as opposed to fresh water, produces greater hardness.

TEMPERING. The *tempering process* is employed as a method of relieving the strains that are brought about in steel during the hardening process. Tempering makes the metal tougher and less brittle. Tempering is accomplished by heating the hardened steel to a temperature below the critical range, holding this temperature for a sufficient time to penetrate the whole piece, and then cooling the piece. In this process, ductility and toughness are improved but tensile strength and hardness are reduced.

CASE HARDENING. *Case hardening* is a process of heat treating by which a hard skin is formed on metal, while the inner part remains relatively soft and tough. A metal that is originally low in carbon is packed in a substance high in carbon content, and heated above the critical range. The case hardening furnace must give a uniform heat. The length of time the piece is left in the oven at this high heat determines the depth to which carbon is absorbed. A commonly used method of case hardening is to (1) carburize the material (an addition of carbon during the treatment), (2) allow it to cool slowly, (3) reheat, and (4) harden in water. Small pieces such as bolts, nuts, and screws, however, can be dumped into water as soon as they are taken out of the carburizing furnace.

Hardness Tests

A number of tests are used to measure the physical properties of metals and to determine whether a metal meets specification requirements. Some of the more common tests are hardness tests, tensile strength tests, shear strength tests, bend tests, fatigue tests, and compression tests. Of primary importance to the worker are the hardness tests.

Most metals possess some degree of hardness, that is, the ability to resist penetration by another material. Many tests for hardness are used, the simplest being the *file hardness test.* While fair estimates of hardness can be made by an experienced workman, more consistent quantitative measurements are obtained with standard hardness testing equipment. Such equipment eliminates the variables of size, shape, and hardness of the file selected, and of the speed, pressure, and angles of the file used by a workman when conducting a test. Before discussing the hardness test equipment, let us consider hardness itself, and the value of such information to the worker.

Hardness has been defined in various ways: resistance to penetration, resistance to abrasion, resistance to machine tool cutting, and resistance to bending (stiffness) by wrought products. Except for resistance to penetration, these characteristics of hardness are not readily measurable. Consequently, most hardness tests are based on the principle that a hard material will penetrate a softer one. In a scientific sense, hardness is a measure of the resistance of a material to penetration or indentation by an indenter of fixed size and geometrical shape, under a specific load.

The information obtained from a hardness test has many uses. It may be used to compare alloys and the effects of various heat treatments on them. Hardness tests are also useful as a rapid, nondestructive method for inspecting and controlling certain materials and processes, and to ensure that heat-treated objects have developed the hardness desired or specified. The results of hardness tests are useful not only for comparative purposes, but also for estimating other properties. *For example,* the tensile strength of carbon and low-alloy steels can be estimated from the hardness test number. There is also a relationship between hardness and endurance or fatigue characteristics of certain steels.

Hardness may be measured by many types of instruments. The most common are the Rockwell and the Brinell hardness testers. Other hardness tests include the Vickers, Eberbach, Monotron, Tukon, and Scleroscope. Since there are many tests, and since the hardness numbers derived are not equivalent, it is essential that the hardness number be designated according to the test and the scale employed in the test. Since you are more likely to have access to a Rockwell tester than any other, this method is discussed in detail. The essential differences between the Rockwell and Brinell tests will also be discussed in the sections which follow. In addition, the Scleroscope and Vickers hardness tests will be covered briefly.

ROCKWELL HARDNESS TEST. Of all the hardness tests, the *Rockwell* is the one most frequently mentioned. The basic principle of the Rockwell test (like that of the Brinell, Vickers, Eberbach, Tukron, and Monotron tests) is that a hard material will penetrate a soft one. This test operates on the principle of measuring the indentation, in a test piece of metal with specified pressure. In the Rockwell tester the hardness number is obtained by measuring the depression made by a hardened steel ball or a spheroconical diamond penetrator of a given size under a given pressure.

With the normal Rockwell tester, the 120° spheroconical penetrator is used in conjunction with a 150-kilogram (kg.) weight to make impressions in hard metals. The hardness number obtained is designated Rockwell C (Rc). For softer metals, the penetrator is a 1/16-inch steel ball in conjunction with a 100-kilogram weight. A hardness number obtained under these conditions is designated Rockwell B (Rb). Figure 18 illustrates the principle of indenter hardness tests. Although the conical penetrator is shown, the principle is the same for a ball penetrator. (The geometry of the indentions would, of course, differ slightly.)

With the Rockwell tester, a deadweight, acting through a series of levers, is used to press the ball or cone into the surface of the metal to be tested. Then

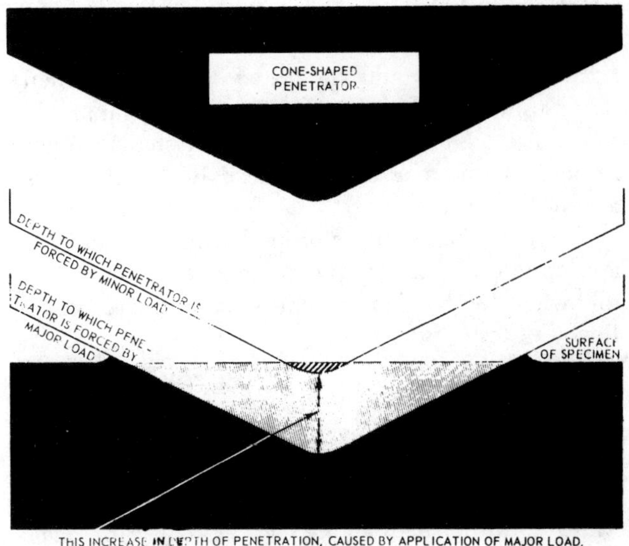
CONE-SHAPED
PENETRATOR
SURFACE
OF SPECIMEN
THIS INCREASE IN DEPTH OF PENETRATION, CAUSED BY APPLICATION OF MAJOR LOAD, FORMS THE BASIS FOR THE ROCKWELL HARDNESS TESTER READINGS.

Figure 18.

the depth of penetration is measured. The softer the metal being tested, the deeper the penetration will be under a given load. The average depth of penetration on samples of very soft steel is only about 0.008 inch. The hardness is indicated on a dial, calibrated in the Rockwell B and the Rockwell C hardness scales. The harder the metal, the higher the Rockwell number will be. Ferrous metals are usually tested with the spheroconical penetrator, with hardness numbers being read from the Rockwell C scale. The steel ball is used for nonferrous metals and the results are read on the B scale.

With most indenter-type hardness tests, the metal being tested must be sufficiently thick to avoid bulging or marking the opposite side. The specimen thickness should be at least 10 times the depth of penetration. It is also essential that the surface of the specimen be flat and clean. When hardness tests are necessary on thin material, a superficial Rockwell tester should be employed.

The Rockwell superficial tester differs from the normal Rockwell tester in the amount of load applied to perform the test, and in the kind of scale used to interpret the results. Where the major loads on the normal tester are 100 and 150 kilograms, the major loads on the superficial tester are 15, 30, and 45 kilograms. One division on the dial gage of the normal tester represents a vertical displacement of the indenter of 0.002 millimeter. One division of the dial gage of the superficial tester represents a vertical displacement of the indenter of 0.001 millimeter. Hardness scales for the Rockwell superficial tester are the N and T scales. The N scale is used for materials of such hardness that, were they of sufficient thickness, they would be tested with the normal tester using the C scale. The T scale is comparable to the B scale used with the normal tester. In other respects the normal and superficial Rockwell testers are much alike.

Assuming the sample is properly prepared and the appropriate penetrator and weights are selected, the following step-by-step procedure will indicate how a Rockwell tester is used.

1. Place the piece to be tested on the testing table or anvil.

2. Turn the wheel elevating the testing table until the piece to be tested comes in contact with the testing cone or ball. Continue to turn the elevating wheel until the small pointer on the indicating gage is nearly vertical and slightly to the right of the dot.

3. Watching the long pointer on the gage, continue raising the work with the elevating wheel until the long pointer is nearly upright (within approximately five divisions, plus or minus, on the scale). This step of the procedure sets the minor load.

4. Turn the zero adjuster, located below the elevating wheel, to set the dial zero behind the pointer.

5. Tap the depressor bar downward to release the weights and apply the major load. Watch the pointer until it comes to rest.

6. Turn the crank handle upward and forward, thereby removing the major but not the minor load. This will leave the penetrator in contact with the specimen but not under pressure.

7. Observe where the pointer now comes to rest and read the Rockwell hardness number on the dial. If the test has been made with the 1/16 inch ball and a 100 kilogram weight, the reading is taken from the red, or B, scale. If the test has been made with the spheroconical penetrator and a weight of 150 kilograms, the reading is taken from the black, or C, scale. (In the first example the number is prefixed by Rb, in the latter instance by Rc.)

8. Turn the handwheel to lower the anvil. Then remove the test specimen.

BRINELL HARDNESS TEST. The *Brinell hardness testing machine* provides a convenient and reliable hardness test. The machine is not suitable, however, for small or thin pieces. This machine has a vertical hydraulic press design and is generally hand operated, a lever being used to apply the load which forces a 10-millimeter diameter hardened steel or tungsten-carbide ball into the test specimen. For ferrous metals, a 3000-kilogram load is applied. For nonferrous metals, the load is 500 kilograms. In general, pressure is applied to ferrous metals for 10 seconds, while 30 seconds are required for nonferrous metals. After the pressure has been applied for the appropriate time, the diameter of the depression produced is measured with a microscope having an ocular scale.

The Brinell hardness number (Bhn) is the ratio of the load in kilograms to the impressed surface area in square millimeters. This number is found by measuring the distance the ball is forced, under a specified pressure, into the test piece. The greater the distance, the softer the metal, and the lower the Brinell hardness number will be. The width of the indentation is measured with a microscope and the hardness number corresponding to this width is found by consulting a chart or table.

The Brinell hardness machine is of greatest value in testing soft and medium-hard metals, and in testing large pieces. On hard steel the imprint of the ball is so small that it is difficult to read.

SCLEROSCOPE HARDNESS TEST. If you were to place a mattress on the floor and drop two rubber balls from the same height, one on the mattress and one on the floor, the one dropped on the floor will bounce higher. The reason is that the floor is the harder of the two surfaces. This is the principle upon which the Scleroscope works. When using the Scleroscope hardness test, a diamond-pointed hammer is dropped through a guiding glass tube onto the test piece and the rebound (bounce) is checked on a scale. The harder the metal being tested, the higher the hammer will rebound and the higher will be the number on the scale. The Scleroscope is portable and can be used to test the hardness of pieces too large to be placed on the anvil or tables of other machines. Another advantage of the Scleroscope is that it can be used without damaging finished surfaces. The chief disadvantage of this machine is its inaccuracy. The accuracy of the Scleroscope is affected by the following factors.

1. Small pieces do not have the necessary backing and cannot be held rigidly enough to give accurate readings.

2. If large sections are not rigid, if they are oddly shaped, if they have overhanging sections, or if they are hollow, the readings may be in error.

3. If oil-hardened parts are tested, oil may creep up the glass tube and interfere with the drop of the diamond-pointed hammer in the instrument, thus causing an error.

VICKERS HARDNESS TEST. The Vickers test measures hardness by a method similar to that used in the Brinell test. The indenter, however, is not a ball, but a square-based diamond pyramid, which makes it accurate for testing thin sheets as well as the hardest steels.

Up to an approximate hardness number of 300, the results of the Vickers and the Brinell tests are about the same. Above 300, Brinell accuracy becomes progressively lower. This divergence represents a weakness in the Brinell method; a weakness that is the result of the tendency of the Brinell indenter ball to flatten under heavy loads. It is for this reason that the Brinell numbers over 600 are considered to be of doubtful reliability.

If a shop has one type of hardness tester and the specifications indicated by the blueprint are for another type, a conversion table, such as Table 2A, may be used to convert the reading.

TABLE 2A
HARDNESS CONVERSION

BRINNEL HARDNESS NUMBER		STANDARD ROCKWELL		BRINNELL HARDNESS NUMBER		STANDARD ROCKWELL	
		B	C			B	C
500 kg	3000 kg	1/16" Ball 100 kg	Brale 150 kg	500 kg	3000 kg	1/16" Ball 100 kg	Brale 150 kg
---	---	---	70.0	---	352	(110.0)	37.9
---	---	---	69.0	---	341	(109.9)	36.6
---	---	---	68.0	---	331	(108.5)	35.5
---	---	---	67.5	---	321	(107.5)	34.3
---	---	---	67.0	---	311	(107.0)	33.1
---	767*	---	66.4	---	302	(106.0)	32.1
---	757*	---	65.9	---	293	(105.5)	30.9
---	745*	---	65.3	---	285	(104.5)	29.9
---	733*	---	64.7	---	277	(104.0)	28.8
---	722*	---	64.0	---	269	(103.0)	27.6
---	710*	---	63.3	---	262	(102.0)	26.6
---	698*	---	62.5	---	255	(101.0)	25.3
---	682*	---	61.7	---	243	100.0	24.2
---	670*	---	61.0	201	241	99.0	22.8
---	353*	---	60.0	195	235	98.2	21.7
---	638*	---	59.2	189	229	97.3	20.5
---	627*	---	58.7	184	223	96.4	(18.8)

(TABLE 2A CONTINUED)

BRINNEL HARDNESS NUMBER		STANDARD ROCKWELL B	C	BRINNELL HARDNESS NUMBER		STANDARD ROCKWELL B	C
---	601*	---	57.3	179	217	95.5	(17.5)
---	578*	---	56.0	175	212	94.6	(16.0)
---	555*	---	54.7	171	207	93.8	(15.2)
---	534*	---	53.5	167	201	92.8	(13.8)
---	524*	---	52.1	164	197	91.9	(12.7)
---	495*	---	51.0	161	192	90.7	(11.5)
---	477	---	50.3	158	187	90.0	(10.0)
---	461	---	48.8	156	183	80.0	(9.0)
---	444	---	47.2	153	179	87.8	(8.0)
---	429	---	45.7	149	174	86.8	(6.4)
---	415	---	44.5	146	170	86.0	(5.4)
---	401	---	43.1	143	167	85.0	(4.4)
---	388	---	41.8	140	163	82.9	(3.3)
---	375	---	40.4	135	156	80.8	(0.9)
---	363	---	39.1	130	149		

* Tungsten-carbide ball.
() Values beyond normal range for scale.
500 kg—non ferrous 3000 kg—ferrous

Plastics

Plastic materials are being used increasingly; in some respects, they tend to surpass structural metals. Plastic has proved to be shock resistant, not susceptible to salt water corrosion, and in casting it lends itself to mass production and uniformity of end product.

CHARACTERISTICS. Plastics are formed from organic materials generally with some form of carbon as their basic element. Plastics are referred to as synthetic material, but this does not necessarily mean that they are inferior to natural material. On the contrary, they have been designed to perform particular functions that no natural material can perform. Plastics can be obtained in a variety of colors, shapes, and forms. Some plastics are as tough, but not so hard as steel; some are as pliable as rubber; some are more transparent than glass; and some are lighter than aluminum.

Plastic materials fall into two major divisions—*thermosettings* and *thermoplastics*—and it is necessary, if you are going to perform any kind of work on plastics, to know which of these two you are using.

Thermosettings are tough, brittle, and heat hardened. When placed in a flame, they will not burn readily, if at all. Thermosettings are so hard they resist the penetration of a knife blade, and any such attempt will dull the blade. If the plastic is immersed in hot water and allowed to remain, it will neither absorb moisture nor soften.

Thermoplastics, on the other hand, when exposed to heat, become soft and pliable, or even melt. When cooled, they retain the shape that they took under the application of heat. Some thermoplastics will even absorb a small amount of moisture, if placed in hot water. A knife blade will cut easily into thermoplastics.

When testing a plastic by inserting it into a fire, you should exercise caution, because thermoplastics will burst into sudden intense flame, and give off obnoxious gases. If you use the fire test, be sure to hold the plastic piece a considerable distance away from you.

MAJOR GROUPS OF PLASTICS. While it is not necessary for you to know the exact chemical composition of the many plastics in existence, it will be helpful to have a general idea of the composition of the plastics you are most likely to use. Table 2B provides information on various groups of plastics.

Laminated plastics are made by dipping, spraying, or brushing flat sheets or continuous rolls of paper, fabric, or wood veneer with resins, and then pressing several layers together to get hard, rigid, structural material. The number of layers pressed together into one sheet of laminated plastic will depend upon the thickness desired. The choice of paper canvas, wood veneer, or glass fabric will depend upon the end use of the product. Paper-base material is thin and quite brittle, breaking if bent sharply, but canvas-base material will be difficult to break. As layers are added to paper-base material, it gains in strength, but it is never as tough and strong in a laminated part as layers of glass fabric or canvas.

Machining Operations

Machining operations on *plastics* include cutting parts from sheet or rod stock, using various metal cutting saws; removing stock from parts by rotating tools such as in the drill press or the milling machine; cutting moving parts by stationary tools, as on the lathe; and finishing operations.

TABLE 2B
MAJOR GROUPS OF PLASTICS

Plastic Trade Names in ( )	Advantages and Examples of Uses	Disadvantages
	THERMOPLASTICS	
Acrylic (Lucite, Plexiglass)	**Formability; good impact strength; good aging and weathering resistance; high transparency, shatter-resistance, rigidity. Used for lenses, dials, etc.**	**Softening point of 170° to 220°F; low scratch resistance.**
Cellulose nitrate (Celluloid)	**Ease of fabrication; relatively high impact strength and toughness; good dimensional stability and resilience; low moisture absorption. Used for tool handles, mallet heads, clock dials, etc.**	**Extreme flammability; poor electrical insulating properties; harder with age; low heat distortion point.**
Polyamide (Nylon)	**High resistance to distortion under load at temperatures up to 300°F; high tensile strength, excellent impact strength at normal temperatures; does not become brittle at temperatures as low as minus 70°F; excellent resistance to gasoline and oil; low coefficient of friction on metals. Used for synthetic textiles, special types of bearings, etc.**	**Absorption of water; large coefficient of expansion; relatively high cost; weathering resistance poor.**
Polyethylene (Polythene)	**Inert to many solvents and corrosive chemicals; flexible and tough over wide temperature range, remains so at temperatures as low as minus 100°F; unusually low moisture absorption and permeability; high electrical resistance; dimensionally stable at normal temperatures; ease of molding; low cost. Used for wire and cable insulation, and acid resistant clothing.**	**Low tensile, compressive, flexural strength; very high elongation at normal temperatures; subject to spontaneous cracking when stored in contact with alcohols, toluene, and silicone grease, etc.; softens at temperatures above 200°F; poor abrasion and cut resistance; cannot be bonded unless given special surface treatment.**
	THERMOPLASTICS	
Polytetrafluoroethylene (Teflon)	**Extreme chemical inertness; high heat resistance; nonadhesive; tough; low coefficient of friction. Used for preformed packing and gaskets.**	**Not easily cemented; cannot be molded by usual methods; generates toxic fumes at high temperatures; high cost.**

(TABLE 2B CONTINUED)

Plastic Trade Names in ( )	Advantages and Examples of Uses	Disadvantages
	THERMOSETTING PLASTICS	
Phenolformaldehyde (Bakelite, Durez, Resinox)	Better permanence characteristics than most plastics; may be used at temperatures from 250° to 475°F; good aging resistance; good electrical insulating properties; not readily flammable, does not support combustion; inserts can be firmly embedded; strong, light; low water absorption; low thermal conductivity; good chemical resistance; economical in production of complex shapes; free from cold flow; relatively insensitive to temperature; low coefficient of thermal expansion; no change in dimensions under a load for a long time; does not soften at high temperatures or become brittle down to minus 60°F; inexpensive. Used for handles, telephone equipment, electrical insulators, etc.	Difficult to mold when filled for greatest impact strength, or when in sections less than 3/32-inch thick; can be expanded or contracted by unusually wet or dry atmosphere.
Urea-formaldehyde (Beetle, Bakelite Urea, Plaskon)	High degree of translucency and light finish; hard surface finish; outstanding electrical properties when used within temperature range of minus 70° to plus 170°F; complete resistance to organic solvents; dimensionally stable under moderate loadings and exposure conditions. Used for instrument dials, electric parts, etc.	Low impact strength; slight warping with age; poor water resistance.

SAWING. Several types of saws (bandsaw, jigsaw, circular saw) may be used to cut blanks from plastic stock. Speeds should be watched carefully; since almost none of the best generated will be carried away by the plastic, there is always danger that the tool will be overheated to the point where it will burn the work.

DRILLING. In drilling plastics, back the drill out frequently to remove the chips and cool the tool. A liberal application of kerosene will help keep the drill cool. To obtain a smooth, clean hole, use paraffin wax on the drill; for the softer plastics, a special coolant may be preferred.

LATHE OPERATIONS. Lathe operations are substantially the same for plastics as for metals, except for type of tool, and the manner in which contact is made with the work. For plastics, set the tool slightly below center. Use cutting tools with zero or slightly negative back rake.

For both thermosettings and thermoplastics, recommended cutting speeds are 200 to 500 fpm with high speed steel tools, and 500 to 1500 fpm with carbide-tipped tools.

FINISHING OPERATIONS. Plastic must be given a finishing process to remove tool marks and produce a clean, smooth surface. Usually sanding and buffing are sufficient for this purpose.

Surface scratches and pits can be satisfactorily removed by hand sandpapering with dry sandpaper of fine grit. Wet sanding can also be done by hand, with water and abrasive paper of fine grade. If a large amount of material must be removed, it will be more advantageous to use sanding wheels or discs.

After pits and scratches have been removed, the plastic should be buffed. This can be done on a wheel made of loose muslin buffs. Buffing compounds in common use are tripoli and rouge. A layer of the compound is deposited on the outside of the buffing wheel. The compound must be renewed frequently.

When large flat sheets are being buffed, be careful not to use too much pressure, nor to hold the work too long in one position. In buffing small plastic parts, be careful that the wheel does not seize the piece and pull it out of your grasp.

Chapter 2

Measuring Tools and How to Use Them

In metalworking, the common measurements are those of length, area, and volume. Many of these must be made with such exactness that a number of measuring tools are available for the purpose. However, the accuracy of the measurements will depend on the measuring tools used and one's ability to use them correctly.

Measuring tools are also used for inspecting a finished or partly finished product. Inspecting operations include testing or checking a piece of work by comparing dimensions given on a drawing or sketch.

Rules and Tapes

There are many different types of measuring tools. Where exact measurements are required, a micrometer caliper (mike) is used. Such a caliper, when properly used, gives measurements to within .001 of an inch accuracy. On the other hand, where accuracy is not extremely critical, the common rule or tape will do for most measurements.

Figure 1 shows some of the types of rules and tapes commonly used. Of all measuring tools, the simplest and most common is the steel rule. This rule is usually 6 or 12 inches in length, although other lengths are available. Steel rules may be flexible or nonflexible, but the thinner the rule, the easier it is to measure accurately, because the division marks are closer to the work.

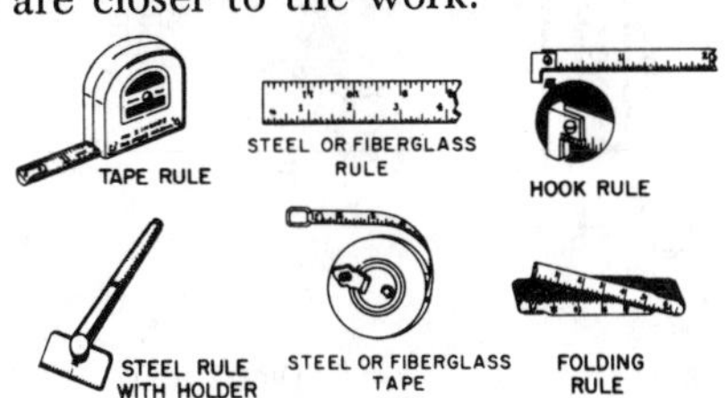

Figure 1. Types of rules.

Generally a rule has four sets of graduations, one on each edge of each side. The longest lines represent the inch marks. On one edge, each inch is divided into eight equal spaces, so each space represents 1/8 inch. The other edge of this side is divided into sixteenths. The 1/4 and 1/2-inch marks are commonly made longer than the smaller division marks to facilitate counting, but the graduations are not, as a rule, numbered individually, as they are sufficiently far apart to be counted without difficulty. The opposite side is similarly divided into 32 and 64 spaces per inch, and it is common practice to number every fourth division for easier reading.

There are many variations of the common rule. Sometimes the graduations are on one side only, sometimes a set of graduations is added across one end for measuring in narrow spaces, and sometimes only the first inch is divided into 64ths, with the remaining inches divided into 32nds and 16ths.

A *metal* or *wood folding rule* may be used for measuring purposes. These folding rules are usually 2 to 6 feet long. The folding rules cannot be relied on for extremely accurate measurements because a certain amount of play develops at the joints after they have been used for a while.

Steel tapes are made from 6 to about 300 feet in length. The shorter lengths are frequently made with a curved cross section so that they are flexible enough to roll up but remain rigid when extended. Long, flat tapes require support over their full length when measuring, or the natural sag will cause an error in reading.

The *flexible-rigid tapes* are usually contained in metal cases into which they wind themselves when a button is pressed, or into which they can be easily pushed. A hook is provided at one end to hook over the object being measured so a worker can handle it without assistance. On some models, the outside of the case can be used as one end of the tape when measuring inside dimensions.

Measuring Procedures

To take a measurement with a *common rule,* hold the rule with its edge on the surface of the object being measured. This will eliminate parallax and other errors which might result due to the thickness of the rule. Read the measurement at the graduation which coincides with the distance to be measured, and state it as being so many inches and fractions of an inch (Fig. 2). Always reduce fractions to their lowest terms, *for example,* 6/8 in. would be called 3/4 in. A hook or eye at the end of a tape or rule is normally part of the first measured inch.

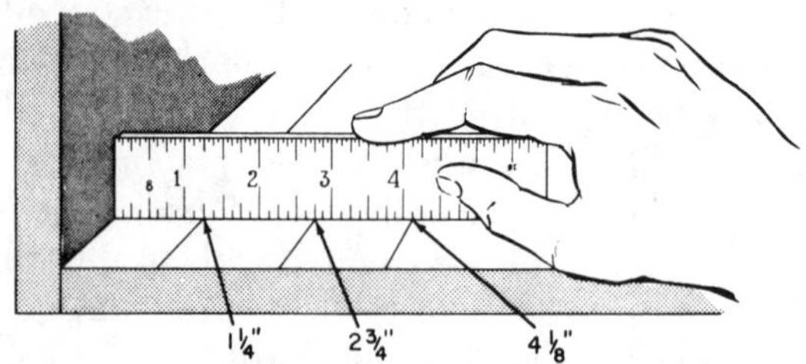

Figure 2. Measuring with and reading a common rule.

Bolts or Screws. The length of bolts or screws is best measured by holding them up against a *rigid rule* or *tape.* Hold both the bolt or screw to be measured and the rule up to your eye level so that your line of sight will not be in error in reading the measurement. As shown in Fig. 3, the bolts or screws with countersink-type heads are measured from the top of the head to the opposite end, while those with other type heads are measured from the bottom of the head.

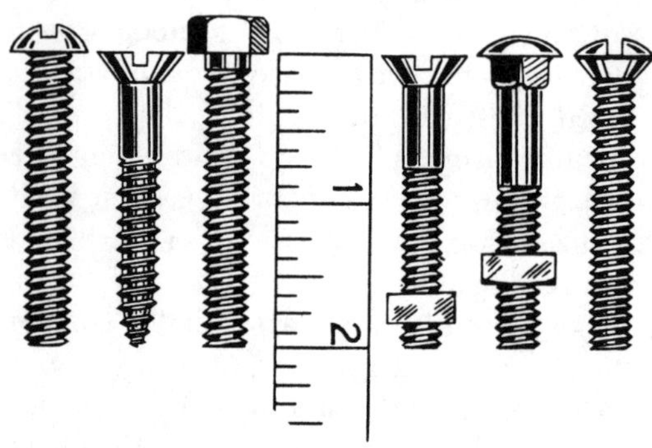

Figure 3. Measuring length of a bolt or screw.

Outside Pipe Diameters. To measure the outside diameter of a pipe, it is best to use some kind of rigid rule. A *folding wooden rule* or a *steel rule* is satisfactory for this purpose. Line up the end of the rule with one side of the pipe, as shown in Fig. 4, using your thumb as a stop. Then with the one end held in place with your thumb, swing the rule through an arc and take the maximum reading at the other side of the pipe. For most practical purposes, the measurement obtained by using this method is satisfactory. It is necessary that you know how to take this measurement, as the outside diameter of the pipe is sometimes the only dimension given on pipe specifications.

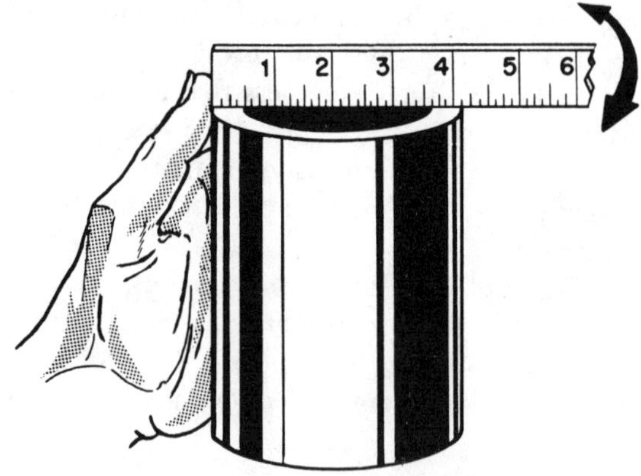

Figure 4. Measuring outside diameter of a pipe.

Inside Pipe Diameters. To measure the inside diameter of a pipe with a rule, as shown in Fig. 5, hold the rule so that one corner of the rule just rests on the inside of one side of the pipe. Then, with one end thus held in place, swing the rule through an arc and read the diameter across the maximum inside distance. This method is satisfactory for an approximate inside measurement.

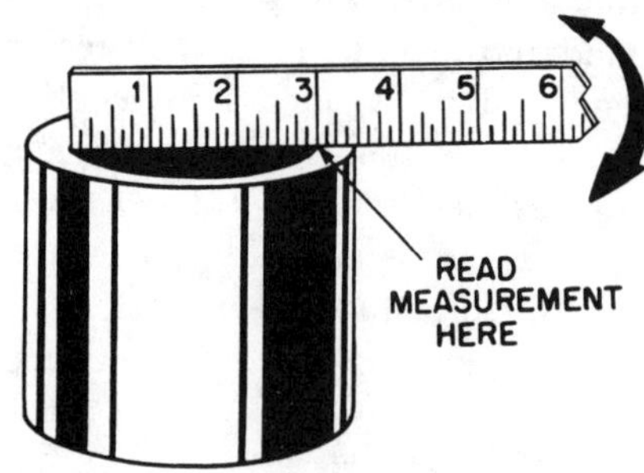

Figure 5. Measuring inside diameter of a pipe.

Pipe Circumferences. To measure the circumference of a pipe, a flexible-type rule that will conform to the cylindrical shape of the pipe must be used. A tape rule or a steel tape is adaptable for this job. When measuring pipe, make sure the tape has been wrapped squarekly around the axis of the pipe (measurement should be taken in a plane perpendicular to the axis) to ensure that the reading will not be more than the actual circumference of the pipe. This is extremely important when measuring large diameter pipe.

Hold the rule or tape as shown in Fig. 6. Take the reading, using the 2-inch graduation, *for example,* as the reference point. In this case, the correct reading is found by subtracting two inches from the actual reading. In this way the first two inches of the tape, serving as a handle, will enable you to hold the tape securely.

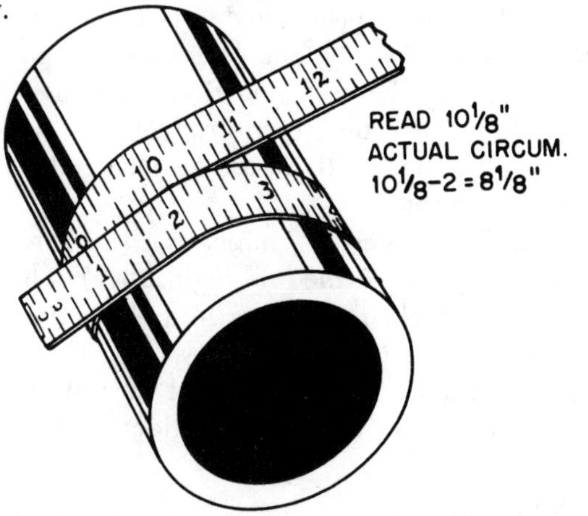

Figure 6. Measuring circumference of a pipe with a tape.

INSIDE DIMENSIONS. To take an inside measurement, such as the inside of a box, a folding rule that incorporates a 6- or 7-in. sliding extension is one of the best measuring tools. To take the inside measurement, first unfold the folding rule to the approximate dimension. Then extend the end of the rule and read the length that it extends, adding the length of the extension to the length on the main body of the rule (Fig. 7). The main body of the rule in Fig. 7 is 13 in. and the extension is pulled out 3 3/16 in. In this case the total inside dimension being measured is 16 3/16 in.

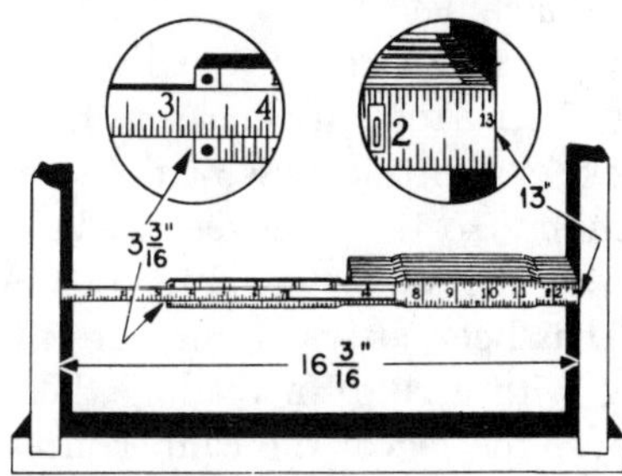

Figure 7. Using folding rule to measure an inside dimension.

In Fig. 8 note in the circled insert that the hook at the end of the particular rule shown is attached to the rule so that it is free to move slightly. When an outside dimension is taken by hooking the end of the rule over an edge, the hook will locate the end of the rule even with the surface from which the measurement is being taken. By being free to move, the hook will retract away from the end of the rule when an inside dimension is taken. To measure an inside dimension using a tape rule, extend the rule between the surfaces as shown, take a reading at the point on the scale where the rule enters the case, and add two inches. The two inches are the width of the case. The total is the inside dimension being taken.

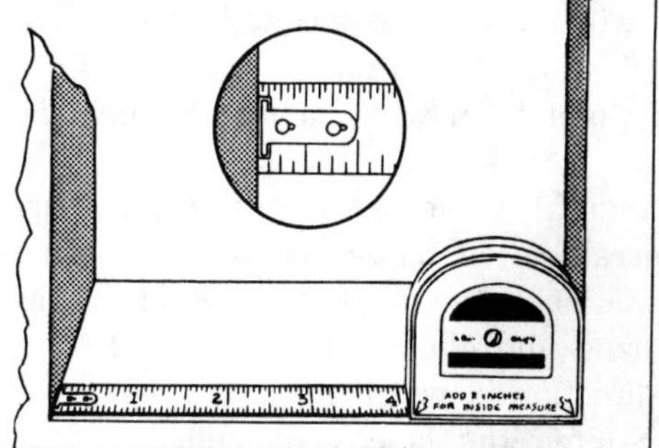

Figure 8. Measuring an inside dimension with a tape rule.

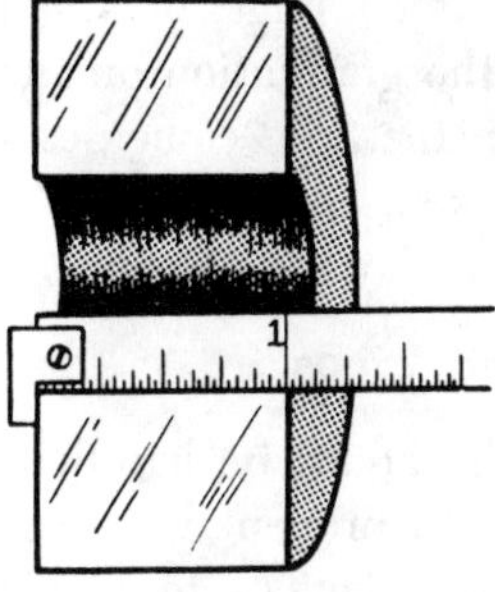

Figure 9. Measuring thickness of stock through a hole.

To measure the thickness of stock through a hole with a *hook rule,* insert the rule through the hole, hold the hook against one face of the stock, and read the thickness at the other face (Fig. 9).

OUTSIDE DIMENSIONS. To measure an outside dimension using a *tape rule,* hook the rule over the edge of the stock. Pull the tape out until it projects far enough from the case to permit measuring the required distance. The hook at the end of the rule is designed so that it will locate the end of the rule at the surface from which the measurement is being taken (Fig. 10). When taking a measurement of length, the tape is held parallel to the lengthwise edge. For measuring widths, the tape should be at right angles to the lengthwise edge. Read the di-

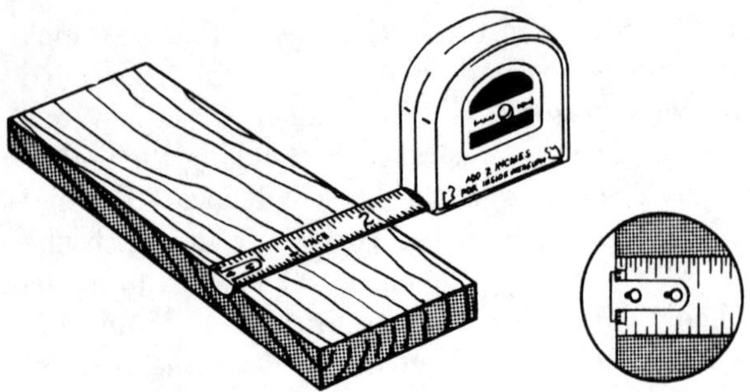

Figure 10. Measuring an outside dimension with a tape rule.

mension of the rule exactly at the edge of the piece being measured.

It may not always be possible to hook the end of the tape over the edge of stock being measured. In this case, it may be necessary to butt the end of the tape against another surface or to hold the rule at a starting point from which a measurement is to be taken.

DISTANCE MEASUREMENTS. Steel or fiberglass tapes are generally used for making long measurements. Secure the hook end of the tape. Hold the tape reel in the hand and allow it to unwind while walking in the direction in which the measurement is to be taken. Stretch the tape with sufficient tension to overcome sagging. At the same time make sure the tape is parallel to an edge or the surface being measured. Read the graduation on the tape by noting which line on the tape coincides with the measurement being taken.

Care of Rules and Tapes

Rules and tapes should be handled carefully and kept lightly oiled to prevent rust. *Never* allow the edges of measuring devices to become nicked by striking them with hard objects. They should preferably be kept in a wooden box when not in use.

To avoid kinking tapes, pull them straight out from their cases; do not bend them backward. With the *windup-type tapes,* always turn the crank clockwise (turning it backward will kink or break the tape). With the *spring-wind type tapes,* guide the tape by hand. If it is allowed to snap back, it may be kinked, twisted, or otherwise damaged. *Do not* use the hook as a stop. Slow down as you reach the end.

Calipers

Simple calipers are used in conjunction with a scale to measure diameters. The calipers most commonly used are shown in Fig. 11.

Outside calipers for measuring outside diameters are bow-legged; those used for inside diameters have straight legs with the feet turned outward. Calipers are adjusted by pulling or pushing the legs to open or close them. Fine adjustment is made by tapping one leg lightly on a hard surface to close them, or by turning them upside down and tapping on the joint end to open them.

Spring-joint calipers have the legs joined by a strong spring hinge and linked together by a screw and adjusting nut. For measuring chamfered cavities (grooves), or for use over flanges, *transfer calipers* are available. They are equipped with a small auxiliary leaf attached to one of the legs by a screw (Fig. 11). The measurement is made as with ordinary calipers; then the leaf is locked to the leg. The legs may then be opened or closed as needed to clear the obstruction, then brought back and locked to the leaf again, therefore restoring them to the original setting.

A different type of caliper is the *hermaphrodite* (sometimes called the odd-leg caliper). This caliper has one straight leg ending in a sharp point, sometimes removable, and one bow leg. The hermaphrodite caliper is used chiefly for locating the center of a shaft or for locating a shoulder.

Using Calipers

A caliper is usually used in one of two ways. Either the caliper is set to the dimension of the work and the dimension transferred to a scale, or the caliper is set on a scale and the work machined until it checks with the dimension set up on the caliper. To adjust a caliper to a scale dimension, one leg of the caliper should be held firmly against one end of the scale and the other leg adjusted to the desired dimension. To adjust a caliper to the work, open the legs wider than the work and then bring them down to the work.

Caution: Never place a caliper on work that is revolving in a machine.

MEASURING THE DIAMETER OF ROUND OR THE THICKNESS OF FLAT STOCK. To measure the diameter of round stock, or the thickness of flat stock, adjust the *outside caliper* so that you feel a slight drag as you pass it over the stock (*see* Fig. 12). After the proper "feel" has been attained, measure the setting of the caliper with a rule. In reading the measurement, sight over the leg of the caliper after making sure the caliper is set squarely with the face of the rule.

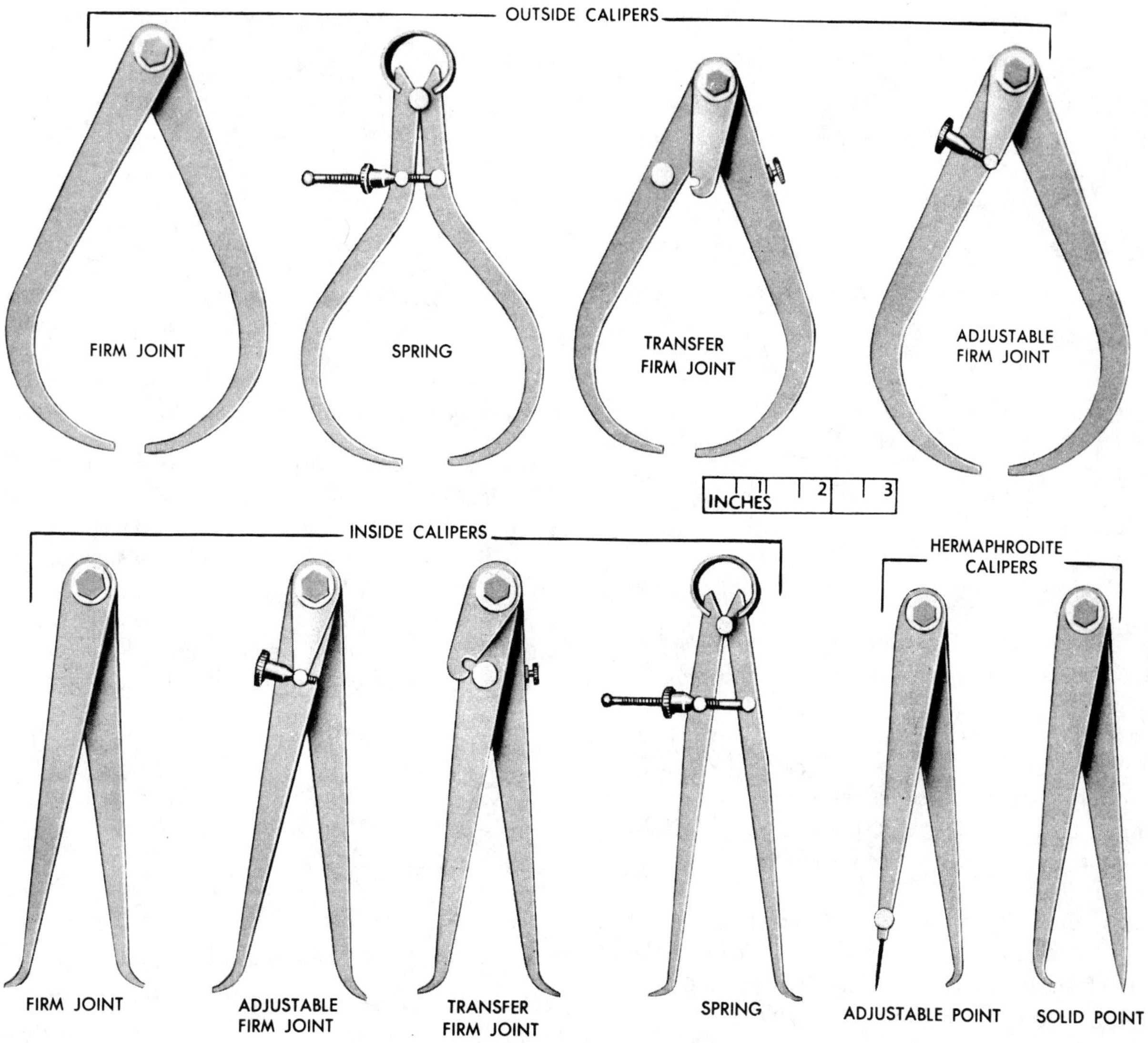

OUTSIDE CALIPERS
FIRM JOINT
SPRING
TRANSFER FIRM JOINT
ADJUSTABLE FIRM JOINT
INCHES 1 2 3
INSIDE CALIPERS
FIRM JOINT
ADJUSTABLE FIRM JOINT
TRANSFER FIRM JOINT
SPRING
HERMAPHRODITE CALIPERS
ADJUSTABLE POINT
SOLID POINT

Figure 11. Simple (noncalibrated) calipers.

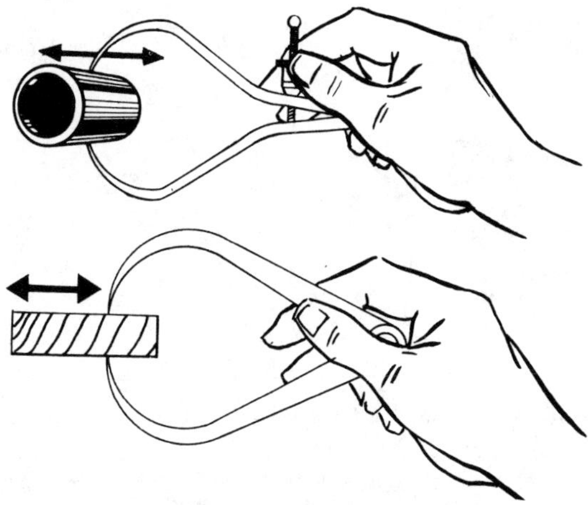

Figure 12. Using outside caliper.

MEASURING HARD-TO-REACH DIMENSIONS. To measure an almost inaccessible outside dimension, such as the thickness of the bottom of a cup, use an *outside transfer firm-joint caliper*, as shown in Fig. 13. When the proper "feel" is obtained, tighten the lock joint. Then loosen the binding nut and open the caliper enough to remove it from the cup. Close the caliper again and tighten the binding nut to seat in the slot at the end of the auxiliary arm. The caliper is now at the original setting, representing the thickness of the bottom of the cup. The caliper setting can now be measured with a rule.

To measure a hard-to-reach inside dimension, such as the internal groove shown in Fig. 14, a *lock-joint*

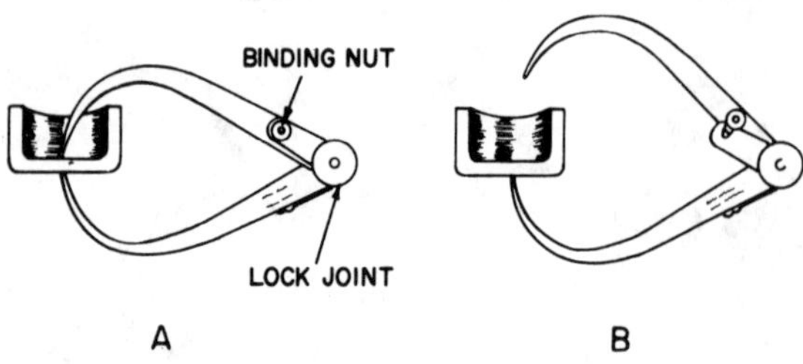

Figure 13. Measuring thickness of bottom of a cup.

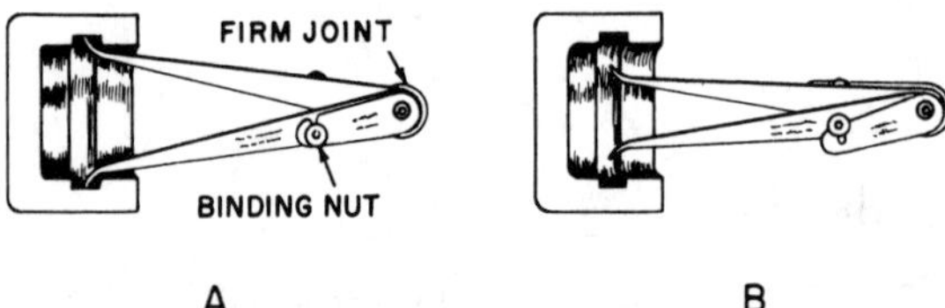

Figure 14. Measuring hard to reach inside dimension with an inside caliper.

inside caliper should be used. The procedure followed for measuring a hard-to-reach outside dimension is used.

MEASURING THE DISTANCE BETWEEN TWO SURFACES. To measure the distance between two surfaces with an *inside caliper,* first set the caliper to the approximate distance being measured (Fig. 15). Hold the caliper with one leg in contact with one of the surfaces being measured. Then, as you increase the setting of the caliper, move the other leg from left to right. Feel for the slight drag indicating the proper setting of the caliper. Then remove the caliper and measure the setting with a rule.

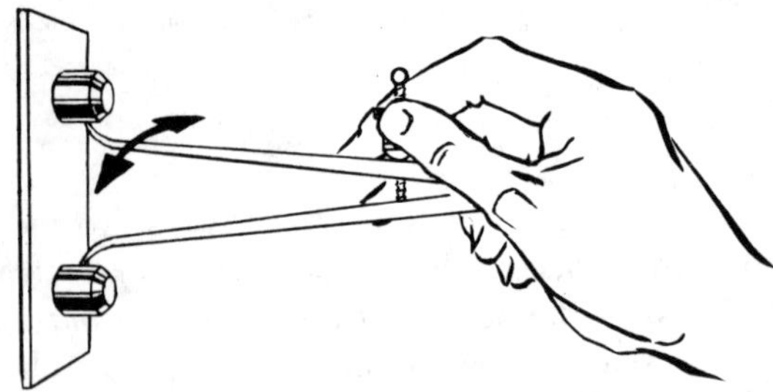

Figure 15. Measuring distance between two surfaces with an inside caliper.

MEASURING HOLE DIAMETERS. To measure the diameter of a hole with an inside caliper, hold the caliper with one leg in contact with one side of the hole (Fig. 16) and, as you increase the setting, move the other leg from left to right, and in and out of the hole. When you have found the point of largest diameter, remove the caliper and measure the caliper setting with a rule.

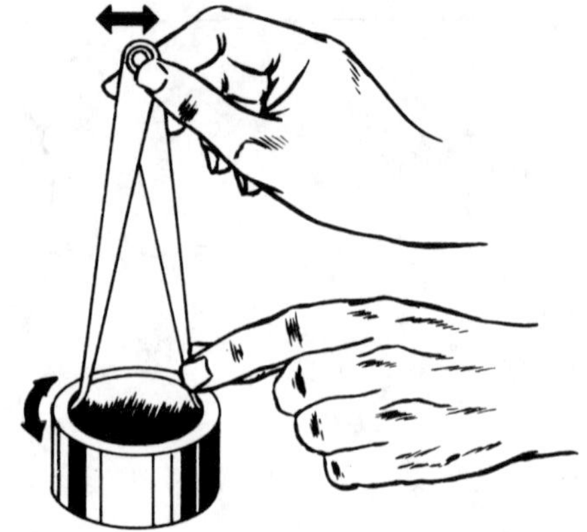

Figure 16. Measuring inside diameter with an inside caliper.

SETTING A COMBINATION FIRM-JOINT CALIPER. To set a combination firm-joint caliper with a rule, when the legs are in position for outside measurements, grasp the caliper with both hands, as shown in A, Fig. 17, and adjust both legs to the approximate setting. By adjusting both legs, the shape of the tool will be approximately symmetrical. Thus, it will maintain its balance and be easier to handle.

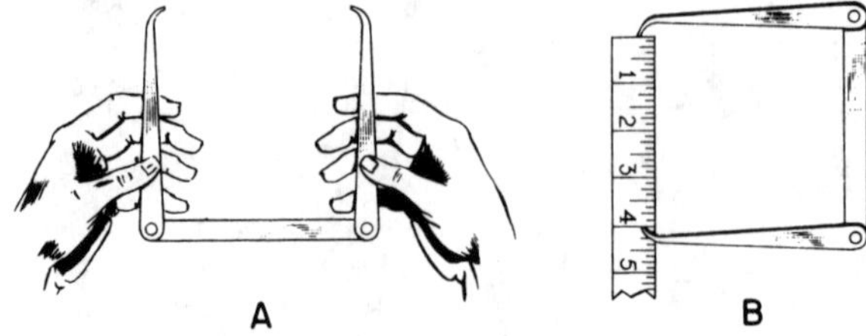

Figure 17. Setting a combination firm-joint caliper.

Check this approximate setting as shown in B, Fig. 17. Sight squarely across the leg at the graduations on the rule to get the exact setting required.

If it is necessary to decrease or increase the setting, tap one leg of the caliper, as shown in Fig. 18. The arrow indicates the change in setting that will take place.

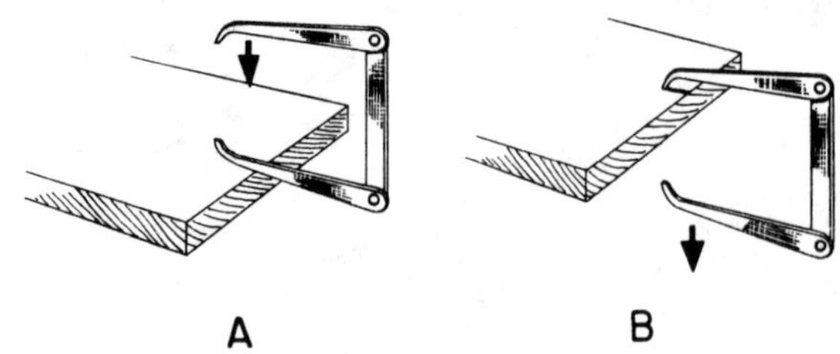

Figure 18. Decreasing and increasing setting of a firm-joint caliper.

When the caliper is set for inside measurements, the same directions for adjusting the setting apply. Figure 19 shows how the end of the rule and one leg of the caliper are rested on the bench top so that they are exactly even with each other when the reading is taken.

SETTING OUTSIDE AND INSIDE SPRING CALIPERS. To set a particular reading on an *outside spring caliper,* first open the caliper to the approximate setting. Then, as shown in Fig. 20, place one leg over the end of the rule, steadying it with the index finger. Make the final setting by sighting over the other leg of the caliper, squarely with the face of the rule at the reading, and turning the knurled adjusting nut until the desired setting is obtained.

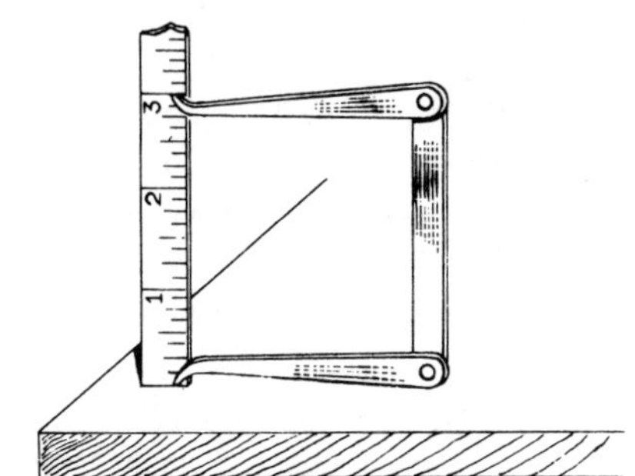

Figure 19. Setting combination firm-joint caliper for inside measurements.

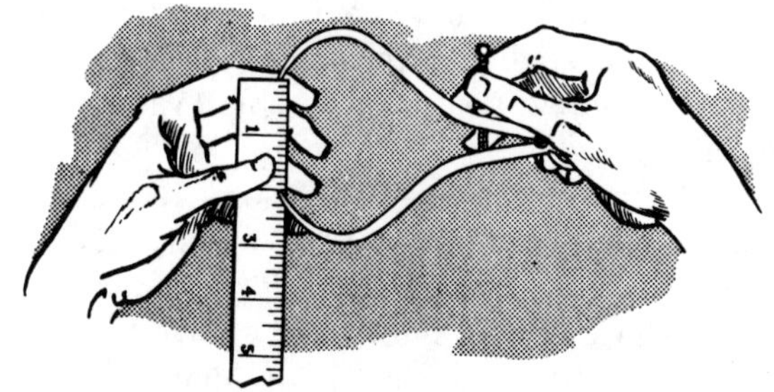

Figure 20. Setting outside spring caliper.

To set an inside spring caliper to a particular reading, place both caliper and rule on a flat surface, as shown in Fig. 21. The rule must be held squarely or normally (90 degrees in both directions) to the surface to ensure accuracy. Adjust the knurled adjusting nut, reading the setting on the rule with line of sight normal to the face of the rule at the reading.

TRANSFERRING MEASUREMENTS FROM ONE CALIPER TO ANOTHER. To transfer a measurement from one spring caliper to another, hold the calipers as shown in Fig. 22. *Note* that one finger is extended to steady the point of contact of the two lower caliper legs. In this illustration the inside caliper is being adjusted to the size of the outside caliper. As careful measurements with caliper depend on one's sense of touch ("feel") calipers are best held lightly. When a slight drag is noticed, the caliper is at the proper setting.

Figure 21. Setting inside spring caliper.

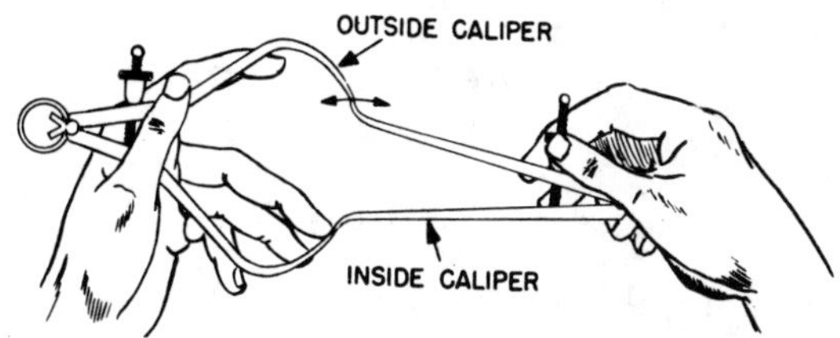

Figure 22. Transferring measurement from an outside to an inside caliper.

Care of Calipers

Keep calipers clean and lightly oiled, but do not overoil the joint of firm-joint calipers or you may have difficulty in keeping them tight. Do not throw them around or use them for screwdrivers or pry bars. Even a slight force may spring the legs of a caliper so that other measurements made with it are never accurate. Remember, calipers are measuring instruments and must be used only for the purpose for which they are intended.

Slide Calipers

The main disadvantage of using ordinary calipers is that they do not give a direct reading of a caliper setting. As explained previously, you must measure a caliper setting with a rule. To overcome this disadvantage, use slide calipers (Fig. 23). This instrument is sometimes called a caliper rule.

Slide calipers can be used for measuring outside, inside, and other dimensions. One side of the caliper is used as a measuring rule, while the scale on the opposite side is used in measuring outside and inside dimensions. Graduations on both scales are in inches and fractions thereof. A locking screw is incorporated to hold the slide caliper jaws in position during use. Stamped on the frame are two words, "IN" and "OUT," which are used in reading the scale while making inside and outside measurements, respectively.

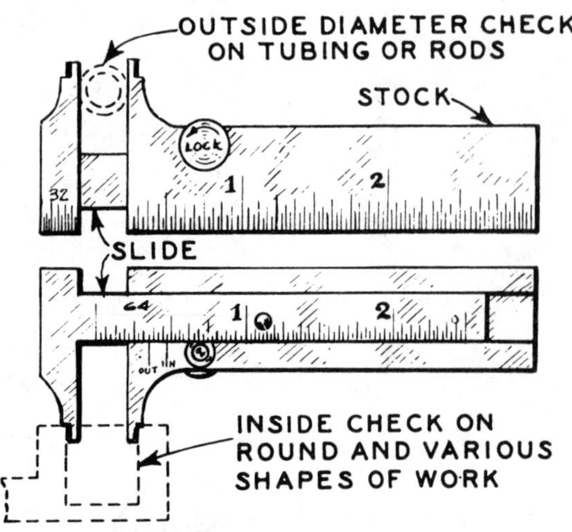

Figure 23. Pocket slide or caliper rule.

To measure the *outside diameter* of round stock, or the thickness of flat stock, move the jaws of the caliper into firm contact with the surface of the stock. Read the measurement at the reference line stamped OUT (Fig. 24).

When measuring the *inside diameter* of a hole, or the distance between two surfaces, insert only the rounded tips of the caliper jaws into the hole or between the two surfaces (Fig. 25). Read the measurement on the reference line stamped IN.

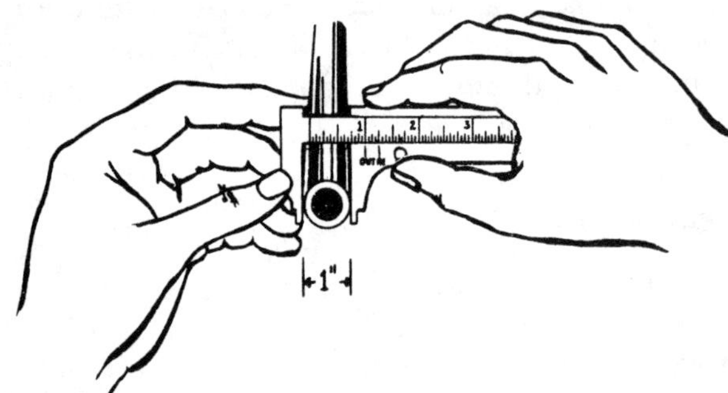

Figure 24. Measuring outside dimension with a pocket slide caliper.

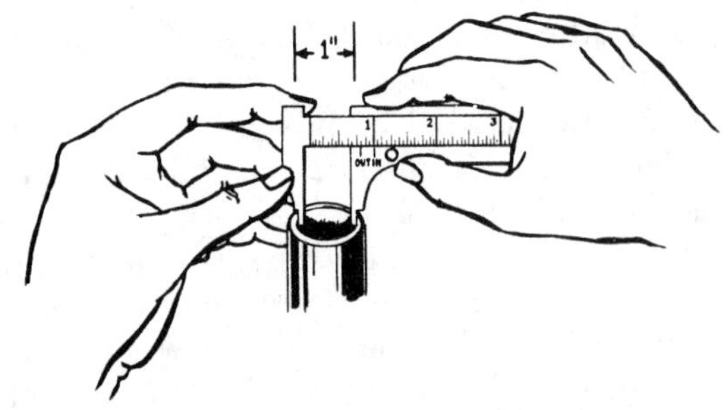

Figure 25. Measuring inside dimension with a slide caliper.

Note that two reference lines are needed if the caliper is to measure both outside and inside dimensions, and that they are separated by an amount equal to the outside dimension of the rounded tips when the caliper is closed.

Pocket models of *slide calipers* are commonly made in 3- and 5-in. sizes and are graduated to read in 32nds and 64ths. Pocket slide calipers are valuable when extreme precision is not required. They are frequently used for duplicating work when the expense of fixed gages is not warranted.

Vernier Caliper

A *vernier caliper* (Fig. 26) consists of an L-shaped member with a scale engraved on the long shank. A sliding member is free to move on the bar and carries a jaw which matches the arm of an L. The vernier scale is engraved on a small plate that is attached to the sliding member.

The most distinct advantage of the vernier caliper, over other types of calipers, is its ability to provide very accurate measurements over a large range. It can be used for both internal and external surfaces. *Pocket models* usually measure from zero to 3 inches, but sizes are available all the way to 4 feet. In using the vernier caliper, you must be able to read a vernier scale.

Principles of the Vernier Scale. It would be possible to etch graduations 1/1000 inch (0.001 in.) apart on a steel rule or sliding caliper, as shown in Fig. 27. The enlarged illustration shows two graduated scales; the top scale has divisions which are 0.025 inches apart, and the small sliding lower scale has 25 divisions, each equal to 0.001 inch graduations which can divide any of the main scale divisions of 0.025 inch into 25 parts. When the first graduation marked "0" on this small scale aligns with a graduation on the main scale, the last or 25th will also align with a graduation on the main scale as shown in Fig. 27. Therefore, the small 0.00 graduations are not significant in this position. But when the zero graduation does not align with a graduation on the main scale, it can be readily determined how many thousandths the zero missed the 0.025 inch graduation by counting the misaligned graduation at either end of the small scale. When the zero or index line on the sliding scale does not quite reach the graduation, the amount of misalignment must be subtracted, but when it passes the 0.025 graduation from which the reading is made, it must be added. This illustrates the simple arrangement to increase

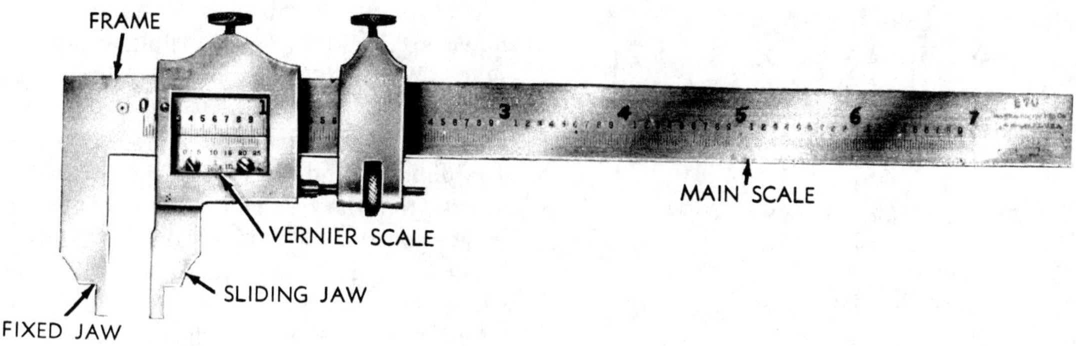

Figure 26. Vernier caliper.

the accuracy of a common scale. Unfortunately, the 0.001 inch graduations are not too legible and so the system is not practical. A vernier arrangement overcomes this problem.

VERNIER SCALE ARRANGEMENT. The main difference between the vernier scale and the arrangement shown in Fig. 27 is the spacing of the 25 divisions. Instead of 25 graduations crowded within the space of one main scale division, the vernier graduations are arranged at intervals exactly 0.001 inch less than the main scale graduations as shown in Fig. 28. This arrangement results in an accumulation of misalignments, starting with the first vernier graduation past the zero so that each may be marked as shown with a number representing the space in thousandths to the next upper scale graduation. *For example,* if the zero index line would be moved past the 8 inch graduation until the vernier graduation number 5 aligned with the next main scale graduation, the exact reading would be 8 inches plus 0.005 or 8.005 inches.

READING A VERNIER CALIPER. Figure 29 shows a bar 1 inch long divided by graduations into 40 parts so that each graduation indicates one-fortieth of an inch (0.025 inch). Every fourth graduation is numbered; each number indicates tenths of an inch (4 x 0.025 inch). The vernier, which slides along the bar, is graduated into 25 divisions which together are as long as 24 divisions on the bar. Each division of the vernier is 0.001 inch smaller than each division on the bar. Verniers that are calibrated as just explained are known as English-measure verniers. The metric-measure vernier is read the same, except that the units of measurement are in millimeters.

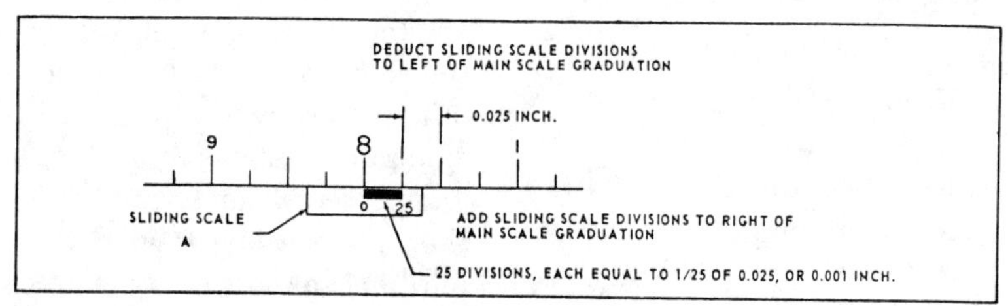

Figure 27. Vernier scale principle.

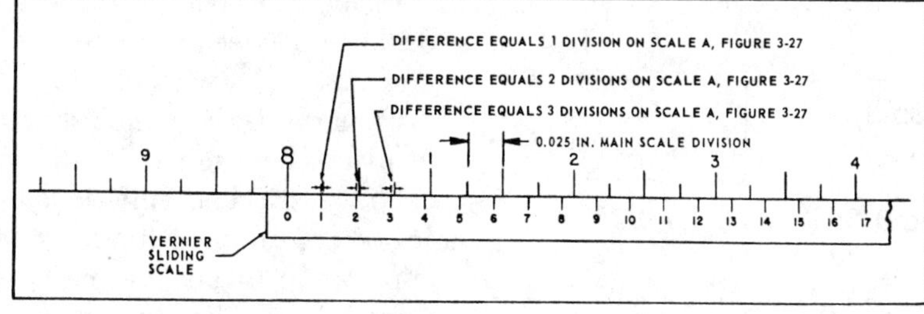

Figure 28. Expanded view of vernier scale.

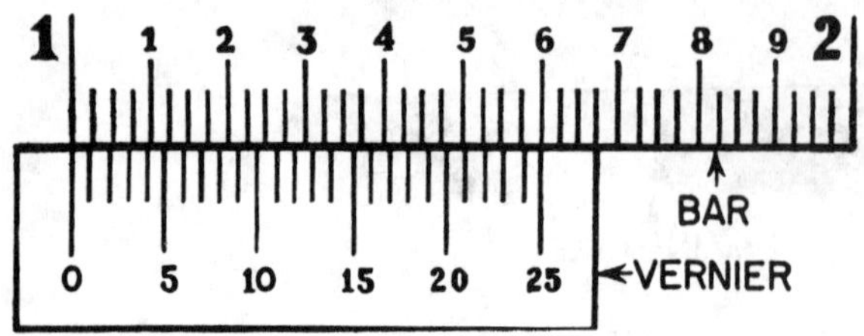

Figure 29. English measure vernier scale.

A, Fig. 30 shows the English measure vernier caliper. B, Fig. 30 shows an enlarged view of the vernier section. As you can see in the illustration, when the zero on the vernier coincides with the 1-inch mark, no other lines coincide until the 25th mark on the vernier.

To read the caliper in C, Fig. 30, write down in a column the number of inches (1.000 in.), of tenths of an inch (0.400 in.), and of thousandths of an inch that the zero mark on the vernier is from the zero mark on the rule. Because the zero mark on the vernier is a little past a 0.025 in. mark, write down the 0.025 in., and then note the highest number on the vernier where a line on the vernier coincides with one on the rule. In this case it is at the 0.011 in. line on the vernier, so you also write the 0.011 in. in the column, which will then look like the following.

1.000 in.
.400 in.
.025 in.
.011 in.
———
1.436 in.

The reading on the caliper shown in C, Fig. 30 is 1.436 in. and was obtained by adding four separate *readings*. After a little practice you will be able to make these calculations mentally.

TABLE 3
MEASURING POINT ALLOWANCES

Size of Caliper	English Measure	Metric Measure
6" or 150 mm .	Add 0.250"...	Add 6.35 mm.
12" or 300 mm .	.300"...	7.62 mm.
24" or 600 mm .	.300"...	7.62 mm.
36" or 600 mm .	.500"...	12.70 mm.

Now try to read the settings of the two verniers shown in D and E, Fig. 30. Follow the above procedure. You should read 2.350 in. on D and 2.368 in. on E.

To read a *metric-measure vernier,* note the number of millimeters and the 0.25 millimeter, if the setting permits, that the zero on the vernier has moved from the zero on the scale. Then add the number of hundredths of a millimeter indicated by the line on the vernier that coincides with a line on the scale.

For example, A, Fig. 31 shows the zero graduation on the vernier coinciding with a 0.5-mm graduation on the scale resulting in a 38.50 mm reading. The reading in B, Fig. 31 indicates that 0.08 mm should be added to the scale reading and results in 38.00 mm + 0.50 mm + 0.08 mm = 38.58 mm.

If a vernier caliper is calibrated in either English measure or in metric measure, usually one side will be calibrated to take outside measurements and the other to take inside measurements directly. The vernier plate for inside measurements is set to compensate for the thickness of the measuring points of the tools. But if a vernier caliper is calibrated for both English and metric measure, one of the scales will appear on one side and one on the other. Then it will be necessary, when taking inside measurements over the measuring points, to add certain amounts to allow for their thickness. *For example,* Table 3 shows the amounts to be added for various sizes of vernier calipers.

OUTSIDE SURFACE MEASUREMENTS. To measure the distance between outside surfaces or the outside diameter of round stock with a vernier caliper, steady the stock with one hand and hold the caliper in the other, as shown in Fig. 32. In the illustration, the clamping screws are at A and B; the horizontal adjusting screw nut is at C. With A and B loose, slide the movable jaw toward the piece being measured until it is almost in contact. Then tighten A to make C operative. With C, adjust the movable jaw to the proper feel and secure the setting with B. The reading can then be taken as previously explained.

INSIDE SURFACE MEASUREMENTS. To measure the distance between inside surfaces, or the inside diameter of a hole, with a vernier caliper, use the scale marked *inside.* Figure 33 shows the measuring points in place. Remember that if you are using a vernier caliper with both metric and English scales, the scales appear on opposite sides of the caliper and apply only to outside measurements. Then, to get correct inside measurements, you add to the actual reading the measuring point allowance for the size

Figure 30. Vernier caliper and enlarged vernier divisions.

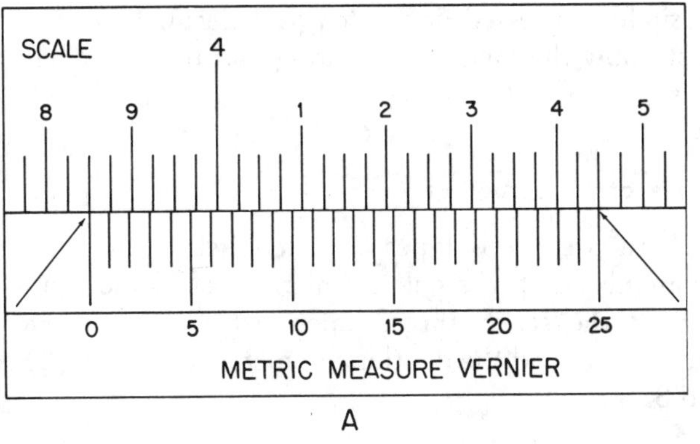

A

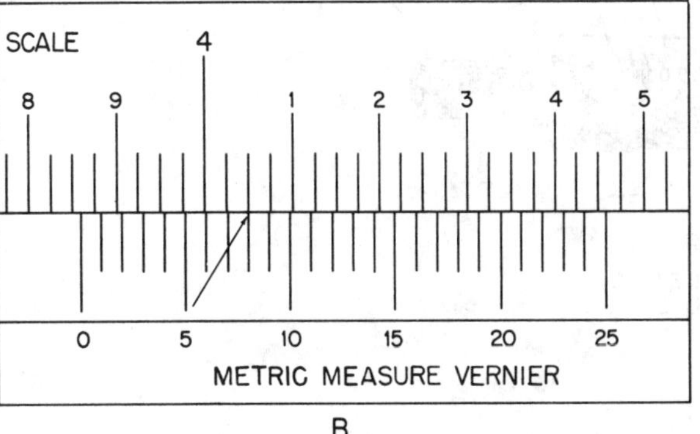

B

Figure 31. Metric-measure vernier scales.

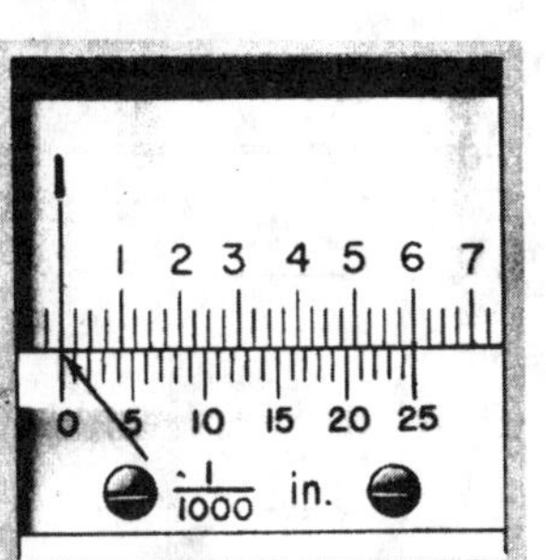

B

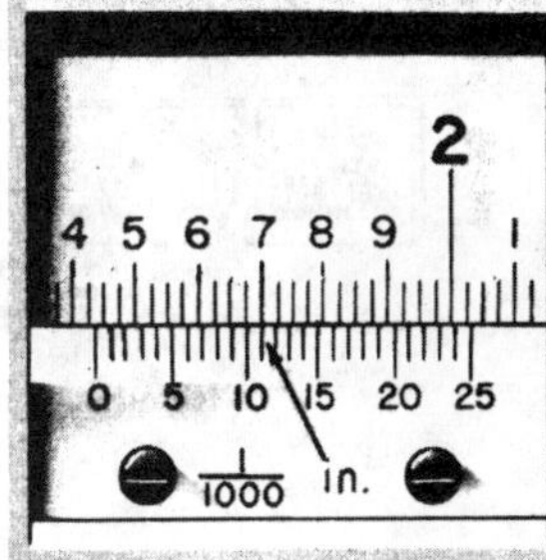

C

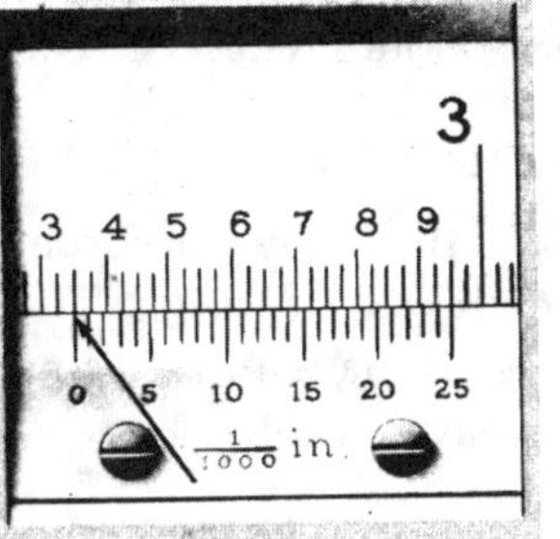

D

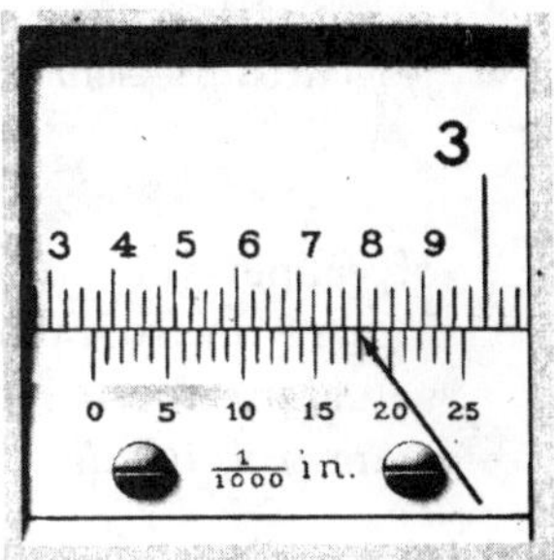

E

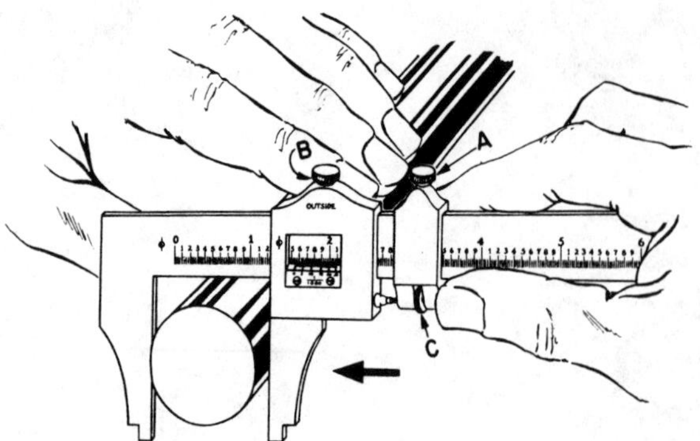

Figure 32. Measuring outside diameter with a vernier caliper.

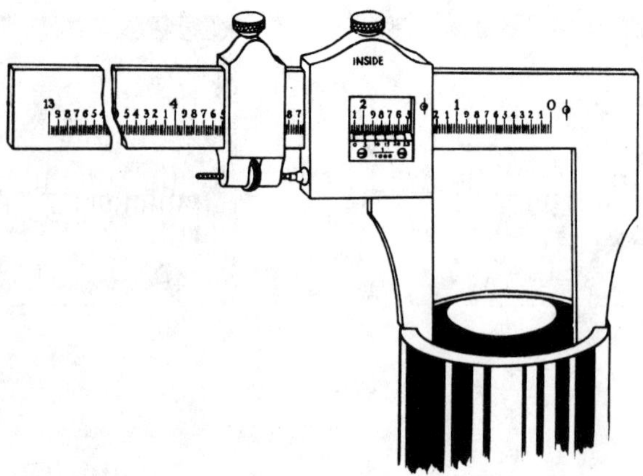

Figure 33. Measuring inside diameter with a vernier caliper.

of caliper you are using. Take this allowance from Table 3, or from the manufacturer's instructions. The actual measurement in this case is made in the same manner as taking an outside measurement.

Care of Vernier Calipers

The inside faces of the jaws and the outside of the tips must be treated with great care. If they become worn, or the jaws bent, the tool will no longer give accurate readings. The accuracy of vernier calipers should be checked periodically by measuring an object of known dimension. Vernier calipers can be adjusted when they are not accurate, but the manufacturer's recommendations for this adjustment must be followed. Keep vernier calipers lightly oiled to prevent rust and keep them stored away from heavy tools.

Micrometers

In much wider use than the vernier caliper is the micrometer commonly called the *mike*. It is important that a person who is working with machinery or in a machine shop thoroughly understands the mechanical principles, construction, use, and care of the micrometer. Figure 34 shows an *outside micrometer caliper* with the various parts clearly indicated. Micrometers are used to measure distances to the nearest one thousandth of an inch. The measurement is usually expressed or written as a decimal; so you must know the method of writing and reading decimals.

Types of Micrometers

There are three types of micrometers that are commonly used: the outside micrometer caliper (including the screw thread micrometer), the inside micrometer, and the depth micrometer. (*See* Figs. 34 and 35.)

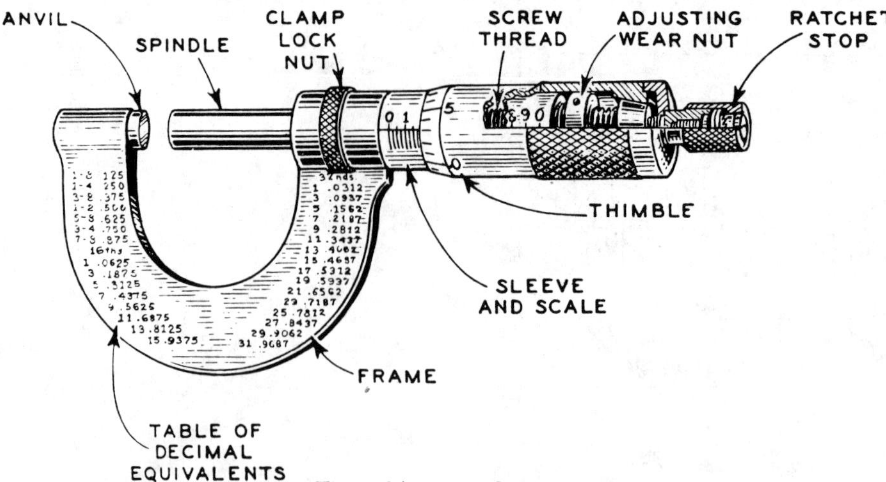

Figure 34. Nomenclature of outside micrometer.

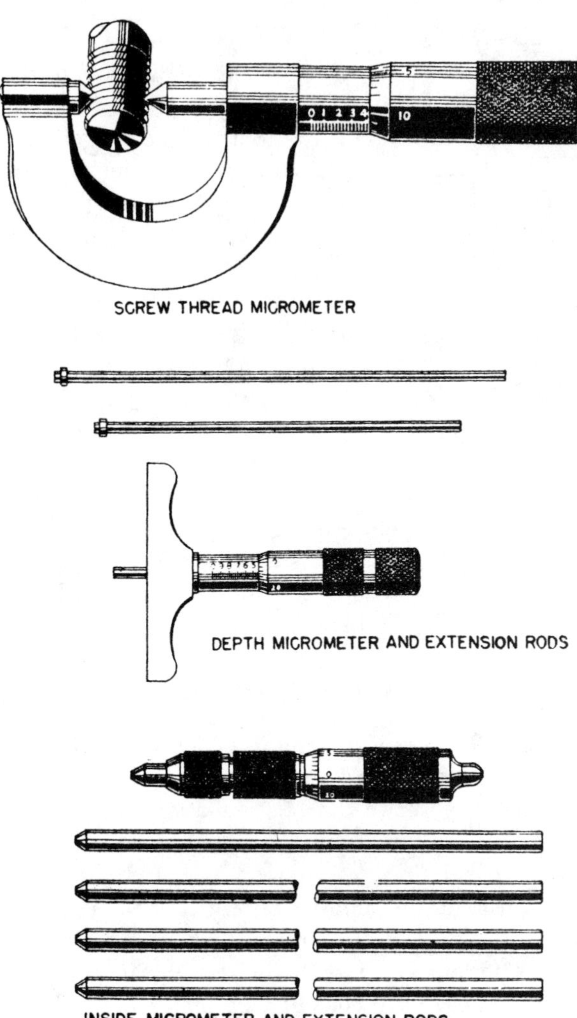

Figure 35. Types of micrometers.

The *outside micrometer* is used for measuring outside dimensions, such as the diameter of a piece of round stock. The *screw thread micrometer* is used to determine the pitch diameter of screws. The *inside micrometer* is used for measuring inside dimensions, as for example, the inside diameter of a tube or hole, the bore of a cylinder or the width of a recess. The *depth micrometer* is used for measuring the depth of holes or recesses.

Selecting the Proper Micrometer

The types of micrometers commonly used are made so that the longest movement possible between the spindle and the anvil is one inch. This movement is called the *range*. The frames of micrometers, however, are available in a wide variety of sizes, from one inch up to as large as 24 inches. The range of a one inch micrometer is from 0 to 1 inch. In other words, it can be used on work where the part to be measured is one inch or less. A two inch micrometer has a range of from 1 to 2 inches, and will measure only work between one and two inches thick; a six inch micrometer has a range of from 5 to 6 inches, and will measure only work between five and six inches thick. It is necessary, therefore, when you are selecting a micrometer, that you first find the approximate size of the work to the nearest inch, and then select a micrometer that will fit it. *For example*, to find the exact diameter of a piece of round stock, use a rule and find the approximate diameter of the stock. If it is found to be approximately 3 1/4 inches, a micrometer with a 3 to 4 inch range would be required to measure the exact diameter. Similarly, with inside and depth micrometers, rods of suitable lengths must be fitted into the tool to get the approximate dimension within an inch, after which the exact measurement is read by turning the thimble. The size of a micrometer indicates the size of the largest work it will measure.

READING A MICROMETER CALIPER. The sleeve and thimble scales of the micrometer caliper have been enlarged in Fig. 36. To understand these scales, you need to know that the threaded section on the spindle, which revolves, has 40 threads per inch. Therefore, every time the thimble completes a revolution, the spindle advances or recedes 1/40 inch (0.025 inch).

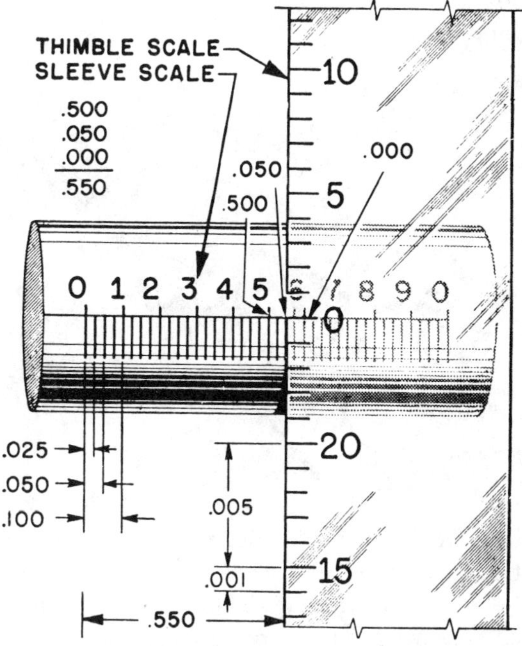

Figure 36. Enlarged sleeve and thimble scales of a micrometer.

Note in the illustration that the horizontal line on the sleeve is divided into 40 equal parts per inch. Every fourth graduation is numbered 1, 2, 3, 4, and so on, representing 0.100 in., 0.200 in., and so on. When you turn the thimble so that its edge is over the first sleeve line past the "0" on the thimble scale, the spindle has opened 0.025 in. If you turn the spindle to the second mark, it has moved to 0.025 in. plus 0.025 in. or 0.050 in. You use the scale on the thimble to complete your reading when the edge of the thimble stops between graduated lines. This scale is divided into 25 equal parts, each part representing 1/25th of a turn; and 1/25th of 0.025 in. is 0.001 in. As you can see, every fifth line on the thimble scale is marked 5, 10, 15, and so on. The thimble scale, therefore, permits you to take very accurate readings to the thousandths of an inch, and, since you can estimate between the divisions on the thimble scale, fairly accurate readings to the ten thousandth of an inch are possible.

Figure 37 will help you understand how to take a complete micrometer reading. Count the units on the thimble scale and add them to the reading on the sleeve scale. The reading in the illustration shows a sleeve reading of 0.250 in. (the thimble having stopped slightly more than halfway between 2 and 3 on the sleeve) with the 10th line on the thimble scale coinciding with the horizontal sleeve line. Number 10 on this scale means that the spindle has moved away from the anvil an additional 10 x 0.001 or 0.010 in. Add this amount to the 0.250 in. sleeve reading, and the total distance is 0.260 in.

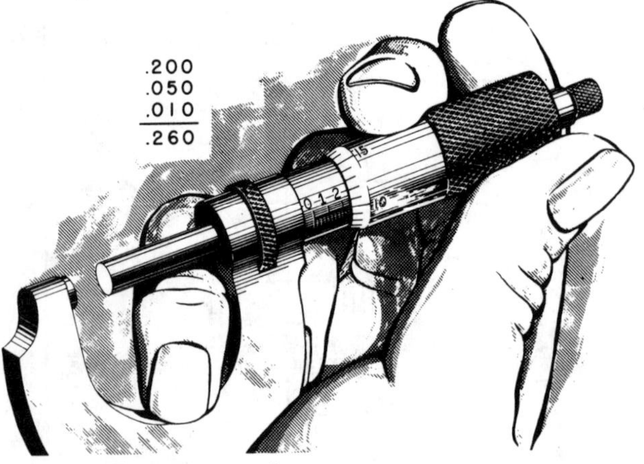

Figure 37. Reading a micrometer caliper.

Read each of the micrometer settings in Fig. 38 so that you can be sure of yourself when you begin to use this tool on the job. The correct readings are given following the figure so that you can check yourself.

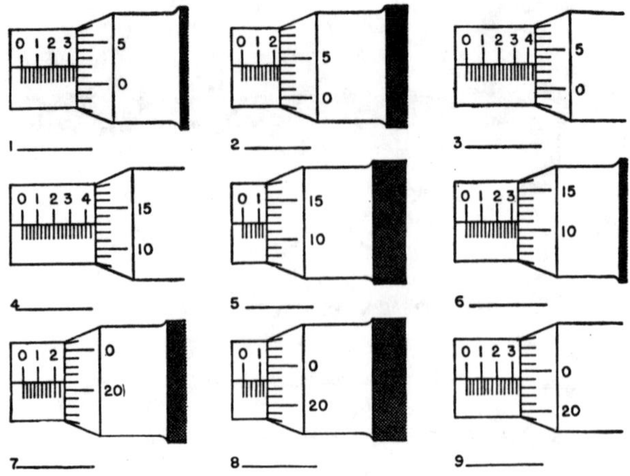

Answers for checking—

1. = 0.327	4. = 0.438	7. = 0.246
2. = 0.229	5. = 0.137	8. = 0.148
3. = 0.428	6. = 0.336	9. = 0.349

Figure 38. Micrometer-reading exercises.

Figure 39 shows a reading in which the horizontal line falls between two graduations on the thimble scale and is closer to the 15 graduation than it is to the 14. To read this to *three* decimal places, see Fig. 39 and calculation A. To read it to *four* decimal places estimate the number of tenths of the distance between thimble-scale graduations the horizontal line has fallen. Each tenth of this distance equals one ten-thousandth (0.0001) of an inch. Add the ten-thousandths to the reading as shown in the calculations of B, Fig. 39.

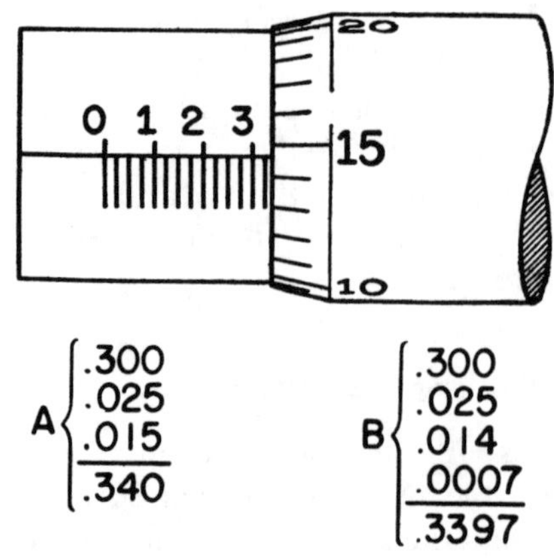

Figure 39. Interpolating a micrometer reading.

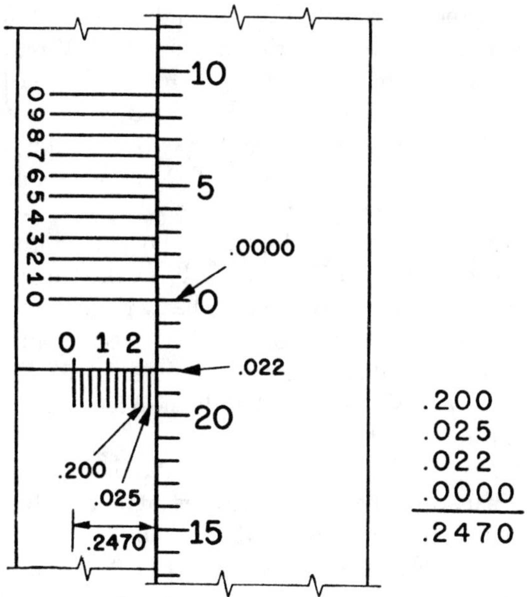

Figure 40. Vernier scale on a micrometer.

READING A VERNIER MICROMETER CALIPER. When working under exceptionally precise dimensions, use a micrometer that is accurate to ten-thousandths of an inch. This degree of accuracy is obtained by the addition of a vernier scale. Figure 40 shows a vernier scale on a micrometer that furnishes the fine readings between the lines on the thimble rather than making you estimate. The 10 spaces on the vernier are equivalent to 9 spaces on the thimble. Therefore, each unit on the vernier scale is equal to 0.0009 in. and the difference between the sizes of the units on each scale is 0.0001 in.

When a line on the thimble scale does not coincide with the horizontal sleeve line, you can determine the additional space beyond the readable thimble mark by finding which vernier mark coincides with a line on the thimble scale. Add this number, as that many ten-thousandths of an inch, to the original reading. *Note* in Fig. 41 how the second line on the vernier scale coincides with a line on the thimble scale.

This means that the 0.011 mark on the thimble scale has been advanced an additional 0.0002 in. beyond the horizontal sleeve line. When you add this to the other readings, the reading will be 0.200 + 0.075 + 0.011 + 0.0002, or 0.2862 in., as shown in Fig. 41.

MEASURING HOLE DIAMETERS WITH AN INSIDE MICROMETER CALIPER. To measure the diameter of small holes from 0.2 to 1 inch in diameter, an inside micrometer caliper of the jaw-type, as shown in A,

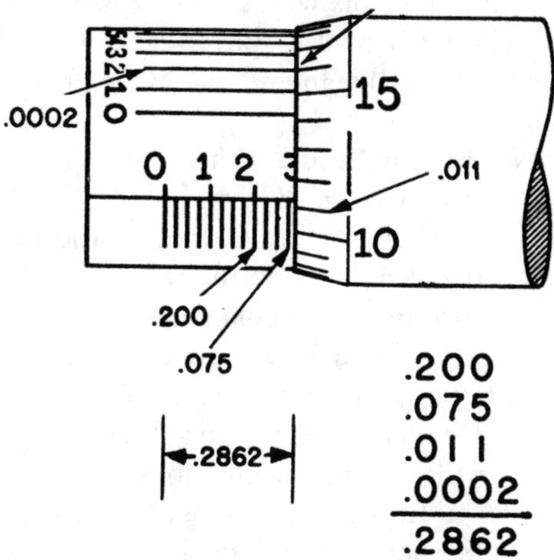

Figure 41. Reading a vernier micrometer caliper.

Fig. 42, may be used. *Note* that the figures on both the thimble and the barrel are reversed, increasing in the opposite direction from those on an outside micrometer caliper. This is because this micrometer reads inside measurements. Therefore, as you turn the thimble clockwise on this micrometer, the measuring surfaces move farther apart and the reading increases. (On an outside micrometer caliper, as you turn the thimble clockwise, the measuring surfaces move closer together and the reading decreases.)

For holes from two inches up to several feet in diameter, select the inside micrometer having extension rods whose range includes the required dimension. The extension rod marked 6-7, *for example,* when inserted into the head of the micrometer, will measure inside diameters from 6 to 7 inches. The shoulder on the rod must seat properly to ensure a correct reading. For large measurements, B, Fig. 42, shows how both hands are used to set the micrometer for checking a diameter. Hold one end in place with one hand as you *feel* for the maximum possible setting by moving the other end from left to right,

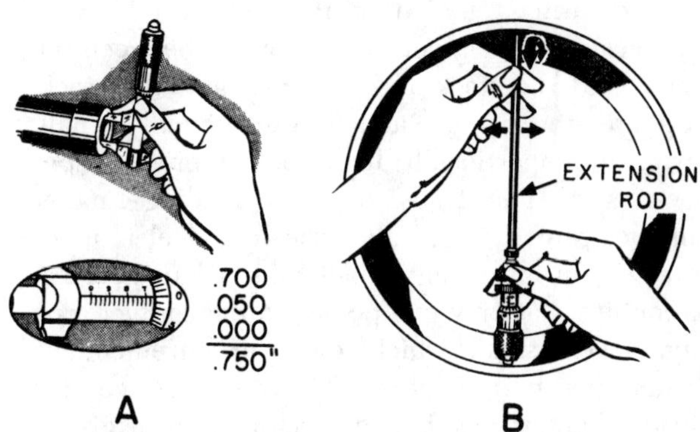

Figure 42. Measuring inside diameter with an inside caliper.

and in and out of the hole with the other hand. When no left-to-right movement is possible, and a slight drag is noticed on the in-and-out-swing, take the reading.

MEASURING ROUND STOCK. When measuring the diameter of a small piece of round stock, hold the stock to be measured in one hand. Hold the micrometer in the other hand so that the thimble rests between the thumb and the forefinger (*see* Fig. 43). The third finger is then in a position to hold the frame against the palm of the hand. The frame is supported in this manner and makes it easy to guide the work over the anvil. The thumb and forefinger are in position to turn the thimble either directly or through the ratchet and bring the spindle over against the surface being measured.

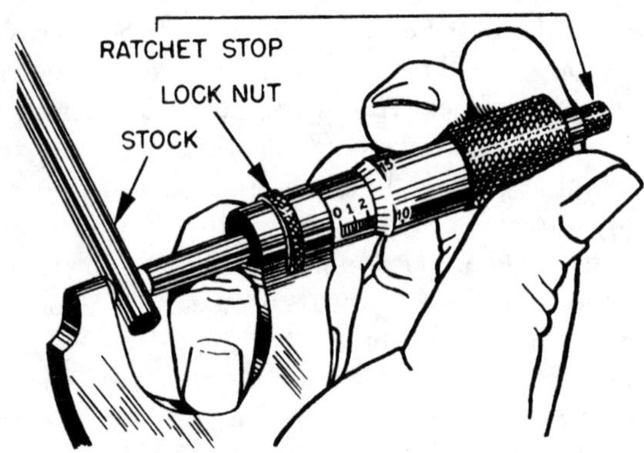

Figure 43. Measuring round stock with a micrometer caliper.

Turn the spindle down to contact by *feel,* or else use the ratchet stop. Your feel should produce the same contact pressure and therefore the same reading as that produced when the ratchet stop is used. Develop your *feel* by measuring a certain dimension both with and without the aid of the ratchet stop. When you have the correct feel, you will get the same readings by both methods.

In measuring round stock the feel must be very light because there is only a line contact between the spindle and the stock and the anvil and the stock. Therefore, the contact area is exceptionally small, causing a proportionally high contact pressure per unit of area. This tends to give a reading smaller than the true reading, unless the light feel is used. Moreover, in measuring a ball from a ball bearing, the contact is at only two points, so the contact area is again very small, which results in a tremendous pressure per unit of area. This condition requires only the lightest possible contact pressure to give a true reading.

Hold the micrometer lightly and for only as long as is necessary to make the measurement. Wrapping the hand around it or holding it for too long a time will cause expansion of the metal and will introduce errors in measurement. Read the setting on the thimble scale (if the object is small) without removing the micrometer caliper from the object.

MEASURING A FLAT SURFACE. When *measuring* a *flat surface* with a micrometer caliper, the entire area of both the anvil and the spindle is in contact with the surface being measured. This causes a proportionally low contact pressure per unit of area. Therefore the *feel* should be slightly heavier than when measuring round stock.

On *large flat work,* it is necessary to have the work stationary and positioned to permit access for the micrometer. The proper method of holding a micrometer when checking a part too large to be held in one hand is shown in Fig. 44. The frame is held by one hand to position it and to locate it square to the measured surface. The other hand operates the thimble either directly or through the ratchet. A large, flat surface should be measured in several places to determine the amount of variation. It is good practice to lock the spindle in place with the locknut before removing the micrometer from the part being measured. After removal of the micrometer the measurement indicated on the thimble scale can then be read.

To retain a particular setting, in cases where several pieces are to be gaged, lock the spindle in place with the locknut. When a piece is *gaged* with a micrometer whose spindle is locked to a particular setting, the piece can quickly be identified as oversize, correct size, or undersize.

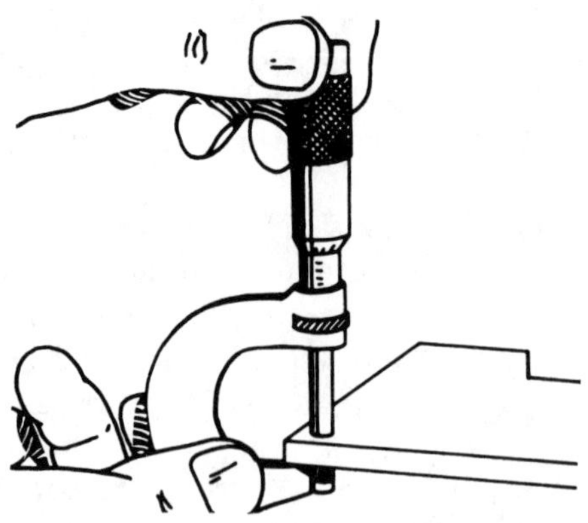

Figure 44. Measuring flat stock with a micrometer caliper.

Care of Micrometers

Keep micrometers clean and lightly oiled. Make sure they are placed in a case or box when they are not in use. Anvil faces must be protected from damage and must not be cleaned with emery cloth or other abrasive.

Squares

Squares are primarily used for testing and checking trueness of an angle or for laying out lines on materials. Most squares have a rule marked on their edge. As a result they may also be used for measuring. There are several types of squares commonly used.

Carpenter's Square

The size of a carpenter's steel square is usually 12 inches x 8 inches, 24 inches x 16 inches, or 24 inches x 18 inches. The flat sides of the blade and the tongue are graduated in inches and fractions of an inch. (The square also contains information that helps to simplify or eliminate the need for computations in many woodworking tasks.) The most common uses for this square are laying out and squaring up large patterns, and for testing the flatness and squareness of large surfaces. Squaring is accomplished by placing the square at right angles to adjacent surfaces and observing if light shows between the work and the square.

One type of carpenter's square (framing) has additional tables engraved on the square. With the framing square, the craftsman can perform calculations rapidly and lay out rafters, oblique joints, and stairs.

Try Square

The *try square* (Fig. 45) consists of two parts at right angles to each other—a thick wood or iron stock and a thin steel blade. Most try squares are made with the blades graduated in inches and fractions of an inch. The blade length varies from 2 inches to 12 inches. This square is used for setting or checking lines or surfaces which have to be at right angles to each other.

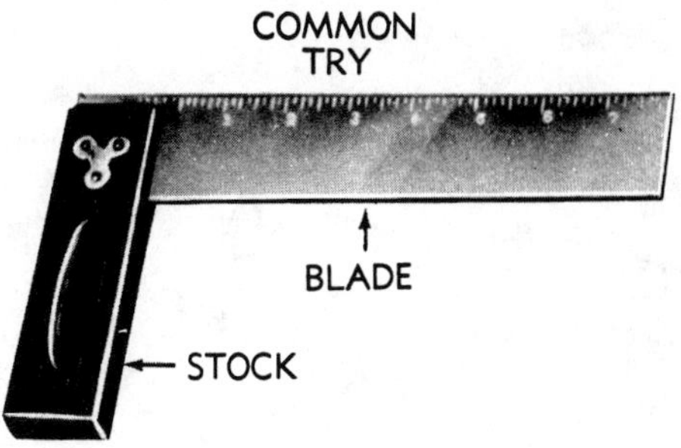

Figure 45. Try square.

Sliding T-Bevel

The *sliding T-bevel* (Fig. 46) is an adjustable try square with a slotted beveled blade. Blades are normally six or eight inches long. The sliding T-bevel is used for laying out angles other than right angles, and for testing constructed angles such as bevels. These squares are made with either wood or metal handles.

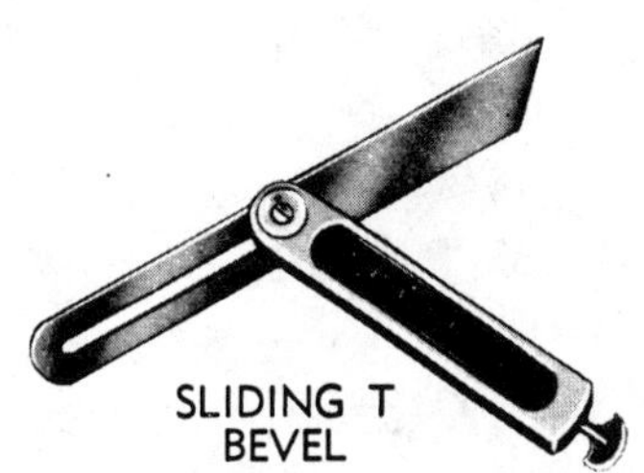

Figure 46. Sliding T-bevel.

Adjustments. To adjust a sliding T-bevel to a desired setting, loosen the blade screw, at the round end of the handle, just enough to permit the blade to slide along its slot and to rotate with slight friction.

To set the blade at a 45-degree angle, hold the handle against a framing square as shown in A, Fig. 47, with the blade intersecting equal graduations on the tongue and blade of the square; or hold the bevel against the edges of a 45-degree drafting triangle, as shown in B, Fig. 47. When using drafting triangles for setting a sliding T-bevel, different size triangles must be used for each different setting. A 45-degree angle can also be set by using the squaring head of a combination set as shown in C, Fig. 47.

A sliding T-bevel can be set to any desired angle by using a protractor. Loosen the blade screw as before, and hold the bevel with the blade passing through the graduation selected and the center of the protractor as shown in D, Fig. 47.

Constructed Angle Verification. To test a chamfer or bevel for trueness, set the T-bevel to the required angle, and hold the handle to the working face of the stock being tested. Face a source of light,

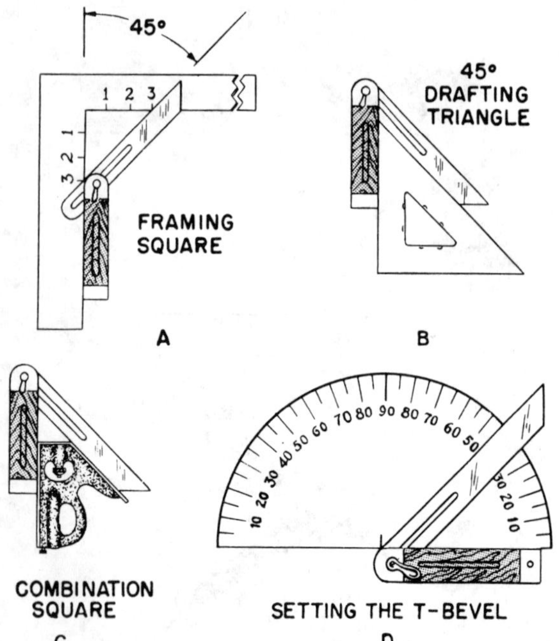

Figure 47. Adjusting sliding T-bevel to a desired setting.

and with the blade brought into contact with the surface to be tested, pass the blade along the length of the surface (Fig. 48). The appearance of light between the blade and the surface of the stock indicates where the angle is not correct. Figure 48 indicates the checking of a bevel, but testing the trueness of a chamfer is accomplished in the same way.

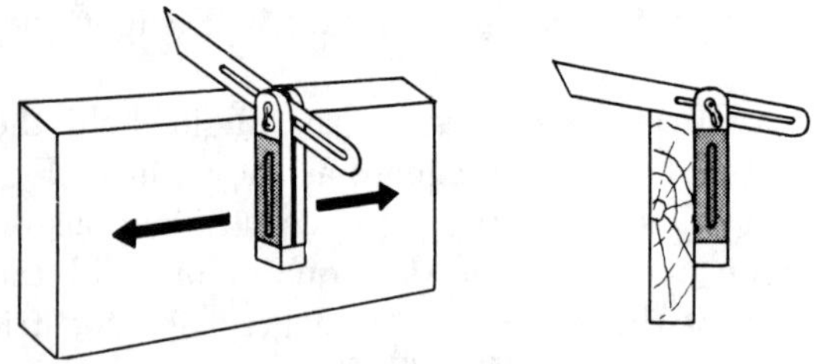
Figure 48. Testing trueness of a bevel.

Combination Square

A combination square is equipped with moving heads called a *square head, protractor head,* and a *center head.* These combine the functions of several tools, and serve a wide variety of purposes. (*See* Figs. 49 and 50.) Normally only one head is used at a time.

The *square head* may be adjusted to any position along the scale and clamped securely in place. The combination square can thus serve as a depth gage, height gage, or scribing gage. Two of the faces of the head are ground at right angles to each other, and a third face at 45 degrees. A small spirit level is built into the head for checking whether surfaces are plumb, and a small scriber is housed in a hole in the end of the head for marking layout lines.

The *center head* can be slid onto the blade in place of the square head. This is a V-shaped member so designed that the center of the 90-degree V will lie exactly along one edge of the blade. This attachment is useful when locating the exact center of round stock.

The *protractor head,* commonly called a bevel protractor, can be attached to the scale, adjusted to any position on it, and turned and locked at any desired angle. Angular graduations usually read from 0 to 180 degrees both ways, permitting the supplement of the angle to be read. A spirit level may be included on some models, forming, in effect, an adjustable level to show any required degree.

Care of Squares

Make certain that the blades, heads, dials, and all accessories are clean. Apply a light coat of oil on all metal surfaces to prevent rusting when not in use. *Do not* use squares for purposes other than those intended. When storing squares or bevels for long periods of time, apply a liberal amount of oil or rust-preventive compound to all surfaces, wrap in oiled paper or cloth, and place in containers or on racks away from other tools.

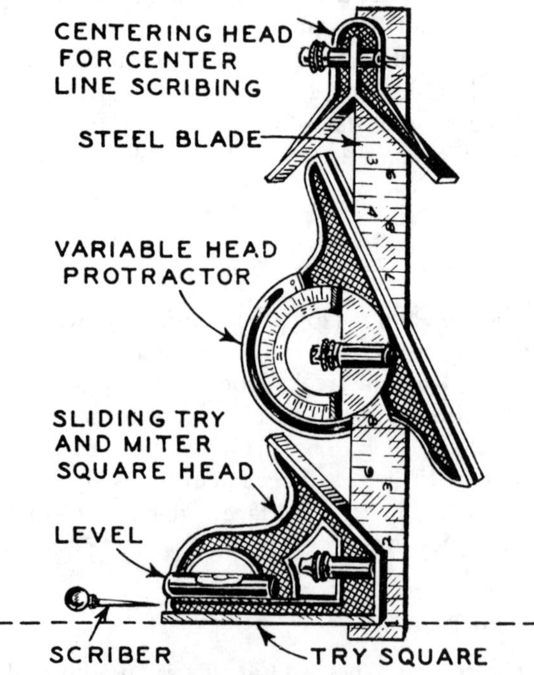

Figure 49. Combination square set.

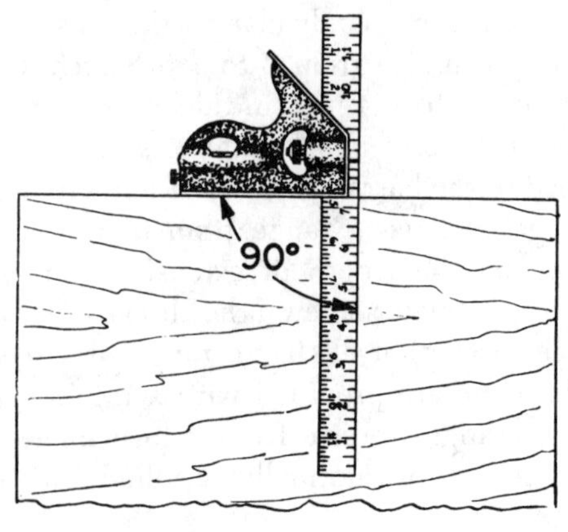

A—SQUARING A LINE ON STOCK

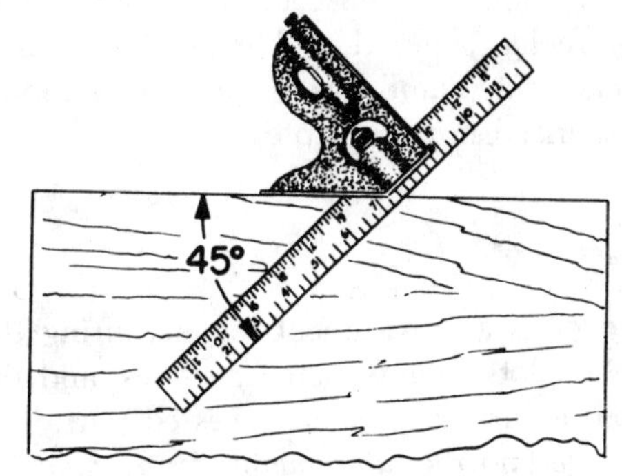

B—LAYING OUT A 45° ANGLE.

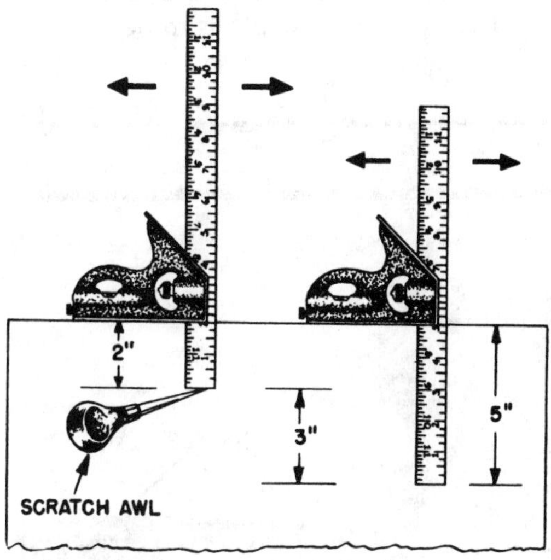

C—DRAWING PARALLEL LINES

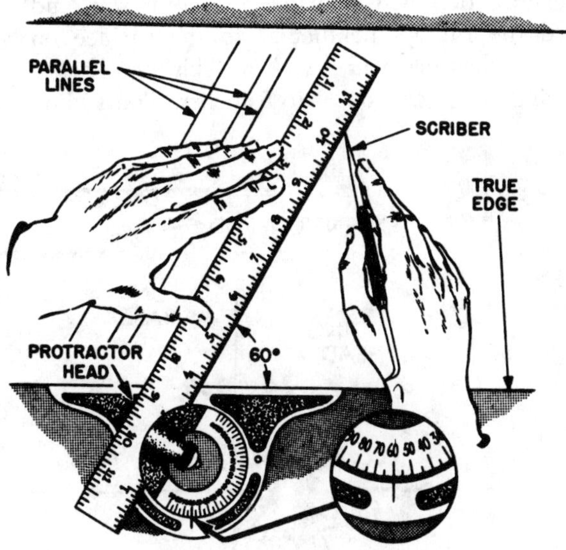

D—DRAWING ANGULAR LINES

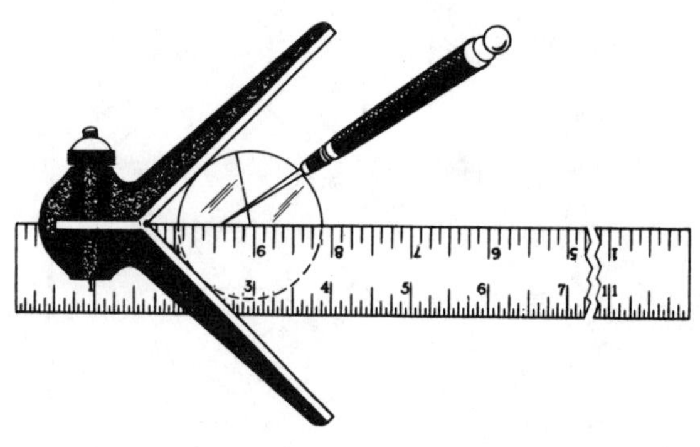

E—LOCATING A SHAFT CENTER

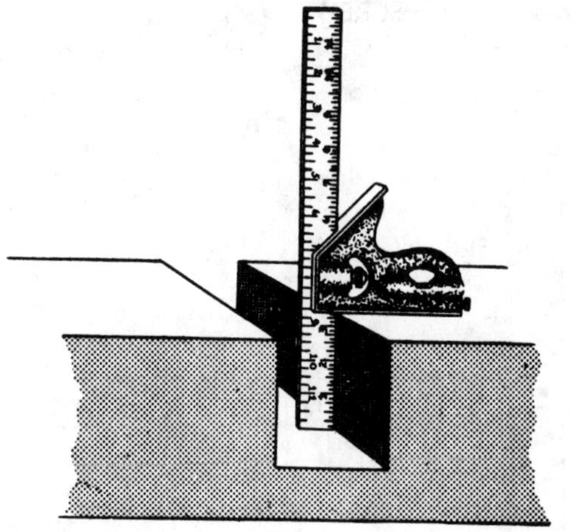

F—MEASURING THE DEPTH OF A SLOT

Figure 50. Combination square.

Miscellaneous Gages

There are a number of miscellaneous gages. The depth gage, feeler gage, thread gage, telescoping gage, dividers, and plumb bob are among some of the gages discussed in this chapter.

Depth Gage

A *depth gage* is an instrument for measuring the depth of holes, slots, counterbores, recesses, and the distance from a surface to some recessed part. The *rule depth gage* and the *micrometer depth gage* are the most commonly used (Fig. 51).

The *rule depth gage* is a graduated rule with a sliding head designed to bridge a hole or slot, and to hold the rule perpendicular to the surface on which the measurement is taken. This type has a measuring range of from 0 to 5 inches. The sliding head has a clamping screw so that it may be clamped in any position. The sliding head has a flat base which is perpendicular to the axis of the rule and ranges in size from 2 to 2 5/8 inches in width and from 1/8 to 1/4 inch in thickness.

The *micrometer depth gage* consists of a flat base attached to the barrel (sleeve) of a micrometer head. These gages have a range from 0 to 9 inches, depending on the length of extension rod used. The hollow micrometer screw (the threads on which the thimble rotates) itself has a range of either 1/2 or 1 inch. Some are provided with a ratchet stop. The flat base ranges in size from 2 to 6 inches. Several extension rods are normally supplied with this type of gage.

To measure the depth of a hole or slot with reasonable accuracy, use a depth gage as shown in A, Fig. 52. Hold the body of the depth gage against the surface from which the depth is to be measured and

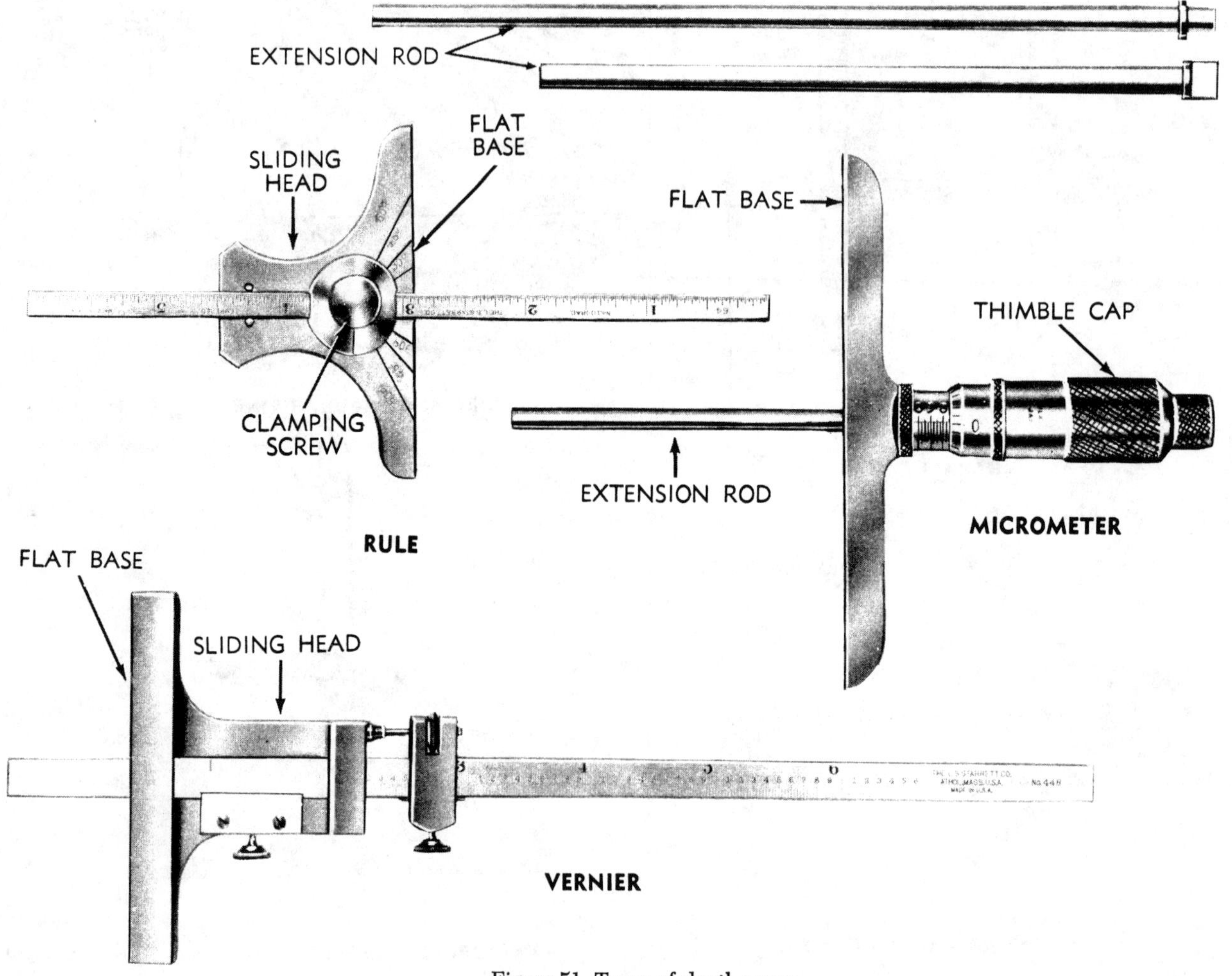

Figure 51. Types of depth gages.

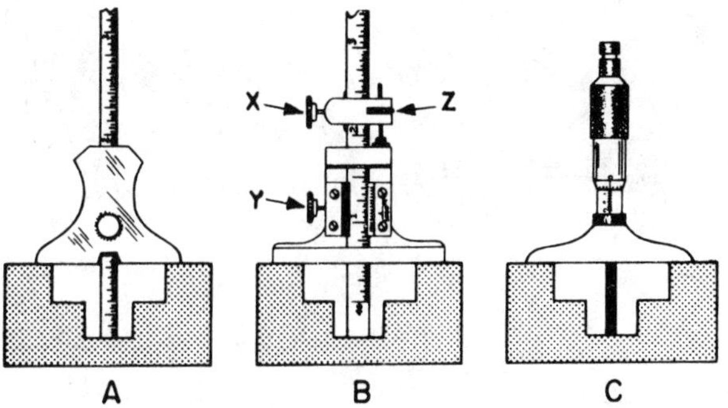

Figure 52. Using depth gages.

extend the scale into the hole or slot. Tighten the setscrew to maintain the setting. Withdraw the tool from the work and read the depth on the scale.

To measure the depth of a hole or slot with more accuracy than is possible with an ordinary depth gage, place a vernier depth gage over the slot, as shown in B, Fig. 52. *Note* that the clamping screws are at X and Y; and the horizontal adjusting screw nut is at Z. With X and Y loose, slide the scale down into the slot being measured until it is almost in contact. Then tighten X to make Z operative. With Z, adjust the scale to the *proper feel* and secure the setting with Y. (By proper feel is meant the adjustment at which you first notice contact between the end of the scale and the bottom of the slot.) Then read the setting as previously described under Reading a Vernier Scale.

To set the vernier depth gage to a particular setting, loosen both setscrews at X and at Y and slide the scale through the gage to the approximate setting. Tighten the setscrew at X, turn the knurled nut at Z until the desired setting is made, and tighten the setscrew at Y to hold the setting.

To measure the depth of a hole or slot, as shown in C, Fig. 52, with more accuracy than is possible with either an ordinary depth gage or a vernier depth gage, place a micrometer depth gage over the slot and adjust the thimble until the contact of the spindle causes the ratchet stop to slip. Remove the micrometer from the work and read the micrometer. Remember, if extension rods are used, the total depth reading will be the sum of the length of the rods plus the reading on the micrometer.

Surface Gage

A *surface gage* is a measuring tool generally used to transfer measurements to work by scribing a line, and to indicate the accuracy or parallelism of surfaces.

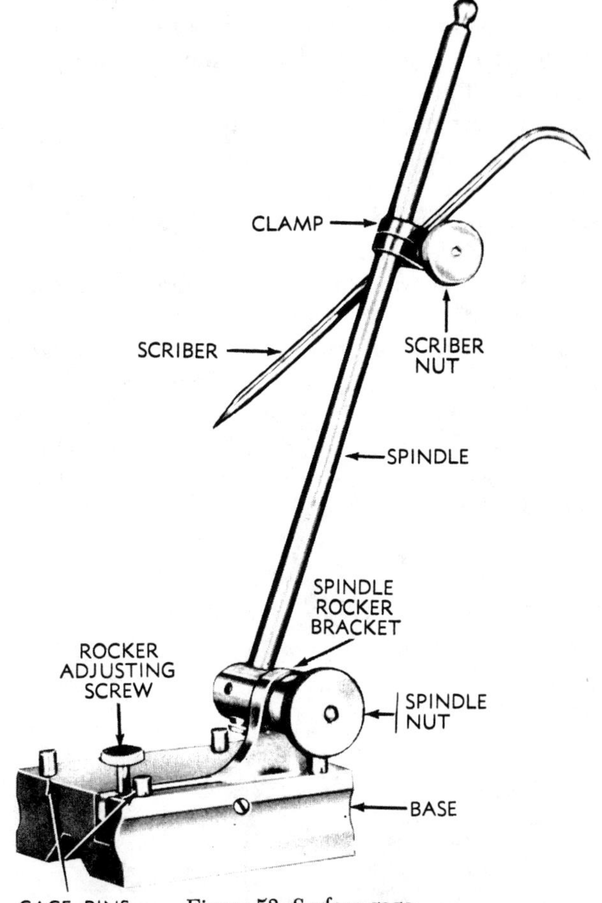

Figure 53. Surface gage.

The surface gage (Fig. 53) consists of a base with an adjustable spindle to which may be clamped a scriber or an indicator. Surface gages are made in several sizes and are classified by the length of the spindle, the smallest spindle being 4 inches long, the average 9 to 12 inches long and the largest 18 inches. The scriber is fastened to the spindle with a clamp. The bottom and the front end of the base of the surface gage have deep V-grooves cut in them, which allow the gage to be seated on a cylindrical surface.

The spindle of a surface gage may be adjusted to any position with respect to the base and tightened in place with the spindle nut. The rocket adjusting screw provides for the finer adjustment of the spindle by pivoting the spindle rocket bracket. The scriber can be positioned at any height and in any desired direction on the spindle by tightening the scriber nut. The scriber may also be mounted directly in the spindle nut mounting, in place of the spindle, and used where the working space is limited and the height of the work is within range of the scriber.

To set a surface gage for height, first wipe off the top of a layout table or surface plate and the bottom of the surface gage. Use either a combination square or a rule with rule holder to get the measurement. A rule alone cannot be held securely without wobbling and consequently an error in setting generally results. Because a combination square is generally available, its use for setting a surface gage is explained in this section.

Place the squaring head of a combination square on a flat surface, as shown in Fig. 54, and secure the scale so that the end is in contact with the surface. Move the surface gage into position and set the scriber onto the spindle. Make the final adjustment for the exact height required (4 1/2 inches in this case) with the adjusting screw on the base of the gage.

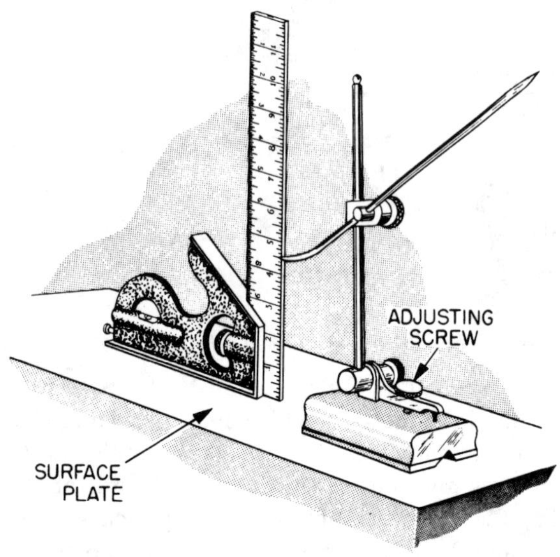

Figure 54. Setting a surface gage to height.

Surface Plate

A *surface plate* provides a true, smooth, plane surface. It is a flat-topped steel or cast iron plate that is heavily ribbed and reinforced on the underside (Fig. 55). It is often used in conjunction with a surface gage as a level base on which the gage and part to be measured are placed to obtain accurate measurements. The surface plate can also be used for testing parts that must have flat surfaces.

To test a surface for flatness, carefully clean it and remove all burrs. Then place the surface of the object on a flat area such as the surface plate in Fig. 56. Any rocking motion that is apparent will indicate a variance from flatness of the piece being tested.

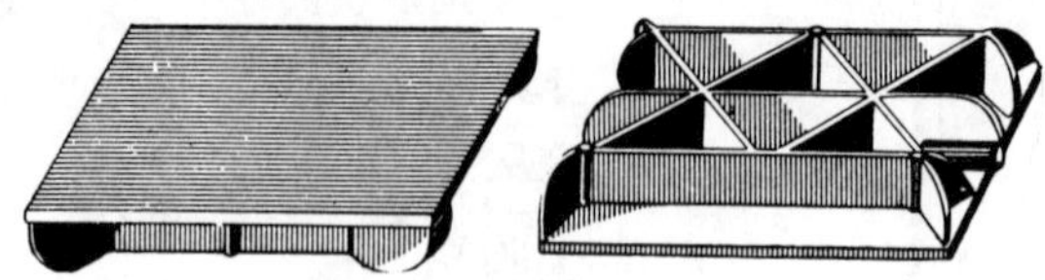

Figure 55. Surface plate.

Figure 56. Testing a surface for flatness.

For very fine work, lightly coat the surface plate with prussian blue (bearing blue) and move the piece being tested across the blue surface (Fig. 57). The low spots on the surface being tested will not take the blue; the high spots will take the blue (Fig. 57).

To determine how much variation there is from flatness—and where it is—you can insert leaves of a thickness gage to determine the amount of variation of flatness. Remember to add the thickness of all leaves together to get the total variation (Fig. 58).

A surface also may be tested for flatness with a straightedge. To do this, clean the surface thoroughly and hold the straightedge on the surface in several places as you look toward a source of light. The light showing between the surface being tested and the straightedge will reveal the low spots.

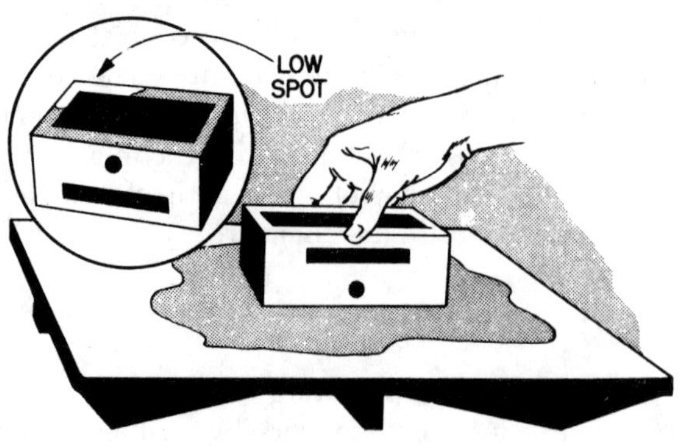

Figure 57. Using prussian blue to aid in testing a flat surface.

Figure 58. Checking conformity of a flat surface.

Care of Surface Plates

The surface plate should be covered when not in use to prevent scratching, nicking, and denting. It must be handled carefully to prevent warping (twisting). *Never* use the surface plate as an anvil or workbench—except for precision layout work (marking and measuring).

Thickness (Feeler) Gage

Thickness (feeler) gages are used for checking and measuring small openings such as contact point clearances, narrow slots, and the like. These gages are made in many shapes and sizes (Fig. 59), and also with multiple blades (usually 2 to 26). Each blade is a specific number of thousandths of an inch thick. This enables the application of one tool to the measurement of a variety of thicknesses. Some thickness gage blades are straight, while others are bent at 45- and 90-degree angles at the end. Thickness gages can also be grouped so that there are several short and several long blades together. Before using a feeler gage, remove any foreign matter from the blades. You cannot get a correct measurement unless the blades are clean.

When using a feeler gage consisting of a number of blades, insert various blades or combinations of blades between two surfaces until a snug fit is obtained. The thickness of the individual blade or the total thickness of *all the blades used* is the measurement between the surfaces.

Care of Thickness Gages

Handle the blades with care at all times. Keep from forcing the blades into openings that are too small for them. Some blades are very thin and can be bent or kinked easily. Blade edges and polished surfaces are also easy to damage. When not using a thickness gage, keep it closed.

Thread Gage

Thread gages (screw-pitch gages) are used to determine the pitch and number of threads per inch of threaded fasteners (Fig. 60). They consist of thin leaves whose edges are toothed to correspond to standard thread sections.

To measure the unknown pitch of a thread, compare it with the standards of the screw pitch gage. Hold a gage leaf to the thread being measured (Fig. 61), substituting various sizes until you find an exact fit. Look at the fit toward a source of light for best results.

The number of threads per inch is indicated by the numerical value on the blade which is found to fit the unknown threads. Using this value as a basis, correct sizes of nuts, bolts, tap cutters, and die cutters are selected for use.

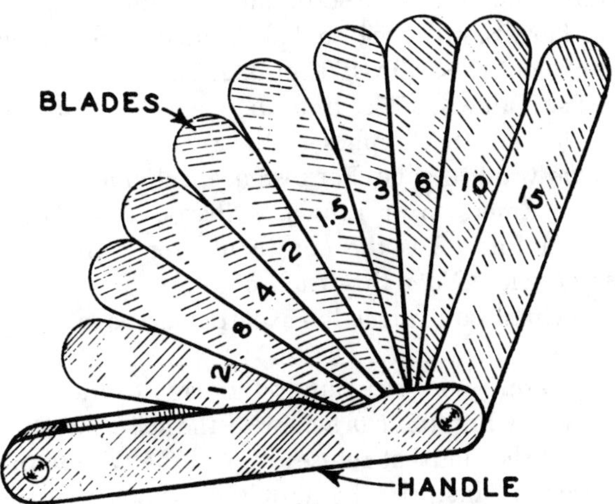

Figure 59. Thickness gage.

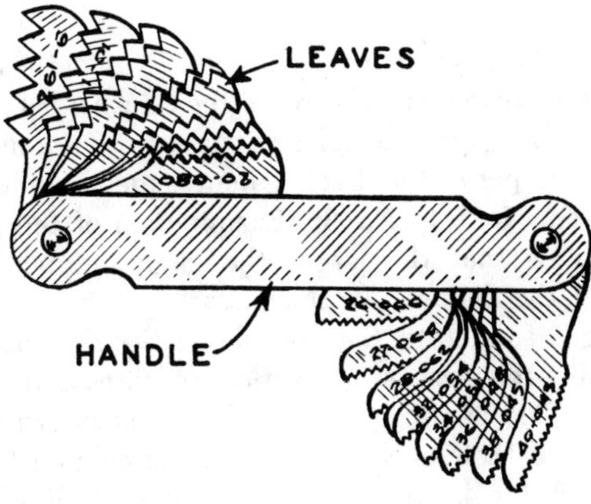

Figure 60. Screw pitch gage.

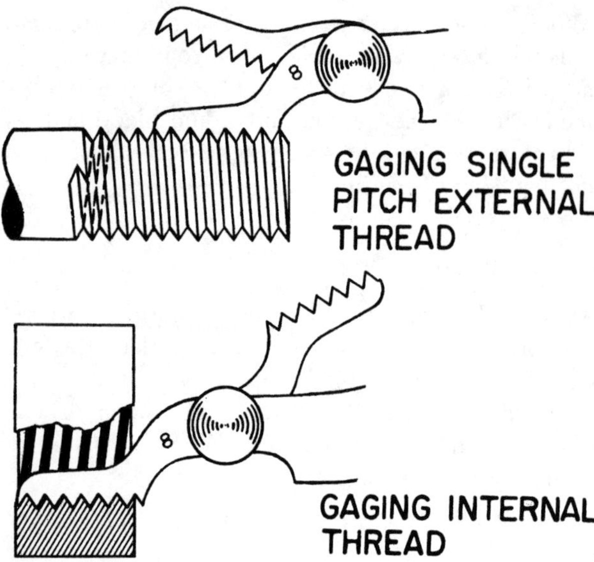

Figure 61. Using a screw pitch gage.

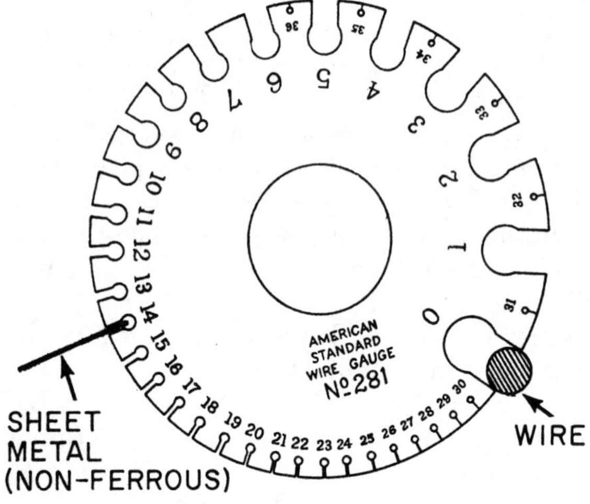

Figure 62. Using a wire gage to measure wire and sheet metal.

Wire Gage

The *wire gage* shown in Fig. 62 is used for measuring the diameters of wires or the thickness of sheet metal. This gage is circular in shape with cutouts in the outer perimeter. Each cutout gages a different size from No. 0 to No. 36. Examination of the gage will show that the larger the gage number, the smaller the diameter or thickness.

Gages similar to the one shown in Fig. 62 are available for measuring a variety of wires and sheet metals. The names of some common standard wire gages and their uses are given in the column headings of Table 4. The body of this table contains gage numbers and their corresponding equivalents in decimal fractions of an inch.

TABLE 4
DIFFERENT STANDARDS FOR WIRE GAGES IN USE IN THE UNITED STATES

Number of Wire Gage	American or Brown & Sharpe	Birmingham, or Stubs' Iron Wire	Washburn & Moen, or Steel Wire Gage	American S.&W. Co.'s Music Wire	Imperial Wire	Stubs' Steel Wire	U. S. Standard Gage for Sheet and Plate Iron and Steel	Number of Wire Gage
00000000	....	....	....	....	....	....	....	00000000
0000000	....	....	.4900	....	....	....	....	0000000
000000	....	....	.4615	.004	.464	....	.46875	000000
00000	....	....	.4305	.005	.432	....	.4375	00000
0000	.460	.454	.3938	.006	.400	....	.40625	0000
000	.40964	.425	.3625	.007	.372	....	.375	000
00	.3648	.380	.3310	.008	.348	....	.34375	00
0	.32486	.340	.3065	.009	.324	....	.3125	0
1	.2893	.300	.2830	.010	.300	.227	.28125	1
2	.25763	.284	.2625	.011	.276	.219	.265625	2
3	.22942	.259	.2437	.012	.252	.212	.250	3
4	.20431	.238	.2253	.013	.232	.207	.234375	4
5	.18194	.220	.2070	.014	.212	.204	.21875	5
6	.16202	.203	.1920	.016	.192	.201	.203125	6
7	.14428	.180	.1770	.018	.176	.199	.1875	7
8	.12849	.165	.1620	.020	.160	.197	.171875	8
9	.11443	.148	.1483	.022	.144	.194	.15625	9
10	.10189	.134	.1350	.024	.128	.191	.140625	10
11	.090742	.120	.1205	.026	.116	.188	.125	11
12	.080808	.109	.1055	.029	.104	.185	.109375	12
13	.071961	.095	.0915	.031	.092	.182	.09375	13
14	.064084	.083	.0800	.033	.080	.180	.078125	14
15	.057068	.072	.0720	.035	.072	.178	.0703125	15
16	.05082	.065	.0625	.037	.064	.175	.0625	16
17	.045257	.058	.0540	.039	.056	.172	.05625	17
18	.040303	.049	.0475	.041	.048	.168	.050	18
19	.03589	.042	.0410	.043	.040	.164	.04375	19
20	.031961	.035	.0348	.045	.036	.161	.0375	20
21	.028462	.032	.0317	.047	.032	.157	.034375	21
22	.025347	.028	.0286	.049	.028	.155	.03125	22
23	.022571	.025	.0258	.051	.024	.153	.028125	23
24	.0201	.022	.0230	.055	.022	.151	.025	24
25	.0179	.020	.0204	.059	.020	.148	.021875	25
26	.01594	.018	.0181	.063	.018	.146	.01875	26
27	.014195	.016	.0173	.067	.0164	.143	.0171875	27
28	.012641	.014	.0162	.071	.0149	.139	.015625	28
29	.011257	.013	.0150	.075	.0136	.134	.0140625	29
30	.010025	.012	.0140	.080	.0124	.127	.0125	30
31	.008928	.010	.0132	.085	.0116	.120	.0109375	31
32	.00795	.009	.0128	.090	.0108	.115	.01015625	32
33	.00708	.008	.0118	.095	.0100	.112	.009375	33
34	.006304	.007	.0104	....	.0092	.110	.00859375	34
35	.005614	.005	.0095	....	.0084	.108	.0078125	35
36	.005	.004	.0090	....	.0076	.106	.00703125	36
37	.004453	....	.0085	....	.0068	.103	.006640625	37
38	.003965	....	.0080	....	.0060	.101	.00625	38
39	.003531	....	.0075	....	.0052	.099	....	39
40	.003144	....	.0070	....	.0048	.097	....	40

Wire diameters may also be expressed in mils as well as by gage numbers. One mil equals one thousandth of an inch. Each decimal equivalent in the table can be converted to mils by multiplying by 1,000. *For example,* the circled decimal in the table is equivalent to .0640 x 1000 or 64 mils.

To use Table 4, select from the gages listed in the table the one that applies to the sheet of metal or wire you want to gage. For instance, column 2 states that the American or Brown & Sharpe Wire Gage shown in Fig. 62 is the one to use for nonferrous sheet or wire. *Note* that each of the gages has its own decimal equivalent for a particular gage number.

To measure wire size, apply the gage to the wire as shown in Fig. 62. *Do not* force the wire into the slot. Find the slot that refuses to pass the wire without forcing. Then, try the next larger slot until one is found that passes the wire. This is the correct size.

Remember, your measurements are taken at the slot portion of the cutout rather than the inner portion of the gage. Now that you have the gage number turn your gage over and read the decimal equivalent for that number.

To measure the gage of a piece of metal, first remove any burr from the place where you intend to apply the gage. Then select the appropriate gage for the metal to be measured.

After the right gage has been selected, apply the gage to the wire, or to the edge of the sheet, as shown in Fig. 62. The number opposite the slot that fits the wire or sheet is its gage number. The decimal equivalent is stamped on the opposite face of the gage.

Telescoping Gage

Telescoping gages are used for measuring the inside size of slots or holes up to six inches in width or diameter. They are T-shaped tools in which the shaft of the T is used as a handle, and the crossarm used for measuring (Fig. 63). The crossarms telescope into each other and are held out by a light spring. To use the gage the arms are compressed, placed in the hole to be measured, and allowed to expand. A twist of the locknut on top of the handle locks the arms. The tool may then be withdrawn and the distance across the arms measured.

These tools are commonly furnished in sets, the smallest gage for measuring the distances from 5/16 to 1/2 inch, and the largest for distances from 3 1/2 to 6 inches.

To measure the diameter of a hole from 1/2 to 6 in. in diameter, select from a set of telescoping gages the one whose range includes the size you need. Loosen the knurled nut at the end of the handle, and telescope the adjustable end of the gage to a size slightly smaller than the hole and retighten the nut. Insert the gage into the hole, as shown in Fig. 64, loosen the nut to permit the spring-loaded adjustable end to expand to the hole diameter, and tighten the nut. The spring-loaded contact of the adjustable end will assure proper contact. Make sure that the gage is held with the telescoping end at right angles to the axis of the hole to measure the true, maximum diameter. Remove the gage and measure the setting with an outside micrometer caliper.

Small Hole Gage

For measuring smaller slots or holes than the telescoping gages will measure, *small hole gages* can be used. These gages come in sets of four or more and will measure distances of approximately 1/8 to 1/2 inch.

The *small hole gage* (Fig. 63) consists of a small, split, ball-shaped member mounted on the end of a handle. The ball is expanded by turning a knurled knob on the handle until the proper feel is obtained (the slight drag of the ball end on the sides of the hole). The gage is then withdrawn (Fig. 65) and the size of the ball-shaped member on the end of the gage can be measured with an outside micrometer caliper. On some types of small hole gages, the ball is flattened at the bottom near the centerline to permit use in shallow holes and recesses.

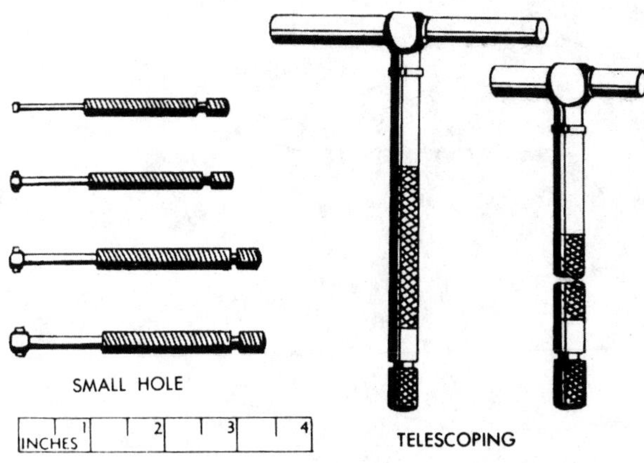

Figure 63. Small hole and telescoping gages.

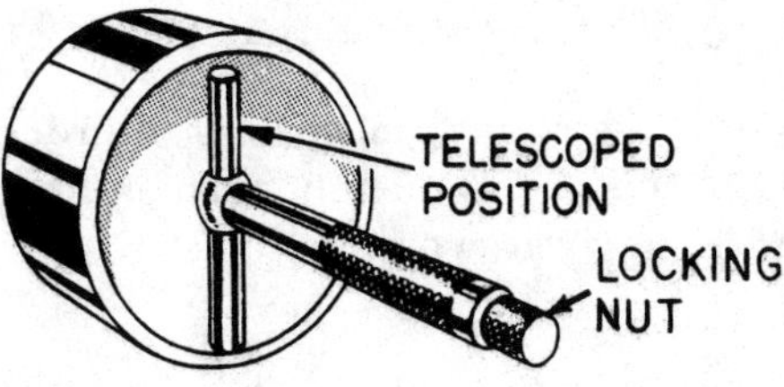

Figure 64. Using telescoping gage.

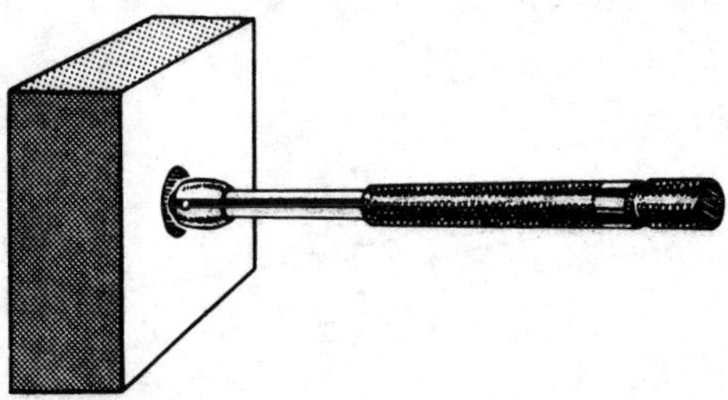

Figure 65. Measuring diameter of a hole with a small hole gage.

Marking Gages

A *marking gage* is used to mark off guidelines parallel to an edge, end, or surface of a piece of wood or metal. It has a sharp spur or pin that does the marking.

Marking gages (Fig. 66) are made of wood or steel. They consist of a graduated beam about eight inches long on which a head slides. The head can be fastened at any point on the beam by means of a thumbscrew. The thumbscrew presses a brass shoe tightly against the beam and locks it firmly in position. The steel pin or spur that does the marking projects from the beam about 1/16 inch.

To draw a line parallel to an edge with a marking gage, first determine the distance the line must be from the edge of the stock. Adjust the marking gage by setting the head the desired distance from the spur. Although the bar of a marking gage is graduated in inches, the spur may work loose or bend. If this occurs, accurate measurement should be made with a rule between the head and spur (A, Fig. 67). To draw a line after setting the gage, grasp the head of the gage with the palm and fingers, as shown in B, Fig. 67; then extend the thumb along the beam toward the spur. Press the head firmly against the edge of the work to be marked, and with a wrist motion tip the gage forward until the spur touches the work. Push the gage along the edge to mark the work, keeping the head firmly against the edge of the work.

Dividers

Dividers are useful instruments for transferring measurements and are frequently used in scribing arcs and circles in layout work.

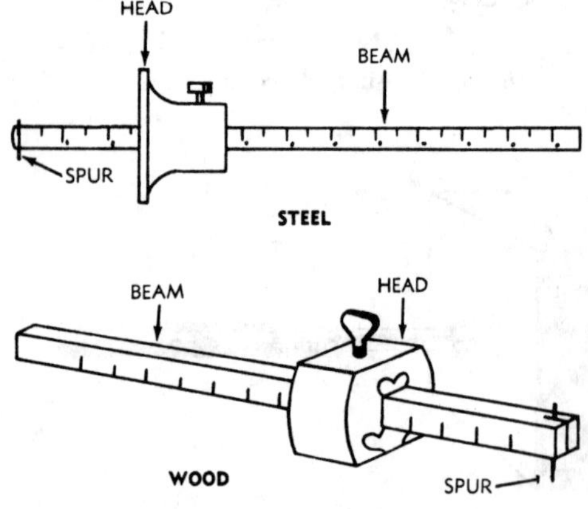

Figure 66. Marking gages.

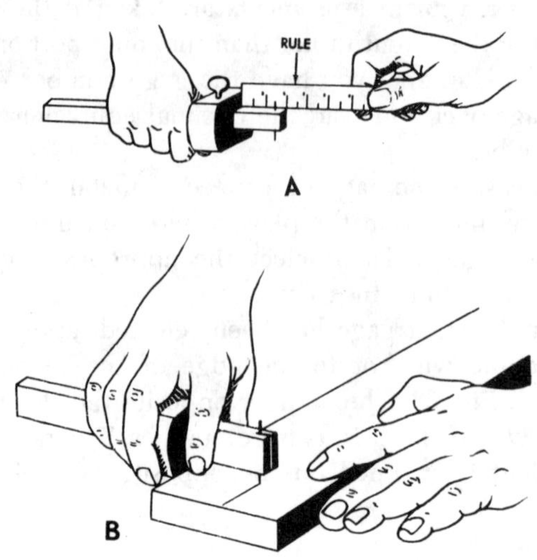

Figure 67. Using marking gage.

To lay out a circle with a divider, set the divider at the desired radius, using a rule as shown in Fig. 68. *Note* that the 3-inch radius being set here is being taken at a central portion rather than at the end of the rule. This reduces the chance of error, as each point of the dividers can be set on a graduation.

Place one leg of the divider at the center of the proposed circle, lean the tool in the direction it will be rotated, and rotate it by rolling the knurled handle between your thumb and index finger (Fig. 69).

Vernier calipers, which have two center points similar to prick punchmarks, are particularly useful in setting a divider to exact dimensions. One center point will be found near the zero end of the scale on the rule. The other point is in line with the first and to the left of the zero on the vernier scale (Fig. 70).

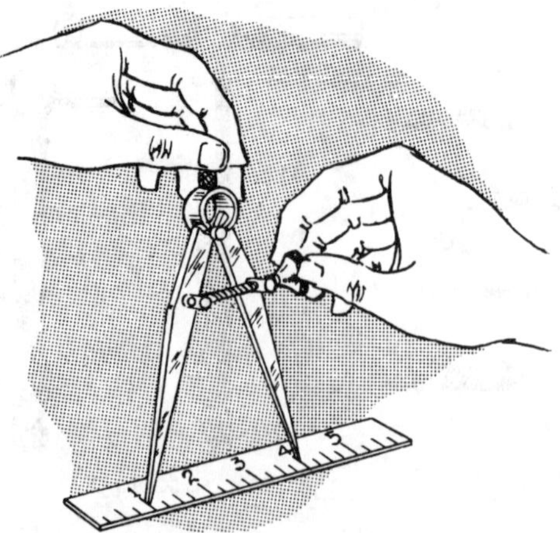

Figure 68. Setting a divider to a desired radius.

Figure 69. Scribing a circle with a divider.

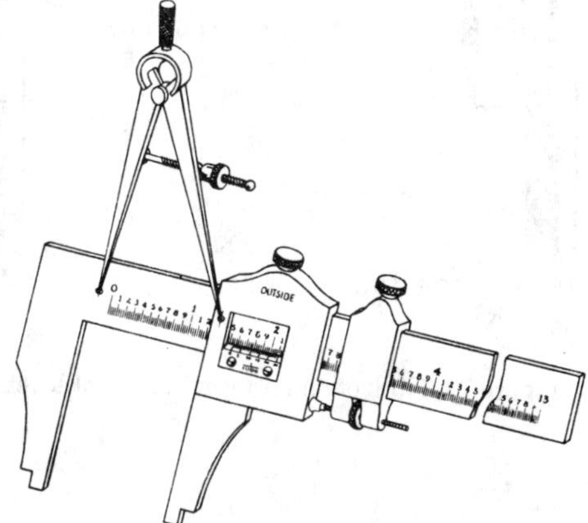

Figure 70. Setting a divider with a vernier caliper.

Set and secure the desired setting on the vernier caliper and adjust the divider until both points readily enter the center points on the vernier caliper, as shown in Fig. 70.

Plumb Bob

A *plumb bob* is a pointed, tapered brass or bronze weight which is suspended from a cord for determining the vertical or plumb line to or from a point on the ground. Common weights for plumb bobs are 6, 8, 10, 12, 14, 16, 18, and 24 ounces.

A plumb bob is a precision instrument and must be cared for as such. If the tip becomes bent, the cord from which the bob is suspended will not occupy the true plumb line over the point indicated by the tip. A plumb bob usually has a detachable tip so that if the tip should become damaged it can be renewed without replacing the entire instrument.

The cord from a plumb bob can be made more conspicuous for observation purposes by attachment of a red-and-white target (Fig. 71).

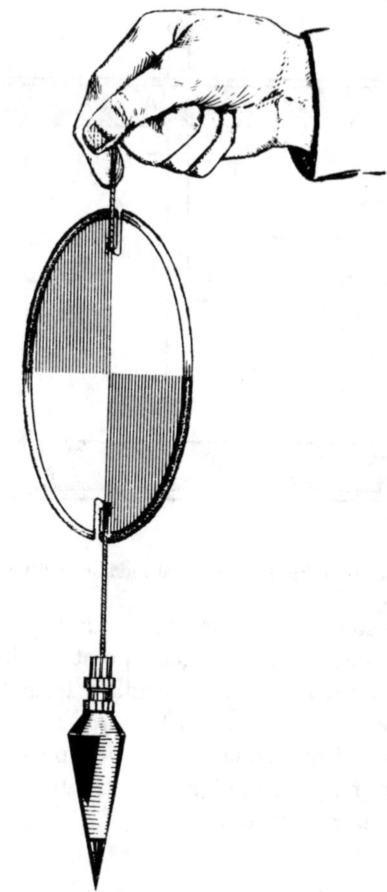

Figure 71. Plumb bob, cord, and target.

The plumb bob is used in carpentry to determine true verticality when erecting vertical uprights and corner posts of framework. Surveyors use it for transferring and lining up points.

To locate a point which is exactly below a particular point in space, secure the plumb bob string to the upper point, such as is shown in A, Fig. 72. When the plumb stops swinging, the point as indicated at B, Fig. 72 will be exactly below A.

To plumb a structural member, or an electrical conduit, secure the plumb line A, Fig. 73 so that you can look at both the line and piece behind the line. Then, by sighting, line up the member or conduit with the plumb line.

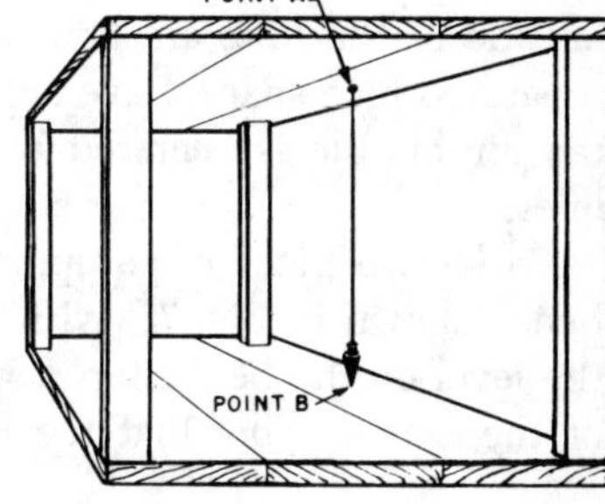

Figure 72. Locating a point with a plumb bob.

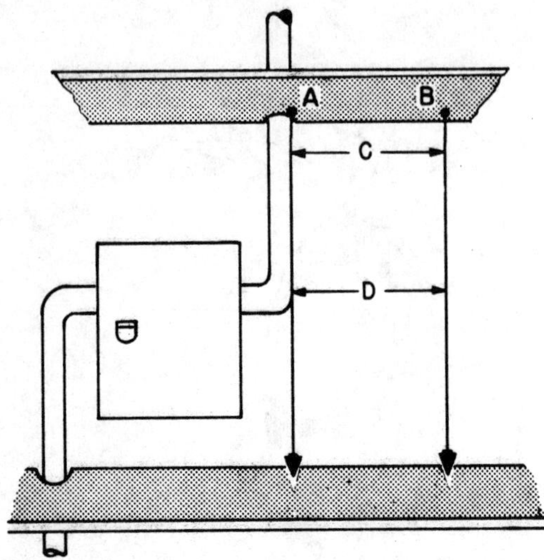

Figure 73. Plumbing a structural member with a plumb bob.

If this cannot be done, it may be necessary to secure the plumb line at some point, such as shown at B, and then measure the offset from the line to the piece at two places so that, *for example,* C and D in Fig. 73 are equal. If the distances between C and D are not equal, adjust the structural member or conduit until they are.

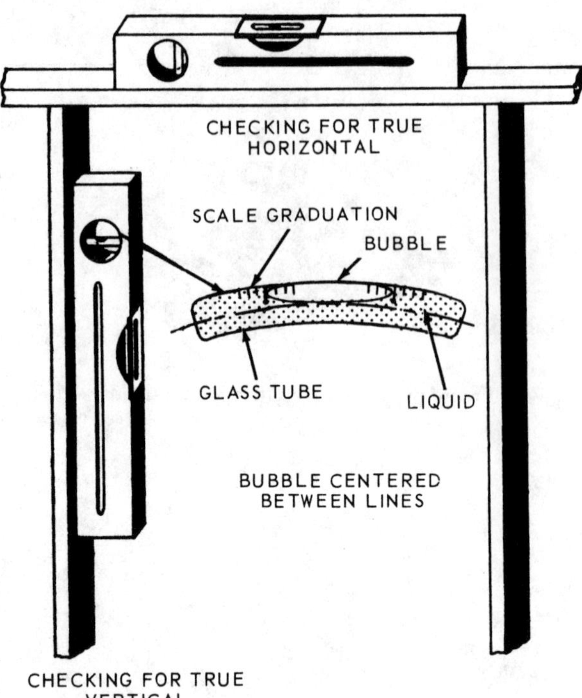

Figure 74. Horizontal and vertical use of level.

Levels

Levels are tools designed to prove whether a plane or surface is true horizontal or true vertical. Some precision levels are calibrated so that they will indicate in degrees, minutes, and seconds the angle inclination of a surface in relation to a horizontal or vertical surface.

The level is a simple instrument consisting of a liquid, such as alcohol or chloroform, partially filling a glass vial or tube so that a bubble remains. The tube is mounted in a frame which may be aluminum, wood, or iron. Levels are equipped with one, two, or more tubes. One tube is built in the frame at right angles to another (Fig. 74). The tube shown in Fig. 74 is slightly curved, causing the bubble to seek always the highest point in the tube. On the outside of the tube are two sets of graduation lines separated by a space. Leveling is accomplished when the air bubble is centered between the graduation lines.

To level a piece of equipment, such as the workbench shown in Fig. 75, with a carpenter's level, set the level on the bench top parallel to the front edge of the bench. *Note* that the level has several pairs

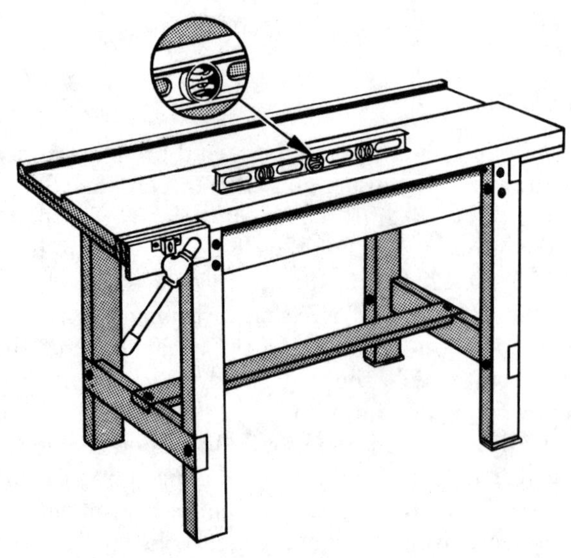

Figure 75. Leveling a bench.

of glass vials. Regardless of the position of the level, always watch the bubble in the bottom vial of a horizontal pair. Shim or wedge up the end of the bench that will return that bubble to the center of its vial. Recheck the first position of the level before securing the shims or wedges.

To plumb a piece of equipment, such as the drill press (Fig. 76), place the level on the side and on the front of the main column of the press. Figure 76 shows the level on the side. Use shims as necessary to bring the bubble in the lower vial of either pair of the horizontal vials to the center in each case.

Levels must be checked for accuracy. This is readily accomplished by placing the level on a true horizontal surface and noting the vial indication. Reverse the level end for end. If the bubble appears on one side of the graduations with reference to the operator on the first reading and on the other side for the second reading, the level is out of true and must be adjusted.

Do not drop or handle a level roughly. To prevent damage, store it in a rack or other suitable place when not in use.

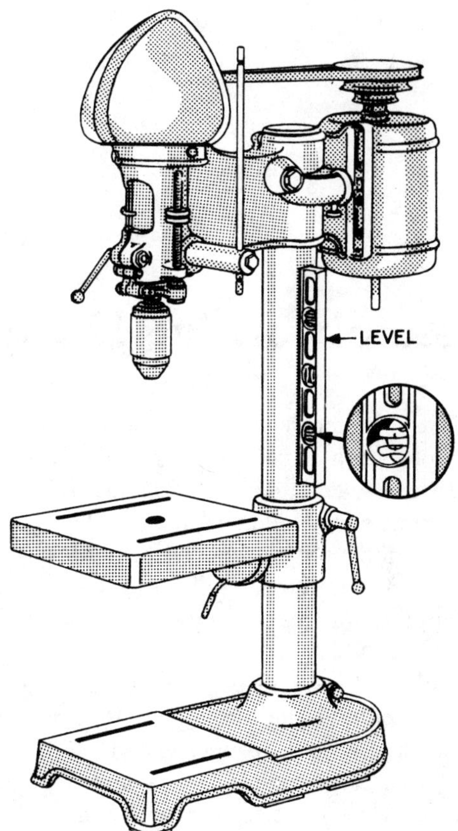

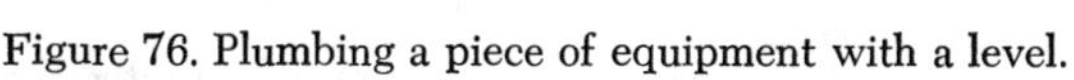
Figure 76. Plumbing a piece of equipment with a level.

Chapter 3

Metalworking Hand Tools and How to Use Them

Tools are the mechanic's best friend. They are indispensable servants, performing innumerable tasks beyond the power of your own hands. Like friends, tools become more valuable to you the better you are acquainted with them. The term "bench work" covers filing, chipping, polishing, hand reaming, hand tapping, all the many jobs done at the bench or in a vise.

Regardless of the type of job to be done, a worker should choose and use the correct tools in order to do the work accurately, properly, and quickly. Metalworking tools are carefully made and demand particular care if they are to work and last as the manufacturer intended.

Classes of Tools

The tools described in this book are classified as *hand tools, measuring* and *layout tools,* and *hand power tools.* Each type of tool has its special characteristics and purposes and should be used accordingly.

HAND TOOLS. Hand tools are usually small and are used with the hands to perform mechanical operations.

MEASURING AND LAYOUT TOOLS. Measuring and layout tools are precision made tools used for measuring and for laying out work accurately. (*See* Chap. 2.)

HAND POWER TOOLS. Hand power tools are operated entirely or partly by power, such as electricity and compressed air, in order to make an operation easier or faster, or more accurate.

Hammers and Mallets

Types of hammers used in the sheet-metal shop are the machinist's or ball-peen, the cross-peen, the tinner's riveting, the tinner's peening, the setting, the raising, the soft-face, and the brass-head (Figs. 1 and 2).

The essential parts of a machinist's or ball-peen hammer, the all-purpose hammer used in working metal, are shown in Fig. 1. This hammer is used for bending and forming sheet metal and brass strip.

When it is desirable to leave no marks on the metal being formed, the soft-face or the brass-head hammer is used (Fig. 1). There are several varieties of soft-face hammers, some of which are made with a plastic head, while others are equipped with a renewable face of either rawhide or lead inserted in a steel head.

The cross-peen or tinner's riveting hammer is used to flatten tinner's rivets on furnace pipes, ducts, and similar material (Fig. 1).

The square, flat face of the setting hammer (Fig. 2) is used for setting or flattening metal seams without marking or damaging the material. The single tapered peen on this hammer has a beveled end and is used for peening.

The raising hammer shown in Fig. 2 is used for raising doors and cornice ornaments and for other raising and bumping work.

Mallets made either of all wood or with rawhide faces are generally used on light gauge materials to prevent marring or damaging the metal (Fig. 2).

When a large number of sheets of heavy-gauge metal are to be bent or shaped at angles, machines called brakes are used. These machines are described in Chap. 4. Sheet metal up to 24 in. in width that is not too thick can be bent by hand.

HOW TO USE A METAL-WORKING HAMMER. In bending metal, only the face of the ball-peen hammer or mallet is used. To bend a piece of sheet metal, get two straight strips of hardwood, measuring approximately 1 in. thick by 3 in. wide and slightly longer than the width of the sheet metal, and a third strip of hardwood of the same length

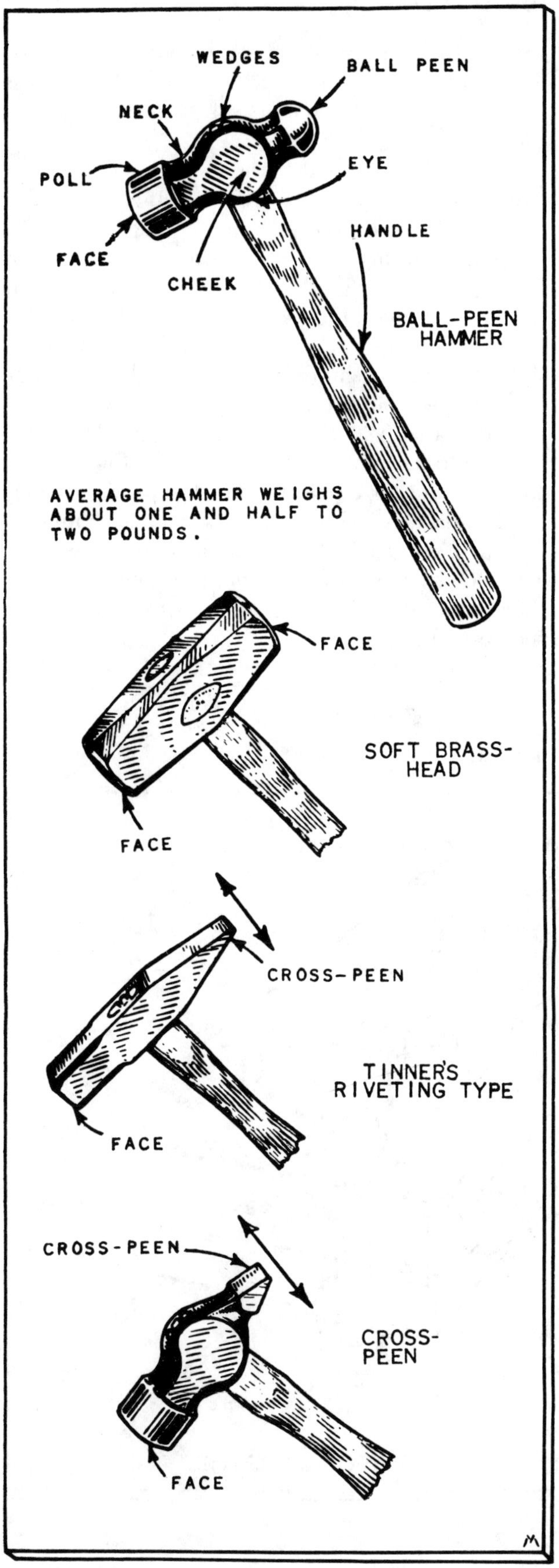

WEDGES
BALL PEEN
NECK
POLL
EYE
FACE
CHEEK
HANDLE
BALL-PEEN HAMMER

AVERAGE HAMMER WEIGHS ABOUT ONE AND HALF TO TWO POUNDS.

FACE
SOFT BRASS-HEAD
FACE

CROSS-PEEN
TINNER'S RIVETING TYPE
FACE

CROSS-PEEN
CROSS-PEEN
FACE

Figure 1.

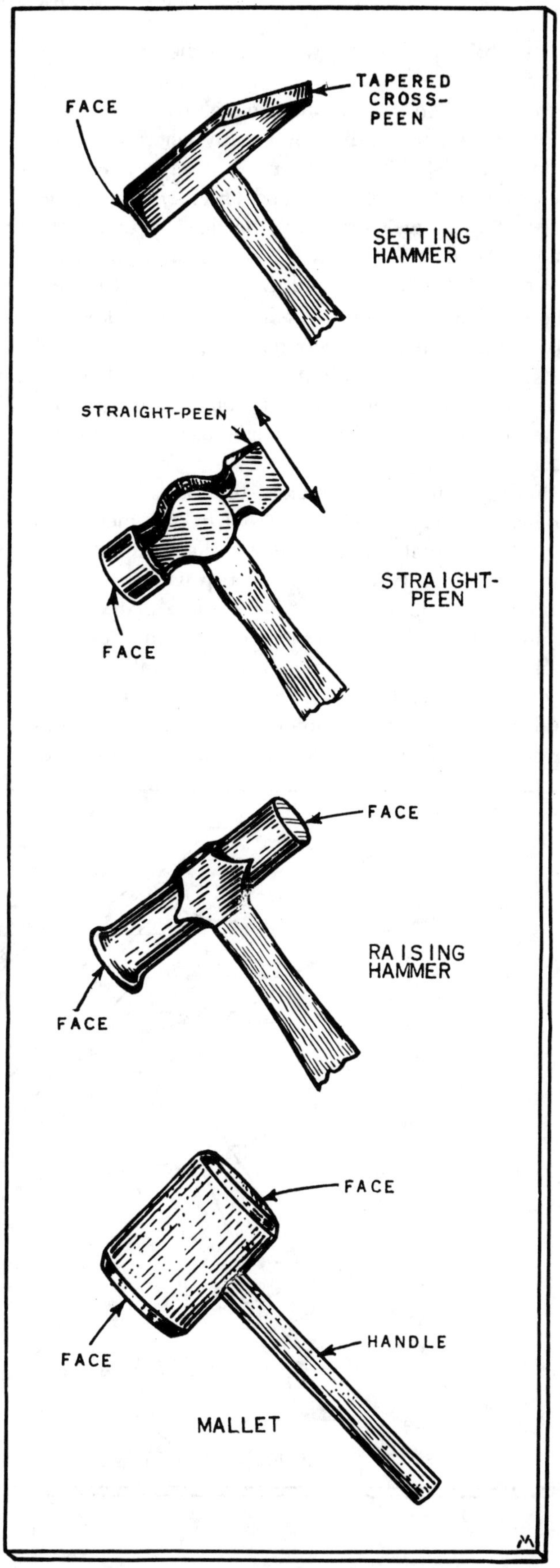

FACE
TAPERED CROSS-PEEN
SETTING HAMMER

STRAIGHT-PEEN
STRAIGHT-PEEN
FACE

FACE
RAISING HAMMER
FACE

FACE
FACE
HANDLE
MALLET

Figure 2.

but slightly thicker and wider than the others (Fig. 3).

Scribe a line on the sheet metal with the sharp point of a scriber, indicating exactly where the bend is to be made (Fig. 4). Place the sheet between the two shorter strips of hardwood (Fig. 3). The upper edge of the lower strip must be directly under the line of bend and the lower edge of the upper strip must be on the line of bend. Both strips must project about ½ in. beyond the edge of the workbench. Using the third strip, press down on the sheet metal to start the bend. With this strip in contact, strike the strip a series of blows all along the length and continue until the desired angle has been formed (Fig. 3).

For bending metal brackets or braces of ⅛ in.—or heavier-gauge steel or brass strip, the method is slightly different. Figure 4 shows the correct procedure for bending steel or brass strip with a vise and a ball-peen hammer. In laying out the material for bending ⅛ in.—or heavier-gauge steel, an allowance must be made for the amount of metal taken up by the bend, depending upon the thickness of the metal and the type of seam or joint. A simple rule is to add approximately one-half the thickness of the metal to the length of the piece to be bent. For example, if a 2 in. x 3 in. corner brace is to be made of ⅛ in.-gauge metal, a piece of material 5/16 in. long must be provided (Fig. 4).

Scribe a line across the strip exactly 2 in. from one end. Place the metal to be bent in the vise so that the scribed line is even with the top edge of the vise jaw and is clamped tightly. Using the face of the ball-peen hammer, strike the metal as close to the vise as possible (Fig. 4). To avoid objectionable toolmarks as far as possible, the hammer blows should overlap each other and extend the full width of the piece being bent.

Where a strip is to be bent at right angles with a rounded rather than a sharp corner (Fig. 4), the amount of metal lost in the bend depends not only on the thickness of the metal but on the radius of the curve made. When a strip is to be shaped with a rounded corner, the material must be cut longer than required, and after bending, trimmed down to the desired size.

FASTENING RIVETS. To fasten rivets with a ball-peen hammer, use the ball-peen part to flatten and expand the ends of the rivets to form the rivetheads. The face of the hammer is used to shape the tails of

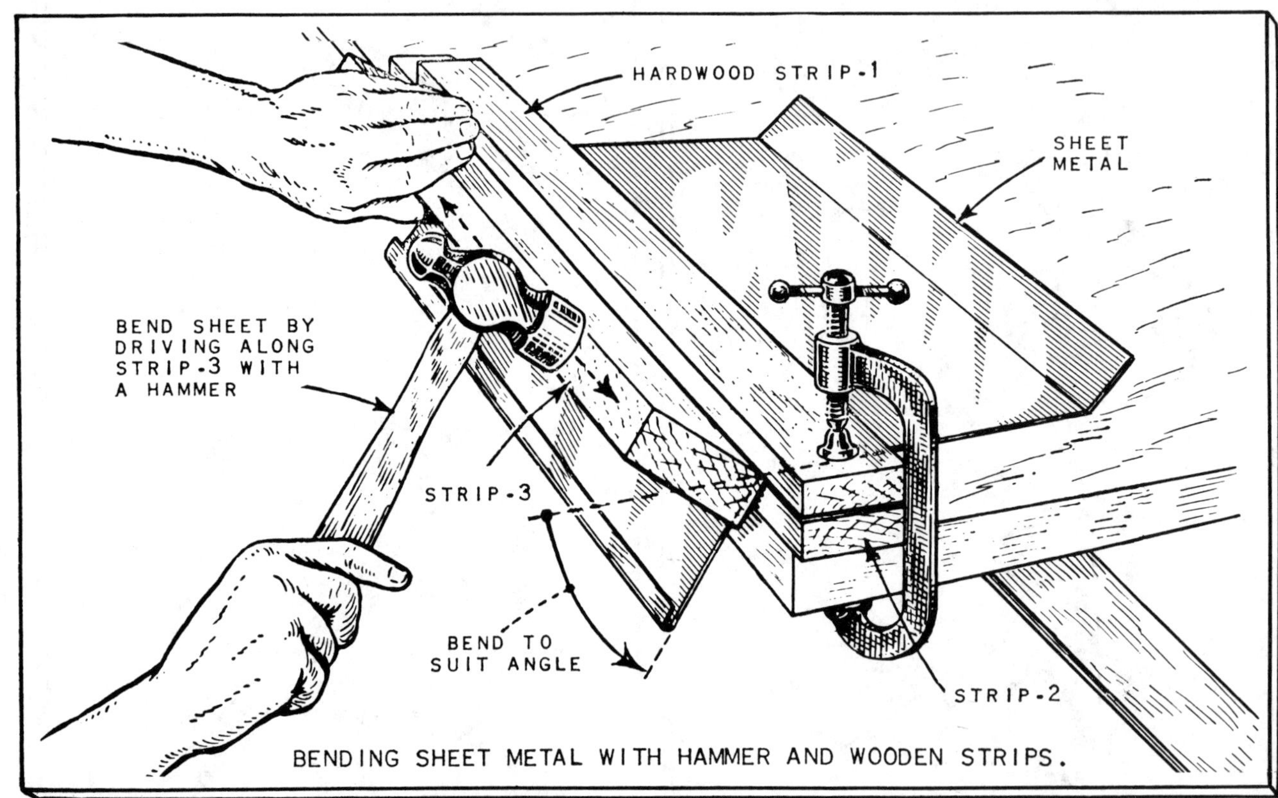

Figure 3.

rivets and for driving the rivet set and the header. A rivet set or header is merely a short piece of hardened and tempered tool steel with a hole in one end and a conical depression alongside the hole (Fig. 5). The hole is used to force the metal pieces down on the rivet shank before the end of the rivet is flattened. The conical depression is then set over the rivet end with the header held in a vertical position, and the header is struck with the hammer to shape the rivet after it has been flattened. For detailed information on rivets and riveting, see Chap. 7. Machinist's hammers of various sizes or weights are used in riveting, depending on the type and size of the rivets.

Replacing Broken Hammer Handles. Machine-made hickory handles in various sizes can be secured at most hardware stores. The portion of the broken handle that remains in the hammer head must be removed. The simplest and most effective method of doing this is to drill through it with a twist drill to remove as much wood as possible. It is then easy to split out several small pieces and thus remove the old wedged-in handle.

The end of a new handle is usually larger than required and must be scraped or pared slightly before it will fit into the head of the hammer. However, do not pare it too much, since it must fit very tightly. After the small fitted end of the handle is inserted

Figure 4.

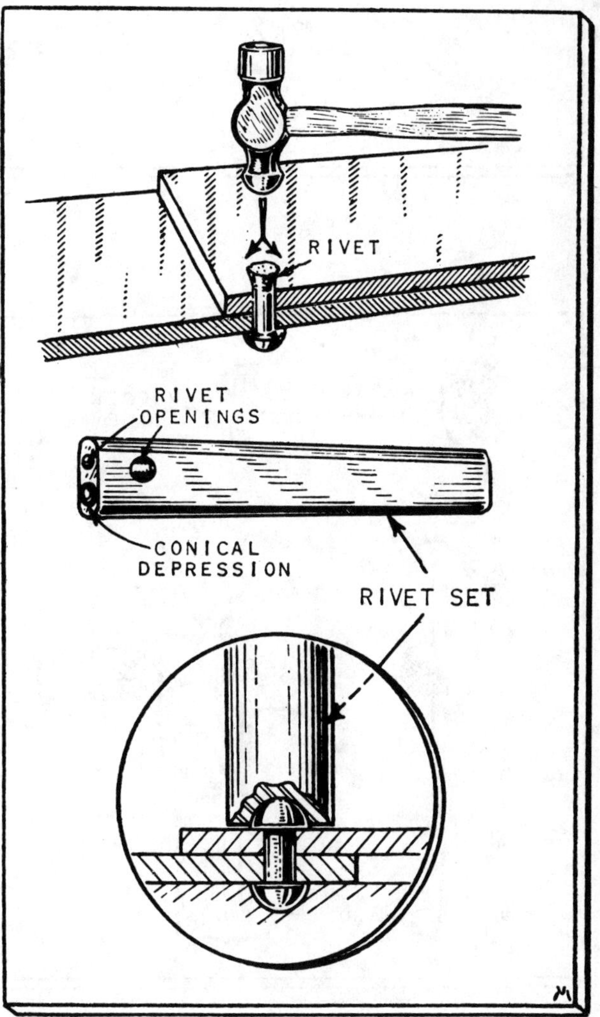

Figure 5.

into the opening in the head of the hammer, tamp the other end of the handle against a solid surface until the head is in place (Fig. 6). To prevent the head of the hammer from flying off, the end of the handle must be expanded, after it is in place in the hammer head, by inserting several wooden or metal wedges (Fig. 7). Wooden wedges can be made of either maple or hickory wood. Metal wedges can be secured at any hardware store and are preferable. Do not insert the wedges until the head is on the handle as far as it can go. When using wooden wedges, make a saw cut about as long as the wedge in the end of the handle before inserting it into the head of the hammer. Saw cuts are not necessary when using metal wedges (Fig. 7).

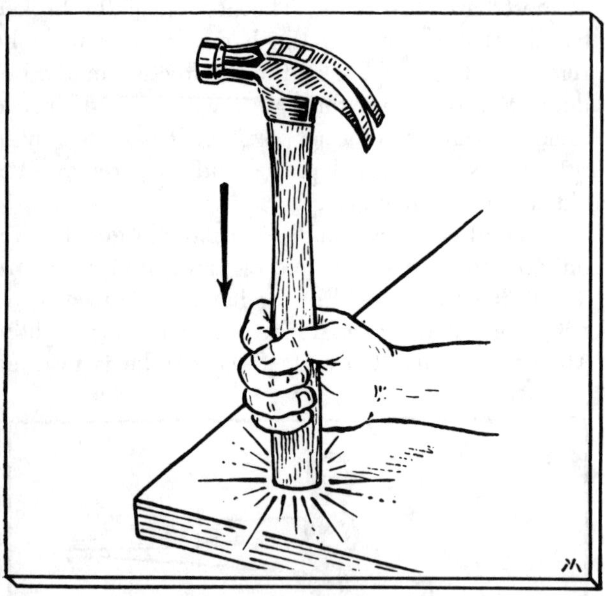

Figure 6.

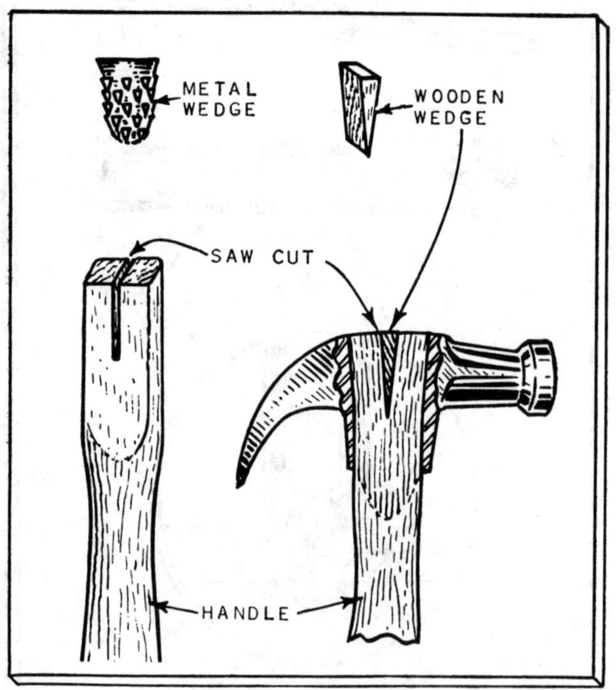

Figure 7.

Screwdrivers

The several types of screwdrivers used in the sheet metal shop are the common screwdriver, ratchet, spiral ratchet, offset, and Phillips. Screwdrivers are available in various sizes. The size is always given by the length of the blade: a 6 in. screwdriver has a 6 in. blade, and so on. Narrow-tipped blades are designed for small screws, and blades with larger tips for heavier screws.

Common Screwdriver. The various parts of a common screwdriver are shown in Fig. 8.

Ratchet and Spiral Ratchet Screwdrivers. The two variations of the common screwdriver are the ratchet

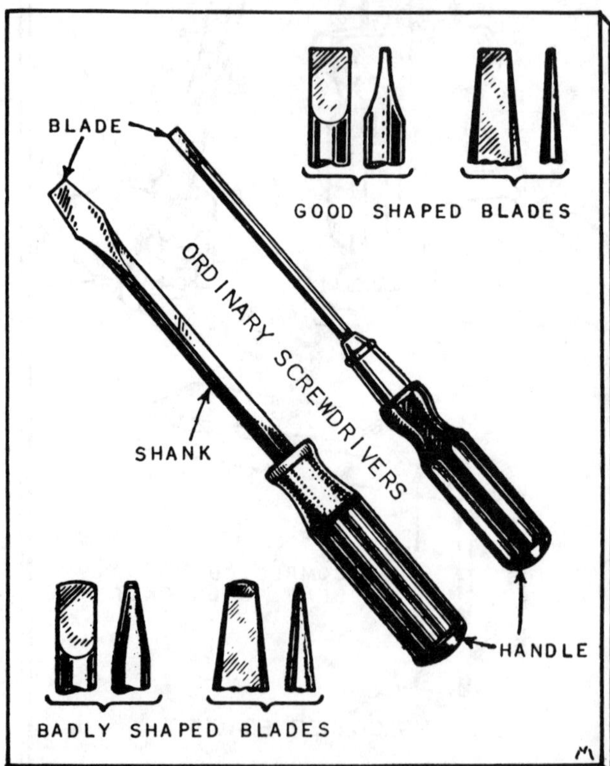

Figure 8.

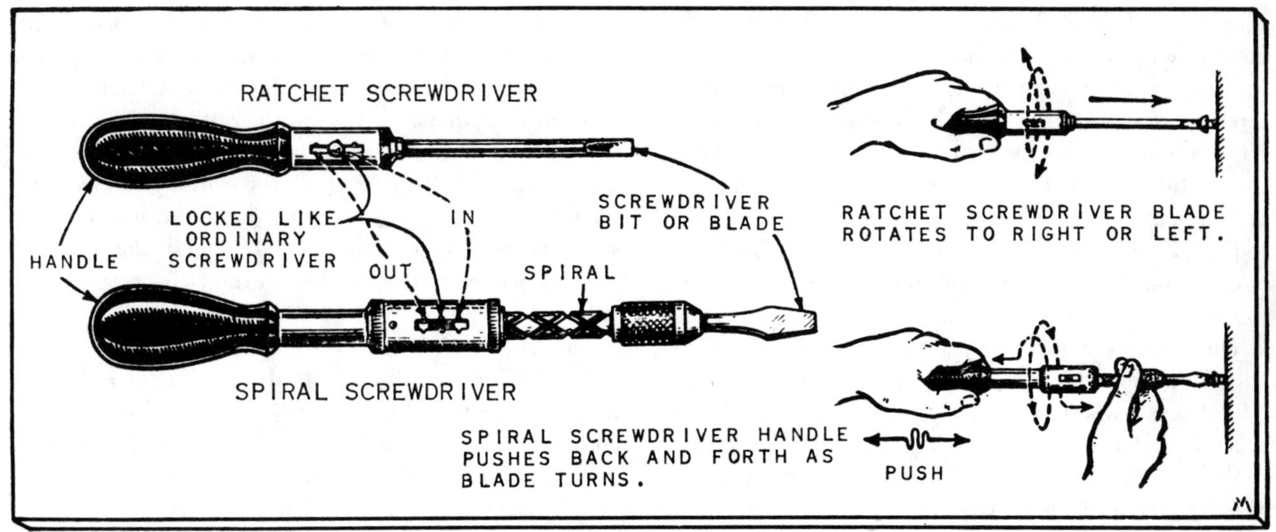

Figure 9.

and the spiral ratchet types (Fig. 9). Similar in operation to the common screwdriver, the ratchet type drives screws in much faster and works semiautomatically. Blades of various sizes can be secured for both types of ratchet screwdriver, and both types can be set for driving screws in or extracting them. The handle of the ratchet screwdriver turns back and forth in the direction set.

The spiral ratchet screwdriver operates even faster than the ratchet. It can be set for either in or out. To drive the screw, set the blade in the screw slot and push on the handle, steadying the blade with the other hand. The blade makes several turns for each push.

Offset Screwdriver. Offset screwdrivers are designed for driving screws where there is insufficient space to use the conventional type of screwdriver (Fig. 10). The offset screwdriver is made from a piece of either round or octagonal steel with two blades at opposite ends at right angles to one another and to the shaft. When screws have to be driven in or extracted in inaccessible places, it is sometimes necessary to use both ends of the offset screwdriver, turning the screw a short distance with one end and then with the other.

Phillips Screwdriver. The Phillips screwdriver is used only for driving the Phillips screw (Fig. 11). Phillips screws have a head with two V-slots which cross at the center. The tip of the Phillips screwdriver blade is shaped like a pointed or beveled cross to fit into these slots. To keep the blade in the cross slots of the screw, more downward pressure is used.

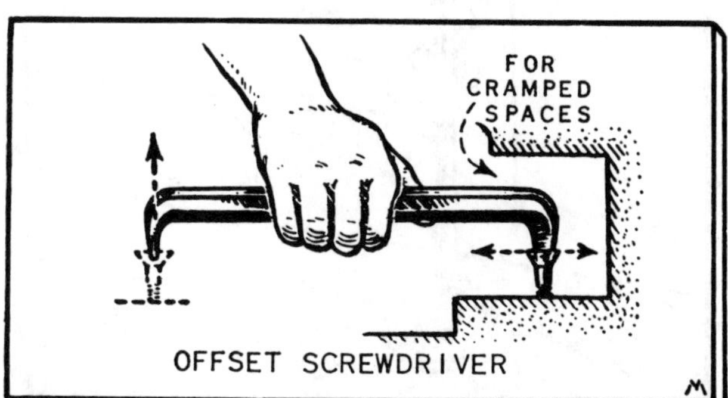

Figure 10.

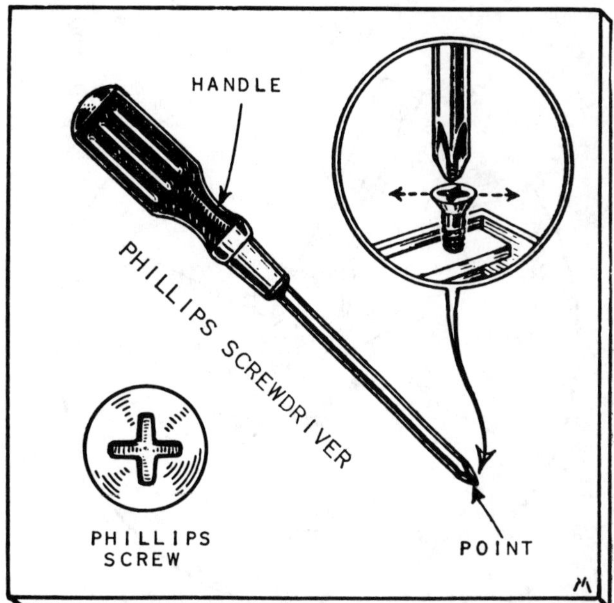

Figure 11.

This type of screwdriver cannot slip out of the slot or otherwise damage finishes.

USING A SCREWDRIVER. Choose the right size of screw and screwdriver, and be sure to use the longest screwdriver that is available and convenient for the particular job. The blade of the screwdriver must fit the screw slots. It must be neither too small nor too large. If it is too small, the blade may break. If it is too large, it may slip out and mar the surface of the wood.

The end of a screwdriver blade must be square and flat, and the sides slightly curved. A round-edged screwdriver is dangerous; it is apt to slip when driving a screw, causing serious injury (Fig. 12).

When driving screws with a common screwdriver, grasp the handle with the thumb side of the hand toward the blade. Use automatic screwdrivers according to directions given by the manufacturer of each type. Place the screw in the pilot hole, hold it straight with the left hand, set the blade in the slot, and start turning the screwdriver, exerting pressure with the right hand (Fig. 13). As soon as the screw has taken hold of the wood, remove the left hand, and continue driving the screw in. Hold the screwdriver steady, with the blade in a direct, straight line with the screw.

REMOVING TIGHT SCREWS. To remove a tight screw, use a screwdriver that has a blade with parallel sides that fit the screw slot perfectly. If the right size and shape of screwdriver is not used, the screw becomes "chewed," making the job more difficult. A tight screw sometimes can be started by giving it a slight twist in a clockwise direction, that is, the same direction which drives it in. If this does not help, twist the screw both ways, backing it out as far as it will go easily, and then turning it part way back in again. Each time this is repeated, the screw usually will back out a little farther until it is all the way out. In some cases, a screw with a damaged slot can be backed partly out, and then turned the rest of the way with a pair of pliers.

DRESSING SCREWDRIVER BLADES. A screwdriver is not a cutting tool and for that reason does not have to be sharpened, but it must be dressed or kept in condition. This is done by occasionally grinding it on an emery wheel or by filing the blade with a flat file. Correct and incorrect shapes for a screwdriver are shown in Fig. 8.

When dressing a screwdriver with a file, hold the screwdriver in a vise and file the tip absolutely

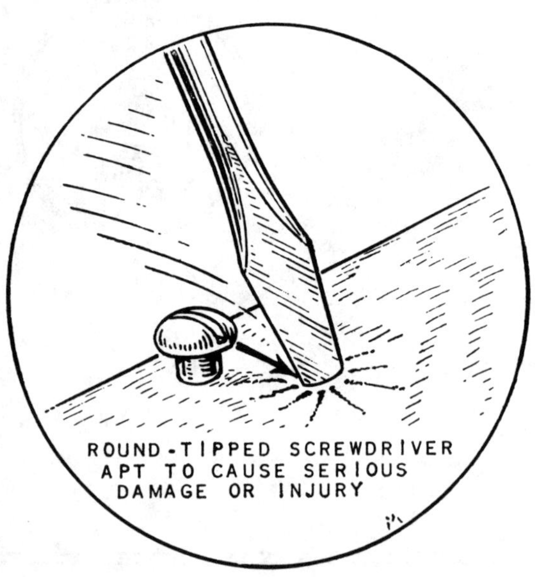

Figure 12.

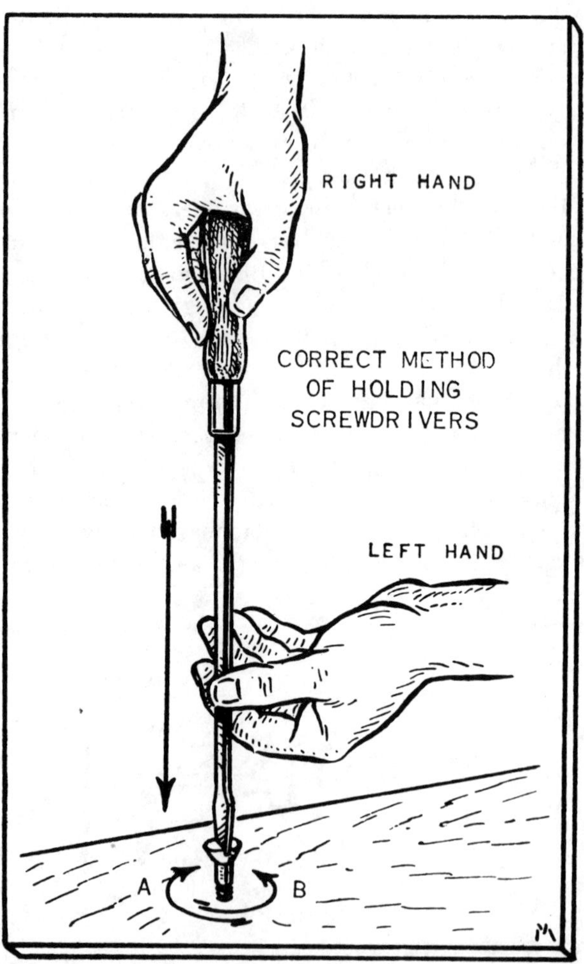

Figure 13.

straight across both ends, at right angles to the shank and the sides, with the faces near the tip as parallel as possible to each other (Fig. 14). Never bevel or round the blade of a screwdriver.

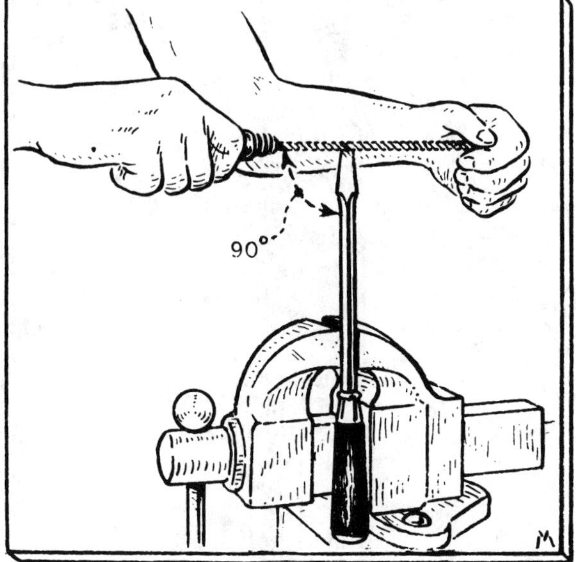

Figure 14.

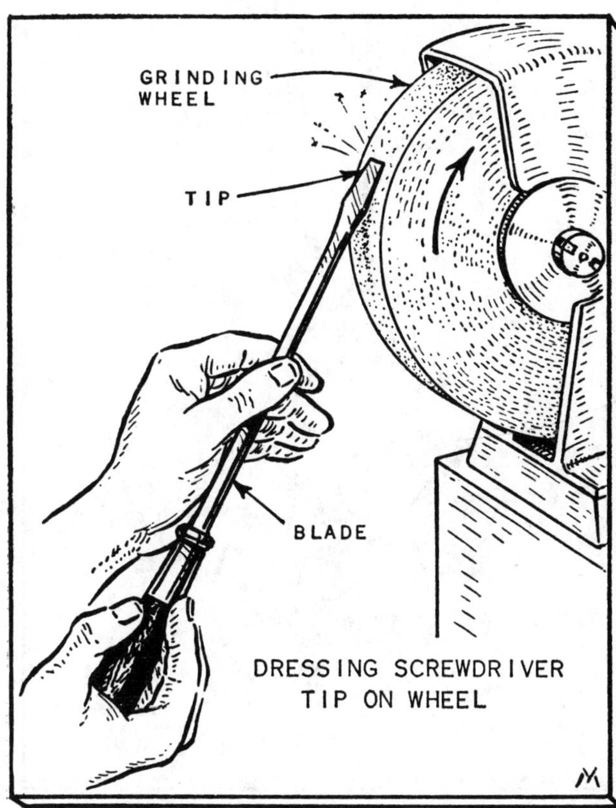

Figure 15.

When using an emery wheel for dressing a screwdriver, hold at angle shown in Fig. 15. Do not hold the blade against the wheel too long, or the friction wheel will heat the steel and draw the temper or soften the blade. When dressing a screwdriver, dip the blade in water at frequent intervals.

Drills

To drill holes in sheet metal, either the hand or breast drill shown in Figs. 16 and 17 is used with a twist drill of the required type and size. The chuck of the hand drill (Fig. 16) has a drill size capacity of up to ¼ in. Where a larger size twist drill up to 1 in. maximum is required, the breast drill must be used (Fig. 17).

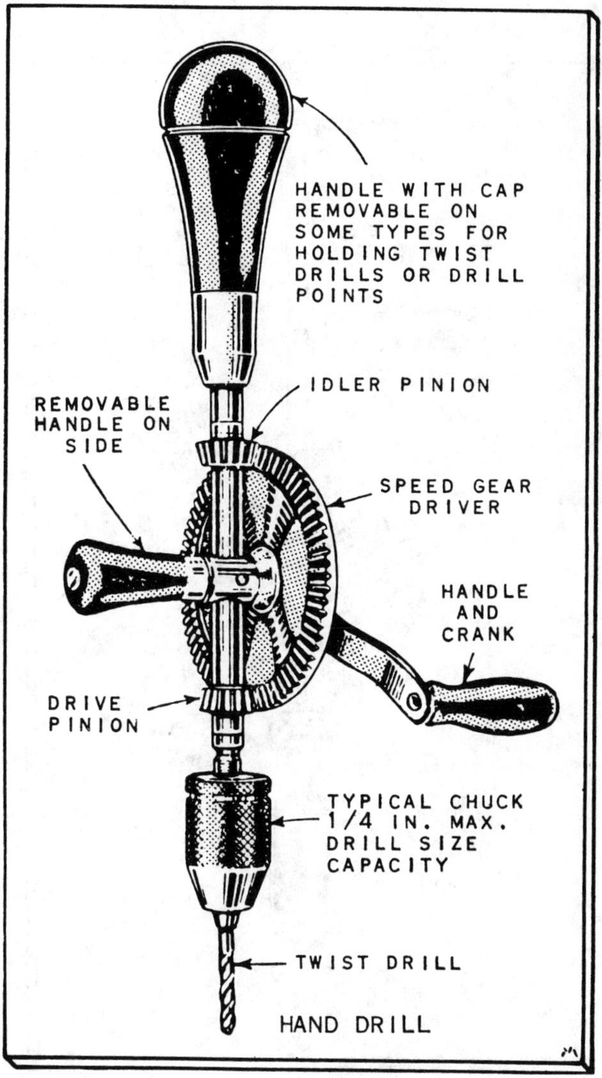

Figure 16.

The twist drill, more specifically known as the Morse twist drill, is designed for drilling holes in metal and other hard materials (Fig. 18). The several types of twist drills are the square-shank, straight-shank, and taper-shank (Fig. 19).

All twist drills, irrespective of type, have two cutting edges, or *lips*, as they are called (Fig. 18). The upper faces of these two cutting edges are formed by milling, or grinding, two opposite spiral grooves (flutes) into a cylinder of tool steel. The bottom ends of these cutting edges are ground at an angle of approximately 60 degrees with the axis. After considerable research and experimentation, the makers of twist drills have found that the best angle at the point for both centering the drill and keeping it centered without any tendency to wedge or stick is about 120 degrees. These angular faces are backed

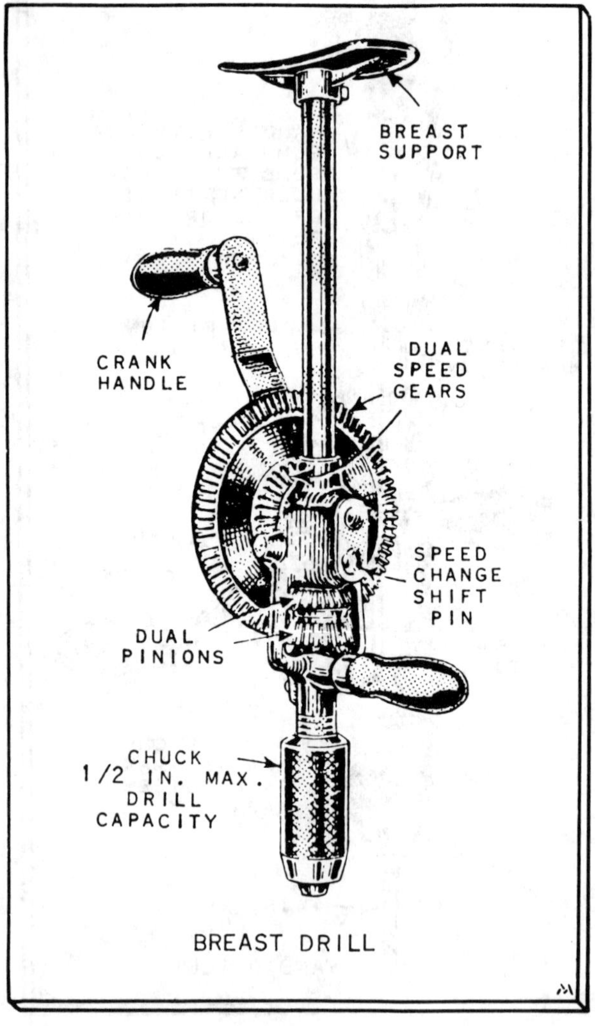

Figure 17.

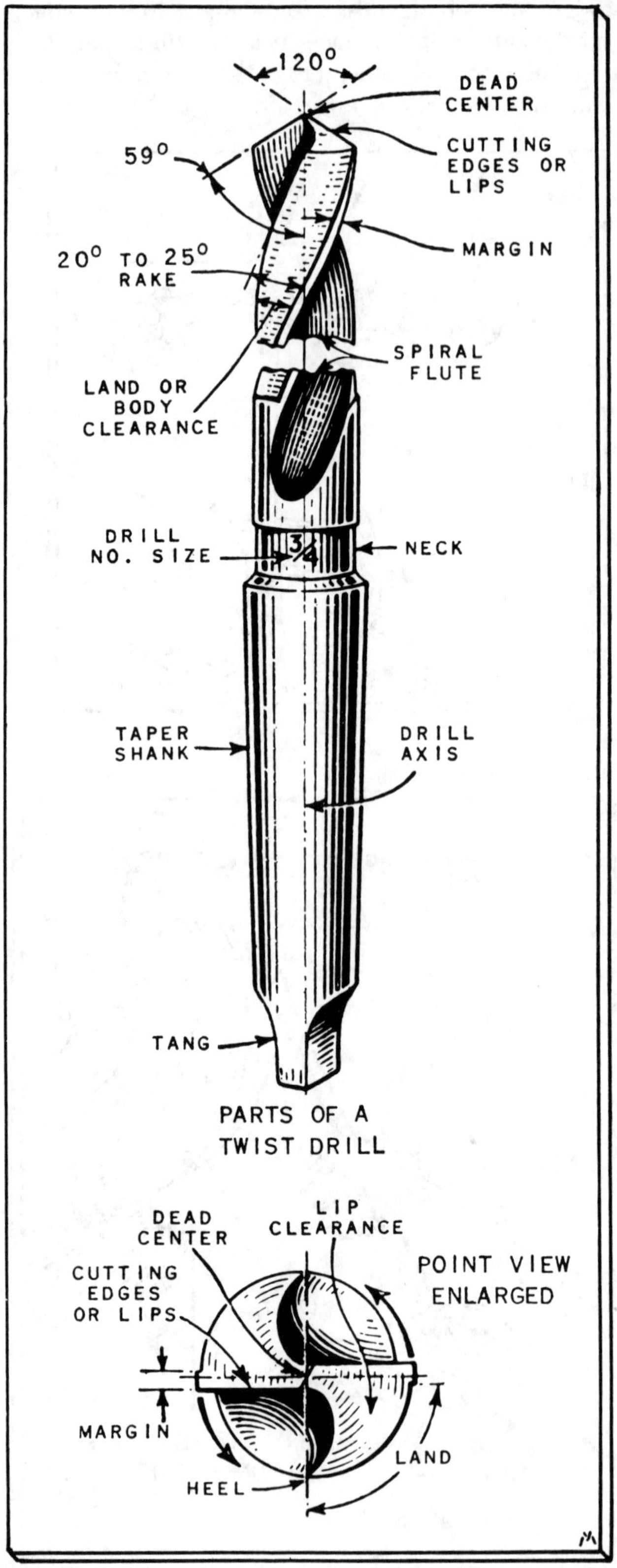

120°
DEAD CENTER
59°
CUTTING EDGES OR LIPS
MARGIN
20° TO 25° RAKE
SPIRAL FLUTE
LAND OR BODY CLEARANCE
DRILL NO. SIZE
NECK
TAPER SHANK
DRILL AXIS
TANG
PARTS OF A TWIST DRILL
DEAD CENTER
LIP CLEARANCE
CUTTING EDGES OR LIPS
POINT VIEW ENLARGED
MARGIN
LAND
HEEL

Figure 18.

off for clearance, and when the cutting edges become dull, only these faces have to be ground.

The flute in the twist drill is milled at an angle of about 20 to 25 degrees with the axis to give the drill the necessary rake, or clearance, between the cutting edge and the work (Fig. 18). When this cutting edge is properly ground, it has a relief angle of about 10 to 12 degrees on the end; consequently the cutting angle of a twist drill ranges usually from 55 to 60 degrees. The flute in a twist drill is designed so that the chips work out easily while cutting. This is an added advantage when drilling a fairly deep hole. They also serve as leads for lubricants.

Figure 18 shows that, after the flute in the twist drill has been cut, the remaining portion of the surface of the body of the drill is relieved, or cut away, and a narrow *land*, or body clearance, remains. This reduces the friction of the drill in the hole. The thinner section of the body of the drill, between the bottoms of the flutes, is called the *web*.

When properly sharpened, the cutting edges of a twist drill produce a hole that is fairly round, straight, and of the same diameter as the drill. However, a twist drill is considered essentially a roughing tool. Holes are made more accurate by subsequent reaming or grinding.

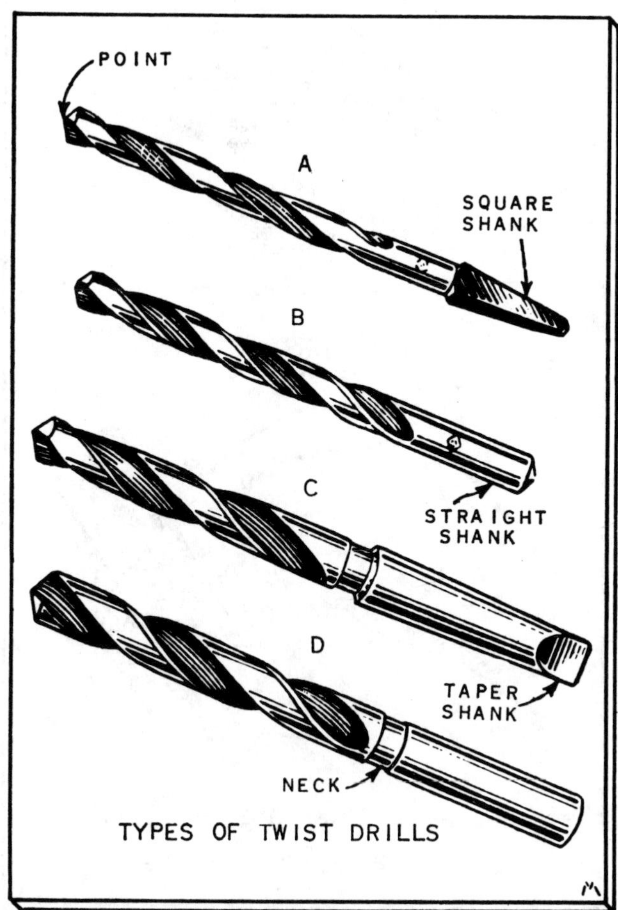

Figure 19.

Square-shank Twist Drills. The square-shank twist drill is designed to fit into the chuck of a wood-working ratchet brace (A, Fig. 19). It is made of metal that has been tempered for use in soft metal. A wood-working brace is not ideal for driving a twist drill and should be used only if a hand or breast drill is not available, or when hidden nails or other unexpected metal may be encountered in the work. Square-shank drills are available in diameters ranging from 1/16 in. to 3/4 in. in gradations of 1/32 in.

Straight-shank Twist Drills. Straight-shank twist drills up to 1/2 in. in diameter are used in either hand or breast drills, small power drills, and the lighter type of drill presses fitted with either a two-jaw or a three-jaw chuck.

There are two types of straight-shank twist drills: those with a neck or ring-shaped groove in the shank, and those without a neck (B and D, Fig. 19). The small sizes, up to 1/4 in. in diameter, have no neck, and are inserted in the small hand and breast drills by turning the sleeve outside the chuck to open the jaws wide enough, and then tightening in the opposite direction. Chucks used for drills larger than 1/4 in. in diameter are usually opened and closed by means of a wrench called a key.

Taper-shank Twist Drills. Taper-shank twist drills of more than 1/2 in. diameter are used only in power drills. Hand drills or breast drills do not have sufficient power to drive larger sizes efficiently. The small end of a taper-shank drill is machined flat to form a tang which fits into a slot in the end of the spindle socket in a power drill press (C, Fig. 19).

CLASSIFICATION OF TWIST DRILLS. All types of Morse twist drills are made of either carbon-tool steel or high-speed steel. Carbon-tool-steel drills are used in hand and breast drills and where low-speed drilling is required on power drill presses. They are less expensive than high-speed-steel drills.

High-speed-steel drills are used on high-speed, power driven drill presses. They can be operated at much higher cutting speeds and will retain their cutting edges longer than carbon-tool-steel drills.

The sizes of Morse twist drills are arranged in four groups: numerical, alphabetical, fractional or machinist's, and metric. The numerical sizes are numbered from 1 to 80, ranging in diameter from 0.0135 in. to 0.228 in. The number is stamped on the shank of the large sizes only; a drill gauge is used to identify the small sizes. A drill gauge is a flat piece of steel in which sixty marked holes have been drilled (Fig. 20). The number above the hole into which a drill fits snugly is the number size of that particular drill. Sizes 61 to 80 are seldom used, and are too small to gauge accurately without a micrometer caliper. As a rule, the diameter in decimal parts of an inch also is marked on the gauge. If this is not the case, the diameter of the particular drill can be ascertained by referring to a standard table of drill sizes.

The fractional sizes are available in diameters ranging from 1/64 in. to 4 in. or more in gradations of 1/64 in.

The metric sizes range from 0.5 mm (millimeter) to 10.0 mm in gradations of 0.1 mm, and from 10.0 mm to 25.5 mm in gradations of 0.5 mm.

Laying Out and Indenting the Hole. The exact location of the hole to be drilled must be marked and indented to prevent the point of the drill from walking around the metal before it takes hold. This is called laying out a hole for drilling. With the point of a scriber, mark the spot accurately and locate the center of the hole with an X. Make an indentation at this point with a center punch and hammer (Fig. 21).

Center punches are pointed tools made from either round or octagonal steel rod. Two types of punches are used (Fig. 21): the prick or dot punch, with a 60 degree point, and the center punch, sometimes called the octagonal type, with a 90 degree point. Both punches are ground to a true taper point central with the shank of the tool. The dot punch is used to make the first indentation locating the center of the hole. The center punch is used to widen and deepen the indentation.

To make the indentation at the exact spot required, the punch must be held at a slight angle while the point is placed. Then straighten it up until it is exactly perpendicular to the surface of the metal. Hold the shank of the punch between the thumb and the first and second fingers as shown in Fig. 21. Using the machinist's hammer, make several quick firm taps in line with the punch.

Drilling with a Hand or Breast Drill. A hand drill can be used to drill holes up to 1/4 in. in diameter in soft steel, brass, zinc, aluminum, cast iron, and other die-cast alloys. When holes from 1/4 in. to 1 in. in diameter have to be drilled in these materials, a breast drill must be used. The average type of hand drill available is equipped with a three-jaw chuck, which takes straight-shank twist drills up to 1/4 in. in diameter.

Only the shank of the drill should be gripped by

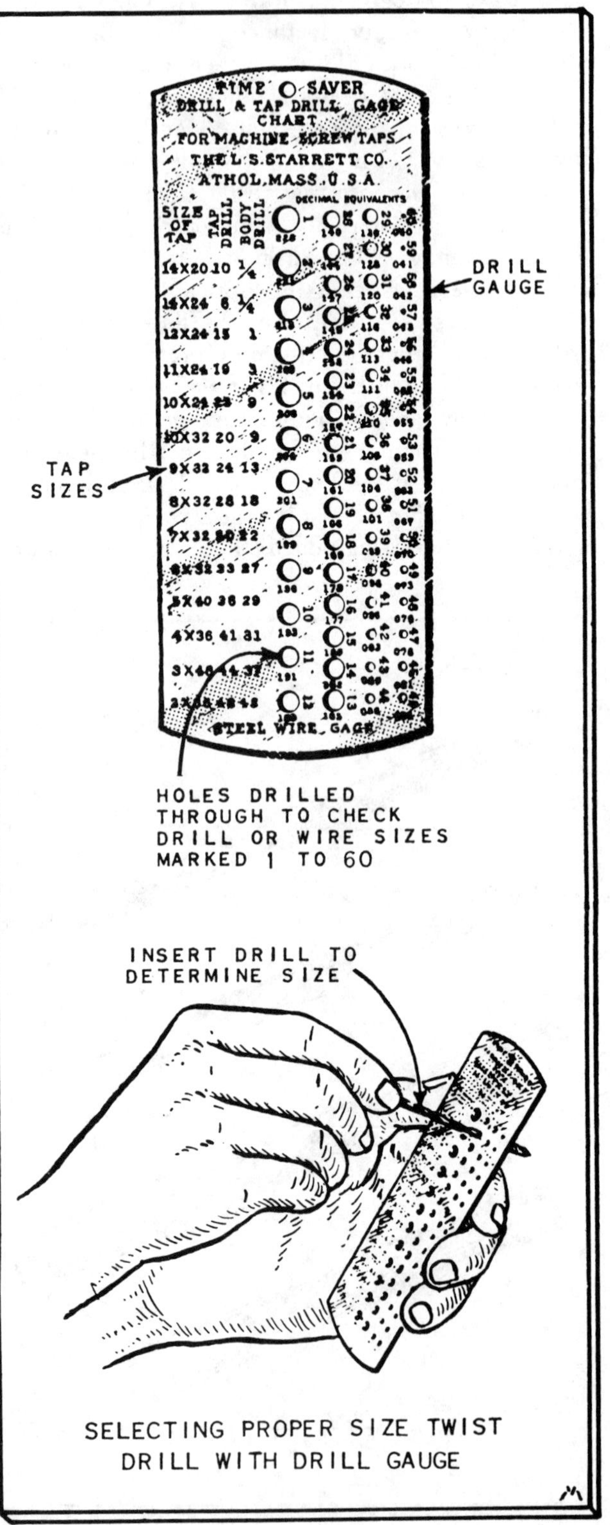

Figure 20.

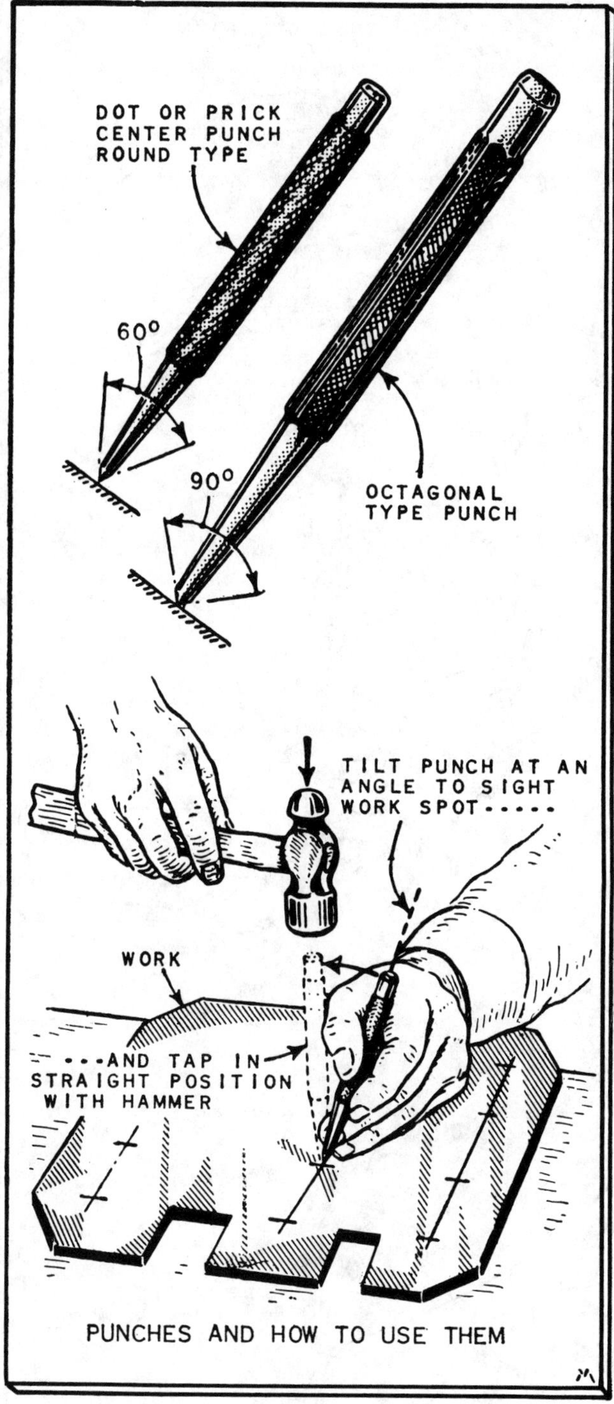

Figure 21.

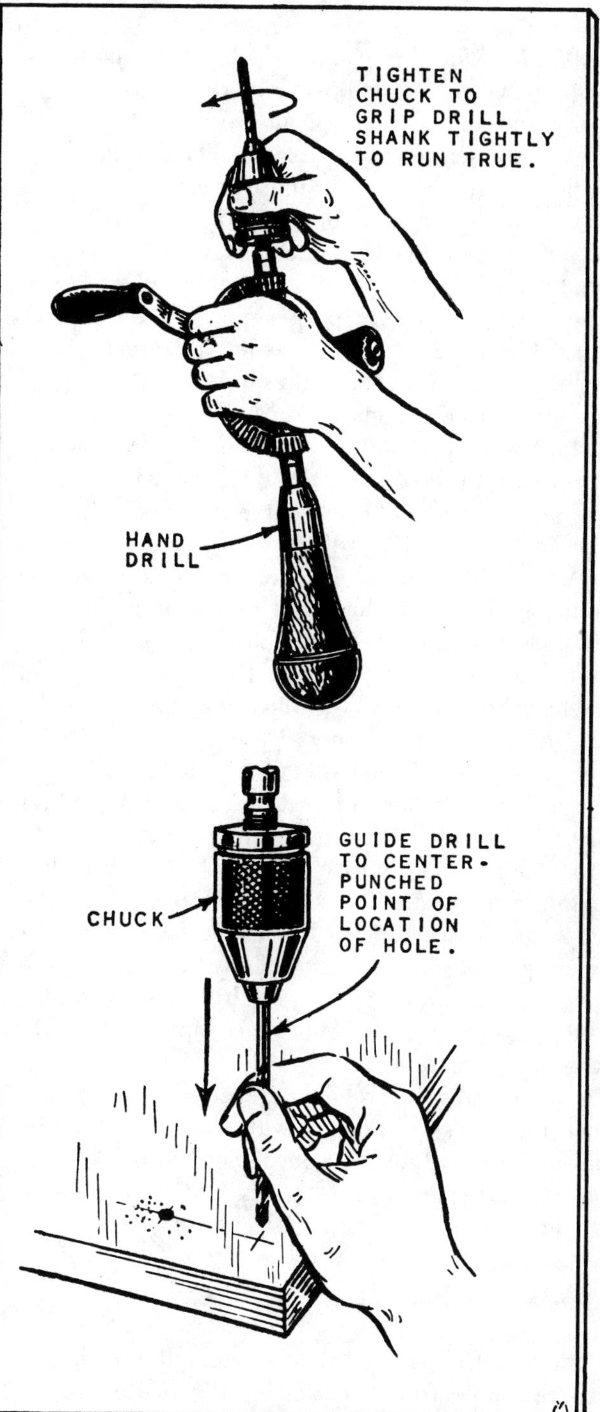

Figure 22.

the chuck (Fig. 22). The shank is softer than the fluted part of the drill, and the jaws of the chuck grip it more tightly, which lessens the danger of breaking the drill. Do not insert the entire length of the shank in the chuck (Fig. 22), but leave a portion of it outside to take up some of the strain. If the shank is set in all the way up to the fluted portion, the drill may snap.

Before drilling a hole, check the drill to find out if it is gripped tightly in the chuck and if it runs straight and true (Fig. 22). When a drill runs out of true, a bent shank probably is responsible. A drill wobbles if there is a burr on the shank. An out-of-true drill will not bore a hole to the exact size required and is liable to break.

After marking the metal with the center punch at the point where the hole is to be drilled, secure the work firmly in a vise. If it is not secured firmly, drill breakage or serious injury may result (Fig. 23).

The hand or breast drill must be held steady and in an absolutely straight line with the twist drill once the hole is started. Too much pressure on the drill may bend or break it. As you turn the drill, maintain an even motion and the proper speed for the type of material (Fig. 23). Never attempt to force a drill; feed it with even pressure and speed.

Drills of small diameter do not clear themselves of chips so readily as the larger ones. When drilling small-diameter holes, withdraw the twist drill from the hole occasionally to clear the flutes of chips.

Do not use twist drills smaller than 1/16 in. in diameter with hand drills. Smaller sizes than this should be used in a motorized hand tool of the type shown in Fig. 24.

Drilling Speeds and Feeds. The type of material in which holes are to be drilled and the size of the drill determine the proper speed and feed of the drill. A general rule governing speed and feed is that, in a given material, small drills must be turned faster and fed into the work more rapidly than larger drills.

In drilling a hole in mild or soft steel, the drill should be run and fed slowly. For harder metals, the speed and feed of the drill must be faster than for the softer material. In copper, brass, bronze, aluminum, and aluminum alloys, the drill must turn at a greater speed and be fed more rapidly than for either mild iron or steel.

Drill squeaks occur when a drill is fed too fast, when the flutes are clogged with chips, or when the drill has become dull. A squeaking drill quickly becomes overheated and loses its cutting edge and temper.

Hacksaws and Blades

The essential parts of a hacksaw are the blade and the adjustable frame that holds the blade. An efficient hacksaw is equipped with a frame adjustable for 8 in., 10 in., or 12 in. blades, and has either a pistol-grip or a straight handle (Fig. 25).

Hacksaws can be used to cut practically all types of metals, with the exception of tempered steel.

To ascertain whether a metal can be cut with a hacksaw, test it with a file. If the metal cannot be filed, it cannot be cut with a hacksaw.

Inserting a Hacksaw Blade. To insert the blade in the frame of the saw, first adjust the frame to fit

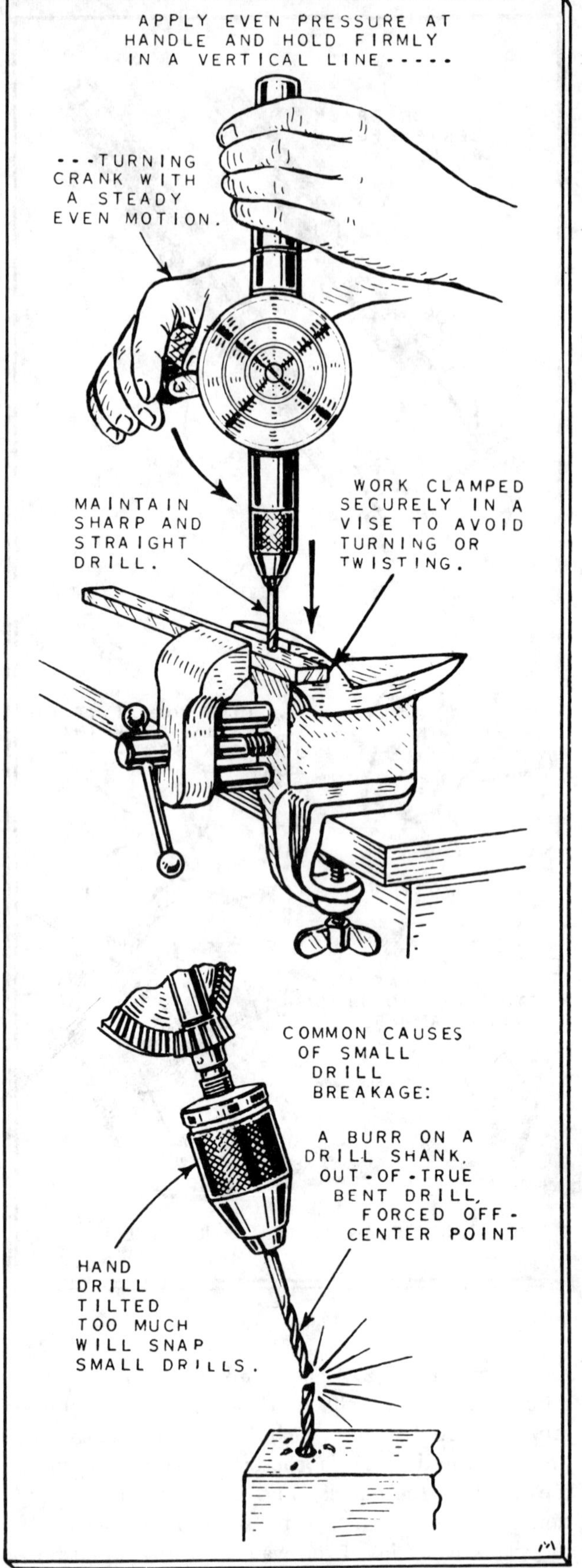
APPLY EVEN PRESSURE AT HANDLE AND HOLD FIRMLY IN A VERTICAL LINE-----
---TURNING CRANK WITH A STEADY EVEN MOTION.
MAINTAIN SHARP AND STRAIGHT DRILL.
WORK CLAMPED SECURELY IN A VISE TO AVOID TURNING OR TWISTING.
COMMON CAUSES OF SMALL DRILL BREAKAGE:
A BURR ON A DRILL SHANK, OUT-OF-TRUE BENT DRILL, FORCED OFF-CENTER POINT
HAND DRILL TILTED TOO MUCH WILL SNAP SMALL DRILLS.

Figure 23.

the length of the blade. All hacksaw blades have a hole in each end to fit over pins in the stretchers at each end of the saw frame. When a blade is set in the frame, the teeth must point away from the handle (Fig. 26). When the blade is in position, tighten the wingnut until the blade is under strong tension.

A hacksaw blade cannot be reset, sharpened, or ground, and when dull or broken it must be replaced with a new one. To replace a blade, turn the wingnut on the frame of the hacksaw until the tension is re-

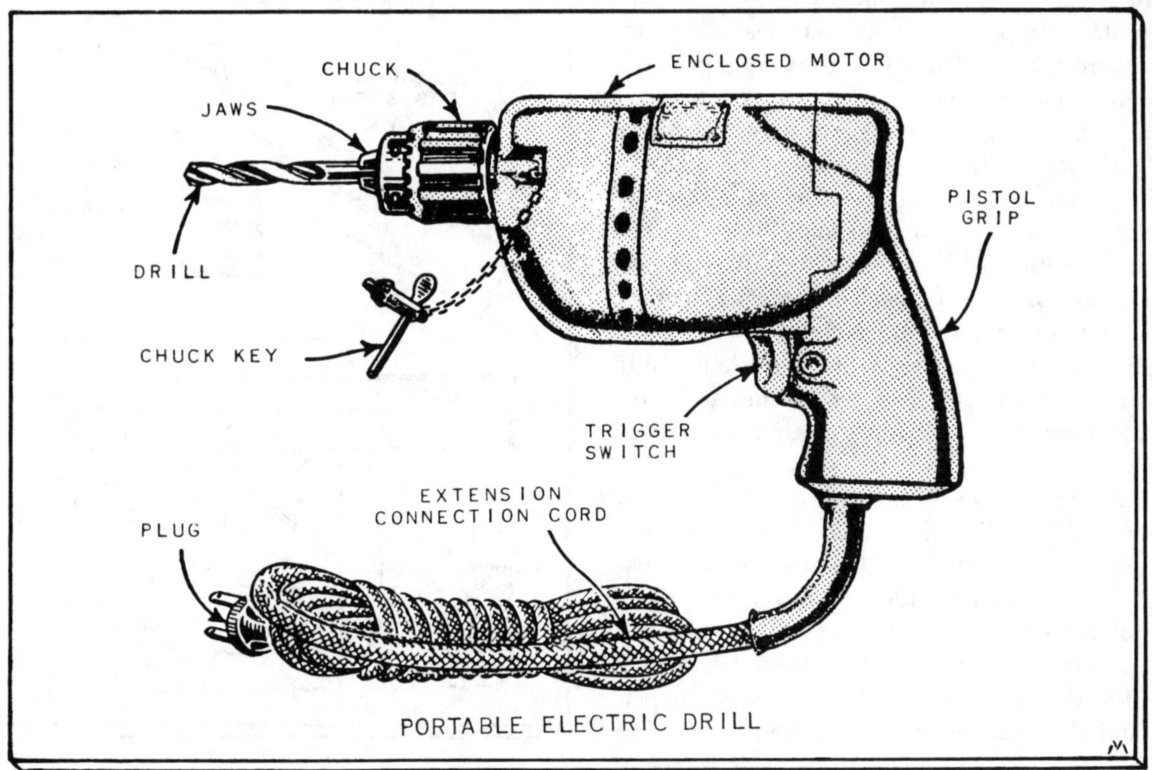

Figure 24.

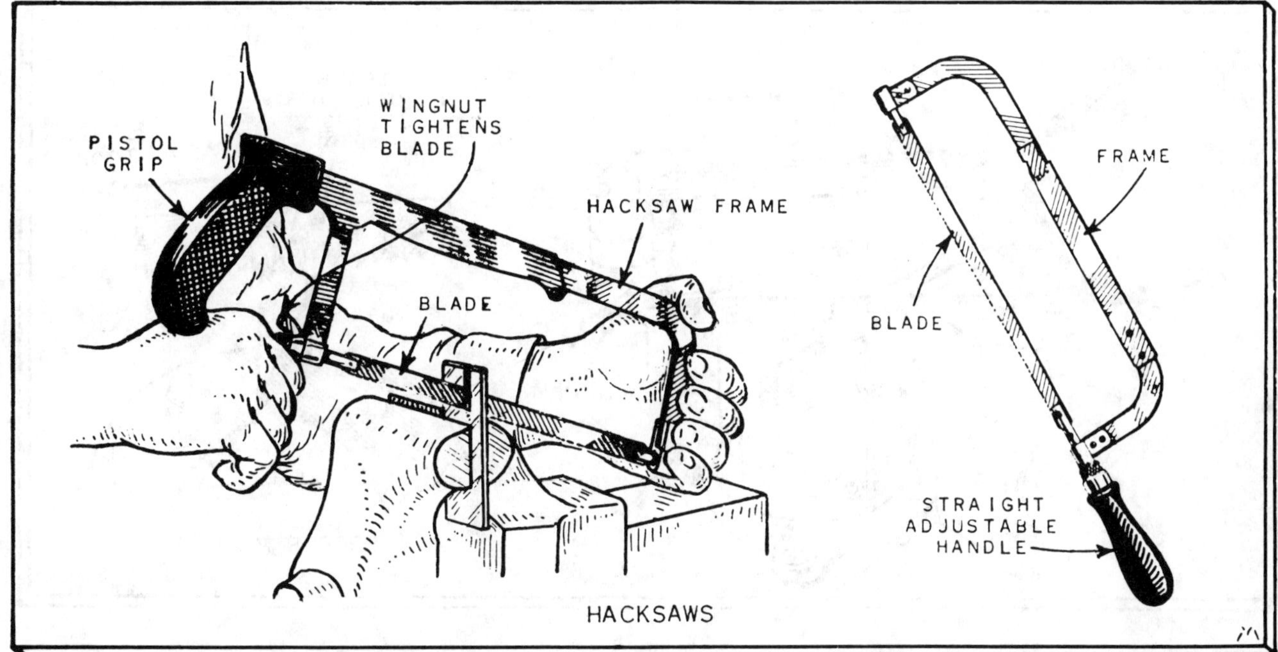

Figure 25.

leased, then remove the old blade. Insert a new blade, and tighten the wingnut.

SELECTING THE HACKSAW BLADE. Hacksaw blades are classified according to the number of teeth per inch, or pitch, as it is sometimes called. They range from 14 to 32 teeth per inch, in gradations of 4. The 14- and 18-teeth-per-inch blades are classified further as hard blades. The 24- and 32-teeth-per-inch blades are termed flexible.

Three rules govern the choice of a correct blade for metal cutting. The first is known in the trade as the three-tooth rule, which means that at least three consecutive teeth of the blade should be in contact at all times with the work (Fig. 26). Although the type and size of blade depend to a great extent on the material to be cut, the three-tooth rule also serves as a guide in selecting the size of the blade tooth. It is a proved fact that coarse-toothed blades are faster cutters than fine-toothed blades, but they break more easily.

Two other rules for selecting the correct blade are: a fine-toothed blade plus light, steady pressure should be used on tubing and thin sections of material; a coarse-toothed blade with heavy, even pressure should be used on thick stock or material.

When cutting tool steel and drill rod, use an all-hard 18-teeth-per-inch blade. For soft steel, copper, brass, and aluminum, with the exception of very thin material, a 14-teeth-per-inch all-hard blade is recommended. For steel trim, wrought-iron pipe, and electrical conduit use a 24-teeth-per-inch flexible blade. Thin metal and tubing should be cut with a 32-teeth-

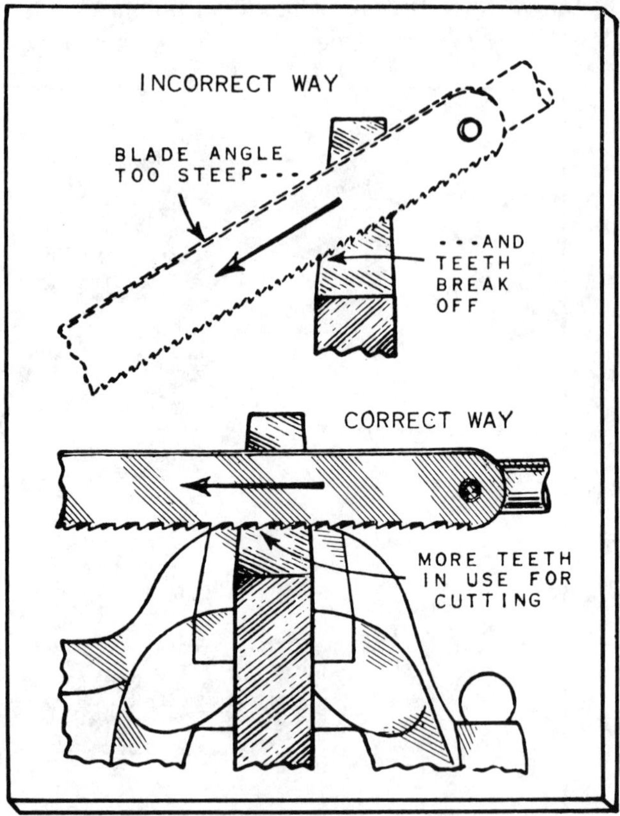

Figure 27.

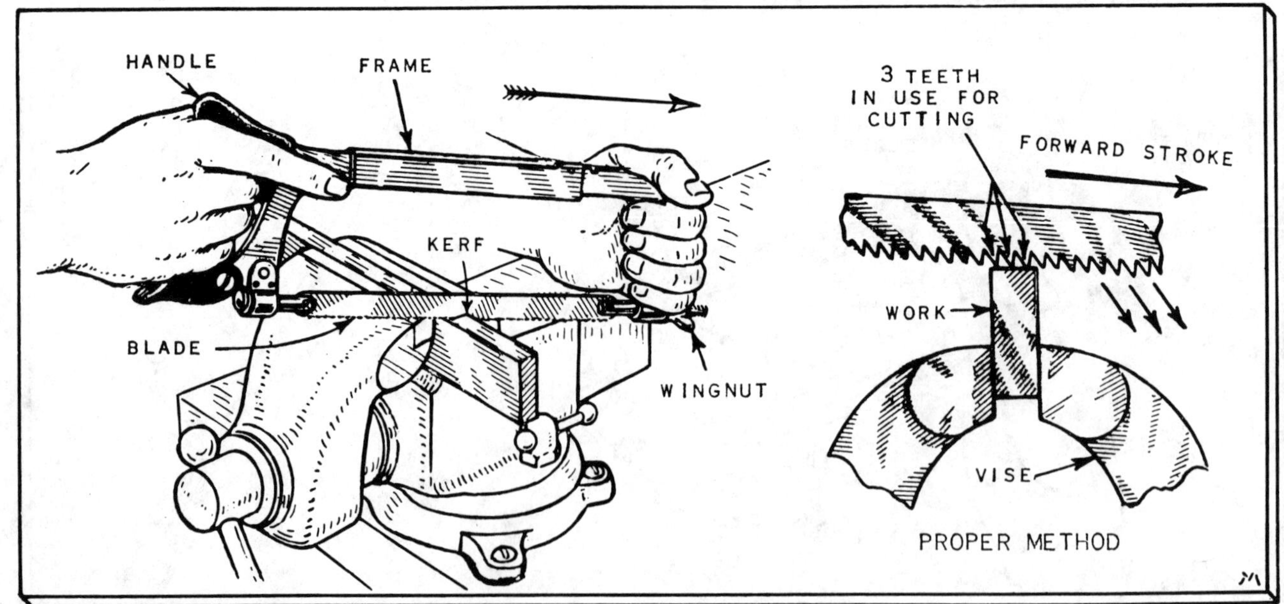

Figure 26.

per-inch flexible blade and light angle pieces with an 18-teeth-per-inch all-hard blade. When cutting very thin sheet metal, the work must be clamped between two pieces of wood.

Figure 28.

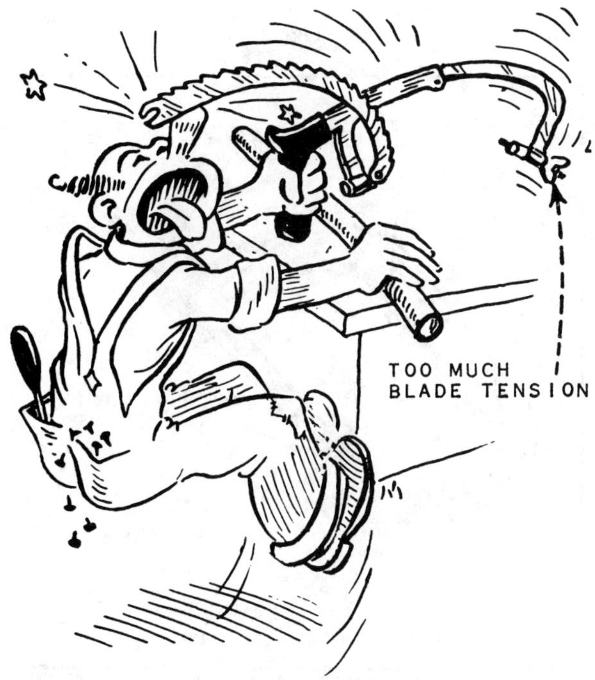

Figure 29.

USING A HACKSAW. To prevent the blade from breaking and to assure a good clean cut, the material must be securely fastened in a vise (Figs. 26 and 27). Always start the cut at a slight angle, guiding the blade with the thumb of the left hand until the cut, or kerf, is of sufficient depth so that both hands can be used on the frame of the saw.

When starting the cut, it is not necessary to lift the blade off the work on the return stroke. After the cut has been started, grasp the frame of the hacksaw with both hands, one hand on the handle and the other hand on the far end of the frame (Fig. 26). Because the hacksaw cuts only on the forward stroke, use a little pressure on the forward stroke, but on the return stroke, lift the saw slightly so that the teeth scarcely touch the metal work (Fig. 26). All strokes must be long and steady so that nearly all the teeth on the blade are in use (Fig. 27).

The amount of pressure used on the forward stroke is governed by the type of material plus the experience of the mechanic. Light pressure is used on soft metals and on thin sections of metals, but more pressure is necessary on the harder metals and heavier sections.

Do not saw too rapidly. A rate of approximately 60 strokes per minute should be the top speed. Slow, steady strokes with the proper pressure are far more effective than fast, uneven cutting. Always keep the blade of the saw moving in a straight line and use sufficient pressure to keep the blade from becoming either jammed or pinched, since this tends to break the teeth or the blade.

BLADE BREAKAGE, CAUSES AND PREVENTION. If you examine a new hacksaw blade, you will see that the teeth are set, that is, alternately pushed out in opposite directions from the blade, similar to the teeth of a wood-working saw. This makes the slot, or kerf, cut by the teeth slightly larger or wider than the blade, and thus provides the clearance necessary to prevent the blade from sticking in the material.

With constant use, the points of the teeth wear down and become dull, and at the same time straighten out so that the kerf becomes narrower. Thus, a dull blade has a tendency to stick considerably more than a new one, and forcing it through a cut will cause the blade to break.

If a blade breaks while a cut is being made and a new blade is necessary to continue the work, always start the new cut in line with the first one, if possible. If the piece of work is round or square, it should be rotated 90 to 180 degrees and a new cut started to meet the old one. If the piece is flat, turn it over and start the new cut from the opposite edge. When this is impossible and it is necessary to use a new blade before the cut is finished, work the new blade into the old slot very gradually and with extreme care.

Aside from normal use, the teeth can become dull and the points rounded for other reasons. The cutting speed may be too fast. The frame of the saw may not have been lifted slightly on the return stroke. This is easily remedied by remembering to apply a slight lift to the frame on the return stroke. Or you may not be using the proper blade. In that event, select the proper blade for the type of material that is being cut. The blade may have been in the frame with the teeth pointed backward. If so, simply reverse it. Teeth sometimes can be dulled when the pressure is too light; exert a firmer pressure when cutting.

Hacksaw blades will also snap or break for the following reasons: There may not be enough tension on the blade (Fig. 28), or there may be too much tension (Fig. 29), or the teeth on the blade may have been too coarse for the material being cut. A new blade may have been started incorrectiy in a kerf cut by an old blade. Too much pressure may have been used on a blade. The frame of the saw may have been twisted while sawing.

If a blade twists (Fig. 30) or bends slightly before it snaps, not enough tension was put on the blade when it was inserted in the frame. The tension must be increased when a new blade is inserted. If the blade broke at the holes, too much tension was put on it when it was inserted. If a breakage is caused by using a new blade in a kerf started by an old blade, the work must be turned around, and a new cut started to meet the old one. When a break occurs because the material is too hard, a finer blade must be selected. If too much pressure on the blade causes a break, do not bear down so hard with a new blade. A break caused by twisting the frame of the saw can be avoided by pushing the saw steadily back and forth in a straight line so that there is no wobbling or twisting.

Breaking or twisting of the saw teeth may be caused by too much downward pressure when cutting. Sometimes breaking or stripping of the teeth is caused by starting the cut at the corner of the material. Always start a cut at a slight angle with the surface, not at the corner, and keep off all sharp corners.

Clamps

The two types of clamps used for sheet metalworking are the C-clamps and the parallel clamp.

C-CLAMPS (Fig. 31). C-clamps are available in a variety of sizes. The threaded movable part of this clamp is equipped with a non-rotating swivel head which advances as the screw is turned.

Using C-clamps (Fig. 32). Clamps are secured on the work with the swivel head on the underside. If more than one clamp is used, clamps are tightened alternately.

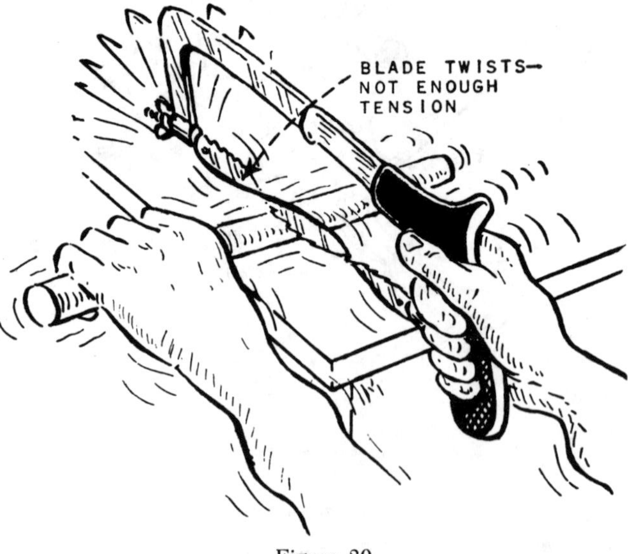

Figure 30.

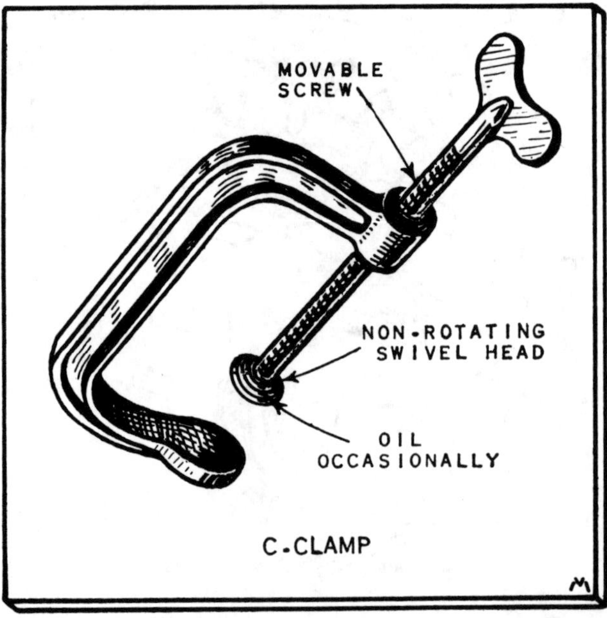

Figure 31.

Parallel Clamp (Fig. 33). Parallel clamps are equipped with two knurled screws. The outer screw is used to push the jaws apart, and the inner screw holds the jaws together. To be effective the jaws of these clamps must always be parallel, otherwise the work will slip.

Using Parallel Clamps (Fig. 33). To open the clamps, turn both screws. Place the clamps on the work, making sure that as large a surface of the work as possible is in contact with the jaws of the clamp. Adjust the clamps until they are slightly opened (A, Fig. 33). Proceed to close the jaws parallel with the work by turning the outer screw. When jaws are properly closed and tightened, they should rest flat on the work as shown at B, Fig. 33.

Pliers and Nippers

Pliers generally used in the sheet metal workshop are combination, round-nose, flat-nose, long-nose, and cutting pliers or nippers. The types of cutting pliers are side-cutting, end-cutting, diagonal-cutting, and Bernard side-cutting. Never use pliers on hardened steel surfaces, because this will dull the teeth, causing the pliers to lose their gripping power.

Combination Pliers. Combination pliers can be used in many instances as a general purpose tool (Fig. 34). The slip joint of these pliers permits the jaws to be opened wide at the hinge pin when gripping work of large diameter. Combination pliers are used for gripping small rods, pipes, and studs, and sometimes can be used in place of a small wrench. They must never be used for loosening or tightening nuts.

Round-nose Pliers. Both jaws of round-nose pliers are rounded and tapered to a tip toward the end. Round-nose pliers are used for bending and holding curves in wire and in metal strips of small width. The tips of the jaws are used to bend curves of small radius, and the base of the jaws is used in making curves of greater radius (Fig. 35).

Long-nose Pliers. The jaws of long-nose, sometimes called chain-nose pliers, are considerably longer than those of round-nose pliers, and they taper to a blunt point. These pliers are generally

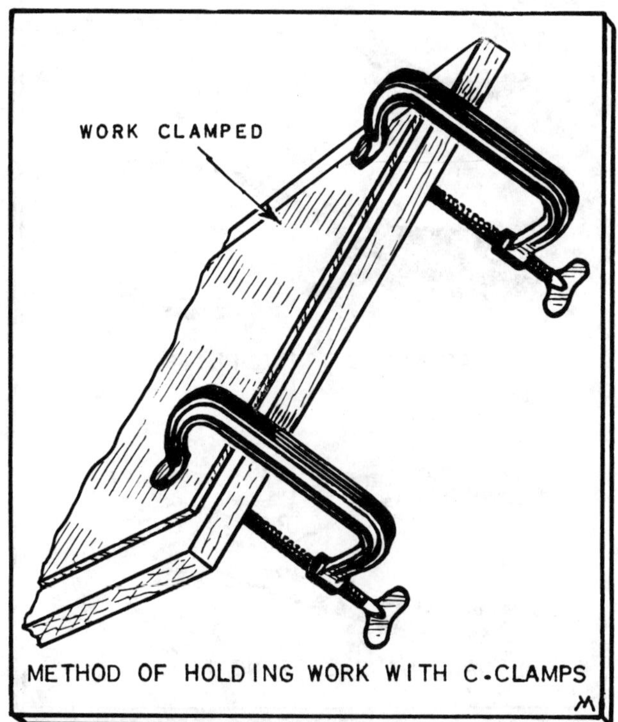

Figure 32.

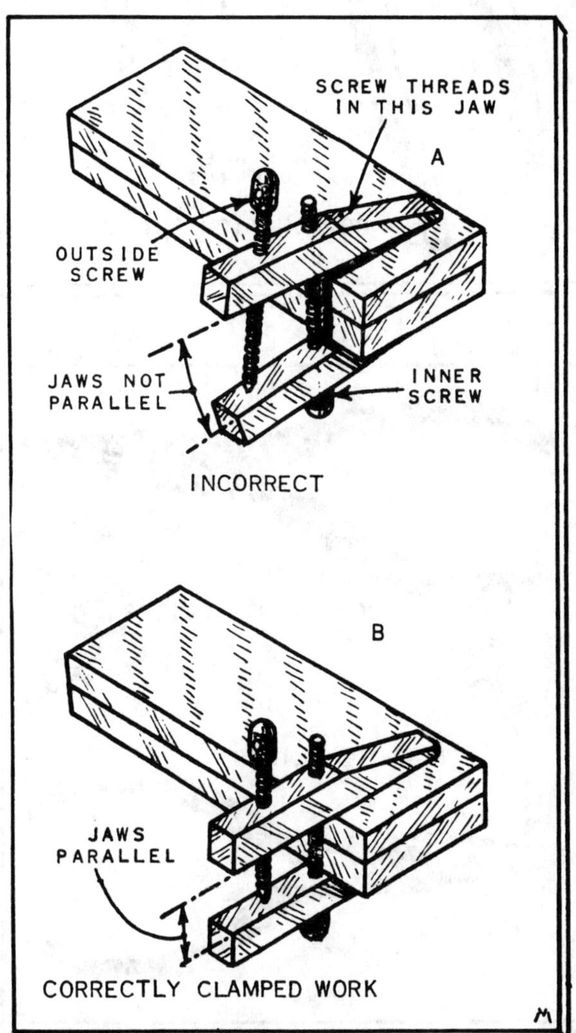

Figure 33.

used for holding parts that are too small to be held with the fingers. The flat surface between the jaws makes long-nose pliers extremely useful as a small wrench when bending angles either in strips of metal or in wires. The length of the jaws makes them particularly useful for recovering nuts, washers, and similar parts, where there is not sufficient room to pick them up with the fingers (Fig. 35).

FLAT-NOSE PLIERS. Unlike the round-nose and long-nose pliers, the jaws of flat-nose pliers do not taper to a point, but have a flat gripping surface between the jaws which is particularly useful for holding and bending angles in strips of metal and in wires (Fig. 36).

DIAGONAL-CUTTING PLIERS OR NIPPERS. Diagonal-cutting pliers are sometimes called diagonal nippers. The angle of the jaws is specially designed to cut close to the surface. They are handy for cutting small wires, screws, rivets, and similar material (Fig. 36).

BERNARD SIDE-CUTTING PLIERS. The parallel jaws hold flat objects firmly so that these pliers can be used both as a vise and as a wrench. Their compound leverage gives them great holding and cutting power. Six-inch Bernard cutting pliers will cut an 8-penny nail with ease (Fig. 36).

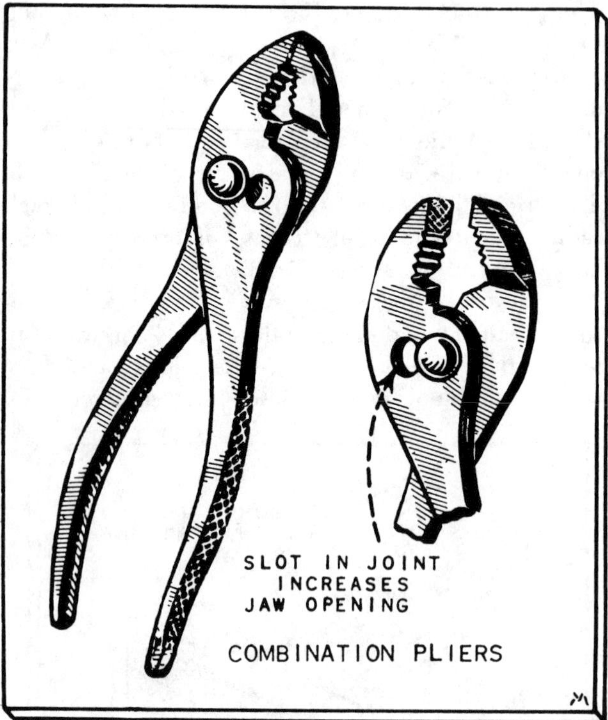

Figure 34.

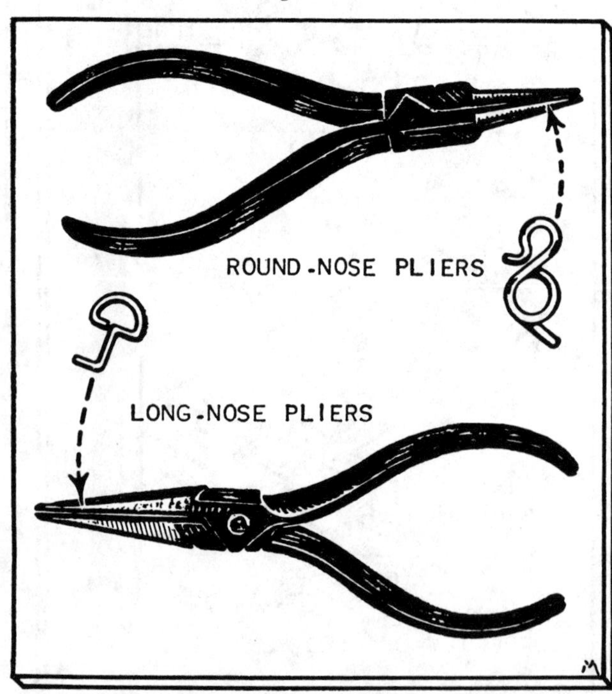

Figure 35.

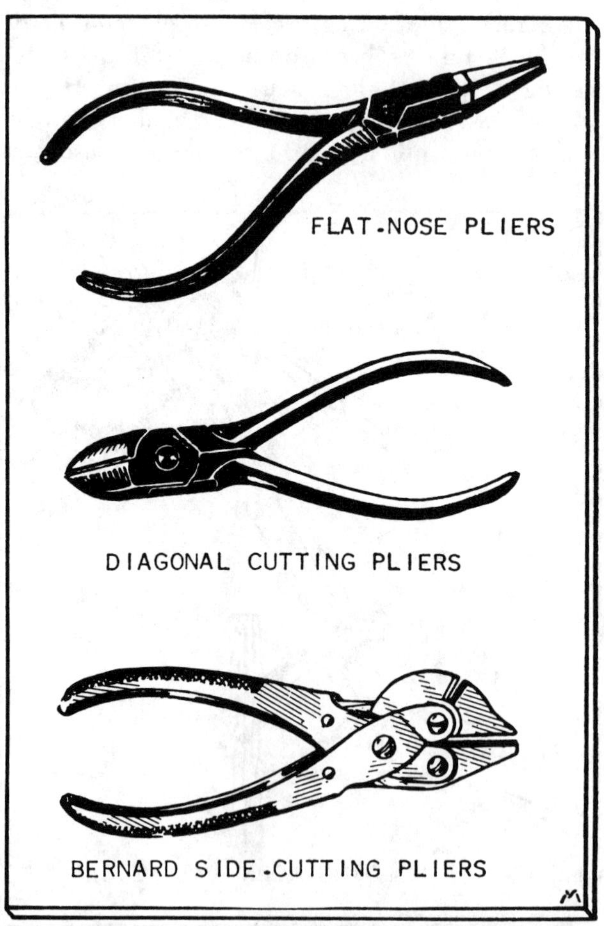

Figure 36.

Wrenches

Of the many types of wrenches, those used most frequently in sheet metal shops are the monkey, adjustable, open-end, pipe and Stillson, socket, and Allen wrenches. There are many other specially designed combination and offset box wrenches, and, of course, many types of wrenches designed for specific industries.

To keep a wrench in good working condition, apply a few drops of light machine oil to all the moving parts.

MONKEY WRENCHES. The monkey wrench is adjustable and is designed specifically for turning the octagonal and square heads of bolts and nuts. Because its jaws are designed for gripping only flat surfaces, this wrench is never used for turning pipe, rods, or other round objects.

Monkey wrenches are equipped with wooden-faced metal handles (Fig. 37). They have two jaws: one is fixed, the other movable. A nut adjusts the opening of the jaws to the required size.

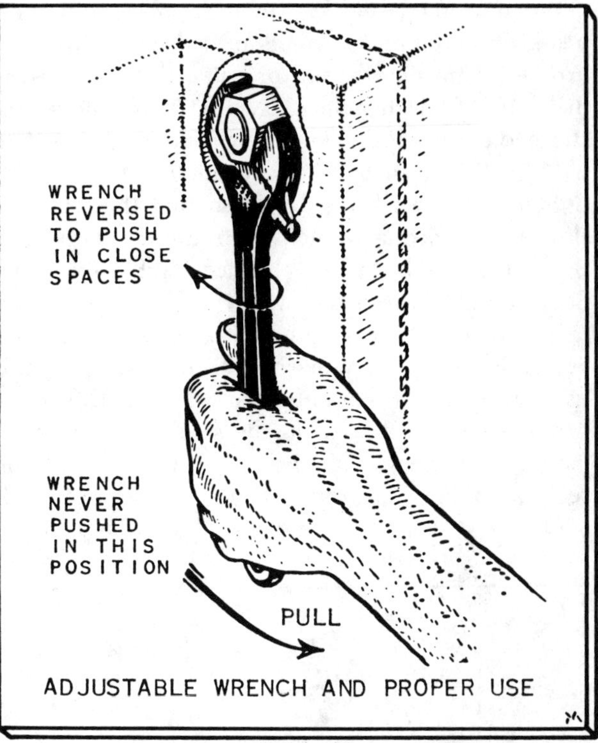

Figure 38.

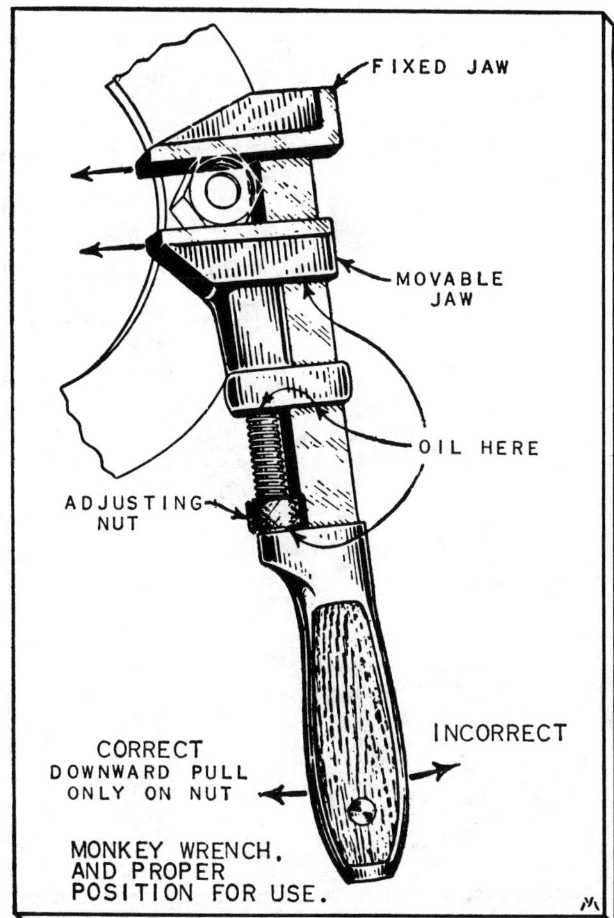

Figure 37.

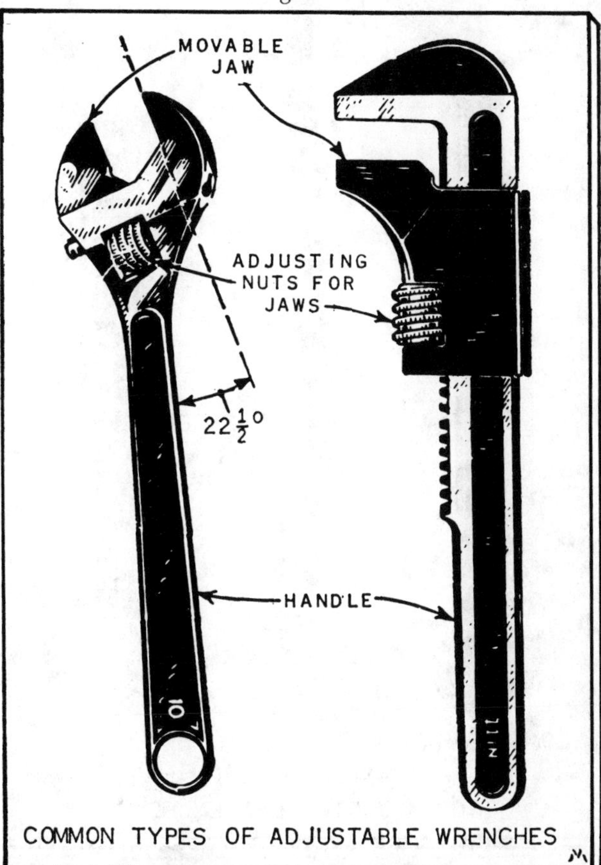

Figure 39.

When using a monkey wrench, place it on the head of the nut or bolt to be turned so that the force exerted in turning the nut or bolt will be applied to the back of the handle (Fig. 37). This relieves the strain on the adjustable jaw, which is the weakest part of the wrench. Before turning a nut or bolt, tighten the wrench jaws on it so that they will not slip. A loose-fitting wrench will round the corners of the nut or bolthead being turned, and make it difficult to tighten or loosen further.

Adjustable Wrenches. Adjustable wrenches are available in a variety of sizes. The most commonly used are 4 in., 8 in., and 12 in. (Fig. 39). The adjustable wrench is used in the same manner as the monkey wrench and for the same purposes. The correct method of using this wrench is shown in Fig. 38.

Open-end Wrenches. Open-end wrenches have a fixed opening between the nonadjustable jaws. They are usually double-ended, that is, they have an opening on either end. The size of the opening between the jaws determines the size of the wrench, and this size is stamped on its side. However, the openings are really from .005 in. to .015 in. larger than the stamped size, to ensure an easy fit.

All types of open-end wrenches are available in many different sizes (Fig. 40). They are sold usually in sets of ten to twelve, in sizes ranging from 5/16 in. to 1 in. Those with large-sized openings are longer, to provide the proper leverage. If all open-end wrenches were made with the same size handle, too much force might be applied on small-sized nuts and bolts, resulting in stripped threads or twisted bolts or studs.

Before using an open-end wrench, make certain that it fits snugly on whatever it is to turn. If the wrench is too loose, it will slip and round the corners. Pull on the wrench to move it in the desired direction—never push on a wrench. In a cramped or tight space, turn the wrench over after each turn of the nut or the bolt (Fig. 41).

Pipe and Stillson Wrenches. Pipe and Stillson wrenches have two toothed jaws, one of which is

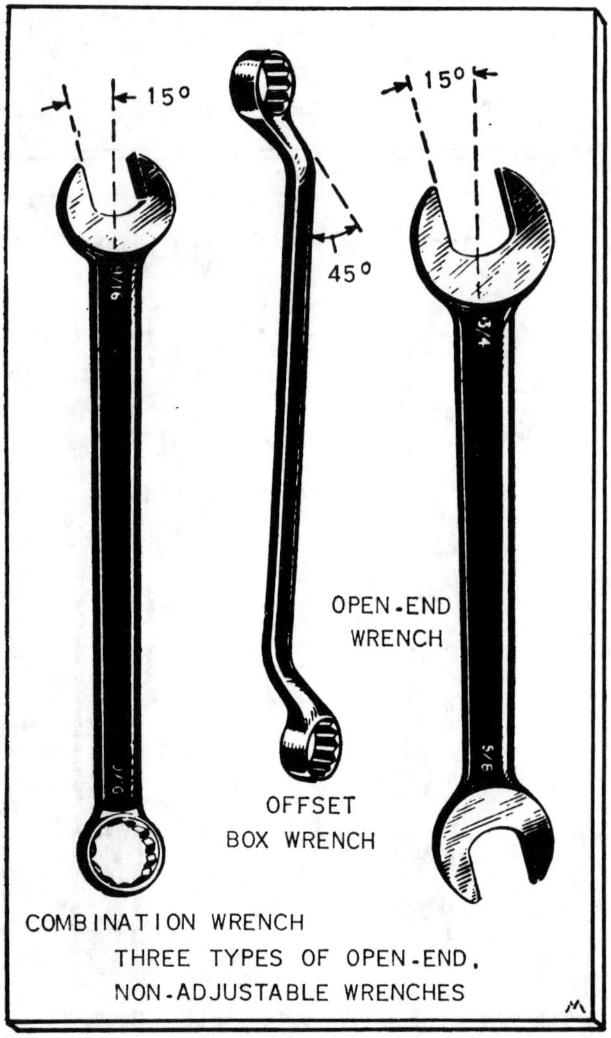

15°
15°
45°
OPEN-END WRENCH
OFFSET BOX WRENCH
COMBINATION WRENCH
THREE TYPES OF OPEN-END, NON-ADJUSTABLE WRENCHES

Figure 40.

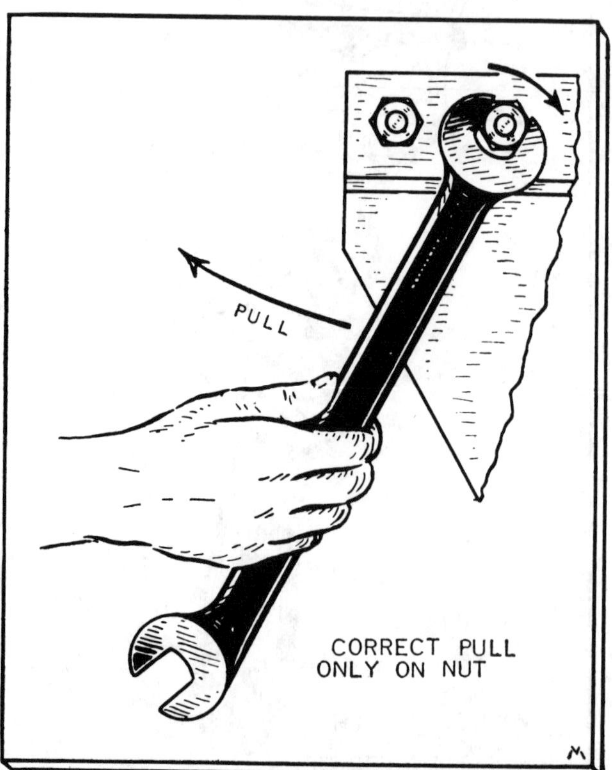

Figure 41.

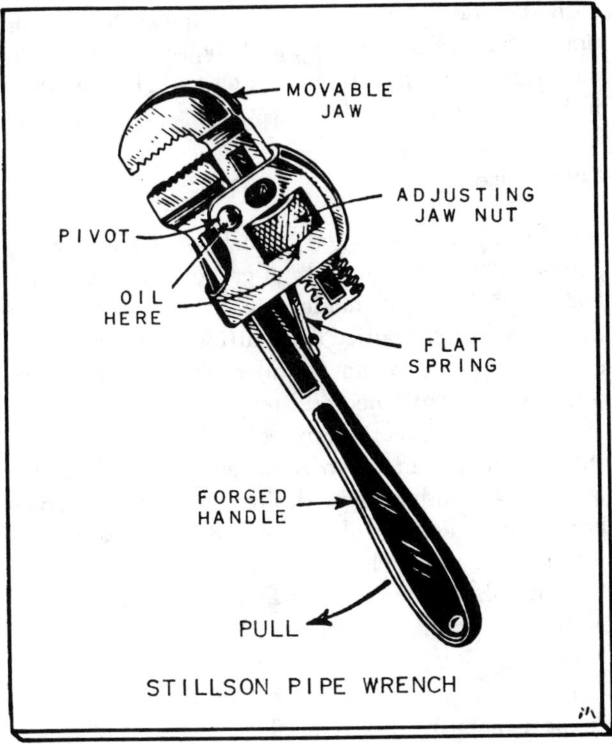

STILLSON PIPE WRENCH

Figure 42.

movable, and a nut for adjusting the opening between them (Fig. 42). The pipe wrench is the only type used on round objects, such as pipes and shafting, and it works in one direction only.

A pipe wrench must never be used on a nut or a bolthead unless the corners have been rounded so that they cannot be turned with any other type of wrench. A pipe wrench will chew a nut or bolt so that it can never be used again. Because of the gripping action of a pipe or Stillson wrench, it is necessary to apply the force to the back of the handle of the wrench.

Socket Wrenches. Socket wrenches come in sets or kits (Fig. 43). These kits consists of several handles and a number of high-strength alloy steel sockets, which fit nuts of different sizes. There are two openings in every socket: one is a square hole to fit the handle, and the other a circular hole with twelve notches that slip over a hexagonal nut or the head of a bolt. Socket wrenches are used extensively in automobile repairs.

Allen Wrenches. Allen wrenches are L-shaped bars of hexagonal tool steel (Fig. 44). They are specially designed to fit the hexagonal sockets in Allen headless setscrews, which are used to fasten pulleys or collars in place on the moving parts of revolving machine shafts and other places where screws or bolts with protruding heads cannot be used. Two other L-shaped screw wrenches are made of round

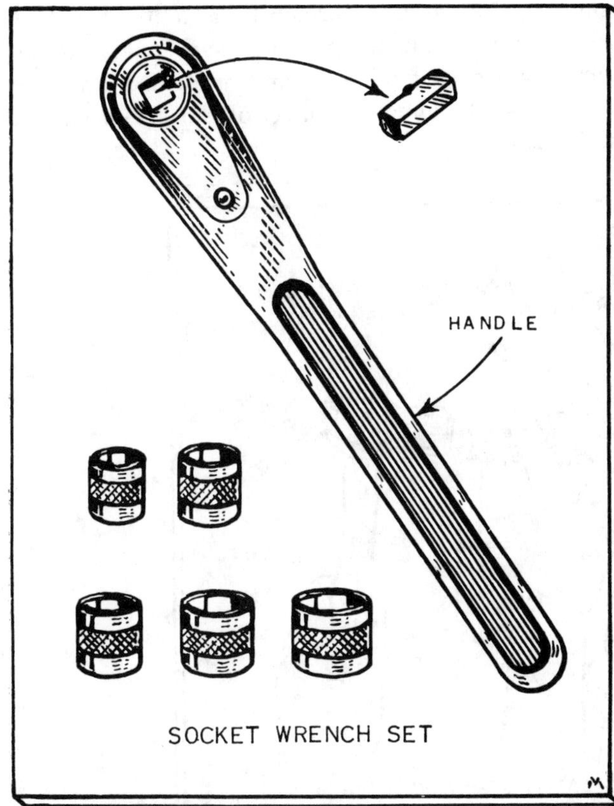

SOCKET WRENCH SET

Figure 43.

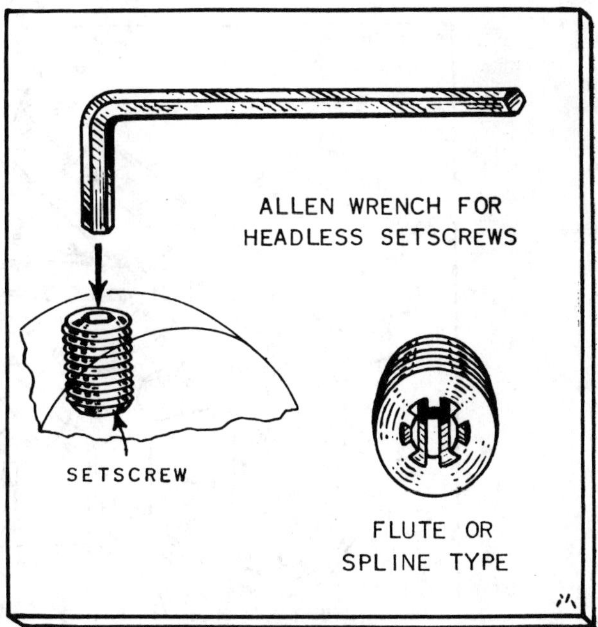

Figure 44.

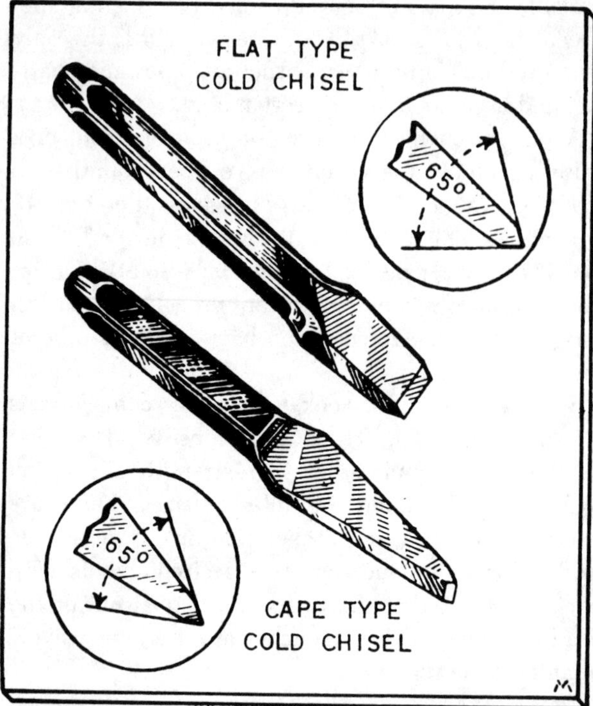

Figure 45.

tool steel with little flutes or splines to fit into other types of headless setscrews, but the Allen screw and wrench are used more extensively.

The short end of the wrench is inserted in the head of the Allen setscrew when the screw is to be tightened or taken out. After loosening the screw with the short end of the wrench, very little additional leverage is required, and the screw can be removed faster by inserting the long end of the wrench in the screwhead.

Cold Chisels

Cold chisels are forged from bars of silicon-manganese alloy steel, tough high-carbon steel, and similar alloys. They are made stubby and blunt to give them greater strength. The cutting edge of a cold chisel is ground to an included angle of about 60 degrees, then hardened and tempered.

In the sheet metal shop, cold chisels are used to cut or split the metal to required sizes and shapes, to cut rods and bars to desired sizes, to cut rivet-heads, and to split obstinate nuts that cannot be moved with a wrench.

Cold chisels are available in sizes ranging from 1/8 in. to 1 in. The size indicates the width of the cutting edge.

The two types of cold chisels most commonly used in sheet metal work are the flat and cape chisels.

FLAT CHISELS. The flat cold chisel is the type most commonly used. The flat chisel has a slightly rounded cutting edge, formed by a double bevel. It is used for cutting heavy gauge sheet metal or for chipping a considerable amount of metal from large surfaces that cannot be filed or surface-machined (Fig. 45).

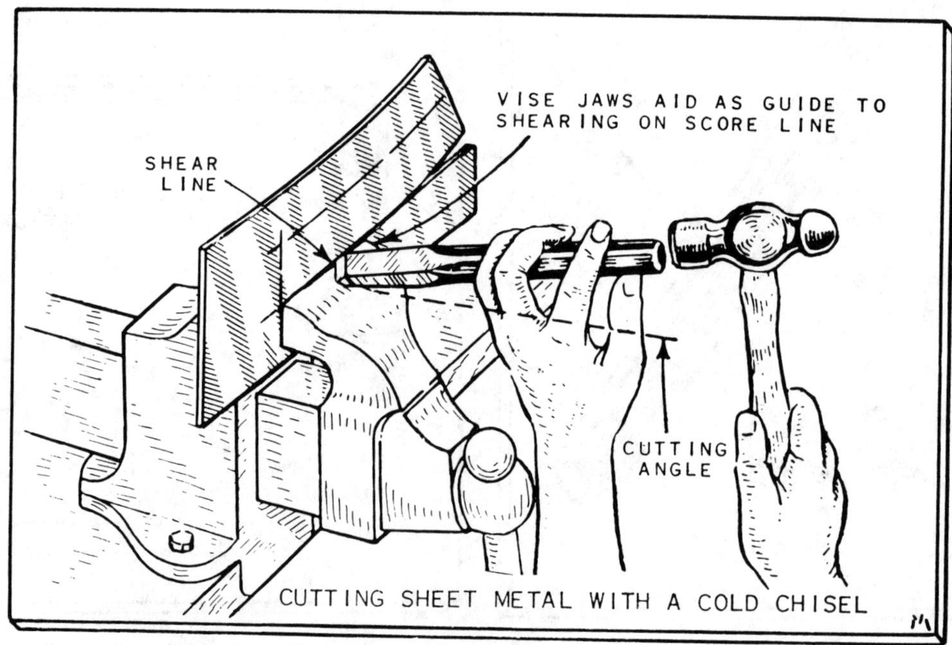

Figure 46.

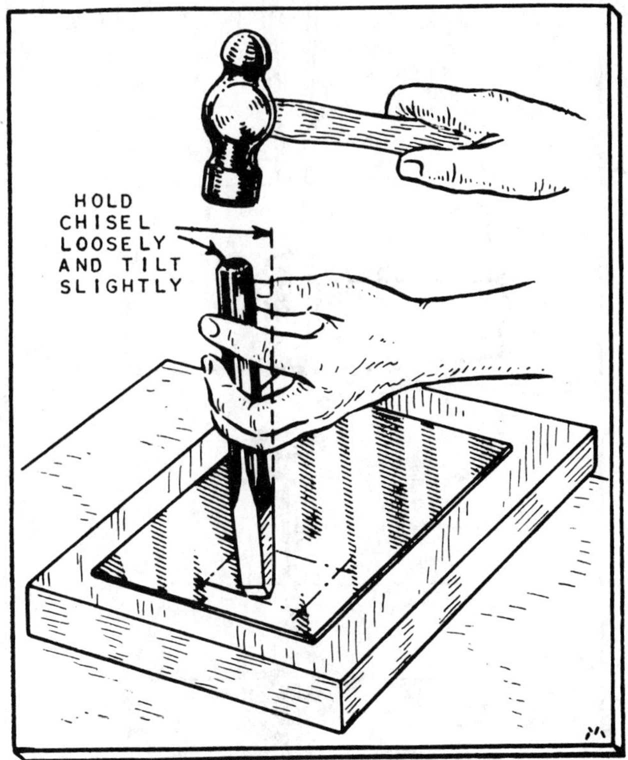

Figure 47. Position of cold chisel for cutting sheet metal.

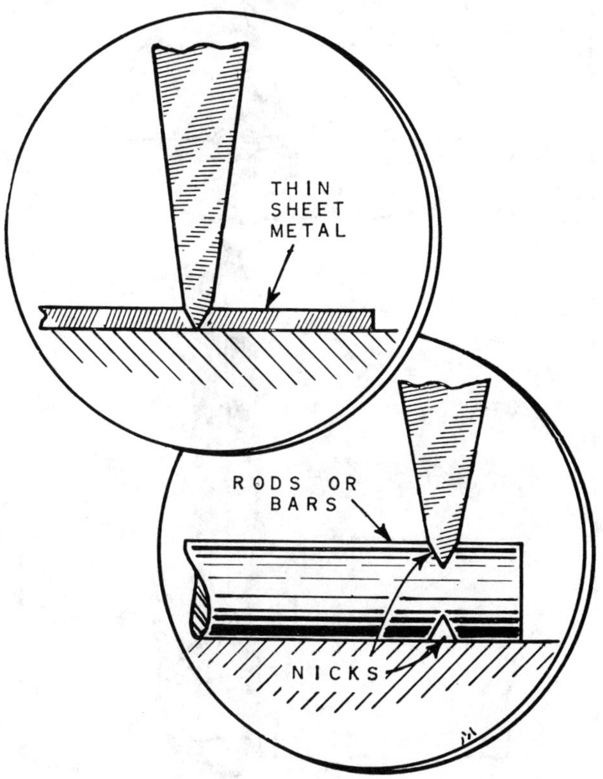

Figure 48. Cutting thin sheet metal and rods on block or anvil.

Cape Chisels. The cutting edge of a cape chisel has a double bevel similar to that of a flat chisel, but is narrower for cutting narrow grooves and square corners (Fig. 45). However, it is slightly wider than the shank, so that there will be no binding in narrow grooves. Cape chisels range from 1/8 in. to 1/2 in. in width.

Cutting with a Cold Chisel. A machinist's hammer is always used to drive a cold chisel. The size of the chisel determines the size of the hammer. The cold chisel is always held loosely between the thumb and the first finger of the left hand (Fig. 46). The remaining fingers must hold the shank of the tool loosely. With the hammer in the right hand, strike sharp, quick blows with the flat face of the hammer and gradually increase the force of the blows as the work progresses.

Cutting Sheet Metal Held in a Vise. Before placing sheet metal in a vise to be cut, mark the metal with a scriber to indicate the cutting line; then, using the scriber or a sharp-pointed tool, deepen the line. Clamp the sheet in the vise above the jaws so that the scribed line is just visible and parallel to the top edge of the vise.

Hold the chisel at an angle to the sheet metal so that the cutting edge shears it across the top of the vise jaw. Strike sharp, quick blows with the flat face of the hammer, and drive the chisel forward along the line to be cut. Always start a cut at the right-hand edge of the metal, and drive the chisel to the left and toward the solid stationary jaw of the vise (Fig. 46).

Cutting Sheet Metal on a Metal Block or Anvil. To cut sheet metal on a block or anvil, first mark and deepen the cutting line on the metal with a scriber. To get a clean-cut edge, always lay the sheet on a block or anvil of soft iron or soft steel. Never use a wood block. The metal block must be placed directly under the point where the cut is to be made.

Hold the chisel vertically to the surface of the sheet (Fig. 47). On plate or heavy sheet metal, the cut deepens gradually, and it is necessary to go over the line several times before it is cut through. On thin sheet metal, the cut is made almost immediately (Figs. 47 and 48).

To cut along a curved line, a chisel of narrow width must be used so that the shape of the cut will conform more closely to the curved line.

Cutting Rods or Small Bars. To cut a rod or a small bar, mark the metal to indicate the cutting point. Lay the rod or bar on a block of steel or iron (Fig. 47). Hold a flat cold chisel in vertical position

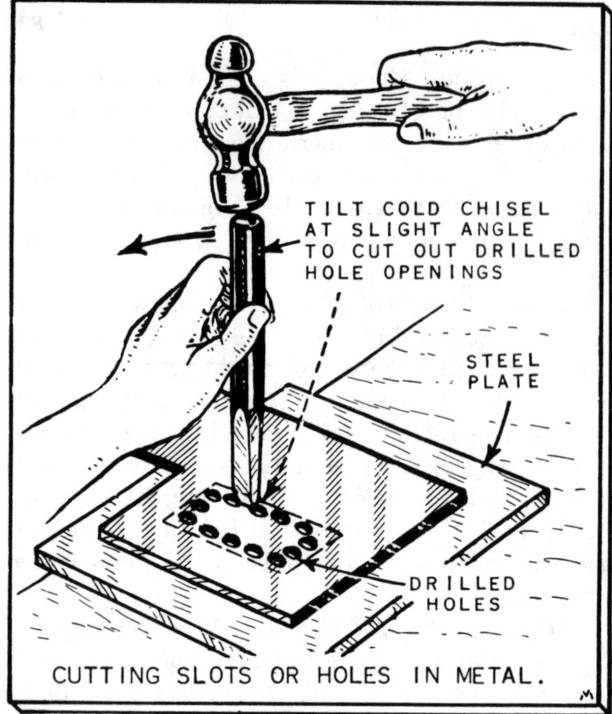

Figure 49.

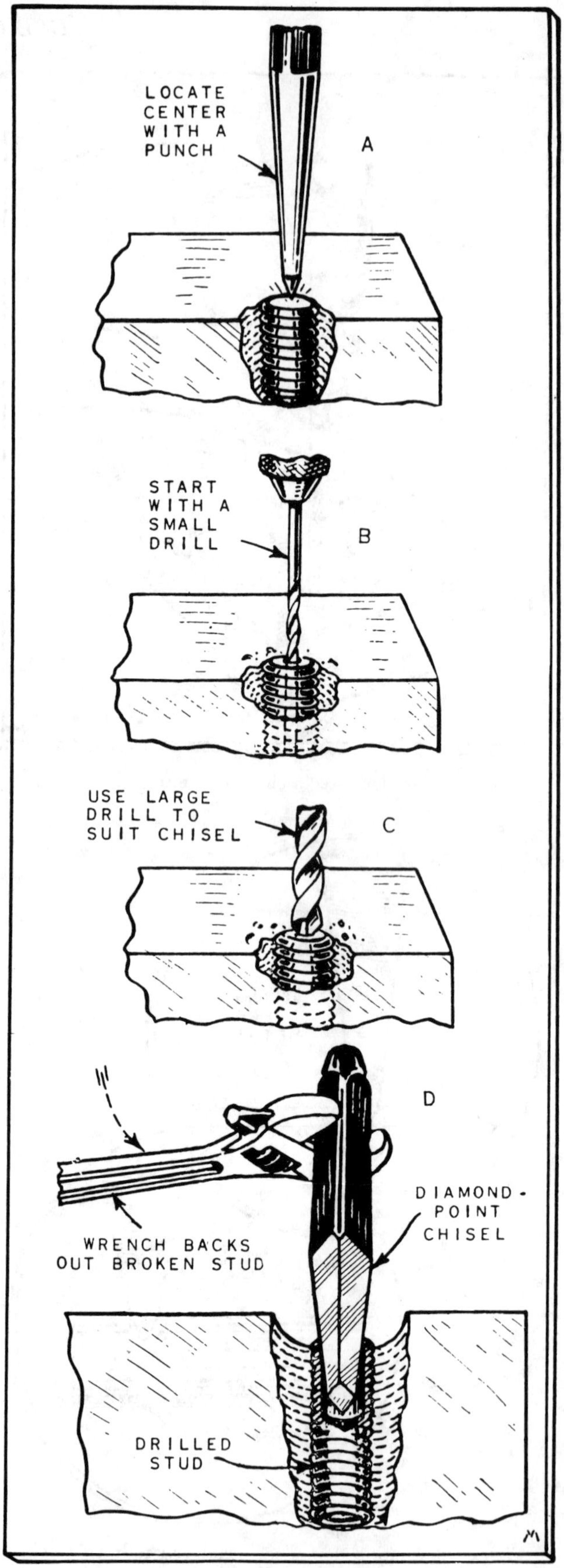

on the cutting point, and, with a few taps of the hammer, cut a deep nick on opposite sides of the rod. Bend the rod slightly at the nicks, and it will snap apart (Fig. 48).

Cutting Slots or Holes in Sheet Metal. To cut a slot or hole in sheet metal, first mark a line on the metal to indicate the hole. Deepen the line with a scriber. Drill a series of holes, using a twist drill, in the metal as close together as possible inside the scored line. Lay the sheet on a steel plate, and, with the chisel held at a slight angle, cut through the metal (Fig. 49).

Removing Broken Screws, Studs, and Frozen Nuts. To remove a broken screw or stud, first mark its exact center with a center punch (A, Fig. 50). Then drill a hole with a small-sized twist drill (B, Fig. 50) into the full length of the screw or stud. Next, enlarge this hole by drilling it through again with a drill just a fraction under the size of the stud (C, Fig. 50). After this, all that should remain of the screw or stud is a thin-walled threaded sleeve (D, Fig. 50).

Insert a cold chisel into the hole and drive it in lightly. Then fit a wrench onto the shank of the chisel and turn it in a counterclockwise direction to back out the broken screw or stud (D, Fig. 50). If the threads of a screw or stud are rusted, insert a few drops of kerosene or thin oii after the hole is drilled. Allow some time for the oil to penetrate, and then remove the screw or stud. Stubborn screws

Figure 50. Procedure for removing broken screws and studs.

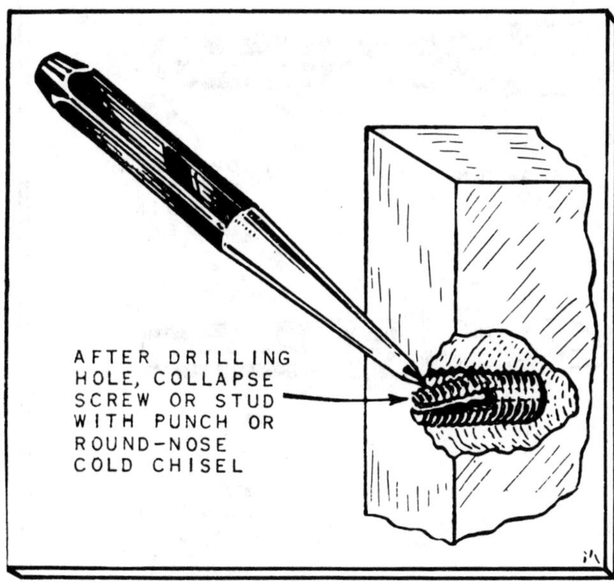

Figure 51. Final step for removal of screws or studs.

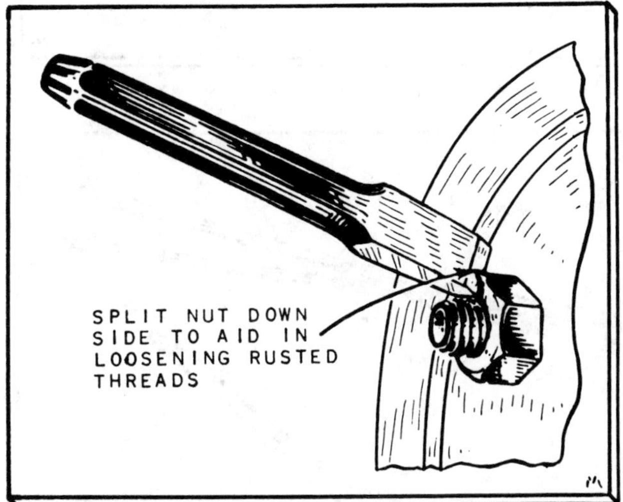

Figure 52. Removing frozen nut and loosening rusted threads.

or studs may be collapsed with a punch or round nose cold chisel (Fig. 51).

To remove a frozen or rusted nut or one with rounded corners, apply some kerosene or thin oil and allow sufficient time for it to work into the threads. Then, with a sharp flat cold chisel, split the nut and remove it (Fig. 52).

Sharpening Cold Chisels. The cutting edges of carbon-steel cold chisels are kept in good condition by grinding them on a dry emery wheel or a wet grindstone. Cold chisels made of chromium vanadium steel or a similar alloy, though extremely tough, are soft enough to be filed rather than ground. This eliminates the danger of burning the edges of the tool.

Flat cold chisels should be ground so that they have a slightly convex edge (A, Fig. 53). Chisels to be used on hard or tough metal should be ground to an included angle of approximately 70 degrees. For use on softer metals, they can be ground to angles ranging from 40 to 60 degrees, depending on the metal (B, C, Fig. 53). Recommended angles are 60 degrees for cast iron; 50 degrees for wrought iron, bronze, duralumin, and manganese; and 40 degrees for aluminum, aluminum alloys, copper, zinc, and brass. A small sheet-metal template, or pattern, can easily be made for checking and maintaining the angle of the cutting edge that is being filed or ground (Fig. 53).

If a dry emery wheel is used, the chisel should be held against it with very little pressure, and the cutting edge should be dipped into cold water frequently to retain its temper. When a wet grinding wheel is used, dipping is not necessary.

The incessant hammer blows on the end of the handle of a cold chisel eventually upset or mushroom it, and this will cause splinters to fly when the chisel is being hammered. It is very dangerous to use a cold chisel in this condition. To prevent possible splinters, grind off all the spread-out metal so that the end is flat and set slightly tapering (A, B, C, Fig. 53).

Roofing and Gutter Tongs, Seamers and Beaders

TONGS. Roofing and gutter tongs are used for turning up the edges of sheet metal preparatory to the forming of standing seams or locks. The various types of roofing and gutter tongs in general use are shown in Fig. 54. The conventional roofing tongs shown at A, Fig. 54 can be used to turn only a specified size seam or lock. They are available in sizes ranging from ½ in. to 2 in., and in gradations of ¼ in.

The clamp tongs shown at B, Fig. 54 have a jaw depth of 3 in. This type has the advantage of being equipped with a special clamp.

A type of gutter tong in general use is shown at C, Fig. 54. This type has a jaw depth of 14 in.

"Reese's" patent tongs, shown at D, Fig. 54, are adjustable and can be used to turn any required size of seam or lock ranging from ¾ in. to 3 in. in depth.

"Stow's" improved tongs, shown at E, Fig. 54, are adjustable. They can only be adjusted to turn five

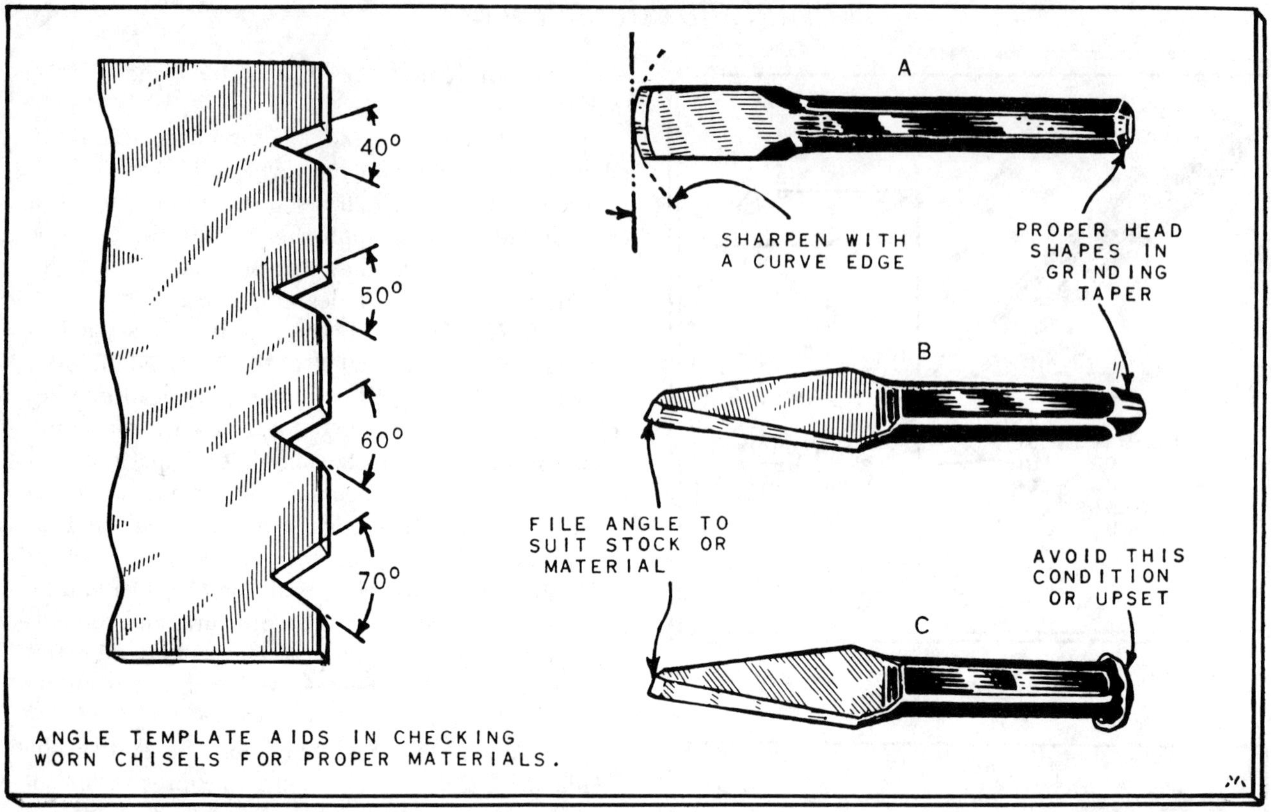

ANGLE TEMPLATE AIDS IN CHECKING WORN CHISELS FOR PROPER MATERIALS.

40°

50°

60°

70°

A

SHARPEN WITH A CURVE EDGE

PROPER HEAD SHAPES IN GRINDING TAPER

B

FILE ANGLE TO SUIT STOCK OR MATERIAL

AVOID THIS CONDITION OR UPSET

C

Figure 53. Sharpening, shaping, and checking angles of cold chisels.

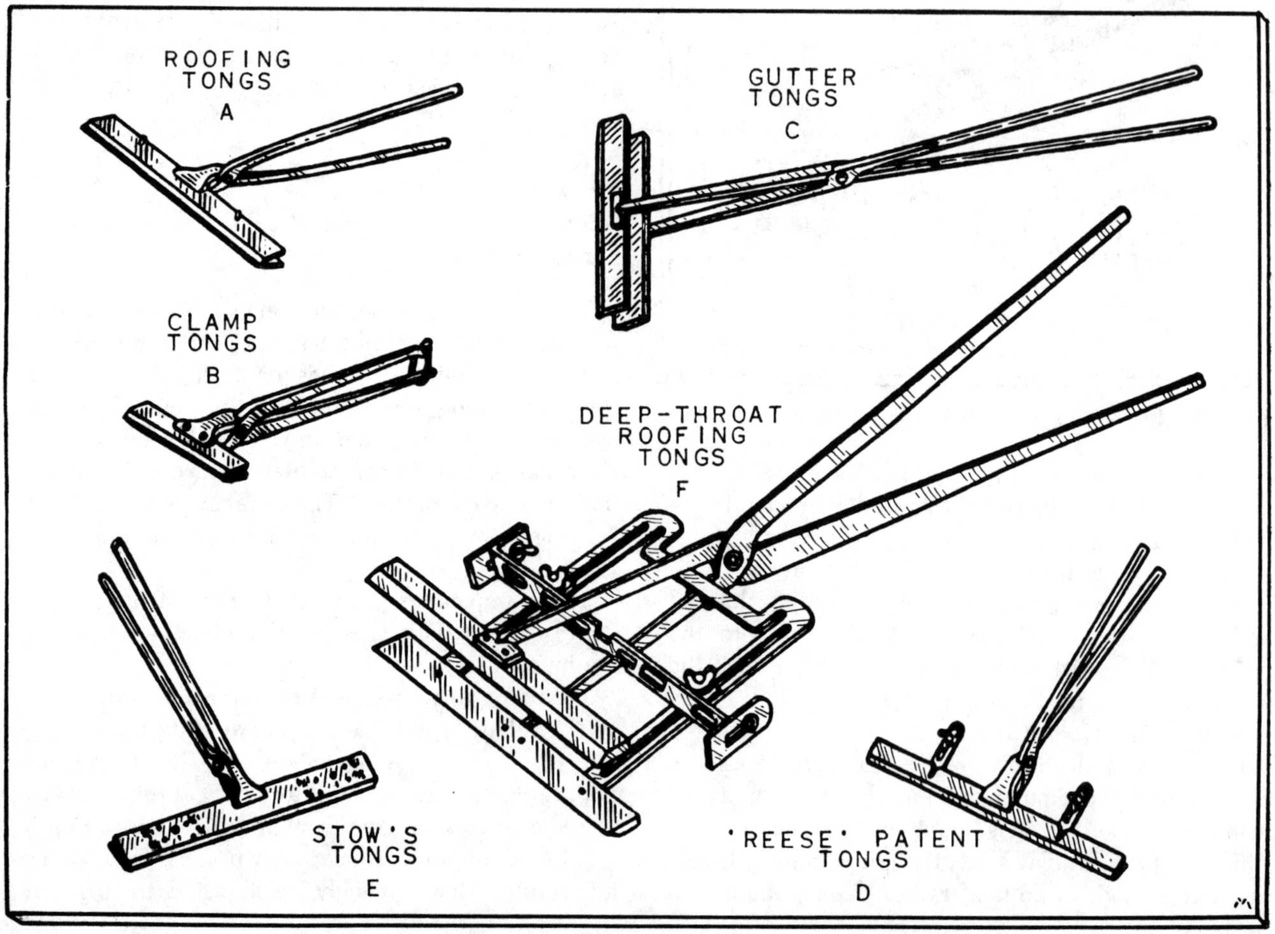

ROOFING TONGS A

GUTTER TONGS C

CLAMP TONGS B

DEEP-THROAT ROOFING TONGS F

STOW'S TONGS E

'REESE' PATENT TONGS D

Figure 54.

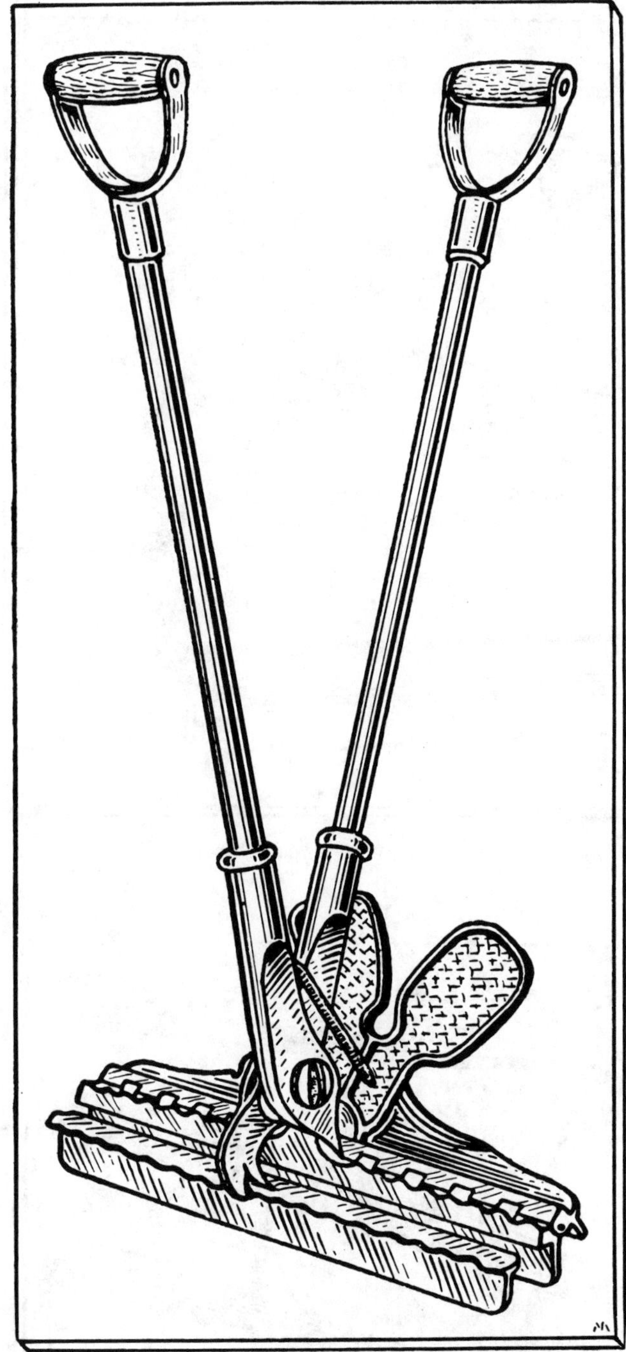

Figure 55. "Burritt's" patent double seamer.

widths or depths of locks or seams ranging from ½ in. to 1½ in. in ¼ in. gradations.

The deep throat roofing tongs shown at F, Fig. 54 are equipped with an adjustable gauge and can be used for turning edges from ½ in. to 10½ in. in ¼ in. gradations.

Figure 56.

Seamers. After turning the edges of the roofing with the roofing tongs, a tool called a double seamer is used. The "Burritt's" patent double seamer is a type generally used for this purpose (Fig. 55). This type of seamer, used to form a double seam in standing seam roofing, is further classified as a common- and wide-gauge seamer. The common-gauge type is used to follow and complete the seam made by the standard 1 in. and 1¼ in. roofing tongs. The wide-gauge roofing double seamers are used for the same purpose as the common-gauge type, but they will finish a standing seam 1 in. in height. The hand roofing double seamer shown in Fig. 56 is used for the same purpose as the type shown in Fig. 55. When using the hand roofing double seamers the seams are finished by hand with blows of a mallet against both sides of their flat surfaces.

Gutter Beading Tools. Gutter beading tools or gutter beading machines, as they are called, are used for forming a bead on the edge of gutter sheet metal (A, Fig. 57). The two types generally used are the adjustable and plain beader.

The adjustable beader shown at B, Fig. 57 forms beads in gutters up to 30 in. in length. The various-sized metal rods necessary for forming beads ranging from ⅜ in. to ⅞ in. can be inserted in this beader. The metal that is to be formed into a gutter bead is inserted into a slot that is milled in the forming rod. Using the hand crank, the sheet metal is wound around the forming rod, thus completing the bead. The rod with the sheet of metal and the formed bead can easily be lifted out of the tool and the beaded work slipped from the forming rod. This tool is adjustable and can be set so that it will form any number of beads of exactly the same size without additional adjustment.

The plain gutter beading machine shown at C, Fig.

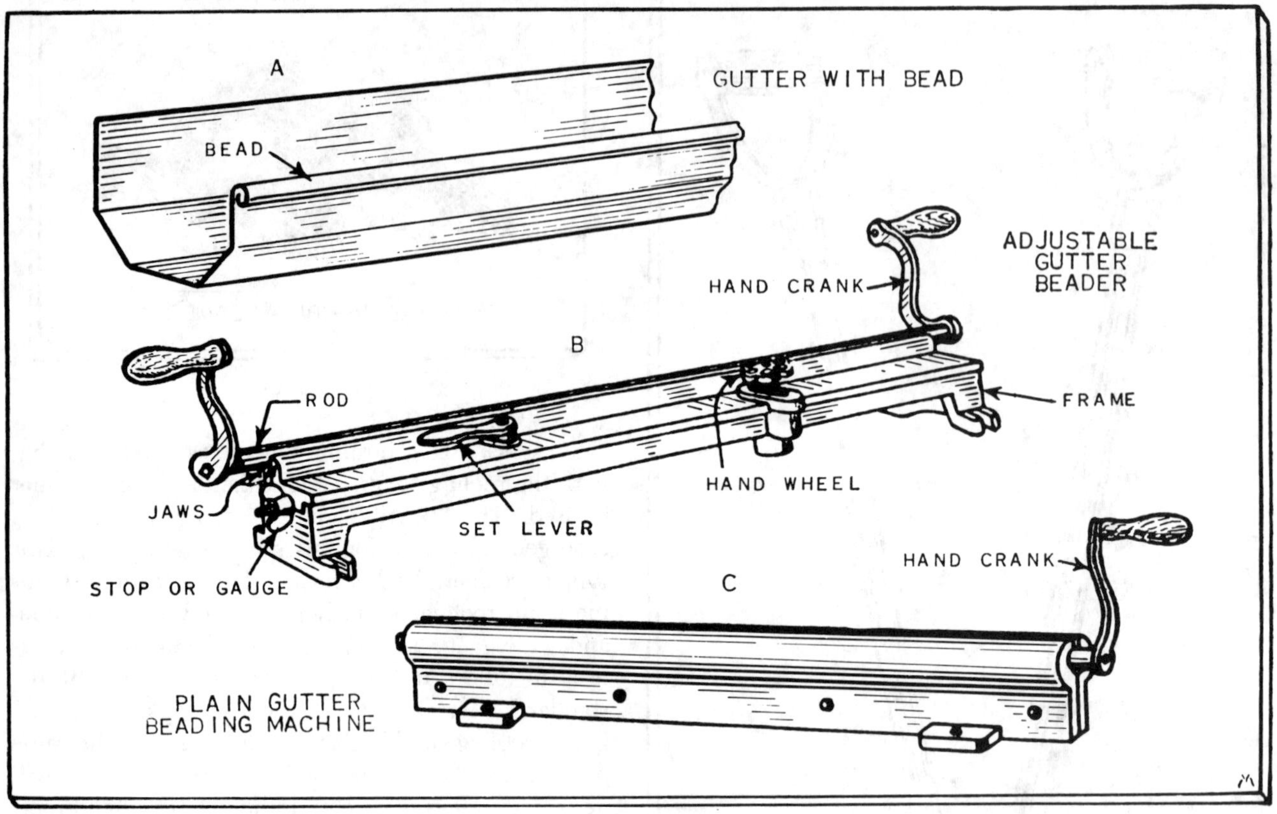

Figure 57.

57 is available in two sizes, 30 in. and 42 in. It is not adjustable, and each tool can hold only one size rod and can be used to make a bead of only one size, necessitating the use of individual beaders for each required size of bead. Plain gutter beading machines are available in a range of ⅜ in. to 1 in. rod diameters.

Punches

The six types of punches used in the sheet metal shop are shown in Figs. 58 and 59.

Prick Punches (A, Fig. 58). These punches are used in layout work. Prick punches are made of hardened, tool steel with ground ends and are available in various sizes.

Center Punches (B, Fig. 58). Center punches are used in layout work prior to drilling. They are hardened and the ends are tempered. Points are ground carefully at an angle which will give maximum strength and penetration and provide a punch mark in which drills will start easily. They are available in sets of various sizes.

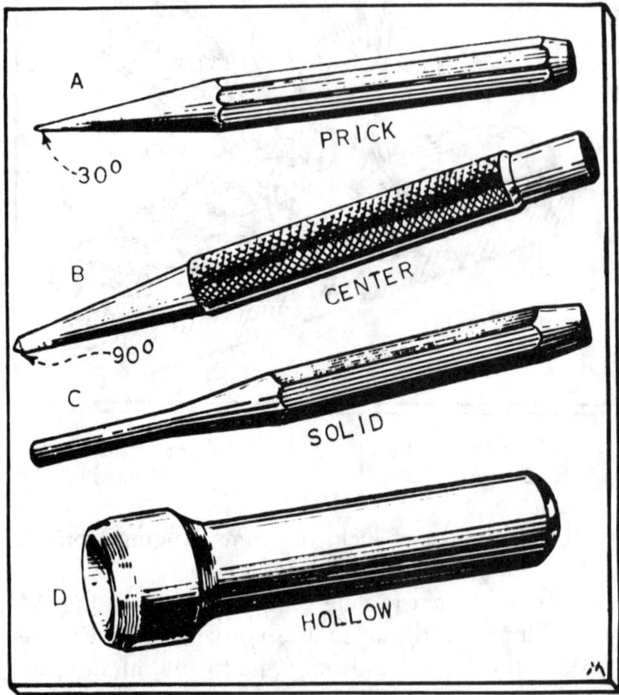

Figure 58. Punches.

Solid Punches (C, Fig. 58). Solid punches are used to punch small holes in light sheets. Metal should be backed up with end grain hardwood or a lead slab. They are available in sets containing various sizes.

Hollow Punches (D, Fig. 58). Hollow punches are used to cut round holes in light sheet metal. The shank is lathe turned and knurled to facilitate gripping. The cutting edge is beveled and ground to give sharpness and durability. Hollow punches should be used against a slab of lead. They are available in sets of various sizes.

Tinner's Hand Punches (E, Fig. 59). These punches are equipped with interchangeable dies and punches and are operated with a hand lever. They are used for punching small holes in light and medium gauges of sheet metal. The punches and dies have a range of sizes and are easily changed. The punch size must always be changed with the die and they must always be mates, otherwise, if a punch is forced with a smaller-sized die, one or both of the parts will break. Keep the punch well lubricated to ensure ease of working. This type of punch usually has a gauge which consists of a guide mark and an adjustable scale. However, the gauge is seldom used, because a center punch is generally used to mark the position of the hole to be punched.

Iron Hand Punches (F, Fig. 59). Iron hand punches are similar to tinner's hand punches, and are used to cut holes in heavier-gauge sheet metals. They are equipped with interchangeable punches and dies in gradations of 1/32 in.

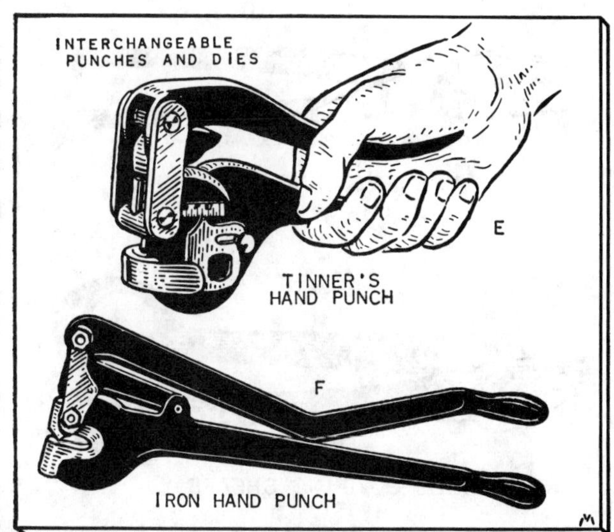

Figure 59.

Snips and Shears

Snips and shears are used to cut thin sheet brass, copper, sheet aluminum, iron, tin, and galvanized soft and medium steel. They cannot be used to cut tempered steel. All snips and shears are of two general classifications, the regular straight and the circular, and they come in various types and sizes. Those most commonly used are the straight, curved, aviation, combination scroll and circular, bull-dog, hawk's bill, double cutting, and compound lever. All these are available in lengths ranging from 6 in. to 16 in. (Figs. 60 and 61).

All snips and shears have tapered blades with an inlaid steel cutting edge and sloping shoulders. The grips or handles are designed to fit the hand, and are formed and centered to give the maximum leverage required for cutting.

The type of metal to be cut and the gauge of the metal determine the correct size of snips to use. Mild steel requires a larger pair of snips than aluminum, and hard brass requires larger snips than soft brass. These snips and shears, with the exception of the compound lever shears, can be used to cut sheet metal only up to 20 gauge. Compound lever shears of the type shown in Fig. 60 can be used to cut up to 12 gauge. Heavy-gauge metals must be cut with either a hacksaw, a cold chisel, or heavy power equipment.

Snips should never be used in place of pliers or wire cutters. To avoid springing the blades, do not attempt to cut material of heavier gauge than that for which the snips are intended. Snips that have been sprung are useless and cannot be repaired.

Regular or Straight Snips. Regular or straight snips are used for cutting straight lines or circles of large diameter (Fig. 60). Straight snips are available for both right-handed and left-handed users.

Double Cutting Snips. Double cutting snips have a top blade with a double cutting edge into which the lower blade works (Fig. 60). They are used in the same manner as regular or straight snips, but principally for cutting light sheet-iron pipe, stacks, and thin-gauge cylinders.

Circular or Curved Snips. Circular snips have curved blades and are used for cutting inside scrolls or circles of small diameter (Fig. 60). To cut a circular opening in a sheet of metal, it is necessary first to punch a hole on the inside of the outline of the desired opening so that the blades of the snips may be started.

BULL-DOG SNIPS. Bull-dog snips have short blades with long handles (Fig. 60). They are used for cutting both straight and irregular lines.

TINNER'S BENCH SHEARS. Tinner's bench shears are used for cutting sheet metal of 20 to 16 gauge (Fig. 60). These large shears are designed so that the lower shank of the handle fits into a hole in the bench plate, and thus only one hand is required to raise and lower the upper shank.

HAWK'S BILL SNIPS. Hawk's bill snips can be used to cut either straight lines or curves in any direction (Fig. 60). They are used in the same manner as the other types described in the preceding paragraphs.

DOUBLE CUTTING SHEARS. Double cutting shears of the type shown in Fig. 60 are equipped with forged steel blades and specially hardened cutting edges. They are used for cutting pipe of various shapes and sizes.

COMPOUND LEVER SHEARS. Compound lever shears of the type shown in Fig. 60 are used for cutting the heavier gauges of sheet metal. The long handles are designed to give the necessary additional leverage. They are equipped with removable blades that can be easily replaced.

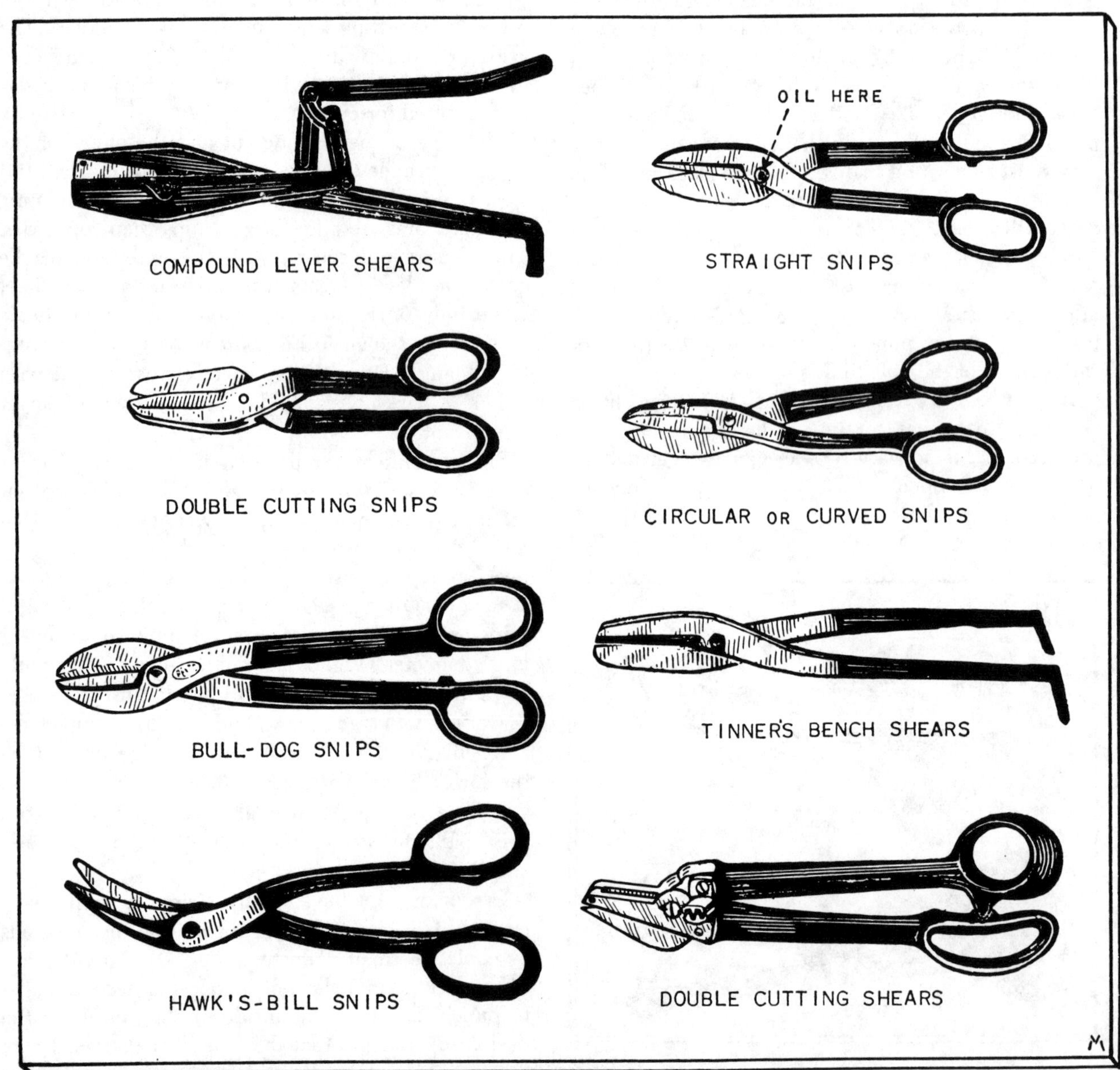

Figure 60.

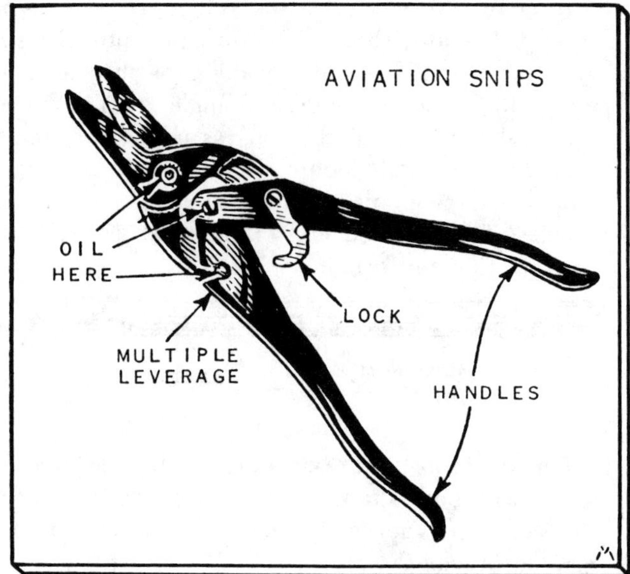

Figure 61.

Aviation Snips. Aviation snips are designed and constructed specifically for cutting heat-treated aluminum alloys and stainless steel. The blades of these snips have small teeth on the cutting edges, and the handles are made to give greater leverage for heavy cutting. This tool usually cuts up to 0.050 in. stock (Fig. 61).

Correct Method of Using Snips and Shears. All types of snips and shears are used in approximately the same manner. If the material is light-gauge sheet metal, hand snips will be used. For 22 gauge or lighter mild steel, use straight or combination snips. For 16 to 20 gauge mild steel, use bulldog snips. Always place the cutting edge of the upper blades exactly on a guideline marked on the metal, and insert the sheet as far back as possible between the blades (Fig. 62). Hold the snips so that the flat sides of the blades are at all times perpendicular, or at right angles, to the surface of the work. The waste metal or the smaller piece should curl on the upper side of the lower blade.

All cuts, and especially curved cuts, must be continuous. Complete every cut with the point of the snips to avoid cutting beyond the required point.

When it is necessary to cut a hole or an opening in sheet metal, lay the metal on a hardwood block and punch a hole in it with a hollow punch or a small cold chisel, so that the point of the snips can be inserted to start the cut.

The pivot point on snips must be oiled frequently, and the nut on the pivot must be adjusted so that the handles are not too tight and can be moved with ease (Fig. 62).

An outside circle as well as a straight line can be cut with the combination snips. Cut off the corners of the metal to make it easier to handle. Then make a continuous cut, turning the metal as the cut is being made. If possible, remove the waste material in one piece. Use a hawk's bill, aviation, or pivoter snips to cut an inside circle. To start the cut, punch a hole in the center of the circle to be cut, work out to the line, and then follow the line around until the cut is completed. The pivoter snip is one of the handiest hand cutting tools, because it will cut irregular curves as well as straight lines.

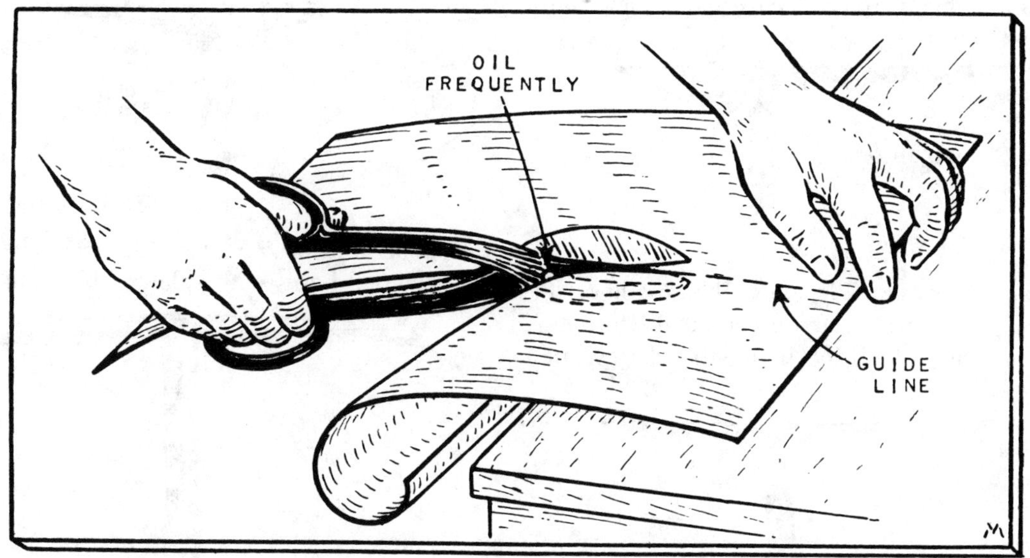

Figure 62. Cutting with snips and shears.

Stakes

Stakes of various types and shapes are used by the sheet metal worker for bending and shaping, riveting, and seaming sheet metal by hand. They are available in a great variety of shapes and sizes. All stakes consist of three parts (Fig. 63): the shank, which as a rule is standard size, and the head and the horn, which vary with each type. Types of stakes generally used in the sheet metal shop are:

beakhorn	conductor
blowhorn	bevel edge
candlemold	teakettle
hollow mandrel	hatchet
solid mandrel	commonsquare
creasing	coppersmith
double seaming	bottom
double seaming with interchangeable heads	hand dolly

Beakhorn Stake (Fig. 63). This stake is used for general forming, riveting, and seaming operations.

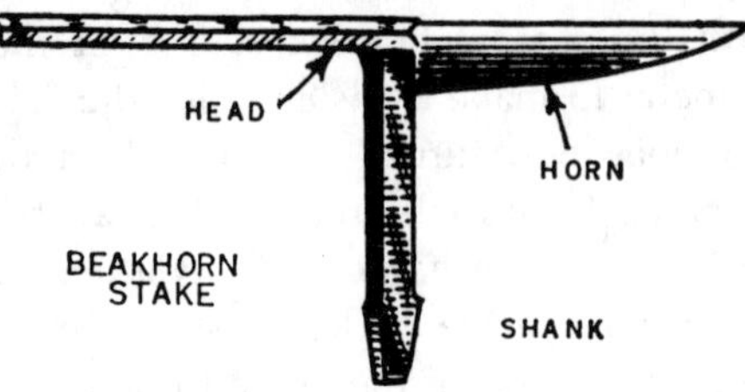

Figure 63.

Blowhorn Stake (Fig. 64). Both the short tapered horn at one end of this stake and the longer horn at the other end are used for forming, seaming, and riveting funnels, pitched covers, lids, and similar tapered objects.

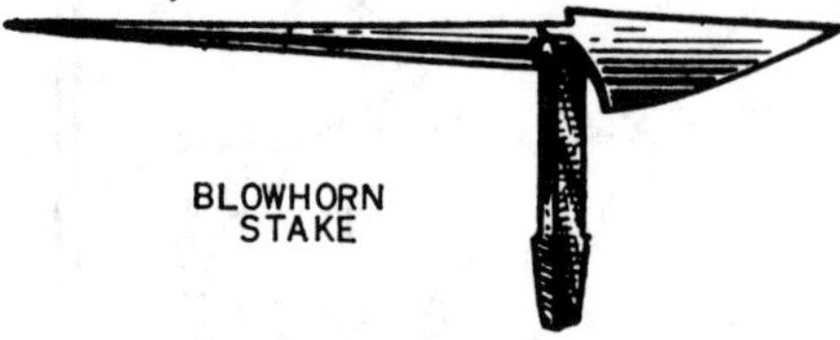

Figure 64.

Candlemold Stake (Fig. 65). The two horns of different tapers on this stake are used for forming, seaming, and riveting objects with either flaring lines or ends.

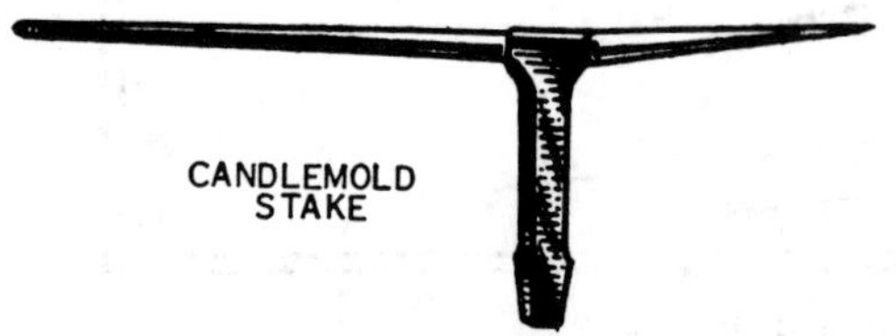

Figure 65.

Hollow Mandrel Stake (Fig. 66). A slot equipped with a sliding bolt runs the entire length of this stake. This feature enables the mechanic to secure the stake at any desired angle or length. The square-shaped end of the stake is used for forming laps, riveting, and double seaming corners of rectangular-shaped objects such as boxes and similar articles. The rounded end of the stake is used for pipe riveting and seaming.

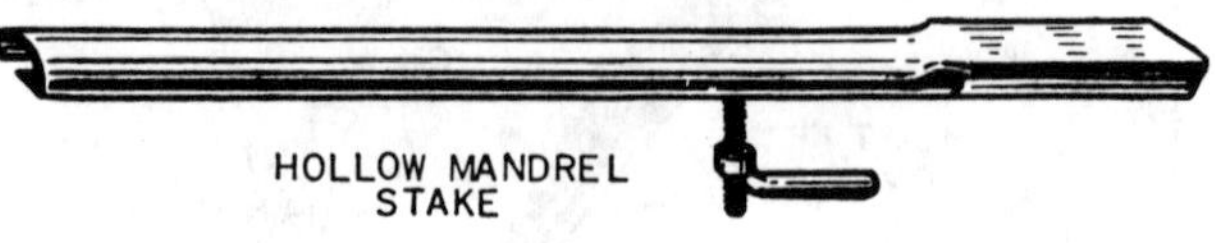

Figure 66.

Solid Mandrel Stake (Fig. 67). The double shank with both a rounded and a flat side is used for the same operation as the hollow mandrel type described previously.

Figure 67.

Creasing Stake (Fig. 68). Two types of creasing stakes are available. The several grooved slots in the double rectangular-shaped horn of one of these types is used for bending wire and creasing sheet metal. The other type of creasing stake has a rectangular-shaped horn on one end and a round tapering one on the other end. This type is generally used for forming and riveting small rounded and tapered work.

Figure 68.

Double Seaming Stake (Fig. 69). The two elliptical-shaped horns with enlarged knobs at both ends

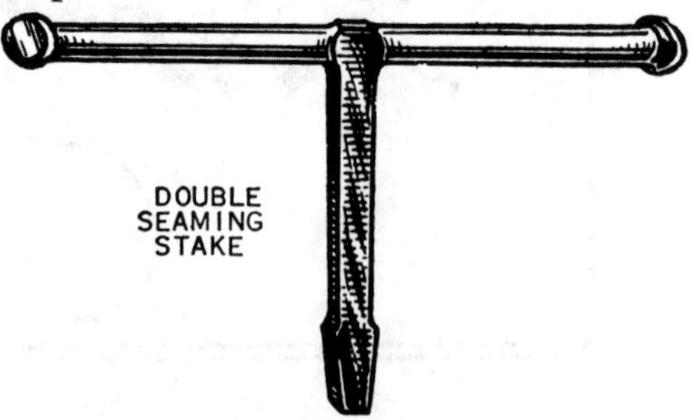

Figure 69.

of this stake are used for double seaming small cylindrical work.

DOUBLE SEAMING STAKE WITH INTERCHANGEABLE HEADS (Fig. 70). The double shank of this stake enables the mechanic to use it in either a horizontal or vertical position. The interchangeable heads are used for double seaming all types of large work.

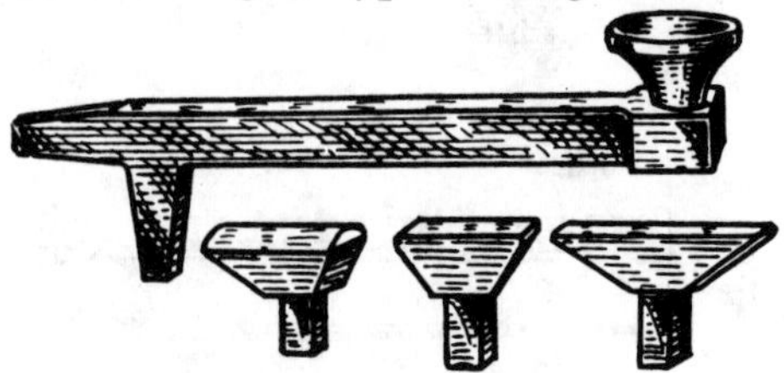

DOUBLE SEAMING STAKE WITH INTERCHANGEABLE HEADS
Figure 70.

CONDUCTOR STAKE (Fig. 71). The two cylindrical-shaped horns of different diameters on this stake are used for forming, riveting, and seaming small sized pipes and tubes.

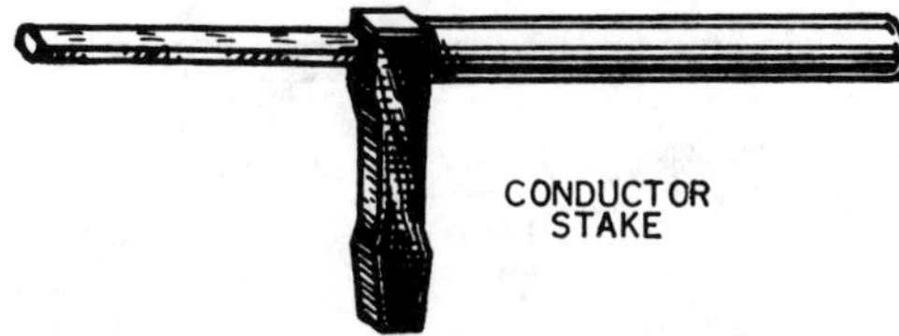

Figure 71.

BEVEL EDGE STAKE (Fig. 72). The offset shank of this stake permits the work to clear the bench. The flat, square head with beveled edges is used for double seaming operations.

Figure 72.

TEAKETTLE STAKE (Fig. 73). The four different-shaped interchangeable heads of this stake are used for many forming operations for which other stakes cannot be used.

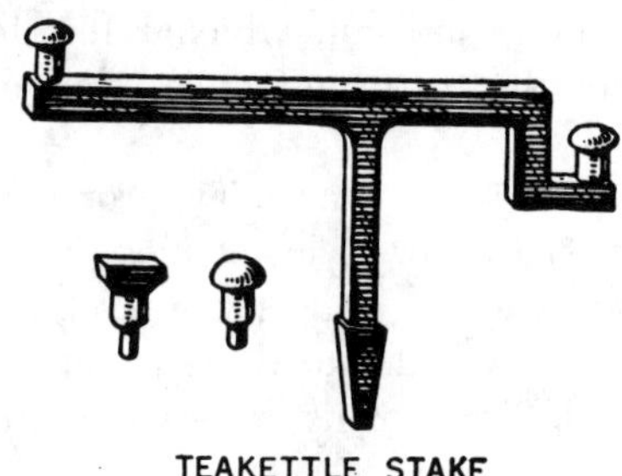

TEAKETTLE STAKE
Figure 73.

HATCHET STAKE (Fig. 74). The sharp straight edge that is beveled on one side of this stake is used for bending edges, making sharp bends, and for forming pans, boxes, and similar work.

COMMONSQUARE STAKE (Fig. 75). The flat square head and long shank of this stake are used for general operations.

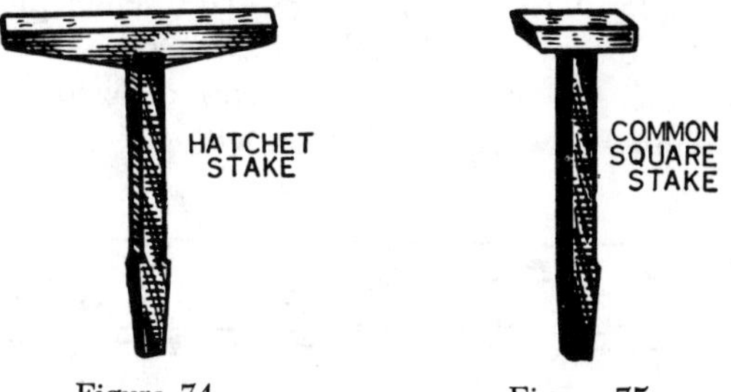

Figure 74. Figure 75.

COPPERSMITH STAKE (Fig. 76). One side of the head of this stake has a sharp rectangular edge and the other side a rounded edge. It is also a general purpose stake.

BOTTOM STAKE (Fig. 77). The fan-shaped, slightly rounded, and beveled edge of this stake is used for turning small flanges, for double seaming, and for dressing burred edges on discs.

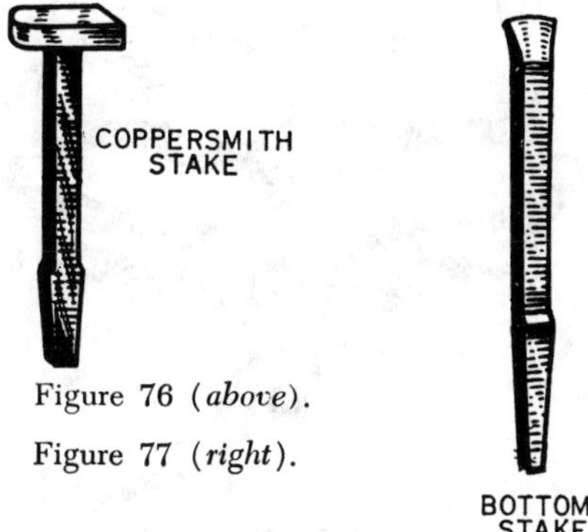

Figure 76 (*above*).

Figure 77 (*right*).

BOTTOM STAKE

HAND DOLLY STAKE (Fig. 78). The flat face of this stake has two straight edges, one concave edge and one convex edge. It is available in various sizes and shapes, and is used for bucking rivets and double seaming.

HAND DOLLY STAKE
Figure 78.

Stakeholders

The three types of stakeholders used in the sheet metal shop are: bench plate, revolving bench plate, and universal stake holder.

Bench Plate (Fig. 79). The bench plate is a flat iron rectangular plate pierced with a number of various-sized square tapered holes. The bench plate is fastened to the workbench and the shanks of the stakes are set securely in the correct-sized square hole while the work is being formed.

BENCH PLATE

Figure 79.

Revolving Bench Plate (Fig. 80). This type of stake holder consists of a revolving plate pierced with a number of square tapered holes. It can be set in any desired position by clamping it to the workbench.

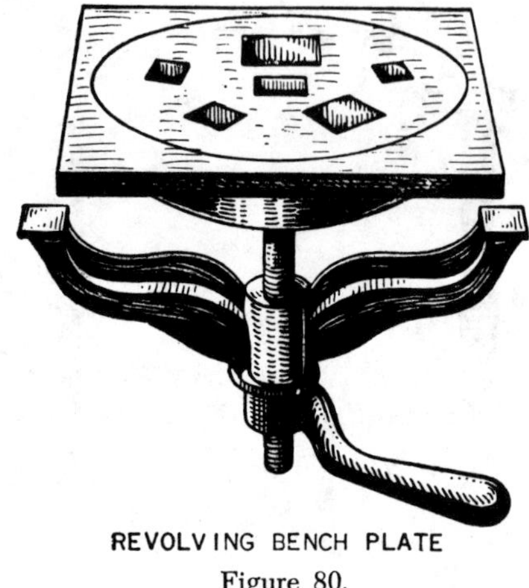

REVOLVING BENCH PLATE

Figure 80.

Universal Stake Holder (Fig. 81). The universal stake holder is clamped to the workbench in any desired position and is available with a complete set of interchangeable stakes.

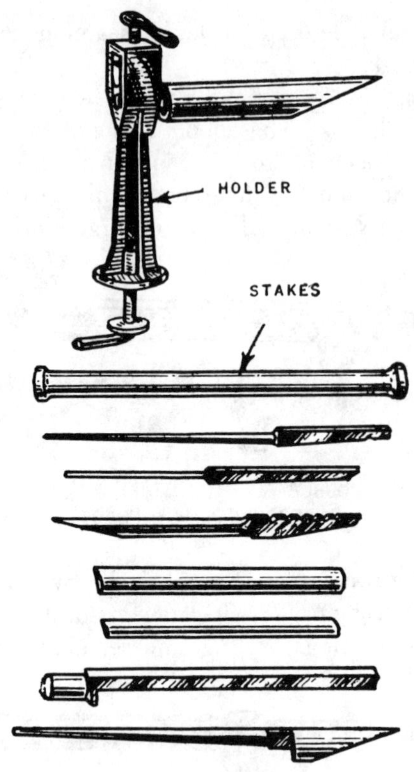

UNIVERSAL STAKE HOLDER

Figure 81.

Files and Filing Procedures

Files are used for finishing and shaping all metals, and for the sharpening and maintenance of all other tools. The hundreds of types of files that are manufactured cannot be described here, but a description of the types most commonly used will be sufficient for the sheet metal worker. Parts of a typical file are shown in Fig. 82. Files have either single-cut or double-cut teeth or a combination of both, in a wide range from smooth to very coarse.

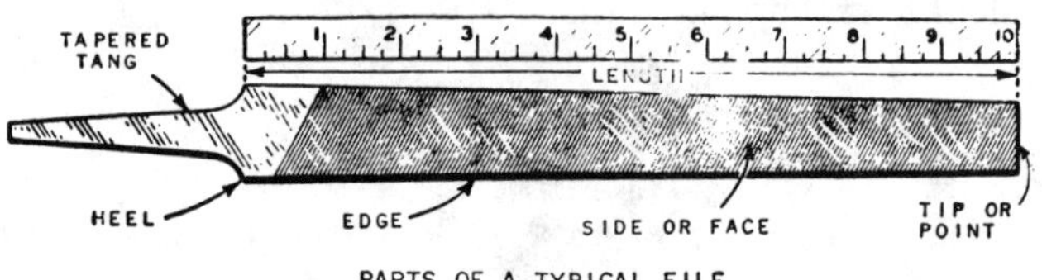

PARTS OF A TYPICAL FILE

Figure 82.

All files have three distinguishing features: length, which is always measured exclusive of the tang or tapered part inserted in the handle (Fig. 83); type, kind, or name, which refers to the shape or style of the file section; and cut, which refers to both the character of the teeth and their relative degree of coarseness.

Classifications of Files. Type or kind refers to the various shapes or styles of files as distinguished by such terms as flat, mill, half-round, and the like. Each type is divided into three general classes, according to the form of its cross section; quadrangu-

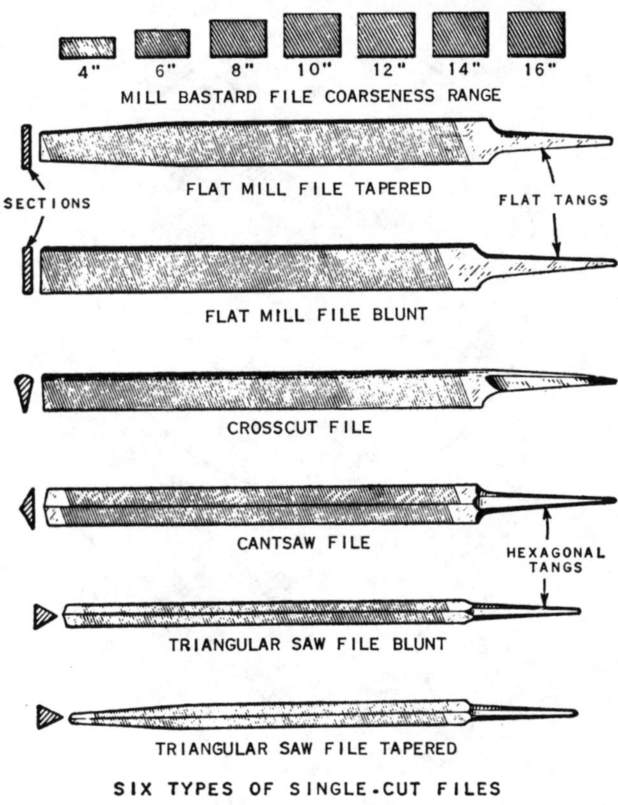

Figure 83.

lar, circular, and triangular (Fig. 84). From these three classes are derived all the odd and irregular forms classified further as miscellaneous, which are subdivided into taper and blunt, again according to general contour or outline.

Taper designates a file whose cross section gradually narrows in width and thickness for one-half to two-thirds of its length; blunt designates a file that keeps the same cross-section size throughout its length (Fig. 85).

Files are classified also according to the cut of teeth, as single-cut, double-cut, rasp-cut, and curved;

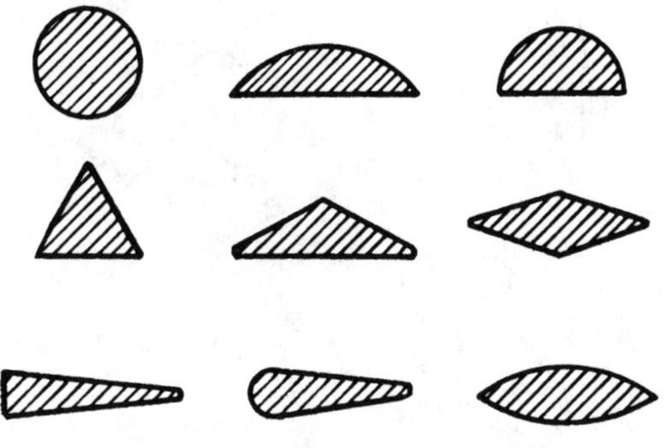

FILE PROFILES

Figure 84.

Figure 85.

and according to the coarseness of the teeth, as rough, coarse, bastard, second-cut, smooth, and dead-smooth (Fig. 86).

Single-cut files are used generally with light pressure to produce a smooth surface finish or a keen edge on knives, shears, saw teeth, or other cutting tools (Fig. 86).

Double-cut files are used generally under heavy pressure for fast metal removal and where a rough finish is permissible (Fig. 86).

Rasp-cut files have a series of individual teeth cut by a sharp and narrow punchlike cutting chisel. The rasp-cut file produces an extremely rough cut and is used principally on wood and leather, and on aluminum, lead, and similar soft metals, for fast removal of waste material (Fig. 86).

A special curved-tooth single-cut file is used on the flat surface of aluminum and steel sheets.

Rough, coarse, and bastard cuts of files are used on heavy work, and second-cut, smooth, and dead-smooth files are used for finishing or on more exacting work.

The teeth of a file are cut into its face at an angle, and sometimes they are cut into one or both edges of a flat or rectangular file. When a file has no teeth on one edge, it is called a safe-edge.

Filing Aluminum. Aluminum is difficult to file with ordinary files because it is a soft, ductile, and malleable metal. The file teeth soon become clogged, even under moderate, even pressure. Filing of aluminum consists of filing roughness from aluminum castings, filing sheet and bar aluminum, and filing aluminum alloys. For fast, rough metal removal, a special aluminum rasp is often used, but the aluminum file (A, Fig. 87), a recent manufacturing development, cuts aluminum rapidly, yet leaves a good finish. Its special tooth construction is very effective in eliminating clogging (B, Fig. 87). Compare this with the regular flat file shown at A. The upcut of the teeth is deep with an open throat, and the overcut is fine, producing small scallops on the upcut, which break up the filings, allow the file to clear itself, and prevent taking too large a bite from the metal. By using this file with a shearing stroke to-

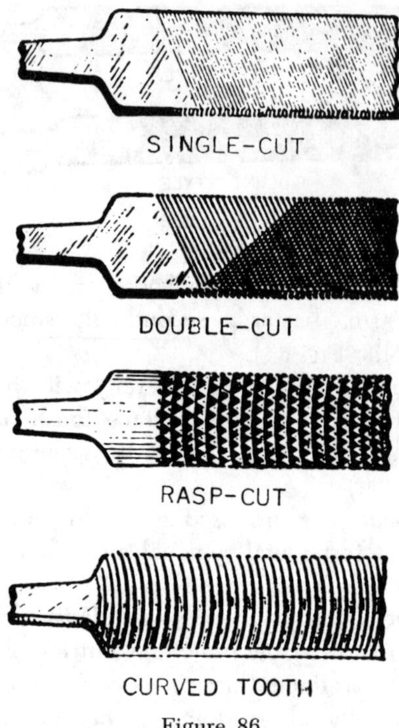

Figure 86.

ward the left, a good finish can be obtained easily. This type of file is available in both flat and half-round shapes.

Filing Brass. Brass has a structure all its own and is a difficult metal to file. Though softer than steel, brass is both tough and ductile. These characteristics demand a file with teeth that are sturdy, very sharp, and cut to an angle that prevents grooving and running the file off the work. Still more important, the file must not clog. In addition to a short upcut angle, the teeth of a brass file, like those of the aluminum file, have a fine long-angle overcut that enables the file to clear itself of chips. This brass file is so designed that the sharp high-cut teeth bite deep into the metal with little pressure, and their short upcut angle produces a smoothing effect (C, Fig. 87).

Filing Stainless Steel. The tremendous increase in the use of stainless steel and similar alloy steels has created a new and distinct filing problem. The hard chromium and nickel content of these types of steel makes them extremely tough, dense, and difficult to file. Their abrasive action greatly shortens the life of a general-purpose file.

The special stainless-steel file shown in Fig. 88 has overcome this problem. It is a file of exceptional wearing qualities. When properly used, with a light pressure combined with a slow steady stroke, this new file removes metal rapidly, requiring but little effort, and leaves a good finish. It is available in the same shapes and sizes as general-purpose files.

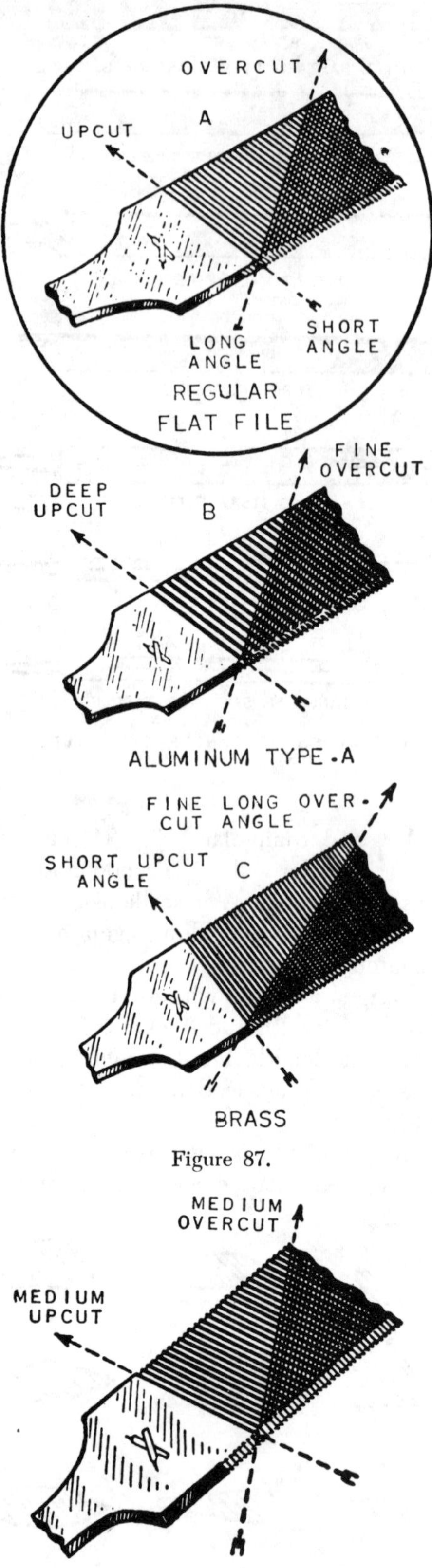

Figure 87.

Figure 88.

Filing Lead. Extra-soft metals, such as lead, babbitt, and pure copper, present filing conditions quite distinct from the others previously mentioned. Metal removal, in normal filing jobs on extra-soft metals, is done on virtually a shaving principle. For lead, the lead float file shown in Fig. 89 is used. Its coarse, short-angle, single-cut teeth are really a series of stubby blades which shear away the metal rapidly under ordinary pressure. Light pressure with the same file produces a smoothing effect. This file is used extensively on lead pipe fittings, solder joints, and similar work. It is used also on soft bearings, shims, and molded metal parts.

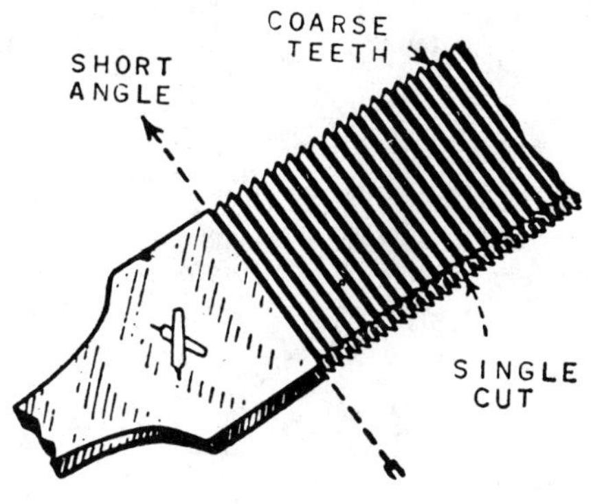

SINGLE-CUT LEAD FLOAT FILE

Figure 89.

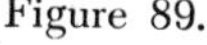

Smooth-finishing Soft Metals. For smooth-finishing soft metals; alloys, such as aluminum, brass, and copper; and other materials, such as plastics, hard rubber, and wood, a special shear-tooth file has been designed (Fig. 90). This file combines fast removal of material with excellent smoothing qualities. The coarse, long-angle, single-cut teeth help the shear-tooth file to clear itself of chips, thus minimizing clogging. Its coarseness provides fast cutting, while the long angle gives the shearing cut which leaves a smooth finish.

Under certain conditions, as on narrow surfaces, the shear-tooth file has a tendency to run to the left because of its long angle. To overcome this tendency, it should be used with a somewhat diagonal stroke to the right.

Inserting a File in a Handle. It is extremely dangerous to use a file without a handle. Wooden handles of various sizes are available and are easily installed. Before inserting the tang of the file in the handle, make certain that the hole is large enough. Grasp the handle and insert the tang into the hole so that the file is pointing upward (Fig. 91). Holding it in this position, hit the bottom end of the handle against the workbench or other solid surface. This drives the file tang down into the handle. Although the ferrule or metal sleeve on the handle should keep the wood from splitting, do not try to drive the tang in too far. To remove a file from the handle, hold

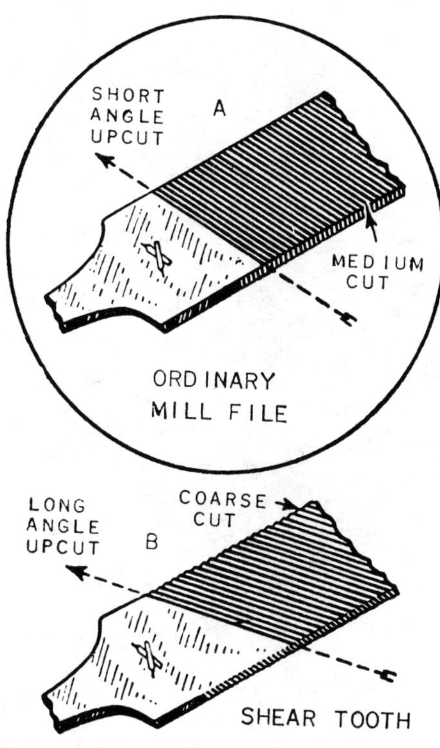

SINGLE-CUT FILES FOR SMOOTH-FINISHING SOFT METALS

Figure 90.

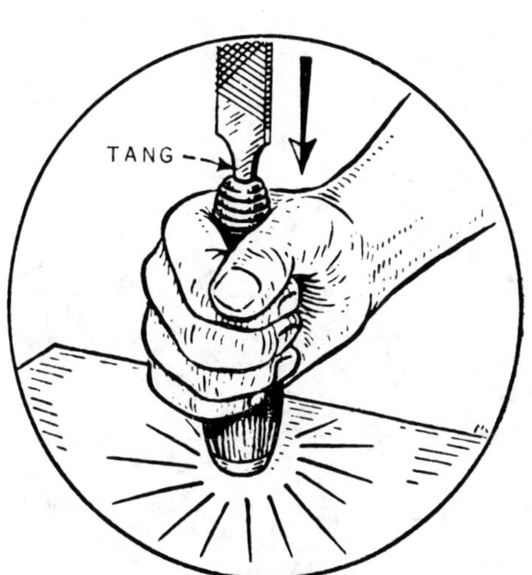

DRIVING TANG OF FILE INTO HANDLE

Figure 91.

the file in the right hand and tap the ferrule end sharply against the edge of any hard surface to loosen it.

Selecting the Right File. It is important to select the file that will do the work quickly and efficiently. Many factors enter into the selection of the right file. As a general rule, it is safe to assume that different files are required to file a flat or a convex surface, to file a concave surface, to file an edge, to file a notched flat square, or to file a round hole. These considerations, plus the type of material to be filed, the amount of material to be removed, and the degree of smoothness or accuracy required, are important in choosing a file for a specific job.

Manual or hand filing consists of straight filing and draw filing. Straight filing is done by pushing the file lengthwise, straight ahead, or slightly diagonally. Draw filing is done by grasping the file at each end and pushing and drawing it sideways across the work.

Most work that is to be filed is secured firmly in a vise. For general filing, the vise should be about elbow height (C, Fig. 93). If a great deal of filing is to be done, the work should be fastened in a lower position. If the work is of a fine or delicate nature, it should be raised nearer eye level.

Correct Methods of Holding a File. A generally accepted method of holding the handle of a file intended for operation with both hands is to allow the end of the handle to fit into and up against the fleshy part of the palm below the joint of the little finger, with the thumb lying parallel over the top of the handle and the fingers pointed upward toward the worker's face. Grasp the point of the file by the thumb and first two fingers of the other hand. With the ball of the thumb of this hand pressed on top of the file, bring the thumb in line with the handle when heavy strokes are required.

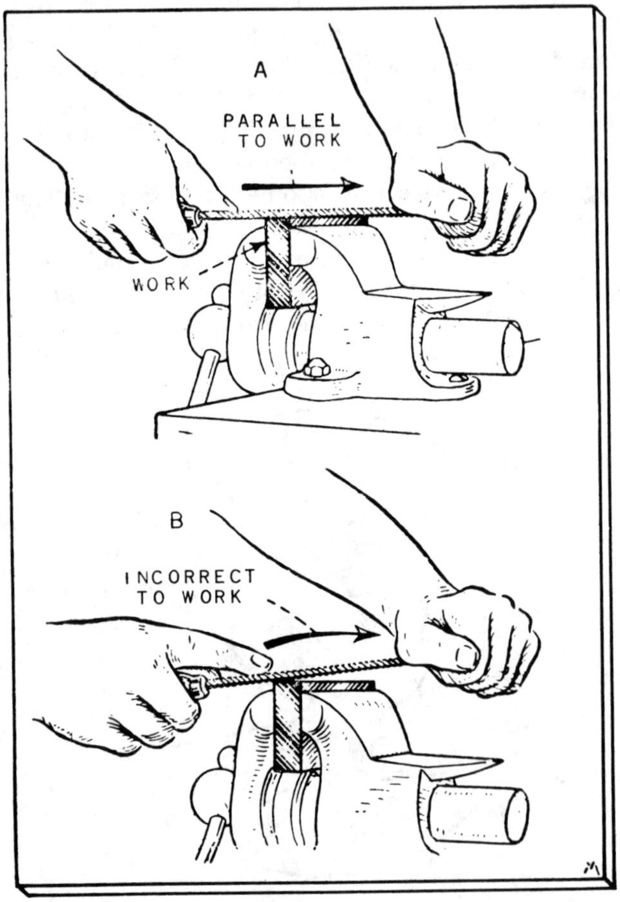

Figure 92.

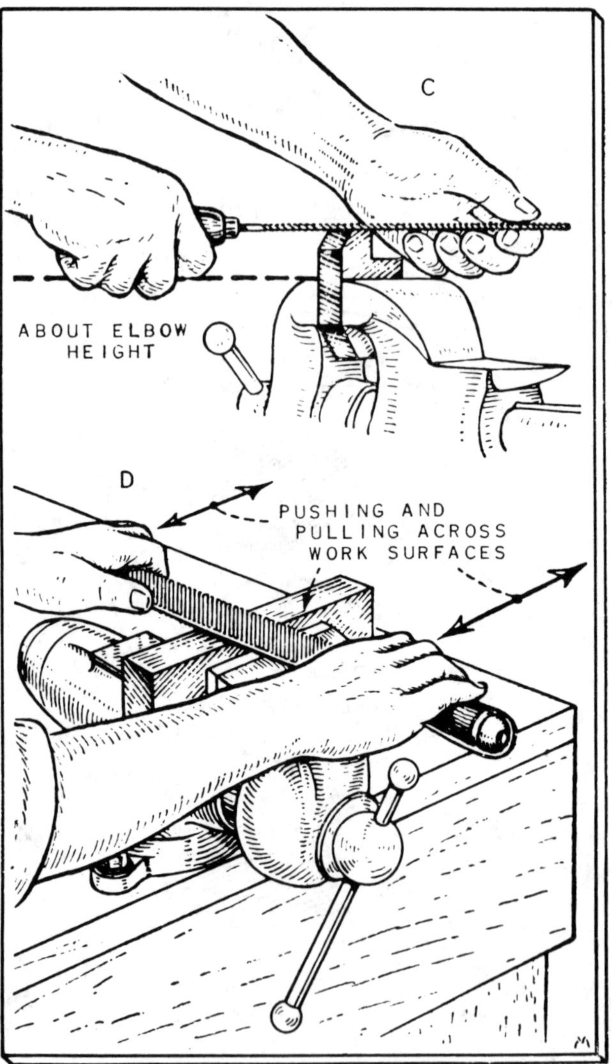

Figure 93.

Where light strokes and less pressure are required, the thumb and fingers of the point-holding hand may change their direction until the thumb lies at right angles with the length of the file, their position changing as required to increase the downward pressure (A, Fig. 92). In holding the file with one hand to file pins, dies, small parts, and edged tools, which cannot be secured in a vise and which must be held in the other hand, the forefinger instead of the thumb is generally placed on the top of the file and as nearly parallel with the blade as possible.

The natural rocking movement of the hand and arm would carry the stroke of the file across the work in a curved line, which would produce a curved surface where a level surface is desired. Therefore, for the usual flat filing, try to carry the file forward on an almost straight line, changing its course just enough to prevent grooving the material (A, Fig. 92). A wrong method of carrying the file is shown in B, Fig. 92. Here too much pressure is evident, the grip is too desperate, the file is not being held level, the motion is curved, and a rounded instead of a square surface will inevitably result.

One of the quickest ways to ruin a good file is to use too much or too little pressure on the forward stroke. Different materials, of course, require different pressures, but, in general, apply only enough pressure to keep the file cutting at all times. If the file is allowed to slide over the harder metals with little pressure, the teeth soon become dull. If the teeth are overloaded by too much pressure, they are likely to chip or clog.

On the reverse strokes, lift the file clear off the work except when filing on very soft metal. Even then, the pressure on the return stroke must be extremely light, never more than the weight of the file itself.

Draw Filing. Draw filing is the finish filing which assures a perfectly smooth and level surface on a piece of metal that has been filed roughly to the size and shape desired. Since files are designed primarily to cut on a longitudinal forward stroke, a file with a short angle cut must never be used for draw filing because it may score or scratch the surface of the work instead of shaving or shearing it.

A smooth file is generally used for draw filing, and the work is secured in a vise. Hold the file in both hands with the thumbs on the edge toward you and the other fingers on the rear edge. Grasp the file firmly at each end as indicated, and alternately push

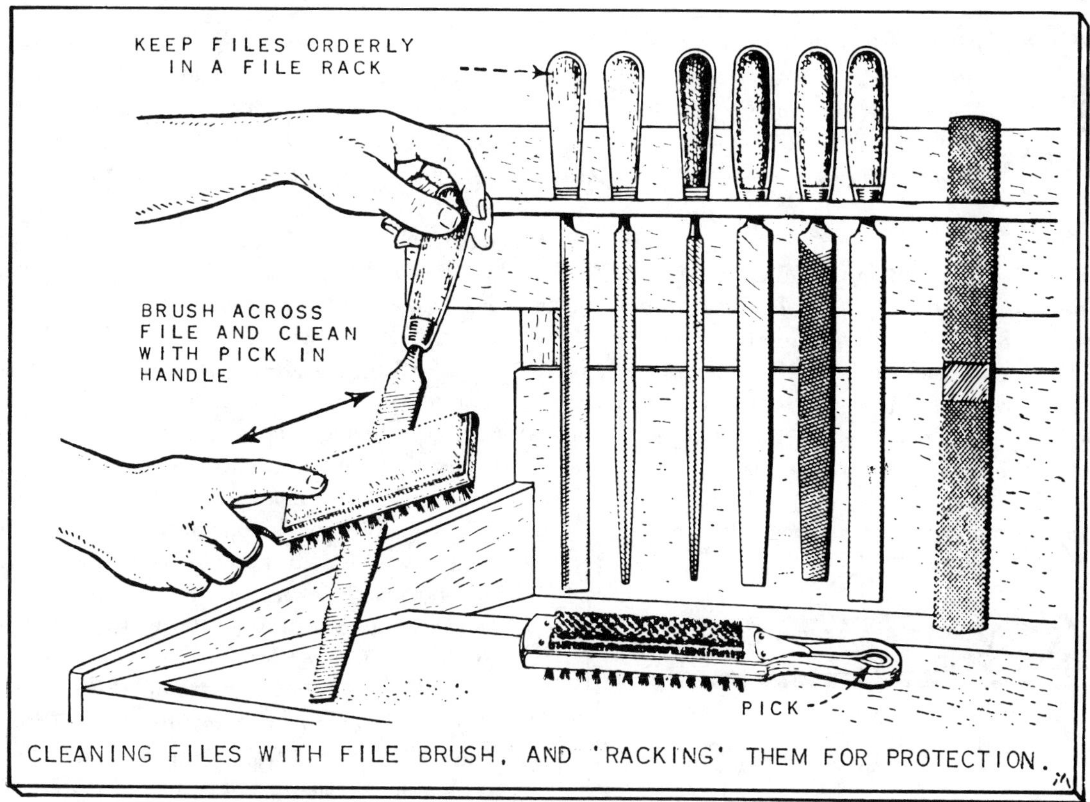
KEEP FILES ORDERLY IN A FILE RACK
BRUSH ACROSS FILE AND CLEAN WITH PICK IN HANDLE
PICK
CLEANING FILES WITH FILE BRUSH, AND 'RACKING' THEM FOR PROTECTION.

Figure 94.

and pull it sideways across the work with an even pressure (D, Fig. 93).

All work that has to be filed true and square must be tested frequently, while filing, with either a straightedge or a square. Hollow or uneven spots on the work can be detected by light shining under the straightedge. When angles are being filed, they must be tested with either a bevel or a try square.

CARE OF FILES. Files are ruined by improper care as well as by improper use and improper selection. Files should never be thrown into a drawer or toolbox or be laid on top of each other. Such treatment will ruin the cutting edges of the teeth. Keep them separate, standing with the tangs in a row of holes or hung on a rack by the handles. Keep them in a dry place so that rust does not corrode the teeth points (Fig. 94).

It is important to keep files clean of filings or chips which collect between the teeth during use. After every few strokes, a good mechanic taps the end of the file on a workbench to loosen the chips. The teeth of a file should be brushed frequently with either a file card or a brush. The file brush combines brush, card, and pick or scorer.

The scorer is made of soft iron and is used especially on fine-cut files to remove the "pins" which fill up and clog the file teeth, causing scratches in the work if not removed. It is sometimes necessary to use the point of a scriber to remove material that brushing does not clean out.

Rivet Sets

Rivet sets are used to form and draw rivets (Fig. 95). They are made of tool steel and are available in a variety of sizes. The cup-shaped hole in the bottom of the tool is used to form the finished head of a rivet. The deeper hole is used to draw the rivet. The large hole in the side is used to smooth out the burrs that are punched through the metal by the rivet. Riveting procedures detailing the use of rivet sets are given in Chap. 7.

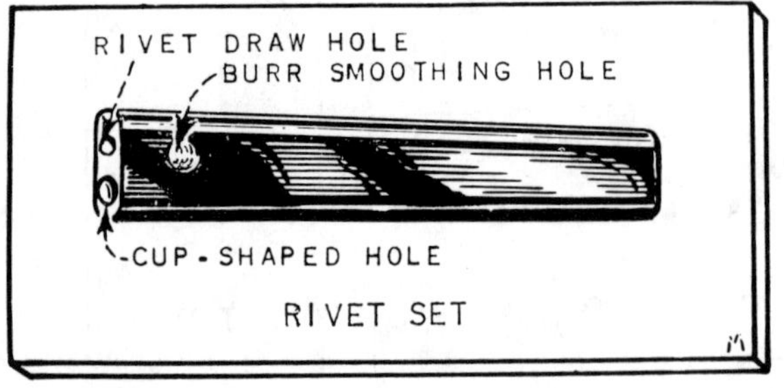

Figure 95.

Hand Groovers

Hand groovers are used to groove seams by hand (Fig. 96). They are available in sizes to fit grooves ranging from 3/32 in. to 19/32 in. The recessed end of the groover fits over the lock of the seam to form the grooved seam. The methods of using hand groovers are detailed in Chap. 5.

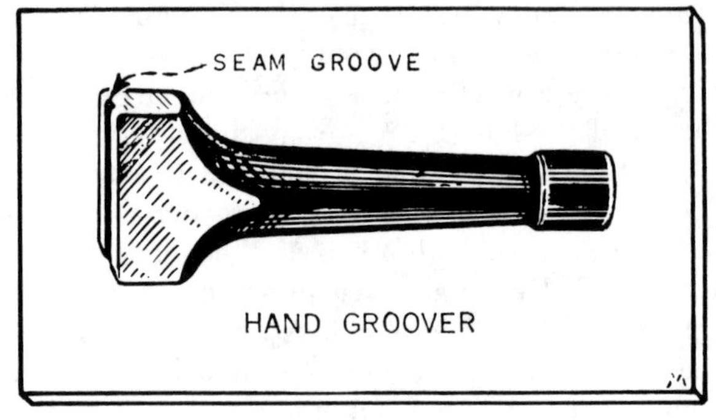

Figure 96.

Soldering Coppers

Two general types of soldering coppers or irons are used in the sheet metal shop; the fire-heated type and the electric type. The essential parts of each of these types are shown in Fig. 97. While fire-heated coppers are generally used in sheet metal work, the electric type is occasionally used for making minor repairs and for soldering the lighter-gauge metals.

Soldering coppers vary in weight and shape, and are classified according to their shape and size or weight. The fire-heated types are marked with a figure indicating the weight per pair. For example, if a copper is marked with a 6, single coppers will weigh 3 lb. each, exclusive of the handle and shank. Fire-heated coppers are available in weights ranging from 1 to 16 lb. per pair.

Electric soldering coppers are classified according to their wattage and range from 50 to 500 watts. Each 50 watts is equal to a 1/2 lb. fire-heated iron. Electric coppers rating at 100 watts or less are used only for soldering electric wires and for extremely light soldering operations. For sheet metal work, those rated at 150 to 250 watts (3 to 5 lb.) should be used. Electric coppers are available with interchangeable plugs and screw tips (Fig. 97). The plug-tip slips into the head of the copper and is held in

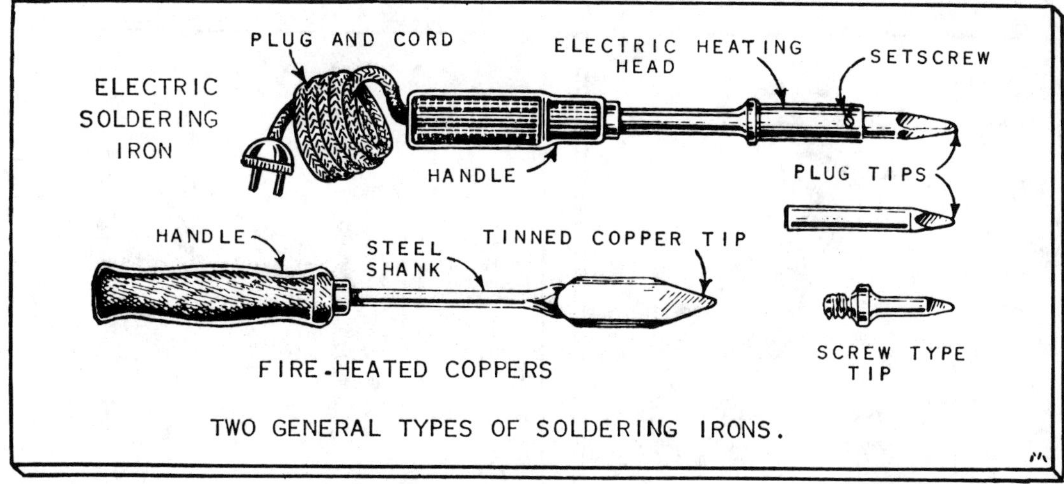

Figure 97.

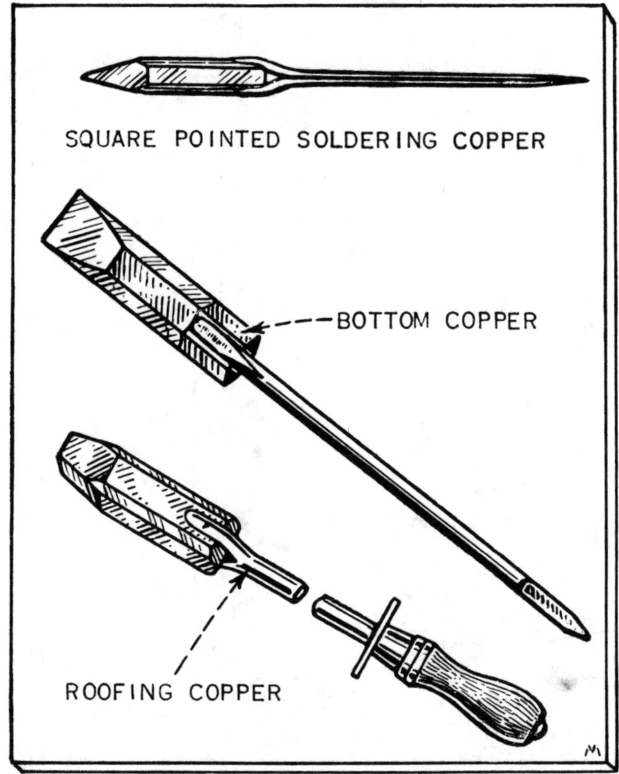

Figure 98.

place by a set screw. The screw tip is threaded and screwed directly into the heater head.

The tips of all types of soldering coppers are made of copper because it is considered the best conductor of heat.

The three types of soldering coppers generally used in the sheet metal shop are the square point, bottom, and roofing (Fig. 98).

Square Pointed Copper (Fig. 98). The square pointed copper is the type commonly used for all types of sheet metal soldering. To do the various soldering jobs in the sheet metal shop, the points of these coppers are sometimes forged to various shapes. Detailed procedures for forging and using soldering coppers are given in Chap. 6.

Bottom Soldering Copper (Fig. 98). As its name implies, the bottom soldering copper is employed for soldering the bottoms of pails, tanks, receptacles, and similar articles.

Roofing Soldering Copper (Fig. 98). This copper is used for soldering all types of metal roofing.

Handles (Fig. 99). Soldering copper handles are made of either wood or fiber, with a metal ferrule at the end where the rod is to be inserted. The ferrule prevents burning of handles when the copper is heated. Handles for roofing soldering coppers and other heavy coppers are usually equipped with a large metal flange at the point where the rod of the copper is inserted into the handle (Fig. 98).

Method of Attaching Handles (Fig. 100). To attach a handle to the copper, heat the point of the rod red hot. Push the heated point into the hole of the handle to a depth of several inches (A, Fig. 100). Quickly remove the rod and permit it to cool. Then replace the rod into the handle. To get a tight fit, strike the end of the handle with a mallet as shown at B, Fig. 100.

Firepots and Blowtorches

The various types of heating equipment used in sheet metal shops for heating fire-heated soldering

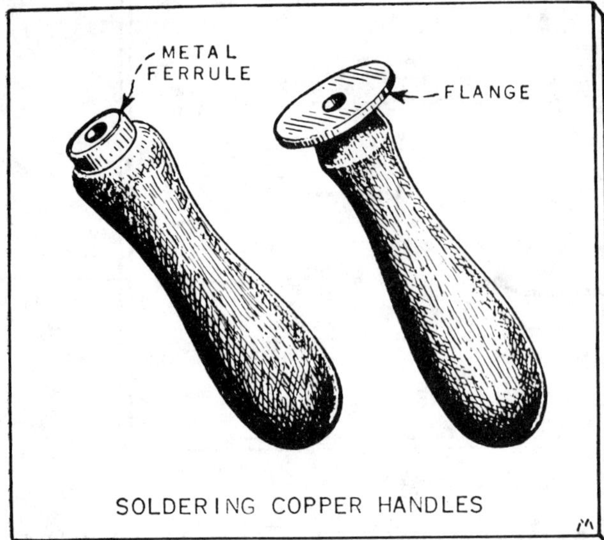

Figure 99.

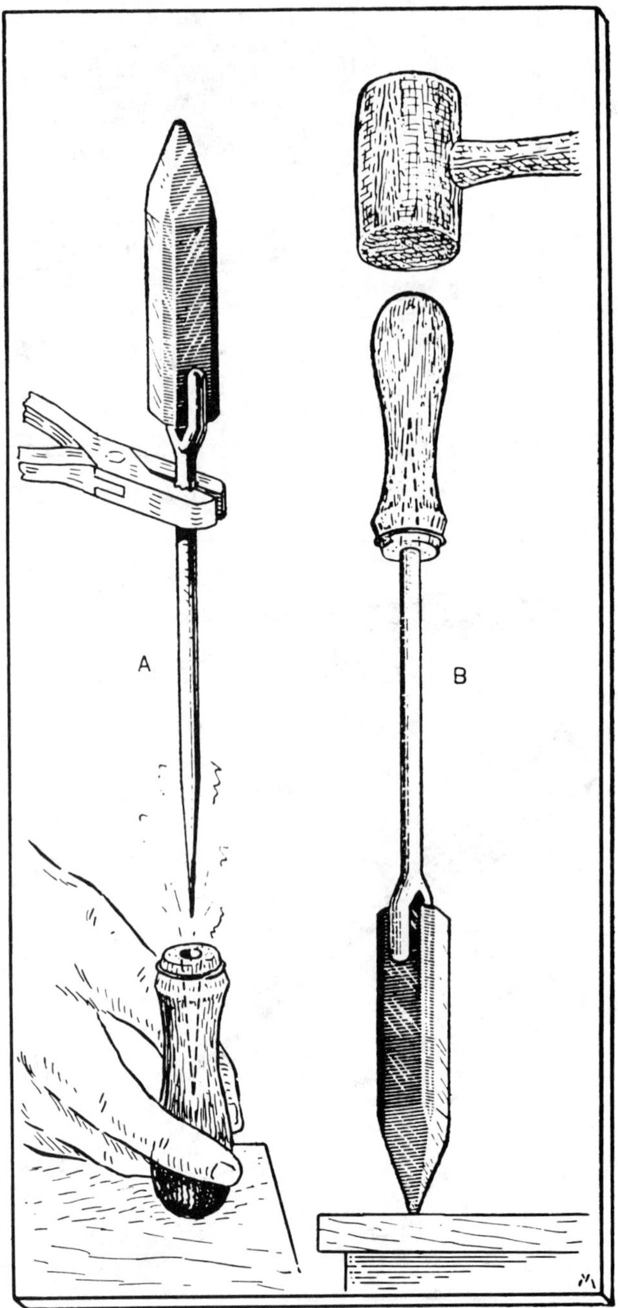

Figure 100.

irons are bench gas furnaces, gasoline firepots, and tinner's charcoal pots. Blowtorches are used principally for necessary preheating of heavy gauge sheet metal or rods for various procedures, such as shaping and bending.

Gas Furnaces. Single or double gas furnaces of the bench type, shown in Fig. 101, are used generally in the sheet metal shop. Single burners are used for heating 6 lb. coppers or less. Double burners are used for heating heavier coppers. All commercial gas furnaces are equipped with shut-off valves and pilot lights. Both bases and covers of these furnaces are asbestos lined.

Operation of Gas Furnace. These gas furnaces burn either natural or artificial gas. Properly operated, they will produce the blue hot flame necessary for proper heating of soldering coppers. All gas furnaces are operated in practically the same manner.

When lighting gas furnaces, the following procedures and precautions should be taken: Clean out all dirt from inside the furnace. Make certain that the shut-off valve is closed. Place a small piece of lighted paper inside the mouth of the furnace; at the same time turn the handle usually located on the front of the furnace. This lights the furnace. Adjust the burner by working the valve handle until the required blue flame appears. The small pilot light near each burner automatically relights the gas burners when the valve handle is turned to the "on" position.

Gasoline Firepots (Fig. 105). The portability of gasoline firepots makes them particularly useful for heating soldering coppers on all types of indoor and outdoor jobs. Firepots are available in a variety of sizes and types. Working parts of a typical gasoline firepot are shown in Fig. 102.

In the gasoline firepot, air pressure is used to force the fuel into the generating coil or chamber. The chamber is kept just hot enough to vaporize the fuel.

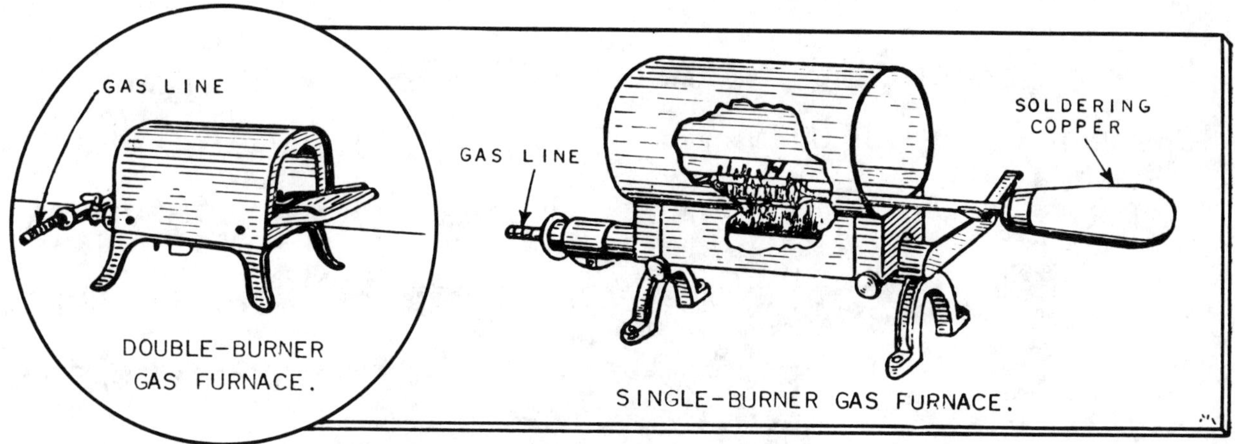

Figure 101.

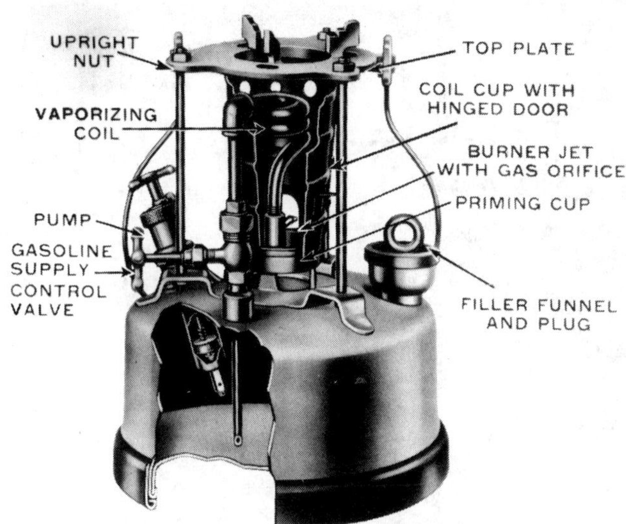

Figure 102. Cutaway view of firepot.

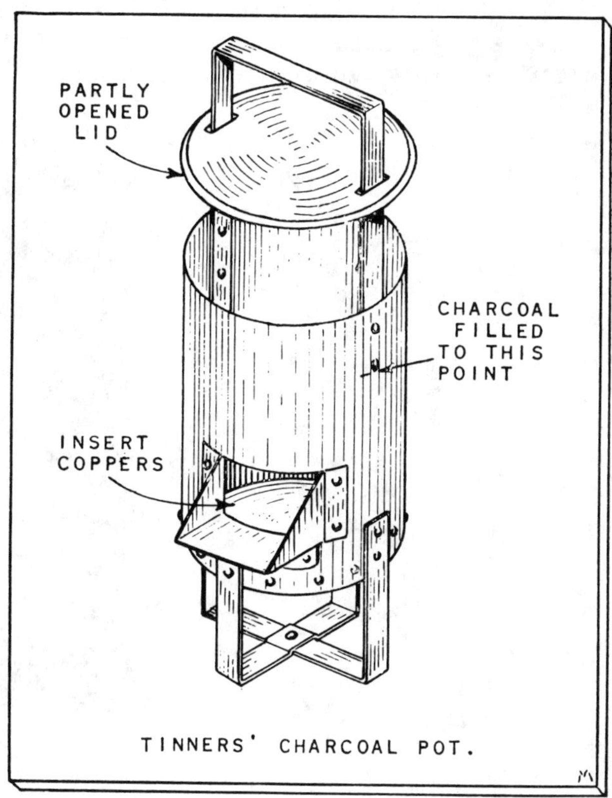

Figure 103.

The gas is then forced through a small opening, drawing in the required amount of air to produce a combustible mixture.

Although specific directions for filling and using firepots are usually furnished by the manufacturer, the methods of filling the gasoline firepot, regardless of type, are generally identical. Extreme care should always be exercised to avoid serious burns.

As an additional precautionary measure, do not fill the firepot in a closed room. To fill the torch, remove the filler plug (Fig. 102). Fill the tank with white gasoline. Close the valve, unscrew the pump plunger, and use the pump to build up the required air pressure. Hold the hand over the coil or combustion chamber and turn on the gasoline-supply control valve to permit the gasoline to drip into the priming cup. Light the gasoline that has dripped into the priming cup. This supplies the heat required to preheat the gasoline in the combustion chamber. Preheating the gasoline in the combustion chamber vaporizes it. Before all of the gasoline in the priming cup is consumed, turn on the control valve slowly and carefully to permit the flame from the priming cup to ignite the vapor produced in the combustion chamber.

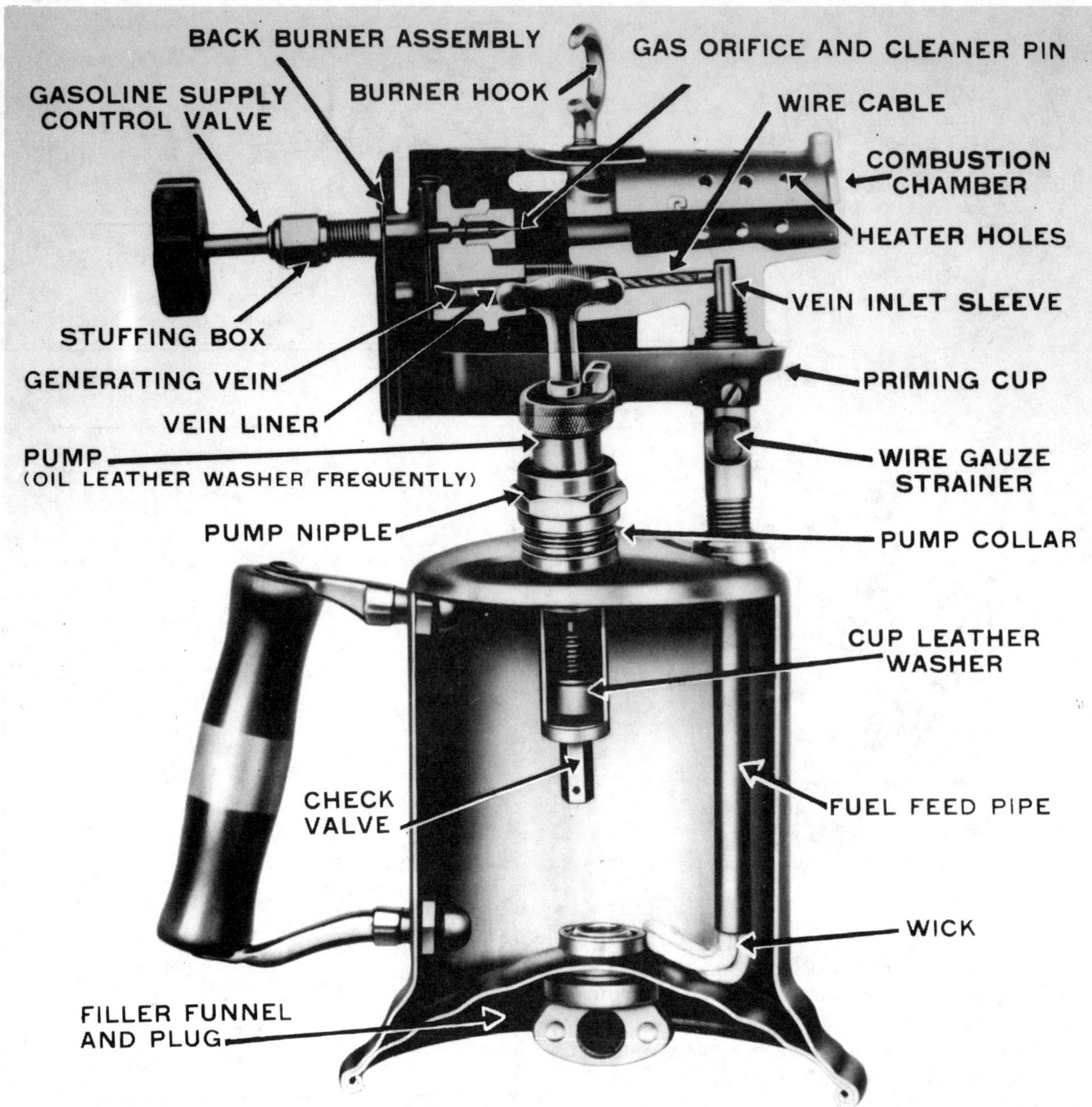

Figure 104. Cutaway view of blowtorch.

To prevent accidents, follow carefully specific directions furnished by the manufacturer for its operation, care, and maintenance.

Tinner's Charcoal Pot. The tinner's charcoal pot shown in Fig. 103 is generally used on roofing and similar outdoor jobs. It will produce a clean, uniform heat if kept nearly filled with burning charcoal. Coppers are heated in the charcoal pot by placing them in the red hot charcoal.

Blowtorches (Fig. 105). Blowtorches are available in a variety of types and sizes. Working parts of a typical blowtorch are shown in Fig. 104. The procedures for filling, lighting, and adjusting blowtorches are similar to those for gasoline firepots.

Figure 105. Blowtorch and firepot.

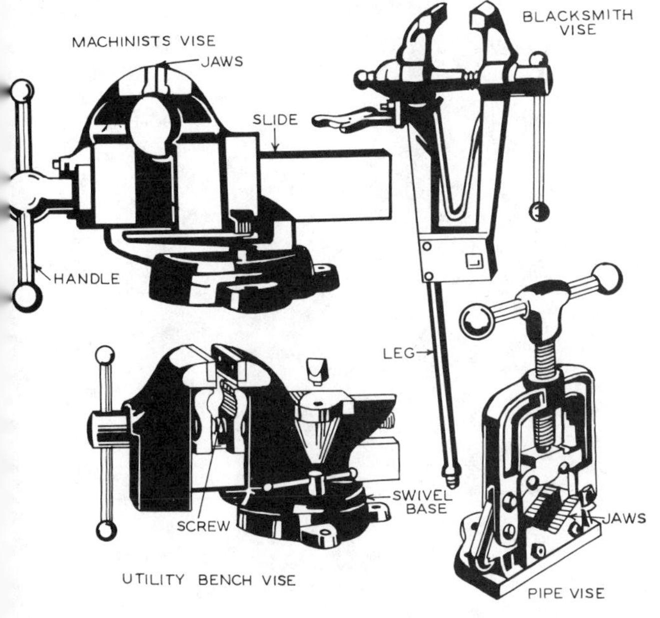

Figure 106.

Vises

Vises are used for holding work when it is being planed, sawed, drilled, shaped, sharpened, or riveted, or when wood is being glued.

A *machinist's bench vise* (Fig. 106) is a large steel vise with rough jaws that prevent the work from slipping. Most of these vises have a swivel base with jaws that can be rotated, but there are others that cannot be rotated. A similar light duty model is equipped with a cutoff. These vises are usually bolt-mounted onto a bench.

The *bench* and *pipe vise* (Fig. 106) has integral pipe jaws for holding pipe of from 3/4 inch to 3 inches in diameter. The maximum working main jaw opening is usually 5 inches, with a jaw width of from 4 to 5 inches. The base can be swiveled to any position and locked. These vises are equipped with an anvil and are also bolted onto a workbench.

The *clamp base vise* usually has a smaller holding

capacity than the machinist's or the bench and pipe vise and is usually clamped to the edge of a bench with a thumbscrew. These type vises can be obtained with a maximum holding capacity varying between 1 1/2 inches and 3 inches. These vises normally do not have pipe holding jaws.

The *blacksmith's vise* (Fig. 106) is used for holding work that must be pounced with a heavy hammer. It is fastened to a sturdy workbench or wall, and the long leg is secured into a solid base on the floor.

The *pipe vise* (Fig. 106) is specifically designed to hold round stock or pipe. The vise shown has a capacity of from 1 to 3 inches. One jaw is hinged so that the work can be positioned and then the jaw brought down and locked. This vise is also used on a bench. Some pipe vises are designed to use a section of chain to hold down the work. *Chain pipe vises* range in size from 1/8 to 2 1/2 inch pipe capacity up to 1/2 to 8 inch pipe capacity.

Drill Press Hand Vise (Fig. 106). This vise is usually used for holding small pieces of material, in conjunction with a motor-powered drill press. It is equipped with several sets of jaw blocks for holding irregular-shaped pieces.

Care of Vises

Keep vises clean at all times. They should be cleaned and wiped with light oil after using. Never strike a vise with a heavy object and never hold large work in a small vise, since these practices will cause the jaws to become sprung or otherwise damage the vise. Keep jaws in good condition and oil the screws and the slide frequently. Never oil the swivel base of a swivel jaw joint, as its holding power will be impaired. When the vise is not in use, bring the jaws lightly together or leave a very small gap. (The movable jaw of a tightly closed vise may break due to the expansion of the metal in heat.) Leave the handle in a vertical position.

Safety Precautions

When closing the jaw of a vise, avoid getting any portion of your hands or body between the jaws or between one jaw and the work.

When holding heavy work in a vise, place a block of wood under the work as a prop to prevent it from sliding down and falling on your foot.

Do not open the jaws of a vise beyond their capacity, as the movable jaw will drop off, causing personal injury and possible damage to the jaw.

Chapter 4

Sheet Metalworking Machines

Many types of machines are used in industrial metal-working shops for squaring, cutting, forming, crimping, seaming, and other operations. Some of these machines are operated by foot-power, and/or by electric motors. In certain industries, machines specially designed to manufacture specific articles are used. As a rule, these machines are combinations of two or more standard machines. For obvious reasons, these special machines cannot be described here.

Squaring Shears

Two general types of squaring shears are used in the sheet metal workshop: foot-power operated and motor driven. Squaring shears are used for shearing, cutting, trimming, and squaring to required sizes, the large-sized sheets of tin plate, sheet iron, brass, copper, or aluminum that are delivered from the mill. Although some squaring shears will differ slightly in design and construction, the operations of all are similar.

FOOT-POWERED SQUARING SHEARS. The principal parts of a typical foot-powered squaring shear are shown in Fig. 1. All standard squaring shears of this type are equipped with two transverse T-slots on top of the bed for the front and bevel gauges and a large depression in the center of the bed for necessary clearance (Fig. 1). Two graduated scales for setting gauges are located on the top of the bed (Fig. 2). The two extension arms are used for supporting the front gauge, which can be fastened in the T-slots of these front brackets for making either straight or angular cuts (Fig. 1). A special bevel gauge for making angular cuts is attached to the bed. The side gauges, located on each side of the bed, are used for squaring the corners of the material, and the back gauge, mounted on the rear of the shears, is used when cutting large sheets. Two blades are used in this machine: a lower blade that moves upward and an upper cutting blade that descends simultaneously when the foot treadle is employed to force the cutting blades together (Fig. 1). The holddown is a double service part used both for holding the metal in place and as a safety guard (Fig. 1). Foot-powered squaring shears are usually used for cutting metals up to and including 16-gauge (U.S. Standard) sheets in sizes 22, 30, 36, 42, and 52 in. Larger machines are available, similar in design, but slightly different in construction, for sizes ranging up to 120 in. For cutting materials heavier than 16-gauge, powered squaring shears must be used.

Operation. It is usual practice to insert material to be squared or cut between the cutting blades from the front of the machine. When it is necessary to cut short pieces from very long sheets that ordinarily would interfere with the operation of the foot treadle, the metal is inserted from the rear. When the sheet is inserted from the rear, the front bed gauges are employed. When the material to be cut is larger than the bed of the machine, the bed gauge is extended out on the front bed gauge arms that are provided for this purpose (Fig. 1). When squaring and trimming smaller pieces that do not interfere with the operation of the foot treadle, the material is always inserted between the cutting blade from the front of the machine and the work is gauged to the required size on the bed, using either the short or the long bed gauge.

The usual procedure for squaring and cutting sheet metal to required size is as follows: place one side of the material against the left-side gauge, with the edge of the material that is to be trimmed extending 1/8 in. over and beyond the lower blade (Fig. 3). Clamp the sheet in place by pulling down the holddown handle. Hold the metal sheet down with both hands and with the fingers away from the blade. Step on the foot treadle to cut the metal (Figs. 1

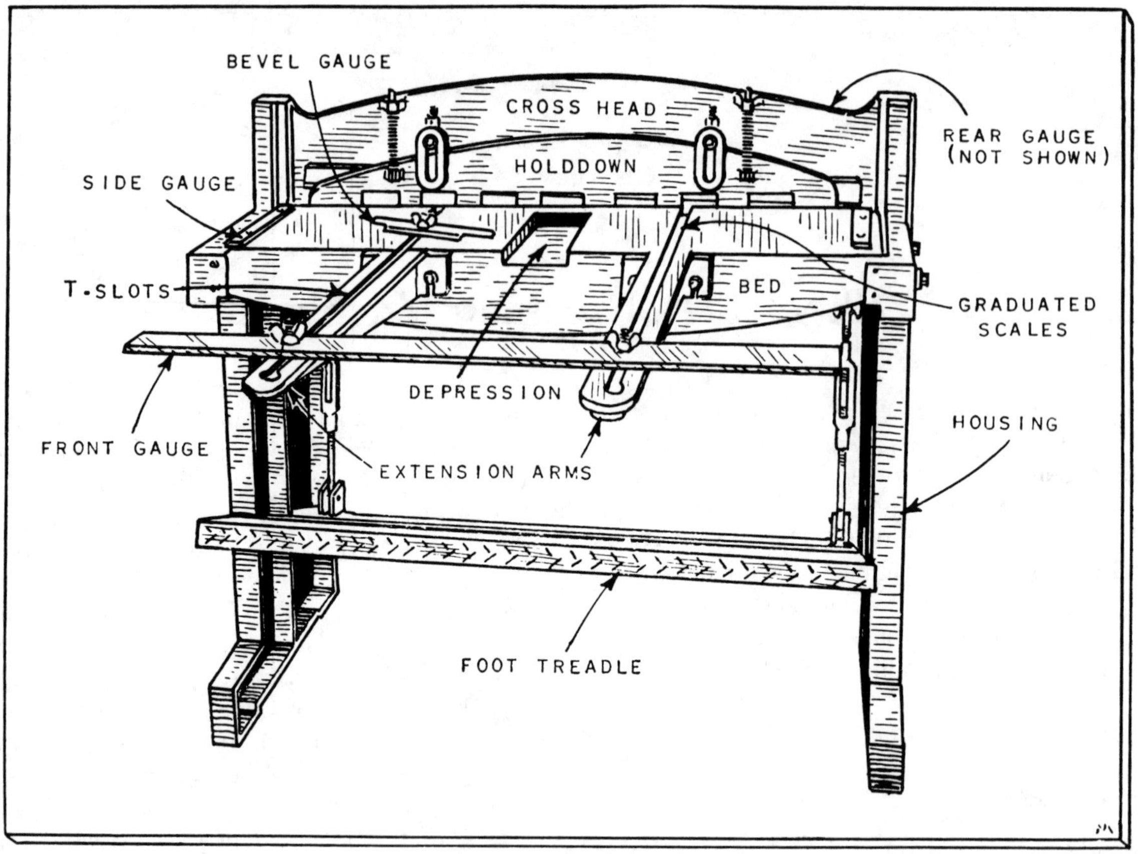

Figure 1. Foot-powered gap squaring shears.

and 4). Keep the foot on the treadle and release it gradually. Remove the metal by releasing the hold-down handle. Proceed by placing the newly trimmed edge against the left-side gauge and repeating the first cutting operation. Place the two squared edges against the front and left-side gauges and set the front gauge to required size. Repeat the cutting operation. Reset the gauge and cut the remaining edge.

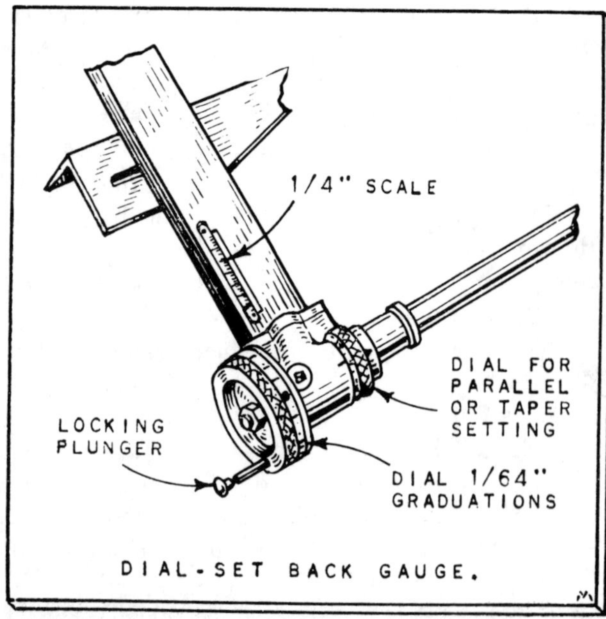

Figure 2.

Power Driven Shears. Power driven shears of the overhead or over-driven type shown in Fig. 5 are generally used when sheet metal of 16, 14, or heavier gauges is to be squared and cut. They are available in lengths of 30, 36, 48, 60, 72, 96, 120, and 144 in. and in a wide variety of capacities and types. Although they differ in size and type, setting up and operation are to a great extent similar for all power shears.

Necessary Adjustment. Before attempting to use one of these machines, the operator should be familiar with all of the working parts shown in Fig. 5.

The accuracy of this machine depends upon the proper adjustment of the bed and the lower cutting knife. To make the necessary adjustments, proceed as follows:

LOWER CUTTING BLADE
LEFT-SIDE GAUGE
1/8"
PLACING ONE SIDE OF MATERIAL AGAINST LEFT-SIDE GAUGE.

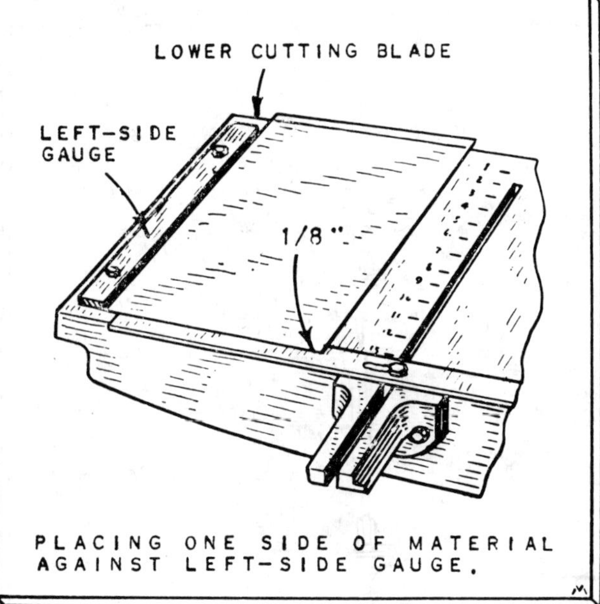

Figure 3.

Facing the front of the machine, two adjusting screws will be found at both the left and right ends where the bed and legs meet. Loosening one of these screws and tightening the other, the bed which holds the lower knife will move inward or outward.

It is essential that the operator acquaint himself with the action of these screws and the movement of the bed before attempting to adjust the shear knives. Hereafter we will refer to these screws as bed adjusting screws.

Before turning bed adjusting screws, loosen all bolts holding the bed to the end legs about one-quarter turn. If there is a center leg attached to the bed, loosen this also.

Proceed to trip the shear through by depressing the foot treadle. *Turn the flywheel slowly by hand and always in one direction as indicated by arrow on*

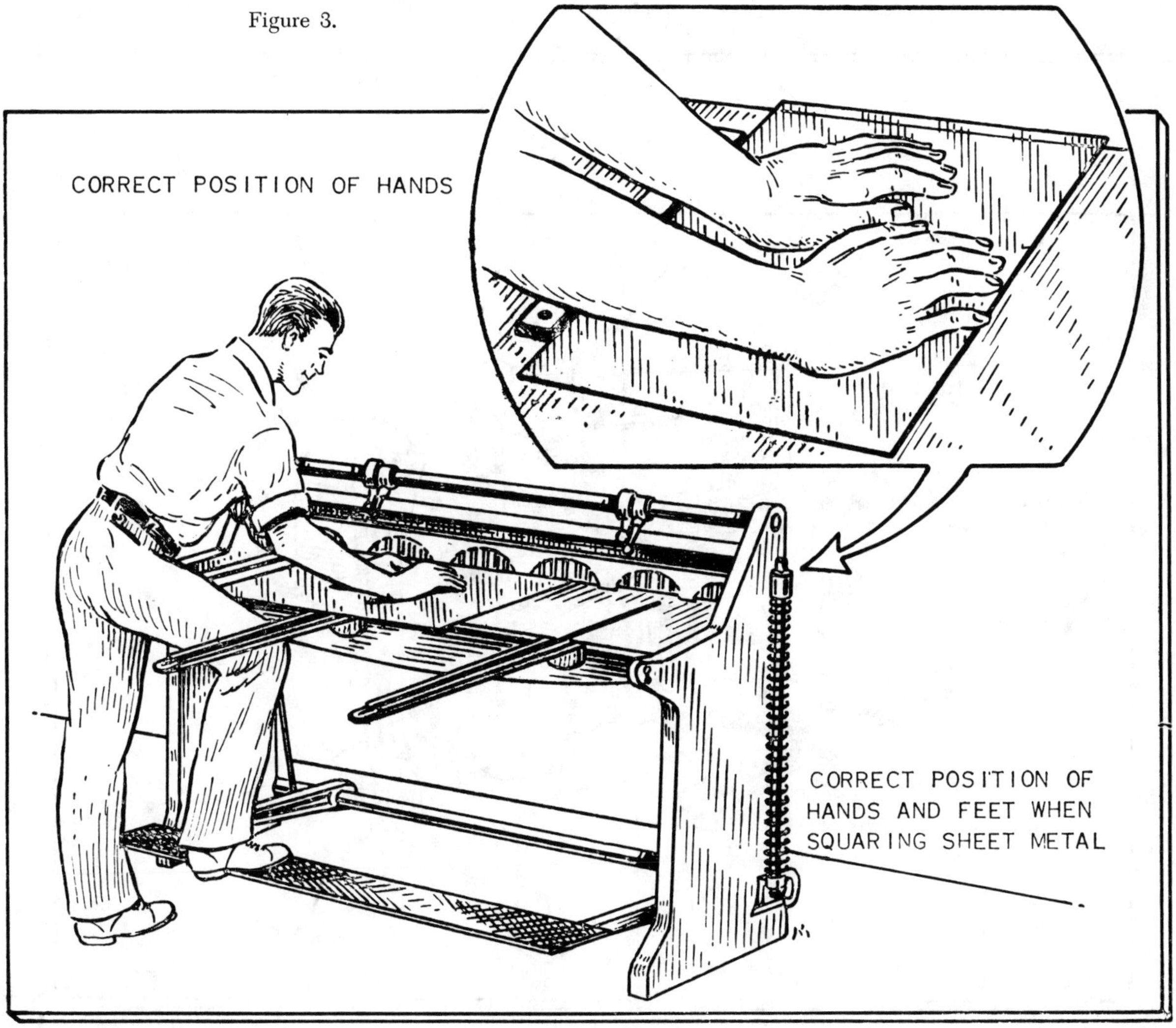

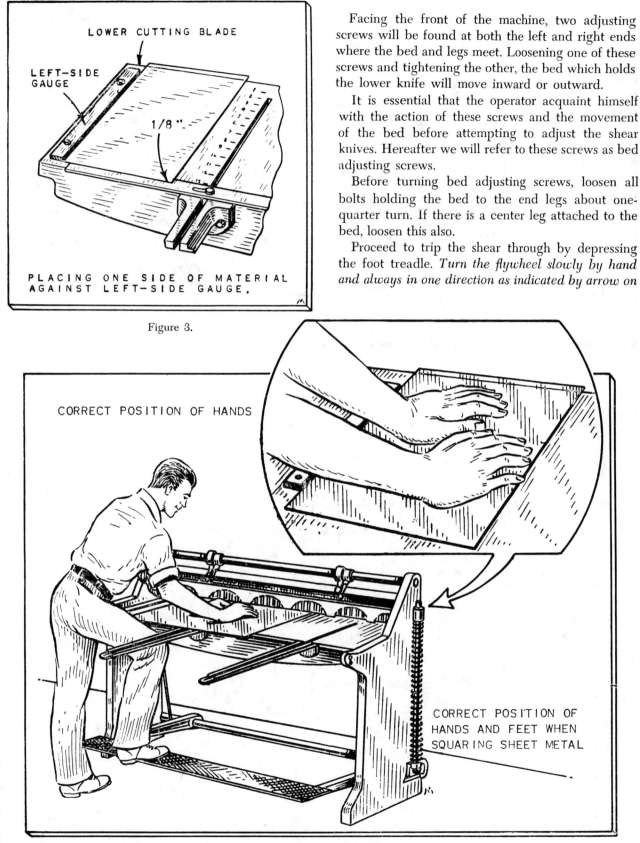

CORRECT POSITION OF HANDS
CORRECT POSITION OF HANDS AND FEET WHEN SQUARING SHEET METAL

Figure 4.

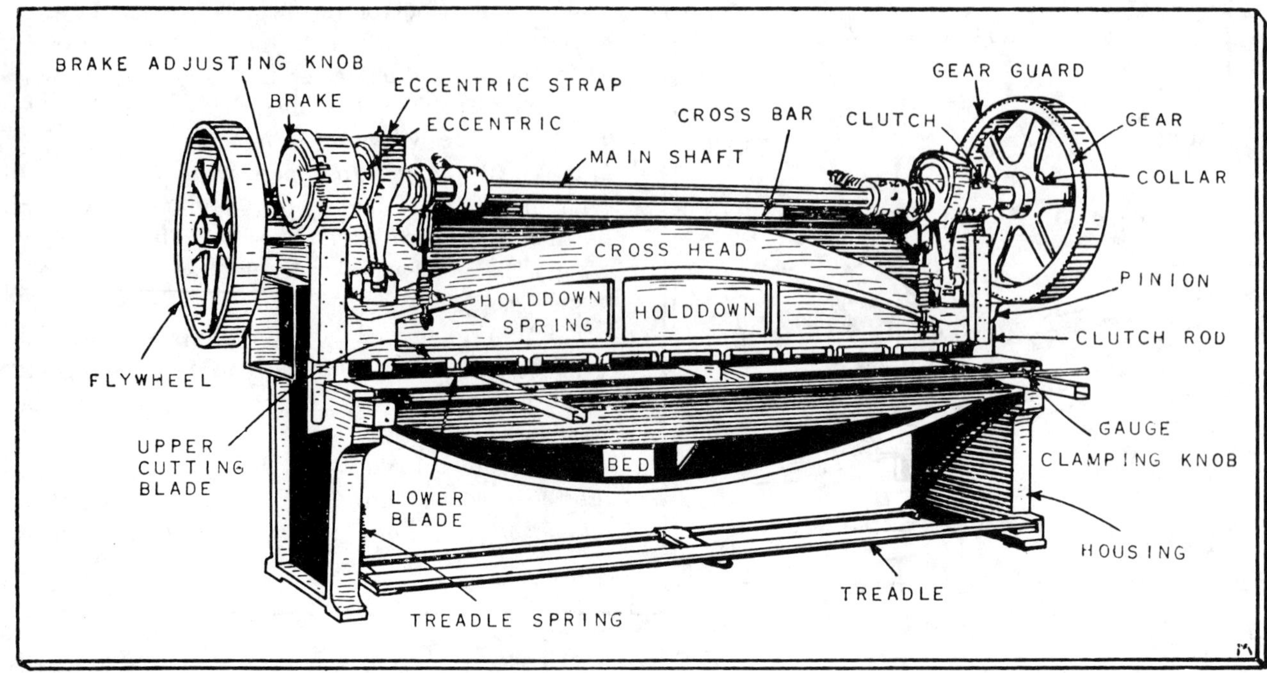

Figure 5. Power-driven shears.

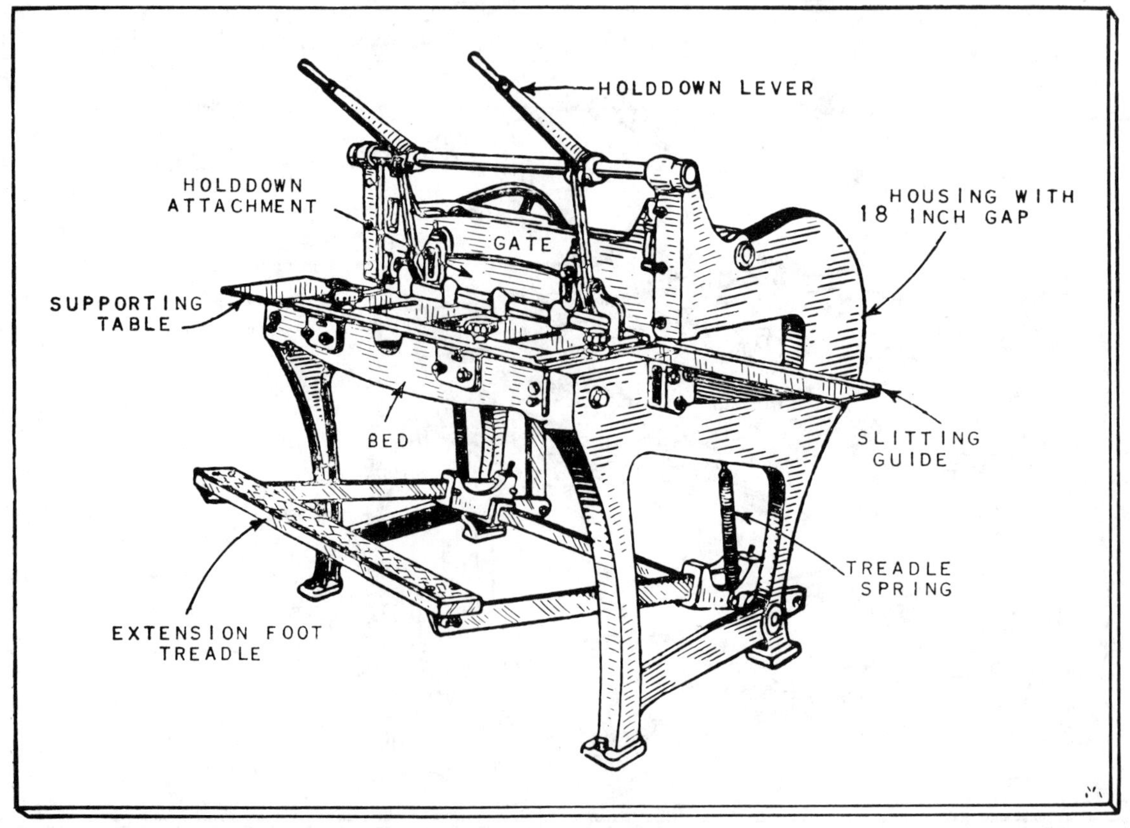

Figure 6. Gap squaring shears.

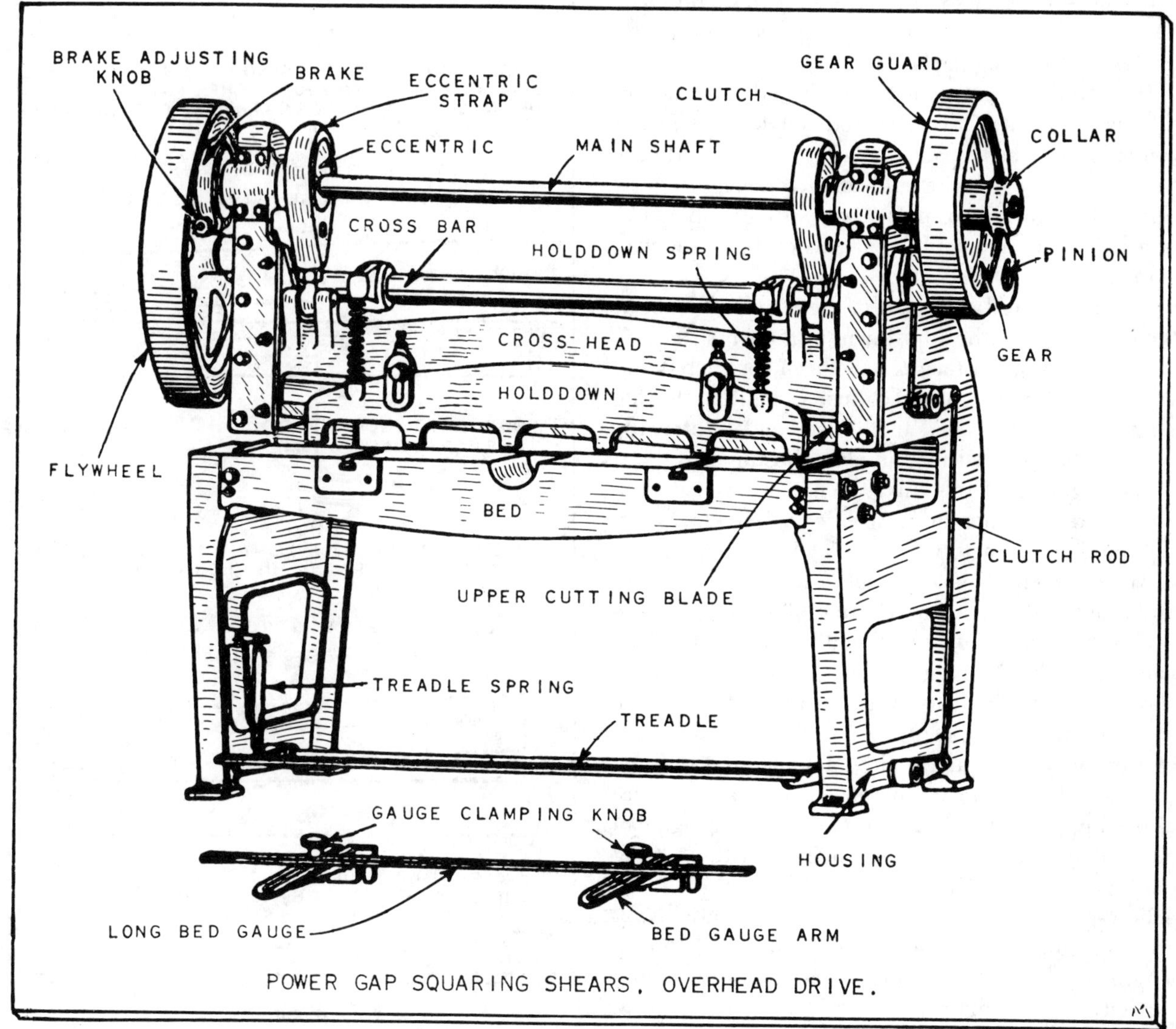

Figure 7.

flywheel—serious damage will result to the clutch if the flywheel is turned backward. When the upper knife passes the lower knife at the start of cut, move that end of the bed inward by turning the bed adjusting screws in the proper direction until the knives are about 1/32 in. apart. Proceed to let the cross head down, watching for a 1/32 in. clearance all the way across the knives. Move the bed inward at that end until the knives are uniformly 1/32 in. apart along the full length of the knives. Now raise the cross head to its highest point. Never turn the flywheel backward, but always in one direction.

Depress the treadle again, trip the shear as before, and turn the flywheel by hand, bringing the cross head down as before until the knives are in a position to start with the cut. Insert two pieces of wrapping paper between the knives. With paper between the knives, turn the flywheel slowly and watch carefully the clearance of the knives all the way across. Proceed to move the bed inward, observing that the knives are the same distance apart at the start of cut as at the extreme other end. Now raise the cross head to the highest point as before.

Test the adjustment just made to ascertain if the knives have been set at a uniform clearance by placing a heavy sheet of paper between the full length of the knives. Depress the treadle again and turn the flywheel *by hand,* bringing the cross head down to make a cut of the paper. If the knives do not cut the paper, adjust the bed inwardly by turning the bed adjusting screws evenly at each end of the bed. Test each adjustment of bed movement until the knives start cutting paper.

If shears will cut paper at both ends and not in the center, tighten the truss rod nut located in the center of the back part of the cross head. Always turn the nut clockwise and about one-eighth of a turn. After this adjustment, try cutting paper and repeat if necessary until paper cuts clean all the way across.

If paper should cut clean in the center and not at the ends, reverse the adjustment of the truss rod nut.

When these adjustments have been completed and you are ready to cut sheet metal, tighten the leg screws holding the bed to the legs and tighten the check nuts provided for the bed adjusting screws.

Packing behind the knives is not necessary when knives are new nor in most cases when knives are reground at the factory.

Always keep oil holes or lubricating fittings clean and filled with a good lubricating oil or light grease.

Gap Squaring Shears. An additional cutting advantage gained in the use of the gap squaring shears shown in Fig. 6 is that the construction of this type of shears permits the cutting and squaring of sheets of varying lengths and widths. It is limited only by the size of the gap or throat. These machines are also equipped with a slitting gauge. This gauge can be used for slitting material longer than the cutting blades of the machine.

Foot-powered gap squaring machines are available for cutting sheet up to and including 52 in. in length, with an 18 in. gap or throat and a maximum capacity for cutting up to No. 16 gauge metal (U.S. Standard).

Operation and Maintenance. The general procedures for the operation and maintenance of these machines are similar to those previously given for squaring shears.

Power Gap Squaring Shears. The new type of power gap squaring shears shown in Fig. 7 is available in lengths ranging from 30 to 144 in. and in a varied range of cutting capacities. It is powered by an overhead drive.

Operation. Although procedures for the operation of these shears are similar to those previously given, it is sometimes necessary to make additional cutting adjustments prior to cutting.

These machines are usually delivered and adjusted for cutting to the full length of the machine (Fig. 7). The nominal cutting length of the shear thus adjusted is somewhat longer than the cutting

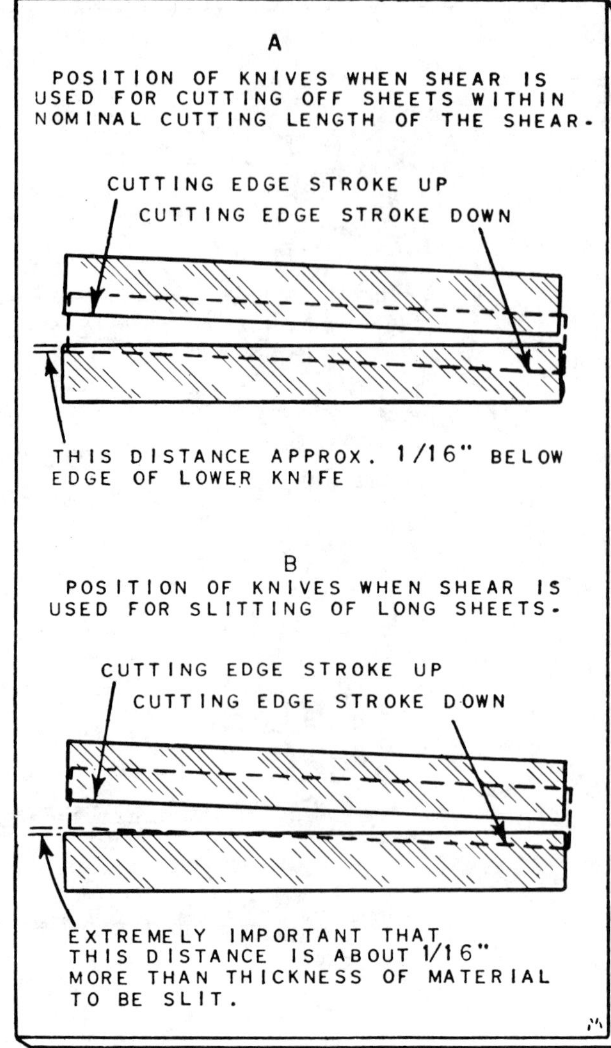
A
POSITION OF KNIVES WHEN SHEAR IS USED FOR CUTTING OFF SHEETS WITHIN NOMINAL CUTTING LENGTH OF THE SHEAR.
CUTTING EDGE STROKE UP
CUTTING EDGE STROKE DOWN
THIS DISTANCE APPROX. 1/16" BELOW EDGE OF LOWER KNIFE
B
POSITION OF KNIVES WHEN SHEAR IS USED FOR SLITTING OF LONG SHEETS.
CUTTING EDGE STROKE UP
CUTTING EDGE STROKE DOWN
EXTREMELY IMPORTANT THAT THIS DISTANCE IS ABOUT 1/16" MORE THAN THICKNESS OF MATERIAL TO BE SLIT.

Figure 8.

length of blades when set for slitting (A, Fig. 8). Cutting length should be decreased when the shear is to be used for slitting long sheets (B, Fig. 8).

Convenient adjustment is provided on connection screws for this purpose. The most popularly used is shown in Fig. 9.

To lower or raise the upper knife, first loosen nuts "A" on both the left and right sides of the shear. Turning connecting screw "B" in a clockwise direction (looking from the top) will lower the upper shear knife. Turning screw "B" in the opposite direction will raise the upper knife. Care must be used to make the adjustment on each side intermittent; not to make a large adjustment on one side and then on the other, but a little at a time on each side until the desired adjustment is obtained. The ends of the gate or top knife holder and the ways in the

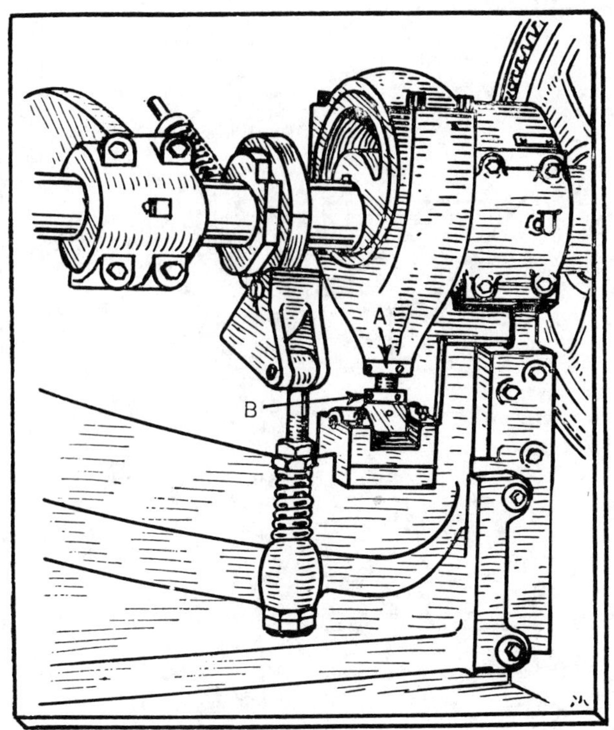

Figure 9. Adjustment of connecting screws.

side housings are machined to provide from 1/32 to 1/16 in. clearance between them, and unless the gate or top knife holder is raised or lowered uniformly at each end, the shear or rake of the knives will be reduced and a binding of the gate in the guides will result.

When adjustment is made, be sure to tighten nuts "A" securely on each end of the shear.

This adjustment is of further value in that it allows grinding down the upper knife as much as the tool steel edge will permit, while still maintaining full nominal cutting length of shear.

Ring and Circle Shears. Ring and circle shears are used to cut discs or rings, or for irregular cutting to a line, when the clamping arm is removed or pushed back out of the way. The type shown in Fig. 10 can also be used for slitting operations. The parts of a typical modern ring and circle shears are shown in Fig. 10. They are either hand or power operated.

The cutting head is provided with cutters of various diameters according to the capacity of the machine. The cutter shafts are at an angle to each other to allow for inside as well as outside cutting. The upper cutter may be moved vertically, and is raised and lowered by means of a hand wheel or crank. Cutters should be set to give a clean cut with no burr, but should never be allowed to rub. When cutting light-gauge materials, the cutters should just touch but not rub against each other (Fig. 10). For heavy-gauge material (18 gauge or heavier), the cutters should be separated slightly (Fig. 10). In this respect, specific directions for adjustment of cutters given by the manufacturer of the equipment should be followed. On the hand machine, adjustment is accomplished by means of threaded collars on the lower angular shaft, and on power shears of 16 gauge capacity and heavier, adjustment is accomplished by means of lateral movement of the upper shaft in the same manner.

The circle arm is provided with a pair of clamping discs. The lower disc is provided with a center point and a vertical adjustment (Fig. 11).

In the type of machine shown in Fig. 10, the front and rear circle arm adjusting screws position the circle arm in relation to the cutting head. If the circle arm is improperly positioned, the circles will:

1. Have a "rolled-over" edge if *rear* circle arm adjusting screw is in too far.
2. Form an ellipse if *front* circle arm adjusting screw is in too far.

The optimum position of the circle arm is between these extreme settings. Loosen the circle arm clamping screw when making adjustments. The upper clamping disc is lowered to a clamping position by means of a lever or hand wheel. This arm is also provided with two swinging gauges (Figs. 12 and 13) which may be set to center blanks and which are locked in place by means of setscrews. On hand machines, the circle arm is locked in place on its ways by means of a screw with a lever handle. On power ring and circle shears, the movement of the circle arm is accomplished through a rack and pinion; the circle arm is secured to the ways through the use of two bolts and nuts which can be loosened with a wrench.

Operation. When cutting circles, proceed as follows: Determine the center of the square blank and prick punch the center point (Fig. 14). With a pair of dividers, scribe a circle of desired size on the blank. Scribing the circle can be eliminated if the graduated bed shown in Fig. 12 is used for setting the sliding circle arm. Loosen the circle arm on its ways by releasing the locking screw or bolts provided, then sliding it until it is in the proper position to cut the disc required. There is an indicator on the circle arm graduated in fractions of inches. Therefore, if a circle 5 in. in diameter is to be cut, draw the circle arm backward or forward so that the indicator on the circle arm is pointing to 5 in. on the

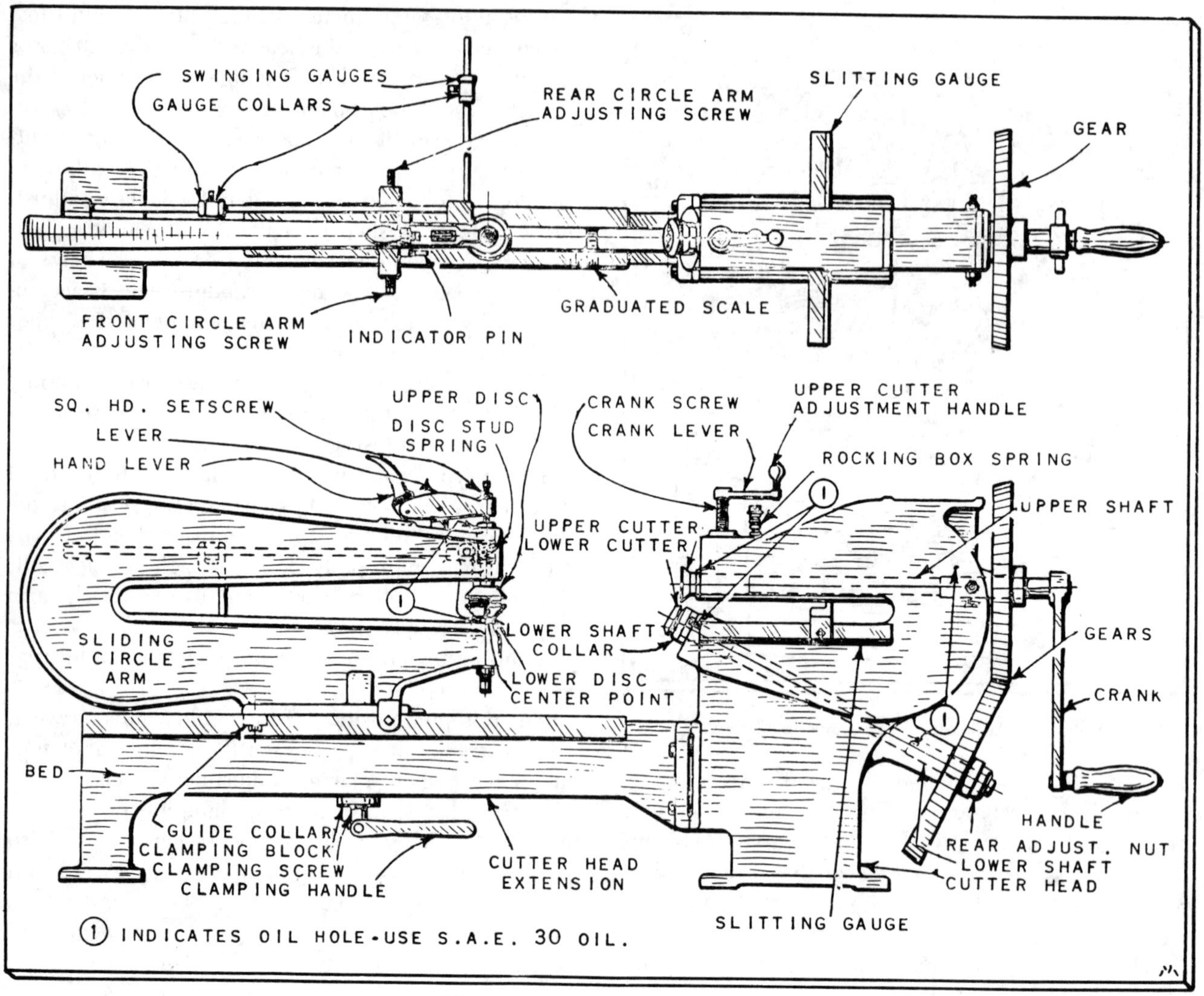

Figure 10. Ring and circle shears.

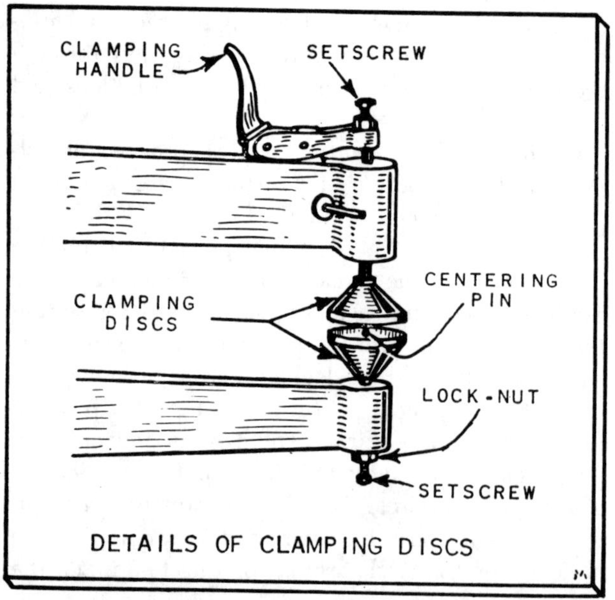

Figure 11.

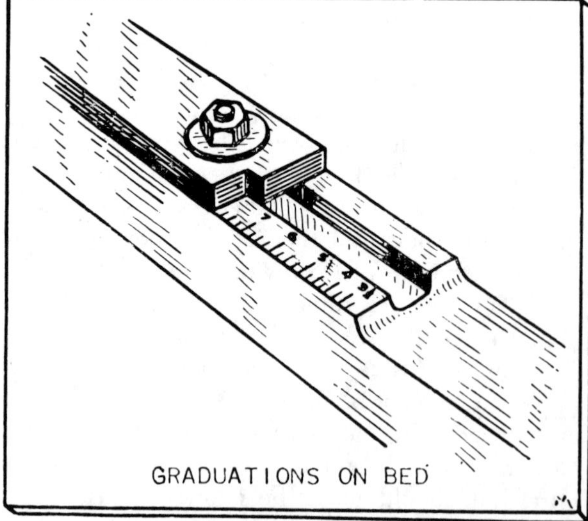

Figure 12.

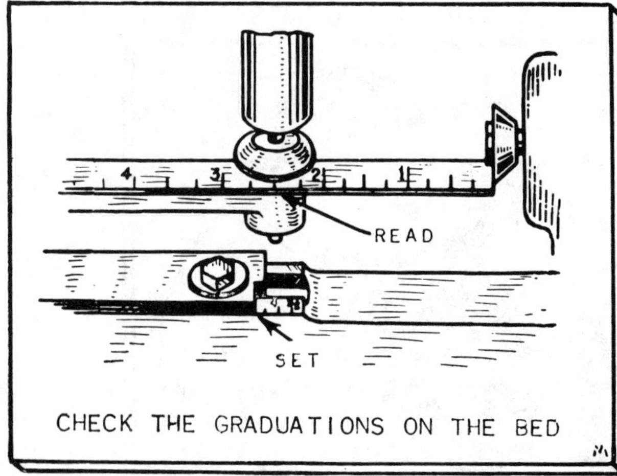
READ
SET
CHECK THE GRADUATIONS ON THE BED

Figure 13.

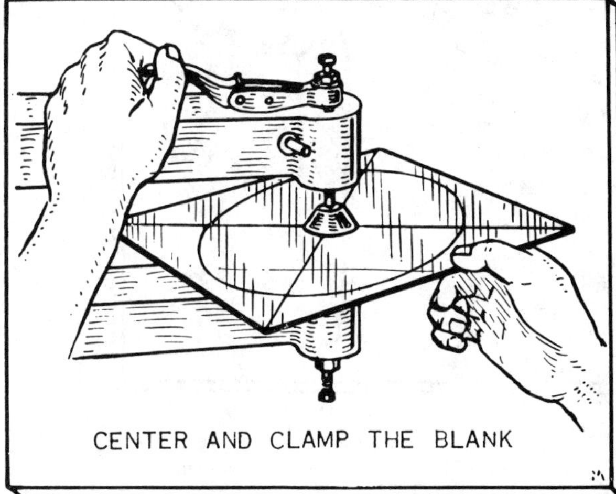
CENTER AND CLAMP THE BLANK

Figure 14.

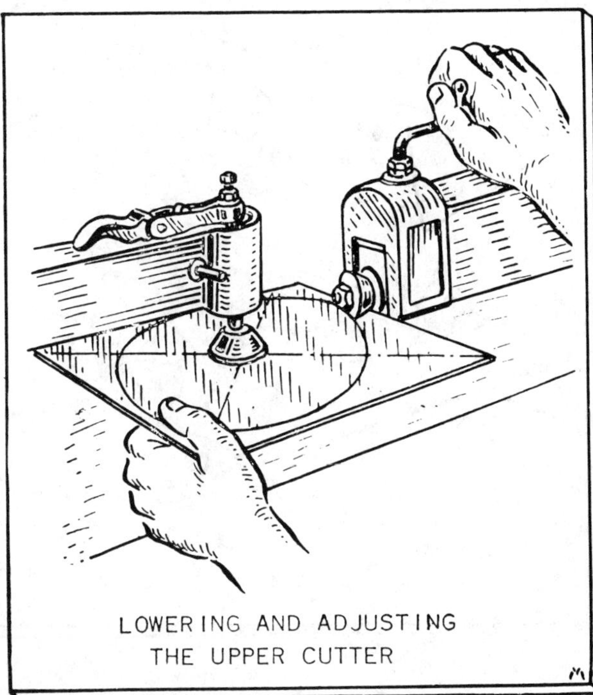
LOWERING AND ADJUSTING
THE UPPER CUTTER

Figure 15.

scale, then lock the circle arm securely through the locking lever. Using the prick punch mark as a guide, place the square blanks between the clamping discs in position and clamp (Fig. 14). Tighten the lock-nut on the circle arm to check that the cutters are in line with the previously scribed circle, then turn the blank by hand.

Lower the upper cutter and make adjustment if necessary (Fig. 15). Turn the operating handle on hand machines or switch on the power on power machines to cut the disc (Fig. 16). When the circle has been cut, release the clamping handle to remove the disc. If a quantity of the same size is to be cut, the swinging gauges can be adjusted so that they will strike the edge of the square blanks and center them (Fig. 17).

To make a ring, or to cut a circle from the inside of a square sheet of metal, the blank is clamped between the clamping discs in the usual way and the sliding circle arm, with the sheet metal blank inserted, is brought toward the cutters, permitting as much of the edge of the sheet to slide between the cutters as is necessary, according to the size of the inside of the circle that is to be cut. With the proper alignment of the blank in the machine secured, bring the upper cutter down on the material by turning the crank screw hard enough that the cutters will cut the material without burring or buckling the edge.

If a tendency to buckle or pull a disc is noted, it indicates that the center of the clamping disc is not properly located. The center of the clamping disc, when properly set, is slightly off center of the vertical center line of the cutters on the side toward which the metal is fed. It is in line with the edge of the cut. This adjustment is made on hand machines by means of setscrews on either side of the ways. On means of setscrews which rest against the circle arm to the slide are loosened and the arm adjusted by means of setscrews which rest against the circle arm casting just back of the lower clamping disc bearing. When the proper setting is made, the bolts are locked and no further adjustment except of the cutters should be required.

To slit material on this machine, proceed as follows: Set the slitting gauge to the required width of slit with a rule as shown in Fig. 17. Set and clamp the upper cutter and proceed to make the cut as shown in Fig. 18.

Irregular cuts can be made on this machine by setting and clamping the upper cutter, feeding the material into the machine, and guiding the material with the left hand so that the cutter will cut along the scribed line (Fig. 19).

Lubrication. For efficient operation, hand operated

TURN HANDLE IN DIRECTION SHOWN
WHEN CUTTING DISCS

Figure 16.

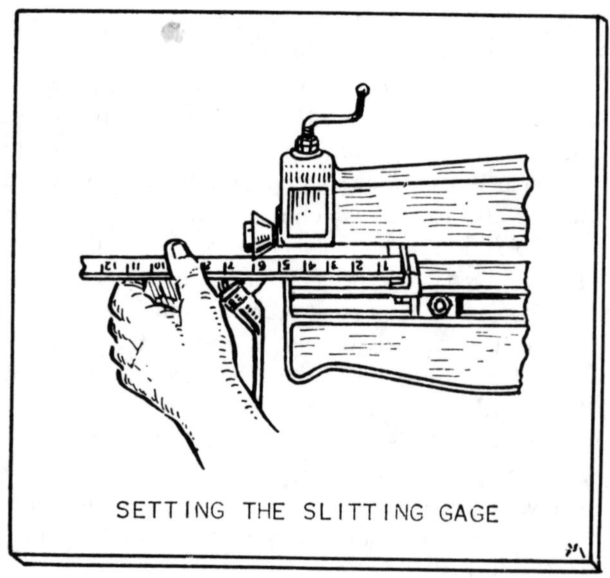
SETTING THE SLITTING GAGE

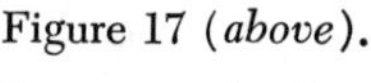

Figure 17 (*above*).

Figure 18 (*right*).

SLITTING A SHEET

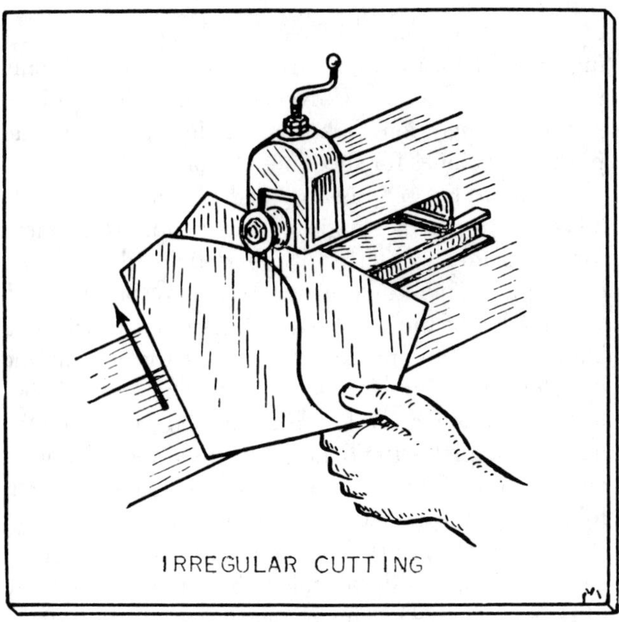

Figure 19.

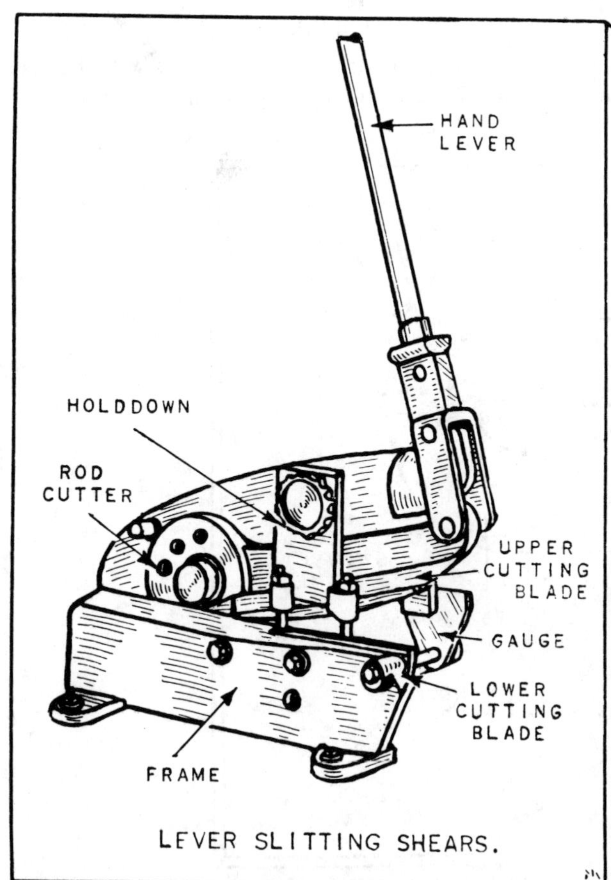

Figure 20.

machines must be lubricated with SAE30 oil once each working day at points shown in Fig. 10.

On the power machines, lubrication is provided for through the means of alemite fittings, and a grease gun is always furnished with each power machine. For any points on the power machine where oil is needed but where no fittings are provided, a high grade of oil will suffice.

Lever Slitting Shears. The lever slitting shears shown in Fig. 20 are usually used for straight slitting, notching, and irregular cutting. Unlike the other shears previously described, these shears cannot cut on the inside of sheets without cutting the outer edge. They are, however, designed to permit the slitting of sheet metal in any desired length or width up to the capacity of the machine. All of the working parts are shown in Fig. 20.

Proper adjustment of blades is maintained by means of two headless setscrews which bear against the lower blade.

To make the necessary blade adjustments, blade attaching screws are loosened and the headless setscrews are turned until the proper clearance between the blades is attained. Then the blade holding screws are tightened. This adjustment will allow the sheet to pass without any obstruction.

Operation. The holddown attachment should be adjusted to hold the metal in the cutting operation and to prevent it from tipping up and wedging between the blades. This adjustment is made by means of the knob screw at the top of the shear.

Scroll Shears. Scroll shears of the type shown in Fig. 21 are designed for cutting irregular shapes and for cutting inside of sheets.

The lower blade is attached to a slide which works in V-shape guides and is operated by the hand lever.

The slide is held in the frame by a cap which has holding and push screws for adjustment. This cap should be adjusted to hold the slide firmly without binding.

The upper blade is stationary and is attached to a plate which is adjustable for lining up this blade with the lower.

Adjust the upper blade to the lower by loosening slightly the two cap screws holding the plate in the frame, and adjust the blade by the two adjusting screws back of the plate in the frame (Fig. 21).

Keep blades sharp and properly adjusted.

For irregular cutting and inside cuts, the shape to be cut is marked out on the blank. When cutting to the line, best results are obtained by making short cuts. The length of cut is controlled by a check nut on the stud which is screwed in the lower end of the slide holding the lower blade (Fig. 21).

The gauge (Fig. 21) is used for straight cutting. The slide must be oiled frequently.

Folding and Bending Machines

The two classes of folding machines used in the sheet metal shop are folders and brakes. They are used for bending or forming straight pieces of sheet metal for insertion of wire, for turning flanges to various angles, and for making necessary locks or joints. When the width of the edge, lock, or angle being formed is limited, folders are used; when it is unlimited, brakes are employed.

FOLDERS. The three types of folders used are the bar, sheet iron, and pipe folding machines.

Bar Folders

Bar folders of the type shown in Figs. 22 and 23 are employed for bending edges of mild steel sheets 20 gauge or lighter to form various angles, for preparing folds for lock seams and wired edges, and for double right angle folds (channel shapes). As a general rule, bar folders are hand operated. They are available in various sizes with working lengths ranging from 21 in. to 42 in. Power folders are used only for mass production. Universal adaptability and rapidity of operation make bar folders the most important machines for sheet metal work.

A gauge (Fig. 24) is provided for narrow or wide folds. Stops fix the angle of the bend. Adjustment can be made for sharp or rounded bends required for wiring. Thick or thin material may be clamped.

The edge of the sheet is inserted under the folding blade and is automatically clamped the instant the handle is pulled upward toward the operator. Clamping is maintained while the continued motion of the handle completes the bend. Clamping and folding in one motion of the operating handle makes the bar folder highly productive on duplicating work.

The *gauge*, adjusted by a knurled thumb screw, indicates the width of fold on a graduated scale (Figs. 22 and 24). The Gauge bar and slide are of steel.

The *jaw*, raised by the clamping mechanism, grips the sheet under the blade. It is adjustable for various thicknesses of material.

The *wing*, pivoted to the folding bar (Figs. 22 and 23), turns with it to produce the bend. It is adjustable by a rack and pinion mechanism for sharp

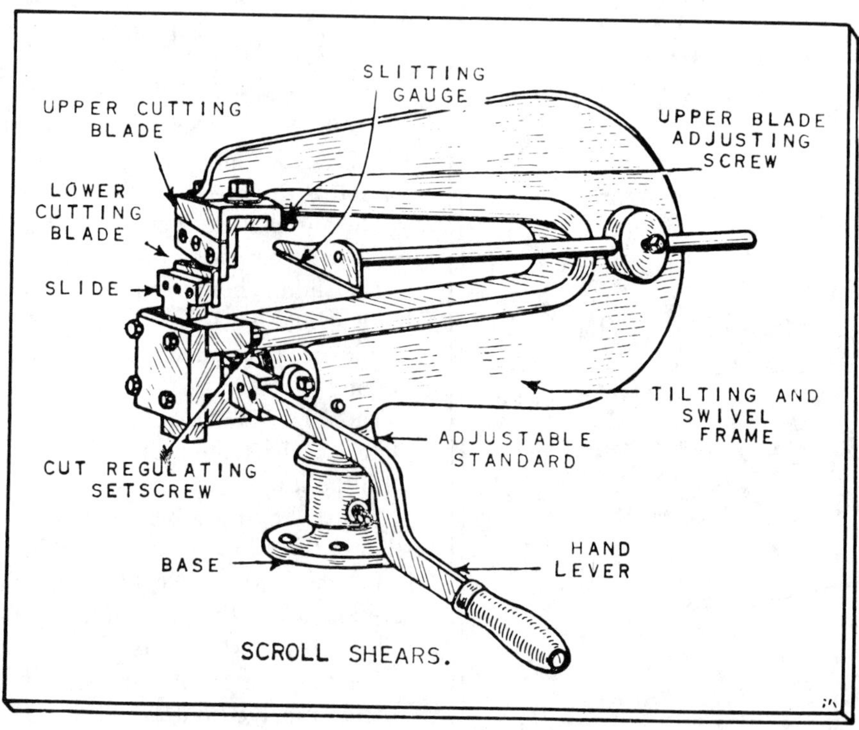

Figure 21.

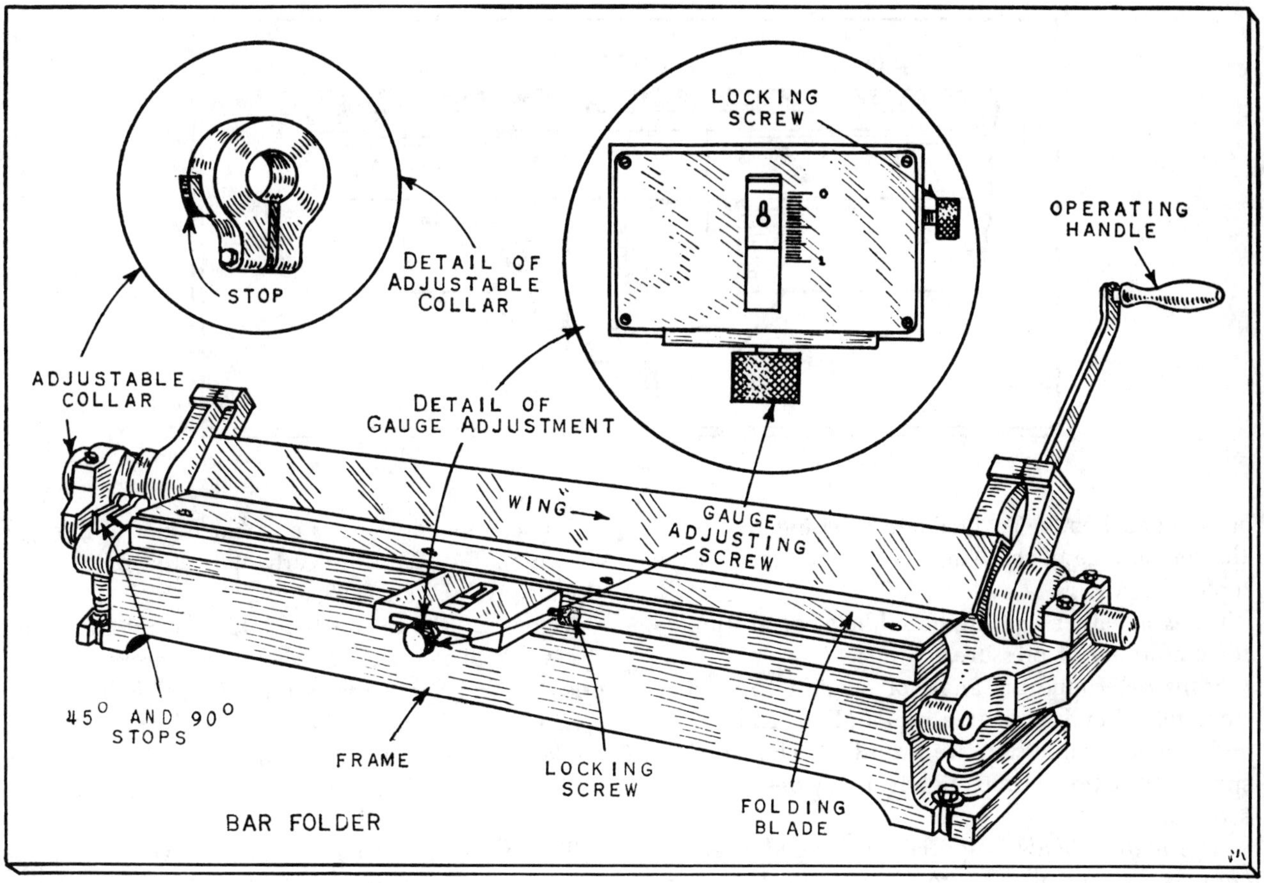

DETAIL OF
ADJUSTABLE
COLLAR
STOP
LOCKING
SCREW
OPERATING
HANDLE
ADJUSTABLE
COLLAR
DETAIL OF
GAUGE ADJUSTMENT
WING
GAUGE
ADJUSTING
SCREW
45° AND 90°
STOPS
FRAME
LOCKING
SCREW
FOLDING
BLADE
BAR FOLDER

Figure 22.

FINGERS
45° AND 90°
STOPS
WEDGE
LOCK-NUT
WEDGE
ADJUSTING
SCREW
WING
TURNED
BACK
ADJUSTABLE
COLLAR
REAR VIEW OF BAR FOLDER

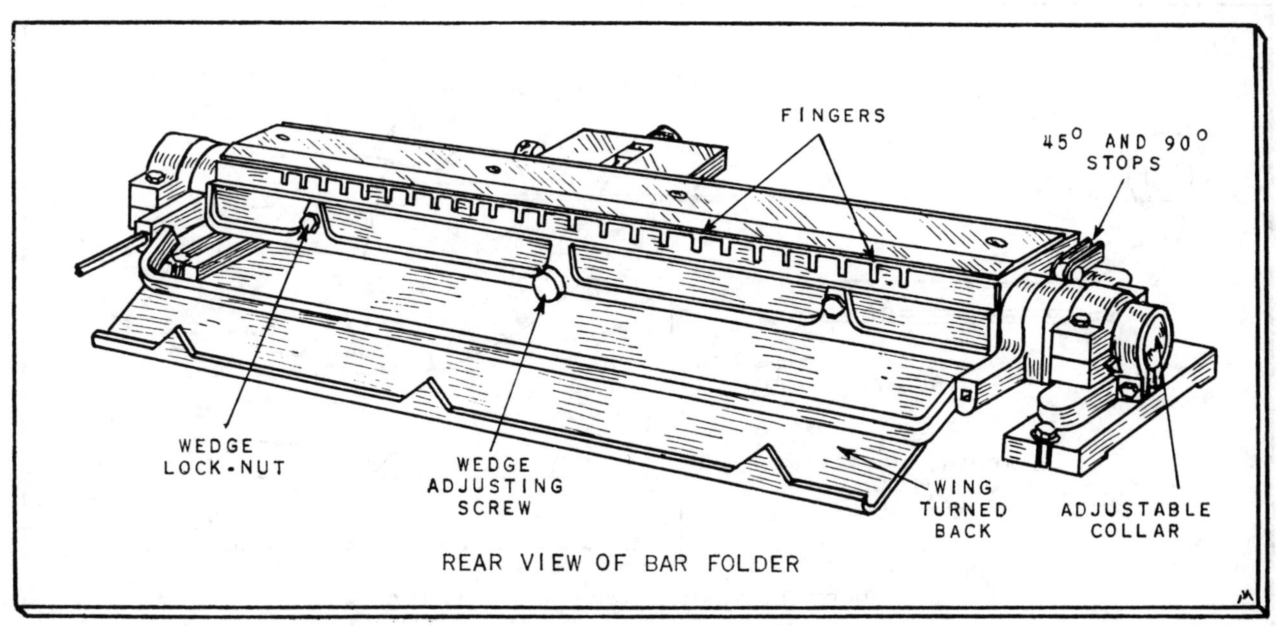

Figure 23.

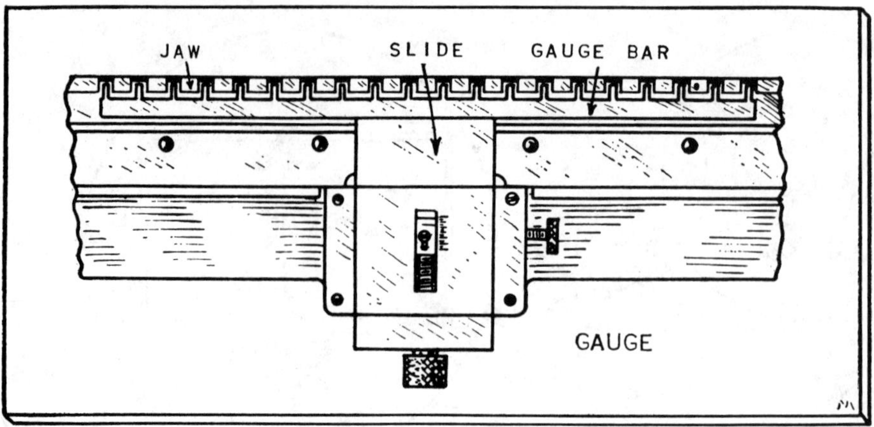

Figure 24.

or rounded bends. To facilitate inserting the work, the top surface of the wing is always flush with the top of the jaw.

Cams at either end of the folding bar are milled for uniformity of pressure.

Stops determine the angle of bend. Two positive stops for 45 and 90 degree bends (Figs. 22 and 23) and one adjustable stop are furnished. The latter, of split construction, clamps tightly at any desired angle setting.

The *folding blade* is special hard rolled steel, accurately ground all over to an even thickness and straight edge.

These component parts of a bar folder of the type shown in Fig. 22 are clearly indicated on the sectional views, Figs. 22, 23, and 24.

Figure 25 shows the bar folder ready to receive the work. The sheet, as shown, is inserted in the opening or space between the folding blade and the jaw. It is held against the gauge with the left hand, while, with the right hand, the operating handle is brought forward toward the operator as indicated by the arrow (Fig. 26).

The jaw automatically raises (Fig. 26) to grip the sheet between it and the folding blade, holding it tightly while the remainder of travel of the folding

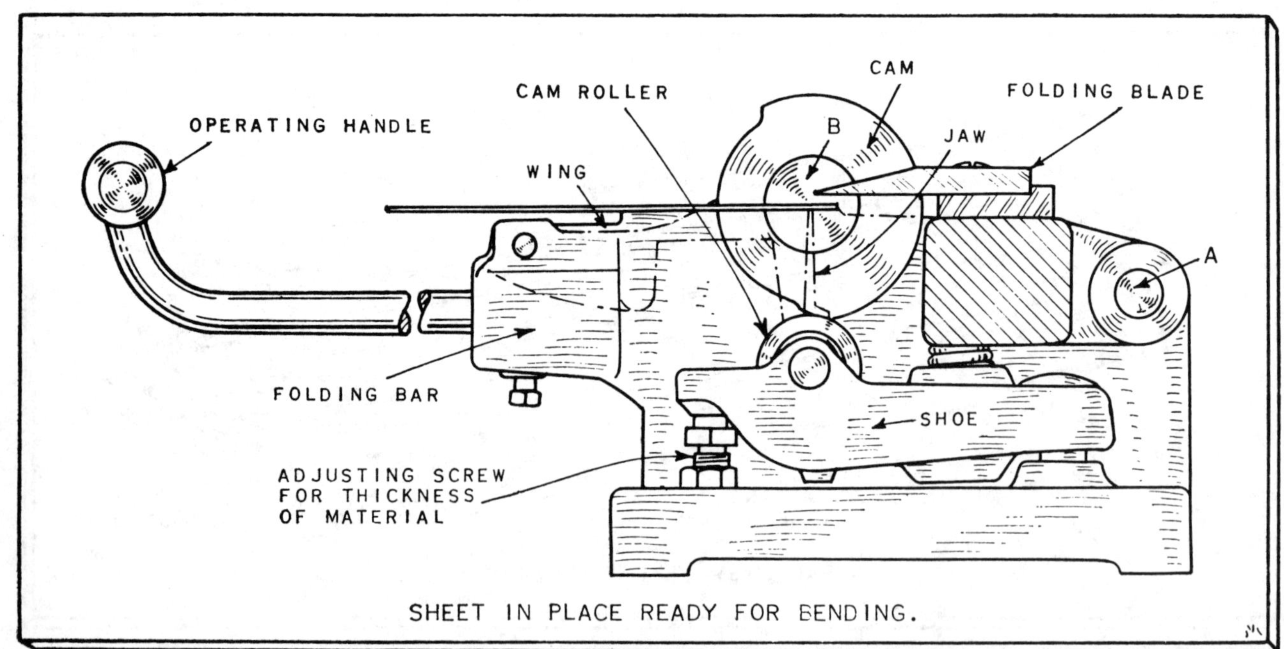

Figure 25.

bar and wing produces the bend. A stop limits the motion of the folding bar and determines the angle of the bend.

When the operating handle is returned to its starting point, the parts assume their original position (Fig. 25). This releases the clamping pressure so that the finished work can be quickly and easily removed.

The folding blade is rigidly fastened to the main frame. The jaw is pivoted at both ends of the machine at point A, Fig. 25. It carries the two large bearings for the trunnions (B, Fig. 25), on which the folding bar turns. A pivoted adjustable wing is mounted on the folding bar and moves with it. The cams at both ends of the folding bar are concentric with the trunnions.

Cam rollers are carried in two shoes at either end of the machine as indicated. The weight of the folding bar and jaw assembly keeps a constant pressure of the cams against the cam rollers.

The low part of the cam is in contact with the cam roller when the machine is in the open or starting position (Fig. 25). As the operating handle is pulled toward the operator in the direction indicated by the arrow, the folding bar turns on its trunnions, rotating the cams. The high parts of the cams roll into position on the cam rollers, raising the folding bar and jaw and causing the latter to clamp the sheet between the jaw and the stationary folding blade. A continued motion of the operating handle turns the folding bar and wing, forming the bend. The cams maintain a constant clamping pressure on the sheet.

Either of the positive stops can be set to limit the motion of the folding bar and the angle of bend. An adjustable stop of split construction pivots on the left hand trunnion, and can be clamped for any desired angle of bend.

Clamping pressure or clearance for various thicknesses of metal is regulated by raising or lowering the cam rollers carried in the shoes. This is accomplished by means of the adjusting screws shown in Figs. 25 and 26.

Sharp bends, such as those commonly required for lock seams, are produced when the wing is adjusted as shown in Fig. 26. Rounded bends, such as are made when a wire is to be inserted in the edge for stiffening, are produced if the wing is lower. The wing is raised and lowered by a wedge adjustment,

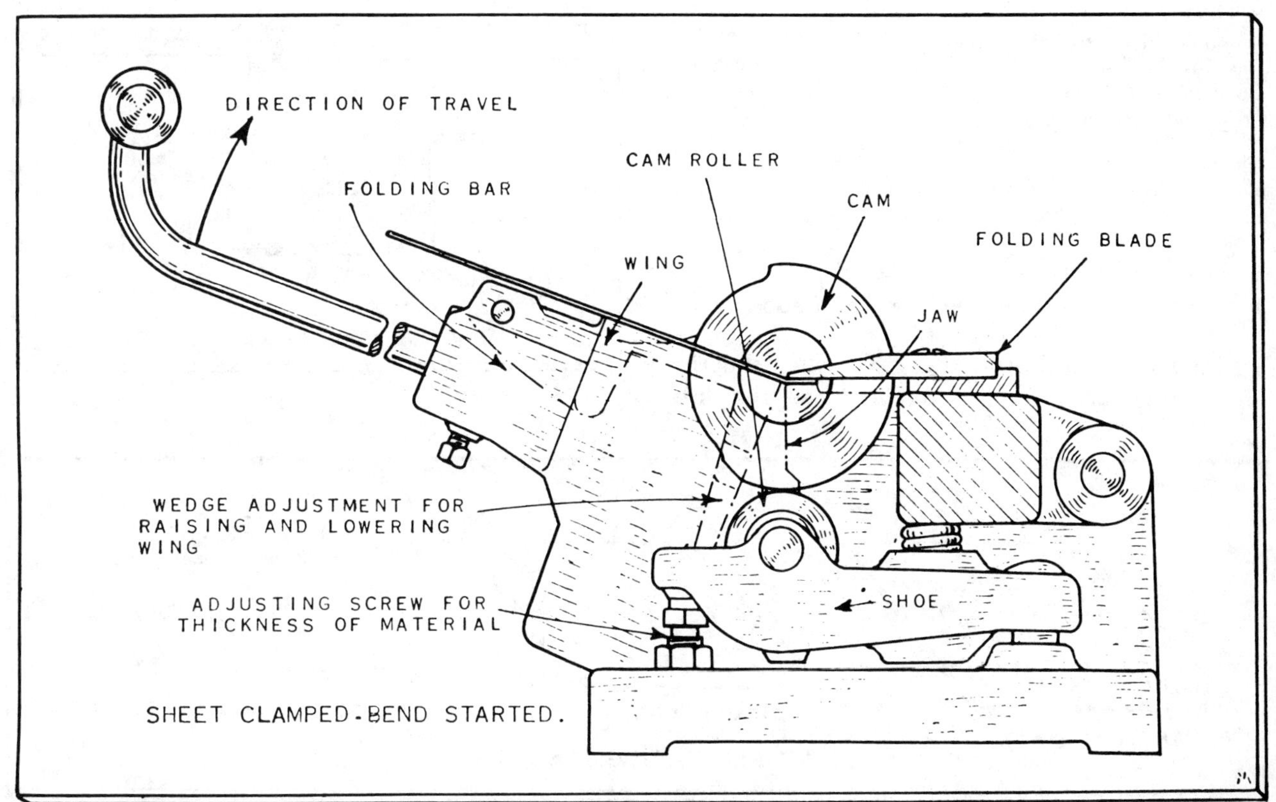

Figure 26.

which is actuated by a rack and pinion mechanism. Locking nuts are provided. The top of the wing is always flush with the top of the jaw when the bar folder is in open or starting position, regardless of the position of the supporting wedges. This alignment is obtained by a guide pin under the wing.

The gauge under the folding blade (Fig. 24), against which the sheet is placed, is adjustable for various widths of folds by a large thumb screw. The setting is plainly visible on a scale graduated to sixteenths of an inch. The gauge setting may be locked by means of a small thumb screw (Figs. 25 and 26).

The steel gauge bar, which has a series of gauging points, is mounted on a steel slide. The knurled adjusting screw acts on the slide directly, without linkage or other mechanical elements likely to wear and develop lost motion or inaccuracies. Springs below the gauge slide keep the gauge in close contact with the underside of the folding blade so that the edge of the sheet to be folded cannot override the gauge.

The width of folds that can be made on the bar folder depends upon the gauge of the material. Use the following table as a guide.

TABLE 5

Working lengths of bar folders	21″ to 42″
Capacity, mild steel	Gauge No. 20
Gauging range	3/32″ to 1″
Widths of folds at capacity	3/16″ to 1″
Widths of folds No. 28 gauge mild steel and lighter	3/32″ to 1″
Round folds for wire, maximum diameter	1/4″

Procedures for Basic Bar Folder Operations

MAKING SINGLE FOLDS (Fig. 28). After squaring and cutting the material to required size, the three progressive steps for making single folds are: marking the edge, folding, and completing the fold, as shown in Fig. 28. The procedure is as follows: Mark the sheet for the required width of fold (A, Fig. 28), loosen the locking screw (Fig. 27), set the gauge (Fig. 27), and tighten the locking screw. Place the edge of metal between the folding blade and the jaw of the bar folder (Fig. 29). With one hand, hold the metal firmly against the gauge fingers and place the other hand on the operating handle of the folder (Fig. 30). Keeping the hand on the sheet throughout the operation, pull the operating handle as far as it will go. Return the handle to its original position. Keep the hand on the handle until the wing is in its original position. Remove the folded material. This completes the second step (B, Fig. 28). Proceed with the third and final step for making single folds (C, Fig. 28) by placing the folded material with the fold facing upwards on the beveled part of the blade and set snugly against the wing of the folder as shown in Fig. 31. Pull the operating handle to flatten the fold, return the operating handle to its original position and remove the material from the machine.

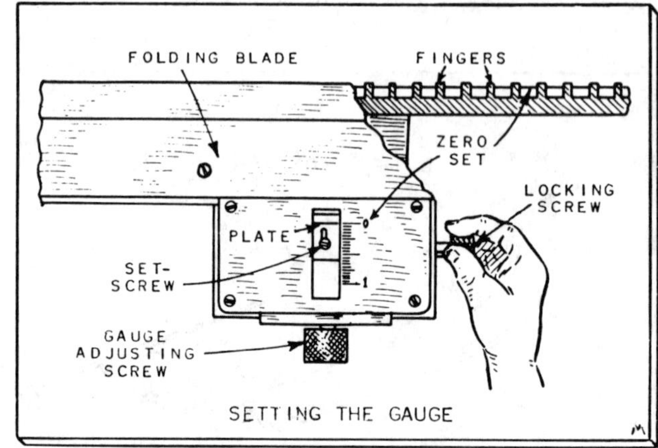

Figure 27.

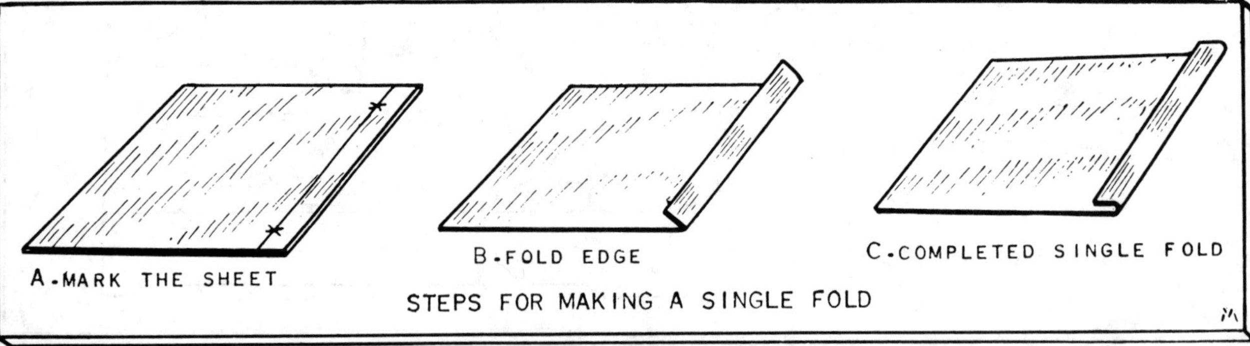

Figure 28.

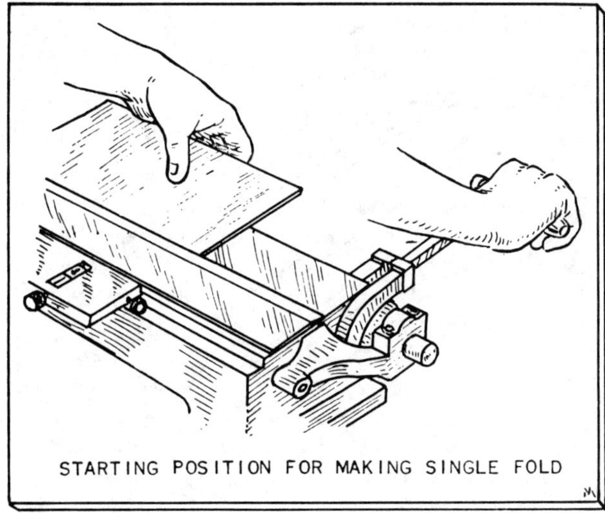

Figure 29.

Making Double Folds. To make double folds (Fig. 32), proceed as follows: After squaring and marking the metal, make a single fold as previously outlined, then insert the single folded edge between the jaw and folding blade of the folding machine. To make the second fold (A, Fig. 32) and to complete the double fold (B, Fig. 32), follow folding and flattening procedure previously given for making single folds.

Making Folds for Grooved Locks or Seams (Fig. 33). After squaring and marking the width of the grooved seam on the metal, set the gauge of the bar folder slightly less than the required width of the grooved seam. Insert the edge of the metal between the folding blade and the jaw, and proceed to make the first fold shown at A, Fig. 33 in the usual manner. After the first fold is made, insert the other edge of the second piece of sheet metal in the machine and make the fold shown at B, in the same way. Connect both pieces and close the grooved lock with a soft-faced mallet.

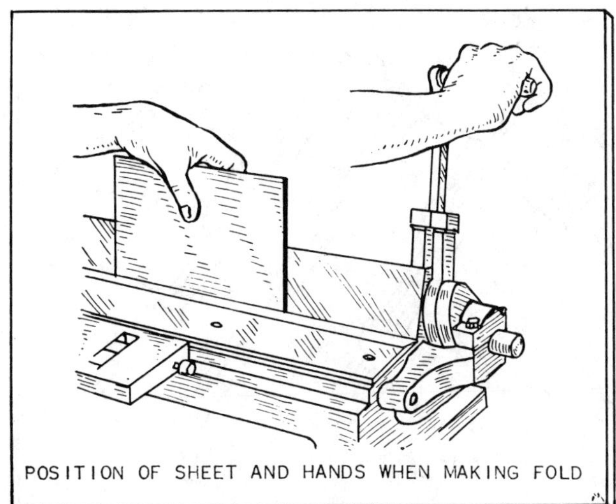

POSITION OF SHEET AND HANDS WHEN MAKING FOLD

Figure 30.

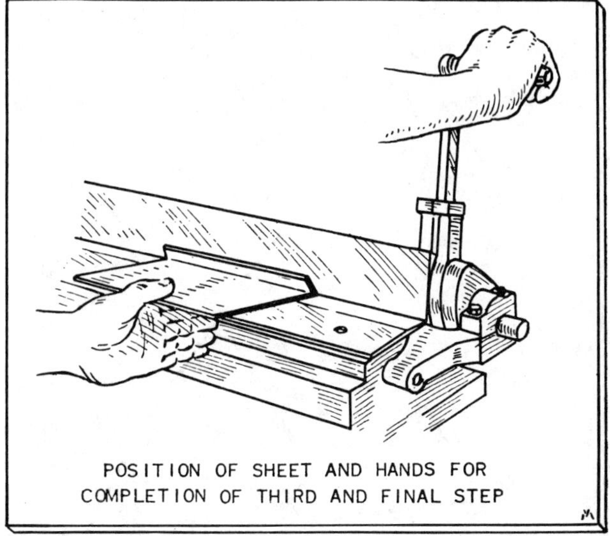

POSITION OF SHEET AND HANDS FOR
COMPLETION OF THIRD AND FINAL STEP

Figure 31.

Making Rounded Folds for Wired Edges (Fig. 34). Prior to making rounded folds or folds for wired edges, special wing adjustments must be made in the following manner: Move the wing back while it

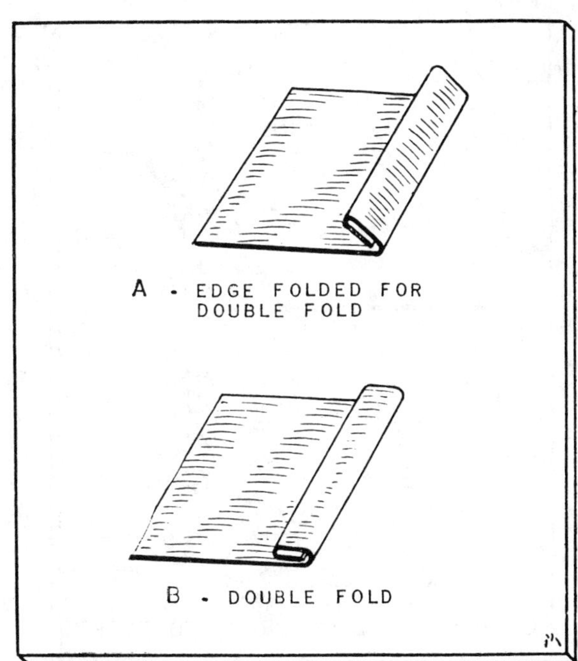

Figure 32.

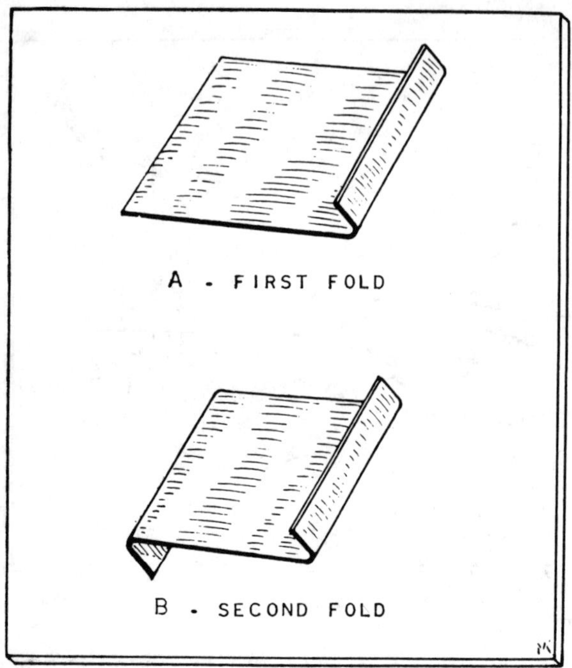

Figure 33.

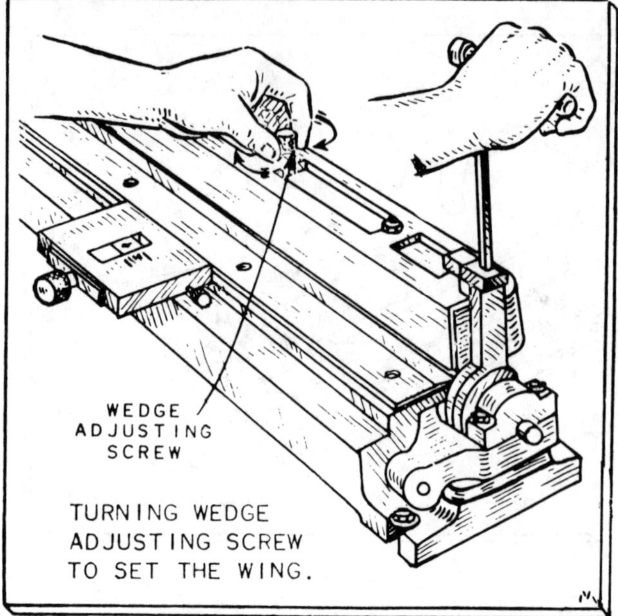

Figure 35.

is held in vertical position (Fig. 35), and turn it back so that the rear of the bar folder is exposed. With an open end wrench, loosen the wedge lock-nuts (Fig. 36). Turn the wedge adjusting screw and lower the wing until the wedge is as far to the right as possible, then raise the operating handle to put the wing into a vertical position. Proceed by turning the wedge adjusting screw to set the required distance between

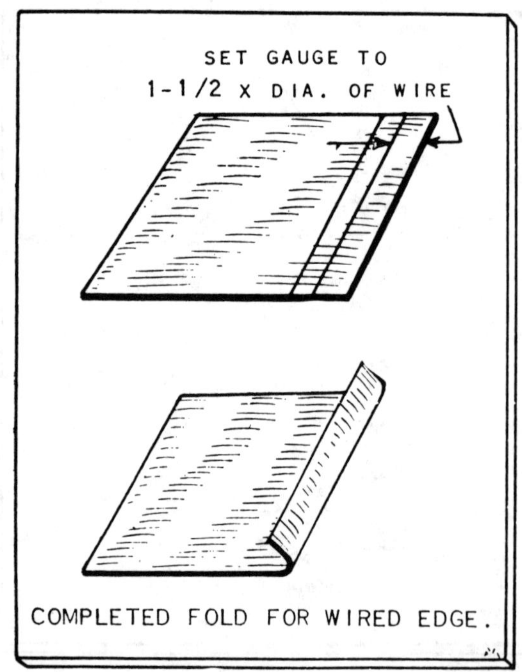

Figure 34.

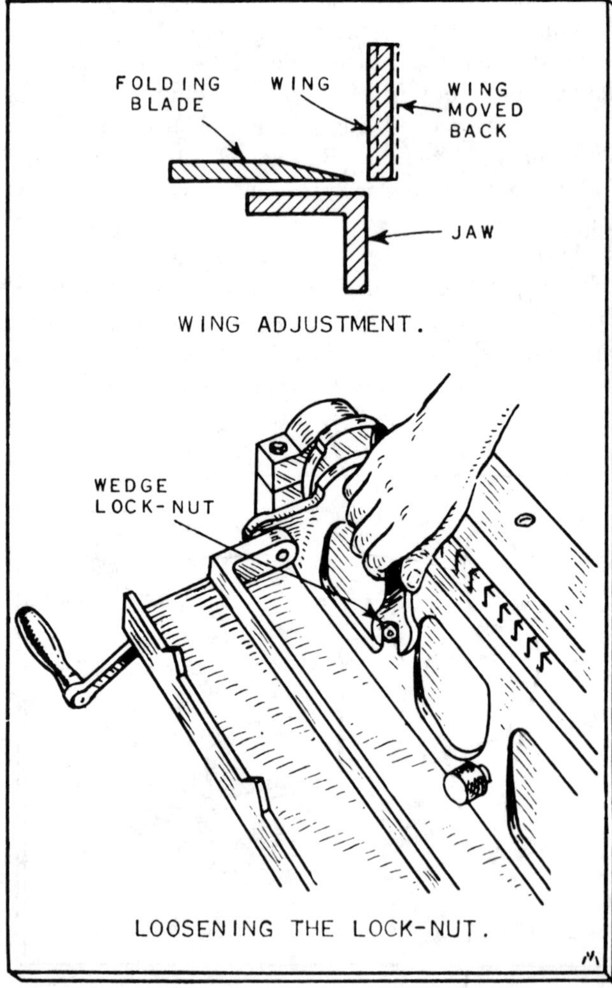

Figure 36.

the wing and the edge of the folding blade (Fig. 35). For proper clearance this distance should be about $\frac{1}{32}$ in. more than the diameter of the wire to be used. It can be checked easily by holding a piece of the wire that is to be used in the position shown in Fig. 37. After checking the clearance, tighten the wedge lock-nuts, place the operating handle in its normal position, and proceed as follows: Square the material and set the gauge to the diameter of wire $\times 1\frac{1}{2}$ as shown in Fig. 34. Place the edge of the metal between the blade and jaw of the folder. Hold the metal firmly against the gauge fingers with one hand and pull the handle as far as possible with the other. Remove the folded sheet after returning the operating handle to its original position.

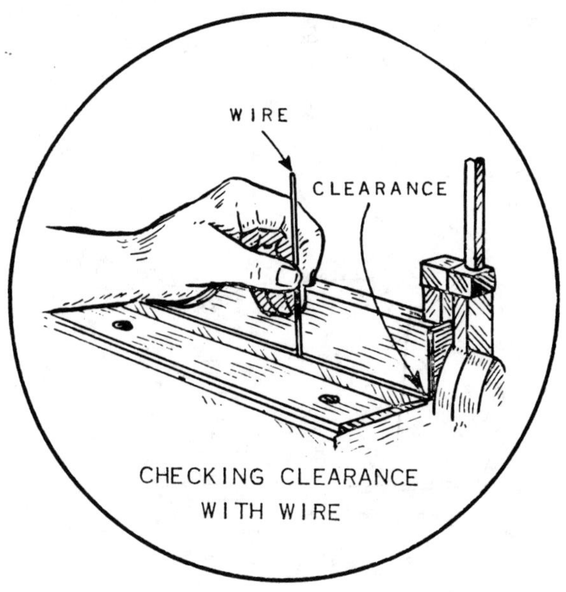

Figure 37.

Making 45 Degree, 90 Degree, or Special Angle Folds. The wing of the bar folder must be set as previously described before rounded angle folds may be made. For sharp folds this preliminary procedure is not necessary. The various types of angle folds that can be made on the bar folder are shown in Fig. 38.

When 45 or 90 degree angles are to be formed, proceed by moving the desired angle stop in place (Fig. 39).

When angles other than these two are to be formed, it is necessary to set the adjustable collar to produce the required angle. To do this, a metal template cut to the degree of angle required is held between the wing and the folding blade (Fig. 40). The adjustable collar is then set so that the stop just touches the frame and the gauge is set for the required width of the fold. Insert the sheet and proceed in the usual manner.

Making Double Right Angle Folds. After determining the size of right angle folds desired, scribe a line on squared material for the first fold shown at A-A, then scribe a line for the second fold B-B (A, Fig. 41). If rounded bends are desired, the wing of the bar folder must be set as previously described.

Place the 90 degree angle stop in correct position (Fig. 39) and set the gauge to line A-A. Insert the material and proceed to make the first fold (B, Fig. 41) in the usual manner. If several identical pieces are to be folded, make all of these A-A folds before proceeding with the second fold.

To complete the double angle fold, re-set the gauge to scribed line B-B, insert the material, and proceed to make the second fold in the usual manner (C, Fig. 41).

Figure 42 shows the edges and folds that may be formed on a bar folder.

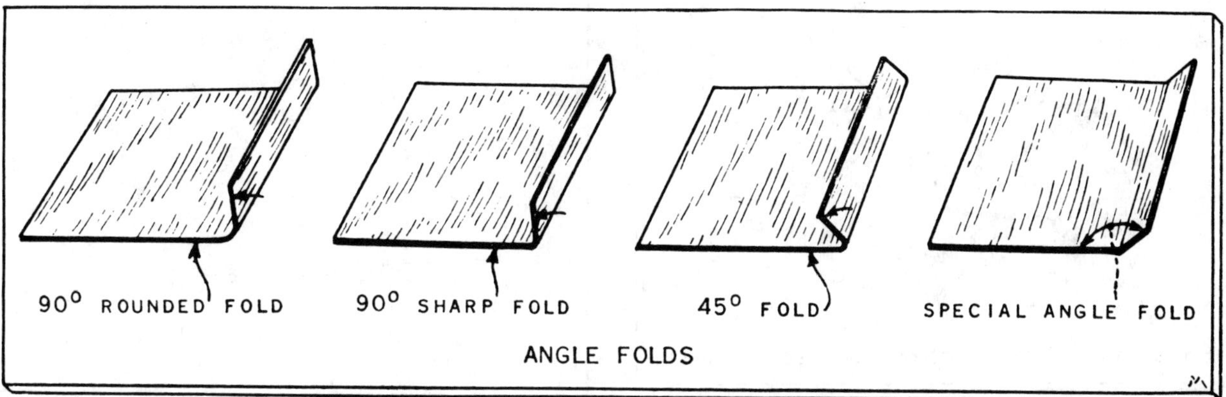

Figure 38.

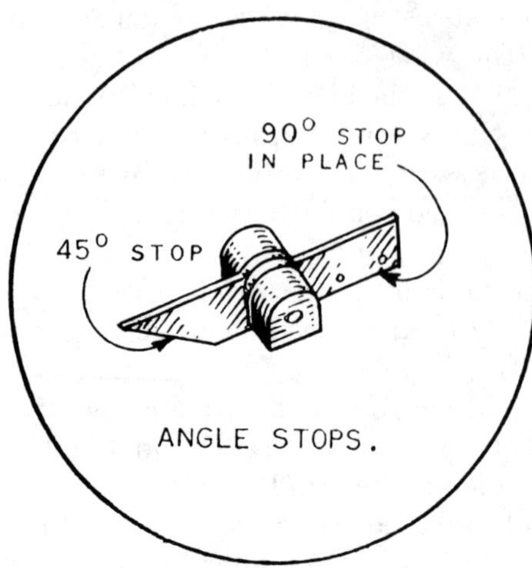

Figure 39.

Note: Always keep one hand on the metal sheet in the machine until the sheet is clamped.

After pulling the handle to make the required folds, keep one hand on the handle until it has returned to its original position.

Caution: When operating a bar folder, be sure to keep fingers and loose clothing away from the folding blade.

Sheet Iron Folders

Sheet iron folders of the type shown in Figs. 43 and 44 are generally used for making bends and locks that do not require extreme accuracy and uniformity. Sheet iron folders are available in several sizes and have a capacity of No. 20 gauge iron or lighter (U.S. Standard).

The construction of this machine consists of a milled cast-iron frame that is hinged to a machined cast-iron folding bar equipped with a steel folding blade. A slotted steel strip that moves parallel to the folding strip is used as a gauge, and its gauging capacity is limited to producing closed locks of $\frac{1}{4}$ in. to $\frac{1}{2}$ in.

Procedures for the use and maintenance of these machines are approximately the same as those given for bar folders.

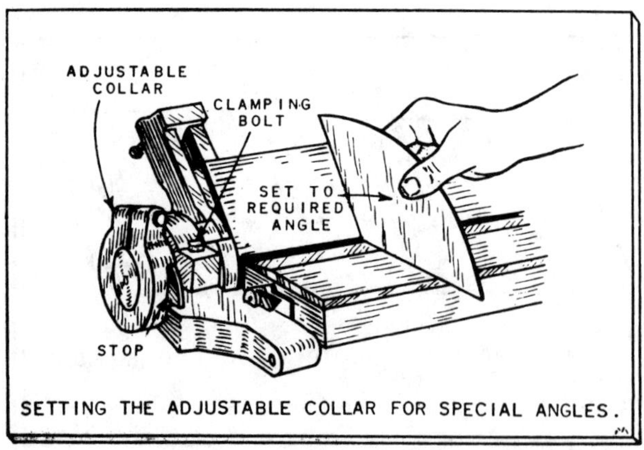

Figure 40.

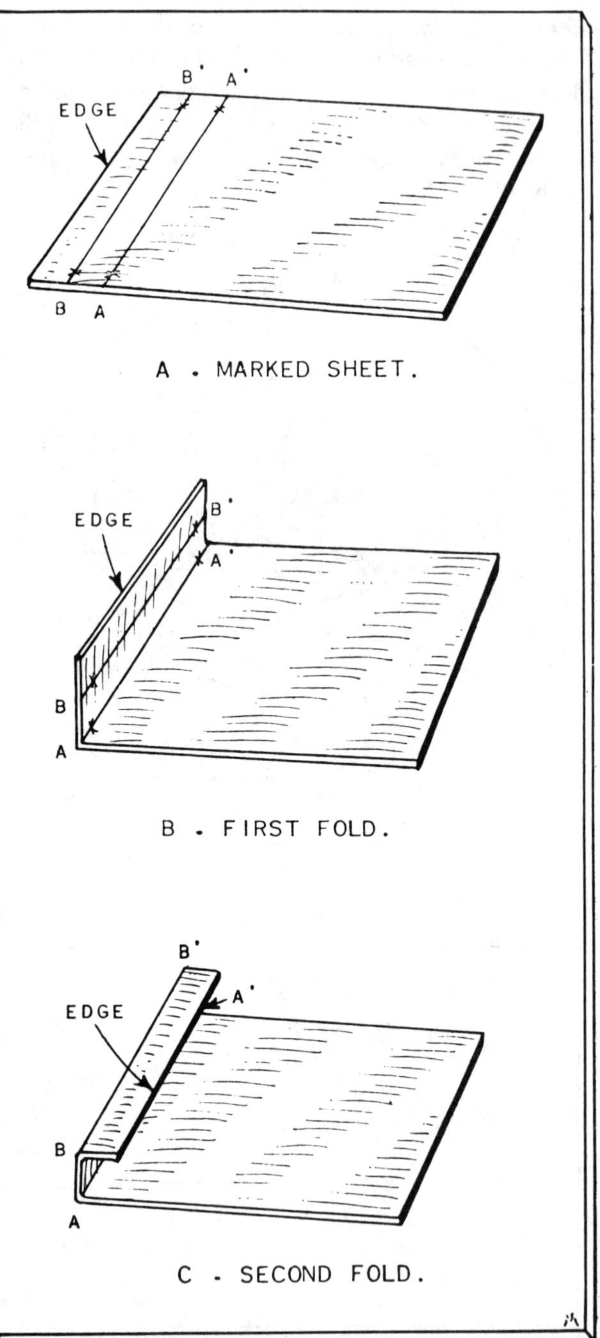

Figure 41.

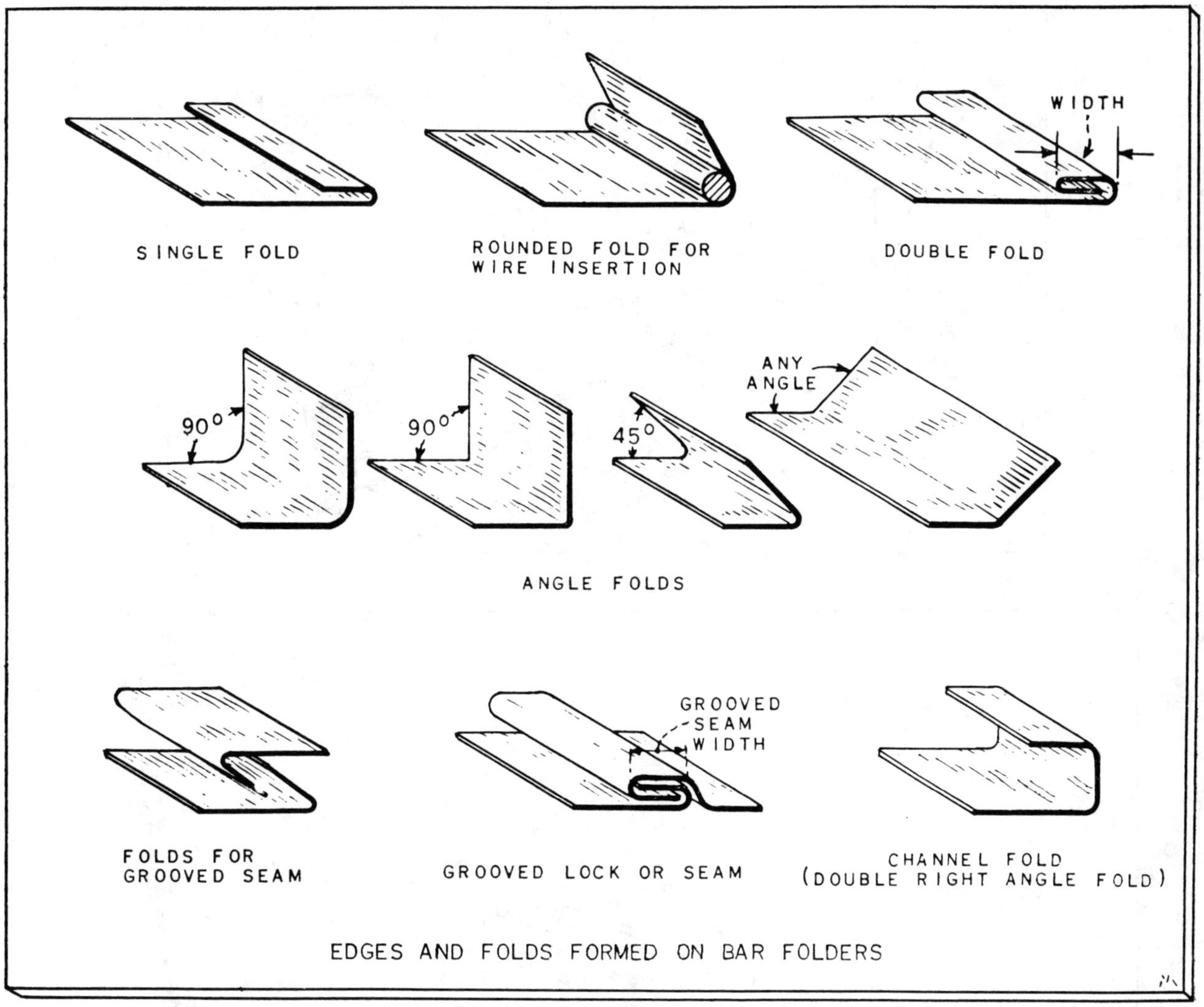

SINGLE FOLD

ROUNDED FOLD FOR WIRE INSERTION

WIDTH

DOUBLE FOLD

90°

90°

45°

ANY ANGLE

ANGLE FOLDS

FOLDS FOR GROOVED SEAM

GROOVED SEAM WIDTH

GROOVED LOCK OR SEAM

CHANNEL FOLD (DOUBLE RIGHT ANGLE FOLD)

EDGES AND FOLDS FORMED ON BAR FOLDERS

Figure 42.

Figure 43.

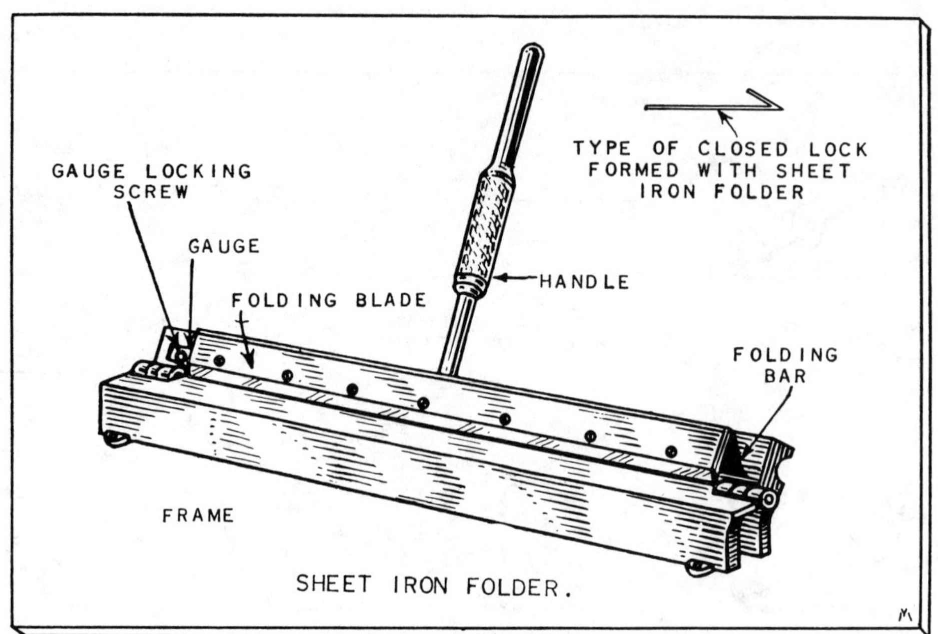

Figure 44.

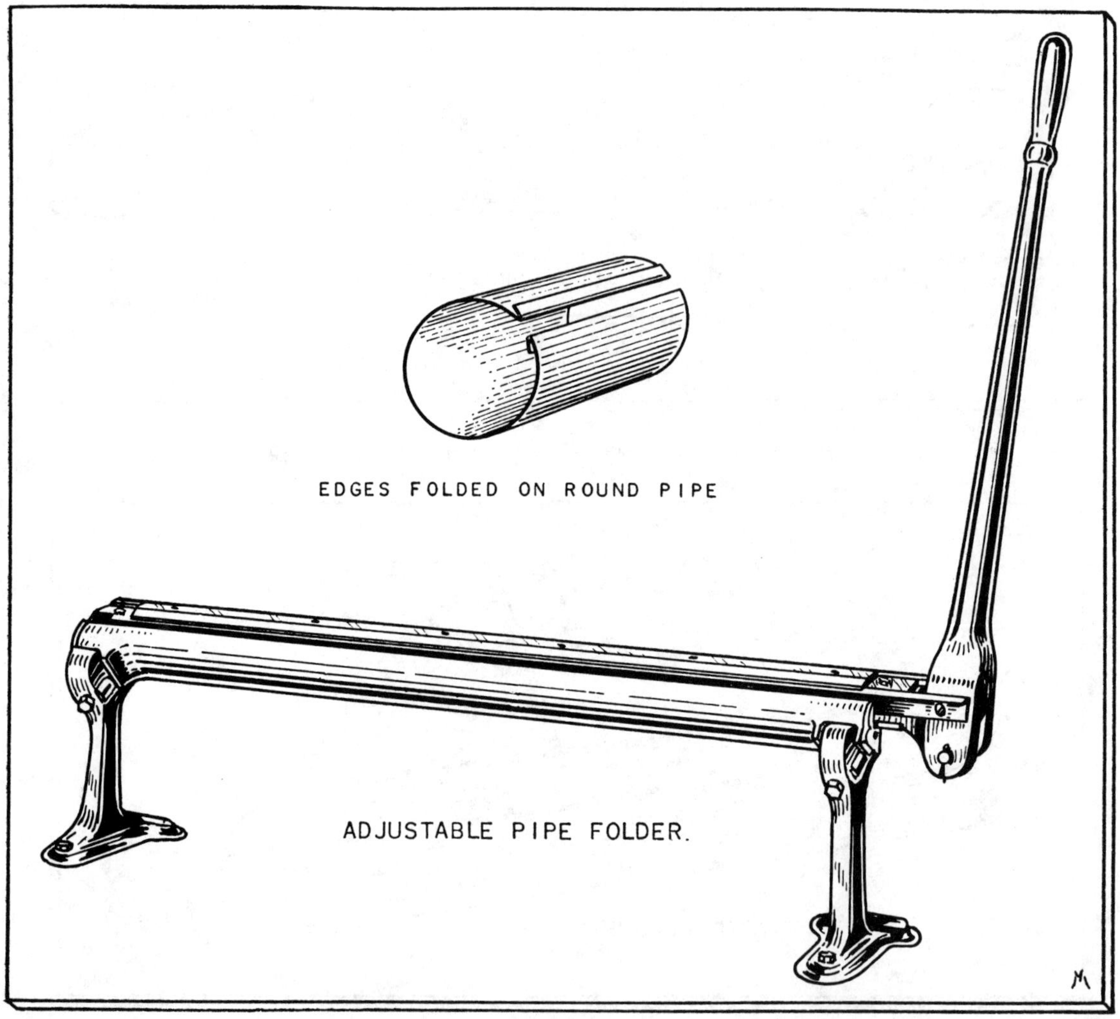

EDGES FOLDED ON ROUND PIPE

ADJUSTABLE PIPE FOLDER.

Figure 45.

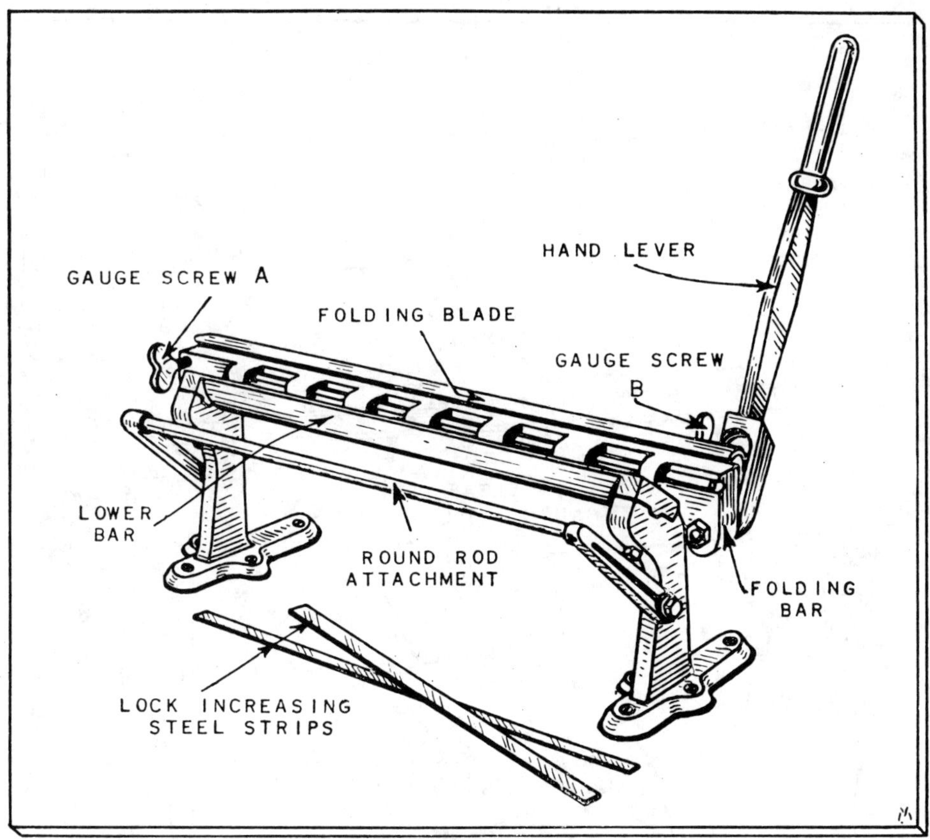

Figure 46.

Pipe Folders

Pipe folders (Figs. 45 and 46) are used in edging or forming locks on cylinders after the cylinders have been formed. The pipe folder shown in Fig. 46 has a capacity of No. 22 gauge iron and lighter (U. S. Standard), and will turn a lock $\frac{1}{4}$ in. and $\frac{3}{8}$ in. Locks of larger sizes, $\frac{1}{2}$ in. and $\frac{5}{8}$ in., can be formed by the use of lock increasing steel strips (Fig. 46). These are inserted under the work and between the folding blade (Fig. 46).

Using the Pipe Folder. To edge or form a lock on a cylinder, proceed as follows: Insert one edge of the cylinder between the folding bar and the lip of the folding blade, and clamp the work by moving the hand lever to the left (Fig. 46). Pull the folding bar over toward you until the lock is completed (Fig. 45). Push the folding bar back and release the work by pushing the hand lever to the right (Fig. 46). Form the corresponding edge by inserting the other edge of the cylinder over instead of under the folding bar (Fig. 46) and complete the operation as previously outlined.

When changing the gauge to secure $\frac{1}{4}$ in. and $\frac{3}{8}$ in. locks, be careful not to turn in the gauge screw (B, Fig. 46) so far that it strikes against the folding bar. This will draw the folding blade out of line. By the same token the gauge screw (A, Fig. 46) must not be turned so far that it pushes the gauge and folding blade out of line. These two gauge screws (A and B, Fig. 46) hold or release a concealed gauge that is under the folding blade. The correct adjustment of these gauges is extremely important when the pipe folder is adjusted for these two sizes of locks. When gauge screw B is screwed in and gauge A is unscrewed, the gauge is held up against the folding blade and will turn a $\frac{1}{4}$ in. lock. When gauge screw B is unscrewed and gauge A is screwed in, the gauge is held down and will turn a $\frac{3}{8}$ in. lock. Before changing the gauge, push the hand lever toward the left as far as possible. After making the adjustments, return the lever to its original position.

Screws securing the cap and folding blades must be inspected frequently. If they are loose, tighten them to prevent springing the folding blade. Lubricate as directed by the manufacturer of the machine.

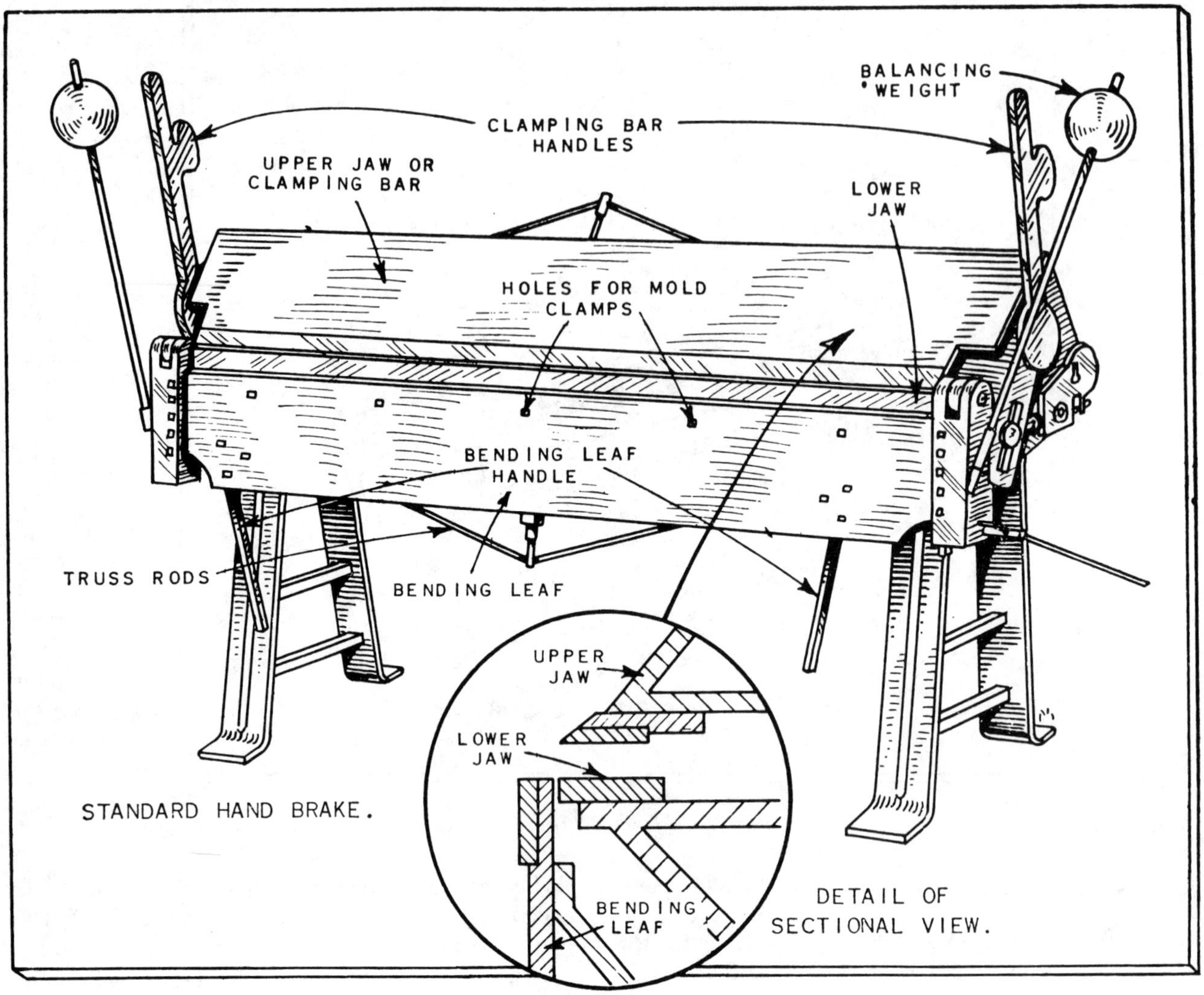

Figure 47.

Brakes

Of the many types of brakes used in the sheet metal shop, the standard hand brake shown in Fig. 47 is the type generally used for making unlimited folds in sheet metal. A combination brake and bar folder is available (Fig. 48) which comprises some of the features of both of these machines.

The standard hand brake shown in Fig. 47 is a versatile machine used to make both sharp and rounded angle brakes or folds. The various types of brakes made on this machine are shown in Fig. 49. Various curved shapes can be made by using molds (Fig. 50).

The essential parts of a standard hand brake are shown in Fig. 47. An upper jaw or clamping bar and

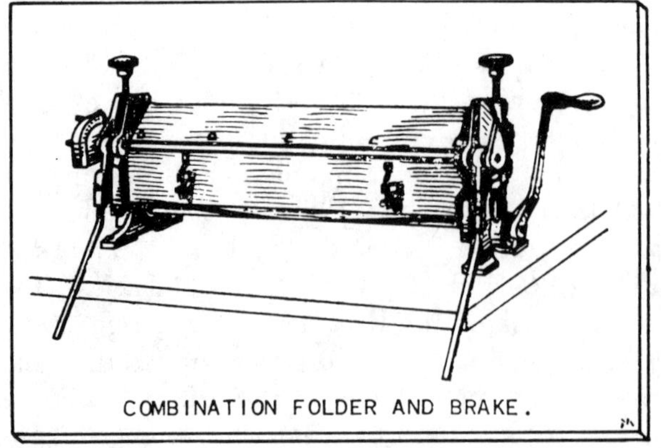

Figure 48.

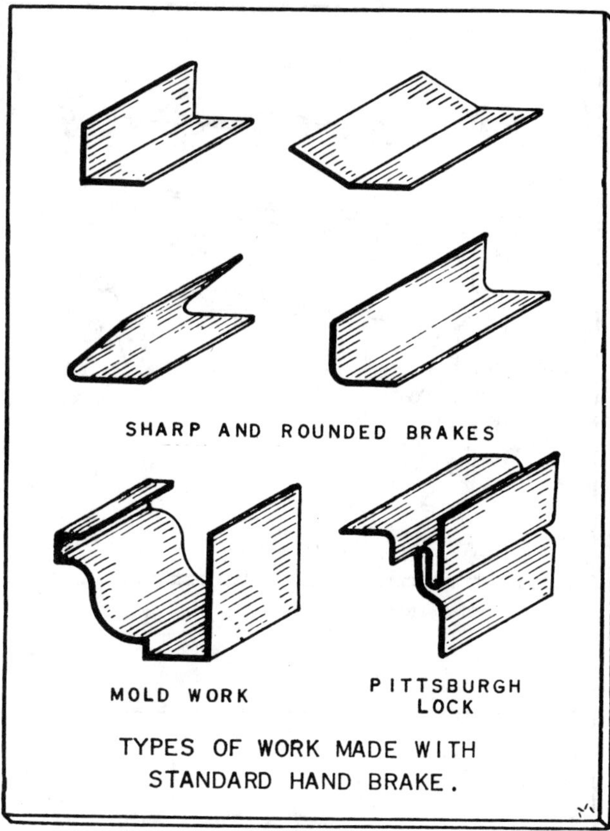

Figure 49.

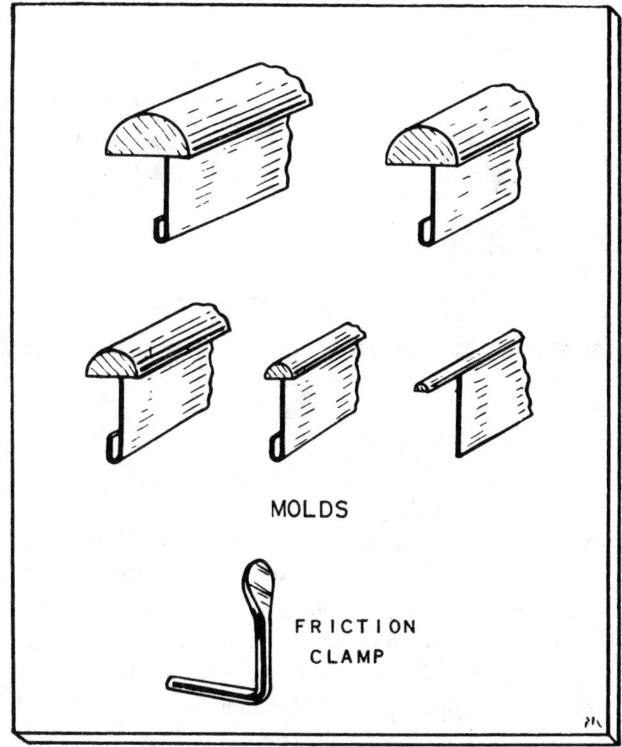

Figure 50.

a lower jaw, between which the metal is clamped, are attached to the frame of the machine (Fig. 47). The bending leaf handles are used to move the bending leaf, which forms the metal to required fold or form (Fig. 47). The bending leaf is recessed to hold a ¼ in. steel bar (Fig. 47). This bar can be removed when making narrow, reverse bends.

The two clamping bar handles are employed to move the upper jaw, which clamps or releases the work. Each of these handles can be moved independently of the other.

To form curved shapes, molds (Fig. 50) are clamped to the bending leaf with the special friction clamps shown in Fig. 50. Molds are available in diameters ranging from ⅝ in. to 3 in. Brakes operated by hand or power are available in various lengths ranging from 3 ft. ½ in. to 10 ft. 1 in. in capacities of more than 1 in. width bends or brakes.

Basic Operating Procedures of Standard Hand Brakes

A standard hand brake of the type shown in Fig. 47 is usually operated by the mechanic from the right side of the machine. When operating a hand brake, be sure that the fingers of the operator and the helper are clear of both clamping bars and balancing weights.

Do not attempt to bend or brake more than a single thickness of sheet metal within the capacity specified by the manufacturer of the brake at any one time. Wire, rod, band iron, or seamed pieces of metal must not be bent or formed on this machine.

Fill oil holes and lubricate all sliding surfaces at least once a week, using machine oil specified by the manufacturer. Strict adherence to these precautionary measures is necessary to assure efficient and accurate performance of this machine.

Preliminary Procedures. Before proceeding to make any sharp bends or brakes on this or any type of machine, it is important to determine and plan the proper sequence of braking operations. The reason for this is that sheet metal, irrespective of the type of metal used, will either be weakened or will break if it is bent up at a 90 degree angle or bent over square and then straightened and rebent in the opposite direction. This condition will vary in degree with the type of material used. The characteristics of the various metals used in the sheet metal industry are fully described in Chap. 1.

Adjustments and Procedures for Making Sharp Bends. After planning the sequence of bending operations, mark the material with a prick punch on the right and left-hand corners at points where the bend is to be made, and proceed as follows: On short pieces the right hand clamping bar is opened by pushing back the handle of this bar with the right hand. When long pieces are to be bent, both the left and right hand clamping bars must be pushed back. Stand in front of the machine and insert the material between the upper and lower jaws of the machine. Proceed to place the material in the required position with the prick punch mark, previously made on the left hand side of the material, flush with the edge of the clamping bar. Holding the sheet in place with the left hand, pull the clamping bar handle with the other hand until the left side of the material has been firmly clamped as shown in Fig. 51. To clamp the right side of the material, move the sheet metal until the prick punch mark on the right side is flush with the clamping bar and finish clamping the sheet in place by pulling the clamping bar handle as far as possible (Fig. 52). With the right hand on the balancing weight arm of the machine, and with the other hand on the bending leaf handle, proceed to make the required bend by raising the bending leaf of the machine to the correct position for the required angle of the bend as shown in Fig. 53. Because of the spring-back or elasticity of some metals, it may be necessary to raise the bending leaf several degrees more to attain the required angle. After the bend has been made, keep the left hand on the bending leaf handle until the bending leaf is slowly re-

Figure 51.

Figure 52.

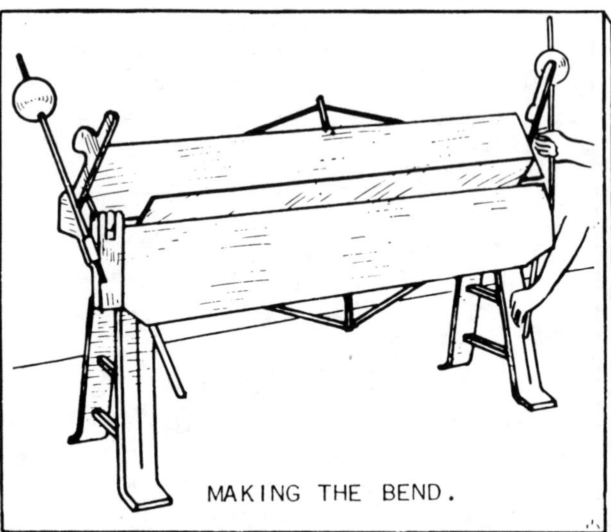

Figure 53.

turned to its original position. Remove the sheet from the machine by opening the clamping bars.

Adjustments and Procedures for Forming Pocket for Pittsburgh Lock or Seam (Fig. 54). To form the pocket for a Pittsburgh lock or seam, proceed as follows: Lay out and prick mark points on material for the progressive bends as shown at *a*, *b*, *c*, on A, Fig. 54. Insert the sheet in the brake and close the upper jaw of the machine flush with the prick mark *a*. Raise the bending leaf to make the first bend at an angle slightly under 90 degrees as

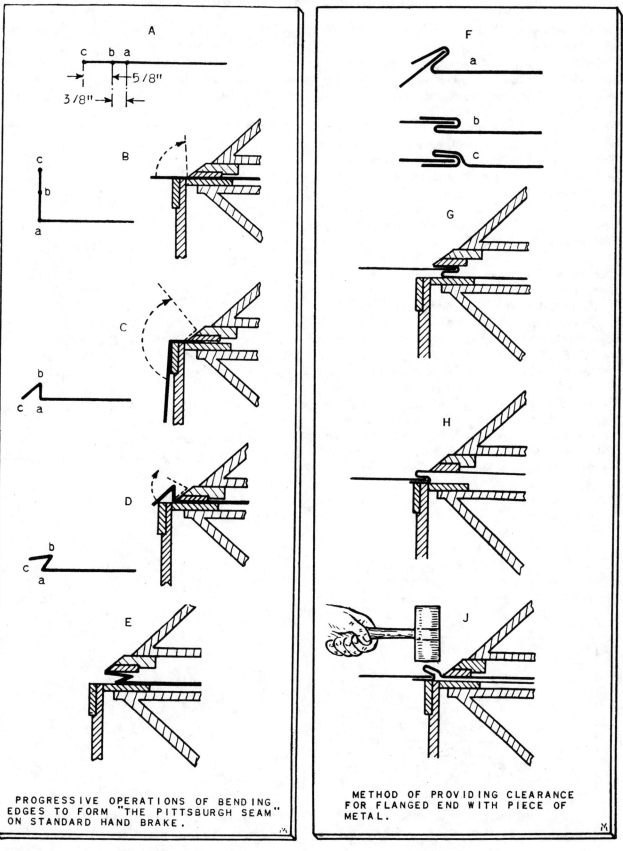

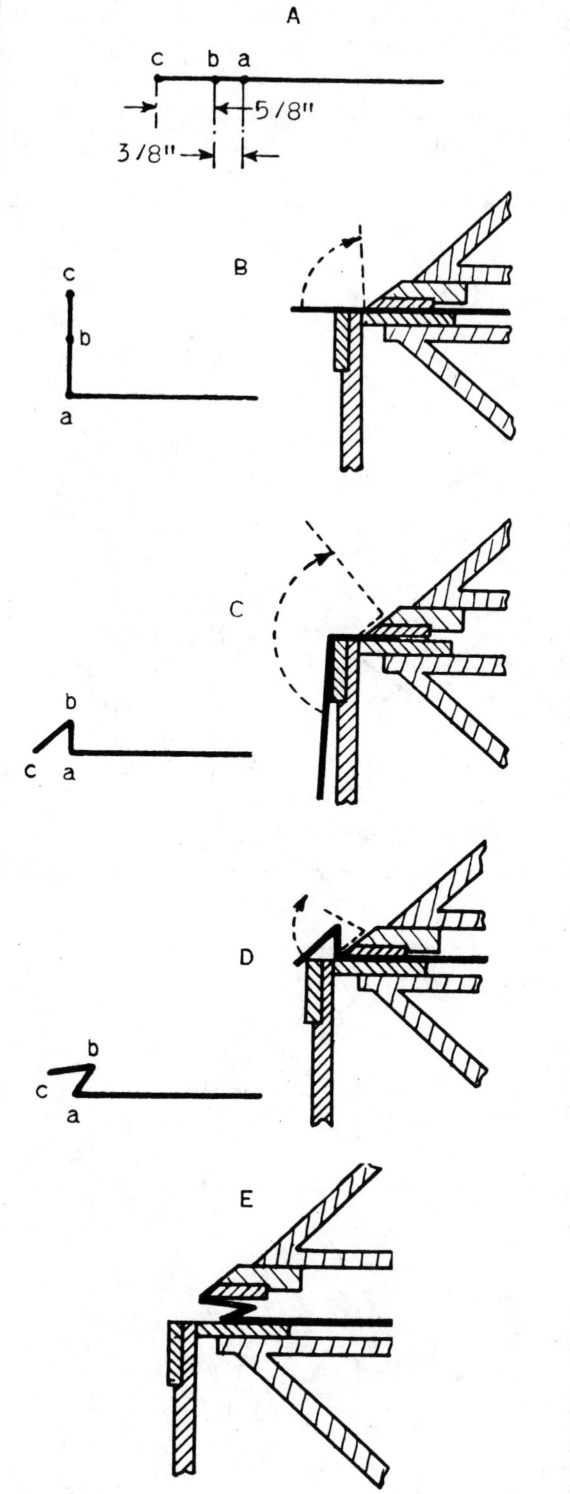

A

c b a

5/8"

3/8"

B

c

b

a

C

b

c a

D

b

c

a

E

PROGRESSIVE OPERATIONS OF BENDING EDGES TO FORM "THE PITTSBURGH SEAM" ON STANDARD HAND BRAKE.

Figure 54.

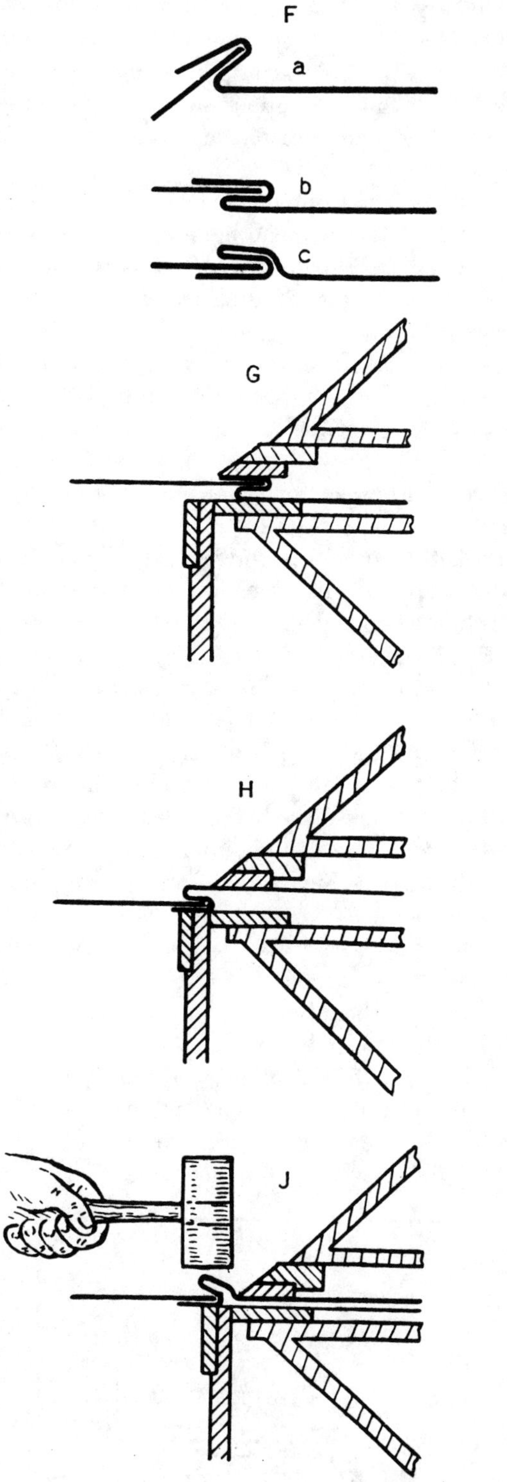

F

a

b

c

G

H

J

METHOD OF PROVIDING CLEARANCE FOR FLANGED END WITH PIECE OF METAL.

Figure 55.

shown at B, Fig. 54. Remove the sheet from the machine. The sheet is now turned over. Place the edge in the brake and close the upper clamp down on prick mark *b*. Close the upper jaw and raise the bending leaf as far as possible to form this second bend as shown at C, Fig. 54.

Remove the sheet from the machine, then insert again with the 90 degree bend held against the edge of the upper jaw as shown at D, Fig. 54. Close the upper jaw and raise the bending leaf as far as possible to form the third bend.

Remove the work from the machine and reinsert it in the brake with the upper edge of the work flush with the outer edge of the upper jaw as shown at E, Fig. 54.

To provide clearance for a flanged edge, a piece of scrap metal should be inserted in the upper fold of the pocket before it is squeezed together. The progressive steps for this procedure are shown at F, Fig. 55. After the metal is inserted, close the upper jaw (G, Fig. 55).

Open the upper jaw and remove the work from the machine, turn the work over and reinsert it in the machine with the outer bent edge flush with the outer edge of the bending leaf, and close the upper jaw (H, Fig. 55). Raise the bending leaf slightly and strike the outer edge with a mallet to offset the pocket as shown at J, Fig. 55. Remove the completed pocket from the brake.

Procedures for Using Forming Molds. After the work that is to be formed has been bent to a right angle, remove the bent sheet from the brake, select the desired mold, and lay it along the edge of the bending leaf (Fig. 56). Holding the mold in place, insert friction clamps in the holes provided for this purpose in the bending leaf. Strike each of the clamps a slight blow with a mallet (Fig. 57). To insert the previously bent sheet, release the clamping bar handles, insert the work, and close both clamping bar handles (Fig. 58). Stand in front of the brake, place both hands on the work, and bend the work over the mold as far as necessary (Figs. 58 and

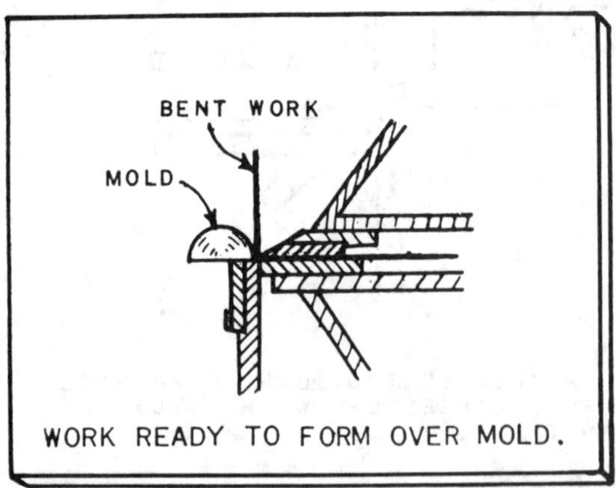

Figure 56.

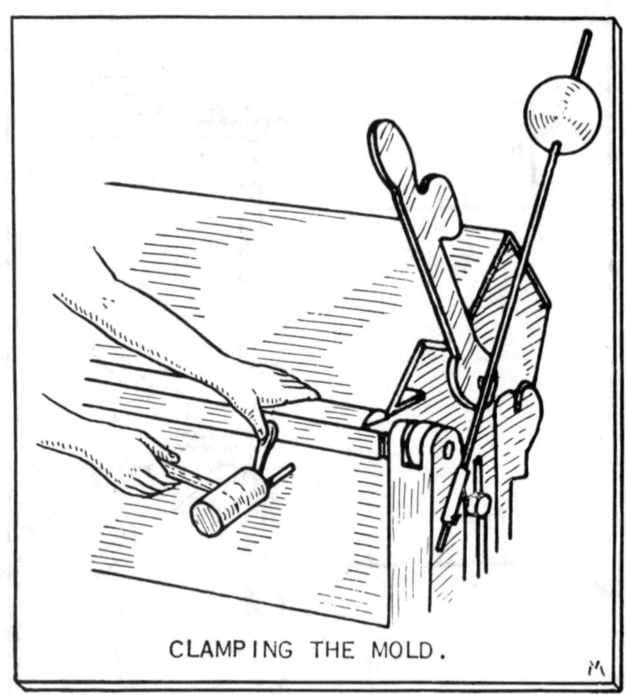

Figure 57.

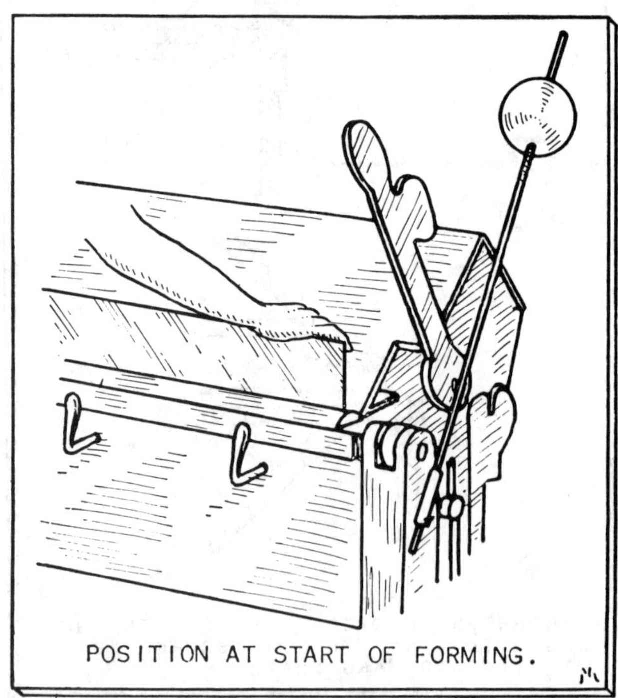

Figure 58.

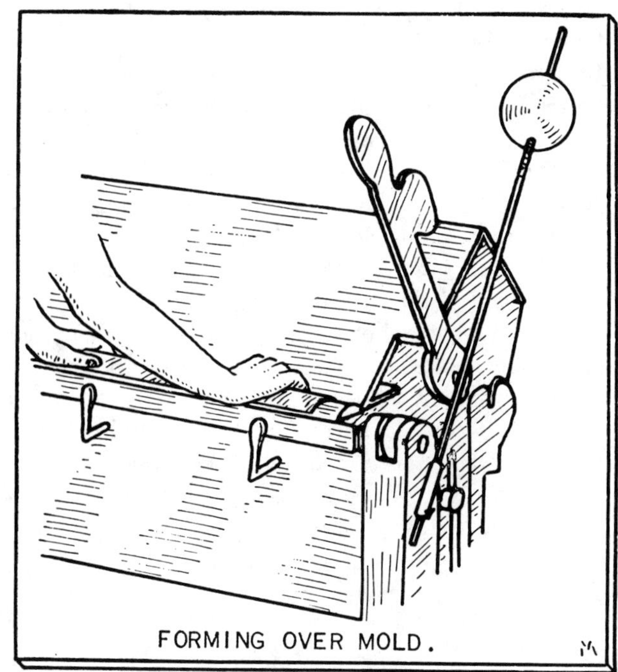

Figure 59.

59). To remove the formed sheet, release both clamping bar handles.

Remove clamps and mold with an upward blow of the mallet on the bottom of the clamps.

Combination Folders and Brakes

Combination folders of the type shown in Figs. 60 and 61 are available in sizes ranging from 36 in. to 60 in. with capacities varying from 18 to 22 gauge.

These machines are designed to fold locks as they are folded or bent on regular bar folders, and to make bends or brakes at any point on sheets as is done on brakes. They will also do a variety of other forming operations with the sheet remaining stationary as the bends are made.

Operating Procedures (Figs. 60 and 61). The upper clamping bar with the folding blade is operated by a hand crank through eccentrics and connections and may be adjusted for the various thicknesses of material by the hand screws on top of the side frames (Fig. 60).

Adjust the bar so that the material is held securely when the crank is at its highest position.

The front gauges are used for forming narrow bends (Fig. 60). For wide bends, the rear gauge is used (Fig. 61). For bends wider than can be made with the rear gauge, scribe the sheet at the point of bend and bend to the line.

In forming sharp bends or locks, the edge of the folding bar should be even with the top of the bed. Rounded bends or open locks for wire with a radius

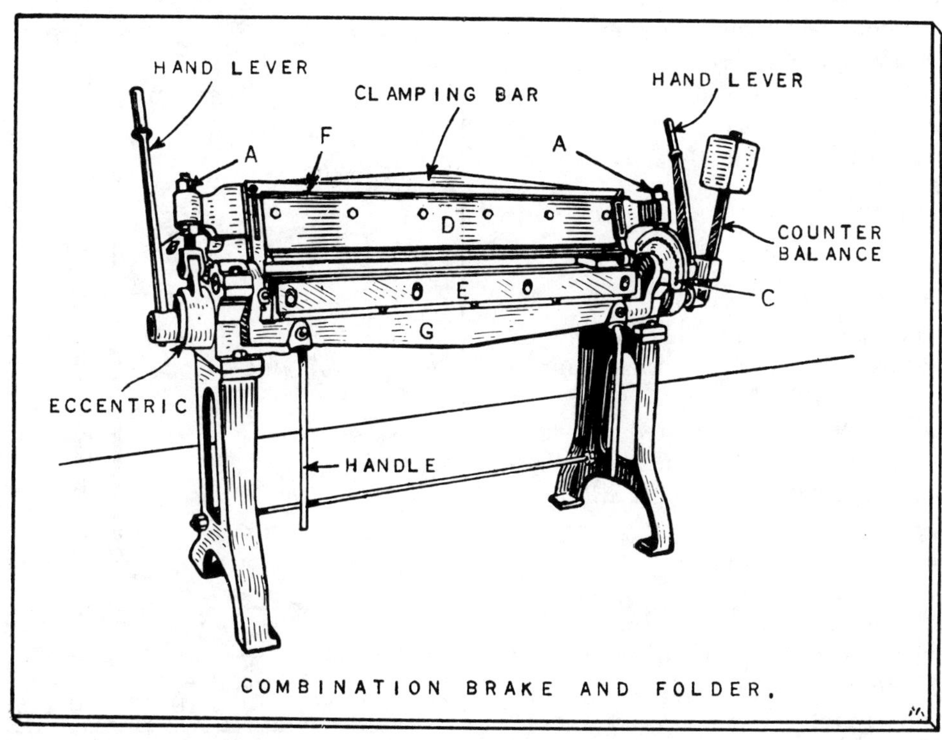

Figure 60.

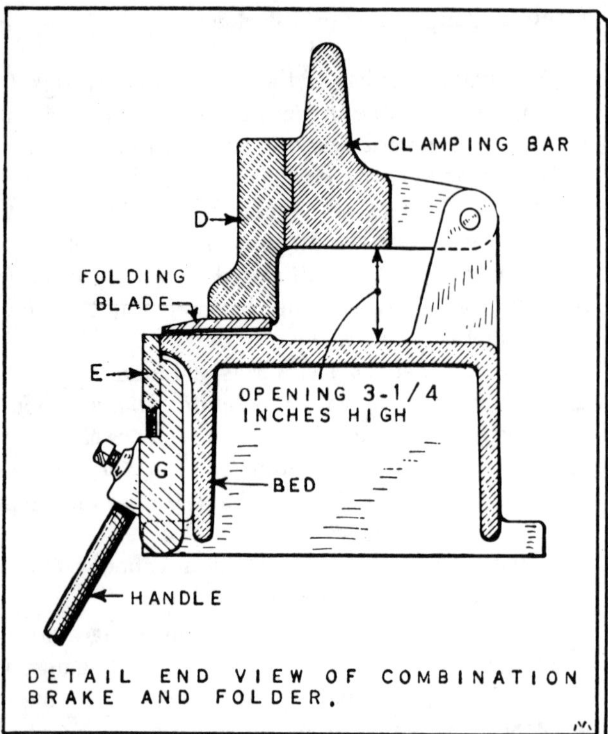

Figure 61.

of not more than ¼ in. can be made by dropping the folding bar in the folding bar holders by means of the setscrew in the underside.

The adjustable stop on the left hand end permits the making of bends to the desired angle (Fig. 60).

The clamping bar can be raised to 3 in. above the bed, and, by removing the folding blade, will permit the use of special-shaped bars for special bending and forming (Fig. 61).

Drill Press

Two types of drill presses used for sheet metal work are the bench and floor types. The bench type is secured to the work bench in the usual manner. The floor drill press does not have to be secured to the floor, but can be set wherever desired. The floor model, however, should always stand on a level place in the workshop. The essential parts of a drill press are shown in Fig. 62.

The table must be readily adjustable for height over the entire range of the column, and should not have a tendency to become shaky or to spring when work is done up to the full capacity of the tool. It should be tiltable to any desired angle, and should be furnished with several slots for securing various fixtures and accessories to the table. The table should be sufficiently rigid to permit the attachment of a larger additional top required for various operations. It should be equipped with a device enabling it to be set quickly and accurately in any desired position.

The spindle of the drill press should revolve in bearings that are entirely independent of those carrying the belt pulley. If work other than drilling holes is to be done, the spindle must be easily removable, so that other spindles can be substituted.

The head of the drill press should be reversible so that the tool can be driven from below the table, giving all the advantages of a separate shaper in conjunction with the drill press.

The drive should be as direct as possible, to prevent excessive vibration and loss of power.

Installation of the Drill Press. The instructions given here for the installation, adjustment, and

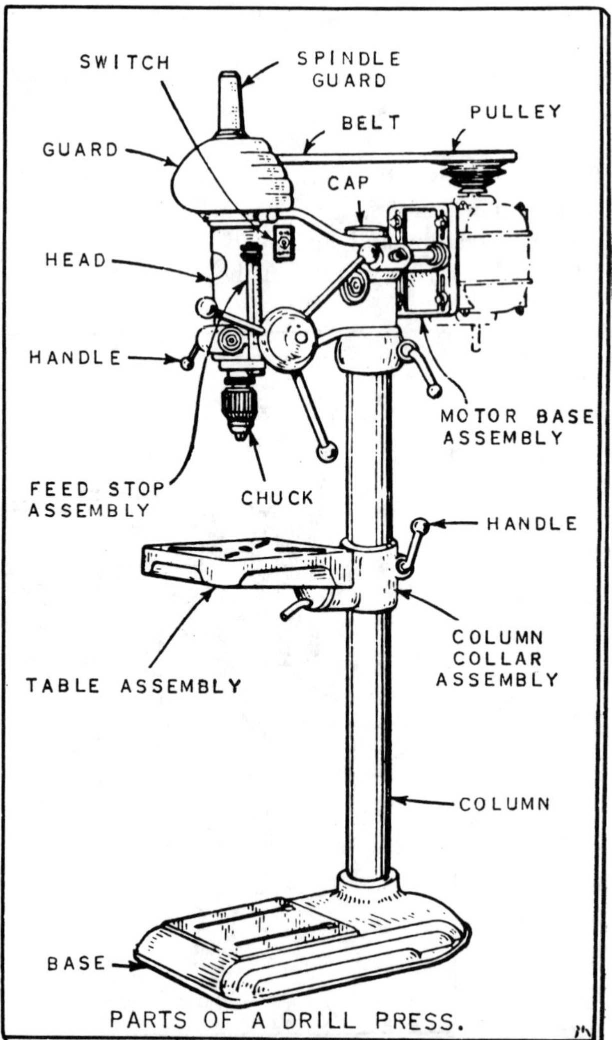

Figure 62.

operation of a drill press are applicable to all standard types. Before making any adjustments, however, be sure to check the manufacturer's printed instructions.

The type of drill press shown in Fig. 62 should be equipped with a ⅓ or ½ hp, 1740 rpm ball-bearing motor, for efficient operation with any required accessory. The following speeds will be obtained: (1) With the spindle, motor, and pulley in direct line—580, 1300, 2440, and 5200; (2) with the motor and pulley raised one step—760, 1800, and 4000; (3) with the motor and pulley lowered one step—1000, 1800, and 3300 rpm.

Mount the motor on the motor bracket and place the pulley on the shaft with the large step away from the motor. With a straightedge, line up the motor pulley with the spindle pulley. The motor should rotate in a clockwise direction when viewed from the pulley end. If motor rotates in the wrong direction, reverse its action according to manufacturer's instructions.

Adjustments and Controls. To move the drill-press head or the table to a different position on the column, loosen the clamp by turning the lever located next to the column.

The quill of the drill press is locked in position by turning the small handle usually located at the lower front part of the head (Fig. 62). A quill is a hollow shaft that revolves on a solid shaft, carrying pulleys or clutches. When clutches are closed, the quill and shaft revolve together.

The two knurled nuts on the spindle stop gauge can be set at any desired position and locked. By means of this control, a definite amount of spindle travel can be obtained, and any number of consecutive holes can be drilled to a desired depth.

If longitudinal play develops in the spindle, it can be eliminated as follows: (1) Remove the two locknuts on the feed stop bracket. (2) Remove the spring housing by loosening the setscrew on the underside of the boss. (3) Remove feed lever and pinion shaft after loosening the setscrew in the collar adjacent to the head. (4) Pull spindle and quill downward and remove from drill head. (5) Loosen setscrew in collar directly above the quill and, while forcing the spindle up against the bottom of the quill, tighten the collar up against the inner race of the quill bearing. Be careful not to make this adjustment too tight. (6) Put spindle back into drill head and reassemble.

When it is necessary to remove the chuck from the spindle, use the wedge provided for this purpose by the manufacturer. Handle the drill-press chuck with respect. Never strike it with a hammer, bump it, or drop it. Use no tools on a chuck other than the wedge or the chuck wrench.

When it is necessary to adjust the tension on the quill-return spring, turn the spring housing counterclockwise to increase the tension, or pull upward on the ratchet-pawl to release the tension.

To tilt the table of the drill press, pull out the knurled handle located directly beneath it (Fig. 62). If the table is tilted 90 degrees right or left, the knurl pin can be inserted in the holes provided in the column. For any intermediate angle the table must be locked in place by tightening the nut.

Tools and Accessories Used. The tools used for drilling, reaming, boring, counterboring, countersinking, and spot facing are shown in Fig. 63. All of these operations can be accomplished with either a straight-shank or tapered-shank tool. All sizes of drills and reamers under ½ in. are usually provided with straight shanks which can be conveniently and firmly held in the chuck of the drill press. The additional cost of taper-shank tools for these small sizes is therefore not necessary. In larger sizes, the difference in cost between the straight and the taper type is trifling. It is always more convenient to hold the

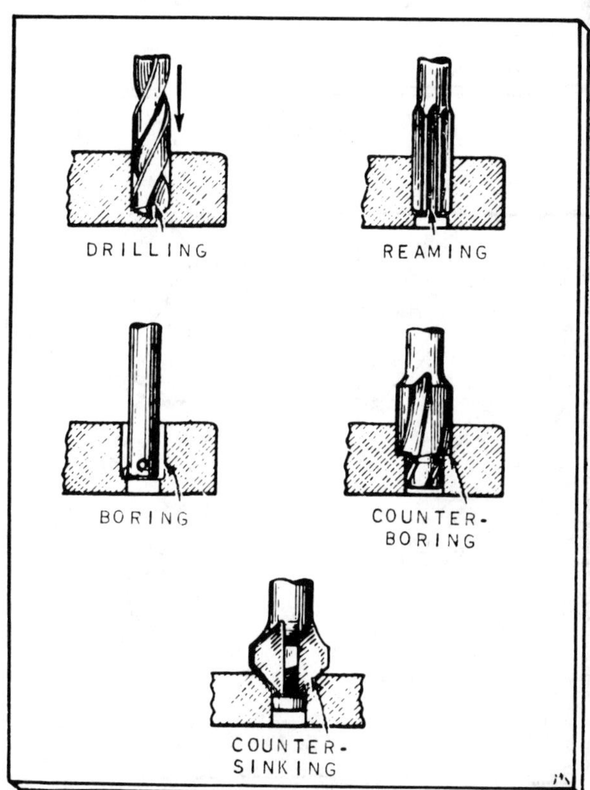

Figure 63.

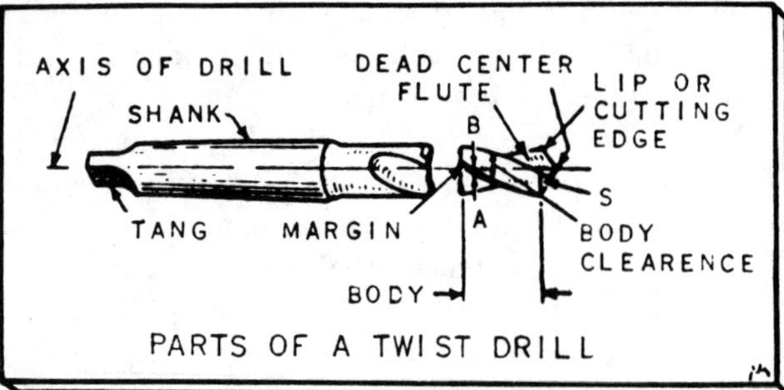

Figure 64.

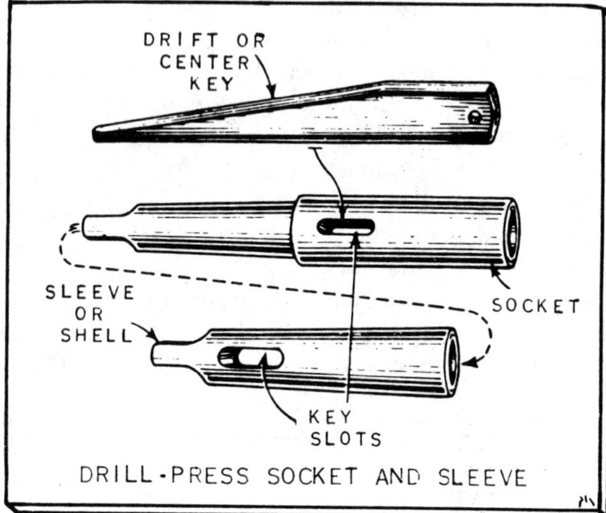

Figure 65.

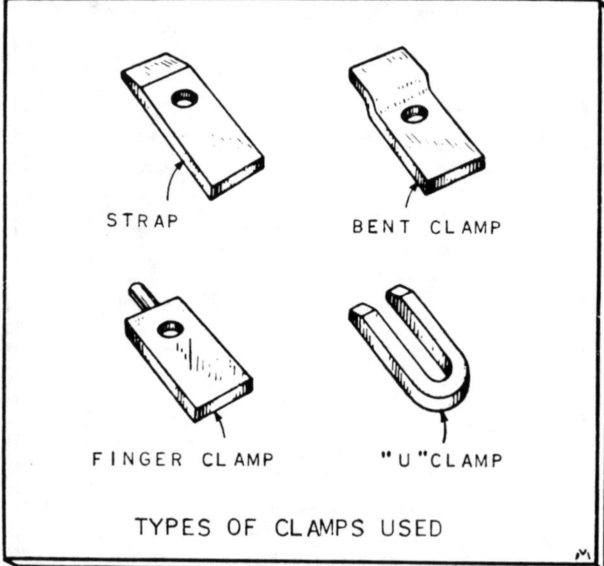

Figure 66.

larger sizes in the drill press by means of the taper shank.

Drilling is the operation of producing a circular hole by the removal of solid material. For this the *twist* drill is used (Fig. 64).

Reaming consists of both sizing and finishing a drilled hole. A *reamer* is a tool with several cutting edges (Fig. 63).

Enlarging a drilled hole by means of an adjustable tool is called *boring*. A boring tool which has only one cutting edge is used (Fig. 63).

Cylindrically enlarging only the end of a drilled hole to a predetermined distance is called *counterboring*. The tool used for this operation is shown in Fig. 63.

A *countersink* is used to form or cut a cone-shaped enlargement at the end of a previously drilled hole, to form a recess for a flatheaded screw (Fig. 63).

A *spot-facing tool* is used for smoothing and squaring the surface around the ends of a previously drilled hole to seat a nut or the head of a capscrew.

Tools with taper shanks too small to fit the taper hole in the drill-press spindle are held in a special socket. The shank of this special socket fits into the standard spindle hole. The attachment is called a *drill-press socket and sleeve* (Fig. 65). Note that the taper-shank socket and sleeve has a flattened end forming a tang. This tang fits into a slot at the end of the taper hole of the spindle and helps drive the drill (the hold of the taper alone is not sufficient).

HOLDING THE WORK. With the exception of very heavy pieces, all work must be firmly secured to the table of the drill press to assure accuracy and to avoid injury to the operator. If a vise is used to hold the work, this vise must also be clamped to the table. The four types of clamps generally used are the strap, bent, finger, and U-clamps (Fig. 66).

If the work is small, a single clamp can safely be used to hold it securely in place. For larger work, two or more clamps must be used. An ideal setup is shown in Fig. 67.

Tables of all drill presses are provided with T-slots. These slots are used for the location of the necessary bolts to secure the clamp or other holding fixture used. Several types of bolts are used for various kinds of work. The square-head bolt is used for ordinary clamping purposes; however, to place it in position it must be pushed along the T-slot from one end (Fig. 68). The T-head bolt is more convenient to use. It is set in place by simply dropping the head lengthwise in the slot and turning it to the right.

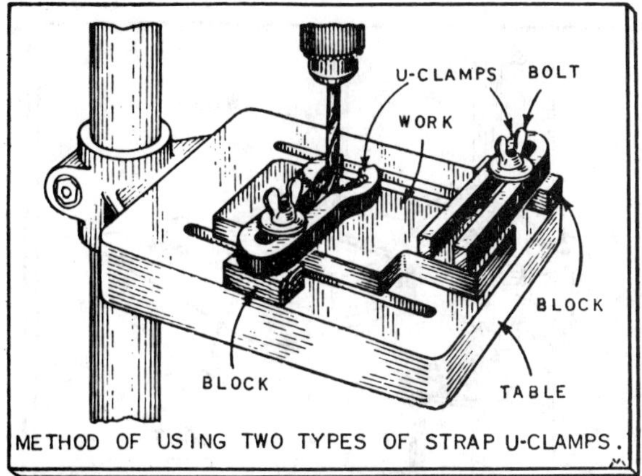

Figure 67.

This type of bolt is especially convenient when it is necessary to clamp the inside of work that otherwise would have to be lifted over the bolt (Fig. 68). The tapped T-head bolt is sometimes preferred because the stud of this bolt can be removed and the head

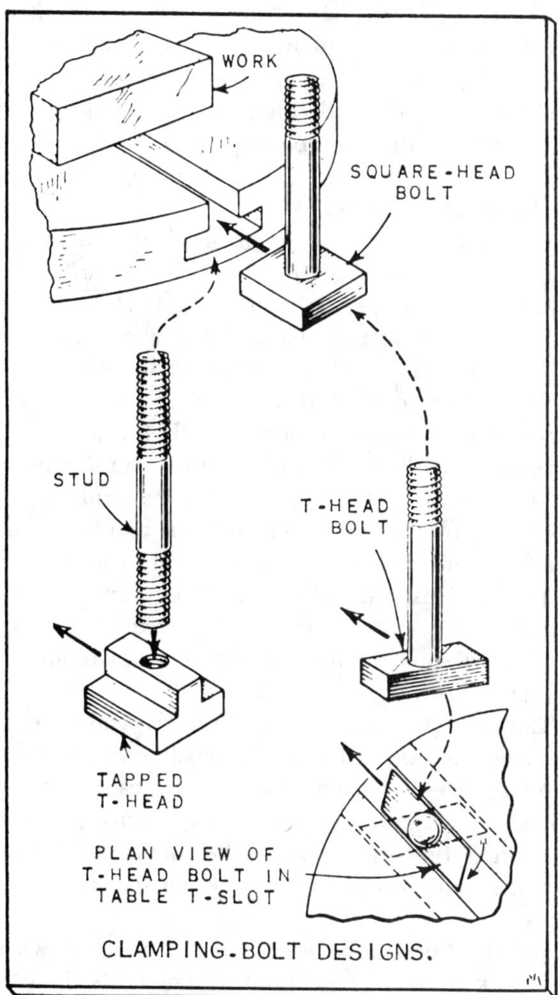

Figure 68.

Figure 69.

pushed along the slot under the work to the required position. Mechanics usually have a supply of studs of various lengths with a few heads to be used when required. This obviates the need for a supply of different types of bolts of varying sizes.

Step blocks are used in conjunction with bolts and clamps to secure the work to the drill-press table. These are available in various sizes, and with various numbers of steps (Fig. 69). Note that the block used under the outer end of the clamp can be made of either scrap metal or hardwood. If wood is used, be sure that it is of sufficient cross section to give it the needed stiffness. Set it under the clamp with the pressure against the grain of the wood.

The arrangement of the work when step blocks are used is shown in Fig. 70. The setups shown in these illustrations are merely suggestions and can be altered to suit varying conditions. The most important factor to consider is that the work must be firmly secured at all times.

If the work is fastened directly onto the table of the drill press, it must be located so that the drill or tool used will pass through one of the table openings. If the work cannot be centered over one of the openings, it must be mounted on either wood blocks or pieces of machined bar stock called *parallels* (Fig. 70).

When a light piece of metal is supported at points too far apart, it will spring under the pressure of the drill, resulting in an inaccurate hole and often a broken drill. To prevent the work from springing, use a V-support or block made of hardwood (Fig. 71).

A *V-block* is used in conjunction with a step block, clamp, and bolt to secure round work for drilling; *angle plates* are used to secure odd-shaped work (Fig. 70).

Other methods of securing the work are shown in Figs. 67 and 70.

Layout of work. Use the following procedure for laying out work prior to drilling: By means of intersecting lines, show the position of the center of the hole that is to be drilled. With a center punch, make a slight mark at the point of these intersections. If the work is rough, rub some chalk on it. If the surface of the work has been machined or is smooth,

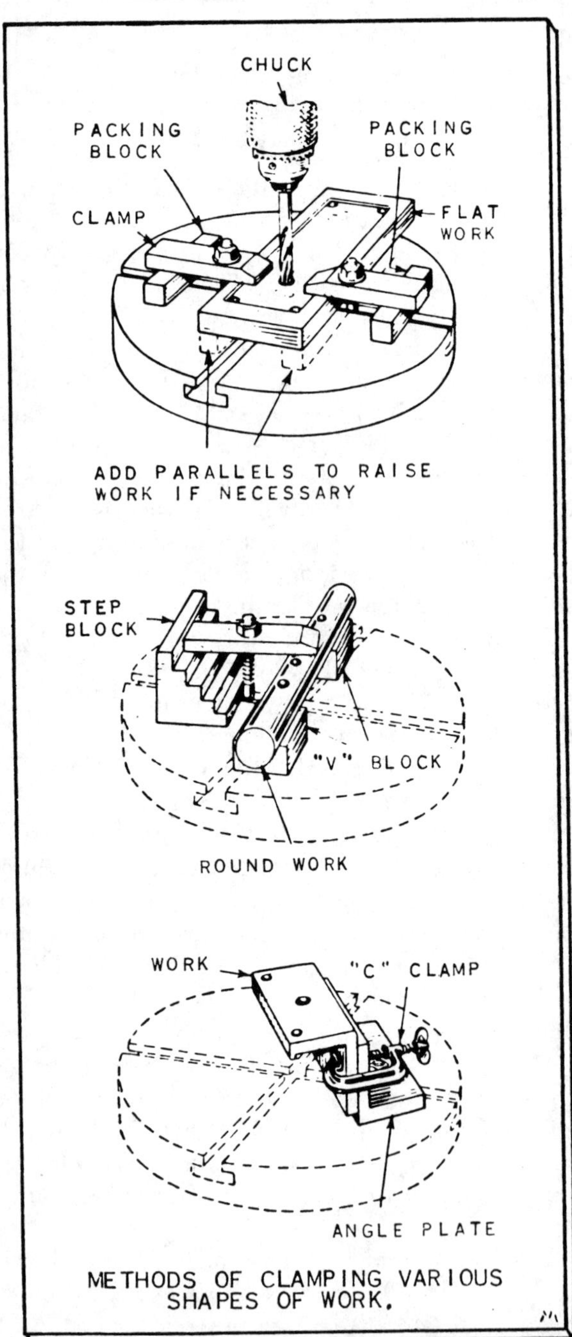

Figure 70.

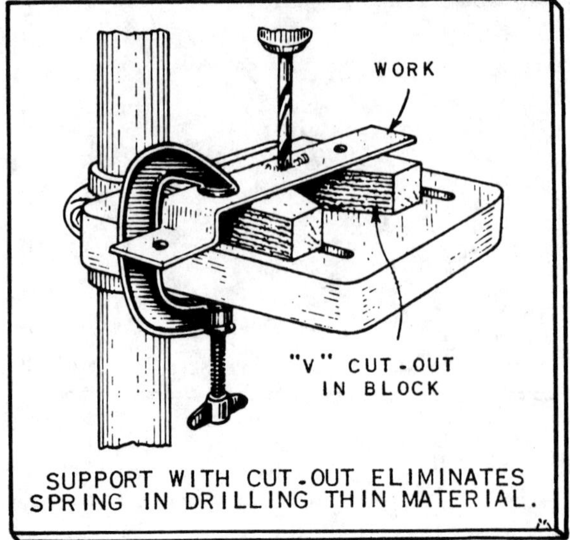

Figure 71.

use a coating of blue vitriol solution instead of chalk. Let it dry for a few minutes before scribing the surface. Using the punch mark as a center, scribe a circle with a pair of dividers indicating the size of the hole to be drilled. Before proceeding to drill the hole, use a larger center punch to make a larger indentation at the center.

Speeds and Feeds. Speed, as applied to a drill, is the speed at the circumference of the drill. This speed is called the peripheral speed and is the speed at which the drill would travel if it were laid on its side and rolled. In other words, a drill with a stated peripheral speed of 30 ft. a minute would roll a distance of 30 ft. in one minute. Speed of a drill, therefore, as generally used, does not refer to rotation per minute unless so stated specifically. As a rule, a drill does not pull itself into the work but requires a constant pressure behind it to advance it. This advance is always measured in fractions of an inch per revolution, and is called *feed.* Feed pressure, therefore, is the pressure required in order to maintain the necessary feed.

The correct speed and feed are dependent upon so many conditions that it is impossible to give hard-and-fast rules regarding them. They can be determined only by judgment resulting from experience. The suggestions given should be considered only as a guide and as a point from which to start operations.

Starting Speeds. To start a drill, bring it down to the work by hand feed until it centers itself in the work; then, and only then, apply the power feed. As previously mentioned, no definite rules can be given for the speed at which a drill should run and the correct amount of feed per revolution. The composition and hardness of material, the depth of hole required, the lubricant used, the type of machine used, the condition of the machine, the setup, point grinding, quality of the holes desired, and many other items have a distinct influence on the speeds and feeds required. The following speeds are given only as suggestions. The correct speeds and feeds should, as previously mentioned, be determined by good judgment and trial in each instance.

TABLE 6

SUGGESTED SPEEDS FOR HIGH-SPEED DRILLS *

Metal	*Speed in rpm*
Aluminum and its alloys	200–300
Brass and bronze, ordinary	200–300
Cast iron, soft	100–150
Cast iron, hard	70–100
Malleable iron	80– 90
Magnesium and its alloys	250–400
Monel metal	40– 50
Steel, annealed	60– 70
Steel forgings	50– 60
Steel alloy	50– 70

* If carbon-steel drills instead of high-speed drills are used, they should be run at speeds from 40 to 50 per cent of those given in this table.

When the extreme outer corner of the cutting edges of the drill wears away too rapidly, it is evidence of too much speed.

High speed in cast iron tends to wear away the margin of the drill. The maximum speed suggested for carbon drills in cast iron is 50 ft. per minute peripheral speed.

Starting Feeds. The starting feed is largely governed by the size of the drill used and the material to be drilled. The general rule is to use a feed of .001 in. to .002 in. per revolution for drills smaller than 1/8 in.; .002 in. to .004 in. for drills 1/8 in. to 1/4 in.; .004 in. to .007 in. for drills 1/4 in. to 1/2 in.; .007 in. to .015 in. for drills 1/2 in. to 1 in.; and .015 in. to .25 in. for drills larger than 1 in.

Start the drill with a moderate speed and a moderate feed. Increase either one or both after careful observation of the condition of the drill. The following suggestions should be carefully observed.

If the drill chips out at the cutting edge, it is a certain indication of either too heavy a feed or too much lip clearance. Before deciding that it is too heavy a feed, check the lip clearance of the drill. (See Chap. 3 for detailed description of parts of twist drills.)

A drill that splits up the web may have been given too much feed for the amount of lip clearance. Either decrease the feed or increase the lip clearance, or both.

Failure to give sufficient lip clearance at the center of a drill will also cause it to split up the web. On the other hand, too much lip clearance at the center (or at any other point on the lip) will cause the lip to chip. Therefore, before blaming the feed, make certain that the drill has been properly ground. If it has been properly ground, decrease your feed.

It is better to err on the side of too much speed than on the side of too much feed. This is true for all metals, with the exception of cast iron. The nature of this material permits an unusually heavy feed. Speed can be increased to the point where the outside corners of the drill commence to show signs of wearing away. The speed should then be reduced slightly.

LUBRICATION FOR DRILLING. It is very important to use the proper lubricant when drilling metals of gauges heavier than 1/16 in. Lubricants are used to cool both the edges of the tool and the work that is being machined. Lubricants used for drilling are called *coolants*. As large a volume as possible of the coolant should be directed onto the cutting edges of the tool, and allowed to flow onto and around the work. Proper lubrication aids in chip clearance. It also materially improves the finish of the hole.

Suggested lubricants for various metals are:

Aluminum and its alloys—Soluble oil, kerosene, and lard-oil compound; kerosene and soluble oil mixtures.

Brass—Soluble oil, kerosene, and lard compound; light non-viscous neutral oil.

Copper—Soluble oil.

Cast iron—No lubricant required.

Malleable iron—Soluble oil.

Monel metal—Soluble oil; mineral oil.

Steel (ordinary)—Soluble oil; mineral oil.

DRILLING SHEET METAL. Sheet metal must be backed against a wooden base block or preferably sandwiched between two blocks of wood and clamped. A bottom support must be used to prevent burring and crushing the metal.

Drilling Small Holes. Holes 1/16 in. in diameter and smaller should be drilled at high speed.

Drilling Large Holes. A smaller-sized lead hole must be drilled before completing the drilling of a large hole in metals heavier than 1/16 in. gauge. Proceed as follows: Start to drill with the full-size drill, check, and draw the drill if necessary. After the drill has started to cut full size, change to the small drill and proceed to run it through the work to make the lead hole (Fig. 72). This smaller lead hole will now be exactly in the center of the layout circle. Then set the larger drill into the spindle and drill the hole full size.

The diameter of the small drill used for the lead hole should be approximately the same as or a little larger than the web thickness of the larger drill. Because there is less tendency for a small drill to run off center than a large one, this procedure will result in a hole that is usually a good deal more accurate than if it were drilled by any other method (Fig. 72).

Drilling Round Stock. When it is necessary to drill round stock, a thin disc the same size as the work and preferably cut from the end of the work should be used in setting up the stock for drilling (Fig. 73). This disc must be carefully laid out and center-drilled the required diameter. Clamp both work and disc in a vise (Fig. 73). The disc will guide the drill directly to the center of the work and will prevent drifting. Drifting often occurs when round stock is drilled by any other method.

Countersinking. Various types of countersink drills must be used to countersink the work for the heads of the various types of machine screws, so that these heads come either flush with or below the surface of the material. This is done after the hole has been drilled to the depth required.

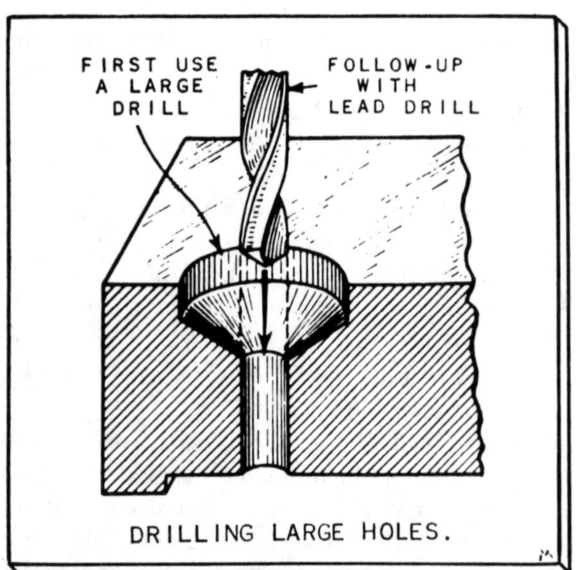

Figure 72.

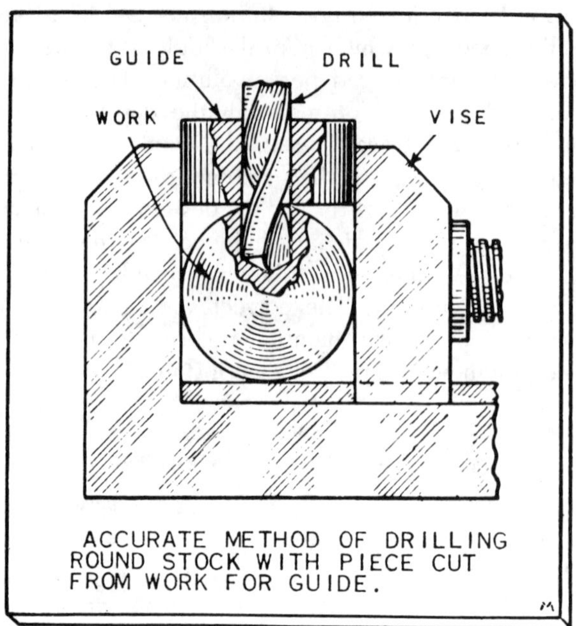

Figure 73.

Portable Electric Hand Drills

A well-designed portable electric hand drill is an excellent tool that can frequently be used in lieu of the drill press. It is especially valuable for work that cannot be moved to the workshop. Portable drills are available in various sizes; the ½ in. size is recommended for all general purposes. Figure 74 shows the various parts of a standard well-constructed and practical powered hand drill.

The drill shown is equipped with a universal-type motor that will operate on either d.c. or a.c. of 25, 40, 50, or 60 cycles, of a specified voltage. Thus a 110-volt universal motor will operate on either d.c. or a.c. 110-volt current and must be used only on that specified voltage. If the drill is used on a low-voltage line, it will not operate at normal speed, will lack the necessary power, and will heat up quickly. If used on too high a voltage, it will run at very high speed, and the motor will overheat and probably suffer serious damage. Always check voltage specifications on the nameplate of the hand drill with the voltage of the supply line used. Do not plug the drill in if they do not correspond. If drill runs slowly, gets hot, or smokes, disconnect it immediately and check the supply line with a voltmeter. Peak loads and off-peak loads will often cause a wide variation in supply lines that are supposed to carry a standard voltage. If the drill is being used more than four or five feet from the source of power supply, be sure

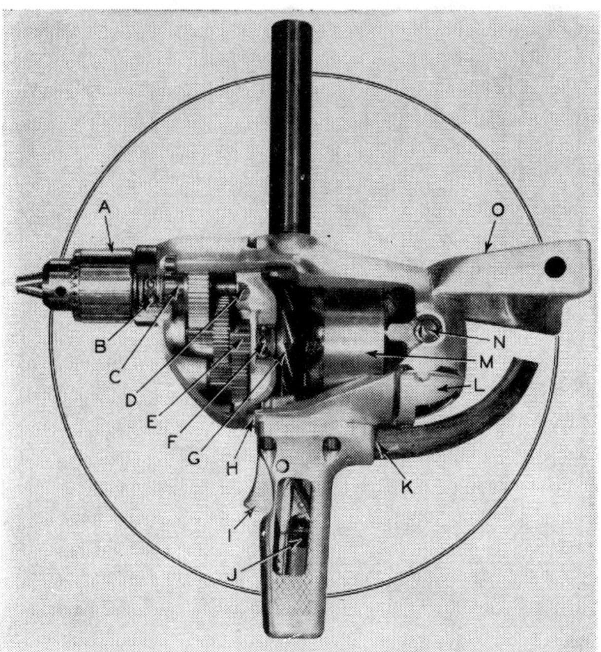

Figure 74. Cutaway view of a ½ in. standard drill.
A. Jacobs three-jaw geared chuck, threaded on spindle.
B. Deep-groove ball bearing on chuck spindle with inner and outer faces locked in place.
C. Splined mounting of spindle increases strength, facilitates inspection, and minimizes noise, friction, and wear.
D. Needle roller bearing at back end of spindle.
E. Full Size armature pinion with 13 teeth.
F. Double grease-sealed ball bearing on armature shaft.
G. Steel fan ensures cool operation.
H. Ample ventilating slots.
I. Instant release switch control, convenient for right- or left-hand use.
J. Two-pole automatic release switch mechanism.
K. Patented rubber sleeve cord protector and cord clamp prevent kinking.
L. Removable commutator inspection plate facilitates inspection and cleaning of commutator and brushes.
M. Full-powered universal-type motor, operates on either alternating or direct current.
N. Brushes easily accessible for inspection and replacement.
O. Removable spade handle with convenient chuck-key holder.

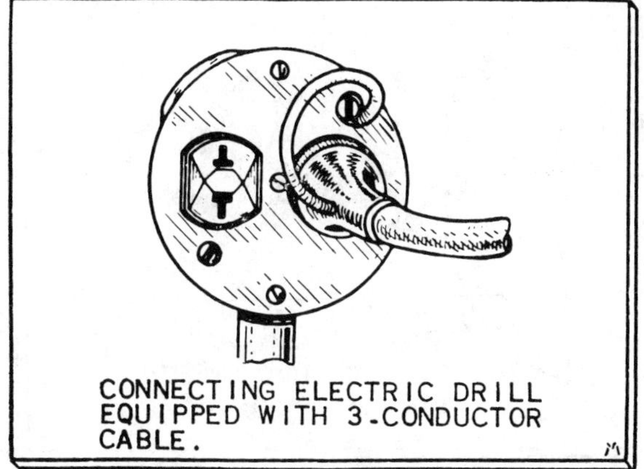

Figure 75.

that the wire used for the extension cable is large enough to carry the current to the tool without too great a drop in voltage. Use the table that follows as a guide for correct sizes of wire to be used.

TABLE 7

SIZE OF EXTENSION CABLE FOR PORTABLE ELECTRIC TOOLS

Based on current equivalent to 150 per cent of full load of tool and a loss in voltage of not over 5 volts. This table is for 110-volt tools. For 220-volt tools use wire size corresponding to an extension length of one-half the contemplated length.

Full-load Ampere Rating of Tool	0–2.0	2.1–3.4	3.5–5.0	5.1–7.0	7.1–12.0	12.0–16.0
Distance in Feet (one way)	Wire Size (B & S gauge)					
25	18	18	18	18	16	14
50	18	18	18	16	14	12
75	18	18	16	14	12	10
100	18	16	14	12	10	8
200	16	14	12	10	8	6
300	14	12	10	8	6	4
400	12	10	8	6	4	4
500	12	10	8	6	4	2
600	10	8	6	4	2	2
800	10	8	6	4	2	1
1000	8	6	4	2	1	0

Note: If voltage is already low at source (outlet), have voltage increased to standard, or use a much larger cable than listed in order to prevent any further drop.

To protect the mechanic against shock, the portable drill must always be grounded when in use. Well-designed drills are usually equipped with a three-conductor cable. The green or red conductor is usually the ground wire and is attached to the frame of the tool inside the case. The other end of this ground wire extends through the side of the attachment plug (Fig. 75). If the wire terminals at the switch are disconnected, reconnect the ground wire to the tool frame and not to a switch terminal.

Where a number of power tools are to be grounded, install a permanent grounding wiring system with three-wire receptacles and equip the tools with three-pole attachment plugs. A tool is then automatically grounded when plugged in (Fig. 76).

PORTABLE-DRILL CHUCKS. Standard electric hand drills, as shown in Fig. 74, are equipped with chucks to hold drills and other tools. These chucks are precision instruments and, like all accurate mechanisms, they should never be abused.

To permit the chuck jaws to grip the shank of the drill properly, always bottom the drill in the chuck.

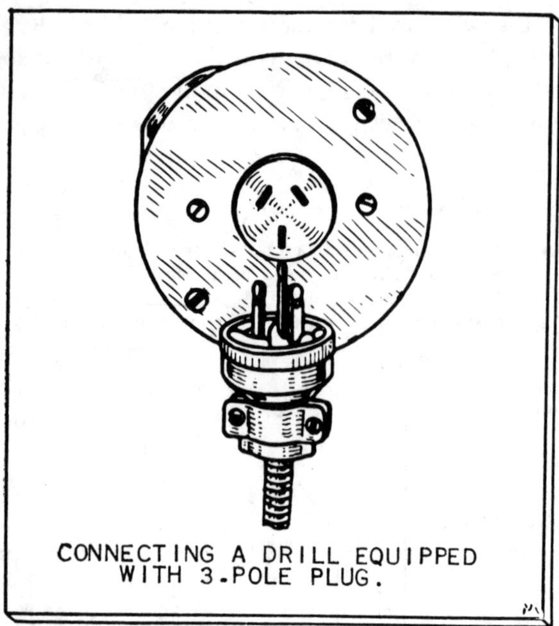

CONNECTING A DRILL EQUIPPED
WITH 3-POLE PLUG.

Figure 76.

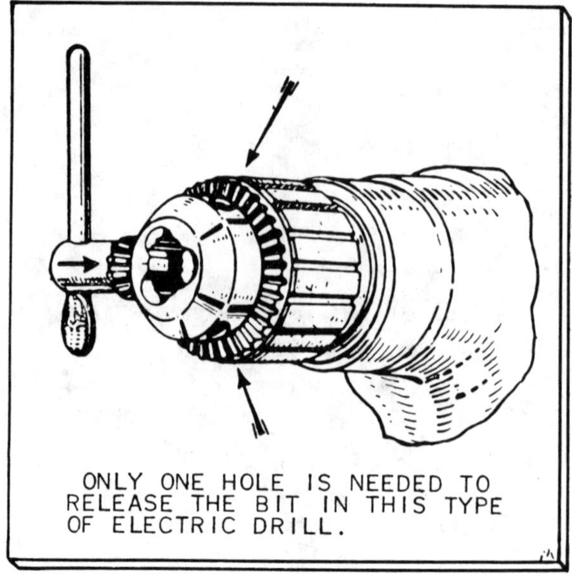

ONLY ONE HOLE IS NEEDED TO
RELEASE THE BIT IN THIS TYPE
OF ELECTRIC DRILL.

Figure 77.

To insure a uniform grip on the shank and to prevent slippage or unequal strain on the jaws, be sure to use all three holes in the chuck body to tighten the jaws. Insert the chuck key furnished with the drill in each of the holes in rotation and tighten as much as possible. To release the bit, loosen only one hole (Fig. 77). Never use a wrench, hammer, or any other tool but the correct sized chuck key to tighten or loosen the chuck jaws—otherwise the mechanism might be damaged. In the event of loss, order a new chuck key from the manufacturer by the number stamped on the body of the chuck.

Some drills are equipped with keyless chucks. These are opened and tightened by using the patented gear-locking pin in the gear case (Fig. 78). On other drills, the keyless chuck is opened and tightened by holding the locking collar just behind the chuck (Fig. 74).

Portable drills equipped with Morse taper socket spindles use bits with corresponding Morse taper shanks. When inserting tapered-shank bits in the spindle, tap the end of the drill lightly with a soft-faced mallet to be sure the tang fits in the socket correctly.

Tools Used. Portable electric drills are most frequently used with twist drills of the required size for drilling holes in metal. These twist drills are identical with those used in the drill press. The electric drill supplies the power for turning, but the mechanic must exert the forward pressure to feed the bit into the work. In metal, high speed and light feed are recommended.

The bit and the metal must be lubricated when drilling all types of ferrous metal except cast iron. The lubricants previously specified for use with the drill press are recommended.

A special bit for cutting large holes in thin sections or sheets of metal, wood, or composition is called the *hole saw* (Fig. 79). One-quarter inch electric drills will drive up to 1½ in. hole saws; ½ in. drills up to 3 in. hole saws, and ⅝ in. or larger drills will easily drive the largest (4 in.) hole saw bit.

Wood augers equipped with special shanks are available to fit the drill chuck. They are used to bore holes in structural timbers and other heavy wood members.

Although reaming, counterboring, and other sim-

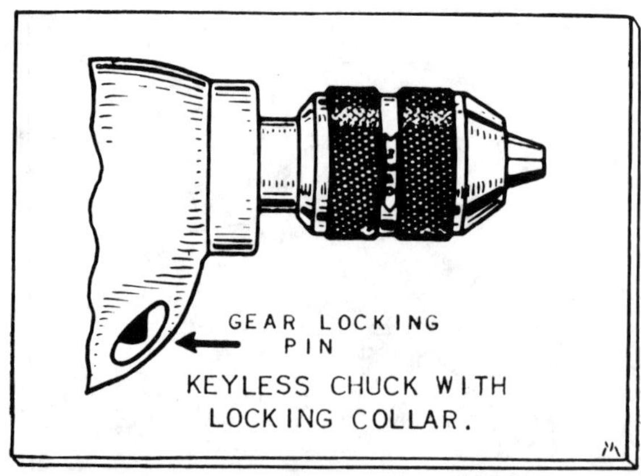

Figure 78.

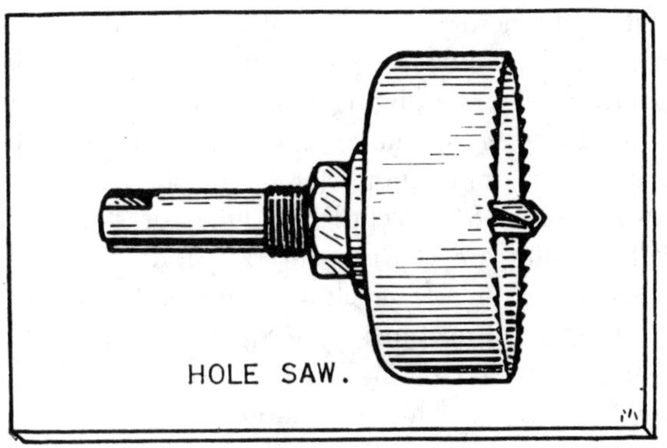

Figure 79.

ilar operations can, if necessary, be accomplished with a portable electric drill, it must be remembered that its spindle speed, power, and bearings have been designed primarily for drilling holes.

Operation. Lay out the work carefully and mark the exact center of the hole with a center-punch to provide a start in the metal for the point of the drill. To prevent damage or injury, be sure that the work is firmly secured.

Always grasp the control handles firmly and aim the drill in the same manner as a pistol or a gun. The small end-handle drills must be held with the hand and wrist in position to apply pressure in a straight line with the drill spindle. The other hand is used to balance and support the drill (Figs. 80 and 81).

The larger side-handle drills with auxiliary pipe handles are held with the spade handle against the shoulder, chest, or abdomen and with both hands firmly holding the switch and pipe handles. When using these larger drills, you must always be braced

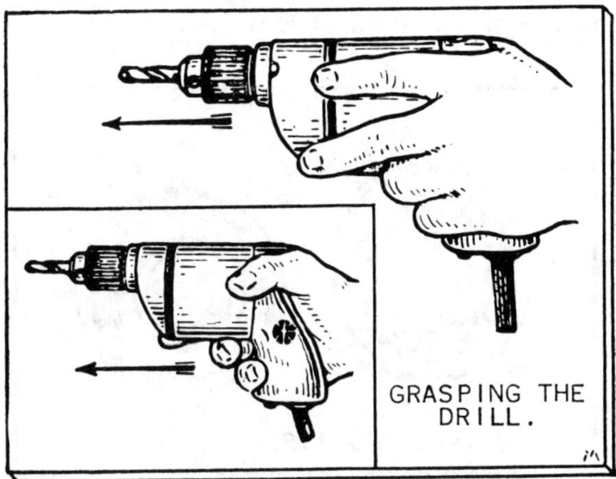

Figure 80.

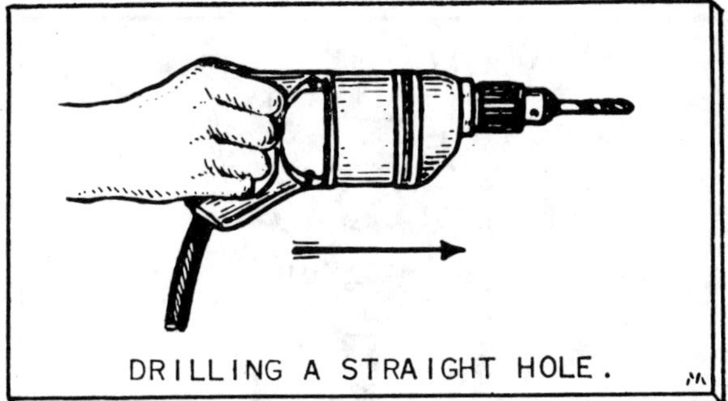

Figure 81.

against their torque or twisting action (Fig. 82). When drilling in a downward direction, the switch and pipe handles must be braced against your legs for additional support (Fig. 83).

All manufacturers of standard portable drills furnish detailed information on the limitations of their tools. Do not make the mistake of overloading; if the drill stalls it is being seriously overloaded or otherwise improperly used. Never try to force a drill. Turn the switch off and remove the drill from the work. Don't click the switch off and on in an effort to start a stalled drill. This will ultimately damage the switch, overheat the motor, and may break the bit. To avoid stalling it is good practice to relieve the feed pressure as the drill bit breaks through the finished hole.

Maintenance and Lubrication. To maintain an electric drill in top operating condition, frequent inspection and careful attention to first signs of wear are necessary (Fig. 84).

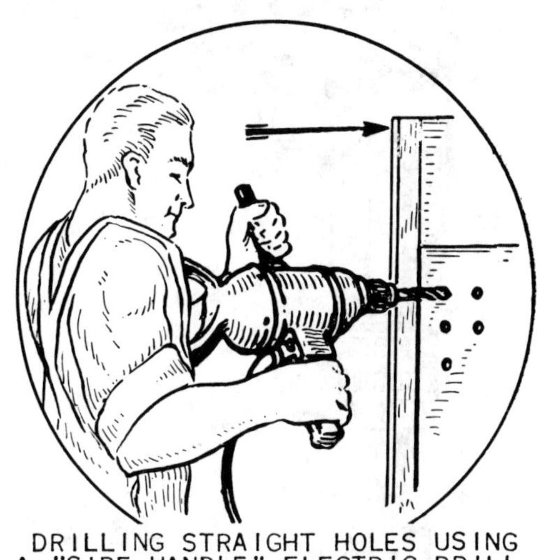

DRILLING STRAIGHT HOLES USING
A "SIDE-HANDLE" ELECTRIC DRILL.

Figure 82.

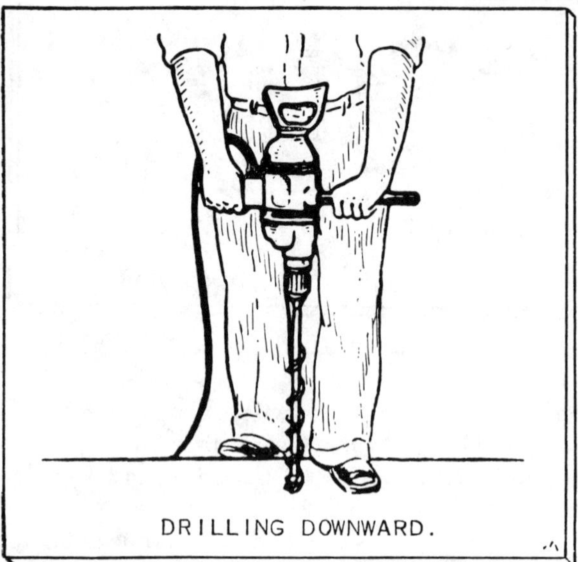

Figure 83.

All drill motors are air cooled. They depend on a constant abundant circulation of air for efficient operation. The ventilating fans, which are mounted on the front end of the armature shaft, are designed to draw an ample supply of air through the motor housing (Fig. 84). Ventilating holes or slots in the drill housing are of "non-clog" design to permit a constant stream of air flow. Keep this ventilating system clear at all times by frequently and regularly forcing a stream of air through the slots with the motor running. This precautionary measure will eliminate one cause of grounding and damage to motor and bearings. In a well-designed and properly constructed drill, most of the ball bearings are of the grease-sealed or closed type (B, Fig. 85). Both sides of this type of bearing are permanently lubricated and sealed. They have sufficient lubrication packed in them to last the normal life of the bearing. Never immerse closed bearings in any solvent whatsoever because this will dilute the lubricant. Wipe them clean but otherwise leave them alone. In open-type ball bearings (A, Fig. 85) having no seals of any kind or only one plate seal, the balls and ball retainers are visible. All open-type ball bearings, sleeve bearings, and needle roller bearings require periodic relubrication at regular intervals, depending on the use of the tool. Before refilling gear case, gears, and bearings with fresh lubricant, wash off all old grease, using any good commercial solvent. Use lubricant recommended by the manufacturer of the drill. Fill gear case only half full with lubricant—too much is just as bad as too little. The lubricant will expand when warm and any excess will be forced through the bearings into the motor, damaging the windings of the motor and clogging the ventilating holes.

COMMUTATORS AND CARBON BRUSHES. The commutator of a drill motor is the nerve center of the

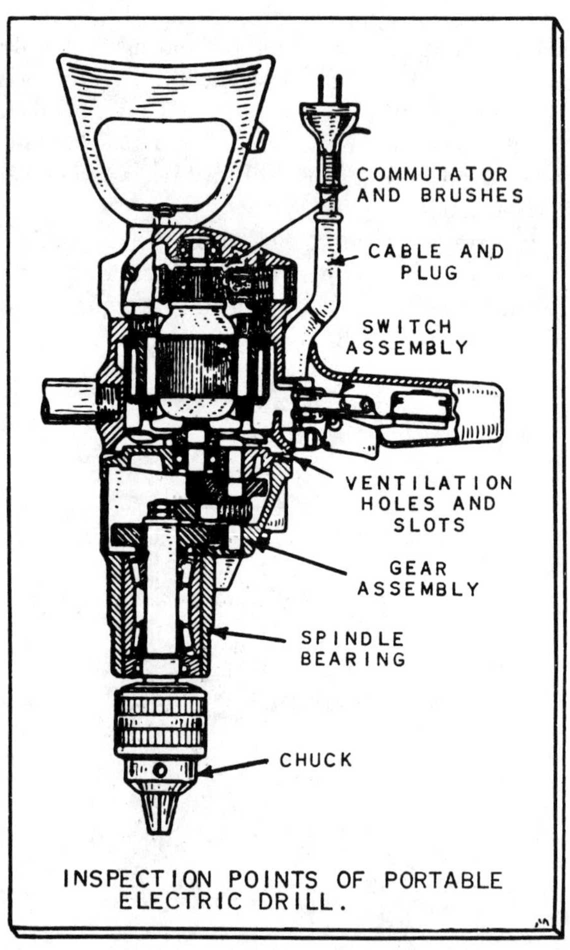

Figure 84.

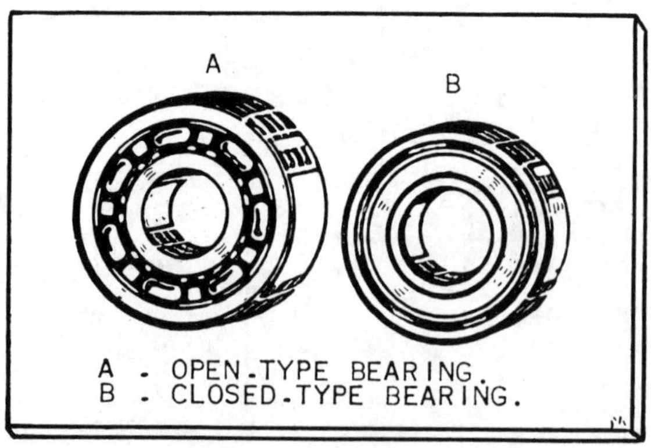

Figure 85.

entire tool (A, Fig. 86). It should be inspected frequently and, if greasy or rough, cleaned lightly and smoothed with very fine sandpaper. Do not use emery cloth. If a groove has been cut by the brushes, the commutator should be turned down on a lathe until a smooth surface is obtained again. If the mica insulation was originally undercut, it must be re-undercut after the turning operation. Inspect the soldered connection slots carefully; if solder has loosened, resolder before the leads break loose.

If there is excessive arcing at the commutator, check the following: *Weak brush springs:* Brushes not contacting properly. Undercut mica may have worn flush, causing brushes to jump. *Worn brushes:* If brushes for undercut mica are used on a flush-mica commutator, they will wear excessively; if flush-mica brushes are used on undercut-mica commutators, there will be excessive commutator wear. *Bearing wear:* If armature shaft bearings are badly worn, end and lateral play will cause vibration, commutator wear, and arcing.

Since the commutator is such a vital part of the drill, its inspection and care should be trusted only to a skilled mechanic or to the service department of the manufacturer.

Carbon brushes on the motor should be inspected frequently and kept free from dirt and dust, and should always operate freely in their guides, without sticking. There should be enough spring tension to keep the brushes in firm contact with the commutator.

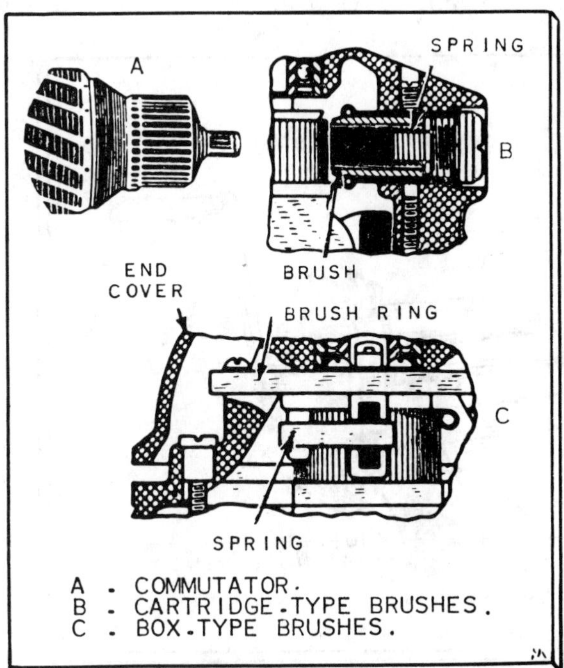

Figure 86.

Badly worn brushes should be replaced immediately, because they can cause serious damage to the armature and can necessitate expensive repairs or replacements.

In replacing worn brushes, do not use just any kind of brush. Extensive tests have been made to find the correct brush for each motor, and these are always available in the stocks of genuine replacement parts at all factory service branches. The "brush rigging" on all universal motor tools is at the rear (handle) end of the unit. In some cases (cartridge type), the brush holders and caps are visible in the outer housing (B, Fig. 86). In others (box type), the end cap must be removed to get at the brushes and commutator (C, Fig. 86).

Forming Machines

Forming machines, or *rolls*, as they are sometimes called, are used extensively in every sheet metal shop for curving sheet metal or forming cylinders of various diameters.

A modern forming machine similar to that shown in Fig. 87 consists of a left and right end frame or housing and three solid steel rolls connected with driving gears and operated by means of a hand crank, by a belt, when fitted with pulleys for power drive, or by a motor, when arranged for individual motor drive.

All forming machines are similar to the general type shown in Fig. 87. They are made in many sizes and capacities, the capacity depending on the diameter and length of the three forming rolls.

The two front rolls (Fig. 87) grip the sheet of metal and force it against the rear roll, which bends it upward around the rear of the front upper roll, curving the sheet and forming the cylinder.

The rear or forming roll can be adjusted in an angular vertical position by adjusting screws on the rear of left and right end housings (Fig. 89). Three inch and smaller diameter forming machines have hand adjusting screws, and on 4 in. and larger forming machines, the adjusting screws are fitted with sprockets connected with a chain for parallel adjustment of the rear roll.

For forming tapered cylinders, one end of the rear forming roll can be adjusted somewhat higher or

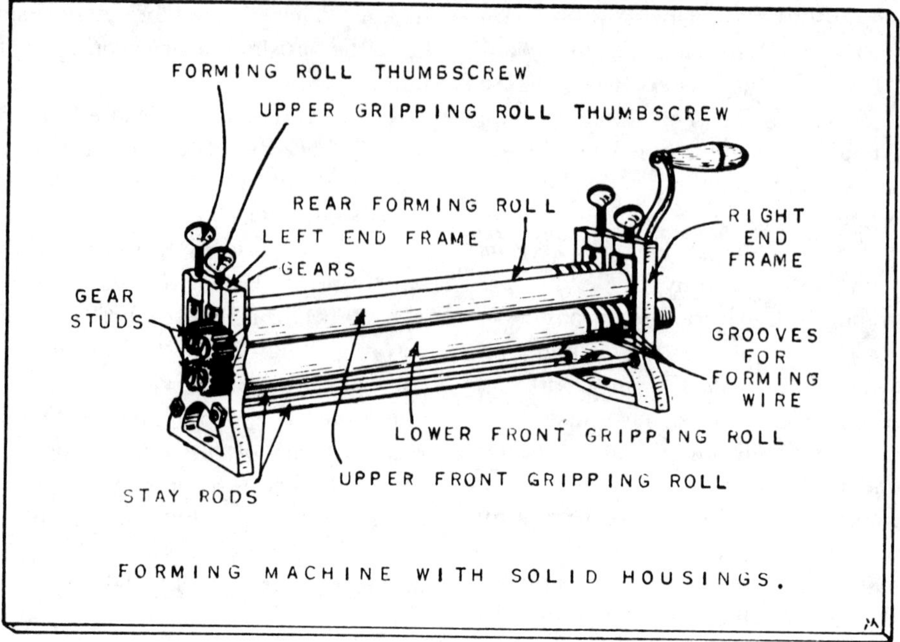

Figure 87.

lower than the opposite end by means of these adjusting screws. The chain on the 4 in. and larger diameter rolls can be readily disconnected for setting the rear roll in a tilted position (Fig. 90).

The radius of curve or diameter of cylinder that can be formed on a forming machine depends on the position of the rear roll in relation to the front upper roll.

There is no set rule that may be applied for the setting of the rear roll to secure any desired radius of curve, because the spring in the metal will affect this setting. For instance, soft copper or brass have less spring than does steel in its varying degrees of hardness or uniformity of quality. Therefore, when forming soft sheet metal, the rear forming roll should be set slightly lower than when forming the same

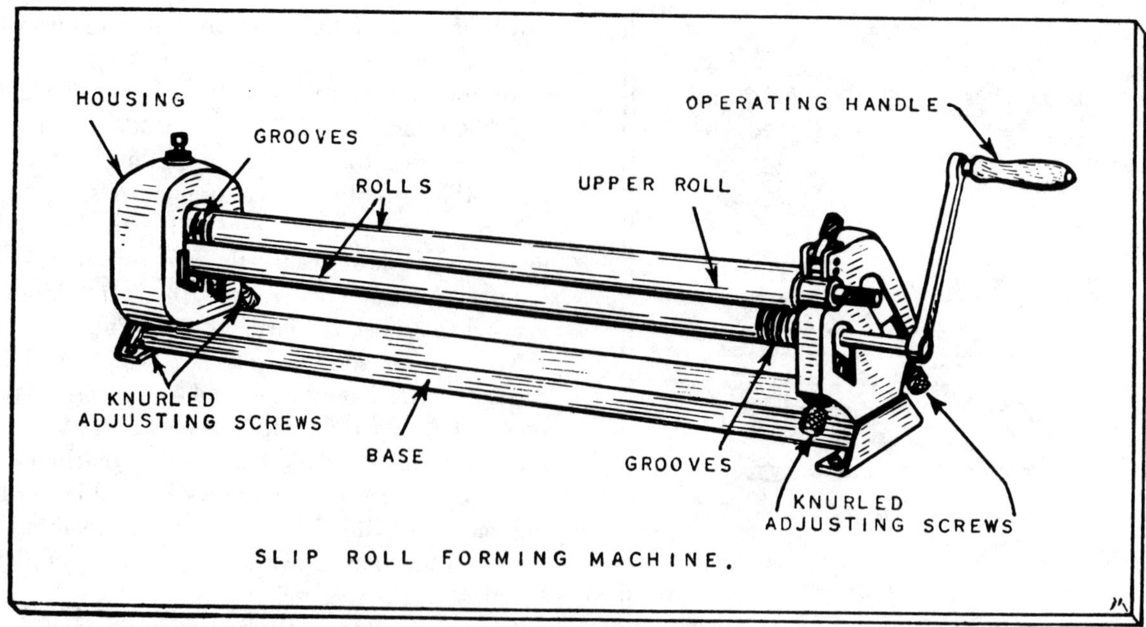

Figure 88.

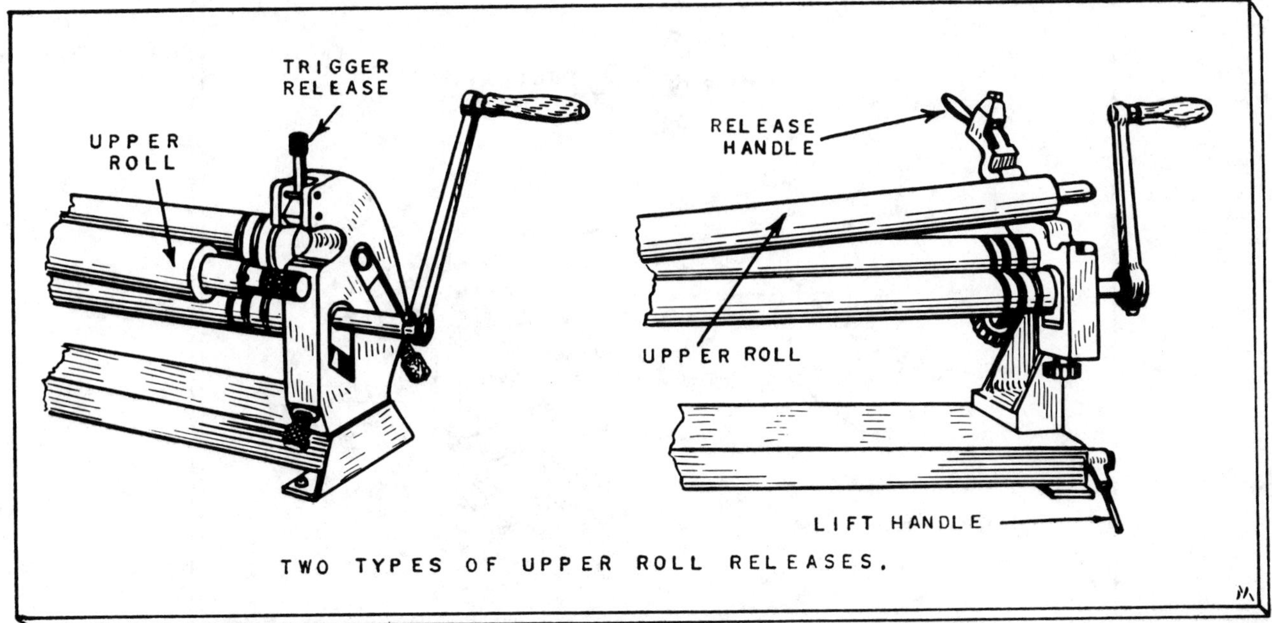

Figure 89.

diameter of cylinder in sheet metal possessing more spring or of stiffer quality. The adjustment of the rear roll can best be obtained through experiments with the material to be formed.

The adjustment of the two front or gripping rolls is obtained through a hand adjusting screw on each left and right end housing under each end of the lower front roll. The lower front roll is adjusted up or down for sufficient clearance between the two gripping rolls for the thickness of material to be formed, so material will pass through the rolls freely when the hand crank is turned or power applied (Fig. 87). Forcing the material through the gripping rolls without sufficient clearance for the thickness of metal may cause serious damage and breakage of left or right end housings.

Operating Forming Machines. The sheet of metal to be formed is inserted from the front of the machine between the two front gripping rolls after the two front rolls have been properly adjusted. Turn

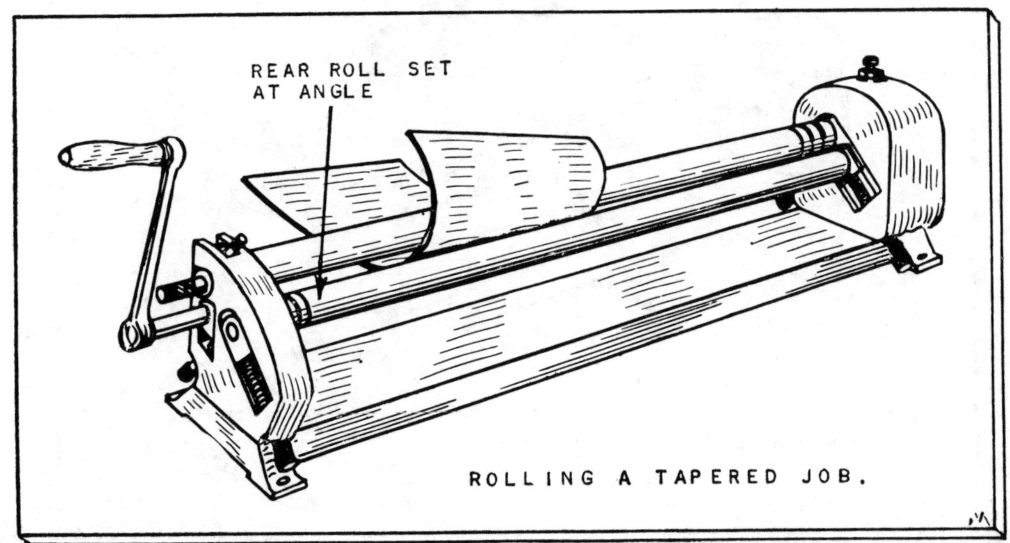

Figure 90.

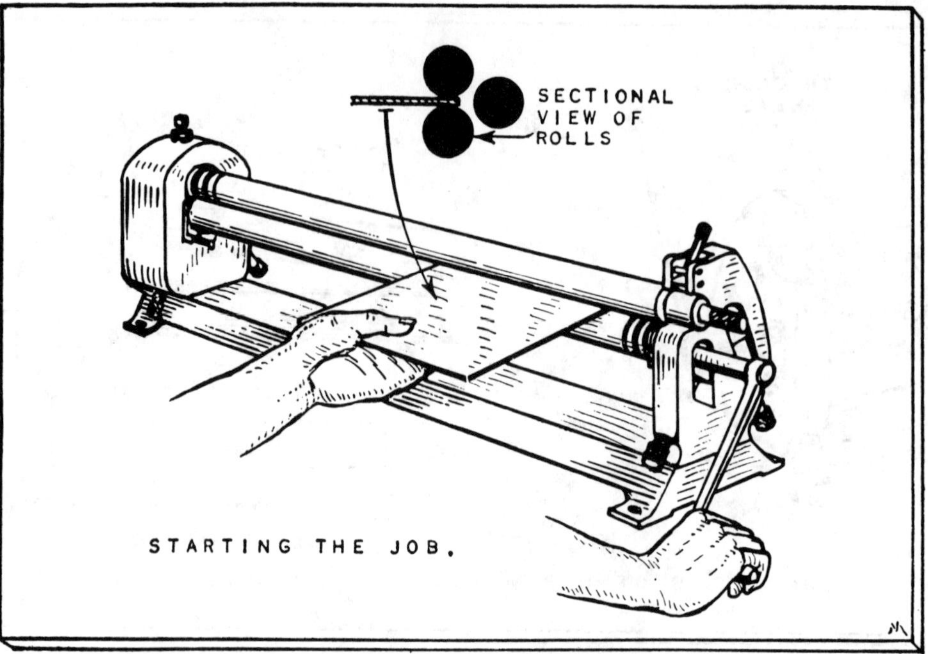

Figure 91.

the hand crank or apply power (Fig. 91), feeding the sheet metal through the gripping rolls against the upper side of the rear forming roll, which bends the metal upward, thereby forming the curve or cylinder (Fig. 92). If the radius of curve in the first experiment should not prove to be the desired radius, lowering the rear forming roll will increase the diameter of the cylinder, or raising the rear forming roll will decrease the diameter of the cylinder (Fig. 93).

The capacity ratings of forming machines of the type shown in Fig. 87 are based on forming mild steel the full length of the rolls, and are considered as standard by the sheet metal trade for forming rolls of a specified diameter and length. Definite capacities, however, would depend upon the diameter and length of the cylinder to be formed and the number of passes through the rolls to obtain a given diameter, the stiffness of the material, and the uniformity desired. When a forming machine is over-

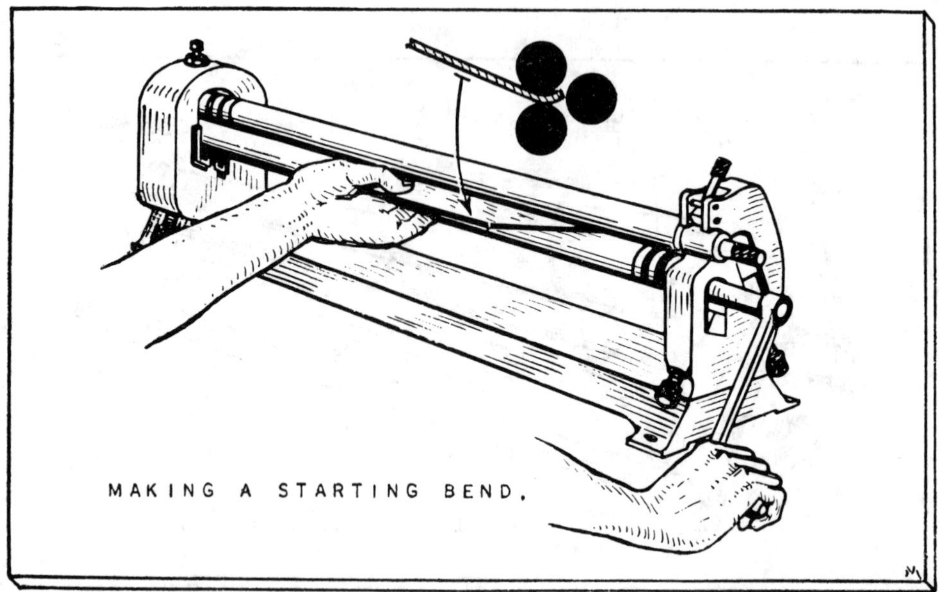

Figure 92.

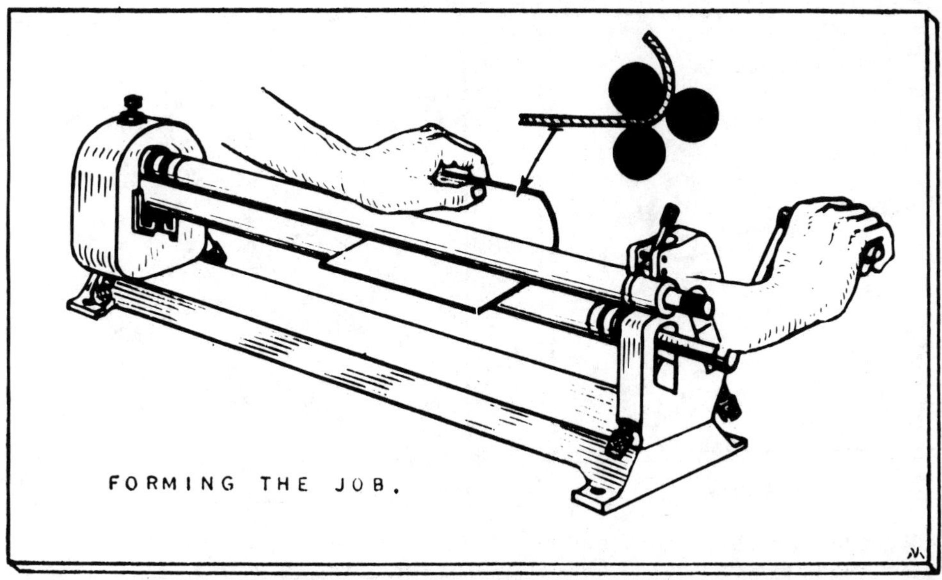

Figure 93.

loaded the immediate result will be deflection in the center of the rolls, resulting in cylinders bulged in the center.

When forming small diameter cylinders up to the full rated capacity, it will be necessary to pass the metal through the rolls several times. After the rear roll is properly adjusted, the first pass forms a semi-cylinder. The rear roll is then raised somewhat higher and the metal passed through again. The rear roll is then raised to form the complete cylinder. A little practice will enable the operator to determine just how high the rear roll can be raised for the first pass and have the rear roll bend up the metal upward. Three inch and larger diameter forming rolls have longitudinal grooves in the rear forming roll to prevent slippage of the edge of the sheet against the rear roll and to assist in bending the metal upward. On these forming machines, the rear roll is also driven, to assist in pulling the metal through the rolls.

On heavy gauges of metal it is common practice to reverse the metal after the first pass through the rolls when forming small diameter cylinders—to feed the edge of the curved sheet that passed through the rolls last in the first pass through the gripping rolls first in the second pass. This will reduce to a minimum the flat spot on the edge of the sheet after the initial pass, resulting from the space between the center of the gripping rolls and the forming side of the rear forming roll.

To reduce the number of rear roll adjustments in forming small diameter cylinders when working light-gauge metal, it is common practice to insert the edge of the sheet between the two feed or gripping rolls from the front of machine, pinching the metal between the two gripping rolls and bending the sheet slightly upward around the top gripping roll, then continuing to pass the sheet through the machine by hand crank or power operation (Fig. 93). This will reduce the flat spot on the initial edge of the sheet to a minimum and will enable the operator to form a cylinder of the desired diameter with fewer adjustments of the rear forming roll, or in one pass through the rolls.

Modern forming rolls of the type shown in Fig. 88, are of the *slip roll* type. On these machines the right hand housing is provided with a hinged journal cap and locking lifting latch, commonly called open-end formers (Fig. 88).

On these machines, after the cylinder is formed around the top front gripping roll, the latch is lifted, then the lever on the right end of the base of the machine is pulled down, lifting the top roll so that the work can be slipped off the end of the top roll without distorting the formed cylinder. The roll-raising lever is then pulled up and the top roll drops back into its bearing. The hinged journal cap is then dropped back in position, the latch automatically locks, and the former is ready for the next forming operation. The roll-raising lever should never be forced down when the journal cap and latch are in a locked position because this may distort the roll-raising mechanism, causing damage to the machine.

Forming machines are provided with grooves of

Figure 94.

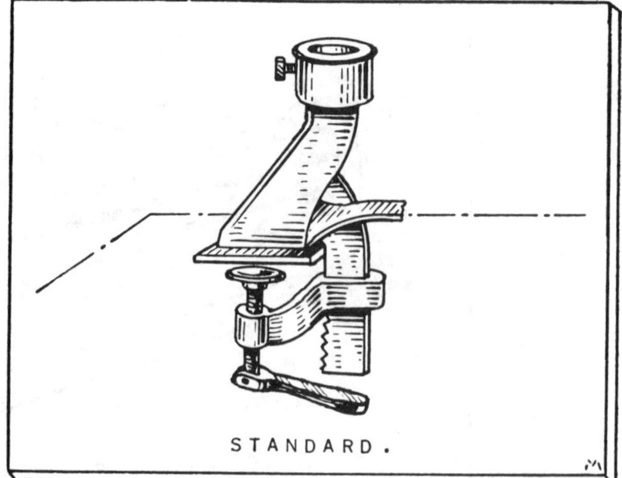

Figure 95.

varying sizes in the right end of the lower and rear rolls to allow for forming cylinders on which the metal has a wired edge (Fig. 94). The previously wired metal is inserted while the sheet is in the flat.

Note that when rolling wired material heavier than 20 gauge, the rear roll of the forming machine must be set at a distance that is slightly greater at the wired end than at the opposite end (Fig. 94). When rolling wired material lighter than 20 gauge, the distance between the rear roll and both the upper and lower rolls must be greater at the wired end than at the opposite end.

MAINTENANCE. Lubricate forming machines with oil specified by the manufacturer. To prevent scratches, dents, or damage, the highly polished special purpose rolls that are available for forming monel metal, aluminum, stainless steel, and similar metals must be kept covered or otherwise protected when not in use.

Bench Machines

Bench machines of various types, each of which is designed for a specific purpose, are used extensively in the sheet metal shop. These machines consist mainly of a rigid cast iron frame fitted with shafts, gears, and rolls or faces of various sizes and shapes which are operated by a hand crank. Bench machines are generally classified as turning, wiring, burring, and setting-down machines. The design of the rolls or faces of each of these machines varies in shape and size in accordance with the type of machine and specific type of work it performs. Individual bench machines are usually fastened to the work bench on individual machine standards of the type shown in Fig. 95. Revolving machine standards

Figure 96. Revolving standard for bench tools.

of the type shown in Fig. 96 are used where it is necessary to perform a series of consecutive operations to complete a job. On revolving machine standards, the problem of setting up individual machines and taking them down is eliminated, time is saved, and the danger of damage to bench tools due to mishandling and neglect is obviated. Standards of this type occupy less than 28 in. of floor space and are being used extensively in most modern shops.

TURNING MACHINES. As its name implies, the turning machine shown in Fig. 98 is generally used to turn or form rounded edges into which wires are inserted. The shape of the edges formed is shown in Fig. 98. After the wire is inserted, these rounded edges are closed by a wiring machine (Fig. 103). All the parts of a standard turning machine are shown in Fig. 97. The rolls shown in detail A, Fig. 97 can be removed for adjustment, alignment and replacement. The machine shown in Fig. 97 is operated by means of an operating handle and has a capacity of a 20 gauge mild steel. For turning heavier-gauge material, power driven turning machines are generally used (Fig. 99). The operation is identical for both machines.

Various sizes of rolls are available, and the size nearest to the size of wire to be inserted should be used. Adjust the upper roll to groove in the lower roll as shown in Fig. 100, so that when the upper roll is depressed, it is centralized in the groove of the lower roll as shown in detail A, Fig. 101. This adjustment is secured by a knurled lock-nut on the rear end of the upper arbor. The gauge should then be adjusted for the required amount of metal that is to be turned over to cover the wire when it is closed down by the wiring machine (Fig. 103).

Place the edge of the work between the rolls with the edge of the job firmly against the gauge (Fig. 102). Bring the upper roll down by turning down the crank screw, so that when work is revolved the upper roll will make a slight crease or depression on the first pass. On the second pass, turn down on the crank screw and bear down on the work so that at the end of the second pass the edge has begun to turn over slightly. To prevent buckling, it is advis-

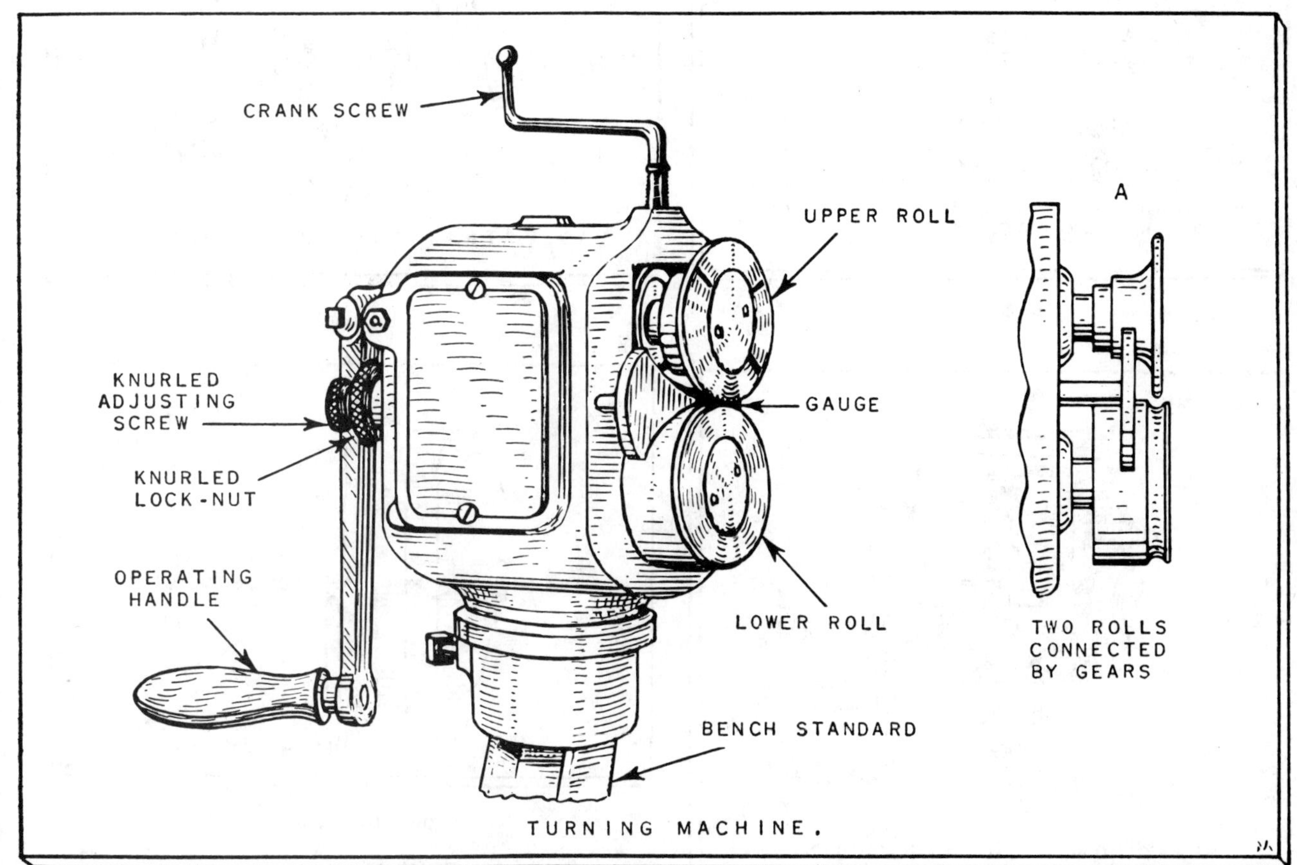

Figure 97.

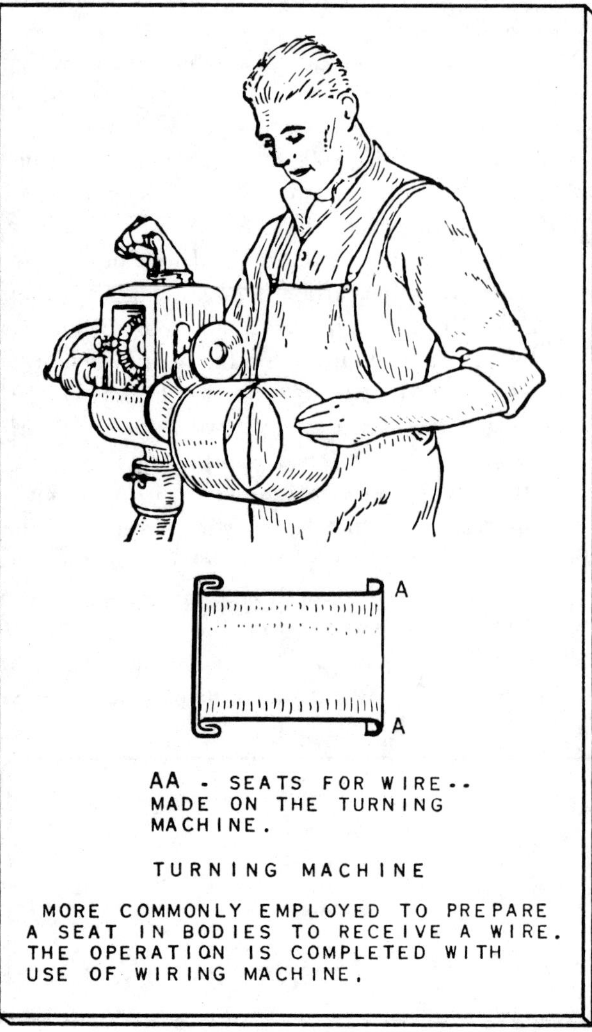

A
A
AA - SEATS FOR WIRE--
MADE ON THE TURNING
MACHINE.
TURNING MACHINE
MORE COMMONLY EMPLOYED TO PREPARE
A SEAT IN BODIES TO RECEIVE A WIRE.
THE OPERATION IS COMPLETED WITH
USE OF WIRING MACHINE.

Figure 98.

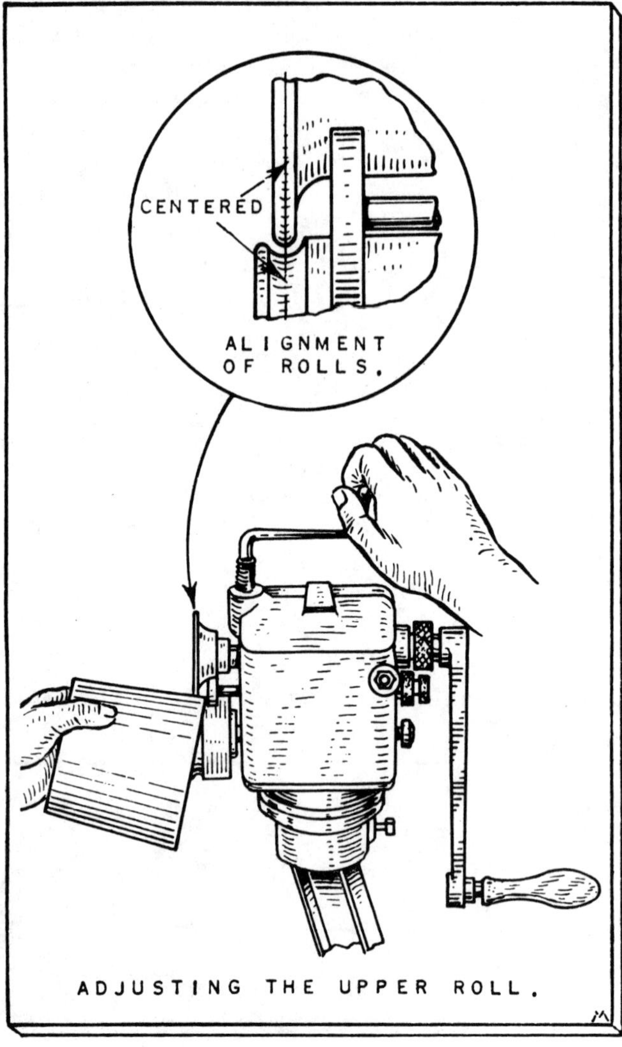

Figure 100.

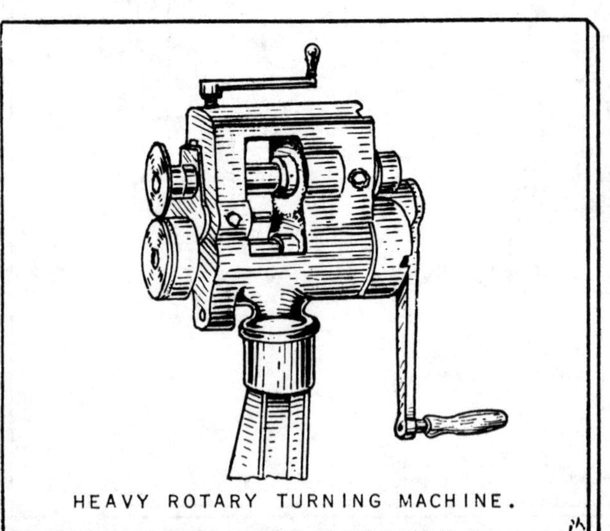

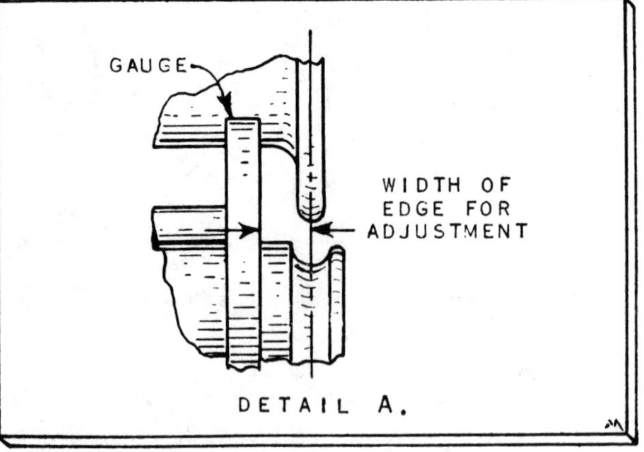

Figure 101 (*above*).

Figure 99 (*left*).

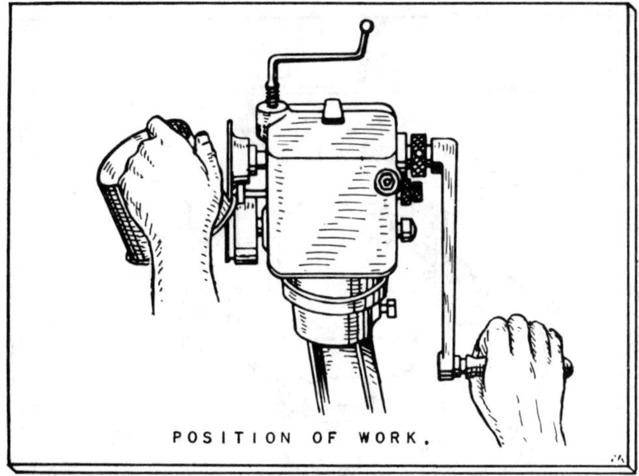

Figure 102.

able not to attempt to form a completed edge in one or two passes. Usually, a successful edge turning operation requires at least three or four complete passes.

WIRING MACHINES. The wiring machine shown in Fig. 103 is used in conjunction with the turning machine previously described (Fig. 98) to close the turned edge over the wire. All parts of a wiring machine are shown in Fig. 104. Before the wire is inserted onto the job, it must be formed into a circle by running the straight wire through the groove in the rolls of the forming machine. The formed wire

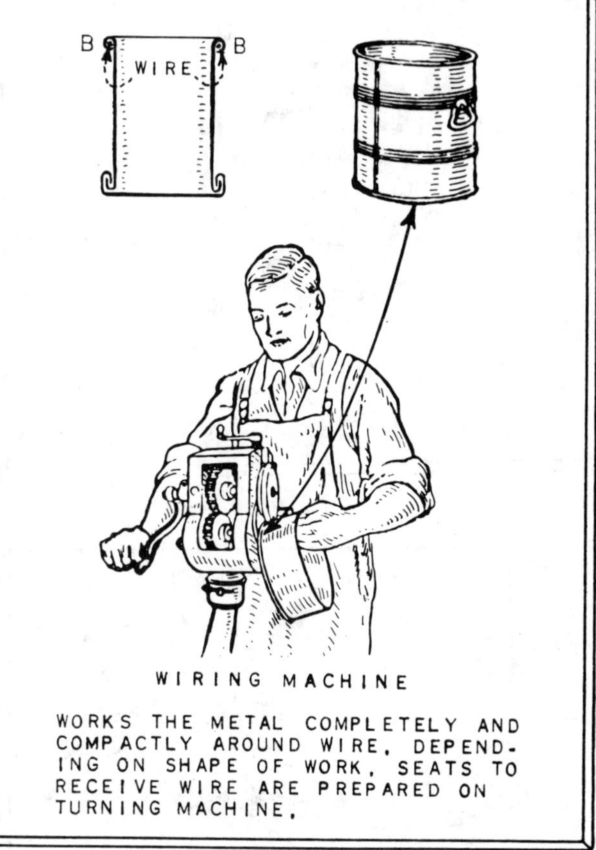

B
WIRE
B
WIRING MACHINE
WORKS THE METAL COMPLETELY AND COMPACTLY AROUND WIRE. DEPENDING ON SHAPE OF WORK, SEATS TO RECEIVE WIRE ARE PREPARED ON TURNING MACHINE.

Figure 103.

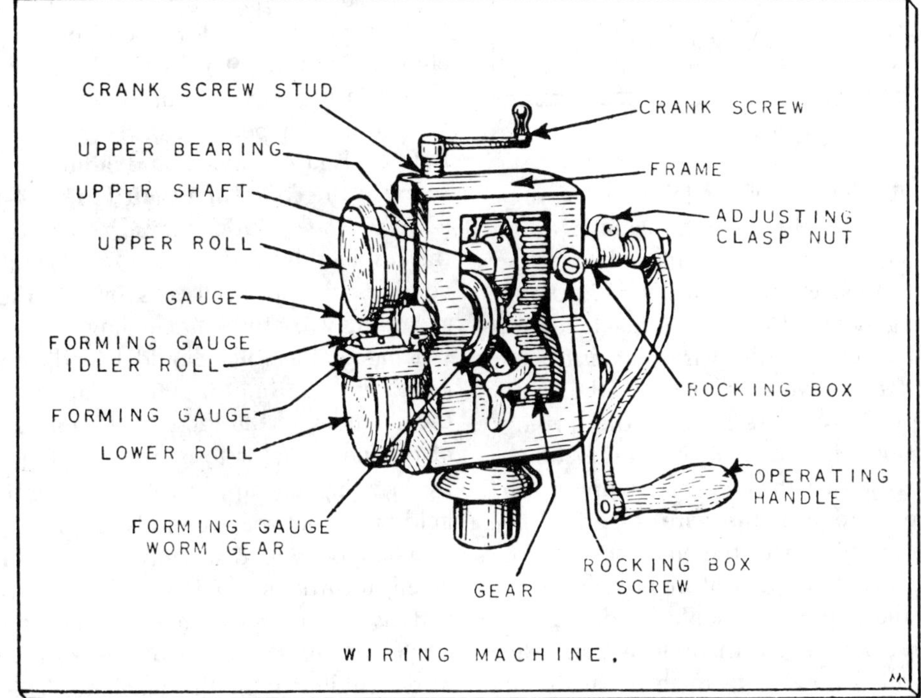

Figure 104.

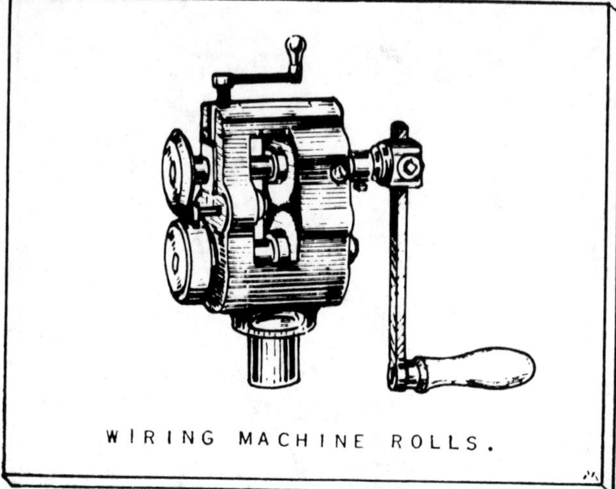

Figure 105.

WIRE RETAINED TEMPORARILY
IN POSITION BY CLOSING THE
GROOVE IN SPOTS WITH MALLET.

Figure 106.

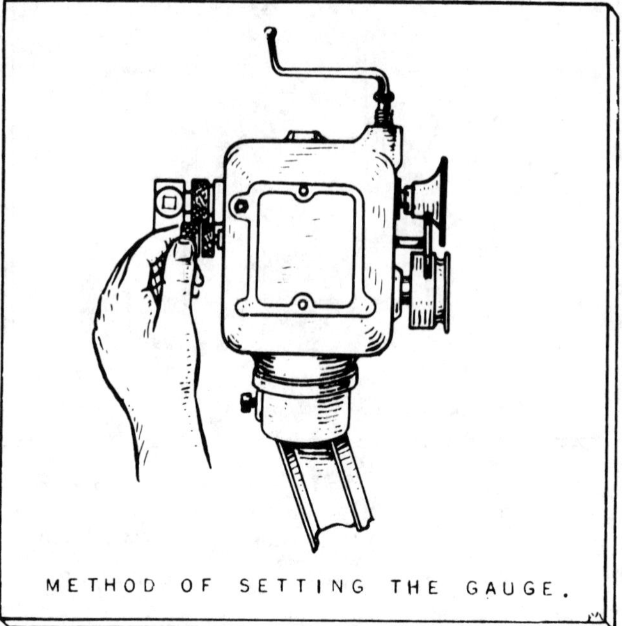

METHOD OF SETTING THE GAUGE.

Figure 107.

is then slipped into the seat of the job that has previously been formed by the turning machine (Fig. 98). The wire is held temporarily in place by closing the metal in several places with a mallet (Fig. 106). Adjust the forming gauge of the wiring machine and place the job, together with the wire that has been temporarily inserted, between the rolls in the same manner as that previously described for the turning machine. The gauge in the rear of the machine should be adjusted so that the edge of the upper roll will clear the outer edge of the wire. Depress the upper roll of the machine with the crank screw. For the first pass, depress the upper roll slightly; for each succeeding pass the upper roll should be depressed a little more, and on the fourth or fifth pass, the work should be tilted upward to force the material completely in and around the wire (Fig. 107).

Burring Machines. Burring machines of the type shown in Fig. 108 are employed to form narrow edges on discs, covers, pails, boilers, cans, and similar jobs, and for preparing circular edges of bottoms and bodies of jobs for double seaming and set-in bottoms.

The construction of a burring machine is similar to that previously described for other bench machines. The type of rolls usually used for burring is shown in Fig. 108. The upper roll is disc shaped and the lower is shaped with a recess near the outer end. Both rolls are aligned and adjusted by a knurled screw at the end of the shaft (Fig. 108).

To set the width of the burr to be turned, measure the distance from the face of the gauge to the inner edge of the upper roll, as shown in Fig. 109, and set accordingly. Before proceeding with the work, the spacing of the rolls should be adjusted so that the edge of the upper roll is at a distance from the shoulder of the lower roll equal to the thickness of the metal that is to be burred (Fig. 110). Proceed by bringing the upper roll down until the metal is held firmly between the rolls (Fig. 111).

When burring discs, take a small piece of light metal, form it into a U-shape as shown in Fig. 112, and use it in the crotch between the thumb and forefinger for the edge of the disc to rub against when guiding it in the machine. This will prevent cutting or injuring the operator's hand. Use the two

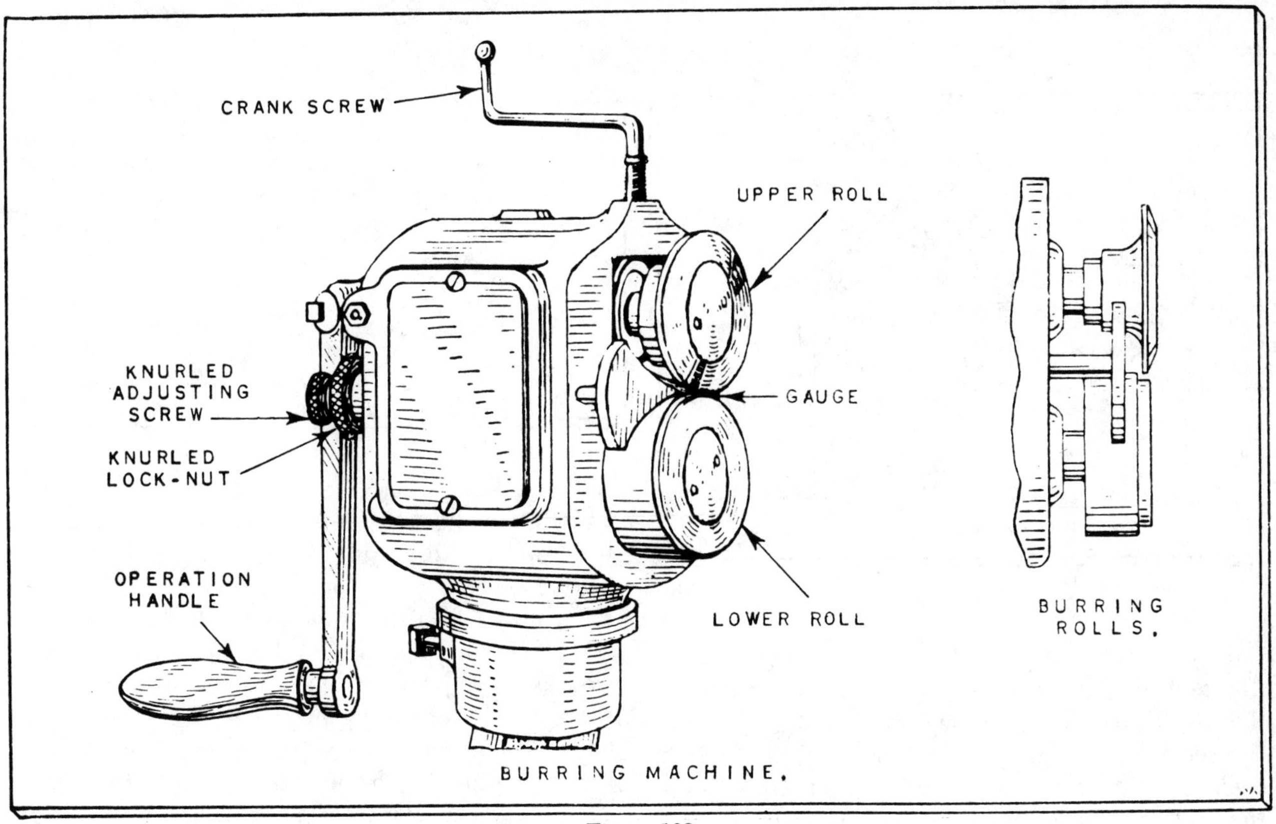

CRANK SCREW
UPPER ROLL
KNURLED ADJUSTING SCREW
GAUGE
KNURLED LOCK-NUT
OPERATION HANDLE
LOWER ROLL
BURRING ROLLS.
BURRING MACHINE.

Figure 108.

GAUGE
THICKNESS OF METAL
SPACING ROLLS.

Figure 109.

FIRST PASS OF BURRING OPERATION.

Figure 111.

GAUGE
WIDTH OF EDGE
GAUGE SETTING.

Figure 110.

2"
HAND GUARD

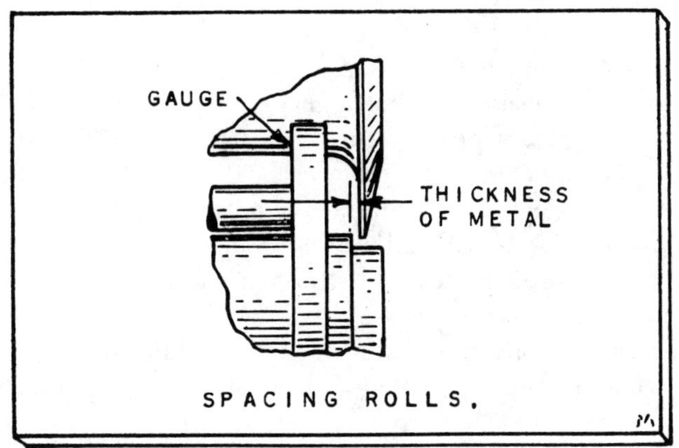

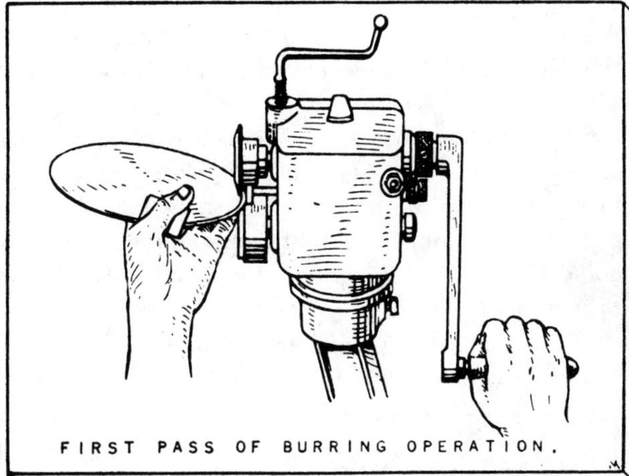

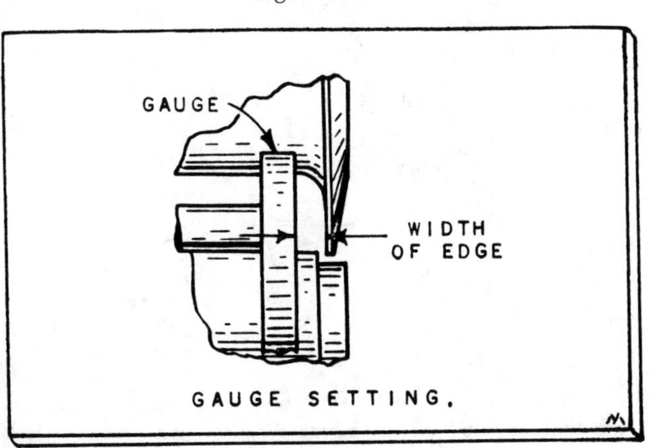

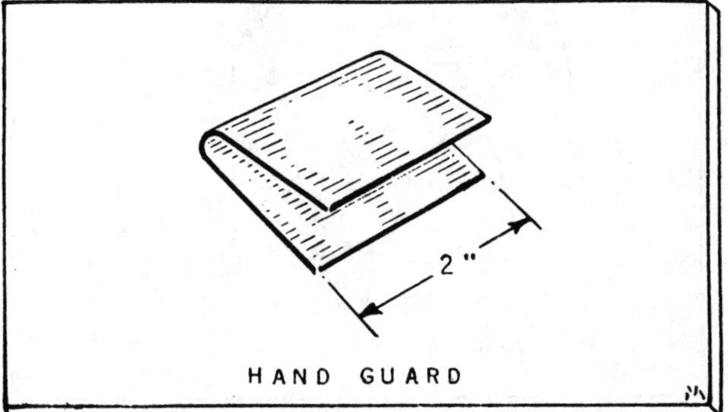

Figure 112.

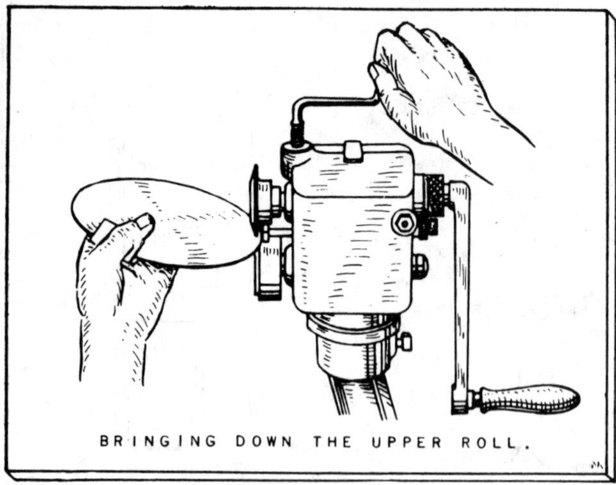

Figure 113.

forefingers for supporting the disc as shown in Fig. 113, and turn the operating handle rapidly, allowing the disc to pass freely through the hand guard. For the second pass, raise the material slightly, and at each succeeding pass continue to raise the disc until the edge has been burred to the required position or angle (Fig. 114). The burring of cylinders is similar to that described for discs, with the exception that the material is held in the position shown in Fig. 116.

SETTING-DOWN MACHINES. The setting-down machine shown in Fig. 117 is used to close the seams or locks made by the burring or turning machine preparatory to double seaming operations. This machine is used principally for the setting-down operations of can or tank bottoms.

The setting-down machine shown in Fig. 117 is available in two sizes: for seams up to $\frac{3}{8}$ in. on No.

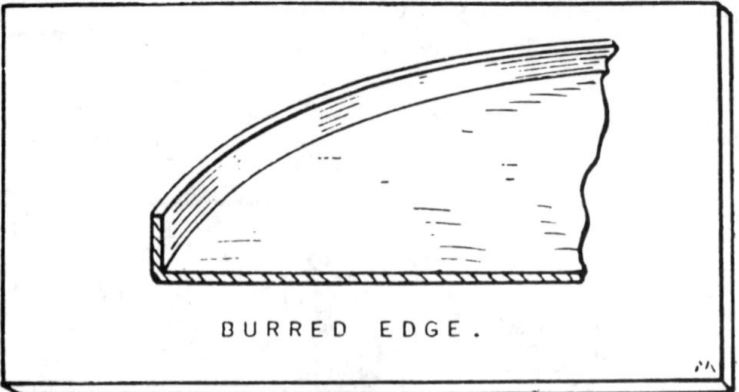

Figure 115.

24 gauge or lighter weight metal, and for seams up to $\frac{1}{2}$ in. on No. 18 gauge metal or lighter. Figure 115 shows the edges of the work as they appear after having been put through the burring machine. Note that the edges of the bottom must be burred over as far as possible, but not so far that the burred sides cannot be sprung in on the setting-down machine. If the set down seam has been bent toward the side walls of the job during the setting-down operation, as shown in Fig. 117, it will facilitate the final double seaming operation that is always necessary on jobs of this type.

Note that, in the machine shown in Fig. 117, the inclined position of both the upper and the lower rows or faces permits the work to be held bottom up or down, and the seam can easily be started inward during the setting-down operation. This machine is fitted with adjustable idler roll gauges that serve to guide the work through the setting-down roll. The roller gauges are set to allow the work to enter the rolls only to the width of the burr edge.

To operate the machine, bring the lower face or

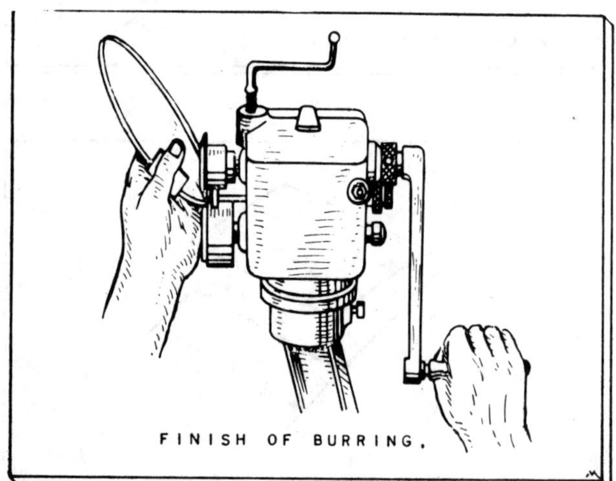

Figure 114.

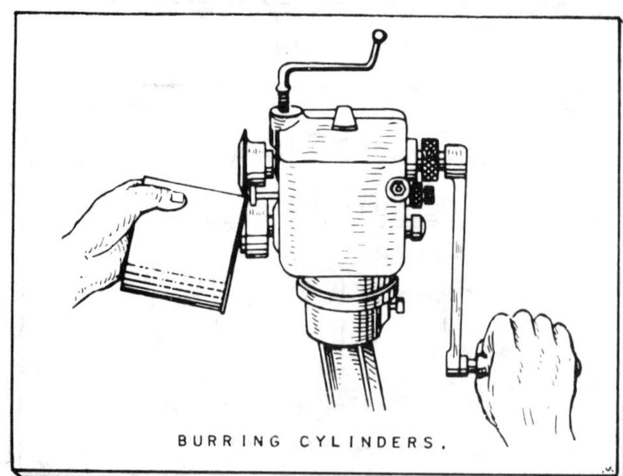

Figure 116.

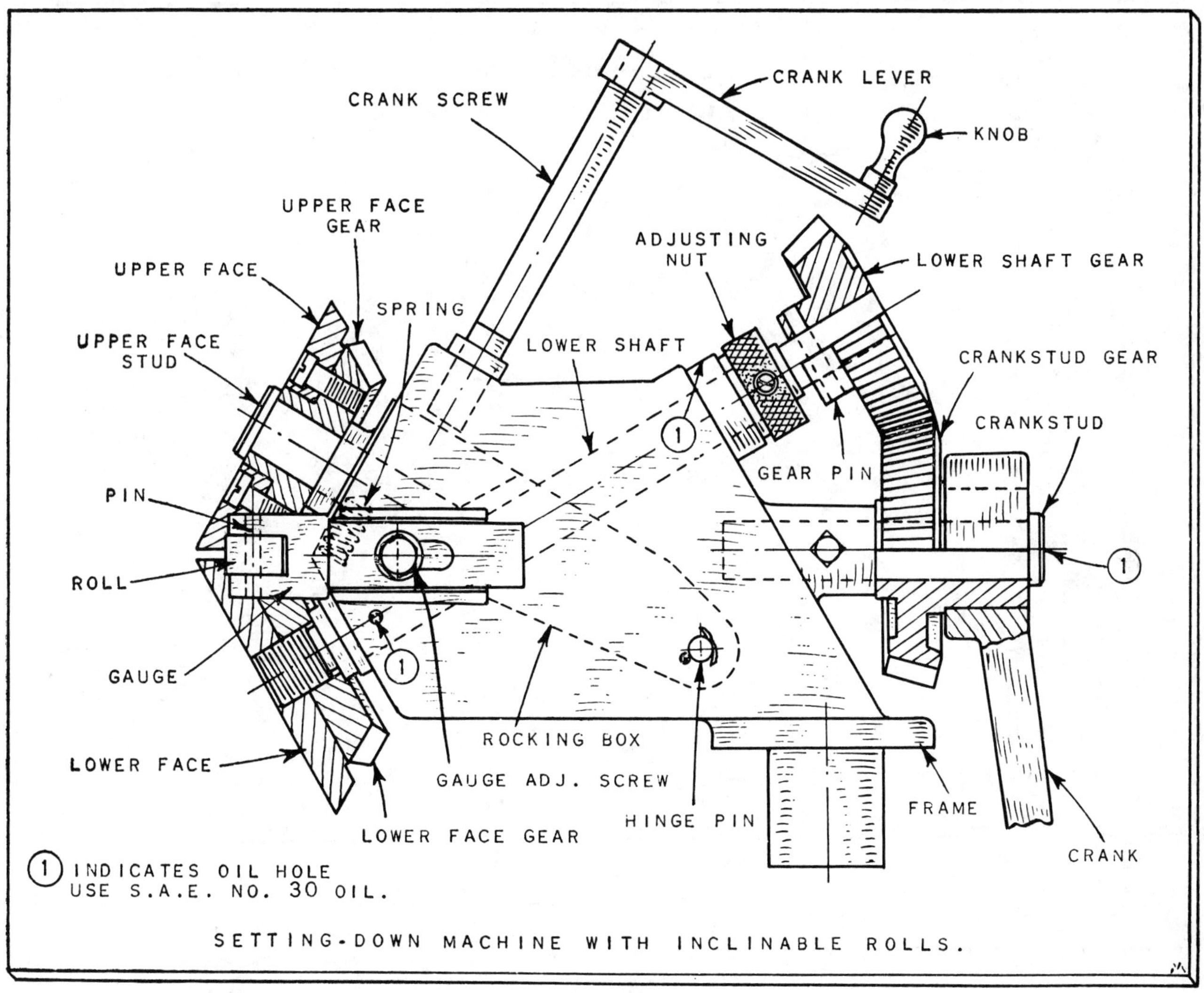

Figure 117.

lower setting-down roll in alignment with the upper face by loosening the setscrew in the adjusting nut, and rotate adjusting nut in or out for required tightening or loosening. When adjusting the nut in the desired position relative to the lower face, lock the setscrew securely and proceed to operate the machine in the usual manner.

Double Seaming Machines. The double seaming machine shown in Fig. 118 is known in the trade as "Moore's Patent Double Seamer." This machine is used for double seaming edges that have been prepared by the setting-down machine previously described. After the edges have been prepared and set down, the work is placed over the horn against the lower face. The upper shaft and face are moved outward laterally by a hand wheel on the side of the frame. The crank screw brings the angular surface of the upper face against the upright edge. At this time, the small wheel backs up the metal, taking a position as shown in Fig. 118. By rotating the crank handle, the edge is deflected and is ready for flattening. A turn of the hand wheel shifts the upper face so the flat portion of the upper roll will squeeze down the deflected edge as the crank screw is lowered (Fig. 118), thus completing the double seam.

The lower gear is wide, so that it remains in mesh with the upper gear when the shaft is in either position. The frame is one piece, enclosed, protecting all working parts. The machine is operated by the operating crank handle after the work is inserted.

Crimping and Beading Machines. A great deal of descriptive detail is not necessary in connection with the crimping and beading machine. Crimping and beading machines are intended to facilitate the

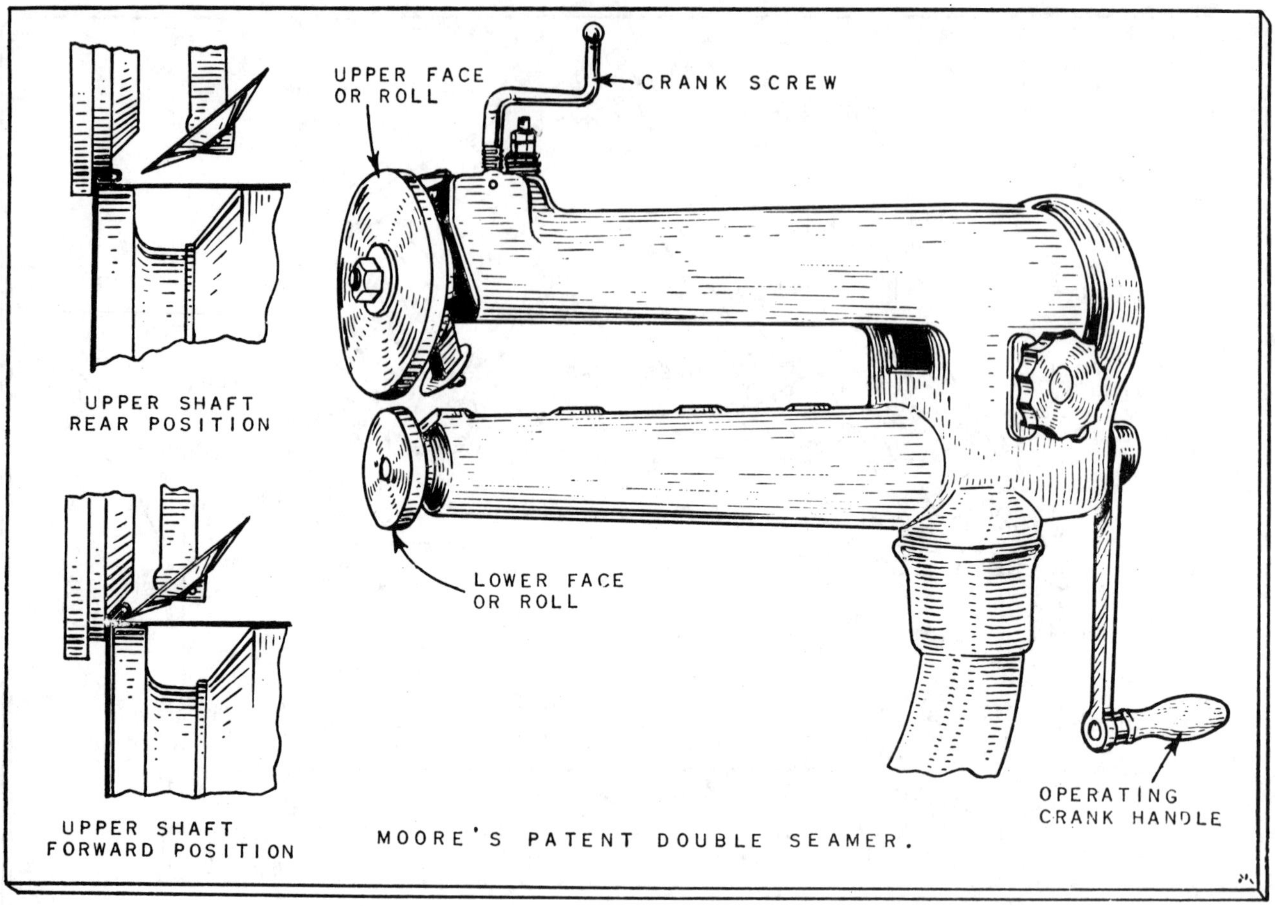

UPPER FACE
OR ROLL
CRANK SCREW
UPPER SHAFT
REAR POSITION
LOWER FACE
OR ROLL
OPERATING
CRANK HANDLE
UPPER SHAFT
FORWARD POSITION
MOORE'S PATENT DOUBLE SEAMER.

Figure 118.

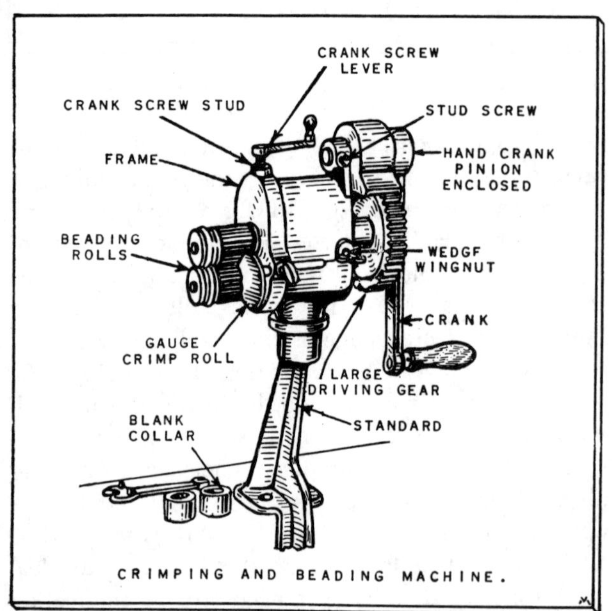

CRANK SCREW
LEVER
CRANK SCREW STUD
STUD SCREW
FRAME
HAND CRANK
PINION
ENCLOSED
BEADING
ROLLS
WEDGF
WINGNUT
CRANK
GAUGE
CRIMP ROLL
LARGE
DRIVING GEAR
BLANK
COLLAR
STANDARD
CRIMPING AND BEADING MACHINE.

Figure 119.

CRIMP AND BEAD MADE WITH CRIMPING AND BEADING MACHINE.

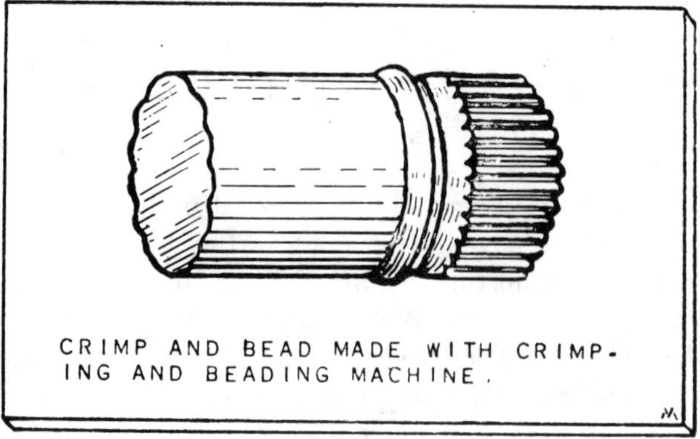

Figure 120.

making and putting together of sheet iron pipes of different diameters, by contracting the edge of the pipe so that one joint of pipe will enter another (Fig. 119). In putting together the pipe, the ogee bead next to the crimp prevents the joints slipping beyond the impression made with the beading rolls.

The working parts of a crimping and beading machine are easy to operate (Fig. 119). The joint of pipe to be crimped is laid over the lower rolls, with one edge of the pipe pressed against the gauge. By means of a crank screw, a depression of the upper crimping and beading rolls is made, and by turning the hand crank with the right hand and guiding the work with the left hand, the pipe in the machine revolves around the rolls, making an impression around the edge of the pipe called a crimp and bead (Fig. 120).

The wedge between the rear bearings in the frame provides an adjustment for regulating the relative depth of crimp and bead. This wedge is adjusted by wingnuts in the front and back of the frame. By turning these wingnuts, the upper shaft can be tipped as desired, making a deep crimp and shallow bead, or shallow crimp and deep bead. Blank collars are included in the regular equipment furnished with the crimping and beading machine, and may be substituted in place of beading, where crimping alone is desired.

Chapter 5

Working with Metal

When you start working with metal there are several things you always have to think about before you can actually begin the work. Some of these are: materials, layout procedures, forming processes, and tools needed. In other words, you have to know what you have to work with, how you are going to plan the job, how you are going to do it once it has been planned, and just what tools are going to be required to do the job.

Edges and Seams

Seaming or joining is an important process in the fabrication of sheet metal. The type of seam and method of joining are dependent on the strain and stress the fabricated article must withstand, and the tools or equipment available. The various machine tools used and procedures employed for the forming of desired bends or seams have been described in other chapters. This chapter describes the procedures for the fabrication of seams generally used in the sheet metal shop where machine equipment is not available.

Single Edges. Single edges or hems of the type shown in Fig. 1 are used in hemming the edges of sheet metal and in constructing single seams. They are formed either on a wood block or on a hatchet stake (See Chap. 3). The desired width is marked on the metal. The material is then set on the block or stake and formed with a ball peen hammer or mallet (Fig. 2). The bar folder (Chap. 4) is used where machine equipment is available.

Folded Seams. Folded seams are produced by turning single edges on the two pieces of sheet metal that are to be joined, hooking the edges together as shown in Fig. 3, and hammering them flat with a

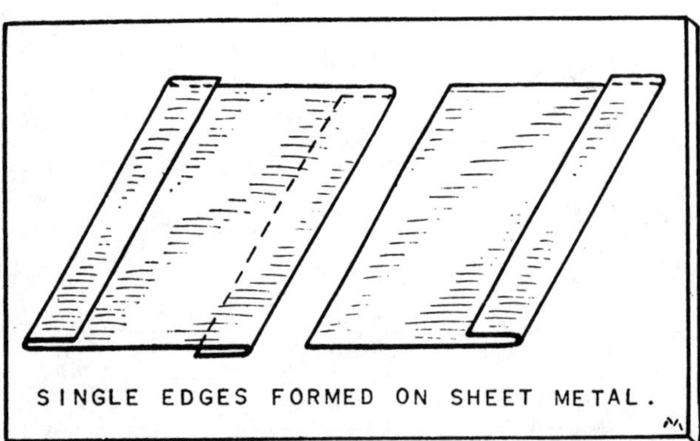

Figure 1.

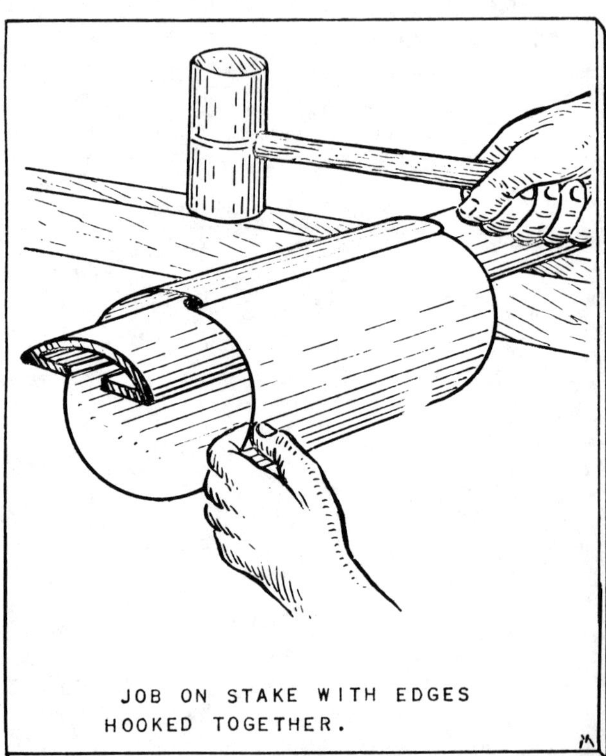

Figure 2.

Figure 3.

wooden mallet. Folded seams are generally used when laying flat seam metal roofing.

LAP SEAMS. The simple lap seam shown in Fig. 4 is generally used in the construction of square pipes, small diameter cylinders, and similar fabrications. When used on rectangular forms, the edges must be formed in the same manner as described for single edges (A, Fig. 4). Lap seams are usually soldered or riveted. (Riveting and soldering procedures are given in Chaps. 6 and 7).

DOUBLE EDGES. The double edge, double lock, or double hemmed edge, as it is variously called, is shown in Fig. 5. It is generally used to reinforce the strength of sheet metal forms. It is produced in the same manner as the single edge described in the previous paragraph, with the exception that, after

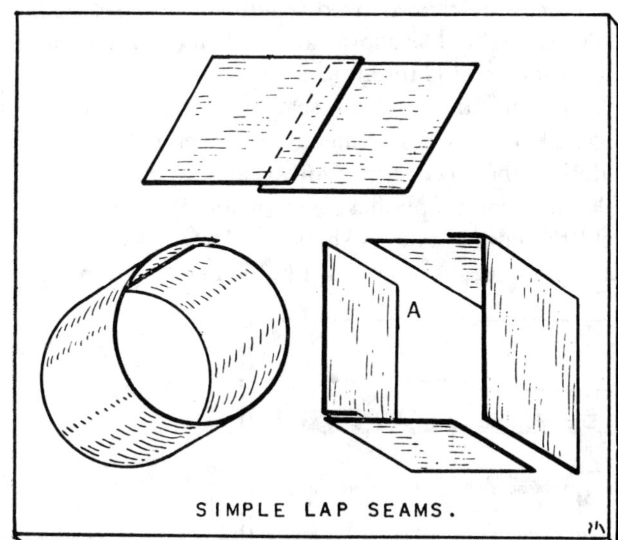

Figure 4.

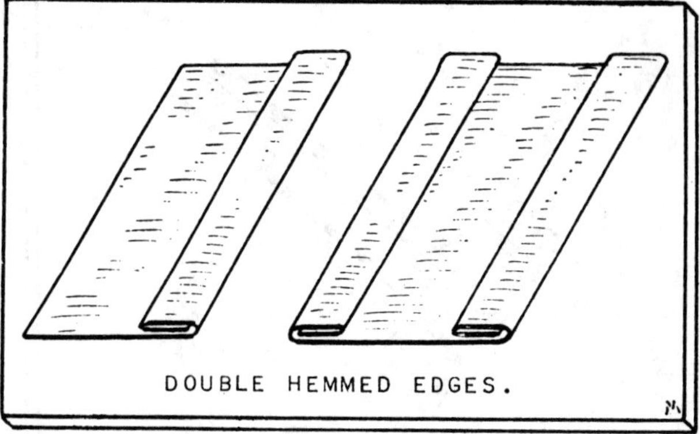

Figure 5.

the single edge has been formed, the work is turned over and the second bend is made.

GROOVED SEAMS. Grooved seams or locks of the type shown in Fig. 6 are usually used in joining or splicing flat pieces of sheet metal, making vertical side seams in flaring or cylindrically-shaped articles, and making longitudinal seams in either square or round sheet metal piping. They are produced by hooking and offsetting two folded edges (Fig. 3). As a general rule, where machines are available the bar folder (Chap. 4) is used for small articles, and the combination or cornice brake (Chap. 4) for larger work. Where machines are not available, grooved seams are fabricated with a hand groover (Fig. 7), a grooving rail (Fig. 7), or a mandrel stake (Fig. 8).

Hand groovers are used to offset outside grooved seams and are available in groove widths of various sizes, ranging from $\frac{3}{32}$ to $\frac{19}{32}$ in. Always use a hand groover approximately $\frac{1}{16}$ in. wider than the width of the finished lock or seam.

Grooving rails are used to offset inside grooved

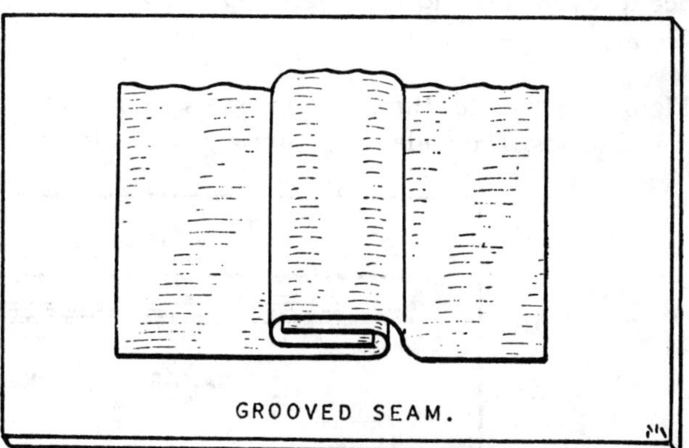

Figure 6.

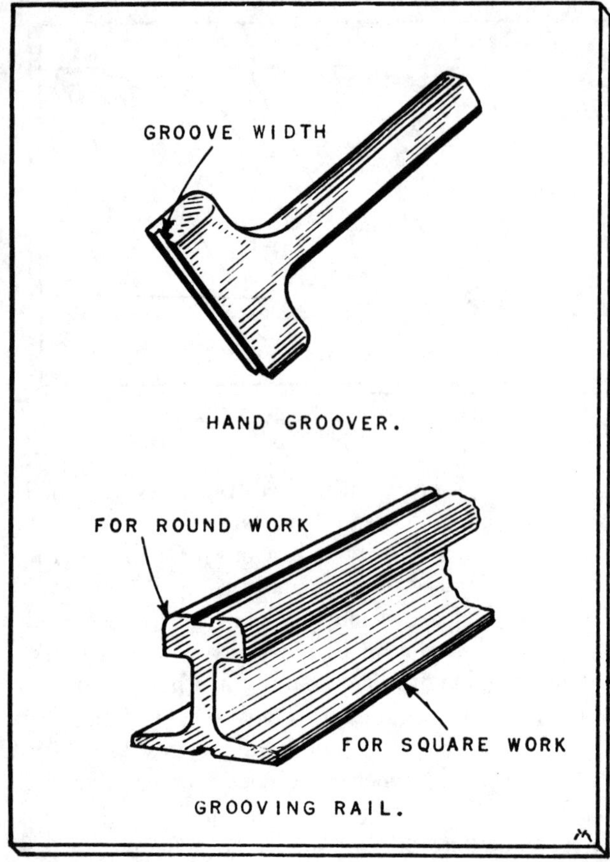

Figure 7.

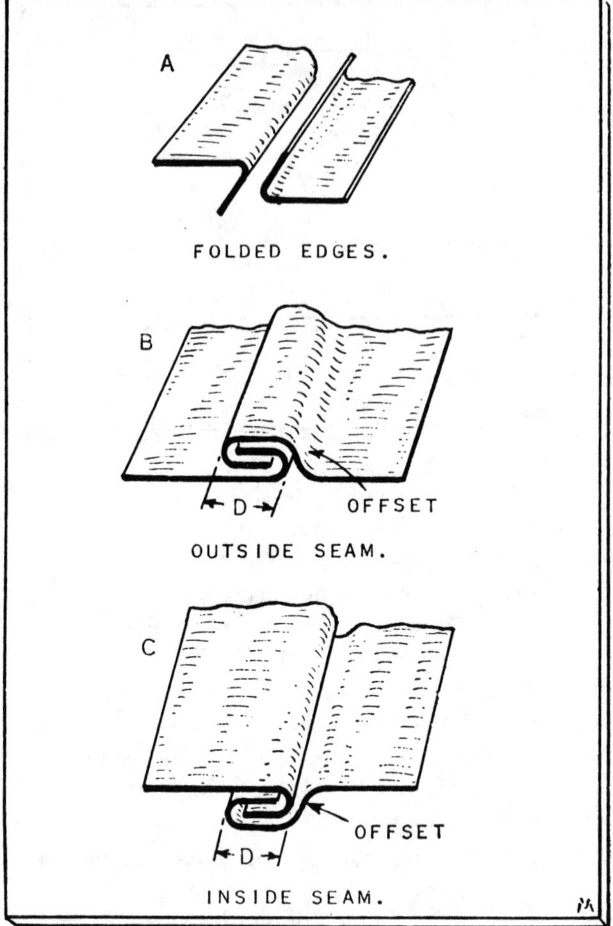

Figure 9.

seams. They are pieces of railroad rail with a formed groove on top that is used for round work and a similar groove milled in the bottom that is used for flat or square work. Grooving rails are available in a range of sizes corresponding to those given for hand groovers.

Mandrel stakes are used in combination with hand groovers to finish grooved seams on cylindrical work.

Procedures for Making and Finishing Grooved Seams

Figure 9 illustrates the necessary steps in making grooved seams. The folded edges for a grooved seam in the two pieces of sheet metal must be uniform in width and folded or bent as shown at A, Fig. 9. The two pieces are then hooked together and offset with the grooving tool as shown at B for an outside seam, and as shown at C for an inside seam.

When making grooved seams, be sure that the edges of both pieces of metal have been cut straight and that the necessary allowance described in the following paragraph has been made for the seam. Fold the edges scant as shown at A, Fig. 4 and pull the folded edges together tightly before grooving.

Figure 8.

It is important to use a hand groover or grooving rail that is slightly larger than the size of the lock, and to use a wooden mallet to fasten the seam after it is grooved.

REQUIRED ALLOWANCES FOR GROOVED SEAMS. When laying out patterns for grooved seams, allowances must be made for the metal used in forming these seams. When using 24 gauge or lighter material it is necessary to add three times the width (Fig. 9) of the grooving lock to the pattern or layout. Add one-half of this allowance to each side of the lock. When using 22 or 20 gauge material it is necessary to add three times the width (Fig. 9) of the grooving lock plus four times the thickness of the metal to the pattern or layout. Grooved seams are rarely used on material exceeding 20 gauge.

MAKING AND FINISHING OUTSIDE GROOVED SEAMS (B, Fig. 9). To make and finish outside grooved seams, proceed as follows:

Mark the width of the edges to be folded on each of the two pieces to be joined and fold them to the required width, then form the job. If the work is cylindrical, place it on a mandrel stake of the required curvature, if it is flat, place it on a flat stake or plate. Proceed to hook the edges together as shown in Fig. 2 and slightly flatten the seam with a mallet. Select a hand groover of the correct size (1/16 in. or slightly larger than the width of the seam). Holding the groover in the left hand, place it over one end of the seam and strike it with a hammer as shown in Fig. 10. Repeat this operation at the other end of the work. Start at the first point and proceed to groove by moving and striking the hand groover along the entire length of the seam. The seam is finished by flattening it down with a mallet.

MAKING AND FINISHING INSIDE GROOVED SEAMS (C, Fig. 9). Mark the edges, fold and form the job as previously outlined, and proceed as follows:

Select a grooving rail of the required size and make sure that the width of the groove in the selected rail is approximately 1/16 in. larger than the width of the seam. Secure the rail to the bench, hook the edges of the work together and place it on the rail. If the work is rectangular in shape, the work is placed on the bottom part of the rail; if cylindrical, the work is placed on the top or curved surface of the rail and the seam is held in the groove with the left hand. Using the other hand, strike an end of the seam with a mallet (Fig. 2). Repeat at the other end of the seam. Proceed to groove the entire length of the seam by striking the work with the mallet evenly along the seam. Strike it hard enough to force the folded metal into the groove. Remove the work from the groove, place it on the rail with the grooved

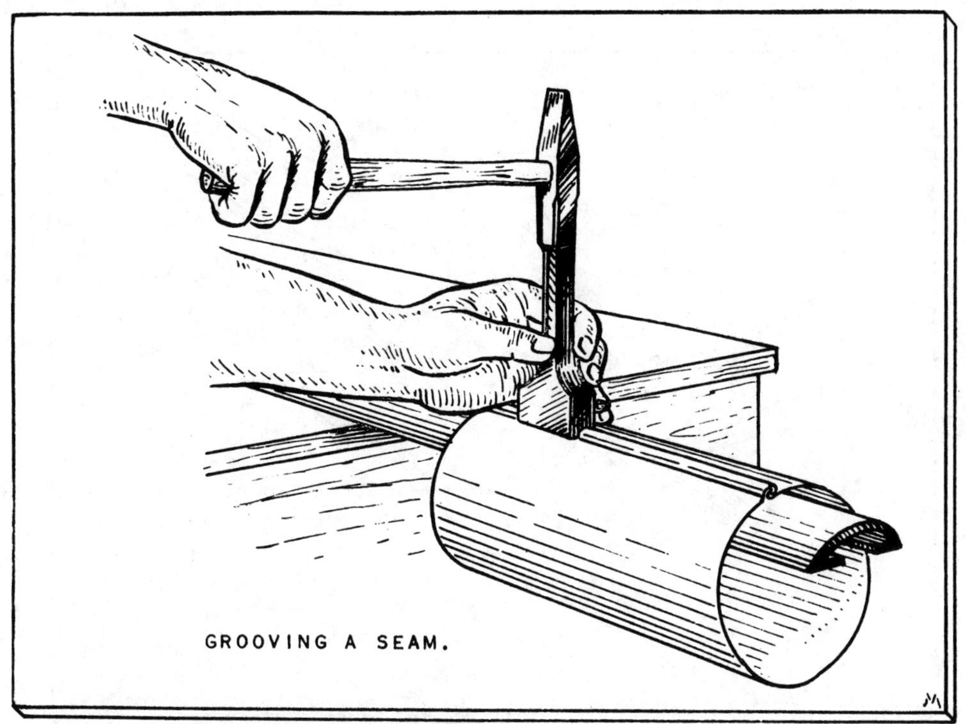

Figure 10.

seam in the position shown in Fig. 11, and finish or close the seam with the mallet as shown in Fig. 12.

PLAIN, ROUND, DOVETAIL SEAMS. Dovetail seams are an easy and convenient method for joining collars and similar sheet metal fittings to other parts without soldering or riveting.

The plain, round, dovetail seams shown in Fig. 13 are made by slitting the collar, shown at A, with the

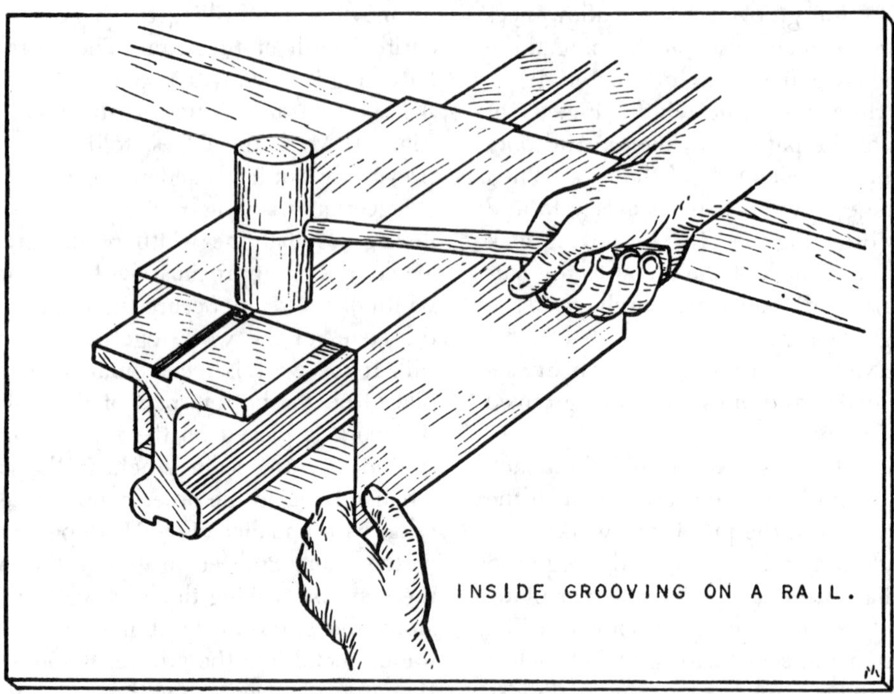

INSIDE GROOVING ON A RAIL.

Figure 11.

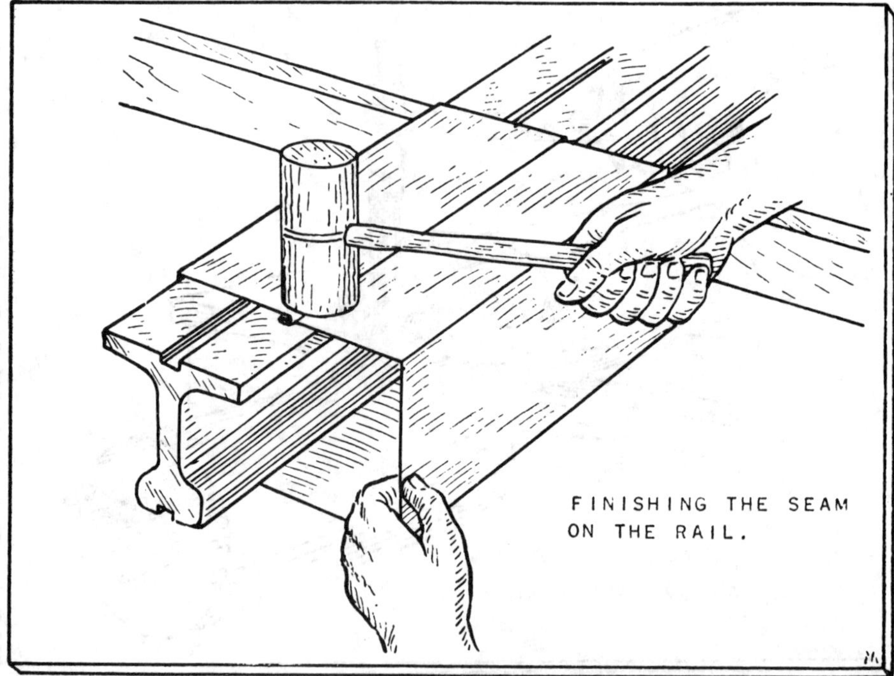

FINISHING THE SEAM
ON THE RAIL.

Figure 12.

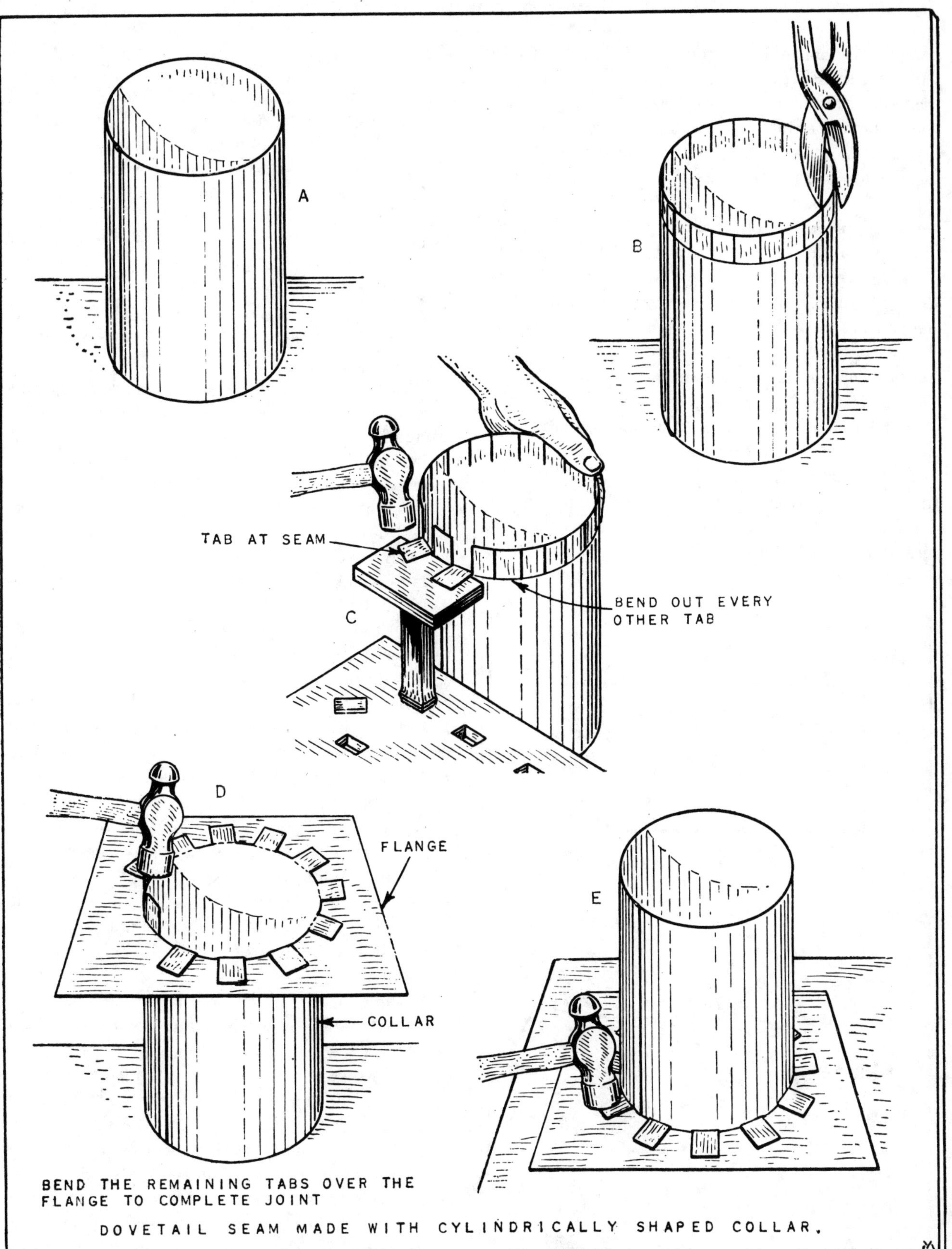
A
B
TAB AT SEAM
BEND OUT EVERY
OTHER TAB
C
D
FLANGE
COLLAR
E
BEND THE REMAINING TABS OVER THE
FLANGE TO COMPLETE JOINT
DOVETAIL SEAM MADE WITH CYLINDRICALLY SHAPED COLLAR.

Figure 13.

combination shears to the required width of the tabs (B), and then bending out alternate tabs with a ball peen hammer and a square stake, as shown at C. These bent out tabs act as stops for the flange or fitting. If a flange is to be fitted over the collar, cut an opening in the flange the size of the collar, using a pair of circular shears. (See Chap. 3.) To complete the seam, place the collar with the notched and bent-out tabs in the cut-out opening and bevel the remaining tabs over the flange as shown at D. Flatten the stops by placing the flange on a flat surface and hammering as shown at E, Fig. 13.

The width of a dovetail is usually ⅝ in. The spacing between the slits ranges from ½ to 1 in., depending on the size of the work.

Watertight dovetail seams must be soldered. For detailed soldering procedures see Chap. 6.

To facilitate the even marking of tab-widths on the collar, a marking gauge is used, which is made from a piece of scrap metal and cut out to the pattern shown at A, Fig. 14. The method of using this gauge is shown at B.

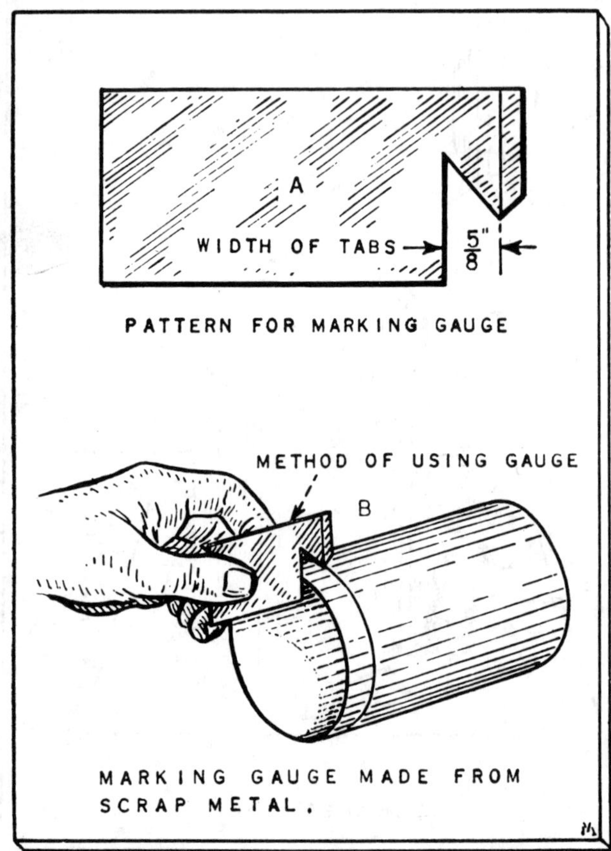

Figure 14.

Flanges

Flanges are bent edges made on the edges of cylindrically-shaped parts (Fig. 15). The are used to provide additional stiffening or to make connections to other sheet metal parts. Flanges of the type shown in Fig. 15 are usually made with the turning or burring machine described in Chap. 4. Where watertight flange connections are required, they must be soldered, using the soldering procedures outlined in Chap. 6.

Where turning or burring machines are not available, or where flanges on irregularly shaped jobs are required, they can be made by hand.

When flanges are turned on the outside of jobs, as shown in Fig. 16, the metal must of necessity be stretched. When turned on the inside of jobs, as shown in Fig. 17, the metal is of course shrunk.

In addition to the riveting hammer and mallet described in Chap. 3, both square and conductor stakes, described in Chap. 2, are used when flanging edges by hand.

Turning Outside Flanges. To form a flanged edge on the outside of a job, proceed as follows:

With the gauge shown in Fig. 14, mark the width of the required flange on the inside of the job (Fig. 18). Note that the flange should be made as small as possible. The reason for this is obvious, because flanging by hand requires the working or hammering of the metal. Excessive hammering will harden the metal and make it brittle. A large flange necessitates more hammering than a smaller one and will, in a great many cases, result in cracking of the metal.

Proceed by placing the square stake in the bench plate and holding the work with edge to be flanged in the position shown at Fig. 19. Strike the edge with the peen end of the hammer and revolve the work until the flange on the entire edge has been started.

As the flange forms and the metal stretches, lower the work gradually, continuing to hammer the flange with the peen end of the hammer until the required angle is formed (Fig. 19). After the flange has been formed to the required angle, it should be smoothed on a conductor stake by holding the flange on the stake and smoothing it with the flat face of the riveting hammer, as shown in Fig. 20.

Turning Inside Flanges. To turn inside flanges, proceed as follows: With the marking gauge, mark the required width of the flange on the outside of the work (Fig. 21). Place the work on a conductor

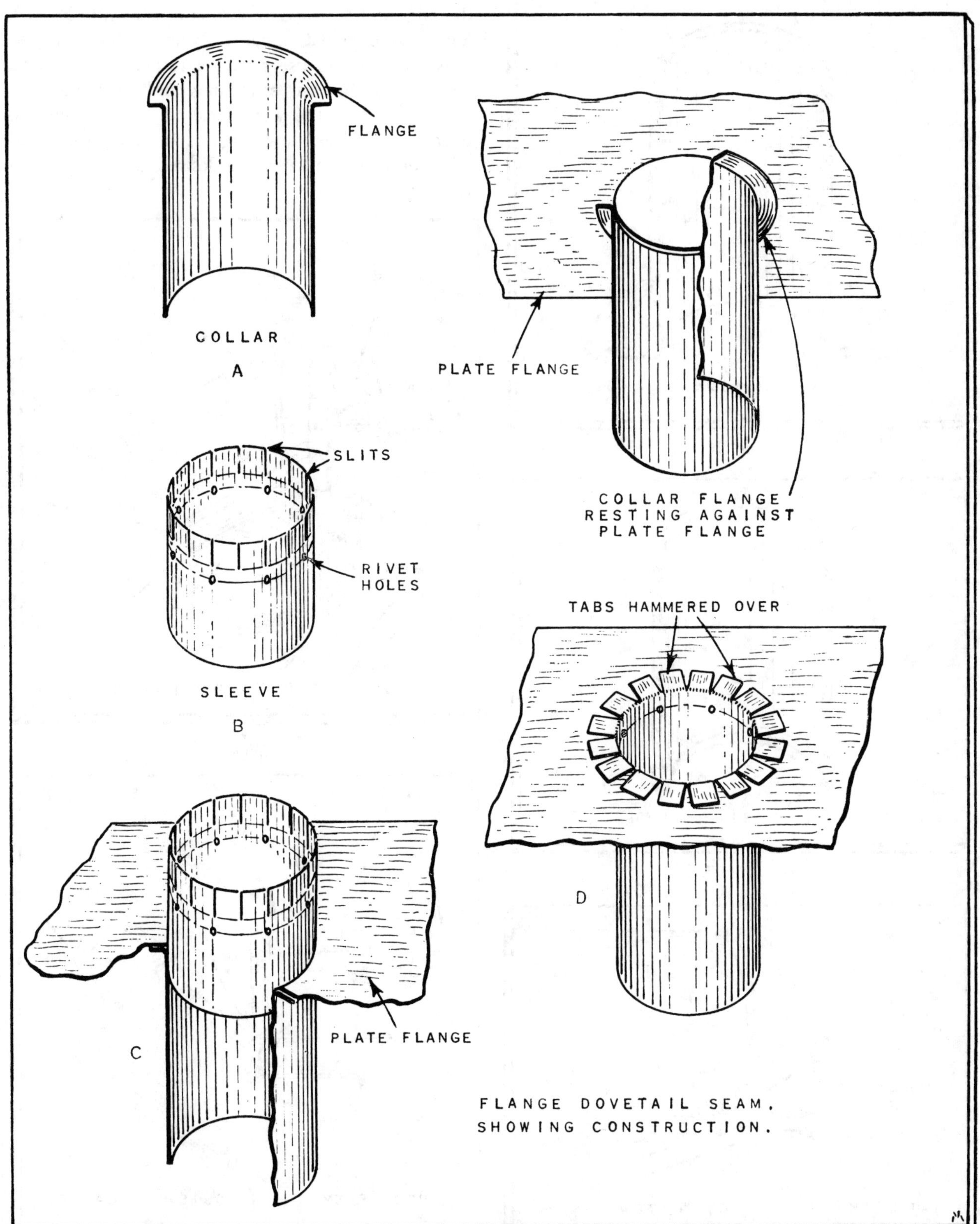
FLANGE
COLLAR
A
PLATE FLANGE
SLITS
COLLAR FLANGE
RESTING AGAINST
PLATE FLANGE
RIVET
HOLES
SLEEVE
B
TABS HAMMERED OVER
D
C
PLATE FLANGE
FLANGE DOVETAIL SEAM,
SHOWING CONSTRUCTION.

Figure 15.

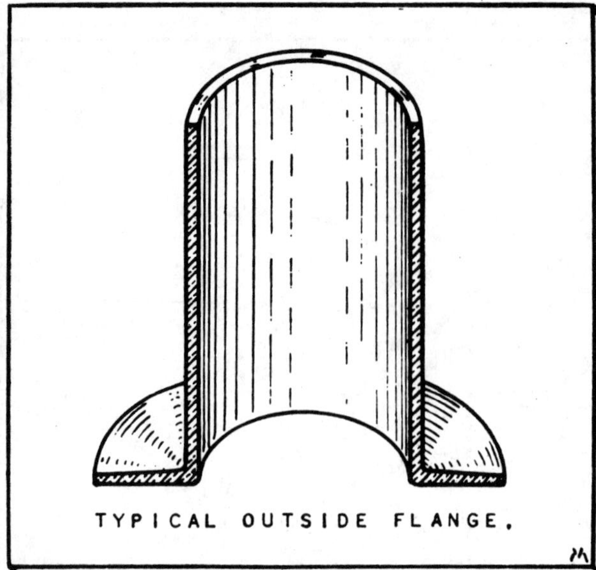

Figure 16.

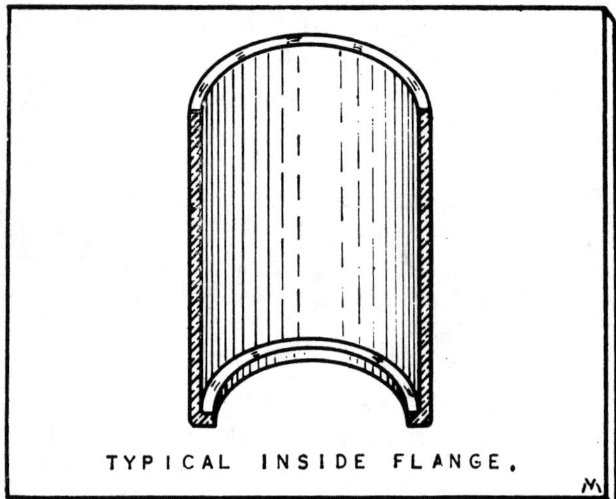

Figure 17.

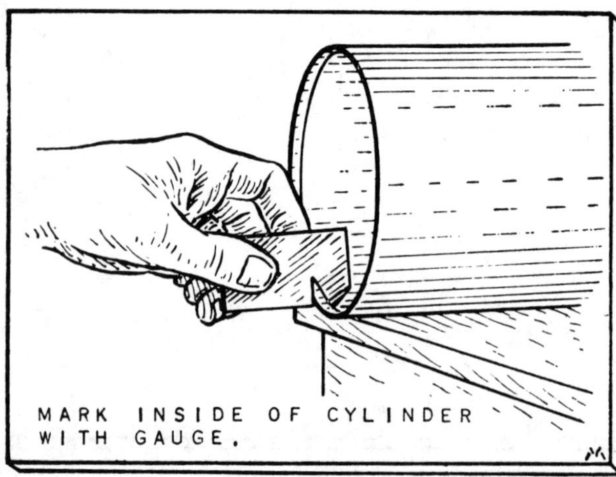

Figure 18.

(or any round stake of the correct curvature) with the edge to be turned or shrunk as shown in Fig. 22, and strike edge with a mallet. When shrinking metal, it is advisable to use a mallet rather than a metal hammer, to prevent stretching and buckling. Proceed to revolve the work until the entire edge has been formed. Keep lowering the job and striking the edge until a flange of the desired angle has been formed.

Figure 19.

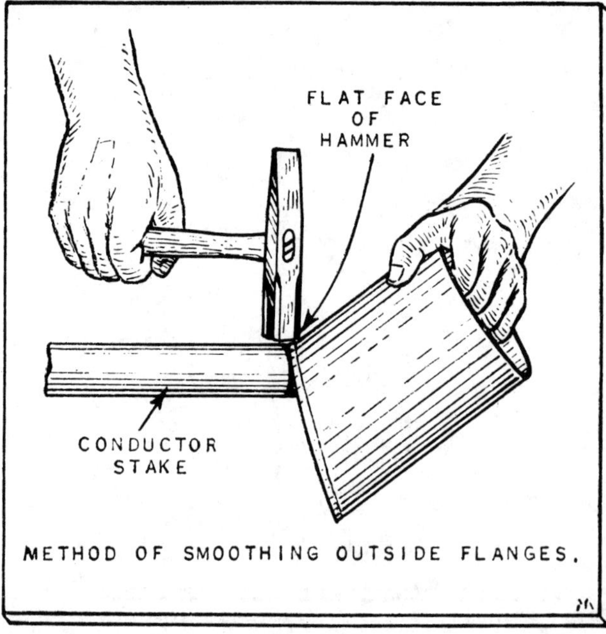

Figure 20.

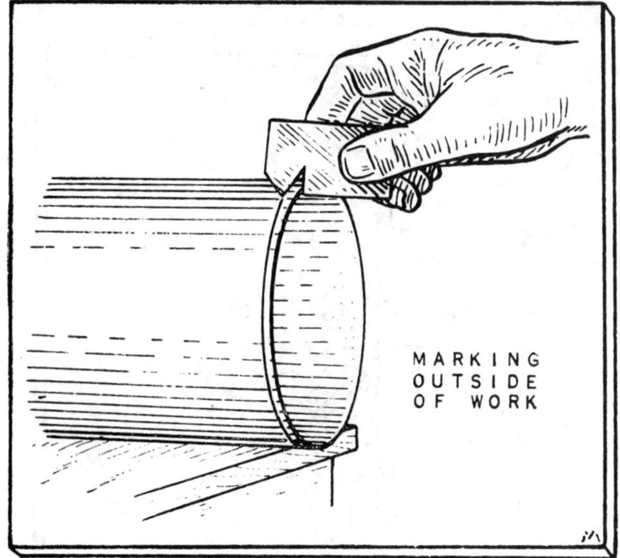

Figure 21.

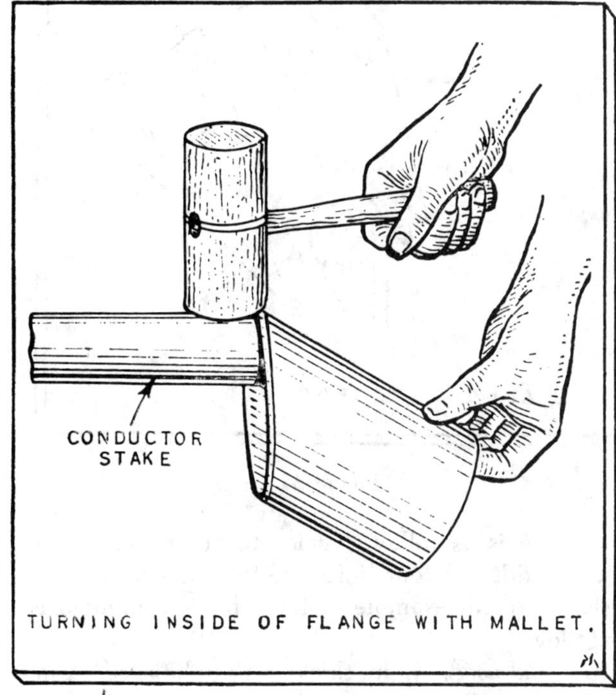

Figure 22.

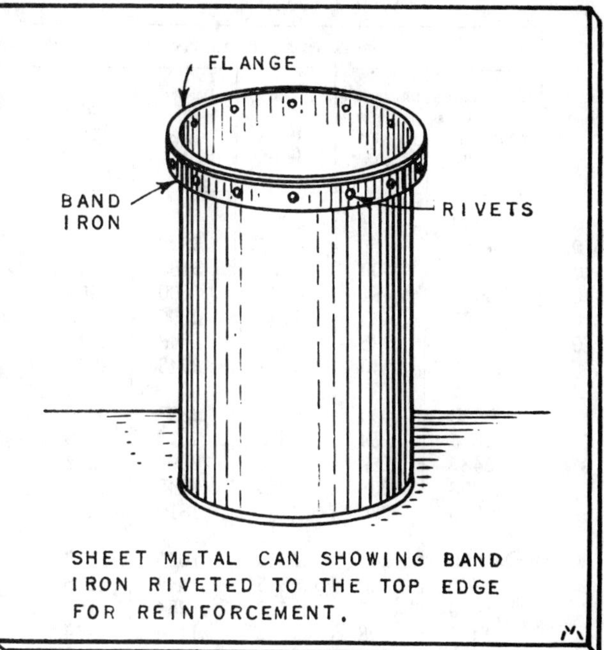

Figure 23.

Wired and Reinforced Edges

In sheet metal fabrication of small articles, wire of various types and diameters is used to reinforce the edges of the work, and in some cases to fabricate hinges and handles. The edges of large sheet metal articles are usually reinforced by riveting band iron to the top edge (Fig. 23).

Types of Wire Used. As a general rule, uncoated wire is used on articles made of black iron, tinned or copper coated wire on tin articles, copper or copper coated wire on those made of copper, and galvanized wire on galvanized articles. It is good policy, however, to use coated wire, because this type of wire resists corrosion and is considerably easier to solder.

Sizes of Wire. Wire is available either in coils of various weights or in rods of straight 10 ft. or 20 ft. lengths. Rods are used only for reinforcing straight edges. Both wire and rods are sold by the pound. Sizes or diameters of wire are usually designated by a series of gauge numbers, corresponding to the diameter of the wire in decimals of an inch. Table 8 gives the standard gauges and weights of wire.

Allowance for Wiring. When making a pattern for a wired job, it is essential to determine the exact amount of material to add to the pattern for the take-up of the wire. As a general rule, the amount that is added is equal in width to 2½ times the diameter of the wire (See A, Fig. 24).

When using material of 24 gauge or lighter, no allowance is made for the thickness of the metal. However, when reinforcing edges of articles made of heavier material, and additional allowance must be made to compensate for the thickness of the material used. The formula usually used for computing this

TABLE 8
WIRE GAUGES

Gauge Numbers	American Steel & Wire Co.'s STEEL WIRE GAUGE	Birmingham or Stubs' Gauge	U. S. Standard Gauge	American Wire Gauge (B. & S.)	British Imperial Standard*
	DECIMAL EQUIVALENTS				
7/0	.4900	....	.5000	....	.500
6/0	.4615	....	.4687	.5800	.464
5/0	.4305	.500	.4375	.5165	.432
4/0	.3938	.454	.4062	.4600	.400
3/0	.3625	.425	.3750	.4096	.372
2/0	.3310	.380	.3437	.3648	.348
1/0	.3065	.340	.3125	.3248	.324
1	.2830	.300	.2812	.2893	.300
2	.2625	.284	.2656	.2576	.276
3	.2437	.259	.2500	.2294	.252
4	.2253	.238	.2344	.2043	.232
5	.2070	.220	.2187	.1819	.212
6	.1920	.203	.2031	.1620	.192
7	.1770	.180	.1875	.1442	.176
8	.1620	.165	.1719	.1284	.160
9	.1483	.148	.1562	.1144	.144
10	.1350	.134	.1406	.1018	.128
11	.1205	.120	.1250	.0907	.116
12	.1055	.109	.1093	.0808	.104
13	.0915	.095	.0937	.0719	.092
14	.0800	.083	.0781	.0640	.080
15	.0720	.072	.0703	.0570	.072
16	.0625	.065	.0625	.0508	.064
17	.0540	.058	.0562	.0452	.056
18	.0475	.049	.0500	.0403	.048
19	.0410	.042	.0437	.0358	.040
20	.0348	.035	.0375	.0319	.036
21	.0317	.032	.0344	.0284	.032
22	.0286	.028	.0312	.0253	.028
23	.0258	.025	.0281	.0225	.024
24	.0230	.022	.0250	.0201	.022
25	.0204	.020	.0219	.0179	.020
26	.0181	.018	.0187	.0159	.018
27	.0173	.016	.0172	.0142	.0164
28	.0162	.014	.0156	.0126	.0148
29	.0150	.013	.0140	.0112	.0136
30	.0140	.012	.0125	.0100	.0124
31	.0132	.010	.0109	.0089	.0116
32	.0128	.009	.0101	.0079	.0108
33	.0118	.008	.0094	.0070	.0100
34	.0104	.007	.0086	.0063	.0092
35	.0095	.005	.0078	.0056	.0084
36	.0090	.004	.0070	.0050	.0076
37	.0085	....	.0066	.0044	.0068
38	.0080	....	.0062	.0039	.0060
39	.0075	....	....	.0035	.0052
40	.0070	....	....	.0031	.0048

* Also called English Standard Gauge. Full name is Legal Standard Wire Gauge, common designation Standard Wire Gauge, abbreviation S.W.G.

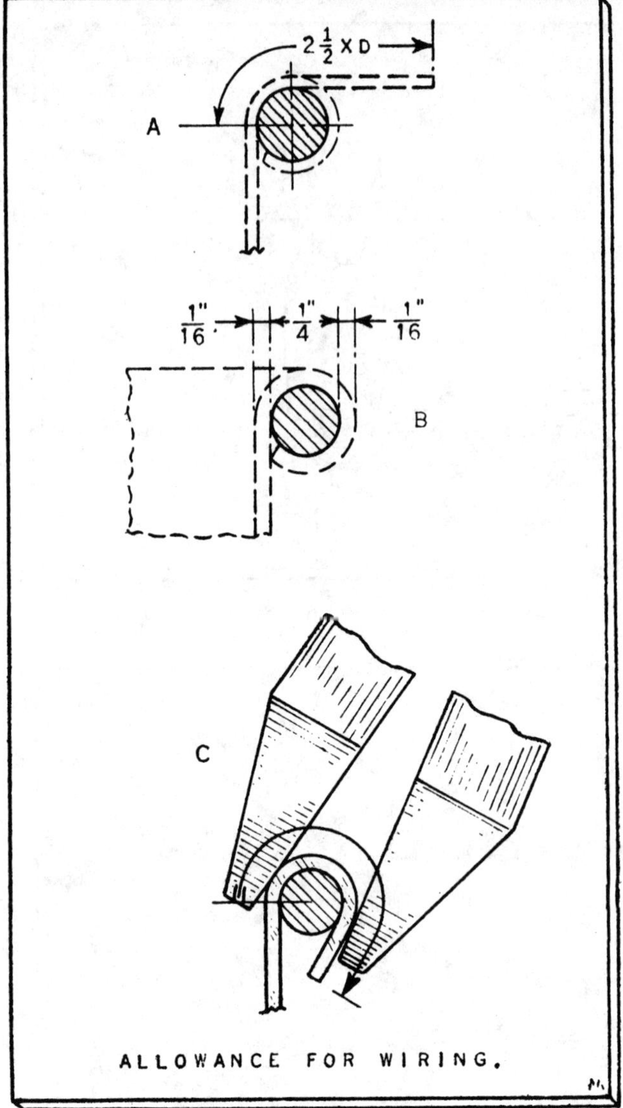

Figure 24.

allowance is as follows: twice the diameter of the wire is added to four times the thickness of the material used. An example of how this is computed is as follows:

Material used, 1/16 in. thick; wire to be used, 1/4 in. in diameter (B, Fig. 24).

1/4 in. × 2 + 1/16 in. × 4 = 3/4 in.

Another method of determining the necessary allowance for wiring is to secure a small strip of the material used, and, with a pair of pliers, bend this material closely around the wire (C, Fig. 24).

CALCULATING REQUIRED LENGTH OF WIRE. The established rules and formulas for calculating the length of wire required to wire the edges of circular, square, and rectangular jobs are as follows:

Circular. The length of wire required for wiring the edge of a circular job is equal to the diameter of the job plus the diameter of the wire multiplied by Pi (π) which equals 3.1416. The formula is expressed as follows:

L.W. = π (D + d)

D = diameter of job in inches

d = diameter of wire in inches.

Example. For a job $17\frac{3}{4}$ in. in diameter, find the length of $\frac{1}{4}$ in. wire needed (Fig. 25).

L.W. = 3.1416 ($17\frac{3}{4} + \frac{1}{4}$)

L.W. = 3.1416 × 18

L.W. = 56.5488 in. = $56\frac{17}{16}$

Answer $56\frac{17}{16}$ in. of wire required.

Square. The length of wire required for wiring the edge of a square job is equal to 4 times one side of the work plus twice the diameter of the wire. The formula is expressed as follows:

L.W. = 4S + 2d

L.W. = length of wire in inches

S = length of one side of rectangle in inches

d = diameter of wire used in inches

Example. For a rectangular job with sides measuring $20\frac{1}{4}$ in., find the length of $\frac{1}{4}$ in. wire needed (Fig. 26).

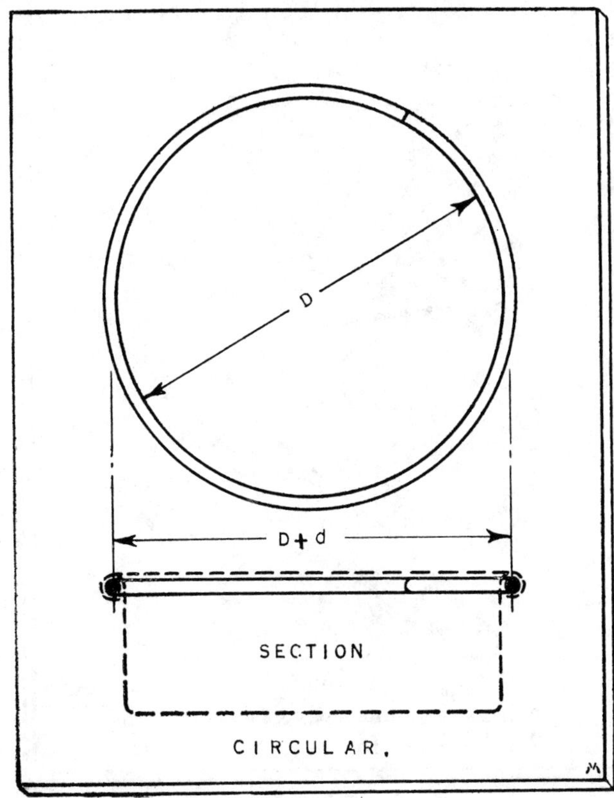

Figure 25.

L.W. = 4 × $20\frac{1}{4}$ + 2 × $\frac{1}{4}$

L.W. = 81 + $\frac{1}{2}$ = $81\frac{1}{2}$ in.

Answer $81\frac{1}{2}$ in. of wire required.

Rectangular. The length of wire required for wiring the edge of a rectangular job is equal to 2 times the length of the job plus 2 times its width and plus 2 times the diameter of wire used. The formula is expressed as follows:

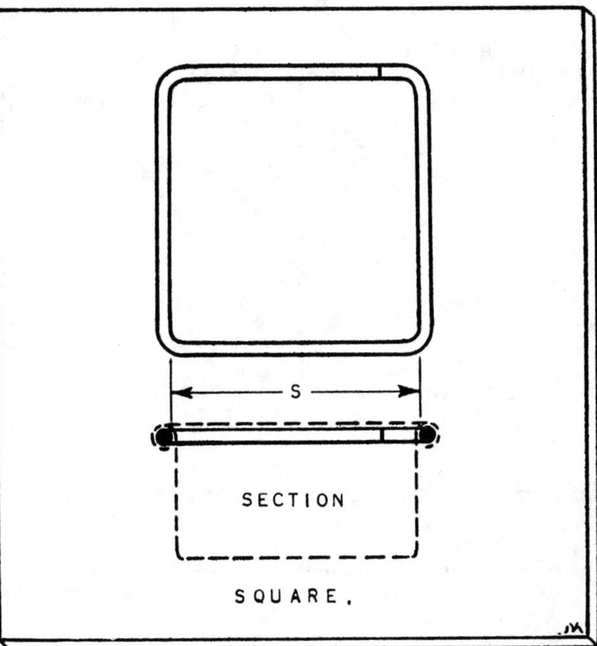

Figure 26.

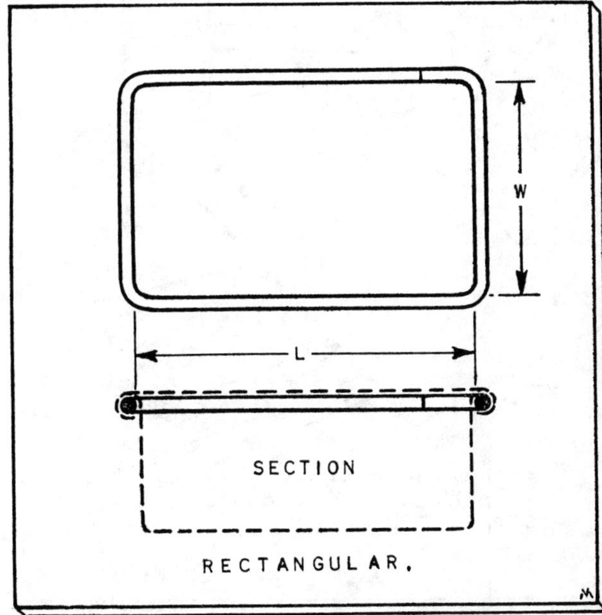

Figure 27.

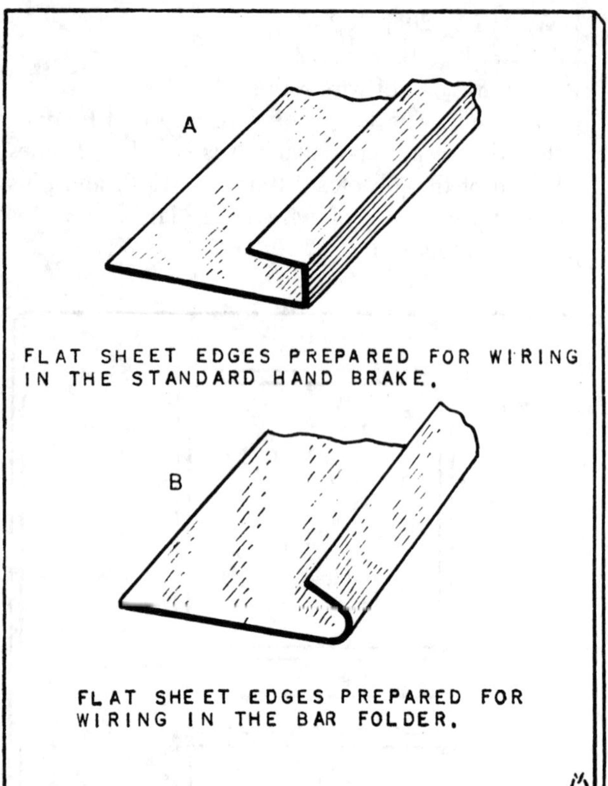

Figure 28.

L.W. = 2L + 2W + 2d
L. = length of job in inches
W. = width of job in inches
d = diameter of wire in inches

Example. Find length of ¼ in. wire required for wiring the edge of a job measuring 21 in. × 9 in. (Fig. 27).

L.W. = 2 × 21 + 2 × 9 + 2 × ¼
L.W. = 42 + 18 + ½ = 60½
Answer 60½ in. of wire required.

PROCEDURES FOR FINISHING WIRED EDGES. All edges of sheet metal articles that are cylindrically-shaped with straight sides (such as tanks, cans, and similar jobs), and the small ends of tapered jobs, are usually wired while the material used is in the flat sheet;

Figure 29.

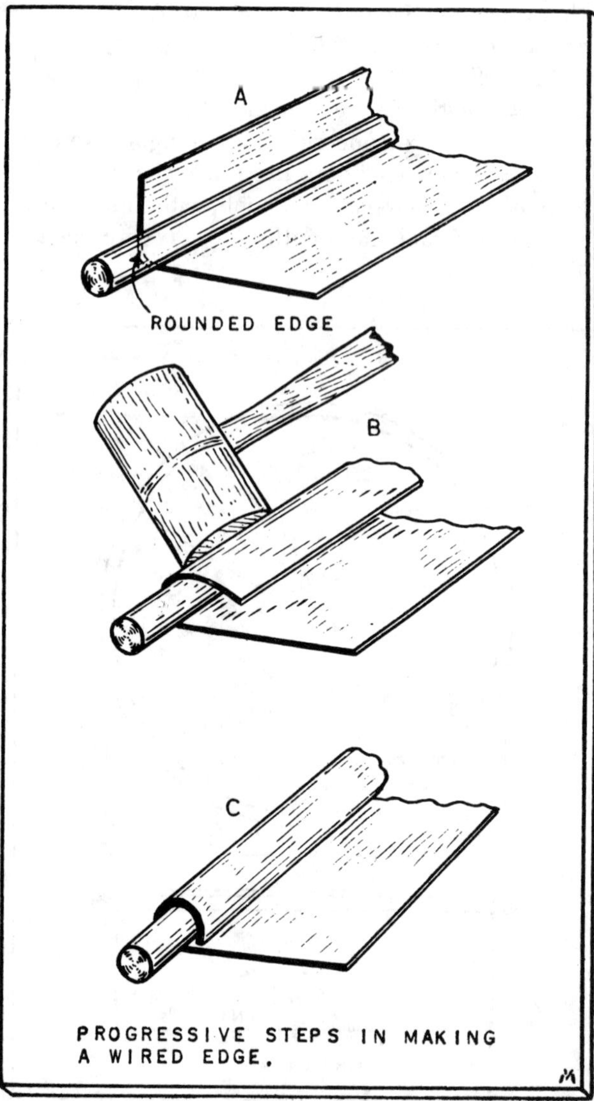

Figure 30.

that is, before the articles are formed. Boxes of various shapes, box shaped articles, and the large ends of tapered jobs are usually wired after the metal has been formed to the required shape.

Where machines are available, the edges are prepared for wiring on either the standard hand brake or the bar folder (Chap. 4), and the edge is wired on the wiring machine as described in Chap. 4.

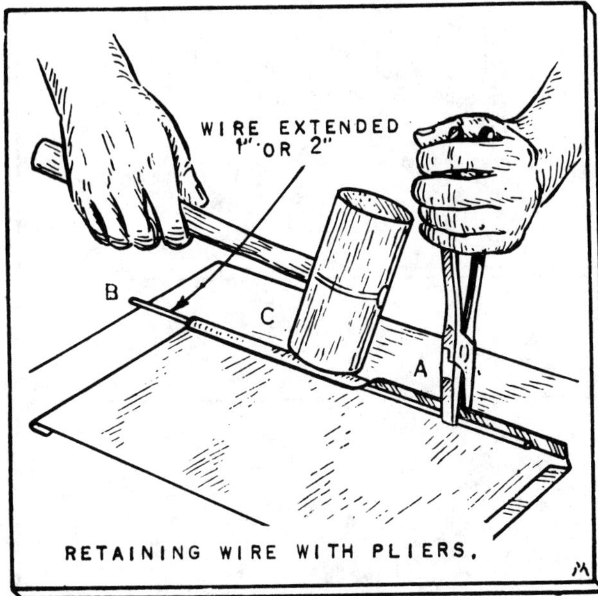

Figure 31.

Figure 32.

Flat sheet edges prepared for wiring on the standard hand brake and the bar folder are shown at A and B, Fig. 28. To wire straight edges on flat sheets where these machines are not available, proceed as follows:

With a micrometer or wire gauge, measure the diameter of wire to be used and mark the edge to a width equal to 2½ times the diameter of the wire. Bend the edge over as shown in Fig. 29. The completed bend is shown at A, Fig. 30. Cut the wire to the required length with wire nippers or pliers,

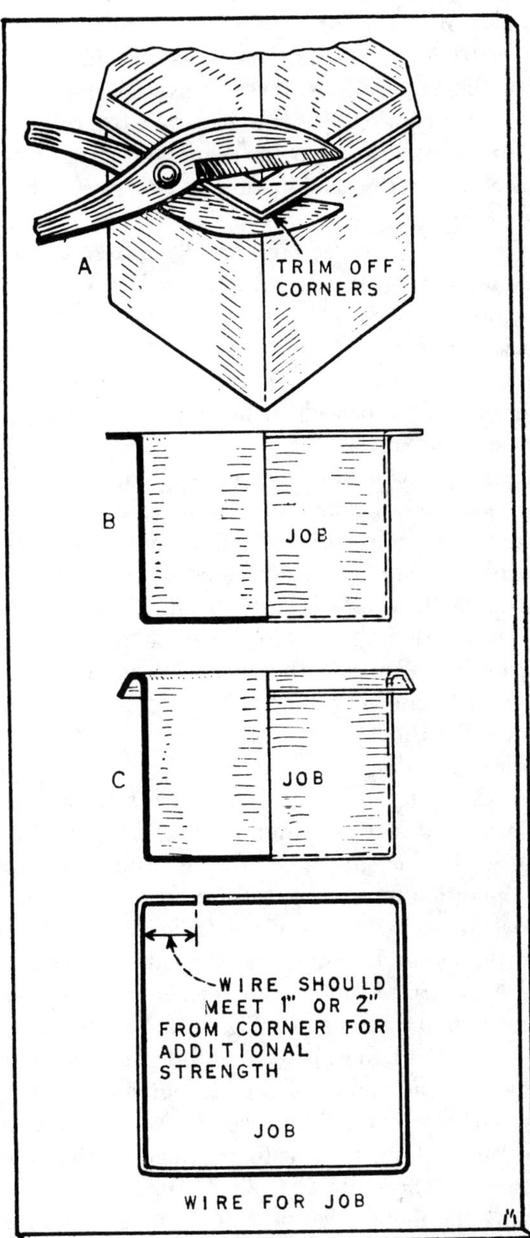

Figure 33.

straighten the wire, and set it in the folded edge, holding the wire in place with pliers as shown at A, Fig. 31. When sheet is to be cylindrically formed, it is necessary to extend the wire 1 to 2 in. from one end to strengthen the seam as shown at B, Fig. 31. Still holding wire in place, start closing the fold with a mallet as shown at A and C, Fig. 31. Continue to bend the metal over the wire with the mallet as far as possible. The edge completed up to this stage is shown at B, Fig. 30. Using the peen of a setting hammer, proceed as shown in Fig. 32 to complete the wired edge. A completed wired edge on a flat sheet is shown at C, Fig. 30.

When wiring an inside or outside radius on a flat sheet, the procedure is the same as that given above, with the exception that the wire must be rolled in a slip roll forming machine or shaped on a round stake to the required shape before inserting it into the turned edge.

When making wired edges on flat material, always back up the work with either a rail stake or a flat plate, and always use pliers to hold the wire to avoid injury to fingers.

Wiring Formed Rectangular or Square Jobs. To wire edges of formed rectangular or square jobs, proceed as follows:

Mark the width of edge on all four sides of the job equal to 2½ times the diameter of wire. With shears, cut each corner to the width of edge as shown at A, Fig. 33. Form the edge with a mallet on a suitable stake as shown at B and C. To ascertain the correct length of wire, use the formula given previously and cut to the required length. To form the wire to the shape shown in Fig. 33, proceed as follows. Set the wire in a vise with one or two inches of wire extending at one end of the vise (Fig. 34). Form this extended end of the wire to a 90 degree angle with a setting hammer (Fig. 35), measure a point in the wire for the following bends, and repeat the operation until the wire is formed to the required shape. After the wire has been formed, place it on the job and lay the job on a flat stake as shown at A, Fig. 36. Holding the formed wire frame in place with the pliers (B, Fig. 36), proceed to fold the edges with the mallet, bending the metal over the wire as far as possible on all four sides of the job (Fig. 36). Bend the folded edges over as far as possible on all four sides with the face of the setting hammer as shown in Fig. 35. Complete the job by peening the metal edge down over as tightly as possible with the peen of the setting hammer as shown in Fig. 37.

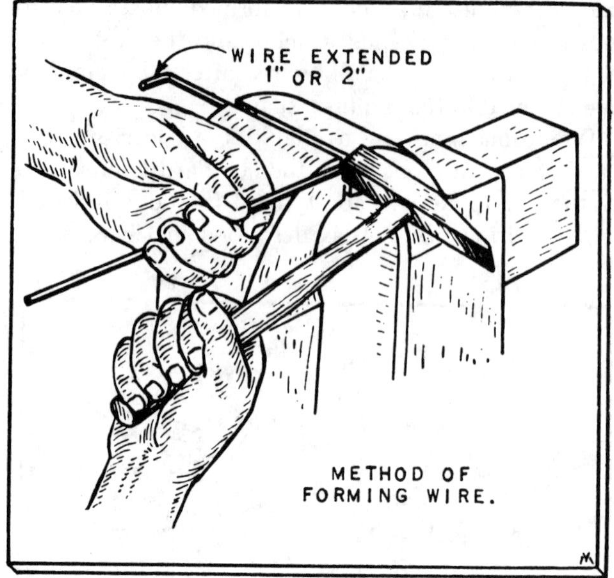

Figure 34.

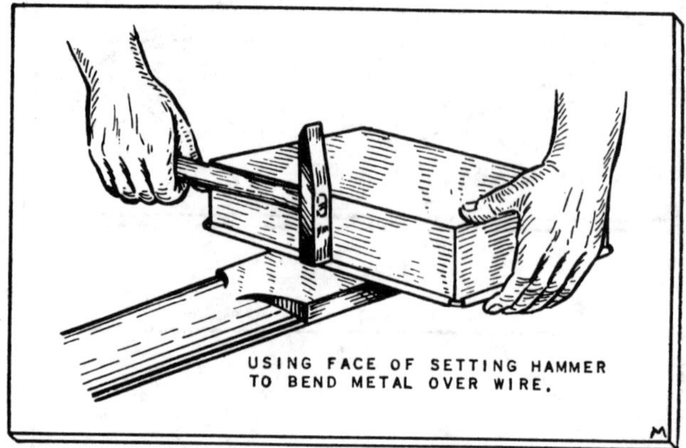

Figure 35.

Figure 36.

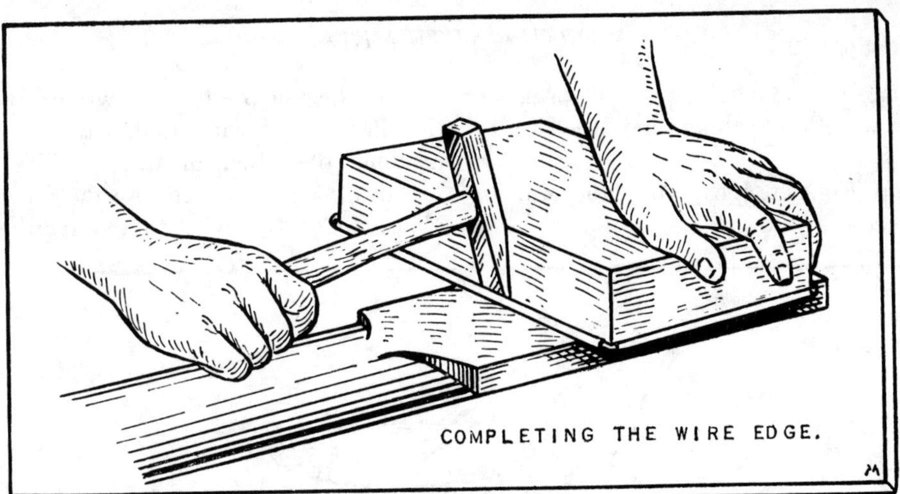

Figure 37.

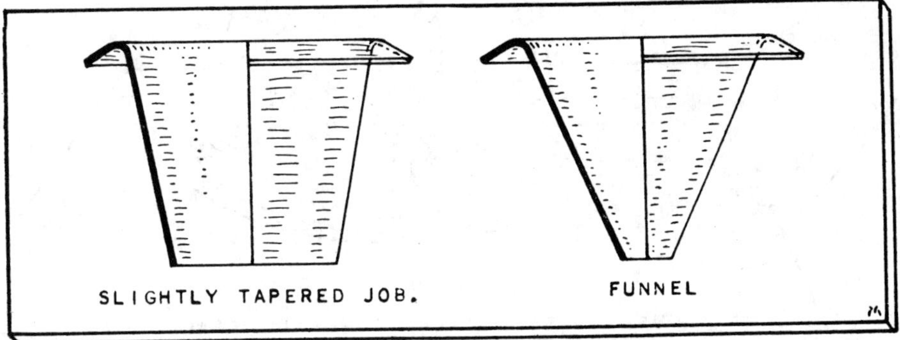

Figure 38.

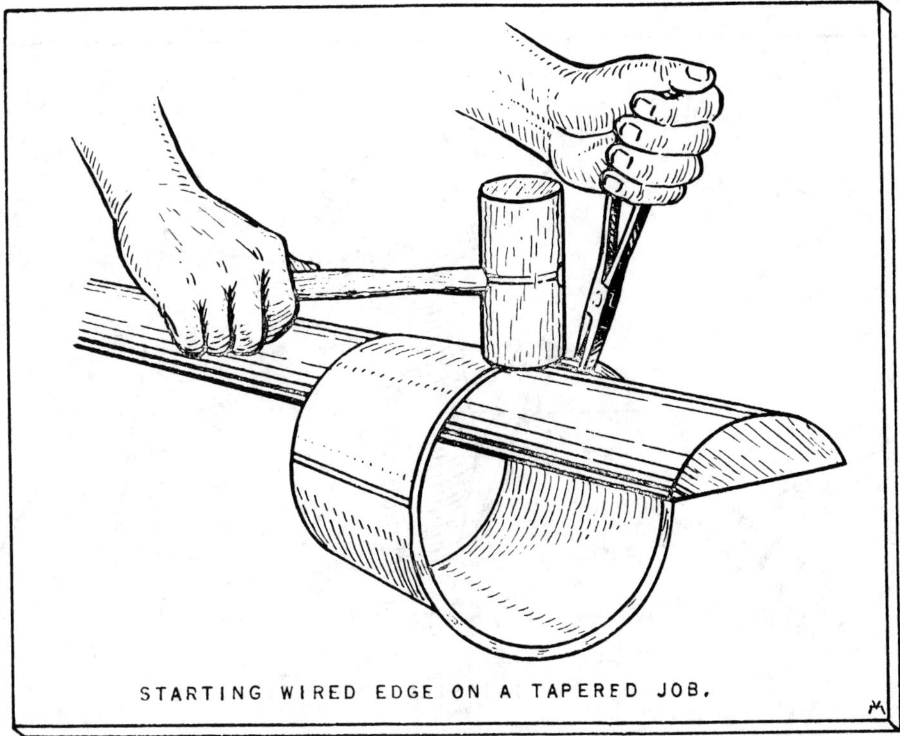

Figure 39.

Corners of square or rectangular jobs are usually soldered and filed smooth. (For soldering procedures see Chap. 6.)

WIRING FORMED TAPERED JOBS. To wire formed tapered jobs, proceed as follows:

For edges of the type shown in Fig. 38, 2½ times the diameter of wire used is turned on the turning machine described in Chap. 4. To ascertain the length of wire required, use the formula given previously. Cut the wire to the required length and

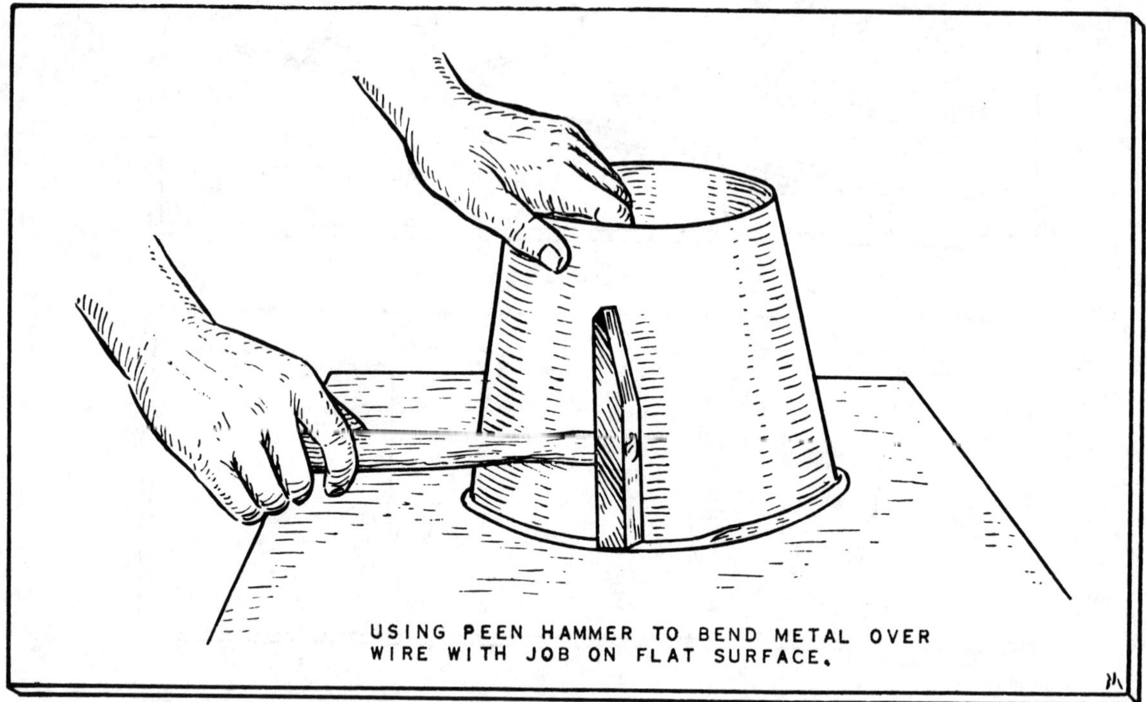

USING PEEN HAMMER TO BEND METAL OVER
WIRE WITH JOB ON FLAT SURFACE.

Figure 40.

FINISHING THE WIRE EDGE.

Figure 41.

form it into a circular shape on the slip roll forming machine described in Chap. 4. Place the job on a suitable mandrel. For slightly tapered jobs use a hollow mandrel stake; for funnels use a blow-horn stake. (For types of stakes see Chap. 3.) Hold the wire in place with pliers and start folding the metal over the wire with a mallet about one or two inches from the seam (Fig. 39). Work all around the circumference of the job. Remove the job from the stake and place it on a flat surface. Using the flat face of the setting hammer, bend the metal as far around the circumference of the job as possible (Fig. 40). Complete the job by peening the metal down tightly with the peen of the hammer as shown (Fig. 41).

Metal Cutting Operations

Many hand tools and power tools have been designed for the specific purpose of cutting metals quickly and accurately. Metal cutting operations can be performed with chisels, drills, taps, dies, reamers, and pipe and tubing cutters. (*See also* Chap. 3.)

Metal Cutting with Chisels

When struck with a heavy hammer, a cold chisel is capable of cutting metal. With chisel and hammer, you can cut wires, bars, rods, and other shapes of metal and also cut off the heads of rivets and bolts.

Cutting Wire or Round Stock. Mark off a guideline on the stock and place the work on the top face of an anvil or other suitable working surface. Place the cutting edge of the chisel on the mark in a vertical position and lightly strike the chisel with a hammer. Check the chisel mark for accuracy. Continue to strike the chisel until the cut is made. The last few blows of the hammer should be made lightly to avoid damage to the anvil, supporting surface, or to the chisel.

Heavy stock is cut in the same manner except that the cut is made halfway through the stock. Then turn the work over and finish the cut from the opposite side.

Cutting Off a Rivet or Bolt Head. Hold the work in a heavy vise or secure it in some other way so that the work will not move (A, Fig. 42). Hold the cold chisel with one face of the bevel flat on the surface of the job. Strike the head of the chisel with the hammer as you loosely hold and guide the chisel.

To cut off a rivet head with a cape chisel, select a chisel of about the same size as the diameter of the rivet. Cut through the center of the rivet head, holding one face of the bevel flat on the surface of the job, and then sever the center of the head from the shank or body (B, Fig. 42).

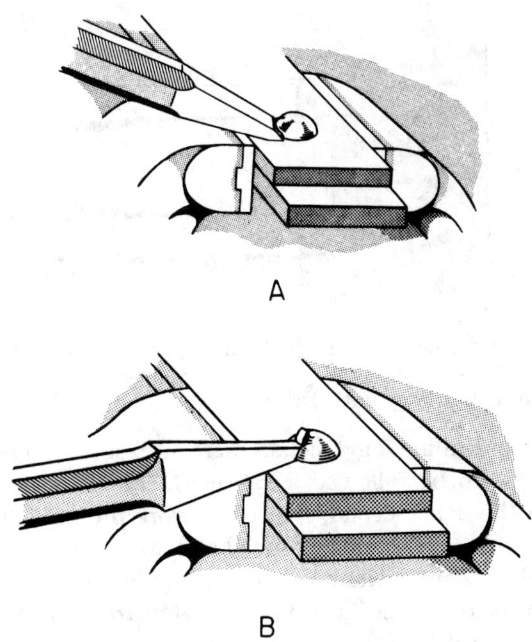

Figure 42. Cutting off a rivet head with a chisel.

To cut off a rivet head with a side cutting chisel, place the chisel nearly flat on the surface of the work with its single bevel upward. Drive the cutting edge under the edge of the rivet head just as you would if you were using a cold chisel (A, Fig. 43). *Note* in B, Fig. 43 that the cutting edge of the chisel has a slight radius which will tend to prevent the corners from cutting undesirable grooves in the surface of the work.

To remove a rivet head (Fig. 44) when there is not room enough to swing a hammer with sufficient force to cut the rivet, first drill a hole about the size of the body of the rivet in and almost to the bottom of the rivet head; then cut off the head with a cold chisel.

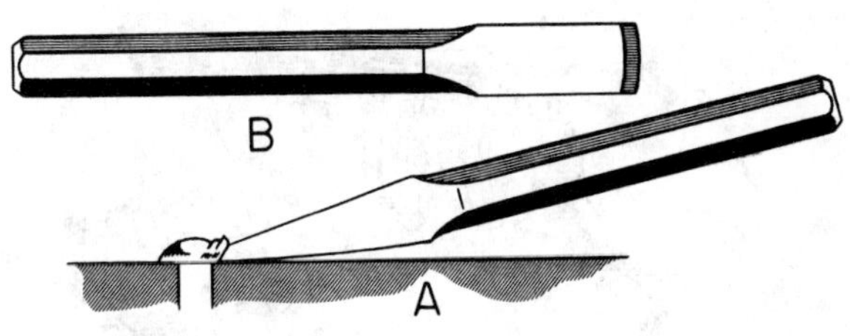

Figure 43. Cutting off a rivet head with a side cutting chisel.

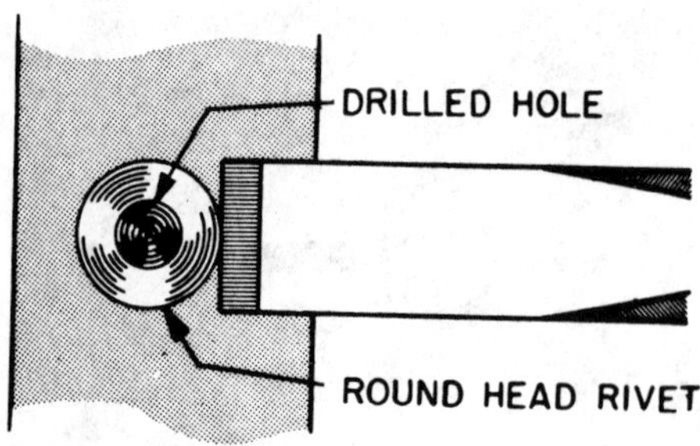

Figure 44. Removing a rivet head in a hard to reach position.

Metal Cutting with Drills

In drilling any metal, there are several general steps to be followed. First, mark the exact location of the hole. Second, secure the work properly. Then, use the correct cutting speed and appropriate cutting oil or other coolant, where applicable. Finally, apply pressure on the drill properly. *Be sure* to select the correct drill size.

LOCATING THE HOLE. The exact location of the hole must be marked with a center punch. The punch mark forms a seat for the drill point, thus ensuring accuracy. Without the punch mark, the drill may have a tendency to *walk off* before it begins to cut into the metal.

HOLDING THE WORK FOR DRILLING. Most work is held for drilling by some mechanical means, such as a vise or clamps. It is *important* that the work be *well secured,* or the work or stock may rotate at high speed or fly loose, becoming a high-speed projectile endangering all persons within range. Various securing procedures are discussed in the following paragraphs.

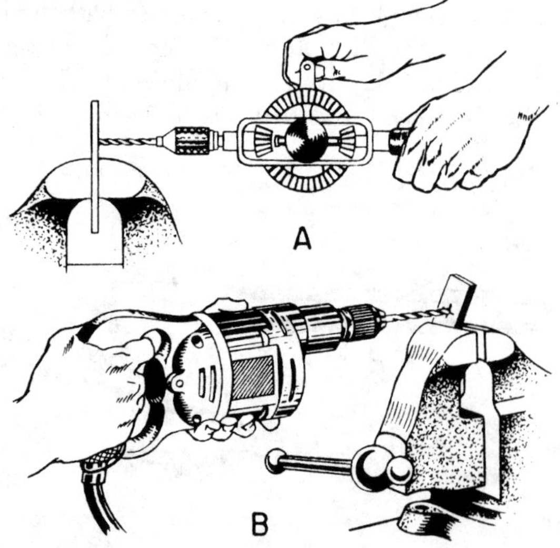

Figure 45. Holding small pieces in a vise for drilling.

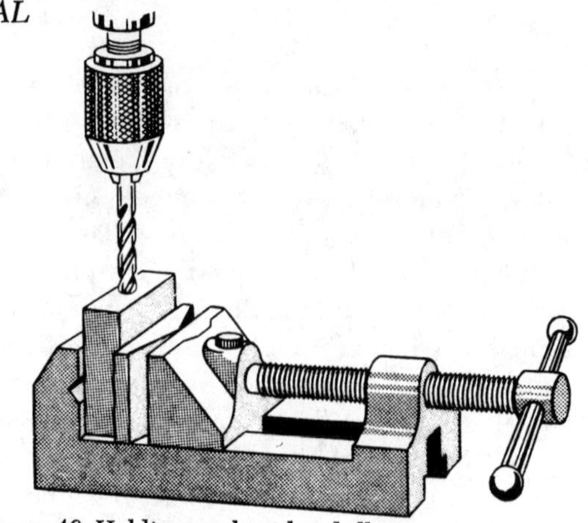

Figure 46. Holding work with a drill press vise.

When drilling in small pieces with a *hand drill,* it is best to hold the work in a *vise* so that the axis of the drill is horizontal (Fig. 45). This position provides better control of the drilling operation and will tend to ensure a hole which will be square with the surface of the work.

When drilling in small pieces with a *drill press,* hold the work either in a *drill press vise* (Fig. 46), or between *V-blocks* (Fig. 47). *Caution: Be sure* to fasten the drill press vise or V-block to the drill press table.

When using a drill press to drill holes in the end of round stock, place the stock in one of the *V-grooves* in the stationary jaw of the *drill vise,* as shown in Fig. 48. These V-grooves will hold the work perpendicular to the table of the drill press. The drilled hole will then be parallel with the axis of the round stock.

Drilling holes in large pieces can be accomplished by holding the work with a *step block* and *clamps* (Fig. 49).

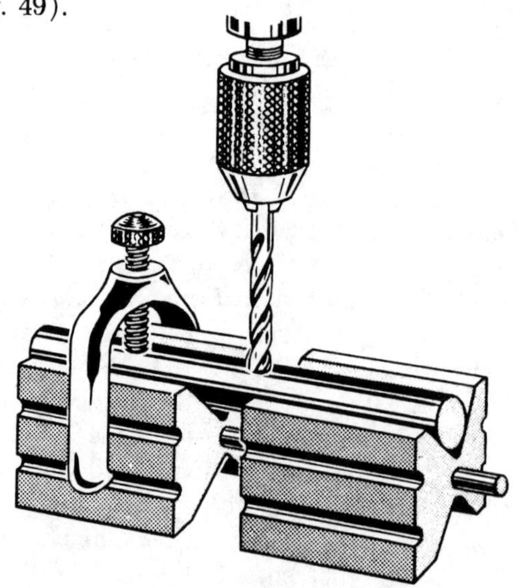

Figure 47. Holding work in V-blocks.

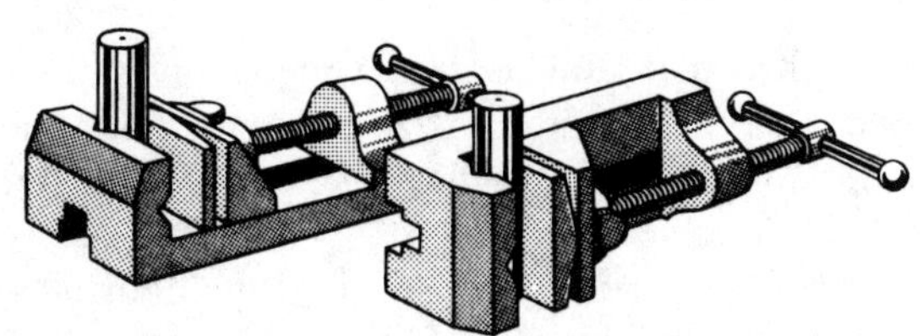

Figure 48. Holding work to drill holes in the end of round stock.

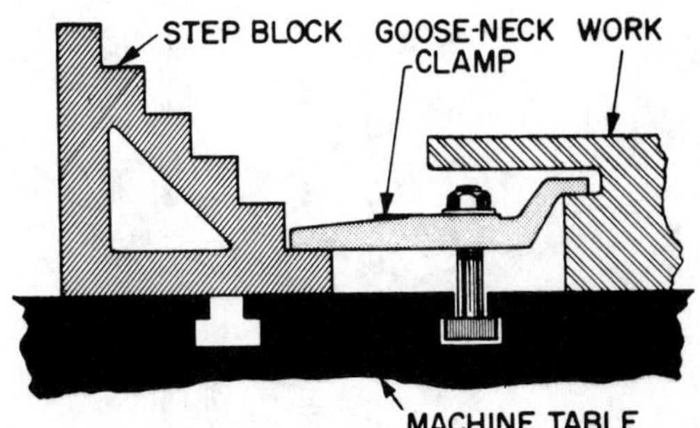

Figure 50. Holding work with step block and clamp for drilling.

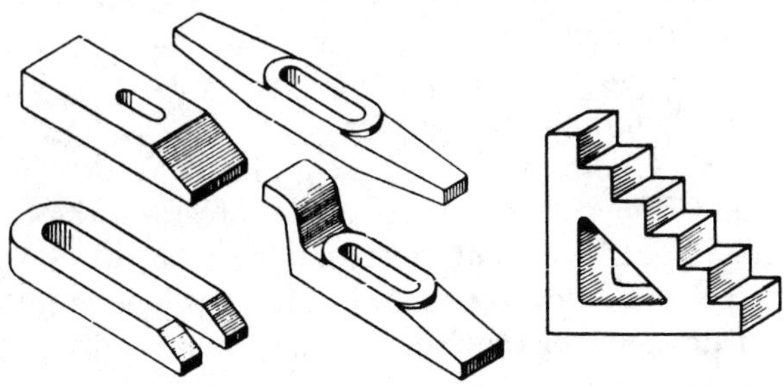

Figure 49. Step block and clamps.

When holding work with step blocks and clamps, you may use a gooseneck clamp, as shown in Fig. 50. *Note* that the body of the clamp is approximately parallel with the surface of the drill press table and that the bolt is held close to the work rather than close to the step block. This setup provides the most favorable mechanical advantage. As a rule, two or more clamps are used on each setup.

If you are required to hold thin metal, place it on a block of wood to provide support directly beneath the intended hole. This support will also help minimize drill breakage when the feed pressure is applied. Secure the *C-clamp* (Fig. 51) and drill through the metal and into the wood. Stop drilling when wood chips appear, to avoid damage to the drill table.

Cutting Speed. The correct cutting speed for metal drilling depends upon the type of metal and its properties, plus the diameter and type of drill (high speed or carbon). (*See* Table 9.)

Table 9

Drill Speeds in R.P.M.

Diameter of Drill	Soft Metals 300 F.P.M.	Annealed Cast Iron 140 F.P.M.	Mild Steel 100 F.P.M.	Malleable Iron 90 F.P.M.	Hard Cast Iron 80 F.P.M.	Tool or Hard Steel 60 F.P.M.	Alloy Steel Cast Steel 40 F.P.M.
1/16 (No. 53 to 80)	18320	8554	6111	5500	4889	3667	2445
3/32 (No. 42 to 52)	12212	5702	4071	3666	3258	2442	1649
1/8 (No. 31 to 41)	9160	4278	3056	2750	2445	1833	1222
5/32 (No. 23 to 30)	7328	3420	2444	2198	1954	1465	977
3/16 (No. 13 to 22)	6106	2852	2037	1833	1630	1222	815
7/32 (No. 1 to 12)	5234	2444	1745	1575	1396	1047	698
1/4 (A to E)	4575	2139	1527	1375	1222	917	611
9/32 (G to K)	4071	1900	1356	1222	1084	814	542
5/16 (L, M, N)	3660	1711	1222	1100	978	733	489
11/32 (O to R)	3330	1554	1110	1000	888	666	444
3/8 (S, T, U)	3050	1426	1018	917	815	611	407
13/32 (V to Z)	2818	1316	939	846	752	563	376
7/16	2614	1222	873	786	698	524	349
15/32	2442	1140	814	732	652	488	326
1/2	2287	1070	764	688	611	458	306
9/16	2035	950	678	611	543	407	271
5/8	1830	856	611	550	489	367	244
11/16	1665	777	555	500	444	333	222
3/4	1525	713	509	458	407	306	204

Figures are for High-Speed Drills. The speed of Carbon Drills should be reduced one-half. Use drill speed nearest to figure given.

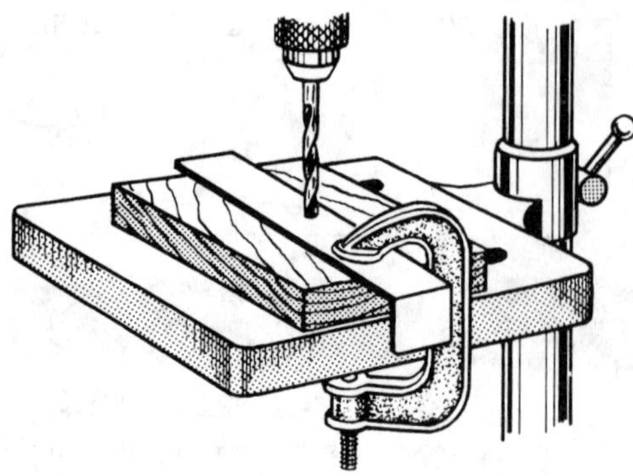

Figure 51. Holding thin gage metal for drilling.

Threads and Thread Cutting

Threads are helical ridges cut into screws, nuts, bolts, or the walls of a hole, so that the action of turning the screw, nut, or bolt gives it endwise as well as rotary motion.

THREAD NOMENCLATURE. The outside diameter of a thread is known as the *major diameter*. The diameter across the roots of the thread is called the *minor diameter*. The *pitch* is defined as the distance from any point on the thread of a screw to the corresponding point on an adjacent thread. It is usually measured from crest to crest and is expressed by a specific quantity of threads per inch. (*See* Fig. 52.)

Tap Drill Determination

If a threaded hole is to be made in a piece of metal, a hole of suitable size must first be drilled. The hole must be somewhat smaller than the size of the bolt to be screwed into it.

Figure 53 shows the system used for figuring how to determine how much smaller to drill the hole. The resultant thread is known as a *75 per cent thread* because the diameter of the hole is 75 per cent of the difference between the major and minor diameters, subtracted from the major diameter.

When the *tap hole* is the right size, it is a little larger than the *root diameter* of the tap, as shown in Fig. 54. The tap will cut a thread in the work which is only 75 per cent as deep as the thread on the tap. The other 25 per cent of the depth of thread on the tap provides clearance between the tap hole and the root diameter of the tap (Fig. 54). This makes tapping easier.

If the tap drill selected is oversize, the tap hole will be oversize, and the tap can cut only shallow threads in the work (Fig. 55). With less than a full 75 per cent depth of thread, stud or capscrew threads usually strip.

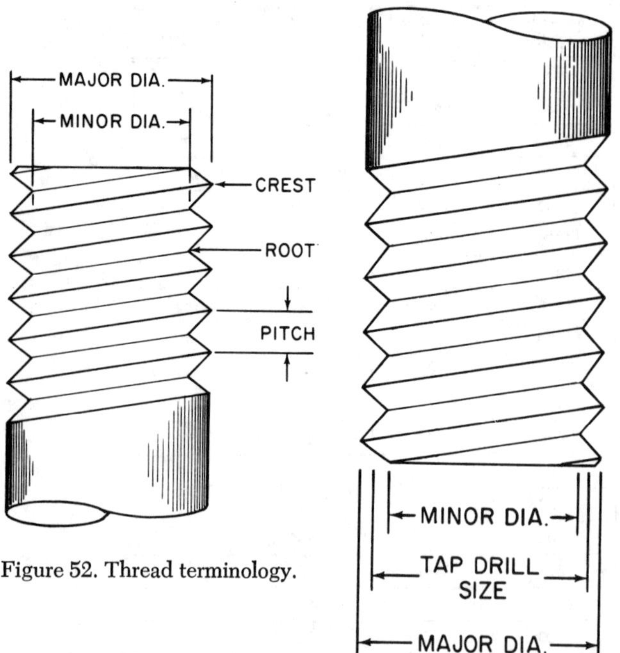

Figure 52. Thread terminology.

Figure 53. Tap drill size determination.

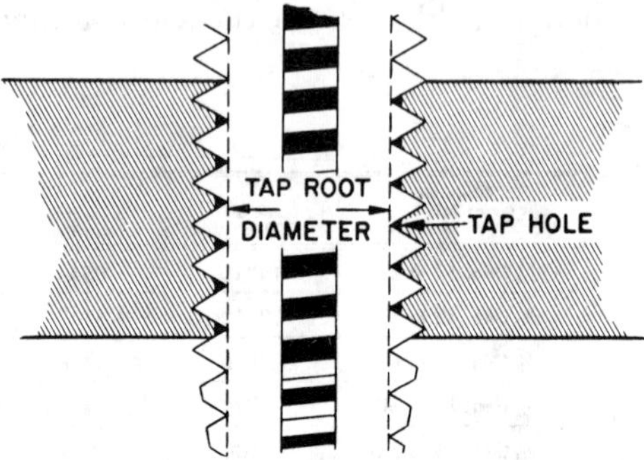

Figure 54. Proper size drilled hole for tapping.

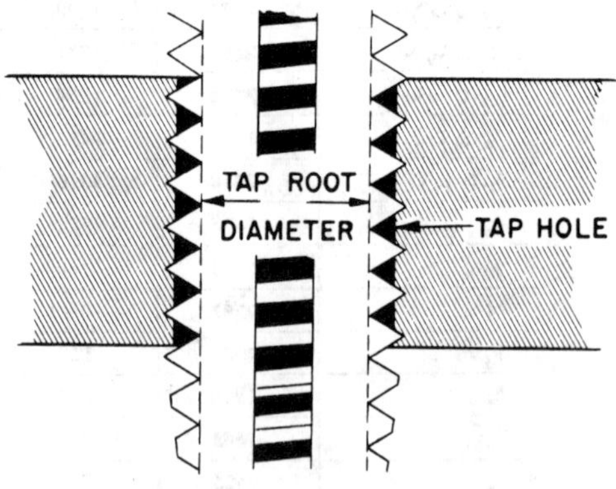

Figure 55. Oversize drilled hole for tapping.

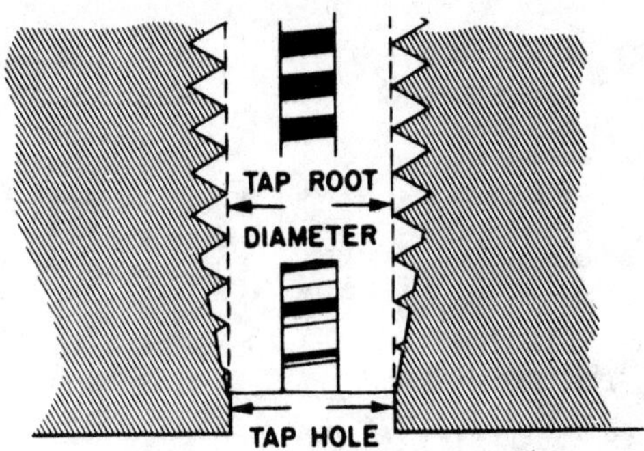

Figure 56. Undersize drilled hole for tapping.

If the *tap drill* selected is *undersize,* the tap hole will be undersize, being perhaps equal to the root diameter of the tap (Fig. 56). Then there will be no clearance, the tap will turn hard, tear the threads, and probably break.

Table 10 will help to determine exactly which size of tap drill to use. A similar chart is generally included with a set of taps and dies by the manufacturer. (*See* Fig. 57.)

TABLE 10
AMERICAN NATIONAL FORM THREADS

Nominal size	Thr'd series	Major diameter, inches	Root diameter, inches	Tap drill to produce approx. 75% full thread	Decimal equivalent of tap drill
0–80	N. F.	.0600	.0438	3/64	.0469
1–64	N. C.	.0730	.0527	53	.0595
72	N. F.	.0730	.0550	53	.0595
2–56	N. C.	.0860	.0628	50	.0700
64	N. F.	.0860	.0657	50	.0700
3–48	N. C.	.0990	.0719	47	.0785
56	N. F.	.0990	.0758	45	.0820
4–40	N. C.	.1120	.0795	43	.0890
48	N. F.	.1120	.0849	42	.0935
5–40	N. C.	.1250	.0925	38	.1015
44	N. F.	.1250	.0955	37	.1040
6–32	N. C.	.1380	.0974	36	.1065
40	N. F.	.1380	.1055	33	.1130
8–32	N. C.	.1640	.1234	29	.1360
36	N. F.	.1640	.1279	29	.1360
10–24	N. C.	.1900	.1359	25	.1495
32	N. F.	.1900	.1494	21	.1590
12–24	N. C.	.2160	.1619	16	.1770
28	N. F.	.2160	.1696	14	.1820
1/4–20	N. C.	.2500	.1850	7	.2010
28	N. F.	.2500	.2036	3	.2130
5/16–18	N. C.	.3125	.2403	F	.2570
24	N. F.	.3125	.2584	I	.2720
3/8–16	N. C.	.3750	.2938	5/16	.3125
24	N. F.	.3750	.3209	Q	.3320
7/16–14	N. C.	.4375	.3447	U	.3680
20	N. F.	.4375	.3726	25/64	.3906
1/2–13	N. C.	.5000	.4001	27/64	.4219
20	N. F.	.5000	.4351	29/64	.4531
9/16–12	N. C.	.5625	.4542	31/64	.4844
18	N. F.	.5625	.4903	33/64	.5156
5/8–11	N. C.	.6250	.5069	17/32	.5312
18	N. F.	.6250	.5528	37/64	.5781
3/4–10	N. C.	.7500	.6201	21/32	.6562
16	N. F.	.7500	.6688	11/16	.6875
7/8– 9	N. C.	.8750	.7307	49/64	.7656
14	N. F.	.8750	.7822	13/16	.8125
1– 8	N. C.	1.0000	8376	7/8	.8750
14	N. F.	1.0000	9072	15/16	.9375

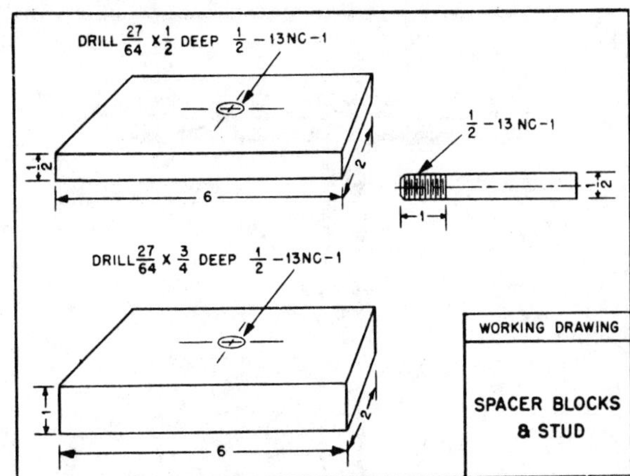

Figure 57. Working drawing for tapping and cutting threads.

Cutting Machine Threads with Taps

A 50-50 mixture of white lead and lard oil, applied with a small brush, is recommended as a lubricant when tapping in steel. When using this lubricant, tighten the tap in the tap wrench and apply the lubricant to the tap. Start the tap carefully with its axis on the center line of the hole. The tap must be square with the surface of the work (Fig. 58).

To continue tapping, turn the tap forward two quarter turns, back it up a quarter turn to break the chips, and then turn forward again to take up the slack. Continue this sequence until the required threads are cut. After you cut for the first two or three full turns, you no longer have to exert downward pressure on the wrench. You can tell by the *feel* that the tap is cutting as you turn it. Do not permit chips to clog the flutes or they will prevent the tap from turning. If the tap will not turn, and you notice a springy feeling, stop trying to turn it. Back the tap up a quarter turn to break the chips, clean

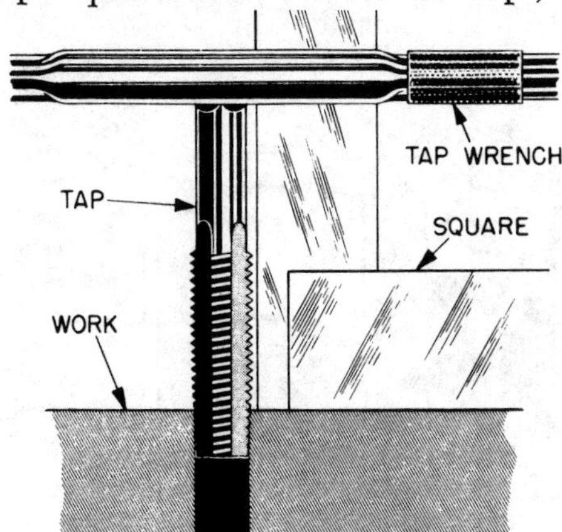

Figure 58. Using a square to ascertain a tap is square with the work.

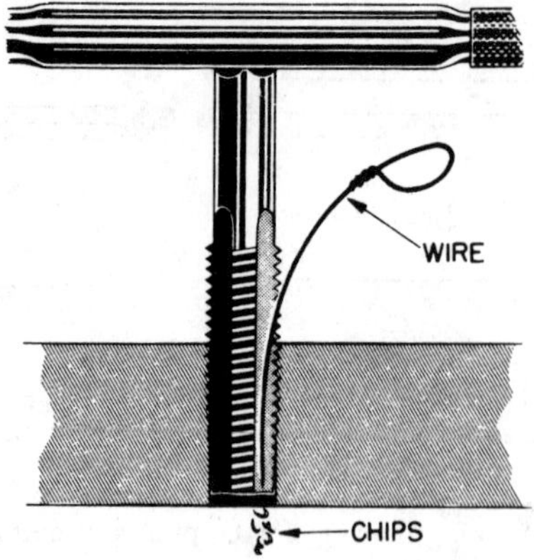

Figure 59. Using a wire to clear chips from flute of a tap.

them out of the flutes with a wire (Fig. 59), then add some more lubricant and continue tapping. When the tap has cut threads through the hole, the tap will turn with no resistance.

To tap a blind hole, start with the taper tap. For a blind hole you will need all three types of taps—the taper, the plug, and the bottoming taps. *Be sure* they are the size and thread series you need, and that the tap hole is the size called for by the working drawing shown in Fig. 57 and Table 10.

Begin with the taper tap, and handle it as previously described. A, Fig. 60 shows the taper tap just starting to cut. In B, Fig. 60 it has cut a little farther. In C, Fig. 60 it has bottomed in the hole after having cut several full threads near the top of the hole. This completes the work done with the taper tap.

In A, Fig. 61 the plug tap has entered the few full threads cut by the taper tap. In B, Fig. 61 it has continued these threads a little farther down into the hole. In C, Fig. 61 it has bottomed in the hole. This is all the work that you can do with the plug tap, as it has cut full threads about halfway down the tap hole before bottoming.

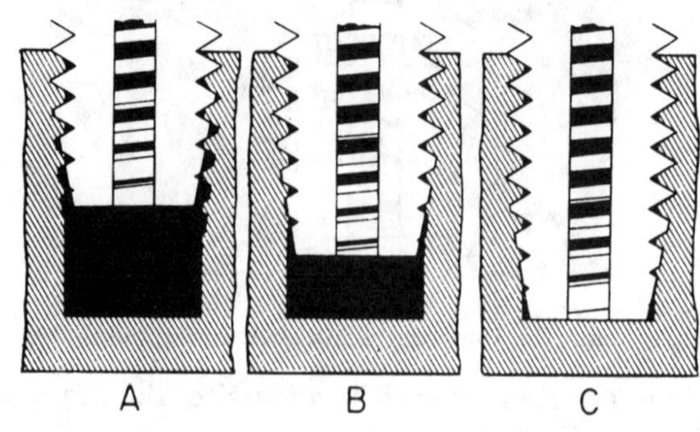

Figure 61. Tapping a blind hole with a plug tap.

In Fig. 62 the bottoming tap has been substituted for the plug tap. In A, Fig. 62 it has been run down the full threads cut by the plug tap and is ready to cut more full threads. In B, Fig. 62 it has cut a few more threads, and in C, Fig. 62 it has bottomed in the hole. The blind hole has now been completely tapped.

Because these threads are being tapped in a blind hole, chip removal must be done differently. To remove chips, back the tap completely out of the hole very frequently, invert the stock, if possible, and jar out the chips or work them out of the hole with a wire while the stock is in the inverted position. If the work cannot be inverted, blow out the chips with air. Whenever you use air, *be sure* to use safety goggles. Chip removal in tapping blind holes is much more difficult to do and is very important because chips will fall ahead of the tap through the flutes and accumulate in the bottom of the blind hole. Until these chips are removed, none of the three taps can complete its work. In tapping blind holes, alternate with tapping and chip removal until each of the three taps bottom in the blind hole.

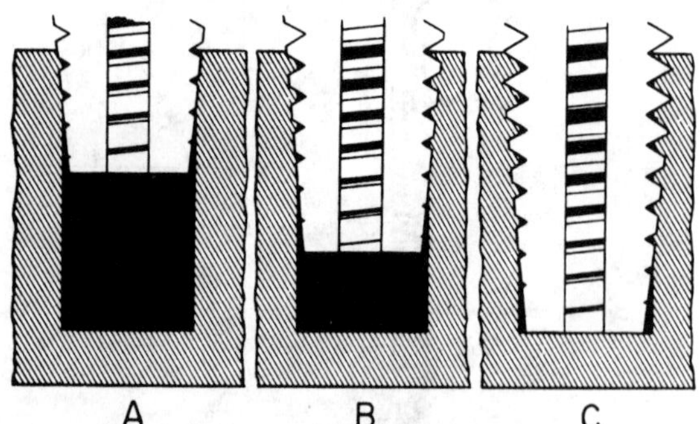

Figure 60. Tapping a blind hole with a taper tap.

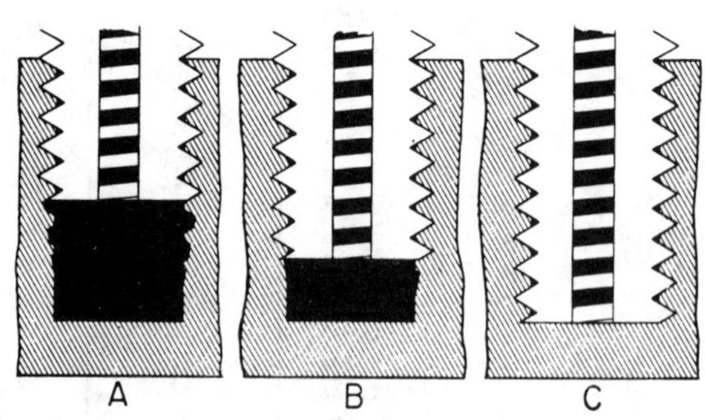

Figure 62. Finish tapping a blind hole with a bottoming tap.

After using the three taps, brush the chips out of their teeth, oil them with lubricating oil, wipe off the surplus oil, and replace them in the threading set.

Cutting Machine Threads with Dies

To cut threads on a piece of round stock, first grind a chamfer on the end of the rod, as shown in Fig. 57. Then hold the rod vertically in the vise to cut the threads. The illustration calls for a 1/2 – 13 National Coarse (N.C.) – 1 thread. The 1/2 signifies diameter and the 13 the number of threads per inch. The figure 1 after the N.C. indicates that a class 1 fit is required. A class 1 fit is a loose fit. The fit is controlled while threading the round stock. Tap the threads in the hole first, as there is no way to adjust a tap. However, as threading dies are usually adjustable, control the fit of the threaded rod in the tapped hole by adjusting the threading die.

The adjustable round split die shown in A, Fig. 63 has an adjustable screw. By tightening this screw and spreading the die slightly, it will cut less deeply into the rod and the fit in the tapped hole will be tighter. The shallow hole (B, Fig. 63) is placed in the die stock opposite the adjustable handle (E, Fig. 63), and serves as a drive hole. Also, when the adjustable handle is tightened, it holds the split die together and against the adjusting screw to maintain the setting while the die is cutting. The threads or cutting teeth of the die are chamfered or relieved (C, Fig. 63) to help start the die squarely on the round stock. The die is put into the die stock with the face of the unchamfered teeth against the shoulder (D, Fig. 63).

Figure 64 shows a plain round split die and die

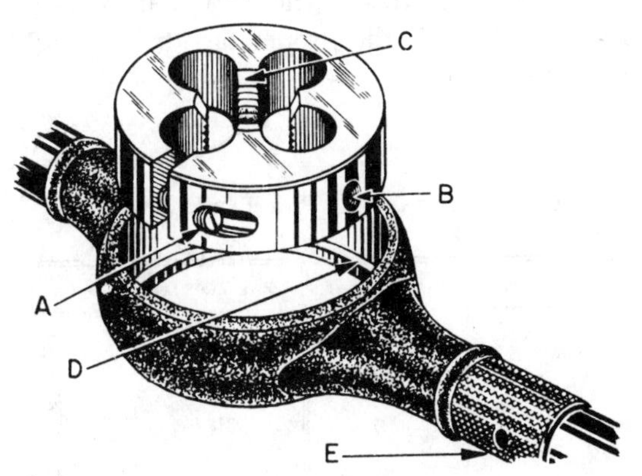

Figure 63. Assembling an adjustable round split die to diestock.

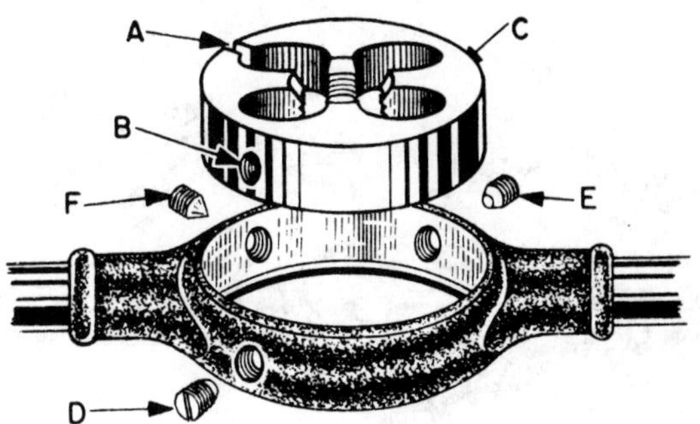

Figure 64. Assembling a plain round split die to diestock.

stock. At A, where the die is split, there is no adjusting screw. There are shallow holes at B and C, on both sides of the split, opposite which there are setscrews in the die stock at D and E. In F, Fig. 64 is the adjusting screw which is pointed and enters the split A in the die. D and E are the holding setscrews. They have flat points and are tightened after the setting is made with F. D and E hold the adjustment and furnish the drive as they enter the shallow holes B and C, as shown in Fig. 64.

Figure 65 shows a section of the die in the die stock and its relation to the chamfer on the end of the work. The taper on the face of the die will accept the chamfer on the end of the work to start the threads square with the common center line.

To thread the work, brush some 50-50 white lead and lard oil on the rod. Start the die square with the work. Hold one handle with each hand, apply downward pressure, and turn clockwise until you feel the thread has been started. When the die has started to cut, rotate the die stock two quarter turns, back it off one quarter turn to break the chips, and repeat the cutting (Fig. 66). When you have cut enough threads so that the rod comes through the back of the die, remove the die and try the rod in the tapped hole.

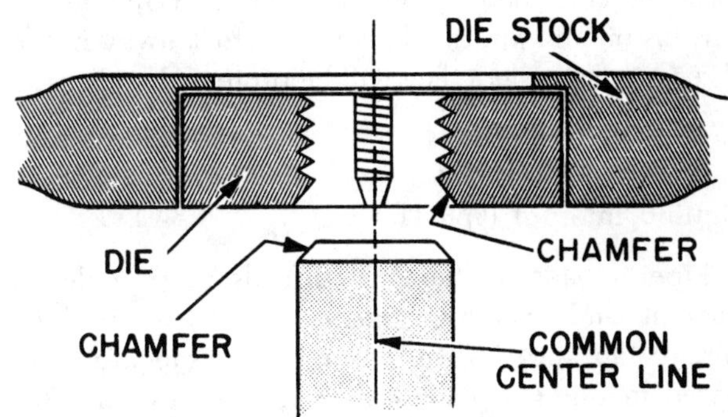

Figure 65. Position of diestock in relation to chamfer on end of work.

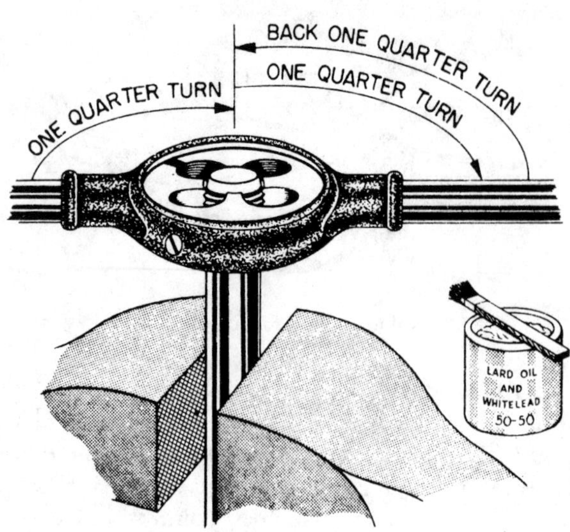

Figure 66. Cutting outside threads on round stock.

Adjusting a threading die to produce a thread of the proper fit is a trial-and-error procedure. This was a trial run. If the fit is too loose, cut off and discard the portion of the rod that you threaded. Then expand the die by tightening the pointed setscrews (or the adjusting screw) so that the die will cut shallower threads on the rod and produce a tighter fit.

If the fit is too tight, it will not be necessary to discard the threaded portion of the rod. Contract the die by backing off (loosening) the pointed setscrew (or the adjusting screw) to decrease the size of the split in the die. This will cause the die to remove more metal, when cutting, and produce a looser fit. Then run the die down the cut threads that were too tight. Now test the fit again by turning the threaded end into the tapped hole.

When you have finished the threading job, remove the die from the die stock, carefully clean out all the loosened chips, and apply plenty of oil. Wipe off the surplus oil and put the die and die stock away in the threading set where they will be protected and ready for the next job.

Cutting Internal Pipe Threads

Pipe threads are tapered threads to provide an airtight and liquidtight joint. A 3/8 in. machine thread tap and a 3/8 in. pipe thread tap are compared in Fig. 67 to show their differences. The 3/8 in. machine thread tap will cut machine threads in a hole so that a 3/8 in. cap screw having the same

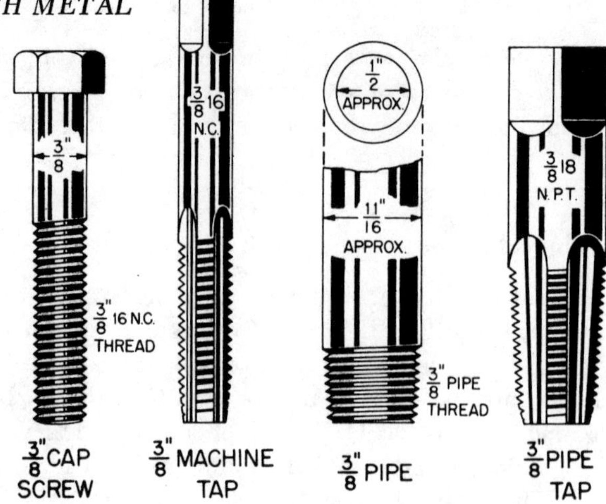

Figure 67. Comparison of machine thread tap and pipe thread tap.

thread can be screwed into the hole. The 3/8 in. pipe thread tap will cut pipe threads in a hole so that a 3/8 in. threaded pipe can be screwed into the hole. Because pipe diameters are measured and given as inside diameters, and the wall thickness of the pipe must be taken into consideration, the 3/8 in. pipe thread tap in Fig. 67 is noticeably larger than the 3/8 in. machine thread tap. It should also be noted that the pipe thread tap is tapered, but the machine thread tap is not.

The N.P.T., which formerly stood for National Pipe Thread, is still used as a carryover and now refers to the new name (American Standard Taper Pipe Thread) for the same thread. This standard taper is 3/4 in. per foot.

To select the proper tap drill for the pipe tap that you will use to tap a hole to take a given size of threaded pipe, see Table 11. *For example*, if you want to drill and tap a hole to take a 3/8 in. pipe thread, find the 3/8 in. pipe tap in the Pipe Tap Size column. Opposite this in the Tap Drill Size column is 19/32 in. This is the proper tap drill to use for a 3/8 in. pipe tap.

TABLE 11

AMERICAN STANDARD PIPE TAP DRILL SIZES

Pipe Tap Size	Tap Drill Size	Pipe Tap Size	Tap Drill Size
1/8	11/32	2	2 3/16
1/4	7/16	2 1/2	2 5/8
3/8	19/32	3	3 1/4
1/2	23/32	3 1/2	3 3/4
3/4	15/16	4	4 1/4
1	1 5/32	4 1/2	4 3/4
1 1/4	1 1/2	5	5 5/16
1 1/2	1 23/32	6	6 3/8

To *cut internal pipe threads,* drill a tap hole in the stock to be tapped, and following the suggested procedure for tapping machine threads as previously described in this chapter under the heading Cutting Machine Threads with Taps, run the pipe tap into the tap hole. *Note* that the first few threads on the pipe tap are ground away. This makes starting easier. Plenty of lard oil is the standard lubricant for steel. Tap copper and brass with no lubricant. The depth to which it is desirable to tap pipe threads is usually determined by turning the threaded pipe into the tapped hole for a trial. As shown in Fig. 68, the last few threads on the pipe should still be visible when the pipe is drawn up tight in the tapped hole. Figure 68 shows the values of dimension A (the length of thread on pipe required to make a tight joint) for various sizes of pipe up to 12 in.

The general practice in tapping holes for pipe threads is to drill the proper size tap hole and then start the pipe tap right into the tap hole. Some workers recommend using a pipe reamer, especially when large, deep holes are to be tapped. A pipe reamer has the same 3/4 in. per foot taper as a pipe tap. A reamed pipe tap hole would have the same shape as the pipe tap, and therefore would make tapping easier and reduce wear on the tap.

Cutting External Pipe Threads

Usually, both ends of a pipe are threaded with external pipe threads. (*Note* in all the illustrations showing pipe threads that they are V-shaped.) The standard 3/4 in. taper per foot of pipe threads is equal to 1/16 in. per inch. Therefore, the taper of the threads on each side of the pipe is 1/32 in. taper per inch. This taper cannot be changed, and this produces a tight joint. The angle between sides of the threads is 60 degrees, and several threads on the end of the pipe are perfect threads. The next few have V-bottoms but flat tops, and the last few threads have both flat tops and bottoms. Each size of the pipe has a certain number of threads per inch, built into the pipe taps and dies.

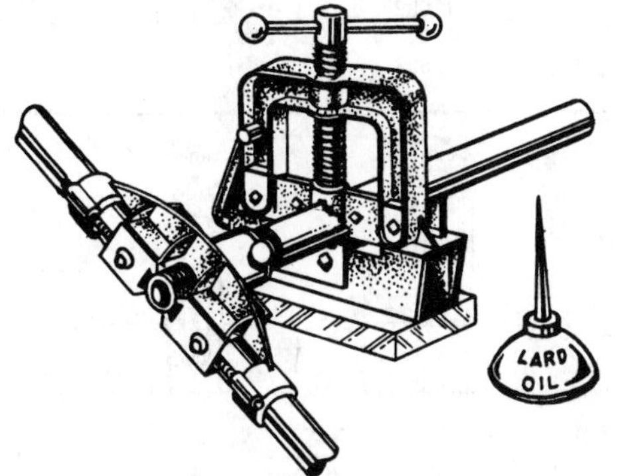

Figure 68. Length of thread on pipe required to make a tight joint.

Adjustable pipe dies have a reference mark on each die which when lined up with the corresponding reference mark on the die stock will give a standard-size thread. You adjust the dies one way or the other from the reference mark to cut a thread with the fit you want.

To cut external threads on iron pipe, first determine its nominal size. Nominal size means the *name size* of the pipe, such as 1/8 in., 3/4 in., and so on. Except in the sizes below 1 in., nominal sizes correspond closely to inside diameters. For 1 in. pipe and larger, measure the inside diameter (I.D.) with your rule, to the closest 1/32 in., and you will have nominal size. For sizes below 1 in. you can determine nominal size by measuring the outside diameter (O.D.) to the nearest 1/32 in. and reading the corresponding nominal size in Table 12. This method can also be employed for sizes 1 in. and above in lieu of the I.D. measurement.

TABLE 12

APPROXIMATE O.D. OF STANDARD WROUGHT IRON PIPE

NOMINAL SIZE	OUTSIDE DIAMETER	NOMINAL SIZE	OUTSIDE DIAMETER
1/8	13/32	3 1/2	4
1/4	17/32	4	4 1/2
3/8	11/16	4 1/2	5
1/2	27/32	5	5 9/16
3/4	1 1/16	6	6 5/8
1	1 5/16	7	7 5/8
1 1/4	1 21/32	8	8 5/8
1 1/2	1 29/32	9	9 5/8
2	2 3/8	10	10 3/4
2 1/2	2 7/8	11	11 3/4
3	3 1/2	12	12 3/4

To begin cutting, put the die stock on the pipe so that the pipe passes through the guide and enters the tapered face of the pipe die. Turn the die stock clockwise for right-hand threads, applying pressure only when starting. It is not necessary to turn the die back and forth as you do when cutting machine threads. Pipe-threading dies can cut continuously because they cut only as many threads on the pipe as there are on the die itself and because there is plenty of room in a pipe die for the chips to escape. After the die has taken hold, it will feed itself. When cutting threads on steel pipe, apply lard oil to the pipe and die where the cutting is actually taking place. Continue turning until the end of the pipe has gone through the die and is flush with the near face. (*See* Fig. 68.)

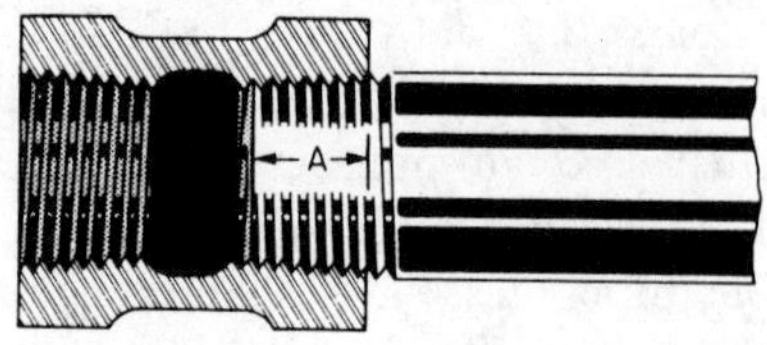

Size of Pipe, Inches	Dimension A, Inches	Size of Pipe, Inches	Dimension A, Inches	Size of Pipe, Inches	Dimension A, Inches
1/8	1/4	1 1/2	11/16	5	1 1/4
1/4	3/8	2	3/4	6	1 5/16
3/8	3/8	2 1/2	15/16	7	1 3/8
1/2	1/2	3	1	8	1 7/16
3/4	9/16	3 1/2	1 1/16	9	1 1/2
1	11/16	4	1 1/8	10	1 5/8
1 1/4	11/16	4 1/2	1 3/16	12	1 3/4

Figure 69. Threading an external pipe thread with a pipe die.

This will give you the length of thread called for in the table shown in Fig. 69. *Note* that in the assembled pipe joint in Fig. 69 several threads remain on both pipe and fitting to permit further tightening should a leak develop.

Reaming Operations

Reaming operations are jobs that smoothly enlarge drilled holes to an exact size and finish the hole at the same time. A hole that has been made by drilling is usually slightly oversize. This is quite satisfactory for holes in which bolts or rivets are placed. When greater accuracy and a smooth finish are required, the hole is first drilled undersize and then finished by reaming. Reamers are also used to remove burrs from the insides of pipe.

STRAIGHT HOLES. A solid straight-hole reamer is used for most work, since it is the most accurate and rugged reamer. The straight-hole hand reamer is turned by means of a tap wrench that is tightened on the square end of the reamer shank (Fig. 70). Secure the work in a vise so that the hole to be reamed is perpendicular to the top of the vise jaws. Position the reamer at the top of the hole (Fig. 71). Straight-hole reamers have a slight taper at the end so that they will fit into the hole easily. Turn the wrench clockwise very slowly until the reamer is centered in the hole.

After the reamer is centered in the hole, turn the wrench clockwise with a steady firm pressure until the reamer has been turned all the way through the hole. When reaming steel, use cutting oil or machine oil to lubricate the tool. When reaming soft iron, do

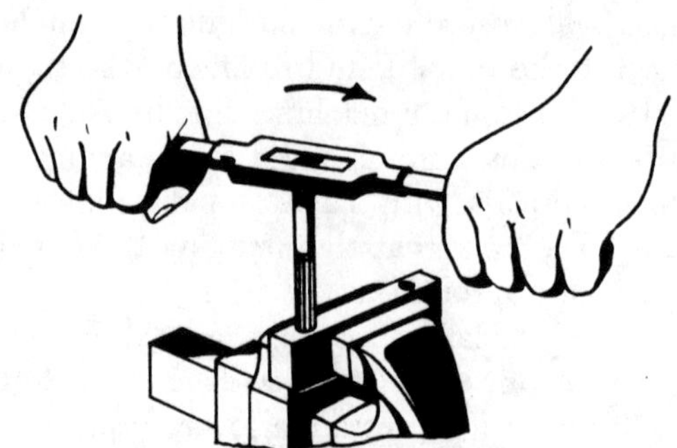

Figure 70. Using a tap wrench to turn a hand reamer.

not lubricate the tool. To remove the reamer from the hole, turn the wrench clockwise and raise the reamer simultaneously.

Note, turning the wrench too fast or too slowly will cause the reamer to chatter, producing an unevenly reamed hole.

TAPERED HOLES AND PIN INSTALLATION. When installing a tapered pin, be sure you have the proper size of pin to use. The size will be given as a number and length in inches. (*See* Table 13.) For in-

TABLE 13
STANDARD TAPER PIN DIMENSIONS

No. of Pin	Diameter at Large End D	Diameter at Large End D	Max. Length L
00000	0. 094	3/32	3/4
0000	. 109	7/64	7/8
000	. 125	1/8	1
00	. 141	9/64	1 1/8
0	. 156	5/32	1 1/4
1	. 172	11/64	1 1/4
2	. 193	3/16	1 1/2
3	. 219	7/32	1 3/4
4	. 250	1/4	2
5	. 289	19/64	2 1/4
6	. 341	11/32	3
7	. 409	13/32	3 3/4
8	. 492	1/2	4 1/2
9	. 591	19/32	5 1/4
10	. 706	23/32	6
11	. 860	55/64	7 1/4
12	1. 032	1 1/32	9
13	1. 241	1 15/64	11
14	1. 523	1 33/64	13

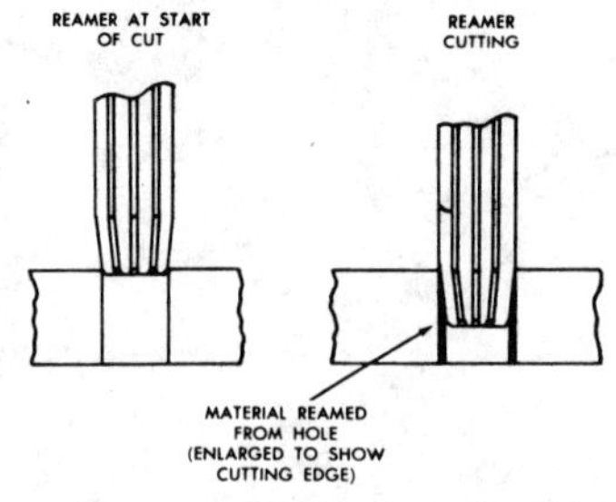

Figure 71. Reaming a hole with a straight hole reamer.

stance, a No. 3 pin 1 3/4 in. long might be specified. Then when you have the proper pin, measure the diameter of its small end and drill a hole of that size through, for example, the hub of a flange and a shaft while the flange is in place on the shaft (Fig. 72). Then select the same number of tapered pin reamer—a No. 3 in this case.

TABLE 14
TAPER REAMER DIMENSIONS

No. of Taper Pin Reamer	Diameter at Large End of Reamer	Diameter at Small End of Reamer	Length of Flute
7/0	0.0666	0.0497	13/16
6/0	0.0806	0.0611	15/16
5/0	0.0966	0.0719	1 3/16
4/0	0.1142	0.0869	1 5/16
3/0	0.1302	0.1029	1 5/16
2/0	0.1462	0.1137	1 9/16
0	0.1638	0.1287	1 11/16
1	0.1798	0.1447	1 11/16
2	0.2008	0.1605	1 15/16
3	0.2294	0.1813	2 5/16
4	0.2604	0.2071	2 9/16
5	0.2994	0.2409	2 13/16
6	0.3540	0.2773	3 11/16
7	0.4220	0.3297	4 7/16
8	0.5050	0.3971	5 3/16
9	0.6066	0.4805	6 1/16
10	0.7216	0.5799	6 13/16

See Table 14 for specifications of various sizes of reamers. The specifications given opposite the reamer numbers in the left-hand column of Table 14 are the dimensions of the reamers. The small end of the reamer should just enter the hole you drill and if the proper size of reamer has been selected the pin will fit exactly. Turn the tapered pin reamer with a tap wrench slowly and in a clockwise direction only, lifting it out of the hole to clean away the chips while it is still turning. If you reverse the direction of the reamer, chips may be wedged behind its cutting edges, causing them to break. Ream brass dry but apply cutting oil when reaming steel. Try the taper pin in the hole several times as the reaming progresses. Stop reaming when the pin protrudes the same amount on both sides of the hub of the gear.

BURR REMOVAL. After a piece of pipe has been cut, the ends should be reamed to remove the burr that is left on the inside of the pipe. This burr, if not removed, will restrict the flow of fluid in the pipe. Besides the pipe reamer you will need a vise to hold the pipe steady. After making sure the pipe is held firmly in the vise, insert the reamer in the end of the pipe and turn the handle (Fig. 73). Rotate the handle of the reamer clockwise in short, even strokes until the burrs inside the cut piece of pipe are completely removed. Remove the reamer from the pipe by rotating it clockwise and reducing applied pressure.

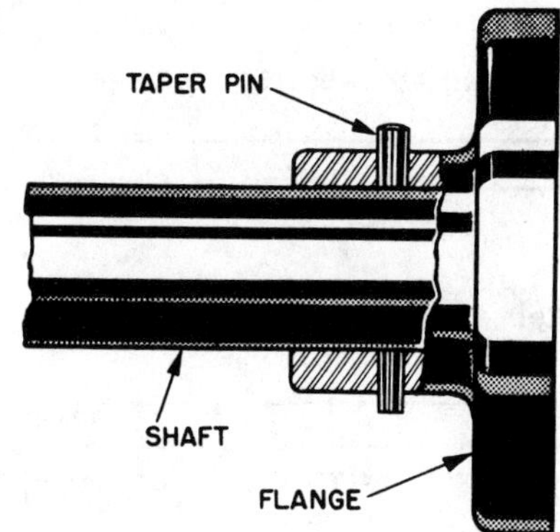

Figure 72. A tapered pin installed in a shaft and flange.

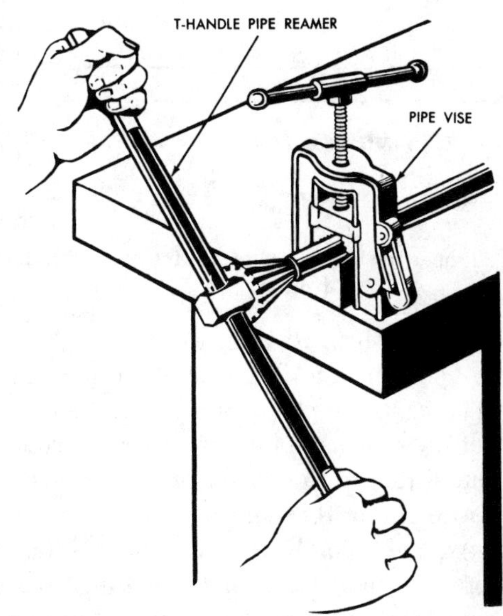

Figure 73. Using a pipe reamer to remove burrs from pipe.

Cutting Piping and Tubing

The main difference between pipe and tubing lies in their wall thicknesses: Pipe has thicker walls than tubing. Though pipe cutters are larger than tube cutters, they work on the same principle.

PIPE. Before cutting a pipe to length, *be sure* you have the correct measurement. Figure 74 shows methods of measuring threaded pipe to desired lengths.

The *end-to-end method* includes measuring the threaded portions of the pipe and measuring the pipe from end to end. The *end-to-center method* is used on a section of pipe that has a fitting screwed

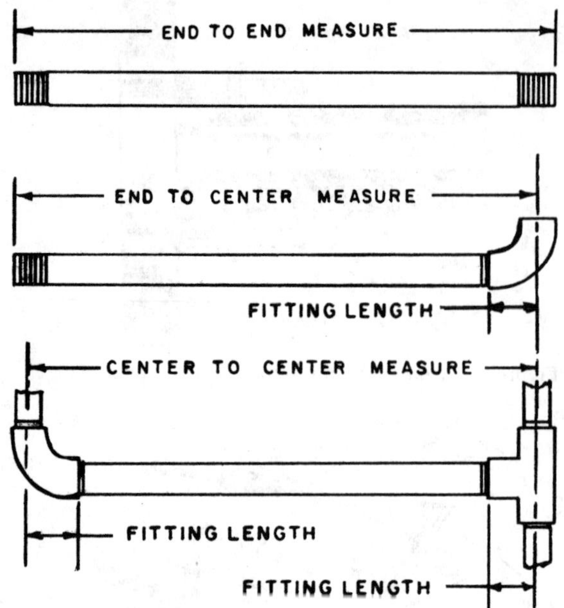

Figure 74. Proper methods for measuring pipe to desired lengths.

on one end only. Measure from the free end of the pipe to the center of the fitting at the other end of the pipe. The *center-to-center method* is used when both ends of the pipe have fittings. Measure from the center of one fitting to the center of the other fitting at the opposite end of the pipe.

The approximate length of thread on 1/2 in. and 3/4 in. wrought iron or steel pipe is 3/4 in. On 1 in., 1 1/4 in., and 1 1/2 in. pipe the length of the thread is approximately 1 in. long. On 2 in. and 2 1/2 in. pipe the length of thread is 1 1/8 in. and 1 1/2 in., respectively.

To determine the length of pipe required, take the measurement of installation such as center to center of the pipe requiring two fittings. Measure the size of the fittings as shown in Fig. 74. Subtract the total size of the two fittings from the installation measurement. Multiply the approximate thread length by 2 and add the result to the length obtained. This will give the length of pipe required.

After the length of the pipe has been determined, measure the pipe and mark the spot where the cut is to be made with a scriber or crayon. Lock the pipe securely in a pipe vise.

Inspect the cutter to make sure that there are no nicks or burrs in the cutting wheel. Open the jaws of the cutter by turning the handle counterclockwise. Position the cutter around the pipe at the marked point. Make sure the cutting wheel is exactly on the mark and close the jaws of the cutter lightly against

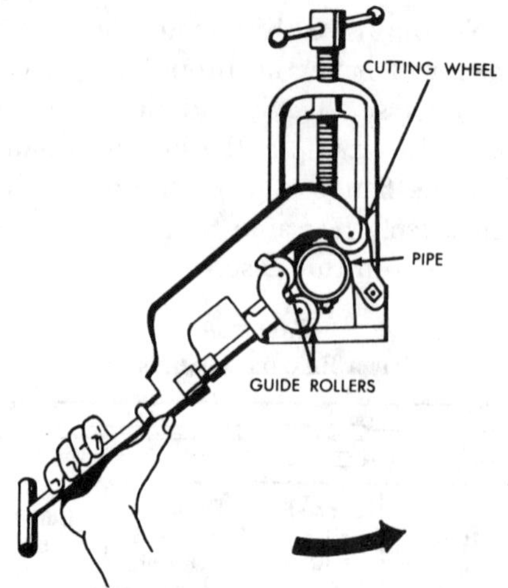

Figure 75. Cutting pipe with a pipe cutter.

the pipe by turning the cutter handle clockwise. After making contact, turn the cutter handle clockwise one-fourth of a turn more. This will put a bite on the pipe.

Grasp the cutter handle and rotate the cutter as a whole one complete revolution, swinging it around the pipe in the direction indicated in Fig. 75. Turn the cutter handle clockwise one-fourth of a turn more to take another bite on the pipe and rotate the cutter another complete revolution. Keep the cutter perpendicular to the pipe at all times or the wheel will not track properly. Repeat this operation until the pipe is cut. Remove the small shoulder on the outside of the pipe with a file and remove the burr on the inside with a reamer.

TUBING. Copper tubing is one kind of metallic tubing that you can cut readily with a tube cutter. To cut tubing, place the tube cutter with the cutting wheel on the mark where the cut is to be made. Move the cutting wheel into light contact with the tubing. (*See* step 1 in Fig. 76.) Then swing the handle around the tubing as you feed the cutting wheel a little for each revolution by turning the screw adjustment. Different wall thicknesses, kinds, and diameters of metallic tubing require different feeds. Step 2, Fig. 76 indicates the direction of rotation. The feed pressure is correct when it keeps the wheel cutting but does not flatten the tubing.

The design of some tubing cutters will permit cutting off a flared end close to the base of the flare. *Note* the groove in the backup roller in Fig. 77. Place the flare in this groove so that the cutting wheel rides at the base of the flare. Then cut off the flare as you would cut tubing.

Burrs that form may be similar to those formed in

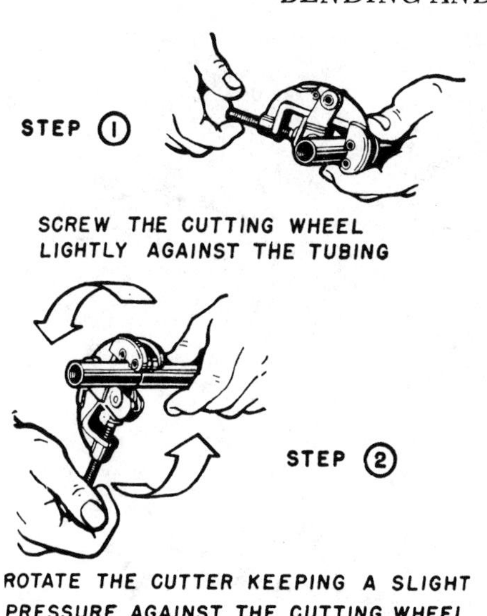
STEP ①
SCREW THE CUTTING WHEEL LIGHTLY AGAINST THE TUBING
STEP ②
ROTATE THE CUTTER KEEPING A SLIGHT PRESSURE AGAINST THE CUTTING WHEEL WITH THE SCREW ADJUSTMENT

Figure 76. Steps in cutting tubing with a tube cutter.

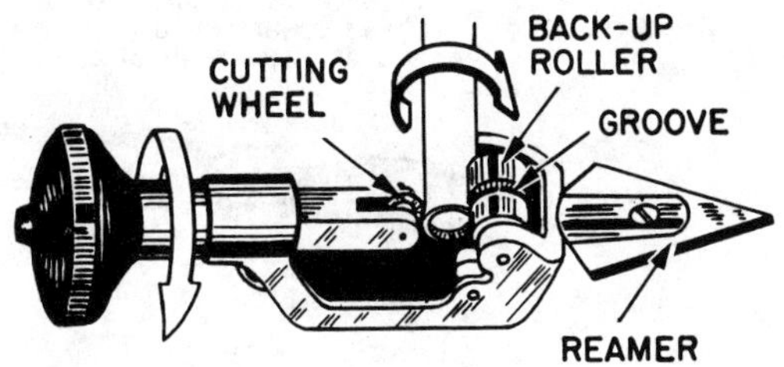
CUTTING WHEEL
BACK-UP ROLLER
GROOVE
REAMER

Figure 77. Cutting tubing close to the base of a flare.

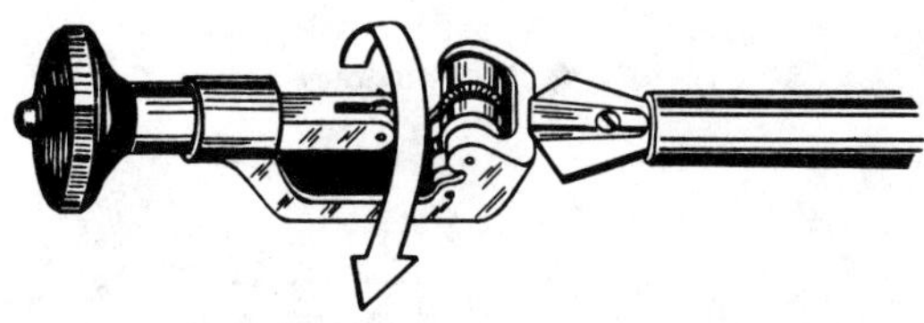

Figure 78. Reaming the burrs from a piece of tubing.

pipe cutting. Remove the inside burr with the reamer attached to the tubing cutter opposite the handle (Fig. 78). In some cases, a three-cornered scraper, pocketknife blade, or round file may work better than the reamer. After reaming, clean out the chips. Then remove any outside burr with a file.

Bending and Flaring Metallic Tubing

The objective in tube bending is to obtain a smooth bend without flattening the tube. Tube bending is usually accomplished with one of the tube benders discussed in this chapter. In an emergency, aluminum tubing with a diameter of less than 1/4 inch may be bent by hand.

Spring Benders. *External spring-type benders* (A, Fig. 79) come in sizes to bend 1/4 in., 5/16 in., 3/8 in., 7/16 in., 1/2 in., and 5/8 in. outside-diameter soft copper, aluminum, and other soft metallic tubing. To bend tubing with this type of bender, first select the size that will just slip over the size of tubing you want to bend. Then slip it over the tubing so that it centers at the middle of the proposed bend. Grasp the bender with both hands and make the bend (B, Fig. 79). The restraining action of the bender will prevent the tubing from collapsing at the bend and will produce a smooth curve. To remove the bender, grasp the belled end and pull it off the tubing.

Internal spring-type benders (C, Fig. 79) are available in sizes to bend 3/8 in., 1/2 in., and 5/8 in. outside-diameter tubing. This type can be used when both ends of a length of tubing are flared and the external type cannot be applied. To bend tubing with an internal spring-type bender, select the proper size bender and slip it inside the tubing. Insert the bender so that the center of its length is at the center of the proposed bend. Grasp the tubing with both hands and make the bend. If the bender sticks out of the end of the tubing, remove it by pulling it out. If not, remove it with a fish wire or other simple means.

Hand Tube Bender. The hand tube bender (Fig. 80) consists of four parts—handle, radius block (mandrel), clip, and slide bar. The radius block is marked in degrees of bend ranging from 0 to 180. The slide bar has a mark which is lined up with the zero mark on the radius block. The tube is inserted in the tool, and after lining up the marks, the slide bar is

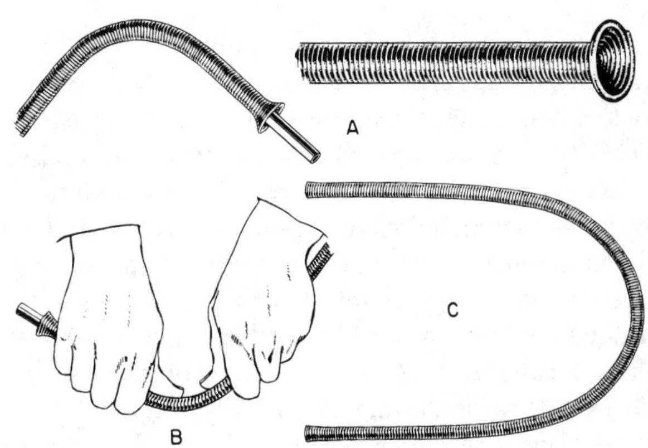
A
B
C

Figure 79. Bending tubing with spring type tube benders.

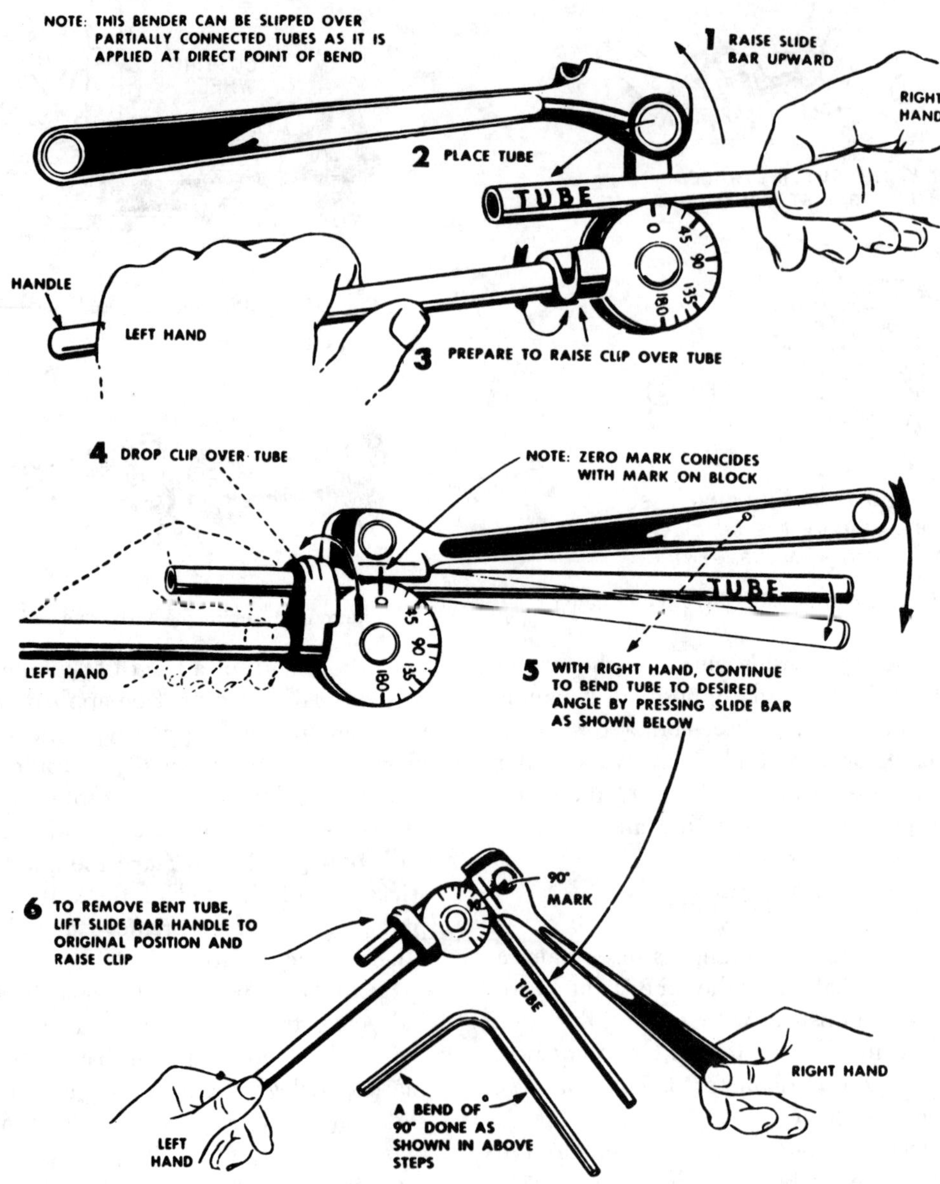
NOTE: THIS BENDER CAN BE SLIPPED OVER PARTIALLY CONNECTED TUBES AS IT IS APPLIED AT DIRECT POINT OF BEND
1 RAISE SLIDE BAR UPWARD
RIGHT HAND
2 PLACE TUBE
TUBE
HANDLE
LEFT HAND
3 PREPARE TO RAISE CLIP OVER TUBE
4 DROP CLIP OVER TUBE
NOTE: ZERO MARK COINCIDES WITH MARK ON BLOCK
TUBE
LEFT HAND
5 WITH RIGHT HAND, CONTINUE TO BEND TUBE TO DESIRED ANGLE BY PRESSING SLIDE BAR AS SHOWN BELOW
6 TO REMOVE BENT TUBE, LIFT SLIDE BAR HANDLE TO ORIGINAL POSITION AND RAISE CLIP
90° MARK
TUBE
RIGHT HAND
A BEND OF 90° DONE AS SHOWN IN ABOVE STEPS
LEFT HAND

Figure 80. Tube bending.

moved around until the mark on the slide bar reaches the desired degrees of bend on the radius block. Follow the procedure shown in Fig. 80.

This type of bender is furnished in 3/16 in., 1/4 in., 5/16 in., 3/8 in., 1/2 in. sizes. For larger sizes of tubing, similar mandrel-type benders are used. The only difference is that these larger benders are geared for greater mechanical advantage.

Flaring. Tube flaring is a method of forming the end of a tube into a funnel shape so that it can be held by a threaded fitting. A partially threaded flare nut is slipped over the tube, the end of the tube is flared, the flare is seated with the inside of the flare against the end of a fitting which has threads on the outside, and then the flare nut is screwed onto the fitting, pushing the outside of the flare against the seating surface of the fitting.

The tube-flaring tool shown in Fig. 81 is one type which is commonly used to flare copper tubing. To flare the end of tubing, first check to see that it has been cut off squarely and has the burrs removed from both inside and outside. Remember to slip the flare nut on the tube before you make the flare. Then, as shown in A, Fig. 81, open the flaring tool at the die which corresponds to the size of the tubing being flared. Insert the end of the tubing to pro-

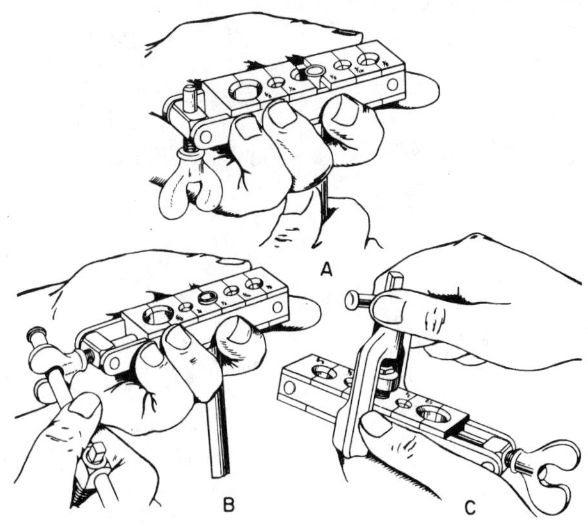

Figure 81. Flaring metallic tubing.

trude slightly above the top face of the die blocks. The amount by which the tubing extends above the blocks determines the finished diameter of the flare. The flare must be large enough so that it will seat properly against the fitting, but small enough so that the threads of the flare nut will slide over it. You determine the correct size by trial-and-error. Then, as shown in B, Fig. 81, close the die block and secure the tool with the wing nut. Use the handle of the yoke to tighten the wing nut. Then place the yoke over the end of the tubing (C, Fig. 81), and tighten the handle to force the cone into the end of the tubing. The completed flare should be slightly visible above the face of the die blocks.

Removing Broken Bolts and Studs

When the removal of a broken bolt or stud is required, flood the part being worked on with plenty of penetrating oil or oil of wintergreen. Time permitting, soak the area for several hours or overnight. A week's soaking may loosen a bolt which would otherwise have to be drilled out.

If enough of the broken piece protrudes, take hold of it with vise-grip pliers as shown in Fig. 82 and carefully try to ease it out. If the bolt cannot be turned, further soaking with penetrating oil may help. Or, try removing the pliers and jarring the bolt with light hammer blows on the top and around the sides. This may loosen the threads so that the bolt can then be removed with the vise-grip pliers.

If a bolt has been broken off flush with the surface as shown in Fig. 83, it is sometimes possible to back it out with light blows of a prick punch or center

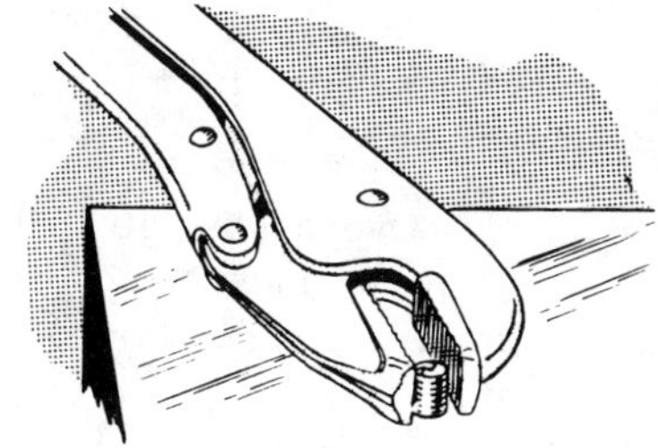

Figure 82. Removing a broken stud with vise-grip pliers.

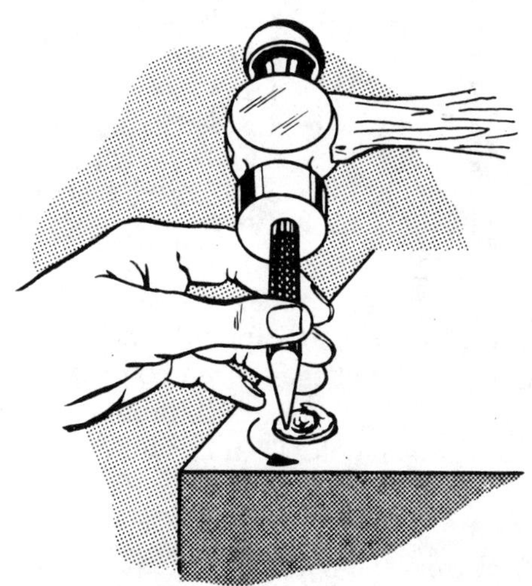

Figure 83. Removing a broken bolt with a prick punch.

punch. If the bolt was broken due to rusting, this method will not remove it. If it cannot be removed by careful punching first on one side and then on the other, a screw and bolt extractor (B, Fig. 84) may remove it.

When using a bolt extractor, file the broken portion of the bolt to provide a smooth surface at the center for a punch mark, if possible. Then carefully center punch the exact center of the bolt (A, Fig. 84).

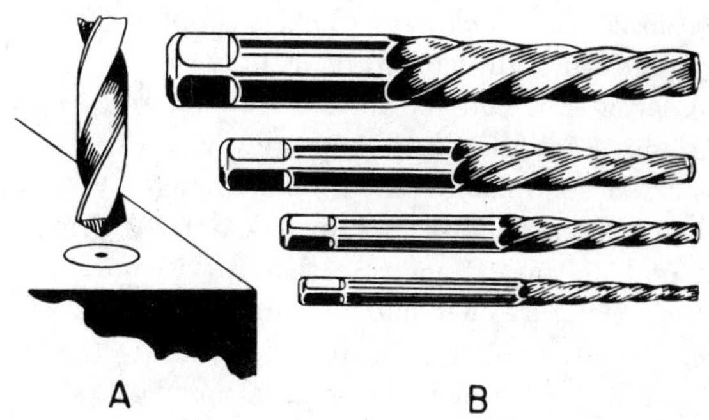

Figure 84. Screw and bolt extractors for removing broken studs.

TABLE 15

CHART FOR SCREW AND BOLT EXTRACTORS

Extractor		Used For—		Use Drill Size Dia., Inches
Size No.	Overall Length, Inches	Nominal Screw And Bolt Size, Inches	Nominal Pipe Size, Inches	
1	2	3/16 - 1/4	--------	5/64
2	2 3/8	1/4 - 5/16	--------	7/64
3	2 11/16	5/16 - 7/16	--------	5/32
4	3	7/16 - 9/16	--------	1/4
5	3 3/8	9/16 - 3/4	1/4	17/64
6	3 3/4	3/4 - 1	3/8	13/32
7	4 1/8	1 - 1 3/8	1/2	17/32
8	4 3/8	1 3/8 - 1 3/4	3/4	13/16
9	4 5/8	1 3/4 - 2 1/8	1	1 1/16
10	5	2 1/8 - 2 1/2	1 1/4	1 5/16
11	5 5/8	2 1/2 - 3	1 1/2	1 9/16
12	6 1/4	3 - 3 1/2	2	1 15/16

See Table 15 to select the proper drill size to use according to the size of the broken bolt that you are trying to remove. If possible, drill through the entire length of the broken bolt. Then carefully work some penetrating oil through this hole so that it fills the cavity beneath the bolt and has a chance to work its way upward from the bottom of the bolt. The more time you let the penetrating oil work from both ends of the broken bolt, the better are your chances of removing it.

When drilling a hole in a stud which has broken off below the surface of the piece which it was holding, as shown in A, Fig. 85, a drill guide will center the drill and may be preferred rather than a center punch mark.

When the hole has been drilled, and additional penetrating oil has had time to soak, put the spiral end of the screw and bolt extractor into the hole. Set it firmly with a few light hammer blows and secure the tap wrench as shown in B, Fig. 85. Carefully try to back the broken bolt out of the hole. Turn the extractor counterclockwise. (This type of extractor is designed for right-hand threads only.)

A screw and bolt extractor can sometimes be used to remove an Allen head capscrew when the socket has been stripped by the Allen wrench (Fig. 86). When attempting this removal, carefully grind off the end of the extractor so that it will not bottom before the spiral has had a chance to take hold. B, Fig. 86 shows this end clearance. In doing this kind of grinding operation, great care must be taken to keep the temperature of the extractor low enough so that the tip can be handled with the bare hands. If the hardness is drawn from the tip of the extractor by overheating during the grinding, the extractor will not take hold.

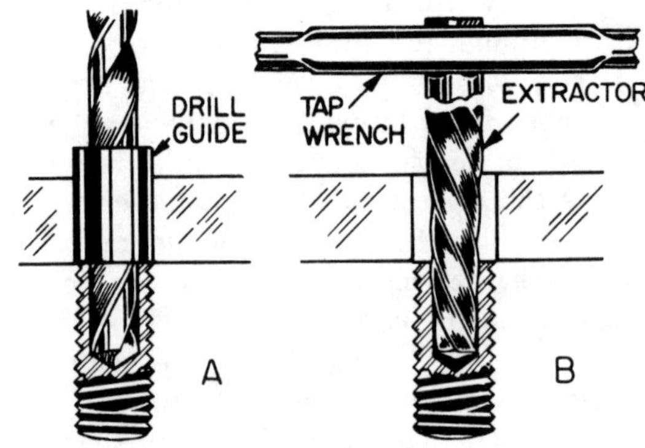

Figure 85. Removing a stud broken off below the surface.

REMOVING A BROKEN BOLT AND RETAPPING HOLE. To remove a broken bolt and retap the hole, file the bolt smooth, if necessary, and center punch it for drilling.

Then select a twist drill which is a little less than the tap drill size for the particular bolt that has been broken. As shown in Fig. 87, this drill will just about but not quite touch the crests of the threads in the threaded hole or the roots of the threads on the threaded bolt. Carefully start drilling at the center punch mark, crowding the drill one way or the other as necessary so that the hole will be drilled in the exact center of the bolt. The drill shown in Fig. 87 has almost drilled the remaining part of the bolt away and will eventually break through the bottom of the bolt. When this happens, all that will remain

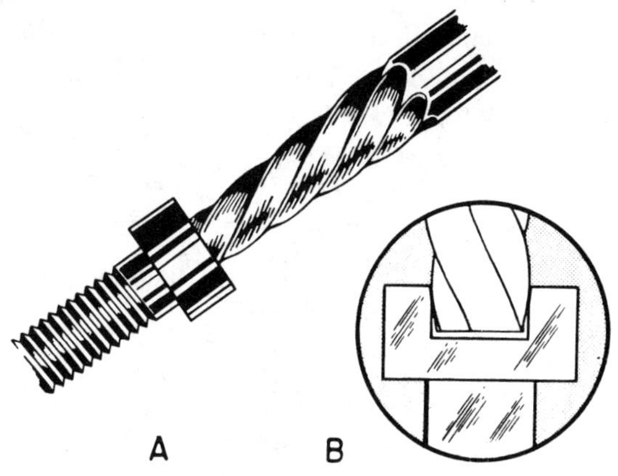

Figure 86. Removing an Allen head capscrew with a bolt extractor.

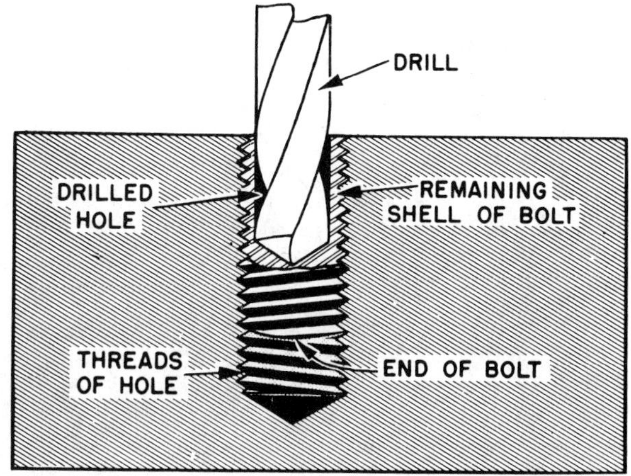

Figure 87. Removing a broken bolt and retapping hole to same size.

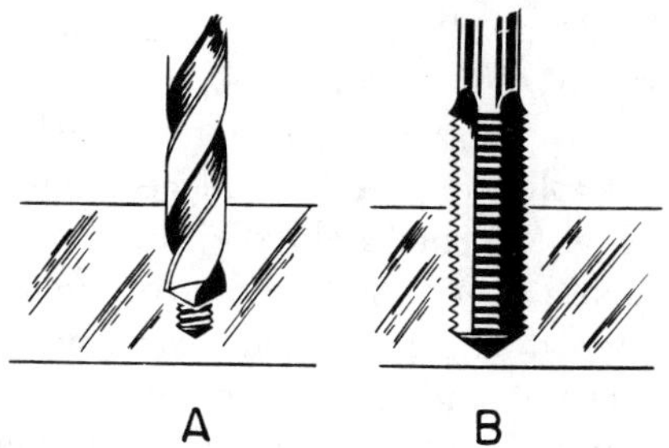

Figure 88. Removing broken bolt and retapping hole to larger size.

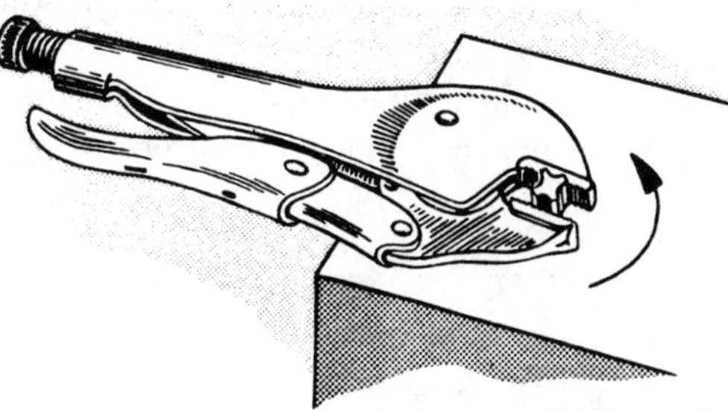

Figure 89. Removing a broken tap with vise-grip pliers.

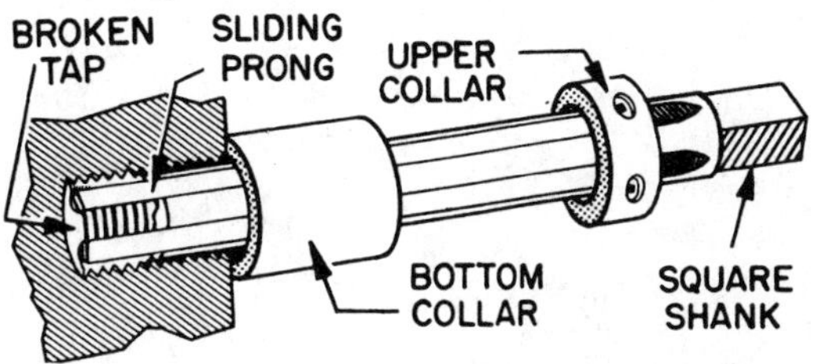

Figure 90. Removing a broken tap with a tap extractor.

of the bolt will be a threaded shell. With a prick punch or with a suitable tool, chip out and remove the first two or three threads, if possible, at the top of the shell. Then start a tapered tap into these several clean threads and continue tapping until the shell has been cut away and the original threads restored.

In cases where the identical size of capscrew or bolt is not necessary as a replacement, center punch and drill out the old bolt with a drill larger than the broken bolt as shown in A, Fig. 88. Tap the hole first and then finish it with a bottoming tap as shown in B, Fig. 88. Replace with a larger size capscrew or stud.

Removing a Broken Tap from a Hole

To remove a broken tap from a hole, apply penetrating oil to the tap, working it down through the four flutes into the hole. Then grasp the tap across the flats with vise-grip pliers (Fig. 89). Adding penetrating oil as necessary, ease the tap out of the hole.

If the tap has broken off at the surface of the work, or slightly below the surface of the work, use a tap extractor to remove it (Fig. 90). Again, apply a liberal amount of penetrating oil to the broken tap. Place the tap extractor over the broken tap and lower the upper collar to insert the four sliding prongs down into the four flutes of the tap. Then slide the bottom collar down to the surface of the work so that it will hold the prongs tightly against the body of the extractor. Tighten the tap wrench on the square shank of the extractor and carefully work the extractor back and forth to loosen the tap. It may be necessary to remove the extractor and strike a few sharp blows with a small hammer and pin punch to jar the tap loose. Then reinsert the tap remover and carefully try to back the tap out of the hole.

Each size of tap will require its own size of tap extractor. Tap extractors come in the following sizes:

1/4 in., 5/16 in., 3/8 in., 7/16 in., 1/2 in., 9/16 in., 5/8 in., 3/4 in., 7/8 in., and 1 in.

When a tap extractor will not remove a broken tap, try the following method. Place a hex nut over the tap (Fig. 91) and weld the nut to the tap. *Be sure* to choose a nut with a hole somewhat smaller than the tap diameter to reduce the possibility of welding the nut and the tap to the job. Allow the weld to cool before trying to remove the tap. When the nut, the tap, and the job have come to room temperature, it is often helpful to heat quickly the immediate area around the hole with an oxyacetylene torch. This quick heating expands the adjacent metal of the work after which the removal of the tap may be less difficult. If the heating is too slow, the tap will expand with the adjacent metal of the work and there will be no loosening effect.

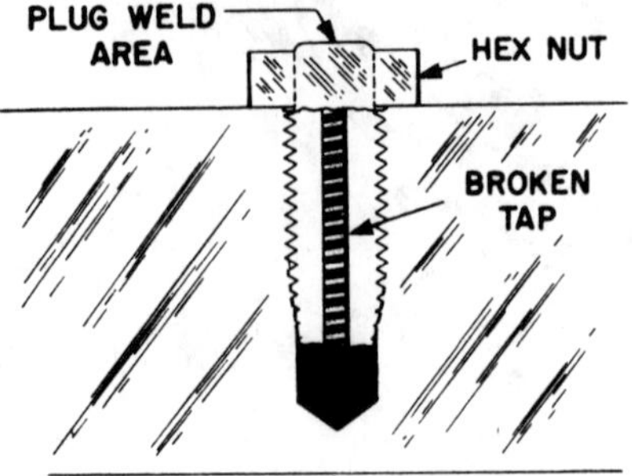

Figure 91. Using a plug weld to remove a broken tap.

Chapter 6

Soldering Materials and Procedures

Soldering is the process of joining two pieces of like or unlike metals together by means of an alloy having a lower melting point than that of the pieces being joined.

The strength of soldered points depends largely upon the nature of the solder used and the temperature at which the soldering is done. Therefore, the degree of strength required for joints must be kept in mind in choosing a solder for a given class of work. A large percentage of soldered joints are defective due to improper cleaning and fitting of the parts to be joined. Selection of the proper flux (which is used to prevent and remove oxides) when necessary, is important. The metal surfaces must be kept chemically clean and free from oxide throughout the operation. If the base metal is one that oxidizes slowly, and if it is kept at the correct soldering temperature, it is usually sufficient to coat the freshly cleaned surface with tallow, rosin, or some other similar substance. For such soldering, the only requirement of the flux is that it should be present during the actual soldering process. If, however, either the metal surface or the solder is covered with an oxide film or coating, some method must be used to remove it. Most of the metal fluxes meet this requirement, thus enabling clean metal surfaces to come together and alloy. In soldering sheet metal parts that must be kept free from corrosion, rosin or some other noncorrosive flux should be used.

Soft and hard soldering are the two general classifications of soldering materials and procedures used. Soldering coppers (Chap. 3) are used for soft soldering and occasionally for aluminum soldering. Blow torches are always used for hard soldering, and often for aluminum soldering. Various types of soldering coppers are shown in Fig. 1.

Because soft soldering is the type of soldering used extensively by the sheet metal worker, the soldering procedures described in this chapter will be confined to that particular method.

The most important points for the student to consider in all soft soldering operations are: thorough cleaning of the parts to be joined, careful fitting together of the parts, application of the proper flux, heating and tinning of the soldering copper, and application of the solder to the seam or joint. The parts may be cleaned by scraping, filing, or brushing with a wire brush. This removes all scale, dirt, and oxides.

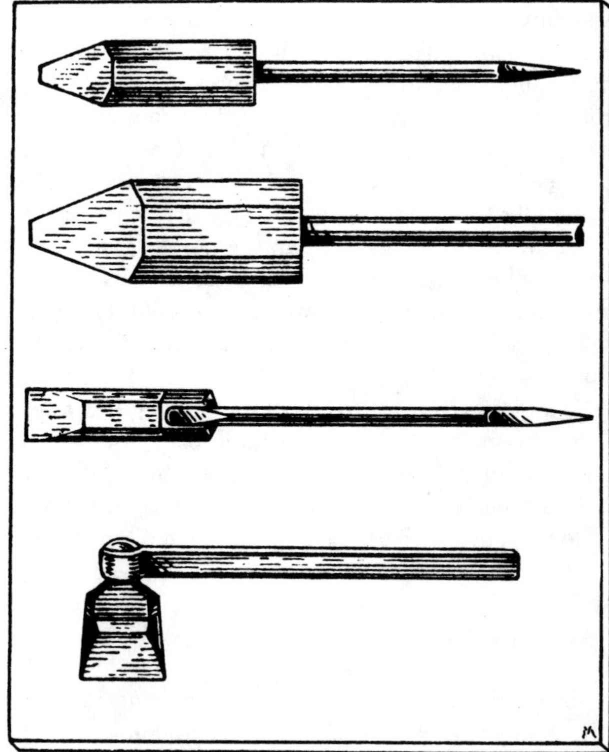

Figure 1. Soldering coppers. *Top to bottom:* regular, roofing, bottom, and hatchet.

After the surfaces of the parts to be joined have been cleaned, they should be fitted and secured in place, then coated with a suitable flux (*see* Table 16). After this, the application of the hot soldering copper and the proper amount of melted solder to the adjoining parts will cause them to adhere.

FLUXES. There are two classes of fluxes: Corrosive and noncorrosive. The corrosive fluxes eat away the soldered metals unless they are thoroughly washed off after soldering. The fluxes ordinarily used for soft soldering are solutions or pastes that contain zinc chloride. Zinc chloride and sal ammoniac are corrosive fluxes.

TABLE 16
USUAL FLUXES FOR COMMON METALS

Metal	Flux
Brass, copper, tin	Rosin
Lead	Tallow, rosin
Iron, steel	Borax, sal ammoniac
Galvanized iron	Zinc chloride
Zinc	Zinc chloride
Aluminum *	Stearine, special flux

* Stearic acid or stearine may be used in soldering aluminum, but a special aluminum solder is now available which makes the use of flux unnecessary.

Practically all clean metals when exposed to the atmosphere acquire a film of rust or tarnish. The thickness of this film increases as time goes on. Moisture and heat help speed it up. This film or oxide is present even though it is invisible. It is difficult to get solder to adhere to such metal, because the solder must "wet" and penetrate into the pores of the metal to be soldered. A chemical material is used to prepare the metal for the wetting or alloying with molten solder. This chemical is called a soldering flux.

A soldering flux is used for the following purposes: first, it removes tarnish or metallic oxide; second, it prevents further oxide from forming while the metal is being heated to soldering temperature; and third, it lowers the surface tension of the molten solder, enabling it to spread about the area and penetrate where it should.

Although there are many commercially prepared fluxes available, sheet metal workers generally prefer to prepare their own flux by "cutting" zinc in muriatic acid (also known as HCl or hydrochloric acid), thus producing zinc chloride. This flux is also called "cut" or "killed" acid. It is used as a flux when soldering clean galvanized iron, zinc, lead, copper, brass, and tin plate that has been exposed to the weather.

To make zinc chloride flux, proceed as follows: Drop pieces of zinc into a glass or earthenware jar containing muriatic acid until the acid stops boiling and bubbles have stopped rising to the surface. When all boiling has stopped, the solution is strained. Note that zinc chloride must be prepared outdoors or near an open window and away from heat or flames of any kind, because the fumes are injurious and inflammable. Zinc chloride, when not in actual use, must be kept in closed containers.

Muriatic acid is often used in its raw or original state as a flux for soldering galvanized iron and zinc.

Both raw and "cut" or "killed" acid fluxes are corrosive and must be washed off when the soldering job is completed.

When soldering tin plate, bright copper, or pewter, rosin is used as a flux. Rosin is the most commonly used non-corrosive flux of this type, and it does not have to be washed off. It is available in either paste, powder, or liquid form. Rosin does not clean the surface of the work, but it does prevent oxidation during soldering by covering the surface with a protective film. Liquid fluxes are usually applied by a brush. The flux is spread lightly along the seam or joint that is to be soldered as shown in Fig. 2. When either powdered or paste rosin flux is used, it is either spread, sprinkled, or melted on the work with a hot soldering copper.

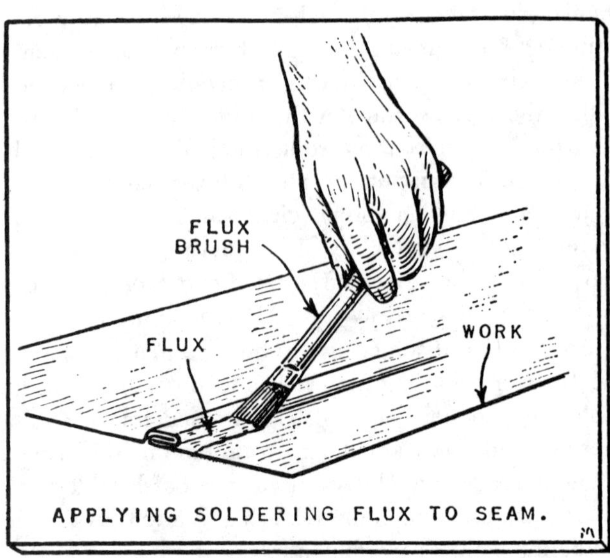

Figure 2.

SOLDER. Solders used by sheet metal workers are made of varying percentages of tin and lead. Solder should always be secured from a reliable source, because a good soldering job is largely dependent on the quality of the solder being used.

Tin is a metal endowed with a few unique physical and chemical properties. In the molten state, tin dissolves and alloys readily with many metals. A soldering flux, as previously explained, helps to do this.

It is this property of tin, coupled with its low melting point (450 deg. F.), that creates the fusible alloy we call soft solder, or just solder.

If pure tin, which melts at 450 deg. F., and lead, which liquefies at 620 deg. F., are mixed in the proportion of 63 parts of tin by weight to 37 parts of lead by weight, the surprising result will be a fusible alloy that will melt at a temperature even lower than the melting points of the two metals—361 deg. F. This is the lowest melting composition of tin-lead mixtures.

Tin mixes with lead in all proportions. The most common compositions are 40/60, 50/50, and 60/40. Tin, contrary to popular belief, is an expensive metal. There are no tin mines in the United States; consequently, it must be imported from countries in Asia, Africa, and South America.

Lead, on the other hand, is a cheap metal, ordinarily selling for about one-sixth the price of tin. Of course, the more tin in the solder, the more costly it will be.

A good solder is 40/60. It is an all-round solder and contains 40 per cent tin and 60 per cent lead (the first number mentioned is always tin). This solder starts to soften at 361 deg. F., goes through a mushy or plastic stage, and becomes completely liquid and mobile at 460 deg. F.

Some prefer 50/50 solder, also called "half and half." It has a narrower plastic range, becoming completely molten at 414 deg. F.

An excellent solder, the 60/40 composition, is more expensive, very fluid, and is used where a low melting solder is required; for example, on pewter ware. 60/40 is liquid at 370 deg. F.; its plastic range is very narrow, from 361 to 370 deg. F.

Solders of these varying percentages of tin and lead are available in bars weighing from ½ to 1½ lb. each, or in wire form ranging from .009 in. to .250 in. gauge or thickness.

SOLDERING COPPERS (Fig. 1). Successful soldering requires enough heat to raise the area of the metals to be joined to a solder-melting temperature.

There are many ways of transmitting heat to a metal surface or joint. The most popular and preferred method of transferring heat is by means of a soldering copper.

Not only does a soldering copper deliver heat to the metals to be soldered and melt the solder, but it also enables the user to sweat seams, smooth out the wrinkles in pasty solder, and make a neater appearing job.

Soldering irons are available in many weights or sizes. Gas or forge-heated soldering irons or coppers, as they are often called, are sold singly, or by the pair, because sometimes it is desirable to have one of these irons heating up while the other is in use, to avoid interruption of the work.

A copper weighing ½ lb. is suitable for light work, a 1 lb. iron for medium weight soldering, and a 1½ lb. iron for heavier soldering. Coppers may be purchased that weigh 4 and 5 lb. to the pair for even heavier work. See Chap. 3 for a description of the various types of soldering coppers used in the sheet metal shop.

It is not enough to have a high temperature capable of melting solder, but there must be also a great enough volume of heat transmitted by the iron to the work to raise quickly the temperature of the metals to be joined to solder-melting temperature.

Not only must a soldering iron be hot enough, but its faces must be smooth and well "tinned" (solder-coated). It is the tinning that provides for the quick transfer of heat into the metals to be joined and also enables the iron to glide along smoothly.

If the faces of the soldering iron tips are oxidized (black spots) or pitted so as to prevent the rapid flow of heat, they must be filed flat and smooth, down to the bare bright copper, before tinning.

Filing and Tinning Coppers. To file the copper before tinning, proceed as follows:

Heat the copper to a cherry red and clamp it in a vise. Using a single cut bastard file, file all four sides of the copper until they are bright and smooth (Fig. 3). With the copper held in the position shown in Fig. 4, round off all of the sharp corners.

To tin the soldering copper, proceed as follows: Reheat the copper just hot enough to melt the solder. After applying a little solder, rub the tip of the copper back and forth on a cake of sal ammoniac until the tip is tinned or coated with a coat of the solder (Fig. 5).

After tinning, the copper is ready for use.

Forging the Soldering Copper. It is sometimes necessary to forge a soldering copper. Coppers are

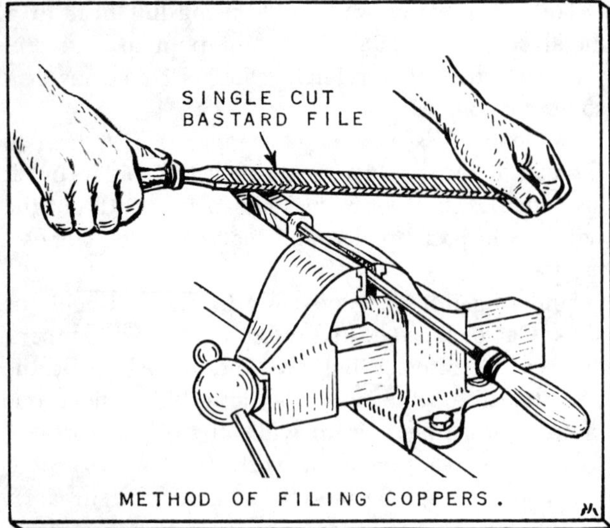

METHOD OF FILING COPPERS.

Figure 3.

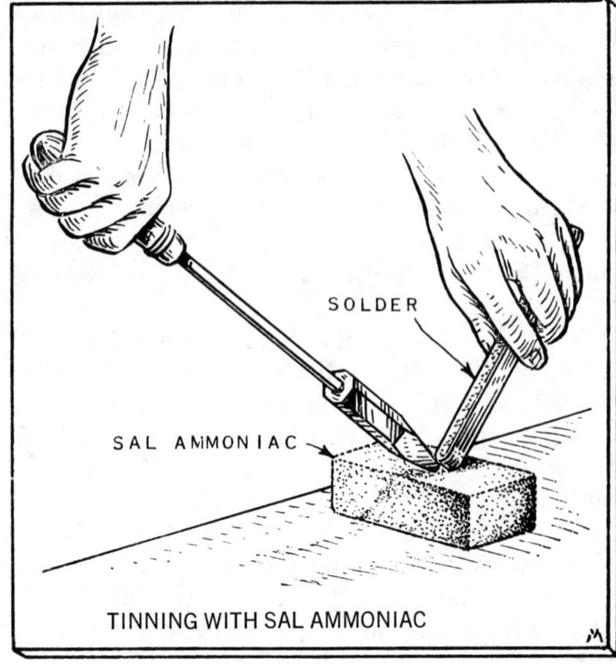

Figure 5.

easily forged to the required shape, on either an anvil or a metal block, by the following procedure: Heat the copper to a dark cherry red, clamp it in a vise in the position shown in Fig. 3, and file off pitmarks and any dross, scale or other imperfections that may be found on the copper (Fig. 6). Remove the copper from the vise, reheat it, and place it as shown in Fig. 7. With a heavy machinist's hammer, hammer the misshaped point back into the body (Fig. 7). Remove the copper from the vise and reheat it. Hold the copper on an anvil iron plate and forge to the required shape by striking solid blows with the flat face of a heavy hammer as shown in Fig. 8, turning the copper frequently to forge a square surface. When forging a copper, reheat it as often as is found necessary.

Using a Dipping Solution. A dipping solution is used to keep the tinned part of the soldering copper bright and clean. This solution is made by dissolving ½ ounce of powdered sal ammoniac in a quart of clean water. The soldering copper is dipped into this

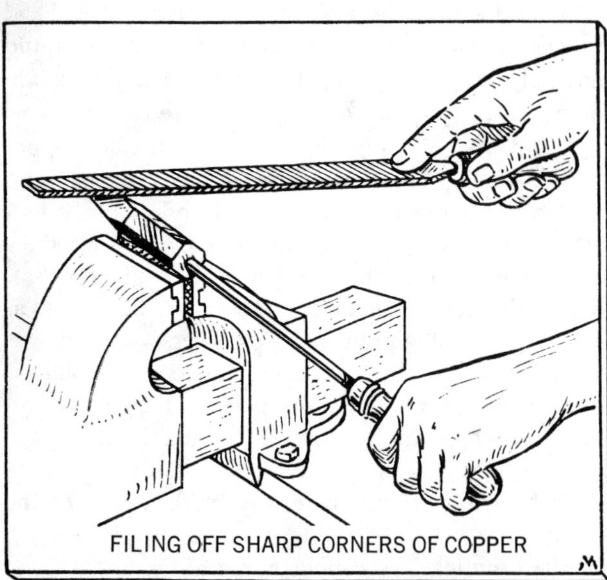

Figure 4.

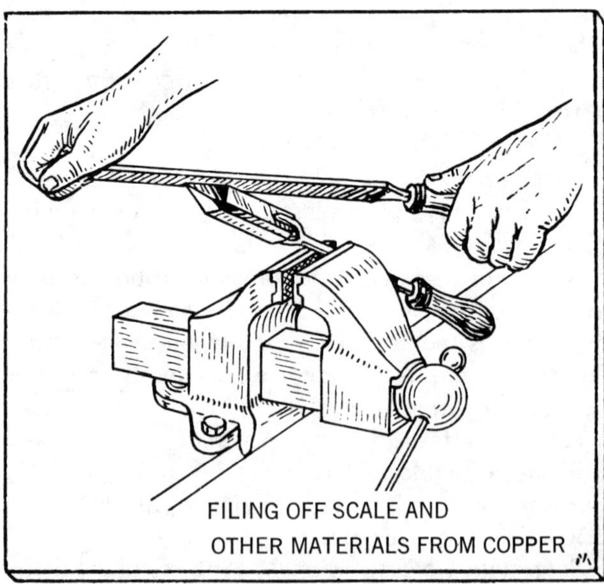

FILING OFF SCALE AND
OTHER MATERIALS FROM COPPER

Figure 6.

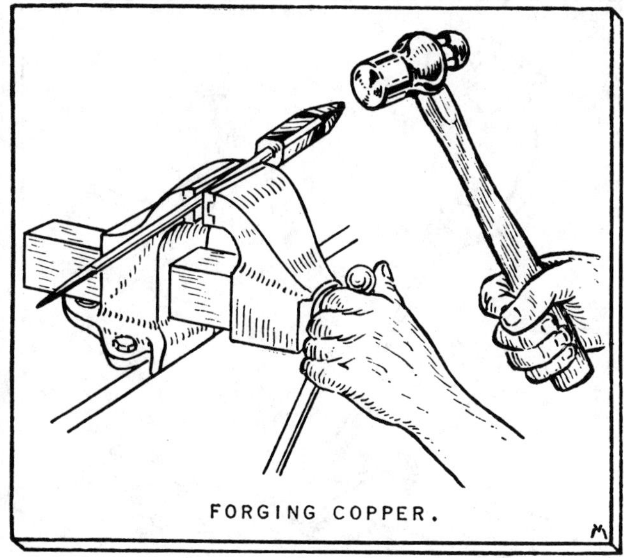

Figure 7.

solution immediately after removing it from the flame or heat. When a dipping solution is not available, the copper should be wiped lightly and quickly with a cotton rag. Never use a woolen rag for wiping, nor any solution other than sal ammoniac for dipping.

Soldering Procedures

SOLDERING LAP SEAMS. To solder lap seams, proceed as follows: Place the work on a suitable support as shown in Fig. 9. A sheet of black sheet iron or a piece of glass or marble ½ to 1 in. in thickness is excellent for this purpose. Heat the tinned copper. Apply the flux as shown in Fig. 2. Dip the heated copper into the dipping solution and touch a bar of solder to the heated tip of the copper (Fig. 10). With the drops of solder that adhere to the copper, tack the seam at a number of points to hold the sheets in position while soldering. The method of holding the sheets in position is called tack welding and is shown at A, Fig. 11. A properly tacked seam is shown at B, Fig. 11.

After tacking, apply a hot, well-tinned soldering copper, with the point extending over the seam on the single thickness of the metal and the heel or back of the copper over the seam proper, at about a 45 degree angle. Touch a bar of solder to the hot copper while it is in this position. As the solder melts, draw the copper slowly along the work, keeping it at an angle and allowing it to draw or sweat the solder the full width of the seam (Fig. 9). Make as long a stroke as possible before the soldering copper becomes too cold. When it will no longer melt the solder freely, change it for a hot one. Beginning at the point where the soldering was stopped, hold the second hot copper on the seam long enough to remelt the solder at that point, then move it along just fast enough to make a smooth seam.

If an acid flux has been used, be sure to wash off all traces of the flux after soldering has been completed.

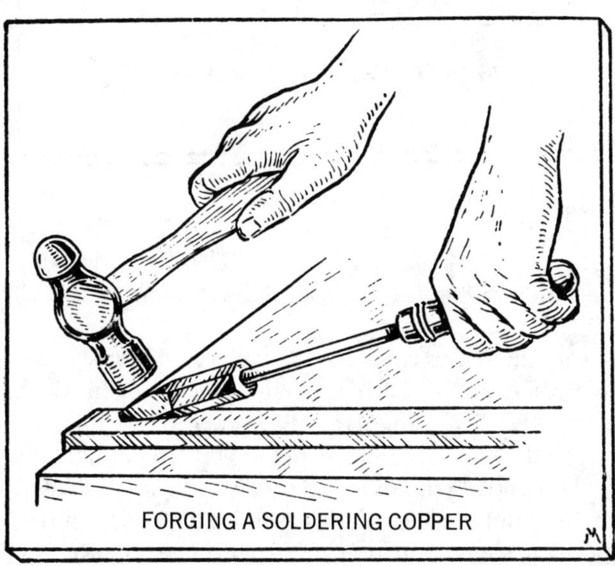

Figure 8.

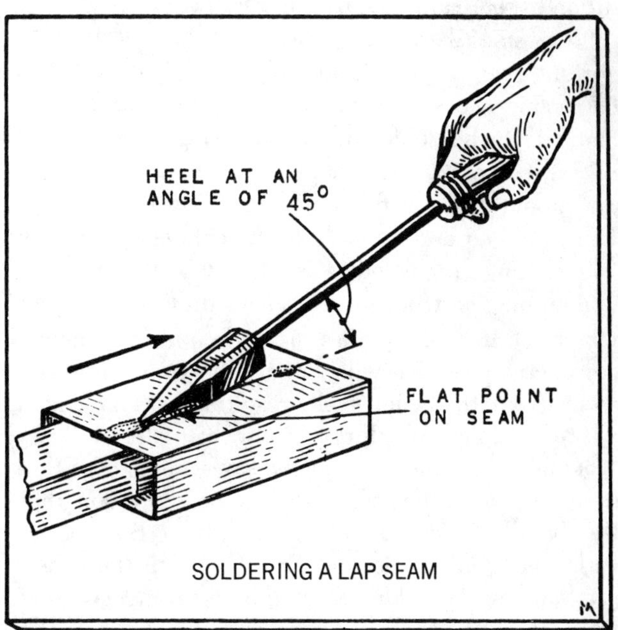

Figure 9.

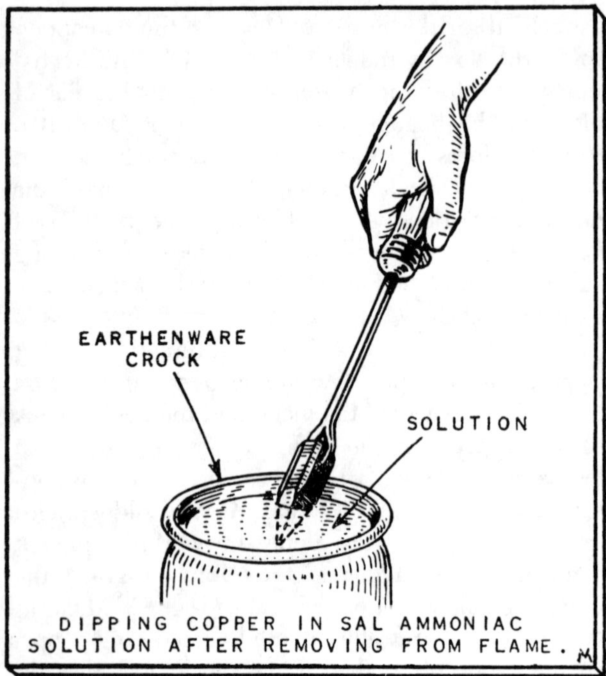

Figure 10.

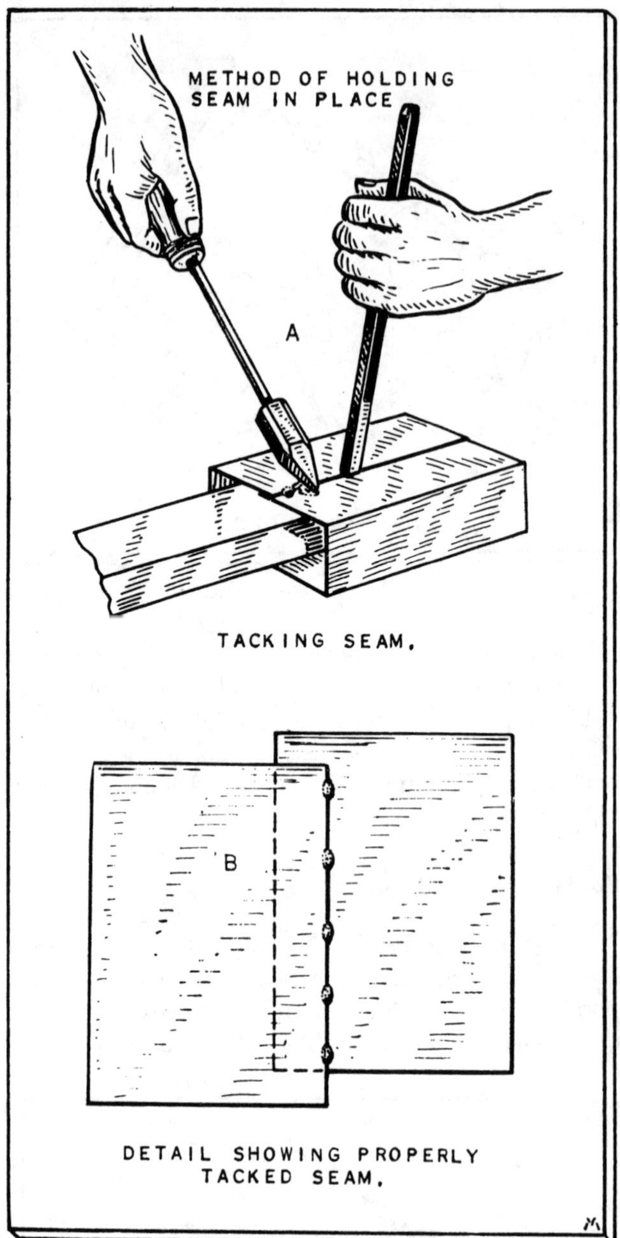

Figure 11.

Soldering Grooved or Riveted Seams. Tacking is not necessary when soldering either grooved or riveted seams. When soldering these types of seams, apply the proper flux and solder the seam in the same manner as for the lap seams previously described. However, when a water-tight job is required on a riveted seam, the rivets must be soldered in addition to the seam, as shown in Fig. 12.

Soldering Vertical Seams. To solder vertical or upright seams, such as are frequently encountered in roofing work and similar jobs, no matter what metal is to be soldered, the soldering copper must be forged to a wedge shape as shown at A, Fig. 13 and about ¾ in. wide and ¼ in. thick at the point. Only the end and top side of the copper are tinned. The tinning area is indicated at B, Fig. 13. (Forging and tinning instructions are given previously in this chapter.) If all four sides of the copper are tinned, considerable solder will run to the underside and away from the seam itself, resulting not only in a waste of time and effort but also of material. After tacking, solder the seam in the same manner as that described for other seams, with the exception that the handle must be held higher than the copper (Fig. 9) to allow the solder to flow until the necessary amount of solder is on the seam and sweated into the joint. This is accomplished by heating the copper thoroughly and moving it alternately to the right and left on the seam itself, thus drawing the solder into the seam as shown in the detail C, Fig. 13.

Soldering Bottoms of Cylindrical, Square, and Rectangular Jobs. To solder bottoms of cylindrical, square, and rectangular jobs, proceed as follows: Tin and heat a bottom copper. Make a number of solder beads by holding the solder against the heated copper and letting the melted solder drop onto a piece of sheet iron or marble as shown in Fig. 14. With a brush apply the required flux to the seam of

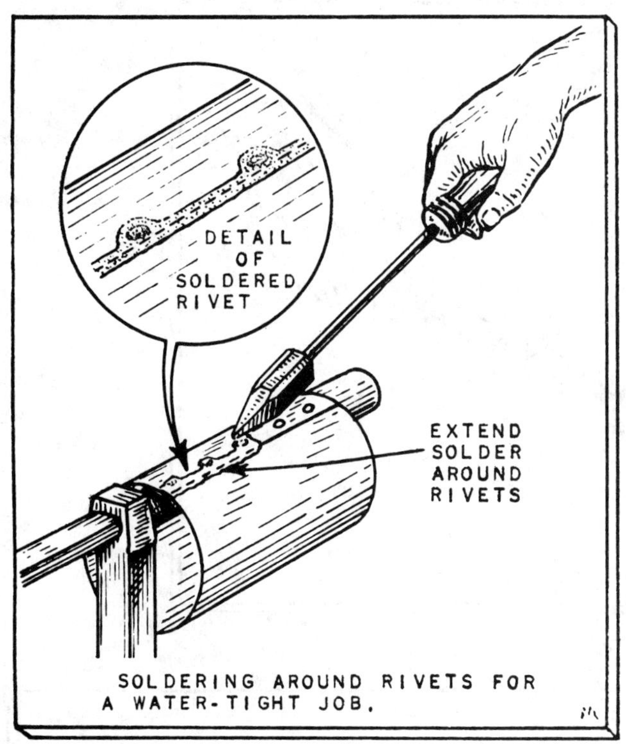

Figure 12.

the job, as shown in Fig. 15, then place one of the cold solder beads in the bottom of the work as shown in Fig. 16. After heating the soldering copper, dip it into the dipping solution and hold it in contact with the cold bead until the solder begins to flow smoothly into the seam. The seam is finished by drawing the soldering copper slowly along the seam, adding additional beads as required and reheating the copper when necessary (Fig. 17).

Cooling and Cleaning Soldered Seams. Once the job has been completed, the work should be allowed to cool *undisturbed* until the solder has had an opportunity to solidify. Movement of the parts during this cooling or pasty stage may result in a weak joint. Tiny fractures sometimes set themselves up inside the joint and weaken it. Do not apply water to speed up the chilling of a soldered joint until after the solder has had ample opportunity to reach the solid stage. Never use water on soldered seams or joints that have been fluxed with a rosin type flux. There is no danger of corrosion if the residues of rosin are left behind.

Clean water, warm, if available, should be used

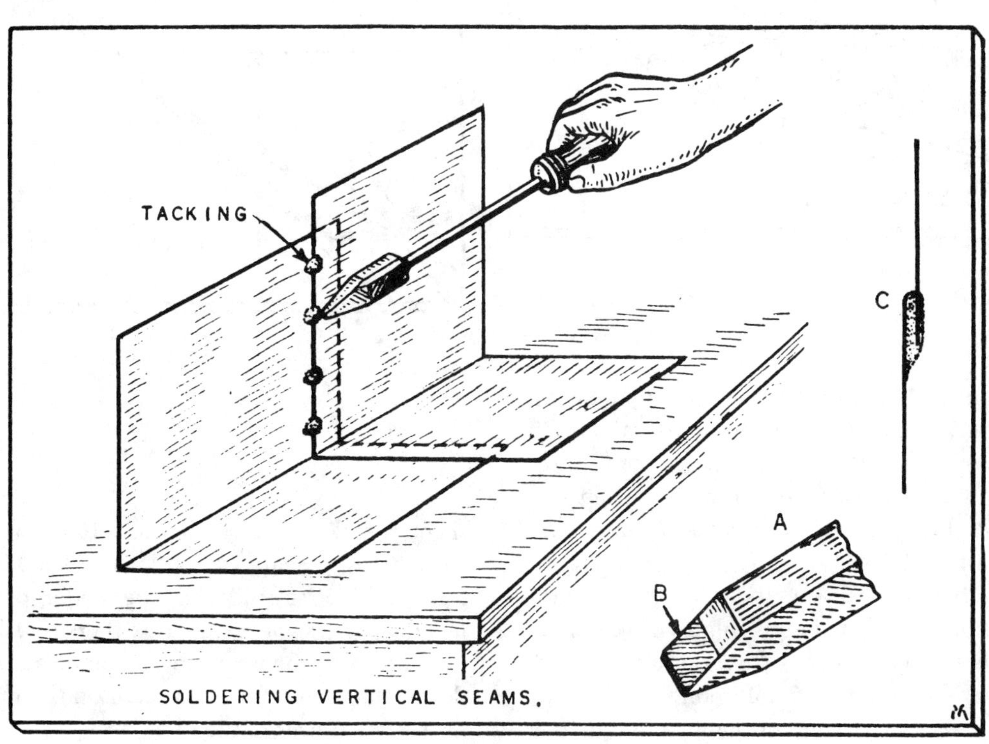

Figure 13.

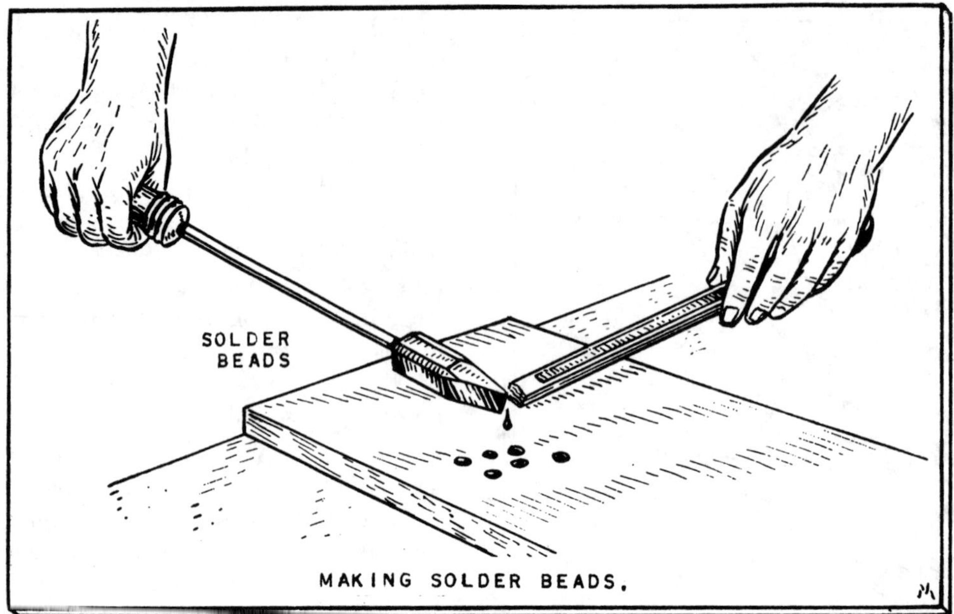

Figure 14.

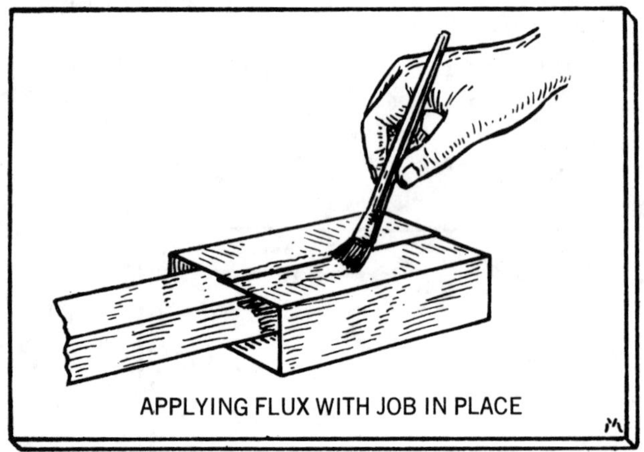

Figure 15.

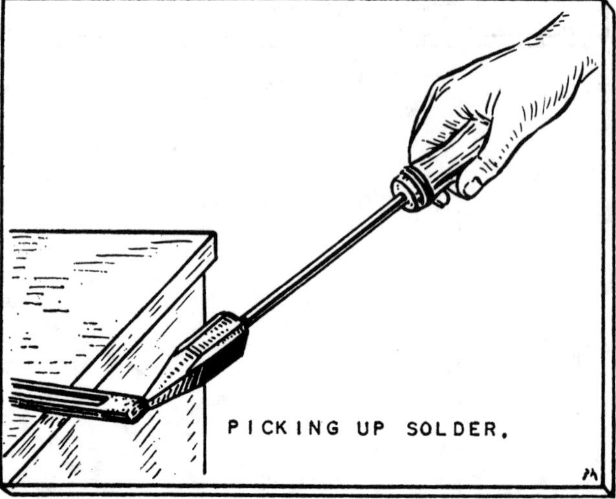

Figure 16.

to remove the residues of all types of acid fluxes. These residues, if allowed to soften for about 15 minutes after soldering, can be more readily removed with a final rinse in clean water. Then dry with a clean rag as extra insurance against flux streaks and water stains.

SOLDERING REINFORCED JOINTS IN SHEET METAL. Where it is impractical or impossible to make interlocking bends in sheets or rods that are to be joined, there are several methods of reinforcing a butt joint. Figure 18 shows butt seams or joints that do not have enough strength and have to be reinforced.

A simple method of reinforcing a butt joint on sheet metal is shown in the left drawing, Fig. 18. This type of seam or joint, called a bead seam, is formed by first soldering the under portion of the metal in the same manner as that used for an interlocked bend, then forming a reinforced strip of solder in the form of a bead seam on the upper portion of the two pieces of metal.

To make a bead seam, paste a piece of masking tape or "cellotape" on each of the sheets parallel to the two edges and approximately half of the width of the bead from each edge (Fig. 18). Apply flux to the space between the pasted-down strips. With a hot soldering iron, apply enough solder to form a bead. Place the edge, not the flat side, of the soldering iron in the center of the seam, and move it along as fast as the solder melts. The adhesive strips serve to keep the molten solder from spreading. Making a bead requires a little practice. At first the solder will be quite rough. Run the iron over the seam several times, until a smooth bead is formed.

Another method of reinforcing seam joints is with a lap seam shown in the right drawing, Fig. 18. The two pieces of metal to be joined are overlapped and soldered in the position shown. The solder flows between the two pieces and along each of the edges. This type of joint is considered stronger than either the butt or the bead seam. When making a lap seam, use the flat side of the iron.

Another method of reinforcing a butt joint is to solder an additional strip of metal between the two sheets of metal lengthwise with the joint.

SOLDERING REINFORCED JOINTS IN RODS AND BARS. Rods and bars, whether circular, square, or rectangular, must be reinforced with a collar of metal when butt-jointed. A short section of brass or copper tubing just large enough to slip over the rod can be used as a collar for a circular rod. For a square or rectangular rod, bend a piece of sheet metal to the proper shape to form the reinforcing collar. When fitting the collar, allow enough space to permit the solder to flow freely between the collar and the rod.

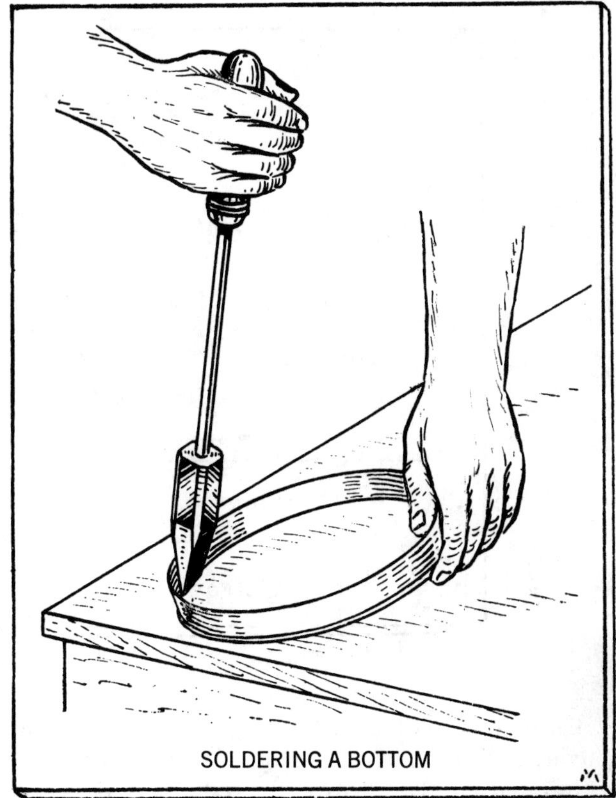

Figure 17.

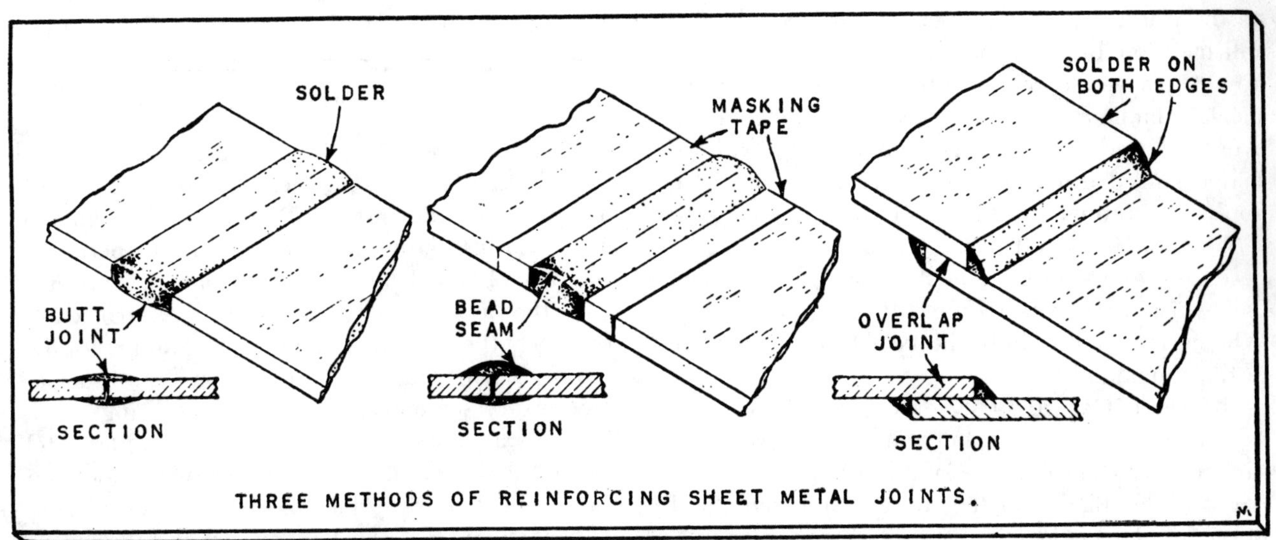

Figure 18.

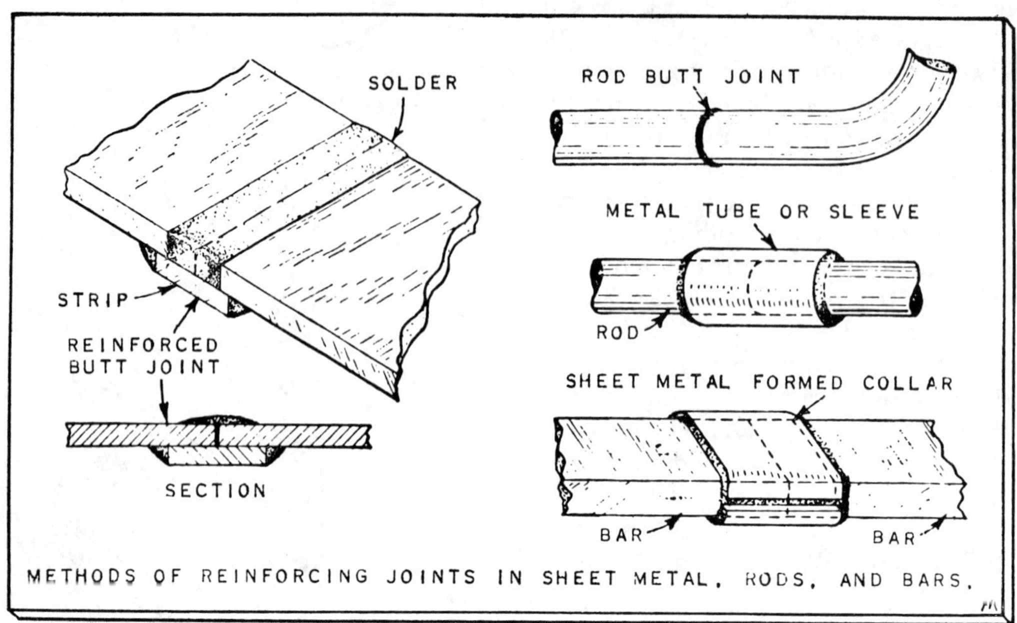

Figure 19.

Clean and polish both the rod and the collar thoroughly with emery paper, and apply the flux to both before putting the collar on the rod. Then solder the work in the usual manner (Fig. 19).

Soldering Aluminum. To solder aluminum, a special flux and solder must be used. The aluminum flux, which is available in powder form, must be immediately sprinkled over the previously cleaned surface to prevent the formation of oxide. If an electric soldering copper is used, it should be at least a 200-watt iron.

Hold the flat surface of the iron on the fluxed area. As the iron attains the proper temperature, the flux will melt, bubble, and then smoke. When it smokes, do not remove the iron from the work, but apply the special aluminum solder to the copper and melt it over the fluxed surface of the aluminum. If additional solder is needed to reinforce or strengthen the joint, apply it with the tip of the iron in the usual manner.

When soldering other metals to aluminum, it is necessary to use aluminum flux for the aluminum and whichever flux is required for the other metal. Wherever possible, apply the heat to the underside of the aluminum.

Soldering Cast Iron. Soldering cast iron is not especially recommended, but sometimes it is necessary to make temporary repairs in cracked cast-iron parts. Widen the top of the crack with a cold chisel or a file, or by grinding it into a V-shaped groove. The groove should be made wide and deep enough

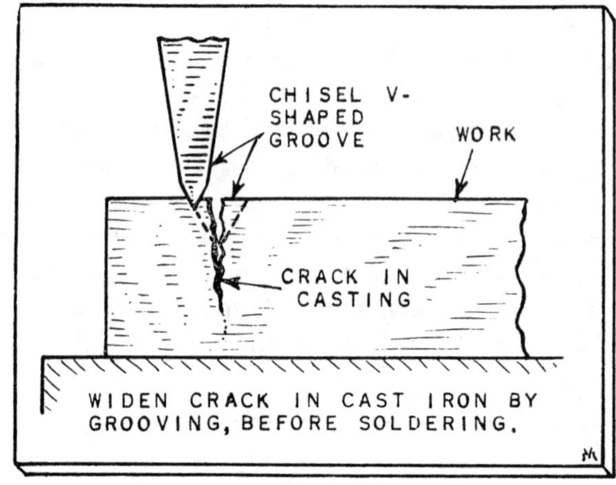

Figure 20.

to permit a sufficient amount of solder to enter and close the crack (Fig. 20). Clean all grease, dirt, rust, or paint from the cast iron. Most of the aluminum fluxes can also be used for cast iron, but better results are obtained by using a special cast-iron flux. Place the flux in the groove and on the surface surrounding the groove. Apply heat until the flux smokes. The peculiar structure of iron castings makes it necessary sometimes to repeat the fluxing operation several times before applying the solder. Melt the solder and run it into the groove with a hot copper until the entire surface has been soldered.

Soldering Brass and Bronze. Brass is an alloy of copper with zinc or another metal. A flux of zinc chloride or rosin is used for brass, and is applied in the usual manner to the cleaned surface. Be careful not to use too much heat. Then solder the parts in the manner described previously for the type of work. If zinc chloride has been used as a flux, the joined parts must be washed clean of all traces of it with water containing soap and washing soda.

Bronze is the general term used for various alloys of copper and tin. Some types of bronzes also contain zinc, silicon, lead, and nickel. Bronze is fluxed and soldered by the method just described for brass.

SOLDERING IRON AND STEEL. Zinc chloride flux and tin-lead solder are satisfactory for soldering iron and steel, but the special commercial aluminum solders and fluxes give better results. The soldering procedure is the same as that for other metals, according to the type of work.

SOLDERING STAINLESS STEEL. Stainless steel can be soldered satisfactorily if certain important factors are considered. Because stainless steel is a poor heat conductor, a relatively heavy copper must be used, and it must be held in one place on the stainless steel considerably longer than is necessary when soldering other metals.

Special commercial stainless-steel fluxes are available, but muriatic acid used undiluted is considered the best flux for the purpose. After cleaning the metal, brush the acid on the surfaces to be soldered and allow it to remain there for several minutes before beginning to solder. The ordinary half-and-half type of solder can be used on stainless steel.

After the acid has been allowed to bite into the material, apply the solder with the heated iron, moving the iron along the joint or seam very slowly. In fact, the iron should be held on each spot before moving it along. After the soldering has been completed and the metal has cooled, wash off the excess flux with a solution of washing soda and soapy water.

SOLDERING LEAD, TIN, PEWTER, AND ZINC. Lead has a very low melting point—621 deg. F.—so the soldering copper must not be too hot. The flux and solder also must have a low melting point.

In lead soldering, the joints must be scraped bright and fluxed before the solder is applied. An ideal flux for lead is ordinary tallow. Scrape a few shavings of tallow on the joint and melt it into the joint. A special commercial tin-lead-bismuth solder, which has an extremely low melting point, must be used. Keep the soldering copper moving to avoid melting the surrounding metal.

Tin has a low melting point, and the procedure given for lead soldering should be followed in soldering this metal.

Pewter is an alloy of tin, lead, and other metals. It also has a low melting point, very near that of lead, and the procedure for soldering pewter is the same as for lead.

Zinc also has a low melting point, approximately 775 degrees. Use zinc chloride as a flux, and the same solder and procedure as the lead. After soldering zinc, wash off the excess flux with a solution of soapy water and washing soda.

SOLDERING WHITE METALS. White metals are usually combinations of lead, tin, antimony, and other metals that have a very low melting point. They vary to such an extent that specific directions for soldering them cannot be given without knowing which metals have been combined. As a rule, no flux is used on white metals. Clean the metal by sanding or scraping. Apply commercial tin-lead-bismuth solder with a wire brush before using the soldering copper. The general procedure for soldering white metals is approximately the same as for lead.

Chapter **7**

Riveting Materials and Procedures

Rivets are made of brass, copper, wrought iron, tinned iron, mild steel, aluminum, and Allegheny metal. It is customary to use rivets of the same metal as the parts that are being joined. Rivets have either solid, hollow, or split shanks, and they have a variety of heads. Types generally used for sheet metal work are shown in Fig. 1.

Round-head and flat-head solid rivets are more commonly used. Round-head and countersunk-head soft-steel rivets are available in fractional sizes, ranging from 1/8 in. to 7/16 in. in diameter, and in various lengths. Flat-head copper rivets are obtainable in seven sizes, ranging in length from 1/4 in. to 1½ in.

Tinner's rivets are available in twenty-four sizes, from .070 in. to .293 in. in diameter, and from 1/8 in. to 17/32 in. in length.

Copper-plated steel and solid copper rivets are sold by weight in half-pound boxes, each containing an assortment of lengths and a burr, or washer, for each rivet. The burr is necessary when copper rivets are used, but it is optional with other types. It is slipped over the tail or end of the rivet—that part of the rivet shank which projects through the work before the end is flattened or mushroomed.

Rivet Setting Procedures

The usual tools required for setting rivets are a ball-peen or a tinner's hammer, a rivet set, and a rivet header. (*See* Figs. 3, 4, and 5.)

Use the flat face of a tinner's riveting hammer to flatten small tinner's rivets. The flattened ends of either tinner's or small rivets are never shaped with the tinner's riveting hammer, but only with the rivet set and cup tool, or header. A rivet set is a small piece of hardened and tempered steel with a hole in one end for the rivet head and either a conical or hemispherical depression alongside the hole, for shaping the rivet end after it has been flattened with the hammer.

Small rivets made of aluminum, copper, brass, or similar soft metals must be hammered lightly, and, naturally, will require a smaller hammer. Larger rivets made of the harder types of metals will require a heavier hammer. No set rule can be given for the correct size of hammer. A little experience or practice will quickly determine whether a hammer is too small or too large for the job.

Holes must be either punched or drilled in the

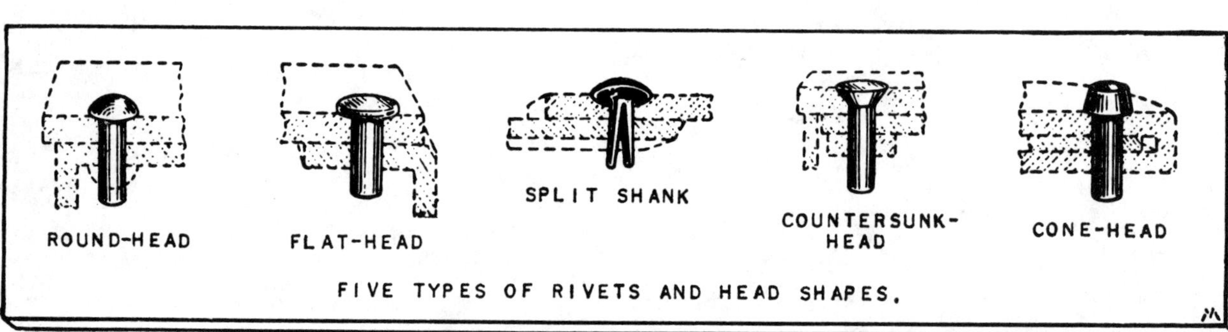

Figure 1.

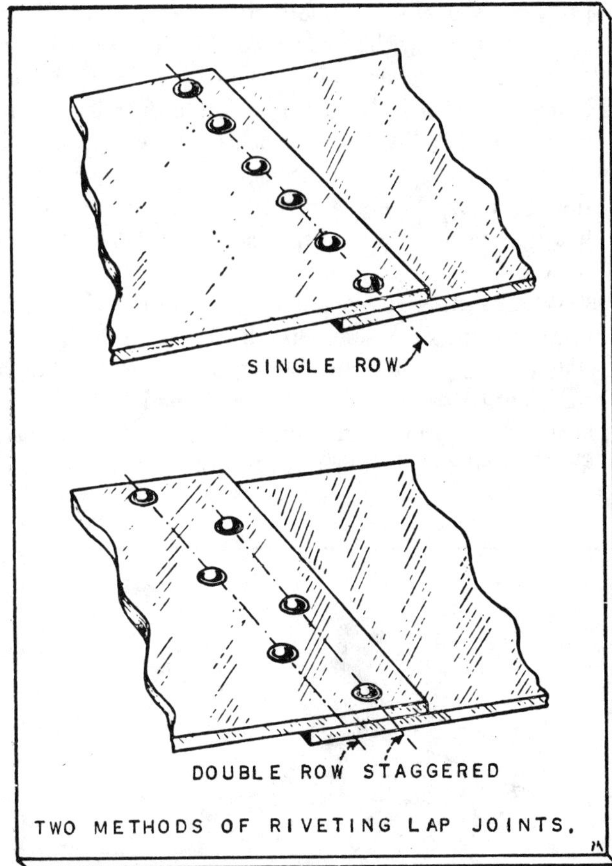

Figure 2.

metal before riveting. Drills and punches used and methods of using them are described in Chaps. 3 and 4.

When more than one rivet is used, all of the holes must be properly spaced and lined up. The spacing of rivets is determined by the nature of the work and the type of material used. In general, a good rule is that the minimum distance between rivets should be three diameters of the rivet stem, and the maximum, eight diameters. The minimum distance from the edge of the work should be two diameters of the rivet stem. Rivets that are placed too close to the edge will cause the metal to stretch and tear. Too great a distance from the edge causes buckling and loosening of the joint.

The length of rivet necessary to form a head sufficient for the work depends on the clearance between the rivet and the rivet hole, the type of rivet used, and the type of metal being riveted. In general, the rivet should extend from one to two diameters of its shank beyond the material. The diameter of the rivet should not be less than the combined thickness of the sheets that are being riveted.

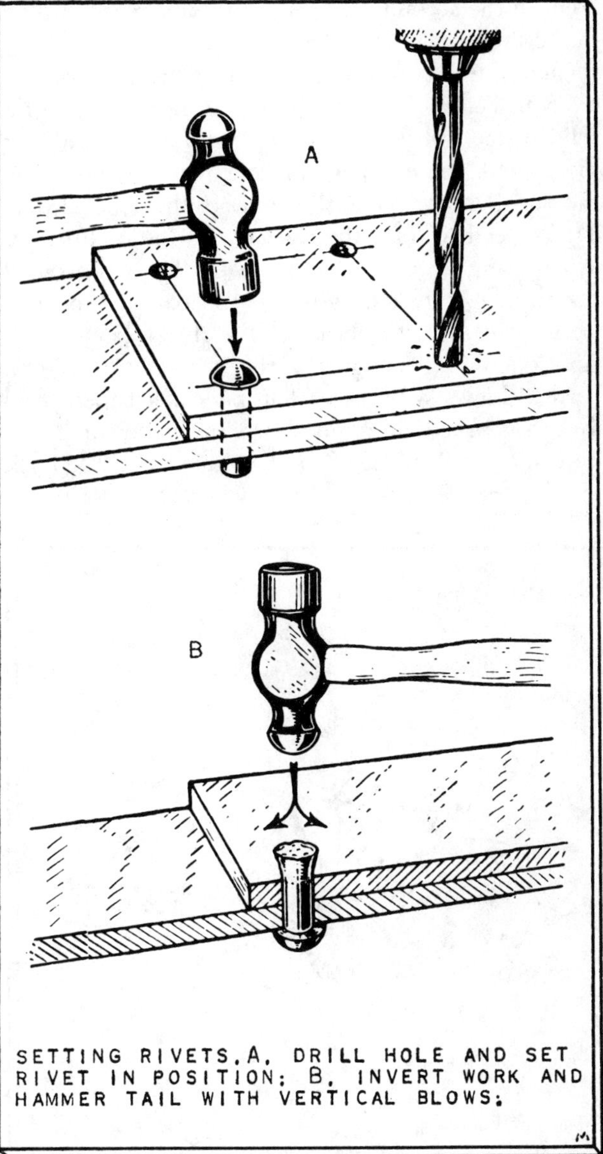

Figure 3.

Rivets can be set in either a single row or a double row, staggered as shown in Fig. 2. Narrow seams or joints are usually riveted with a single row in a straight line, while heavier material is usually riveted with a double row of staggered rivets, especially when the joint of the seam is to be reinforced with solder. Unless the rivets are staggered, there is a tendency for the hot solder to expand the metal between them, causing the gaps and buckles in the work. To prevent errors, drill all of the holes in one of the pieces, and only one hole in the second piece. Secure the two pieces together with either a rivet or a temporary bolt (A, Fig. 3). Drill the rest of the holes in the second piece, using those already drilled in the first as guides.

Clamp the two pieces together tightly. Set the rivet in the first hole with the head resting against a solid surface. Strike the tail of the rivet several direct blows with the ball-peen of your hammer to expand the tail slightly beyond the edges of the hole (B, Fig. 3). Proceed to form the rivet to the required shape, by working around its edge with the ball-peen at the proper angle (C, Fig. 4). Proceed in the same manner to form the head of the rivet (D, Fig. 4). Continue to strike angular rather than vertical blows; vertical blows will form a flat, pancake-shaped head that is weaker than a round or a conical head. Then, by using the flat face of the hammer, as in E, Fig. 5, properly shape and smooth the head. Rivets can be easily shaped with a rivet set of the correct size. Place the depression in this tool over the rivet end, hold the tool in a vertical position, and strike it with a hammer (F, Fig. 5). One or two blows will usually shape a small rivet; large ones require several additional blows. While a rivet is being flattened and headed, back it up with a suitable stake set in a bench plate.

When setting rivets, particularly copper rivets that require burrs or washers, the burr should fit the rivet shank snugly and must be slipped over the tail of the rivet before it is flattened or shaped. When rivets larger than ½ in. in diameter are used, they are usually heated to a bright red in a forge or a gas flame,

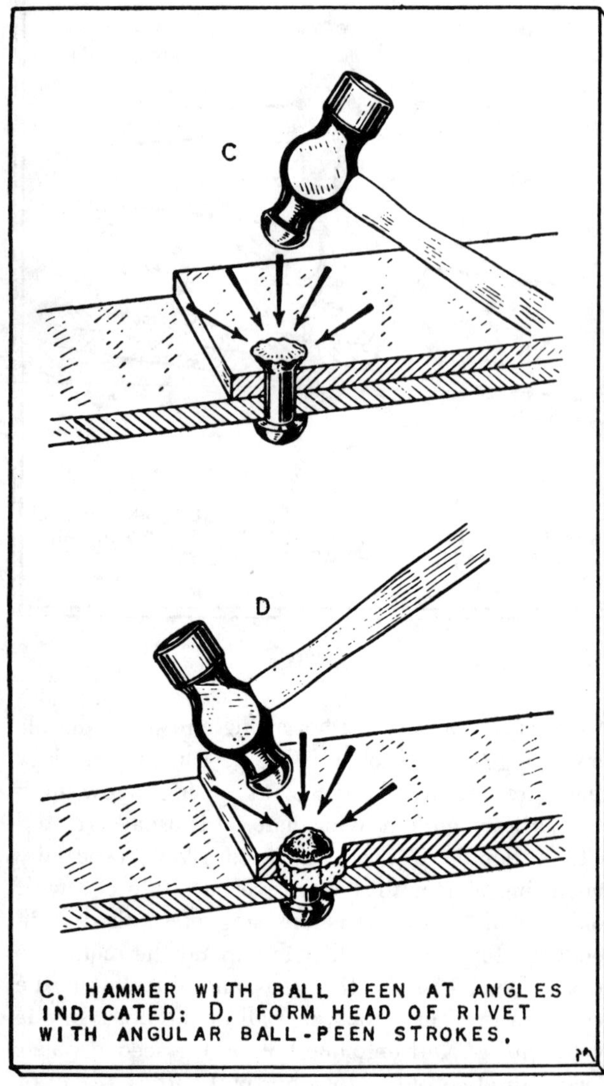

C, HAMMER WITH BALL PEEN AT ANGLES INDICATED; D, FORM HEAD OF RIVET WITH ANGULAR BALL-PEEN STROKES.

Figure 4.

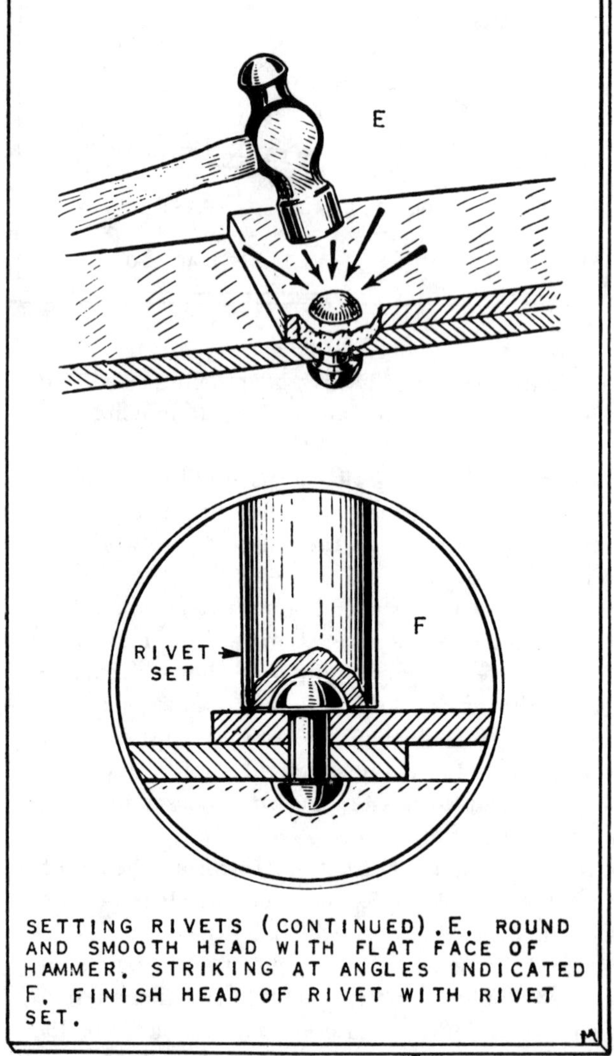

SETTING RIVETS (CONTINUED). E, ROUND AND SMOOTH HEAD WITH FLAT FACE OF HAMMER, STRIKING AT ANGLES INDICATED F, FINISH HEAD OF RIVET WITH RIVET SET.

Figure 5.

slipped through the holes, and headed before they cool. This type of riveting is called hot riveting and is never done by hand. A jack hammer or a riveting gun driven by compressed air is used for driving hot rivets. Hot rivets are used only on heavy construction work and will not be discussed in this book.

Riveting Aluminum and Its Alloys

Aluminum and its various alloys are used extensively in industry, and almost exclusively in the fabrication of aircraft and its many components.

Riveting is the most commonly used method for joining aluminum, particularly the structural alloys used to a great extent in the fabrication of tanks, disposal and chemical containers, laboratory equipment, aircraft fuselages, spars, and wing members, which depend upon heat treatment for their high mechanical properties. In the smaller gauges or thicknesses, aluminum alloy rivets are always used. For the thicker sections used in larger structures, either aluminum alloy or steel rivets may be used, the choice depending upon conditions attending the erection and use of the structure.

Steel rivets are stronger than aluminum alloy rivets and offer certain advantages in ease of driving from the standpoint of equipment required. However, their use is limited to those applications in which the structure can be protected adequately against corrosion. Aluminum alloy rivets make possible the maximum saving in weight and offer the greatest resistance to corrosion.

The riveting of aluminum and its alloys differs in many ways from the ordinary riveting of steel or iron. The former operation must always be done in a way to produce the greatest strength possible, and any distortion of the material must be avoided.

Types of Rivets. The factors governing the selection of rivets depend largely on the job to be done and the location of the seam. Figure 6 shows the common types of solid shank rivets and Table 17 gives their general specifications.

In many cases where the rivets are to be subjected to shear stresses only, the appearance of the heads may well be the determining factor. However, where it is possible that some tensile stress may be induced in the rivet, other points must be considered. In such cases, a type of rivet should be used in which the height or thickness of the head is not less than one-half the diameter of the rivet shank.

Round-head (A, Fig. 6). This type of rivet is used in relatively thick sheets where strength is required. The size of the head is such that it covers sufficient area to strengthen the sheet around the hole and at the same time offers considerable resistance to tension.

Brazier-head (B, Fig. 6). The brazier-head covers sufficient area to strengthen the sheet around the

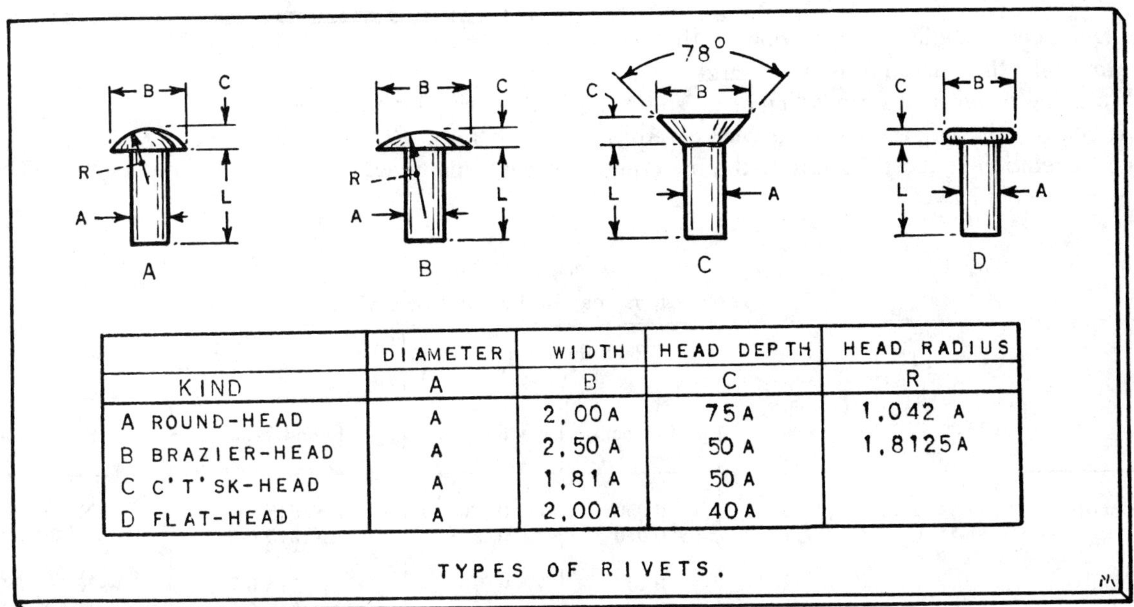

KIND	DIAMETER A	WIDTH B	HEAD DEPTH C	HEAD RADIUS R
A ROUND-HEAD	A	2.00 A	75 A	1.042 A
B BRAZIER-HEAD	A	2.50 A	50 A	1.8125 A
C C'T'SK-HEAD	A	1.81 A	50 A	
D FLAT-HEAD	A	2.00 A	40 A	

TYPES OF RIVETS.

Figure 6.

TABLE 17

RIVET SPECIFICATIONS

Type	Material	Identification	Shearing strength (lb. per sq. in.)	Remarks
A	Aluminum alloy No. 2.	Plain.	10,000	Do not heat treat before using.
AD	Aluminum alloy No. A-17S.	1 dimple in head.	25,000	Do not heat treat before using.
D	Aluminum alloy No. 17S.	1 raised tit on head.	30,000	Heat treat before using.
DD	Aluminum alloy No. 24S.	2 raised dashes on head.	35,000	Heat treat before using.
	Iron (cadmium plated).	Plain.	35,000	

hole and at the same time offers considerable resistance to tension.

Countersunk-head (C, Fig. 6). This type is used for riveting thick sheets over which other plates must fit. Countersunk-head rivets may also be used, in some cases, for riveting thin sheets.

Flat-head (D, Fig. 6). The flat-head type of rivet is sometimes used for internal riveting where increased clearance is required.

Special Rivets. Two special rivets are used to a certain extent in aircraft construction (Figs. 7 and 8).

Steel Tubular Rivet. Rivets shown in Fig. 7 are not in the true sense tubular. The portion of the rivet shank through the material is solid and is only drilled to a depth sufficient for heading or up-setting. For this reason, the lengths must be very carefully matched in relation to the thickness of the materials through which they go.

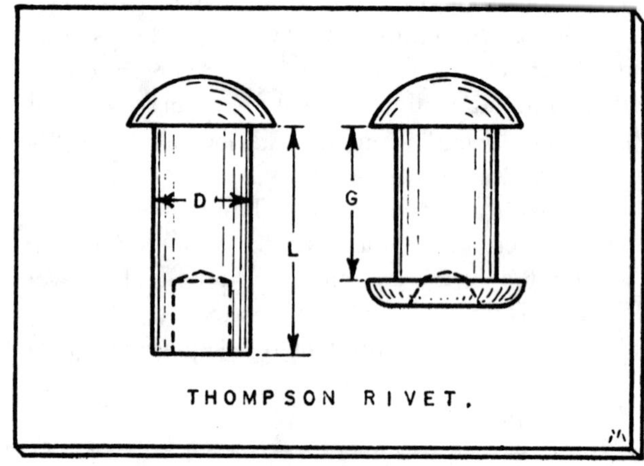

Figure 7.

Rivnuts. Rivnuts, shown in Fig. 8, are threaded rivets manufactured from alloy number 53. They are

TABLE 18

SPECIFICATIONS FOR THE USE OF RIVNUTS

Type	Rivnuts length (inches)	Total thickness of joint (inches)		Type of screw	
		Maximum	Minimum	Round head	Flat head
Open end	3/8	0.050	0.020	AN 515-6-5	AN 505-6-5
	7/16	0.070	0.050	AN 515-6-6	AN 505-6-6
Blind end	1/2	0.130	0.070	AN 515-6-7	AN 505-6-7
	9/16	0.130	0.070	AN 515-6-7	AN 505-6-7

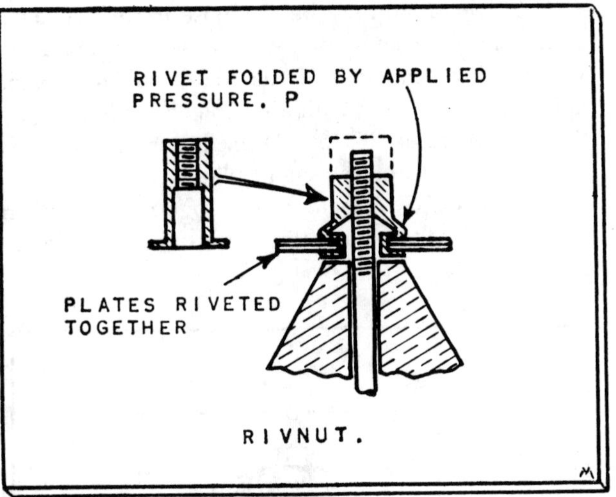

Figure 8.

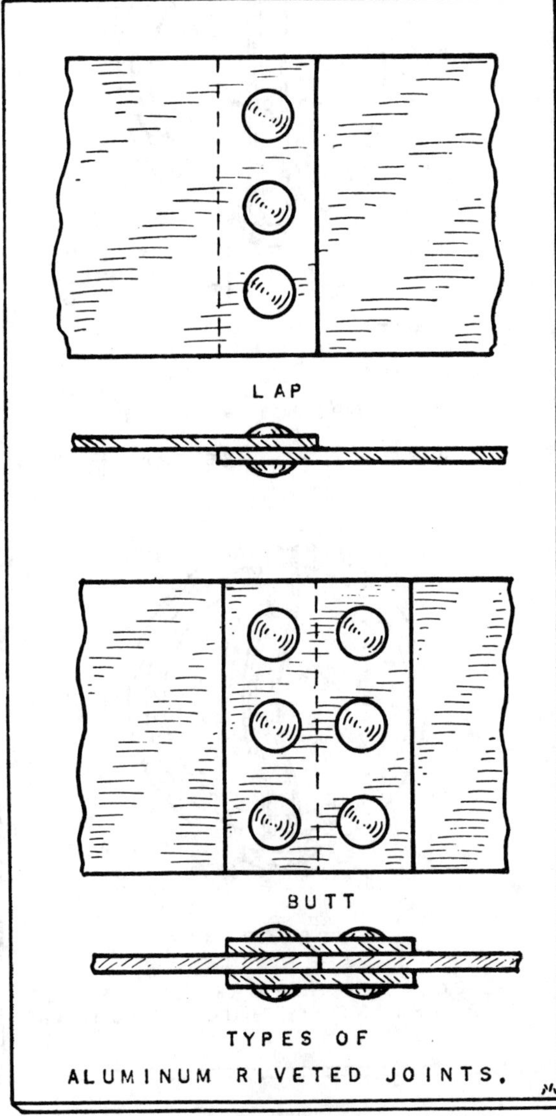

Figure 9.

used in places that are impossible to reach with a bucking iron. The rivet is hollow and the end opposite the head has an internal thread for approximately one-half its length. The remaining length is counterbored to a somewhat larger diameter than the thread. The rivet is headed by means of a special tool with a threaded mandrel which is screwed into the threaded portion of the rivet. The tool bears against the head of the rivet and withdraws the mandrel which upsets the counterbored portion as shown in Fig. 8. Table 18 gives the general specifications for its use.

Rivnuts manufactured from 2, A-17, and 53 alloys have been heat treated by the manufacturer and no further treatment is necessary.

Types of Joints (Fig. 9). The two standard joints used for riveting aluminum are the lap joint and the butt joint. Either type may be made with one or more rows of rivets. In joints using more than one row, the rivets are usually staggered to distribute the stresses.

General Aluminum Riveting Procedures. A large percentage of the riveting of aluminum is done on thin gauge aluminum alloy, and the work must be so accomplished that the material is not distorted by hammer blows or injured with the riveting tools. This is done by up-setting, or heading the rivets against a bucking tool of the type shown in Fig. 10, instead of striking the shank with a hammer.

To prevent deforming of its head, a rivet set must be selected to fit each type. The depth of this set must be such that it does not touch the material being riveted.

When solid rivets go completely through hollow tubes, their diameter should be at least one-eighth of the outside diameter of the tube. Rivets through hollow tubes which are loaded only in shear should be hammered just enough to form a small head. No attempt should be made to form the standard round head, because the amount of hammering required often causes the rivet to buckle inside the tube, with resultant injury to the member. Correct and incorrect examples of this type of installation are shown in Fig. 11.

The selection of the proper rivet for the various operations is very important and must be given careful consideration. Table 19 gives the application of standard rivets.

The rivets must be of the proper length for the total thickness of the pieces being riveted. Ordinarily, from 1½ to 2 times the diameter of the rivet is about the right amount for the rivet shank to pro-

TABLE 19

SELECTION OF RIVETS

Rivet type	Use
A	Parts fabricated from 2S and 3S alloys.
AD	Parts fabricated from 17S and 24S alloys.
D	Parts fabricated from 17S and 24S alloys.
DD	Parts fabricated from 24S alloy and as a substitute for types AD and D rivets.

trude through the material to form the head (Fig. 4). For heavy material, such as plates or fittings, from 2 to $2\frac{1}{2}$ times the diameter may be used. Where the two edges of thin sheet are lapped and riveted together, about one diameter of the rivet will prove sufficient.

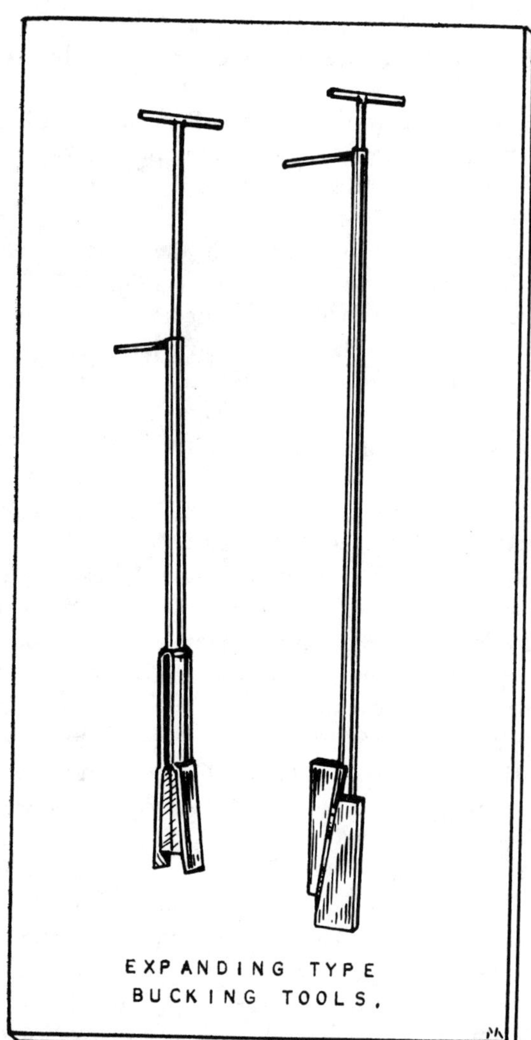

Figure 10.

The rivet should not be too loose in the previously drilled hole, because this will cause it to bend over while being headed, and the shank will not be sufficiently expanded to fill the hole completely (Fig. 3). A drill from .002 to .004 in. larger than the rivet should be used for sheet and plate riveting.

Pieces should be held firmly together by clamps, screws, or bolts while they are being drilled and riveted.

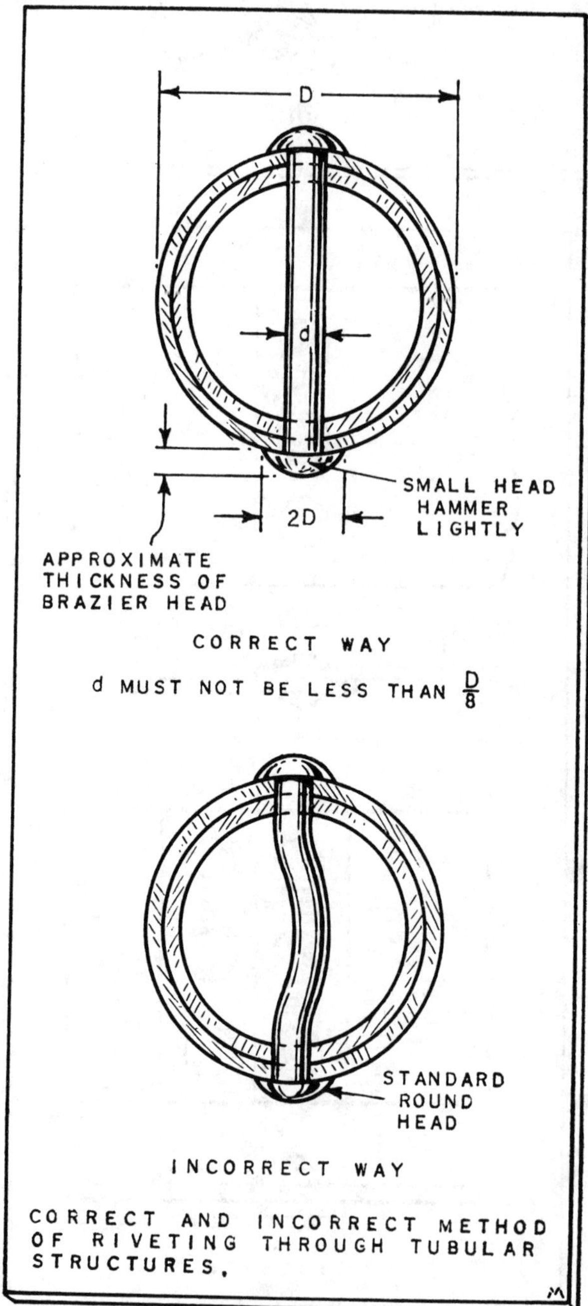

Figure 11.

Where rivets are headed on the inside of the structure, the bucking tool is held against the end of the rivet shank. Care must be exercised during this operation to prevent unseating the rivet by the application of too much pressure. For the first few blows, the bucking tool should be held lightly against the rivet shank, so that it will receive the impact of the blow through the rivet. The tool must be held square with the rivet to avoid turning the rivet over.

Only a sufficient number of blows should be struck to up-set a rivet properly. The blows must be as uniform as possible; not too hard or too light.

SPACING AND DIAMETER OF RIVETS. There are no specific rules that are applicable to every case or type of aluminum riveting. There are, however, certain general rules which should be understood and followed.

Rivets are never placed closer than two diameters of the rivet, measured from the edge of the sheet or plate to the center of the rivet hole.

The spacing between rivets, when in rows, depends upon several factors; principally, the thickness of the sheet, the diameter of the rivets, and the manner in which the sheet will be used or stressed. This spacing is seldom less than four diameters of the rivet, measured between the centers of the rivet holes. Rivets spaced four diameters apart are found in certain seams of airplane fuselages, webs of built-up spars, various plates or fittings, and floats or pontoons.

Where there are two rows of rivets they are usually staggered. The transverse pitch, or distance between rows, should be slightly less than the pitch of the rivets, 75 per cent of the rivet pitch being the usual practice.

The best practice in repair jobs, when possible, is to make the pitch of the rivets equal to those in the original structure.

The spacing of rivets in aluminum or aluminum alloy tubes, when they are spliced, or when the rivets go completely through them, is as follows: When adjacent rivets are at right angles, they are placed from four to seven diameters apart. The first rivet on each side of the joint should be not less than two and one-half times the diameter of the rivet from the end of the tubes, and the last rivet not less than two diameters from the ends of the sleeve.

When the rivets are in line, they should be spaced from five to seven diameters apart.

The diameter of the rivets should never be less than the combined thickness of the parts being riveted.

In tubular members, where the rivets go completely through the tubes, a minimum diameter is established by taking one-eighth of the outside diameter of the tube. Where one tube sleeves over another, the outside diameter of the outer tube is taken. A good practice, in many cases, is to use the next larger size of rivet than that obtained in the calculation for the minimum size.

Hand and Machine Riveting Methods

There are numerous places in the original fabrication of structures where machine riveters cannot be used, and where the rivets have to be headed-up by hand, as described previously in this chapter. A large percentage of all repair work must also be accomplished by hand methods, although mechanical riveters should be used wherever possible. In order to be able to do good work, using any of the riveting methods, considerable skill is required together with a general knowledge of riveting practices. Figure 12 shows both properly and improperly applied rivets and brings out many common faults that must be avoided.

HAND OPERATED SQUEEZE RIVETERS. Numerous types of hand operated squeeze riveters are manufactured and are used successfully for heading rivets not over 1/8 in. in diameter. Riveters of this type are often used in the application of the cover on aircraft using the stressed skin type of construction. Specific directions for their use are furnished by the manufacturer.

For bucking rivets inside of round or oval-shaped tubular members and straight channel sections, an expanding tool is used. Two such bucking tools are shown in Fig. 10.

SQUEEZE RIVETING. Many machine riveters in general use are of the squeeze type operated by air pressure. They are manufactured both as portable and stationary units, although the portable riveter is the most satisfactory for general work. The air pressure required to operate these riveters is between 80 and 100 lb. per sq. in. Squeeze riveting is the most efficient method insofar as the strength of riveted joints in aluminum is concerned. The rivet is up-set with a single operation, all rivets are headed over with uniform pressure, the heads are all formed alike, and the rivet shank is sufficiently expanded to fill the hole completely. A rivet which has been swelled or expanded all the way through the total thickness of the material ensures a good bearing surface. A portable squeeze riveter is shown in Fig. 13.

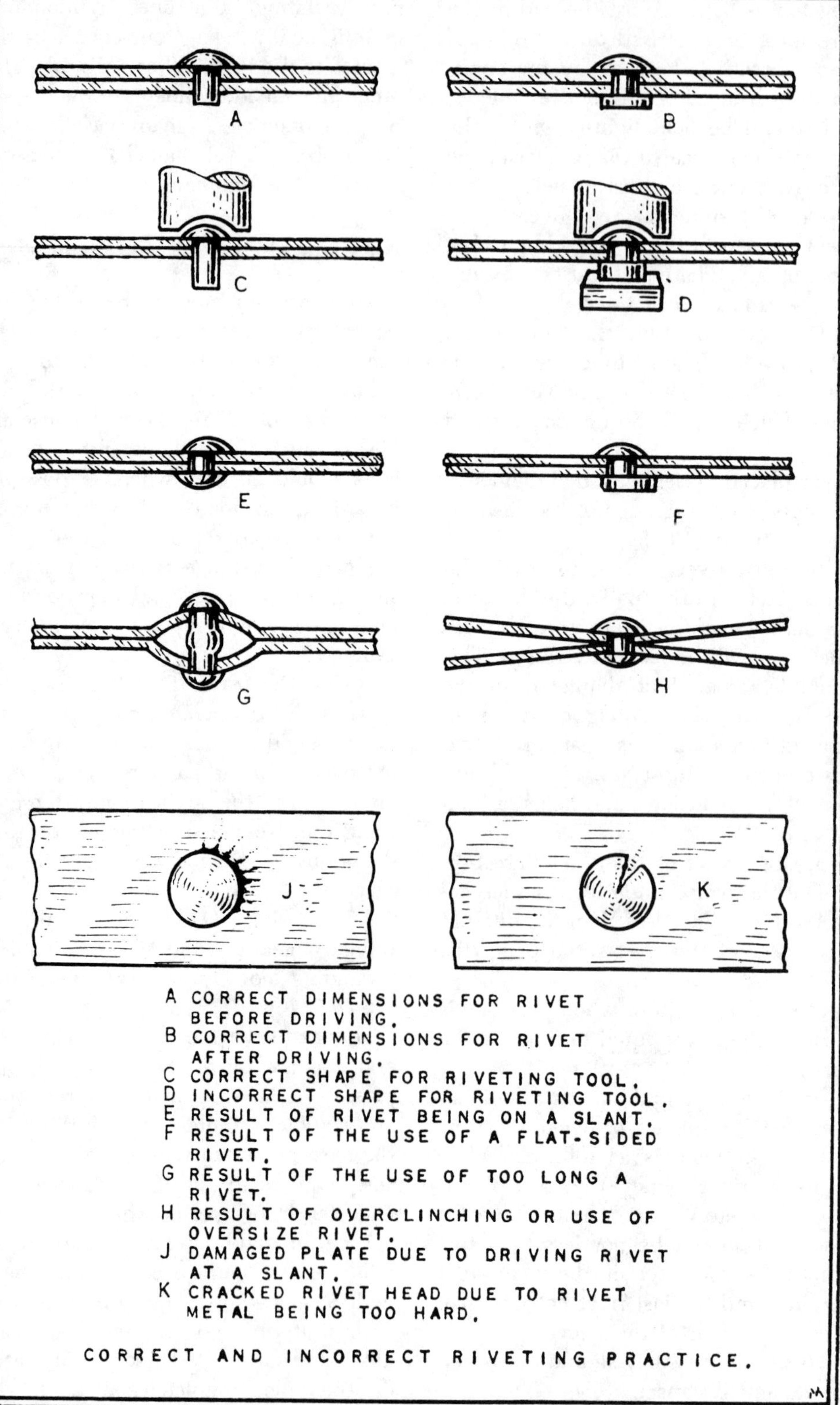
A
B
C
D
E
F
G
H
J
K
A CORRECT DIMENSIONS FOR RIVET BEFORE DRIVING.
B CORRECT DIMENSIONS FOR RIVET AFTER DRIVING.
C CORRECT SHAPE FOR RIVETING TOOL.
D INCORRECT SHAPE FOR RIVETING TOOL.
E RESULT OF RIVET BEING ON A SLANT.
F RESULT OF THE USE OF A FLAT-SIDED RIVET.
G RESULT OF THE USE OF TOO LONG A RIVET.
H RESULT OF OVERCLINCHING OR USE OF OVERSIZE RIVET.
J DAMAGED PLATE DUE TO DRIVING RIVET AT A SLANT.
K CRACKED RIVET HEAD DUE TO RIVET METAL BEING TOO HARD.
CORRECT AND INCORRECT RIVETING PRACTICE.

Figure 12.

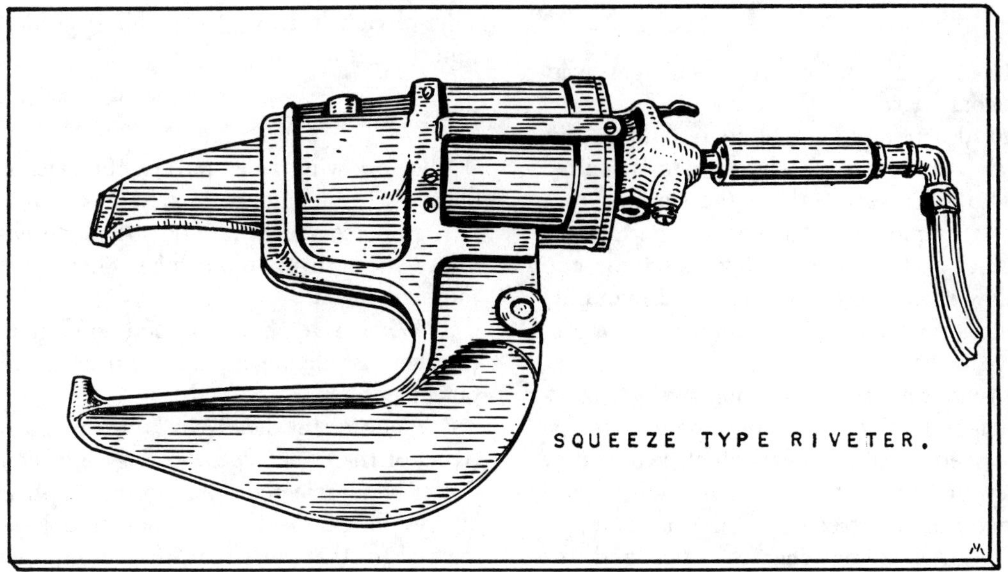

Figure 13.

A deep throated type is the most satisfactory for general work, although a shallow throated one has the greatest squeezing capacity.

Pneumatic Riveters (Fig. 14). Assembly and repair work can often be done more efficiently with the use of the portable pneumatic riveter. Because most aircraft riveting is comparatively light and is often done in limited spaces, the riveters for this purpose should be small, light, and compact. The pneumatic riveter operates on compressed air, which is supplied from a compressor or air storage tank through a hose line to the tool. When the throttle or trigger is opened, the compressed air causes a plunger in the cylinder to be blown back and forth with great rapidity and force. As the air passes through the main valve the plunger is forced down, where it strikes a rivet header, which in turn imparts the impact to the rivet. Rivet headers are supplied with different sizes of cups to make the various shaped heads. The return stroke of the piston, or plunger, is cushioned by air, reducing the jar to the operator.

Most of the essentials outlined under general riveting practices should be followed in machine riveting. It is very essential that the pieces, sheets, or plates be held in close contact while being riveted. When two pieces of metal are drilled together, as is the case in most riveting work, the drill has a tendency to raise the first piece away from the lower or second piece if they are not held together tightly. This allows burrs or chips to wedge between the two pieces and prevents them from being drawn close together when the rivets are headed up.

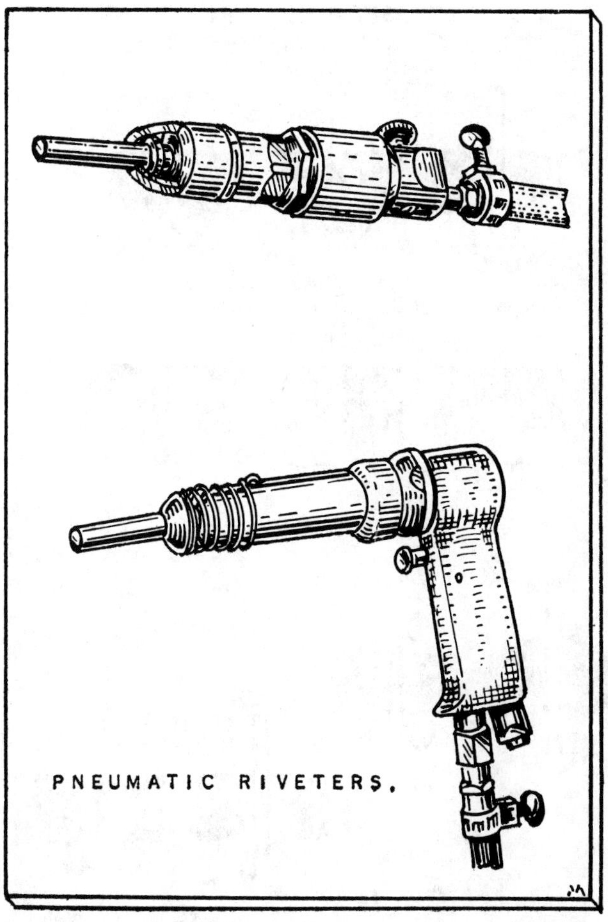

Figure 14.

Pop Rivets

Pop rivets (Fig. 15) have two advantages compared to standard rivets in that they can be set by one man and also be used for blind fastening. This means that they can be used where there is limited or no access to the reverse side of the work.

Operation is simple. Drill holes in the parts to be riveted together and align the holes. Insert the pop rivet (a hollow rivet assembled on a solid mandrel) and set it with a pop riveter (Fig. 16) using the procedure shown in Fig. 17.

There are two basic designs for pop rivets: closed-end and open-end (Fig. 15). The *closed-end* type rivet fills the need for blind rivets which seal as they are set. They are gas- and liquidtight, when used properly, since a high degree of radial expansion provides excellent hole-filling characteristics and the mandrel head is within the core of the rivet body.

The *open-end* type is not liquidtight because the mandrel head which remains in the rivet body is not enclosed within that body as is the closed-end type. This obviously leaves room for possible seepage of liquid or gas.

Rivet Selection

The following rules govern the selection and use of rivets in making a repair:

1. Replacements must not be made with rivets of lower strength material unless they are larger than those removed.

2. When rivet holes become enlarged, deformed, or otherwise damaged, use the next larger size as replacement.

3. Countersink head rivets are to be replaced by rivets of the same type and degree of countersink.

4. Rivets selected for specific applications must always be of the type recommended in the repair manual for that particular piece of equipment. Rivets are available in a variety of metals and alloys having specific shear strength and hardness characteristics. Selection of the wrong alloy-type rivet could produce hazardous results.

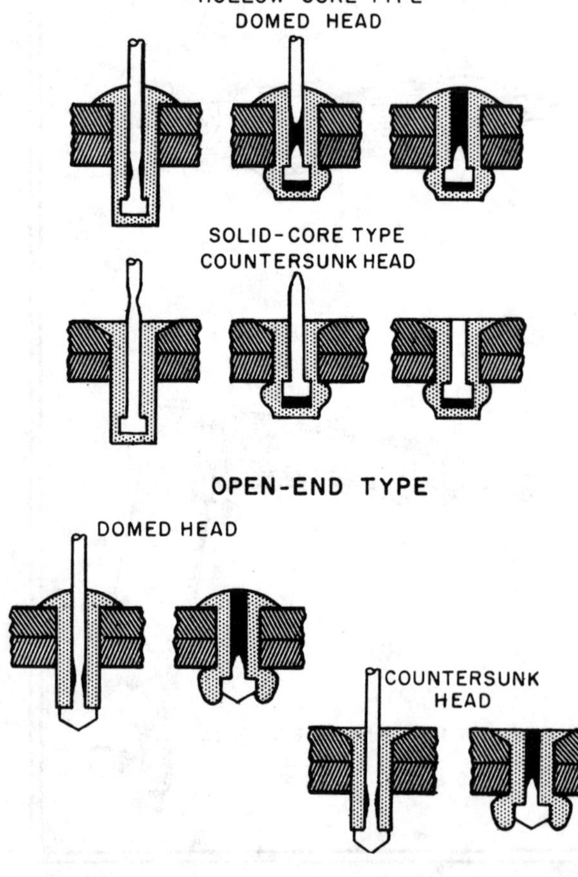
CLOSED-END TYPE
HOLLOW-CORE TYPE
DOMED HEAD
SOLID-CORE TYPE
COUNTERSUNK HEAD
OPEN-END TYPE
DOMED HEAD
COUNTERSUNK
HEAD

Figure 15. Pop rivets.

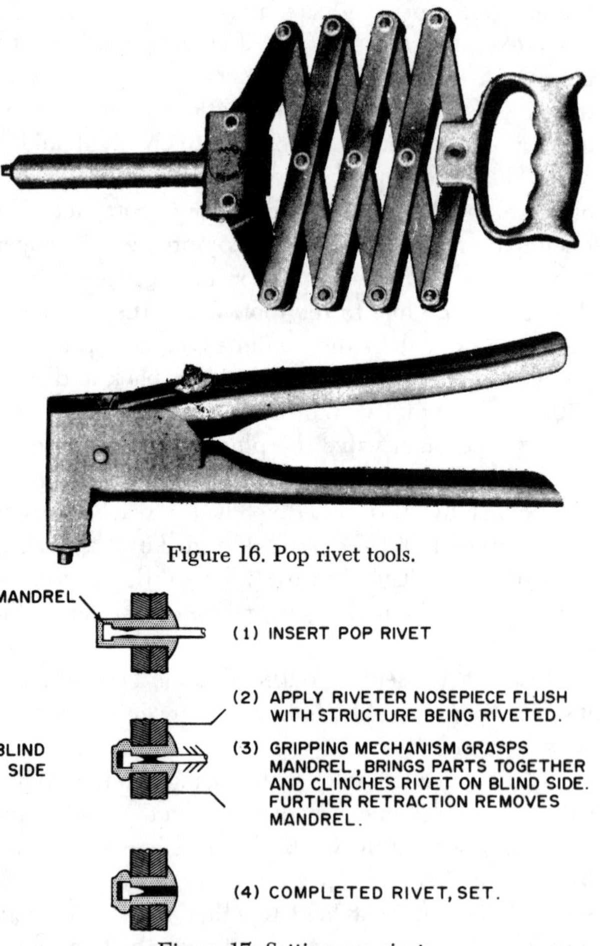
MANDREL
(1) INSERT POP RIVET
(2) APPLY RIVETER NOSEPIECE FLUSH WITH STRUCTURE BEING RIVETED.
BLIND
SIDE
(3) GRIPPING MECHANISM GRASPS MANDREL, BRINGS PARTS TOGETHER AND CLINCHES RIVET ON BLIND SIDE. FURTHER RETRACTION REMOVES MANDREL.
(4) COMPLETED RIVET, SET.

Figure 16. Pop rivet tools.

Figure 17. Setting pop rivets.

Chapter 8

Sheet Metal Fasteners

Many mechanisms and devices are held together with metal fasteners. Only the more commonly used fasteners will be discussed here so you will know when, where, and how they should be used. Use the fastening device that is best suited for the job.

Sheet Metal Screws

Hardened sheet metal screws are used for fastening or joining sheet metal parts that cannot be riveted. These screws are known in the trade as "self-tapping" screws (Fig. 1). The following tables give the sizes of screws and drills to be used for metal of different thicknesses.

As shown in Fig. 1, both blunt and sharp pointed screws are available. In general, the blunt end screws will be found most satisfactory, but the pointed type is used if alignment of the holes is difficult. In all "self-tapping" screws, the letter Z denotes the blunt or square end while *A* indicates the gimlet or sharp point.

Type *A* screws are usually used for joining materials lighter than .050 in.

Type Z screws are usually used for sheets from .015 to .203 in. thick.

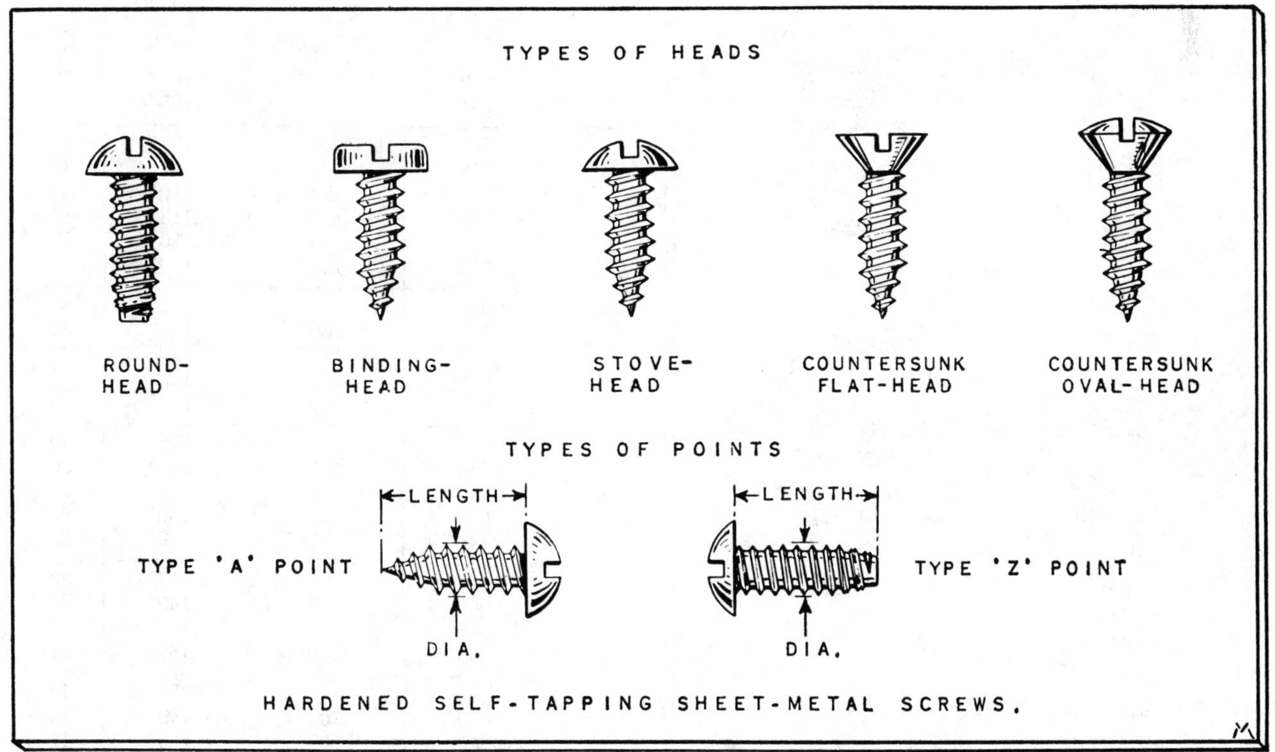

Figure 1.

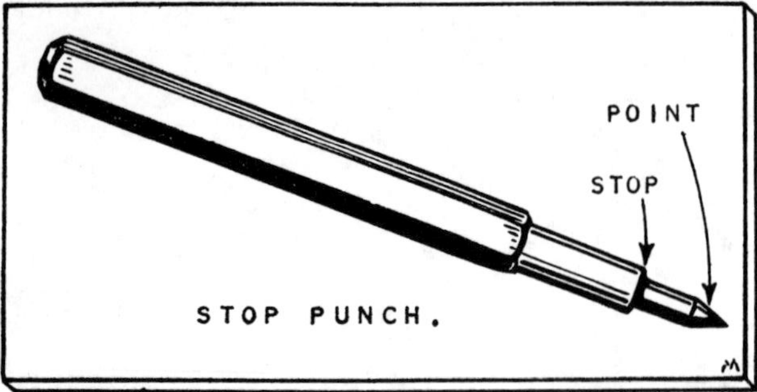

Figure 2.

are also available in approximately the same size range as the "self-tapping" screws. These screws require a special screw driver for each size of head.

PROCEDURE FOR USING TYPE *A* SHEET METAL SCREWS. When two parts made of light gauge sheet metal are to be joined, the holes in both may be drilled or clean-punched with a stop punch (Fig. 2) the same size, using the hole size recommended for the total metal thickness (A, Fig. 3), or the holes in both thicknesses may be pierced at the same time in a nested form (B, Fig. 3), which results in a stronger fastening. When a part in which a clearance hole is provided is to be fastened to light gauge sheet metal, it is desirable to pierce or extrude the hole in the latter (C, Fig. 3). Recommended hole sizes are given in Table 20.

PROCEDURES FOR USING TYPE Z SELF-TAPPING SCREWS. The type Z, hardened, self-tapping screw, shown in Fig. 4, was designed to extend the many advantages of the original sheet metal screw (the type *A*) to a broader range of applications. With the type Z, secure fastenings are made simply and inexpensively to light and heavy gauge sheet metal, nonferrous castings, and sheet metal parts to rosin

TABLE 20

RECOMMENDED HOLE SIZES FOR TYPE *A* HARDENING SELF-TAPPING SCREWS

SCREW DIAM.	Steel, Stainless Steel, Monel Metal, Brass, Aluminum Alloy			
	Metal Thickness	Pierced or Extruded Hole	Drilled or Clean-Punched Hole	
		Hole Required	Hole Required	Drill Size No.
No. 4	.015″	....	.086″	44
	.018″	....	.086″	44
	.024″	.098″	.093″	42
	.030″	.098″	.093″	42
	.036″	.098″	.098″	40
No. 6	.015″	....	.099″	39
	.018″	....	.099″	39
	.024″	.111″	.099″	39
	.030″	.111″	.101″	38
	.036″	.111″	.106″	36
No. 7	.015″	....	.104″	37
	.018″	....	.104″	37
	.024″	.120″	.110″	35
	.030″	.120″	.113″	33
	.036″	.120″	.116″	32
	.048″	.120″	.120″	31
No. 8	.018″	....	.113″	33
	.024″	.136″	.113″	33
	.030″	.136″	.116″	32
	.036″	.136″	.120″	31
	.048″	.136″	.128″	30
No. 10	.018″	....	.128″	30
	.024″	.157″	.128″	30
	.030″	.157″	.128″	30
	.036″	.157″	.136″	29
	.048″	.157″	.149″	25
No. 12	.024″	....	.147″	26
	.030″	.185″	.149″	25
	.036″	.185″	.152″	24
	.048″	.185″	.157″	22
No. 14	.024″	....	.180″	15
	.030″	.209″	.189″	12
	.036″	.209″	.191″	11
	.048″	.209″	.196″	9

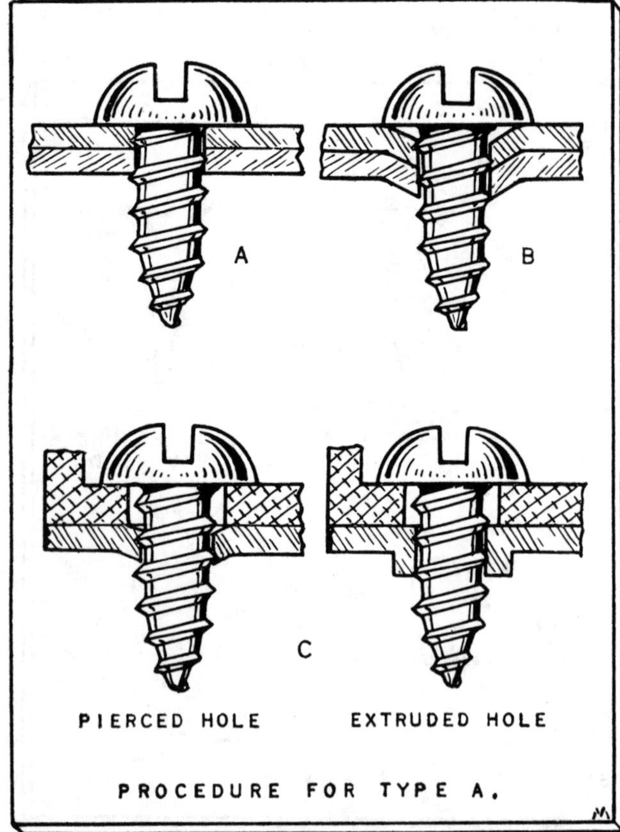

Figure 3.

impregnated plywood, hard rubber, or slate.

The type Z is hardened, so that it *forms* a mating thread as it is driven into a drilled or punched hole of suitable size. Fastenings made with type Z resist vibration, tension, and shear stresses. To drill the necessary hole, any conventional hand or power screw driver can be used, and type Z can be removed and replaced repeatedly without impairing security.

Because they eliminate tapping and threading and because of the obvious saving in time, trouble, and costs, these type Z screws have replaced machine screws, bolts, rivets, and other devices for many metal assemblies throughout the sheet metal industry. They are available with both the conventional slotted head and the Phillips recessed head (Fig. 5).

When two parts made of sheet metal are to be joined with type Z screws, the holes in both may be drilled or clean-punched the same size, using the hole size recommended in Table 21 for the *total metal thickness* (A, Fig. 4), or the holes in both thicknesses may be pierced at the same time in a nested form (B, Fig. 4), which results in a stronger fastening. When a part in which a clearance hole is provided is to be fastened to light gauge sheet metal, it is desirable to pierce or extrude the hole in the latter (C, Fig. 4). Pierced or extruded holes are not necessary when the screws are used in relatively heavy gauges of sheet metal as indicated in the hole size (see Table 21.)

Nails

Many types of conventional nails made of zinc coated and tinned copper are still used for fastening sheet metal work to wood and masonry. However,

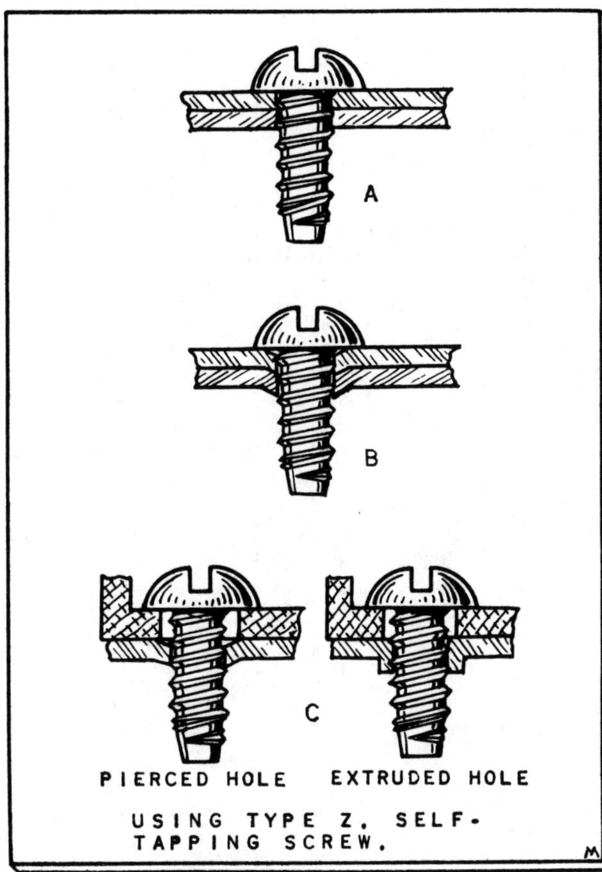

Figure 4.

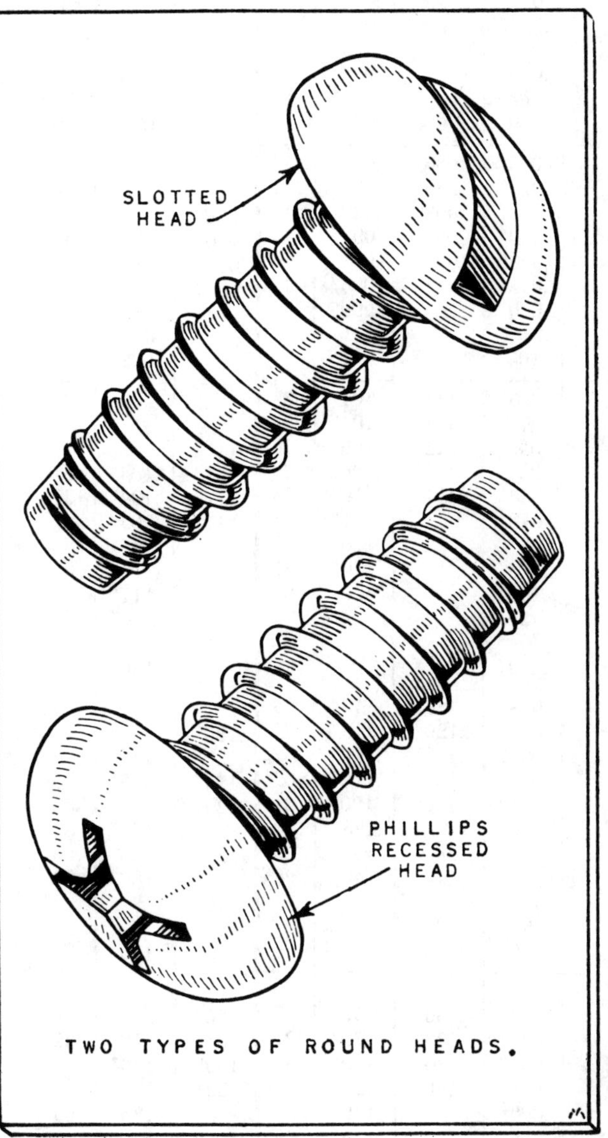

Figure 5.

the type of tinner's nails shown in Fig. 6 are gradually being discarded.

The problem of fastening sheet metal economically and securely to wood is solved by the hardened screwnail (Fig. 7), which combines the easy driving qualities of a nail with the strong holding property

TABLE 21

RECOMMENDED HOLE SIZES FOR TYPE Z HARDENED SELF-TAPPING SCREWS IN SHEET METAL

Screw Diameter	Metal Thickness	Steel, Stainless Steel, Monel, Brass: Pierced or Extruded Hole — Hole Required	Steel, Stainless Steel, Monel, Brass: Drilled or Clean-Punched Hole — Hole Required	Drill Size No.	Aluminum Alloy: Pierced or Extruded Hole — Hole Required	Aluminum Alloy: Drilled or Clean-Punched Hole — Hole Required	Drill Size No.
No. 2	.015″	....	.063″	52	....	....	..
	.018″	....	.063″	52	....	....	..
	.024″	....	.067″	51	....	.063″	52
	.030″	....	.070″	50	....	.063″	52
	.036″	....	.073″	49	....	.063″	52
	.048″	....	.073″	49	....	.067″	51
	.060″	....	.076″	48	....	.070″	50
No. 4	.015″	.086″	.086″	44	....	....	..
	.018″	.086″	.086″	44	....	....	..
	.024″	.098″	.089″	43	.086″	....	..
	.030″	.098″	.093″	42	.086″	.086″	44
	.036″	.098″	.093″	42	.086″	.086″	44
	.048″	....	.096″	41	.086″	.086″	44
	.060″	....	.099″	39	....	.089″	43
	.075″	....	.101″	38	....	.089″	43
	.105″	....	....	..	....	.093″	42
No. 6	.015″	.111″	.104″	37	....	....	..
	.018″	.111″	.104″	37	....	....	..
	.024″	.111″	.106″	36	.111″	....	..
	.030″	.111″	.106″	36	.111″	.104″	37
	.036″	.111″	.110″	35	.111″	.104″	37
	.048″	....	.111″	34	.111″	.104″	37
	.060″	....	.116″	32	....	.106″	36
	.075″	....	.120″	31	....	.110″	35
	.105″	....	.128″	30	....	.111″	34
	.128″ to .250″	....	....	..	....	.120″	31
No. 7	.018″	.120″	.113″	33	....	....	..
	.024″	.120″	.113″	33	.120″	....	..
	.030″	.120″	.116″	32	.120″	.113″	33
	.036″	.120″	.116″	32	.120″	.113″	33
	.048″	.120″	.120″	31	.120″	.116″	32
	.060″	....	.128″	30	....	.120″	31
	.075″	....	.136″	29	....	.128″	30
	.105″	....	.140″	28	....	.136″	29
	.128″ to .250″	....	....	..	....	.136″	29
No. 8	.018″	.136″	....	..	....	....	..
	.024″	.136″	.116″	32	.136″	....	..
	.030″	.136″	.120″	31	.136″	.116″	32
	.036″	.136″	.120″	31	.136″	.120″	31
	.048″	.136″	.128″	30	.136″	.128″	30
	.060″	....	.136″	29	....	.136″	29
	.075″	....	.140″	28	....	.140″	28

Screw Diameter	Metal Thickness	Steel, Stainless Steel, Monel, Brass: Pierced or Extruded Hole — Hole Required	Steel, Stainless Steel, Monel, Brass: Drilled or Clean-Punched Hole — Hole Required	Drill Size No.	Aluminum Alloy: Pierced or Extruded Hole — Hole Required	Aluminum Alloy: Drilled or Clean-Punched Hole — Hole Required	Size No. Drill
	.105″	....	.149″	25	....	.147″	26
	.125″	....	.149″	25	....	.147″	26
	.135″	....	.152″	24	....	.149″	25
	.162″ to .375″	....	....	..	....	.152″	24
No. 10	.018″	.157″	....	..	....	....	..
	.024″	.157″	.144″	27	.157″	....	..
	.030″	.157″	.144″	27	.157″	....	..
	.036″	.157″	.147″	26	.157″	.144″	27
	.048″	.157″	.152″	24	.157″	.144″	27
	.060″	....	.152″	24	....	.144″	27
	.075″	....	.157″	22	....	.147″	26
	.105″	....	.161″	20	....	.147″	26
	.125″	....	.169″	18	....	.154″	23
	.135″	....	.169″	18	....	.154″	23
	.164″	....	.173″	17	....	.159″	21
	.200″ to .375″	....	....	..	....	.166″	19
No. 12	.024″	.185″	.166″	19	....	....	..
	.030″	.185″	.166″	19	....	....	..
	.036″	.185″	.166″	19	....	....	..
	.048″	.185″	.169″	18	....	.161″	20
	.060″	....	.177″	16	....	.166″	19
	.075″	....	.182″	14	....	.173″	17
	.105″	....	.185″	13	....	.180″	15
	.125″	....	.196″	9	....	.182″	14
	.135″	....	.196″	9	....	.182″	14
	.164″	....	.201″	7	....	.189″	12
	.200″ to .375″	....	....	..	....	.196″	9
No. 14	.030″	.209″	.185″	13	....	....	..
	.036″	.209″	.185″	13	....	....	..
	.048″	.209″	.191″	11	....	....	..
	.060″	....	.199″	8	....	.199″	8
	.075″	....	.204″	6	....	.201″	7
	.105″	....	.209″	4	....	.204″	6
	.125″	....	.228″	1	....	.209″	4
	.135″	....	.228″	1	....	.209″	4
	.164″	....	.234″	15/64″	....	.213″	3
	.187″	....	.234″	15/64″	....	.213″	3
	.194″	....	.234″	15/64″	....	.221″	2
	.200″ to .375″	....	....	..	....	.228″	1

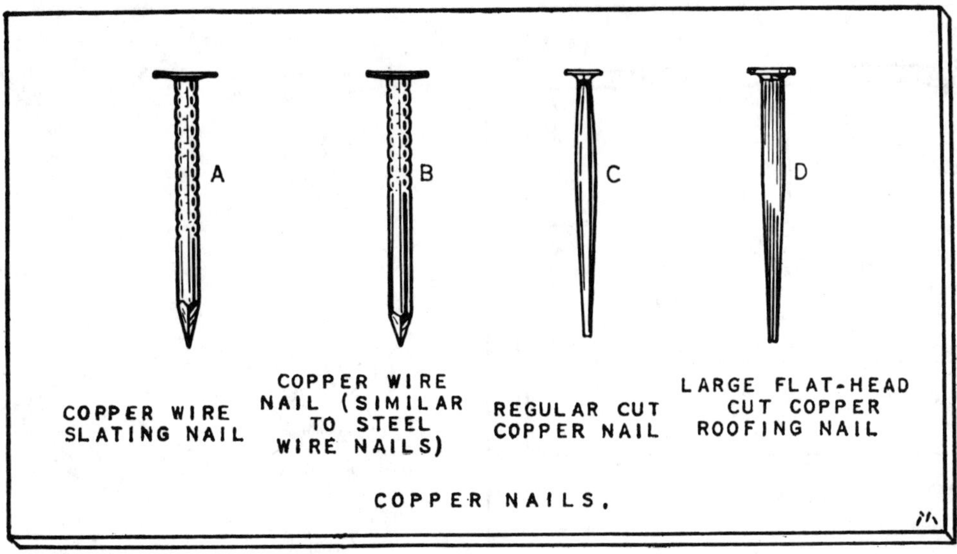

Figure 6.

of a screw. Unlike ordinary nails, these screwnails do not break or bend, nor do they work loose, back out, or pull out. The hardened spiral threads cut into the burr formed in the sheet metal by the pilot (smooth portion above the point) (Fig. 7) and worm their way into the wood, holding the sheet metal and wood together as though they were clamped in a vise.

Due to the greater strength of the fastenings they make, fewer screwnails are needed to do a job, thus speeding up the work and lowering the cost. Screwnails are used extensively by tinsmiths and roofers, and by manufacturers of automobiles, buses, railway cars, refrigerators, signs, billboards, and other products involving sheet metal-to-wood fastenings.

They are also available with cement coating, for increased holding power in wood. In such applications, the cement acts as a bonding agent between the wood fibers and the threads of the screwnail.

PROCEDURES FOR USING SCREWNAILS. Drive the screwnails through sheet metal into wood the same as ordinary nails are hammered into wood. If the sheet metal is too heavy for the screwnail to pierce it easily, a hole should first be punched with a screwnail punch (Fig. 8). An ordinary prick punch can be used if a screwnail punch is not available, but care must be exercised to avoid making the hole too large.

Note how the hardened spiral threads of the screwnail cut into the metal and worm into the wood like a screw (A, Fig. 9). No punch was used to make the hole—the hardened needle point pierced the metal with ease. Now observe the fit of the *ordinary nail* in metal and wood (B, Fig. 9). The hole in this metal was punched, because the nail would not pierce it without bending. The holding power of the ordinary nail is by friction alone; there is no engage-

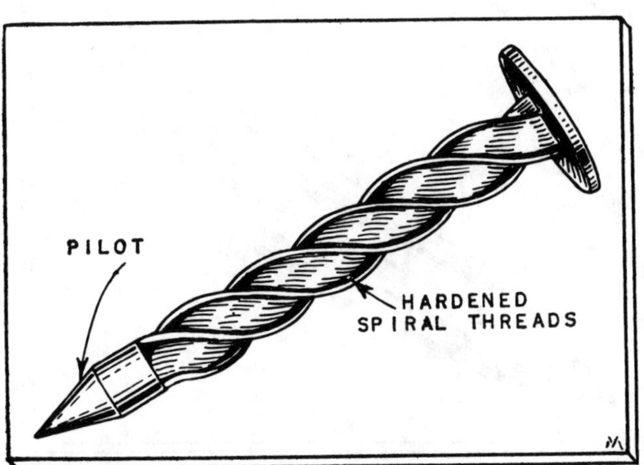

Figure 7.

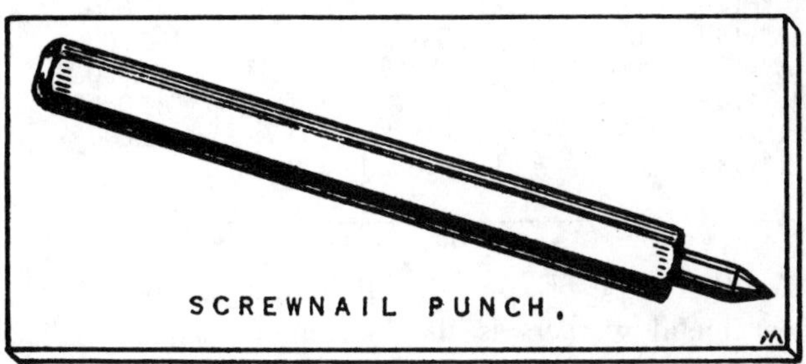

Figure 8.

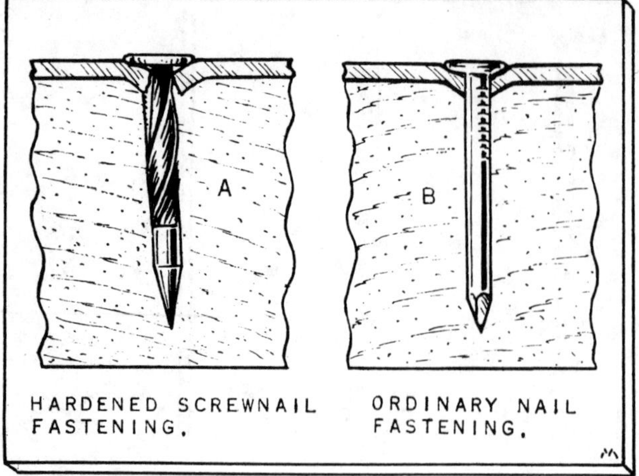

Figure 9.

ment in the metal. Eventually, vibration or expansion and contraction will cause the nail to loosen and will weaken the structure.

Screwnails are available in the standard head styles shown in Fig. 10, and sizes and weights shown in Table 22.

TABLE 22

STANDARD SIZES AND WEIGHTS

Standard Sizes	Decimal Equivalent of Gauge Number	Style of Head	Weight Per 1000 in Pkgs.	Approximate Quantity in a 100 lb. Keg
¾″x15	.072″	plain flat	1 lb.	105,000
¾″x13	.091″	" "	1¾ "	60,000
⅞″x13	.091″	" "	2 "	50,000
1″x12	.105″	" "	2¾ "	37,000
1¼″x11	.120″	" "	4⅔ "	22,000
1½″x11	.120″	" "	5⅔ "	20,000
1¾″x10	.135″	" "	7⅝ "	15,000
2″x10	.135″	" "	8⅔ "	12,000
2½″x10	.135″	" "	10⅔ "	10,000
¾″x15	.072″	countersunk flat	⅞ "	105,000
¾″x14	.080″	" "	1⅛ "	92,000
1″x14	.080″	" "	1½ "	70,000
1¼″x14	.080″	" "	1¾ "	55,000
1½″x14	.080″	" "	2⅛ "	45,000
¾″x15	.072″	small round	1 "	105,000
½″x14	.080″	" "	¾ "	120,000
¾″x14	.080″	" "	1³⁄₁₆ "	85,000
1″x14	.080″	" "	1½ "	65,000
1″x13	.091″	large round	2½ "	45,000

Another type of special nail used extensively by sheet metal workers is the hardened masonry nail (Fig. 11).

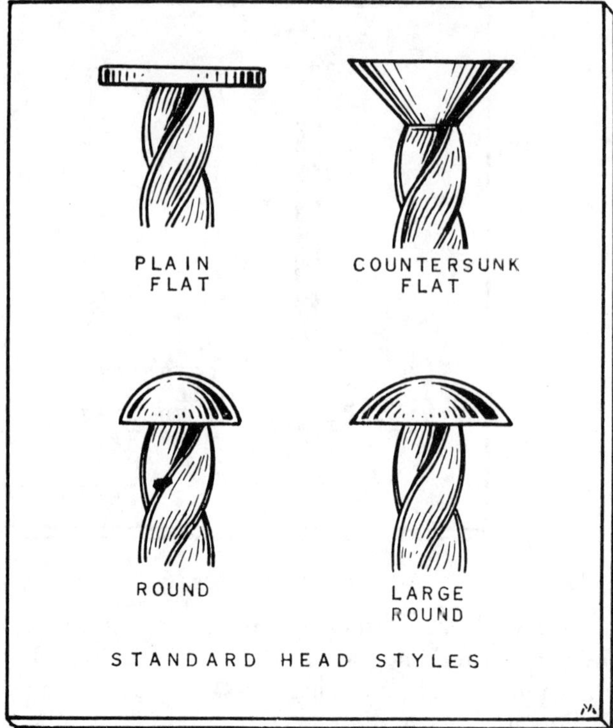

Figure 10.

These unique nails provide a simple, inexpensive, yet thoroughly satisfactory means of fastening sheet metal to brick, concrete, and other masonry. Made of special grade steel and heat-treated, they will not easily bend or break. Furthermore, the ribs become embedded in the masonry, thus strengthening the fastenings.

Masonry nails are available in the standard sizes shown in Table 23.

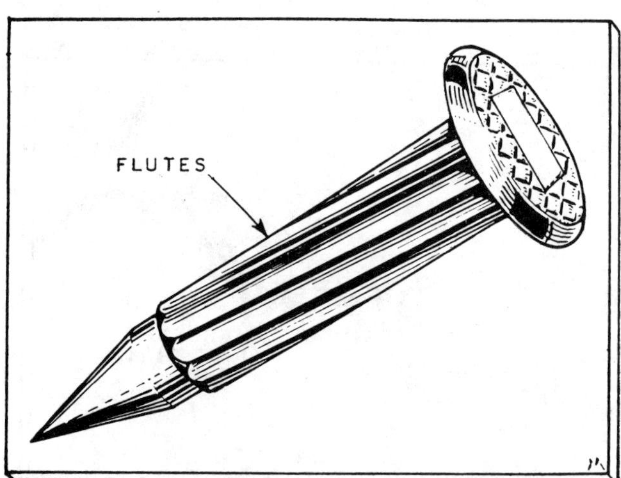

Figure 11. Hardened masonry nail.

TABLE 23

STANDARD SIZES AND WEIGHTS

Diameter	Length	Approximate Weight per 100	Approximate No. in a Pound	Approximate Quantity in a 100 lb. keg
1/8"	3/4"	1/2 lb.	207	20,700
5/32"	1"	2/3 "	120	12,000
3/16"	1 1/4"	1 2/3 "	72	7,200
1/4"	1 1/2"	2 1/2 "	40	4,000
1/4"	2"	3 1/8 "	32	3,200
1/4"	2 1/2"	4 "	26	2,600

Hardened masonry nails are simple to use. They can be hammered into mortar, cinder blocks, and other comparatively soft masonry the same way ordinary nails are hammered into wood. When used in concrete, brick, or other hard substances, it is necessary first to drill a hole of the proper size about two thirds of the length of the nail. For making the holes, masonry drills are recommended.

The *drill-bit-holder* of the masonry nail drill shown in Fig. 12 is made of tool steel, heat treated to resist "mushrooming" of the hammer end. The drill-bits (Fig. 12), forged of vanadium tool steel, stand up unusually well. The spiral flutes prevent binding and, when the drill is rotated slightly between blows, they serve to extract the pulverized material from the base of the hole. When dulled, the drill-bits are easily reground like twist drills. They are furnished in the following sizes:

1/8" For use with 1/8" x 3/4" Masonry nails
5/32" For use with 5/32" x 1" Masonry nails
3/16" For use with 3/16" x 1 1/4" Masonry nails
1/4" x 1 1/2" Masonry nails
1/4" For use with 1/4" x 2" Masonry nails
1/4" x 2 1/2" Masonry nails

Light, rapid blows increase the cutting speed of a drill, prevent binding, and extend the life of the drill.

Fasteners for Copper Sheet Metal

Because the right types of fastenings are essential to the proper installation of all sheet-copper work, these definite rules should be followed:

1. All fastenings should be of copper or a copper alloy.
2. Never secure sheets in any way that will prevent some free movement.
3. All pieces of copper forming parts of roofs, tanks, or other large units, should be cleated.
4. Fasten copper flashings more than 12 in. wide with cleats.

Rule 1 merely is an application of the principle that dissimilar metals must never be in contact. This applies not only to nails, but to hangers, brackets, braces, and screws and rivets. This basic rule is especially important when working with copper.

Rules 2, 3, and 4 are corollary to the fundamental rule that provision must be made for expansion and contraction when working with copper. Cleats permit such movement, and also restrict it to each sheet, so the movement is not multiplied throughout the entire copper work.

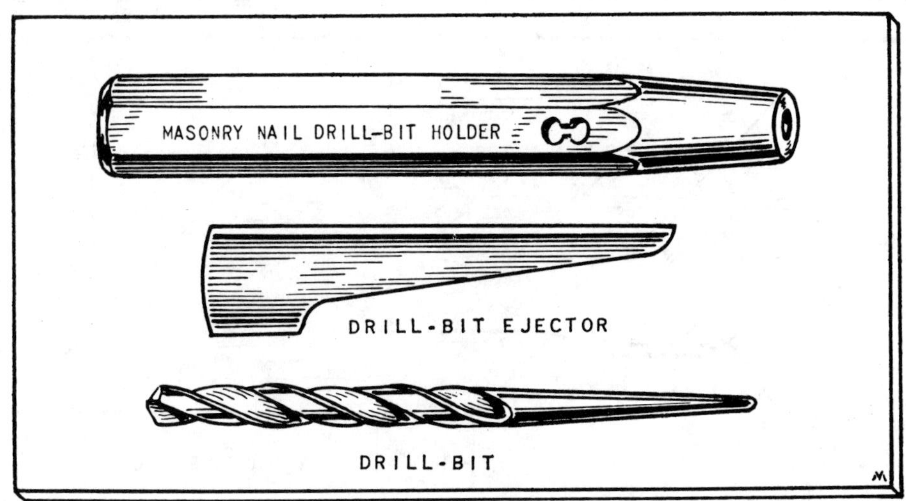

Figure 12.

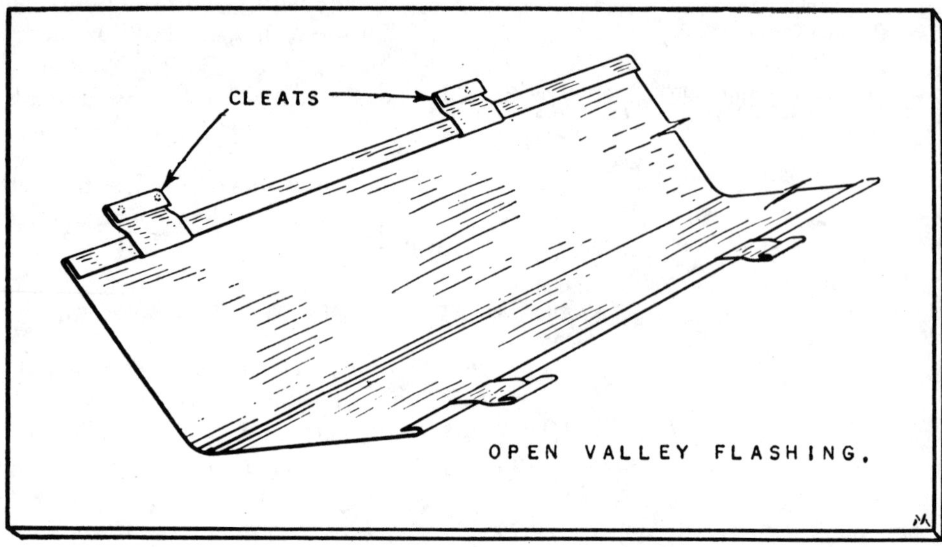

Figure 13.

Strips less than 12 in. wide, such as flashings and edge strips, may be secured by nails. In such instances, the nailing should be restricted to one edge. Nails should be near the edge and evenly spaced, not more than 4 in. apart.

A common source of flashing trouble derives from failure to observe rules 2 and 4 in valley flashings. These, by their very nature, are usually from 16 to 24 in. wide, and must be secured on both sides. Figure 13 shows a valley flashing. If such a flashing is nailed, two things may result from movement through extreme temperature ranges: the flashing may tear at the nails and become loose, or the sheet may buckle along the edge of the roofing material. With the first, water works under the loose flashing; with the second, splitting or cracking occurs from fatigue of the metal.

Cleats for Copper Work

Cleats should be made of 16-ounce cold-rolled copper, not less than 2 in. wide, and should be fastened with two copper or copper-alloy nails as shown in Fig. 14. A width of 2 in. is preferable, because it gives a stronger cleat and minimizes the possibility of the nails tearing out. The nails are placed parallel to the edge to prevent turning. The end of the cleat is bent back over the nails to prevent the nail heads from cutting the sheet. The length is determined by the kind of seam with which it is used.

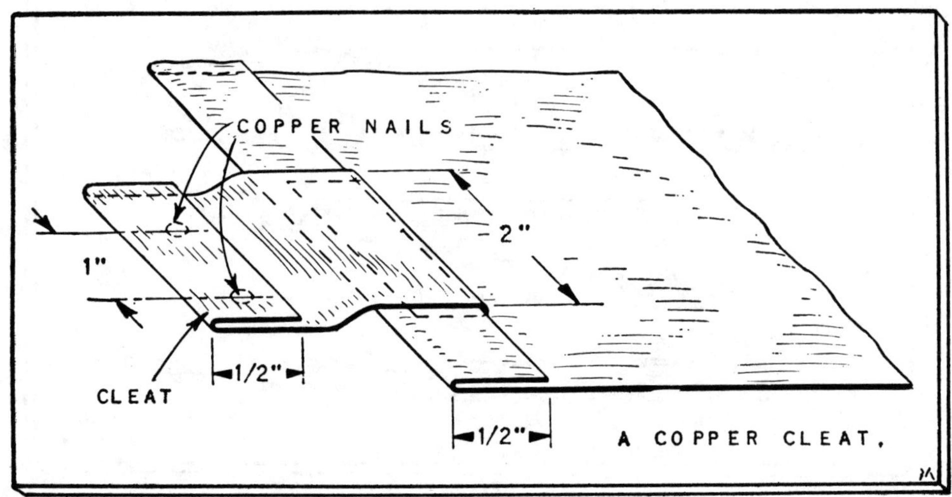

Figure 14.

Maximum spacing should not exceed 12 in.; a spacing of 6 or 8 in. is recommended. This does not apply to concealed valley flashings, where the sheet or strip is held by the roof covering. Under these conditions the spacing may be increased considerably; a maximum of 24 in. is recommended.

The cleat holds the sheet as shown in Fig. 13. If it also secures a second sheet, it is folded in with the sheets as the seam is formed. In such cases, the cleat must be nailed down before the sheets are brought together.

COPPER AND COPPER-ALLOY NAILS AND SCREWS. Many flashings, such as gravel stops, those around window and door openings, and some eave strips, must be nailed. In these cases, the four rules for fastening previously given in this chapter are still observed, for the copper strip is fastened along one edge only, and is free to move in a direction normal to the line of nailing. The longitudinal movement is taken care of by placing the nails a short distance (4 in. is the recommended maximum spacing) apart. As the total movement, through a temperature of 170 deg. F., between nails spaced even as much as 12 in. will be less than 1/50 in., there is little danger of tearing or splitting because of strain.

The cost of nailing with nails spaced 4 in. is not enough to justify risking failure of flashings at such vulnerable places as wall openings and roof edges.

The folly of using iron or steel nails with sheet copper cannot be over-emphasized. No economy results from saving a few dollars in nails that quickly corrode and thereby bring about failure.

The proper nails to use with sheet copper are large flat-head wire nails, not less than 12 gauge, with barbed shanks and diamond heads (A, Fig. 6). These are known as "copper wire slating nails," and differ from ordinary wire nails in the design of the head and the shank immediately under the head. The barbs at these points act like diminutive fish hooks in the wood fibers. As can be seen in B, Fig. 6, the ordinary wire nail has a ridge or shoulder under a smaller head. This makes it impossible to drive the nail home without tearing the sheet around the clean hole formed by the shaft. Moreover, the smaller head does not have enough gripping surface to hold well.

Cut nails regularly used for shingles and tile roofing are shown at C and D, Fig. 6. These nails have a greater holding power (2 or 3 times) than wire nails of the same length, but their disadvantages for use in sheet copper work are obvious. The shank tears the sheet, and the head, if driven home, punches through. For ordinary use in wood sheathing, the holding power of the large flathead wire slating nail is satisfactory.

In exposed locations, or wherever a special holding power is required, heavy (10 gauge) wire nails with barbs the full length of the shank are recommended. Cement-coated nails and etched nails also develop tremendous gripping power when the metal is nailed to wood.

The list of copper wire slating nails given in Table 24 has been set forth by the U.S. Department of Commerce, with the approval of the industry, through the National Bureau of Standards, under *Simplified Practice Recommendation* R150-34.

TABLE 24

COPPER WIRE SLATING NAILS

Length (Inch)	Stubs' Gauge	Decimal Equivalent (Inch)	Aprox. Number to the Pound
1	12	0.109	292
1¼	12	0.109	240
1¼	11	0.120	208
1¼	10	0.134	164
1½	12	0.109	204
1½	11	0.120	164
1½	10	0.134	132
1¾	10	0.134	116
2	10	0.134	108

Cut slating or roofing nails of brass and Naval brass are standard for slate and tile roofs, where large nails (2 in. or longer) of considerable holding power are required. The length of the nail necessary to give sufficient penetration into the nailing base, which is often gypsum or nailing concrete, demands an alloy harder than copper.

Cut slating and roofing nails of brass and other copper alloys are also used to attach slate and composition shingles to roof. They are like ordinary cut copper nails, except that, to get more holding power, they are made from heavier-gauge material and with larger heads.

Special Fasteners for Metal Gutters, Leaders, and Roof Drainage Systems

The drainage systems of all roofs are designed to carry water away quickly and to avoid pockets in which snow and ice can collect. The basic designs of roofs, flashings, and valleys are unaffected by the type of material used. They should shed water directly and speedily to gutters, the outlets of which transfer their horizontal flow into vertical leader flow with maximum efficiency. Sheet metal units comprising a complete drainage system are available in various styles and sizes and require only assembly and correct fastening (Figs. 15 and 16).

Installation of Gutters and Leaders. When installing gutters, leaders and other parts of the roof drainage system, the use of copper is recommended. While the initial cost of copper is slightly more than that of other metals, it is non-corrosive and will be found more economical over a period of years.

Copper gutters, leaders, hangers, hooks, and other

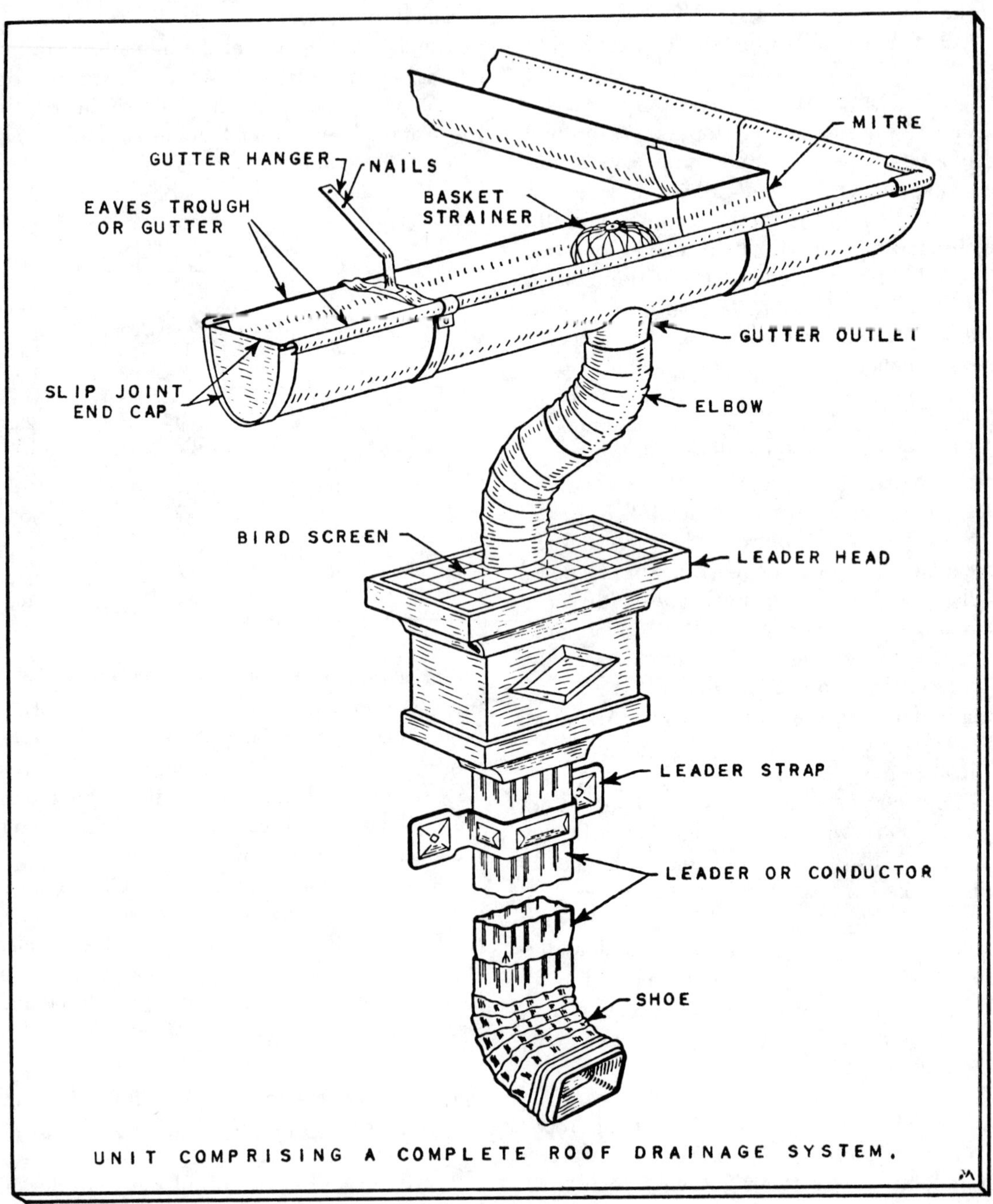

Figure 15.

necessary accessories are available in different sizes and forms at local dealers, ready for installation (Fig. 16).

The different types of gutters that are fabricated of 16-ounce cold-rolled copper in various sizes are shown in Fig. 17. The moulded copper gutters illustrated conform with the *Simplified Practice Recommendations* R 29-42 (United States Department of Commerce) made effective February 1, 1942, and generally followed by the trade. The gutters shown in the two upper left illustrations of Fig. 17 are made to rest upon the roof near the eaves, and the pitch or fall of the gutter is farther away from the eaves at the high point than at the low point. Attach light copper bars at the front, nail to the roof at the top, and cap with copper to prevent leakage.

There are many kinds of copper hangers on the market, and most of them are satisfactory for the special conditions for which they are made. The several varieties shown in Fig. 18, by no means a complete selection of those available, will serve for all ordinary purposes.

Figure 18 illustrates some of the bronze and copper shank-and-circle-type hangers, which may be made of either cast or wrought metal. They can be adjusted to give the gutter the necessary pitch by attaching the circular part to the shank at different heights. If the exterior is to be painted or stuccoed,

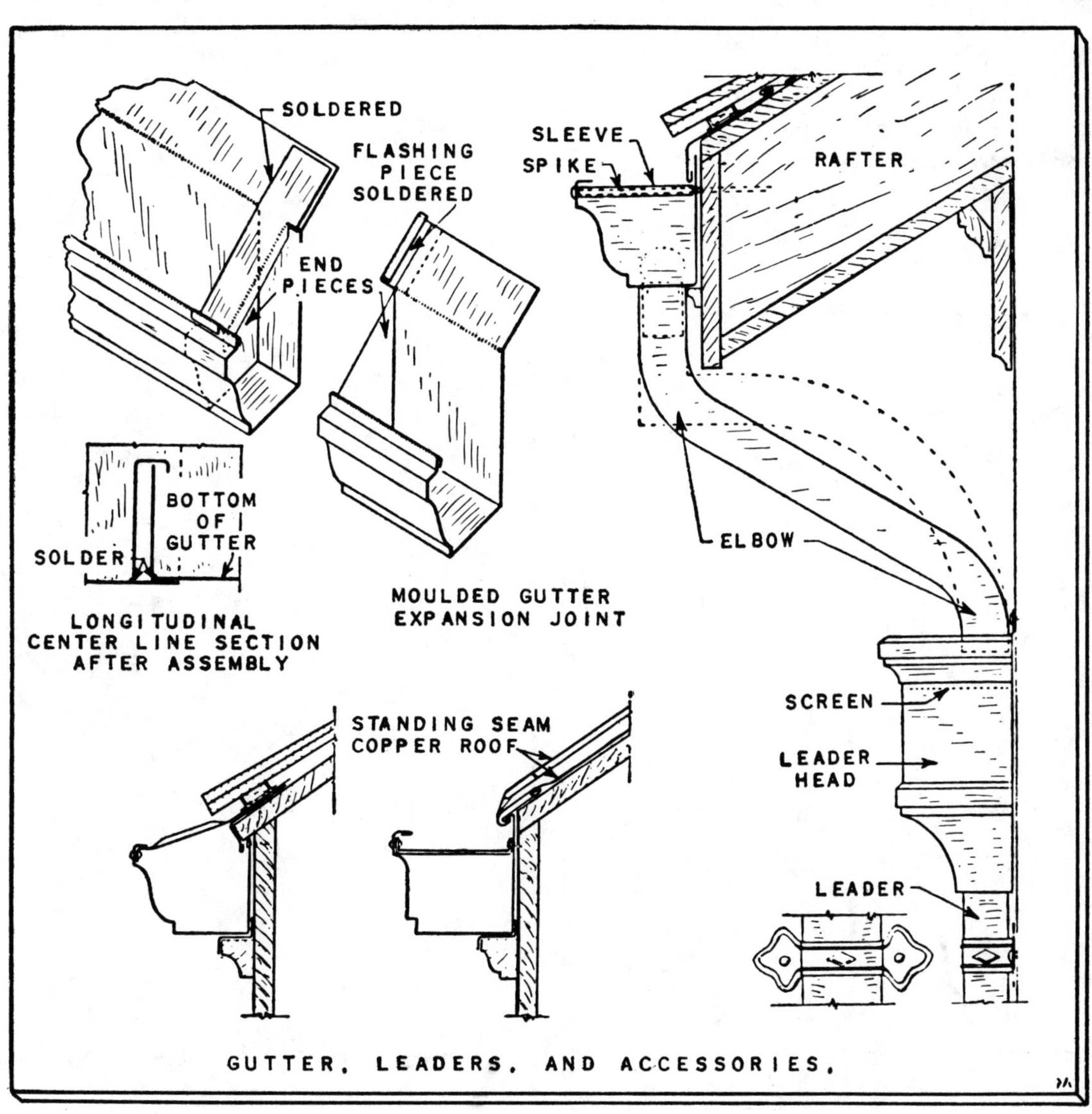

Figure 16.

the shank is normally attached before this work is done and the gutters hung afterward, thus avoiding the chance of damage to the gutters by the necessary scaffolding and ladders.

Figure 18 also illustrates three common types of leader hooks. These, if desired, can be obtained in two pieces—the clasp part separate from the shank. Shanks are available in different lengths, designed either for wood or brick drive. These leader hooks are driven into the wall before the leader is placed. Leader hooks generally should not be spaced farther than 6 ft. apart; in any case there should be at least one to each 10 ft. length.

A special type of ornamental cast brass leader strap with removable front is available. This can be put in position before the wall is repainted or stuccoed and the leaders set in place later.

Leaders or conductors are made and stocked in four different shapes. Plain round leaders do not resist freezing as well as do the corrugated ones. Moreover, the latter are more pleasing in appearance than are the plain ones. Sixteen-ounce leaders are regularly furnished in 10 ft. lengths.

All outlets should be provided with strainers. Strainers are essential when the leaders are small, or when they have elbows where leaves are likely to stick and clog. Wire basket strainers of stock design are generally carried by jobbers and sheet metal contractors. Strainers of heavier design, however, can readily be made up to desired specifications. Heavier-cast brass strainers should be used for drainage outlets on promenade tile or composition roofs.

One illustration in Fig. 16 shows the adjustable copper gutter shank nailed to the facia board, and the other shows it nailed on the roof. Proper placing of flashing strips is also shown in the same illustration.

A copper rod ⅜ in. in diameter may be driven into a ½ in. bead of a stock gutter for reinforcement. These rods are recessed 2½ in. at one end of a

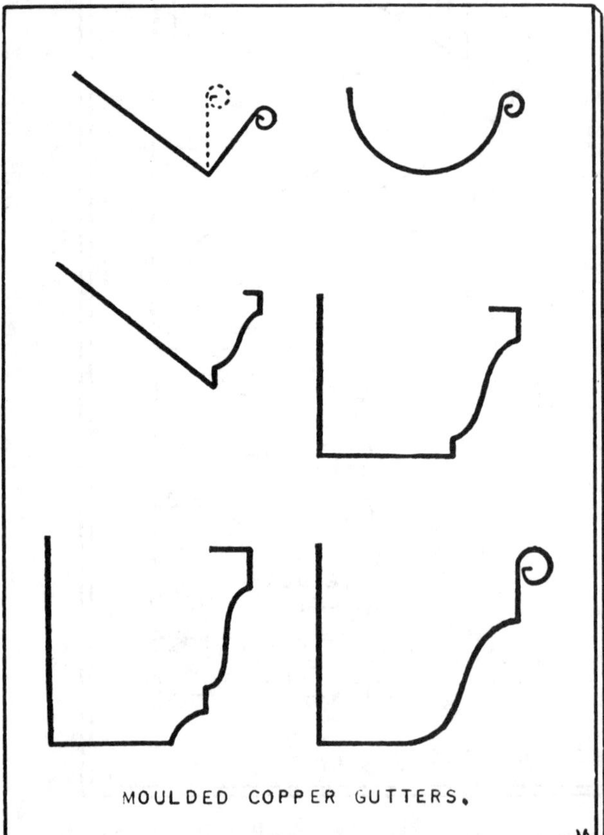

Figure 17.

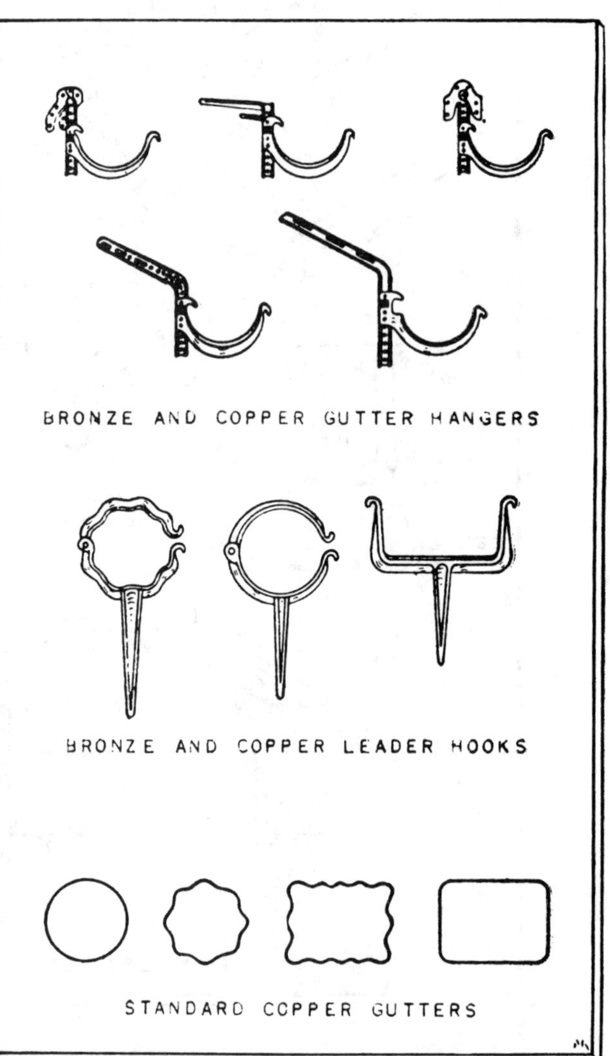

Figure 18.

section of gutter and extended 1½ in. at the other end to form an interlock between sections with 1 in. lap.

The strap hanger shown in Fig. 19 is clamped at the back of the gutter and is spaced not over 30 in. on centers. The sustaining strap regulates the pitch of this gutter. An expansion joint for long sections is also shown.

Moulded gutters (Fig. 16) are set in a position to receive the drainage, but low enough to prevent snow slides from injuring the outer edge. They are usually set level because of architectural considerations. Where the brass spikes are used, they should be nailed into rafter ends. Pressed sheet copper straps are available to fasten gutters back to the roof. Expansion joints, shown in Fig. 16, should be used in long lengths of this type of gutter. It is important to keep leaders ¾ in. from the wall to avoid staining in case freezing causes breaks in the seams.

Cold-rolled copper is frequently used for the lining of wooden gutters. Two typical designs are shown in Fig. 20. Note that the outer edge of the copper gutter lining is loose-locked over an edge strip, which also forms a drip. The inner edge is loose-locked into a flashing strip along the sheathing. Flashing strips are attached with narrow cleats to prevent nailing through the copper.

INSTALLING CIRCULAR GUTTERS. Half-round gutters are installed on circular towers, or on bay windows with large radii, by using short sections of straight gutter formed without the bead. Section a brass rod covered with a strip of copper into long lengths, and solder it to the circular gutter. Arrange the adjustable copper gutter hangers to conceal the cross joints in the gutter.

If, however, the radius is not large enough to permit the use of small sections of straight gutter, make a circular gutter by joining front and back sections throughout with a bottom strip cut to a radius slightly larger than that of the wall line (Fig. 21). Obtain the radii of the two conical pieces by extending the dotted lines *a-b* and *c-d* to a vertical line in the center of the tower. Stretch the blank piece of the rear section over a mandrel. Raise the other on a block that has been cut to profile.

Draw the bottom member of the rectangular gutter to the radius of the wall line, adding ½ in. for thickness of the gutter hangers, and draw the second curve in front of this to the exact projection of the gutter. The vertical member in the back of the gutter has an edge hemmed at the top, and a small edge turned at 90 degrees at the bottom as a lap for soldering. The bottom front member has a quarter-round bend at the top, which is stretched to the proper curvature before it is soldered at the bottom. The next strip has two edges turned in as soldering laps, and the flat strip at the top is cut radially. This gutter is supported by copper bar hangers, which are nailed to the woodwork in the back.

In the left illustration of Fig. 22, an opening is cut into the stone cornice to permit the leader to run in a straight line. A little clearance between the leader and the stone may prevent discoloration of the stone cornice.

The center illustration in Fig. 22 shows the proper

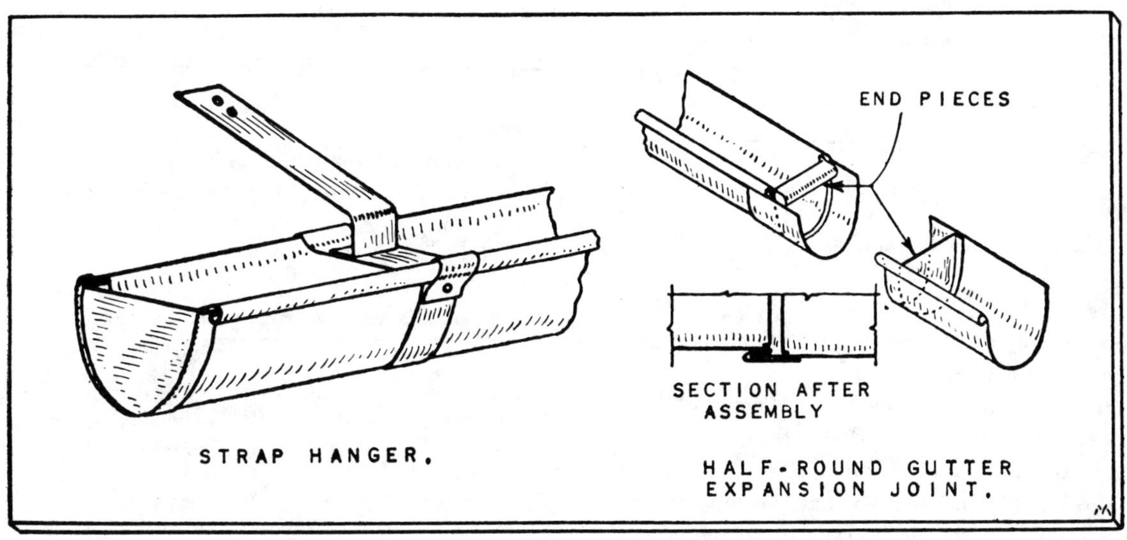

Figure 19.

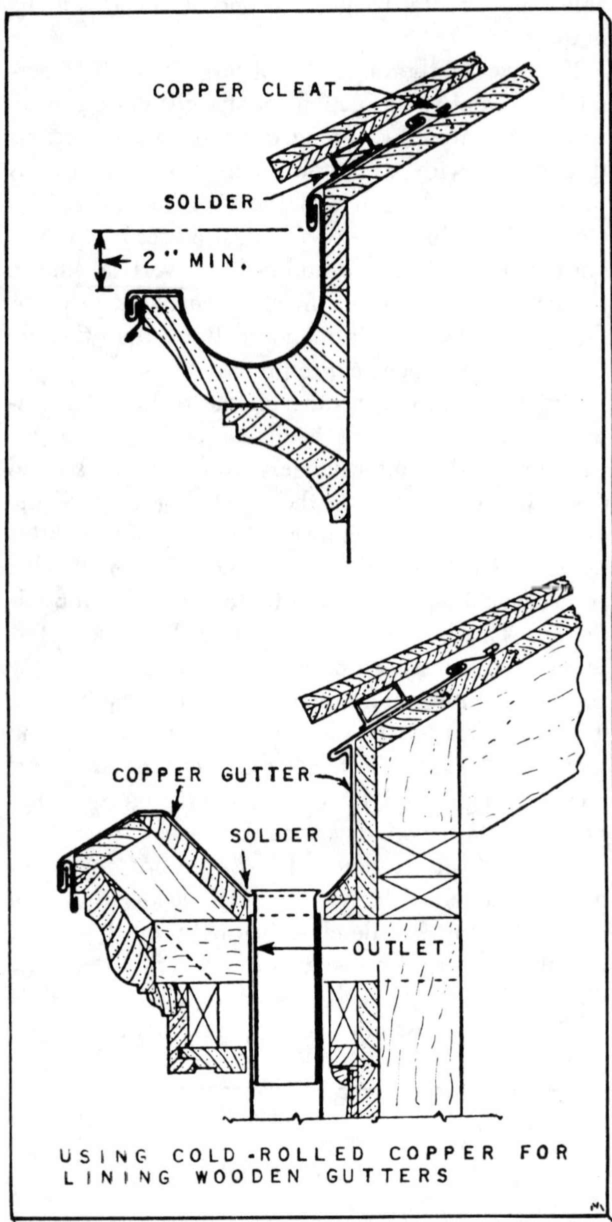

Figure 20.

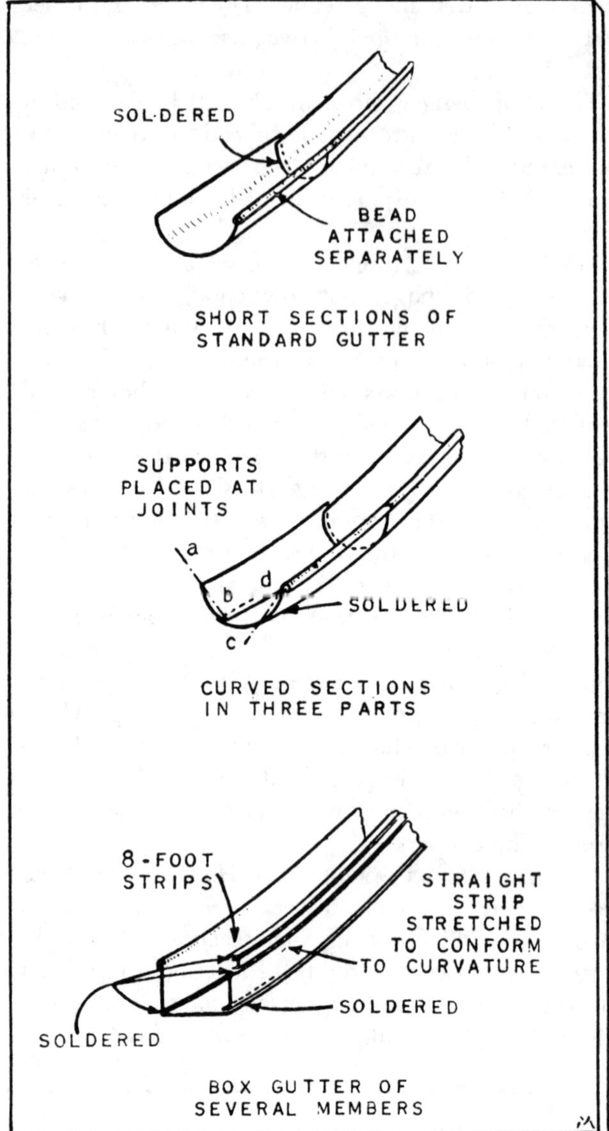

Figure 21.

method of elbowing to conform to the profile of a stone belt course.

The right illustration in Fig. 22 shows the leader on the front of a building connected to a drain located on the side of the building.

Figure 23 illustrates a method of fastening gutter hangers to concrete-and-wood sheathing where roofs are covered with composition roofing. The hangers should be let into the slab so that the tops are flush with the deck, and should be secured to the concrete slab by brass nails or bolts in expansion sleeves.

The center illustration shows provision for nailing the eave strip where the concrete is covered with insulation.

Table 25

Approximate Area of Leader in Square Inches

Nominal Leader Size in Inches	Plain Round	Corrugated Round	Corrugated Rectangular
3	7	6	8
4	13	11	12
5	20	18	19
6	28	26	—

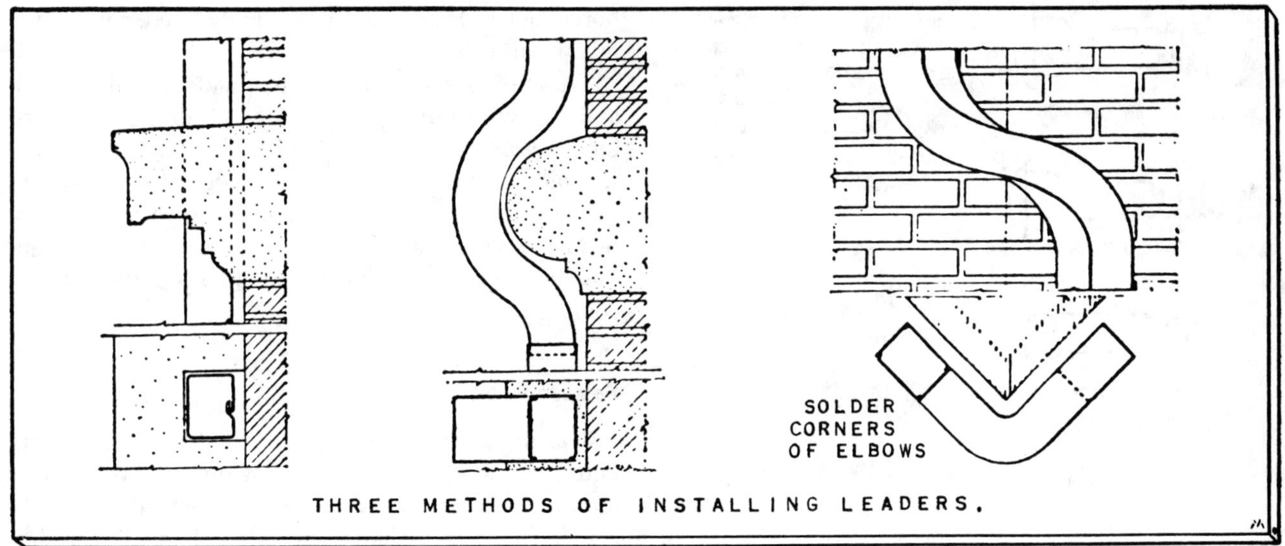

Figure 22.

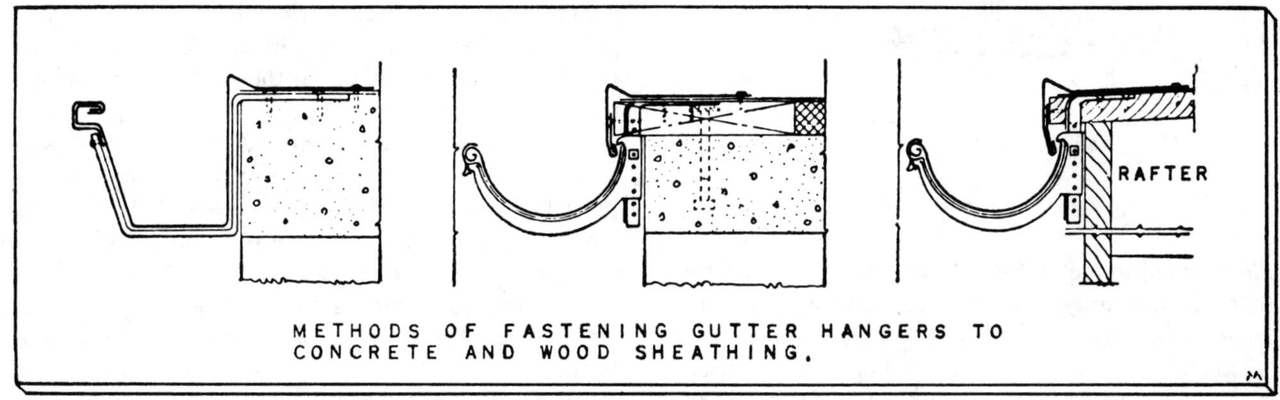

Figure 23.

The left illustration shows the gutter attached to wood sheathing.

Leaders are usually located near the corners of the building to avoid retarding the flow of drainage, and to eliminate sharp turns in the gutters. The approximate required leader area is given in Table 25

One square inch of leader area will serve approximately 200 sq. ft. of actual computed roof area for an average 6 in. intensity of rainfall.

Bolts

Machine Bolts. Machine bolts (Fig. 24) are made with National Fine (N.F.) or National Coarse (N.C.) threads extending in length from twice the diameter of the bolt plus 1/4 inch (for bolts less than 6 inches in length), to twice the diameter of the bolt plus 1/2 inch (for bolts over 6 inches in length). They are precision-made and are generally applied metal-to-metal where close tolerance is desirable. The head may be square, hexagon, rounded, or flat countersunk. The nut usually corresponds in shape to the head of the bolt with which it is used. Machine bolts are externally driven only. Selection of the proper machine bolt is made on the basis of head style, length, diameter, number of threads per inch, and coarseness of thread. The hole through which the bolt is to pass is bored to the same diameter as the bolt. Machine bolts are made in diameters from 1/4 inch to 3 inches and may be obtained in any length desired.

Stove Bolts. Stove bolts (Fig. 24) are less precisely made than machine bolts. They are made with either flat or round slotted heads and may have threads extending over the full length of the body, over part of the body, or over most of the body. They are generally used with square nuts and ap-

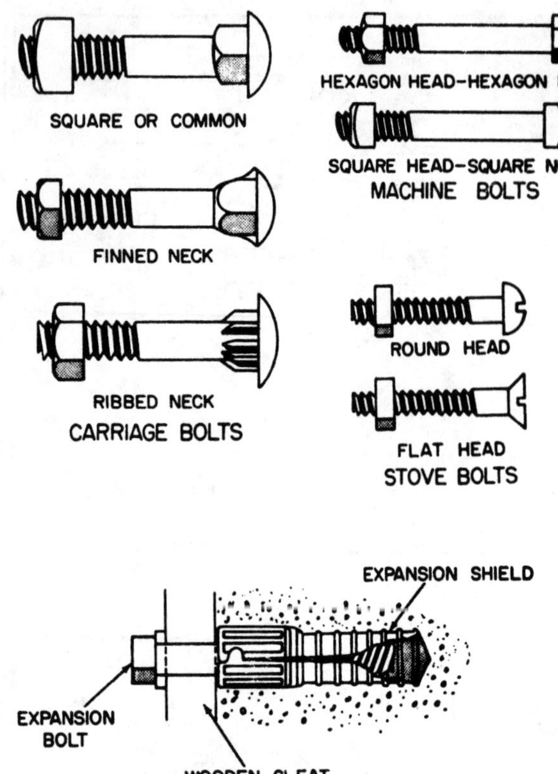

Figure 24. Types of bolts.

plied metal-to-metal, wood-to-wood, or wood-to-metal. If flatheaded, they are countersunk; if roundheaded, they are drawn flush to the surface.

EXPANSION BOLT. An expansion bolt is a bolt used in conjunction with an expansion shield (Fig. 24) to provide anchorage in substances in which a threaded fastener alone is useless. The shield, or expansion anchor, inserted in a predrilled hole expands when the bolt is driven into it and becomes wedged firmly in the hole, providing a secure base for the grip of the fastener.

Capscrews

Capscrews perform the same functions as machine screws, but come in larger sizes for heavier work. Sizes range up to 1 inch in diameter and 6 inches in length.

Capscrews are usually used without nuts. They are screwed into tapped holes, and are sometimes referred to as tap bolts. Threads may be either N.F. or N.C.

Capscrews may have square, hex, flat, button, or fillister heads. Fillister heads are best for use on moving parts when such heads are sunk into counterbored holes. Hex heads are usually used where the metal parts do not move.

The strongest capscrews are made of alloy steel and can withstand great stresses, strains, and shearing forces. Capscrews made of Monel metal are often specified on machinery that is exposed to salt water.

Some capscrews have small holes through their heads. A wire, called a *safety wire,* is run through the holes of several capscrews to keep them from coming loose.

Setscrews

Setscrews are used to secure small pulleys, gears, and cams to shafts, and to provide positive adjustment of machine parts. They are classified by diameter, thread, head shape, and point shape. The point shape is important because it determines the holding qualities of the setscrew.

Setscrews hold best if they have either a *cone point* or a *dog point,* shown in Fig. 25. These points fit into matching recesses in the shaft against which they bear.

HEADLESS SETSCREWS. Slotted, Allen, or Bristol types of headless setscrews are used with moving parts because they do not stick up above the surface. They are threaded all the way from point to head.

COMMON SETSCREWS. Common setscrews, used on fixed parts, have square heads. They have threads all the way from the point to the shoulder of the head.

THUMB SCREWS. Thumb screws are used for setscrews, adjusting screws, and clamping screws. Because of their design they can be loosened or tightened without the use of tools.

Nuts

SQUARE AND HEXAGONAL NUTS. Square and hexagonal nuts are standard, but they are supplemented by special nuts (*see* Fig. 26). One of these is the *jam nut* used above a standard hex nut to lock it in position. It is about half as thick as the standard hex nut, and has a washer face.

CASTELLATED NUTS. Castellated nuts are slotted so that a safety wire or *cotter key* may be pushed through the slots and into a matching hole in the bolt. This provides a positive method of preventing the nut from working loose. *For example,* you will see these nuts used with the bolts that hold the two halves of an engine connecting rod together.

WING NUTS. *Wing nuts* are used where the desired

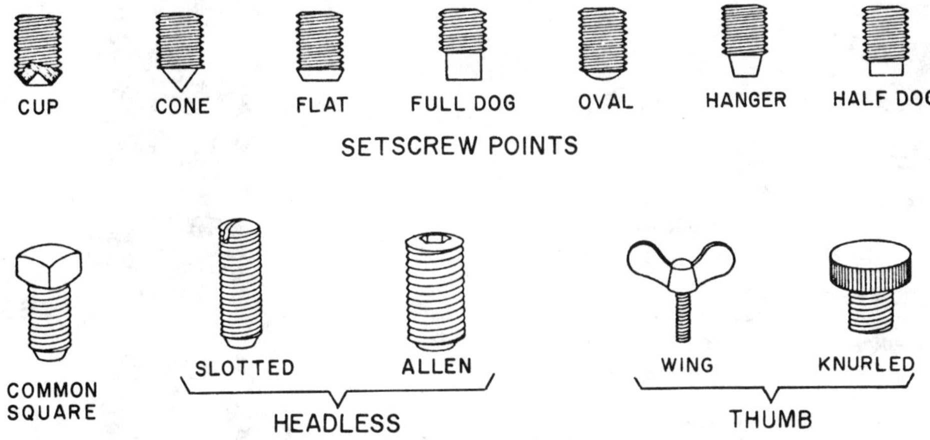

Figure 25. Setscrews and thumbscrews.

degree of tightness can be obtained by the fingers. *Cap nuts* are used where appearance is an important consideration. They are usually made of chromium plated brass. *Thumb nuts* are knurled, so they can be turned by hand for easy assembly and disassembly.

ELASTIC STOP NUTS. *Elastic stop nuts* are used where it is imperative that the nut does not come loose. These nuts have a fiber or composition washer built into them which is compressed automatically against the screw threads to provide holding tension. They are used extensively on radios, sound equipment, fire control equipment, and on aircraft.

Washers

Figure 27 shows the types of washers commonly used.

FLAT WASHERS. *Flat washers* are used to back up bolt heads and nuts and to provide larger bearing surfaces. They prevent damage to the surfaces of the metal parts.

SQUARE HEXAGONAL JAM CASTELLATED

WING CAP THUMB STOP

Figure 26. Types of nuts.

SPLIT LOCK WASHERS. *Split lock washers* are used under nuts to prevent loosening by vibration. The ends of these spring-hardened washers dig into both the nut and the work to prevent slippage.

SHAKEPROOF LOCK WASHERS. *Shakeproof lock washers* have teeth or lugs that grip both the work and the nut. Several patented designs, shapes, and sizes are obtainable.

Keys and Pins

COTTER KEYS. *Cotter keys* (Fig. 28) are used to secure screws, nuts, bolts, and pins. They are also used as stops and holders on shafts and rods.

SQUARE KEYS AND WOODRUFF KEYS. *Square keys* and *Woodruff keys* (Fig. 28) are used to prevent hand wheels, gears, cams, and pulleys from turning on a shaft. These keys are strong enough to carry heavy loads if they are fitted and seated properly.

TAPER PINS. *Taper pins* (Fig. 28) are used to locate and position matching parts. They are also used to secure small pulleys and gears to shafts. They usually have a taper of 1/4 in. per foot. Holes for

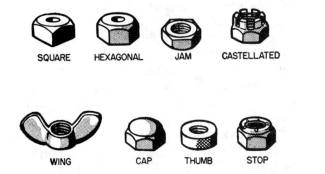

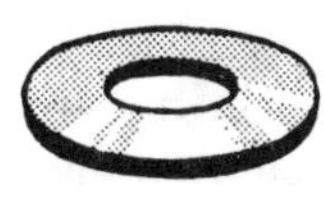

FLAT WASHER SPLIT LOCK WASHER SHAKE PROOF WASHER

Figure 27. Washers.

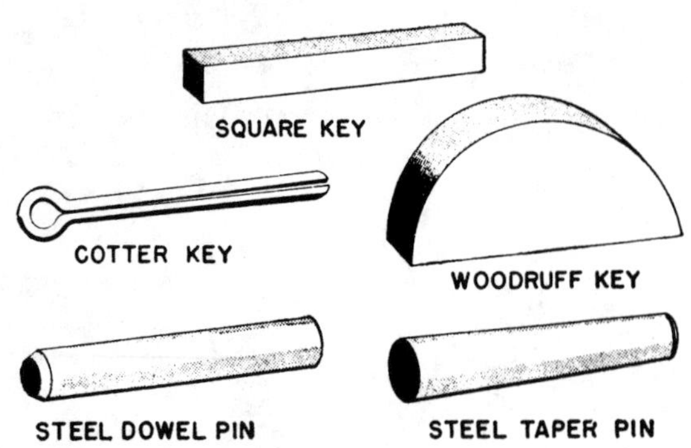

Figure 28. Keys and pins.

taper pins must be reamed with tapered reamers, or the taper pin will not fit properly.

DOWEL PINS. *Dowel pins* (Fig. 28) are used to position and align the units or parts of an assembly. One end of a dowel pin is chamfered, and it is usually .001 to .002 inch greater in diameter than the size of the hole into which the pin will be driven.

Turnlock Fasteners

Turnlock fasteners are used to secure doors, inspection plates, and other removable panels on items of support equipment and aircraft. These fasteners are also referred to by such terms as quick-opening, quick-acting, and stress panel fasteners. The most desirable feature of these fasteners is that they permit quick and easy removal of access panels and doors for inspection and servicing.

Turnlock fasteners are manufactured and supplied by a number of manufacturers under various trade names. Some of the more common trade names are the Camloc and Dzus (pronounced zoo's) types.

CAMLOCK FASTENERS. *Camlock fasteners* are made in a variety of styles and designs. Regardless of the particular style or shape, the Camloc fastener consists of a stud assembly, receptacle, and a grommet (Fig. 29).

The *stud assembly* consists of a stud, a cross pin, spring, and spring cup. The assembly is so designed that it can be quickly inserted into the grommet by compressing the spring. Once installed in the grommet the stud assembly cannot be removed unless the spring is again compressed.

The *grommet* is a flanged sheet metal ring made to fit into a hole in the access door or panel. It is ribbed and can be pressed or dimpled into place.

The *receptacle* consists of a metal forging mounted

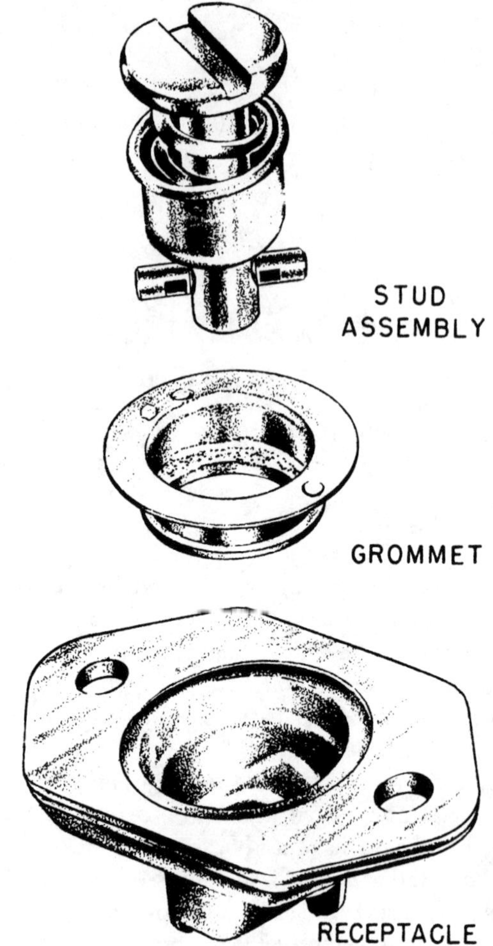

Figure 29. Camlock fastener.

in a stamped sheet metal. It is riveted to the access opening frame attached to the structure or equipment.

A quarter turn clockwise of the stud screw locks the cross pin into the grooved receptacle. Conversely, a counterclockwise rotation releases the connection between the stud assembly and the receptacle.

DZUS FASTENERS. The *Dzus fastener* (Fig. 30) consists of a rotatable stud, which may have a slot for a screwdriver or a winged fitting on it for hand operation. It also has a permanently mounted spring and a grommet. The stud and grommet are mounted in the door or other removable part, and the spring is riveted to the frame of the access on which the door fits.

Cams on the stud engage with the spring to lock the fastener in the engaged position. The purpose of the grommet is to retain the stud in the access door. In some installations, the grommet is not used as a

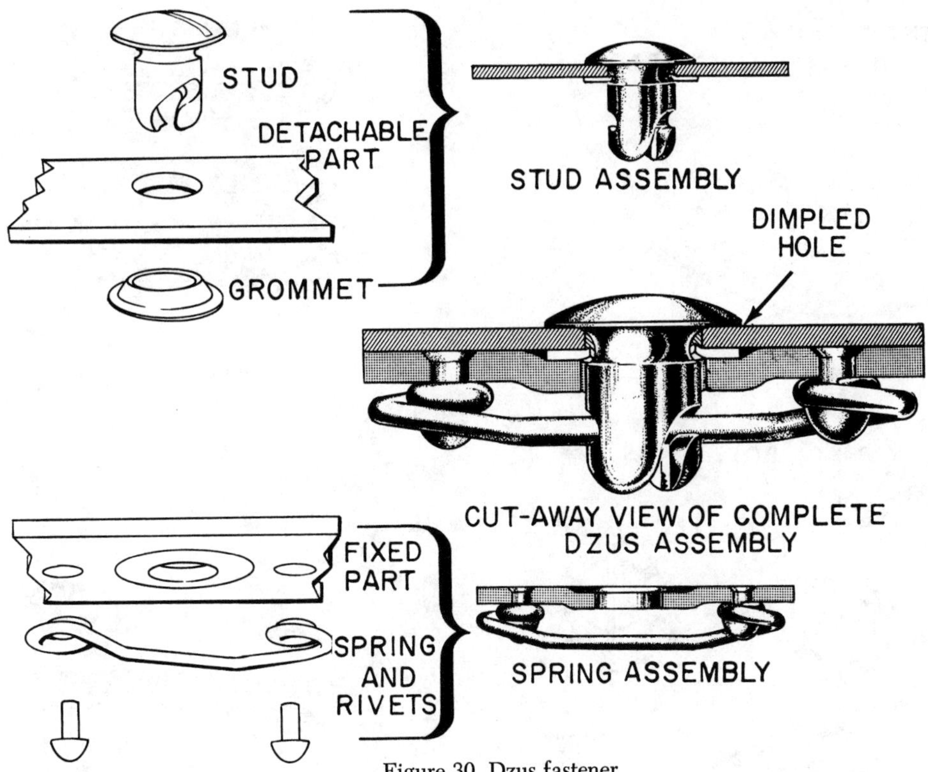

Figure 30. Dzus fastener.

retainer; the stud is secured to the access door by a snapring, cup washer, or by dimpling of the metal around the stud.

The quick action of the Dzus fastener is achieved when a quarter turn rotation of the stud causes its engagement or disengagement with the spring.

Safetying Methods

Safetying is a process of securing fasteners and other equipment so they do not work loose due to vibration. Loose bolts, screws, and nuts or other parts can ruin delicate equipment or endanger life when they fall off equipment.

Various methods for safetying parts exist. The most widely used are safety wire and cotter pins. *Be sure* to learn the proper techniques and *use* them.

Safety Wiring

Safety wiring is the most positive and satisfactory method of safetying capscrews, studs, nuts, and bolt heads which cannot be safetied by any other practical means. It is a method of wiring together two or more units in such a manner that any tendency of one to loosen is countered by the tightening of the wire and the other unit. Components are safety wired by the single wire plain method or the twist method (Fig. 31).

The *single wire plain method* may be used on small components in a closely spaced, closed geometrical pattern, and in places that are difficult to reach. When safety wiring closely spaced components, take advantage and safety wire the whole series. The number of parts in the series safely wired together by this method depends upon the application; but the maximum number in the series is limited by a maximum 24 inch wire length.

The *twist method* is the most common method of safety wiring. The technique is shown in Fig. 32. A group of three should be the maximum in the series when safety wiring widely spaced components by this method.

The following general rules should be followed when using the safety wire method to secure components.

1. The safety wire must be new upon each application.

2. All safety wires must be tight after installation, but not under such tension that normal handling or vibration will break the wire.

3. The wire must be applied so that all pull exerted by the wire tends to tighten the nut.

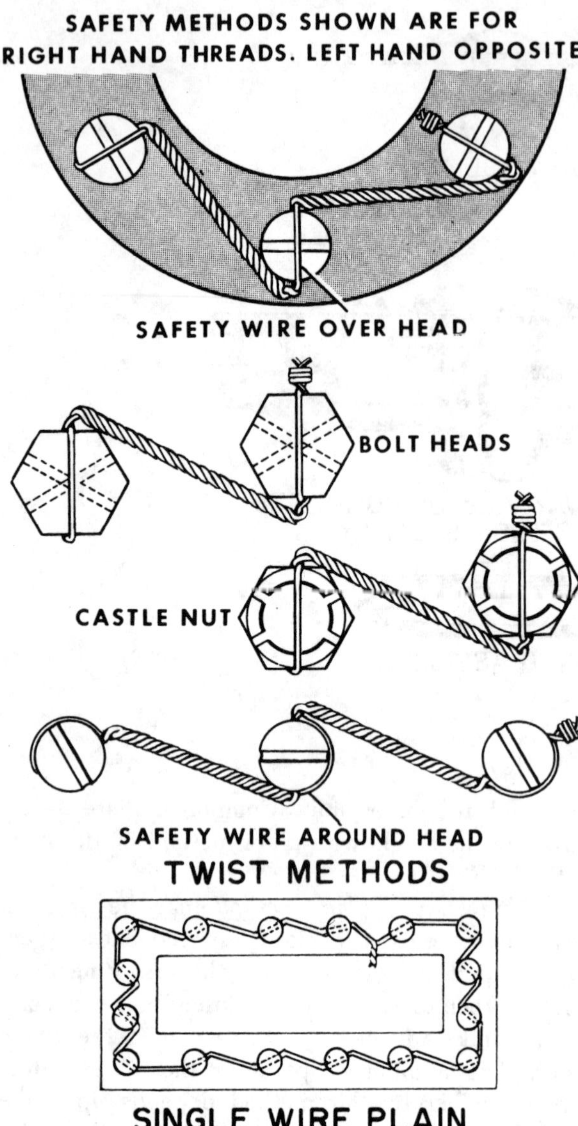

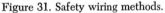

Figure 31. Safety wiring methods.

4. Twists should be tight and even and the wire between the nuts as taut as possible without over-twisting. Wire twister pliers should be used if available; otherwise, wire between nuts should be twisted with the hands. The use of regular pliers for twisting will damage the wire. Regular pliers may be used only for the final twist, prior to cutting off the excess wire.

5. When castellated nuts are to be secured, tighten the nut to the low side of the selected torque range, unless otherwise specified and, if necessary, continue tightening until a slot aligns with a hole.

Cotter Pins. Some cotter pins are made of low-carbon steel, while others consist of stainless steel

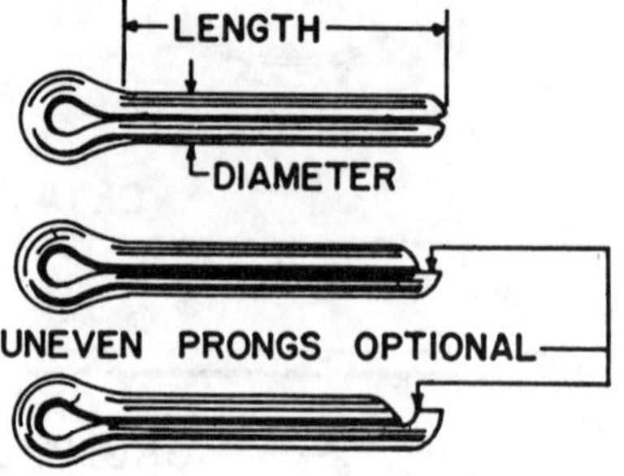

Figure 33. Types of cotter pins.

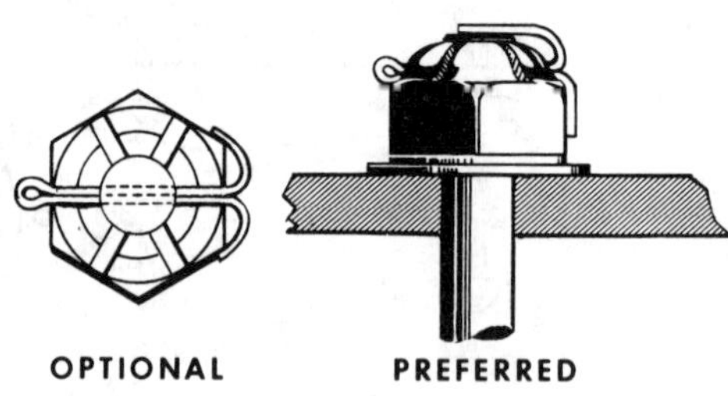

Figure 34. Cotter pin installation.

and thus are more resistant to corrosion. Regardless of shape or material, all cotter pins are used for the same general purpose—safetying.

Dimension perimeters of a cotter pin are shown in Fig. 33. Whenever uneven prong cotter pins are used, the length measurement is to the end of the shortest prong.

A cotter pin installation is shown in Fig. 34. The cotter pin should fit neatly into the hole with very little sideplay.

In the preferred installation method, the bent prong above the bolt end should not extend beyond the bolt diameter. Additionally, the bent prong should not rest against the surface of the washer. Cut the prongs down to size if necessary.

If the optional wraparound method is used, the prongs should not extend outward, but should be bent over a reasonable radius to the sides of the nut. Sharp-angled bends invite breakage. Usually the initial bending of the prongs of a cotter pin is accomplished with needle nose or diagonal pliers and the best tool for final bending of the prongs is a soft faced mallet.

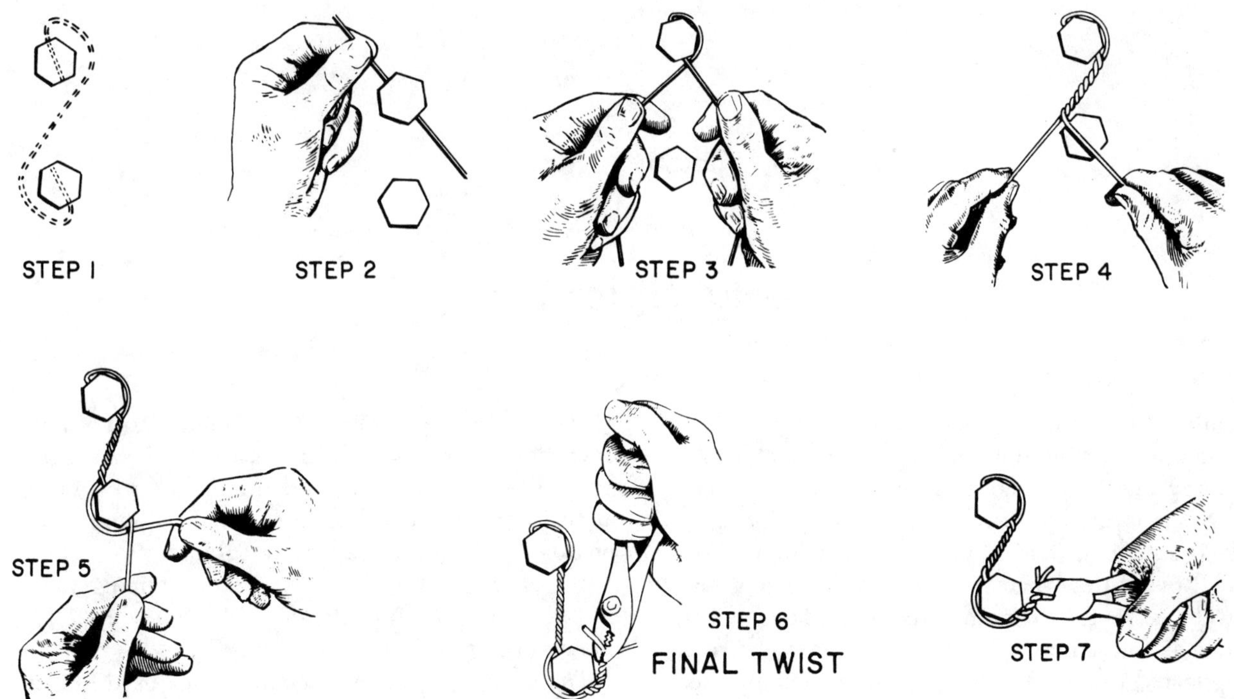

Figure 32. Standard twist safety wire installation procedure.

Chapter 9

Metal Spinning

Spinning is one of the oldest of the metal-working arts and has been used in making circular metal ware for many years. Although in recent years it has been largely replaced by draw press forming for large scale production, it is still widely used for forming limited quantities when tool costs must be kept low, as well as in the manufacture of products which cannot be formed on a draw press because of size or complicated design. Spinning is also commonly used in combination with drawing for economy in finishing and trimming operations.

In the spinning process, a lathe similar to the type shown in Fig. 1 is used to rotate a circular metal blank or shell at high speed while it is pressed against a rotating chuck whose shape the metal blank being formed is to take. The blank is forced against the chuck by means of suitable forming tools, which are manipulated either by hand or mechanically (Fig. 2). With an experienced operator, spun articles can be held to reasonably close dimensional accuracy and will be uniform in size and identical in appearance.

Since the metal is formed over a chuck rotating in a lathe, the process is limited to symmetrical articles that are circular in cross section, normal to the axis of rotation. Typical spun articles are cooking utensils, lighting reflectors, processing kettles, and ornaments of many different types made of silver, aluminum, copper, pewter, and similar metals.

The Lathe for Metal Spinning

The first requirement of the lathe for spinning is a substantial headstock spindle. Suitable bearings must be provided to take up the heavy end and lateral thrusts. There must be absolutely no end play. The speed range should be between 900 and 1400 rpm for average work. Speeds somewhat lower than this are useful but not necessary. A speed range above 1400 rpm is useful for polishing and finishing operations, but is seldom necessary for actual spinning. The power unit should preferably be a ½ hp motor, although a wide range of light spinning can be done with an even less-powerful motor.

Tools. There are many shapes of spinning tools, and the more or less standardized types used are shown in Fig. 3.

The beading tool is a specialized type used to turn the rim of the disk into a lip or a true bead. It is also useful to start bending the metal where the edge is to be folded to a double thickness. The pulley, which rotates freely within the holder, is interchangeable with other sizes to suit a wide variety of work.

The flat tool is the most important tool in the metal-spinner's kit. It is double-surfaced; round on one side and flat on the other. The round side is used to "break down" the metal blank almost to the chuck surface, and the flat side completes the operation of smoothing the metal snugly to the chuck.

The point tool is both a forming and finishing tool that is particularly useful on small work. Its pointed end surface is useful in shaping fillet corners or forming sharp internal bends in the metal surface.

The cutting-off tool, parting tool, or graver, is simply what its name implies—a tool for cutting. It is used to trim away surplus metal at the neck of the spinning; also, it makes an excellent tool for scraping down high spots on the metal.

The ball tool is used to break down the surface of hard metals. It is not a finishing tool and should not be used to bring the metal snug to the chuck surface.

The back stick is an auxiliary aid to the various spinning tools. Its purpose is to back up the metal on one side as the pressure of the spinning tool is brought to bear on the opposite side. The stick should be made from hard wood, either rectangular

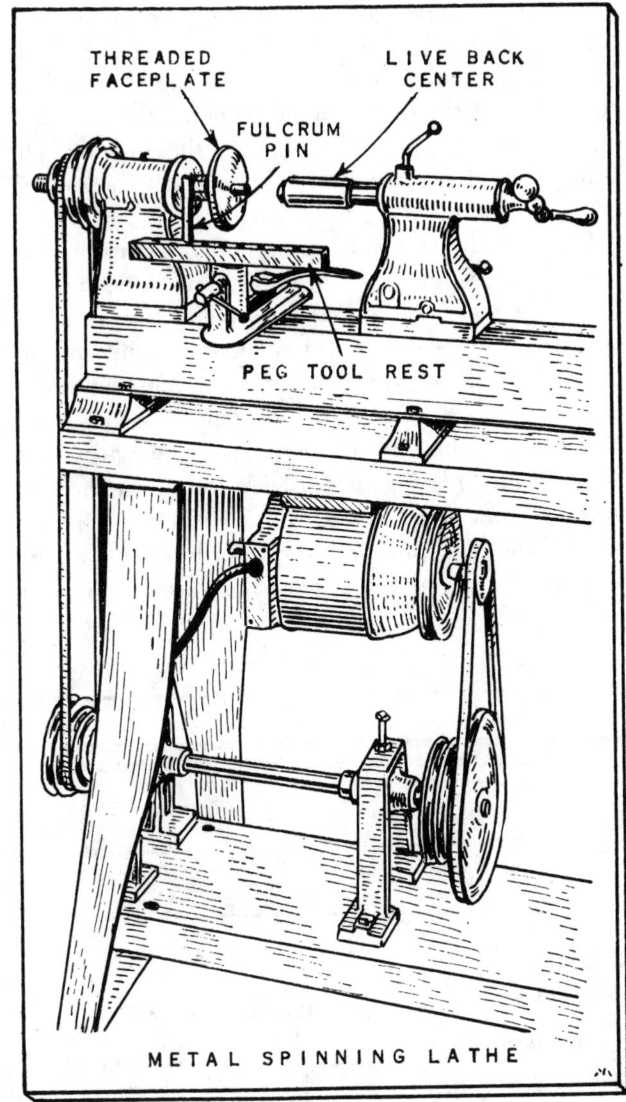

Figure 1.

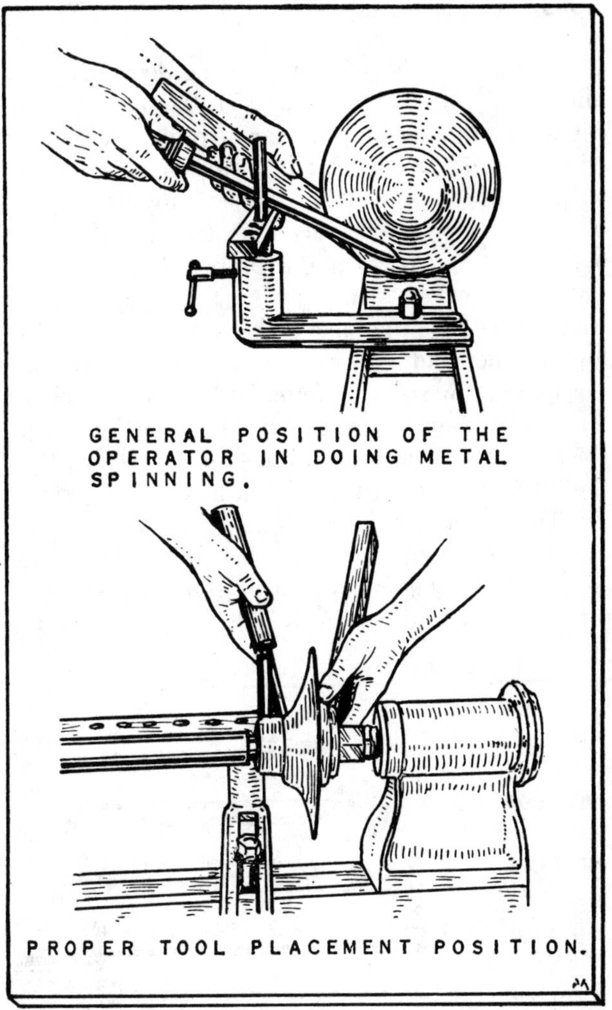

Figure 2.

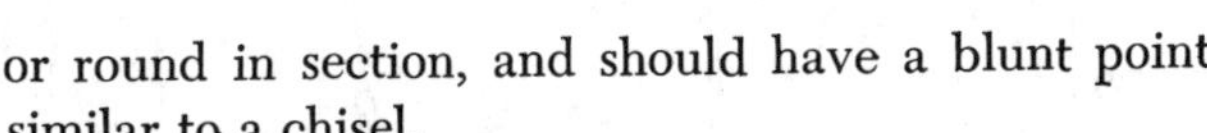
or round in section, and should have a blunt point similar to a chisel.

All spinning tools should be properly tempered and then polished to reduce friction. The overall length of each tool should be about 2 ft., in order to give the required leverage necessary for spinning.

The Tool Rest (Fig. 3). The tool rest or support for the spinning tools is a peg or fulcrum type of tee rest. It should have a shank to fit the tool-support base. The tool rest is drilled with a number of holes, as shown, to permit various settings of the fulcrum pin to suit the work.

Tailstock Center (Fig. 3). The tailstock center for metal spinning must revolve with the work. Three different types are shown in the illustration. Each features a tapered shank which fits the tailstock spindle. This portion of the center is fixed. The rotating center is housed within the fixed body, and is given a free movement by some form of ball-bearing. A good spinning center is essential.

Arbors and Faceplates (Fig. 3). Metal spinning is faceplate work, the wood or metal form or chuck over which the metal is spun being fastened to a suitable plate or arbor. A 3 in. faceplate with screw-fastenings into the chuck can be used, but the threaded nose type faceplate offers a quicker and more substantial form of mounting for this particular work. The threaded nose can be either straight or tapered. Straight and tapered screw arbors are also used extensively, especially for small work.

Spinning Procedures

SETTING-UP (Fig. 4). Any spinning demands (1) a chuck, (2) a follow block, (3) the metal blank. Figure 4, 1A shows a typical simple project—a shallow tray. A wood chuck must be made up to the exact shape of the proposed object, using any good-grade hardwood. It is good practice to turn the chuck an inch or so longer than the proposed spinning, so that there will be some space between the finished spinning and the faceplate. The follow block or follower is now turned to shape, either on a separate faceplate or by simply gripping it between the chuck and the spinning center. It should be at least 1 in. thick, and of a diameter from 1/8 to 1/4 in. less than the base diameter of the project, as shown in Fig. 4, 1B. The drawing shows the base of the chuck slightly concave and the end of the follower slightly convex. This form of shaping should be followed wherever practical, because it affords better gripping of the metal blank while adding to the stability of the finished spinning. Figure 4, 1C shows the metal blank for this particular spinning. In all metal spinning, the radius of the blank should be equal to the radius of the project plus the depth of the project. The blank should form a perfect circle with a smooth edge all around.

Figure 5 shows other representative forms of shallow chucks or forms. Figure 5, 3 shows a deep form, such as would be required for a metal cup. It is evident that the deeper form is more difficult to spin than the shallow form since the metal must be drawn to a greater extent. A series of chucks is sometimes employed in spinning deep forms, as shown in Fig. 5, 4, the metal being successively spun over three or four different shapes gradually to result in the finished form. The purpose is to afford a positive support for the metal throughout the various stages of spinning.

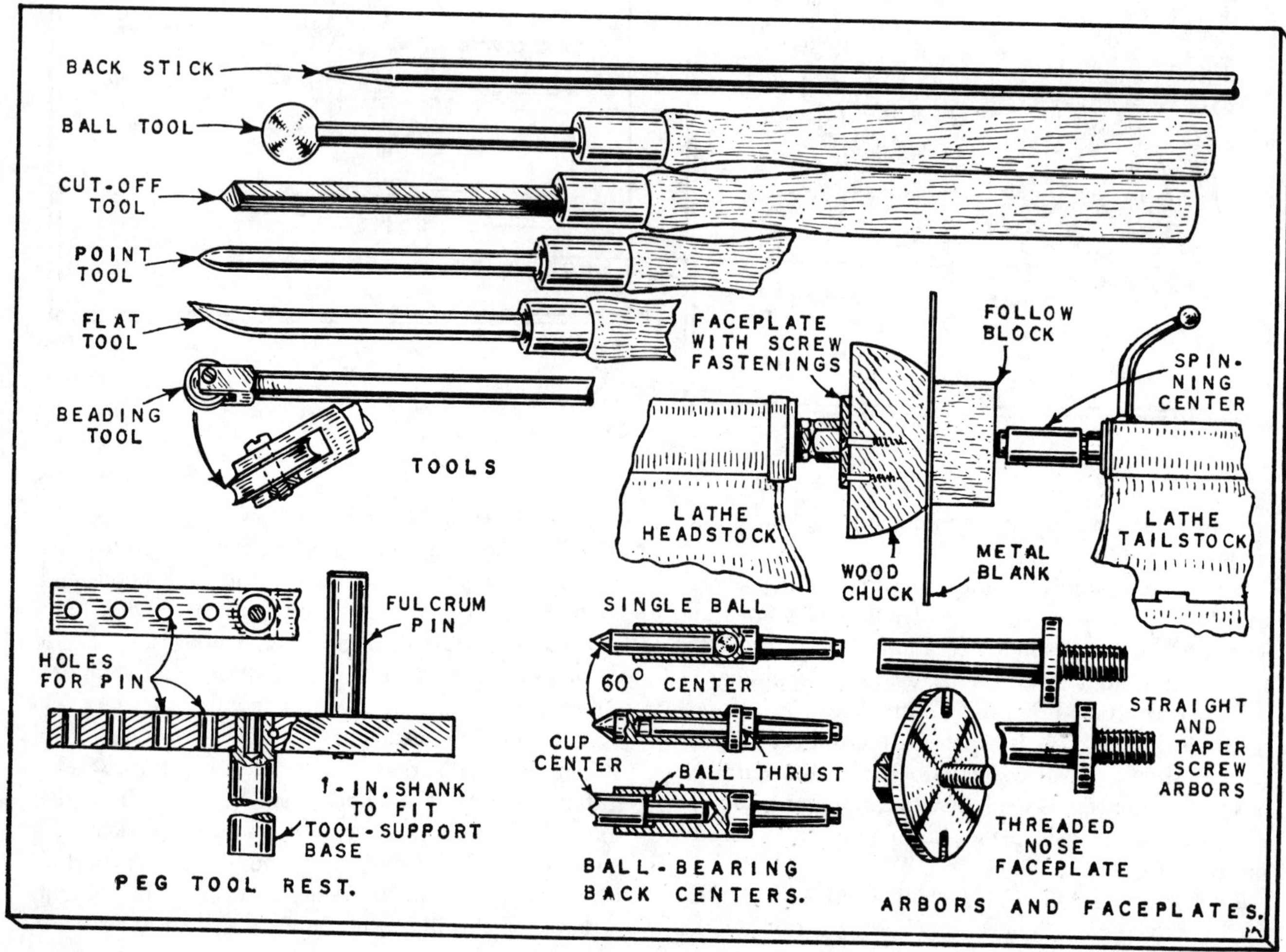

Figure 3.

All wood chucks should be glazed with soap or beeswax (Fig. 5, 5). This is done after sanding, the soap or wax being forced into the pores of the wood with the flat tool while the chuck is revolving.

CENTERING. The final operation before spinning is to center the metal blank. Where a hole in the center of the spinning is permissible, the blank can be fastened directly to the chuck (Fig. 5, 6). In another method, an indentation is made in the center of the blank, the indentation fitting over a round-head nail driven in the center of the chuck (Fig. 5, 7). This readily locates the center of the blank, after which the follow block is brought up firmly to clamp the disk in place. In the ordinary method of centering, the disk is inserted between the chuck and follower, centering as closely as possible by eye. The tailstock is run forward to clamp the blank firmly but not too tightly in place. The lathe is then started on low speed, and the back stick is placed on the rest, to the left of the fulcrum pin (Fig. 1). The tailstock is then backed off slightly, and the stick advanced to touch the edge of the revolving disk. If the edge of the blank is smooth, the disk will center itself perfectly, after which the follower is again set firmly against the metal. After the disk is centered, lubricate the metal on each side with laundry soap. The disk is now ready to spin.

SPINNING THE METAL. Spinning the metal over the wooden form is not at all difficult, providing a few hard and fast rules are observed. The work cannot be hurried. Practically all craftsmen realize that it takes time to finish a wood or metal turning, yet some think that a similar operation in spun metal can be done in a few minutes. The beginner should keep this important point in mind.

The first operation in actual spinning calls for the flat tool. This is placed on the rest, to the left of the fulcrum pin, the pin being placed in the hole, which will set it slightly to the right of the metal blank. Now, with one or two sweeping strokes of the flat tool (the rounded edge contacts the metal), the disk is "seated" against the base of the chuck. The back stick is now brought into play, holding up the metal on one side while the flat tool presses against the opposite side. The general position of the operator at this point can be seen in Fig. 2. The tool contacts the work well below center, as can be seen in Fig. 2. Notice, also, in this illustration, that there is a fairly wide gap between the metal disk and the tool rest. Figure 2 shows the same tool position as viewed

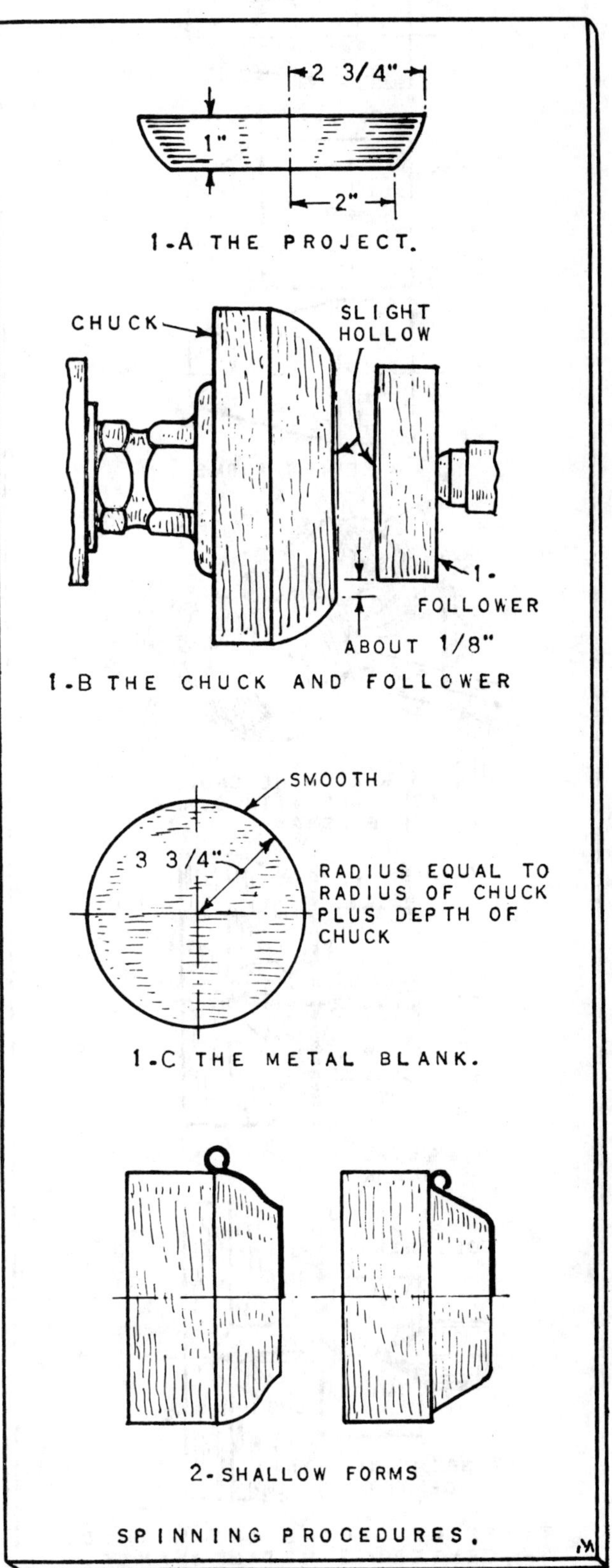

Figure 4.

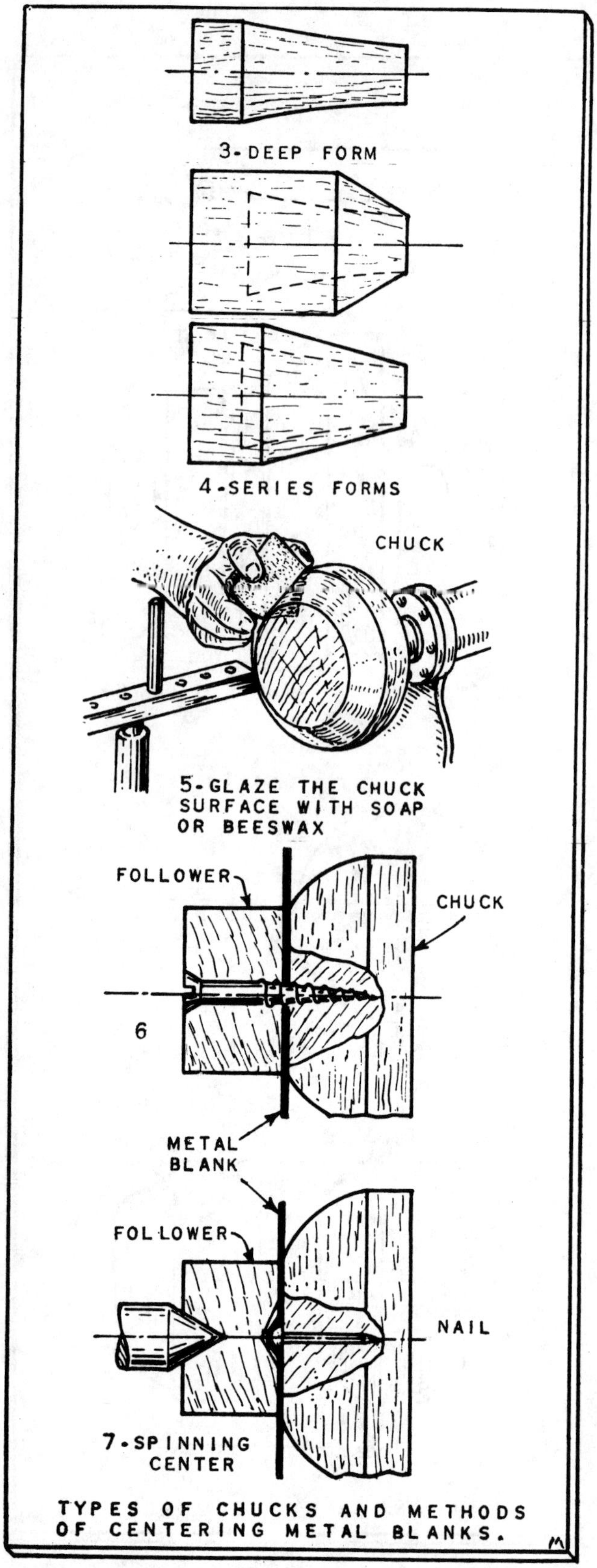

3-DEEP FORM

4-SERIES FORMS

CHUCK

5-GLAZE THE CHUCK SURFACE WITH SOAP OR BEESWAX

FOLLOWER

CHUCK

6

METAL BLANK

FOLLOWER

NAIL

7-SPINNING CENTER

TYPES OF CHUCKS AND METHODS OF CENTERING METAL BLANKS.

Figure 5.

from the front. Note how the fulcrum pin is located so that the tool can bear against the disk without the point digging into the metal. The back stick follows the point of the tool, leading it slightly.

The forming action of the tool becomes readily apparent when attempting actual work. The object is to force the metal around the chuck, and to do this the tool is simply brought to bear, with considerable pressure, against the revolving metal surface. The tool must not remain in any one spot because of the liability of burning right through the metal. Instead a sweeping action of the tool takes place, the tool moving constantly from the center to the rim of the disk. This movement is effected by a "hunching" movement of the shoulders, the body of the operator moving to the right. Since the action is quite natural, there is little difficulty encountered on this score.

Various points essential to good spinning are shown in Fig. 6. At A is shown the initial operation,

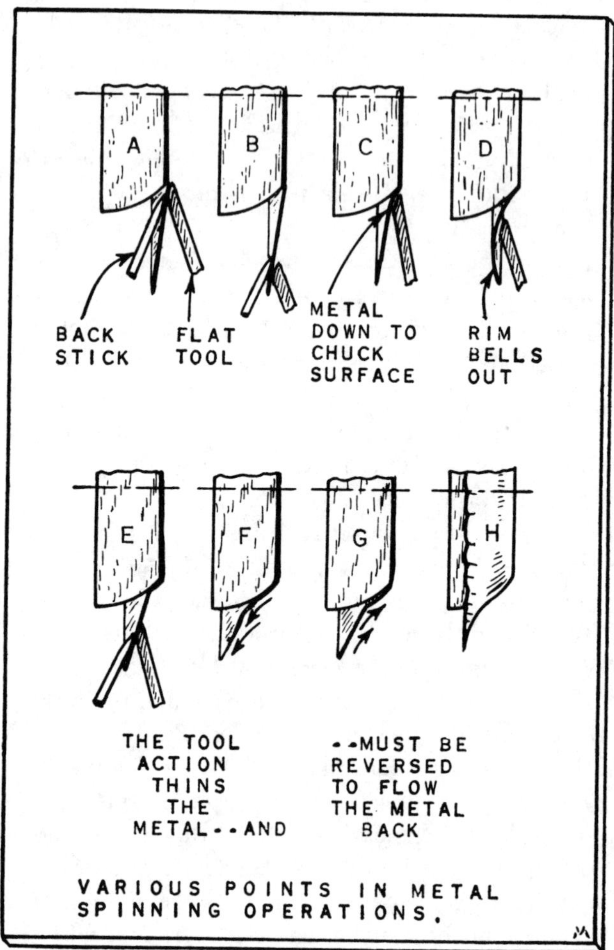

Figure 6.

the flat tool pressing against the disk while the back stick supports the opposite side. The closer the tool is to the chuck, as in C, the less need there is for the support of the back stick; the farther the tool from the chuck, as at B, the more necessary it becomes to properly "back up" the metal. The first stage of the spinning brings the metal to the shape shown at B. The metal should be kept straight, like a shallow funnel, and should not be allowed to bell out, as shown at D. After the position shown at B has been attained, the flat tool alone can be used to force a small portion of the metal closer to the chuck surface, as shown at C. This action should not be too prolonged or over too much territory, either of which will result in the rim of the disk turning out, as shown at D. As soon as the rim begins to bell, the back stick should be used and the metal again spun to a true funnel shape, as shown at E. Note that the funnel-shape is much sharper than shown at B. These two essential operations—crowding a small portion of the metal to the chuck surface and keeping the rest of the disk funnel-shaped—are carried out in successive operations, until the whole shape has been made.

F, Figure 6 illustrates a point which can only be learned completely from experience. It can be seen that the constant stroking of the tool towards the left has a tendency to thin the spun portion of the metal. If carried to extremes, the metal will burn completely through. To avoid this, the stroking action of the tool must be reversed, stroking in the direction

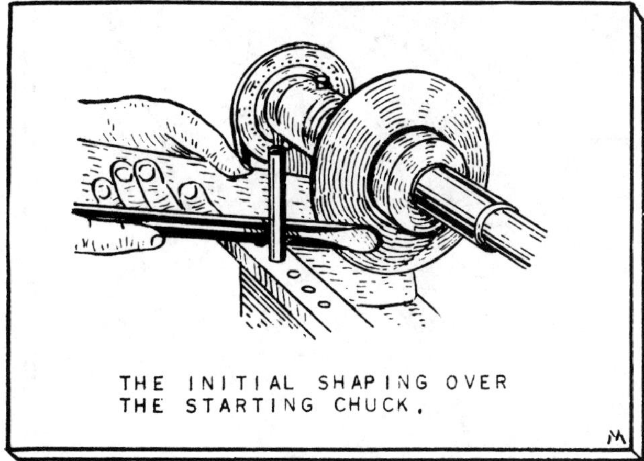

Figure 7.

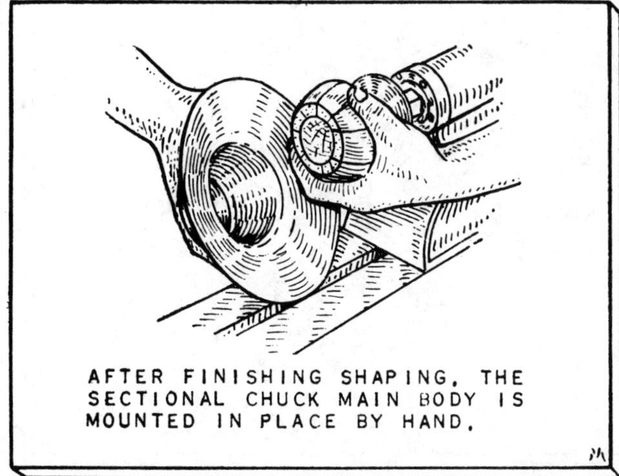

AFTER FINISHING SHAPING, THE
SECTIONAL CHUCK MAIN BODY IS
MOUNTED IN PLACE BY HAND.

Figure 8.

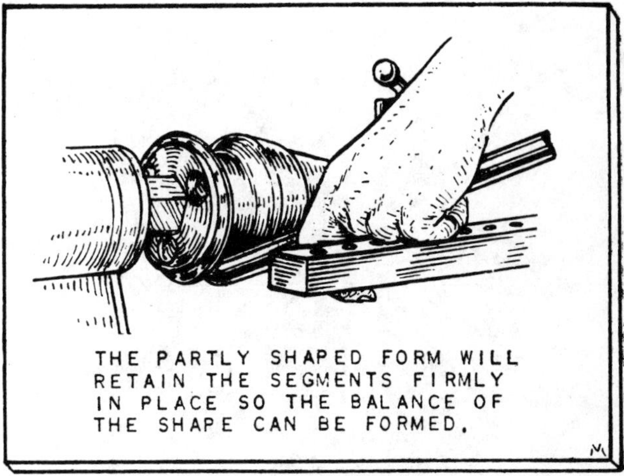

THE PARTLY SHAPED FORM WILL
RETAIN THE SEGMENTS FIRMLY
IN PLACE SO THE BALANCE OF
THE SHAPE CAN BE FORMED.

Figure 9.

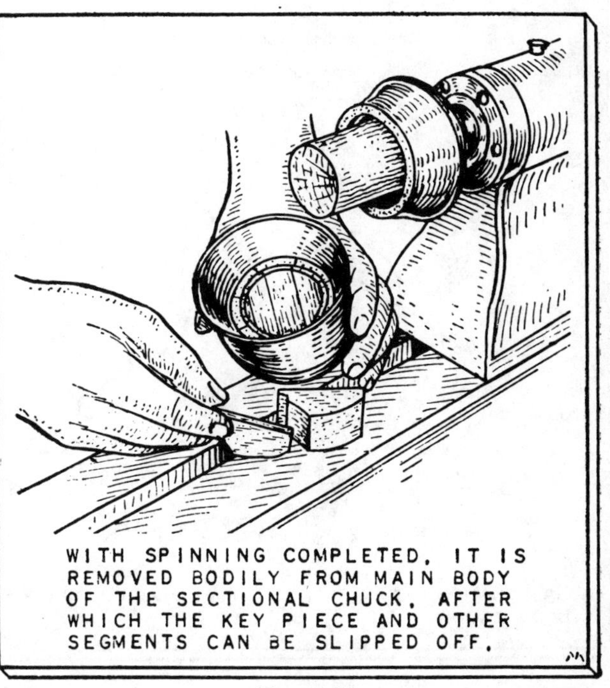

WITH SPINNING COMPLETED, IT IS
REMOVED BODILY FROM MAIN BODY

SEGMENTS CAN BE SLIPPED OFF.

Figure 10.

shown by the arrows in G, Fig. 6 to flow the metal back to normal thickness. This operation is especially important where the metal is to be spun around any sharp bend. Buckling, a common difficulty in spinning, is shown at H. Buckling is caused largely by forcing the work. That is, in attempting to get an immediate finished shape, the operator will press the work hard at the position shown at *D*. This causes the rim to bell out, and later attempts to spin it back to a true funnel-shape usually result in a buckled edge instead of a smooth metal edge.

CUTTING-OFF. Figures 7 through 10 show operations in trimming off the surplus metal as performed with the hand cut-off tool and with the slide rest. In either case, the point of the tool should be on center.

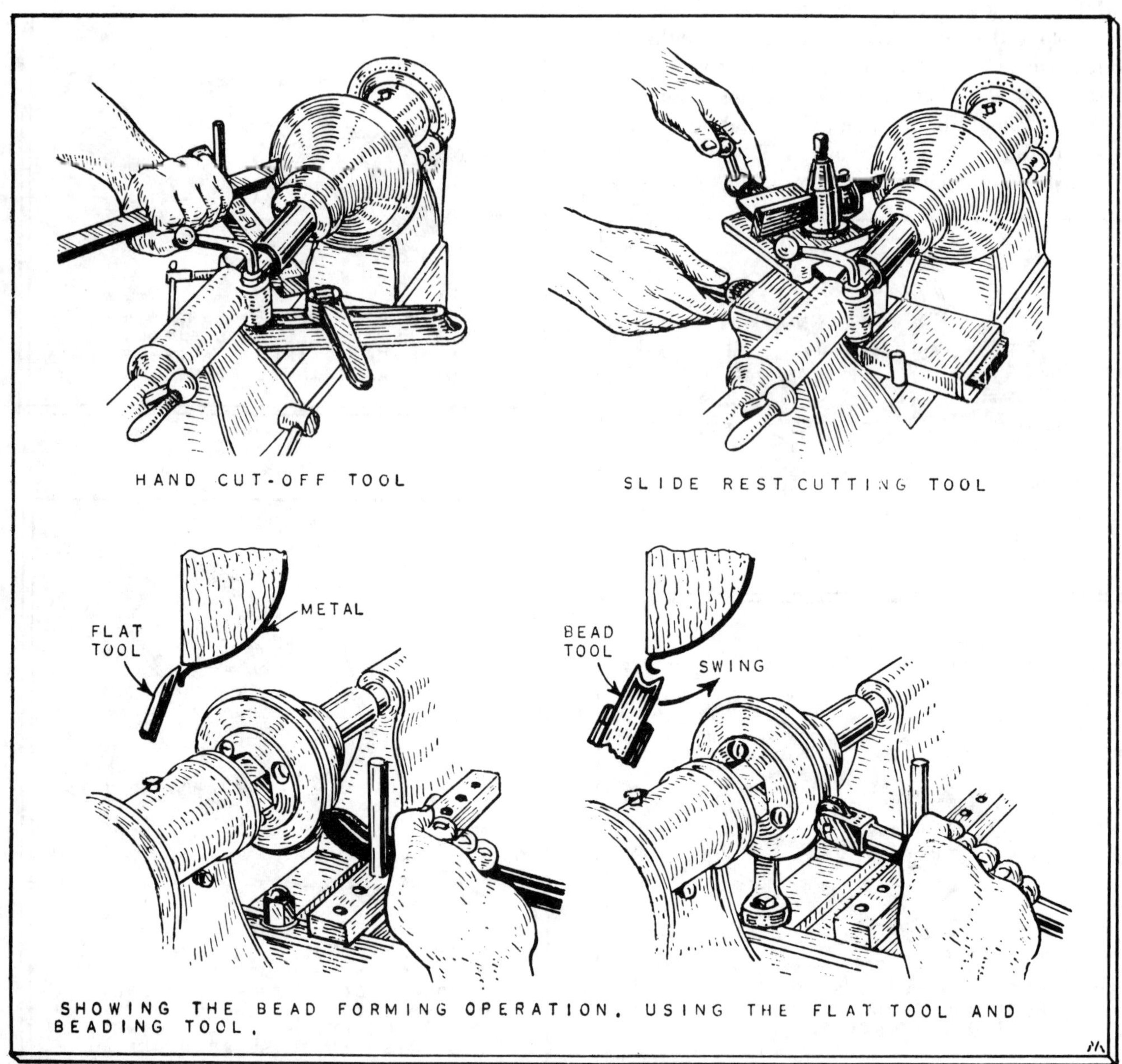

Figure 11.

BEADS. The trimmed edge of the metal is frequently turned over to form a bead. This operation is performed with the beading tool. As shown in Fig. 11, the point of the flat tool is first used to lift a small portion of the metal from the chuck surface. The beading tool is then used to work the metal into a true bead.

Using Special Spinning Chucks

SPINNING A SPHERE. The spinning of a sphere differs somewhat from work previously described, the essential difference resting in the fact that the curved surface of the spherical chuck does not permit the immediate use of a follow block. Instead, a starting chuck must be made up (A, Fig. 12). This has a recessed rim to take the metal blank snugly, while the center portion is turned out to the same spherical shape as the intended finished spinning. The metal is spun into this recessed center portion (B, Fig. 12), the recessed rim holding the blank quite firmly. The partly-formed disk can then be placed over the regular chuck (C, Fig. 12) for finishing. Note that the follow block is concave, so that it will fit snugly against the metal. If the spinning is to be a perfect ball, two hemispheres must be made up and then soldered together. (Soldering procedures are given

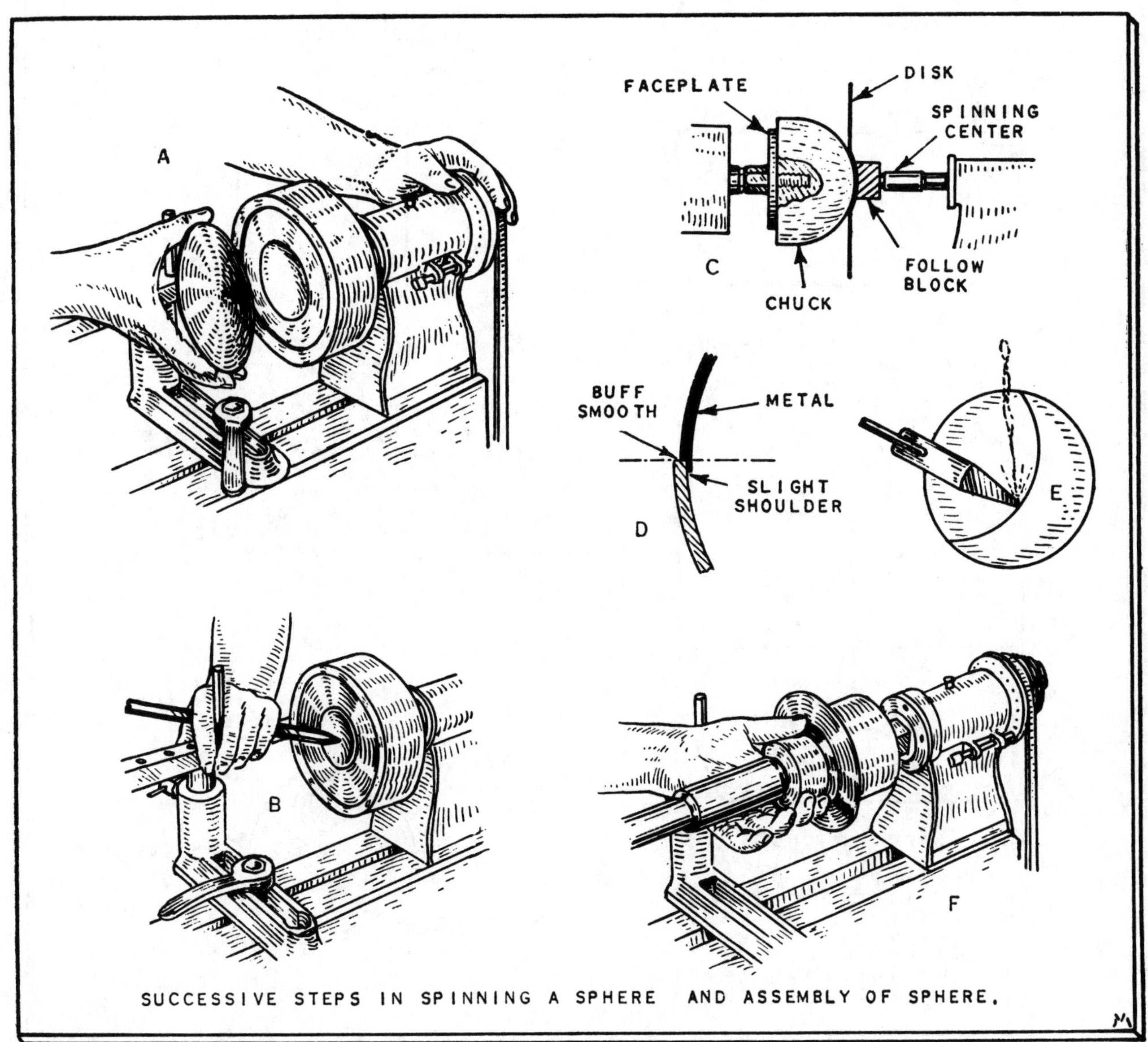

Figure 12.

in Chap. 6.) The joint can be butted and buffed smooth after soldering (D, Fig. 12), or a very slight rim can be cut on one portion of the ball (E, Fig. 12), as an aid in making the joint.

In a similar manner, any other spinning with either a round or pointed end surface must be started by first using a concave starting chuck. Where the end curvature is very slight, the follower can sometimes be forced against the metal to give sufficient traction for spinning the metal (F, Fig. 12).

Sectional Chucks. Any form having a neck or opening smaller in diameter than some other portion of the work (Fig. 13) must be spun on a sectional chuck. The sectional chuck, as its name implies, is a built-up form, so arranged that the various pieces can be removed one by one from the inside of the finished work. The typical example shown covers, in a general manner, the basic rules that must be observed in the making of any simple sectional chuck.

A starting chuck is always used in connection with

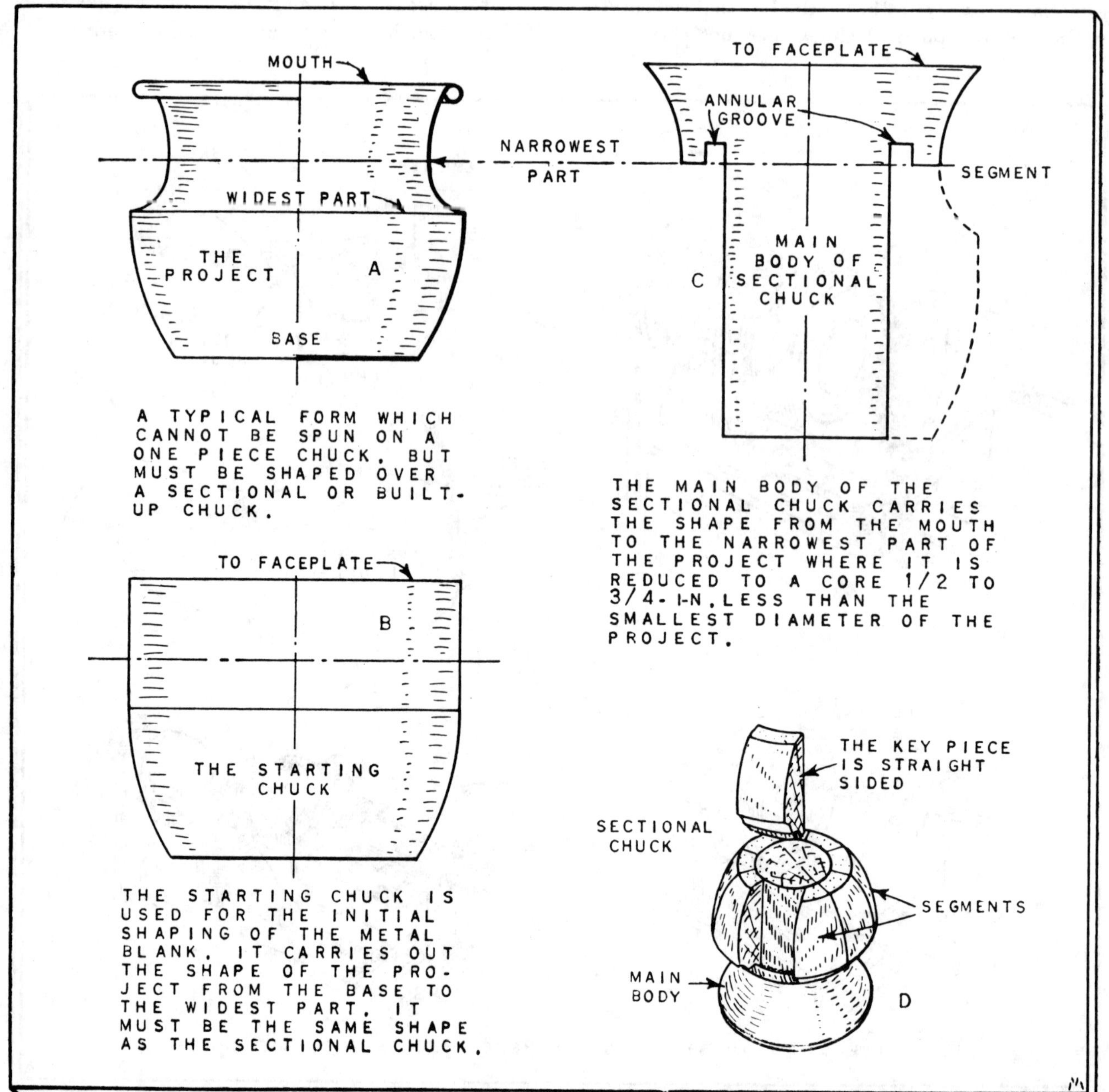

Figure 13.

the sectional chuck, the metal being spun over this and then switched to the built-up form. As far as it goes, which is to the widest part (A, Fig. 13) of the proposed project, the shape of the starting chuck must be identical with the shape of the sectional chuck. The sectional chuck itself consists of a main body, which carries the shape from the mouth of the project to its narrowest part (B, Fig. 13). At this point, the main body is reduced to a cylindrical core having a diameter from ½ to ¾ in. less than the smallest diameter of the project. Around this core are grouped the various segments, all of which are wedge-shaped, with the exception of the key piece, which is straight sided. The annular groove in the main body of the chuck takes a corresponding rim turned on the segment portion.

In making a sectional chuck, the main body is turned first (C, Fig. 13). The segment portion, in a solid block, is then rough turned to approximate dimensions. A ¾ in. hole is drilled through the center. The turning is then removed from the lathe for the cutting of the various segments. These range in number from 6 to 12 pieces, depending upon the size of the opening through which they must be withdrawn. The saw cuts are then sanded smooth and the segments glued back in their original position, using glazed paper at the joints. The turning is then finished to exact size, carrying out the shape of the project externally and fitting the main body of the chuck internally. After sanding and glazing, the various segments are again separated.

Spinning over a sectional chuck is carried out in much the same manner as spinning over a one-piece chuck. B, Figure 13 shows the initial shaping over the starting chuck. After this is finished, the sectional chuck main body is mounted in place, with the segments held in place by hand (C, Fig. 13). It is apparent that the partly-formed spinning will hold the segments securely in place, so that the rest of the shape can be formed (Fig. 13). After the spinning is completed, it can be slipped bodily from the main body of the sectional chuck, after which the key piece and then the other segments can be withdrawn (D, Fig. 13).

For average work, the gluing of the sectional chuck can be dispensed with by turning the segment portion to finished size and then sawing it apart with a very fine scroll saw or band saw blade. By allowing a little for the various saw kerfs, a sufficiently accurate form can be made in this manner. If the chuck is to be made in metal, the same general procedure as first described is followed, sweating the segments together with solder.

Chapter 10

Portable Metalworking Power Tools

With the machines and power tools available today, hand operations are practically eliminated in ordinary jobs. Such work is generally performed only to correct errors or where proper power tools are not available. This chapter will be devoted to the more common types of portable electric and air-driven power tools and equipment.

Portable Electric Power Tools

Portable power tools are tools that can be moved from place to place. Some of the most common portable power tools used are drills, disc sander, grinders, saber saw, and impact wrench.

Drills

The *portable electric drill* (Fig. 1) is probably the most frequently used power tool. Although it is especially designed for drilling holes, by adding various accessories it can be adapted for different jobs. Sanding, sawing, buffing, polishing, screw-driving, wire brushing, and paint mixing are examples of possible uses.

Portable electric drills commonly used have capacities for drilling holes in steel from 1/16 inch up

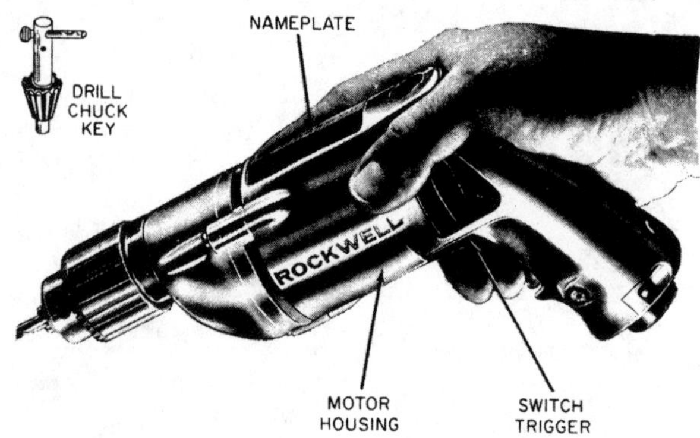

Figure 1. ¼ inch portable electric drill.

to 1 inch in diameter. The sizes of portable electric drills are classified by the maximum size straight shank drill they will hold. That is, a 1/4 inch electric drill will hold a straight shank drill up to and including 1/4 inch.

The revolutions per minute (rpm) and power the drill will deliver are most important when choosing a drill for a job. You will find that the speed of the drill motor decreases with an increase in size, primarily because the larger units are designed to turn larger cutting tools or to drill in heavy materials, and both these factors require slower speed.

If you are going to do heavy work, such as drilling in masonry or steel, then you would probably need to use a drill with a 3/8 or 1/2 inch capacity. If most of your drilling will be forming holes in wood or small holes in sheet metal, then a 1/4-inch drill will probably be adequate.

The chuck is the clamping device into which the drill is inserted. Nearly all electric drills are equipped with a three-jaw chuck. Some of the drill motors have a hand-type chuck that you tighten or loosen by hand, but most of the drills have gear-type, three-jaw chucks which are tightened and loosened by means of a chuck key (Fig. 2). Do not apply further pressure with pliers or wrenches after you hand-tighten the chuck with the chuck key.

Always remove the key *immediately* after you use it. Otherwise the key will fly loose when the drill motor is started and may cause serious injury to you. The chuck key is generally taped on the cord of the drill; if it is not make sure you put it in a safe place where it will not get lost.

Portable electric drills have controls similar to the ones shown on the 1/4-inch drill in Fig. 1. This drill has a momentary contact trigger switch located in the handle. The switch is squeezed to start the electric drill and released to stop it.

The trigger latch is a button in the bottom of the

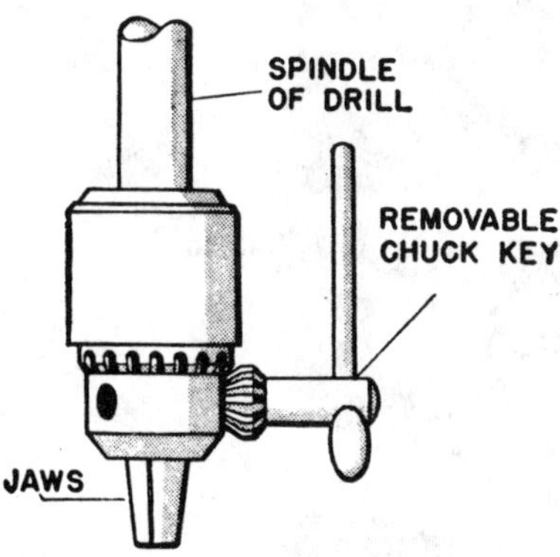

Figure 2. Three-jaw chuck and chuck key.

drill handle. It is pushed in, while the switch trigger is held down, to lock the trigger switch in the ON position. The trigger latch is released by squeezing and then releasing the switch trigger.

Sanders

Portable sanders are tools designed to hold and operate abrasives for sanding metals, plastics, and wood.

Disc Sander

Electric disc sanders (Fig. 3) are especially useful on work where a large amount of material is to be removed quickly, such as scaling surfaces in preparation for painting. This machine must not be used where a mirror-smooth finish is required.

The disc should be moved smoothly and lightly over the surface. Never allow the disc to stay in one place too long because it will cut into the metal and leave a large depression.

Figure 3. Disc sander.

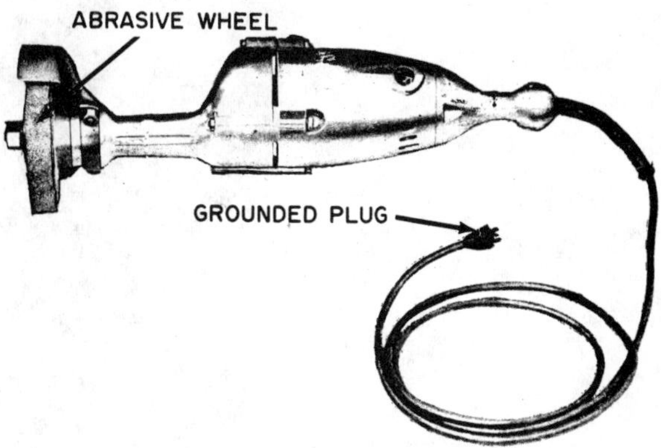

Figure 4. Portable grinder.

Portable Grinders

Portable grinders are power tools for rough grinding and finishing of metallic surfaces. They are made in several sizes (Fig. 4).

The abrasive wheels are easily replaceable so that different grain size and grades of abrasives can be used for varying types of surfaces to be ground and the different degrees of finish desired.

A flexible shaft attachment is available for most portable grinders. This shaft is attached by removing the grinding wheel, then attaching the shaft to the grinding wheel drive spindle. The grinding wheel can then be attached to the end of the flexible shaft. This attachment is invaluable for grinding surfaces in hard to reach places.

The wheel guard on the grinder should be positioned so that abrasive dust and metal particles will be deflected away from your face.

Before you turn the grinder on, make sure the abrasive grinding wheel is properly secured to the grinder spindle and not cracked or damaged.

Saber Saw

The *saber saw* (Fig. 5) is a power-driven jigsaw that will let you cut smooth and decorative curves in light metal and wood. Most saber saws are light duty machines and are not designed for extremely fast cutting.

There are several different blades designed to operate in the saber saw, and they are easily interchangeable. A blade with fine teeth is designed for cutting metal. For fast cutting of wood, a blade with coarse teeth may be used.

The best way to learn how to handle this type of tool is to use it. Before trying to do a finished job

Figure 5. Saber or bayonet saw operations.

with the saber saw, clamp down a piece of scrap plywood and draw some curved as well as straight lines to follow. You will develop your own way of gripping the tool, and this will be affected somewhat by the particular tool you are using. On some tools, *for example,* you will find guiding easier if you apply some downward pressure on the tool as you move it forward. If you are not firm with your grip, the tool will tend to vibrate excessively and this will roughen the cut. *Do not* force the cutting faster than the design of the blade allows or you will break the blade.

Electric Impact Wrench

The *electric impact wrench* (Fig. 6) is a portable hand-type reversible wrench. The wrench shown has a 1/2-inch square impact driving anvil over which 1/2-inch square drive sockets can be fitted. Wrenches also can be obtained that have impact driving anvils ranging from 3/8 to 1 inch. The driving anvils are not interchangeable from one wrench to another.

The electric wrench with its accompanying equipment is primarily intended for applying and removing nuts, bolts, and screws. It may also be used to drill and tap metal, plastic, wood, and the like, and drive and remove socket-head Phillips-head, or slotted-head wood, machine, or self-tapping screws.

Before you use an electric impact wrench, depress the on-and-off trigger switch and allow the electric wrench to operate a few seconds, noting carefully the direction of rotation. Release the trigger switch to stop the wrench. Turn the reversing ring located at the rear of the tool; it should move easily in one direction (which is determined by the current direction of rotation). Depress the on-and-off trigger again to start the electric wrench. The direction of rotation should now be reversed. Continue to operate for a few seconds in each direction to be sure that the wrench and its reversible features are functioning correctly. When you are sure the wrench operates properly, place the suitable equipment on the impact driving anvil and go ahead with the job at hand.

Safety Precautions

Safe practices in the use of power tools cannot be overemphasized. There are several general safety measures to observe in operating or maintaining power equipment.

1. Never operate power equipment unless you are thoroughly familiar with its controls and operating instructions or ask someone who knows.
2. All portable tools should be inspected before use to see that they are clean and in a proper state of repair.
3. Have ample illumination. If extension lights are required, ensure that a light guard is provided.
4. Before a power tool is connected to a source of power (electricity, air, and so on), *be sure* that the switch on the tool is in the OFF position.
5. When operating a power tool, give it your *full* and *undivided attention.*

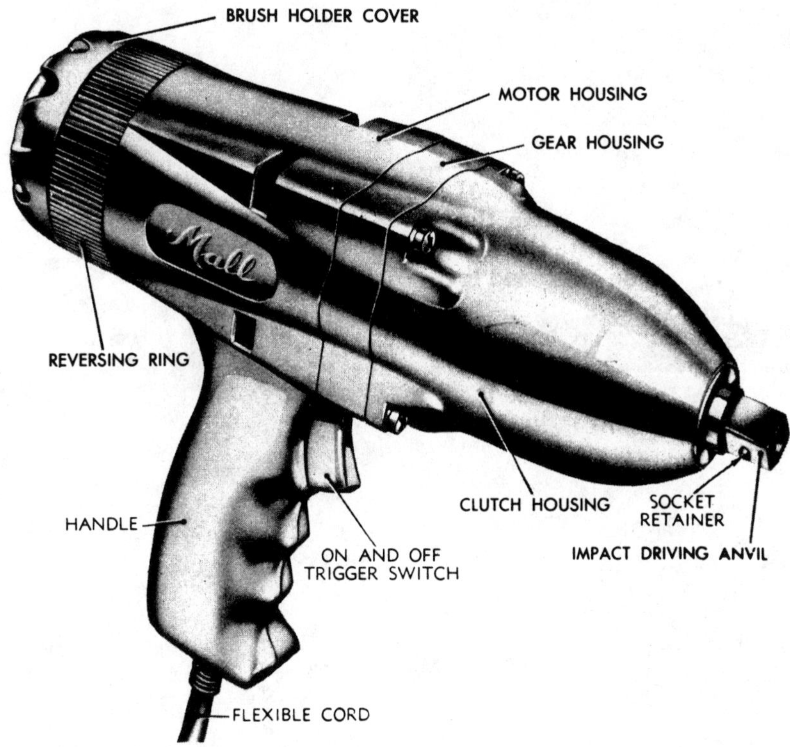

Figure 6. Reversible electric impact wrench.

6. Keep all safety guards in position and use safety shields or goggles when necessary.

7. Fasten all loose sleeves and aprons.

8. Never try to clear jammed machinery unless you remove the source of power first.

9. After using a power tool, turn off the power, remove the power source, wait for all rotation of the tool to stop, and then clean the tool. Remove all waste and scraps from the work area and stow the tool in its proper place.

10. Never plug the power cord of a portable electric tool into an electrical power source before ensuring that the source has the voltage and type of current (alternating or direct) called for on the nameplate of the tool.

11. If an extension cord is required, always connect the cord of a portable electric power tool into the extension cord before the extension cord is inserted into a convenience outlet. Always unplug the extension cord from the receptacle before the cord of the portable power tool is unplugged from the extension cord. (The extension cord and the power cord can each be no longer than 25 feet in length. Extra extension cords should be limited, wherever possible, to maintain allowable resistance to ground.)

Portable Pneumatic Power Tools

Portable pneumatic power tools are tools that look much the same as electric power tools but use the energy of compressed air instead of electricity. They are used most around a shop where compressed air outlets are readily accessible.

Pneumatic Chipping Hammer

The *pneumatic chipping hammer* (Fig. 7) consists basically of a steel piston which is reciprocated (moved backward and forward alternately) in a steel barrel by compressed air. On its forward stroke the piston strikes the end of the chisel, which is a sliding fit in a nozzle pressed into the barrel. The rearward stroke is cushioned by compressed air to prevent any metal-to-metal contact. Reciprocation of the piston is automatically controlled by a valve located on the rear end of the barrel. Located on the rear end of the barrel is a grip handle containing a throttle valve.

The throttle valve is actuated by a throttle lever which protrudes from the upper ear of the grip handle for thumb operation. Projecting from the butt of the handle is an air inlet. The handle is threaded

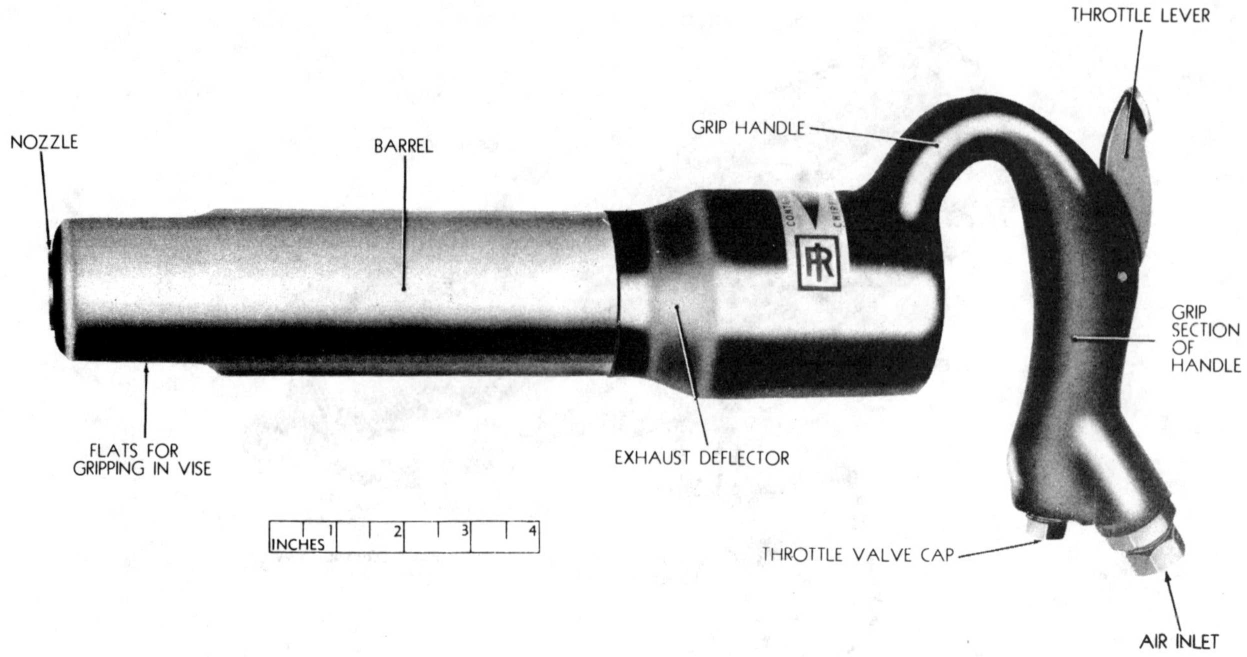

Figure 7. Pneumatic chipping hammer.

onto the barrel and is prevented from unscrewing by a locking ring. Surrounding and retaining the locking ring is an exhaust deflector. This deflector may be located in any of four positions around the barrel in order to throw the stream of exhaust air to the desired direction.

The pneumatic hammer may be used for beveling, calking, or beading operations, and for drilling in brick, concrete, and other masonry.

Chipping hammers should not be operated without safety goggles and all persons in the immediate vicinity of the work should wear goggles.

While working, never point the chipping hammer in such a direction that other people might be struck by an accidentally ejected tool. When chipping alloy steel or doing other heavy work, it is helpful to dip the tool in engine lubricating oil about every six inches of the cut and make sure the cutting edge of the tool is sharp and clean. This will allow faster and easier cutting and will reduce the possibility of the tool breaking.

When nearing the end of a cut, ease off on the throttle lever to reduce the intensity of the blows. This will avoid any possibility of the chip or tool flying.

If for any reason you have to lay the chipping hammer down, always remove the attachment tool from the nozzle. Should the chipping hammer be accidentally started when the tool is free, the blow of the piston will drive the tool out of the nozzle with great force and may damage equipment or cause injury.

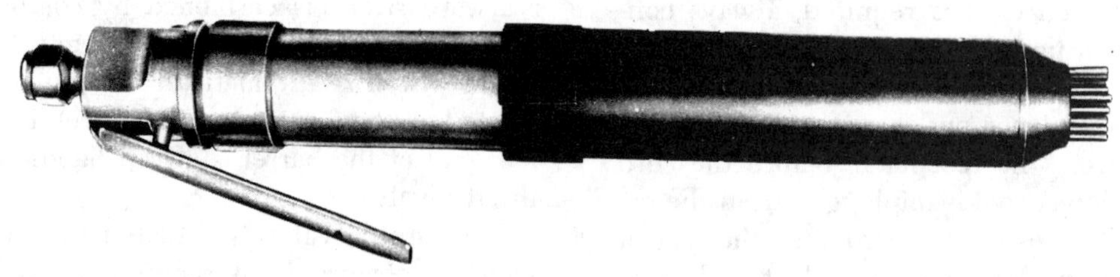

Figure 8. Needle impact scaler.

Figure 9. Rotary impact scaler.

Needle and Rotary Impact Scalers

Needle and rotary scalers (Figs. 8 and 9) are used to remove rust, scale, and old paint from metallic and masonry surfaces. You must be especially careful when using these tools, since they will *chew* up anything in their path. Avoid getting the power line or any part of your body in their way.

Needle scalers accomplish their task with an assembly of individual needles impacting on a surface hundreds of times a minute. The advantage of using individual needles is that irregular surfaces can be cleaned readily.

The rotary scaling and chipping tool, sometimes called a *jitterbug*, has a bundle of cutters or chippers for scaling or chipping (Fig. 9). In use, the tool is pushed along the surface to be scaled and the rotating chippers do the work. Replacement bundles of cutters are available when the old ones are worn.

Portable Pneumatic Impact Wrench

The *portable pneumatic impact wrench* (Fig. 10) is designed for installing or removing nuts and bolts. The wrench comes in different sizes and is classified by the size of the square anvil on the drive end. The anvil is equipped with a socket lock which provides positive locking of the socket wrenches or attachments. The wrench has a built-in oil reservoir and an adjustable air valve regulator which adjusts the torque output of the wrench. The torque regulator reduces the possibility of shearing or damaging threads when installing nuts and bolts to their required tension.

Nearly all pneumatic wrenches operate most efficiently on an air pressure range of from 80 to 90 pounds per square inch (p.s.i.). A variation in excess of plus or minus five pounds is serious, because lower pressure causes a decrease in the driving speeds, while higher pressure causes the wrench to overspeed, with subsequent abnormal wear of the motor impact mechanisms.

The throttle lever located at the rear of the pneumatic wrench provides the means for starting and stopping the wrench. Depressing the throttle lever starts the wrench in operation. Upon release, the lever raises to its original position stopping the wrench.

The valve stem is seated beneath the pivot end of the throttle lever. Most wrenches have a window cut in the throttle lever so that the markings on the upper surface of the valve stem will be visible. Two letters, F and R, have been engraved on the head of the valve stem to indicate the forward (clockwise) and reverse (counterclockwise) rotation of the anvil. To change from forward to reverse rotation, or vice versa, turn the valve stem 180 degrees until the desired marking is visible through the window in the throttle lever. When the valve stem is in proper position, the valve stem pin engages a recess on the underside of the valve stem, preventing accidental turning of the stem.

The air valve regulator is located at the bottom and toward the rear of the wrench. Using a screwdriver and altering the setting of the air regulator up to 90 degrees, either to the right or left, reduces the torque from full power to zero power.

Before operating the pneumatic impact wrench make sure the socket or other attachment you are

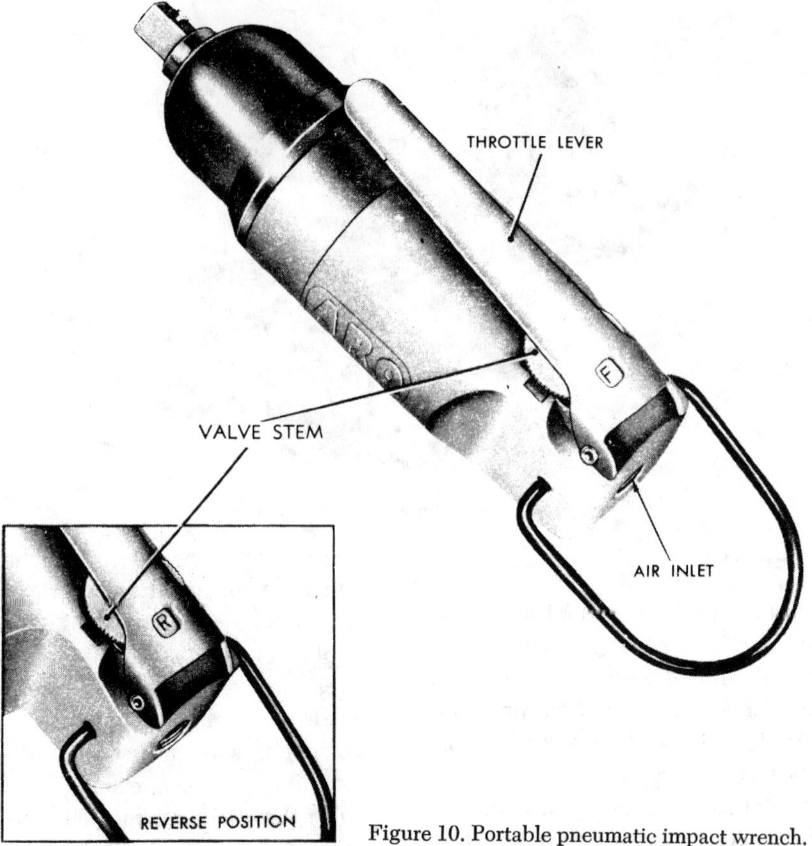

Figure 10. Portable pneumatic impact wrench.

using is properly secured to the anvil. It is always a good idea to operate the wrench free of load in both forward and reverse directions. To see that it operates properly, check the installation of the air hose to make sure it is in accordance with the manufacturer's recommendation.

Bench Grinder

The *electric bench grinder* (Fig. 11) is designed for hand grinding operations, such as sharpening chisels or screwdrivers, grinding drills, removing excess metal from work, and smoothing metal surfaces. It is usually fitted with both a medium grain and fine grain abrasive wheel. The medium wheel is satisfactory for rough grinding where a considerable quantity of metal has to be removed, or where a smooth finish is not important. For sharpening tools or grinding to close limits of size, the fine wheel should be used, as it removes metal more slowly, gives the work a smooth finish, and does not generate enough heat to anneal the cutting edges.

When a deep cut is to be taken on work or a considerable quantity of metal removed, it is often practical to grind with the medium wheel first and finish up with the fine wheel. Most bench grinders are so made that wire brushes, polishing wheels, or buffing wheels can be substituted for the removable grinding wheels.

To protect the operator during the grinding operation an eyeshield and wheel guard are provided for each grinding wheel. A tool rest is provided in front of each wheel to rest and guide the work dur-

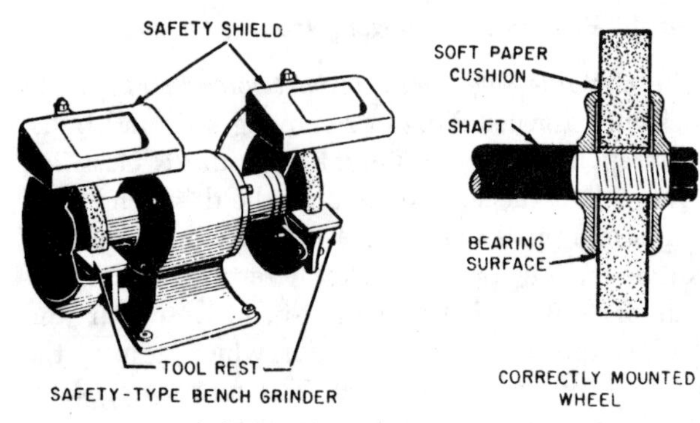

Figure 11. Bench grinder and wheel.

ing the grinding procedure. The rests are removable, if necessary, for grinding odd-shaped or large work.

When starting a grinder, turn it on and stand to one side until the machine comes up to full speed. There is always a possibility that a wheel may fly to pieces when coming up to full speed. *Never* force work against a cold wheel; apply work gradually to give the wheel an opportunity to warm, thereby minimizing the possibility of breakage.

Handle grinding wheels carefully. Before replacing a wheel always check it for cracks. Make sure that a fiber or rubber gasket is in place between each side of the wheel and its retaining washer. Tighten the spindle nut just enough to hold the wheel firmly. If the nut is tightened too much the clamping strain may damage the wheel. When selecting a replacement wheel, ascertain that the grinder will not exceed the manufacturer's recommended speed for the wheel.

When grinding, always keep the work moving across the face of the wheel. Grinding against the same spot on the wheel will cause grooves to be worn into the face of the wheel. Keep all wheel guards tight and in place. Always keep the tool rest adjusted so that it just clears the wheel and is at or just below the center line of the wheel, to prevent accidental jamming of work between tool rest and wheel.

Wear goggles, even if eyeshields are attached to the grinder. Keep your thumbs and fingers out of the wheel.

Safety Precautions

In operating or maintaining air-driven tools, take the following precautionary measures to protect yourself and others from the damaging effects of compressed air.

1. Inspect the air hose for cracks or other defects. Replace the hose if found defective.

2. Before connecting an air hose to the compressed air outlet, open the control valve momentarily. Then, make sure the hose is clear of water and other foreign material by connecting it to the outlet and again opening the valve momentarily.

Caution: Before opening the control valve, see that nearby persons are not in the path of the air flow. *Never* point the hose at another person.

3. Stop the flow of air to a pneumatic tool by closing the control valve at the compressed air outlet before connecting, disconnecting, adjusting, or repairing a pneumatic tool.

Chapter 11

Layout and Benchwork

Laying out is the method of placing lines on the stock to correspond to the lines and dimensions of the blueprint. These layouts are full size and must be measured and marked accurately on the stock. Limits and allowances must be observed.

Mechanical Drawings and Blueprints

A *mechanical drawing*, made with special instruments and tools, gives a true representation of an object to be made, including its shape, size, description, specifications as to material to be used, and method of manufacture. A *blueprint* is an exact duplicate of a mechanical drawing.

The following paragraphs cover briefly some important points in connection with working from sketches and blueprints. Of the many types of blueprints, the simplest one is the *plan view*. This is a blueprint which shows the position, location, and use of the various parts of the object.

In addition to plan views, you may use other blueprints, called assembly prints, unit or subassembly prints, and detail prints. These prints show various kinds of machinery and mechanical equipment.

Assembly prints show the various parts of the mechanism and how the parts fit together. Individual mechanisms, such as motors, pumps, and others, will be shown on *subassembly prints*. These show location, shape, size, and relationships of the parts of the subassembly unit. Assembly and subassembly prints are used to learn operation and maintenance of machines and equipment.

Detail prints give you the information required to make a new part. They show size, shape, kind of material, and method of finishing. You will find them indispensable in your work.

Working from Drawings

Detail prints usually show only the individual part or piece you must produce. They show two or more orthographic views of the object, and, in special cases, they may show an isometric projection, without dimension lines, near the upper right corner. An isometric projection shows how the part will look when made.

Each drawing or blueprint carries a number, located in the upper left-hand corner and in the title box in the lower right-hand corner of the print. The title box also shows the part name, the scale used, the pattern number, the material required, the assembly or subassembly print number to which the part belongs, the job order number, the quantity and date of the order, and the names or initials of the persons who drew, checked, and approved the drawings.

Accurate and satisfactory fabrication of a part described on a drawing depends upon the following:

1. Correctly reading the drawing and closely observing all data thereon;
2. Selecting the correct material;
3. Selecting the correct tools and instruments for laying out the job;
4. Using the baseline or reference line method of locating the dimensional points during layout, thereby avoiding cumulative errors (described later in this chapter);
5. Strict observance of tolerances and allowances;
6. Accurate gaging and measuring of work throughout the fabricating process;
7. Giving due consideration, when measuring, for expansion of the workpiece by heat generated by the cutting operations. This is especially important when checking dimensions during finishing operations, if work is being machined to close tolerance.

Accurate Measurement

It is to your advantage to always strive for the

greatest amount of accuracy. You can work many hours on a project and if it is not accurate, you will often have to start over. With this thought in mind you would do well to study carefully the following information about both the English and metric systems of measurement.

ENGLISH SYSTEM. With the *English system* the standard unit of measurement is the *inch.* The inch can be broken down into smaller parts for finer measurements. One breakdown is the *common fraction* such as 1/2 inch, 1/4 inch, 1/8 inch, 1/32 inch, or 1/64 inch. The inch may also be divided into decimal fractions, such as 1/10, 1/100, or 1/1000. *Decimal fractions* can be expressed with a numerator and denominator, but in most machine shop work and on blueprints or drawings they are frequently expressed in decimal form such as 0.1 in., 0.01 in., and 0.001 in. Decimal fractions are expressed in the following manner.

One-tenth inch = 0.1
One-hundredth inch = 0.01
One-thousandth inch = 0.001
One ten-thousandth inch = 0.0001

A breakdown from 1/64 in. to 1 in. is shown in Table 26.

METRIC SYSTEM. The *metric system* is used by many countries other than the United States, and you should have an understanding of this system of measurement. The standard unit of measurement for the metric system is the *meter.*

In the metric system, the meter is subdivided into the following parts:

1 meter = 10 decimeters (dm)
1 decimeter = 10 centimeters (cm)
1 centimeter = 10 millimeters (mm)

From this we can say that one decimeter is one-tenth meter, one centimeter is one-hundredth meter, and one millimeter is one-thousandth meter. Other subdivisions of the meter are also included in the metric system. One meter is equal to 2.54 centimeters.

TABLE 26

LENGTH—INCHES AND MILLIMETERS—EQUIVALENTS OF DECIMAL AND FRACTIONS OF AN INCH IN MILLIMETERS

From 1/64 to 1 Inch

½'s	¼'s	8ths	16ths	32ds	64ths	Millimeters	Decimals of an inch	Inch	½'s	¼'s	8ths	16ths	32ds	64ths	Millimeters	Decimals of an inch
					1	= 0.397	0.015625							33	=13.097	0.515625
				1	2	= .794	.03125						17	34	=13.494	.53125
					3	= 1.191	.046875							35	=13.891	.546875
			1	2	4	= 1.588	.0625					9	18	36	=14.288	.5625
					5	= 1.984	.078125							37	=14.684	.578125
				3	6	= 2.381	.09375						19	38	=15.081	.59375
					7	= 2.778	.109375							39	=15.478	.609375
		1	2	4	8	= 3.175	.1250				5	10	20	40	=15.875	.625
					9	= 3.572	.140625							41	=16.272	.640625
				5	10	= 3.969	.15625						21	42	=16.669	.65625
					11	= 4.366	.171875							43	=17.066	.671875
			3	6	12	= 4.762	.1875					11	22	44	=17.462	.6875
					13	= 5.159	.203125							45	=17.859	.703125
				7	14	= 5.556	.21875						23	46	=18.256	.71875
					15	= 5.953	.234375							47	=18.653	.734375
	1	2	4	8	16	= 6.350	.2500			3	6	12	24	48	=19.050	.75
					17	= 6.747	.265625							49	=19.447	.765625
				9	18	= 7.144	.28125						25	50	=19.844	.78125
					19	= 7.541	.296875							51	=20.241	.796875
			5	10	20	= 7.938	.3125					13	26	52	=20.638	.8125
					21	= 8.334	.328125							53	=21.034	.828125
				11	22	= 8.731	.34375						27	54	=21.431	.84375
					23	= 9.128	.359375							55	=21.828	.859375
		3	6	12	24	= 9.525	.3750				7	14	28	56	=22.225	.875
					25	= 9.922	.390625							57	=22.622	.890625
				13	26	=10.319	.40625						29	58	=23.019	.90625
					27	=10.716	.421875							59	=23.416	.921875
			7	14	28	=11.112	.4375					15	30	60	=23.812	.9375
					29	=11.509	.453125							61	=24.209	.953125
				15	30	=11.906	.46875						31	62	=24.606	.96875
					31	=12.303	.484375							63	=25.003	.984375
1	2	4	8	16	32	=12.700	.5	1	2	4	8	16	32	64	=25.400	1.000

Limits of Accuracy

You must work within the limits of accuracy specified on the drawing. A clear understanding of *tolerance* and *allowance* will help you to avoid making small, but potentially dangerous errors. These terms may seem closely related, but each has a very precise meaning and application. The following paragraphs point out the meanings of these terms and the importance of observing the distinctions between them.

TOLERANCE. Working to the absolute or exact basic dimension is impracticable and unnecessary in most instances. The designer calculates, in addition to the basic dimensions, an allowable variation. The amount of variation or limit of error permissible is indicated on the drawing as a given amount, such as = 0.005; = 1/64. The difference between the allowable minimum and the allowance maximum dimension is *tolerance*. *For example*, in Fig. 1:

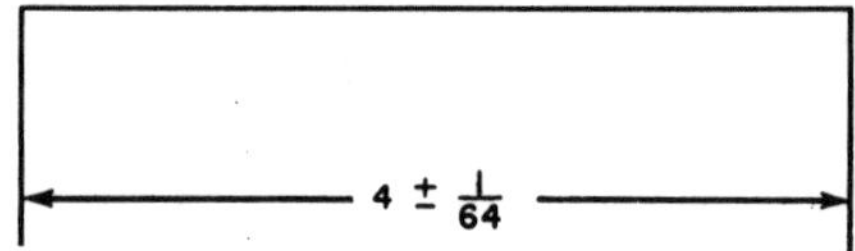

Figure 1. Basic dimension and tolerance.

Basic dimension = 4
Long limit = 4 1/64
Short limit = 3 63/64
Tolerance = 1/32

When tolerances are not actually specified on a drawing, fairly concrete assumptions can be made concerning the accuracy expected by using the following principles. For dimensions which end in a fraction of an inch, such as 1/8, 1/16, 1/32, 1/64, consider the expected accuracy to be to the nearest 1/64 inch. When the dimension is given in decimal form, the following applies.

If a dimension is given as 3.000 in. the accuracy expected is ± 0.0005 in. or, if the dimension is given as 3.00 in., the accuracy expected is ± 0.005 in. The ± 0.0005 is plus or minus five ten-thousandths of an inch. The ± 0.005 is plus or minus five thousandths of an inch.

ALLOWANCE. *Allowance* is an intentional difference in dimensions of mating parts to provide the desired fit. A *clearance allowance* permits movement between mating parts when assembled. *For example,* when a hole with a 0.250 in. diameter is fitted with a shaft that has a 0.245 in. diameter, the clearance allowance is 0.005 in. An *interference allowance* is the opposite of a clearance allowance. The difference in dimensions in this case provides a tight fit. Force is required when assembling parts which have an interference allowance. If a shaft with a 0.251 in. diameter is fitted in the hole identified in the preceding example, the difference between the dimensions will give an interference allowance of 0.001. As the shaft is larger than the hole, force is necessary to assemble the parts.

What is the relationship between tolerance and allowance? In the manufacture of mating parts, the tolerance of each part must be controlled so that the parts will have the proper allowance when assembled. *For example,* if a hole 0.250 inch in diameter with a tolerance of 0.005 in. (± 0.0025) is prescribed for a job, and a shaft to be fitted in the hole is to have a clearance allowance of 0.001 in., the hole must first be finished within the limits, and the required size of the shaft determined exactly, before the shaft can be made. If the hole is finished to the upper limit of the basic dimension (0.2525 in.), the shaft would be machined to 0.2515 in. or 0.001 in. smaller than the hole. If the dimension of the shaft was given with the same tolerance as the hole, it is obvious that there would be no control over the allowance between the parts. As much as 0.005 in. allowance (either clearance or interference) could result.

To provide a method of retaining the required allowance while permitting some tolerance in the dimensions of the mating parts, the tolerance is limited to one direction on each part. This single direction (unilateral) tolerance stems from the basic hole system. If a clearance allowance is required between mating parts, the hole may be larger but not smaller than the basic dimension. The part that fits into the opening may be smaller, but not larger than the basic dimension. Therefore, shafts and other parts that fit into a mating opening have a minus tolerance only, while the openings have a plus tolerance only. If an interference allowance between the mating parts is required the situation is reversed. The opening can be smaller but not larger than the basic dimension, while the shaft can be larger, but not smaller than the basic dimension. Therefore, you can expect to see a tolerance such as +.005, −0, or +0, −.005, but with the required value not necessarily .005. One way to get a better understanding of a clearance allowance, or an interference allowance, is to make a rough sketch of the piece and add dimensions to the sketch where they apply.

Precautions

Be sure you have the correct print for the part to be made or repaired. You want the print which has not only the correct title, but also the correct assembly number.

Never take a measurement with a rule directly from the print because the tracing from which the print was made may not have been copied from the original drawing perfectly, and may contain scaling errors. Also, paper stretches and shrinks with changes in atmospheric conditions. Dimensions must be taken only from the figures shown on the dimension lines.

Be very careful in handling all blueprints and working drawings. When they are not in use, place them on a shelf, in a cabinet, or in a drawer. Return them to the blueprint file as soon as the job is done. Blueprints and working drawings are always valuable and often irreplaceable. Make it a point never to mutilate, destroy, or lose a blueprint.

Layout

Layout is the term used to describe the marking of metal surfaces that provides an outline for machining. A layout is comparable to a single view (end, top, or side) or a part which is sketched directly on the workpiece. The difficulty experienced in making layouts depends on the intricacies of the part to be laid out and the number of operations required to make the part. A flange layout, *for example,* is relatively simple, as the entire layout can be made on one surface of the blank flange. However, an intricate casting may require layout lines on more than one surface. This requires careful study and concentration to ensure that the layout has the same relationships as those shown on the drawing (or sample) that you are using.

When a part must be laid out on two or more surfaces, it may be necessary to lay out one or two surfaces and machine them to size before further layout lines can be used. This prevents removal of layout lines on one surface while machining another. In other words, it would be useless to lay out the top surface of a part and machine the layout lines off while cutting the part to the layout lines of an end surface.

Through the process of computing and transferring dimensions, you will become familiar with the relationship of the surfaces. Understanding this relationship will be of benefit when planning the sequence of machining operations.

Accuracy in making layouts depends on your ability. You should be capable of holding the dimensions of a layout to within a tolerance of 1/64 in. Sometimes you must work to a tolerance of even less than that.

A layout of a part is made when the directional movement or location of the part is controlled by hand or aligned visually without the use of precision instruments (such as when the work is done on bandsaws or drill presses). When cutting irregular shapes on shapers, planers, lathes, or milling machines, layout lines are made, and the tool or work is guided by hand. When making a part with hand cutting tools, layout is essential.

Mechanical drawing and layout are closely related subjects. Knowledge of one will help you understand the other.

MATERIALS AND EQUIPMENT. A scribed line on the surface of metal is usually hard to see; therefore a *layout liquid* is used to provide a contrasting background. Commercially prepared *layout dyes* or *inks* are available. Chalk can be used occasionally, although it does not stick to a finished surface as well as does layout dye. The layout dyes, commonly used, color the metal surface with a blue or copper tint. A line scribed on this colored surface reveals the color of the metal through the background.

The tools generally used for making layout lines are the combination square set, machinist's square, surface gage, scriber, straightedge, rule, divider, and caliper. Tools and equipment used in setting up the part to be laid out are surface plates, parallel blocks, angle plates, V-blocks, and sine bar. Surface plates have very accurately scraped flat surfaces. They are used to provide a mounting table for the work to be laid out so that all lines in the layout can be made to one reference surface. Angle plates are commonly used when the lines in the layout are at an angle to the reference surface. These plates may be fixed or adjustable. Fixed angle plates are considered to be more accurate because one surface is machined to a specific angle in relation to the base. Adjustable angle plates are convenient to use because the angular mounting surface may be adjusted to meet the requirements of the job. V-blocks are used for mounting round stock on the surface plate. Parallel blocks are placed under the work to locate the work at a convenient height.

The sine bar is a precision tool used for determining angles which require accuracy within five minutes of arc. The sine bar may be used to check angles or establish angles for layout and inspection work. The sine bar must be used in conjunction with a surface plate and gage blocks if accuracy is to be maintained. Using the sine bar will be covered later in this chapter. (*See also* Chap. 2, Measuring Tools and How to Use Them.)

Layout Methods

To ensure complete accuracy when making layouts, establish a reference point or line on the work. This line, called the baseline, is located so that it can be used as a base from which you can measure dimensions, angles, and lines of the layout. A machined edge or centerline may be used as a reference line. Circular layouts, such as flanges, are usually laid out from a center point and a diameter line.

Inaccuracy in layouts can be held to a minimum when the reference method is used, because errors can be made only between the reference line and one specific line or point. Making a layout with each line or point referenced to the preceding one causes compounding of any existing error and thus results in an inaccurate layout.

Making a layout on stock that has one or more machine finished surfaces is usually easy. Laying out a casting presents special problems because the surfaces are too rough and not true enough to permit the use of squares, surface plates, or other mounting methods with any degree of accuracy. A casting usually must be machined on all surfaces. Sufficient material must be left outside the layout line to permit truing up the surface by machining. *For example,* a casting might have only 1/8 inch machining allowance on each surface (or a total of 1/4 inch oversize). It is obvious in this example that taking more than 1/8 inch off any surface can mean the loss of the casting. The layout procedure is especially important when there are irregular surfaces or cored holes in the casting. The layout lines then must be within the machining allowance on all surfaces. *Do not* attempt to make the layout so that a maximum amount of material is removed from one surface and a minimum amount from another surface.

MAKING LAYOUT LINES. The following information is applicable to practically all layouts. Layout lines are formed by using a reference edge or point on the stock or by using the surface plate as a base.

LINES SQUARE OR PARALLEL TO EDGES. When scribing layout lines on sheet metal, hold the scratch awl, or scriber, as shown in Fig. 2, leaning it toward the direction in which it will be moved and away from

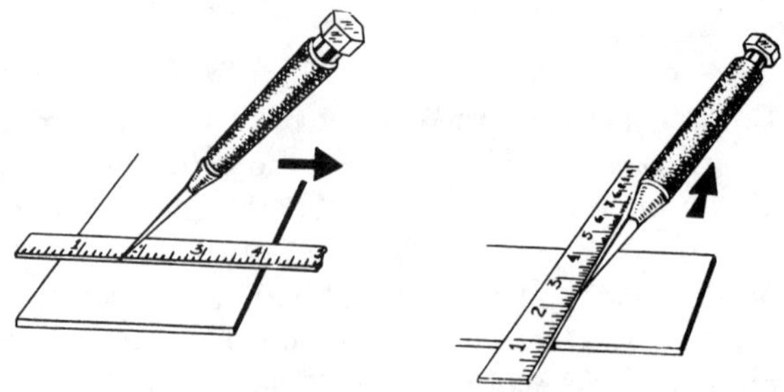

Figure 2. Using a scribe.

the straightedge. This will help scribe a smooth line which will follow the edge of the straightedge, template, or pattern at its point of contact with the surface of the metal.

To square a line on stock with a combination square, place the squaring head on the edge of the stock (Fig. 3). Draw the line along either edge of the blade. The line will be square with the edge of the stock against which the squaring head is held, that is, the angle between the line and the edge will be 90 degrees.

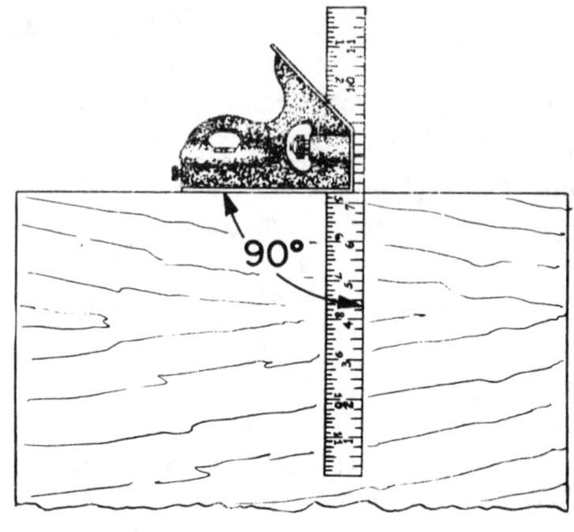

Figure 3. Using a combination square.

To draw lines parallel to an edge using a combination square, extend the blade from the squaring head the required distance, such as the 2-inch setting shown in Fig. 4. Secure the blade at this position. Scribe a line parallel to the edge of the stock by holding the scratch awl or scriber at the end of the blade as you move the square along the edge. All lines so scribed with different blade settings will be parallel to the edge of the stock and parallel to each other.

To scribe a line parallel to an edge with a hermaphrodite caliper, hold the caliper as shown in Fig. 5, so that the curved leg maintains contact with the edge while the other leg scribes the line. Hold the

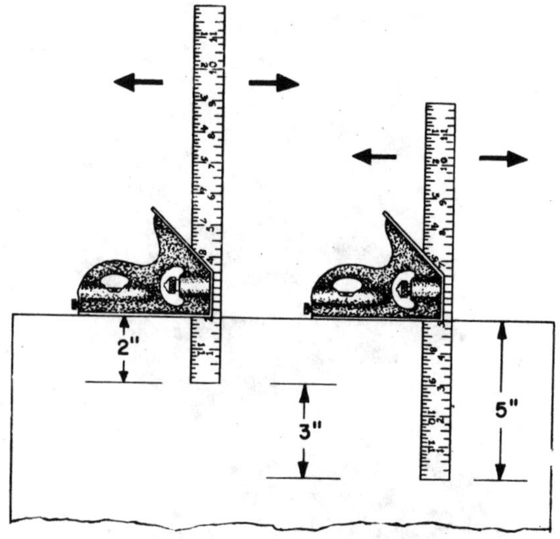

Figure 4. Laying out parallel lines with a combination square.

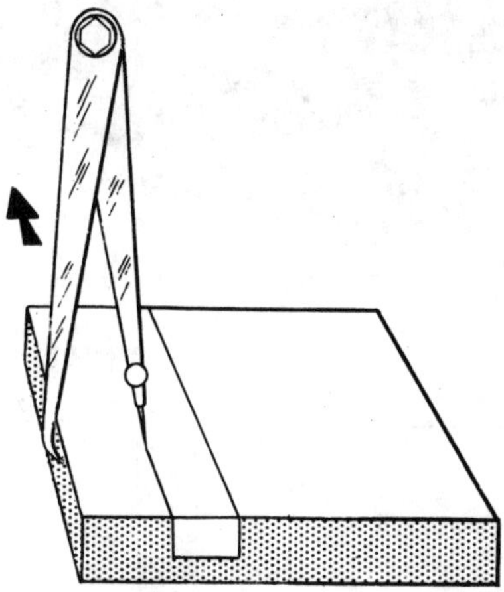
Figure 5. Laying out a parallel line with a hermaphrodite.

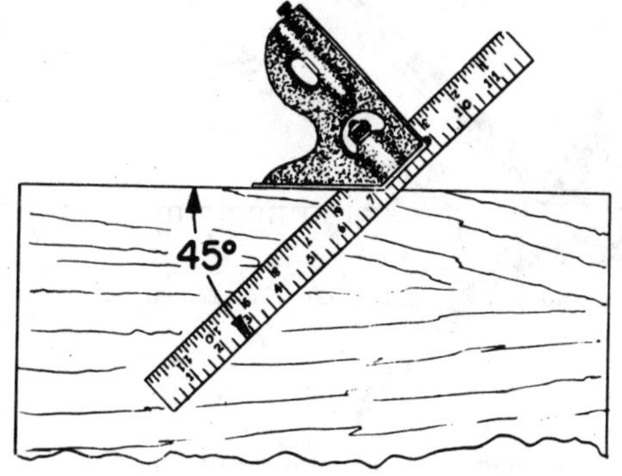

Figure 6. Laying out a 45-degree angle.

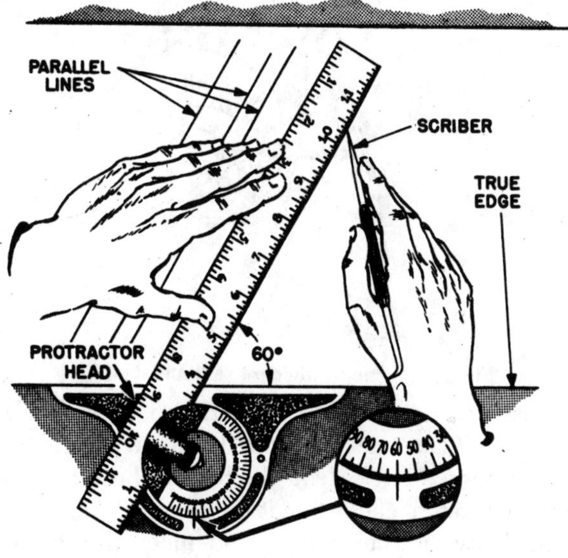

Figure 7. Laying out angular lines.

caliper in such a way that the line will be scribed at the desired distance from the edge of the stock.

Forming Angular Lines. To lay out a 45 degree angle on stock, using a combination square, place the squaring head on the edge of the stock as shown in Fig. 6, and draw the line along either edge of the blade. The line will form a 45 degree angle with the edge of the stock against which the squaring head is held.

To draw angular lines with the protractor head of a combination square, loosen the adjusting screw and rotate the blade to where the desired angle lines up with the index mark on the body of the protractor head. The setting shown in Fig. 7 is 60 degrees. Tighten the screw to hold the setting.

Hold the body of the protractor head in contact with a true edge of the work with the blade resting on the surface. Scribe the lines along the edge of the blade on the work. The angle set on the scale determines the angle laid out on the work. All lines drawn with the same setting, and from the same true edge of the work, will be parallel lines.

Laying Out Circles and Irregular Lines. Circles or segments of circles are laid out from a center point. To ensure accuracy, the center point is prick punched to keep the point of the dividers from slipping out of position. Use the center head and rule, as shown in Fig. 8, to locate the center of round stock. To find the center of square and rectangular shapes, scribe straight lines from opposite corners of the workpiece. The intersection of the lines locates the center.

To lay out a circle with a divider, take the setting of the desired radius from the rule, as shown in Fig. 9. *Note* that the 3 inch setting is being taken *away* from the end of the rule. This reduces the chance of

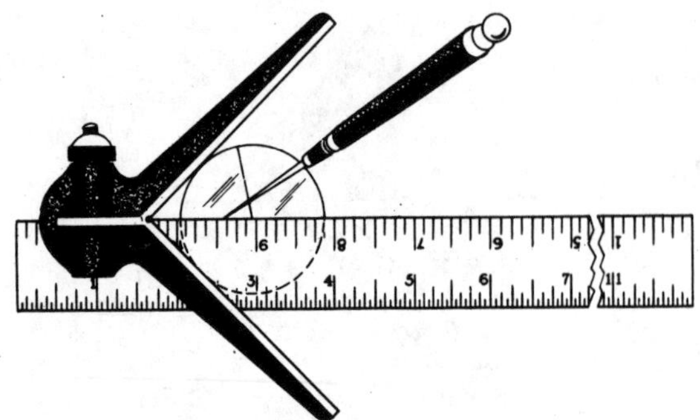

Figure 8. Using a center head and rule.

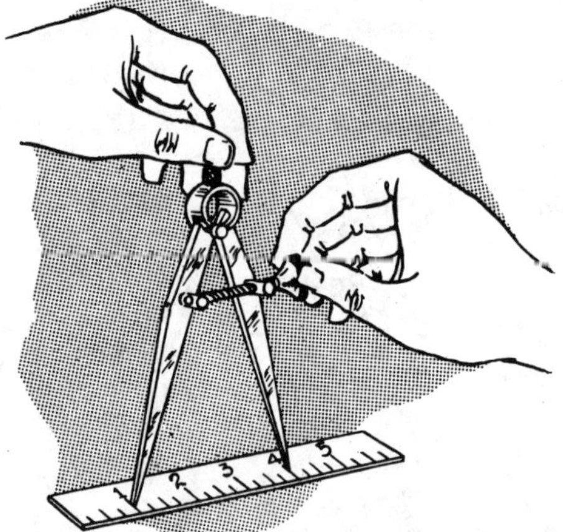

Figure 9. Setting a divider to a dimension.

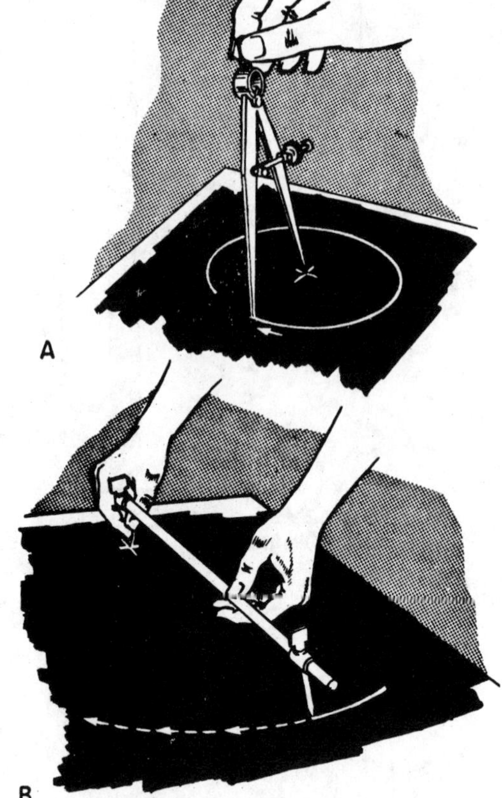

Figure 10. Laying out circles.

error as each point of the dividers can be set on a graduation. Place one leg of the divider at the center of the proposed circle, lean the tool in the direction it will be rotated, and rotate it by rolling the knurled handle between your thumb and index finger (A, Fig. 10).

When setting trammel points (B, Fig. 10), follow the same direction as for a divider; a steel tape may be required to set the trammel points.

To lay out a circle with trammel points, hold one point at the center, lean the tool in the direction you propose to move the other point, and swing the arc or circle (B, Fig. 10).

To transfer a distance measurement with trammel points, hold one point as you would for laying out a circle and swing a small arc with the other point opened to the desired distance.

Scribing an irregular line to a surface is a skill used in fitting a piece of stock (Fig. 11) to a curved surface. A, Fig. 11 shows the complete fit. In B, Fig. 11, the divider has scribed a line from left to right. When scribing horizontal lines, the legs of the divider must be kept plumb (one above the other). When scribing vertical lines, the legs must be kept level. To scribe a line to an irregular surface, set the divider so that one leg will follow the irregular surface and the other leg will scribe a line on the material that is being fitted to the irregular surface (B, Fig. 11).

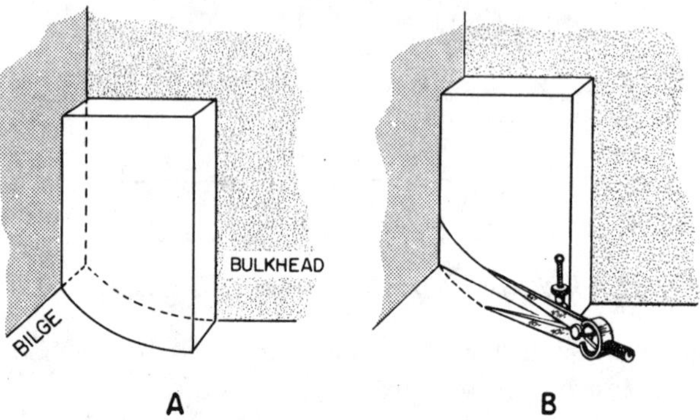

Figure 11. Laying out an irregular line from a surface.

Using the Surface Plate. The surface plate is used with such tools as parallel squares, V-blocks, surface gages, angle plates, and sine bar in making layout lines. Angle plates similar to the one shown in Fig. 12 are used to mount work at an angle on the surface plate. The angle of the angle plate is set by using a protractor and rule of the combination square set, or by using a vernier protractor.

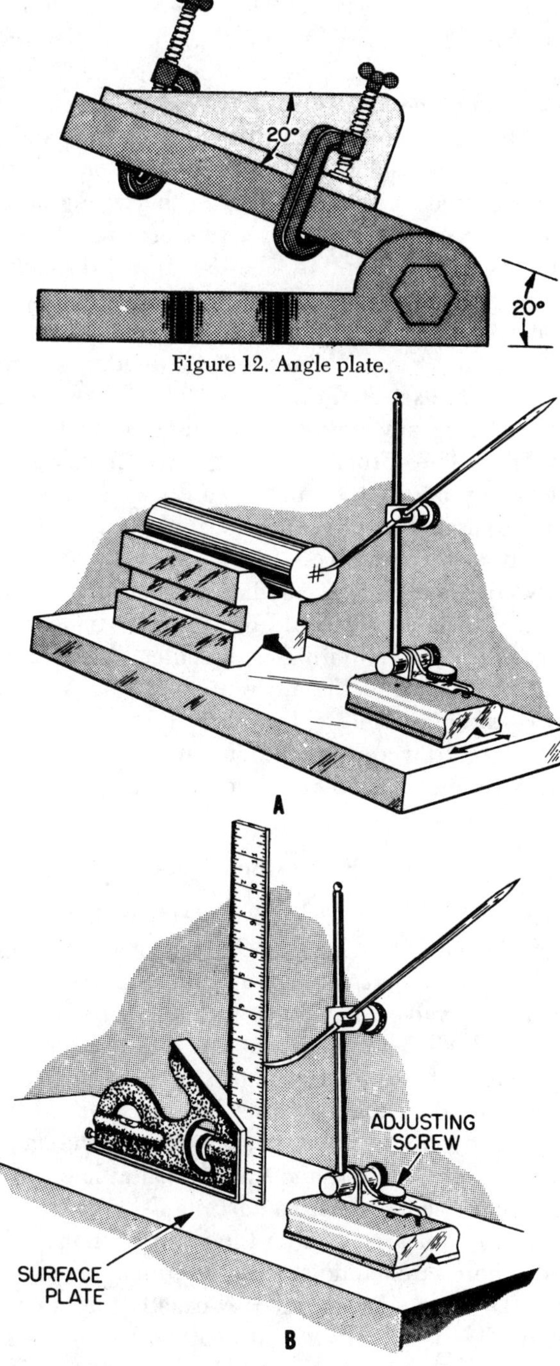

Figure 12. Angle plate.

Figure 13. Setting and using a surface gage.

A, Fig. 13 shows the use of a surface gage V-block combination in laying out a piece of stock. To set a surface gage for height, first clean the top of the surface plate and the bottom of the surface gage. Then place the squaring head of a combination square as shown in B, Fig. 13. Secure the scale so that the end is in contact with the surface of the plate. Move the surface gage into position. Set the scriber to the approximate height required, using the adjusting clamp that holds the scriber onto the spindle. Make the final adjustment for the exact height required (4 1/2 inches in this example) with the adjusting screw on the base of the surface gage.

USING THE SINE BAR. The sine bar is used in conjunction with the surface plate. The sine bar is not used as often as other layout tools, but it would be advantageous to know how to use the sine bar. Sine bars, such as the one shown in Fig. 14, are available in various sizes with lengths of 5 in., 10 in., and 20 in. The length is taken from the center line of the rolls. To be able to use the sine bar, you must be familiar with natural trigonometric functions. In Fig. 14 we have a desired angle A, and to achieve this angle we must find dimension X. This is done in the following manner. Dimension X = length of sine bar times the sine of angle.

Example:

Length of sine bar = 5 in.
Angle A = 23 degrees 35 ft.
Sine of angle A = 0.4000
X = 5 x 0.40008
X = 2.00040 in.

By reversing the procedure you can find the angle. The formula for finding the angle is as follows.

$$\text{Sine of angle} = \frac{\text{Distance X}}{\text{Length of Sine Bar}}$$

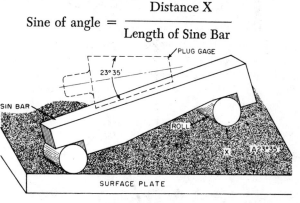

Figure 14. Sine bar.

GEOMETRIC CONSTRUCTION OF LAYOUT LINES. It is sometimes necessary to scribe in a layout which cannot be made using conventional layout methods. *For example,* making straight and angular layout lines on sheet metal with irregular edges cannot be done readily by using the combination square set. Neither can sheet metal be mounted on angle plates in a manner that permits scribing angular lines. Geometric construction is the answer to this problem.

Use a *divider* to lay out a perpendicular *from* a point *to* a line, as shown in Fig. 15. Lightly prick

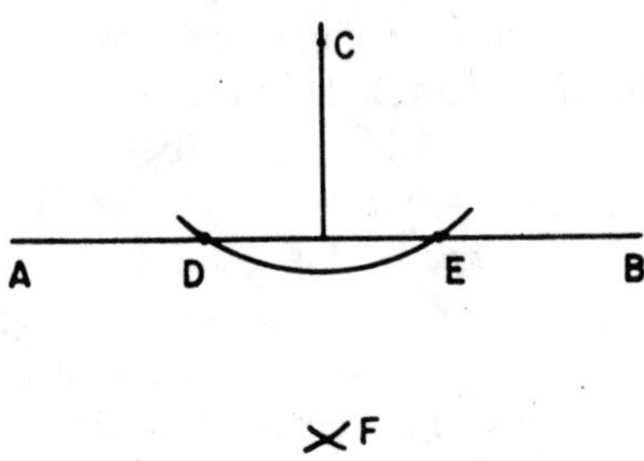

Figure 15. Layout of a perpendicular from a point to a line.

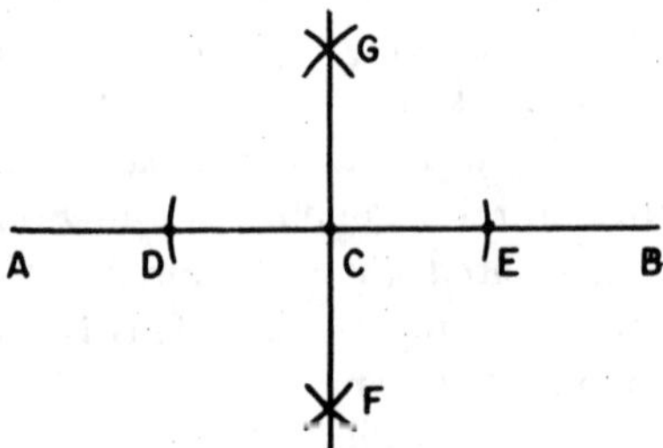

Figure 16. Layout of a perpendicular from a point on a line.

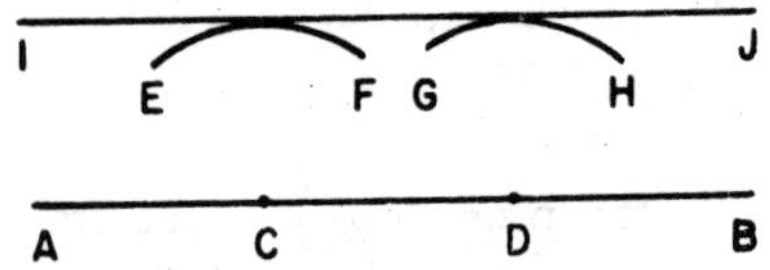

Figure 17. Layout of a parallel line.

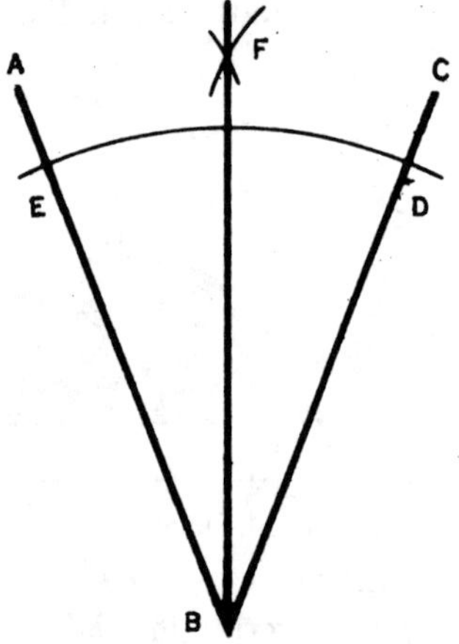

Figure 18. Bisecting an angle.

punch the point, C, then swing any arc from C which will intersect the line AB, and prick punch the intersections D and E, as shown in the illustration. With D and E as centers, scribe two arcs which intersect at a point such as F. Place a straightedge on points C and F. The line drawn along this straightedge from point C to line AB will be perpendicular (90 degrees) to the line AB.

Use a *divider* to lay out a perpendicular *from* a point *on* a line, as shown in Fig. 16. Lightly prick punch the point which is identified in the illustration as C on line AB. Then set the divider to any distance to scribe arcs which intersect AB at C and E with C as the center. Punch D and E lightly. With D and E used as centers, and with the setting of the divider increased somewhat, scribe arcs which cross at points such as F and G. The line drawn through F and G will pass through point C and be perpendicular to line AB.

To lay out parallel lines with a divider, set the divider to the selected dimension. Then, referring to Fig. 17, from any points prick punched such as C and D on line. From AB swing arcs EF and GH. Then draw line IJ tangent to these two arcs, and it will be parallel to line AB and at the selected distance from it.

Bisecting an angle is another geometric construction with which you should be familiar. Angle ABC (Fig. 18) is given. With B as a center, draw an arc cutting the sides of the angle at D and E. With D and E as centers, and with a radius greater than half of arc DE, draw arcs intersecting at F. A line drawn from B through the point F bisects the angle ABC.

Laying Out Valve Flange Bolt Holes

Before describing the procedure for making valve flange layouts, it is best to clarify the terminology involved in the description that will be given. Figure 19 shows a valve flange with the bolt holes marked on the bolt circle. The straight line distance between the centers of two adjacent holes is called the *pitch chord.* The bolt hole circle itself is called the *pitch circle.* The vertical line across the face of the flange is the *vertical bisector,* and the horizontal line across the face of the flange is the *horizontal bisector.*

The bolt holes' centers on the pitch circle and the pitch chord are equidistant. The pitch chord between any two adjacent holes is exactly the same as the pitch chord between any other two adjacent holes. *Note* that the two top holes and the two bottom holes straddle the vertical bisector. The vertical bisector cuts the pitch chord for each pair exactly in half. This is the standard method of placing the holes for a 6-hole flange. In the 4-, 8-, or 12-hole flange, the bolt holes straddle both the vertical and horizontal bisectors. This system of hole placement permits a valve to be installed in a true vertical or horizontal position, provided that the pipe flange holes are also in standard location on the pitch circle. Before proceeding with a valve flange layout job, find out definitely whether the holes are to be placed in standard position. If you are working on a *per sample* job, follow the layout of the sample. The procedure for setting up the layout for straight globe or gate valves is as follows.

1. Fit a fine grain wood plug in the opening in each flange (Fig. 19). The plug should fit snugly and be flush with the face of the flange.

2. Apply layout dye to the flange faces, or if dye is not available, rub chalk on the flange faces to facilitate the drawing of lines which will be clearly visible.

3. Locate the center of each flange with a surface gage, or with a center head and rule combination, if the flange diameter is relatively small. (*See* Fig. 13 and A, Fig. 8.) After you have the exact center point located on each flange, mark the center with a sharp prick punch.

4. Scribe the pitch or bolt circle, using a pair of dividers. Check to see that the pitch circle and the outside edge of the flange are concentric.

5. Draw the vertical bisector. This line must pass through the center point of the flange and it must be visually located directly in line with the axis of the valve stem (Fig. 19).

6. Draw the horizontal bisector. This line must also pass through the center point of the flange and must be laid out at right angles to the vertical bisector. (*See* Figs. 16 and 19.)

Up to this point the layout is the same for all flanges regardless of the number of holes. Beyond

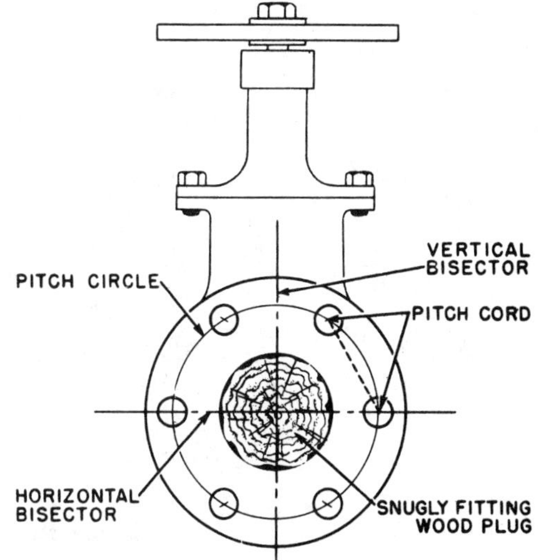

Figure 19. Flange layout terminology.

this point the layout differs with the number of holes. The layout for a 6-hole flange is the simplest one.

Six-Hole Flange. Set your dividers exactly to the dimension of the pitch circle radius. Place one leg of the dividers on the point where the horizontal bisector crosses the pitch circle on the right-hand side of the flange, point (1) in A, Fig. 20, and draw a small arc across the pitch circle at points (2) and (6). Next, place one leg of the dividers at the intersection of the pitch circle and horizontal bisector on the left-hand side of the flange point (4), and draw a small arc across the pitch circle line at points (3) and (5). These points (1) to (6) are the centers

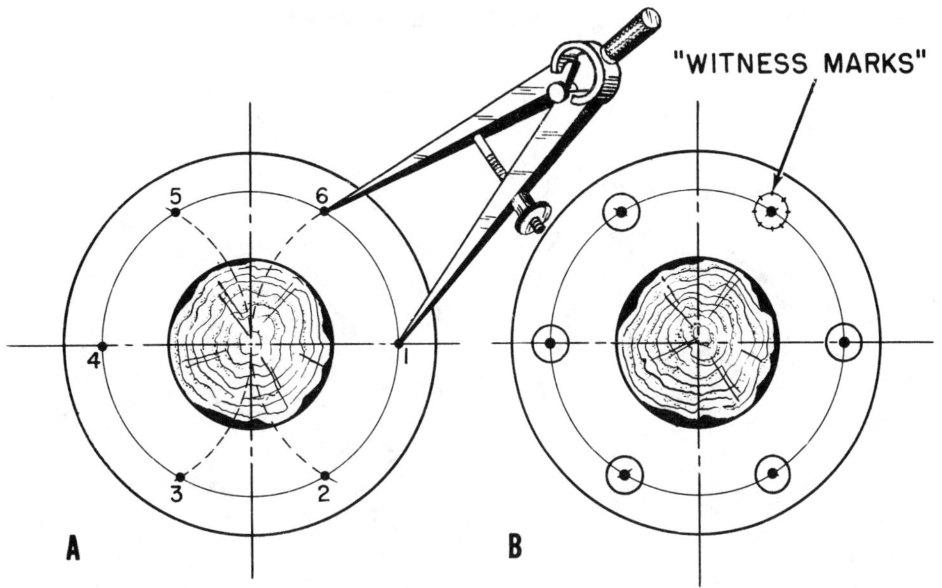

Figure 20. Development of a 6-hole flange.

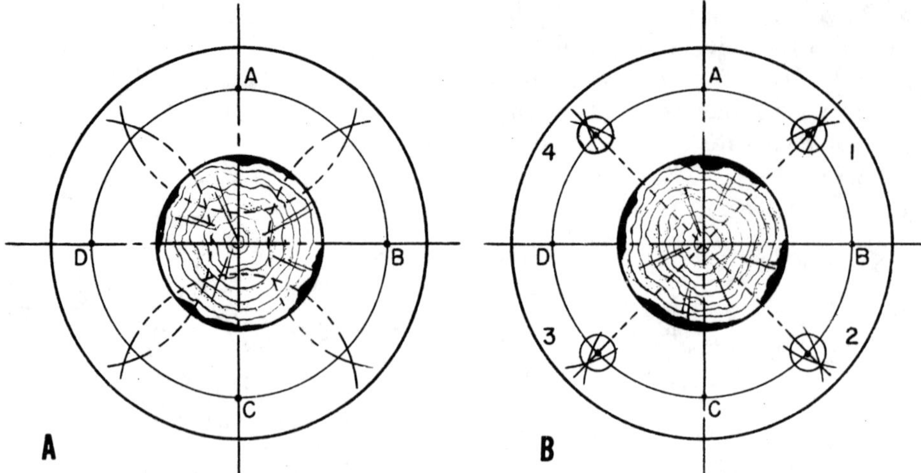

Figure 21. Four-hole flange development.

for the holes. Check the accuracy of the pitch chords. To do this, leave the dividers set exactly as you had them set for drawing the arcs. Starting from the located center of any hole, step around the circle with the dividers. Each pitch chord must be equal to the setting of the dividers. If it is not, you have an error in hole mark placement that must be corrected before you can center punch the marks for the holes. After you are sure the layout is accurate, center punch the hole marks and draw a circle of appropriate size around each center punched mark and prick punch *witness marks* around the circumference, as shown in B, Fig. 20. These witness marks will be cut exactly in half by the drill to verify a correctly located hole.

Four-Hole Flange. Figure 21 shows the development for a 4-hole flange layout. Set your dividers for slightly more than half the distance of arc AB, and then scribe an intersecting arc across the pitch circle line from points A, B, C, and D, as shown in A, Fig. 21. Next, draw a short radial line through the point of intersection of each pair of arcs, as shown in B, Fig. 21. The points where these lines cross the pitch circle, (1), (2), (3), and (4), are the centers for the holes. To check the layout for accuracy, set your divider for the pitch between any two adjacent holes and step around the pitch circle. If the holes are not evenly spaced, find your error and correct it. When the layout is correct, follow the center punching and witness marking procedure described previously under the 6-hole flange layout.

Eight-Hole Flange. Figure 22 shows the development of an 8-hole placement. The procedure is as follows. First locate point E by the same method as described for locating point (1) in the 4-hole layout. Then divide the arc AE in half by the same method.

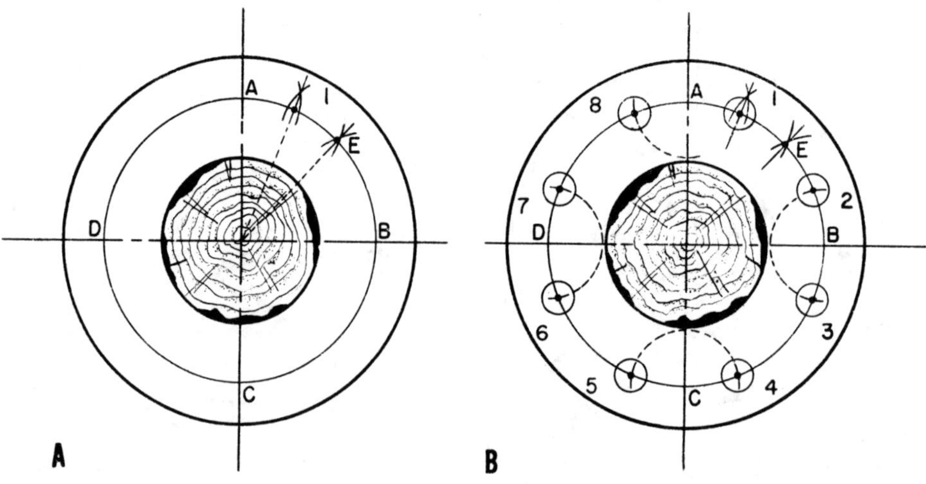

Figure 22. Eight-hole flange development.

The mid-point of arc AE is the location for the center of hole (1) (A, Fig. 22). Next set your dividers for distance A (1), and draw an arc across the pitch circle line from A at point (8); from B at points (2) and (3); from C at (4) and (5); and from D at (6) and (7) (B, Fig. 22). Now set your calipers for distance AE and gage the pitch chord for accuracy. Then finish the layout as described in the preceding paragraphs.

MATHEMATICAL DETERMINATION OF PITCH CHORD LENGTH. In addition to the geometric solutions given in the preceding paragraphs, the spacing of valve flange bolt hole centers can be determined by simple multiplication provided a constant value for the desired number of bolt holes is known. The *diameter* of the pitch circle multiplied by the constant equals the length of the pitch chord. The constants for specified numbers of holes are given in Table 27.

TABLE 27
CONSTANTS FOR LOCATING CENTERS OF FLANGE BOLT HOLES

No. bolt holes	Constant
3 - - - - - - - - - -	0.866
4 - - - - - - - - - -	.7071
5 - - - - - - - - - -	.5879
6 - - - - - - - - - -	.5
7 - - - - - - - - - -	.4338
8 - - - - - - - - - -	.3827
9 - - - - - - - - - -	.342
10 - - - - - - - - - -	.309
11 - - - - - - - - - -	.2817
12 - - - - - - - - - -	.2588
13 - - - - - - - - - -	.2394
14 - - - - - - - - - -	.2225
15 - - - - - - - - - -	.2079
16 - - - - - - - - - -	.195
17 - - - - - - - - - -	.184
18 - - - - - - - - - -	.1736
19 - - - - - - - - - -	.1645
20 - - - - - - - - - -	.1564

Here is an example of the use of Table 27. Suppose a flange is to have 9 bolt holes, laid out on a pitch circle with a diameter of 10 inches. From the table, select the constant for a 9-hole flange. The pitch *diameter* (10 inches) multiplied by the appropriate constant (.342) equals the length of the pitch chord (3.420 inches). Set a pair of dividers to measure 3.420 inches, from point to point, and step off around the circumference of the pitch circle to locate the centers of the flange bolt holes. *Note* that the actual placement of the holes in relation to the vertical and horizontal bisectors is determined separately. (This is of no concern if the layout is for an unattached pipe flange rather than for a valve flange.)

Benchwork

Benchwork includes practically all repair work other than actual machining.

There are specific techniques that can be used in assembly and disassembly of equipment which will improve the effectiveness of a repair job. You should note such things as fastening devices, fits between mating parts, and the uses of gaskets and packing when repairing equipment. Noting the positions of parts in relation to mating parts or the unit as a whole is extremely helpful in ensuring that the parts are in correct locations and positions when the unit is reassembled.

Inspecting the equipment before and during the repair procedure is necessary to determine causes of defects or damage. The renewal or replacement of a broken or worn part of a unit may give the equipment an operational status. Eliminating the cause of damage prevents recurrence.

Repairs are made by replacement of parts, by machining the parts to new dimensions, or by using hand tools to overhaul and recondition the equipment. Hand tools are used in repair procedure in jobs such as filing and scraping to true surfaces, and to remove burrs, nicks, and sharp edges.

Assembly and Disassembly

Equipment should be disassembled in a clean, well-lighted work area. With plenty of light, small parts are less likely to be misplaced or lost, and small but important details are more easily noted. Cleanliness of the work area as well as the proper cleaning of the parts as they are removed decreases the possibility of damage due to foreign matter when the parts are reassembled.

Before starting any disassembly job, select the tools and parts that you think will be necessary and take them to the work area. This procedure will permit you to concentrate on the work without unnecessary interruptions during the disassembly and reassembly processes.

Have a container at hand for holding small parts to prevent loss. Use tags or other methods of marking to identify the parts with the unit from which they are taken. Doing this prevents mixing parts of one piece of equipment with parts belonging to another

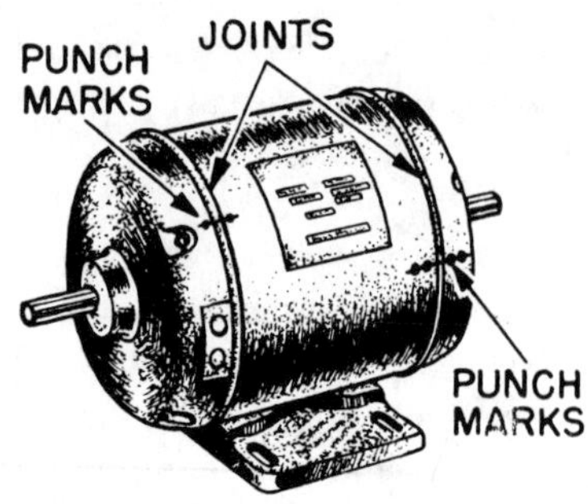

Figure 23. Mating parts location marks.

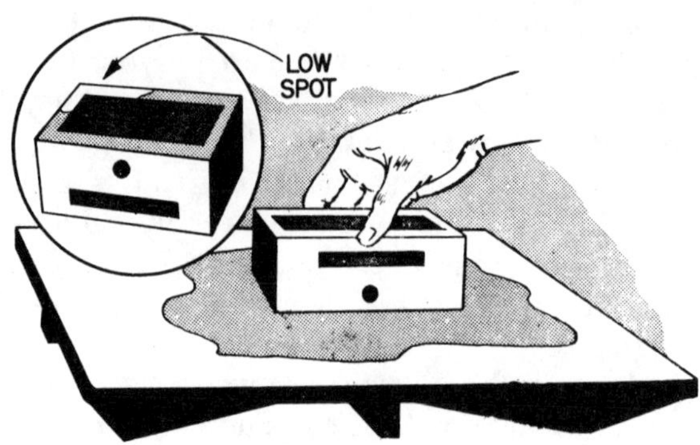

Figure 24. Checking a surface.

similar unit, especially if several pieces of equipment are being repaired in the same area. Use a scriber or prick punch to mark the relative positions of mating parts that are required to mark in a certain position (Fig. 23). You must pay close attention to details of the equipment you are taking apart to fix in your mind how the parts fit together. When overhauling equipment, use no more force than necessary to disassemble and reassemble the parts. Double check for overlooked fastening devices if heavy pressure is required to separate parts. An overlooked pin, key, or setscrew that locks parts in place can cause extensive damage if pressure is applied to the parts. If hammers are required to disassemble parts, use a mallet or hammer with a soft face (lead, plastic, or rawhide) to prevent distortion of surfaces. If bolts or nuts or other parts are stuck together due to corrosion, use penetrating oil to free the parts.

Precision Work

In the repair of equipment, it is usually necessary to do a certain amount of precision hand finishing of parts. This requires the use of file, scrapers, precision portable grinders, and hydraulic and arbor presses. Machined parts are likely to have burns, wire edges, and small irregularities that must be removed by filing or offhand grinding. It is sometimes necessary to *scrape in* flat surfaces and bearings so that true surfaces and correct clearances are maintained. Hydraulic and arbor presses are used to force-fit mating parts.

Scraping. Scraping requires the use of cutting tools, similar to files without serrated edges, to accomplish precision work. A great deal of experience is necessary to become proficient in scraping a true surface. Scraping produces a more accurate surface than machining.

To scrape a flat surface, a surface plate and prussian blue are required. Lightly coat the surface plate with blue and move the workpiece over this surface. The blue will stick to the high spots on the workpiece, thus revealing the areas to be scraped (Fig. 24). Scrape the areas of the workpiece surface that are blue and check again. Continue this process until the blue coloring shows on the entire surface of the workpiece. To reduce frictional *drag* between mating finished scraped surfaces, solid surfaces are usually rotated so that each series of scraper cuts is made at an angle of 90 degrees to the preceding series. This action gives the finished scraped surface a cross-hatched or basket weave appearance.

A shell-type split bearing, or a bushing, can be scraped, if necessary, to fit a shaft. To do this, a mandrel the same size as the shaft, or the shaft itself, is blued and placed in the bearing. Turning the mandrel or shaft slightly will mark the high spots which then can be scraped down. Scraping a bearing is more difficult than scraping a flat surface, because longitudinal as well as radial clearance must be maintained. Scraping is not often required in most repair work, but when it is needed there is no other way to do the job.

Removal of Burrs and Sharp Edges. An important but often forgotten item in the repair of machinery is the removal of burrs and sharp or marred edges from the parts before reassembly. Removal of burrs and sharp edges, in addition to being the *mark of a craftsman,* makes parts safer to handle, prevents interference in the fitting of mating parts, and prevents the possibility of having chips break off edges when the part is back in operation. Inspect parts of an assembly carefully, and when necessary, remove corners and burrs or marred edges with a file.

Classes of Fits. The fit of a part is the dimensional relationship of one part with its mating part. Types of fits may be placed in three general categories: the clearance fit, the transition fit, and the interference fit. The type of fit depends on the allowance provided between the mating parts. *For example,* a clearance fit requires that a clearance allowance be provided between the mating parts. The American Standards Association (ASA) has further classified these fits according to use.

Clearance fits (running or sliding fits by ASA standards) have nine classifications varying according to the amount of clearance between the two mating parts. These fits are used when one part moves in relation to its mating part. *For example,* a rotating shaft and bearing relationship, or the sliding action of a shaper ram.

Transitional fits (locational fits by ASA standards) are used for locating one part in relation to its mating part. A transition fit may have a small clearance or a light interference allowance, depending on usage requirements. *For example,* a small clearance allowance would be used between the end bell and housing of a motor. This clearance permits relative ease of assembly and disassembly while retaining good alignment characteristics. A transitional interference fit which would require only light pressure to fit the parts together might be used between an aligning dowel pin and its hole. This type of fit provides better alignment than the clearance allowance, but makes assembly and disassembly more difficult.

Interference fits (force fits by ASA standards) require force to assemble mating parts. There are five classes of interference fits, varying from a light drive fit (class 1) to a shrink fit (class 5). Classes 1, 2, and 3 interference fits can usually be assembled by using mechanical pressure. In classes 4 and 5, heat or a shilling medium may be required to expand or contract one part so that the parts can be fitted together.

Using Hydraulic and Arbor Presses

Hydraulic and arbor presses are simple but useful machines. They are used primarily in force-fitting parts when making repairs. Arbor presses, which consist of a gear and rack arrangement, are used for very light pressing jobs, such as pressing arbor into workpieces for machining. Most hydraulic presses are manually operated.

Regardless of the type of press equipment used, be sure that it is operated correctly. The only method of determining the amount of pressure exerted by a hydraulic press is by watching the pressure gage. A part being pressed can reach the breaking point without any visible indication that too much pressure is being applied. When using the press, you must consider the interference allowance between mating parts, corrosion and marred edges, and overlooked fastening devices, such as pins, setscrews, and retainer rings.

To prevent damage to the work, observe the following precautions when using the hydraulic press.

1. Ensure that the work is adequately supported.
2. Place the ram in contact with the work by hand, so that the work is positioned accurately in alignment with the ram.
3. Use a piece of brass or other material (preferably slightly softer than the workpiece) between the face of the ram and the work to prevent mutilation of the surface of the workpiece.
4. You cannot determine the pressure exerted by *feel.* Watch the pressure gage; if excessive pressure is required, release the pressure and double check the work to find the cause.
5. When pressing parts together, use a lubricant between the mating parts to prevent seizing.

There are no set rules for determining how much pressure will be needed to force-fit two mating parts together. The distance that the parts must be pressed usually increases the required pressures, and increased interference allowances require greater pressures. As a guideline for force-fitting a cylindrical shaft, the maximum pressure, in tons, should not exceed seven to ten times the shaft's diameter in inches.

Using an Oxyacetylene Torch

You may have to use an oxyacetylene torch to heat parts to expand them enough to permit assembly or disassembly. This should be done with great care. The operation of the oxyacetylene torch is not explained in this book, but safety precautions which must be observed when using the torch and equipment are as follows.

1. Use only approved apparatus that has been examined and tested for safety.
2. When cylinders are in use, keep them far enough away from the actual heating area so they will not be reached by the flame or sparks from the object being heated.
3. Never interchange hoses, regulators, or other apparatus intended for oxygen with those intended for acetylene.
4. Keep valves closed on empty cylinders.
5. Do not stand in front of cylinder valves while opening them.
6. When a special wrench is required to open a

cylinder valve, leave the wrench in position on the valve stem while the cylinder is being used, so that the valve can be closed rapidly in an emergency.

7. Always open cylinder valves slowly. (*Do not* open the acetylene cylinder valve more than 1 1/2 turns.)

8. Close cylinder valves before moving the cylinders.

9. Never attempt to force unmatching or crossed threads on valve outlets, hose couplings, or torch valve inlets. The threads on oxygen regulator outlets, hose couplings, and torch valve inlets are right-handed; for acetylene these threads are left-handed. The threads on acetylene cylinder valve outlets are right-handed, but they have a pitch which is different from the pitch of the threads on the oxygen cylinder valve outlets. If the threads do not match, the connections are mixed.

10. Always use the correct tip or nozzle and the correct pressure for the particular work involved. This information should be taken from tables or worksheets supplied with the equipment.

11. Do not allow acetylene and oxygen to accumulate in confined spaces. Such a mixture is highly explosive.

12. Keep a clear space between the cylinder and the work so that the cylinder valves may be reached quickly and easily if necessary.

13. When lighting the torch, open the acetylene valve first and ignite the gas while the oxygen valve is still closed. Do not allow unburned acetylene to escape and accumulate in small or closed compartments.

14. When extinguishing the torch, close the acetylene valve first and then close the oxygen valve.

These precautions are by no means all the safety precautions that pertain to oxyacetylene equipment, and they only supplement those specified by the manufacturer. Always read the manufacturer's manual and adhere to all precautions and procedures for the specific equipment you are going to be using.

Chapter 12

Drills, Drilling, and Drilling Machines

Drilling Procedures

There are many *kinds of drills,* ranging from those for general purposes to specialized types for specific materials or operations. Various lengths and numbers of flutes are available, with straight or various flute angles, with regular or special points, and with straight or tapered shanks. (*See* Chap. 3, section on drills.)

Drilling has been described as "making holes in solid material with a tool called a drill." This is a perfectly good definition, but it is somewhat like describing a donut by the part you do not eat.

The worker would do better to think of *drilling* as "the forming of a workpiece by removing unwanted material with a drill." This sounds like the same thing, but there is one important difference. It makes us concerned with the surface as well as the position and dimensions of what is left, and after all, that is the whole problem of drilling.

There is a wide variety of *drilling machines* for drilling holes in metal, each of which has its particular advantages for certain kinds of work. Among those in most common use are portable drills, sensitive drills, standard drill press, radial drills (traveling head drills), multiple spindle drills, gang drills, and other specially designed machines.

Before proceeding with actual drilling, the work should be securely fastened to the table of the drill press by one of the clamping and holding procedures described later in this chapter.

Checking the Drill

Prior to drilling the hole, be sure that the drill is the correct size, that it is sharp and firmly secured in the chuck of the machine, and that the work has been securely clamped or fastened. Proceed by carefully aligning the point of the drill with the mark previously made when laying out the work and start the machine. After the drill has run a few revolutions, it must be lifted to compare the cuts made with the circle previously laid out on the work. The cuts will sometimes be found to be off center. To correct, proceed as follows: With a small roundnose chisel, cut a small shallow groove (Fig. 1) on the side toward which to draw the hole. Start the drill again and it will drift over to the correct position. Repeat the operation if necessary. Note that this must be done before the drill starts to cut its full diameter. Once the drill is cutting full size nothing can be done to remedy any inaccuracy.

Drilling Small Holes

Holes $\frac{1}{16}$ in. in diameter and smaller should be drilled at a high speed. Use a special bushing to fit

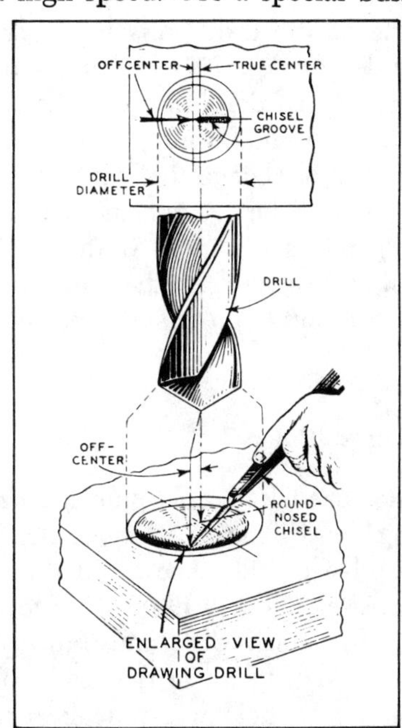

Figure 1. Correcting off-center drill by grooving with chisel.

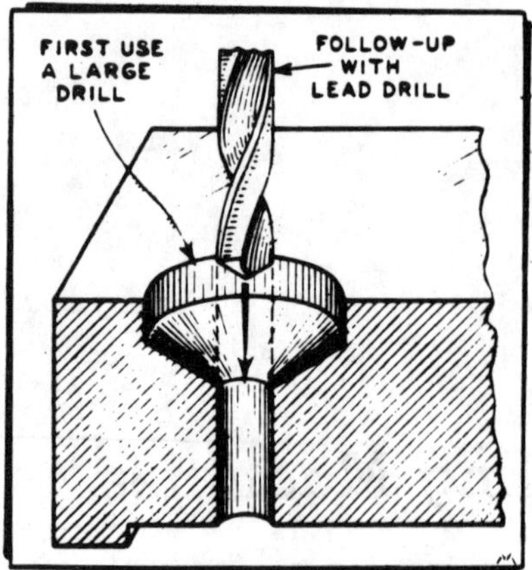

Figure 2. Drilling large holes.

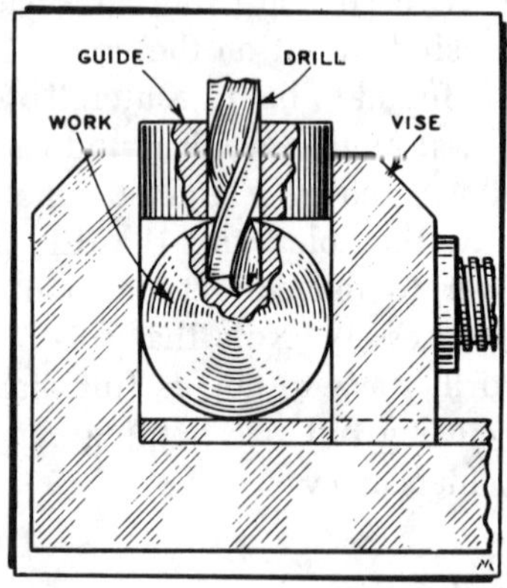

Figure 3. Drilling round stock, with piece cut from work for guide.

the spindle of the drill press when drilling small-diameter, deep holes. This bushing should be sufficiently long so that the drill can be housed almost its full length inside the bushing at the start of the cut. When the drill has cut to the length of this extended portion, it should be set out another short distance and the operation repeated. If the full length of a small drill is extended at the start of the drilling operation, inaccurate holes and breakage of the drill may result.

Drilling Large Holes

A smaller-sized lead hole must be drilled before completing the drilling of a large hole. Start to drill with the full-size drill, check, and draw the drill if necessary. After the drill has started to cut full size, change to the small drill and proceed to run it through the work to make the lead hole (Fig. 2). This smaller lead hole will now be exactly in the center of the layout circle. Then set the larger drill into the spindle and drill the hole full size. The diameter of the small drill used for the lead hole should be approximately the same as, or a little larger than, the web thickness of the larger drill. Since there is less tendency for a small drill to run off center than a large one, this procedure will result in a hole that is usually more accurate than if it were drilled by any other method (Fig. 2).

Drilling Sheet Metal

Sheet metal must be backed against a wooden base block or, preferably, sandwiched between two blocks of wood and clamped. A bottom support must be used to prevent burring and crushing the metal.

Drilling Round Stock

A thin disc the same size as the work and preferably cut from the end of the work should be used in setting up round stock for drilling (Fig. 3). This disc must be carefully laid out and center-drilled to the required diameter. Clamp both work and disc in a vise (Fig. 3). The disc will guide the drill directly to the center of the work and will prevent drifting. Drifting often occurs when round stock is drilled by any other method.

Countersinking

Various types of countersink drills must be used to countersink the work for the heads of the various types of machine screws so that their heads come either flush with or below the surface of the material. This is done after the hole has been drilled to the depth required.

Drilling for Tapped Holes

The drill that is used preparatory to tapping or threading must be a definite size. See the table in the Appendix for accurate sizes of drills to use. The results produced by the use of various sizes of drills are shown in Fig. 4. At *A*, Fig. 4 the previously drilled hole was too small. The black area illustrates the amount of metal that should have been removed by the drill. The removal of this excess metal by the tap produced a rough thread. Tapping a drill hole that is too small may dull the tap and in some cases break it. If the drill is too large, the thread will be only partially cut, and this will necessarily weaken the holding power of the screw (*B*, Fig. 4). A hole

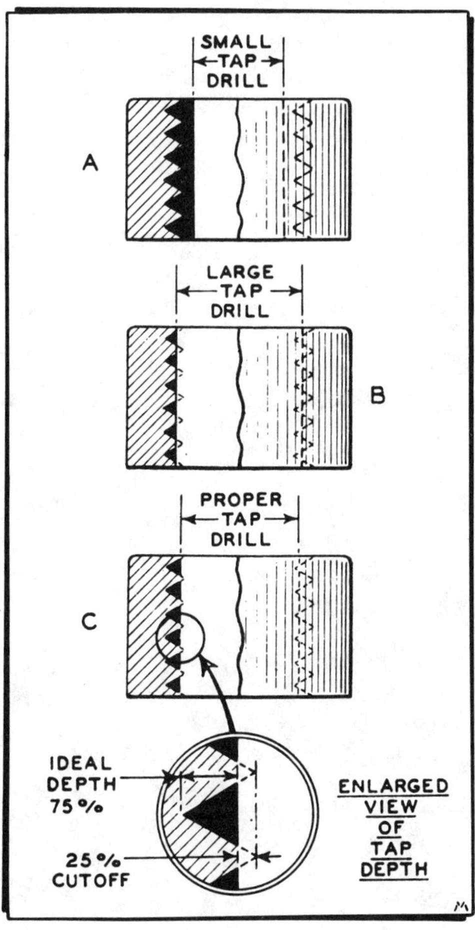

Figure 4

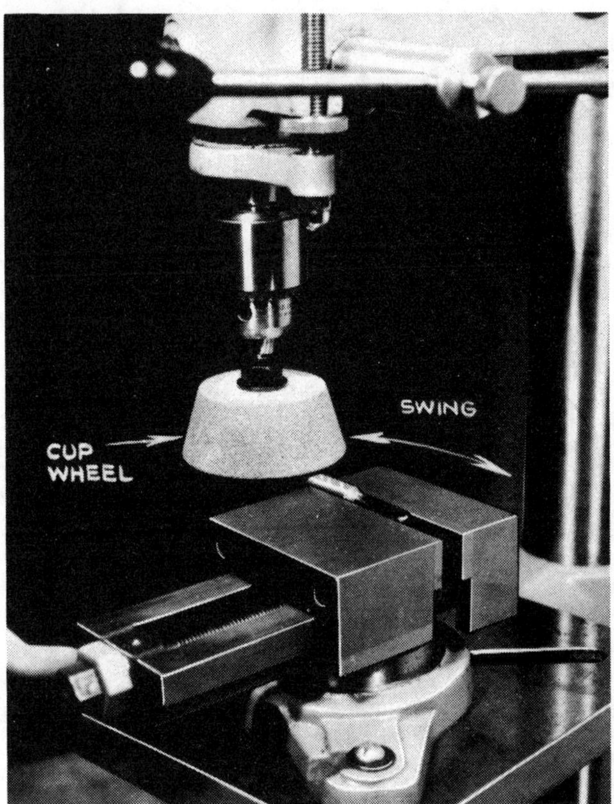

Figure 5

must be drilled that will allow the tap to cut at least 75 per cent of a full thread (*C*, Fig. 4). To tap drilled holes on a drill press, a special tapping attachment must be used. This accessory is attached to the spindle and holds the tap in a solid chuck. Various columns are supplied with the attachment which take a range of tap sizes. The tap is advanced to the hole by means of a V-lever on the attachment. Speeds and feeds for tapping vary with the size of hole and material. Manufacturers of tapping attachments furnish speed-and-feed tables and specific directions for the use of their product. After tapping to the required depth, the tap automatically reverses rotation and extracts itself from the work. The reverse rotation is usually about twice the forward speed.

Miscellaneous Drilling Machine Operations

GRINDING. When a suitable grinding machine is not available, light surface grinding can be done perfectly on the drill press by the use of a cup wheel mounted on a special spindle. The grit and bond of the wheel should be selected to suit the work. Various types of wheels are fully described in Chapter 18. The speed of the drill press should be about 5,000 rpm. The work is projected along the drill press table and under the cup wheel. This wheel must be set to take a suitable bite, and the quill must be locked in position. Heavy cuts should be avoided. A column collar can be used under the drill press head. Clamp the work in place in the vise (Fig. 5), and swing the drill press head back and forth across the work.

POLISHING. The spot finish, sometimes called the engine finish, is an attractive finish for metal and can be done on the drill press. All that is required is a rod of hard rubber or a hardwood dowel. The drill press should run about 1,200 rpm. A paste can be made which consists of abrasive grains such as emery, aluminum oxide, or silicon carbide, of about 150. Grit mixed with oil, or a commercial valve grinding compound mixed with either oil or water, can also be used. Spread the paste lightly and evenly over the suface of the metal and then feed the revolving rod onto the work. The rod tip grinds the abrasive grains into the metal, producing a circular spot.

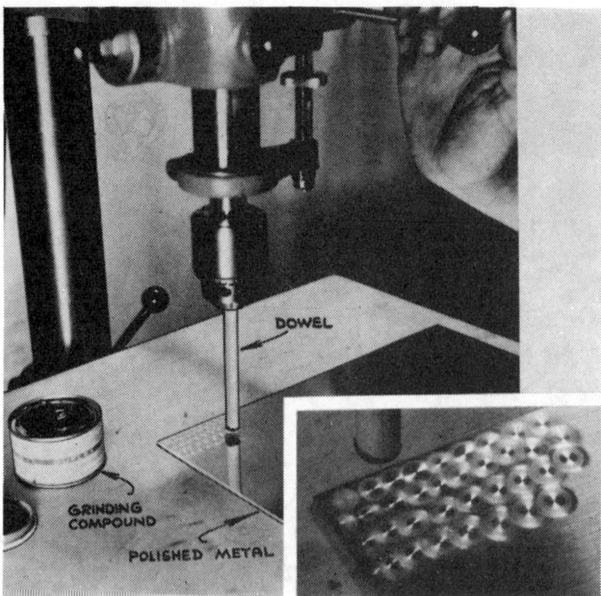

Figures 6 and 7.

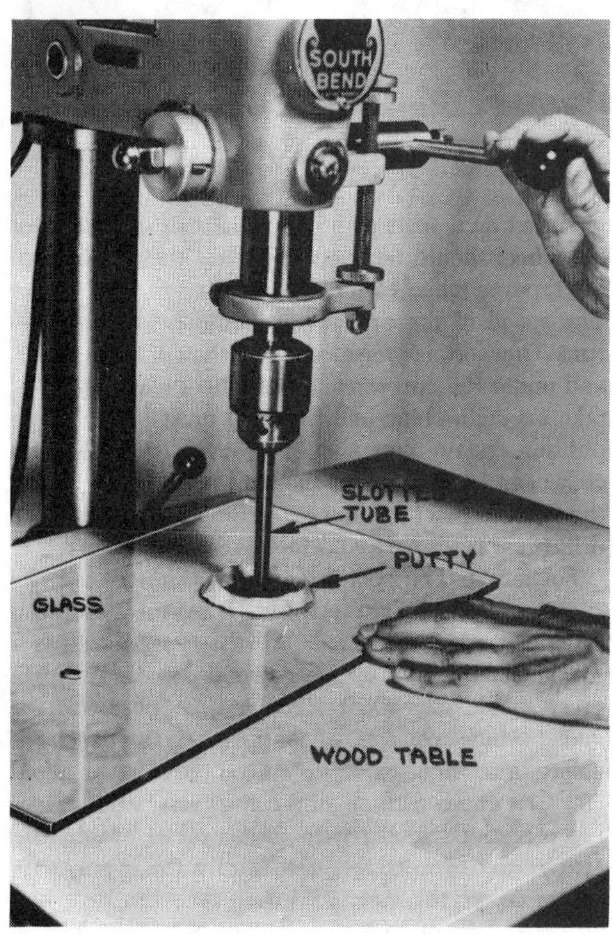

Figure 8

Repeat the operation, overlapping the rings a little, until the whole surface is covered. The line of spots should be regularly spaced and kept even by means of a fence. A uniform feed pressure and duration of contact must be practiced to get good results. Many effective patterns can be worked out (Figs. 6 and 7).

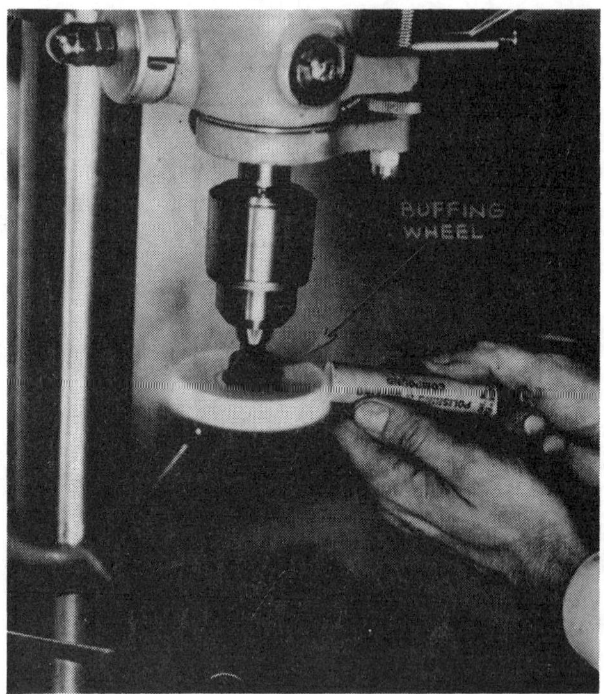

Figure 9

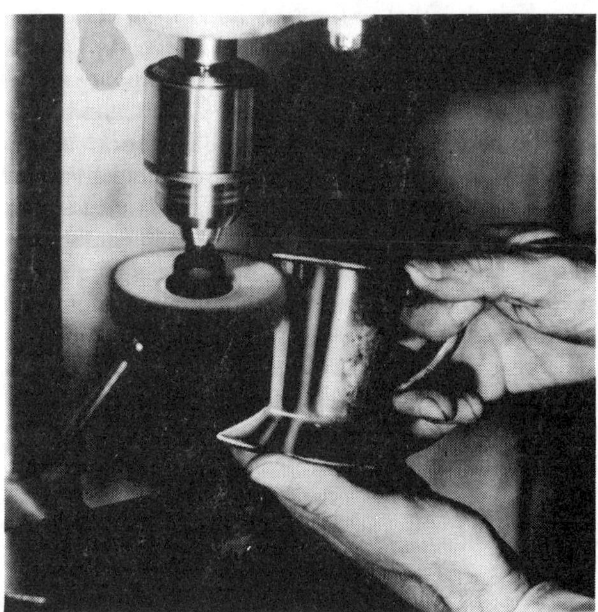

Figure 10

DRILLING IN GLASS. Glass is drilled with the use of a steel or brass tube of the diameter desired for the hole. The tube is slotted at the working end with a saw cut. Mark the glass with a grease pencil and build a dam of putty around the spot where the hole is to be drilled (Fig. 8). The tube drill is fed with a mixture of 80-grit silicon carbide abrasive grains combined with turpentine. The drill speed should be about 500 rpm. Specially designed spear-point carbide-tipped tools are also available for drilling in glass.

BUFFING. When special buffing equipment is not available, polishing and buffing with cloth wheels can be done on the drill press. An inexpensive arbor held in the chuck as shown in Fig. 9 will hold a canvas buffing wheel. With buffing compound applied (Fig. 10), a good job of polishing can be obtained on a variety of materials.

The Radial Drilling Machine

The radial drilling machine shown in Figs. 11 and 12 was so named because the arm which carries the head of the machine swings on a column, and is always radial to the column. This machine is extremely useful when it is necessary to drill several holes in large and heavy pieces. The radial drill, because of its wide range and versatility of operation, has taken the place of the larger upright drills to a certain extent in large production shops. The spindle head of this drill is mounted on a radial arc which is fastened to the column. The head of the radial drill is adjustable along the arm, and the arm of the machine can be swung to any desired position. This adjustment is used when drilling holes in large pieces

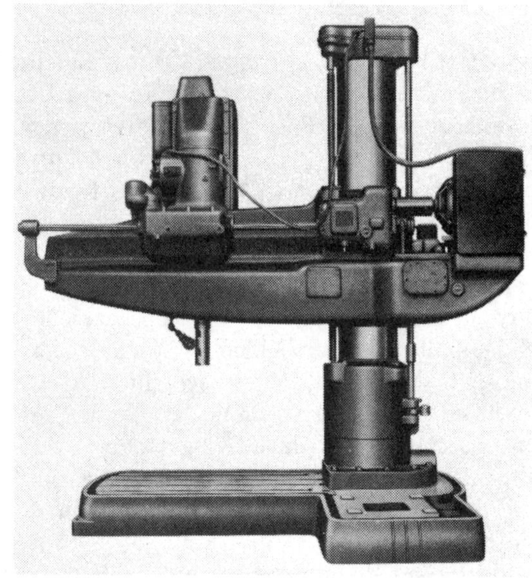

Figure 12. Rear view of standard radial drill.

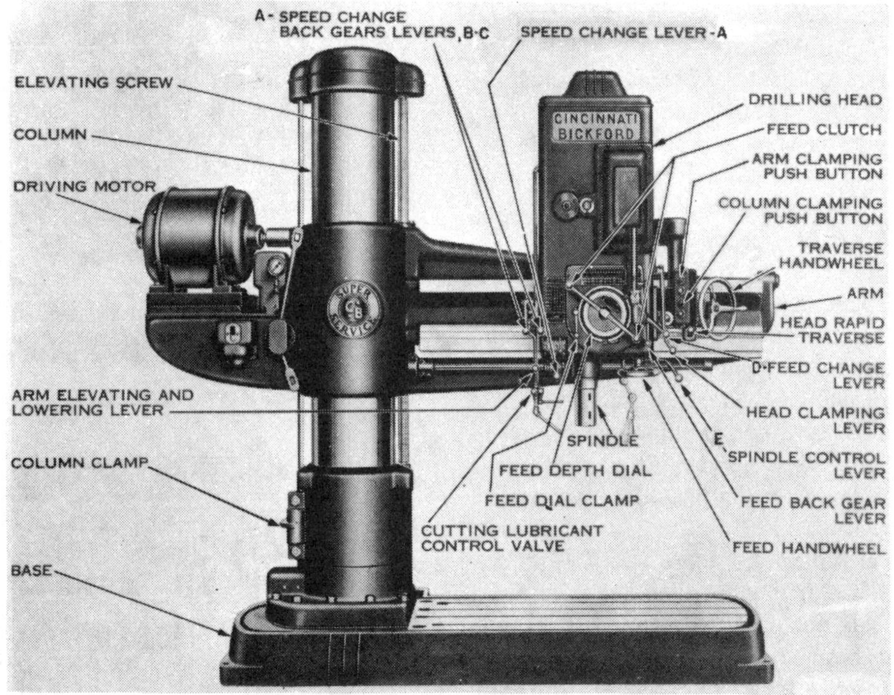

Figure 11. Parts of a radial drill.

which cannot be placed on the table of the machine; it permits the operator to locate the cutting tools quickly over any point of the work within a considerable area. The arm of this drill can be raised or lowered to accommodate quite a range of height in pieces of work. As a rule, radial drills are classified as to size by the length of the radial arc.

Radial Drilling Machine Operation

Before starting the machine, put the driving clutch lever, shown in Fig. 11, in neutral (midway between its extreme positions). Push the quick-return levers toward the head as far as they will go; then turn the machine over by hand so that it revolves freely. By means of temporary connections, check the directions of rotation of the driving motor. When the motor runs in the direction indicated on the machine, these connections can then be made permanent. To run the spindle of the machine right-handed, as in drilling, pull the driving clutch lever forward as far as it will go. To run the spindle left-handed, as in backing out taps, push the driving clutch lever toward the arm as far as it will go. To stop the spindle, put the driving clutch lever midway between these two positions.

Avoid running the spindle of this machine when the driving clutch lever is not in either of the extreme positions. A partially engaged clutch will slip, causing wear on the machine. The super-service type of radial shown in Fig. 11 has 36 spindle feeds. The speed-change lever, *A*, Fig. 11, provides nine changes of speed. The back-gear levers *B* and *C*, Fig. 11, each provide two changes of speeds. The nine speeds obtained through lever *A*, when multiplied by the four speeds obtained through back-gear levers *B* and *C* give a total of 36 spindle speeds. The nine positions of speed-change lever *A* are indicated by an arrow and a numbered plate at the upper end of the lever. These numbers correspond with numbers on the center column of the speed plate (Fig. 13a), usually affixed to the machine by the manufacturer. The back gears *B* and *C* have two positions each; one is the horizontal, the other a downward position. The positions of these levers are indicated by arrows at the top of the speed plate.

All of the 36 changes of spindle speeds are obtained on this machine through sliding gears. To shift these gears, it is only necessary to engage the driving clutch of the machine very lightly, just enough to cause the gears to roll slowly, and then to shift with a quick decisive movement. The speed plate is calibrated for direct reading, and gives the spindle speed in rpm and the corresponding sizes of drills necessary for boring and facing cutters for cast iron and for steel. Drill diameters for cast iron are based on a cutting speed of 100 feet per minute, and are given on the affixed speed plate. The size of the boring and the facing cutters for cast iron is based on a cutting speed of 50 feet per minute, and indicated on the machine.

Drill diameters for steel are based on a cutting speed of 80 feet per minute. The size of the boring and the facing cutters for steel is based on a cutting speed of 40 feet per minute, and is also indicated on the machine. The speeds recommended for both cast iron and steel are also given on the affixed speed plate.

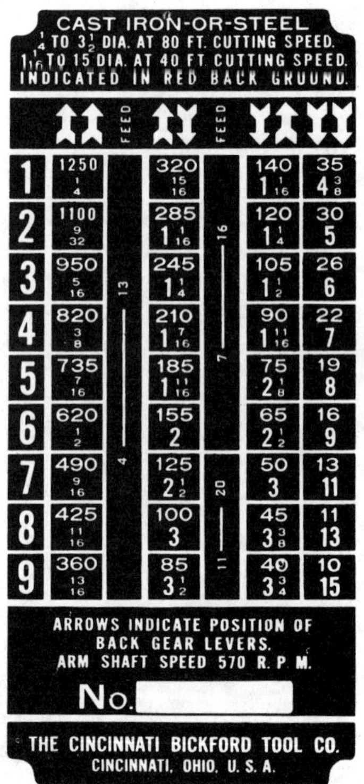

Figure 13a

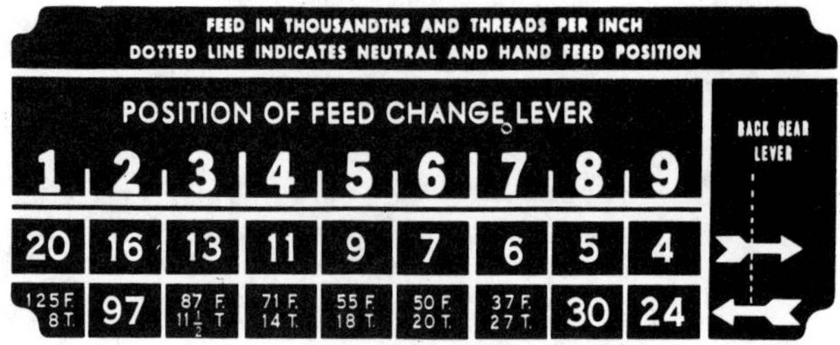

Figure 13b

SELECTION OF FEEDS. The super-service radial (Fig. 11) has 18 feeds. The feed lever *D*, Fig. 11, provides nine changes of feed. These are doubled by the feed lever *E*, Fig. 11, making a total of 18 feeds. The nine positions of lever *D* are indicated by an arrow and a bronze plate at the upper end of the lever, the numbers corresponding with the top row of numbers of the feed plate affixed to the machine. Lever *E* has two positions, between which is a neutral position at which it may be set for hand speeds.

To start the spindle feeding downward, run the spindle in the direction for drilling and set the feed levers *D* and *E* according to the position indicated on the feed plate. Pull the quick-return lever shown in Fig. 11 away from the head as far as it will go. This engages the quick-return clutch. To stop the feed at any time, push the quick-return lever toward the head of the machine.

All of the 18 speed changes are obtained on this machine by means of gliding gears. Speeds can be changed while the spindle is running idle without disengaging the driving clutch, but they should not be changed while drills or tools are actually cutting.

The feed plate (Fig. 13b) furnished by the manufacturer usually gives feeds in thousandths of an inch per revolution of the spindle. For driving pipe taps, select the feed corresponding to the lead of the tap. The spindle will then automatically advance the tap at its required rate. On the type of machine shown in Fig. 11 there is a limit trip that disengages the power feed of the machine when the spindle comes within a half-inch of its lower limit of travel. This prevents the teeth of the rack pinion from running into the spindle sleeve at the end of the rack.

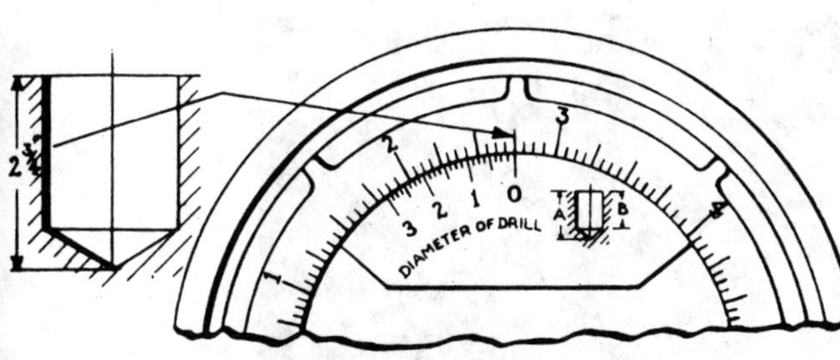

Figure 14

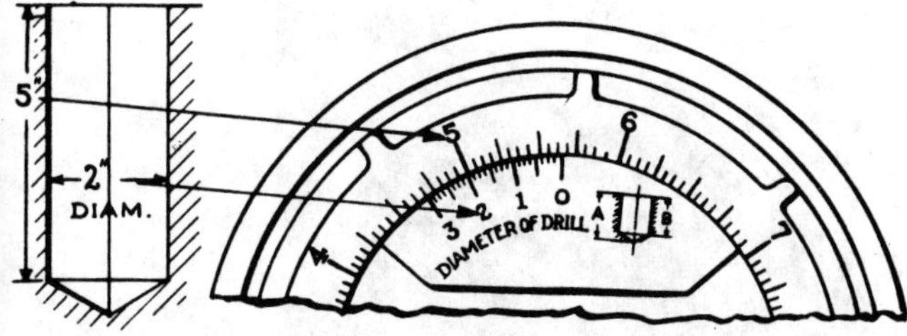

Figure 15

A safety clutch is also provided on this machine which will slip if the feed is overloaded, preventing damage to the mechanism even though the mechanic might become careless in selecting or tripping the feed.

The feed mechanism of a modern radial drill includes a dial and depth gauge of the compensating type. The depth gauge automatically disengages the feed when either the point or the body of the drill has penetrated to the required depth. The graduations on the ring represent spindle travel in sixteenths of an inch. The graduation on the etched plate represents drill diameters in eighths of an inch. To advance the drill to a given depth, set the point of the drill so that it touches the work. Unclamp the graduated ring by swinging the depth-gauge clamping lever in a clockwise direction until it points downward.

To advance the point of the drill to a given depth, revolve the graduated ring until the point on the ring that corresponds to the required depth registers with the zero on the etched plate; this shows the depth gauge set to trip the feed when the drill point has penetrated to a depth of 2¾ in.

To advance the body of the drill to a given depth, revolve the graduated ring until the point on the ring corresponds to the required depth and registers with the drill diameter indicated (Fig. 14). Figure 15 shows the depth gauge set to trip the feed when the body of a two-in. drill has penetrated to a depth of five in. When these settings have been made, swing the depth-gauge clamping lever upward until the graduated ring is firmly clamped and engage the feed; when the drill reaches the required depth, the feed will automatically disengage.

MOVING THE HEAD ON THE ARM. The head of the machine can be moved along the arm with the head-moving hand wheel (Fig. 11) or by the power rapid-traverse lever (Fig. 11). To move the head by the power rapid-traverse lever, pull the traversing lever down to its lowest position and move it to the right or left according to the direction in which the head is to be moved. When the head is in the position required, release the lever, and it will return to neutral. The hand wheel can be used for final close positioning of the head of the machine. In addition to moving the head swiftly and easily along the arm, the power rapid-traverse can be used in the same manner as the traversing motor on an electric crane.

Heavy tools can be placed on a bench or tool stand near the column and carried to and from the work by means of the power traverse. This relieves the mechanic of heavy lifting in getting tools on and off the heavy spindle. To clamp the head on the arm, pull up hard on the head-clamping lever (Fig. 11); to unclamp, push it down.

Raising, Lowering, and Clamping the Arm. Arm clamping and elevating are conveniently and safely controlled at the operating position by a free-moving directional lever, *A*, Fig. 16, at the lower left side of the head. On moving this lever up, the arm clamp is hydraulically released, the multiple-disc clutch for elevating is automatically engaged, and the arm rises. To stop elevation, the lever is moved to the "stop" or center position. This automatically disengages the elevating clutch, and the arm is automatically clamped through a powerful hydraulic clamping mechanism. The cycle for lowering and clamping is similarly automatic and foolproof. Protective limit trips are provided at the upper and lower limits of travel, and, in addition, there is a safety in the mounting of the elevating screw to prevent damage should the arm be lowered onto any obstruction within its limits of travel.

Hydraulic column clamping on the standard machine is controlled from the head as shown at *B*, Fig. 16. Its push-button control at the head marked "clamp" and "release" operate a solenoid controlling the hydraulic mechanism that is built-in at the motor end of the arm. The hydraulic clamp, through two bolts on the cuff of the column sleeve, automatically applies up to 55,000 pounds of pressure on the column and sleeve clamping surfaces, joining these two members as effectively as if they were one solid part.

Adjusting Arm Clamp. To adjust arm clamp, stop the main driving motor of the machine and remove link *J* on the clutch-shifting mechanism in the rear of the arm. Also remove the plate *H* on the front of the arm-clamping mechanism.

The upper and lower limit screws must not be moved or adjusted. They are merely for the purpose of controlling the amount of expansion of the arm when the arm is unclamped and are properly set at the factory.

Now start the main driving motor of the machine, set the arm-control lever mounted on the head of the machine in either up or down position. This will unclamp the arm and, since link *J* has been disconnected from the elevating clutches, the arm will not raise or lower. When clamping or unclamping the arm, the push rod and equalizing bar located in the bracket under plate *H* should travel a total distance of between ½ and 9⁄16 of an inch. Measure this travel by causing the rod to move out when the elevating-control lever is moved to the neutral position. This measurement can be taken from the machine surface on the end of the bracket where plate *H* is fitted. If the clamping rod is not traveling between ½ and 9⁄16 inch, then either one or both of

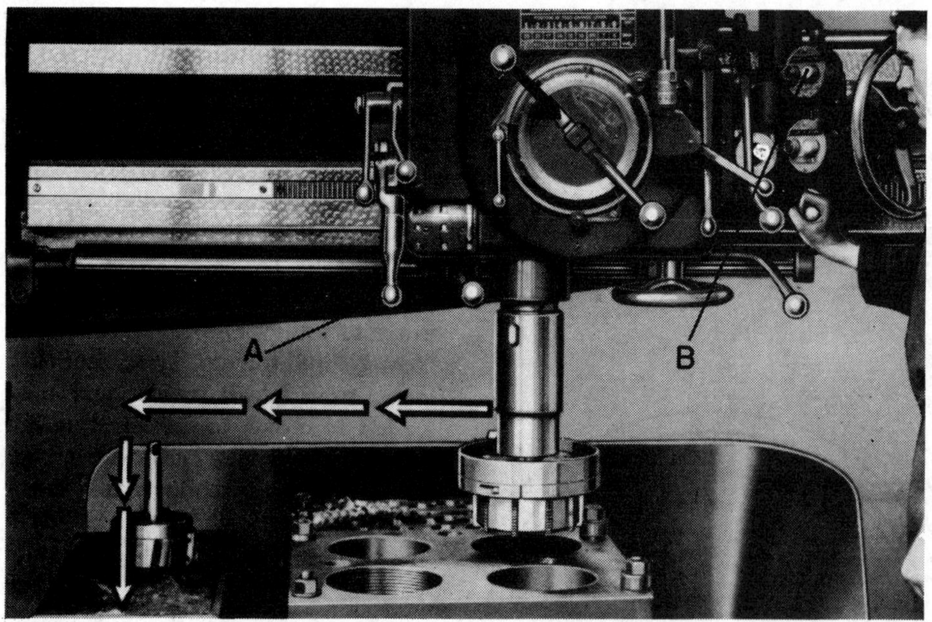

Figure 16

the arm-clamping levers are adjusted too tightly. When this happens, the nuts *G* must be loosened to permit full travel of the clamping rod.

To adjust the clamp, unclamp the arm and adjust the upper and lower adjusting nuts so that the equalizing bar on the end of the push rod is held in a vertical position when the arm is clamped. Make this adjustment between the upper and lower levers slowly, being sure that the equalizing bar remains in a vertical position to insure proper clamping at the upper and lower portions of the arm.

When adjusting the nuts slowly, clamp the arm after each adjustment. If the nuts have been tightened to a point where the push rod fails to travel its full amount, the ½ to 9⁄16 of an inch previously checked, then back off each nut one-half a turn. Check to be sure that the push rod is making its full travel and that the equalizing bar is in a vertical position when the arm is clamped. The arm is now properly adjusted. Stop the driving motor and, with the arm in a clamped position, replace plate *H* and the elevating-clutch connecting link.

Adjusting the Column Clamp. The column clamp is located at the rear of the machine and at the bottom of the column sleeve (Fig. 17). To set this clamp, have the main driving motor of the machine running, and then push the column electric-control button, mounted on the head of the machine, to the unclamped position. This will rotate the vertical clamping shaft approximately 90 degrees. On the lower end of this shaft is mounted an eccentric which rotates against the roller. In the unclamped position of the column, the high point of the eccentric is rotated away from the roller. When the column is adjusted at the factory, the nuts are properly adjusted to control the amount the sleeve cuff will open when the column is in the unclamped position.

To adjust the column clamp, be sure that it is unclamped and that the eccentric is away from the roller. Place a wrench on the end of clamp bolts *B*, and adjust the nuts until an approximate 3⁄16-inch (as indicated on the column-clamp adjusting plate) clearance between the roller and the eccentric is obtained. Care should be taken when adjusting the nuts to see that both the upper and lower nuts have approximately the same tension when clamping. Clamp the mechanism by pushing the column-clamp button on the head of the machine, and then check to see that the high point of the eccentric is against the roller and that the shaft has rotated its full distance. Care should be taken at this point to be sure that the eccentric or shaft has rotated its full distance, otherwise the arm clamp on the machine will not function properly. After the machinist is certain that the eccentric shaft has traveled its full distance, the column clamp thus adjusted should be satisfactory. If the column is not rigidly clamped for any reason, additional adjustments should be made on nuts *A* as previously described. Be sure that the high point of the eccentric will still rotate to its limit against the roller. The machine is now ready for operation.

Figure 17

Drilling Machines

Drilling machines or drill presses of various types are used in the machine shop for drilling holes in metal. Those generally used are the portable drills previously described in Chapter 3, sensitive drills, standard drill presses, floor and bench types of column drills, radial drills (traveling head drills), multiple spindle drills, gang drills and other specially designed machines.

Sensitive Drills

For very light work where it is necessary to feel the action of the drill point as it penetrates the work, the modern sensitive drill shown in Fig. 18 is used. It is used for center drilling in machine shops where a special machine for this purpose is not practicable. No gears are used to drive the spindle. The drive is entirely by belts. Nothing but a hand lever, pinion, and rack on the spindle intervenes between the hand of the operator and the drill point. The spindle is bored out to a No. 1 Morse taper. Drills with shanks of this taper can be used direct, or a drill chuck (with a shank) to fit this taper can be used.

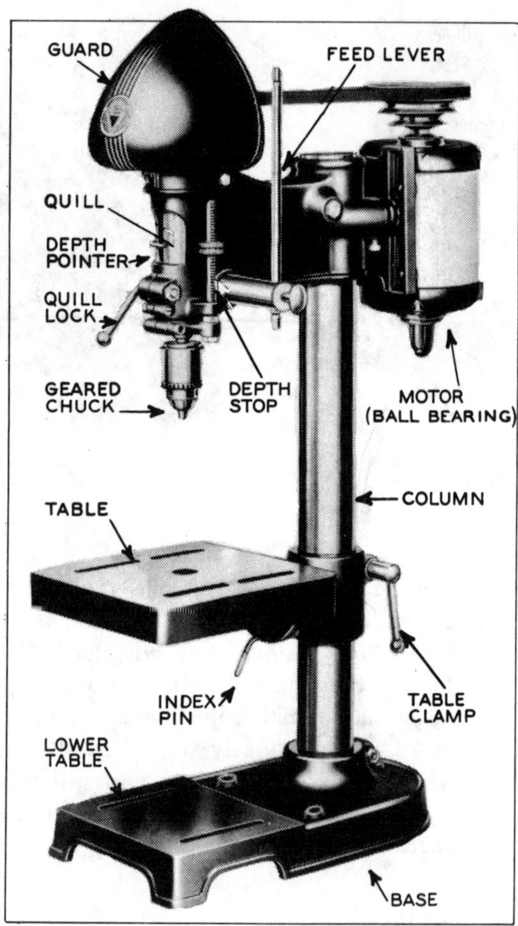

Figure 18. Sensitive bench drill press.

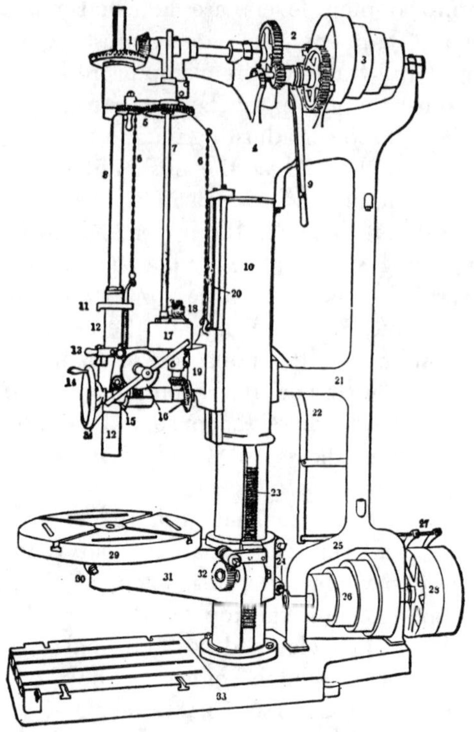

Figure 19. Parts of a drill press: (1) Main driving gears, bevel, (2) Back gears, (3) Upper cone pulley, (4) Frame, (5) Feed gears, (6) Counterweight chains, (7) Feed gear driving shaft, (8) Spindle, (9) Back gear lever, (10) Column, (11) Automatic spindle feed stop, (12) Spindle sleeve, (13) Feed trip lever, (14) Hand feed wheel, (15) Spindle quick return lever, (16) Feed gearing, (17) Feed box, (18) Feed change handle, (19) Sliding head, (20) Sliding head ways, (21) Back brace, (22) Belt shifter, (23) Rack for elevating table, (24) Table arm clamping screws, (25) Pulley stand, (26) Lower cone pulley, (27) Belt shifting fingers, (28) Tight and loose pulleys, (29) Table, (30) Table clamping screw, (31) Table arm, (32) Table elevating gear, (33) Base, (34) Ball thrust spindle bearing.

Standard Drill Press

The standard drill press (Fig. 19) is used for heavier work. It has back gearing similar to a lathe together with a power feed. The principal differences between the standard drill press and the sensitive drill are its greater weight and rigidity, the strength and size of its moving parts, the range of its spindle speeds, its power feed, and its greater power due to the use of cones and back gears.

Radial Drills

In the case of the radial drill, the drill spindle is carried in a traveling head on a horizontal arm. The head that carries the spindle can be located at any point in the range of the machine along the arm. In addition, the horizontal arm can be swung in a horizontal plane, raised or lowered, and clamped rigidly in position. These machines of the type shown in Figure 20 are used for jobs where the work is so heavy that it is more practicable to bring the drill into position by means of the horizontal arm than to move the work.

Universal Radial Drills

Although similar in design to radial drills, these machines have a traveling head that can be swung to any angle in a vertical plane. The horizontal arm can be swung in a horizontal plane, and, in addition, it can be swiveled on its axis, thus enabling the machine to drill holes at any angle (Fig. 20).

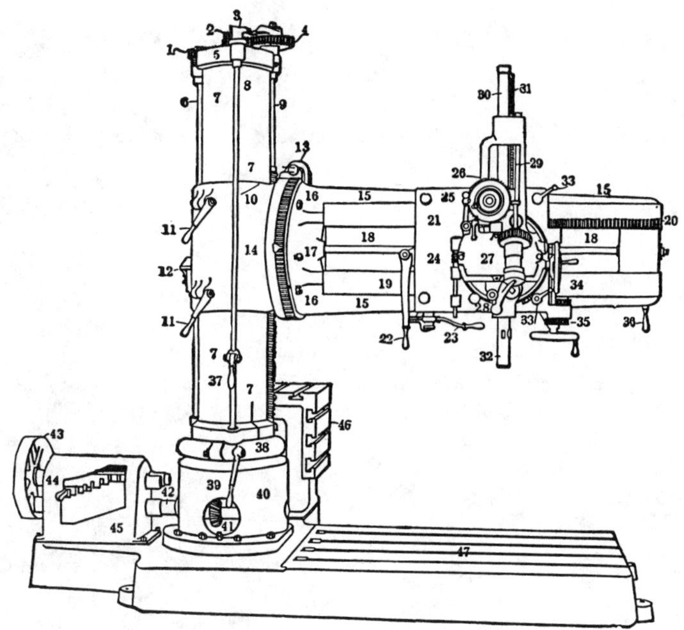

Figure 20. Parts of a Universal Radial Drill: (1) Vertical driving shaft gear, (2) Center driving shaft gear, (3) Elevating tumble plate segment, (4) Elevating screw gear, (5) Column cap, (6) Vertical driving shaft, (7) Column sleeve, (8) Elevating lever shaft, (9) Elevating screw, (10) Arm girdle, (11) Arm clamping lever, (12) Spindle driving miter gear guard, (13) Arm rotating worm, (14) Arm indicating pointer, (15) Full universal arm, (16) Arm clamping nuts, (17) Arm locating pin, (18) Arm driving shaft, (19) Arm ways, (20) Spindle head traversing rack, (21) Saddle, (22) Spindle reversing lever, (23) Back gear lever, (24) Spindle head swiveling worm, (25) Spindle feed trip lever, (26) Depth gage dial, (27) Universal spindle head, (28) Spindle quick return lever, (29) Spindle feed rack worm shaft, (30) Spindle, (31) Spindle feed rack, (32) Spindle sleeve, (33) Saddle clamping lever, (34) Spindle feed handwheel, (35) Spindle head traversing gear, (36) Arm swinging handle, (37) Arm elevating lever, (38) Clamping ring, (39) Clamping ring handle, (40) Column, (41) Main driving miter gears, (42) Driving shaft coupling, (43) Driving pulley, (44) Speed change lever, (45) Speed change case, (46) Box table, (47) Base.

Multiple Spindle Drill

The drill shown in Fig. 21 is used on production work requiring holes of a variety of sizes. Two or more spindles are driven from the same driving shaft by worms and worm gears or belts. The table is not usually adjustable except on certain types. The spindles can be moved along the cross rail (on some machines) and set the required distances apart within the range of the machine. This type of drill is used for plate work, structural iron, or light work requiring a number of holes in a straight line.

Universal Multiple Spindle Drill

This type of drill (Fig. 22) has a cluster of drill spindles held in a head that can be raised or lowered and clamped in position on the column. The spindles are driven by means of universal joints and can be set at variable distances apart. Jigs should be used when work is to be done with spindles driven by universal joints.

Gang Drills

The gang drill shown in Fig. 23 is an assembly of from two to eight single drill presses. They are mounted on a single base with an adjustable work table as shown in Fig. 23. Although combined in a single unit, the vertical adjustment of each of the heads and also the speed and feed units of each spindle can be adjusted individually and independent of one another. This type is a production machine and is used for work held in a jig that can be readily shifted from spindle to spindle as required.

Figure 21. Multiple spindle drill in operation.

means of simple rack-and-pinion gearing worked by the *feed lever*. When the feed handle is released, the quill is returned to its normal position by means of a coil spring. Adjustments are provided for locking the quill and presetting the depth to which the quill can travel.

Construction of a Drill Press

The four basic parts of the drill press are the *base, column, table,* and *head.* The term, head, is used to designate the entire working mechanism which is attached to the upper end of the column. The table of a well-designed, modern drill press can be moved up and down on the column, and it can be swung to one side or tilted if the work requires these movements. The essential part of the head is the *spindle*. This revolves in a vertical position, and is housed in ball bearings at either end of a movable sleeve called the *quill*. The quill, and hence the spindle which it carries, is moved downward by

SIZE. The name size of the drill press is expressed in terms of the diameter of the largest circular piece of work which can be drilled through the center while on the drill press table. Thus, a 14-inch circle can be center drilled on a 14-inch drill press; or, in other words, the distance from the center of the spindle to the front of the column is 7 inches. Another index to size is the distance between the end of the spindle and the table, this being much greater in floor models than in bench models. In both cases, the depth of the hole which can be drilled with one stroke of the feed lever is about 4 inches.

POWER AND SPEED. The drill press is usually fitted with cone pulleys so that selective speeds can be obtained. The average range of speeds is 590, 1,275, 2,450 and 5,000 revolutions per minute. As a general rule, a larger cone pulley is used in the machine shop on the spindle to give speeds of about 390, 745,

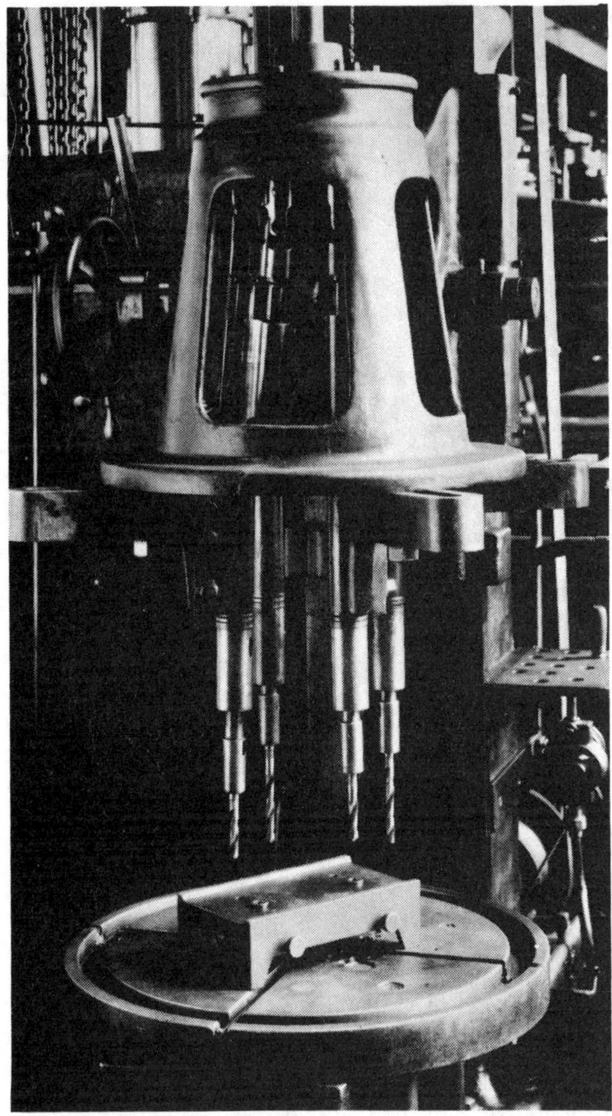

Figure 22. Universal multiple spindle drill.

1,280 and 2,050 rpm. Because the shaft stands vertically, only a sealed ball-bearing motor should be used as a power unit. For average work, a one-third horse power motor is used for all requirements, this being the approximate power required to push a ½-inch drill through high-speed steel.

Belt Tension. The belt tension is adjusted by moving the motor closer or farther from the spindle (Fig. 24), locking the motor bracket at the required position. There should be enough slack in the belt so that it will "blow out" on the slack side (Fig. 25). A belt that is too tight will cause excessive heating and vibration. On the other hand, the belt must be sufficiently tight so that it will not whip against the column when the drill press is in operation.

Figure 23. Gang drill.

Figure 24.

Inserting Drills. Figure 26 shows the method for chucking drills in a keyless chuck. The drill is held in the third and fourth fingers of the left hand, and the chuck is gripped by the thumb and first and second fingers. A pull on the belt with the right hand secures the drill in the chuck. Drills are removed in the same manner, except that the belt is pushed away from the machinist. The insertion of drills and other tools in a spindle which has a hole in the end to receive the shank of the drill is quite simple; the drill is pressed into the hole and the set screws tightened to hold it. Where taper-shank drills are used, the drill is fitted by pressing it into the tapered hole at the ends of the spindle and engaging the tang of the drill in the corresponding slot in the spindle. During the course of the work, the drill becomes tightly wedged in the tapered hole and must be driven out by means of a drift key (Fig. 27). One edge of the drift key is flat and the other round. The round edge fits against the upper round part of the slot in the spindle, and the flat edge fits against the end of the drill being removed.

Centering Table. In average drilling operations, the hole in the center of the table should be directly under the drill, so that the drill, after going through the work, will enter the hole in the table. Where

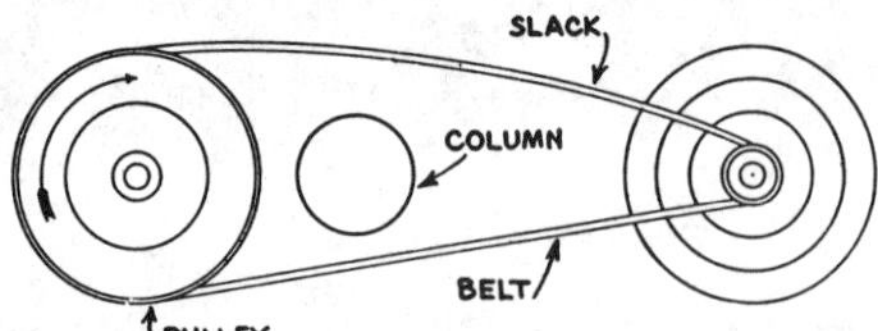

Figure 25

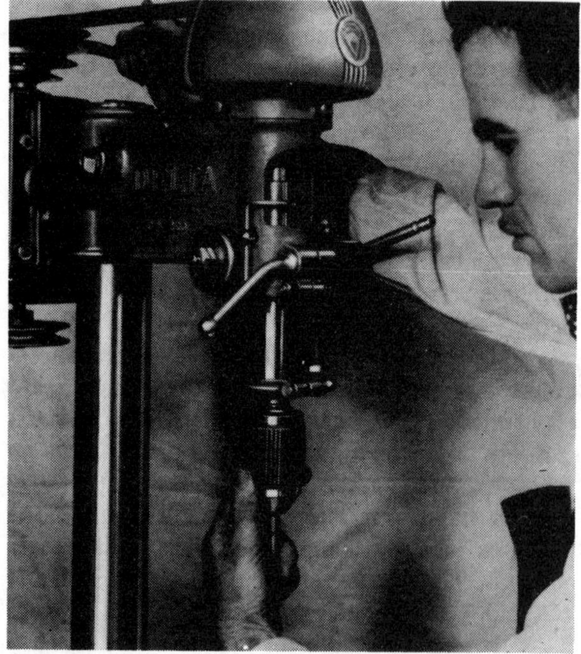
Figure 26. Inserting a drill in a keyless chuck.

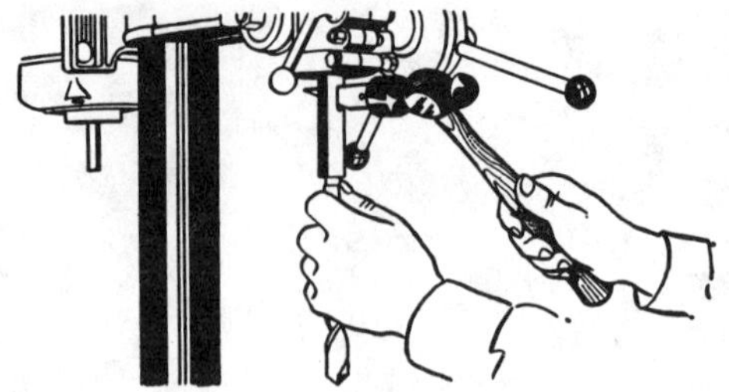
Figure 27

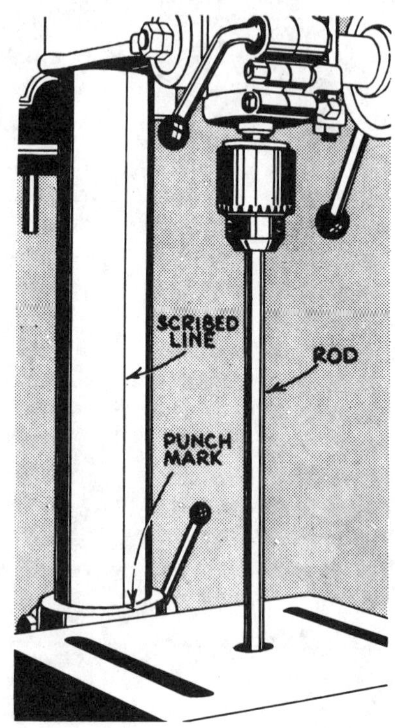

Figure 28. Scribed line centers the table.

through drilling is being done, the feed handle should always be pressed without the work in place to see that the drill enters the table opening. Another method of checking the proper table position is to scribe a line on the column. This should be done with the table properly centered by means of a suitable round rod (Fig. 28). A mark is punched on the table collar in line with the scribed line, and a similar mark is punched on the underside of the head.

Adjusting Spindle Return Spring. For the purpose of automatically returning the spindle upward after a hole has been drilled, a coil spring enclosed in a metal case is fitted to the side of the drill press. This spring is adjusted at the factory and usually requires no subsequent adjustment. If, however, the spindle fails to return to a normal position, or if the return is too violent, the tension should be adjusted accordingly (Fig. 29). This is done by loosening the locknuts which hold the case in place. They should not be completely removed, but backed off about 1/4 inch so that the case can be pulled out to clear the bosses on the head. As the case is pulled out, it must be held tightly to prevent the spring from unwinding. The case is turned clockwise to loosen the spring; counterclockwise to tighten it. When the quill is up, two full turns from a nontension position should give the proper tension. Before adjusting the spring, it is well to slack it off entirely. When this is done, the spindle should be perfectly free. It may be jammed, however, by one or both of two things; first, the bolt beneath the quill lock may be drawn too tight, thus locking the quill; secondly, the screw fastening of the pulley may be turned in so tightly as to bind the spindle. If the spindle does not move freely when released from the tension of the spring, a check should be made at these two points before tensioning. Excessive turning should be avoided when resetting the locknuts holding the spring case because this will also lock the quill.

TILTING TABLE. The table can be tilted by loosening the nut under the table. A pin, fitting through corresponding holes, provides a positive stop at both the level and the vertical positions. A hole can be drilled to locate the 45-degree position, or a punch can be made (Fig. 30) to locate this table position. Whether this is worthwhile or not will depend upon the nature of the work to be done. Where average work requires the setting of the table to various angles, to fit a scale and adjustable pointer to the underside of the table to locate these positions.

TOOLS AND ACCESSORIES USED. The tools used for drilling, reaming, boring, counterboring, countersinking, spot facing, and tapping are shown in Fig. 31. All of these operations, with the exception of tapping, can be accomplished with either a straight-shank or a tapered-shank tool. All sizes of drills and reamers under 1/2 in. are usually provided with

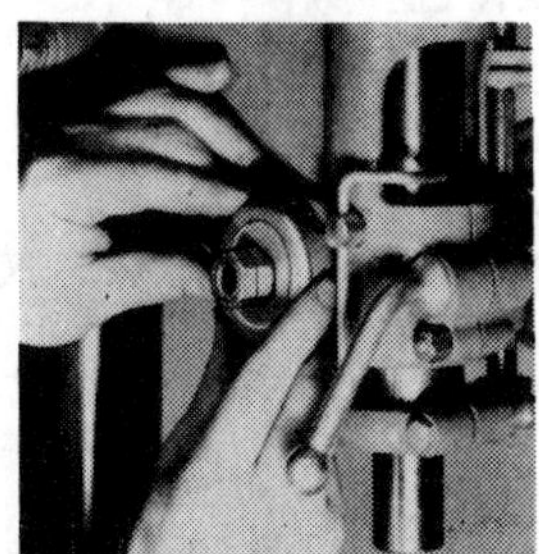

Figure 29. Adjusting spindle return spring.

Figure 30. Table tilts right and left with positive stops at level and vertical positions.

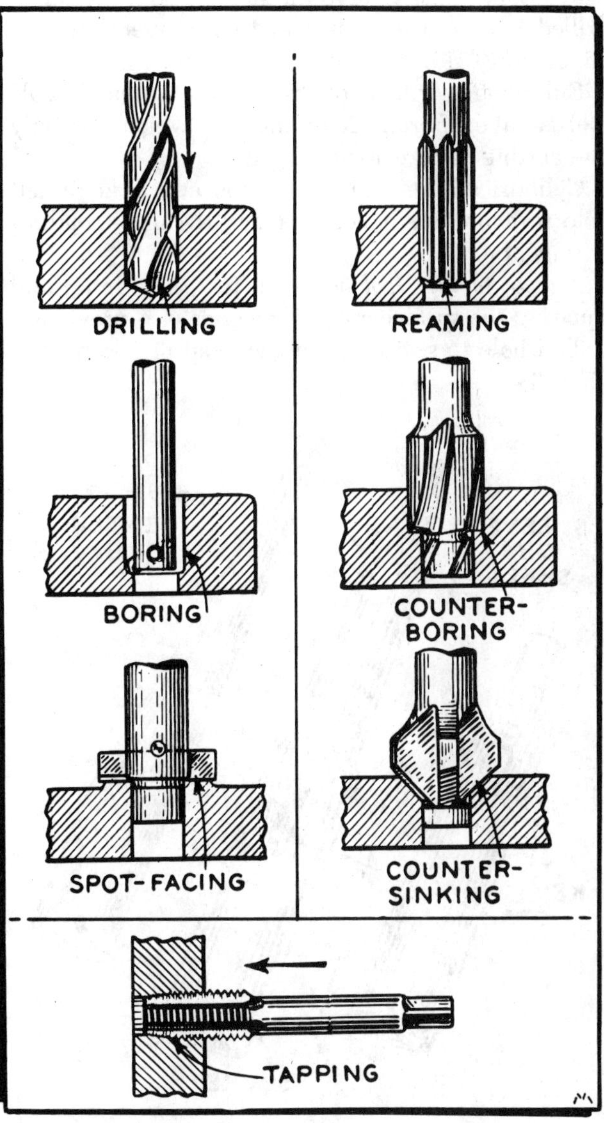

Figure 31

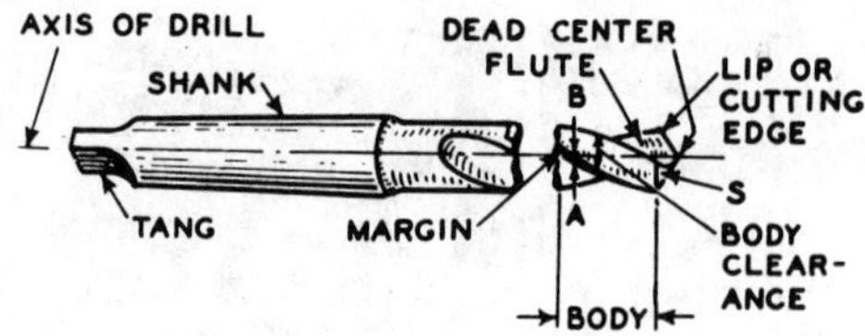

Figure 32. Parts of a twist drill.

straight shanks which can be conveniently and firmly held in the chuck of the drill press. Taper-shank tools for these small sizes are not necessary. Hold the larger sizés in the drill press by means of the taper shank.

Drilling is the operation of producing a circular hole by the removal of solid material for which the twist drill is used (Fig. 32).

Reaming consists of both sizing and finishing a drilled hole. A *reamer* is a tool with several cutting edges (Fig. 31).

Enlarging a drilled hole by means of an adjustable tool is called *boring.* A boring tool which has only one cutting edge is used (Fig. 31).

Cylindrically enlarging only the end of a drilled hole to a predetermined distance is called *counter-boring* (Fig. 31).

A *spot-facing tool* is used for smoothing and squaring the surface around the ends of a previously drilled hole to seat a nut or the head of a capscrew (Fig. 31).

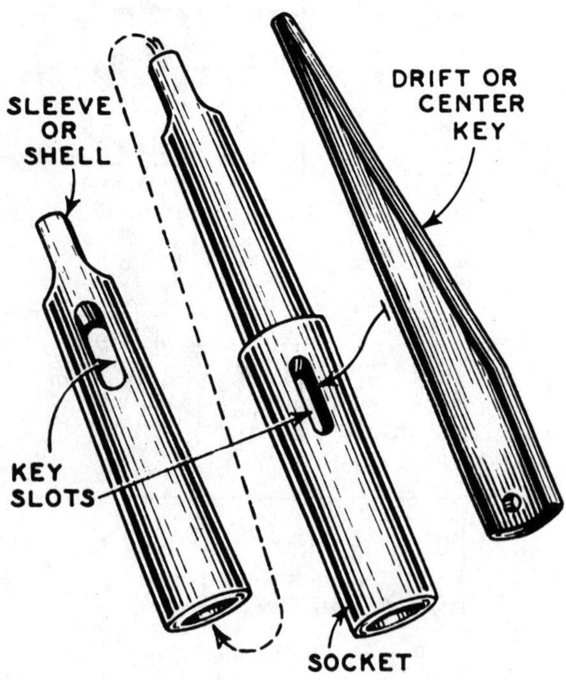

Figure 33. Drill press socket and sleeve.

The forming of internal screw threads in a previously drilled hole is called *tapping,* and the tool used is called a *tap* (Fig. 31). To use the tap, a reversible motor or a reversing accessory called a tapping attachment is necessary.

Tools with taper shanks too small to fit the taper hole in the drill-press spindle are held in a special socket. The shank of this special socket fits into the standard spindle hole. The attachment is called a *drill-press socket* and *sleeve* (Fig. 33). Note that the taper-shank socket and sleeve has a flattened end forming a tang. This tang fits into a slot at the end of the taper hole and helps drive the drill (the hold of the taper alone is not sufficient).

Holding the Work. With the exception of very heavy pieces, all work must be firmly secured to the table of the drill press to assure accuracy. If a vise is used to hold the work, it must be clamped to the table. The four types of clamps generally used are, the strap, bent, finger, and U-clamps (Fig. 34). A single clamp can safely be used to secure small work. For larger work, two or more clamps must be used (Fig. 34). The tables of all drill presses are provided with T-slots. These slots are used for the location of the necessary bolts to secure the clamp or other holding fixture used. Several types of bolts are used for various kinds of work. The square-head bolt is used for ordinary clamping purposes; however, it has to be pushed along the T-slot from one end (Fig. 35) for placement. The T-head bolt is more convenient to use. It is set in place by dropping the head lengthwise in the slot and turning it to the right. This type of bolt is especially convenient

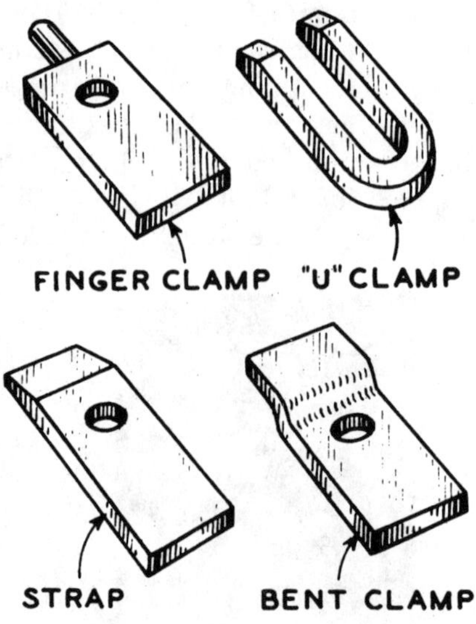

Figure 34. Types of clamp.

when it is necessary to clamp the inside of work that otherwise would have to be lifted over the bolt (Fig. 35). The tapped T-head bolt is sometimes preferred because the stud of this bolt can be removed and the head pushed along the slot under the work to the required position. Machinists usually have studs of various lengths with a few heads to be used when necessary. This practice obviates the need for a supply of different types of bolts of varying sizes.

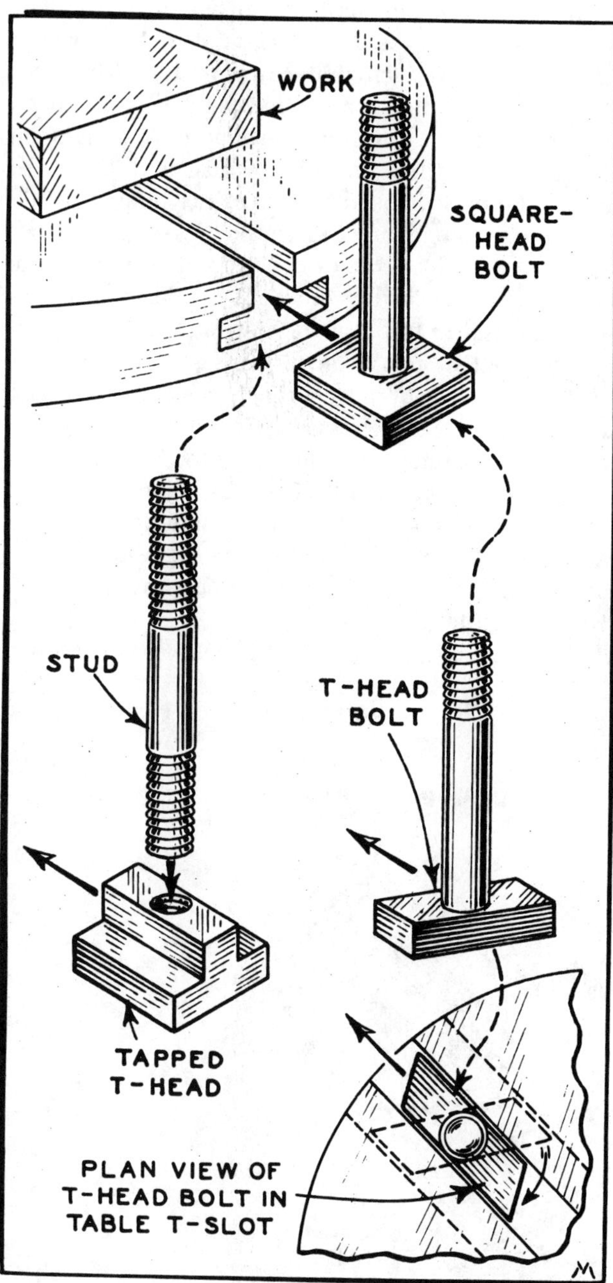

Figure 35. Clamping-bolt designs.

Figure 36. Strap and step block for clamping work.

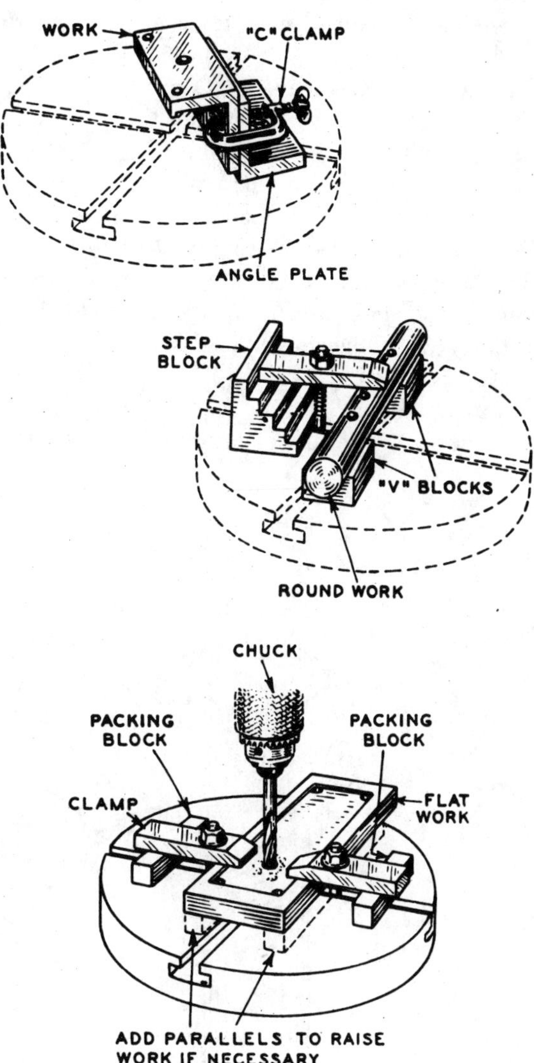

Figure 37. Clamping various shapes of work.

Step blocks are used in conjunction with bolts and clamps to secure the work to the drill-press table. These are available in various sizes and with various numbers of steps (Fig. 36). Note that the block used under the outer end of the clamp can be made of either scrap metal or hardwood. If wood is used, be sure that it is of sufficient cross section to give it the needed stiffness. Set it under the clamp with the pressure against the grain of the wood. The setups shown in these illustrations are merely suggestions; they can be altered to suit varying conditions, but the work must at all times be firmly secured. If the work is fastened directly to the table of the drill press, it must be located so that the drill or tool used will pass through one of the table openings. If the work cannot be centered over one of the openings, it must be mounted on either wood blocks or pieces of machined bar stock called *parallels* (Fig. 37).

When a light piece of metal is supported at points too far apart, it will spring under the pressure of the drill, resulting in an inaccurate hole and often a broken drill. To prevent the work from springing, use a V-support or block made of hardwood (Fig. 37). A *V-block* is used in conjunction with a step block, clamp, and bolt to secure round work for drilling; *angle plates* are used to secure odd-shaped work (Fig. 37). Other methods of securing work are shown in Figs. 38 and 39.

Layout of Work. Lay out the work prior to drilling as follows: By means of intersecting lines, show the position of the center of the hole that is to be drilled. With a center punch make a slight mark at the point of these intersections. If the work is rough, rub chalk on it. If the surface of the work has been machined or is smooth, use a coating of blue vitriol solution instead of chalk. Let it dry for a few minutes before scribing the surface. Using the punch mark as a center, scribe a circle indicating the size of the hole to be drilled with a pair of dividers. Before proceeding to drill the hole, use a larger center punch to make a larger indentation at the center.

Speeds and Feeds. Speed as applied to a drill is the speed at the circumference of the drill. This speed is called the peripheral speed and is the speed at which the drill would travel if it were laid on its side and rolled. In other words, a drill with a stated peripheral speed of 30 feet per minute would roll 30 feet per minute. As generally used, therefore, speed of a drill does not refer to rotation per minute unless it is specifically stated. As a rule, a drill does not pull itself into the work, but requires a constant pressure of feed to advance it. This advance is always measured in fractions of an inch per revolution and is called feed. Feed pressure is the pressure required in order to maintain the necessary feed.

The correct speed and feed are dependent upon so many conditions that it is impossible to give hard-and-fast rules regarding them. The suggestions given should be considered only as a guide and as a point from which to start operations.

Starting Speeds. To start a drill, bring it down

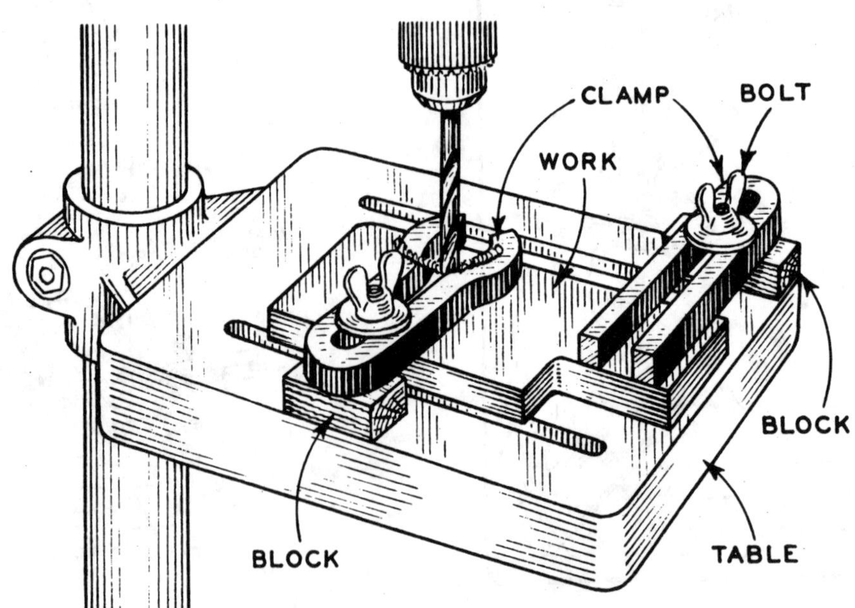

Figure 38. Using two types of strap clamp.

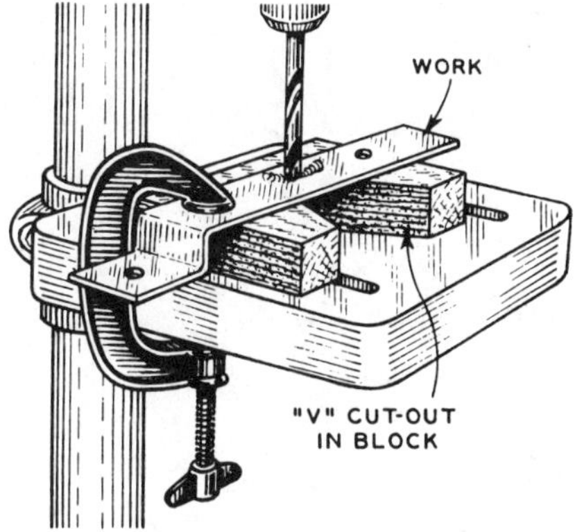

Figure 39. Support with cut-out eliminates spring in drilling thin material.

to the work by hand feed until it centers itself in the work; then and only then, apply the power feed. Composition and hardness of material, the depth of hole required, the lubricant used, the type of machine used, the condition of the machine, the setup, the quality of the point grinding, the quality of the holes desired, and many other items have a distinct influence on the speeds and feeds required. The correct speeds and feeds should be determined by good judgment and trial in each instance.

Suggested Speeds for High-Speed Drills

Metal	*Speed in rpm*
Aluminum and its alloys	200–300
Brass and bronze, ordinary	200–300
Cast iron, soft	100–150
Cast iron, hard	70–100
Malleable iron	80–90
Magnesium and its alloys	250–400
Monel metal	40–50
Steel, annealed	60–70
Steel forgings	50–60
Steel alloy	50–70

If carbon steel drills instead of high-speed drills are used, they should be run at half the speeds given in the table.

When the extreme outer corners of the cutting edges wear away too rapidly, it is evidence of too much speed. High speed in cast iron tends to wear away the margin of the drill. The maximum speed suggested for carbon drills in cast iron is 50 feet per minute peripheral speed.

Starting Feeds. The starting feed is largely governed by the size of the drill used and the material to be drilled. The general rule is to use a feed of .001 in. to .002 in. per revolution for drills smaller than 1/8 in.; .002 in. to .004 in. for drills 1/8 in. to 1/4 in.; .004 in. to .007 in. for drills 1/4 in. to 1/2 in.; .007 in. to .015 in. for drills 1/2 in. to 1 in.; and .015 in. to .025 in. for drills larger than 1 inch. Start the drill with a moderate speed and a moderate feed. Increase either one or both after careful observation of the condition of the drill. The following suggestions should be carefully observed. If the drill chips out at the cutting edge, it indicates either too heavy a feed or too much lip clearance. Before deciding that it is too heavy a feed, check the lip clearance of the drill. A drill that splits up the web may have been given too much feed for the amount of lip clearance. Either decrease the feed or increase the lip clearance, or both.

Failure to give sufficient lip clearance at the center of a drill will also cause it to split up the web. On the other hand, too much lip clearance at the center (or at any other point on the lip) will cause the lip to chip. Make certain that the drill has been properly ground. If it has been properly ground, then decrease the feed.

It is better to err on the side of too much speed than on the side of too much feed. This is true for all metals with the exception of cast iron. The nature of this material permits an unusually heavy feed. Speed can be increased to the point where the outside corners of the drill commence to show signs of wearing away. The speed should then be slightly reduced.

Lubrication for Drilling. Lubricants called coolants are used to cool both the edges of the tool and the work that is being machined. As large a volume as possible of the coolant should be directed onto the cutting edges of the tool and allowed to flow onto and around the work (Fig. 40). Proper lubrication aids in chip clearance and improves the finish of the hole.

Suggested lubricants for various metals are:

Aluminum and its alloys—Soluble oil, kerosene, and lard-oil compound; kerosene and soluble oil mixtures.
Brass—Soluble oil, kerosene, and lard compound; light nonviscous neutral oil.
Copper—Soluble oil.
Cast iron—No lubricant required.
Malleable iron—Soluble oil.
Monel metal—Soluble oil; mineral oil.
Steel (ordinary)—Soluble oil; mineral oil.
Steel (very hard)—Soluble oil; turpentine.

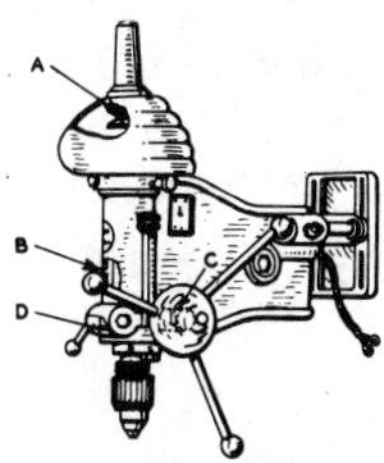

Figure 40. Lubrication points on drill-press head.

Chapter 13

Milling Machines

The milling machine produces one or more machined surfaces on a piece of material—the work piece—by means of one or more rotary milling cutters. The work piece is usually held securely on the work table of the machine or in a fixture or jig that is clamped to the table. It is fed to the cutter or cutters by the motions of the table, or the work and cutters may both be moved in a definite relation to each other.

The existing types of milling machines are very numerous and their designs merge into one another to a great extent. However, the most common are the knee-and-column (including vertical spindle) (Fig. 1), manufacturing, automatic, duplex, planer and drum types, together with special and single-purpose machines. We shall only describe the knee-and-column and manufacturing types because they are the most common. In general, the same principles apply to all types. Figure 2 illustrates the parts of a typical milling machine.

Knee-and-Column Milling Machines

The knee-and-column milling machine has a rigid column, in which is mounted the spindle, and a table supported by a vertically adjustable knee (Fig. 2). Provision is made for horizontal movement of the table both parallel and at right angles to the axis of the spindle. The combination of vertical, transverse, and longitudinal table movements is found only in the knee-and-column machine, thus giving this type advantages on general milling work. Plain, universal, vertical spindle, and some automatic machines are of this design.

Manufacturing Milling Machines

The manufacturing milling machine is characterized by fixed table height (Fig. 3). Vertical adjustment is obtained by an adjustable spindle head, and only slight transverse movement is provided. These machines are noteworthy for their rugged construction and the ease with which they are operated. "Lincoln" type, duplex, and some automatic milling machines come under this classification.

The milling machine shown in Fig. 3 has a complete electrical control for all table feed, speed and spindle movements which aids in exceptional rapidity and precision. The unusual range of feeds and speeds

Figure 1. Vertical knee-and-column type milling machine.

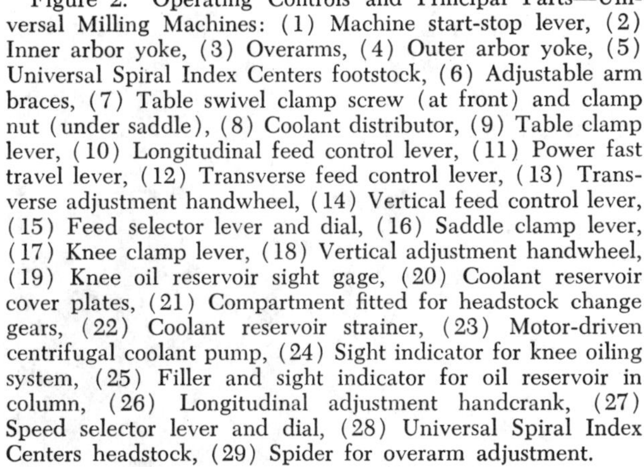
Figure 2. Operating Controls and Principal Parts—Universal Milling Machines: (1) Machine start-stop lever, (2) Inner arbor yoke, (3) Overarms, (4) Outer arbor yoke, (5) Universal Spiral Index Centers footstock, (6) Adjustable arm braces, (7) Table swivel clamp screw (at front) and clamp nut (under saddle), (8) Coolant distributor, (9) Table clamp lever, (10) Longitudinal feed control lever, (11) Power fast travel lever, (12) Transverse feed control lever, (13) Transverse adjustment handwheel, (14) Vertical feed control lever, (15) Feed selector lever and dial, (16) Saddle clamp lever, (17) Knee clamp lever, (18) Vertical adjustment handwheel, (19) Knee oil reservoir sight gage, (20) Coolant reservoir cover plates, (21) Compartment fitted for headstock change gears, (22) Coolant reservoir strainer, (23) Motor-driven centrifugal coolant pump, (24) Sight indicator for knee oiling system, (25) Filler and sight indicator for oil reservoir in column, (26) Longitudinal adjustment handcrank, (27) Speed selector lever and dial, (28) Universal Spiral Index Centers headstock, (29) Spider for overarm adjustment.

Figure 3

available provides for a wide variety of work, and an automatic table reverse makes it possible to rough and finish mill at one chucking by the use of dual feed rates if this is desired. This machine is adapted for climb milling as well as conventional milling.

Size and Power Rating of Milling Machines

The term "size" is generally used in referring to characteristic dimensions of certain main elements of milling machines, their range of movement, if intended to be movable, and the power rating of the main driving motor of the machine.

Thus the range of movement or maximum travel in the longitudinal, cross, and vertical directions of the table, saddle, and knee, respectively, of a knee-and-column machine (Fig. 4) and the corresponding movements of a manufacturing machine (Fig. 5) determine the physical dimensions of the machine and its capacity for doing work. An increase in the size of the machine is determined not only by the need for accommodating larger work, but also by the need for more power.

Size is particularly important in the case of *standard milling machines* because they are designed to handle a variety of work. Rather than fit the machine to the job, the work is assigned to the machine in relation to its capacity.

The power of the driving motor is selected in relation to the probable maximum cutting capacity required of the machine. The power is the same in all machines of a given size.

In the very low range of spindle rpm which is suitable for heavy milling with large-diameter high-speed steel milling cutters, the power of the driving electric motor is automatically reduced to half that

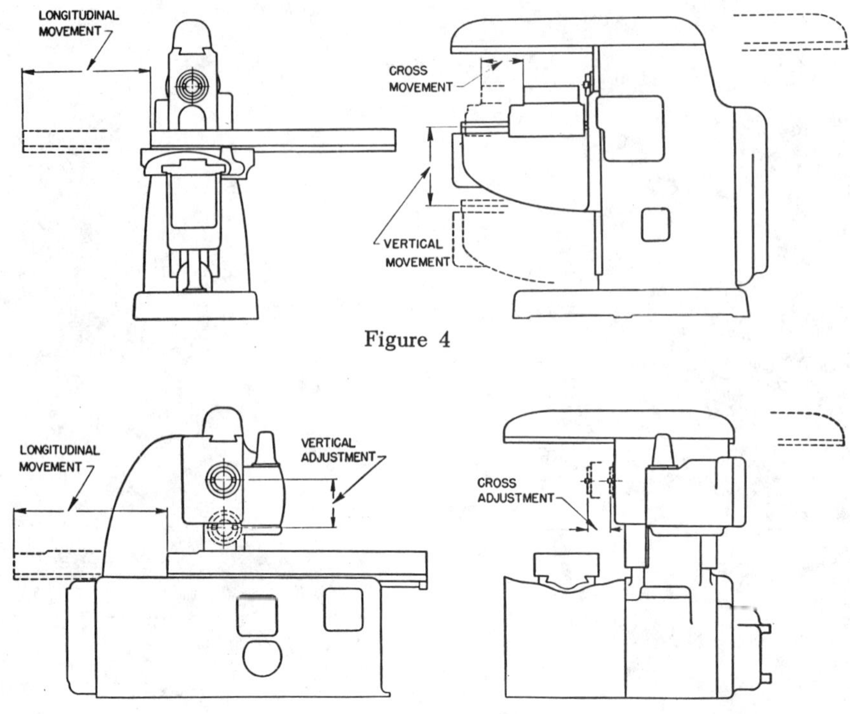

Figure 4

Figure 5

in the higher range of spindle rpm. This range is that commonly used in high-speed milling with carbide-tipped cutters, and the higher power available permits taking advantage of the high productivity of these cutters.

There is no definite size for *special milling machines* which are designed for a specific job or operation. The design of the machine, its range, and the power rating of the main driving motor are determined by the requirements of the job.

Milling Machine Accessories

Attachments, fixtures, and arbors are removable, supplementary devices or accessories made for the purpose of increasing the usefulness and productivity of the milling machine.

Fixtures are attached to the table of the milling machine and are intended for quantity production. They are designed chiefly for holding a specific piece of work while it is being machined, and are classified as special equipment. The design varies in relation to the type of work, the method of holding it, and the method of machining employed.

Attachments are of a more general and standard character. They are designed for application to the spindle, overarm, table, and various slides of milling machines, particularly those of the standard type.

Figure 6 shows the difference between a fixture and an attachment. The work is held in a *fixture*

Figure 6

designed for the purpose, and the fixture, in turn, is bolted on the rotary table of a circular milling *attachment*.

Attachments are divided into two classes, *standard* and *special*.

Special attachments are made for the purpose of adapting a standard milling machine to special milling operations in quantity production. They are used on a machine for an indefinite period of time which may be determined by a change in the design of the part or the method of machining it. When they are removed, the machine can be used for general milling work or, by the use of different special or standard attachments, it can be adapted to perform other milling operations.

Standard attachments are easily removable units for either temporary or semi-permanent application to standard milling machines. The large variety of standard attachments are as follows:

1. Attachments which serve as auxiliary spindle units, mostly connected to and driven by the main spindle of the machine.
2. Attachments for holding the workpiece on the table. Some are stationary; others are capable of imparting additional movements, such as rotary motion or indexing the workpiece held between centers.
3. Attachments for mounting the cutter (arbors, collets, adapters, and others).
4. Attachments for precision measuring the adjustment of various slides of the machine.

Standard attachments are of particular value in toolroom work where a milling machine may be required to perform a variety of machining operations such as the following: cutting helical and spur gear teeth; profiling work on dies, models, and patterns; and other work requiring frequent changes in setup and operation. Standard attachments also find their place in quantity production where they may solve a manufacturing problem quickly and without recourse to special equipment. They reduce, to a large extent, the necessity for having a variety of different or special type machines by providing the means for handling different classes of work and work involving a change in method on a single milling machine.

Heavy Vertical-Milling Attachment. By means of a vertical-milling attachment (Fig. 7) mounted on the face of the column and supported from the overarm, plain and universal types of milling machines can be adapted to operations which are ordinarily done on vertical machines. The speed of the vertical spindle is usually the same as that of the machine spindle. Angular surfaces can be milled by swinging the vertical head in a plane parallel to the face of the column and clamping it at any required angle between zero and 45 degrees on either side of the vertical position.

Figure 7

High-Speed Universal Milling Attachment. The high-speed universal milling attachment (Fig. 8) is used on plain and universal types of milling machines to adapt them to perform milling operations on surfaces in a wide range of positions.

The cutter may be placed in a vertical or horizontal position and at any angle in the plane parallel to the face of the column, but only within 45 degrees on either side of the vertical position in the plane at right angles to the face of the column, or a combination of the two. A quill hand-feed device provides adjustment for the cutter. The wide range of the cutter adjustment is obtained through the compound swivel on which the spindle of this attachment is mounted. The attachment, supported by the overarm, has a limited lengthwise adjustment, and its spindle is driven by the machine spindle. The attachment spindle operates at a higher speed than the machine spindle, and is designed for receiving small- to medium-size cutters such as are used in performing key-seating, die-sinking, and other operations of similar nature.

Unversal Spiral Milling Attachment. The universal spiral milling attachment (Fig. 9) can be

Figure 8

mounted on horizontal milling machines of both the plain and universal types. As in the high-speed universal milling attachment, the spindlehead is mounted on a compound swivel which permits swinging the spindle in both the horizontal and vertical planes. It can then be clamped in the angular positions required by the job. The speeds of the attachment spindle are the same as those of the machine on which it is being used. When a universal spiral milling attachment is used in conjunction with a dividing head on a plain milling machine, this machine can handle milling operations similar to those performed on a universal milling machine. When a universal spiral milling attachment is applied to a universal milling machine, it will make possible the milling of helices having a helix angle of greater than 45 degrees on parts such as gears, worms, screw threads, spiral milling cutters, and twist drills.

Slotting Attachment. Mounted on the column face of a plain or universal milling machine, the slotting attachment (Fig. 10) converts the rotary motion of the spindle into the reciprocating motion of the tool slide. Thus a milling machine can be adapted to perform work with a single-point cutting tool, similar to a slotter, as in the cutting of keyways. The slotting attachment is valuable when a slotter is not available and on work for which a key-seating machine is not adaptable. The tool slide can be set at any angle through 360 degrees; the stroke from zero to four inches.

Universal Dividing Head. The universal dividing head is an exceptionally versatile and accurate indexing attachment which may be employed to support the work between centers (Fig. 11), or hold it

Figure 9. Universal spiral milling attachment set up for milling a large helix angle.

Figure 10. Application of a slotting attachment.

in a chuck. It has an indexing arrangement as well as a gearing which is connected to the driving mechanism for the purpose of imparting such rotary motion to the work as is required when cutting helices. The dividing head is mounted on the milling machine table at the operator's right when facing the machine.

The work may be indexed by any required portion of a revolution, thus providing a means to space notches and grooves on its periphery. These may be either straight (parallel to the axis of the work), as in the milling of spur-gear teeth, or at an angle, as in the flutes of twist drill and helical mills, helical and bevel-gear teeth, cams, and a variety of similar work.

Figure 11. Dividing head mounted on the table of a universal milling machine set up for milling helical gear teeth.

Figure 12. Circular milling attachment.

Accurate spacing is obtained by means of a side index plate mounted on the dividing head, as shown in Fig. 11. This plate is made with a number of holes arranged in circles and equally spaced in each circle. Each successive circle contains a larger number of spacing holes; in addition, interchangeable plates with different arrangements of holes make it possible to obtain a wide range of indexing. Direct indexing for a low number of divisions is obtained by using the front index plate.

Circular Milling Attachment. The circular milling attachment (Fig. 12) can be used on the plain, universal, and vertical types of milling machines. It provides rotary motion to the workpiece in addition to the longitudinal, cross, and vertical motions already available in these machines. It is bolted to the top of the table of the machine, and can be driven either by hand or by power from the table-feed drive shaft. This attachment mounted on the table of a milling machine enables the operator to produce any profile—straight or curved—by using the table and cross feed of the machine and the rotary motion of the attachment. It is also employed in continuous milling operations by using the rotary motion of the table as in the rotary type of milling machine. This feature is valuable in surface milling large numbers of small identical parts.

An indexing attachment can be used in place of the hand crank for work requiring accurately spaced holes, slots, or grooves.

Milling Machine Vises. Vises are used for holding the workpiece while it is being milled. They are bolted to the top of the milling machine table, and are provided with means to locate them properly with respect to the axis of the spindle. Vises are made in three styles known as the plain, the swivel, and the toolmaker universal.

The *plain vise* (Fig. 13) is the simplest of its kind. By means of tongues bolted on the under surface of the vise and engaging the T-slots of the table, it can be set with the jaws parallel to or at right angles to the axis of the machine spindle.

The *swivel vise* is identical to the plain vise with the exception of a swivel base under the vise body, graduated in degrees, on which the vise can be swiveled in a horizontal plane. The swivel vise is used for milling surfaces and boring holes at a given angle with respect to another surface or hole.

Like the swivel vise, the toolmaker universal vise is mounted on a base for swiveling 360 degrees in a horizontal plane. In addition, however, it is hinged for tilting in a vertical position, and may be clamped

Figure 13. Application of a plain vise bolted to the table of a plain milling machine.

at any angle between zero and 90 degrees.

ARBORS, ADAPTERS, AND COLLETS FOR MILLING CUTTERS. Milling cutters are mounted on the spindlenose of a milling machine, or on arbors, adapters, or collets held in the spindlenose. These accessories are provided with various taper sizes for insertion in the milling machine spindlenose. The main function of adapters and collets is to extend the range of sizes and types of tapers that can be used in a milling machine having a hole of a given taper size in the spindlenose.

There also are *quick-change collets* and *shell-end mill arbors* which, used in conjunction with a special clamping assembly known as the *quick-change adapter* mounted on the spindlenose, make it possible to perform a variety of operations such as drilling, milling, and boring without changing the setup of the part being machined.

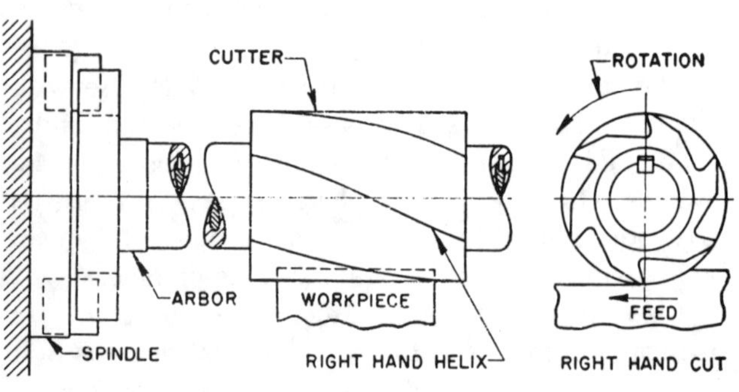

Figure 14

Milling Cutters

The cutting tool used in milling machines is known as the *milling cutter*. It usually has a cylindrical body, rotating on its axis, and provided on the periphery with equally spaced teeth which engage intermittently with the workpiece.

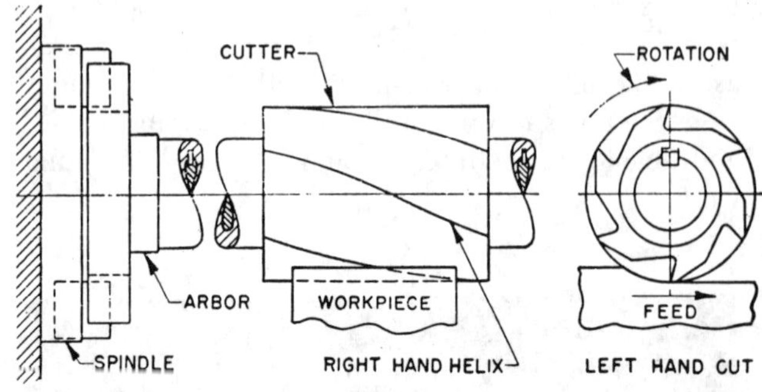

Figure 15

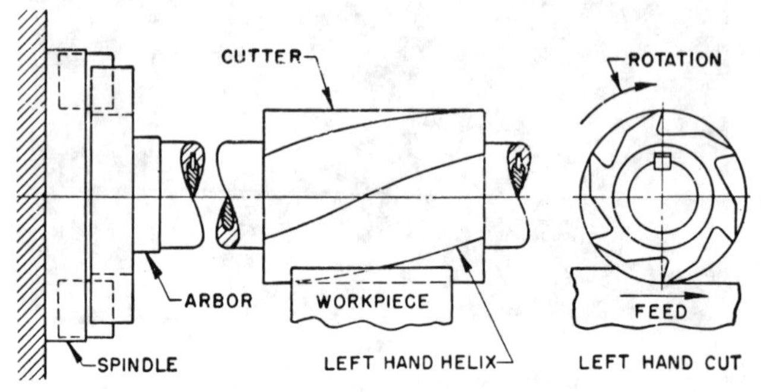

Figure 16

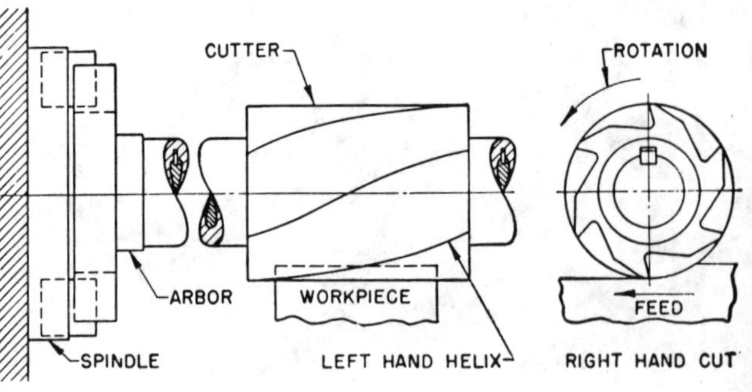

Figure 17

Classification, Types, and Uses. Milling cutters are made in many sizes and types for milling both regular and irregular shaped surfaces on the workpiece. They are classified as follows:

1. They may be of the *solid type,* with teeth and body integral; or of the *inserted-tooth type,* with removable teeth held and rigidly locked in slots or suitable holes in the body.
2. The teeth may be *straight* (parallel to the axis of rotation) or at an *angle* known as the helix angle.
3. Milling cutters may be made with a *center hole* for mounting on an arbor; integral with or mounted on a *shank* for insertion in the end of the milling machine spindle; or with the back *recessed* for bolting directly on the spindlenose.
4. They may be made for either right- or left-hand *rotation,* and with either right- or left-hand *helix.*

The *hand* of a milling cutter refers to the direction of cutting, and may be determined by looking at the front end of the cutter when mounted on the spindle. A *right-hand* cutter requires counter-clockwise spindle rotation; a *left-hand* cutter requires clockwise spindle rotation. These conditions are termed, *right-hand cut* and *left-hand cut.*

The *hand of the helix* may be determined by looking at the teeth or flutes from the cutter end. If they lead to the right, the helix is *right hand* (Figs. 14 and 15); if they lead to the left, the helix is *left hand* (Figs. 16 and 17).

Arbor-type milling cutters are made with either right or left helix. They can be mounted for either right- or left-hand cutting regardless of the direction of the helix. Reversing the position of the cutter on the arbor will change the direction of cutting to the opposite hand. Arbor-type milling cutters having straight teeth can also be mounted for cutting in either direction.

In the *shank-mounted cutters* such as end mills, the hand of the helix and the hand of the cut can easily be determined by the operator by placing the shank of the cutter against his body and noticing whether the helix and the cutting edge lead toward the right or the left. If the helix leads toward the right, the helix is right hand; if it leads toward the left, it is a left-hand helix. Similarly, if the cutting edge is on the right-hand side, the cutter is right hand; if the cutting edge is on the left side, the cutter is left hand.

The same method can be used with *face mills* and *shell-end mills,* holding the back of the cutter against the body and noticing whether the teeth and the cutting edge lead toward the right or the left.

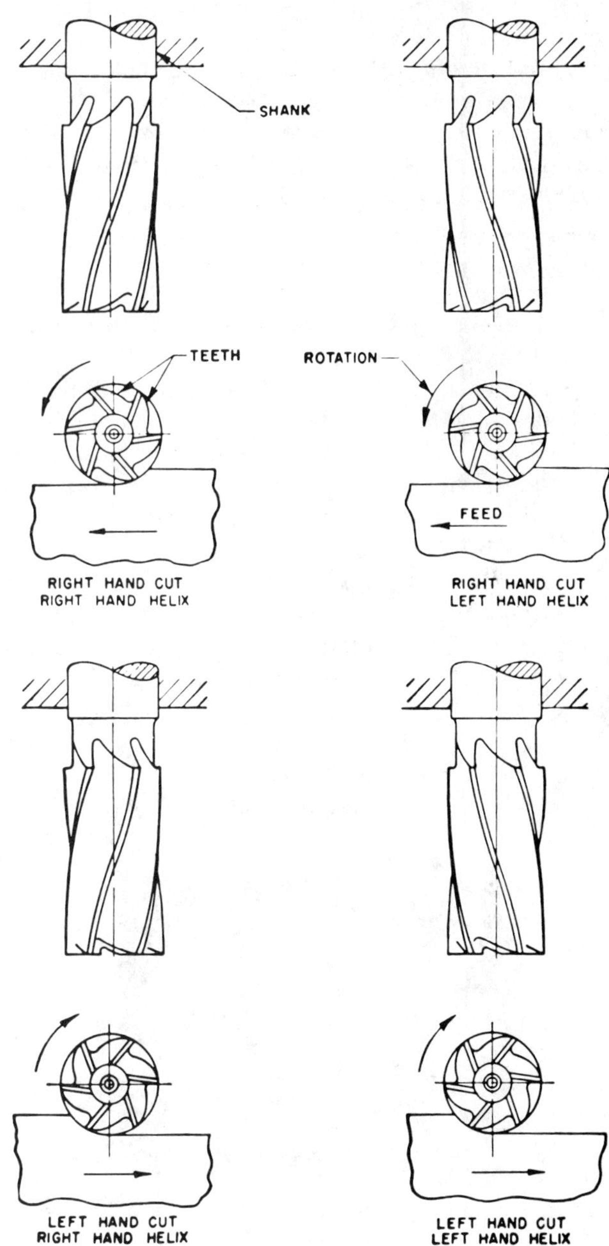

Figure 18

The four combinations of right- and left-hand helix and right- and left-hand cut possible in shank-mounted milling cutters are illustrated in Fig. 18.

Cutters fall into two classifications: *Standard milling cutters* are those which conform to dimensions approved by the American Standards Association. The dimensional standards, relating chiefly to cutter diameter and width, size of center hole, and width and depth of keyway, have been adopted by cutter manufacturers.

Special milling cutters are those designed for work on special jobs. They may or may not have standard dimensions and do not conform to any generally accepted standard; therefore they will not be discussed in this book.

Standard Milling Cutters

The many types of standard milling cutters may be classified as follows:

PLAIN MILLING CUTTERS. Plain milling cutters are cylindrical cutters with teeth on the circumferential surface only, and are used to produce flat surfaces parallel to the axis of the spindle. They are made in a wide variety of diameters and widths for "slab milling" operations, and may be grouped as follows:

Light-duty plain milling cutters of less than ¾ in. in width generally have straight teeth (parallel to the axis of the cutter; those over ¾ in. in width have the teeth on approximately a 25-degree helix angle. These cutters are useful in taking light cuts, but they have too many teeth and insufficient chip space for average milling work.

Heavy-duty plain milling cutters (Fig. 19) are made in larger widths only. The teeth have a helix angle greater than 25 degrees and ranging up to about 45 degrees. Heavy-duty cutters have fewer teeth than the light-duty type and also are termed "coarsetooth milling cutters."

Figure 19. Milling of forged steel part with a heavy-duty plain milling cutter.

As the name indicates, heavy-duty plain milling cutters are designed for applications in which a considerable amount of stock must be removed. Because fewer teeth are used, the spacing is wider, providing ample chip space and permitting greater support to the cutting edge.

Plain milling cutters with helix angles of 45 to 60 degrees and higher are called *helical mills*. They may be of either the hole type or the shank type. Shank-type helical mills (Fig. 20) can be used to advantage for milling intermittent surfaces in contour and profile milling. Shank-type helical mills with pilot (Fig. 21) are commonly used for milling elongated slots through the workpiece and also for milling wide surfaces.

The helical mill is efficient for taking light cuts on soft steel or brass, but is not as efficient as the plain milling cutter for deep cuts in slab milling, although it provides smooth cutter action and a good finish on the milled surface. This is a particularly desirable characteristic which makes shank-type helical mills valuable in profile milling.

END MILLING CUTTERS. End milling cutters are solid-type cutters with teeth on the circumferential surface and one end. All styles except the shell end mill have a straight or tapered shank for mounting and driving. They are used for facing, profiling, and end milling operations. End milling cutters are made in three general types, grouped as follows:

End mills (Figs. 22 and 23) are multiple-tooth cutters with straight or helical teeth like those in plain and helical mills. They are used for light operations such as the milling of slots and the profiling and facing of narrow surfaces.

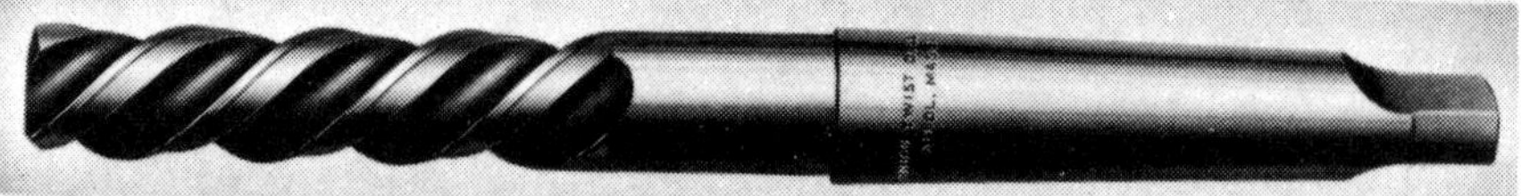

Figure 20. Standard shank-type helical mill.

Figure 21. Standard shank-type helical mill with pilot.

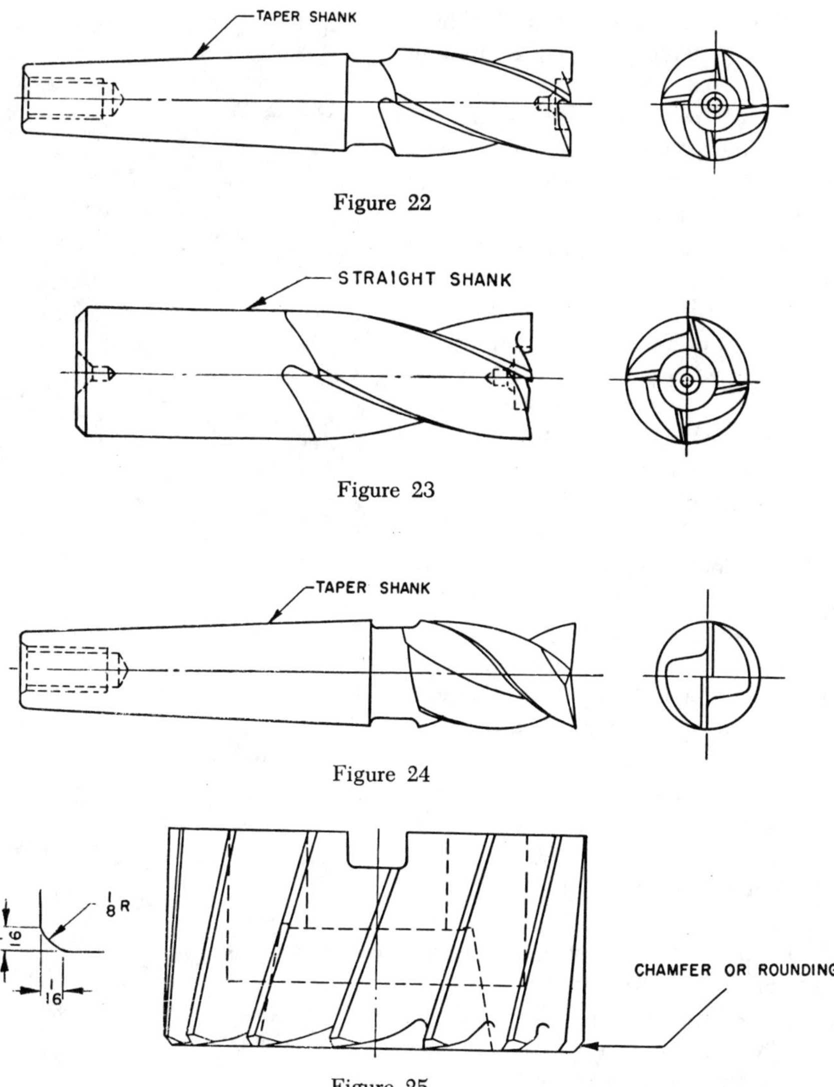

Figure 22

Figure 23

Figure 24

Figure 25

Two-lip end mills (Fig. 24), also known as *slotting mills,* have two straight or helical teeth on the circumferential surface and end teeth cut to the center. In milling grooves, this type of cutter can be sunk into the material like a drill and then fed lengthwise in the groove. A depth of cut equal to the diameter of the mill usually can be taken from solid stock.

Shell end mills (Fig. 25) are solid multiple-tooth cutters without shanks having teeth on the face and periphery. The face is recessed to receive a screwhead or nut for mounting the cutter on a separate shank or *stub arbor* which is driven by keys on the spindlenose. Driving slots across the back of the cutter are engaged by drive collar keys on the arbor.

The teeth are generally helical in modern shell end mills, with either a right- or left-hand helix. They may also be cut straight (parallel to the axis of rotation), although more efficient and satisfactory operation is obtained with the helical tooth form. Shell end mills are used to advantage in face milling operations requiring the milling of two surfaces at right angles to each other.

Side Milling Cutters. Side milling cutters have teeth on one or both sides as well as on the periphery, and are made for mounting on an arbor. The various types are classified as follows:

Half-side milling cutters are used in face milling operations and other applications where only one side of the cutter is required. Half-side mills have either straight or helical teeth on the circumference and one side only. The periphery of the cutter does the actual cutting and the face does the sizing and finishing. The length of the side teeth on half-side mills is greater than on the standard side mill. These cutters are efficient for taking heavy side milling cuts.

Slide mills (Fig. 26) are comparatively narrow cylindrical cutters having teeth on both sides as well as on the periphery; they are used for cutting slots and in face milling operations.

Straddle milling consists of milling the right- and left-hand parallel sides of the workpiece simultaneously. Such operations can be performed with either the half-side or the side milling cutters mounted together on an arbor with one or more spacers between them. When using the half-side mills, it is necessary to use one right- and one left-hand cutter. Cutters used in this way are referred to as "straddle mills."

Interlocking slotting cutters consist of two cutters similar to the side mills but made as a unit with interlocking teeth. Interlocking cutters are used in preference to staggered-tooth cutters because of their flexibility. The cutters can be adjusted to the required width by interposing collars or shims. This also makes it possible to compensate for the changed dimensions resulting from wear and sharpening. Interlocking cutters are effective in accurately sizing slots of shallow or medium depth. If the slots being milled are narrow, however, and the cutters used are consequently thin, the tendency of the cutters to "close in" will result in an undesirable change in the width of the slot.

Staggered-tooth milling cutters (Fig. 27) are narrow cylindrical cutters with alternate teeth of opposite helix angle. To reduce the possibility of dragging or scoring the work, the side portion of the teeth is relieved by leaving a narrow land near the edge of the teeth. Staggered-tooth milling cutters are used for keyway and other slotting operations. They have a free cutting action, even at high speeds and feeds, which makes them effective in milling deep slots. However, their use is limited to slots of narrow width, and the interlocking type of cutter is to be preferred for wide slots. In the solid-type staggered-tooth cutter, the width will change through wear and with each resharpening, thus altering the width of the slot.

METAL SLITTING SAWS. Metal slitting saws are thin, plain milling cutters with the side slightly relieved or "dished" to prevent rubbing or binding. They usually have more teeth for a given diameter than plain milling cutters, and are made in widths from 1/32 to 3/16 in. Saws are used for cutting-off operations and in milling deep, narrow slots.

For heavy sawing in steel, metal slitting saws are

Figure 26. Slide milling cutters, straddle milling both sides of a reverse shifter bracket for an automotive transmission (sample of work shown at right, on top of fixture).

Figure 27. Standard staggered-tooth milling cutter.

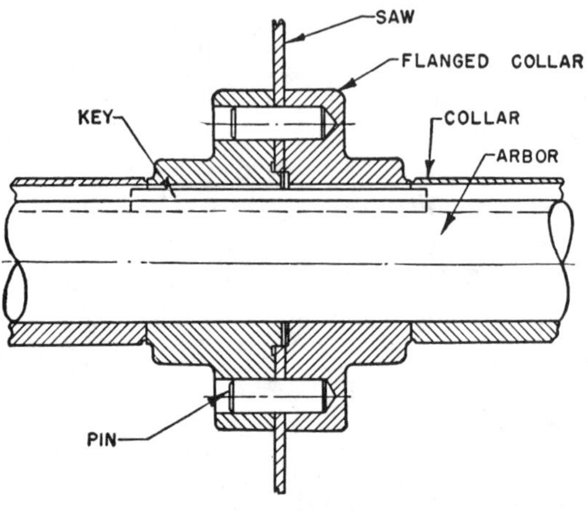

Figure 28

made with staggered teeth and also may have side teeth similar to side milling cutters. Such saws usually range in width from 3⁄16 to 3⁄8 in.

Special saws with form relieved teeth, sharpened by grinding the tooth face, are sometimes used for cutting copper and other similar materials. The teeth are given considerable peripheral clearance, and they are so constructed as to break up and throw out the chips, preventing clogging of the saw to a great extent.

When considering speeds and feeds, metal slitting saws are in a class by themselves. Because of their fragile section, they should be operated at approximately 1⁄4 to 1⁄8 of the feed per tooth used for other types of cutters, except in cutting nonferrous metals, when the speed and feed can be much greater.

It is preferable, especially for thin saws, to use driving means other than the standard key. A desirable mounting utilizing *flanges* is shown in Fig. 28.

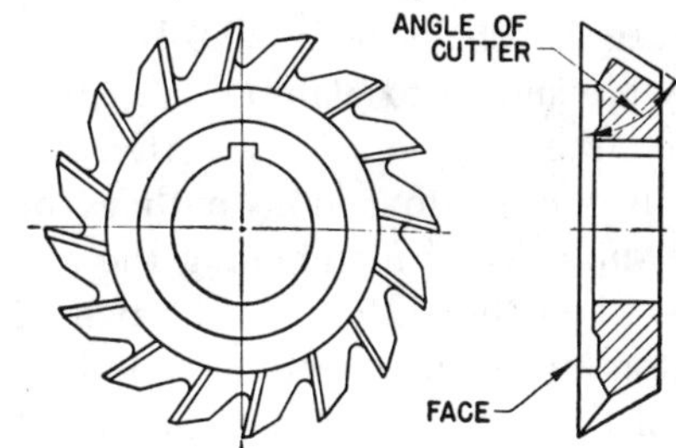

Figure 29

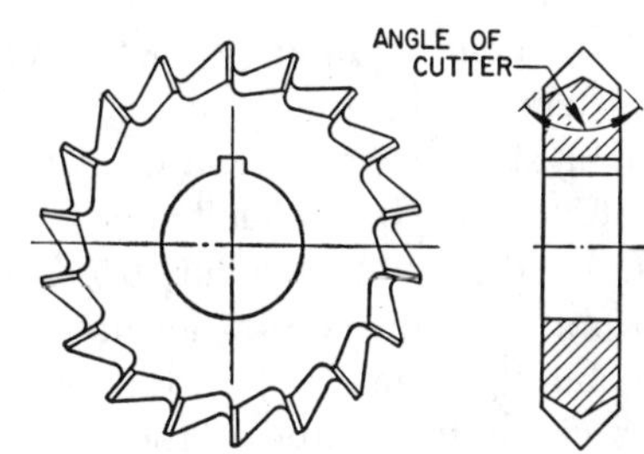

Figure 30

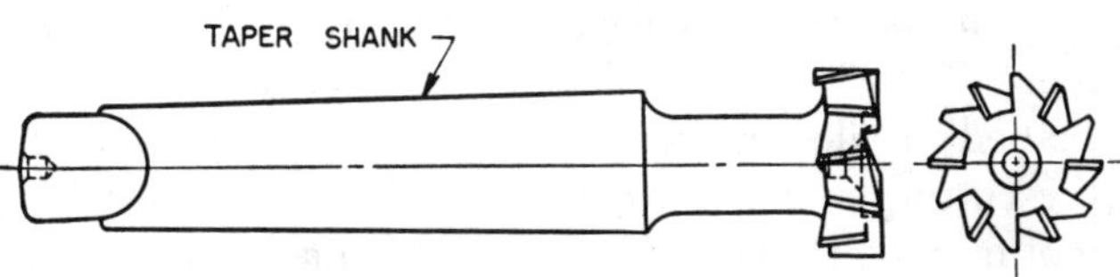

Figure 31

Figure 32. Shaped profile cutter.

ANGLE MILLING CUTTERS. Angle milling cutters shaped like segments of a cone are used for angular milling—cutting of dovetails, grooves, V-notches, serrations, and reamer teeth. They are designed in two general styles:

Single-angle cutters (Fig. 29) have teeth on a conical surface at an angle of 45 or 60 degrees to the plane of the face. In most cases, the face is also provided with teeth.

Double-angle cutters (Fig. 30) have V-shaped teeth with both conical surfaces at an angle to the end faces. The two angles are not necessarily the same. They are usually made with an included angle of 45, 60, or 90 degrees.

T-SLOT MILLING CUTTERS. The T-slot milling cutters are special purpose shank-type cutters (Fig. 31) for milling the wide groove at the bottom of T-slots after the narrow upper groove has been cut with a slotting mill or end mill. Straight or staggered teeth are cut on the circumferential surface and on both sides. Large T-slot cutters are made for mounting on a separate shank.

WOODRUFF KEY MILLING CUTTERS. Woodruff key milling cutters are small standard keyseat cutters which are similar in design to plain and side mills. Sizes up to two inches in diameter are made with a solid shank for mounting in the spindle; the larger sizes are made for arbor mounting. The smaller sizes have straight teeth on the circumferential surface only, with the sides slightly relieved for clearance. The larger-diameter cutters are made with staggered teeth on both the periphery and sides. Woodruff key milling cutters are especially suited for blind cuts such as in milling semi-cylindrical keyways on shafts.

FORMED MILLING CUTTERS. Formed cutters usually have a curved-tooth outline, and are used in milling contours of various shapes. They may be divided into two classes; the shaped or formed profile cutters, and the form or cam relieved cutters. They can also be classified as *profile-ground* and *face-ground* formed cutters, according to the method of sharpening. *Shaped or formed profile cutters* (Fig. 32) have an irregular shape or profile, but in other respects they are similar to plain milling cutters. They may be of either the solid or inserted blade type. Their use is limited to simple outlines or profiles due to the difficulty of maintaining the accuracy of this profile when the cutter is resharpened. Shaped profile cutters are resharpened by grinding a small land back of the cutting edge like that in plain milling cutters. This means that the contour of the cutter must be reproduced every time the cutter is resharpened. There should be no difficulty in accurately reproducing simple geometric profiles like those in cutters of the plain milling type, but the grinding of a shaped profile cutter having a complicated outline may be difficult, and can be done more easily on the cutter contour grinding machine shown. To obtain the necessary accuracy, gauges of the profile should be made. In addition, a template for guiding either the cutter or the grinding wheel will often be required to secure the desired accuracy and speed in the resharpening operation.

Form or cam relieved cutters are of the solid type. They are so-called in contradistinction to shaped profile cutters because the clearance back of the cutting edge is produced by a form or a master tool in a cam relieving machine, giving all the teeth the contour of the master tool. Whereas shaped profile cutters are sharpened by grinding the land along the profile of the tooth, form relieved cutters are sharpened on the *face* of the tooth, thus preserving the contour of the original profile produced in the manufacture of the cutter. Form relieved cutters may be resharpened many times until they have been ground to a point where the teeth are too slender to withstand the strain of the cutting load. The teeth of form relieved cutters may have a *radial face* (zero rake), or may be made with a *rake angle* or "undercut." They may also be either straight (parallel to the axis of rotation) or helical. The helix angle is generally five to ten degrees. As in profile-type cutters, the helical tooth form produces a gradual engagement of the teeth with the work, thus reducing shock and the tendency to "chatter."

In some cases, form relieved cutters are made with an angular gash. This type is easier to sharpen than cutters having the teeth formed on a helix, but it is practical only on narrow cutters. Straight-tooth cutters are used for standard production work when the finish is of secondary importance. Helical-tooth cutters produce a superior finish and have a smooth cutting action which permits higher speeds. Formed cutters are used for the accurate duplication of varying outlines or shapes, and make possible economical

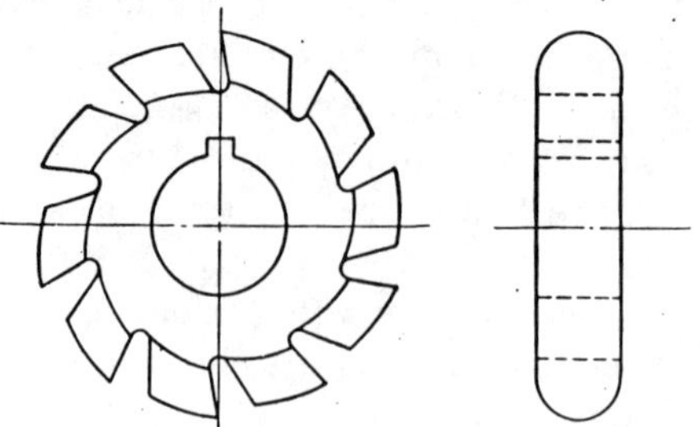

Figure 33

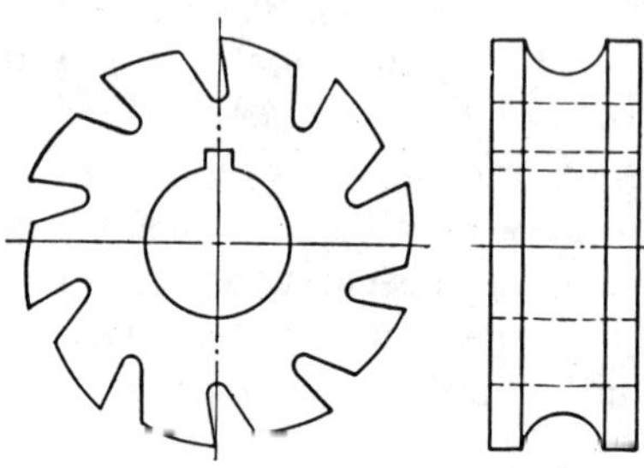

Figure 34

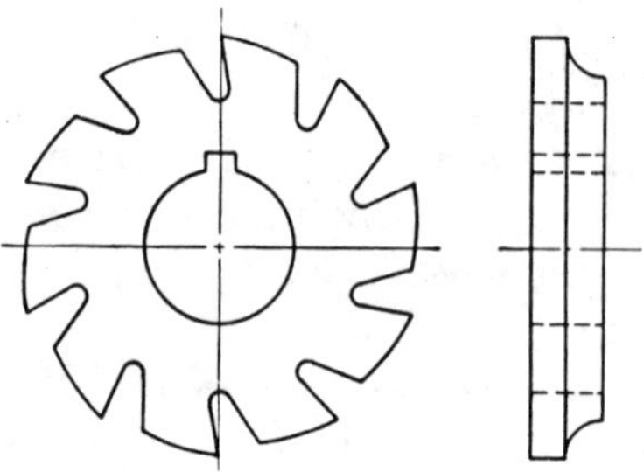

Figure 35

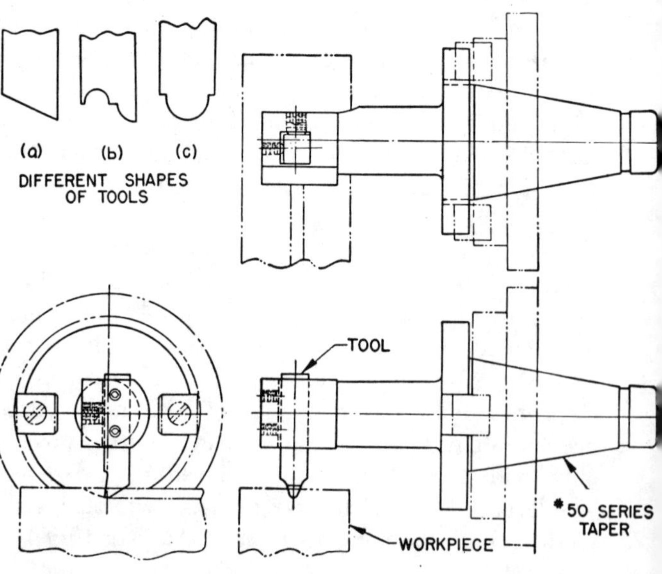

Figure 36

milling of complicated contours. Typical form relieved cutters include gear cutters, chain and sprocket cutters, convex and concave cutters (Figs. 33 and 34), corner rounding cutters (Fig. 35), spline and thread cutters, hobbing cutters, and others which, through wide usage, are now made with standard dimensions.

Fly Cutters. The fly cutter (Fig. 36) is a single-point cutting tool applied to an arbor. The cutting edge can be made in any desired shape. Fly cutters are used mainly in the experimental shop and tool room.

Inserted-Tooth Milling Cutters. Almost all types of milling cutters can be made with inserted teeth. Included are plain milling cutters, end mills (Fig. 37), side mills (Fig. 38), face mills (Fig. 39), shell end mills, and slotting mills. This type of construction is generally applied to large cutters although it is also used in milling cutters as small as two inches in diameter. The object of the inserted-tooth construction is economy in the first cost as well as in maintenance. These cutters are made with a cylindrical body of low-cost steel, an important factor in cutters of large dimensions. Grooves or slots are cut into the body for inserting the cutter teeth or blades. This makes it possible to replace the teeth quickly or adjust them to compensate for wear. It also permits using different materials, such as high-speed steel and sintered carbide, as the conditions of the job may require. In addition, the inserted-tooth construction prevents the loss of the entire cutter due to accidental tooth breakage because the damaged tooth or blade can be readily replaced. Various types of inserted-tooth milling cutters are as follows:

Face milling cutters are the most commonly used cutters of the inserted-tooth type, and are effective for facing wide surfaces. In sizes up to six inches in diameter they are termed *shell end mills* and are mounted on tapered shanks. Larger sizes are called *face mills* and are mounted directly on the spindle-nose. Face mills are made in light-duty and heavy-duty types. The light-duty face mill has a lighter body and a larger number of teeth, being used principally for finishing cuts. The heavy-duty face mill has a stronger, heavier body and fewer blades and is employed for heavy roughing cuts.

The general practice is to obtain the desired quality of finish and accuracy by one cut wherever practicable. This eliminates the additional time involved where the operation is performed in two cuts, known as *roughing* and *finishing* cuts. The combining of two cuts in one is sometimes applied to face

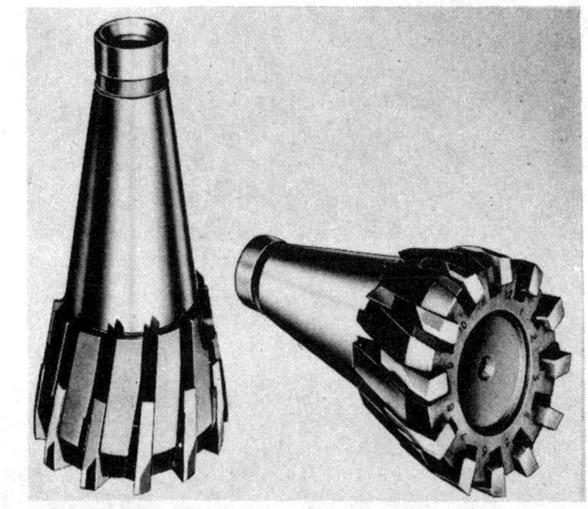

Figure 37. End mill with inserted blades.

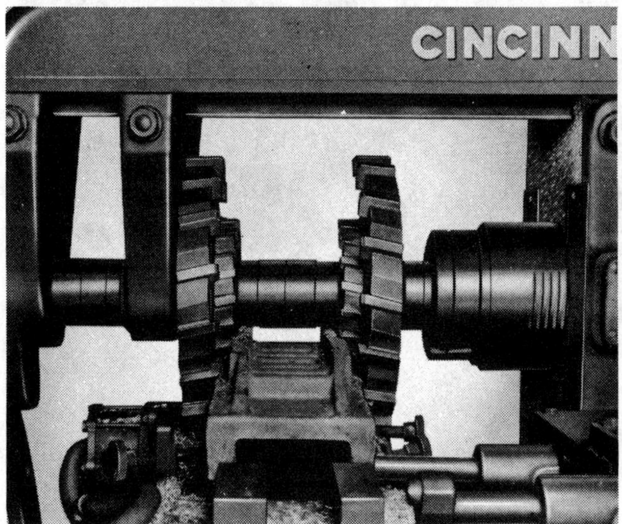

Figure 38. Application of inserted-tooth type half-side milling cutters, performing a straddle milling operation.

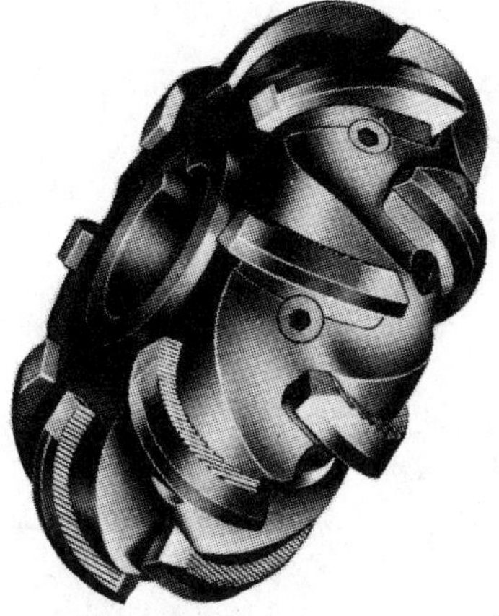

Figure 39. Inserted-tooth type face mill with sintered carbide tipped blades.

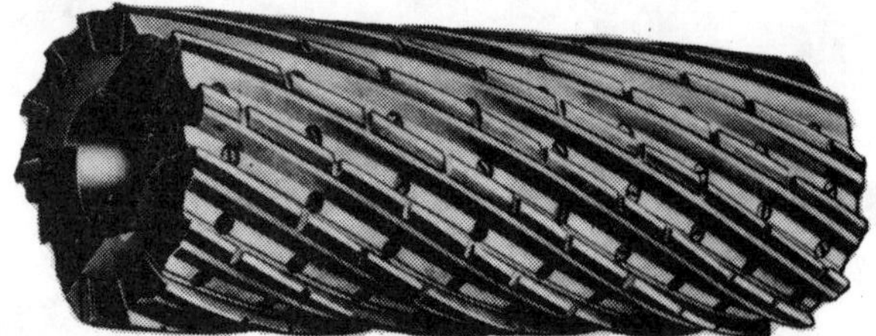

Figure 40. Slab mill with inserted blades.

Figure 41

mills having blades tipped with sintered carbide material. The roughing and finishing blades are mounted on the same body, with a limited number of finishing blades set to a smaller diameter and extending slightly farther from the face than the roughing blades. They also have a wide face to sweep the milled surface effectively.

Face mills with blades of *cast-tool material* are used for milling steel, cast iron, and nonferrous materials at a speed somewhat faster than is practicable with high-speed steel blades. Face mills tipped with *sintered carbide cutting materials* are run much faster than face mills with blades of high-speed steel or cast-tool material, and may be used for milling steel, cast iron, and nonferrous materials.

Inserted-tooth slab mills (Fig. 40) are long, cylindrical cutters of large diameter. The teeth are inserted in helical slots in the cylindrical body and are held in place by wedges and screws.

Notches known as *chip breakers* are often provided on the blades of these cutters, spaced so as to break up the extreme width of the chip into smaller segments of more convenient size (Fig. 40). Where wide surfaces are to be milled, however, it is preferable to use cutters made in short, interlocking sections (Fig. 41).

SOLID MILLING CUTTERS WITH BRAZED-ON TIPS. Milling cutters are also made with the cutting material in the form of tips brazed directly on a solid cutter body. Inserted blades are thereby eliminated. These cutters are usually made with fewer teeth than cutters of high-speed steel. This method of mounting the cutting material offers the advantage of greater rigidity and better performance as well as higher economy resulting principally from the considerable saving in the time required for maintenance.

Chapter 14

Operating Milling Machines

With some milling machines, the machinist may stand either to the left or to the right in front of the table (Figs. 1 and 2), whichever is more convenient for the work under cut. The machinist has at hand, in either position, all controls necessary for the operation of the machine (Fig. 3). As a further aid to operation, the table movements on the type shown in the various illustrations are always in the direction the controlling lever is thrown, and, from both operating positions, as a general rule, a single lever is within reach to stop all machine movements immediately.

Setting Up

METHOD AND CUTTERS. The two important factors, to the successful milling of any job are: the choice of the method to be used, and the selection of the type of cutters to be used. Each is dependent upon the other, to a degree. However a third factor must be taken into account, the matter of feeds and speeds. A feed and speed must be selected, tentatively at least, before any analysis of methods and cutters can be made.

Whatever cutter is used, it should be of as small

Figure 1. Left operating position.

Figure 2. Right operating position.

Figure 3. Operating Controls and principal parts of a vertical milling machine. (A) Machine start-stop lever, (B) Scale for angular setting of spindle head, (C) Spindle feed handwheel and adjustable dial, (D) Swiveling spindle head, (E) Spindle stops, (F) Spindle sleeve clamp lever, (G) Spindle head clamp bolts, (H) Spindle head vertical alignment lever, (I) Adjustable coolant distributor.

a diameter as possible for economy in cost and to avoid unnecessary "run in" allowances. Figure 4 illustrates the relative "run in" required on large- and small-diameter cutters.

Arbors. The cutter arbor selected, if one is used, should be of as large a diameter as possible to get maximum rigidity. The use of too small-diameter arbors is a very common fault, and, unfortunately, their weakness is often emphasized by inadequate supports. If the stocks of cutters on hand make the

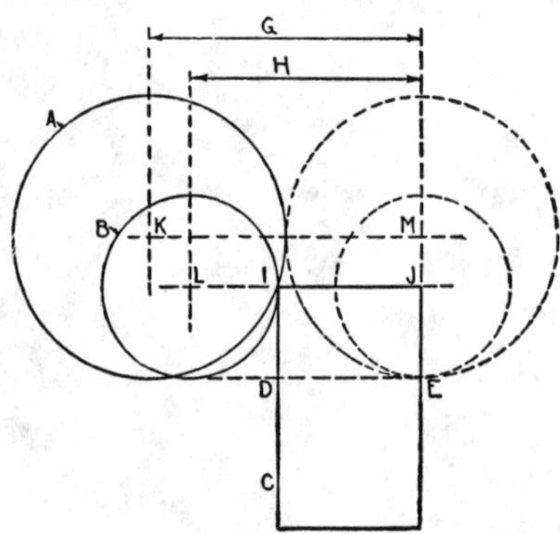

Figure 4

use of small arbors necessary, care should be taken to procure cutters, when replacements are made, large enough to permit the use of substantial arbors.

When an arbor of the proper size has been found and inserted in the machine spindle, the cutter should be mounted as close to the column of the machine as possible, and, if a helical or spiral cutter is used, it should be rotated in such a direction that, as the teeth enter the work, they tend to push the arbor toward the spindle rather than pull it away. Cutters should be securely keyed to the arbor because friction from tightening the arbor nut cannot be relied upon to hold them. Spacing collars and the arbor nut must be perfectly clean before clamping because dirt or chips between any of the members on the arbor are sure to cause a spring when the nut is set up, and, consequently, the arbor will run out. This not only prevents accurate machining, but causes uneven cutter wear, needless stress upon the machine, and severe wear in the bushings of the arbor yokes. On most arbors are hardened and ground sleeves, larger in diameter than the regular collars, that are used as bearings for the arbor yokes. These sleeves should be placed as near to the cutter as is practicable so that the arbor yokes may support the arbor close to the cut. Two arbor yokes are furnished with most machines. The smaller sizes usually have a yoke with a small bushing to fit the pilot on short arbors in cases where support at the extreme end of the arbor only is permissible. The smaller sizes also have a yoke with a larger hole to fit the sleeves mentioned for occasions when the arbor yoke may be placed nearer the spindle end or when both yokes are required. Heavy machines have two yokes with large bushings. Upon some work it is advisable to use both arbor supports, attempting at all times to keep the yokes near the cutters, and whenever possible the arm braces (which tie the overarms and the knee together) should be used. Arbor yoke bushings are adjustable for wear, and a good fit on the arbor sleeves or pilots should be maintained (Fig. 5).

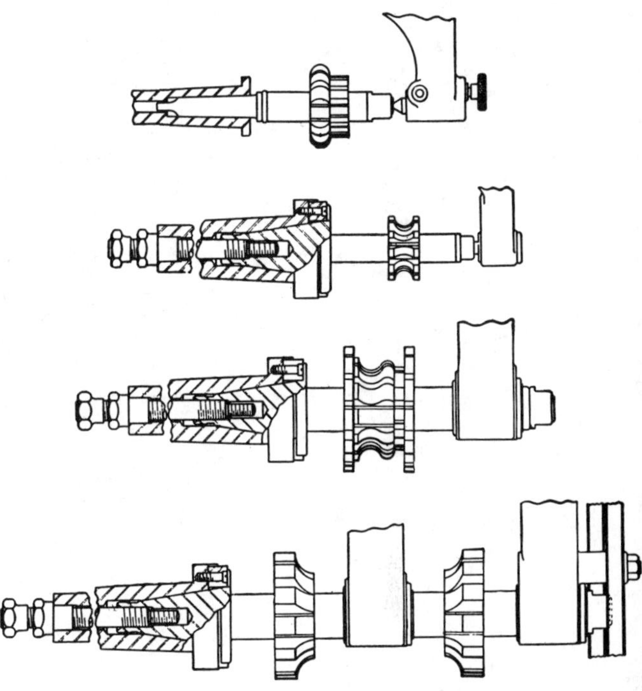

Figure 5. Arrangements of different arbor yokes.

HOLDING METHODS. The most common holding device is the milling machine vise, and it is used extensively for both short- and long-run jobs. Formed vise jaws for irregularly shaped work are inexpensive and frequently offer the only means of handling some parts. Before the work held between the vise jaws can be machined accurately, the vise must be squared up with the machine spindle. To set a plain vise or a vise without tongues so that its jaws are parallel to the spindle, place an arbor in the spindle and bring the vise jaws up to the arbor (Fig. 6). The vise can be set at right angles to the spindle by a square placed against the arbor and the jaws. Swivel vises may be set by the aid of the graduations on their bases. Work that cannot be handled in a vise because of its weight, shape, or other characteristics may be fastened directly to the machine table. An assortment of clamps and straps, jacks, a shim, a step block, and a clamping bolt, are shown in Fig. 7. Whenever clamping a piece to the table, the straps should be placed squarely across, in order to have a good bearing at each end, and, if possible, upon a solid section from table to strap at the work end. If it is necessary to place a strap on an overhanging part, a support should be placed between the work and the table or the lip will be sprung or broken. Another important consideration is the position of the clamping bolt. It should always be placed as near to the work as conditions will allow, for in this position it will exert the greatest pressure in the right place and be easier to set up or loosen.

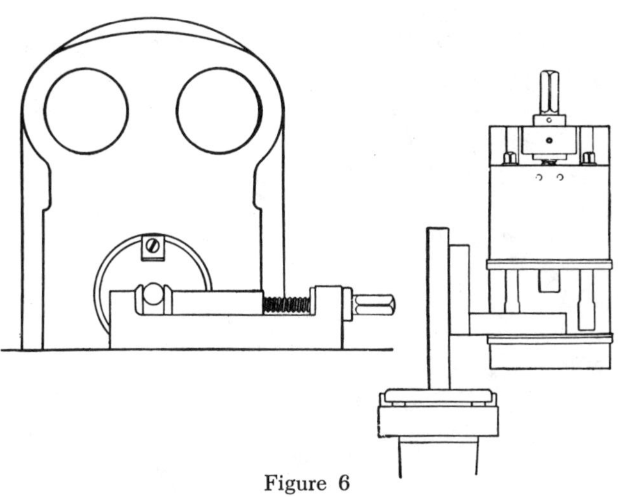

Figure 6

FIXTURES. If a sufficient quantity of pieces warrants the expense, fixtures are usually built to facilitate handling and to increase production. Since these fixtures are made in an endless variety, it is not practical at this time to discuss this phase of milling machine work.

Mounting of Milling Cutters

Milling cutters are mounted on the spindle of a milling machine either directly or by means of arbors

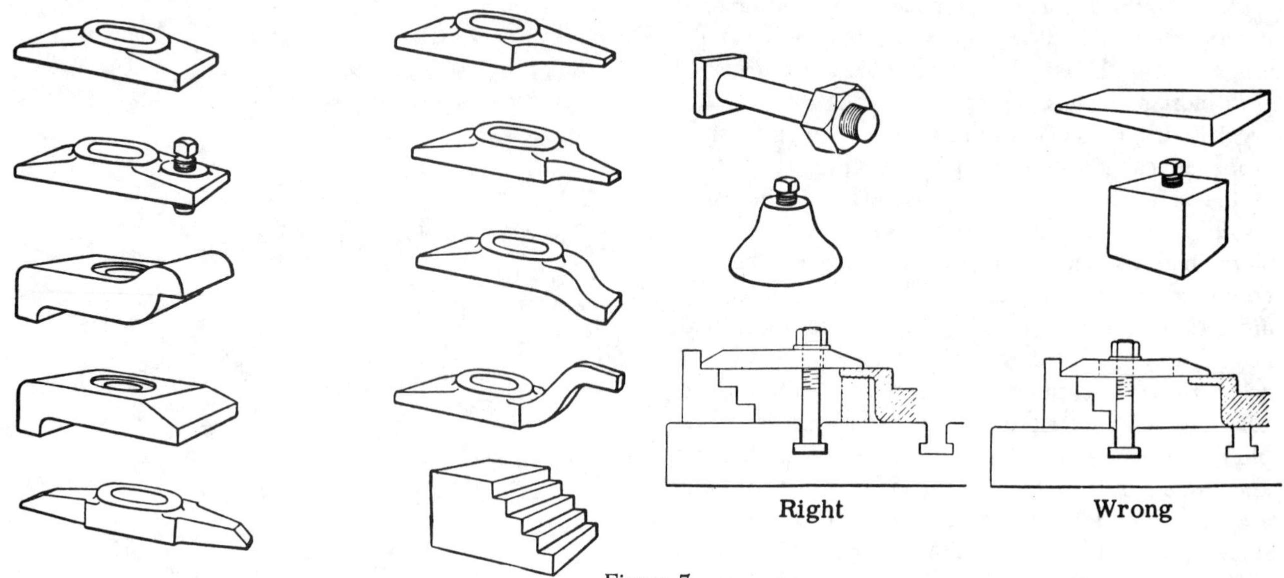

Figure 7

and adapters. For this purpose, the front end of the spindle or "spindlenose" is provided with (Fig. 8):

1. *An accurately ground face* which is square with the outer surface of the spindle.
2. *Four threaded holes and two driving keys* for locating and driving adapters and large face mills.
3. *An accurately machined tapered hole or socket* for locating shank-type cutters, arbors, and adapters, and to align them with the axis of the spindle.

TABLE 28
GENERAL DIMENSIONS OF
STANDARD MILLING MACHINE TAPER
All Dimensions in Inches

No. of Taper	D	d	L	E	B	F
30	1¼	.692	2⅞	½	2.7493	.6255
		.685			2.7488	.6252
40	1¾	1.005	3⅞	⅝	3.4993	.6255
		.997			3.4988	.6252
50	2¾	1.568	5½	¾	5.0618	1.0006
		1.559			5.0613	1.0002
60	4¼	2.381	8⅝	1½	8.7180	1.000
		2.371			8.7175	.999

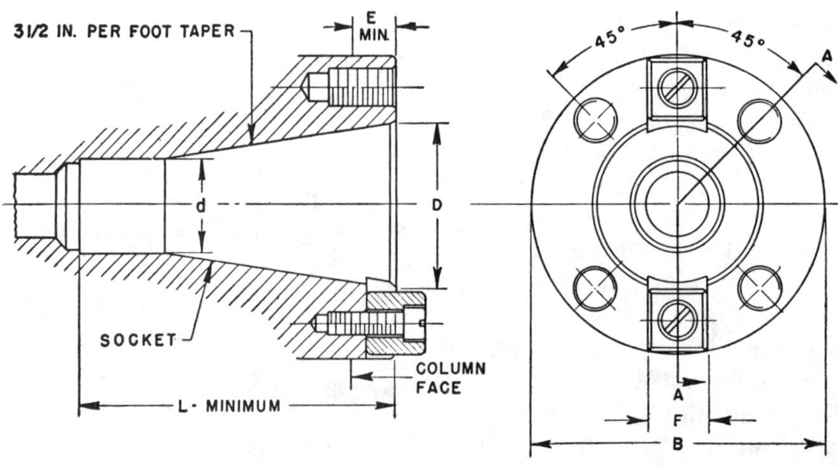

Figure 8

Classification of Tapers and Sizes. The tapers used for mounting milling cutters are conveniently divided into two general groups or classes known as *self-holding* and *self-releasing* or steep tapers, respectively.

Self-holding tapers are characterized by a *small included angle* (generally less than about five degrees) and by the fact that the shank will stay in place without using additional means other than the frictional force between the contacting surfaces when it is firmly seated in the socket.

Self-releasing or steep tapers are characterized by a *large included angle* (generally more than about fifteen degrees). They are dictated by the desirability of achieving uniformity in design; obtaining interchangeability of various devices such as arbors, collets, and adapters while at the same time providing a taper which will permit easy and quick removal of arbors, cutters, and other tools from the spindle of milling machines.

Types of Mounting for Milling Cutters

Milling cutters may be grouped with respect to the method of mounting as follows: face milling cutters, shank-type cutters, and arbor mounted cutters.

Face Milling Cutters. Face milling cutters of seven inches in diameter and over are usually mounted directly on the spindlenose and are held in position by four cap screws (Fig. 9).

Shank-Type Cutters. The shank-type class includes a variety of cutters with an *integral shank,* as in end mills, or a *separate shank,* as in shell end mills and sometimes in smaller face mills. The shank may be straight or tapered, and it is inserted in the spindlenose either directly or with an adapter, depending on the type and the size.

Shank mounted cutters may be classified in two general groups; cutters mounted on a *removable* shank, and cutters having an *integral* shank.

Cutters with Removable Shank. Milling cutters of the *shell end mill* type are not large enough to permit a counterbore which will fit over the spindlenose as in face mills. Consequently, they are mounted on the spindle by means of a short arbor known as a shell end mill arbor or "stub arbor" (Fig. 10).

Large-size face milling cutters may also be mounted on the spindle of a milling machine by means of a face mill arbor or adapter. Figure 11 shows this type of face mill mounting used with a *quick-change adapter* for multiple tooling without flanging the setup of the workpiece.

Standard *single-angle milling cutters* with threaded holes may be included in the group of cutters having a removable shank. The arbor for these cutters has either a right- or left-hand threaded end. The thread is selected in relation to the "hand" or direction of cutting of the cutter and the hand of rotation of the spindle. There are four combinations of hand of rotation, hand of cutter, and hand of thread (Fig. 12).

Cutters with Integral or Solid Shank. This group includes a wide variety of small milling cutters of standard and special shapes, standard end mills, T-slot, and Woodruff key-seat cutters. These cutters are made solid, with either straight or tapered

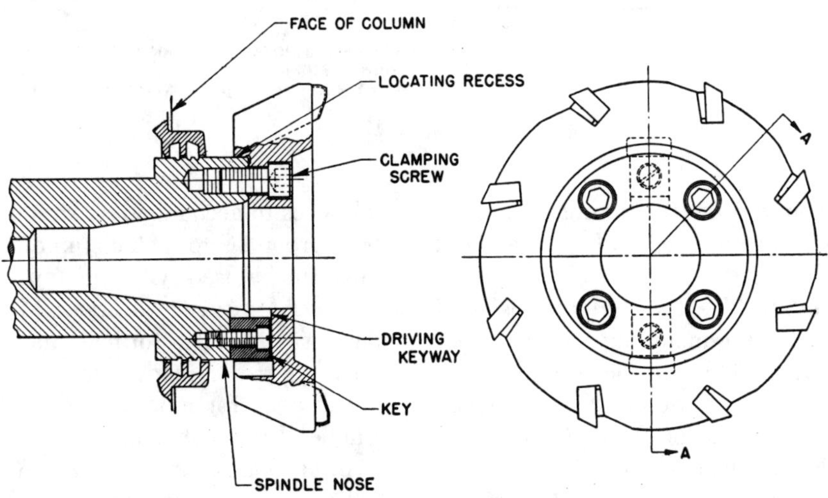

Figure 9

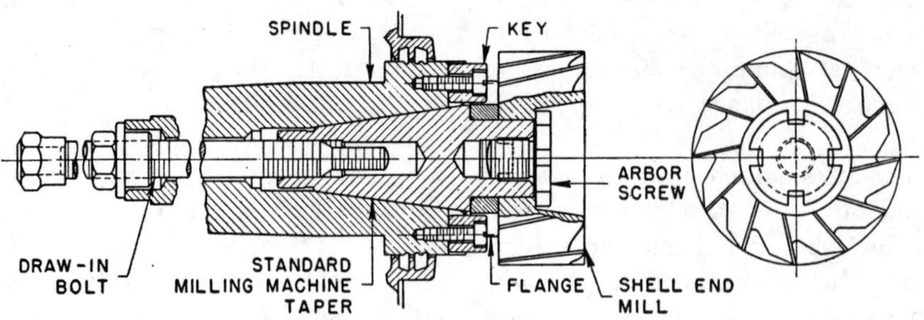

Figure 10

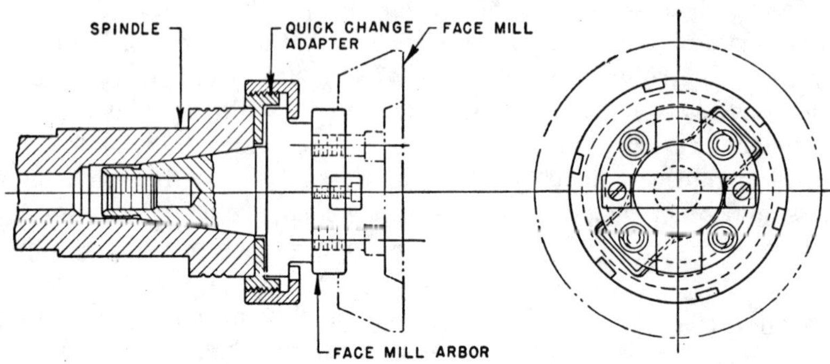

Figure 11

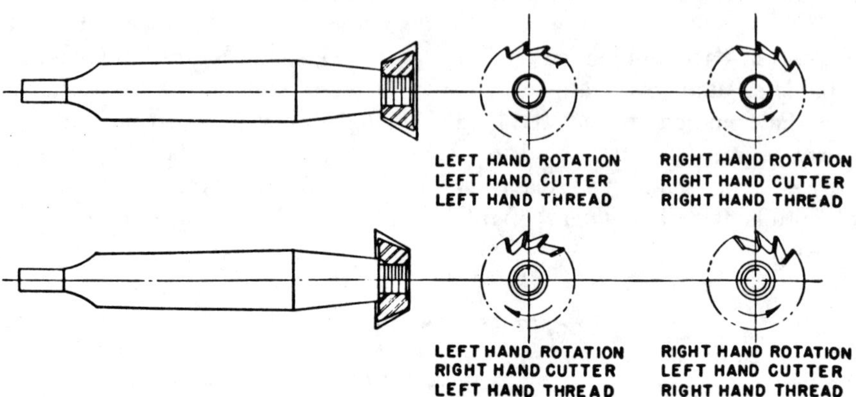

Figure 12

shanks, and are mounted on the standard spindle taper of milling machines by means of adapters and collets.

Adapters and Collets. The term *adapter* is used to denote an accessory for mounting various types and sizes of milling cutters on the spindle of a milling machine. A *collet* is a two-taper sleeve which is used to reduce the taper of the spindle or an adapter to a smaller-size taper (Fig. 13).

The *spring chuck* is actually an adapter with a removable spring collet, and is made in different hole sizes to accommodate straight-shank cutters and drills from $\frac{1}{8}$ to 1 inch in diameter. Double end mills can be used with this type of collet (Fig. 14).

Arbor Mounted Cutters. Milling cutters of the plain, side, angle, formed, metal slitting saw and other types are made with a standard center hole and keyway for mounting on an *arbor* held on the spindle of the machine.

Arbor Shank and Flange. Arbors for hole-type milling cutters are made in various lengths and diameters and in two styles which are identified by

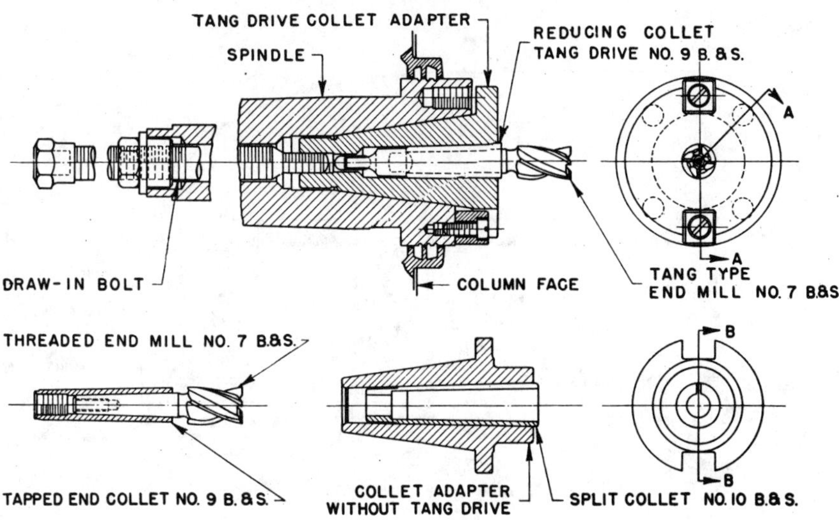

Figure 13

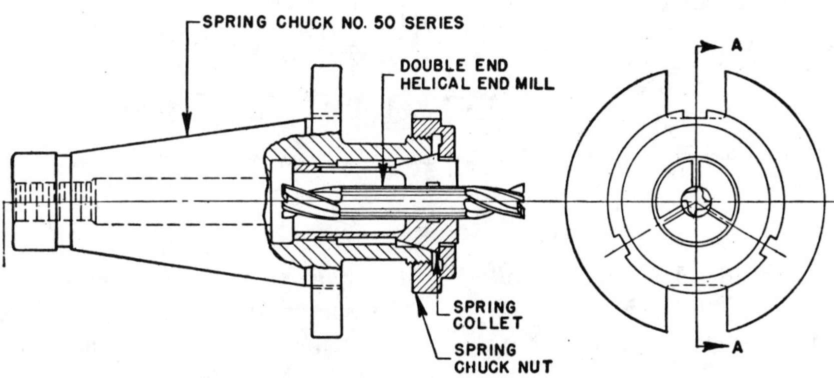

Figure 14

the letters *A* and *B* (Fig. 15). The arbor diameter is ground to close limits throughout its length to insure interchangeability and sliding fit for all milling cutters.

Use of Keys to Drive Cutters. The arbor (Fig. 16) is provided with a full-length *keyway* to accommodate keys for driving the cutters and the bearing collars. A good key material is 0.70 to 0.80 per cent carbon steel, hardened and drawn to a blue. In fitting a key to the cutter and arbor, both the key and key slots should have dimensions corresponding to the standard nominal sizes of arbors and cutters.

Spacing and Bearing Collars. Spacing and bearing collars are used to locate milling cutters on the arbor and maintain them accurately and rigidly in

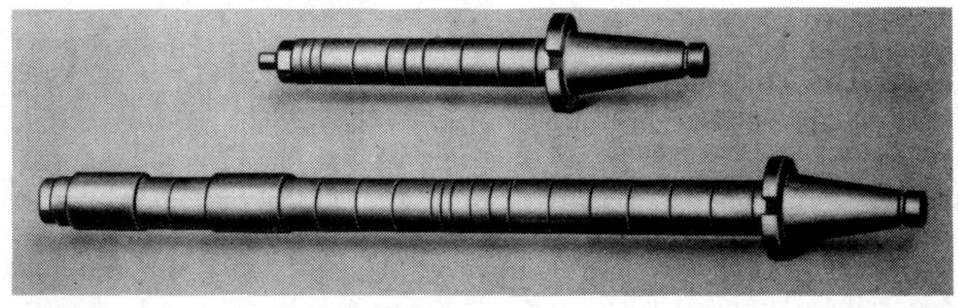

Figure 15

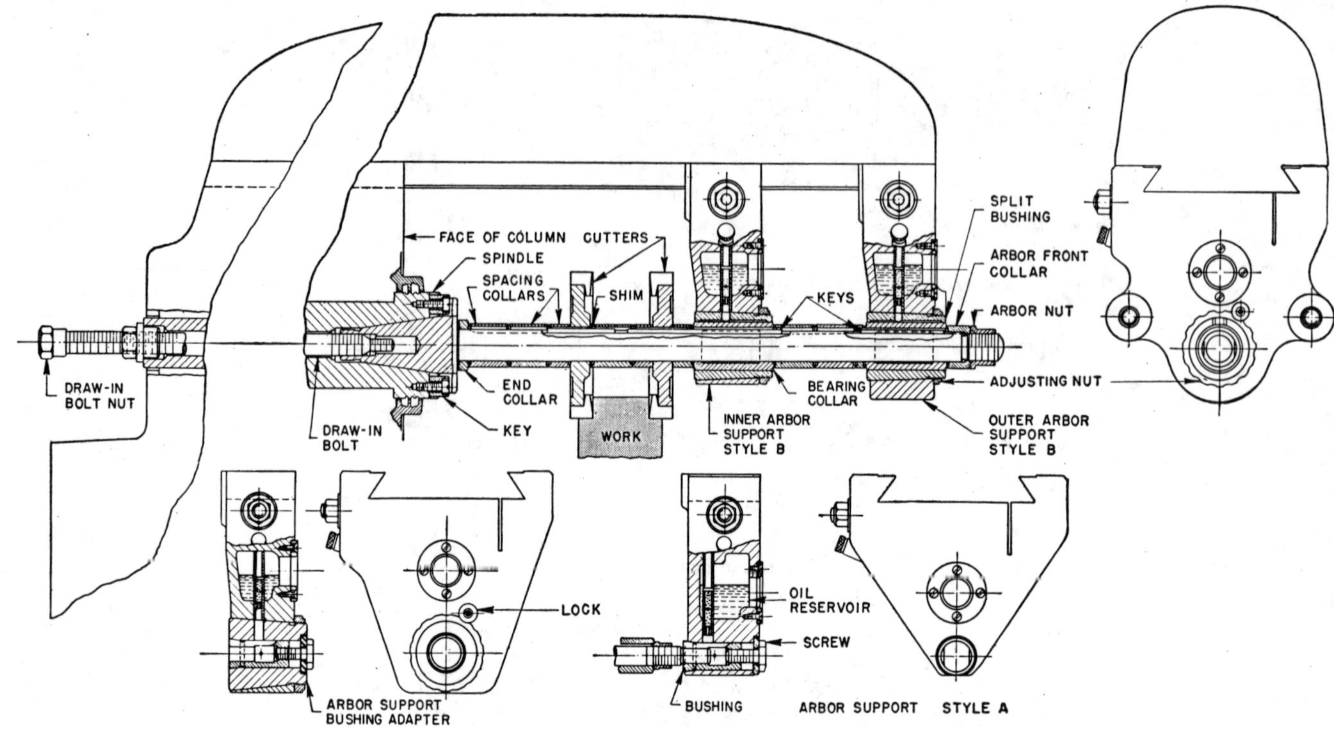

Figure 16

the desired position (Fig. 16). The *spacing collars* are inserted on the arbor on either side of the cutter, and are used in various lengths to permit the required spacing combinations. *Bearing collars* are made in one length and have a slightly larger diameter than spacing collars. They are used in conjunction with arbor supports (style *B*, Fig. 16). The collars and the cutters are tightened by means of the *arbor nut* at the outer end of the arbor.

Use of Style A *Arbors.* The style *A* or short arbor is provided with a shank and flange on one end. The opposite end has a pilot and a threaded portion for the arbor nut. The pilot is used to support the free end of the arbor. This style of arbor is used chiefly in small-size milling machines.

Use of Style B *Arbors.* The style *B* or long arbor, supported by means of one or more arbor supports and bearing collars, is used on both small and large milling machines. Bearing collars fit into the split bushing in the style *B* support (Fig. 16). The bushing is held in the tapered hole of the support by an adjusting nut, thus allowing adjustment of the bushing to the proper fit with the bearing collar. *Too loose* a fit affects the operation of the machine by causing inaccuracy and sometimes chatter; *too tight* a fit generates excessive heat which eventually may damage both the bearing collar and bushing.

A special inner support of the *cap type* permits easy arbor removal from the machine without dismantling the cutters.

SPECIAL ARBORS AND ADAPTERS. It is sometimes necessary, particularly in production jobs, to provide special arbors and adapters which permit the execution of milling operations on parts presenting obstructions or which are not accessible when the cutters are mounted on standard accessories. A special *extended collet adapter* for supporting an end mill to circular mill the bolt lugs of a master rod is shown in Fig. 17.

CUTTER SPEEDS. It is not possible to give definite speeds at which milling cutters should be run because varying conditions make corresponding variations necessary in cutter speeds. The size of cutter, type of cutter, rate of feed required, and the relation between the rate of feed and depth of cut all have a bearing on the speed.

The following surface speeds will be found suitable as a basis from which to work. To achieve the very best results in a particular case, some deviation from the given figures will be, no doubt, advantageous. A plentiful supply of coolant must be used on materials that require it.

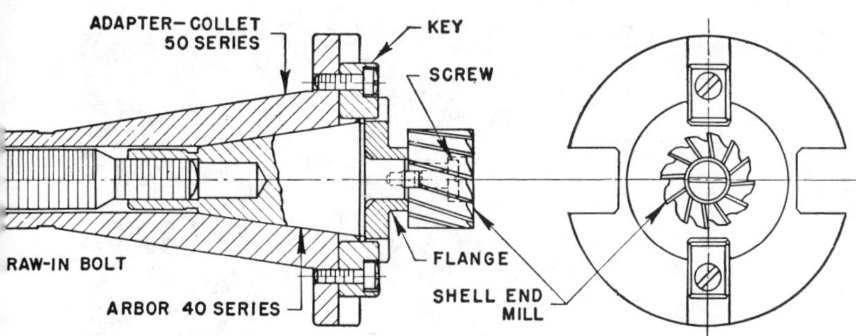

Figure 17. Extended adapter collet for circular milling bolt lugs of a master rod.

Surface Speeds of Cutters

Material	Carbon Steel Cutters	* High-Speed Steel Cutters
Brass	80–100 FPM	150–200 FPM
Cast Iron	40–60 FPM	80–100 FPM
Machinery Steel	30–40 FPM	80–100 FPM
Annealed Tool Steel	20–30 FPM	60–80 FPM

* Considerably higher speeds can be used with cutters of the new fast cutting alloys.

COOLANT. The oil or cutting compound used in milling work is not essentially a lubricant although it is frequently so called, but a cooling agent. In machining some materials, steel for example, considerable heat is generated by the cutting action which, unless dissipated, will soon burn the extreme edges of the cutter, causing it to become dull quickly. An abundance of coolant (Fig. 18) is a positive necessity on most steel jobs if the feeds and speeds that are considered right are to be used. Cutting oils are used mainly on high-speed work and where a good finish is desired. Oils vary somewhat in composition and cutting efficiency, but in general, they should be fairly clean and have no corrosive action and no objectionable odors.

Figure 18

Fundamentals of the Milling Process

Milling is a process of generating machined surfaces by progressively removing a predetermined amount of material or stock from the workpiece which is advanced at a relatively *slow* rate of movement or *feed* to a milling cutter rotating at comparatively *high speed.* The characteristic feature of the milling process is that each milling cutter tooth takes its share of the stock in the form of small individual chips. Milling operations are classified as follows:

PERIPHERAL MILLING. The milled surface generated by teeth located on the periphery of the cutter body, as when milling with a helical mill, is generally in a plane *parallel to the cutter axis.* Milling operations with form-relieved and formed-profile cutters are included in this class. The cross section of the milled surface corresponds to the outline or contour of the milling cutter or combination of cutters used (Figs. 19 and 20).

Figure 19. Combination of peripheral milling cutters for multiple milling operations.

Figure 20. Combination of form relieved cutters for multiple milling operations.

Figure 21. Combination of face mills for milling multiple plane surfaces.

FACE MILLING. The milled surface resulting from the combined action of cutting edges located on the periphery and the face of the cutter is generally *at right angles* to the cutter axis (Fig. 21). The milled surface is flat, there being no relation to the contour of the teeth.

Peripheral milling operations are usually performed on milling machines with the spindle located *horizontally*. The milling cutters are mounted on an arbor supported at the outer end for increased rigidity, especially when the cutter or cutters are located at some distance from the nose of the spindle due to the conditions of the setup.

Face milling is done on both *horizontal* and *vertical* milling machines.

Methods of Milling

In peripheral milling, the workpiece can be fed either *with* or *against* the direction of cutter rotation. In face milling, however, the particular characteristics of the two methods are usually combined because the feeding motion is generally *partly with and partly against* the direction of cutter rotation. The two methods (Figs. 22 and 23) are conventional or *up milling* and climb cut or *down milling*.

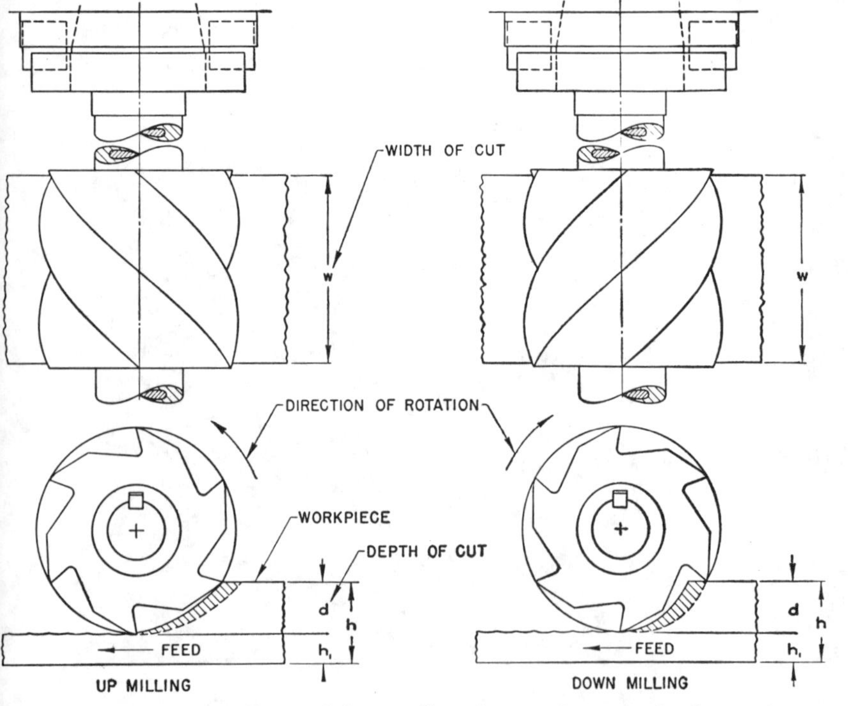

Figure 22. Up milling and down milling showing the principle of operation.

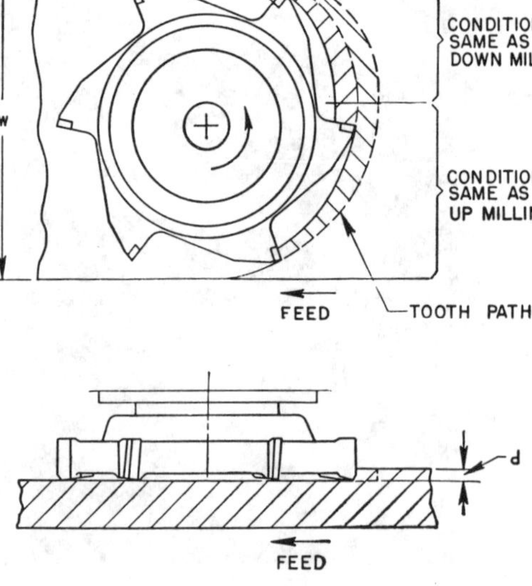

Figure 23. Face milling showing the principle of operation.

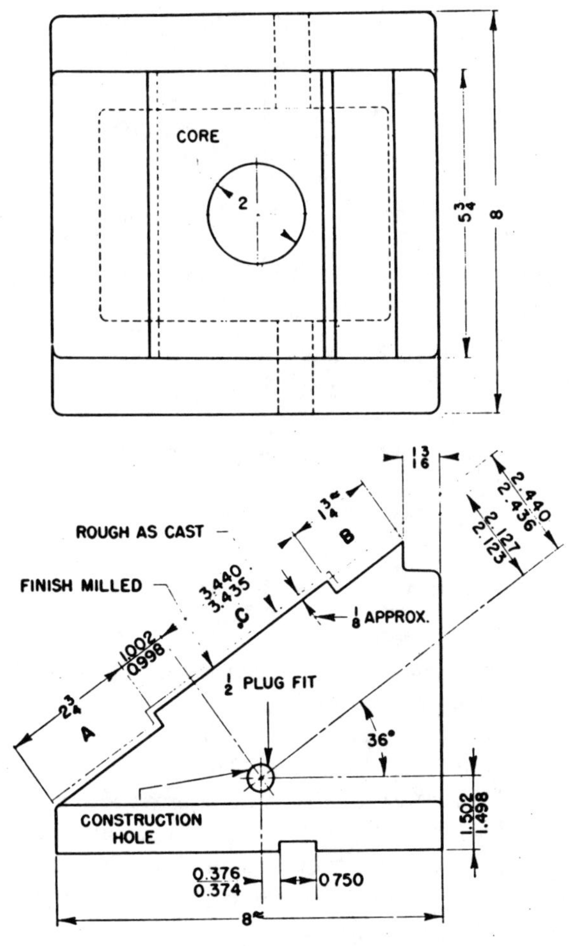

Figure 24. Milling locating surfaces on a milling fixture unit at a 36° angle.

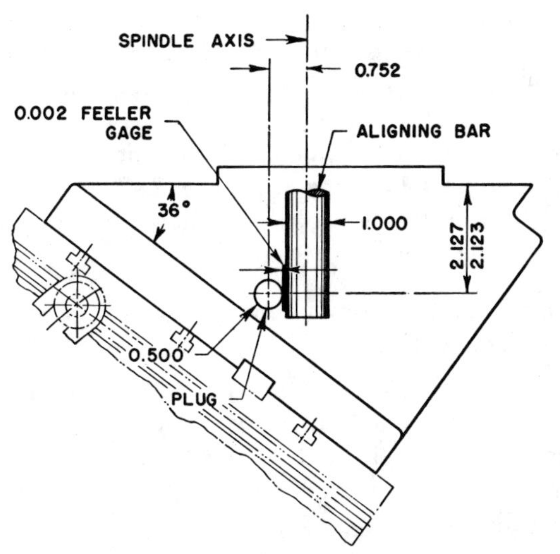

Figure 25. Setting workpiece at a known distance from milling cutter.

Conventional or Up Milling. In conventional or up milling, the cutter rotates against the direction of feed as the workpiece advances toward it from the side where the teeth are moving upward. The separating forces produced between cutter and workpiece oppose the motion of the work.

Climb Cut or Down Milling. In climb cut or down milling, the cutter rotates in the direction of the feed, and the workpiece thus advances toward the cutter from the side where the teeth are moving downward. As the cutter teeth begin to cut, forces of considerable intensity are produced which favor the motion of the workpiece and tend to pull the work under the cutter.

If the workpiece is not held securely on the moving slide, or the slide is not steadily fed by the feeding mechanism, yielding of the work may result in a broken cutter, damaged work and machine, and possible injury to the operator. For this reason, down milling operations are best performed on milling machines which are provided with the necessary equipment to secure positive control of movement of the work, such as the *backlash eliminating devices* used in machines of the screw feed type.

Selection of Setup

Locating the Workpiece with Respect to the Cutter. To locate the workpiece with respect to the cutter, it is necessary to determine the distance of the workpiece from the axis and face of the milling cutter by using a known *reference point* on the workpiece. The ½-in. diameter construction hole indicated in Fig. 24 is used for this purpose. A 1-in. diameter aligning bar is inserted in the spindle of the machine or attachment, and a ½-in. plug is inserted in the construction hole.

Locating the Workpiece with Respect to the Cutter Axis. By manually operating the adjustments of the knee, table, and saddle, the ½-in. plug is placed in light contact with the aligning bar, held in the spindle of the machine, by gauging the distance between them with a 0.002-in. feeler gauge. This thickness must be added when calculating the distance between the axis of the spindle and that of the plug in the workpiece. When contact is finally established, the distance between the axes of the cutter and the plug is 0.752 in. (Fig. 25). This distance is equal to the sum of the aligning bar radius, the plug radius, and the 0.002-in. thickness of the feeler gauge. The micrometer dial in the cross adjustment is set to zero reading, and the machine table is lowered so that the workpiece clears the aligning bar. The bar is then replaced with the 3-in. diameter shell end mill selected for this job.

LOCATING THE WORKPIECE WITH RESPECT TO THE FACE OF THE CUTTER. The table of the machine is adjusted *vertically* so that the reference plug in the workpiece is near the *face* of the cutter. The cross adjustment is not moved, and the cutter *axis* will remain at 0.752 in. from the center of the plug (Fig. 26). The distance, d, between the face of the cutter and the surface of the plug is measured by means of a vernier height gauge (Fig. 26). The difference $(d - \frac{1}{4})$ in. will be the distance between the face of the cutter and the center of the plug. The micrometer dial on the vertical hand adjustment is now set to zero reading. To place the cutter in the plane of surfaces A and C it is necessary to move the knee a distance which is obtained by subtracting the distance $(d - \frac{1}{4}$ in.) from the limits 2.127 in. maximum – 2.123 in. minimum (Fig. 24). If the distance d is 0.500 in., the following results are obtained:

$$2.127 - (0.500 - 0.250) = 1.877 \text{ in.}$$
$$2.123 - (0.500 - 0.250) = 1.873 \text{ in.}$$

Hence the knee will be lowered 1.875 in., which is the *average of the two limits.*

To mill surface A, the table in this case is moved *out* so that the periphery of the cutter lines up with the shoulder at 1.002 in. to 0.998 in. from the center of the plug (Fig. 24). The amount of the adjustment is calculated as follows:

$$1.002 + 0.752 + \frac{3}{2} = 3.254 \text{ in.}$$
$$0.998 + 0.752 + \frac{3}{2} = 3.250 \text{ in.}$$

where 0.752 in. is the center distance between the axis of the plug and the cutter, and $\frac{3}{2}$ is the cutter radius. If the cutter runs out, as determined by indicator check, one-half of the total run-out should be added to the above figures.

After lowering the knee 1.875 in., the table is moved out 3.252 in., which is the average of the calculated limits. These adjustments will place the workpiece in position for milling surface A.

SELECTION OF CUTTING SPEED AND FEED. The cutting speed for the high-speed steel shell end mill is selected from Table 33 in the Appendix. The cutting speed for medium cast iron of 180–220 Brinell hardness is 95 ft per min. Because of the depth of the stock to be removed, the cutting speed is conservatively reduced to about 75 ft per min to avoid premature dulling of the cutter. At this speed, the cutter

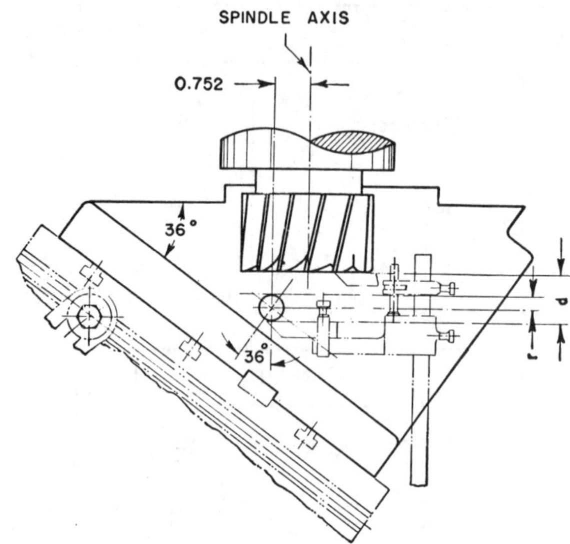

Figure 26. Setting the face of the cutter at a known distance from the locating plug.

rpm is approximately 92, which is the rpm available in the machine. The feed rate, based on a feed per tooth of 0.005 in. (Table 28 in Appendix) is $0.005 \times 10 \times 92 = 4.60$ in. per min. The actual feed will be $4\frac{5}{8}$ in. because this is the nearest feed available in the machine. The rate of stock removal is therefore $2\frac{3}{4} \times \frac{1}{8} \times 4\frac{5}{8} = 1.60$ cu in. per min, and the power at the cutter for a value of $a = 1$ (Table 30 in Appendix, line 2, face mills) is 1.60 horsepower, well within the power capacity of the milling machine. The above calculations can also be made by means of Table 34 in the Appendix.

MILLING SURFACES B AND C. When surface A has been milled, the workpiece is cleared from the cutter and repositioned for milling surface B by reading $1.000 + 3.338 + 3.000 = 7.338$ in. on the dial of the table screw. This is equal to the dimension on the workpiece plus the diameter of the cutter. Surface C is milled by lowering the knee $2.438 - 2.125 = 0.313$ in. from the previous position as indicated by the dimensions on the workpiece.

Milling Surfaces at Compound Angles on Single-Point Tools

Examples of surfaces inclined at compound angles are commonly found in single-point cutting tools, milling cutter teeth, and dovetails. The following cases have been selected for the purpose of illustrating the variety of settings which may be encountered in practice together with the procedure to follow in machining:

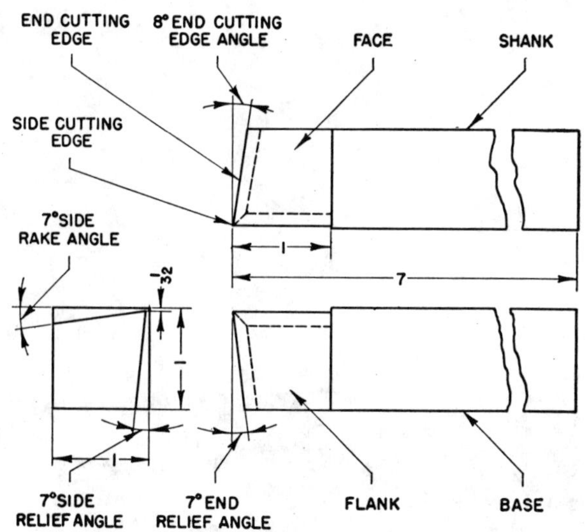

Figure 27. Milling tool point to given angles and dimensions.

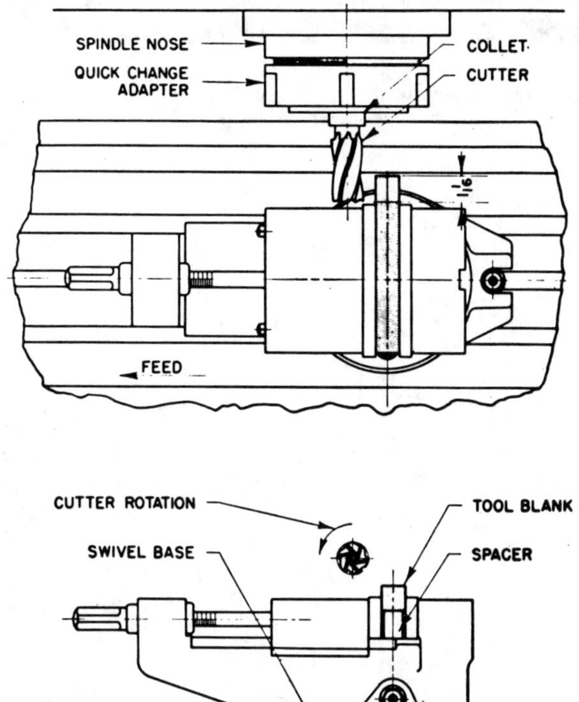

Figure 28. General views of setup used for milling cutting angles of turning tool shown in Figure 27.

MILLING THE CUTTING ANGLES OF A RIGHT-HAND CUT, STRAIGHT, SINGLE-POINT TOOL. (See Fig. 27.) The single-point tool is used for turning a square shoulder. Tool material: 18–4–1 high-speed steel, annealed 200 BHN.

Selection of Setup. The tool blank has been machined on the four sides previous to milling the surfaces on the cutting end of the tool. It is then clamped in a toolmaker universal vise located on the table of a horizontal milling machine. The vise jaws are set in a horizontal plane and parallel to the axis of the machine spindle (Fig. 28). In order to place the work at the proper working distance from the cutter, the vise is aligned with the center T-slot of the table and is bolted near the center portion of the table travel to avoid unnecessary table overhang.

A $1\frac{1}{2}$ in.-diameter standard high-speed steel end mill (8 teeth, right-hand cut, right-hand helix, $\frac{1}{16}$-in. corner radius) is mounted on the spindle of the machine by means of a quick-change adapter.

A cutting speed of approximately 80 ft per min is indicated in Table 33 in the Appendix for the 200 Brinell hardness number of the material to be milled. But this figure is conservatively reduced to about 70 ft per min. The revolutions per minute corresponding to this cutting speed can be determined from Table 34 in the Appendix. Here it is found that for a cutting speed of 70 ft per min and a cutter diameter of $1\frac{1}{2}$ in., the rpm is approximately 175. However, the nearest available rpm in the machine used for this job is 187. Hence, the actual cutting speed will be approximately 75 ft per min.

The feed rate is calculated from the number of cutter teeth, the rpm of the cutter, and the feed per tooth. With a feed per tooth of 0.003 in. for the alloy steel to be milled (see Table 28 in the Appendix) and using an 8-tooth cutter, the feed rate is approximately $3\frac{7}{8}$ in. The actual feed of $4\frac{5}{8}$ in. is selected, however, because it is the nearest feed available in the machine.

First Operation—Milling the Tool Face at a 7-Degree Side Rake Angle. (See Fig. 27.) The tool blank is clamped in the vise with sufficient shank length projecting beyond the jaws toward the cutter (Fig. 28) to allow the cutter to take the width of cut corresponding to the dimension of the tool point. The width of cut should be slightly larger than the final dimension shown in the drawing, thus allowing a small amount of stock for finishing the front end of the tool. In this case, the tool blank is set with respect

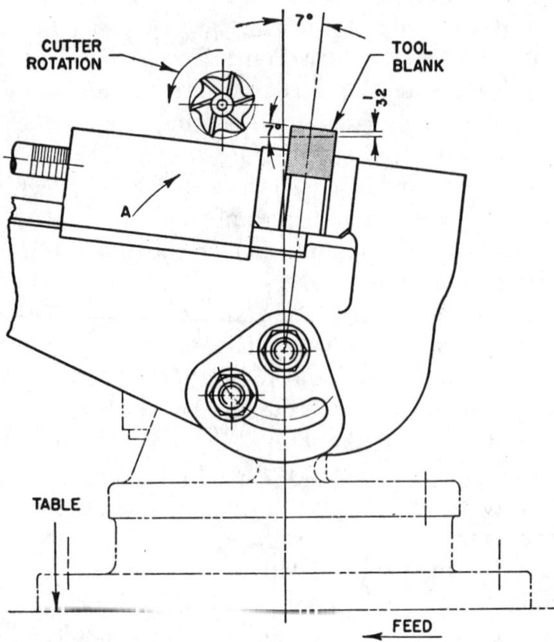

Figure 29. Setup for milling the 7° side rake angle.

Figure 30. Equipment used in milling 7° side rake angle on tool shown in Figure 27.

to the cutter by means of the cross adjustment so that the width of cut taken by the cutter is 1¹⁄₁₆ in.

With a bevel protractor set at a 7-degree angle and resting on the shank at right angles to the vise jaws, the body of the vise is tilted in the direction shown at *A*, Fig. 29 until the air bubble in the level is centered. The angle can also be read on the graduated scale located on one side of the vise body. The vise body is then clamped to the base, and, after raising the machine knee so that the cutter will cut ¹⁄₃₂ in. below the rough edge of the blank (Fig. 29), the table feed is engaged in a right-to-left direction, allowing the cutter to take an *up milling* cut. A close-up view of the equipment used in this operation is shown in Fig. 30.

Second Operation–Milling the Tool Flank at a 7-Degree Side Relief Angle. (See Fig. 27.) The second operation is the same as the first operation, but the surface to be milled (*tool flank*) is now located in a vertical plane at right angles to the face of the tool. The setup is changed as follows: (See Fig. 31.) The vise is indexed 180 degrees on its base, and the tool blank is relocated so as to place the flank of the tool on top. The table is now fed from right to left after raising the knee to take a ¹⁄₃₂-in. depth of cut below the rough edge of the blank.

Third Operation–Milling the Tool End at an 8-Degree End Cutting Edge Angle and 7-Degree End Relief Angle. (See Fig. 27.) The 8-degree end cutting edge angle and the 7-degree end relief

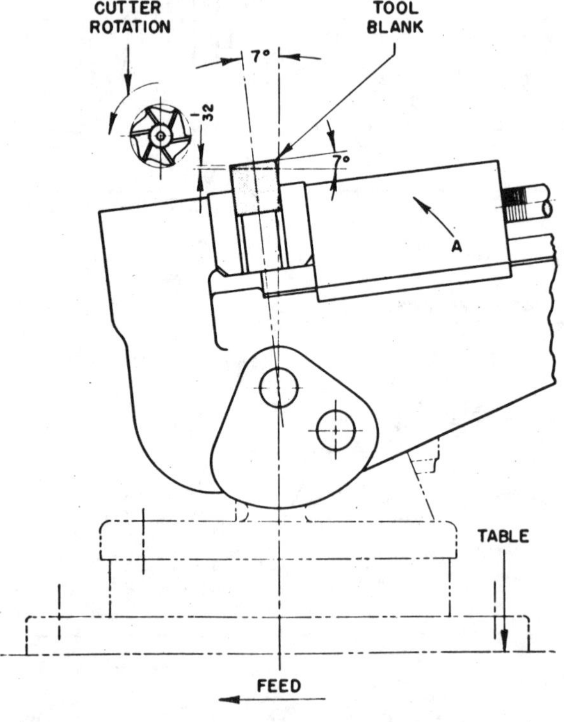

Figure 31. Setup for milling the 7° side relief angle.

angle, measured in two planes at right angles to each other, determine the location of the end surface *DEFG* of the tool point with respect to the tool shank (Fig. 32). In order to mill this surface so that the angles determining it have the given values, the tool blank must be placed with respect to the cutter so that the surface *DEFG* is parallel with the face of the cutter.

For this purpose, two lines *DE* and *DG* are scribed on the tool shank, making angles of 7 and 8 degrees with the end of the tool on the sides corresponding to the end relief and end cutting edge angles, respectively. The vise jaws are placed horizontally and parallel to the spindle axis. The tool blank is placed in the vise with the base of the tool up and with the cutting end of the tool toward the milling cutter. The tool shank is clamped lightly so that, when a bevel protractor, preset to the 7-degree end relief angle, is placed lengthwise on the tool shank, the tool blank can be tilted in a vertical plane in the vise until the air bubble in the level is centered. The line *DE* will now be in a vertical plane and parallel to the face of the cutter (*A*, Fig. 32).

The same result could be obtained by placing a straightedge against the face of the cutter and subsequently tilting the tool shank until the line *DE* lined up with the straightedge. The tool shank is then clamped tightly between the vise jaws.

In order to set the tool for the 8-degree end cutting edge angle without disturbing the previous setting, the vise body is now swiveled in a horizontal plane, parallel to *MM* (*A*, Fig. 32), until the line *DG* is parallel to the face of the cutter. A straightedge held against the face of the cutter can also be used for this setting. This method of setup is generally satisfactory because, in practice, it is not necessary to hold the angles of cutting tools to close tolerances. In some cases, however, it may be required to mill surfaces at compound angles to greater accuracy than this method would provide. In this instance, it is advisable to know the angle *C* (*B*, Fig. 32), at which the tool blank or the vise must be swiveled in a horizontal plane such as *MM*, after tilting it in the vertical plane to the 7-degree end relief angle. This angle is not the same as the 8-degree end cutting edge angle because it is located in a different plane. The tool angles are always given in the orthographic projection of the various views of the cutting end of the tool.

The angle *C* can be calculated by means of the following general formula which is derived from the geometry of Fig. 32:

$$\tan C = \tan b \cos a \qquad (1)$$

where:

C = compound angle, degrees

a = given angle, degrees (first angle used in the setup)

b = given angle, degrees (second angle used in the setup).

Substituting the known values of angles a and b in formula 1 (which in the present case are 7 and 8 degrees, respectively):

$$\begin{aligned} \tan C &= \tan 8 \cos 7 \\ &= 0.141 \times 0.993 \\ &= 0.140 \\ C &= 7^\circ 58' \end{aligned}$$

In this example, the angle *C* differs but slightly from the given 8-degree end cutting edge angle so that no appreciable error is made by swiveling the vise to this angle rather than the 7-degree 58-minute angle *C*.

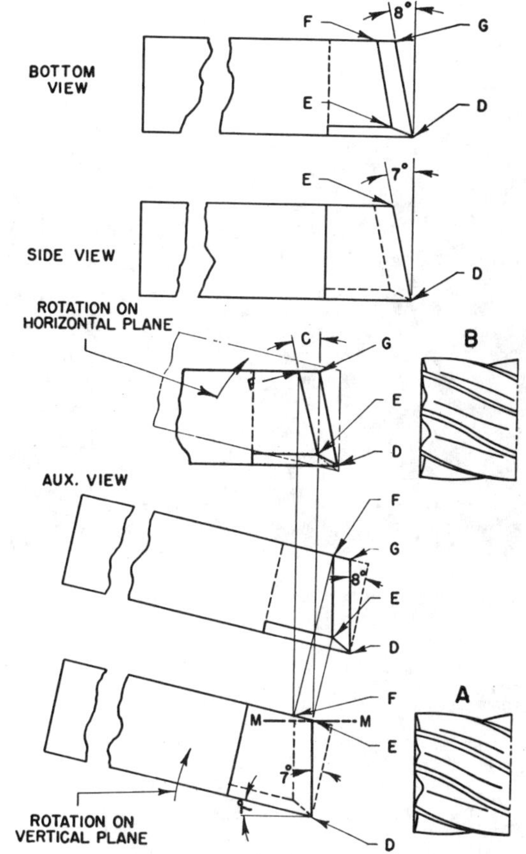

Figure 32. Determining the compound angle for milling the end of cutting tool shown in Figure 27.

In other cases, however, the compound angle may deviate appreciably from the value of the given angle, and the accuracy of machining will be affected if the setup is made by using the given angles instead of the compound angle.

As a general rule, *when the given angles are small* these angles can be used in making the setup, the compound angle being very nearly the same as one of the angles. *When the given angles are large,* the compound angle differs appreciably from either of the given angles.

For example, if $a = 29$ degrees and $b = 30$ degrees:

$$\tan C = \tan 30 \cos 29 = 0.577 \times 0.875 = 0.505$$

and:

$$C = 26^\circ\ 48'$$

In this instance, it would be desirable to use the value of the compound angle in making the setup.

To avoid mistakes which may prove costly, it is preferable to calculate the value of the compound angle in all cases, using the result as a guide in making the setup.

Figure 33. Equipment used in milling the end surface of cutting tool shown in Figure 32.

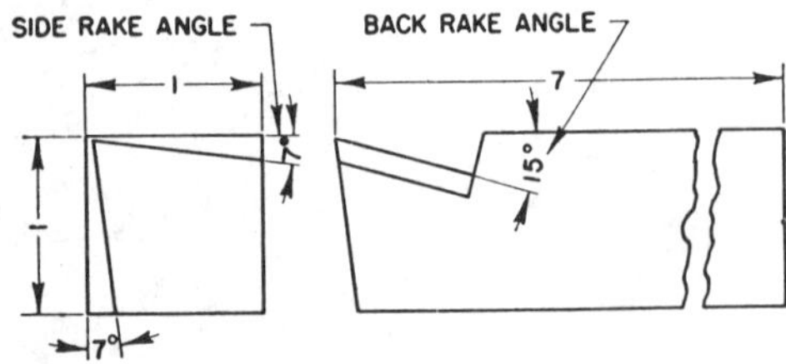

Figure 34

In setting up for machining the end of the cutting tool shown in Fig. 32, the order in which the two angles have been used might be reversed. The tool blank can be set first in the vertical plane at the 8-degree end cutting edge angle, and afterwards swiveled in the horizontal plane at the 7-degree end relief angle. In Formula 1, for determining the compound angle, the functions of the two angles would then be interchanged. The milling operation is completed at one setting of the tool blank by removing the required amount of stock with the end of the cutter (Fig. 33).

MILLING THE FACE OF A LEFT-HAND CUT, SINGLE-POINT TOOL HAVING BACK AND SIDE RAKE ANGLES. (Fig. 34.) Other conditions are the same as for the tool shown in Fig. 27.

Selection of Setup. The setup for machining the faces of tools having back and side rake angles (Fig. 34) is similar to that used in milling the end of a tool as outlined in the third operation for milling the cutting angles of a right-hand cut, straight, single-point tool.

Lines are scribed on the tool blank to indicate the location of the angles. After aligning the vise jaws with the spindle axis, the tool shank is clamped so that the back of the blank is on top. The vise is then tilted at 7 degrees, corresponding to the side rake angle.

To obtain the 15-degree back rake angle, the vise body is swiveled on its base until the scribed line is parallel to the face of the cutter.

The compound angle C is then calculated by substituting the values of the side rake angle (first angle used) and back rake angle (second angle) as in formula 1:

$$\tan C = \tan 15 \cos 7 = 0.268 \times 0.993 = 0.266$$

and:

$$C = 14^\circ\ 54'$$

Therefore, use of the 15-degree back rake angle will provide sufficient accuracy in this setup because the compound angle is nearly the same as the value of the back rake angle. The milling operation is now performed with the periphery of the cutter, using the same feed and speed as described for milling the cutting angles of a right-hand cut, straight, single-point tool. The setup is shown in Fig. 33. The other angles are milled under the same procedure as described previously.

Figure 35. Use of motor-driven universal-milling overarm attachment in milling surfaces at compound angles on a single-point cutting tool.

Setup with Motor-Driven Universal-Milling Overarm Attachment. When the milling machine is equipped with a motor-driven universal-milling overarm attachment (Fig. 35), which is provided with two independent angular adjustments at right angles to each other, the setup can be made by utilizing the angular adjustment of the cutter in conjunction with the angular adjustment of the vise (Fig. 36).

The milling operation is performed with the face of the cutter and using the feed rate previously outlined. However, the cutting speed is changed to approximately 70 ft per min, which corresponds to the 180 rpm available in the motor-driven overarm attachment rather than the 187 rpm of the machine spindle.

The combination of the motor-driven universal-milling overarm attachment and toolmaker universal vise provides a very convenient combination for quick and accurate milling of the cutting angles of single-point tools and face recesses for tips of sintered carbide or other materials (Fig. 37). The various operations, including recesses for carbide tips, can be completed without relocating the tool blank in the vise. The procedure is as follows:

MILLING THE FACE AND CARBIDE TIP RECESS IN A SINGLE-POINT TOOL. The dimensions of the recess and the values of the tool angles when milling the face and carbide tip recess of a single-point cutting tool having negative side and back rake angles are

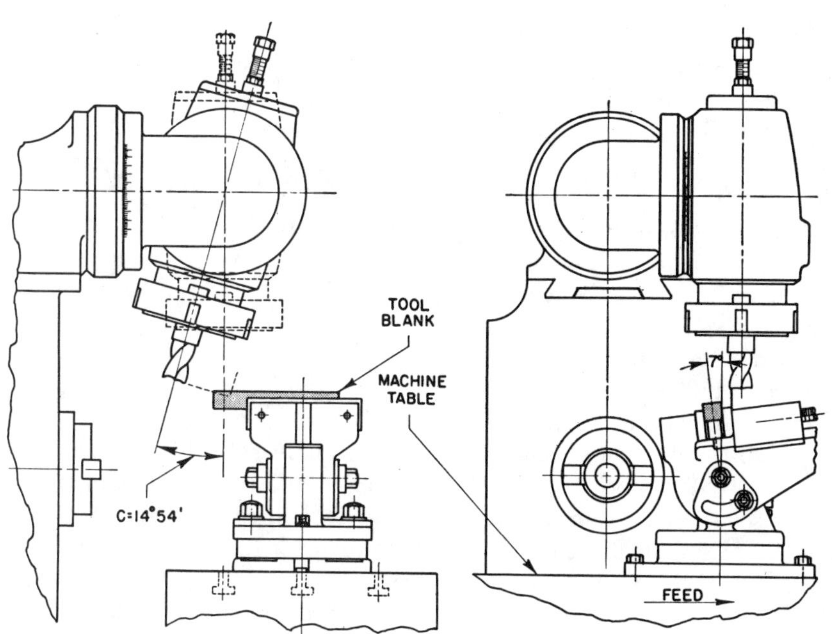

Figure 36

shown in Fig. 38. The tool blank is made of SAE 1040 steel of 170–180 BHN.

First Operation–Milling Tool Flank. In the first operation, the flank of the tool is milled at a 15-degree side cutting edge angle and a 10-degree side relief angle using the periphery of the cutter. The general setup is shown in Fig. 37. The tool blank is clamped in the toolmaker universal vise, and the vise jaws are set in a horizontal plane parallel to the cutter axis.

The vise body is now swiveled on the base to a 15-degree angle. The spindle of the motor-driven universal-milling overarm attachment is swiveled counter-clockwise on the compound bracket, parallel to the face of the column, until the cutter axis is parallel to the scribed line on the tool blank. This line marks the position corresponding to the 10-degree side relief angle (or to the value of the angle C, the compound angle of the 10-degree side relief angle, obtained from formula 1 after substituting the known values):

$$\begin{aligned}\tan C &= \tan 10 \cos 15 \\ &= 0.176 \times 0.966 \\ &= 1.700\end{aligned}$$

and:

$$C = 9° \ 39'$$

Figure 37. Milling the flank of a single-point tool to 10° side relief and 15° side cutting edge angles, by using a motor-driven universal-milling overarm attachment and a toolmaker universal vise.

Selection of Milling Cutter, Cutting Speed, and Feed. The milling cutter for this operation is a 1½-in. diameter, standard, high-speed steel end mill (8 teeth, right-hand helix), mounted for use with a quick-change adapter. The cutting speed is about 70 ft per min, the same as used in the previous operation.

The feed rate is calculated from the assumed value of the feed per tooth, which is taken equal to 0.003 in. for the 180 BHN alloy steel being milled (see Table 28 in Appendix). Hence, for the given number of teeth and actual rpm (see Table 34 in Appendix), it is found that the *approximate* feed rate is 4.49 in. per min. The *actual* feed rate is 4⅝ in. per min because this is the nearest feed rate available in the machine. The work is fed to the cutter by using the cross feed.

To avoid the possibility of the cutter striking the vise, a stop dog should be placed in the cross feed controls to automatically stop the feed as the cutter completes the cut.

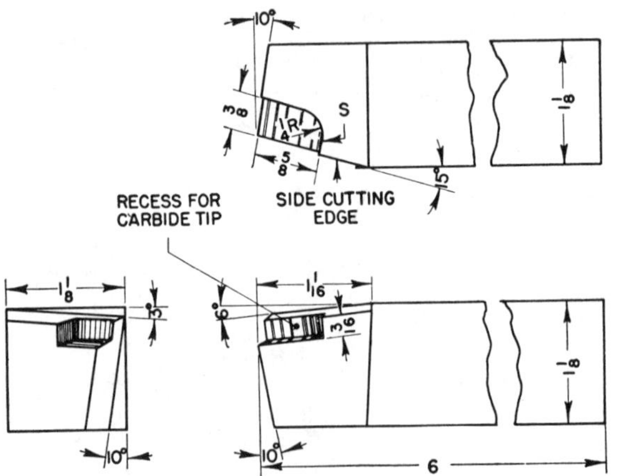

Figure 38. Dimensions of a single-point, right-hand cut carbide tipped turning tool.

RATE OF STOCK REMOVAL IN RELATION TO STRENGTH OF THE CUTTER. In operations with end mills and other small-size milling cutters, the strength of the cutter is a factor in determining the rate of stock removal. Cutter breakage may occur if the selected rate of stock removal is too high for the size of the cutter.

The proper rate of stock removal can be obtained by determining the *allowable horsepower at the cutter* in relation to the cutter size. In end mills this can be calculated by means of the following formula:

$$H_p = \frac{D^3}{336{,}000}\frac{S}{L}\,C \qquad (2)$$

where:

H_p = horsepower allowable at the cutter.
D = neck diameter of cutter in inches (Fig. 39).
S = allowable stress, psi. Depending on operating conditions, this value varies between 10,000 and 20,000 psi for high-speed steel cutters. For end mills tipped with carbides, the allowable stress is that of the material of the shank.
C = cutting speed in feet per minute.
L = distance between neck section and point of load application (Fig. 39) in inches.

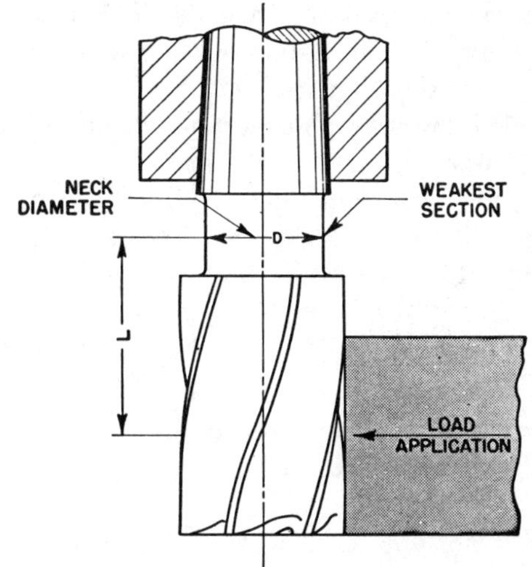

Figure 39. End mill dimensions for calculating allowable horsepower.

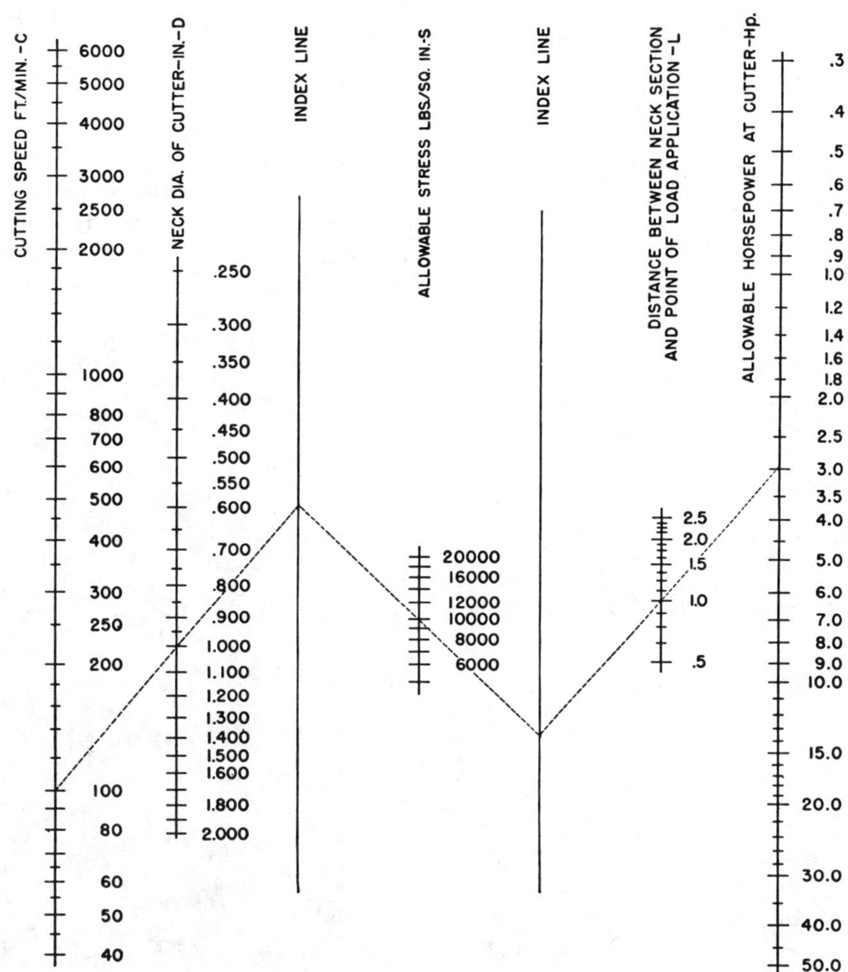

Figure 40. Alignment chart for calculating allowable horsepower for end mills.

When the values of the variables shown in formula 2 are known, the calculation of H_p can also be made by means of the alignment chart shown in Fig. 40.

Knowing the allowable horsepower at the cutter, the rate of stock removal V can be calculated from Table 34 in the Appendix, or from the empirical formula 3 which follows, after selecting the value of the factor a from Table 30 in the Appendix.

$$H_p = a\,V^n \qquad (3)$$

where:

H_p = horsepower at the cutter.
V = rate of stock removal in cubic inches per minute.
a = horsepower at the cutter *when the rate of stock removal is one cubic inch per minute.*
n = slope of the curve, or exponent for the rate of stock removal V.

The application of formula 2 is illustrated by checking the value of the feed rate used in this operation. Standard end mills of 1½ in.-diameter have a neck diameter D of approximately 1 in. The length L is 1 in., the work having been as close as possible to the cutter shank.

The value of the allowable stress S for high-speed steel cutters is assumed equal in this case to 15,000 psi. The cutting speed C is 70 ft. per min. Substituting these values in formula 2:

$$H_p = \frac{15{,}000 \times 70}{336{,}000 \times 1} = \frac{105}{33.6} = 3.13$$

This is the allowable horsepower H_p the cutter. From formula 3, it is found that for an average value of a of 1.25 (Table 30 in the Appendix) the rate of stock removal is:

$$3.13 = 1.25\,V^{3/4}$$

$$V = \frac{3.13^{4/3}}{1.25} = 3.40 \text{ cu. in. per min.}$$

but:

$$V = Fdw$$

In the present case, the feed rate is 4⅝ in. per min., the width of the cut is 1 in., and the maximum depth of the cut approximately 0.267 in. Hence:

$$V = 4\tfrac{5}{8} \times 0.267 \times 1 = 1.24 \text{ cu. in. per min.}$$

This value is well within the maximum allowable value of 3.40 cu. in. per min. obtained in the calculation for the cutter in question. Thus the feed rate of 4⅝ in. per min. is satisfactory and not excessive.

Second Operation—Milling Tool End. In the second operation, the front end of the tool blank is milled to a 10-degree end cutting edge angle and a 10-degree end relief angle.

The vise setting in the horizontal plane is now changed from the 15-degree angle of the previous operation to the 10-degree end cutting edge angle. The table is moved longitudinally to the left to locate the work so that the cutter will cut as in up milling.

To obtain the 10-degree end relief angle, the spindlehead of the attachment is tilted *counter-clockwise* in the plane at right angles to the machine column. The angle to which the spindlehead is tilted is the compound angle C, obtained as previously described by scribed lines or by means of formula 1:

$$\tan C = \tan 10 \cos 10 = 0.176 \times 0.984 = 0.173$$

and:

$$C = 9^\circ\,49'$$

The cut is taken with the teeth on the periphery of the cutter by feeding the table from left to right. The setup used in this operation is shown in Fig. 41.

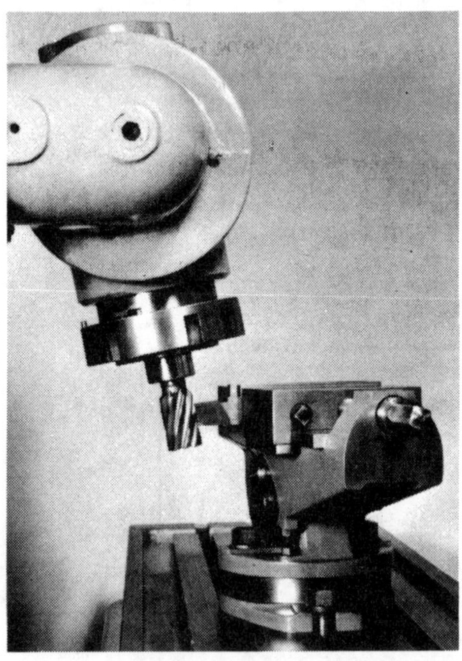

Figure 41. Setup for milling end of single-point tool shown in Figure 38.

Third Operation—Milling Tool Face. When milling the face of the tool to the 3-degree negative side rake angle, the 6-degree negative back rake angle, and the recess for the carbide tip is as shown in Fig. 38.

Setup for Milling the Tool Face. The tool blank is clamped in the vise, and the vise is then tilted in the plane parallel to the face of the column to the 3-degree negative side rake angle. The spindlehead is set at the compound angle of the 6-degree negative back rake angle by tilting it away from the column 6 degrees (Fig. 42); this is approximately the value of the compound angle obtained from formula 1. The cut is taken with the face of the 1½-in. diameter end mill, used in the previous operations, by feeding the table of the machine from left to right.

Setup for Milling the Recess for the Carbide Tip. To mill the recess for the carbide tip (Fig. 38), the 1½-in. diameter cutter is now replaced with a ½-in. diameter standard high-speed steel end mill (4 teeth, right-hand cut, right-hand helix) which will produce the ¼-in. radius on the inner corner of the recess.

At the cutting speed of 95 ft. per min. used to reduce the cutting load on the rather small cutter, this will operate at 726 rpm (see Table 34 in the Appendix). The available rpm in the motor-driven universal-milling overarm attachment is 740. Consequently, the actual cutting speed will be 96.8 ft. per min. With a feed per tooth of 0.002 in., the feed rate would be approximately 5.920 in. The actual feed rate, however, is 5¾ in., this being the nearest feed rate available in the machine.

Checking the Rate of Stock Removal in Relation to the Strength of the Cutter. At the feed rate established, and with depth and width of cuts of 3/16 in. and ⅜ in., respectively, the rate of stock removal is:

$$V = \tfrac{3}{16} \times \tfrac{3}{8} \times 5\tfrac{3}{4}$$
$$= 0.404 \text{ cu. in. per min.}$$

and the corresponding horsepower at the cutter (formula 3) for the average value of a of 1.25 (Table 30 in Appendix is:

$$H_p = a\,V^{3/4}$$
$$= 1.25\,(0.404)^{3/4}$$
$$= 0.633$$

But from formula 2, the allowable horsepower H_p where $D = \tfrac{1}{2}$ in., $S = 10{,}000$ psi, $C = 95$ ft. per min., and $L = \tfrac{3}{4}$ in., becomes:

$$H_p = \frac{(\tfrac{1}{2})^3 \times 10{,}000 \times 95}{336{,}000 \times \tfrac{3}{4}}$$
$$= \frac{95 \times 4}{33.6 \times 3 \times 8}$$
$$= 0.470$$

Since the horsepower corresponding to the selected operating conditions is higher than the allowable horsepower, a modification of the assumed values of the depth, width, and feed rate becomes necessary in order to avoid the possibility of cutter breakage.

By maintaining the same values for the feed rate and width of cut, but reducing the depth of cut to 3/32 in., the rate of stock removal becomes 0.202 cu. in. per min, and the horsepower at the cutter is reduced to 0.377. This value is now lower than the allowable horsepower, and the cut can be taken safely at the selected feed rate.

Figure 42. Setup for milling face of tool shown in Figure 38 at angles of 3° side rake and 6° back rake.

However, two passes will now be required to complete the operation, or one pass can be taken at the full depth of cut but with half the feed rate. If the cut is taken in two passes, the width of cut in the first pass should be 0.010 in. less than the specified value of 3/8 in. to avoid leaving a ridge on the sides of the recess.

Procedure for Locating the Tool Blank in Position for Milling the Recess. The sides of the recess are at right angles to each other, and the side S, Fig. 38, is at right angles to the side cutting edge. Hence the tool blank must be set with the side cutting edge at right angles to the direction of feed. This is done by swiveling the vise on its base to the 15-degree side cutting edge angle. The bottom surface of the recess should be parallel with the face of the tool. Since the tool face was set parallel with the face of the cutter in the previous operation, this condition will not be altered when the vise is swiveled to the 15-degree angle required for the present operation. Therefore it will not be necessary to make any other change in the setup. The workpiece is aligned with the cutter, with sufficient accuracy for this job, by utilizing scribed lines which give the outline of the recess on the surface of the tool.

If the operation is completed in two passes, the position of the saddle at the beginning of the cut is marked on the top of the knee, which has been spotted with red lead, by drawing a pencil line along the edge of the saddle. This mark will be used for relocating the starting position for the second pass. The work is set for the 3/32-in. depth of cut. As the cutter rotates at the selected cutting speed, the table (and consequently the work) is fed to the cutter by hand to the proper width of cut. The cross power feed is then engaged to feed the work away from the column. The second pass is taken in the same manner after the table is moved to the right, and after the saddle is correctly positioned with the help of the pencil mark on top of the knee. A view of the setup used when milling the recess is shown in Fig. 43.

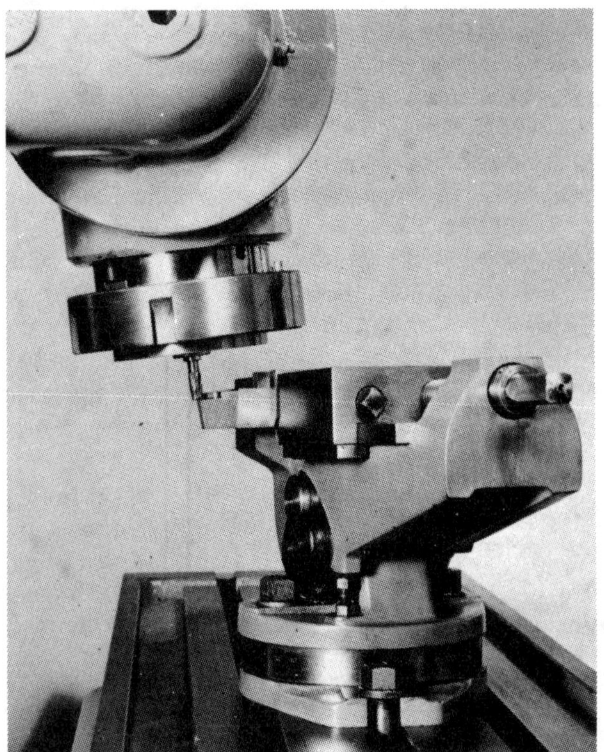

Figure 43. Setup for milling the carbide tip recess on a single-point tool.

Cutting Spirals

The spirals most commonly cut on milling machines are spiral gears, spiral mills, counterbores, and twist drills.

The method of producing the spiral movement of the work has been previously described, and the manner in which the head is geared is shown in Figs. 44 and 45. The four change gears are known as gear on screw, first gear on stud (because it is the first to be put on), second gear on stud, and gear on worm. The screw gear and first gear on stud are the drivers, and the others are the driven gears. By using different combinations of the change gears furnished, the ratio of the longitudinal movement of the table to the rotary movement of the work can be varied; in other words, the leads of the spirals it is possible to cut are governed directly by these gears. Usually they are of such ratio that the work is advanced more than an inch while making one turn; thus the spirals cut on milling machines are designated in terms of inches to one turn, rather than turns, or threads, per inch. For example, a spiral is said to be of 8 inches lead, not that its pitch is 1/8-turn per inch.

The feed screw of the table has four threads to the inch, and 40 turns of the worm make one turn of the headstock spindle; accordingly, if change gears of equal diameter are used, the work will make a complete turn while it is moved lengthwise 10 inches; that is, the spiral will have a lead of 10 inches. This

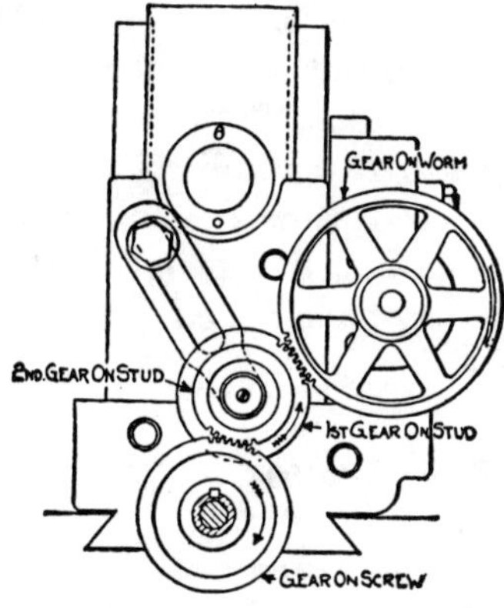

Figure 44. Gearing when no idler is required.

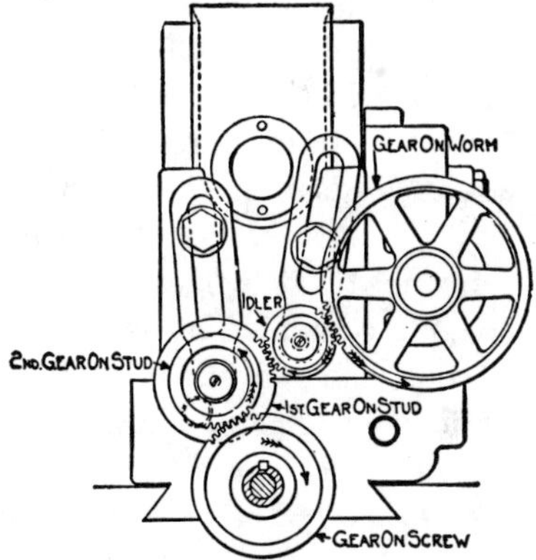

Figure 45. Gearing with idler in use.

is the lead of the machine, and it is the resultant of the action of the parts of the machine that are always employed in this work, and it is so regarded in making the calculations used in cutting spirals.

PRINCIPLE SAME AS FOR CHANGE GEARS OF A LATHE. In principle, these calculations are the same as for change gears of a screw cutting lathe. The compound ratio of the driven to the driving gears equals, in all cases, the ratio of the lead of the required spiral to the lead of the machine. This can be demonstrated readily by changing the diameters of the gears. Gears of the same diameter produce, as explained, a spiral with a lead of 10 inches, the same lead as the lead of the machine. Three gears of equal diameter and a driven gear double this diameter, producing a spiral with a lead of 20 inches, or twice the lead of the machine. With both driven gears, twice the diameters of the drivers, the ratio being compound, a spiral is produced with a lead of 40 inches, or four times the machine's lead. Conversely, driving gears twice the diameter of the driven produce a spiral with a lead equal to $\frac{1}{4}$ the lead of the machine, or $2\frac{1}{2}$ inches.

$$\frac{\text{Driven gears}}{\text{Driving gears}} = \frac{\text{Lead of required spiral}}{\text{Lead of machine}}$$

or, since the product of each class of gears determines the ratio, the head being compound geared, and since the lead of the machine is 10 inches,

$$\text{the } \frac{\text{Product of driven gears}}{\text{Product of driving gears}} = \frac{\text{Lead of required spiral.}}{10}$$

That is, the compound ratio of the driven to the driving gears may always be represented by a fraction whose numerator is the lead to be cut and whose denominator is 10. In other words, the ratio is as the required lead is to 10. For example, if the required lead is 20, the ratio is 20 : 10. To express this in units instead of tens, the ratio is always the same as one-tenth of what the required lead is to 1. And frequently this is a very convenient way to think of the ratio; for example, if the lead is 40, the ratio of the gears is 4 : 1. If the lead is 25, the gears are 2.5 : 1, and so on.

To illustrate the usual calculations, assume that a spiral of 12-inch lead is to be cut. The compound ratio of the driven to the driving gears equals the desired lead divided by 10, or it may be represented by the fraction $\frac{12}{10}$. Resolving this into two factors to represent the two pairs of change gears, $\frac{12}{10} = \frac{3}{2} \times \frac{4}{5}$. Both terms of the first factor are multiplied by such a number (24 in this instance) that the resulting numerator and denominator will correspond with the number of teeth of two of the change gears furnished with the machine (such multiplications do not affect the value of a fraction) $\frac{3}{2} \times \frac{24}{24} = \frac{72}{48}$. The second factor is similarly treated, $\frac{4}{5} \times \frac{8}{8} = \frac{32}{40}$, and the gears with 72, 32, 48 and 40 teeth are selected.

$$\frac{12}{10} = \left[\frac{72 \times 32}{48 \times 40}\right]$$

The first two are the driven, and the last two the drivers, the numerators of the fractions representing the driven gears. The 72 is the worm gear, 40 the first on stud, 32 the second on stud, and 48 the screw gear. The two driving gears might be transposed, and the two driven gears might also be transposed, without changing the spiral. That is, the 72 could be used as the second on stud and the 32 as the worm gear if such an arrangement were more convenient. The following rules express in abridged form the methods of figuring change gears to cut given spirals and also of ascertaining what spirals can be cut with change gears.

Rules for Obtaining the Ratio of the Gears Necessary to Cut a Given Spiral. Note the ratio of the required lead to 10. This ratio is the compound ratio of the driven to the driving gears. Example: If the lead of the required spiral is 12 inches, 12 to 10 will be the ratio of the gears. Or, divide the required lead by 10 and note the ratio between the quotient and 1. This ratio is usually the most simple form of the compound ratio of the driven to the driving gears. Example: If the required lead is 40 inches, the quotient is 40 ÷ 10, and the ratio 4 to 1.

Rule for Determining Number of Teeth of Gears Required to Cut a Given Spiral. Having obtained the ratio between the required lead and 10 by one of the preceding rules, express the ratio in the form of a fraction; resolve this fraction into two factors; and raise these factors to higher terms that correspond with the teeth of gears that can be conveniently used. The numerators will represent the driven and the denominators the driving gears that will produce the required spiral. For example: What gears shall be used to cut a lead of 27 inches?

$$\frac{27}{10} = \frac{3}{2} \times \frac{9}{5} = \left(\frac{3}{2} \times \frac{16}{16}\right) \times \left(\frac{9}{5} \times \frac{8}{8}\right) = \frac{48 \times 72}{32 \times 40}$$

From the fact that the product of the driven gears divided by the product of the drivers equals the lead divided by 10, or one-tenth of the lead, it is evident that ten times the product of the driven gears divided by the product of the drivers will equal the lead of the spiral. Hence the rule:

Rule for Ascertaining what Spiral May be Cut by Any Given Change Gears. Divide ten times the product of the driven gears by the product of the drivers, and the quotient will be the lead of the resulting spiral in inches to one turn. For example: What spiral will be cut by gears with 48, 72, 32, and 40 teeth, the first two being used as driven gears? Spiral to be cut equals

$$\frac{10 \times 48 \times 72}{32 \times 40} = 27 \text{ inches in one turn.}$$

This rule is often of service in determining what spirals may be cut with the gears the machinist chances to have at hand. Combinations of gears that are too small in diameter to reach for right-hand spirals can generally be used for left-hand spirals because the reverse gear is then required and will enable the gears to reach.

As mentioned, the two driving gears or the two driven gears of any combination can be transposed, but a driver must not be substituted for a driven or vice versa. Four different arrangements of the gears of any combination are thus possible without changing the ratio, and when one arrangement interferes or will not reach, the others should be tried. Thus, the gears to give a lead of 3.60 in. are: drivers, 100 teeth and 32 teeth; driven, 24 teeth and 48 teeth. By transposing the gears, the following four arrangements may be obtained:

	1st	*2nd*	*3rd*	*4th*
Drivers				
Gear on screw	100	32	100	32
1st gear on stud	32	100	32	100
Driven				
2nd gear on stud	24	24	48	48
Gear on worm	48	48	24	24

The first arrangement, however, is found by actual test to be the only one available owing to the fact that the interference of the gears in the other combinations prevents their meshing properly.

When very short leads are required, it is preferable to disengage the wormwheel and connect the gearing directly to the headstock spindle (using the differential indexing center). This method gives leads one-fortieth of the leads given in the table for the same combinations of gears. Thus, for a lead of 6.160 in., the table calls for gear on worm, 56 teeth; 1st gear on stud, 40 teeth; 2nd gear on stud, 44 teeth; and gear on screw, 100 teeth. Putting the 56-tooth gear on the spindle instead of on the worm gives the following lead:

$$\frac{6.160}{40} = .154 \text{ in.}$$

By this method, very short leads may be obtained without excessively straining the mechanism, but the regular means of indexing the work cannot be employed. A method that can be used for indexing when using the differential center is to have the number of teeth in the gear on the spindle some multiple of the number required to be indexed. Swing the gears out of mesh and advance the gear on spindle the number of teeth required to index the work one division at each indexing. Thus, if 9 divisions are required with a lead of .261 in., select a lead from the table equal to about .261 in. × 40 = 10.440 in. when the gear on worm (which will not be the gear on spindle) is some multiple of 9, as 72. The nearest lead is 10.467 in., which gives

$$\frac{10.467}{40} = .2617 \text{ in. lead}$$

giving an error of .0007 inch. To index the work, the gear on spindle is advanced $\frac{72}{9} = 8$ teeth at each indexing.

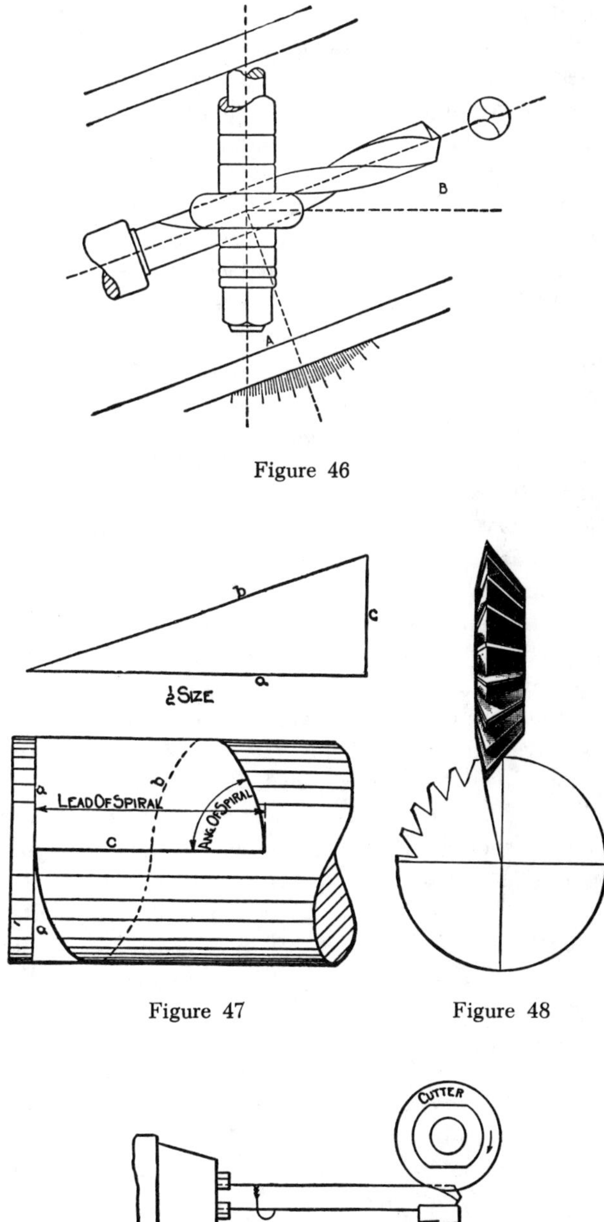

Figure 46

Figure 47

Figure 48

Figure 49

There are also short lead attachments which can be used to cut short leads. An index plate is provided for use in cutting multiple threads.

Position of the Table in Cutting Spirals. The change gears having been selected, the next step in cutting spirals is to determine the position at which the table must be placed to bring the spiral in line with the cutter as the work is being milled. The correct position of the table is indicated by the angle shown at *A*, Fig. 46; note that this angle has the same number of degrees as angle *B*, which is termed the angle of the spiral and is formed by the intersection of the spiral and a line parallel with the axis of the piece being milled. The reason that angles *A* and *B* are alike is that their corresponding sides are perpendicular to each other.

The angle of the spiral depends upon the lead of the spiral and the diameter of the piece to be milled. The greater the lead of a spiral of any given diameter, the smaller the angle, and the greater the diameter of any spiral with a given lead, the greater the spiral angle. The angle desired can be ascertained in two ways, graphically or, more conveniently, by a simple calculation and reference to a table of natural tangents. In determining it graphically, a right triangle is drawn to scale. One of the sides which forms the right angle represents the circumference of the piece in inches, and the hypotenuse represents the line of the spiral. The angle between the lines representing the path of the spiral and the lead of the spiral is the angle of the spiral. This angle can be transferred from the drawing to the work by a bevel protractor, or even by cutting a paper template and winding it about the work as shown in Fig. 47. The machine is then set so that the spiral or groove as it touches the cutter will be in line with the cutter. The angle may also be measured and the saddle set to a corresponding number of degrees by the graduations on the base.

The natural tangent of the angle of the spiral is the quotient of the circumference of the piece divided by the lead of the spiral. The second method of obtaining the angle of the spiral is to divide the circumference of the piece by the lead and note the number of degrees opposite the figures that correspond with the quotients in a table of natural tangents. The angle having been thus obtained, the saddle is set by the graduations on the base. This second method is more satisfactory because it is more accurate and there is less liability of error than with the first. The saddle can be set to the proper angle, but before cutting into the blank, it is well to let the mill just touch the work, then run the work along by hand and make a slight spiral mark, and by this mark see whether the change gears give the right lead. Special care should be taken in cutting spirals that the work does not slip. When a cut is made, it is well to drop the work away from the mill while coming back for another cut or the mill may be stopped and turned to such a position that the teeth will not touch the work while the table is brought back preparatory to another cut.

SETTING CUTTER CENTRAL. In making such cuts that are alike on both sides (for instance, the threads of worms or the teeth of spiral gears), care must be taken to set the work centrally perpendicular with the center line of the cutter before swinging the saddle to the angle of the spiral.

Cuts that have one face radial, especially those that are spiral, are best made with an angular cutter of the form shown in Fig. 48 because cutters of this form readily clear the radial face of the cut, keep sharp for some time, and produce a smooth surface.

TWIST DRILLS. The operation of milling a twist drill is shown in Fig. 49. The drill is held in a collet or chuck, and, if very long, it is allowed to pass through the spindle of the headstock. The cutter is brought directly over the center of the drill, and the table is set at the angle of spiral. The depth of groove in a twist drill diminishes as it approaches the shank in order to obtain increased strength at the place where the drill generally breaks. The variation in depth is conditional, depending mainly on the strength it is desirable to obtain or the usage to which the drill is subject. To secure this variation in the depth of the groove, the spiral head spindle is elevated slightly, depending on the length of the flute and diameter of the drill. The outer end of the drill is supported by the center rest, and when quite small, should be pressed down firmly, until the cutter has passed over the end. The elevating screw of this rest is hollow and contains a small center piece with a V-groove cut therein to aid in holding the work central. This piece may be made in other shapes to adapt it to special work.

Another and very important operation on the twist drill is that of "backing off" the rear of the lip to give it the necessary clearance to prevent excessive friction during drilling. Figure 50 shows the saddle is turned about one-half degree as for cutting a right-hand spiral, but since the angle depends on several conditions, it will be necessary to determine what the effect will be under different circumstances. A slight study of the figure will be sufficient for this if the effects of the different angles, mills, and pitches of spirals are assumed. The object of placing the saddle at an angle is to cause the mill *E* to cut into the lip at *e′*, and have it just touch the surface at *e′*. The line *r* being parallel with the face of the mill, the angular deviation of the saddle is shown at *a* in comparison with the side of the drill. Note that although the drill has a positive traversing and rotative movement, the edge of the mill at *e′* must always touch the lip at a given distance from the front edge, this being the vanishing point. The other surface forming the real diameter of the drill is beyond reach of the cutter and is left to guide and steady it while in use. The point *e*, shown in the enlarged section, shows where the cutter commences and its increase until it reaches a maximum depth at *e*, where it may be increased or diminished according to the angle employed in the operation, the line of cutter action being represented by *ii*.

Before backing off, the surface of the smaller drills in particular should be colored with a solution of sulphate of copper, water, and sulphuric acid. This solution can be applied with a piece of waste; it will give the piece a distinct copper color. The object of this is to show clearly the action of the mill on the lip of the drill. When the action is satisfactory, a uniform streak of coppered surface the full length of the lip from the front edge *g* back to *e* is left untouched by the mill.

The coloring solution can be made by the following formula:

Sulphate of copper (saturated solution)	4 oz.
Water	8 oz.
Sulphuric acid	1 oz.

Some machinists prefer to begin the cut at the shank end. By starting the cut in at this end, the tendency to lift the drill blank from the rest is lessened.

CUTTING LEFT-HAND SPIRALS. For the production of left-hand spirals, the only changes necessary are the swinging of the saddle to the opposite side of the center line and the introduction of an intermediate gear upon the stud (Fig. 45) to engage with either pair of change gears for changing the direction of rotation of the headstock spindle.

CUTTING SPIRALS WITH AN END MILL. When spirals

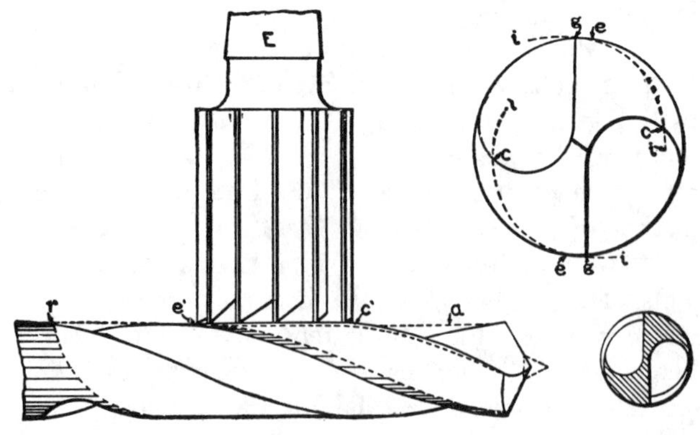

Figure 50

cannot be conveniently cut with side or angular milling cutters, as previously described, it is sometimes convenient to use end mills. Such instances might occur when the diameter of the piece is very large or when the spiral is of such a lead that the table cannot be set at the requisite angle. In such cases, the work is so held that its center and that of the mill will be in the same plane and the saddle is set at zero.

Lubrication and Maintenance Procedures

OILING. It is well to remember when applying oil that ordinary bearings can hold only a few drops at a time, and that this amount applied at regular and frequent intervals is far more beneficial than a flood of lubricant at irregular periods. There are so many good machinery oils on the market that it is hard to specify any one as the best to use for lubricating a milling machine. Any good coal or mineral oil can be used. Animal oil will gum up the bearing surfaces, oil channels, and tubes, and it has a tendency to retard rather than render easy the movements of the different parts. It is cheaper to buy good oil than to run the risk of damage to bearings from overheating or scoring.

CARE OF DRIVING CHAIN OR MOTOR-DRIVEN MACHINES. The chain on motor-driven machines should be kept clean, well lubricated, and properly adjusted. The tension at which the chain should run is obtained by a convenient adjustment on the motor bracket. Properly adjusted, the chain should have a little less tension than would be considered right for a leather belt.

ADJUSTMENTS. As parts and bearing surfaces wear, it becomes necessary to make adjustments from time to time, and, at all important points, convenient means are provided for doing this. Flat bearings are provided with tapered gibs that are easily adjusted, and any cylindrical bearings subject to hard wear have adequate means for readjustment. It is essential that any adjustment required be made promptly, for otherwise the accuracy of the machine is impaired. Furthermore, parts wear much more rapidly as the lost motion becomes greater. By a little examination and adjustment every now and then the efficiency of a machine can be maintained and its life greatly prolonged.

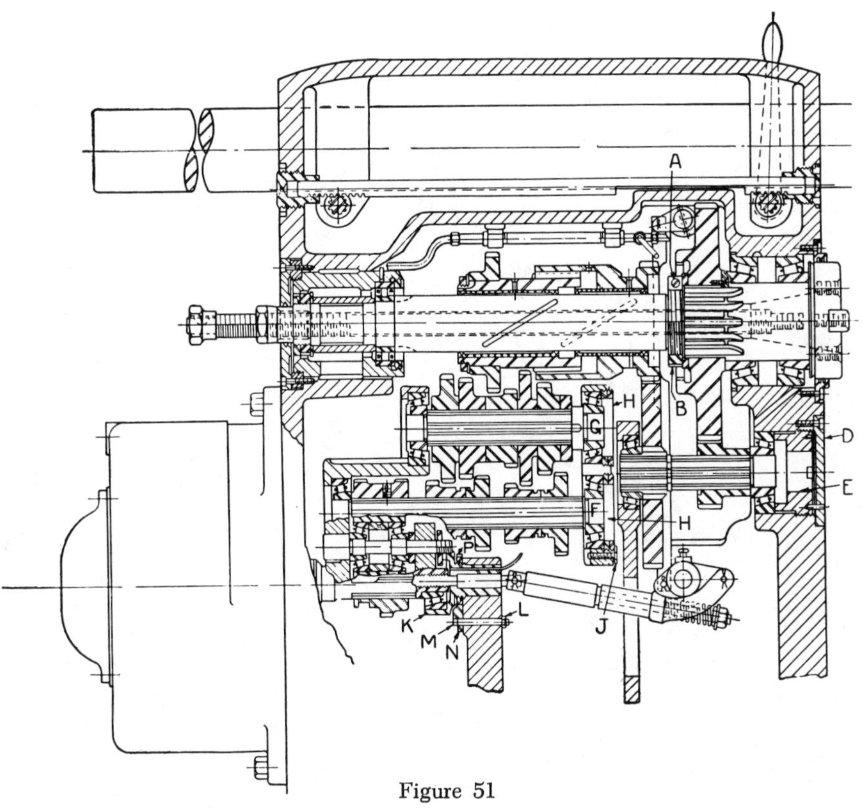

Figure 51

Before proceeding to adjust or take anything apart, it is a good plan to study the machine's construction carefully. Many times this simple precaution will obviate considerable trouble. Manufacturers usually provide detailed instructions regarding important adjustments with each piece of equipment. It is therefore unnecessary to give detailed instructions on adjustments in this book.

Figure 51 will be of interest in showing a typical set of instructions for the adjustment of the spindle bearings of the back gear and sliding gear shafts usually furnished by the manufacturer of the machine.

To adjust the front spindle bearing, loosen screw *A* and tighten nut *B;* tighten screw *A* after the adjustment.

To adjust the back gear bearing, remove cover *D* and adjust nut *E* so that the bearings are snug; then replace cover *D,* making sure that the locking pin registers in the hole in the nut.

To adjust the bearings on shafts *F–G,* remove the locks *J* from the two nuts *H* and adjust to suit. Replace the locks in each nut.

To adjust the bearing in holder *K,* remove nut *L,* bolt *M,* and lock *N.* Adjust nut *P* to suit. Replace lock, bolt, and nut.

When it may be necessary to make adjustments, avoid putting too great a pressure on the bearings.

Chapter 15

Shapers

Shapers are used for the machining of flat or plane surfaces which may be in horizontal, vertical, or angular planes, and for the machining of irregular shapes. This machine is indispensable for the machining of jig, fixture, and other small parts. Figures 1, 2, 3, and 4 show the various parts and adjustment of the shaper. Shapers are classified in several different ways; for example, the name applied to a given design may indicate the action of the machine when in operation, the type of driving mechanism, or other constructional features. The two types of shapers commonly used in machine shops, toolrooms, and production plants are the horizontal and the vertical (Figs. 2 and 4). The size of the shaper is designated by the maximum length of its stroke given in inches.

On shapers, the work is held on a table or knee, and the tool is held in a tool post on the reciprocating ram by means of which it moves across the work. The knee has both transverse and vertical adjustments and is provided with hand and power feeds.

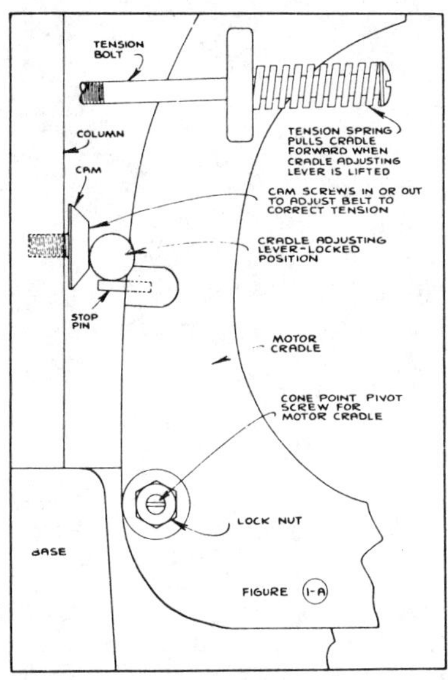

Figure 1

These machines are particularly adapted to small work of the kind usually held in a vise. The length of the ram stroke is adjustable, and the work can be readily shaped close to the shoulder because the length of stroke of the ram is positive.

Vertical Shapers

The vertical shaper (Fig. 5) is generally considered a heavy-duty machine. It is usually used to produce work that cannot be handled on other types of machines. The *rated size* of a vertical shaper is given in terms of the stroke of the ram. Sometimes the diameter of the table is given to ascertain the size of the work a particular machine is able to handle, similar to the swing of a lathe in order to specify its rated size. Since vertical shapers are generally designed and constructed for special operations, it would be impractical to give the procedures for operating this type of shaper. Modern horizontal shapers, however, are in general use, and the operation procedures of this type of shaper are, to a great extent, standardized.

Horizontal Shapers

The horizontal shaper shown in Fig. 6 is a modern universal type. It is equipped with a revolving table with a tilting top that revolves at any angle. The table has one solid face and one tilting face with adjustments up to 15 degrees either way on an axis at right angles to the trunnion of the machine. Each movement is made by a crank wrench through a worm wheel, and all settings are indicated by graduations. The swiveling vise that is usually furnished by the manufacturer permits the machinist to rotate the work around three possible axes.

Power Rapid Traverse. Where some jobs have to be performed at specific speeds, the power rapid

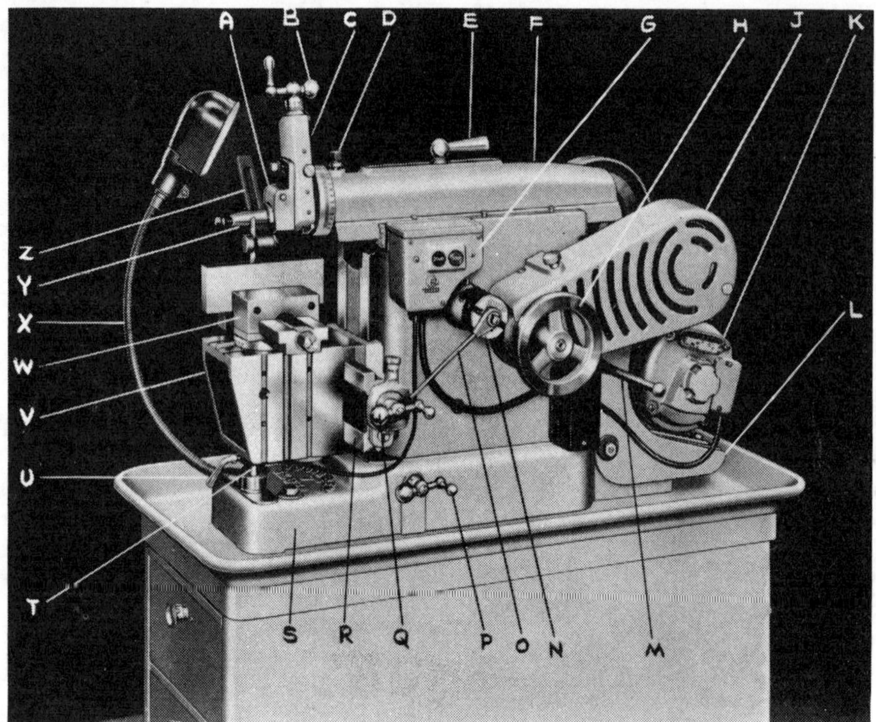

Figure 2. Crank-driven column shaper.

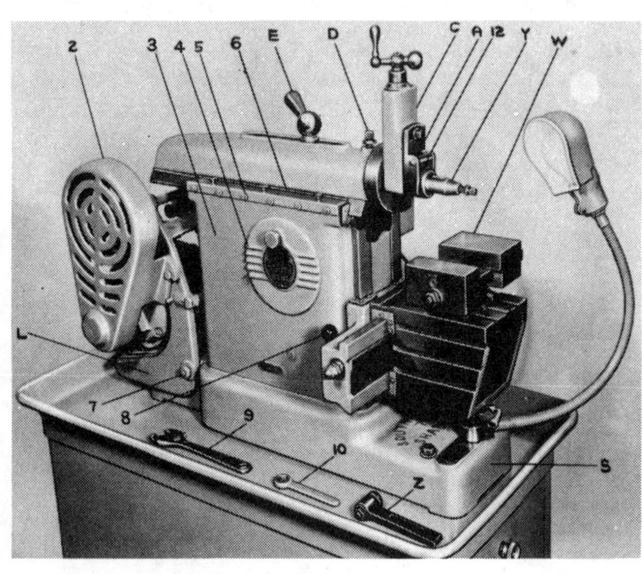

Figure 3

Figure 4

Various parts and adjustments of a shaper shown in Figures 1-4. (A) Clapper Box, (B) Down-feed Handle, (C) Head, (D) Head Swivel Lock Screw, (E) Ram Clamping Handle, (F) Ram, (G) Switch Box, (H) Hand Wheel, (J) Drive-pulley Guard, (K) Motor, (L) Motor Cradle, (M) Tension Release Lever, (N) Eccentric, (O) Feed Rod, (P) Table Elevating Crank, (Q) Cross Feed Crank, (R) Cross-rail, (S) Base, (T) Work-table Support, (U) Support Locking Handle, (V) Work Table, (W) Vise, (X)Lamp, (Y) Tool post, (Z) Tool holder, (2) Motor Pulley Guard, (3) Column, (4) Cover Plate, (5) Gib Adjusting Screw, (6) Gib, (7) Motor Cradle Adjusting Screw, (8) Elevating Lock Handle, (9) Adjustable Wrench, (10) Tail-stock Wrench, (12) Clapper Block, (13) Feed Lock Screw, (14) Feed Pawl, (15) Counter-shaft, (16) Counter-shaft Pulley, (17) Counterbalance Adjusting Screw.

Figure 5. Vertical shaper.

traverse is a valuable addition to any shaper. Time is saved when the piece is finished because the power rapid traverse can be quickly traversed to one side without taking time to crank the table. The work can be unloaded without interference of the tool and the post.

The quick traverse operates directly off the drive pulley of the machine. It is actuated by a lever and is always available to the machinist. Five antifriction bearings are used in mounting the shafts which bring the quick traverse to the table. A safety crank hangs free in place during rapid traverse, ready for instant use in hand feeding; it is also used by the machinist for rail elevating and lowering. The same lever engages and controls the direction of the table during feed and also controls the direction of the power rapid traverse.

Transmission. Changes are made by two levers within easy reach of the operating position. They are on the speed indicator usually attached to the machine. The ease with which speed changes can be made encourages the machinist to use the correct cutting speed. The gears in a modern shaper are placed entirely within the column of the machine. This gives compact and powerful transmission that is practically noiseless and accessible at all times.

Feed. The feeding motion in modern shapers is actuated by a series of cams. This gives a smooth, rather than an abrupt, movement and enables the entire feed under any condition to be confined within the return stroke.

The thrust bearings on each end of the three feed screws reduce the friction at these points and make hand feeding easy. Another feature is the omission of the usual feed box on the end of the cross rail. This is transferred to the side of the column of the machine. Eleven feeds ranging from .010 to .170 inch (.005 to .085 inch optional) are provided. The amount of feed is controlled by the machinist by means of a lever that is mounted on a direct reading dial which indicates the feed in thousandths. Three-quarters of one turn changes the feed from minimum to maximum. A second lever for feed engagement has three positions marked stop, right-hand, and left-hand, indicating the direction of the table movement. All feed changes may be made while the machine is running.

Length of Stroke. In modern machines, the length of the stroke is maintained without the usual clamping nut on the stroke adjusting shaft, the purpose of the nut being fulfilled automatically. The length of the stroke can be changed while the ram is in motion. The indicator dial shows the setting for the length of the stroke at all times, whether the ram is in motion or stopped. A guard covers the stroke adjusting shaft.

Figure 6. Universal shaper.

Ram. The ram is a V-type. Adjustment is made with a full-length taper gib that is controlled by a single screw. The continuous full-length taper gib affords a solid bearing and forces the ram to wear straight. Adjustments can be made quickly and easily. Another advantage is that the length of the ram bearing is the same length as the ram itself. Thus, the extension of the ram bearing out to the swivel head reduces the overhang from the ram to the tool to an absolute minimum. The movement of the ram clamp lever is limited in its open position, and no damage can result to the ram positioning screw.

Column. Both sides of the column top (the ram ways) are built to form a solid part of the column casting, adding to the rigidity of the column. The column throat is closed by a guard so that chips cannot be swept off the work into the shaper.

Tool Slide. The tool slide is solid and fits into the swivel instead of clamping around it, thus avoiding the open or hollow form with its spring and breakage under overload. The guides in the tool slide are fitted with a taper gib having a single-screw adjustment. The tool head is graduated; when it is swiveled to any angle, it can be clamped by using a T-slot in the ram. The feed screw is fitted with a micrometer dial graduated to thousandths. The tool post is made unusually large and is provided with a specially hard screw of the same size as the screw on the vise of the machine. This permits the use of the long vise range when it is necessary to tighten large tools in the tool slide. The tool slide has a clamp screw which assures a set position of the tool for horizontal surfacing and acts against the gib. This prevents burring the tool slide.

Clapper Box. The clapper box in the modern machine is constructed of steel instead of cast iron. The clapper and the serrated tool plate are made in one piece and hold the clapper.

Crank Gear. The crank gear is made in one piece with helical-cut teeth (Fig. 7). This type of construction insures long life to the crank gear plus finishing cuts that are always free from gear-tooth chatter marks. The crank gear is usually located as near as possible in the column of the machine without cutting the ram bearing, and it fits beneath a guard cast with the column.

Rocker Arm. The rocker arm (Fig. 8) is made in one piece, fulcrumed at the bottom, and connected to the ram of the machine by a steel link. Both the fulcrum and the link pins are hardened and ground.

Crank Block. The crank block is held in the dovetail slide of the crank gear by a taper gib and is made of drop-forged steel with a hardened and ground pin (Fig. 9).

Figure 7. Crank gear.

Figure 8. Rocker arm.

Sliding Block. The sliding block is made of gray iron with a hardened and ground steel taper gib on its driving side to compensate for wear. Therefore, there is a hardened steel crank bearing in the gray iron sliding block and a hardened steel crank block gib bearing against the semisteel rocker arm, thus

Figure 9. Crank block.

affording ideal bearing conditions. If the shaper is used on a great variety of work—some long and some short—the wear will be comparatively uniform over the entire sliding surface of the rocker arm, and adjustment for the wear can be made with the taper gib which is on the driving side of the crank block.

Compound Cross Rail. The compound cross rail is square-locked to the column.

Apron. The apron is secured to the long and narrow guide of the cross rail by taper gibs at the top and bottom. It is provided with T-slots for holding the work when necessary. These T-slots do not run across the entire width; they leave reinforcing ribs at the center and the sides, making a solid wall

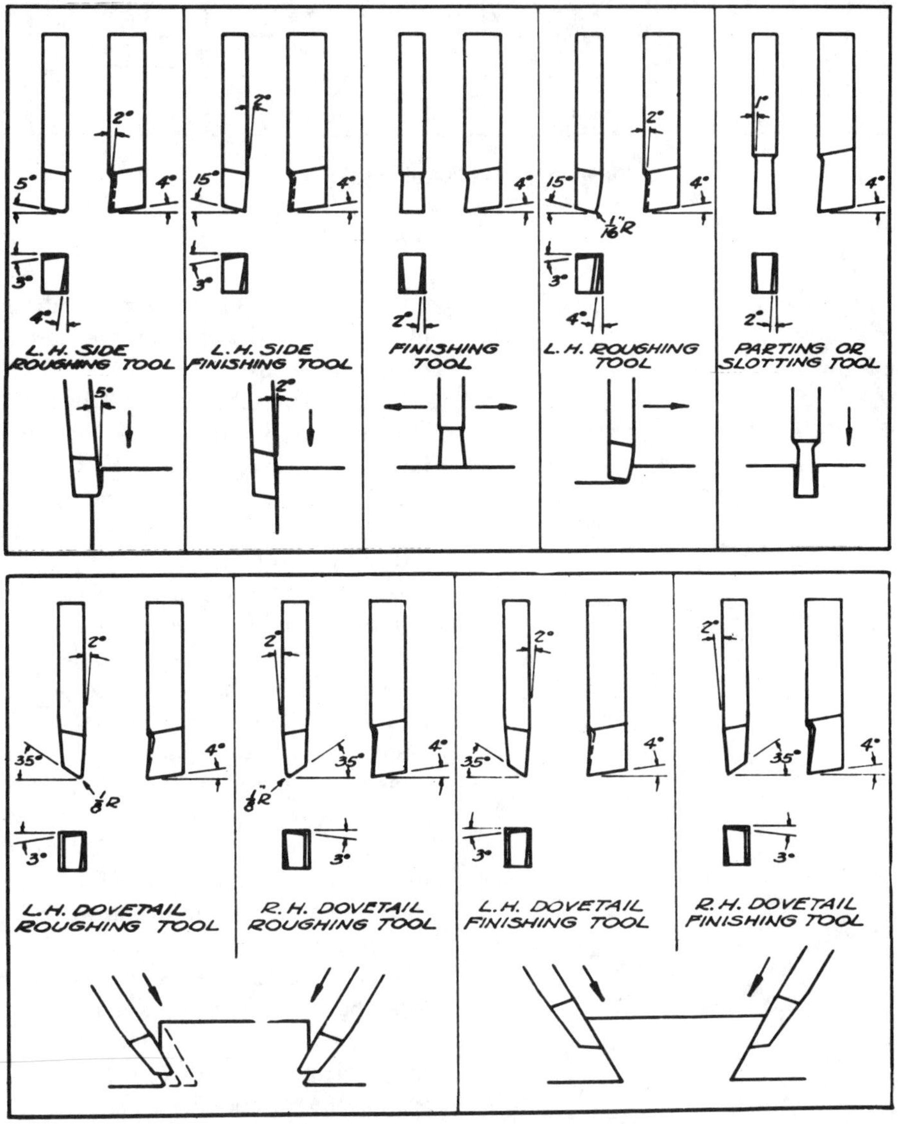

Figure 10. Cast iron cutting tools.

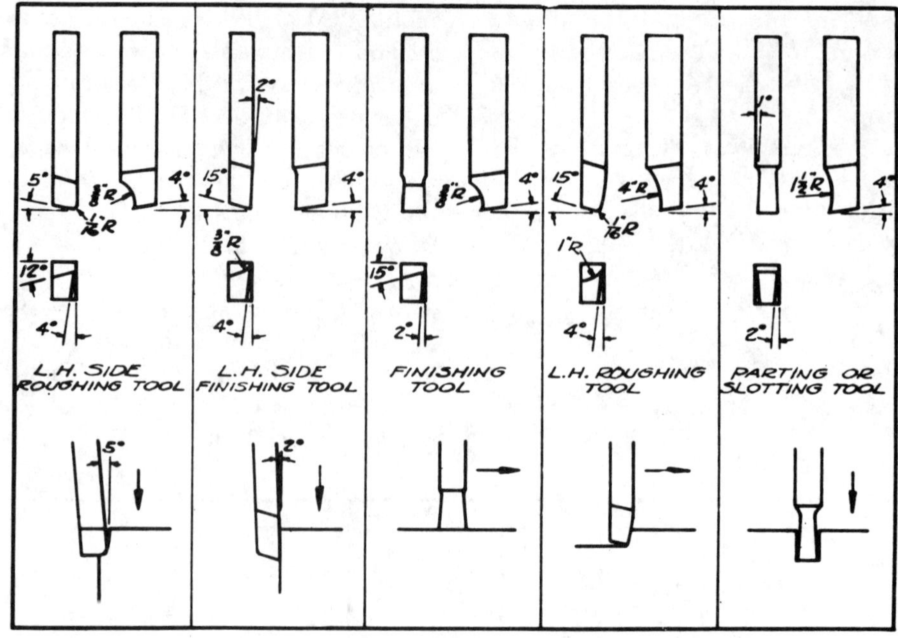

Figure 11. Mild steel cutting tools.

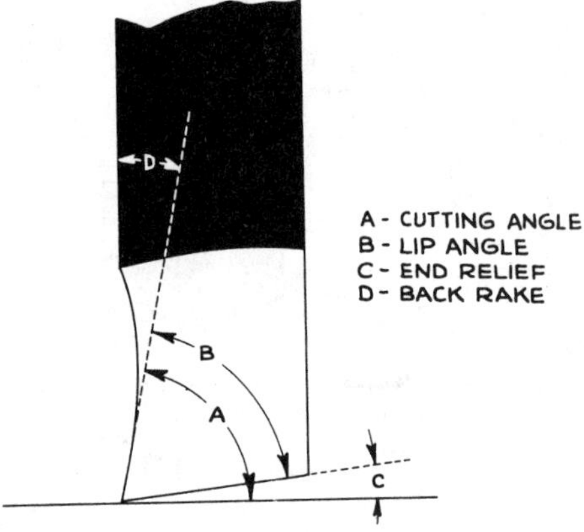

Figure 12

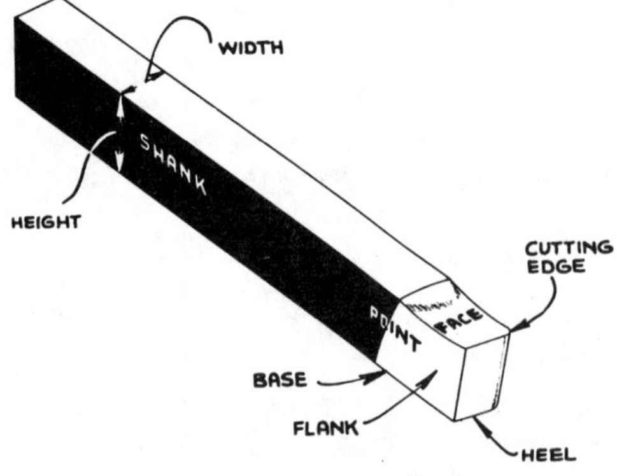

Figure 13

apron and a much stiffer member. A slot is also placed across the face of the apron for the proper alignment of fixtures.

Table. The table is a full box form having small openings in the front and the bottom. Two bolts fasten the table at the top of the apron, and four bolts secure it to the front. The spacing of the T-slots in the table is made so that the vise will fit either the top or the side of the table.

Cutting Tools and Holders. The *straight-shank tool holder* holds the tool parallel with the front and rear surfaces of the tool holder. Since the tool is held parallel with the surfaces, it is at right angles to the direction of the stroke. Thus, the clearance angles which are needed for cutting are easily determined and ground without having to take into consideration the inclined angle of the tool. With the adjustable head of the tool holder, the tool may be turned either to the right or the left, still maintaining the same attack angle to the work. The shape of the tool varies with the character of the work. A number of tools generally used are shown in Figs. 10 and 11. The shape or form of the tool depends upon the shape of the cut, the kind of finish required, and the kind of material to be machined. The rake, the cutting angle, and the clearances depend upon the nature of the material.

Figures 12 and 13 show the terms to designate

the parts of a single-point cutting tool and the working angles used in grinding them. The following terms are accepted standards used in connection with shaper cutting tools:

The *point* is the part of the tool which is shaped to produce the cutting edges and face.

The *shank* is the part of the tool on one end of which the point is formed or the bit is supported. The shank, in turn, is supported in the tool holder of the machine.

The *face* is the surface of the tool on which the chip rolls or flows as it is cut from the work.

The *cutting edge* is the portion of the face edge along which the chip is separated from the work; it consists of the side-cutting edge, the nose radius, and the end-cutting edge.

The *shape* of the tool is the contour of the face when viewed as presented to the work.

The *working angles* are the angles between the tool and the work which depend on the shape of the tool and on its position with respect to the work.

The *cutting angle* is the angle between the face of the tool and the surface to the machined surface at the point of cutting. It equals 90 degrees minus the true-rake angle.

The *lip angle* is the included angle of the tool between the face and the ground flank measured in a plane at right angles to the cutting edge. When measured in a plane perpendicular to the cutting edge at the end of the tool, it is called the *end-lip angle.*

The *back-rake angle* is the angle between the face of a tool and a line parallel to the base of the shank.

The *end-relief* angle is the angle between the portion of the end flank immediately below the cutting edge and a line drawn through that cutting edge perpendicular to the base.

The *side-rake angle* is the angle between the face of a tool and a line parallel to the base.

The *true-rake angle* is the slope of the tool face toward the base from the active cutting edge in the direction of chip flow. This angle will vary with the setting of the tool and with the feed and the depth of cut.

A *right-cut single-point tool,* when viewed from the face, has the cutting edge on the right side (Fig. 10).

A *left-cut tool* has the cutting edge on the left when looking at the face (Fig. 10).

The shape of the tool may be curved, flat, or its sides may converge to a sharp point, depending upon the surface being machined.

There is usually a difference between the roughing and the finishing tool. In addition, a tool may be offset, or bent to the right or to the left, and may feed either in a right-hand or left-hand direction (Fig. 10).

Although the contours of shaper tools are generally similar to lathe tools, they differ in their clearance angles. Lathe turning tools are usually ground with a front clearance of 10 to 12 degrees, and are set above the center so as to have the effect of 2 or 3 degrees of working clearance. Since there is no rocker in the tool post of the shaper, the shaper tool cannot be adjusted for clearance, and the correct clearance angle must be ground on the tool itself. The clearance angles of shaper tools generally used, shown in Figs. 10 and 11, are as follows:

The *roughing tool* is similar in contour to the lathe turning tool. It has a side rake but no top rake, and the amount of side rake depends on the hardness of the metal being cut, the harder the metal the less the rake. They are usually used to cut to the left, but they may be ground with the proper clearance and rake and used to cut to the right.

The *roundnose tool* is used for cutting down; its cutting edge is the widest part of the tool; the corners are slightly rounded for longer life; and it cuts down equally well on either the right or the left side. This tool may be used with a very light chip, a coarse feed, and a slow speed for finishing horizontal cast-iron surfaces.

The *squarenose tool* is available in any desired width for roughing and finishing sides and bottoms of grooves, keyways, and shallow shoulder cuts. The cutting edge of this tool is the widest part of the blade.

The *spring tool* or *"Gooseneck"* is used for finishing cast iron. In using this tool, there is less tendency to chatter and to "dig in" than with the shovel nose.

The *downcutting tool* is made in the shape of a left-hand roughing tool except that it is bent in order to cut down on a vertical surface.

Side tools are made for both right-hand and left-hand cuts. They are used for finishing vertical cuts and occasionally for finishing a narrow, horizontal cut adjacent to the vertical cut.

RIGHT-HAND AND LEFT-HAND TOOLS. Figures 10 and 11 show that some shaper tools are both right-hand and left-hand. When a job is being set up in a machine it is advisable to arrange the work and the cutting tool so that the cut can be observed. When taking a horizontal cut on either a shaper or a planer, start the cut on the side toward the machinist. When shoulder cuts or cuts of a similar nature are made, the work must be arranged so that these cuts will come on the side toward the machinist in order to observe the action of the cutting tools.

A great many shaper jobs include the cutting of tongues, grooves, and angles, and they involve cuts on both sides of the work. To assure greater accuracy and speed in one setting of the work, all the surfaces require right-hand and left-hand tools. The terms, right-hand and left-hand, are derived from lathe tools of similar shapes.

Tool Holders. The forged tool has been superseded to a great extent by the modern tool holder and the modern high-speed steel bit. There are distinct advantages to using the tool holder, for the tool bit can easily be ground to the required shape to accomplish any specific operation. Several types of tool holders are available, and their general construction permits the tool bits to be securely and rigidly held in any position so that right-hand or left-hand horizontal, vertical, or angular cuts can be made. When heavy cuts are to be made, these tool holders can be reversed in the tool post. Tool bits are reversible. The cutting edge will be back of the shank of the tool, and any tendency to dig in or to chatter is eliminated.

Holding the Work

Shaper operations are performed on small pieces; therefore the work is held either in a vise or a chuck. Vises or chucks are auxiliaries to the machine, or specifically to the platen or the table of the shaper. Pieces that are too large to be held in a vise or a chuck must be fastened directly to the platen or table of the shaper. When clamping the work to the table of a machine, tighten the clamp bolts so as to hold the work firmly on the table to avoid any

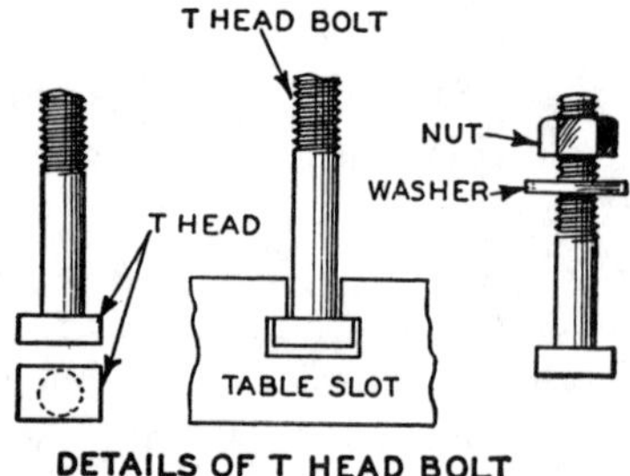

Figure 14

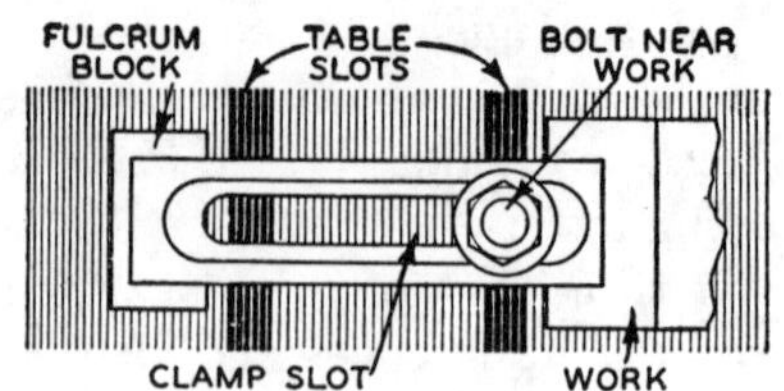

Figure 15

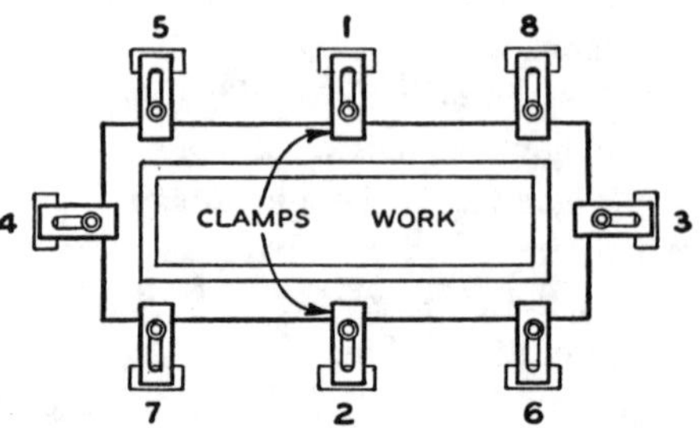

Figuro 16

distortion or spring. The method employed to secure the work is to a great extent dependent upon the type of job to be machined. The work can be fastened by bolts, clamps, stop pins, stop pins and toe dogs, stop pins and strip, special strip pin block and stop pins, or indirectly with a fixture.

Bolts. A complete bolt assembly consists of a bolt, a nut, and a washer (Fig. 14). Table bolts are equipped with T-heads of a size to fit in the table slots. The bolt should always have an ample length of thread to adapt it to work of various thicknesses. A clamping unit consists of a bolt, a bolt assembly, a clamp, and a fulcrum block (Fig. 15).

Clamps. When using clamps, position the work on the table close to the table slot so that the bolt will be as far as is practical from the fulcrum block. Be sure to have the bolt near the work, and screw the nut enough to anchor the work properly. Do not screw the work too tight, for this will have a tendency to spring it.

Where a number of clamps have to be used, proceed as follows: Turn the bolts until the work is lightly clamped. Then tighten the bolts in the sequence as shown in Fig. 16; this will distribute evenly the stress that is brought on the work during clamping.

Select a block of the same thickness as the part that is being clamped when fastening the work to the shaper table. The end of the clamp will then have an even bearing on the work, and the work will be held more securely than if the clamp were bolted

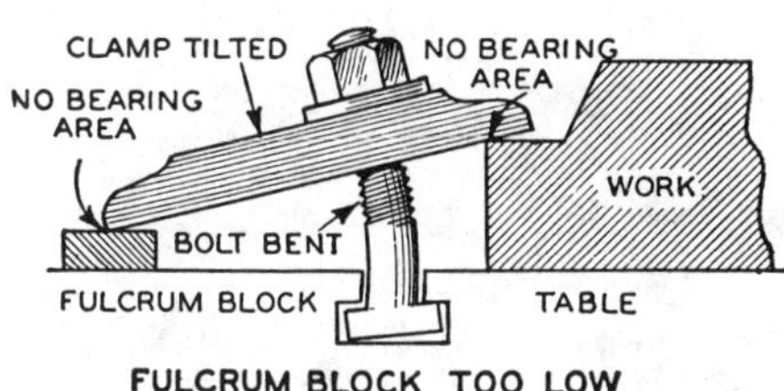

Figure 17

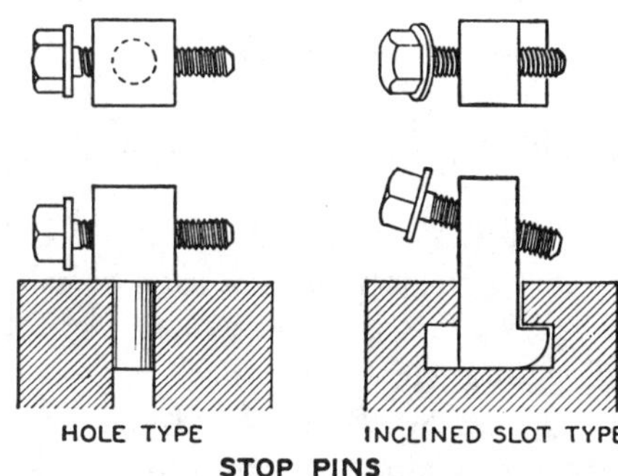

Figure 18

by using a block that was either too high or too low. The effect of low fulcrum blocks is shown in Fig. 17.

STOP PINS. Stop pins are one-leg screw clamps. They are anchored in one of the table holes or slots. The screw can be forced directly against the work or used in conjunction with some other device such as a toe dog to force it against the work (Fig. 18).

STOP PINS AND TOE DOGS. When working on thin stock, stop pins are used in combination with toe dogs as holding units (Fig. 19). A toe dog is a holding device (Fig. 20) similar in shape to a center punch or a cold chisel. It is designed to be forced against the work by a stop pin (Fig. 19). Stop pins are inserted in the table on each side of the work, and the dogs are forced against the work by tightening the stop pin screws. The end of the stop pin screws projects into the short bore in the end of the toe dog, thus connecting the two parts. The work is pressed against the table because of the angular position of the dogs. The angle between the screw and the dog must never be too great. The work must be anchored by a number of stop pin toe dog units to take the thrust properly and secure the work to the table.

STOP PINS AND STRIP. A combination of stop pins and strip is usually adapted to hold down rectangular work of sufficient thickness to project above the strip and stop pin screw (Fig. 21). This combination has a tongue on one side which fits in the table slot and positions the work so that it is parallel to the travel of the tool. Figure 21 shows the strip upside down to illustrate the tongue and holes that are provided for slot bolts.

The procedure for using this combination is as follows: Place the two bolts in the slot, insert the strip tongue side down so that the bolts will pass through the holes with the tongue projecting into the slot, and then secure with the nuts. Put the stop pins into the table holes, and screw them firmly against the work with the strip aligning the work parallel with the tongue of the cutting tool of the shaper. Suitable stops must be provided to take the thrust of the cutting tool.

BRACES. One or more braces are required to take the thrust of the cutting tool where the work that has to be machined projects high above the table of the shaper. When machining work of the type shown

Figure 19

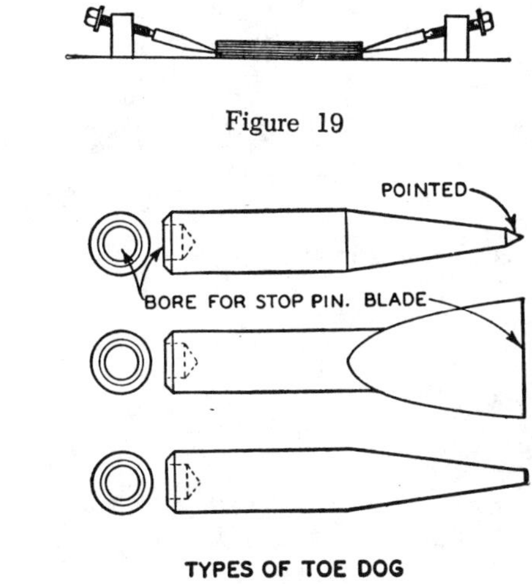

Figure 20

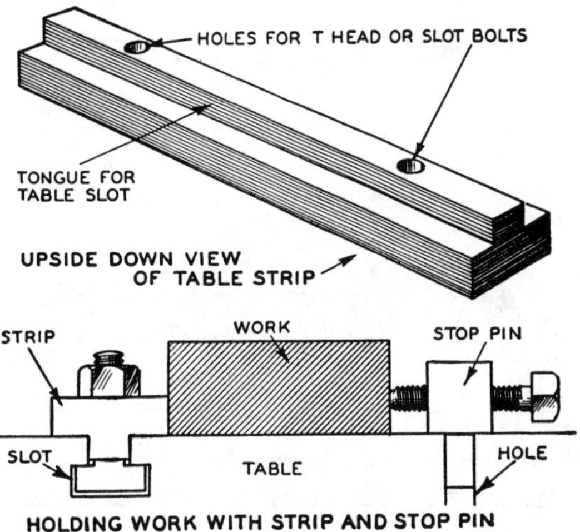

Figure 21

in Fig. 22, the thrust of the cutting tool will tend to rotate the casting around the point marked, *A*, Fig. 22, as the center, indicated by the curved arrow. A properly placed brace will offset that tendency. The clamp at point *A*, Fig. 22, will resist the tendency of the casting to move upward in a circular path around the point marked *B*, Fig. 22, as center. By placing the clamp bolt at point *A* against the lower flange, the clamp will act as a lower stop, and the work will be securely stop-anchored on both the upper and the lower flanges. The number of braces required will depend upon the size and shape of the work.

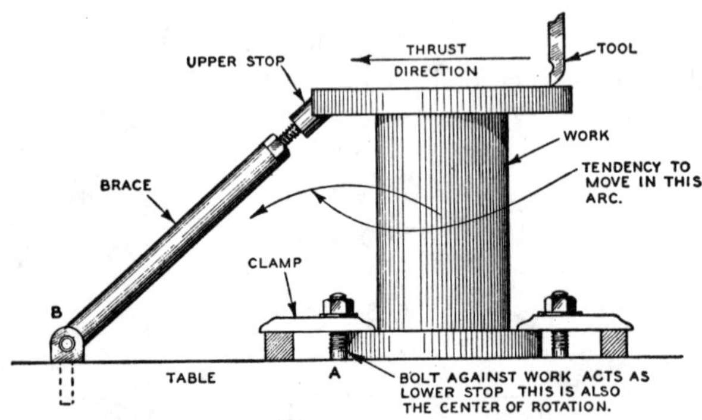

Figure 22

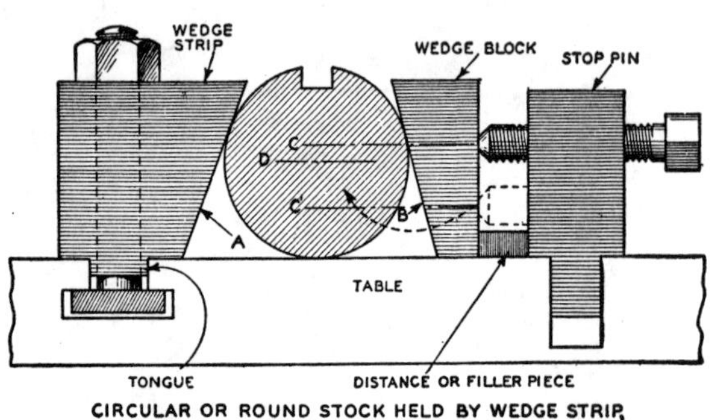

Figure 23

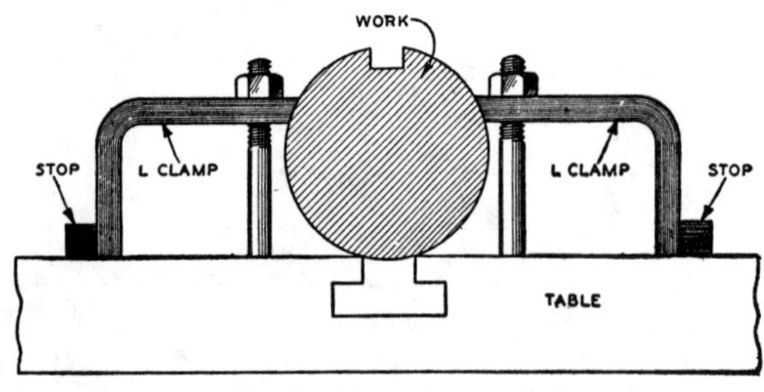

Figure 24

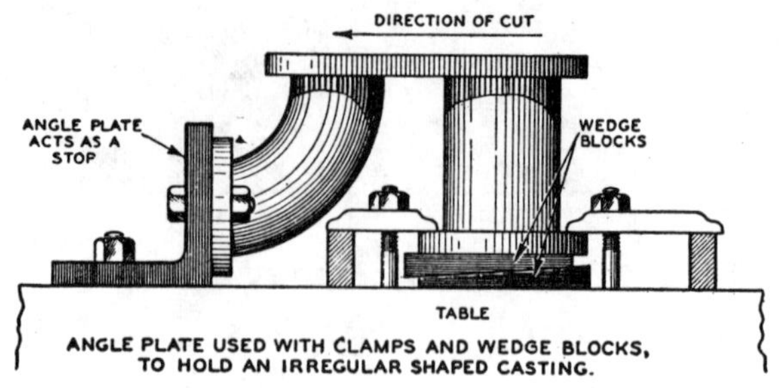

Figure 25

Special Strip Pin Block and Stop Pins. A special strip pin block and stop pins are used to hold circular or round stock. The setup shown in Fig. 23 should provide a rigid anchorage.

In this type of work, a special strip having one side marked *A* inclined toward the work is used. As with the ordinary type of strip, the tongue which fits into the table slot of the machine insures parallelism. The holding unit at the right is a block with one side marked *B* inclined toward the work, with a distance filler piece plus a stop pin. The axis of the stop pin shown at *C*, Fig. 23 must always be higher than the center of the work as shown at *D*, Fig. 23. Under these conditions, the work will be forced firmly against the table at all times when it is clamped with the stop pin. Assume in clamping that the stop pin in axis *C* is at an elevation below *D*, as indicated by *C*. The wedge block would then simply rotate as shown by the dotted curved arrow marked *E*. On general production work where such holding devices as the strip and block are employed, they will be specially designed to give the most efficient clamping. A thrust-resisting stop must always be included in any shaper setup.

Another method of clamping a shaft in which the table slot instead of a strip insures parallelism and L-clamps and stop pins are used is shown in Fig. 24. This method is adapted to shaper tables having transverse slots.

Mounting Irregular Work Indirectly to the Table. A typical example of the setup for mounting irregular work indirectly to the table is shown in Fig. 25. A fixture for holding and positioning the work that is being machined is used. In Fig. 25 the fixture is an angle plate that is fastened to the table on one side, and the work is fastened to the other side of the plate. Since the casting projects a distance from the angle plate, provision is also made in this setup for supporting it on wedge blocks so as to prevent a spring. The clamps are in line with the wedge blocks so that they can be seen by the mechanic, but in an actual machine shop setup they would be shifted about 90 degrees to make the wedge blocks more accessible for any adjustment that might be necessary.

The wedge blocks must not be forced together too tight as to spring the casting, but just tight enough to give adequate support. This condition can be ascertained by testing with a surface gauge and previously scribed marks. Figure 25 shows that the angle plate acts also as an efficient stop.

Holding the Work With a Vise. The machine vise is designed to attach to the machine table. It consists of a base, table, and stationary and adjustable jaws. Two general types are used in the shaper; the plain vise which can be single- or double-screw, and the universal vise.

The plain vise shown in Fig. 26 is equipped with a base that has a tongue to fit in the machine table slot and lugs or open holes for bolting to the table with the T-head bolts. On the base of this vise is a circular gauge that is graduated in degrees to indicate any angular position in which the jaw table is turned. The table of the vise has a stationary jaw at one end and ways on which the adjustable jaw moves.

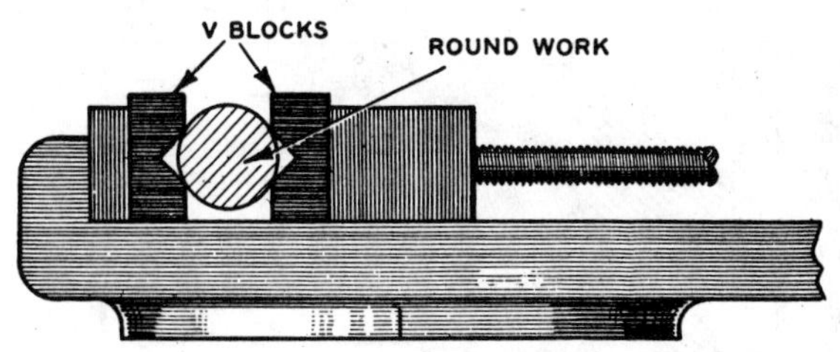

V BLOCKS USED TO CLAMP ROUND STOCK.

Figure 28

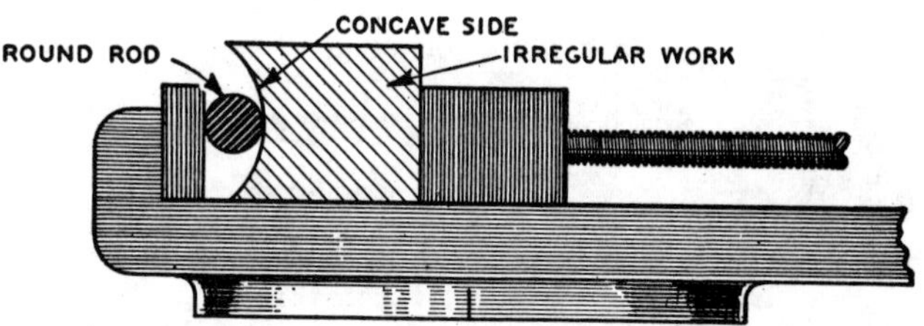

ROUND ROD IS USED IN CLAMPING IRREGULAR WORK.

Figure 29

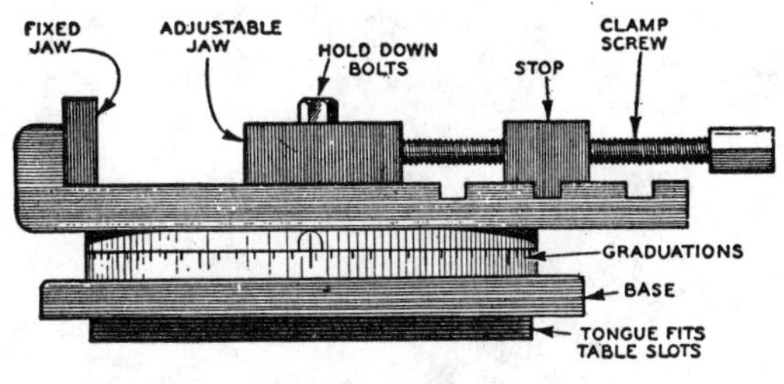

ELEMENTARY PLAIN VISE.

Figure 26

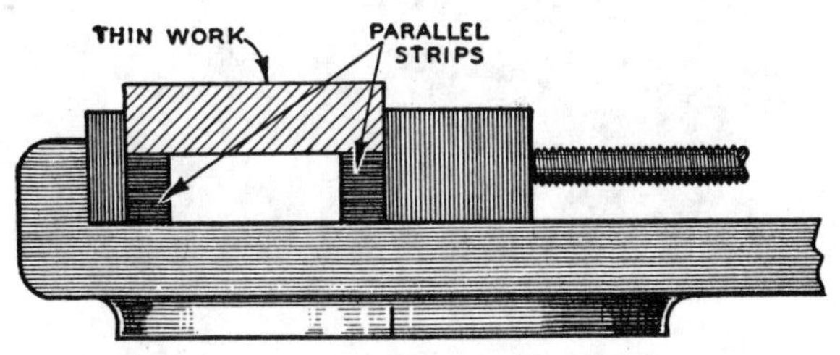

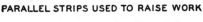

PARALLEL STRIPS USED TO RAISE WORK

Figure 27

It also carries the clamp screw. When clamping the work in the vise, the movable jaw should be brought into position to engage the work.

When a thin piece of work placed in the vise projects above the jaws it has to be raised high enough by resting it on parallel strips so that the jaws of the vise will not interfere with the cutting tool (Fig. 27). If the piece of work is long and narrow, the vise should be turned above 90 degrees so that the cutting tool of the machine will take long strokes rather than a number of short ones.

Where it is necessary to place round work which is too small in diameter to rest on the vise ways, the work can be held in horizontal alignment parallel with the vise table by using suitable V-blocks (Fig. 28).

The procedure for clamping an odd-shaped piece is shown in Fig. 29. Ordinarily, the jaw on the concave side would not get a good grip because it would make contact only as shown at *A*, Fig. 31, and would tilt the work. This condition can be avoided by using a round rod as shown in Fig. 29.

Figure 30 shows a wedge-shaped piece clamped in a vise of the universal type. If the angle of the inclined side of the work is too great, a stop is necessary to prevent the work from shifting sideways.

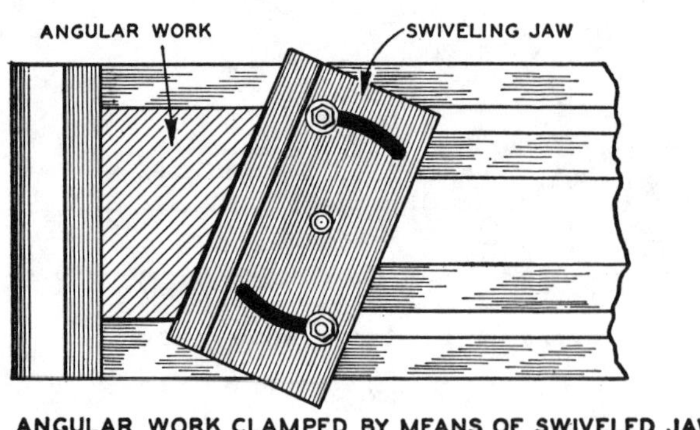

ANGULAR WORK CLAMPED BY MEANS OF SWIVELED JAW.

Figure 30

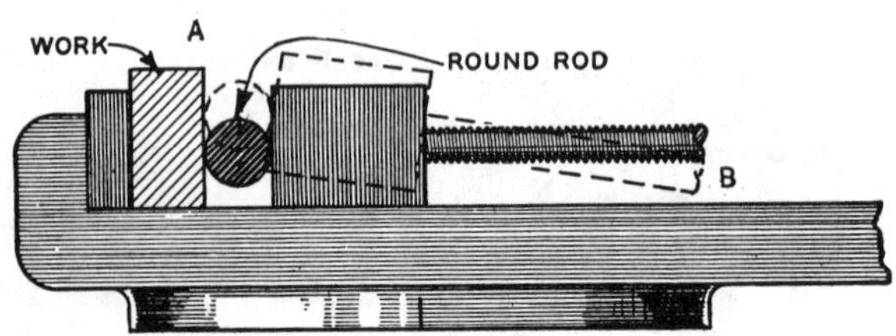

ROUND ROD USED TO PREVENT WORK FROM BEING TILTED BY RAISING OF VISE JAW.

Figure 31

When the movable jaw of a vise is forced against the work, the jaw will raise and lift or even sometimes tilt the work. The jaw will invariably conform to the irregular sides of the casting so that the opposite sides, when machined, will not be true; this can usually be avoided by using a round rod in the clamping setup as shown in Fig. 31. If the jaw drifts, it will cause the rod to roll from position *A*, Fig. 31, to the dotted position B, Fig. 31.

Functions of Special Fixtures. Special fixtures are designed and used in conjunction with the machining of irregularly shaped castings and where the quantity production and machining of a large number of identical pieces is required. The basic requirement is that the fixture must position and support the casting in the right places to prevent any stresses which may spring the casting due to uneven clamping. These fixtures must be constructed so that castings can be attached to them without loss of time and effort.

Functions of Shaper Centers. Shaper centers are employed for finishing work that cannot be completely machined on lathes. They are similar to the headstock and tailstock of a lathe except that the headstock spindle rotates only when turned to a desired angular position as determined by an index head.

Work partly machined in the lathe, when finished in the shaper, is placed between the shaper centers. The same centers are used on the work that were used when it was turned on the lathe. Shaper centers are constructed with a tongue on the base. This tongue fits in the shaper table slots and insures parallelism and correct alignment (Figs. 32 and 33). The alignment of the centers should be carefully checked before the machining operations are started.

Hold-Downs. Hold-downs or grippers are generally used to hold down thin pieces of work in the vise of the shaper. They are made of thin pieces of triangular cross sections of required lengths. The narrow edge of the hold-down is usually rounded, and the opposite edge is beveled to about two degrees toward the bottom as shown in Fig. 34. They are especially valuable when thin material has to be held down on the bottom of the vise or on a parallel. Hold-downs are useful when parallels of a height necessary to raise thinner pieces just above the vise jaws are not available in the machine shop. They are also employed when only two opposite surfaces of a piece require finishing.

Figure 32

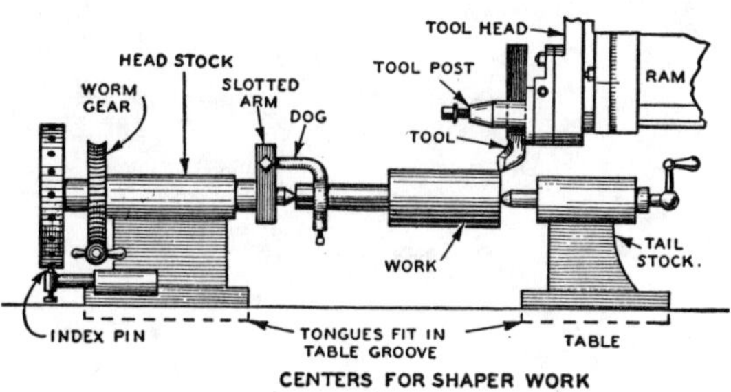

Figure 33

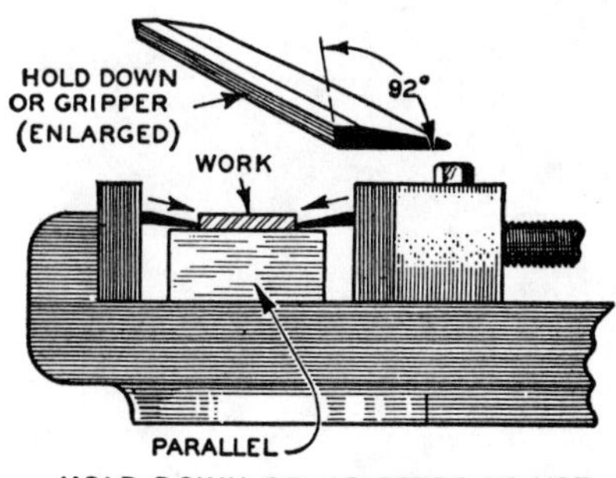

Figure 34

Chapter 16

Fundamental Shaper Operations

To start the modern shaper shown in Fig. 1, put the change gear shift lever in the neutral position. The stroke dial should read zero. Then put the feed lever into neutral. When starting the motor, make certain that it is running in the proper direction. Arrows on the belt and pulley guard show the correct direction. Engage the clutch lever with the gears in neutral and the stroke at zero, allowing the shaper to run from three to five minutes to fill all the oil tubes before the ram is set in motion. Oil should be visible to the machinist in the sight feed station provided at the top of the column of the machine. Be sure that the rocker arm and the sliding block are getting sufficient oil. The oil pressure gauge should read 50 pounds when the clutch is engaged.

General Operating Procedures

In the type of machine shown in Fig. 1, the stroke is adjusted by turning shaft *8* with the crank that is furnished with the machine. The stroke adjusting shaft is self-locking. The length of the stroke is shown on the dial at *5*, Fig. 1 whether the shaper is in motion or has been stopped. When necessary, the ram is unclamped by the lever (*6*, Fig. 1), and is adjusted to the required position by turning the shaft (*2*, Fig. 1). The same crank is used for positioning the ram and for adjusting the stroke.

If the slide has been set at an angle, do not run the ram back into the column until the slide has been set straight again.

There are eight speeds shown on the direct reading selector plate. Four speeds are obtained by means of the lever shown at *9*, Fig. 1. Four additional speeds are obtained through the back-gear control lever shown at *7*, Fig. 1. For all surface cutting speeds, refer to the tables on specific cutting speeds usually furnished by the manufacturer.

The lever shown at *4*, Fig. 1, regulates the amount of feed transmitted to the table. The automatic feed is engaged and disengaged by the lever shown at *3*, Fig. 1. This lever is directional; it shows the direction of the table movement whether employed for feed or for power rapid traverse.

To prevent breakage to the machine in the event that the table should run against an obstruction, a safety clutch is provided for both feed and power rapid traverse.

Vertical Adjustment of the Table. To adjust the table in a vertical direction, unclamp the rail by putting a large wrench on the shaft (*1*, Fig. 1), and pull it toward the front of the machine. Loosen the table support nuts (*13*, Fig. 1). Remove the safety crank (*12*, Fig. 1) from the cross feed shaft and engage it on the elevating shaft (*11*, Fig. 1). Remove the crank by placing the clutch teeth opposite each other and pushing the crank. Raise or lower the table to the desired position and reclamp the rail by turning the shaft *1*. Tighten the front table support by pulling up the nuts, shown at 13, and at the same time be sure that the apron is centered on the rail to prevent cramping. The large hexagon head cap screw holding the rail clamp at each side of the column of the machine must always be tight. The socket-head cap screws should never be disturbed.

Operation of Horizontal and Vertical Power Traverse. To operate the horizontal power rapid traverse (Fig. 2), place the feed lever *J* in the direction of the desired movement and raise lever *KK*.

To operate the vertical power rapid traverse, loosen clamp shaft *L*, Fig. 2, and loosen the table support bolts (*13*, Fig. 1). Place feed lever *J*, Fig. 2, in neutral, place lever *JJ* in the direction of movement, and raise lever *KK*. Always use the head feed for feeding the table.

Operation of Clutch. The shaper shown in Fig. 1 is equipped with a modern electric clutch and brake. Finger-tip control and braking of the ram

Figure 1. Shaper operating points. (1) Rail clamp control, (2) Ram positioning shaft, (3) Cross feed engagement lever, (4) Power cross feed selector, (5) Stroke indicator dial, (6) Ram clamp lever, (7) Back gear lever, (8) Stroke adjusting shaft, 9) Gear shift lever, (10) Power rapid traverse lever, (11) Rail elevating manual control, (12) Cross feed safety crank, (13) Table support clamping nuts, (14) Power elevating engagement lever, (15) Clutch and brake switch lever, (16) Tool post, (17) Clapper clamping nuts, (18) Tool slide crank.

movement is convenient and fast for both setup and operation. No adjustment is required on the electrically operated clutch and brake (Fig. 3).

The control switch furnished by the manufacturer is standard. Duplicate controls are available for the opposite side of the machine. A foot control or portable control can be used if required.

Cutting Speed. The cutting speed on a shaper is governed by the length of the stroke and the strokes per minute. For the same strokes per minute, the cutting speed increases as the stroke is lengthened. Avoid operating the shaper on excessively long stroke at high speeds. A diagram showing a typical full stroke is shown in Fig. 4. The cutting speeds in feet

Figure 2. Power rapid traverse.

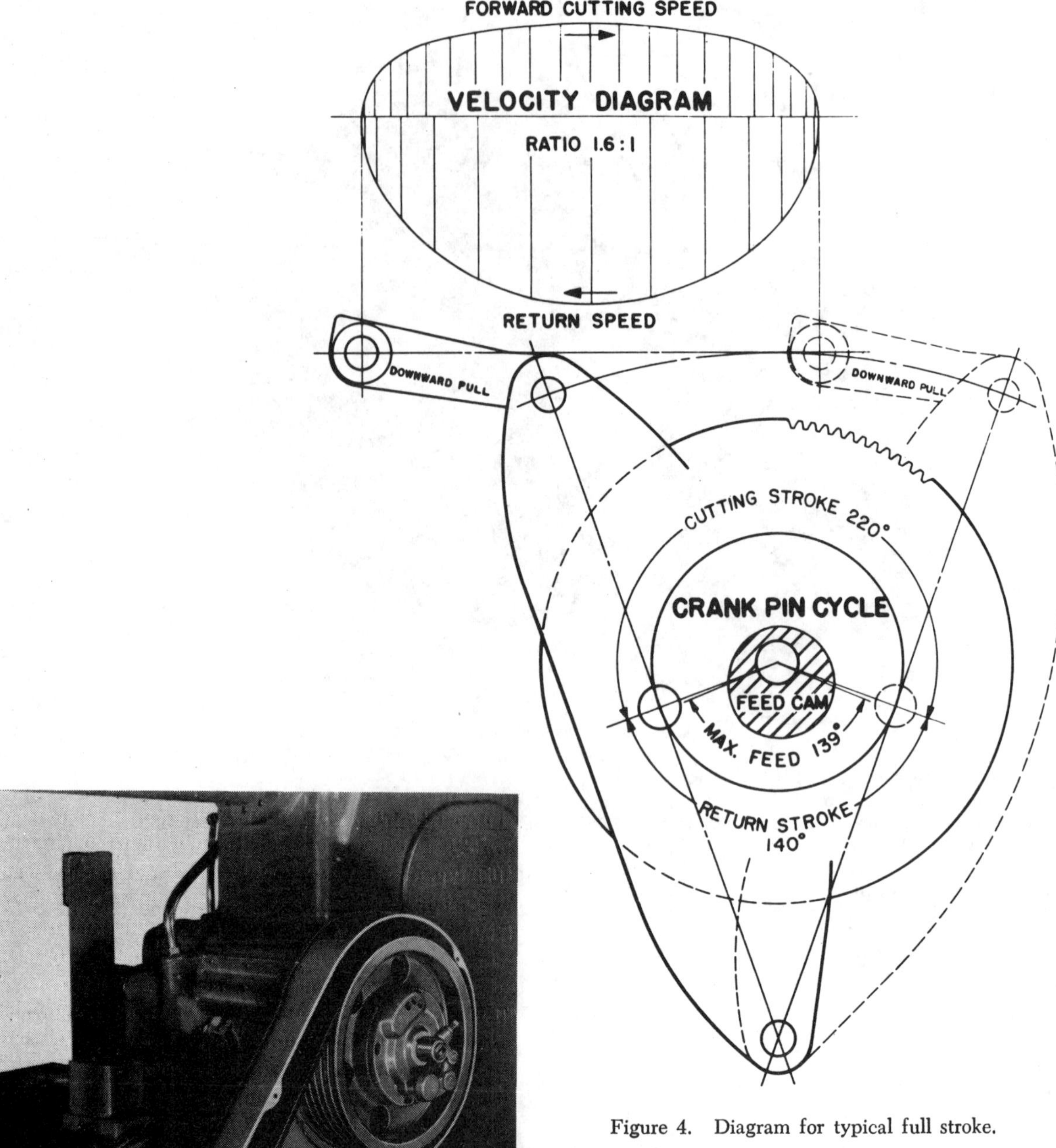

Figure 4. Diagram for typical full stroke.

Figure 3. Clutch and brake.

per minute for the different strokes per minute and various lengths of strokes for various sizes of shapers are shown in Table 29 below and in Table 35 in the Appendix.

TABLE 29

ALLOWABLE CUTTING SPEEDS—FEET PER MINUTE

HIGH SPEED STEEL TOOLS

Material	Roughing	Finishing
Cast Iron	60	100
.10 to .20 C	80	120
.20 to .40 C	60	100
Die Steel	40	40
Hard Bronze	60	100
Brass	150	Max. Speed
Aluminum	150	Max. Speed

Universal Tables

Universal tables in combination with the swivel vise furnished with the machines permit the work to be rotated around all three axes. This type of table is especially useful in tool and die shops. It is rotated by first loosening the four nuts at the front of the table and then operating the shaft (*AA*, Fig. 5). The crank for this shaft is the same as that used for the ram and stroke adjustment. The plain face of the table is brought into position by rotating the table clockwise against the stop. The tilting face is brought into the required working position using the graduations on the front of the table. After the table is rotated to the proper position, tighten the four nuts on the front of the table.

The tilting face of the table is adjusted by first loosening the clamp nuts *BB* and *CC*, Fig. 5. Adjust the face to the desired angle by operating the shaft *DD*, Fig. 5, with the crank. Graduations on the side of the tilting face toward the front show the angle of the tilt. The tilting face should then be secured in position by tightening nut *CC* first and nut *BB* last, as shown in Fig. 5. The nut *CC* operates the wedges to seat the tilting face in its full-scraped bearing, and nut *BB* clamps it securely in position.

For work that requires unusual accuracy, use an indicator, sine bar, or gauges for setting up. Before a final check is made, be sure to draw up the nuts at the front of the table. On universal shapers equipped with table supports, loosen the four table nuts as previously described. Use the socket wrench furnished by the manufacturer to loosen the nuts between the table support brackets. Adjust the table in the same manner as previously described.

SPECIAL OILING PROCEDURES. The worm and the wheel that rotates the table and the gears for the tilting face are packed with grease at the factory.

Figure 5. Universal table.

Oil the sleeve as required around the shaft (*AA*, Fig. 5) at the point marked for oil. Keep the scraped bearing surfaces of tilting face of the table and the scraped bearing between the apron and the rotating table clean and oiled. On the universal shaper with a table support, be sure to keep the slide clean, and oil daily at the point provided near the bottom of the table support.

Operation and Adjustment of the Automatic Power Down Feed to the Head

To set the automatic down feed to the head (Fig. 6), first set the stroke for length and position. Stop the ram at midstroke. Then locate the cam bracket in the approximate position on the column for the end of the return stroke. Alternately stroke the ram and adjust the cam bracket until the required feed graduation coincides with the zero mark on the bracket mounted on the ram. The small clutch lever starts and stops the power down feed. For different depths of cuts, use the positive stop on the head of the machine. Fill the oil pocket in the bracket mounted on ram daily if the power down feed is used daily, otherwise oil as required.

To adjust the power down feed, move the ram out of the column so that the adjusting nuts shown in Fig. 7 are accessible. Loosen the half-nut. Pull the full-nut up to tighten the friction and relock with the half-nut.

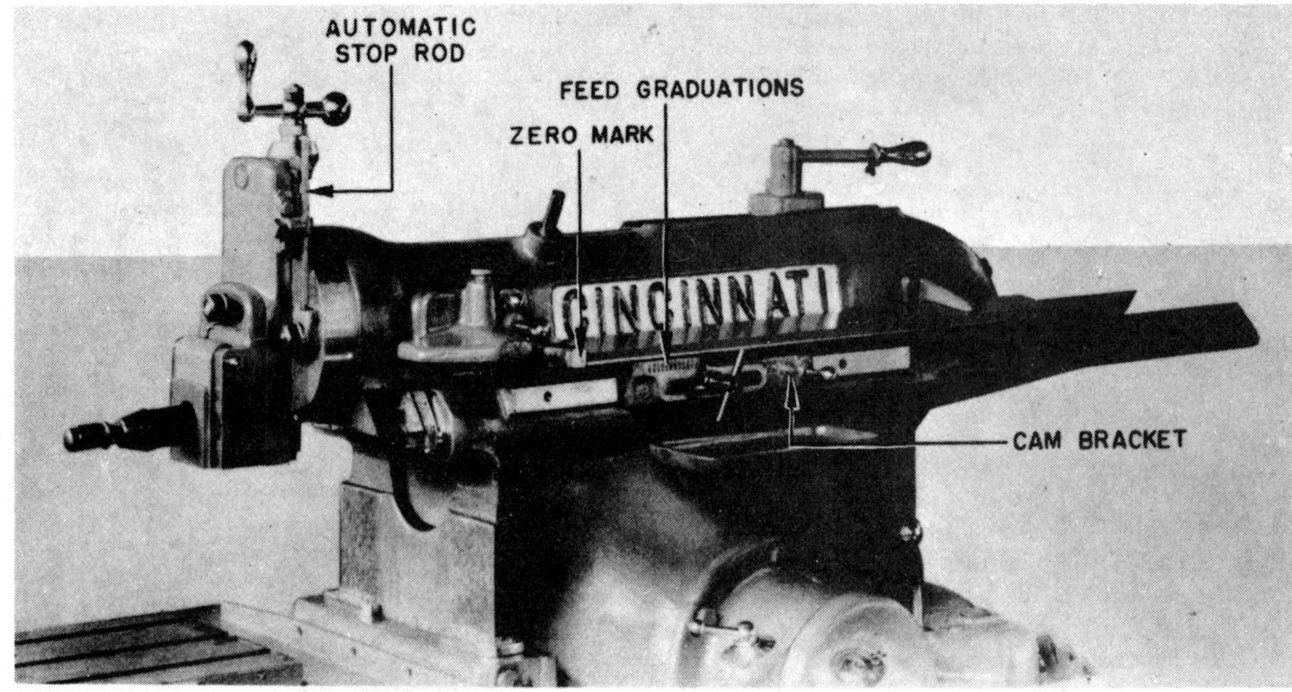

Figure 6. Automatic power down feed to head.

Tool Lifter Operation

To make the tool lifter inoperative, pull out lever *LL* as shown in Fig. 8. To disconnect the tool lifter for removal of the head or for use in a near horizontal position, remove screw *MM*, and pull the rod out of friction. At high ram speeds a slight friction on the rod is necessary, at slow speeds the friction adjustment must be increased. An occasional drop of oil on the indicated hardened bearing surfaces is desirable.

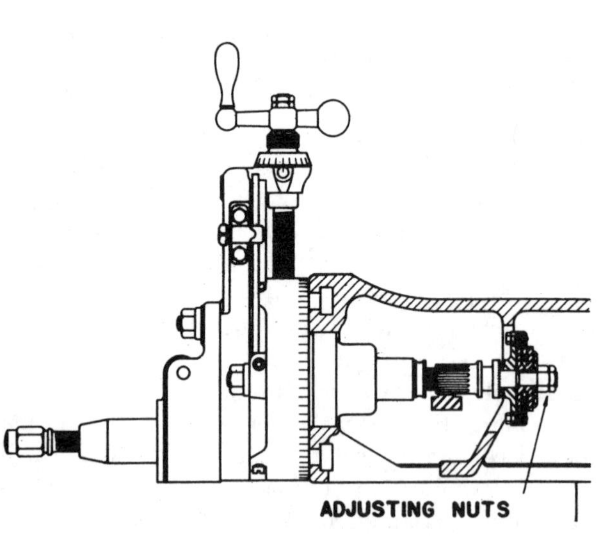

Figure 7. Power down feed.

Figure 8. Tool lifter.

Figure 9. Auxiliary front cross feed.

Auxiliary Front Cross Feed Operation

When using the auxiliary front cross feed (Fig. 9) the locking screw shown at *HH* should be loose, and the locking screw *II* on the feedbox tight. When using the conventional cross feed, loosen locking screw *II* on the feed box and tighten locking screw *HH*. This is also true when using the power rapid traverse.

Adjustments

As a general rule, all the slides with the exception of the table support are provided with adjustable taper gibs in modern shapers. The table support is provided with a flat gib. Accuracy of shaper work depends a great deal upon the proper adjustment of the gibs. Gib adjustment also is important in smoothness of operation and cutting. All gibs should be properly adjusted to eliminate looseness as a source of chatter.

Gib Adjustment. Modern shapers of the type shown in Fig. 1 are gibbed throughout Figures 10 to 14 show the various points of adjustment. In general, gibs should be adjusted with a minimum clearance. A small clearance on a properly fitted bearing is favorable to the formation of a strong oil wedge of film. When making adjustments, be sure that uneven wear has not taken place. That is, movements of the table, ram, and sliding block are usually confined to a certain portion of the entire travel. Accordingly, after a long period of time, there will

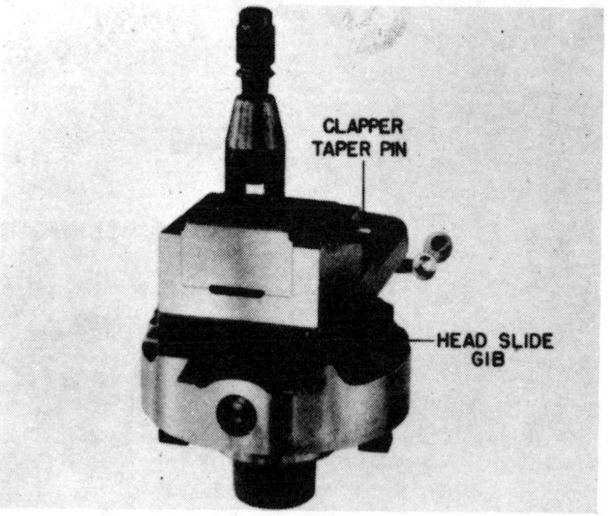

Figure 10. Head adjustments.

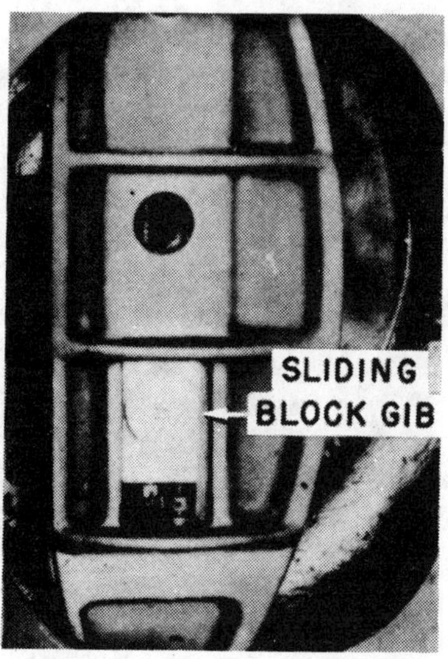

Figure 11. Sliding block adjustment.

be more wear in this portion than elsewhere. If a gib is adjusted for the worn portion it will be tight for the portion that is little used. This condition exists only after a long period of operation and eventually requires refitting. However, in the meantime, the gibs are still useful in keeping proper clearance between the working parts.

When adjustment is necessary, the taper gibs should be drawn up snugly. The gib should then be backed off or relieved until a clearance of not less than .002 in. is obtained between the glazed bearing surfaces. Further adjustment may be required, depending on existing conditions.

Head Slide Gib Adjustment. Adjust the head slide gib (Fig. 10) by the feel of the slide movement. For proper adjustment, the slide should operate snugly. Lock the gib with the screw at the bottom.

Figure 12. Table gib adjustment.

Figure 13. Ram gib adjustment.

Sliding Block Gib Adjustment. With the rocker arm in the vertical position, move the slide block gib shown in Fig. 11 to the bottom of the rocker arm by operating the stroke adjusting shaft. Draw up the gib to the point where it is tight enough to support its own weight, that is, hang in position. Then back off approximately ⅓ of a turn and lock.

Rail Column Gib Adjustment. Adjust the rail column gib shown in Fig. 12 by feel on the rail elevating crank and lock. For proper adjustment, the cross feed crank should operate stiffly.

Ram Gib Adjustment. In general, maintain as small a clearance between the ram and the ram ways as possible. This will give the most accurate work and the best finish. To tighten the ram gib, turn the lock nut shown at *A*, Fig. 13, to move the gib toward the front of the ram. Draw up the gib until snug. Back off half a turn and lock with nut *B*.

Figure 14. Crank block adjustment.

Engage the clutch and feel for the thump at either end of the stroke by laying the hand on top of the ram. If knocking occurs, back off the ram gib in small steps until the thump disappears. Stop the ram when making the adjustment.

Crank Block Gib Adjustment. Adjust the crank block gib shown in Fig. 14 by feel on the stroke adjusting shaft and lock. For proper adjustment, the stroke adjusting shaft should operate stiffly.

Stroke Adjusting Screw. The wear adjusting nuts on the stroke adjusting screw (Fig. 14) should be kept tight. Tighten the inner nut until tight, then lock the outer nut and insert a cotter pin. Finally, back off the inner nut against the outer as far as possible.

Knocking. Knocking can result from poor adjustment. Check the following points: stroke adjusting screw, sliding block gib adjustment, crank block gib adjustment.

Rail Clamp Adjustment. To make any necessary rail clamp adjustments (Fig. 15) proceed as follows: Remove the chip guard from the rail. Apply the wrench to the clamp shaft to loosen the mechanism. Traverse the table toward the left end of the rail to adjust the clamp at the right end. Turn the rail clamp adjusting screw up tight and back off one half a turn. Make the same adjustment at the other end.

It may be necessary to make additional minor adjustments of the rail clamp adjusting screw for the best clamping conditions due to the variations of limits and unequal wear on the mechanism.

Belt Adjustment. When the belt tension must be

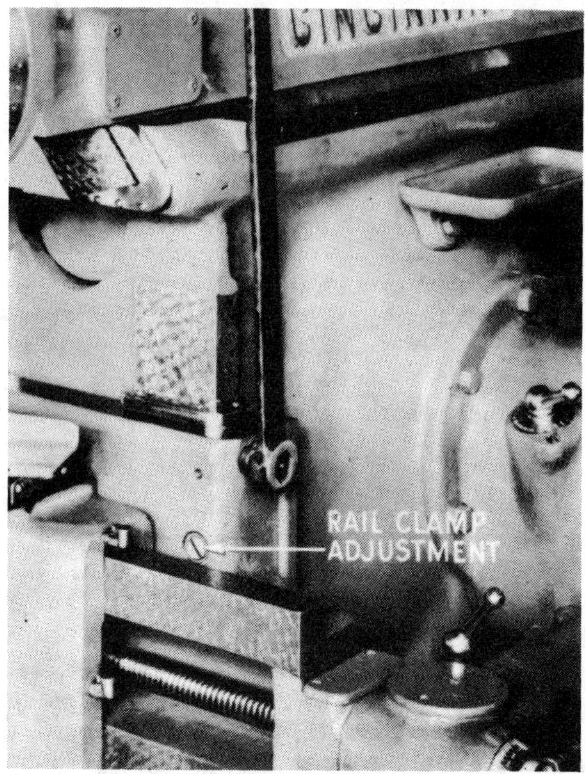

Figure 15. Rail clamp adjustment.

adjusted, proceed as follows: Loosen the four nuts *FF* holding the motor base and tighten the belts by backing off adjusting screw *GG* at the bottom of the base as shown in Fig. 16.

Testing the Work Seat. To test the work seat, the vise should be opened wide. Be sure that the bottom of the vise is clean and smooth. Using a dial test indicator, test the work seat for parallelism. A pair of fair-sized, accurate parallels can be arranged as shown in Fig. 17. Respond indicators are shown at *A* and *C*, Fig. 17; *B* and *D* are for parallelism. If *A* and *D* are low, the work table is sagging, and probably the saddle gib will require tightening or there may be dirt between the vise and the table. If either *A* and *D*, or *B*, or *C* are low, it indicates that the vise is not properly seated on the table and should be corrected.

Testing the Solid Jaw for Squareness. If the face of either vise jaw is scored, dented, or marred, it must be repaired. If the solid jaw is not square with the seat, the work cannot be properly clamped against the jaw and cannot be planed square. To test for squareness, clamp the beam of a square against the solid jaw of the vise with a piece of wood placed between the movable jaw and the square as shown in Fig. 18. Arrange the indicator as shown in Fig. 18, and move the work table the distance from *A* to *B*. If the indicator shows the same registration at both ends of the blade, then the jaw is square. Try the jaw near each end and in the middle; it may be necessary to shim the jaw until it is absolutely square.

Setting the Vise Parallel with the Direction of the Stroke. The graduations on the swivel plate of the shaper are usually accurate enough for practically all jobs. Occasionally, however, a shoulder must be cut exactly parallel with the edge located against the jaw or the work will be spoiled. To make the test for this position, arrange the length of the stroke to the length of the jaw holding the indicator in the tool post, and run the shaper slowly by hand to see if the indicator registers the same at both ends of the jaw. If any adjustment is necessary, the vise should be clamped lightly and tapped with a babbitt hammer until the setting is correct. The vise should then be clamped tight and tested again before proceeding with the actual job.

Setting the Vise Square with the Direction of the Stroke. To set the vise square with the direction of the stroke, and to correct the setting if incorrect, the indicator should be arranged as shown in Fig. 18. The vise is turned 90 degrees, and the worktable is moved by hand to show the movement, if any, of the indicator needle.

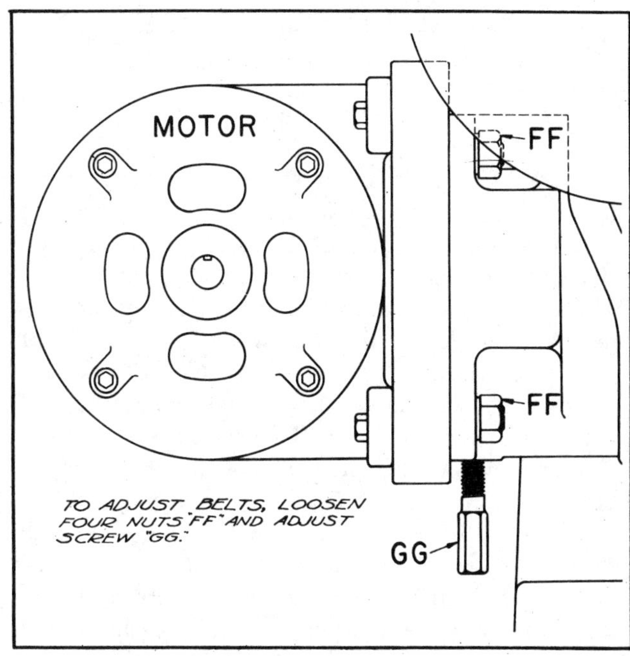

Figure 16. Belt adjustment.

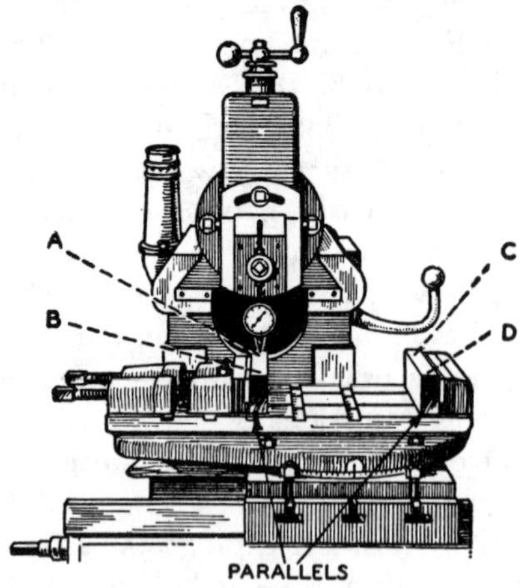

Figure 17

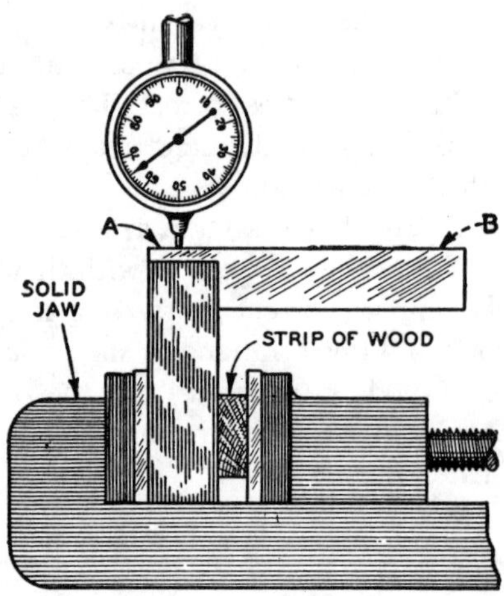

Figure 18

TAKING HORIZONTAL CUTS. When the work is fed in a horizontal direction under the reciprocating cutting tool of the shaper, the result, depending on the tool used, is a horizontal slot or plane surface. The length of the stroke in a shaper is set approximately ¾ in. longer than the work. The position of the stroke is such that ½ in. of this extra length comes at the beginning of the cut to allow the tool block to seat properly for the next cut.

Manufacturers design and construct the clapper block so that it fits the box. The bearing surfaces are scraped to provide the best sliding fits, with the axis of the hinge pin at right angles; the block hinges freely in the box during the return stroke, and it is very rigidly supported during the actual cutting stroke. The bearing surfaces should always be wiped clean, and oiled at least once a week.

The cut is usually started on the right side in order that the depth of the cut, the action of the tool, and the other movements can be readily observed by the machinist. The feed of the table should be arranged to move the work toward the machinist on the return stroke, and the left-hand tool should be used.

Hold small pieces of work, or pieces that will tend to tip up at the pressure of the cut, with the vise jaws at right angles to the thrust. With the exception of the cutting speed, there is practically no difference in roughing steel or cast iron on the shaper. For roughing plain surfaces of cast iron or steel, use the roughing tool or a tool bit that has been ground to a similar shape and held in a suitable holder. The tool should be clamped in a vertical position and pointed a very little in the direction away from the work so that, if the tool moves due to the pressure of the cut, it will move away from the surface instead of undercutting the work.

ADJUSTING THE WORK. After the job has been mounted and properly aligned on the table of the shaper, the first operation is to move out the ram so that the tool post carrying the cutting tool is directly over the work. Then place the tool that is to be used for the job in the tool post, making certain that there is very little overhang. Elevate the table until the work clears the ram of the machine by about one inch. The tool slide should project very little below the bottom of the head, and the overhang of the slide should never be over 1½ inches. If more than this is necessary, the tool rather than the slide should be set for the extra overhang. After this preliminary adjustment, the tool should be clamped firmly. Be sure that it clears the work.

ADJUSTMENT OF THE STROKE. Two necessary adjustments must now be made, those of the length and the position of the stroke. To adjust the length of the stroke, turn the stroke adjustment screw right or left for a longer or a shorter stroke. On modern shaper machines, a handle is provided for the square end of the adjustment screw with a lock nut. To make the necessary adjustment for a longer stroke, the adjustment screw on some types of machines must be turned clockwise. On other machines they are turned counterclockwise. Specific directions for these adjustments are usually supplied by the manufacturer. If they are not available, they can be determined by testing.

After the adjustments have been made, start the machine and note the length of the stroke. The length of the stroke should be readjusted, if it is necessary, until the stroke is long enough to clear the work. This clearance should not be less than approximately 1/4 to 1/2 inch on the forward stroke, with enough on the return stroke to enable the automatic feed of the machine to function before the tool actually comes in contact with the work on the cutting stroke.

The feed should function at the end of the return stroke, rather than at the end of the forward or cutting stroke. After the length of the stroke has been adjusted, position the stroke so that it overtravels the work at both ends as specified above. Then loosen the ram clamp and turn the stroke position adjustment shaft in the required direction. This will move the ram into the required position. After the stroke has been properly positioned, the ram is locked by the ram clamp.

The table must be moved by the hand cross feed screw either to the right or to the left, depending on the type of tool used, until the work is in position transversely to begin the cut. The table should be moved far enough to make one or two test strokes after the stroke is adjusted and before the actual cutting is begun. The tool must then be set to the required depth for the first roughing cut by the vertical feed.

TAKING THE CUTS. After the adjustment of the work to the approximate position has been made, the machinist must decide the number of cuts that will be necessary. This depends largely upon the amount of metal that has to be removed. One or two roughing cuts plus one or more finishing cuts are the usual practice, depending on the nature of the job and the finish desired.

The first cut must be deep enough to remove the seal, thus truing up the surface of the work. This gives the machinist an opportunity to check the setting of the tool. The next step is to take the necessary roughing and finishing cut, but before doing this, the machinist must make certain that the cutting edge does not project too far from the tool post; in other words, the work must be clamped tight. See that the tool head slide has not run down too far, for this position will cause weakness and undue strain. Raise the worktable rather than allow the tool slide to project below the head or have the tool project too far.

When planing cast metal, bevel the edge at the end of the cut with a chisel or an old file to about 45 degrees, practically the depth of the cut that will be taken. Otherwise, it has been found that chunks of the corner break out below the surface, thus leaving the edge of the work ragged. Cast-iron scale is hard and gritty; when working on this type of metal, make certain to set the tool to take a chip that is deep enough to get under the scale of the cast-iron casting. If a portion of the surface is found to be low during the cut and the tool rubs on the scale, the cutting edge of the tool will soon be useless.

Finishing cuts must always be light, especially when finishing either steel or wrought iron. A rather fine feed will give the most satisfactory results. The accepted commercial finish on flat cast-iron pieces is a surface that feels smooth to the hand and shows the feed marks spaced about 3/8 in. or more apart. This type of finish is obtained by the scraping action of a broad square-nosed tool which can be either a forged tool or a tool bit that has been fitted to any one of a number of types of tool holders, and which may be ground to shape. The best tool holder and tool for this purpose is the spring tool because it does not dig into the work; a slow speed and a hand feed should be used with this tool.

Oil should be kept off cast iron; even oily fingers may spoil a good finish.

SELECTING THE PROPER FEED. When setting the automatic feed, the amount of feed will depend upon the kind of metal that is being machined.

PROPER CUTTING SPEED. Similar to lathes and other types of machine tools, a number of speeds are provided on the shaper. High speeds should be used on short stroke operations, and slower speeds should be used for longer strokes. Since the action of a shaper tool is intermittent and not continuous like the tool on a lathe, higher speeds can be used on the shaper, for the heating of the tool is not so severe. (See speed tables in Appendix.)

SETTING THE HEAD OF A SHAPER FOR VERTICAL AND ANGULAR CUTS. A vertical cut is made in the shaper by setting the head on zero and arranging the apron so that the tool will clear the work on the return stroke, always having the tool feeding down. On the shaper, the down feed is used for vertical cuts such as finishing the sides of tongues and grooves, squaring shoulders, squaring ends, and cutting keyways.

Except in the case of cutting-off or a similar operation, or where the surface to be machined is not much over 1/4 inch deep or high, it is necessary to swivel the apron when using the down feed. When the top of the apron is moved in a direction away from the surface of the cut itself, the tool block and the tool will hinge in a direction up and away from the work during the return stroke.

Figure 19 shows the apron swiveled for a vertical

cut, and the axis of the hinge pin is in line on *ab*. The direction in which the tool block will raise on the return stroke is in a plane shown as *xy* which is at right angles to *ab*. If this plane is tipped away as shown in Fig. 19, the tool will raise in a direction away from the surface end and will not run. If the plane were vertical, then the tool would rub along the surface down at *s* on the return stroke.

An angular cut is made by swiveling the head of the shaper and arranging the apron so that the tool will clear the work on the return stroke. Down feed is also used for angular cuts such as those for fairly wide beveled edges and for making dovetails. This movement is also true in angular or beveled cuts as well as vertical cuts (Fig. 20).

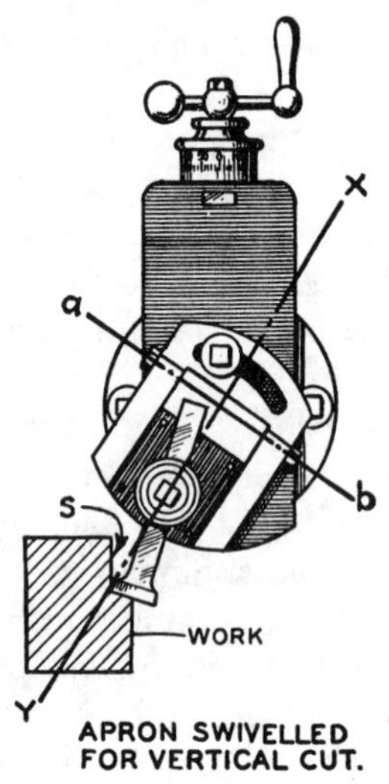

Figure 19

The general setup for an angular cut, with the head of the machine swiveled and the apron also set over, will sometimes appear wrong. Visualizing the angular cut as a vertical cut and setting the apron accordingly will clarify the setup. For all vertical and angular cuts, the top of the apron must be set in a direction away from the surface of the cut to be taken.

Although the construction of the shaper does permit considerable down feed of the head, it is not good practice to use the head of the machine with the slide run down much below the swivel plate because it is not so strong and rigid in this position as when backed up by the ram. Sometimes this procedure may be advisable or necessary, but in no other case should it be used for a finishing cut.

When the head of the machine is set over for an angular cut, and the machinist feeds the tool slide down too far, it is likely to be brought up against the column as the ram slides back into position. Therefore, it is necessary when setting up to have the slide of the machine high enough at the start to make either a vertical or an angular cut, and thus weakness or interference will never result during the actual cutting operation.

Shaping Vertical and Angular Surfaces. It is not always necessary to take an angular cut to produce an angular surface. An angular surface is one that is neither parallel nor square to any given base or to any other surface, and it may be machined in the shaper by several methods.

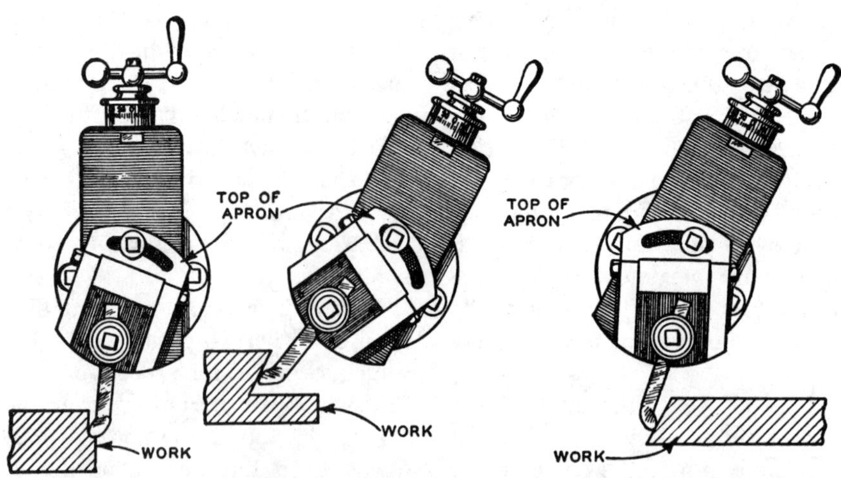

Figure 20

First, the work can be supported on a tapered parallel, often called a taper cut rather than an angular cut. Second, a layout line may be scribed on the work to indicate the position of the surface to be planed; the work can be held in the vise with this line horizontal; and the regular power feed of the machine can be used for either a taper or an angle. Third, the work can be held in angular parallels. Fourth, the vise can be swiveled to the required angular setting. Fifth, when the machine is equipped with a universal table, this table can be used for making necessary adjustments for an angular cut. Sixth, the head of the shaper can be swiveled as shown in Fig. 20.

With the exception of a downcut on a piece that is held in a vise that has been swiveled to a given angle, all of these six methods require only the regular horizontal cut. The sixth method involves the angular setting of the swivel head; this is called an angular cut. Figure 20 shows the setup of the shaper for the downcut for producing a vertical cut as shown at *1*, or an angular cut as shown at *2* or *3*.

PLANING FOUR SIDES OF A RECTANGULAR PIECE. The progressive steps for planing four sides of a rectangular piece in a shaper are shown in Fig. 21. Step *1* is to plane one side of the work, preferably one of the larger surfaces. Using this surface as a seat against the solid jaw of the vise, the adjacent side or edge, step *2*, should be planed. If the vise jaw on the shaper is square and smooth, and if the surface that has been finished first is clean, is free of burrs, and is properly seated against the solid jaw of the vise, the second surface planed will be square with the first step or surface.

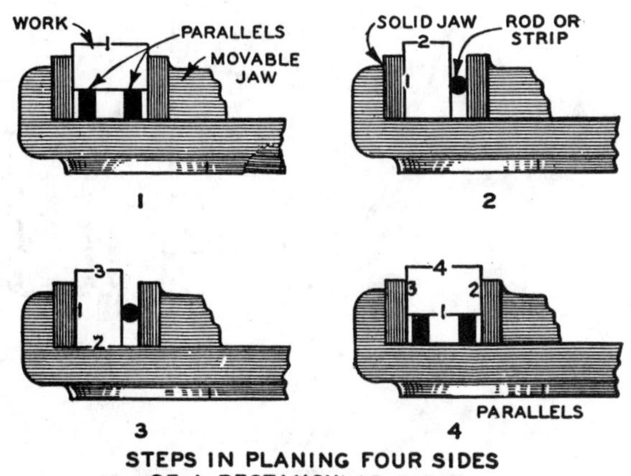

STEPS IN PLANING FOUR SIDES OF A RECTANGULAR PIECE.

Figure 21

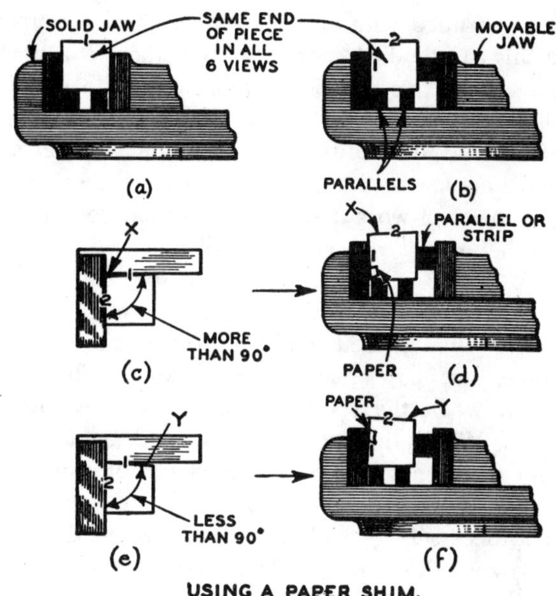

USING A PAPER SHIM.

Figure 22

To make certain that the surface first planed is properly seated against the jaw of the vise, use a rod or a strip between the movable jaw of the vise and the work (*2*, Fig. 21). This will eliminate any tendency for the work to change its position owing to any *give* there might be in the movable jaw. Place the second finished surface down, marked *2*, on the bottom of the vise (*3*, Fig. 21), or if necessary on parallels. Place the first surface against the solid vise jaw (as in the second step) with the rod or strip between the movable jaw and the work, and tighten the vise. Tap the work down in a vise with a babbitt hammer so that it is properly seated on the bottom of the vise and the planed surface marked *3*. If the jaw of the vise is square and the cutting tool is sharp, and if the surfaces of the finished work are clean, the two edges just planed should be parallel and square with the first side planed.

Now, place the first planed surface down on suitable parallels (*1* in step *4*, Fig. 21). Clamp the work between the jaws of the vise *without* the rod or the strip. With the babbitt hammer tap the work until it is properly seated. If the vise is true, and if the work has been seated on both parallels so that neither of the parallels can be moved, then the fourth surface will be parallel with the first surface and square with the other two sides of the work.

Seat the work on two parallels rather than on a single one because it is much easier to judge in this way whether the work is properly seated. At times it may be necessary to measure the piece that is being planed with either a micrometer or caliper, and this can be done more readily if there is a space between the two parallels, or between one parallel and the jaw of the vise.

USING A PAPER SHIM. It is sometimes necessary to have one or more adjacent surfaces planed square with a piece of work that has had one side previously planed. For this reason the work must be properly set up. There will be cases where the work is not square in the vise; in such instances, the adjacent surface, when planed, will not be square with the surface that has already been planed. This may happen when the solid jaw of the vise is *out of square*. When the work is tightened against the faulty surface, it will be as much out of square as the vise jaw itself.

The necessary operations entailed when the solid vise jaw is not square and true have been previously described. However, in many instances these operations are not always practical or possible. In such cases, shim the work in the vise itself rather than shim the vise jaw (Fig. 22).

Unless the *bottom* side of the work is absolutely square with the side against the solid jaw, both of the parallels placed under the work will not be tight. No amount of hammering will *seat* the work on both parallels when the work itself is out of square, or when it is being held out of square, but a few light taps with the babbitt hammer will *seat* the work on both of the parallels when all conditions are correct.

SQUARING THE ENDS OF THE WORK. Two methods are used for planing the ends of work square. Shorter pieces can be planed square by taking the cut horizontally across, and longer pieces by cutting vertically downward. A short piece of work is set either on the bottom of the vise or on suitable parallels; a finished edge or side is set perpendicular by using a machinist's square.

Hold the square down hard on the parallel with the piece of work hard against the blade of the square, and tighten the vise of the machine lightly. Check the setting by tapping the work one way or the other, if necessary, before tightening it securely in the vise. If this has been properly done, and if the vise jaws are clean and square, when the end is planed it should be square with the surfaces that have already been planed. Then seat the work on the finished end, tapping it carefully again with a babbitt hammer, and finish the opposite end to the required length.

If the work happens to be too long for the ends to be finished in this manner, the work should be set lengthwise in the vise with one end projecting in such position that it can be finished by taking a vertical cut. Use parallels to raise the work substantially flush with the tops of the jaws of the vise, allowing it to project from the end only a very short distance. After the vise has been tightened securely, the tool slide should be run well up toward the top, the apron swiveled, and the tool adjusted for the cut. Since the tool has to project a little distance from the tool post in order to take the cut to the bottom of the piece without any interference, a feed somewhat lighter than for horizontal planing is recommended.

Extreme care must be taken not to break out the corners at the end of the cut if the work that is being planed is made of cast metal. When working with cast iron or cast metal, an excellent finish can be obtained by using a side tool. About ¼ in. of the cutting edge of this side tool should be ground straight and set vertically. Take a very light chip with a half turn of the down feed screw of the machine for feed.

Lubrication

Modern shapers are equipped with a pressure oiling system similar to an automobile's (Fig. 23). A gauge shows normal operating pressure when the

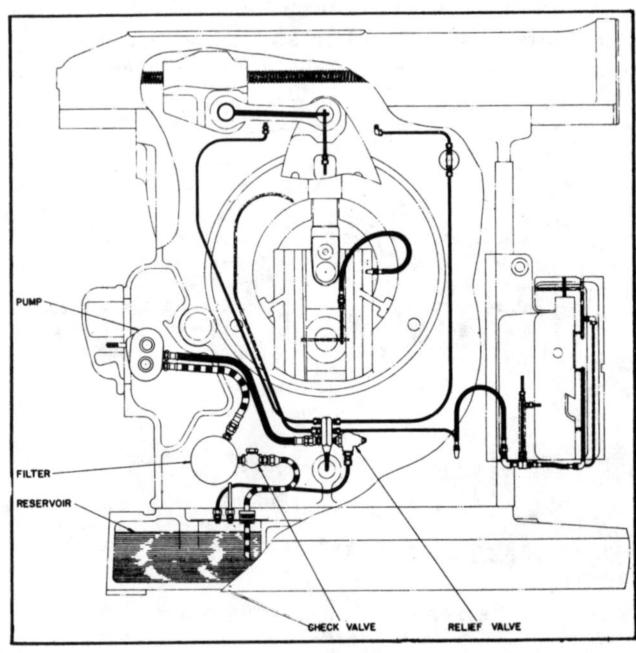

Figure 23. Oiling diagram.

clutch is engaged, and a filter is used to keep the oil clean. The oil should be a high-grade, nonfoaming machine oil; viscosity 220 seconds and 100 degrees F. Once a year, all the oil should be removed, and the shaper should be refilled with fresh oil.

Before starting the shaper, the following steps should be taken: (See Figs. 24 and 25.)

1. Fill transmission reservoir until oil overflows into return basin (Fig. 23).
2. Lúbricate motor according to motor manufacturer's recommendations.
3. After filling the transmission reservoir, open the column door and fill the return basin and main reservoir (Fig. 23). Fill until oil shows in sight window in base.
4. Observe pressure gauge in column near clutch control regularly. If gauge control fails to show pressure, check oil level. Check oil filter every six months.

Daily

5. Clean and oil sliding surfaces of toolhead.
6. Clean surfaces of table support.
7. Clean sliding surfaces of rail.
8. Oil feed screw bearing.
9. Oil feed screw.
10. Clean and oil sliding surfaces of vise. Fill oil holes on single-screw vises.
11. Oil clapper pin; clean frequently.

Weekly

12. Fill oil hole at rear of ram and two oil holes near ram adjustment shaft.
13. Oil ram adjusting screw through opening in ram.
14. Oil speed change lever bearings.
15. Oil crank clutch.

Monthly

16. Remove plug and add oil to feed box.

Note

17. Oil should not be allowed to fall below sight gauge when shaper is stopped.

Figure 24. Lubrication points.

Figure 25. Lubrication points.

Chapter 17

Planers

The planer is used for the production of flat surfaces on work that is too large, impracticable, or impossible to machine in the milling machine or shaper. The work is fastened to the platen or worktable of the planer, which has a reciprocating motion past the toolhead. In the planer, the tool cuts only on the forward or cutting stroke of the planer platen, and it is held stationary except for the feeding movement.

In the planer, the work moves back and forth beneath a stationary tool. In the shaper, the tool moves back and forth above stationary work. The tool is fed to the work for each successive cut in the planer. In the shaper, the work is fed to the tool except for vertical feeding.

The single-point cutting tool used in a planer produces an accurate surface that is better adapted to the scraping operation than a milled surface. In heavy production like parts of steam engines, locomotives, printing presses, lathe carriages, and bottoms of headstocks and tailstocks, the planer is indispensable. A typical modern planer is shown in Fig. 1.

Construction of a Planer

The various parts of a planer are shown in Fig. 2. They are as follows:

The *planer bed* is a strong boxlike stretcher that supports the parts of the machine. The table of the planer is used for holding the work, and arranged to slide back and forth on the bed guided by V-ways.

The *housing* of a planer consists of vertical standards, one on each side, that are attached to the bed. In most types of planers, the upper ends of the standards are connected by a cross member.

Housing ways are form guides upon which the cross rail of the planer is mounted. They can be raised or lowered as desired by the mechanic.

The *cross rail* is mounted on the housing ways of the planer and carries the saddle slide toolhead assembly. It provides guides for the saddle transverse travel and a mounting for the transverse feed screw and gear.

A pair of *bevel gears* are on each housing and connected by a cross shaft so that each pair has the same movement. They form the gear for the raising or the lowering of the cross rail.

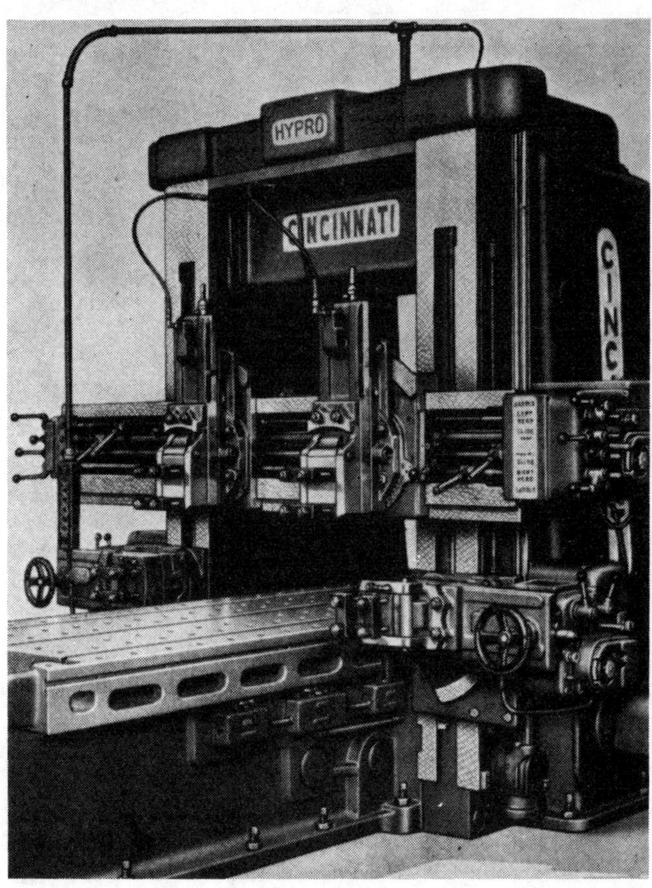

Figure 1. Modern High-speed planer.

Figure 2. Planer, showing different parts. (1) Elevating device, (2) Elevating shaft, (3) Elevating bevel gear, *inside elevating bracket,* (4) Elevating bevel pinion, *inside elevating bracket,* (5) Elevating adjusting nut, *inside elevating bracket,* (6) Elevating shifter fork, *inside elevating device,* (7) Elevating clutch, *inside elevating device,* (8) Horizontal rapid-traverse shaft, (9) Rapid-traverse bracket, (10) Elevating bracket, (11) Arch, (12) Left-hand housing, (13) Right-hand housing, (14) Elevating screw, right hand, (15) Elevating screw, left hand, (16) Slide, (17) Saddle, (18) Down-feed screw, (19) Harp, (20) Clapper-box clamp, (21) Clapper box, (22) Tool block, (23) Tool-block stud, (24) Tool-block clamp, (25) Rail screw, right-hand head, (26) Feed rods, (27) Rail screw, left-hand head, (28) Clapper-box taper pin, (29) Harp gib, (30) Saddle nut, (31) Right-hand head complete, (32) Rail, (33) Rapid traverse and feed-engaging lever, (34) Feed-changing knob, (36) Worm shaft or rail-clamping shaft, (38) Feed solenoid cover, (40) Trigger gear, (41) Right-hand side head complete, (42) Right-hand side-head screw, (43) Bull-wheel shaft, (44) Bull-pinion shaft, (45) Feed-drive box, (51) Table, (52) Bed, (82) Vertical-feed shaft, (83) Vertical rapid-traverse shaft, (84) Vertical-feed shaft bracket, (85) Control rods, (86) Rail-clamping gears, (87) Rail-head stop, (88) Pendant station, (89) Tool-block abutment, (90) Hand wheel, side-head horizontal movement, (91) Side head, clapper-box holding lever, (92) Side-head slide, (93) Side-head slide trigger gear, (94) Magnetic feed switch, (95) Hand adjustment for right-hand side-head saddle up or down, (96) Right-hand side-head saddle gib, (97) Lower side-head screw end bracket, (98) Housing bolt, (99) Housing bearing, (100) Motor-shaft coupling, (101) Main drive motor, (102) Speed-control rheostats, (103) Table-control dogs, (104) Master switch, (105) Leveling blocks, (106) Support for pendant switch arm, (107) Counterweight sheave bracket, (108) Elevated and rapid travel motor, (109) Counterweight cable, (110) Upper-side head-screw end bracket, (111) Air hose for pneumatic tool lift, (112) Outer rail-head saddle gib, (113) Inner rail-head saddle gib, (114) Harp clamp bolts, (115) Slide binder lever, (116) Guard end of rail, (117) Nuts for top and bottom of side-head screw, (118) Rapid-traverse shaft, lower bracket, (119) Right-hand outside rail-clamp unit, (120) Side-head clamp unit.

The *saddle* of a planer is arranged to travel transversely on the cross rail. Other parts of the tool assembly are mounted on the saddle.

The *slide* of a planer is pivoted to the saddle and can be turned to an angular position; it also forms a guide for the head of the planer.

The *head* of a planer moves up or down on the slide by means of the vertical feed screw to provide vertical feed for the cutting tool.

The *apron* or *clapper box* forms the hinged mounting for the clapper which carries the tool, allowing it to turn away from the work on the return, or noncutting, stroke of the table.

The *tool post* is mounted on the clapper of the planer and holds the cutting tool.

The *pawl* is a part of the automatic feed which engages the feed screw gear. It has two teeth, one for forward feed, the other for reverse feed.

Two *feed gears* are used on the planer. The first gear is driven by the reciprocating motion of the rack, and meshes with the second gear on which the pawl is mounted. The pawl engages with the

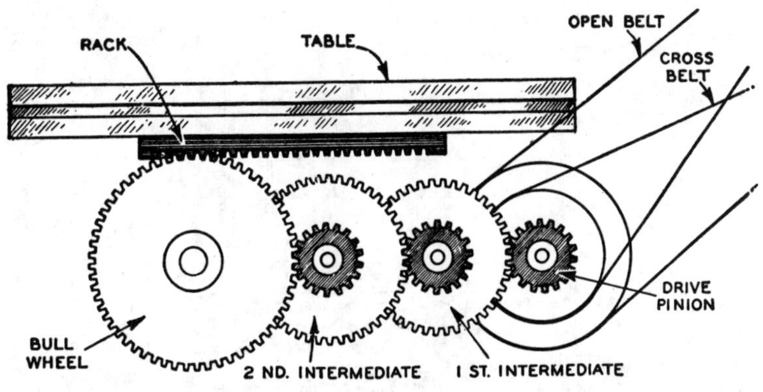

SIMPLE DIAGRAM OF TABLE DRIVE SHOWING OPEN AND CROSS BELTS.

Figure 3

feed screw gear attached to the feed screw of the machine. The feed screw to which the feed screw gear is attached is turned by the motion of the pawl.

The *feed adjustment mechanism* is a disk having an oscillating motion through a small arc. It carries a crankpin with an adjustable arm by means of the feed screw. The crankpin is connected to the rack by a rod. The rack movement controlling the amount of feed may be varied by turning the feed screw.

By clamping the *stroke dogs* in such a position that they come in contact with the reverse lever at desired points on the machine, the amount of table movement of table stroke can be regulated.

By means of the *reverse lever,* the table can be stopped and reversed at the end of each stroke. It is actuated by the stroke dogs.

The power for driving a planer is applied to the *drive shaft* by means of either belt pulleys or an electric motor, depending on the type of machine that is used.

The *table drive mechanism* is obtained by various methods such as rack and spur gears, spiral rack, and worm and crank. In the case of belt and pulley drive it consists of one open and one cross belt, each of which is belted to a loose pulley, which has a belt shifter to shift to a pulley that is keyed to the drive pinion shaft.

The *drive pinion* is the first gear of the reduction by transmission. The tangential speed of the belt must be reduced to obtain the relatively slow speed of the table because of the resistance encountered by the cutting tool. The first intermediate gear (Fig. 3) is the first stage reduction gear; the second intermediate gear is the second stage reduction gear; and the bull wheel is the final gear between the drive pinion and the rack. These gears are needed to obtain the necessary large speed reduction between the belt and the table.

A belt runs at a high velocity, usually 1,000 feet per minute, whereas the table must travel at a much slower speed, especially during the forward or cutting stroke of the tool, which is only 25 to 50 feet per minute. Therefore, big speed reduction is necessary.

Drive Methods

There are two methods of electric motor drive on planers, those with direct, and those with countershaft transmissions. In the direct method, the motor is connected directly or through gearing with the reduction gears of the planer. In the countershaft drive, the motor can either be placed on the housing and connected directly to the countershaft, or it can be placed on the floor and connected to the machine by a belt. Note that all the essential parts in Fig. 2 are identical, that the modern planer shown in Fig. 4 has two toolheads. In specially designed heavy-duty planers, features such as special trips, levers, and safety stops are provided.

Tools and Accessories

Planer tools and accessories are classified as general utility tools and special tools. Where a great many duplicate pieces are to be machined in the planer, it is necessary and practical to design and make a jig or fixture on which a specific job can be quickly set up, correctly aligned, adequately supported, and properly clamped to the worktable. This tool is usually designed to hold one or more pieces,

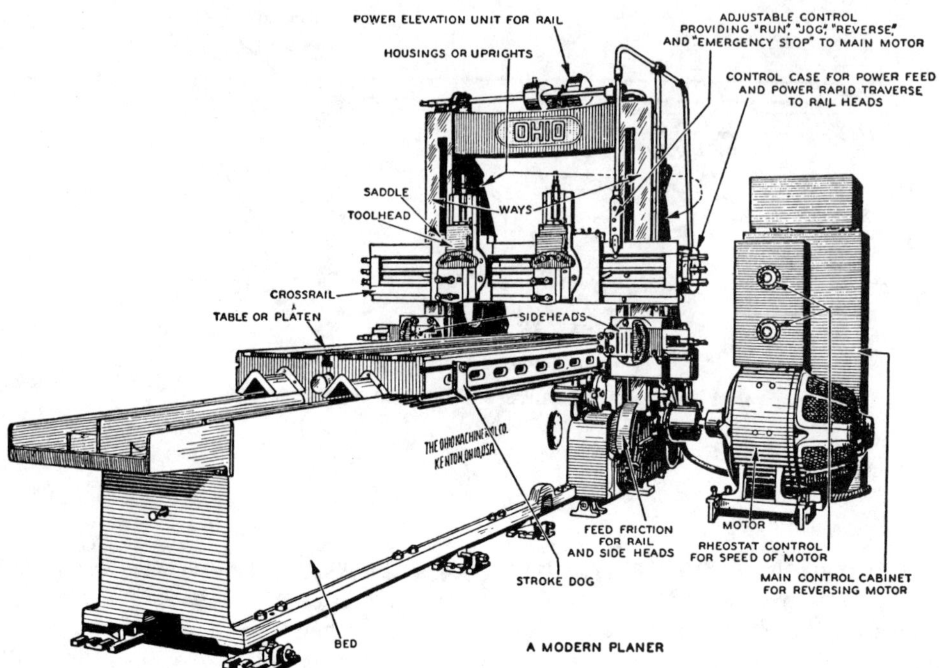

Figure 4

depending upon the layout and size of the job. Most work can be held on the table of the planer with the general utility type of fixtures such as clamps, stops, angle irons, strips, or whatever is adaptable for the particular job.

Vise or Chuck. The planer vise or chuck is made with a plain or a swivel base. By loosening the binding screw, the body of the swivel-type vise shown in Fig. 5 can be set in any desired position. The angle of the setting is indicated by graduation in degrees. To locate the vise when the jaws are parallel or at right angles to the direction of the cut, a taper pin with a squared head is used. One jaw is fixed, and T-slots are provided in the body of the vise for clamping the movable jaw with two bolts. The upper face of the body has cross slots to receive the thrust strips that are held in the backing block. These strips are provided to keep the block from slipping after being located.

Clamping the Work on the Platen of the Machine. The majority of work to be machined must be fastened directly on the platen or table of the planer rather than by the method previously described.

Bolts. The *square head bolt* shown in Fig. 6 is used for ordinary clamping. To place this bolt in position, it must be pushed along the T-slot from one end.

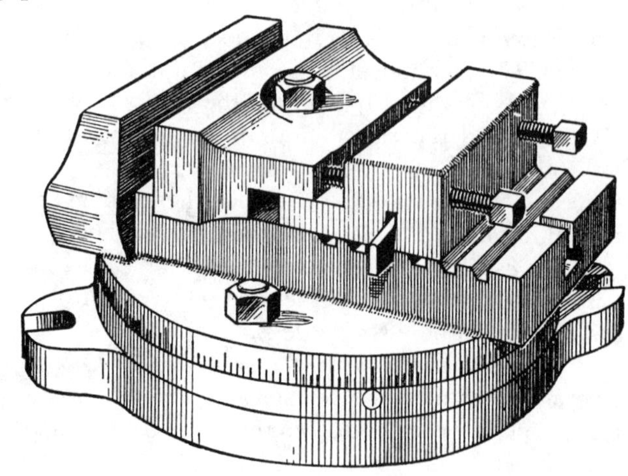

Figure 5

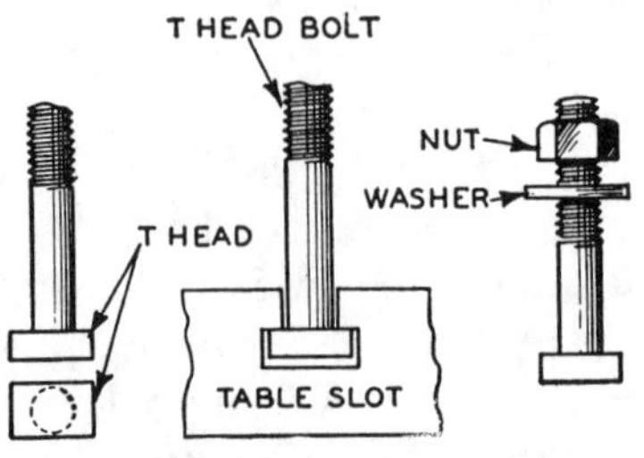

Figure 6

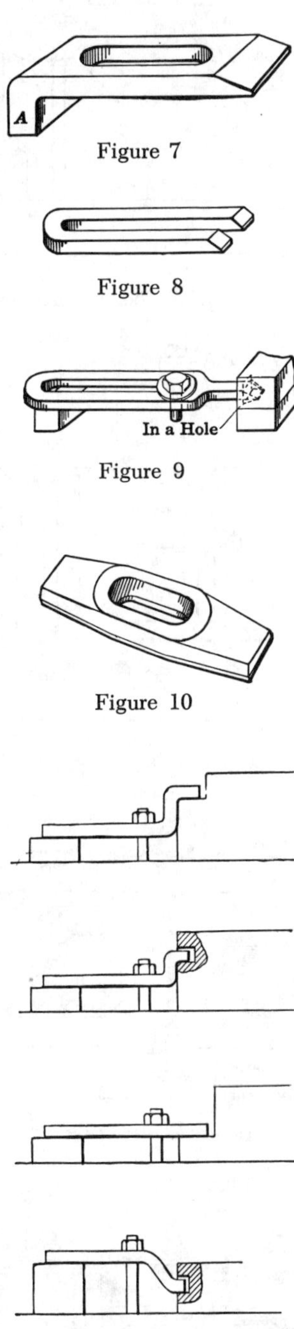

Figure 7

Figure 8

Figure 9

Figure 10

Figure 11

The *T-head bolt* is simple to use and can be placed quickly in position by dropping the head lengthwise in the slot and turning it to the right. This bolt is used when it is necessary to clamp on the inside of a casting which otherwise would have to be lifted over the bolt.

The *tapped T-head* is used when it is necessary to clamp inside a casting; the stud of the bolt can be removed and the head pushed along the slot under the casting to the position that is desired on the machine. Studs of various lengths can be used as needed; thus requiring a small number of tapped T-heads.

CLAMPS. In machine shops where the only clamps available are plain, flat bars with a bolt hole in the center, or perhaps two or three holes to allow the bolt to be placed in different positions, this type of clamp always requires blocking up at the end away from the work. The blocking should be of approximately the same thickness as the work so that the clamp will be flat and bear evenly on both work and block. A few simple clamps are shown in Figs. 7, 8, 9, and 10. The plain hairpin clamp (Fig. 8) is very common and can be used in many places. The clamp shown in Fig. 9 is useful for reaching into holes or recesses in castings, as shown. It is sometimes advisable to drill holes so as to leave the top clear. A plain, forged clamp is shown in Fig. 10. The bent-end clamp (Fig. 7) saves blocking up at the back end and is very convenient. By using clamps with the end *A* of varying lengths, work of different thicknesses can be clamped easily and quickly.

When clamping work, the strap or clamp should be as nearly level as possible, and the bolt must be as near the work as it can be placed. Figure 11 shows several applications of clamps and shows the advantages of keeping the straps level. Figure 11 also shows different applications of plain and bent clamps.

The use of parallel strips on the planer table at times makes it easier to strap the work, for these parallels give good bearing points beneath the clamps and at the same time hold the work level. This may make it necessary to use some sort of an angle plate for an end stop because the parallels raise the work from the table. A cross piece held by stops in the table may serve the same purpose, but some sort of stop must be provided to take the thrust of the tool.

There are clamps and blocks available (commonly known as "CAD" clamps and blocks) that include a variety of clamps, step blocks, packing blocks, wedges, and case-hardened nuts which increase the life of bolts on which they are used. The T-slot forged nut is also useful, for it can be used with any bolt, although T-headed bolts also have their place in setting up work on the planer table. Applica-

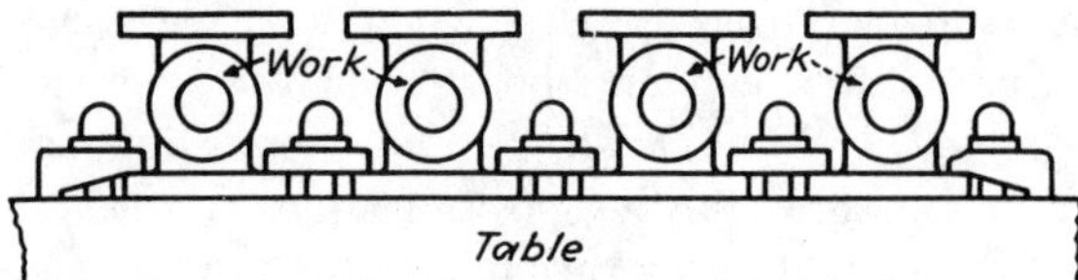

Figure 12. Holding four pieces at once.

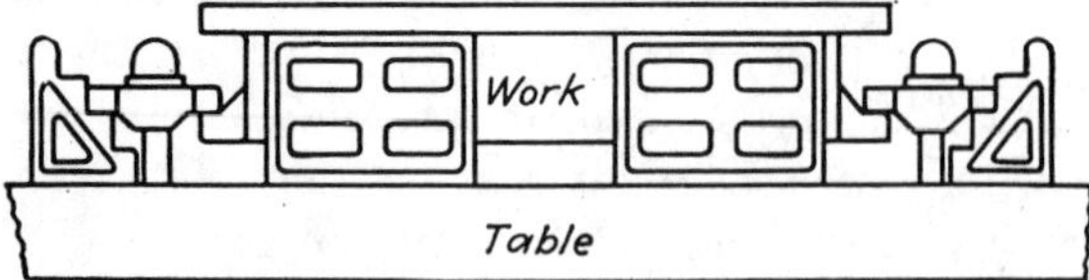

Figure 13. Use of clamps and step blocks.

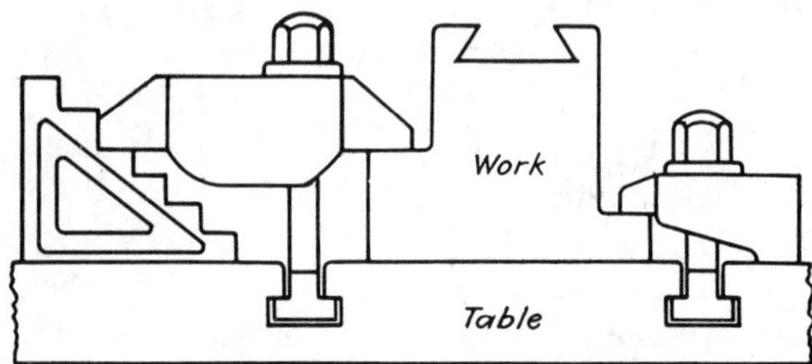

Figure 14. Step blocks keep the clamps level.

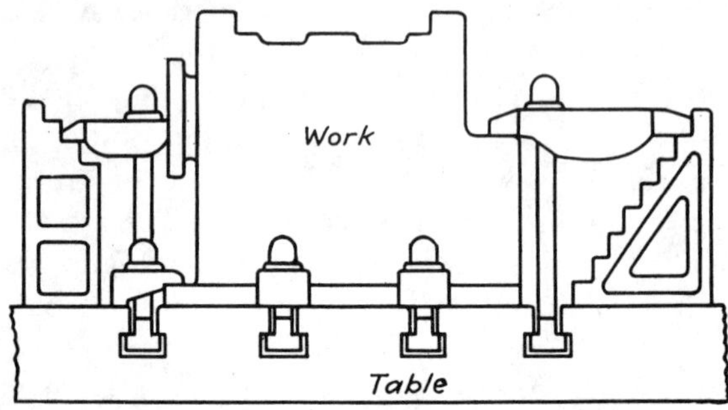

Figure 15. Work clamped at flanged base and on each side.

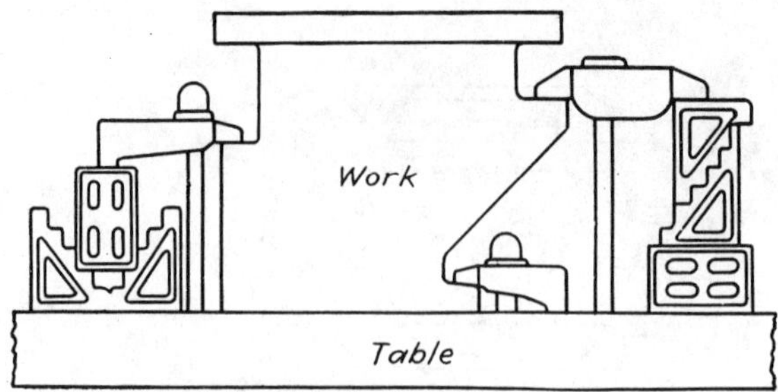

Figure 16. Unusual use of block combinations.

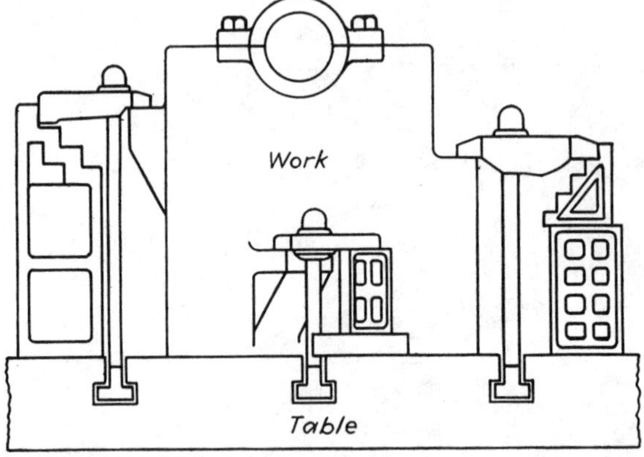

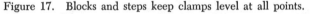

Figure 17. Blocks and steps keep clamps level at all points.

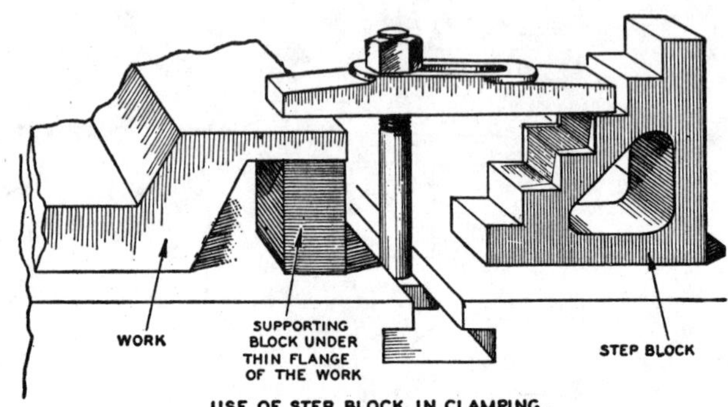

Figure 18

Figure 19a

tions of these blocks and clamps are shown in Figs. 12 to 17. No detailed explanations of the blocks or clamps or the way in which they are used are necessary. Note that the bolt is always placed as near the work end of the clamp as possible.

CLAMPING BLOCKS. The use of a step block in clamping is shown in Fig. 18. The block under the outer end of the clamp is a piece of metal of the required dimensions. If considerable height is required, and if metal of the proper size is not available, pieces of hardwood can be substituted.

The blocks and bolts shown in Fig. 19a will handle a large variety of work. The blocks *A* are planed

Figure 19b

Figure 21. Finishing tool for cast-iron castings.

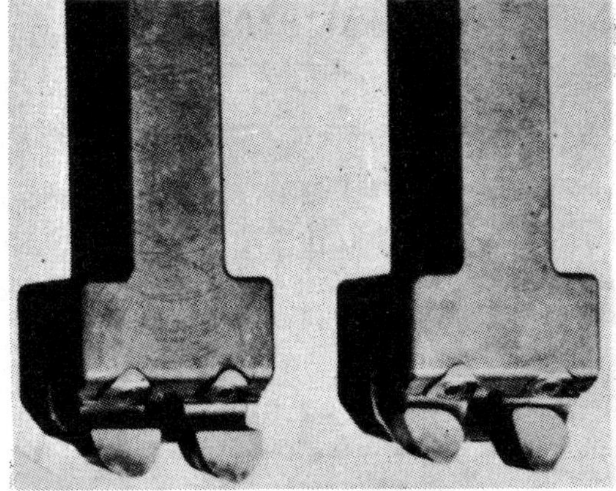

Figure 20. Double tool with forged bits.

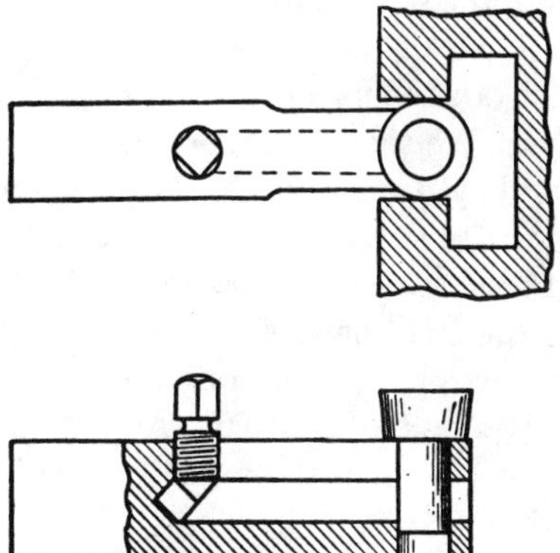

Figure 22. Round tool for T slots.

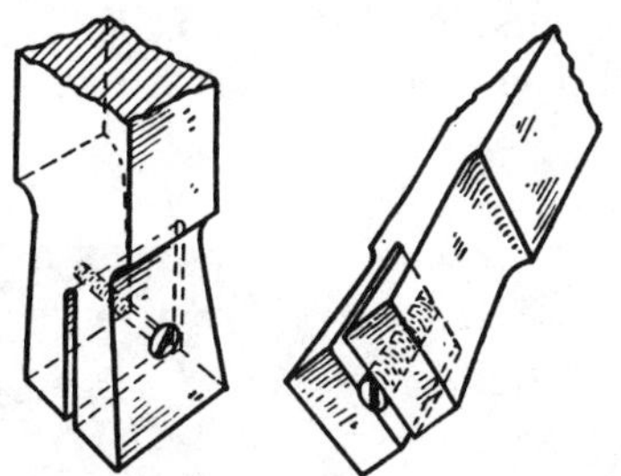

Figure 23. Adjustable tool for T slots.

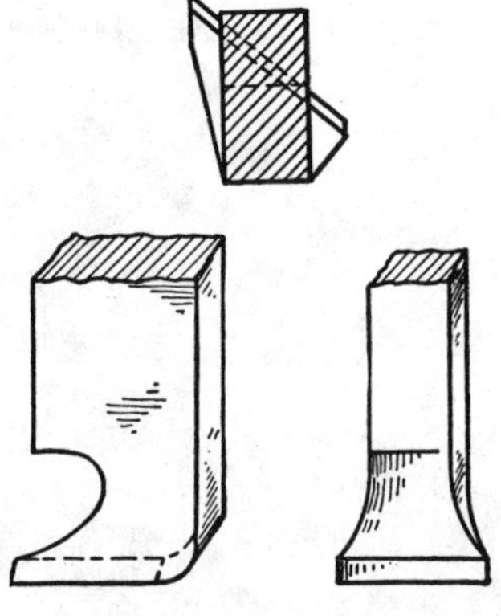

Figure 24. Finishing tool for cast iron.

to hook under the T-slot with the faces all the same distance from it. Blocks *B* are the same, except that they each have a setscrew as shown. Bolts *C* are made in a variety of lengths and have special nuts that fit in the T-slots. Stops *D* are round pieces of soft steel with the ends turned to fit the holes in the planer table. They will be found useful in heights of two to six inches, but should rarely be made longer than this. These also have setscrews. The short stops are used to reinforce the long ones by bearing against the block laid between them.

SHIMS. For fine adjustments or to give added support, shims or thin pieces of material may be placed between the work and the table of the machine, and between any two pieces or parts of pieces. Shims are made of thin pieces of metal, wood, or even paper. Heavier pieces used in the same manner as shims are called *packing blocks*.

JACKS. Planer jacks of the type shown in Fig. 19b are used for leveling the work or for supporting projections under cutting pressure. The base shown at 1 has a diameter of 1¼ inches and a range from 2¼ to 3⅝ inches. With the two extension bases shown at 2 and 3 (provided by the manufacturer), the range is extended to 6½ inches. The base shown at 3 is supplied when such a shape is required. The pointed screw shown at 4 is furnished in place of the screw with the swivel top at 1 for use in such setups as in a corner of the work. When a jack or a base is required for work that is fairly high with a small seating surface, additional braces are used to counteract the tendency of the work to tip under the cutting pressure. A piece of pipe of the required length may be used between the jack shown at 1, Fig. 19, and the base shown at 3, thus giving an adjustable brace to the work.

CUTTING TOOLS. The cutting tools that are used in planer work are similar to those used in the shaper, except that they are larger. There are a number of specialized cutting tools manufactured for specific purposes. The double tools shown in Fig. 20 are special cutters that will handle a large variety of work. Figure 21 shows a double-roughing tool with one tool located behind the other. Forged tool bits of the O.K.-type are used, their size depending largely on the work.

Specially designed tools used for a variety of work are shown in Figs. 22, 23, and 24.

Where a number of T-slots must be planed, use the round tool (Fig. 22), or the adjustable tool (Fig. 23). The round tool can be turned slightly as it wears at the used point. The adjustable tool is manufactured with a screw for locking the size after the adjustment has been made; it can plane a shallower slot than the round tool.

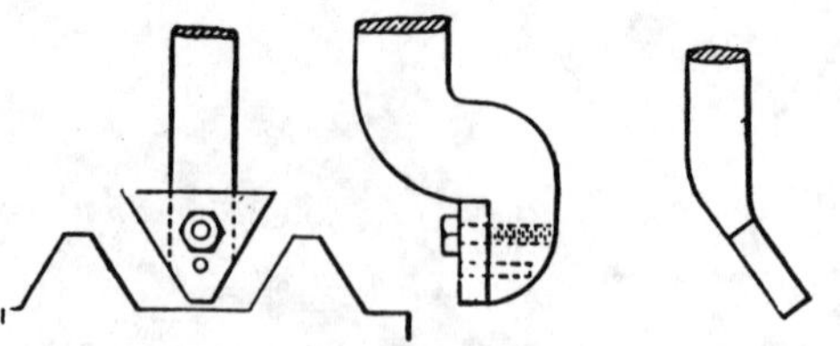

Figure 26. Tool for finishing V's.

Figure 27

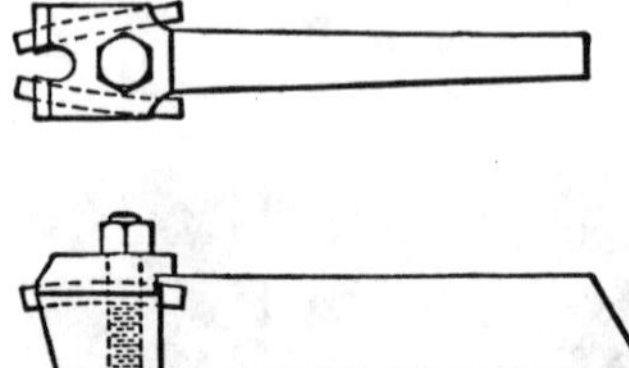

Figure 28. Tool for planing tongues.

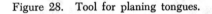

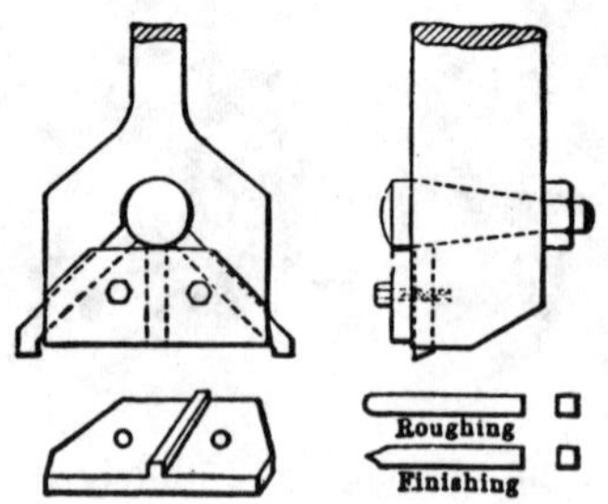

Figure 29. Double tool holder.

Figure 25. Finishing tool for steel.

Figures 22 and 25 show two types of finishing tools; one is used on cast iron, and the other on steel; both give a shearing cut leaving a smooth finished surface.

SPECIAL CUTTING TOOLS AND TOOL HOLDERS. Figures 26 to 30 show a number of special tools and tool holders. Figure 26 shows a cutter used for finishing the V-ways of a lathe or similar machine. The front edge of this cutter is in line with the bottom of the tool shank and prevents digging into the work. The tool shown in Fig. 27 is set at a negative angle to give a scraping cut.

Concave and convex radius tools are shown in Fig. 30; one is a solid cutter, and the other has a removable cutter. The convex tool with the round, coarse corner is made with a central pin or pivot so that it can be turned to present a new cutting edge without making a complete half turn. Where the radius approaches 180 degrees, the design shown in Fig. 30 is the simplest to make.

Figure 30. Radius tool.

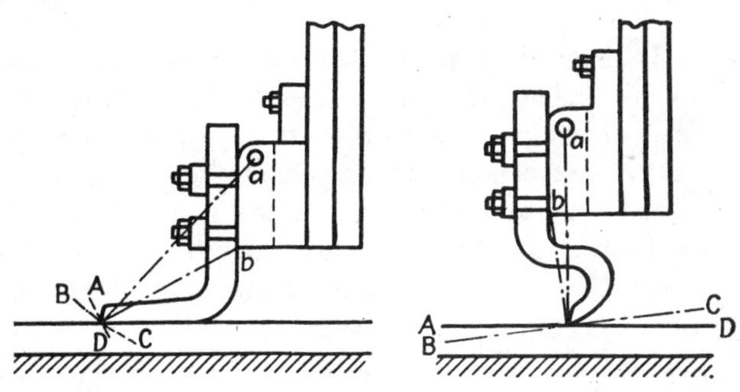

Figure 31. How a tool springs into the cut and out of it.

Figure 32. Special right- and left-hand elling, or undercutting, tools.

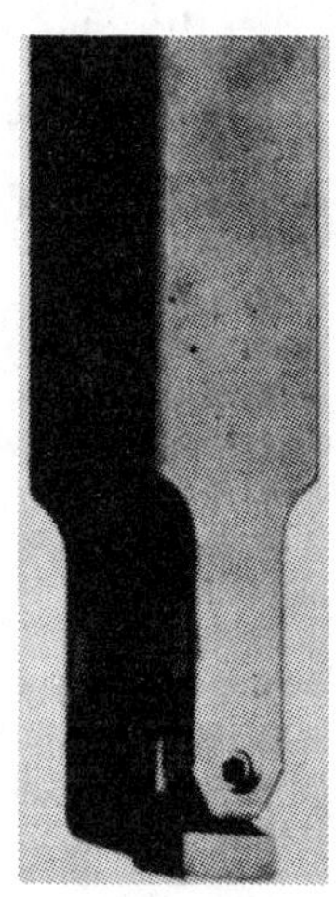

Figure 33. Special slotting tool.

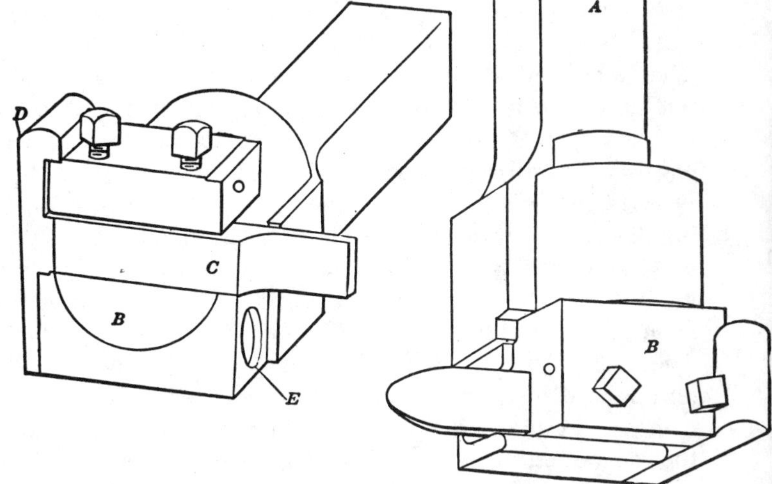

Figure 34. Other types of undercutting tool.

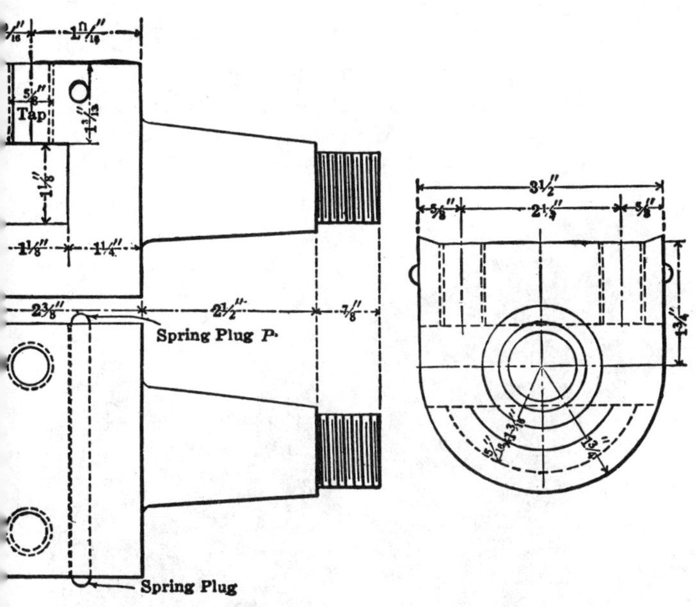

Figure 35. Details of construction of undercutting tool.

Figure 36. Supporting overhanging tools.

Tools used for planing slots of tongues are shown in Figs. 28 and 29, and both use inserted cutters that are held at an angle so that the width of the tongue or the slot can be maintained at the required size. Moving these cutters toward the front of the tool will bring the cutting edges together in the tool for the tongue, and will move them apart in the other tool. The tapered plug (Fig. 29) behind the cutters moves both cutters out an equal amount.

The Whalen planer tool shown in Fig. 30 has an apron, a tool block, and a turret movement that allows the tool to be turned to any angle required in the end of the shank. This makes it possible to cut in any position, across the surface, down the sides, or to do right-hand or left-hand undercutting. The turrethead of this cutter is controlled by the nut at the rear, and there is no dragging on the return stroke. It is used in planing slots in the side of work where the sidehead of the machine cannot be used. A spring tool is used where the tool digs into the work owing to the softness of the material or streaks or spots of hard metal. The primary object of the spring tool is to have the cutting edge away from the work rather than digging into it (Fig. 31). The tool at the left, which has the cutting edge ahead of the center, will dig into the work. The clapper box pin *a* is the block, but the spring of the tool would pivot at the point marked *b;* the arc of movement of the point is shown in both cases at *AD* and *BC*. The spring tool at the right has the cutting edge behind the clapper box pin *a*, and will spring away from the work.

Special Slotting Tools. Forged tool bits held rigidly in suitable holders are used for the planing of slots in tables and similar work. The forged tool bit is beveled at the back end to fit the sloping recess in the holder opening and is held in place by a headless setscrew. The tool bit is supported directly back of the cutting edge, and the holder is made of high-carbon steel. These tools are readily reset after grinding without disturbing the position of the tool shank in the tool block.

Special Tools for Undercutting. Undercutting, or "elling," with a planer tool is a job where the tendency to spring makes it necessary to use a feed of 0.010 to 0.012 inch and a cutting speed in cast iron of approximately 35 feet per minute. Increase of either the feed or the speed usually results in a broken tool. The tool shown in Fig. 32 is used for undercutting. When this tool is used, the feed can be doubled with safety. The tool holders are large and stiff, whereas the supporting end is very deep in the direction of the thrust. The tools are forged O.K. tool bits held rigidly in place with the headless setscrews (Fig. 33). The tool holder is of high-carbon steel, and the bits have serrations on the back by which they can be positioned in the holder so that the depth of cut remains the same.

Other types of undercutting tools are shown in Fig. 34, and their construction is shown in Fig. 35. The holder for this tool has a shank passing through the lower end of the heavy steel body, and the tool block can rock sufficiently to relieve the cutting point on the return stroke (Fig. 35). The tool holder has a large tapered shank which fits into the enlarged portion of the square shank and a straight thread for a round nut and locknut. The bar *A* is 2¼ inches square and 16⅞ inches overall in length, with the tool opening at 1¼ inches square. The rocking tool holder (*B*, Fig. 34) has a substantial bearing in a semicircular seat, and during the cut, the planing tool bears solidly against the shoulder as shown at *C*. This is aided by the spring plugger (*P*, Fig. 35) that bears against the inner face of the hook strap (*D*, Fig. 34). This hook strap also holds the tool against the thrust of the cut. On the return stroke, the spring permits the tool to rock back in its seat far enough to relieve the cutting edge.

Necessary Supports for Overhanging Tools. When cutting metal, the cutting tool must be supported as rigidly as possible, for there are times when the nature of planer work makes it necessary to use very long tools in order to reach the part that is being planed (Fig. 36).

Multiple Planer Tools. When held in proper shanks, the forged tool bits of the O.K. design give excellent satisfaction even on very trying work.

Another tandem or multiple planer tool with forged tool bits held in place by specially designed wedges and hollow-head setscrews is shown in Fig. 37. This tool holder carries seven small forged tool bits set to do its share of the work.

Figure 37. Multiple tool with seven O.K. tool bits used for planing V's.

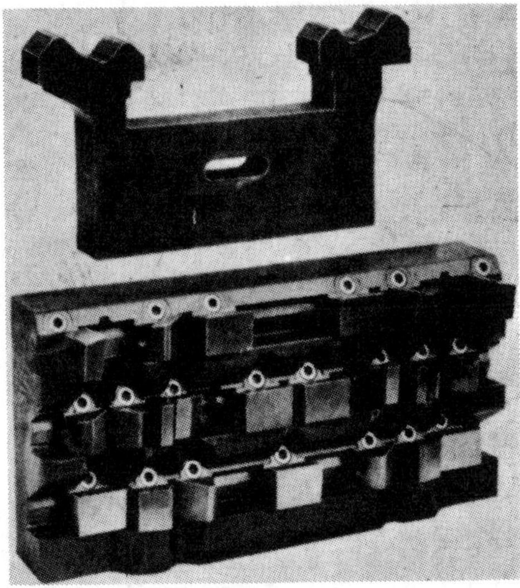

Figure 38. Lathe-bed multiple tool with 21 O.K. tool bits. Cuts profile shown above tool.

Figure 39. Double-housing planer with special tool holders for planing V and flat of a grinder bed.

Figure 38 shows a more complicated form of tool as well as a planer gauge showing the cross section of the lathe bed that this tool finishes. There are 21 tool bits in this holder, and the work of each tool can be traced in the completed section shown above it. This kind of planer tool is closely related to the broach except that there are no successive teeth to act as down feed (in which the last cutting edges of the broach finish the work at one pass). This tool is used only for roughing cuts.

Another tool is shown in Fig. 39 where a lot of roughing work has to be done, the special gang tool. The different tools divide the work. Three tools on each side of the V divide the cut, the side tools flatten the top, and the roundnose tool in the center cuts a clearance groove at the bottom. The other tool holder carries several flat-pointed tools and planes a flat surface at the same time as the other tools are cutting the V. The tool holders are supported by a snug fit against the underside of the tool block to prevent spring. The right-hand tool holder has room for another tool that is not yet in place. Pneumatic tool lifters prevent dragging on the back stroke.

Special Tools and Tool Holders for Heavy Work. The specialized heavy-duty planing that the modern planer performs requires not only the most powerful planers, but also tools and tool holders that will hold the tools and at the same time prevent vibration to the greatest possible degree. This is especially true in the field of railroad manufacturing where rail ends for frog and switch work or locomo-

Figure 40. Tool holder for heavy duty.

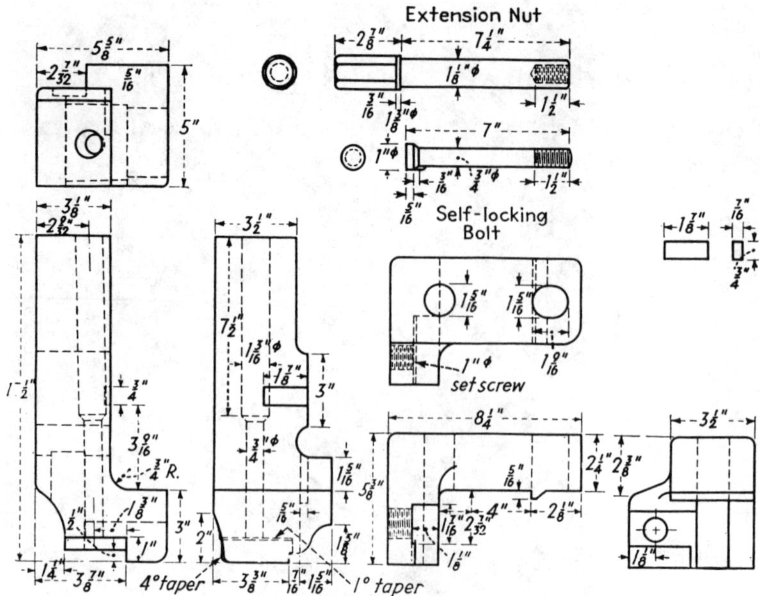

Figure 41. Tool holder and special strap for heavy work.

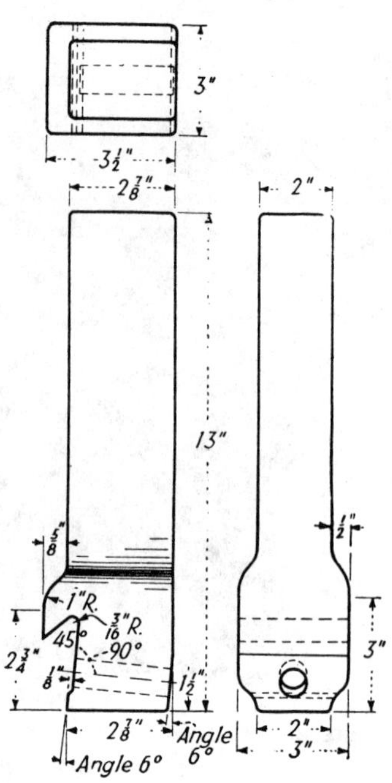

Figure 42. Holder with dovetailed tool support.

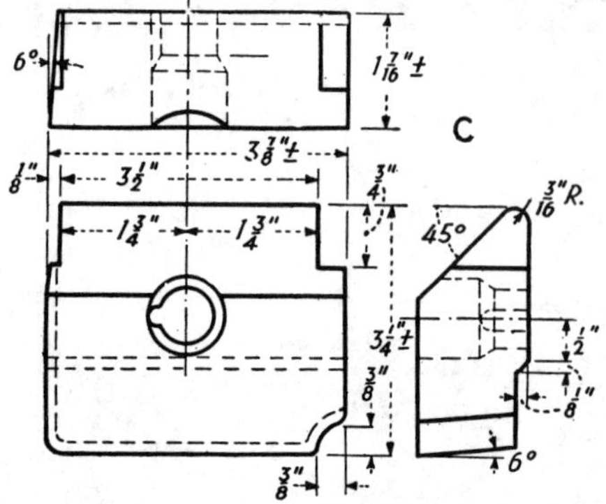

Figure 43. Cutter for tool holder shown in Figure 42.

tive bodies must be planed. One of the special planer tools for heavy work is shown installed in Fig. 40. Details of both tool holder and strap are shown in Fig. 41. The radius on the underside of the tool holder fits the tool block. The tool fits against shoulders behind and at one side and is held in position by the special bolt and nut shown above the clamp (Fig. 41). The tool itself has a countersunk hole with a half-round keyway into which the special self-locking bolthead fits. This bolt draws the cutter solidly against the holder by means of the long, special nut with the hexhead shown with the bolt which reaches down through the tool shank. The head of the bolt can be seen above the strap in the right-hand head (Fig. 40). The main dimensions of the tool holder are given to suggest proportions for similar tools for other work.

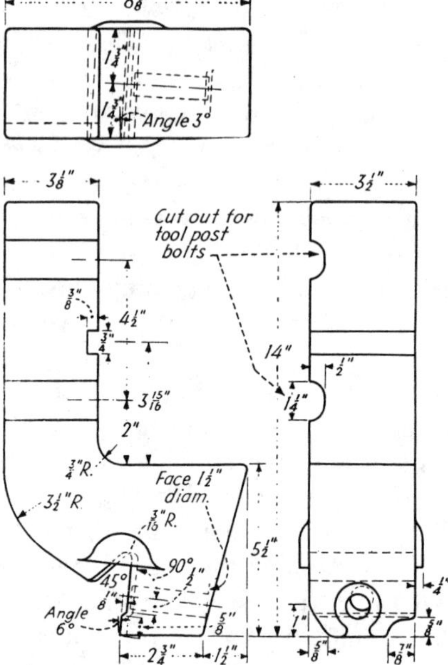

Figure 44. Another tool for dovetail-backed tools that is supported under the clapper block.

The special strap at the right of Fig. 41 holds the tool from both sides against side movement due to the thrust of the cut. It is also recessed at the side for a side tool for special work, this tool being held by a one-inch setscrew at the side. When no side tool is used, it bears directly against the lower end of the tool holder. Another type of tool holder (Fig. 42) was designed for what is known as "short-base planing." It provides a dovetailed support for the cutter against the thrust of the cut as well as the same type of bolt as before, but it has no special nut. A cutter for this holder is shown in Fig. 43. Figure 43 shows how the dovetail fits into the holder and how the cutter is held by the same type of bolt. Figure 44 shows another type of tool. A third design of tool holder is shown in Fig. 45, in which the thrust of the cut is taken by a recess instead of a dovetail. The main dimensions are shown. Figure 46 shows a cutter that fits into the recess and is held by side clamps which grip the sides of the

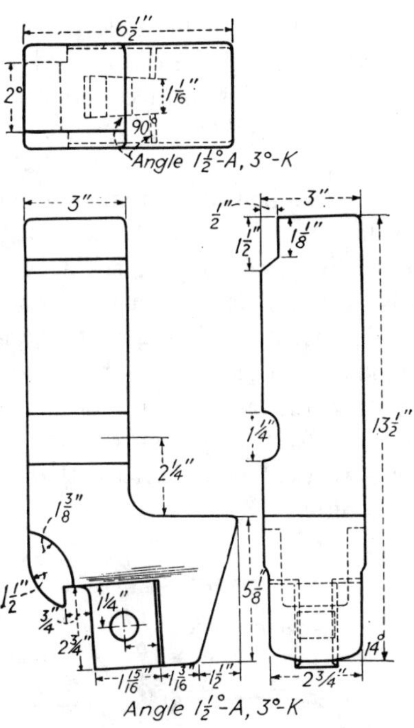

Figure 45. Tool holder with side clamp for tools.

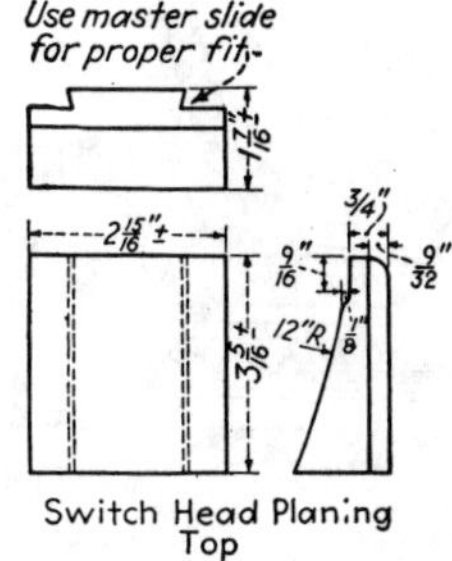

Figure 46. Tool for holder shown in Figure 45.

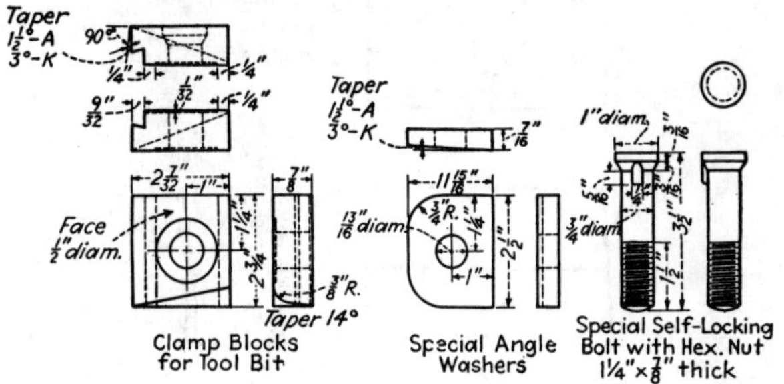

Figure 47. Clamps and bolts for holding cutter by dovetailed edges.

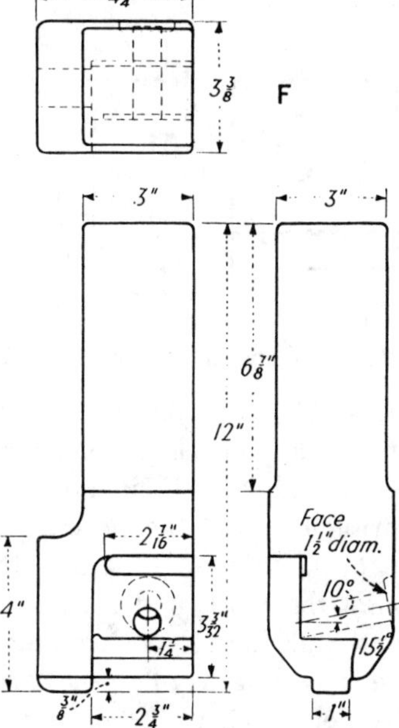

Figure 48. Tool holder for plate planing.

cutter by the dovetails. The clamps (Fig. 47) shown at the left as well as special-angle, or taper, washers may be used when necessary. Care should be taken to have the dovetails at the proper angle to insure solid clamping action. Figure 48 shows another tool holder designed for use in plate planing. This tool holder also uses a cutter with dovetailed sides, but it clamps it in a different manner. The clamp and tool are shown in detail in Figure 49. The clamp fits on the left side of the tool holder, completing the dovetail. The cross tongue at the upper end of the clamp fits into a corresponding recess in the tool holder so that the 15½-degree taper of the dovetail on the tool is held firmly by a cross bolt through both clamps and the tool holder itself.

Leveling the Work. Leveling the work is the setting up of the rough casting that is to be machined. The casting must be supported at the proper

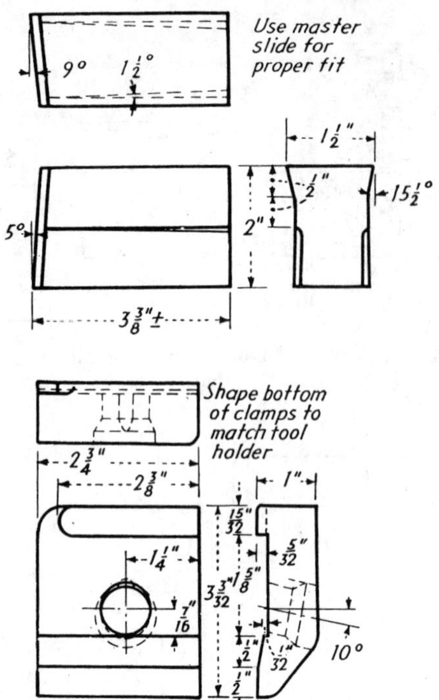

Figure 49. Tool and clamp for Figure 48.

points by blocks or shims so that the work will not buckle or spring under the clamping pressure. The work should be leveled so as to average the corners for height, bearing in mind the necessity for later planing on the other side of the work. It may be necessary to shim the work under two corners, or at times even under all four corners. No matter what clamping device is used, it may be necessary to place shims under the points where the clamping devices are applied because the tremendous screw pressure of bolts and nuts will sometimes spring a heavy casting unless the casting has been solidly supported under the clamp.

In setting up, all work must be leveled with a surface gauge (Fig. 50). Leveling the casting not only means proper blocking, shimming, and clamping, but it also means averaging the surfaces of a casting. Such casting requires a preliminary layout which is done before the job comes to the planer operator; sometimes the planer operator may have to do the preliminary layout himself.

Before cuts are taken, the machinist must ascertain how much stock has to be taken off the surfaces of all castings and from where it should be removed. Check the dimensions of the casting from the base or the edge. The work is leveled on a table, often on the platen of the planer. A tentative layout, the measuring of the casting, is then made. Lines are drawn on the chalked surfaces of the casting to verify the dimensions that have been given to the operator on the working drawing.

Make a tentative leveling with a surface gauge; check any surface that seems to be too low. If the surface is undersized and there is not enough material on it to clean properly, another casting will have to be leveled, and a new temporary layout made. All lines that are parallel to the base should be scribed and used when setting up the base of the casting for planing. After this temporary layout has been completed, the work is beveled to the base surface layout, clamped, and base planed. When the remaining surfaces are planed, they should be measured or gauged from the base or from another finished surface.

TOOLS USED FOR MEASURING AND GAUGING. The testing of a plane surface is done first by gauging its flatness, and secondly by its relation to another surface. When testing for flatness, place a straightedge on the work, and place the planed surface that has to be tested on a flat surface. For the measuring or gauging of the height of a surface, direct scale measurements or a surface gauge that has been tested to a scale can be used. The planer gauge shown in Fig. 51 has two bases and an adjustable slide that is locked by three gauging surfaces which may be extended by the use of various lengths of extension blocks. This tool has a wide range of sizes set by micrometer measurements to gauge the width of the slots, shoulder distances, or similar dimensions. It is also used to set the edge of the cutting tool either a vertical or a horizontal distance from a base or shoulder.

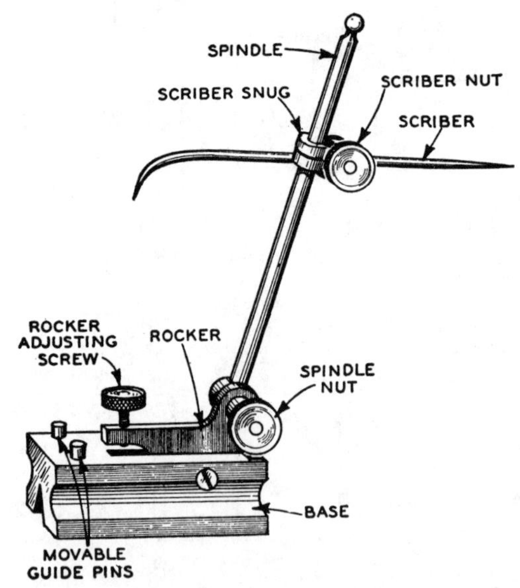

Figure 50. Universal surface gauge.

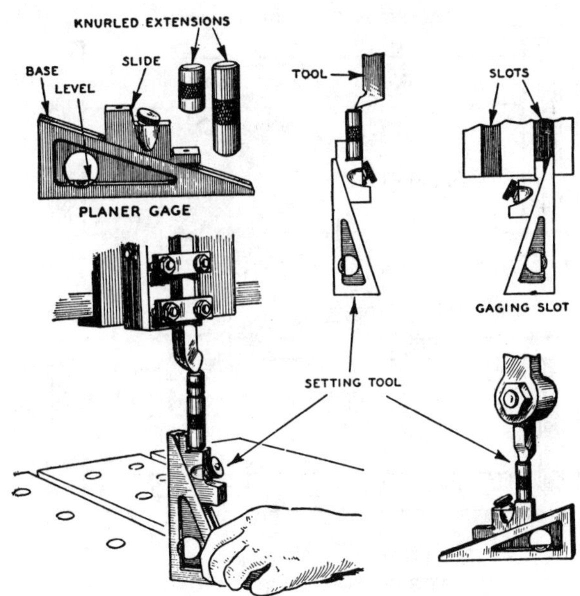

PLANER GAGE AND SOME OF ITS USES.

Figure 51

Planer Operations

Rough Machining a Horizontal Surface. The machining of a horizontal surface is shown in Fig. 52. Place the casting on the table, flange side down, and then align and clamp. The cross rail of the planer should be adjusted to the right height and the clamp screws set up. Select a roughing tool and place it in the tool holder perpendicular to the work. To prevent the tool from shifting, place it against the two clamping bolts on the side to take the lateral thrust. Tighten the tool bolts so that the clamps are parallel with the tool block or clapper.

The first surface of the casting to be machined is at *A*, Fig. 52. The depth of the roughing cuts depends on the amount of metal to be removed. If the casting is hard metal, a deep cut cannot be taken because the metal will break and leave a ragged edge at the end of the stroke. Test for this on the first stroke of the machine and, if the metal tears at the end, set the tool for a lighter cut and take two or more roughing cuts if necessary. Machine the casting until the tool reaches the inside edge of the surface *A*, Fig. 52. Machine surface *D*, Fig. 52 to the inside edge of surface *B*. Position and set the stroke to machine this surface. After machining surface *D*, reset and position the stroke for machining surface *C*. When the tool has reached the inside edge of surface *B*, reset and position the stroke for surface *B*.

For very small work, resetting is not advisable, and the entire surface can be machined with one setting. At this time only the roughing work should be done, up to the point of leaving about .015 inch for the finishing touch.

Finishing a Horizontal Surface. To prepare the work for finishing, break the front edge of the surface with a coarse double-cut file. This prevents the scale on the outside of the casting from destroying the fine cutting edge of the finishing tool. Remove the roughing tool from the tool holder and replace it with a finishing tool. When taking finishing cuts, finish to the dimensions shown on the working drawings. If not enough metal is removed in one cut, an additional light cut should be taken. When the casting has to be reversed for planing on the reverse side, the surfaces that have been ma-

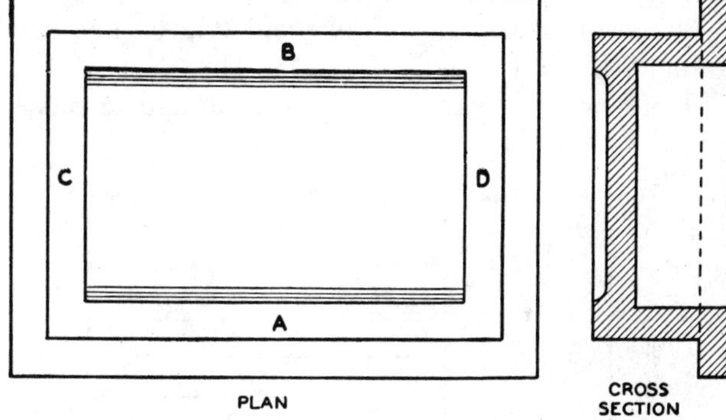

PLANING HORIZONTAL SURFACES ON FLANGED COVER.

Figure 52

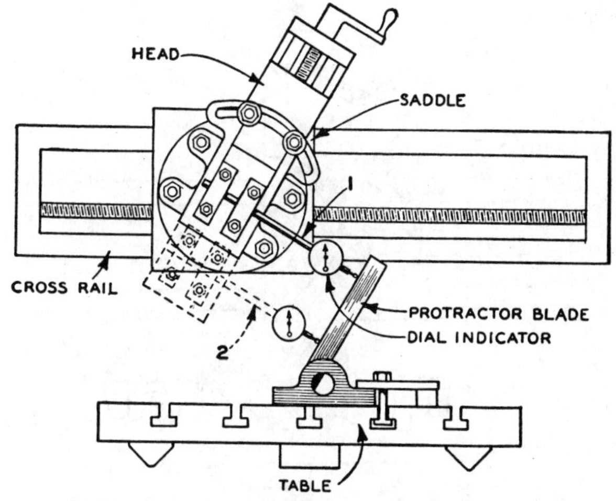

CHECKING ANGULAR SETTING OF SLIDE HEAD WITH A PROTRACTOR.

Figure 53

chined, being in contact with the level table of the planer, will automatically level the casting.

CHECKING ANGULAR SETTING. In dovetail or V-groove planing, the work must be done at a given angle. The toolhead assembly is pivoted to the saddle so that it can swing around a center, and graduations on the circular parts indicate in degrees the angular setting. Check the setting with a protractor (Fig. 53). Mount a dial protractor in the tool holder, clamp a protractor to the table of the machine, and set to the desired angle. Adjust the head until the dial indicator contacts with the protractor in the position at *1*, Fig. 46. Feed downward until the indicator features a position similar to that at *2*, and note the reading. If the readings are identical, the setting is correct; if not, readjustment must be made. The toolhead may be tested in a similar manner for a vertical position by using a square clamped to the table and a dial indicator.

PLANING AT AN ANGLE. For planing at an angle, a table V-block is used (Fig. 54). The sides of the V-block are 45 degrees to the vertical, and to plane

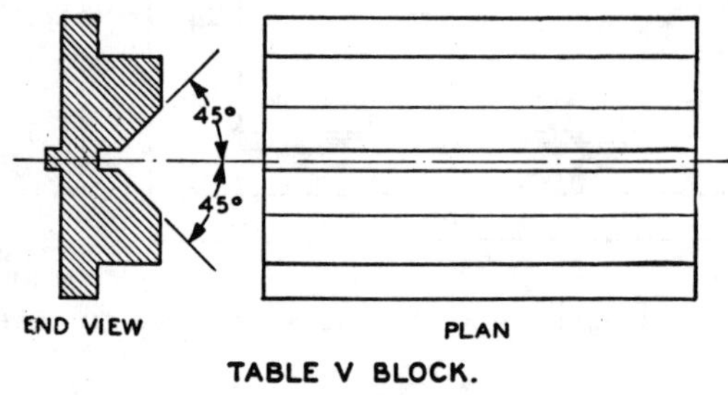

Figure 54

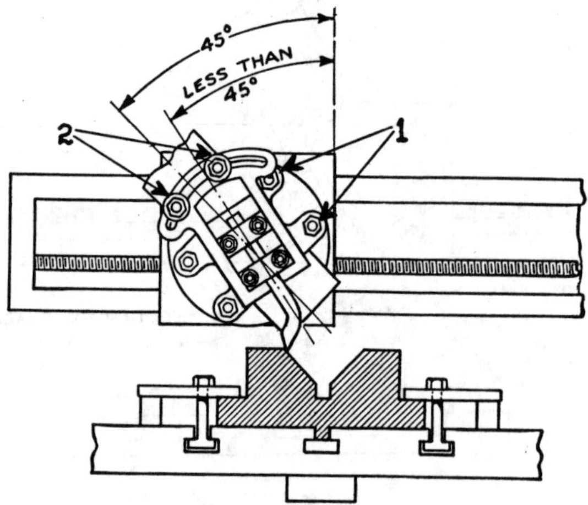

Figure 55

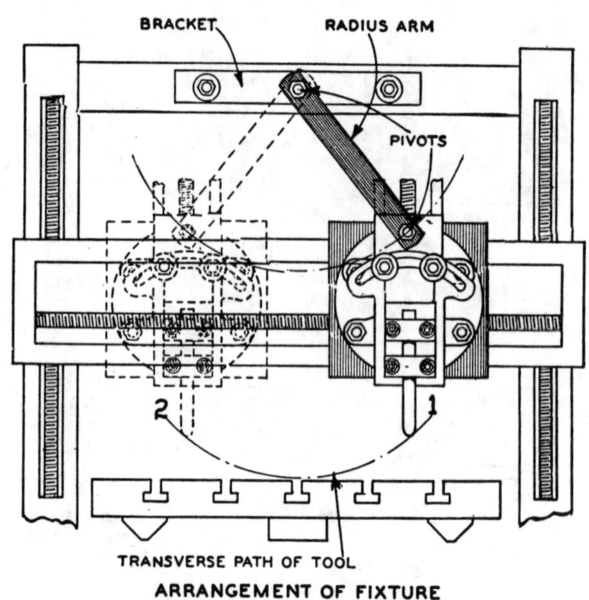

Figure 56

material at this angle, the head of the machine must be set to 45 degrees as shown in Fig. 55. After setting the head, clamp it into position by tightening the bolts shown at *1*, Fig. 55. Set the tool block at less than 45 degrees and clamp it in position by tightening the bolts shown at *2*, Fig. 55. The top of the tool block should be turned away from the work when the surface to be planed is vertical or inclined. In taking the cut shown in Fig. 55, the lower side of this job with its tongue is assumed to have already been machined, placed in a suitable groove, and clamped to the table. Move the saddle into position for the tool to take the first roughing cut beginning at the top. The cut should be started with the hand feed downward, and then the slide feed should be used. This will cause the slide to feed downward a certain amount for each stroke, the saddle always remaining in the same position on the cross rail. After the necessary roughing and finishing cuts have been taken for one side of the V, the angular setting of the slide should not be changed for the other side, but the work should be reversed in the table 180 degrees. It is impossible on a planer to reset the slide to the same angle. By reversing the work, the same angle will be cut, and the V will be in positive alignment with the center axis of the tongue.

PLANING A CURVED SURFACE. Figure 56 shows an elementary method used in planing a concave or arc-shaped surface. This is accomplished with a fixture

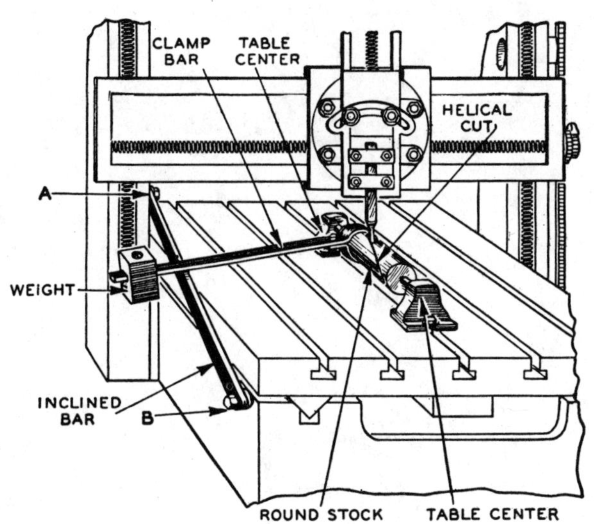

Figure 57

that consists of a radius arm which is pivoted to a bracket and to the slide; the feed screw is removed. When planing with this setup, the cross feed will cause the saddle to traverse the cross rail while the tool being guided by the radius arm planes the circular surface. Figure 56 shows that the elevation of the cutting edge of the tool, as the saddle traverses the cross rail of the planer, depends upon the angular position of the radius arm shown at 1 and 2 and upon the dotted lines showing the traverse part of the cutting tool.

Cutting Helixes on a Planer. Helixes that have a very long pitch cannot be cut on ordinary millers, but they can be produced on a planer by using the table center on the fixture shown in Fig. 57. This fixture has a weighted clamp bar and an inclined bar. The upper end shown at *A* on the inclined bar is attached to the housing, and the lower end *B* is attached to the bed of the planer. The pitch of the helix to be cut depends upon the inclination of the bar. The tool used is formed to produce the desired helical groove required. As the table moves with the clamp bar near the lower end of the inclined bar, the clamp bar is guided to its angular position and gradually rises, turning the work clockwise through the required small arc, and in this manner causing the cutting to cut the required helix.

Chapter 18

Turning

Turning as applied to metalworking is the shaping or forming of a revolving piece by a manipulated tool.

Generally we are referring to operations on a lathe, and the worker will find it so defined in most dictionaries. However, the lathe family has so many diversified relatives today that *turning* has become a rather broad term. Its definition would apply to many types of machine tools: the hand lathe, engine lathe, T-lathe, turret lathe, screw machine, automatic screw machine, polishing and finishing machine, chucking machine, or any other machine where a cutting tool shapes a rotating piece of metal. Even the large multiple spindle automatic screw machine is in effect a multi-axis turning machine.

The Lathe

The *lathe* is the oldest and most universally used machine tool. The earliest lathes were those similar to the ones now termed wood-turning lathes, where the work is supported between centers, and the cutting tool is held in the hand and supported on a tool rest close to the work. In the metalworking industry today this type of machine is still in use for deburring and hand-finishing parts of small quantities.

The most common type of turning machine is the *engine lathe*. A thorough familiarity with the engine lathe is a foundation upon which to build an understanding of all turning machines, regardless of their complexity. The characteristics of a lathe are that the work revolves as the tool feeds (just the reverse, for instance, of the operation of the milling machine). By various combinations of tools, feeds, and cuts, the lathe can probably perform a greater diversity of work than any other single machine tool. Yet a glance will show that the basic operations of the lathe are very simple. (*See* Fig. 1.)

What makes the engine lathe uniquely important

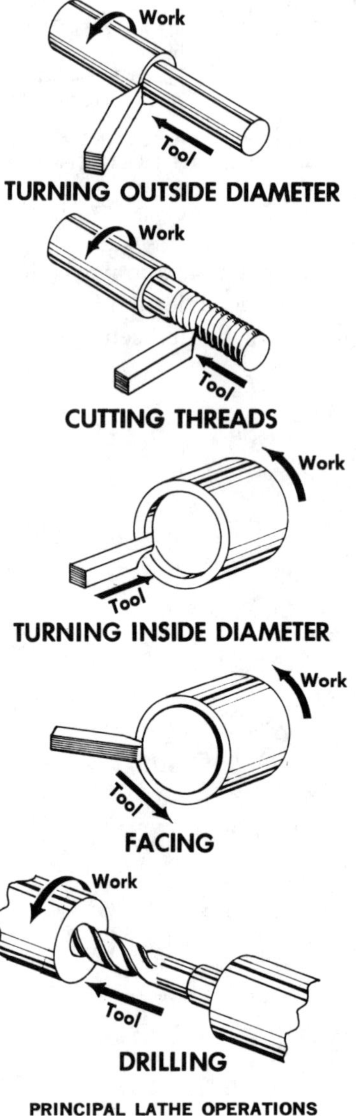

Figure 1. Principal lathe operations.

in metalworking is the precision control of the interrelation between the rotation of the work and feed of the tool.

GEARED HEADSTOCK. The workpiece is rotated on a spindle driven by a geared headstock which provides a wide range of speeds, selected by shifting levers on the headstock. A gear train from the headstock provides power and controlled movement to the carriage carrying the toolpost, which feeds relative to the rotating speed of the work.

LONGITUDINAL AND CROSS FEEDS. Power and interlocked motion are transmitted to the apron of the longitudinal carriage through either (1) the feed rod, or (2) the lead screw. The *feed rod* is a rotating rod, slotted to engage apron gears providing either the longitudinal feed used in turning outside diameters, and the like, or transverse feed to a cross slide used for in-and-out facing of work or depth cuts. The *lead screw*, ordinarily disengaged, is used only in cutting screw threads.

The carriage providing longitudinal and cross feeds is usually furnished with a compound tool slide for added flexibility when turning angular surfaces and similar operations. The work is usually in the form of bar stock or pieces mounted on mandrels which can be supported on centers. Chucks or face plates are also applied to engine lathes to hold workpieces which cannot be held on centers, or where internal operations must be performed such as drilling, boring, and internal threading.

In the United States, the size of a lathe is designated by the diameter of the work which will clear the bed ways when on centers and the length of the bed. A 16 inch by 8 foot lathe will swing work or a face plate over the bed way 16 inches in diameter, and the bed is 8 feet long. In Europe, such a lathe would be regarded as an 8 inch by 8 foot lathe, the work-radius capacity being used rather than the diameter in indicating the lathe size.

In either case, however, the worker must remember that because of the length of the headstock and footstock, and height of the tool rest, the maximum dimensions of the work which can be accommodated between centers and swing over the tool rest are much smaller than the lathe size indicates. Operation of any machine will be hard to understand unless the operator is familiar with the names and functions of the parts. The best way to obtain this knowledge is at the machine itself, although considerable information can be obtained by studying the manufacturers' literature. At this point it might be well to advise the mechanic to form the habit of acquiring useful and up-to-date information on tools of his trade by obtaining literature that is issued free of charge by the manufacturer.

CARE OF THE LATHE. Neatness about a machine is usually characteristic of a good workman. It is a habit acquired by practice. Even while the machine is in use, it should be kept as neat and orderly as possible.

Try to remember not to put tools or work on the ways of the machine. The accuracy of the lathe depends so much on the condition of the ways that they always should be protected from damage. Arrange a wooden tray or receptacle at the end of the machine back of the footstock to hold cutting tools and accessories. Never use the carriage as an anvil. Before starting a job, be sure that all moving parts are lubricated and in good operating condition.

When the work is finished, leave the machine clean and the accessories in good order.

Before You Start To Work

There are a number of elementary things the machinist should know before he puts his first job on the lathe.

TESTING LATHE CENTERS. It is obvious that in any turning process the accuracy of the work begins at the centers. They must be true or the work will be inaccurate. So begin right there—testing the centers.

The large notch in the end of a center gage (Fig. 2) is used to test the center angle, which should be 60 degrees. The smaller notches are used for testing and setting Unified and American, American National or U.S. Standard (60 degrees) threading tools. The point is used primarily to test the cutting angle of inside threading tools. The graduations (14, 20, 24, and 32 parts of an inch) are useful in measuring the number of threads to the inch.

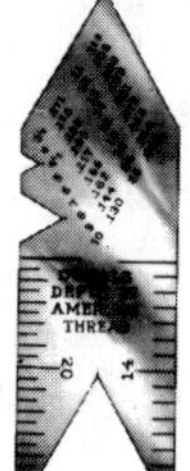

Figure 2. Center gage.

ALIGNMENT OF CENTERS. To test the alignment of centers, put a test bar between centers, and with an indicator (Fig. 3) on the tool carriage, run the indicator along the face of the bar. If it shows no variation from one end of the bar to the other, the centers are in line. If not, they are out of line and should be aligned to the degree of accuracy required of the job.

Three Ways to Align Lathe Centers for Straight Turning. The first two of the following methods will give an approximate degree of accuracy sufficient for ordinary work. If top precision is required, either the first or second should be followed by the third.

1. Release the footstock clamp and move the upper section on the lower section so that the aligning points will coincide. These aligning points are at the end of the footstock under the footstock handwheel.

2. The second method consists in sliding the footstock forward until the centers nearly touch. By turning the adjusting screws in the footstock the centers can be aligned.

3. After the centers have been aligned by one of the previous methods, the third method for greater accuracy is to mount the piece of work that is to be turned (or a piece of stock of similar length) between the centers, using a dog as in a turning operation. At the end of the work near the headstock make a narrow cut deep enough to true the bar, *note* reading on cross slide dial, withdraw tool, and run carriage back to the footstock end. Then take a second cut at the footstock end to the same cross slide dial setting obtained during the first cut at the headstock end. Measure the two cuts thus made with a micrometer caliper and compare the results. If the diameter measures the same at both cuts, the centers are in exact alignment. If not, then by means of the aligning screws in the footstock, set the center over until the diameters become equal. Do not waste time, however, in aligning with great accuracy for short or rough work.

Test Indicator. The *test indicator,* types of which are shown in Figs. 3, 4, and 5, is used to determine the eccentricity of work in motion. To check the *live* center for trueness an indicator can be used as shown in Fig. 4.

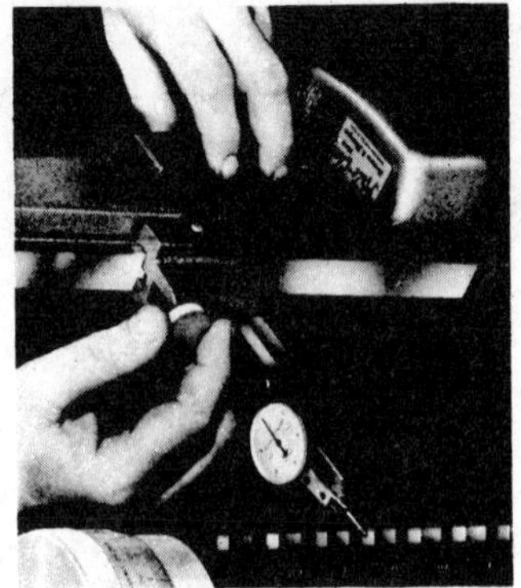

Figure 3. Test indicator.

Figure 4. Testing a long arbor with a dial test indicator.

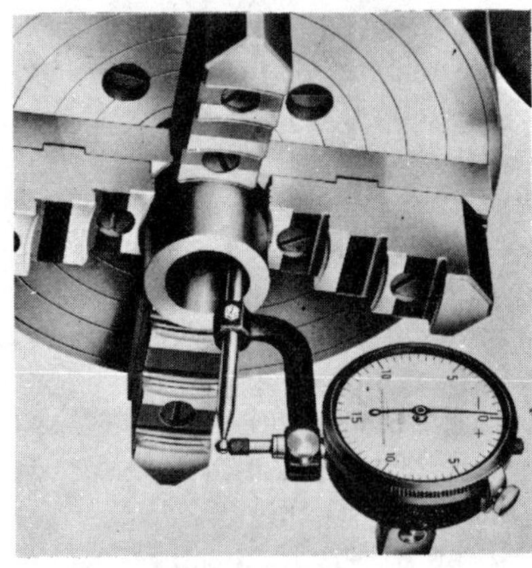

Figure 5. Testing an inside surface with a dial test indicator and hole attachment.

To True Lathe Centers. Before beginning to turn any piece of work requiring accuracy, always be sure that the *live* (headstock) center runs true. First, establish alignment marks on the center and the spindle so that the center can be removed and returned to its original relation with the spindle. Take the *live* center out of the headstock spindle. See that the center and hole in the spindle are clean and free from dirt. Put the center back into the spindle with the aligning marks together and tap it snugly into place with a lead hammer. Revolve the spindle slowly and note the amount of indicated run out which must be corrected by grinding the center point.

Truing Lathe Centers by Grinding. An occasional function which is important in maintaining good quality turning is to true lathe centers by grinding. The same procedure applies whether truing the headstock or footstock center. If both are to be trued,, grind the footstock center first and replace it in the footstock, so that the headstock, or *live* center, after being trued, need not be disturbed.

The headstock center may or may not be hardened. The footstock or *dead* center is usually hardened and tempered.

The usual procedure is to use a portable grinding attachment mounted in the toolpost. *Caution* should be taken to avoid entanglement of the electric cable with moving parts of the lathe when it is started. The compound rest is set at 30 degrees, or one-half the center point angle, and the grinding attachment is positioned with the axis of the wheel spindle parallel to the angle to be ground. With the lathe and the grinding attachment both under power, the grinding wheel is brought in contact with the angular surface of the point.

To perform the grinding operation, the wheel is traversed across the face of the center point slowly to produce a good finish, using the compound slide handwheel. The grinding feed is governed by the cross feed handwheel on the carriage. Several light cuts should be taken, and the angle tested frequently with the center gage.

CENTER HOLES. *Center holes* are the bearing points for work mounted on lathe centers, and are necessary of any work to be turned between centers. They are usually drilled by centering machines, but may be laid out with the aid of the center head and scale of a combination square (Fig. 6), or with hermaphrodite calipers (Fig. 7).

With the center head and scale of the combination square, any two lines scribed at random across the surface of the work will intersect at the approximate center, provided the piece is held snugly within the angle of the head. Lines are usually drawn at right angles.

By using the hermaphrodite calipers and with a radius of about half the diameter of the piece, three or four arcs may be scribed as shown in Fig. 8, the center point located by eye, and prick punched.

Using the combined drill and countersink (Fig. 9) saves time and assures that the countersinking will be concentric with the hole. However, the center holes can be drilled and countersunk in a hand lathe or in a drilling machine having a center in the table arm. The countersink is 60 degrees because the common angle for a lathe center is 60 degrees and a finished center hole should have the same angle.

There is no hard and fast rule for the size of a center hole, but it is advisable to have its diameter in reasonable proportion to the diameter of the work, as indicated in Table 30 (large and deep enough to furnish a good bearing and to prevent undue wear). In any lot of work, the center holes should be of uni-

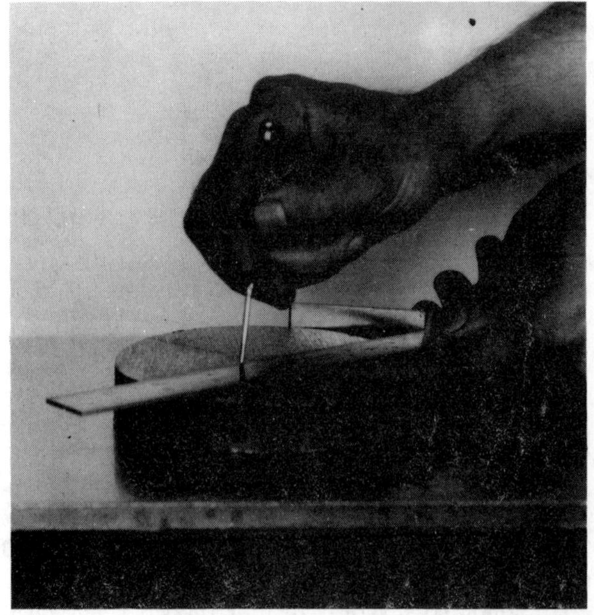

Figure 6. Locating the center of a piece of stock with the center head and scale.

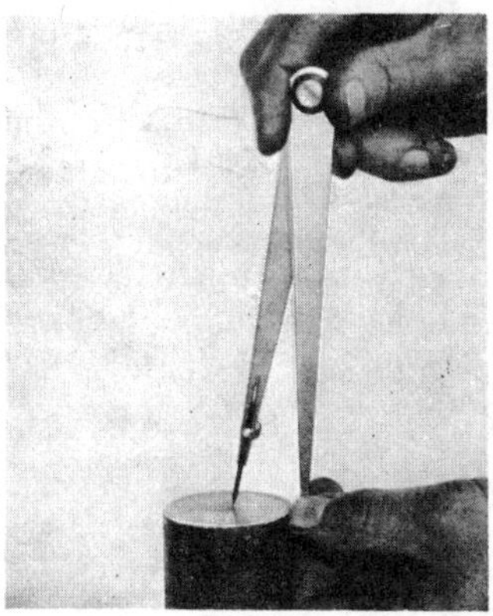

Figure 7. Hermaphrodite caliper scribing arcs to locate a center hole.

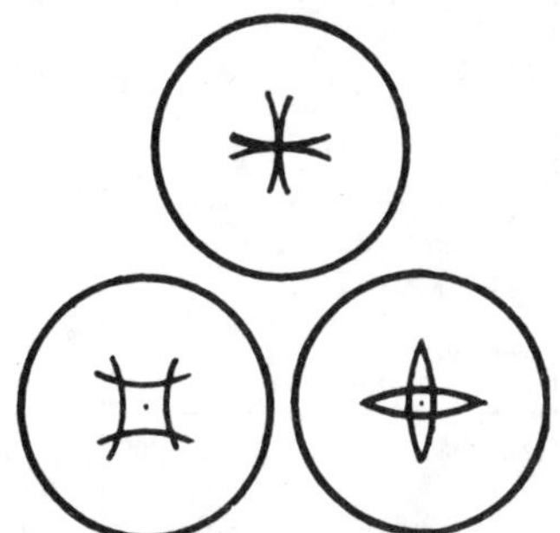

Figure 8. Center holes located by arcs scribed by radii of different lengths.

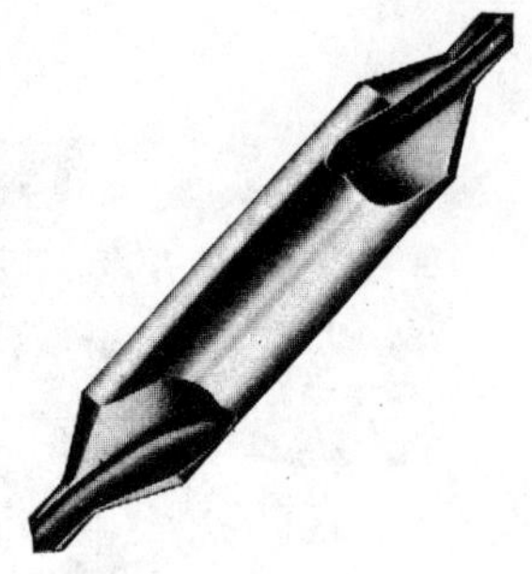

Figure 9. Combined drill and countersink.

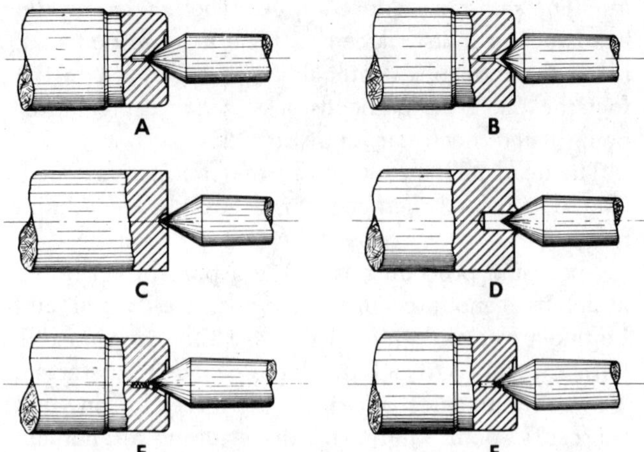

Figure 10. Good and bad center holes. A, Angle of countersink too large; B, Angle of center too large; C, Hole not deep enough; D, Hole not countersunk; E, Chips in center hole; F, Correct center hole, as shown by fit of center.

form diameter. This promotes safety and accuracy, particularly in grinding finishes.

Properly prepared, a center hole will retain oil, and it is of the greatest importance that it be kept well oiled and free from dirt and chips. (*See* Fig. 10 for examples of typical good and bad center holes.)

TO STRAIGHTEN WORK. If after the stock has been centered and rotated between centers in the machine it is perceived to be bent, warped, or otherwise out of line, it should be straightened in the straightening press.

PICKING UP CENTER HOLES. Frequently when rough-turning large or long shafts supported by the dead center in the footstock, the center holes wear eccentric with the turned diameter. When this occurs, the center holes must be *picked up* or restored to their original concentricity with the outside diameter before finishing. The procedure is shown in Fig. 11.

TABLE 30

CENTER HOLE SIZES

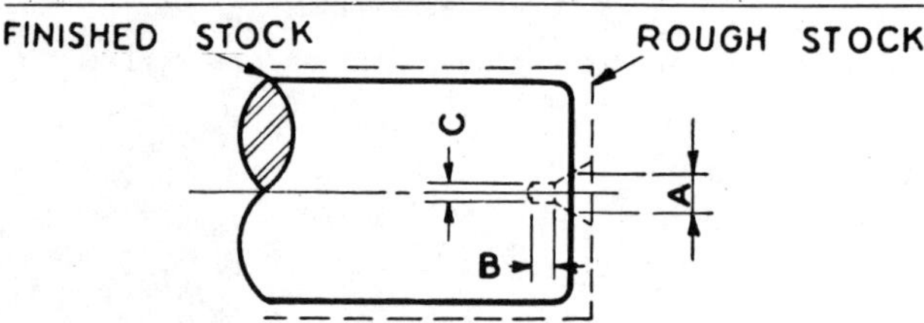

Finished Size of Shaft		Center Drill	A	B	C
From	To	Diam.			
1/8	5/32	1/8	3/64	1/16	3/64
3/16	7/32	1/8	5/64	1/16	3/64
1/4	11/32	1/8	3/32	1/16	3/64
3/8	17/32	13/64	1/8	5/64	1/16
9/16	25/32	15/64	3/16	3/32	5/64
13/16	1 3/32	3/10	1/4	3/32	3/32
1 1/8	1 15/32	7/16	5/16	5/32	5/32
1 1/2	1 31/32	7/16	3/8	5/32	5/32
2	2 31/32	1/2	7/16	3/16	7/32
3	3 31/32	5/8	1/2	7/32	7/32
4	and over	5/8	9/16	7/32	7/32

With a steady rest mounted in position supporting the work close to the footstock end, the lathe dog is strapped securely to the faceplate as in A, Fig. 11. The center hole will then visibly appear to be eccentric with the outside diameter supported in the steady rest. A bell centering tool is now set to the notch in the center gage, as shown in B, Fig. 11. The bell centering tool is presented to the angle of the center hole, as shown in C, Fig. 11, removing only sufficient stock to restore its surface true with the outside diameter. This may be repeated at the opposite end of the work if necessary.

MANDREL. The *mandrel* (Fig. 12), often miscalled an arbor, is used to mount work having a hole in

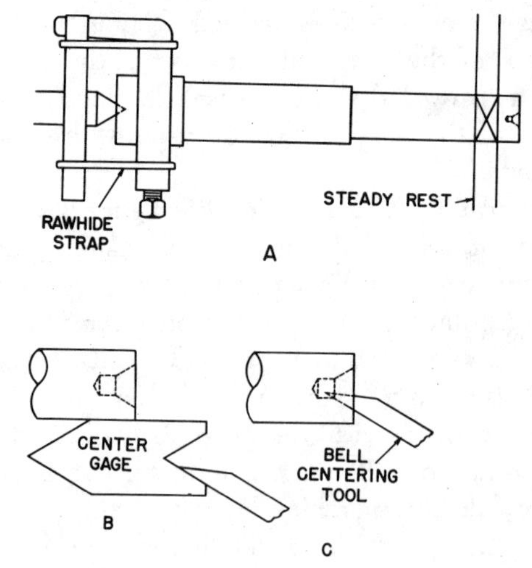

Figure 11. Procedure for picking up center holes.

Figure 12. Mandrel.

Figure 13. Expanding work arbor.

order that the work can be held between centers and machined. It may be pressed, driven, or threaded into the work. The mandrel is made of tool steel, hardened and ground, with a flat milled on each end to provide a seat for a driving dog screw. A mandrel may be .0005 in. to .001 in. or more, smaller on one end than the other so that the work may have a solid bearing when pressed on. For accurate work the mandrel should always be tested for run-out before using.

ARBORS. *Arbors* are used in the same manner as mandrels (Fig. 13). There are two common types of work arbors—*expanding* and *gang*.

Work-Holding Devices

The headstock end of a workpiece on a lathe may be held and secured for turning by either a faceplate and driving dog or a chuck. Generally, the faceplate is used for turning a long piece *between centers,* while a chuck may be more convenient for a piece that is short and stubby.

For turning *between centers* the faceplate is mounted on the lathe spindle at the headstock end with the *live* center projecting through a hole in the faceplate. The faceplate has slots in it for driving the work by means of a dog clamped by a setscrew to the work. When the turning is complete the dog is removed.

Chucks are designed for a wide variety of turning operations, and there are numerous special adaptations.

Chucks and Chucking

Chucking is an expression used to distinguish lathe operations wherein the workpiece is clamped rigidly on the faceplate or chuck and held true in rotation as opposed to where the work is held between centers. The lathe chuck is an adjustable work-holding device that is screwed or otherwise attached to the lathe spindle and rotates with it. The jaws of the ordinary chuck are adjustable to accommodate work of different diameters, and work should be clamped in it firmly before starting, with care being taken not to spring light work by over-tightening the jaws.

TRUING WORK. Because the chuck takes the place of the *live* center in aligning the work, the jaws should be adjusted so that the piece will rotate as nearly concentric as possible with the axis of the spindle. Roughly you can accomplish this by holding a piece of chalk, with the hand resting on the ways of the machine, then moving the hand slowly toward the work so that the high spot will be the first part of the piece to receive a chalk mark. By withdrawing the jaw or jaws opposite the mark and closing the near jaw, the piece can be adjusted sufficiently so that it will rotate truly. If greater accuracy is desired use a dial test indicator (Fig. 4).

Types of Chucks

There are at least five kinds of chucks in common use: universal chucks, independent chucks, combination chucks, drill chucks, and draw-in chucks. Furthermore, chucks are distinguished by four types of jaws: lathe jaws, drill jaws, milling machine jaws, and brass jaws. *Lathe jaws* are used to hold lathe work from the outside or inside, and are usually for larger diameters. *Drill jaws* are made suitable for holding rods and drills, even of very small diameter. *Milling machine jaws* are designed for the requirements of the milling machine. *Brass jaws* are made with contact pieces of brass fitted to the jaws, and which can be readily slipped out.

UNIVERSAL CHUCK. *Universal chucks* (Fig. 14) are made so that when a wrench is applied to move the jaws, all the jaws move simultaneously, inward or outward. Universal chucks are widely used for work of regular shape and are made in several sizes.

INDEPENDENT CHUCK. The jaws of an *independent chuck* (Fig. 15) move independently of each other. This type of chuck is preferred for rough and irregular work, because, by the independent movement of the jaws, irregular pieces can be trued more easily than with the universal chuck. Some have concentric rings to help the operator in setting the jaws.

Combination Chuck. By a device on the back of a *combination chuck* the mechanism can be meshed or unmeshed so that the jaws will move independently, as in the case of the independent chuck, or in unison, as in the case of the universal chuck. This chuck also has concentric rings cut on its face so that when it is desired to use it as a universal chuck, the jaws can be lined up with one of the rings and the mechanism thrown into mesh to furnish the universal action. Combination chucks fulfill the requirements of both independent and universal chucks, but they require more care to keep them in good condition.

Drill Chuck. The *drill chuck* (Fig. 16) is used to hold drills, rods, and work of similar character. It operates like a universal chuck. These are made in a number of sizes, and are usually mounted on a tapered shank.

Draw-In Chuck. The *draw-in chuck* (Fig. 17) is used on some engine lathes and on many turret lathes and screw machines. It is a common type in use on toolmakers' and watchmakers' lathes. In operation, bar or rod stock is usually passed through the spindle into the chuck where it can be held securely. From this bar stock, bolts, nuts, screws, and a variety of shapes may be turned, drilled, and tapped directly without first having to be cut off and handled again. The mechanism for opening and closing the chuck operates while the spindle rotates and is controlled by a handwheel located where the stock enters the spindle, or by a lever on the headstock.

Magnetic Chucks. *Magnetic chucks* of the permanent magnet type (Fig. 18) are now so powerful that substantial cuts can be taken on many types of work, and they can accommodate pieces otherwise difficult to hold.

Care of Chucks. Chucks should receive the care and respect they deserve as precision pieces of ma-

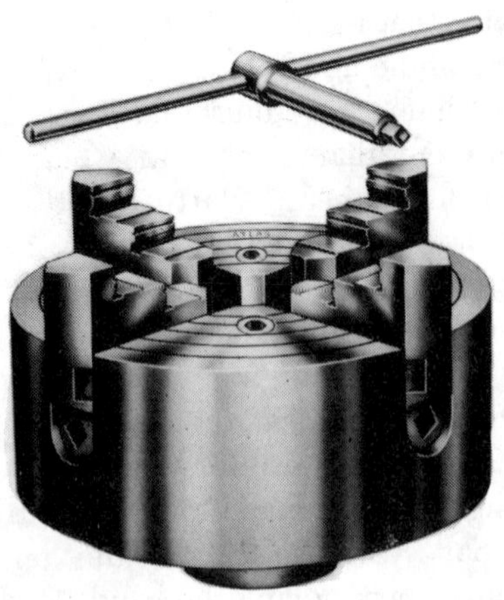

Figure 14. Jaw universal chuck.

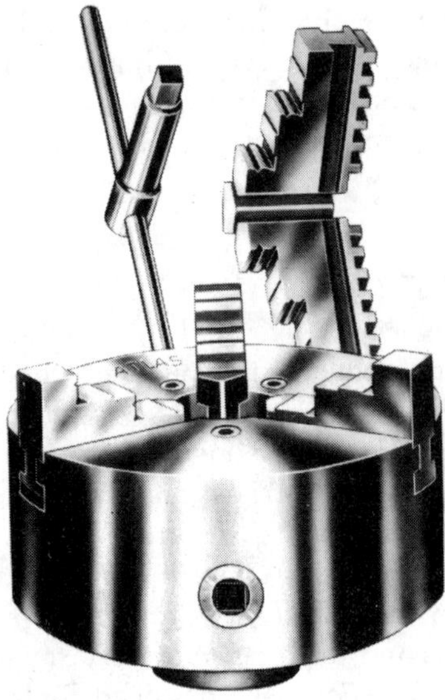

Figure 15. Jaw independent chuck.

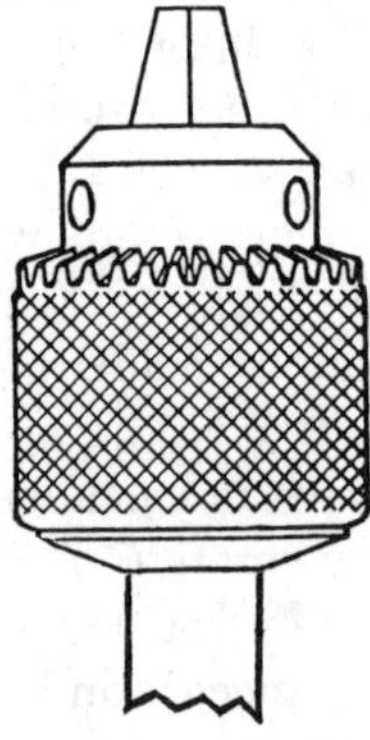

Figure 16. Drill chuck.

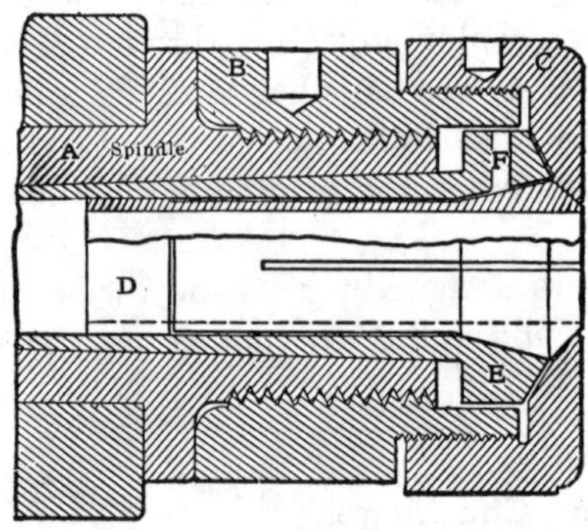

Figure 17. Draw-in chuck or collet. A, lathe spindle; B, sleeve; C, cap; D, collet; E, taper sleeve; F, pin.

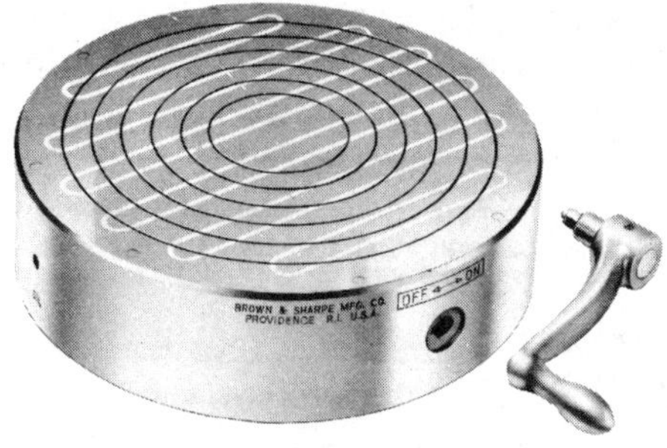

Figure 18. Magnetic chuck.

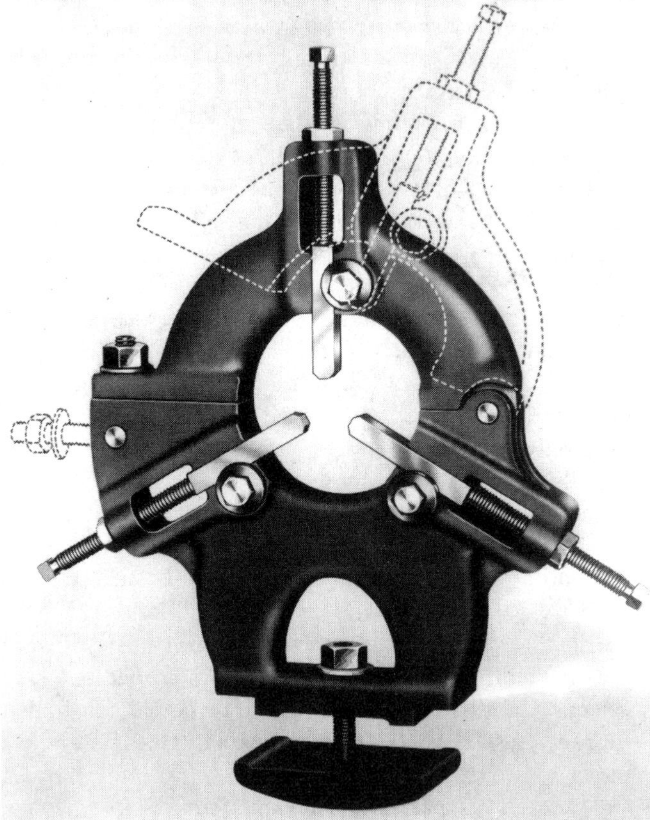

Figure 19. Steady rest.

chinery. In order to preserve their accuracy they should be kept clean and free from grit, and oiled frequently. Exercise particular care in mounting or removing chucks from the spindle of the lathe.

Clean and oil the threaded end of the spindle and the internal thread of the chuck. *Never* use power in screwing on the chuck, nor run the chuck on its thread so fast that it brings up with a shock (this only increases the difficulty of removing it). To remove a chuck, place a monkey wrench on one of the jaws. By a small blow of the hand on the handle of the wrench it can usually be started. For heavier chucks, rotate the chuck against a block of wood held between a jaw of the chuck and the V ways on the back of the machine. When removing or mounting a heavy chuck, it is good practice first to lay a board across the ways of the lathe. The board will serve as a rest for the chuck as it is put on or taken off.

WORK SUPPORTS. Most workpieces of ordinary length and diameter are rigid enough to receive adequate support for turning between centers, or between a proper chuck and a dead center. However, when turning long shafts of small diameter or when boring or threading spindles, it is often necessary to support the work while it is being machined. This is accomplished by the use of a steady rest or a follower rest.

The *steady rest* (Fig. 19), used to support slender work, is bolted to the ways of the lathe and has its bearing on the work at a spot that has been previously finished. If the shaft is to be turned the full length, half of it is turned first, whereupon it is reversed end-for-end and the other half turned. If the work is less than 3/4 inch in diameter and must be machined near the center or more than 5 or 6 inches from the chuck, mount the steady rest near

Figure 20. Facing long work secured in chuck and steady rest.

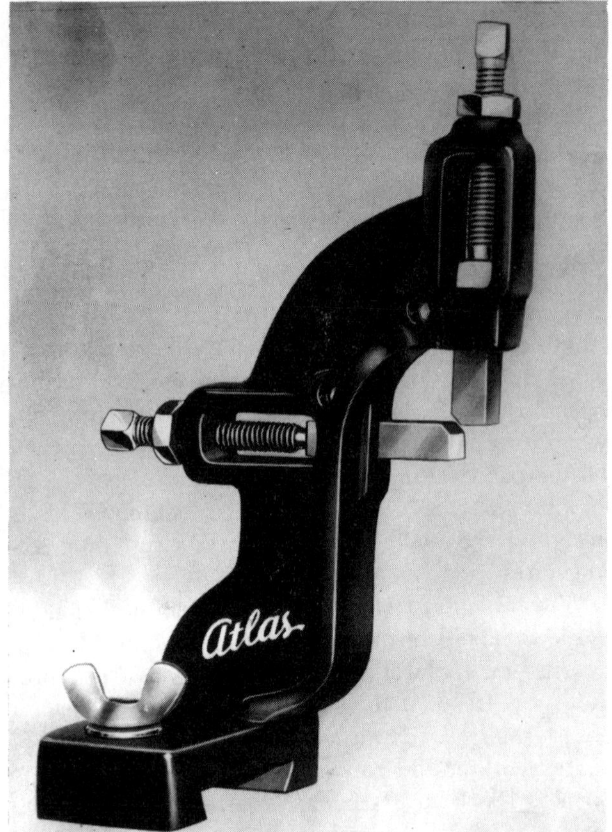

Figure 21. Follower rest.

the portion of the work being machined (Fig. 20).

The *follower* or *traveling rest* (Fig. 21), supporting the work at the cutting point, is usually bolted to the carriage of the lathe and supports the work with the jaws as it moves along with the carriage. It is used primarily when machining slender work requiring greater accuracy than is obtainable with a steady rest. The tool should be slightly in advance of the jaws of the rest. A lubricant should be used on the jaws to prevent any possibility of scoring the surface of the work.

Cutting Operations

Cutting operations are controlled by two interrelated factors, which may be oversimplified as the *machinability* of the *workpiece metal* and the *characteristics* of the *cutting tool.* These primarily determine the speed, the feed, and the depth of cut applied in practice on each individual job.

Any kind of metal cutting operation requires that a tool be forced against the work with sufficient pressure to rupture the metal at the point of cut and thus separate a chip from the workpiece. The amount of force needed depends on the resistance of the metal being torn apart, and the friction of the chip sliding over the face of the tool. Most of the energy used in this process is transformed into heat; and the greater the power required in removing a chip, the higher the temperature is likely to be at the cutting edge of the tool.

Cutting Tools

Materials used in cutting tools must have two main characteristics—sufficient toughness to resist the forces of pressure and impact involved and, sufficient hardness at the temperatures encountered to resist the abrasion of the metal being cut (sometimes called *hot hardness* or *red hardness*). The materials most generally used for cutting tools today are high speed steels, cast nonferrous alloys, and cemented carbides, because they possess the best available combinations of toughness and *hot hardness.*

High Speed Steel. *High speed steel* (HSS) retains its hardness at high cutting speeds and temperatures (up to approximately 1100°F) compared to older types of tool steel.

Cast Nonferrous Alloys. *Cast nonferrous alloys,* marketed under various trade names and grades, consist mainly of cobalt, chromium, and tungsten cast in molds. This type of material, while not as tough as high speed steel, maintains hardness at even higher operating temperatures.

Cemented Carbides. Harder than either HSS or cast nonferrous alloys, cemented carbides are correspondingly less tough. However, the variety of grades available provide a considerable range of hardness and strength, as well as types best suited for machining various materials. By proper grade selection and adherence to good principles of tool design, these carbides can be applied to advantage in a wide range of machining operations.

Straight Tungsten Carbide. *Straight tungsten carbide* is used to machine cast iron and most nonferrous metals which yield discontinuous chips. If used in cutting steel, the chips usually produced in continuous ribbons tend to cause a severe cratering action as they slide across the face. For this reason, steel cutting grades also contain titanium and/or tantalum carbides, which are able to withstand the cratering effectively. Since these grades are less likely to be wear-resistant at the cutting edge, however, they are used only where cratering would be a factor.

Ceramic Materials and Diamonds. Even harder than carbides, *ceramic materials* and *diamonds* resist abrasion at more elevated temperatures, but since their strength is considerably lower, their application is limited at the present time to comparatively light cuts at high speeds.

The development of improved cutting-tool materials has been continuous and there is every reason to expect that the tools of tomorrow will outperform those of today.

Tool Angles

The effectiveness of a cutting tool is measured by the rate at which it removes metal, the power required to drive it, the accuracy and finish it produces, and the length of time it cuts before requiring resharpening. The shape of a tool has an important bearing on how well it performs, and is determined by the tool material, the work material, and the type of cut to be taken.

Figure 22 illustrates the terms used in describing the various angles of a lathe tool. The tool shown has a cutting tip brazed to a steel shank and is typical of a style of carbide tool in general use.

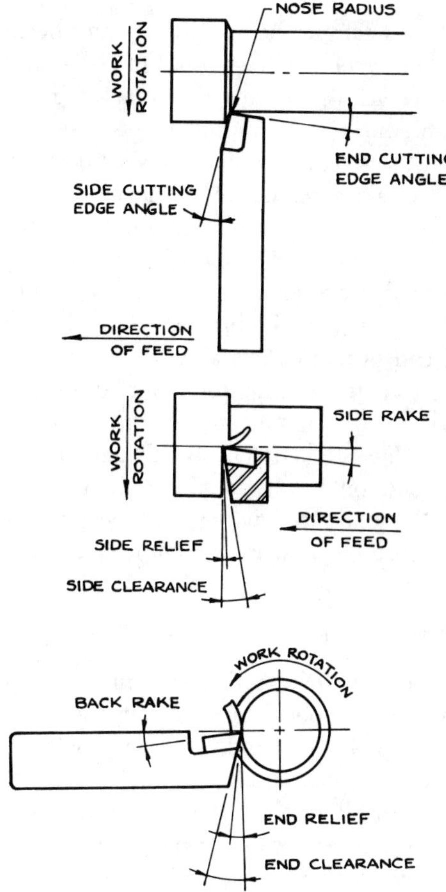

Figure 22. Angles of a lathe tool.

End and Side Relief Angles. The respective *clearance angles* and the *end cutting edge angle* provide that the tool will not rub on the work below or behind the point of cut. These angles may vary from 2 degrees to 15 degrees or more, depending on the tool material and the work material. Generally, large angles will be used with soft materials and strong (such as high speed steel) tools, while hard materials and/or carbide tools (whose edges are more brittle) require smaller angles.

Rake Angles. *Rake angles* influence the manner of chip formation by affecting the shear angle by which the chip is forced to separate from the workpiece (Fig. 23). The smaller the shear angle, the greater the power required to drive the work. *Note,* however, that as the rake angle increases, the point of the tool becomes weaker by reason of the smaller included angle, and for this reason negative rakes are often used, particularly on carbide tools. A disposable insert is clamped in a holder which mechanically provides either positive or negative rake. Where negative rake can be used, the point of impact of the chip is not directly at the cutting edge but behind it, thus in effect making use of a stronger tool section.

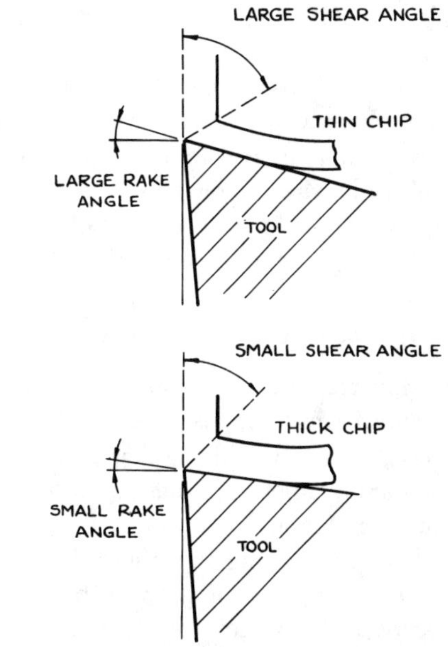

Figure 23. Rake angle influences chip formation.

Side Cutting Edge Angle. The *side cutting edge* must be 0 degree when turning to a square shoulder, but if this is not necessary, an angle of 15 degrees to 45 degrees is of benefit because the work is first brought into contact behind the tip and because the wider, thinner chip allows more of the tool edge to be involved in distributing the force of the cut.

The amount of nose radius affects the strength of the tip of the tool, as obviously a sharp corner would offer the weakest section. Also the surface finish improves with modest increases in nose radii. Too large a nose radius, however, often induces chatter.

An added feature, used on tools cutting a continuous chip, is the chipbreaker. Since long ribbons of steel can be dangerous as well as troublesome to the operator, steel cutting tools can be provided with a groove or step against which the chip is sharply bent and thus broken. The width and depth of the step depend on the type of cut being taken; the heavier the chip, the wider and deeper the chipbreaker must be to snap the chip effectively.

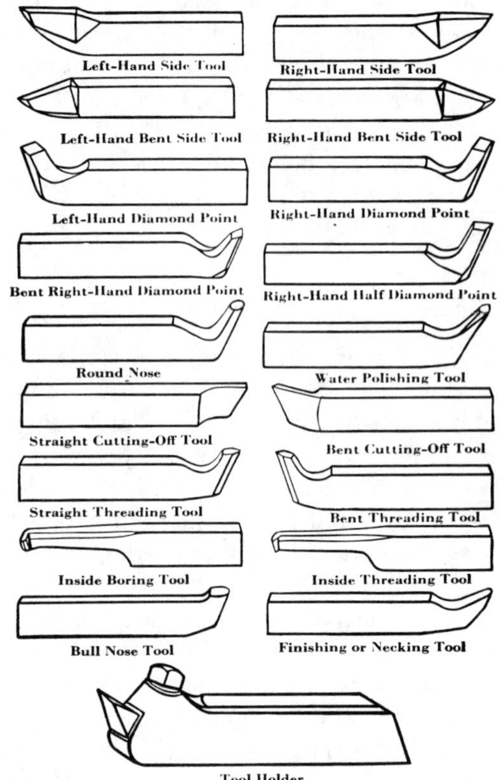

Figure 24. Types of lathe tools.

Grinding Lathe Tools

The worker will learn that care in the preparation of lathe tools—proper angles, keen edges, smooth surfaces—will *pay off* handsomely in better performance, less friction, and longer tool life. High speed steel and cast alloy tools may be ground with an aluminum oxide wheel, while carbide tools are generally roughed out with silicon carbide and finished with diamond wheels. In all cases, grind wet and keep the tool moving across the wheel to avoid heating. After sharpening a finishing tool, it is good practice to use a fine oilstone to remove burrs and give the tool a smooth cutting edge. The cutting edge of a carbide tool may be honed lightly to produce a 45-degree chamfer .002 in. to 005 in. wide. The grinding of carbide tools should be done or closely supervised by skilled workers with experience on special equipment, since there is considerable danger of damaging carbides by the use of improper wheels or faulty techniques. (*See* Fig. 24 for types of lathe tools and Fig. 25 for application of lathe tools.)

Feeds, Speeds, and Depth of Cuts

The time required to remove a given amount of metal from a workpiece is dependent upon the cutting speed, the feed, and the depth of cut. The most efficient metal removal, if not the best finish, results from heavy feeds and deep cuts. In addition to the character of the cutting tool these depend upon the *machinability* of metal of the workpiece.

Materials differ widely in their machinability—in the difficulty of removing stock, the hardness, the malleability or brittleness, and other characteristics—but fortunately there is a wealth of information available to the machinist for his practical guidance. Most useful of these are tables for cutting operations in terms of speeds, feed, and depth of cut.

CUTTING SPEED. *Cutting speed* is the rate at which the surface of the work passes the tool, expressed as *surface feet per minute* (s.f.m.). This is simply the circumference of the work ($\pi \times$ diameter in inches), expressed in feet ($\pi \times D/12$), multiplied by the number of times it revolves in a minute, or:

$$\text{SFM} = \frac{\pi \times \text{D} \times \text{RPM}}{12}$$

where $\pi = \text{Pi} = 3.1416$. The same formula is transposed to calculate the r.p.m. to produce a given surface speed:

$$\text{RPM} = \frac{\text{SFM} \times 12}{\pi \times \text{D}}$$

Table 31 gives cutting speeds for various diameters and spindle r.p.m.'s.

TABLE 31

CUTTING SPEEDS

Feet per Minute	15	17.5	20	22.5	25	27.5	30	35	40	45	50	55
Diam., Inches	REVOLUTIONS PER MINUTE											
1-16	917	1070	1222	1375	1528	1681	1833	2139	2445	2750	3056	3361
1-8	458	535	611	688	764	840	917	1070	1222	1375	1528	1681
3-16	306	357	407	458	509	560	611	713	815	917	1019	1120
1-4	229	267	306	344	382	420	458	535	611	688	764	840
5-16	183	214	244	275	306	336	367	428	489	550	611	672
3-8	153	178	204	229	255	280	306	357	407	458	509	560
7-16	131	153	175	196	218	240	262	306	349	393	437	480
1-2	115	134	153	172	191	210	229	267	306	344	382	420
5-8	91.7	107	122	138	153	168	183	214	244	275	306	336
3-4	76.4	89.1	102	115	127	140	153	178	204	229	255	280
7-8	65.5	76.4	87.3	98.2	109	120	131	153	175	196	218	240
1	57.3	66.8	76.4	85.9	95.5	105	115	134	153	172	191	210
1 1-8	50.9	59.4	67.9	76.4	84.9	93.4	102	119	136	153	170	187
1 1-4	45.8	53.5	61.1	68.8	76.4	84.0	91.7	107	122	138	153	168
1 3-8	41.7	48.6	55.6	62.5	69.5	76.4	83.3	97.2	111	125	139	153
1 1-2	38.2	44.6	50.9	57.3	63.7	70.0	76.4	89.1	102	115	127	140
1 5-8	35.3	41.1	47.0	52.9	58.8	64.6	70.5	82.3	94.0	106	118	129
1 3-4	32.7	38.2	43.7	49.1	54.6	60.0	65.5	76.4	87.3	98.2	109	120
1 7-8	30.6	35.7	40.7	45.8	50.9	56.0	61.1	71.3	81.5	91.7	102	112
2	28.7	33.4	38.2	43.0	47.7	52.5	57.3	66.8	76.4	85.9	95.5	105
2 1-4	25.5	29.7	34.0	38.2	42.4	46.7	50.9	59.4	67.9	76.4	84.9	93.4
2 1-2	22.9	26.7	30.6	34.4	38.2	42.0	45.8	53.5	61.1	68.8	76.4	84.0
2 3-4	20.8	24.3	27.8	31.3	34.7	38.2	41.7	48.6	55.6	62.5	69.5	76.4
3	19.1	22.3	25.5	28.6	31.8	35.0	38.2	44.6	50.9	57.3	63.7	70.0
3 1-4	17.6	20.6	23.5	26.4	29.4	32.3	35.3	41.1	47.0	52.9	58.8	64.6
3 1-2	16.4	19.1	21.8	24.5	27.3	30.0	32.7	38.2	43.7	49.1	54.6	60.0
3 3-4	15.3	17.8	20.4	22.9	25.5	28.0	30.6	35.7	40.7	45.8	50.9	56.0
4	14.3	16.7	19.1	21.5	23.9	26.3	28.7	33.4	38.2	43.0	47.7	52.5
4 1-2	12.7	14.9	17.0	19.1	21.2	23.3	25.5	29.7	34.0	38.2	42.4	46.7
5	11.5	13.4	15.3	17.2	19.1	21.0	22.9	26.7	30.6	34.4	38.2	42.0
5 1-2	10.4	12.2	13.9	15.6	17.4	19.1	20.8	24.3	27.8	31.3	34.7	38.2
6	9.5	11.1	12.7	14.3	15.9	17.5	19.1	22.3	25.5	28.6	31.8	35.0
6 1-2	8.8	10.3	11.8	13.2	14.7	16.2	17.6	20.6	23.5	26.4	29.4	32.3
7	8.2	9.5	10.9	12.3	13.6	15.0	16.4	19.1	21.8	24.5	27.3	30.0
7 1-2	7.6	8.9	10.2	11.5	12.7	14.0	15.3	17.8	20.4	22.9	25.5	28.0
8	7.2	8.4	9.5	10.7	11.9	13.1	14.3	16.7	19.1	21.5	23.9	26.3
8 1-2	6.7	7.9	9.0	10.1	11.2	12.4	13.5	15.7	18.0	20.2	22.5	24.7
9	6.4	7.4	8.5	9.5	10.6	11.7	12.7	14.9	17.0	19.1	21.2	23.3
9 1-2	6.0	7.0	8.0	9.1	10.1	11.1	12.1	14.1	16.1	18.1	20.1	22.1
10	5.7	6.7	7.6	8.6	9.5	10.5	11.5	13.4	15.3	17.2	19.1	21.0
11	5.2	6.1	6.9	7.8	8.7	9.5	10.4	12.2	13.9	15.6	17.4	19.1
12	4.8	5.6	6.4	7.2	8.0	8.8	9.5	11.1	12.7	14.3	15.9	17.5
13	4.4	5.1	5.9	6.6	7.3	8.1	8.8	10.3	11.8	13.2	14.7	16.2
14	4.1	4.8	5.5	6.1	6.8	7.5	8.2	9.5	10.9	12.3	13.6	15.0
15	3.8	4.5	5.1	5.7	6.4	7.0	7.6	8.9	10.2	11.5	12.7	14.0
16	3.6	4.2	4.8	5.4	6.0	6.6	7.2	8.4	9.5	10.7	11.9	13.1
17	3.4	3.9	4.5	5.1	5.6	6.2	6.7	7.9	9.0	10.1	11.2	12.4
18	3.2	3.7	4.2	4.8	5.3	5.8	6.4	7.4	8.5	9.5	10.6	11.7
Feet per Minute	15	17.5	20	22.5	25	27.5	30	35	40	45	50	55

Feet per Minute	60	65	70	75	80	90	100	110	120	130	140	150
Diam., Inches	REVOLUTIONS PER MINUTE											
1-16	3667	3973	4278	4584	4889	...	...	...	...	...	...	...
1-8	1833	1986	2139	2292	2445	2750	3056	3361	3667	3973	4278	4584
3-16	1222	1324	1426	1528	1630	1833	2037	2241	2445	2648	2852	3056
1-4	917	993	1070	1146	1222	1375	1528	1681	1833	1986	2139	2292
5-16	733	794	856	917	978	1100	1222	1345	1467	1589	1711	1833
3-8	611	662	713	764	815	917	1019	1120	1222	1324	1426	1528
7-16	524	568	611	655	698	786	873	960	1048	1135	1222	1310
1-2	458	497	535	573	611	688	764	840	917	993	1070	1146
5-8	367	397	428	458	489	550	611	672	733	794	856	917
3-4	306	331	357	382	407	458	509	560	611	662	713	764
7-8	262	284	306	327	349	393	437	480	524	568	611	655
1	229	248	267	287	306	344	382	420	458	497	535	573
1 1-8	204	221	238	255	272	306	340	373	407	441	475	509
1 1-4	183	199	214	229	214	275	306	336	367	397	428	458
1 3-8	167	181	194	208	222	250	278	306	333	361	389	417
1 1-2	153	166	178	191	204	229	255	280	306	331	357	382
1 5-8	141	153	165	176	188	212	235	259	282	306	329	353
1 3-4	131	142	153	164	175	196	218	240	262	284	306	327
1 7-8	122	132	143	153	163	183	204	224	244	265	285	306
2	115	124	134	143	153	172	191	210	229	248	267	287
2 1-4	102	110	119	127	136	153	170	187	204	221	238	255
2 1-2	91.7	99.3	107	115	122	138	153	168	183	199	214	229
2 3-4	83.3	90.3	97.2	104	111	125	139	153	167	181	194	208
3	76.4	82.8	89.1	95.5	102	115	127	140	153	166	178	191
3 1-4	70.5	76.4	82.3	88.2	94.0	106	118	129	141	153	165	176
3 1-2	65.5	70.9	76.4	81.9	87.3	98.2	109	120	131	142	153	164
3 3-4	61.1	66.2	71.3	76.4	81.5	91.7	102	112	122	132	143	153
4	57.3	62.1	66.8	71.6	76.4	85.9	95.5	105	115	124	134	143
4 1-2	50.9	55.2	59.4	63.6	67.9	76.4	84.9	93.4	102	110	119	127
5	45.8	49.7	53.5	57.3	61.1	68.8	76.4	84.0	91.7	99.3	107	115
5 1-2	41.7	45.1	48.6	52.1	55.6	62.5	69.5	76.4	83.3	90.3	97.2	104
6	38.2	41.4	44.6	47.8	50.9	57.3	63.7	70.0	76.4	82.8	89.1	95.5
6 1-2	35.3	38.2	41.1	41.1	47.0	52.9	58.8	64.6	70.5	76.4	82.3	88.2
7	32.7	35.5	38.2	40.9	43.7	49.1	54.6	60.0	65.5	70.9	76.4	81.9
7 1-2	30.6	33.1	35.7	38.2	40.7	45.8	50.9	56.0	61.1	66.2	71.3	76.4
8	28.7	31.0	33.4	35.8	38.2	43.0	47.7	52.5	57.3	62.1	66.8	71.6
8 1-2	27.0	29.2	31.5	33.7	36.0	40.4	44.9	49.4	53.9	58.4	62.9	67.4
9	25.5	27.6	29.7	31.8	34.0	38.2	42.4	46.7	50.9	55.2	59.4	63.6
9 1-2	24.1	26.1	28.2	30.2	32.2	36.2	40.2	44.2	48.3	52.3	56.3	60.3
10	22.9	24.8	26.7	28.7	30.6	34.4	38.2	42.0	45.8	49.7	53.5	57.3
11	20.8	22.6	24.3	26.0	27.8	31.3	34.7	38.2	41.7	45.1	48.6	52.1
12	19.1	20.7	22.3	23.9	25.5	28.6	31.8	35.0	38.2	41.4	44.6	47.8
13	17.6	19.1	20.6	22.0	23.5	26.4	29.4	32.3	35.3	38.2	41.1	44.1
14	16.4	17.7	19.1	20.5	21.8	24.5	27.3	30.0	32.7	35.5	38.2	40.9
15	15.3	16.6	17.8	19.1	20.4	22.9	25.5	28.0	30.6	33.1	35.7	38.2
16	14.3	15.5	16.7	17.9	19.1	21.5	23.9	26.3	28.7	31.0	33.4	35.8
17	13.5	14.6	15.7	16.9	18.0	20.2	22.5	24.7	27.0	29.2	31.5	33.7
18	12.7	13.8	14.9	15.9	17.0	19.1	21.2	23.3	25.5	27.6	29.7	31.8
Feet per Minute	60	65	70	75	80	90	100	110	120	130	140	150

FEED. *Feed* is the amount of advance made by a tool, usually expressed as thousandths of an inch, per revolution.

DEPTH OF CUT. The *depth of cut* is one-half the amount that a diameter is reduced by a pass of the tool—the distance between the surface of the work-piece and the new surface generated by the particular cut.

The volume of metal removed in cubic inches per minute is therefore the product of the surface speed (the length of the chip in inches), the depth of cut (the width of the chip in inches), and the feed (the thickness of the chip in inches). As this volume increases, more power is required of the drive, more strength of the tool, and more rigidity in support of the work.

Since so many factors must be considered in arriving at suitable speeds, feeds, and depth of cut—power and condition of machine, strength of tool, work machinability, finish, and tool life expected—no exact recommendations can be made. In general, for finishing cuts of 1/64 in. to 1/16 in. depth, feeds are usually in the range of .005 in. to .015 in. per revolution, while for roughing cuts, a rule of thumb is to use a feed of approximately 1/10 of the depth of the cut. As to surface speeds, Table 32 gives some rule of thumb examples for use with high speed tools, keeping in mind the operating characteristics already mentioned.

In general, cast alloy tools can be run at up to twice these speeds, providing there are proper conditions of rigidity, power, and so on. Likewise, carbide tools will run up to four times these speeds if operating conditions are satisfactory.

TABLE 32

SURFACE SPEEDS OF HIGH SPEED TOOLS

Material	*Roughing Cut (SFM)*	*Finishing Cut (SFM)*
Cast Iron	60	80
Machine Steel	90	125
Tool Steel	50	75
Brass	150	200
Bronze	90	100
Aluminum	200	300

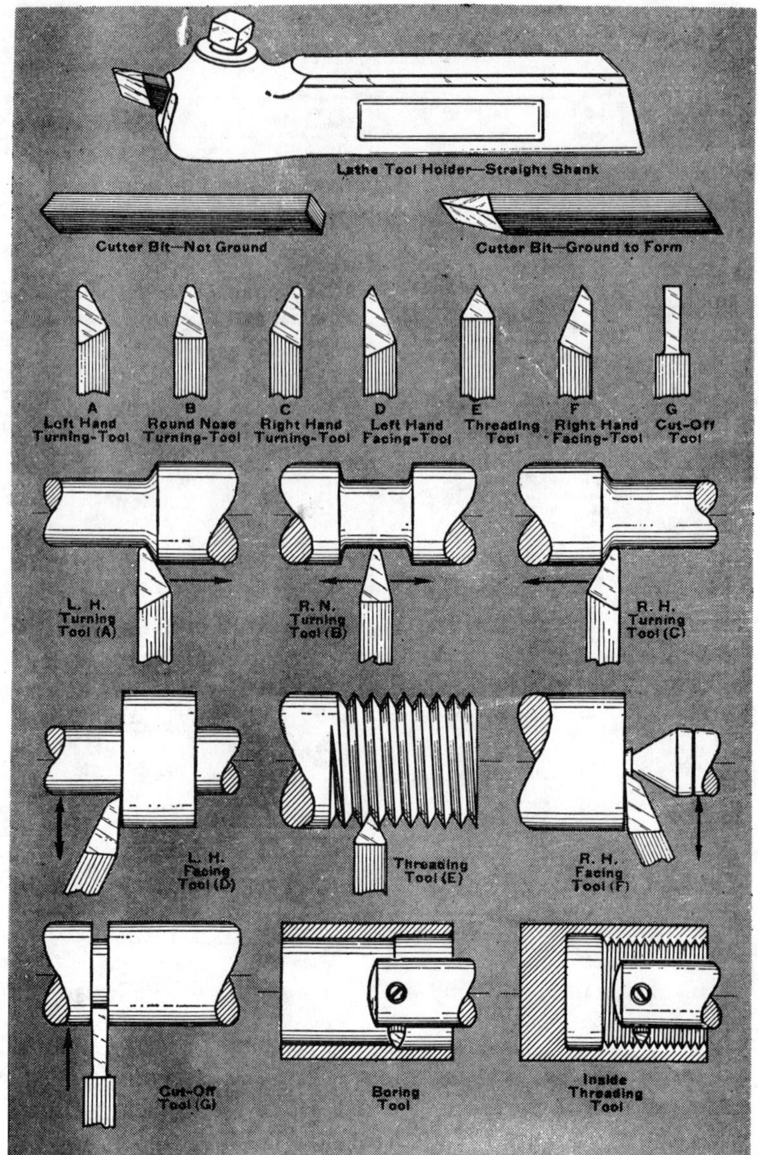

Figure 25. Application of lathe tools.

Tapers and Taper Turning

Tapers are denoted by so many inches or fractions of an inch per foot: as 1 in. per foot or 3/8 in. per foot. They are sometimes indicated by degrees and minutes: as 6°42′ or 2°35′. Certain well-known tapers have become recognized as standard for spindles and shanks of cutting tools. The milling machine standard taper, 3 1/2 in. per foot, is generally used by manufacturers of milling machines and products. The *Brown & Sharpe taper,* which is approximately 1/2 in. per foot (except No. 10 which is .5161 in. per foot), is commonly used on collets, shanks of arbors, and end mills. The *Morse taper,* approximately 5/8 in. per foot, is in use on shanks of drills, sockets, end mills, holes in drill press spindles, and lathe spindles. The taper of pipe threads, 3/4 in. per foot, is considered standard in some shops. (*See* Table 33.)

METHODS IN USE TO TURN TAPERS. There are three ways in common use to turn a taper:

TABLE 33

TAPERS PER FOOT AND CORRESPONDING ANGLES

Taper per Foot	Included Angle	Angle with Center Line	Taper per Foot	Included Angle	Angle with Center Line
1-8″	0°—36′	0°—18′	1″	4°—46′	2°—23′
1-4	1°—12′	0°—36′	1 1-2	7°—09′	3°—35′
5-16	1°—30′	0°—45′	1 3-4	8°—20′	4°—10°
3-8	1°—47′	0°—54′	2	9°—31′	4°—46′
7-16	2°—05′	1°—02′	2 1-2	11°—54′	5°—57′
1-2	2°—23′	1°—12′	3	14°—15′	7°—08°
3-4	3°—35′	1°—47′	3 1-2	16°—36′	8°—18′
15-16	4°—28′	2°—14′	4	18°—55′	9°—28′

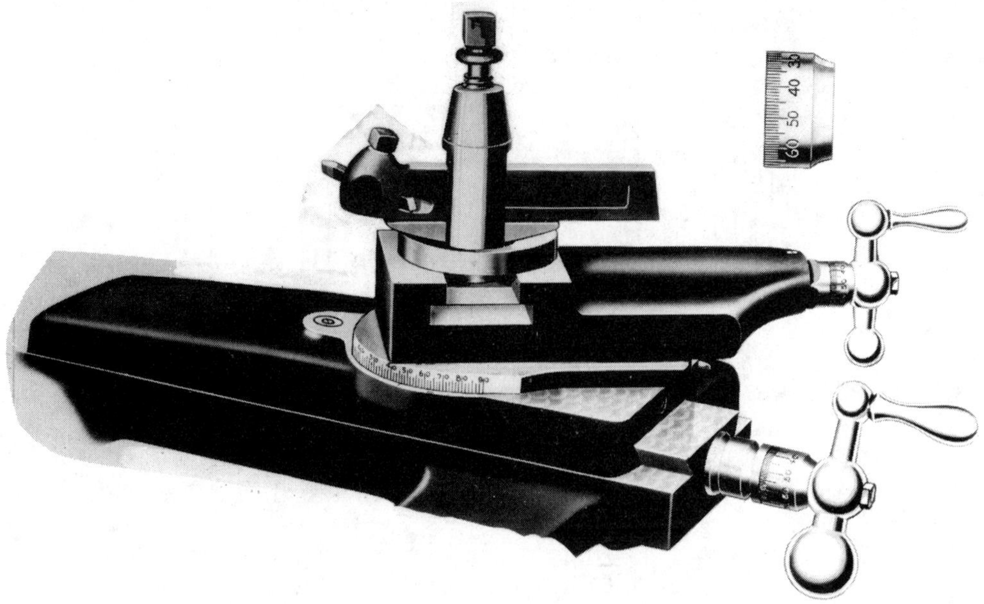

Figure 26. Taper turning attachment.

1. By setting the *dead center* out of line with the *live center*.

2. By using a *taper turning attachment* (Fig. 26).

3. By using a *compound rest* (Fig. 27).

The first method can be used for outside turning only, while the other two methods are applicable to turning and boring. The tool must be kept on a level with the centers to maintain the taper. If the correct taper is provided with the tool on center, raising or lowering the tool will change the taper.

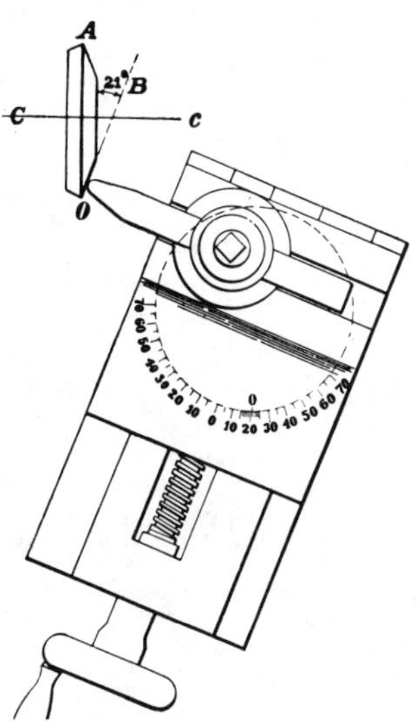

Figure 27. Compound rest set at 21 degrees.

How to Calculate the Set Over of the Footstock. To calculate the set over of the footstock, first take one-half the taper per foot and divide it by 12 to change to taper per inch. Multiply this result by the total length of the work or mandrel in terms of inches. (*Note:* We mention work or mandrel because it is the distance between centers that counts. The work can be much shorter than that distance. The mandrel will be equal to the distance between centers.) (*See* Table 34.) Therefore, with the Brown & Sharpe taper, which is approximately 1/2 in. per foot, we obtain the set over of the footstock for work which requires a center distance of 18 in., as follows. Take one-half of the 1/2 in. taper per foot, which is 1/4 in.; then divide this result by 12 to convert it to taper per inch (1/4 in. x 1/12 in. = 1/48 in.). Multiply the result by the total length of the work, 18 in. (1/48 in. x 18 in. = 3/8 in. or .375 in.). Thus, the set over for the footstock is 3/8 in. or .375 in.

To Set Over The Footstock. To set over the footstock the amount calculated above, loosen the clamping bolts on the footstock and by using the adjusting screw and observing the zero lines in the rear, move the upper part of the footstock until the top zero line is .375 in. from the bottom zero line. Use a pair of dividers set at .375 in. to check this adjustment. (*See* Table 35.)

To Find the Set Over When the Length and Diameters Are Known, but the Taper Per Foot Is Unknown. Suppose the length is 18 in., the larger

Table 34
Brown & Sharpe Tapers

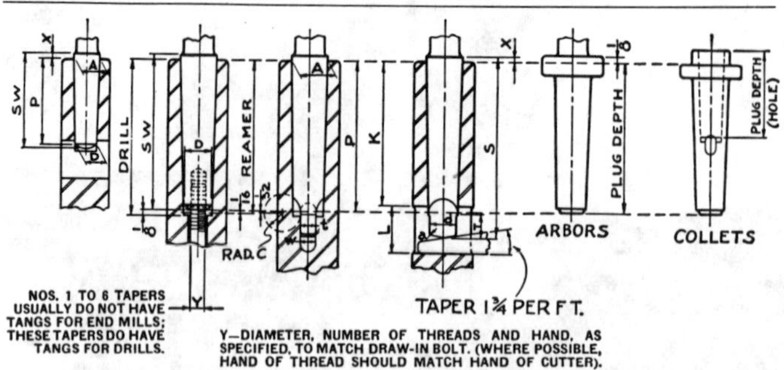

All dimensions are in inches.

No. of Taper	Taper per Foot	Diam. of Plug at Small End	Diam. at End of Socket	Plug Depth P			Key-way from End of Spindle	Shank Length with Tang	Shank Length with-out Tang	Shank Pro-jects from End of Socket	Length of Key-way†	Width of Key-way	Length of Arbor Tongue	Diam-eter of Arbor Tongue	Thick-ness of Arbor Tongue	Radius of Tongue Circle	Radius of Tongue at a
				B & S** Stand-ard	For Mill. Mach.	Miscell.											
		D	A				K	S	SW	X	L	W	T	d	t	c	a
*1	.50200	.20000	.2392	15/16‡			15/16	1 9/32	1 1/16	3/32	3/8	.135	3/16	.170	1/8	3/16	.030
*2	.50200	.25000	.2997	1 3/16‡			1 11/64	1 19/32	1 11/32	3/32	1/2	.166	1/4	.220	5/32	3/16	.030
			.3752	1 1/2‡			1 15/32	1 31/32	1 41/64	3/32	5/8	.197	5/16	.282	3/16	3/16	.040
*3	.50200	.31250				1 3/4	1 23/32				5/8	.197	5/16	.282	3/16	3/16	.040
						2	1 31/32				5/8	.197	5/16	.282	3/16	3/16	.040
4	.50240	.35000	.4023		1 1/4‡		1 13/16	1 3/4	1 25/64	3/32	11/16	.228	11/32	.320	7/32	5/16	.050
				1 11/16			1 41/64				11/16	.228	11/32	.320	7/32	5/16	.050
			.5231		1 3/4‡		1 11/16	2 9/32	1 29/32	3/32	3/4	.260	3/8	.420	1/4	5/16	.060
5	.50160	.45000				2	1 15/16				3/4	.260	3/8	.420	1/4	5/16	.060
				2 1/8			2 1/16				3/4	.260	3/8	.420	1/4	5/16	.060
6	.50329	.50000	.5996	2 3/8‡			2 19/64	2 31/32	2 17/32	3/32	7/8	.291	7/16	.460	9/32	5/16	.060
						2 1/2	2 13/32				15/16	.322	15/32	.560	5/16	3/8	.070
7	.50147	.60000		2 7/8			2 25/32				15/16	.322	15/32	.560	5/16	3/8	.070
			.7254		3‡		2 29/32	3 5/8	3 3/32	3/32	15/16	.322	15/32	.560	5/16	3/8	.070
8	.50100	.75000	.8987	3 9/16‡			3 29/64	4 1/4	3 11/16	1/8	1	.353	1/2	.710	11/32	3/8	.080
9	.50085	.90010	1.0670		4‡		3 7/8	4 3/4	4 1/8	1/8	1 1/8	.385	9/16	.860	3/8	7/16	.100
				4 1/4			4 1/8				1 1/8	.385	9/16	.860	3/8	7/16	.100
				5			4 27/32				1 5/16	.447	21/32	1.010	7/16	7/16	.110
10	.51612	1.04465	1.2892		5 11/16‡		5 17/32	6 17/32	5 13/16	1/8	1 5/16	.447	21/32	1.010	7/16	7/16	.110
						6 7/32	6 1/16				1 5/16	.447	21/32	1.010	7/16	7/16	.110
11	.50100	1.24995		5 15/16			5 25/32				1 5/16	.447	21/32	1.210	7/16	1/2	.130
			1.5318		6 3/4‡		6 19/32	7 19/32	6 7/8	1/8	1 5/16	.447	21/32	1.210	7/16	1/2	.130
12	.49973	1.50010	1.7968	7 1/8	7 1/8‡		6 15/16	8 1/16	7 1/4	1/8	1 1/2	.510	3/4	1.460	1/2	1/2	.150
						6 1/4											
13	.50020	1.75005	2.0730	7 3/4‡			7 9/16	8 11/16	7 7/8	1/8	1 1/2	.510	3/4	1.710	1/2	5/8	.170
14	.50000	2.00000	2.3437	8 1/4‡	8 1/4		8 1/32	9 9/32	8 3/8	1/8	1 11/16	.572	27/32	1.960	9/16	3/4	.190
15	.50000	2.25000	2.6146	8 3/4‡			8 17/32	9 25/32	8 7/8	1/8	1 11/16	.572	27/32	2.210	9/16	7/8	.210
16	.50000	2.50000	2.8854	9 1/4‡			9	10 3/8	9 3/8	1/8	1 7/8	.635	15/16	2.450	5/8	1	.230
17	.50000	2.75000	3.1562	9 3/4‡					9 7/8	1/8							
18	.50000	3.00000	3.4271	10 1/4‡					10 3/8	1/8							

*Adopted by American Standards Association.

**"B & S Standard" Plug Depths are not used in all cases.

†Special lengths of keyways are used instead of standard lengths in some places. Standard lengths need not be used when keyway is for driving only and not for admitting key to force out tool.

‡These lengths are standard for shank cutters.

Table 35
Tapers from 1/16 to 1-1/4 Inches Per Foot

Length Tapered, Inches	Taper per Foot									
	1/16	3/32	1/8	1/4	3/8	1/2	5/8	3/4	1	1 1/4
1/32	.0002	.0002	.0003	.0007	.0010	.0013	.0016	.0020	.0026	.0033
1/16	.0003	.0005	.0007	.0013	.0020	.0026	.0033	.0039	.0052	.0065
1/8	.0007	.0010	.0013	.0026	.0039	.0052	.0065	.0078	.0104	.0130
3/16	.0010	.0015	.0020	.0039	.0059	.0078	.0098	.0117	.0156	.0195
1/4	.0013	.0020	.0026	.0052	.0078	.0104	.0130	.0156	.0208	0260
5/16	.0016	.0024	.0033	.0065	.0098	.0130	.0163	.0195	.0260	.0326
3/8	.0020	.0029	.0039	.0078	.0117	.0156	.0195	.0234	.0312	.0391
7/16	.0023	.0034	.0046	.0091	.0137	.0182	.0228	.0273	.0365	.0456
1/2	.0026	.0039	.0052	.0104	.0156	.0208	.0260	.0312	.0417	.0521
9/16	.0029	.0044	.0059	.0117	.0176	.0234	.0293	.0352	.0469	.0586
5/8	.0033	.0049	.0065	.0130	.0195	.0260	.0326	.0391	.0521	.0651
11/16	.0036	.0054	.0072	.0143	.0215	.0286	.0358	.0430	.0573	.0716
3/4	.0039	.0059	.0078	.0156	.0234	.0312	.0391	.0469	.0625	.0781
13/16	.0042	.0063	.0085	.0169	.0254	.0339	.0423	.0508	.0677	.0846
7/8	.0046	.0068	.0091	.0182	.0273	.0365	.0456	.0547	.0729	.0911
15/16	.0049	.0073	.0098	.0195	.0293	.0391	.0488	.0586	.0781	.0977
1	.0052	.0078	.0104	.0208	.0312	.0417	.0521	.0625	.0833	.1042
2	.0104	.0156	.0208	.0417	.0625	.0833	.1042	.125	.1667	.2083
3	.0156	.0234	.0312	.0625	.0937	.1250	.1562	.1875	.250	.3125
4	.0208	.0312	.0417	.0833	.125	.1667	.2083	.250	.3333	.4167
5	.0260	.0391	.0521	.1042	.1562	.2083	.2604	.3125	.4167	.5208
6	.0312	.0469	.0625	.125	.1875	.250	.3125	.375	.500	.625
7	.0365	.0547	.0729	.1458	.2187	.2917	.3646	.4375	.5833	.7292
8	.0417	.0625	.0833	.1667	.250	.3333	.4167	.500	.6667	.8333
9	.0469	.0703	.0937	.1875	.2812	.375	.4687	.5625	.750	.9375
10	.0521	.0781	.1042	.2083	.3125	.4167	.5208	.625	.8333	1.0417
11	.0573	.0859	.1146	.2292	.3437	.4583	.5729	.6875	.9167	1.1458
12	.0625	.0937	.125	.250	.375	.500	.625	.750	1.000	1.250
13	.0677	.1016	.1354	.2708	.4062	.5417	.6771	.8125	1.0833	1.3542
14	.0729	.1094	.1458	.2917	.4375	.5833	.7292	.875	1.1667	1.4583
15	.0781	.1172	.1562	.3125	.4687	.625	.7812	.9375	1.250	1.5625
16	.0833	.125	.1667	.3333	.500	.6667	.8333	1.000	1.3333	1.6667
17	.0885	.1328	.1771	.3542	.5312	.7083	.8854	1.0625	1.4167	1.7708
18	.0937	.1406	.1875	.3750	.5625	.750	.9375	1.125	1.500	1.875
19	.0990	.1484	.1979	.3958	.5937	.7917	.9896	1.1875	1.5833	1.9792
20	.1042	.1562	.2083	.4167	.625	.8333	1.0417	1.250	1.6667	2.0833
21	.1094	.1641	.2187	.4375	.6562	.875	1.0937	1.3125	1.750	2.1875
22	.1146	.1719	.2292	.4583	.6875	.9167	1.1458	1.375	1.8333	2.2917
23	.1198	.1797	.2396	.4792	.7187	.9583	1.1970	1.4375	1.9167	2.3958
24	.125	.1875	.250	.500	.750	1.000	1.250	1.500	2.000	2.500

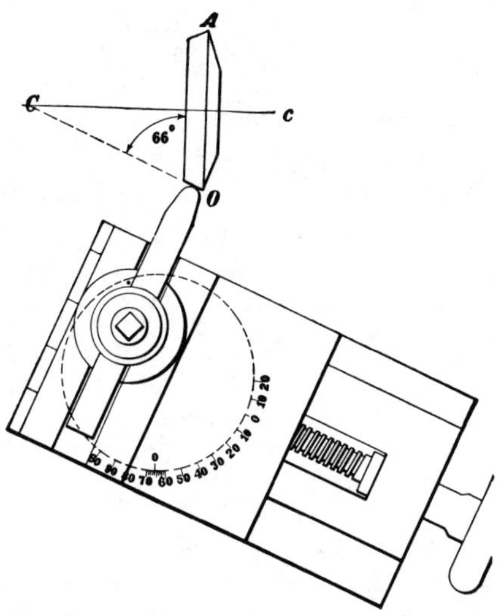

Figure 28. Compound rest set at 66 degrees.

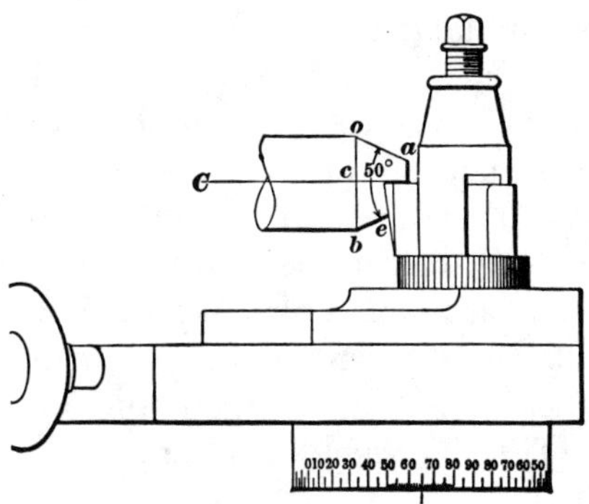

Figure 29. Compound rest set at 65 degrees.

diameter 8 in., the smaller one 7 in., and the length of the tapered surface 12 in. Use the following formula.

$$\text{Larger diameter} - \text{Smaller diameter} \times \frac{\text{Total length}}{\text{Length of part}} = \text{Set over}$$

Thus:

$$\frac{8'' - 7''}{2} \times \frac{18''}{12''} \text{ or } 1/2'' \times 3/2'' = 3/4'' = .750''.$$

SET OVER FROM A SAMPLE PIECE OR PATTERN. It may happen that a piece with the exact taper desired is available. In such a case, mount the piece between the centers, and with a test indicator in the tool post, run the contact point of the indicator along the tapered surface and adjust the screws in the footstock until the *set over* is correct for the sample piece, as shown by the absence of variation as the indicator is moved along the taper. Then clamp the footstock and replace the sample piece with the work to be tapered.

THE TAPER TURNING ATTACHMENT. The *taper turning attachment* can be applied to a lathe to turn either outside or inside tapers, and with this device there is no need for setting over the footstock. The taper required can be obtained by setting the guide bar at an angle corresponding to the taper desired.

THE COMPOUND REST. Very abrupt tapers are usually turned with the *compound rest*. It is simply an extra slide for carrying the tool block, and this extra slide is mounted in the usual position of the tool on the saddle. A circular base is provided for this extra slide so that the slide can be rotated at any angle in a horizontal plane. The base is graduated to degrees, and the extra slide can be set at an angle so that the direction of the movement of the tool will correspond to the desired taper.

Figures 27 and 28 illustrate a compound rest. The zero line of a compound rest is at right angles to the center line, Cc, of the lathe, the zero line being parallel to AO. The flat side of a plate, or disc, can be faced off with the compound rest set at zero.

TESTING THE ACCURACY OF A TAPER. Test the accuracy of tapered work as you go along by trying it in a gage that represents the desired taper. When the work appears to fit solidly in the gage with no rattle or shake, test its bearing by applying a very little prussian blue. If the contact spots are distributed evenly over the surface of the taper it may be considered a good fit.

ANGLES OF BEVEL GEAR BLANKS. These angles are usually figured from a plane perpendicular to the axis, as shown in Figs. 27 and 28. The angles are figured from AO, which is perpendicular to the axis Cc. In turning to angles figured in this way, the setting of the compound rest is just like the figures on the drawing. Therefore, in Fig. 27, the drawing calls for 21 degrees for the angle AOB, and the rest is set to 21 degrees. In Fig. 28, the angle AOC is 66 degrees and the rest is set at 66 degrees on the opposite side of zero from the previous setting. There may, however, be a technical reason for figuring the angles of a bevel gear blank from the axis Cc. In such a case, the compound rest must be set to the complement of the angle. Therefore, if the angle CcO, 69 degrees (Fig. 27) is called for, subtract 69 degrees from 90 degrees and the remainder, 21 degrees, is the setting for the compound rest.

It is better to figure the angles for a bevel gear blank from a line perpendicular to the axis as shown in Figs. 27 and 28, to correspond to the figuring of the compound rest. The angles are also more easily measured from a line perpendicular to the axis than from a line parallel to the axis.

In Fig. 29 a beveled or tapering piece is to be turned, in which the side ao makes 50 degrees with the side eb. In order to set the compound rest, the angle coa must be known. (By a law of geometry coa is the complement to the angle that ao makes with the center line Cc.) The beveled part being symmetrical with the center line, the angle which ao makes with Cc is half of the whole angle 50 degrees, or 25 degrees. So 25 degrees subtracted from 90 degrees gives 65 degrees for the angle coa, which will be the setting of the compound rest.

Screw Threads

It is pretty safe to assume that the machinist knows what screw threads look like, and has a fair general knowledge of what they are and how they are used. There are several kinds of screw threads, and a brief description of the more important ones will help toward a clearer understanding of the distinctions between the various kinds.

A *right-hand thread* is one that has been cut so that either a nut or a bolt so threaded must be turned clockwise to make it engage. A *left-hand thread* turns in the opposite direction, or counterclockwise. Most threads are right-hand threads.

An *external thread* is one that appears on the outside of a piece, as in the case of a bolt. An *internal thread* appears on the inside of a piece, as in the case of a nut.

The threads may be cut single, double, triple, or quadruple (Fig. 30). A *single thread* is a thread made by a single groove; a *double thread* by two parallel grooves, and so on. A piece with more than one thread is referred to as *multiple-threaded.* By inspecting the piece at the beginning of the thread it can be determined readily how many grooves have been cut and how it is threaded.

Most screws are single-threaded, but where the advance per revolution would require such a large pitch as to leave a weak root diameter, multiple threads permit the advance of a coarse pitch with the depth of thread of a fine pitch.

PITCH OF A THREAD. The *pitch of a thread* is the distance from the center of one thread to the center of the next thread. This applies whether the screw has single, double, or multiple threads. Pitch should be expressed in fractions of an inch. For instance, a screw with 16 threads to the inch has threads 1/16 in. from center to center, and the pitch is 1/16 in.

The word *pitch* is sometimes, although improperly, used to designate the *number of threads to the inch.* Plumbers will sometimes colloquially speak of a 12-pitch thread, when 12 threads per inch is what is really meant. The formula for pitch is 1 in. divided by the number of threads to the inch.

LEAD OF A THREAD. The *lead of a thread* is the distance the screw moves in one complete turn. In the case of a single-thread screw the lead is equal to the pitch, but in the case of the double thread, the lead is twice the pitch; in the triple thread, three times the pitch.

Thread Measurements

Threads may be measured in several ways: with a thread micrometer, with a screw pitch gage, by the three wire system, and by the optical measuring system.

SCREW THREAD MICROMETER CALIPER. *Thread micrometers* are fast and conveniently used, but subject to certain limitations. When set to read "O" with the thimble and anvil together, as is usually done, their readings over threads are always slightly distorted, the amount of distortion depending upon the helix angle of the thread being measured. The readings are not distorted when thread micrometers are set to a standard thread plug and used for measuring threads having the same pitch and diameter as the plug. When so set, however, the tool does not read exactly "O" when thimble and anvil are brought together.

The end of the spindle of a screw thread micrometer caliper (Fig. 31) is pointed and the V in the anvil is accurately ground and free to rotate. The end of the spindle point and bottom of the V in the anvil have allowance for clearance so they will not rest on the bottom or top of the thread to be measured. When set at zero, the pitch lines of spindle

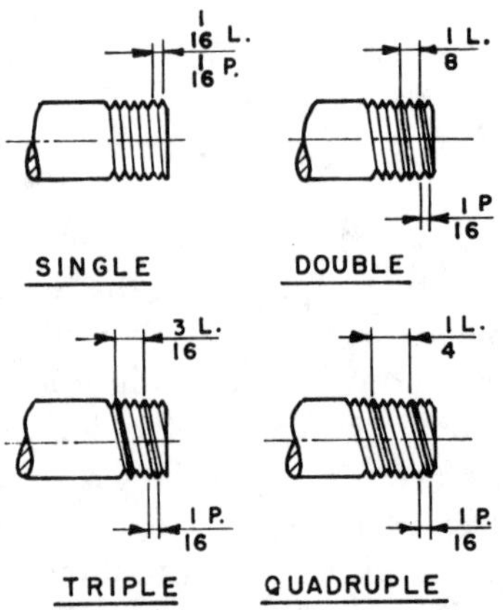

Figure 30. Screw threads.

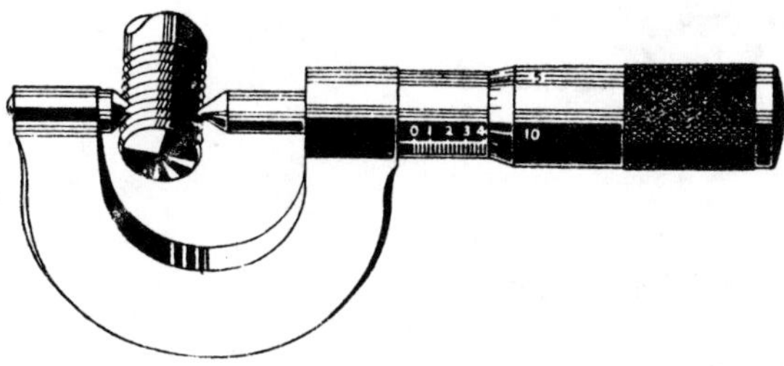

Figure 31. Screw thread micrometer caliper.

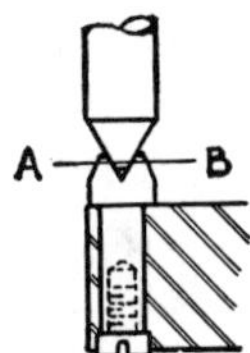

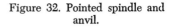

Figure 32. Pointed spindle and anvil.

and anvil coincide as AB, as shown in Fig. 32. When the caliper is opened, the reading represents the distance between the two pitch lines, or the pitch diameter. As the thread itself is measured, the actual outside diameter of the piece does not enter into consideration.

THE THREE WIRE THREAD MEASURING FIXTURE. The *three wire system* of measuring over wires laid in adjacent thread grooves is not as fast or as convenient as the thread micrometer, but is theoretically correct. However, the wires must be held very close to theoretical size, as any error in the wires is multiplied when the thread dimensions are calculated.

Parts to be measured are held between the center, which is adjustable, and the V slide, also adjustable. The micrometer caliper floats on steel balls to insure accurate alignment of measuring surfaces on the measuring wires.

Accurately calibrated wires are used in measuring

TABLE 36

THREAD MEASUREMENT

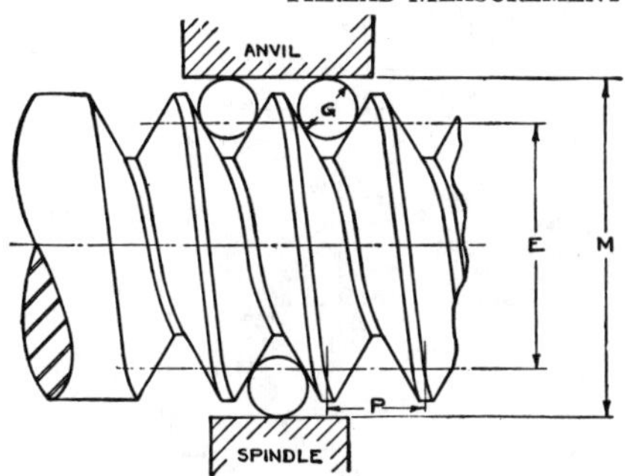

THREE WIRE METHOD FOR MEASURING PITCH DIAMETERS

Wire Sizes and Formulae for 60° Threads

To find the Pitch Diameter (E)

(1) E = M + 0.866025 P − 3G

To Calculate the Measurement over Wires (M)

(2) M = E + 3G − 0.866025 P

E = Pitch Diameter P = Pitch

M = Measurement over Wires G = Diameter of Wires

Example: — Determine (M) Measurement over Wires for ½″—13 Pitch U.N.C.

Nominal Major Diameter	.500000″
Less single Depth of 13 P. UNC Thread	.049962″
Pitch Diameter is	.450038″

Size of Wire to use on 13 P is .044412″ (See Table)

Using Formula (2)

M = .450038″ + (3 × .044412″) − 0.866025 P
M = .450038″ + .133236″ − .066617″
M = .450038″ + .066619″
M = .516657″

By using different formulae, threads of other proportions can be accurately measured.

A wire that comes in contact with the side of the thread at the pitch line is called the " Best Size." Larger wires can be used, but the " Best Size " gives the reading at the important working part of the thread. (Smaller sizes come below the top of the thread.) The " Best Size " of wire for each pitch is given in the following table.

Too much pressure should not be applied when measuring over wires. For pitches finer than 20 threads per inch a pressure of 1 pound is recommended and 2½ pounds for pitches of 20 threads per inch and coarser.

Table 37
Thread Measurement
For Three Wire Thread Measurement of Unified and American Screw Threads

Wire Sizes	Threads Per Inch								
	3	3¼	3½	4	4½	5	5½	6	7
.192450	*.28867	.31088	.32992						
.177646		*.26647	.28551	.31643					
.164957			*.24744	.27837	.30242				
.144339				*.21651	.24057	.25981			
.128300					*.19245	.21169	.22744		
.115470						*.17321	.18895	.20207	
.104973							*.15746	.17058	.19120
.096225								*.14434	.16496
.082479									*.12372

Wire Sizes	Threads Per Inch									
	8	9	10	11	11½	12	13	14	16	18
.096225	.18042									
.082479	.13918	.15121								
.072169	*.10825	.12028	.12990							
.064150		*.09623	.10585	.11372						
.057735			*.08660	.09448	.09790					
.052486				*.07873	.08215	.08529				
.050204					*.07531	.07844	.08400			
.048113						*.07217	.07772	.08248		
.044412							*.06662	.07138	.07911	
.041239								*.06186	.06959	.07561
.036084									*.05413	.06014
.032074										*.04811

Wire Sizes	Threads Per Inch								
	19	20	22	24	26	27	28	30	32
.036084	.06267								
.032074	.05064	.05292							
.030387	*.04558	.04786	.05180						
.028868		*.04330	.04724	.05052					
.026243			*.03937	.04265	.04542				
.024055				*.03608	.03886	.04009			
.022205					*.03331	.03454	.03569		
.021383						*.03208	.03322	.03528	
.020619							*.03093	.03299	.03480
.019245								*.02887	.03067
.018042									*.02706

Wire Sizes	Threads Per Inch									
	34	36	40	44	48	50	56	64	72	80
.019245	.03226									
.018042	.02866	.03007								
.016980	*.02547	.02689	.02929							
.016037		*.02406	.02646	.02843						
.014434			*.02165	.02362	.02526					
.013121				*.01968	.02132	.02204				
.012028					*.01804	.01876	.02062			
.011547						*.01732	.01918	.02111		
.010310							*.01546	.01740	.01890	
.009021								*.01353	.01504	.01624
.008018									*.01203	.01323
.007217										*.01083

* "Best Size" or Wire touching on pitch Diameter.

threads with this fixture, and the *best size* wires are most convenient to use, as these wires come in contact with the side of the thread at the pitch line and are the ones that give the reading at the important working part of the thread. Larger wires can be used but smaller sizes come below the top of the thread. Too much pressure should not be applied when measuring over wires. (*See* Tables 36 and 37.)

Screw Pitch Gages. The *screw pitch gages,* as shown in Figs. 33 and 34, afford one of the easiest and most accurate methods of determining the number of threads to the inch in a screw or a nut. An ordinary scale can be used as shown in Fig. 35. The scale should be placed on the top of the threads with the end coinciding with the point of one thread. The number of grooves included between the inch graduations represents the number of threads to an inch of the screw. (*See* Fractional Thread below.)

Optical Measuring. A precise method of gaging

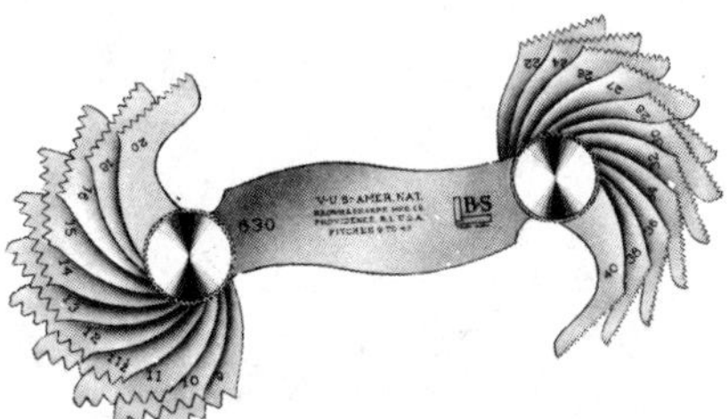

Figure 33. Screw pitch gage.

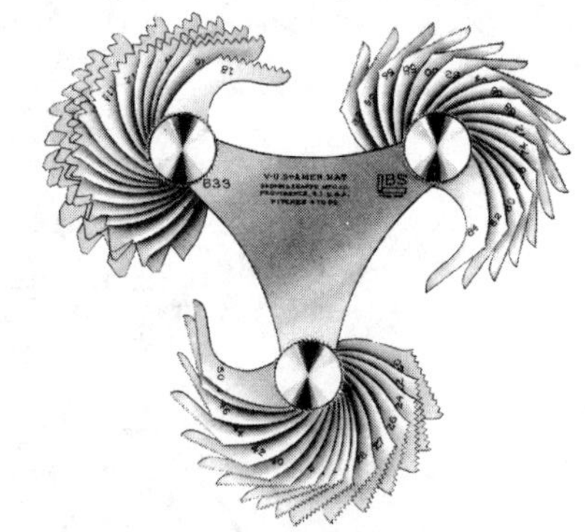

Figure 34. Triangular type screw pitch gage.

the form of a thread, or for that matter, any other contoured part, makes use of an instrument known as an *optical projector* or *comparator.* This system involves placing the object to be gaged in the path of a strong beam of light, and by means of magnifying lenses, projecting an enlarged image on a translucent screen. A properly scaled drawing, which may incorporate the upper and lower limits of tolerance, is held on the screen and the shadow of the part is compared to the drawing.

FRACTIONAL THREAD. A *fractional thread* is the number of threads and fraction of a thread per inch that must be expressed by a fraction or mixed number, as 7/8 of a thread per inch or 5 1/2 threads per inch. An easy way to measure fractional threads is to put the rule across the tops of the threads, read to the nearest exact whole inch mark coinciding with a thread, and divide the number of threads by the number of inches represented.

UNIFIED AND AMERICAN SCREW THREADS. Standardization of screw thread forms and sizes has been a subject of considerable study and investigation since the establishment of the Sellers Standard (1864) and the earlier Whitworth System originally developed by Sir Joseph Whitworth (1841). Later, the National Screw Thread Commission authorized by Congress in 1918 completed a specification which developed a coarse and fine thread American series incorporating the USS, SAE, and ASME diameter and pitch combinations which had been in general use and were outgrowths of the earlier threads.

The Unified and American Screw Threads (Table 38) were adopted by a committee from Canada and the United Kingdom and the United States signalized by the signing of an accord in Washington, D.C., in 1948. These Unified and American Screw Threads find universal application and tend to simplify manufacture and replacement of parts. They replace, or rather embrace, their predecessors, the National Coarse and National Fine Threads, as well as the Whitworth Standard Threads.

These Unified Standards constitute the basic American Standards and incorporate a number of changes resulting from practical experience in manufacture, assembly, and use. (*See* Fig. 36.)

Of particular interest are the thread contours which provide greater fatigue strength, crest clearance, easier assembly, and longer wear life of cutting tools.

Crest clearances permit rounded root forms on both external and internal threads. *Rounded roots*

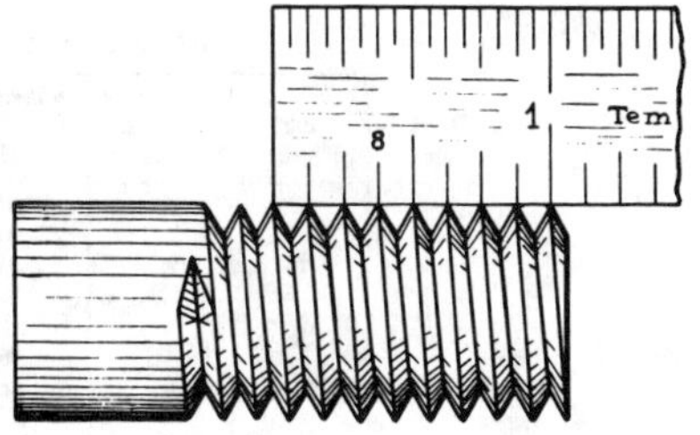

Figure 35. Using a scale to obtain the number of threads per inch.

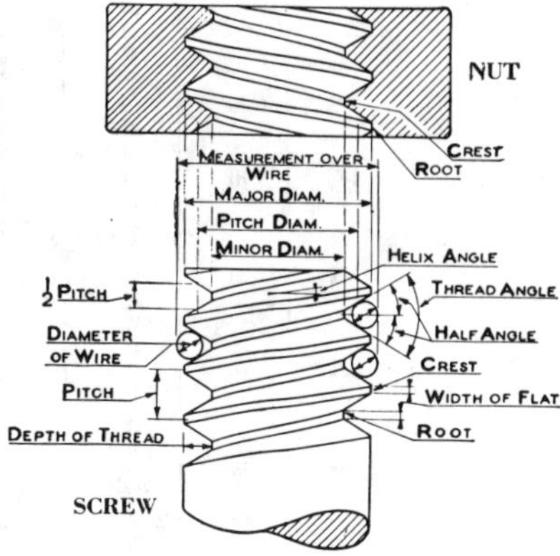

Figure 36. Unified and American screw thread and nut.

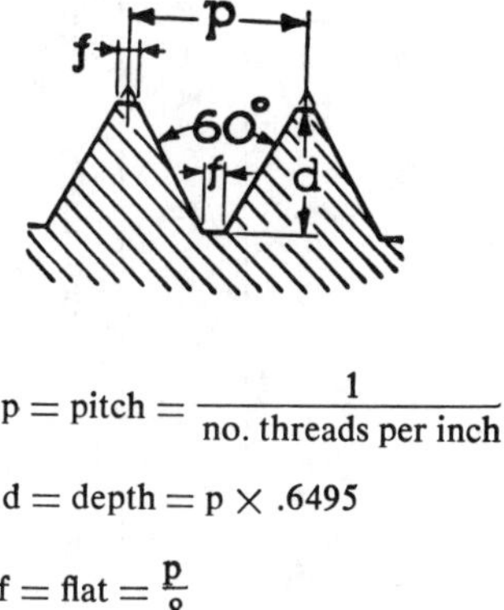

$$p = \text{pitch} = \frac{1}{\text{no. threads per inch}}$$

$$d = \text{depth} = p \times .6495$$

$$f = \text{flat} = \frac{p}{8}$$

Figure 37. American National Standard Thread.

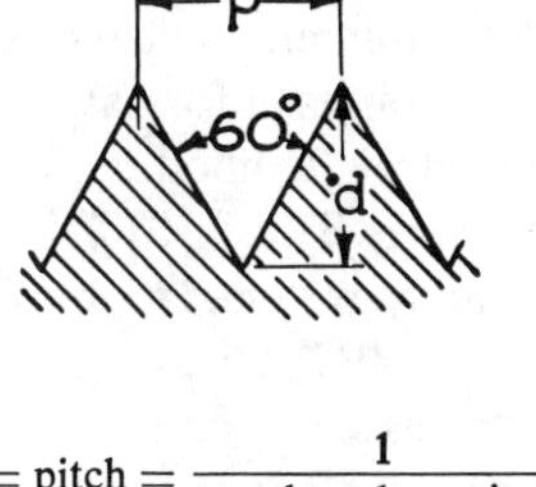

$$p = \text{pitch} = \frac{1}{\text{no. threads per inch}}$$

$$d = \text{depth} = p \times .8660$$

Figure 38. Sharp V thread.

TABLE 38

AMERICAN STANDARD AND UNIFIED FORM THREADS

Thread Size	Pitch Series	Tap Drill Size	Decimal Equivalent of Tap Drill	% of Thread (Approx.)
0–80	NF	56	.0465	83
		3/64	.0469	81
1–64	NC	54	.0550	89
		53	.0595	67
1–72	NF	53	.0595	75
		1/16	.0625	58
2–56	NC	51	.0670	82
		50	.0700	69
		49	.0730	56
2–64	NF	50	.0700	79
		49	.0730	64
3–48	NC	48	.0760	85
		5/64	.0781	77
		47	.0785	76
		46	.0810	67
		45	.0820	63
3–56	NF	46	.0810	78
		45	.0820	73
		44	.0860	56
4–40	NC	44	.0860	80
		43	.0890	71
		42	.0935	57
		3/32	.0938	56
4–48	NF	43	.0890	85
		42	.0935	68
		3/32	.0938	67
		41	.0960	59
5–40	NC	40	.0980	83
		39	.0995	79
		38	.1015	72
		37	.1040	65
5–44	NF	38	.1015	80
		37	.1040	71
		36	.1065	63
6–32	NC	37	.1040	84
		36	.1065	78
		7/64	.1094	70
		35	.1100	69
		34	.1110	67
		33	.1130	62
6–40	NF	34	.1110	83
		33	.1130	77
		32	.1160	68
8–32	NC	29	.1360	69
8–36	NF	29	.1360	78
		28	.1405	65
		9/64	.1406	65
10–24	NC	27	.1440	85
		26	.1470	79
		25	.1495	75
		24	.1520	70
		23	.1540	66
10–32	NF	5/32	.1562	83
		22	.1570	81
		21	.1590	76
		20	.1610	71
12–24	NC	11/64	.1719	82
		17	.1730	79
		16	.1770	72
		15	.1800	67
12–28	NF	16	.1770	84
		15	.1800	78
		14	.1820	73
		13	.1850	67
1/4–20	UNC	9	.1960	83
		8	.1990	79
		7	.2010	75
		13/64	.2031	72
		6	.2040	71
		5	.2055	69
1/4–28	UNF	3	.2130	80
		7/32	.2188	67
5/16–18	UNC	F	.2570	77
		G	.2610	71
5/16–24	UNF	H	.2660	86
		I	.2720	75
		J	.2770	66
3/8–16	UNC	5/16	.3125	77
		O	.3160	73
3/8–24	UNF	Q	.3320	79
		R	.3390	67
7/16–14	UNC	T	.3580	86
		23/64	.3594	84
7/16–20	UNF	W	.3860	79
		25/64	.3906	72
1/2–13	UNC	27/64	.4219	78
1/2–20	UNF	29/64	.4531	72
9/16–12	UNC	15/32	.4688	87
		31/64	.4844	72
9/16–18	UNF	1/2	.5000	87
		0.5062	.5062	78
5/8–11	UNC	17/32	.5312	79
5/8–18	UNF	9/16	.5625	87
		0.5687	.5687	78
3/4–10	UNC	41/64	.6406	84
		21/32	.6562	72
3/4–16	UNF	11/16	.6875	77
7/8–9	UNC	49/64	.7656	76
7/8–14	UNF	51/64	.7969	84
		0.8024	.8024	78
		13/16	.8125	67
1–8	UNC	55/64	.8594	87
		7/8	.8750	77
1–12	UNF	29/32	.9062	87
		59/64	.9219	72
1 1/8–7	UNC	31/32	.9688	84
		63/64	.9844	76
1 1/8–12	UNF	1 1/32	1.0312	87
		1 3/64	1.0469	72
1 1/4–7	UNC	1 3/32	1.0938	84
1 1/4–12	UNF	1 5/32	1.1562	87
		1 11/64	1.1719	72
1 3/8–6	UNC	1 3/16	1.1875	87
		1 13/64	1.2031	79
		1 7/32	1.2188	72
1 3/8–12	UNF	1 9/32	1.2812	87
		1 19/32	1.2969	72
1 1/2–6	UNC	1 5/16	1.3125	87
		1 21/64	1.3281	79
1 1/2–12	UNF	1 13/32	1.4062	87
		1 27/64	1.4219	72
1 3/4–5	UNC	1 17/32	1.5312	84
		1 35/64	1.5469	78
2–4 1/2	UNC	1 25/32	1.7812	76

are required in some applications and are made by tools purposely rounded. Otherwise, rounded roots may result from tool wear.

Various class tolerances have been set up for these threads. Detailed information can be obtained from the brochure "Unified and American Screw Threads No. ASA B1. 1-1949" published by the American Standards Association, 79 East 45th St., New York, N.Y. 10017. Classes of tolerances cannot be defined here as they embrace various formulas, each requiring an explanation for its particular use.

THREADS REPLACED BY UNIFIED AND AMERICAN SCREW THREADS. As the adoption of Unified and American Screw threads is of comparatively recent origin, illustrations of the threads they replace, the American National Standard, Sharp V, and Whitworth Standard threads are also shown. They will be of current use for a number of years, until transition to the Unified and American Screw threads is complete. Table 38 gives the diameters and numbers of threads per inch of the various standard threads.

The *American National Standard thread* (Fig. 37) provides advantages over the Sharp V thread which it replaced.

In the *Sharp V thread* (Fig. 38) the sharp points of the teeth are damaged easily and its taps and dies do not hold their edges as well as those for the Unified and American Screw threads.

The *Whitworth thread* (Fig. 39), formerly standard in England, provides a very strong tooth but re-

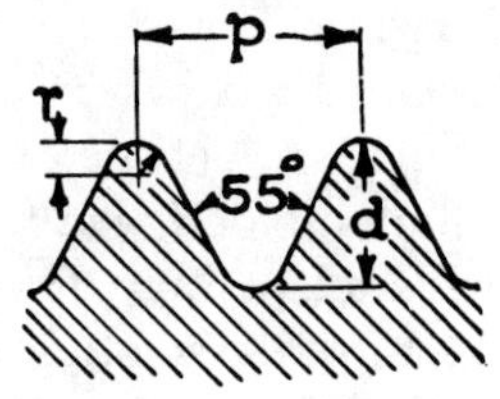

$$p = \text{pitch} = \frac{1}{\text{no. threads per inch}}$$

$$d = \text{depth} = p \times .64033$$

$$r = \text{radius} = p \times .1373$$

Figure 39. Whitworth thread.

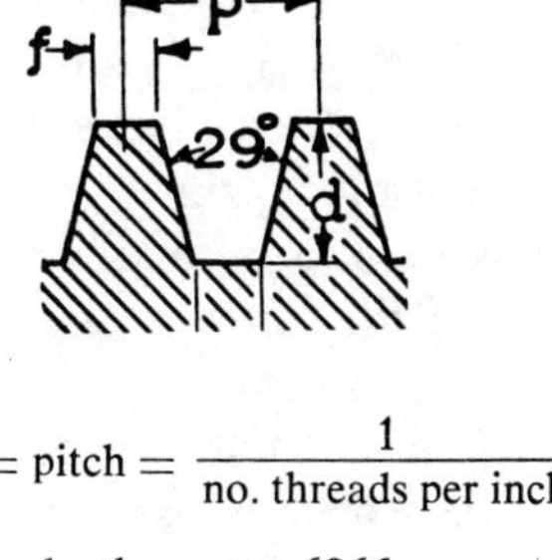

$$p = \text{pitch} = \frac{1}{\text{no. threads per inch}}$$

$$d = \text{depth} = p \times .6866$$

$$f = \text{flat} = p \times .3354$$

Figure 40. Brown & Sharpe 29-degree screw thread.

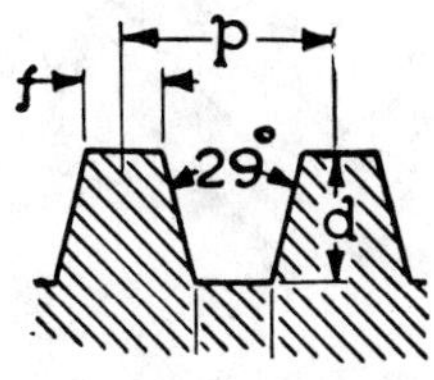

$$p = \text{pitch} = \frac{1}{\text{no. threads per inch}}$$

$$d = \text{depth} = \tfrac{1}{2}\, p + .010$$

$$f = \text{flat} = p \times .3707$$

Above is for 1p only

Figure 41. Acme screw thread.

quires a chasing tool of a different size and shape for each pitch.

Other Threads

The *Brown & Sharpe 29-degree screw thread* (Fig. 40) is used for worms and is much deeper than the Acme thread, which is also 29 degrees. The similarity of these two threads often confuses the mechanic.

The *Acme screw thread* (Fig. 41) is a strong thread used for feed screws, lead screws, and similar purposes. Formula varies with pitch.

THREAD CUTTING ON AN ENGINE LATHE. The spindle of the lathe rotates the work that is to be threaded and, by means of a train of gears, turns the lead screw. The lead screw, while in mesh with the split nut located behind the apron of the carriage, moves the carriage along the bed at a fixed and constant speed. The speed of the carriage in relation to the revolutions of the work naturally determines the lead of the thread. This relation between work rotation and carriage travel is directly controlled by the number of teeth in the change gears.

On modern screw cutting lathes a *quick change gear box* is provided through which a wide range of thread pitches is instantly available. The changes are made through tumbler or sliding gears by placing one or more levers in desired positions. A chart on the gear box usually indicates, in addition to the number of threads per inch, the lead in thousandths of an inch which is the corresponding feed rate when turning. *For example,* if a feed of .031 in. per revolution was required for turning, the levers would be set to cut a 32 pitch thread.

THREADING TOOLS. *Threading tools* are forming tools inasmuch as they shape the threads as the work turns in contact with the tool and the carriage feeds along the work. They are hardened and tempered. The front clearance should be about 15 degrees. In grinding, the top face is ground and the front faces are ground to fit the 60-degree tool notch of the center gage (Fig. 2).

THREAD CUTTING. After the work has been turned to the correct diameter and chamfered on the tailstock end to the depth of the thread to be cut, the threading tool should be mounted in the tool post. Projection of the tool from the post should be kept at a minimum to provide rigidity. Put the point of the tool at the height of the *dead center* and hold the center gage (in a holder if available). Using the cross feed, and tapping the tool to the right or left, bring the tool up to fit the notch in the gage.

When the adjustment is satisfactory, clamp the tool securely in the tool post.

Each cut made by the threading tool should be but a few thousandths of an inch in depth. At the end of each pass over the length of thread, the lead screw split nut is disengaged, the cross slide withdrawn to clear the cut, and the carriage returned to the starting position. The cross slide is then returned to the previous dial reading plus an amount to represent the new depth of cut and the cycle repeated until the thread is finished. Before the threading operation is started, a groove somewhat wider than the pitch and of equal depth is often turned into the shaft at the end of the thread so that the tool may run into it at the end of each pass.

Keep in mind that the proper speed for thread cutting should be about one-half the speed used in turning. Keep the point of the tool sharp, particularly when taking the finishing chip. Use an oilstone on the tool point for the last cut in order to improve the finish.

In threading taper work, such as pipe taps, it is advisable to use the taper turning attachment. Be careful in setting the tool to have it at right angles with the axis of the work instead of at right angles with the taper surface.

CUTTING LEFT-HAND THREADS. In cutting *left-hand threads,* the direction of rotation of the lead screw must be reversed by a reversing gear in the train or by using an extra idler gear.

LUBRICANT FOR THREAD CUTTING. In cutting threads on steel or wrought or malleable iron, use a good grade of cutting oil. On the return travel of the lathe carriage, when the thread tool is withdrawn, clean the threads and thread tool of all chips and then flood the work with the cutting oil. The excess oil will drain into the pan which is usually provided with a strainer to separate the chips.

Turret Lathes and Screw Machines

It has probably occurred to the thoughtful machinist that, although the engine lathe is an ideal machine for individual piecework in the shop, it needs considerable streamlining to adapt its operations to industrial mass production.

It should run continuously, for a machine manufacturing multiple workpieces requiring a number of successive operations has no time to shut down for retooling between each. No time can be wasted in setting up work, or in needless hand-operating. In fact, it becomes clear that there are four basic modifications desirable in redesigning an engine lathe for volume production, varying in degree according to their efficiency: (1) multiple tooling, (2) simultaneous operations, (3) mechanized feeding, and (4) automatic phasing. These modifications of the engine lathe, singly and in various combinations, have led to the design and development of turret lathes and screw machines.

DIFFERENCE BETWEEN TURRET LATHES AND SCREW MACHINES. Sometimes the worker is needlessly perplexed over the difference between turret lathes and screw machines. Both are designed for multiple tooling; both may have adaptations for identical work. Even in name, the turret lathe often is known as the plain screw machine. The best way to think of them is in terms of the work for which they were originally designed.

The *turret lathe* was designed primarily to handle small castings and irregular shaped pieces or cut bar lengths held in a chuck. It gets its name from the fact that the tail stock of the engine lathe is replaced by a multi-faced toolholder resembling a gun turret, indexing on an axis perpendicular to the bed of the lathe. It also has a square turret for tools, mounted on the cross slide. (*See* Fig. 42.)

In contrast to the turret lathe, the *original screw machine* was designed primarily as a bar stock or wire feed machine to form small screw parts from the bar. The turret of the screw machine is generally circular, indexing to bring the tools successively into position. Instead of a square turret on the cross slide, the *screw machine* usually has front and rear single-tool positions. (*See* Fig. 43.)

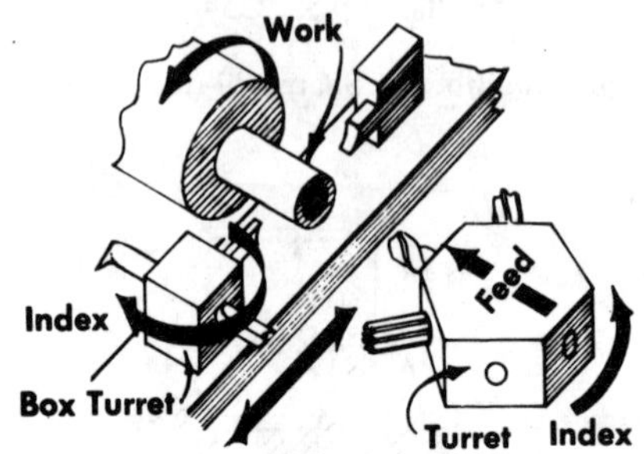

Figure 42. Turret lathe.

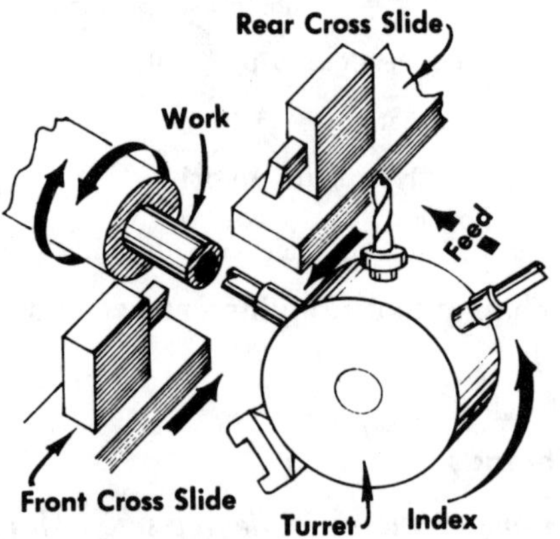

Figure 43. Single spindle automatic screw machine.

Confusion starts entering the picture with the fact that most turret lathes are adapted to bar-fed operation, just as many screw machines are adapted to handle chucked work. Other modifications and degrees of automatic operation are common to both, so that the machinist will do best to consider each basic machine in its simplest form.

HORIZONTAL TURRET LATHE. The *horizontal turret lathe* is the simplest of the adaptations of the engine lathe. It has a square turret in place of the conventional front tool post, indexing to bring tools quickly into cutting position. Another multi-sided turret (usually six-sided), replaces the footstock of the engine lathe, both turrets pivoting about a vertical axis. Each side of each turret accommodates a tool, either simple or specially designed for particular work. Many of the tools employed are similar to those used on automatic screw machines, and as the horizontal turret lathe is now usually equipped to handle work fed from bar stock as well as held in a chuck, the machine is extremely flexible in producing small parts of all kinds in limited quantities.

The two types of horizontal turret lathes are known as the *ram type* and the *saddle type*.

On the *ram type*, the operator moves only the ram and its turret, making for light, fast, and easy operation. However, when the ram is extended from its support in the saddle, the forces on the cutting tool tend to cause vibration, especially when turning a long diameter. For this work the saddle type is preferred.

The *turret* of the *saddle-type lathe* is an integral part of the saddle which traverses on the bed ways. This provides a sturdy support for the cutting tool, for it is constantly close to the saddle for the full travel along the bed.

AUTOMATIC HORIZONTAL TURRET LATHE. The *automatic horizontal turret lathe* makes its place in the turning field between the hand operated turret lathe and the fully automatic screw machine. It gives increased production with less physical effort on the part of the operator because it relieves him from manipulating starting, stopping, speed changing, and reversing of the spindle. All these are controlled with the movement of the turret. Just as in all increases in automation, this machine is more complex, requires a greater investment, and consequently its choice depends upon the lot size necessary for economy and the complexity of machining operations.

HAND SCREW MACHINE. The *hand screw machine* is an even further development of the simple engine lathe. The word *hand* in its name is slightly misleading, because the hand screw machine has all the basic functions of the single-spindle automatic screw machine—except that stock feed, cross-slide feed, turret indexing, and turret feed are hand controlled or engaged. It is principally a *bar stock machine* with means provided to handle *chuck work*.

The hand screw machine is an ideal companion to the single-spindle automatic screw machine for making parts in small lots, ordinarily made in larger volume on the automatic machine. Usually the cross-slide and turret tools, collets, and feed fingers are the same as used in the same corresponding size automatic screw machine. This materially reduces tool inventory and contributes to part-cost economy.

SINGLE-SPINDLE AUTOMATIC SCREW MACHINES. The *automatics,* as the name implies, are capable of automatically producing complete parts of complex form from bar stock. Although there are variations in design, they consist of two basic types, differing in tooling methods and function—the Swiss type and the Brown & Sharpe type.

The *Swiss-type automatic* screw machine has the advantage of being able to turn long slender lengths to extremely close tolerances. This is accomplished by its principle of feeding the stock through a hardened steel or carbide bushing of stock diameter, past an axially stationary single point tool, close to the bushing. Thus the radial force of the cut is close to the support at all times. The surface finish produced can closely approach that of grinding. But although the quality of finish and accuracy are high, the production rate (due to single point turning), is relatively lower than the Brown & Sharpe. Its popularity lies principally with fine instrument makers whose major requirements are surface finish and accuracy, at a sacrifice of productivity. Other limitations are the necessity of using accurately ground stock, and control of wear in the guide bushing.

The *Brown & Sharpe type* is the more common and universally used single-spindle automatic screw machine. Due to its rigidity of design, flexibility, and receptiveness to numerous attachments, its applications are limited only by the ingenuity of the operator. Many operations, such as rear-end drilling, slotting, index drilling, de-burring, and straddle milling, can be performed by standard attachments after the part has been separated from the bar and while the machine is making another part—thus greatly reducing part cost. The tools and tool holders are similar to those used on turret lathes, and are common to those used on hand screw machines. The front and rear cross slides and the turret tools are fed by disc cams designed to gain the last fraction of a second of time. Trip dogs on carriers at the front of the machine index the turret and change spindle speed and direction as well as control feeding the stock to a stop after cutting off a finished piece.

This automatic screw machine, when arranged with automatic bar feed, stores a supply of 10 or 12 foot bars, and automatically restocks the machine with only a few seconds loss of production time. As no assistance is required of the operator, it forms a completely automated unit.

MULTIPLE-SPINDLE AUTOMATIC SCREW MACHINE. The *multiple-spindle automatic* (Fig. 44) is productively the ultimate in engine lathe development. It has four to eight parallel spindles, each rotating a bar of stock. The spindles index simultaneously to successively present the stock to each tool. The reduction in time required per finished piece is the multiple-spindles' advantage over the single-spindle machine; hence its application is in the area of large lot production. Where but one turret tool is working on a part at one time on a single-spindle machine, all tools are working simultaneously on the parts in all spindles on a multiple spindle machine. Therefore, the sum of the time taken for all the turret operations is included in the total time to produce the part on a single-spindle machine. Because operations are usually in sequence, the time required for the longest single cut, plus indexing time, is the total time required to produce the finished part on a multiple-spindle machine. Disadvantages of the multiple-spindle compared to the single-spindle machine are much longer setup time and higher tooling cost. Generally, larger tolerances are required on parts made on multiple-spindle machines, because the relation of turning operations is affected by the accuracy of the index of the spindles.

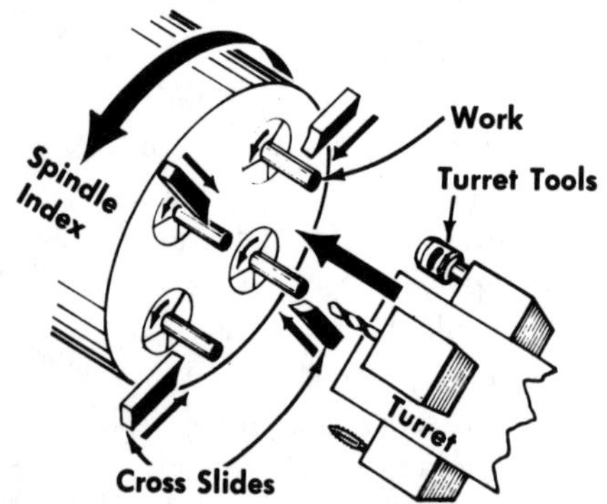

Figure 44. Multiple-spindle automatic screw machine.

Proper Selection and Use of Tools

The success of automatic screw machines in producing highly accurate, well-finished work at a very rapid rate depends to a great extent upon the selection and setting of tools. Accuracy and good finish can be appreciably decreased if selection, grinding, and setting of the tools is not properly done. Experience in *tooling up* is of course advantageous in setting up any job, especially the difficult ones. However, the principles of the tools are simple, and the machinist, even though unfamiliar with this type of machine, should soon be able to get good results with proper care and study of instructions.

TOOLS AVAILABLE FOR ORDINARY OPERATIONS. Owing to the wide variety of work produced on screw machines, a considerable number of different tools are available.

EXTERNAL TURNING TOOLS. Balance turning tools, plain, roller back, and V back tools, hollow mills, swing tools, and knee tools are all used in the turret. Combination centering and facing tools and circular pointing tools are used for operations on the end of the work.

INTERNAL CUTTING TOOLS. Drills, countersinks, and counterbores are held in adjustable holders, and reamers are held in floating reamer holders. Recessing swing tools are also used for internal operations.

THREADING TOOLS. Taps and dies, chasers mounted in opening die holders, and thread rolls held in cross-slide thread roll holders are used to produce threads on parts.

KNURLING TOOLS. Top and side knurl holders are mounted on the cross slides. For knurling from the turret, adjustable knurl holders and knurling swing tools are used.

FORMING AND CUTTING-OFF TOOLS. Circular forming tools and circular cutting-off tools are mounted on the regular cross-slide tool posts and the tool post with worm adjustment. Square tools and thin, straight-blade cutting-off tools are used on the cross slides, while the angular cutting-off tools are utilized in the turret.

SUPPORTING AND AUXILIARY TOOLS. Swing and slide tools, fixed and adjustable guides for operating swing and slide tools, back rests for turret, and spindle brakes add further versatility to operations possible on screw machines.

Chapter 19

Machine Tool Controls

The more familiar you become with machine tools, the more you will discover how greatly their degree of accuracy, versatility, and productivity depends upon the ingenuity and application of devices for their control.

It is only recently that many complex mechanisms used for such functions as reversals, speed and feed changes, braking, and the like have been replaced by simple electrical and hydraulic devices. A new machine is seldom in operation before plans are on the drawing board for further refinements of its controls. While the systems of such controls may sometimes be intricate, the mechanisms operating them are usually easily understood, and the extensive use of such motor drives, electrical controls, hydraulic controls, and electronic elements has made them such integral parts of the machines themselves that the machinist should be familiar with them.

Electrical Components and Controls

The first consideration before touching any electrical device is personal safety. Accidental contact with electrically live parts can result in serious injury or even death. Therefore, the disconnect switch in the machine control enclosure should be turned OFF before any electrical switch compartment is opened.

Control power in a machine is wired with red wire while line voltage devices are wired with black wire. *Machine tool controls* are operated from 110 volt power, obtained from a transformer within the machine. This provides that only a limited voltage and current will be encountered in the red circuits and at the control elements, but due caution should be exercised in dealing with any voltage whatever on a machine.

Power Supply

The common power supply in industrial operations is *alternating current.* In an alternating current (AC) system the current flows alternately in opposite directions, the voltage changing continuously in value from a maximum in one direction to a maximum in the opposite direction. The rate at which the reversals occur is called the *frequency,* measured in cycles per second. A *cycle* is one complete reversal or alternation of the voltage or current.

Phase is the relationship between two or three electrical voltage circuits working together. It is established in any given system by the physical characteristics of the generating equipment in the power house. In a three-phase system, three voltages separately attain their maximums in fixed order of rotation, and this phenomenon is used extensively in motor action. (*See* section on motors in this chapter.)

The common industrial voltages are 220, 440, or 550 volts. The common frequency in the United States is 60 cycles. The majority of industrial power supplies are three-phase, although some areas are two-phase and very small motor-driven equipment may use single-phase power.

Transformers

In alternating current circuits it is possible to change the value of the voltage by means of transformers. A *transformer* (Fig. 1) is a device consisting of a magnetic iron core about which are wound electrical coils for input (primary) and output (secondary) voltages. The number of windings on the input coil is in the same ratio to those of the output coils as the input voltage is to the output (or voltage to be used). This property of transformers makes possible efficient utilization of power for plant power, lighting systems, and so on.

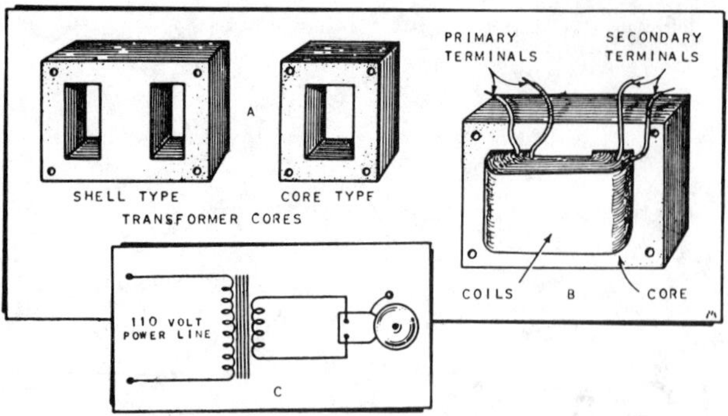

Figure 1. Transformer.

Figure 2. Alternating current squirrel cage induction motor.

Motors

Motors are electrical devices that produce rotating power by means of electromagnetic actions and reactions. They are rated in terms of *horsepower,* which is the measure of the torque the motor will deliver at full load speed.

The most widely used motor for machine tools is the alternating current squirrel-cage *induction motor* (Fig. 2). In an induction motor the rotor does not have any connections to the line. Variations of the current flowing in the stationary member create the effect of a magnetic field between pairs of opposite poles, which in turn induces a magnetic field in the rotor. The speed of the induction motor is therefore dependent upon the frequency of the supply voltage and the number of poles in the motor winding. The synchronous, or theoretical no load, speed is established by the following relationship.

$$\text{R.P.M.} = \frac{60 \times \text{frequency}}{\text{No. of pairs of poles}}$$

The *full load speed* of an induction motor is always some value below this figure. In the case of a 4-pole 60 cycle motor, the no load speed is 1800 r.p.m. while the full-load speed may be 1725 or 1735 r.p.m. Special windings may have slightly different values of full-load speed.

TORQUE. The amount of *torque* that a motor will deliver is determined by the physical size of the components and the grade of insulation used in its construction. The final criterion is the temperature that the motor will reach under full load conditions. An open-type induction motor with class A insulation is rated at 40° centigrade temperature rise above a standard ambient temperature of 40° centigrade. Thus, the total temperature of the motor measured with a thermometer on the outside of the frame may be 80° centigrade or 176° fahrenheit. A totally enclosed 60 cycle motor, class A insulated, has a permissible temperature rise of 55° centigrade or a total temperature of 203° fahrenheit. Special motors with class B, class F, and class H insulations permitting higher total temperatures are used when increased torques from a given frame size motor are desired, or special conditions are encountered.

Motors are made open (Fig. 3), open drip proof or splashproof, totally enclosed nonventilated, or totally enclosed fan cooled (Fig. 4), to suit the conditions of the specific application. Most machine tool motors are built with permanently sealed ball bearings. These require no attention for the life of the bearing.

STARTERS. Motors require some device to permit starting and stopping and provisions for protection against overload. In very simple machines, a *manual starter* with *overload relays* may suffice. This may have toggle or pushbutton operators and a mechanical connection from the overload relays to trip off the starter when an overload occurs.

Figure 3. Open motor.

Figure 4. Totally-enclosed motor.

The majority of machine tools have *magnetic starters* with overload protection. These devices are solenoid operated and use 110 volt control in the coil circuit while controlling the motor at line voltage.

The use of momentary-contact start pushbuttons in a three wire control circuit provides undervoltage protection to the machine. Under these conditions, if power should fail due to fuse failure or line fault conditions, the machine will stop and not restart on restoration of power until the start pushbutton is operated.

OVERLOAD RELAYS. The devices that protect a motor against overload are called *overload relays* (Fig. 5). These are made in numerous forms, but the two most common use solder pots or bimetallic strips as the sensing element, with overload heaters. The heaters are selected on the basis of the motor full load current and may provide up to 15 per cent overload before tripping. Many relays are provided with further adjustments that vary this tripping point from 85 per cent to 115 per cent of standard. Therefore, they provide means for meeting the ambient conditions in many different industrial installations.

When overload relays trip too frequently, the final criterion is the total temperature of the motor. If a larger heater will not permit the motor to exceed its temperature rating then it may be safely used.

Figure 5. Overload relay.

Figure 6. Solenoid.

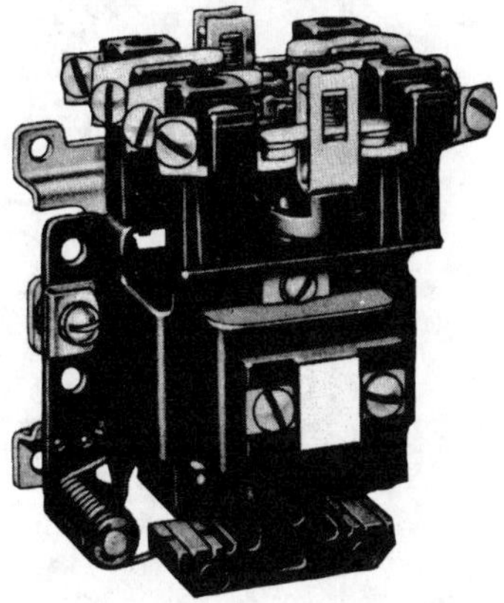

Figure 7. Relay.

Solenoids

A *solenoid* is an electrical device (Fig. 6) made up of magnetic steel laminations and a coil. When the coil is energized, a magnetic field is set up which causes linear motion of the plunger. In alternating current solenoids, a shading coil produces some magnetic effect while the current is passing through zero, therefore preventing chatter of the plunger. Solenoids are used in starters, relays, and in machine elements where linear motion is required to actuate some mechanism.

Relays

Relays (Fig. 7) are electrical devices consisting of a solenoid and contacts. These contacts may be normally open or normally closed and the energizing of the solenoids reverses their state. Relays are used with limit switches to give signals at different points of a circuit, for interlocking, and in general for initiating action by electrical circuits to other electrical controls.

Switches

Any device that closes or opens an electrical circuit when it is operated by contact may be called a *switch*. They are built in open and closed forms and are located throughout a machine to limit mechanical motions, to sense changes and to give signals in the course of the machine cycle. Some are built into the machine, others are mounted on the outside of the machine or upon an attachment. Pushbuttons and selector switches are mounted conveniently accessible to the operator for selection of machine cycles, starting and stopping of motors, control of motions, and selection of other machine features.

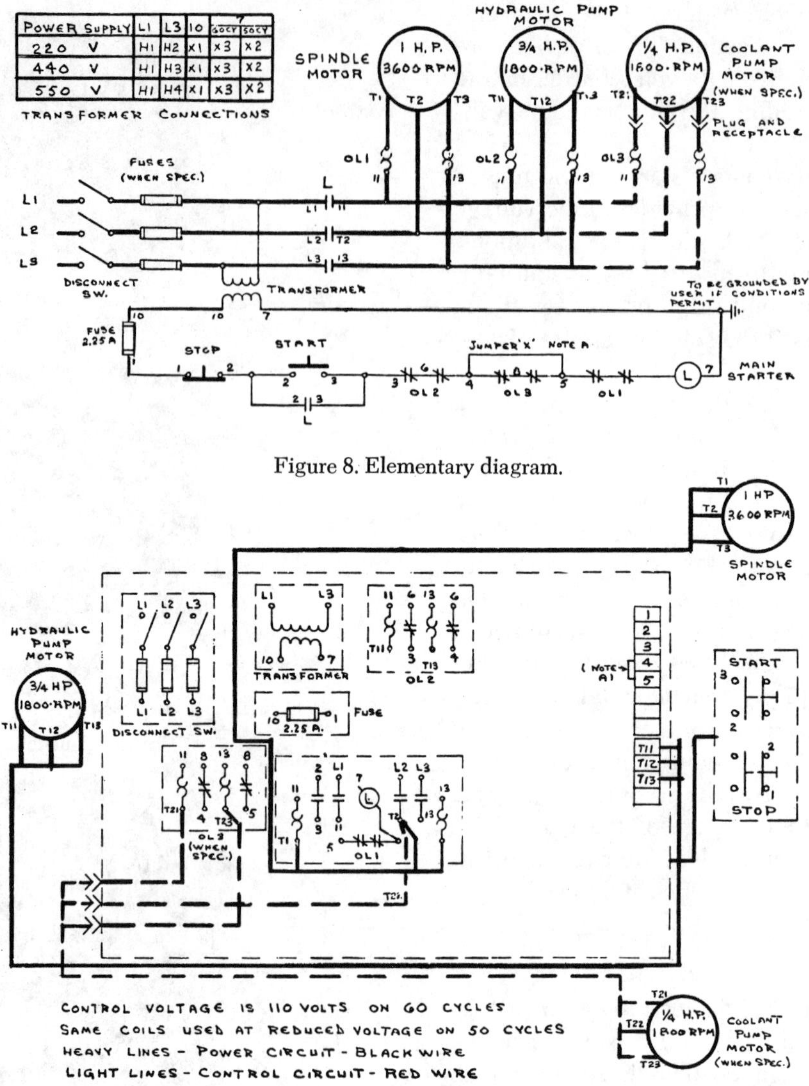

Figure 8. Elementary diagram.

Figure 9. Wiring diagram.

Control Circuits

The arrangement of the various electrical elements previously described, in such a manner as to achieve the desired machine operations, is the machine control circuit. This is shown in diagrammatic form in the machine *elementary diagram* (Fig. 8). The relative location and the actual wiring of each device and their interconnection is shown in the machine *wiring diagram* (Fig. 9).

The *control circuit* of each particular machine is designed for the specific machine. It provides the means for coordinating motions, starting and stopping motors, operating solenoids in hydraulic valves, and causing the proper sequence of events. Each circuit must be studied with the mechanical and hydraulic features of the machine to arrive at an understanding of the machine control.

Many other devices may be utilized for specific functions. Among these, counters, timers, and adjustable speed drives are available in many forms. A great variety are built with electronic components. *For example,* many adjustable speed drive systems use electronic rectifiers to change alternating current to direct current. This is necessary because the speed of a direct current motor can be changed readily while an alternating current motor speed is fixed by the factors previously described. Other means of rectifying alternating current are selenium rectifiers and germanium or silicon diodes. The different means are selected for use in a given circuit on the basis of particular characteristics desired.

The variety and complexity of such devices are beyond the limits of a simple explanation. For further information consult the manufacturer's literature on any particular device.

Hydraulic Components

Most electrical functions can be accomplished by *hydraulic components.* For a better understanding of hydraulic operations, the following list of hydraulic-electrical comparisons is given between corresponding elements, each of which serve similar functions.

Hydraulic	*Electrical*
Pumps	Generators
Pipe	Wires
Motors	
Rotary	Motors
Linear (cylinders)	Solenoids
Valves	
Manual Selector	Switch
Check Valve	Rectifier
Unloading Valve	Voltage Regulator
Pressure Release	Fuse
Servo Valve	Relay
Orifice (throttle)	Resistance with Capacitors
Flow Control	Rheostat
Accumulators	Capacitors, Batteries
Filters	No Equivalent

Figure 10. Gear pump.

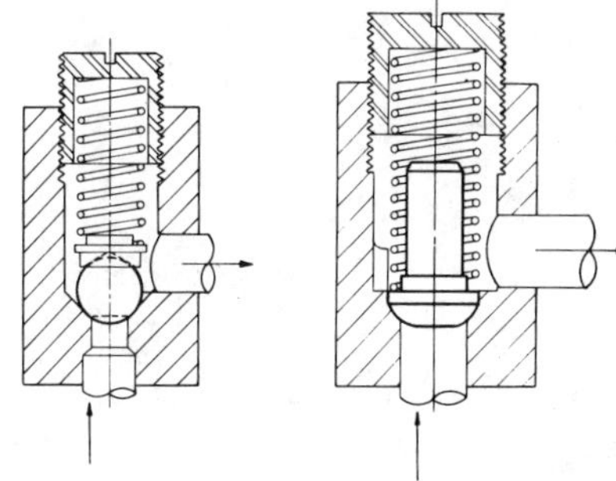

Figure 11. Relief valves.

PUMPS. For converting electrical energy into hydraulic energy, many different types of pumps have been developed, such as *gear, vane, piston,* and *centrifugal*—each type having its advantages and disadvantages.

The most common type is the *gear* pump (Fig. 10). In this type of pump there are two portholes in the housing, for suction and discharge. By rotating the two gears, a vacuum is created at the suction port, drawing the fluid into the pump. The fluid fills the space between the gear teeth and is carried around to the discharge port. There, prevented from returning because the meshing gears act as a seal, pressure forces it into a pipe at the discharge port which carries it to any desired location.

VALVES. Fluid from the pump must be controlled to perform useful functions. *Valves* are used for this purpose to control pressure (p.s.i.), rate of flow (f.p.m.), and direction of flow.

PRESSURE RELIEF VALVES. We must remember that pressure cannot occur without resistance. If the discharge pipe of a pump is blocked off, pressure increases until something gives. A pressure relief or pressure regulating valve is installed in a line to prevent this. Fluid flows through the valve when a set pressure is reached. The construction of this valve is a simple ball and spring, or more generally a poppet and spring, enclosed in a housing. Usually the pressure can be changed by rotating the screw extending from the valve, increasing or decreasing the spring tension which is acting on the poppet. (*See* Fig. 11.)

THROTTLE VALVES. Generally the speed of a moving slide must be variable. A flow control valve, more commonly known as a throttle valve, is employed for this purpose. Its basic function is to open or close the area in the pipeline through which the fluid must pass before it goes to the slide. The simple water faucet is a typical example of a flow control valve. There are two types of throttle valves, *sharp edge orifice* (Fig. 12) and *viscous orifice*. The *sharp edge type* is used to prevent the flow rate from changing due to variations in oil temperature.

DIRECTIONAL CONTROL VALVES. Whenever a slide must move in more than one direction the fluid must change its direction. There are numerous types of direction control valves for performing this function. The most common is called the four-way sliding type

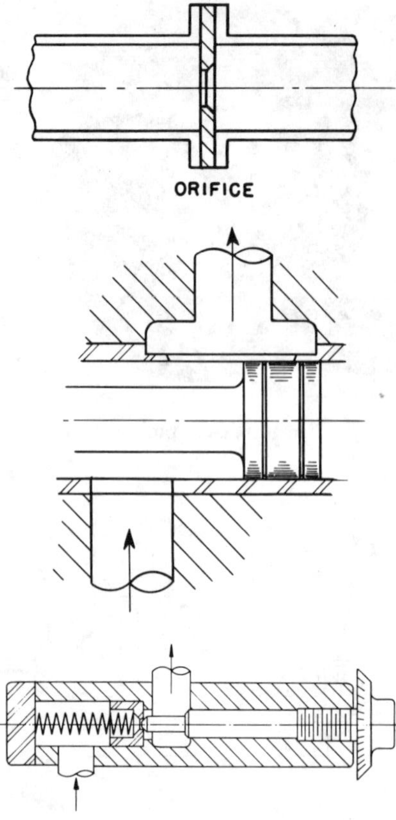

Figure 12. Throttle valves.

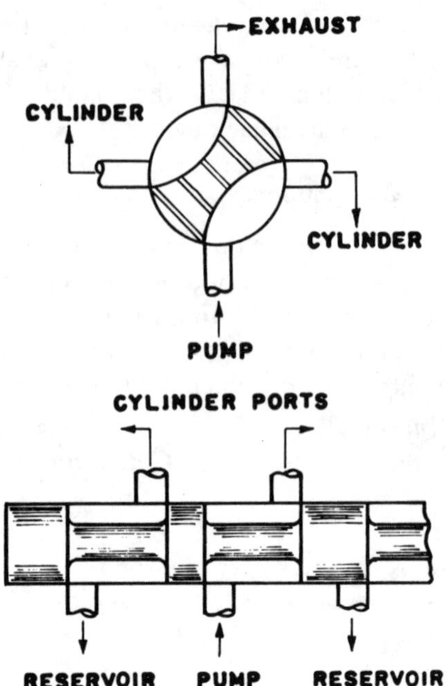

Figure 13. Directional control valves.

Figure 14. Filter.

valve, used to control hydraulic cylinders. It consists of four portholes, one connected to the pump, one connected to a storage reservoir, and the other two leading to opposite ends of the hydraulic cylinder. There is a sliding spool inside the valve body or housing which can be actuated in two positions. One position will connect the pump (high pressure) port to one cylinder lead at the same time the second cylinder lead connects the fluid from the opposite port to the reservoir (low pressure). When the spool is shifted to the second position, the cylinder leads reverse the high and low pressures. Many different versions of direction valves are employed in hydraulic systems by adding more ports and positions. (*See* Fig. 13.)

There are other names given to valves used in hydraulic operations, such as pressure reducing, pressure unloading, sequence, or shut-off, but these all come under one of the previously mentioned categories.

Valves can be actuated in four ways: hydraulically, electrically, manually, or mechanically.

RESERVOIRS. All hydraulic systems use a reservoir or storage tank for the purpose of radiating heat, settling out dirt, and replenishing the system if leakage occurs. The tank may be part of the machine base or a separate unit.

FILTERS. *Filters* (Fig. 14) are used to remove foreign matter from the fluid. These filters can be placed in four different locations in the system: (1) in the high pressure or pump line, (2) the main return line, (3) suction line, or (4) may be bypassed, whereby only a small percentage of the fluid is filtered each time it flows through the system. The *bypass* type is generally preferred because the performance of the machine will not be affected if it clogs. The filter cartridge is made from many materials—cotton, wire screen, paper, and the like.

ACCUMULATORS. Hydraulic energy can be stored in

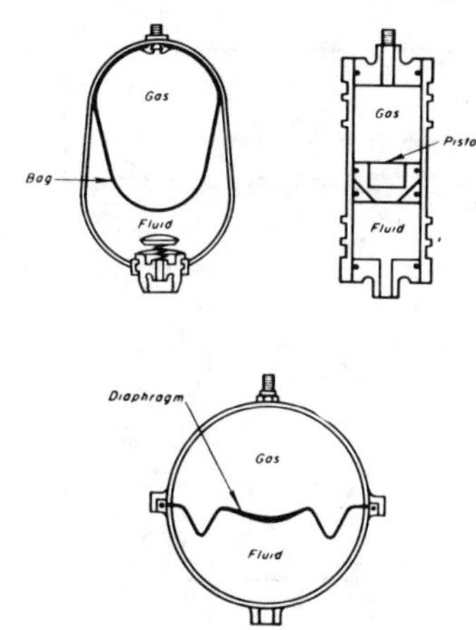

Figure 15. Accumulators.

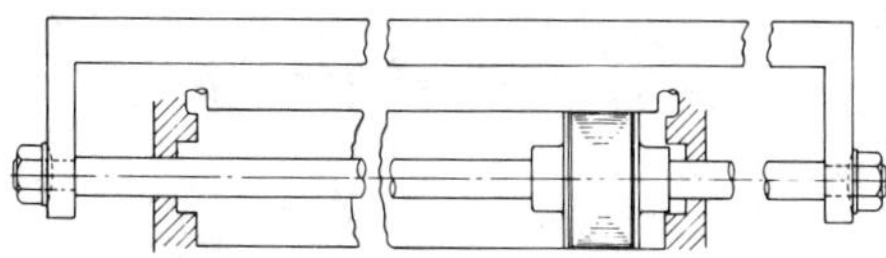

Figure 16. Reciprocating motor.

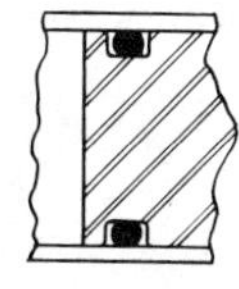

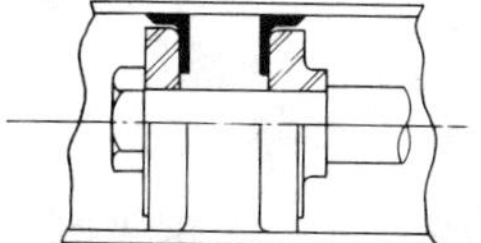

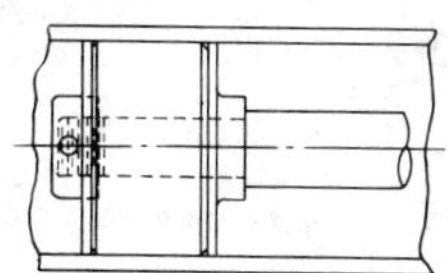

Figure 17. Piston packings.

the system by using an *accumulator* (Fig. 15). Storage is accomplished by compressing air or gas confined in a chamber. The energy thus stored can be later withdrawn. The two main purposes of using an accumulator are the smoothing out of pressure surges or the permissible use of a smaller pump.

MOTORS. Every type of pump can be, and is, used as a hydraulic motor. By far the majority of hydraulic applications use the plain cylinder and piston as a motor. One important factor in the proper operation of a cylinder motor is the removal of all the air. With the air present the motion of the slide that is being moved by the cylinder will be jumpy and erratic. (*See* Figs. 16 and 17.)

POWER TRANSMISSION. Hydraulic power is transmitted from the pump to the control valves and motors through pipes, tubes, and flexible hoses. It is important to use the proper strength pipe to prevent bursting. Care must also be taken to prevent leakage at the fittings. For low pressures, below 200 p.s.i., plastic hose is sometimes used. For high pressures, a wire-braid hose or steel tubing is recommended. Gaskets and seals made of Buna N synthetic rubber are generally used to prevent leakage at the valves, cylinders, and pumps.

HYDRAULIC OIL. Most oil companies produce oil specifically for use in hydraulic systems, which contains additives to prevent rusting and foaming. The most important characteristic of the oil is the viscosity. *Viscosity* is measured by the resistance of the oil to pouring at a certain temperature, and is most commonly rated in Saybolt seconds taken in a standard pour test. Viscosity causes pressure and power losses as oil flows through pumps, valves, and piping. To control these losses, and the heating in the system, it is important to use an oil of the viscosity specified by the machine manufacturer. (*See* Fig. 18.)

Tape or Numerical Control

Tape or numerical control is a growing trend in the control of metalworking machinery (Fig. 19). Punched cards or strips of paper can direct the operations of complex machines with amazing accuracy and economy. Tooling is often simplified, and design of engineering changes in methods of machining can frequently be affected by simply changing the tape.

After the job has been *planned* or *programmed,* the tape is properly perforated in conformance with the programming and placed in a control console. This electronically engages or disengages the various machine functions. Spindle speeds and feeds can be controlled, as well as table movements, work orientation, coolant ON and OFF, and so on.

Numerical control permits machining control in one, two, or three axes. In other words, operations can be performed longitudinally, transversely, or vertically, individually or in combination.

While numerical control can often greatly increase productivity, this must justify the increased overhead costs of these expensive machines, so that the cost per piece is lowered.

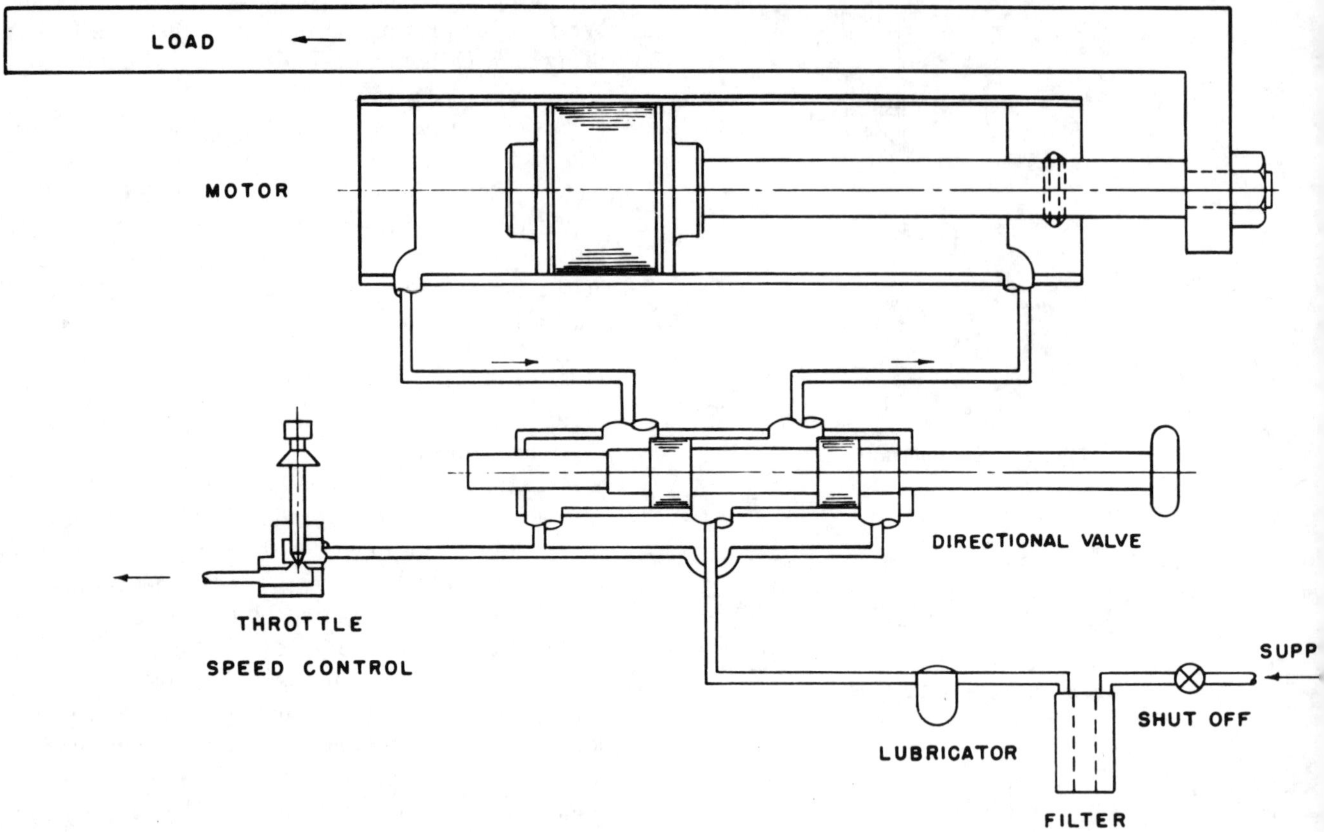

Figure 18. Simple hydraulic circuit.

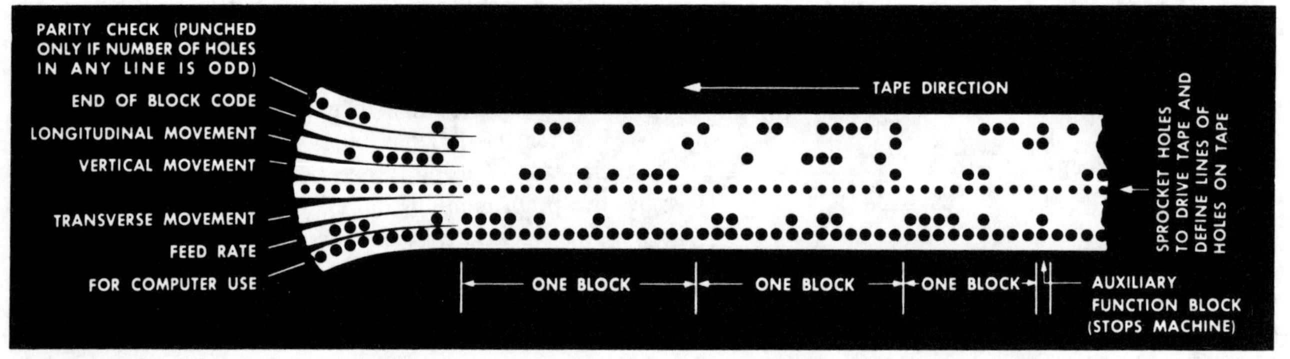

Figure 19. Typical tape with a channel for controlling each desired machine function.

Chapter 20

Grinding and Grinding Machines

Grinding is the process of removing material by contact with an abrasive wheel.

Developments in electronics, aircraft, servo mechanisms, and missiles during recent years have created new dimensions in the realm of accuracy, challenging the capabilities of men and machines. This challenge is being met by modern grinding machines and men with the skill and knowledge of grinding to operate them. A fundamental understanding of grinding is therefore an essential in the foundation upon which to build a career.

Basic Operations of Grinding

The basic operations of grinding are the same as those of many other machine tools, except that by using a high speed abrasive grinding wheel instead of ordinary tools, far greater accuracy and finish may be obtained.

One type of grinder will perform the same operations as the lathe, except that the high speed wheel replaces the single pointed tool. Another type will refine the flat surfaces from the planer with finishes close to perfection. Or cup-type grinding wheels will carry on the finish with the same operation as end milling cutters. Actually, the principle of almost any machine tool operation, except drilling, can be duplicated by grinding. (*See* Fig. 1.)

Grinding Action

A surface that has been ground may appear to be very smooth, but upon magnification you will find that it has a very great number of fine parallel grooves. Each of these has been cut by a particle of abrasive sticking out from the surface of the cutting wheel, and acting as a minute cutting tool. In the process of grinding, each of these *cutting tools,* like

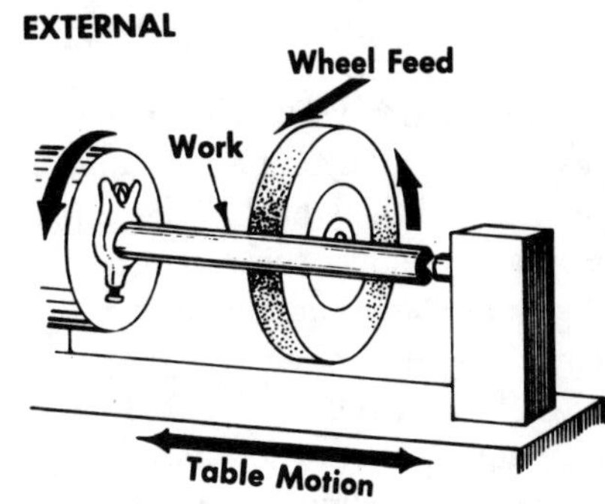

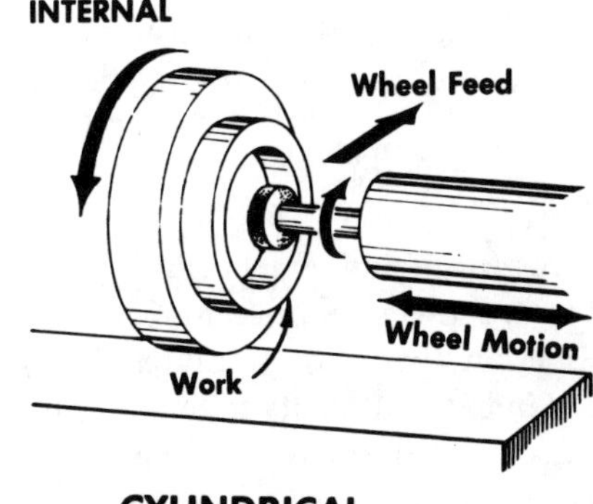

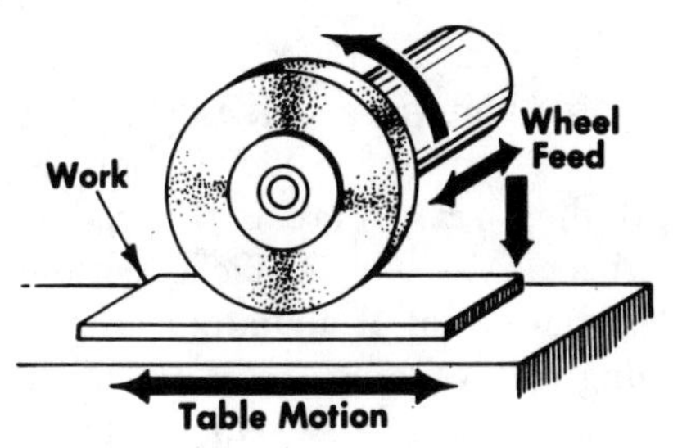

Figure 1. Principle of grinding.

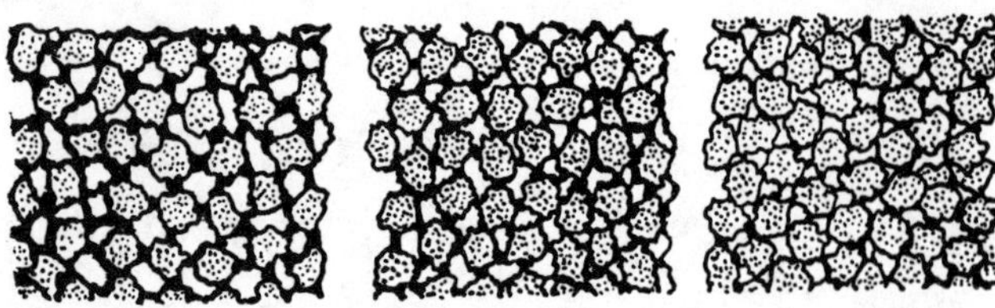

Figure 2. Cross section of three wheels identical in grain size and bond strength, but differing in grain spacing or structure, and providing correspondingly different grinding action.

their larger counterparts, have removed countless tiny chips to form the metal.

As hard as these abrasive grains may be, they are brittle and occasionally break, or wear and become dull and are pulled out of the bond by the force of the wheel against the work. This exposes fresh abrasive grains with new cutting edges and preserves the cutting qualities of the wheel at the expense of wear. If this occurs too slowly the wheel will lose its bite, tend to become shiny and inefficient, and is said to be too *hard.* The ideal wheel for any job will be just hard enough for maximum life, at the point where it is just soft enough to continue to be *self-sharpening.*

This relationship between abrasive grain and bond means that there are five factors to be considered for the selection of a grinding wheel for a particular job —the type of abrasive, the grain size (coarseness), the grade (hardness), the structure (grain spacing in the bond), and the bond itself. (*See* Fig. 2.)

Grinding Wheels

Abrasives. We find emery and corundum, two hard mineral forms of aluminum oxide, ready for use as abrasives in their natural states. These minerals were used in early attempts to make grinding wheels and were collected from many parts of the world. However, since emery may contain anywhere from 40 per cent to 70 per cent of corundum, and since natural corundum itself may vary in hardness up to that of the ruby and sapphire, these posed difficulties in obtaining uniform results in grinding.

The two main types of artificial abrasives used in modern grinding wheels are both products of the electric furnace. The first, artificial corundum, is a more or less pure form of aluminum oxide. The second, seemingly discovered by pure chance in the synthesis of corundum, is extremely hard carborundum—a silicon carbide that does not occur in nature. Both of these products come from the furnace in big chunks which must be crushed, and the resulting abrasive grains sifted for size.

Bonds. Grinding wheels are made by binding these abrasive grains together in circular forms with an adhesive element called the bond. The bond is not an abrasive but a matrix that supports the abrasive grains. The hardness of the wheel varies with the strength of the bond, which may be one of several types—vitrified, silicate, elastic, rubber, or resin.

Vitrified Wheels. Wheels most commonly used today are bonded by the vitrified process. The selected abrasive is mixed with a clay, poured into molds, and exposed to heat until the bonding material is vitrified. These wheels are of even texture and are unaffected by heat, cold, water, oils, or acids. The porous texture of the wheel is advantageous because in grinding the abrasive grains are broken off and thrown away from the wheel, and as a result the wheel does not clog easily with the material being worked. The disadvantage of vitrified wheels is lack of elasticity and their not being able to be used on heavy side cuts.

Silicate Wheels. Silicate wheels derive their name from silicate of soda, which constitutes their bond. These wheels cut smoothly with very little heat. They are adaptable for grinding work requiring a delicate edge, such as for tools and knives. The grinding action is dependable, and the manufacture of these wheels can be easily controlled.

Elastic Wheels. Shellac is the most important bond used for elastic wheels. Such wheels are strong and can be made very thin. This bond makes possible wheels which produce a very smooth finish and can take deep cuts without burning the work. Shellac bonded wheels are also used in cutting-off operations, for finishing chilled iron, cast iron, and steel rolls, and for grinding in narrow spaces. This type of wheel is not intended for heavy duty.

Rubber Wheels. Rubber forms a bond of great strength, and wheels of this type are used to cut grooves or to finish work to high standards. Rubber bonded wheels are capable of running at high speeds, and rapid stock removal is possible at any speed, high or low.

In their manufacture, the rubber bond and the abrasives are mixed and rolled out in a sheet to the required thickness. The wheels are *died out* of this sheet and are heated in molds to vulcanize the rubber. This process makes possible very thin wheels.

Resin Wheels. In the manufacture of resin wheels, the abrasive grains are mixed with resin, a plasticisor added for elasticity, and the mixture is cold molded and baked in an electric oven. This bond is utilized in the larger of the high speed wheels used in foundries. With a rate of stock removal in direct proportion to the operating speed, these wheels are designed to run from 9,000 to 16,000 surface feet per minute.

GRAIN SIZE OF ABRASIVES. Abrasives are numerically classified as to size by passing the particles through screens of various mesh. The fineness of the particles is designated as grain and is indicated by the smallest size of screen mesh through which the particles will pass. *For example,* the grain numbered 36 is one that will pass through a screen which has 36 meshes to the linear inch. In a standard table of abrasive numbers, very coarse abrasives are given a low number and designations become coarse, medium fine, and very fine. Combinations of various size grits are also used in making grinding wheels, depending upon the particular requirements of the grinding operation.

GRADE. Grade refers to the hardness or softness of a wheel and is determined mostly by the strength of the bond used. Wheels whose abrasives tear out or break off easily are termed soft grade wheels, and wheels whose abrasives do not easily break away are known as hard grade wheels. Basically, hard wheels are used to grind soft materials, and soft wheels are used to grind hard materials. Grades are identified by letters, from C (soft) to Z (hard).

WHEEL SPEED. A wheel speed that is too slow wastes the abrasive of the wheel without getting the maximum performance from it, while an excessive speed may retard the cutting or possibly break the wheel. In other words, a wheel running slow acts softer than its rating, and a wheel running faster than its recommended speed acts harder than its rating. All wheels should be run at the speeds recommended by the manufacturer. If a different speed has to be used, a change of grade with the same type of wheel should be used.

Surface feet per minute (s.f.p.m.) is the speed in feet per minute at the outside edge or the periphery of the wheel. It depends upon the diameter of the wheel (D) in inches, the ratio (3.1416) of the circumference (C) to the diameter (D), and the revolutions per minute of the wheel (r.p.m.). Remember that inches must be converted to feet (1/12).

$$\text{S.F.P.M.} = \frac{3.1416 \times D \times \text{R.P.M.}}{12}$$

or

$$\text{S.F.P.M.} = \frac{C \times \text{R.P.M.}}{12}$$

If a wheel is hard and tends to heat or glaze, run it slower. If it is too soft, it can be made to hold its size longer by increasing its speed.

TABLE 39
RECOMMENDED WHEEL SPEEDS

	Surface Feet per Minute
Cylindrical Grinding	5,500 to 6,500
Internal Grinding	2,000 to 6,000
Snagging, Offhand Grinding (Vitrified Wheels)	5,000 to 6,000
Snagging, Rubber Bonded Wheels	7,500 to 9,500
Surface Grinding	4,000 to 6,000
Machine-Knife Grinding	3,500 to 4,000
Wet Tool Grinding	5,000 to 6,000
Cutlery Grinding	4,000 to 5,000
Grinding with Rubber or Shellac Cutting-Off Wheels	9,000 to 16,000

Caution: A crack may not always be noticeable, so it is a good precaution to test a wheel for soundness before starting it. This may be done by tapping the side lightly. If the wheel is sound it will ring clearly.

WORK SPEED. The speed of the work has an effect upon a grinding wheel and this should be considered in making the selection of the wheel. Fast work speed wears the wheel down faster than slower work speed. This becomes clear by considering the effect on each individual abrasive grain of the wheel. An increase in work speed presents more work to each grain per unit of time, increasing the load on the grain and its tendency to pull out sooner.

In general, we may conclude that the work speed should be proportional to the grade and speed of the wheel. It may vary from 50 to 100 feet per minute, depending on the character of the work. Except for special purposes, the surfaces of the wheel and the work pass in opposite directions at the cutting point.

SELECTION OF WHEELS. The proper selection of a grinding wheel is important. Several factors should be considered in wheel selection: the material to be ground, amount of stock to be removed, finish, arc of contact of wheel to work, work and wheel speeds, and the machine on which the wheel is to be used.

Arc of contact of the wheel to the work is a factor affecting the hardness of a grinding wheel. The larger the arc of contact, the longer the individual abrasive grain contacts the work and is subject to dislocation. Therefore, the smaller the angle of contact the softer the wheel acts. To compensate for this (assuming all conditions as shown in Fig. 3 are the

TABLE 40
SUGGESTED WHEELS FOR GRINDING

Suitable for	Material	Grain	Grade
External Cylindrical Grinding			
Good all-round wheels	Alundum	46	L
Best adapted to soft steel		36	L
Hardened steel	Aluminox or Alundum	46	K
Soft steel, small diam.		36	M*
Reamer, drills and general tool work		80	K
Hard steel, dry grinding		100	I
Cast iron and bronze	Crystolon	45	L
Wheels for Facing Shoulders			
Ordinary work	Aluminox	60	H or I
	Alundum	60	H or I
Fine finish	Aluminox or Alundum	80	I*
Wheels for Surface Grinding			
Hardened steel	Alundum or Aluminox	46	H
		46	G†
		60	F†
Hardened high speed steel or very thin pieces of hardened carbon steel	Aloxite	60	U
	Alundum or Aluminox	46	G
Cast iron	Carborundum or Crystolon	36	M
		36	J

*Elastic Wheel †Silicate Wheel

Suitable for	Material	Grain	Grade
Wheels for Internal Cylindrical Grinding			
Automobile cylinders	Carborundum	36	M to P
Automobile cylinders, roughing or fair finish	Carbolite	36	H to I
Automobile cylinders, fine finish		60	H

Wheels for Sharpening Cutters and End Mills

Cutter Material	Operation	Abrasive Material	Grade	Bond	Grain Size
High Speed Steel (regular)	Roughing	Aluminum Oxide	H to K	Vitrified	38 to 46
	Finishing	Aluminum Oxide	I to K	Vitrified	60 to 100
High Alloy High Speed Steel	Roughing	Aluminum Oxide	G to J	Vitrified	38 to 46
	Finishing	Aluminum Oxide	G to K	Vitrified	60 to 100
Cemented Carbides	Roughing	Silicon Carbide	G to K	Vitrified	60
		Diamond	N	Resinoid	100
	Finishing	Silicon Carbide	G-H	Vitrified	100
		Diamond	L-N	Resinoid	100-220

same) if an H wheel is right for A, an I wheel would be better for B, and a J wheel for C.

See Table 40 when selecting wheels for different types of grinding. In some instances it may be advisable to vary from the list in the table somewhat in the selection of a wheel for a particular job because of conditions applicable to that job alone. Otherwise, the wheels suggested should prove satisfactory for the normal uses indicated.

If any grinding wheel acts too hard, decreasing the wheel s.f.p.m. will make it appear softer. It is best to experiment or consult a wheel maker for assistance if problems are encountered.

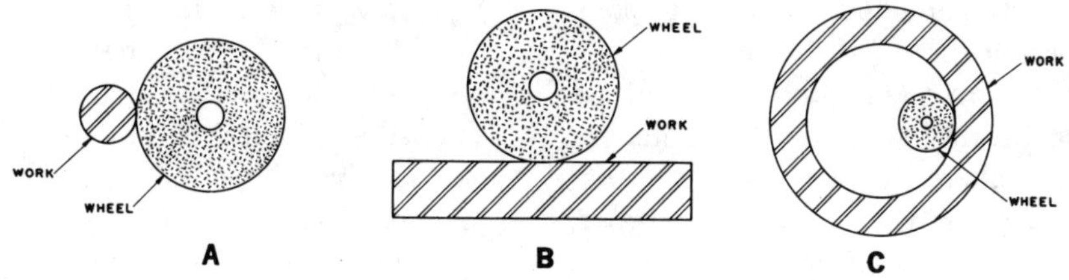

Figure 3. Arc of contact of wheel to work.

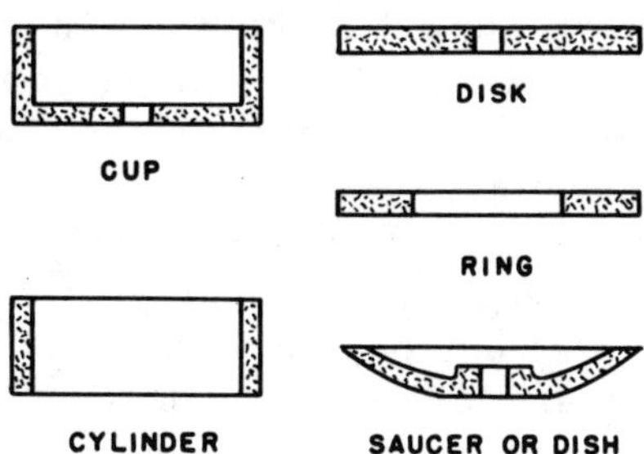

Figure 4. Grinding wheel shapes.

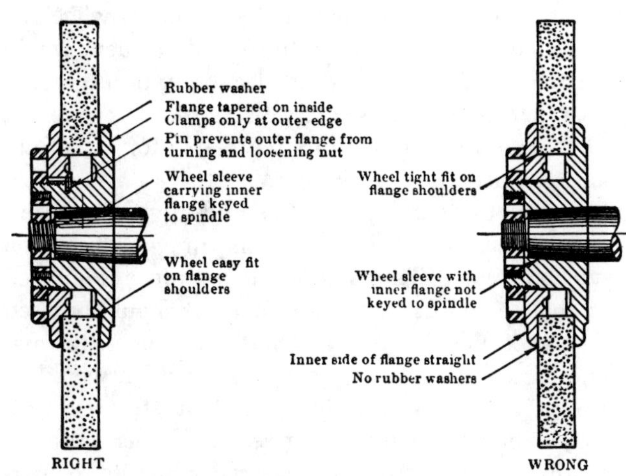

Figure 5. Right and wrong way to mount a grinding wheel.

Grinding Wheel Marking. All grinding wheel manufacturers conform to a system of marking which is standard throughout the industry. Basically the marking consists of letters and numbers, such as A-46 K5-V, although different manufacturers may add prefixes or suffixes to further identify their product.

In this system, the first letter (A above) indicates the kind of abrasive—A (aluminum oxide), C (silicon carbide), or D (diamond). The following number (46 above) gives the grain size—from 10 (coarse) to 600 (very fine). The next letter (K above) is the grade—from C (soft) to Z (hard). Its following number (5 above) gives the structure—from 0 (dense) to 16, and open. The last letter (V above) gives the type of bond—V (vitrified), R (rubber), B (resinoid), E (shellac), or M (metal).

Grinding Wheel Shapes. The type of grinding operation and work requirements frequently necessitate the use of other than a straight-sided wheel. The more common shapes, with their descriptive names, are shown in Fig. 4.

Mounting Wheels. A wheel should fit easily upon the wheel sleeve, yet not loosely, for if loose it cannot be accurately centered and is consequently out of balance. Paper should not be wrapped around the spindle to make a wheel fit when the hole is too large. On the other hand, when a wheel fits too tightly it should never be forced on a spindle, as it may crack. If the hole is only a slight amount undersize it can be scraped out easily; if lead bushed, a jackknife can be used to cut out enough metal to make the wheel fit easily on the spindle.

The flanges should be relieved on their inner sides so that they bear against the wheel only at the outer edge. (*See* Fig. 5.) The inner flange or sleeve should be keyed or otherwise fastened securely to the spindle, and the outer flange should be keyed to the wheel sleeve to prevent it from turning and loosening the clamping nut. Flanges that are straight on their inner sides should never be used, for the tightening of the clamping nut will cause them to become slightly convex, bringing the pressure near the center instead of distributing it over the entire surface of that portion of the wheel enclosed between the flanges. Where the pressure is so concentrated there is danger of the wheel breaking.

Frequent inspection of the flanges and clamping nut is important. If flanges become out of true or out of balance, they should not be used. Careful inspection is also necessary after a wheel has been broken, to guard against reusing damaged flanges.

Washers of leather, pulp, or rubber should be placed between the bearing surfaces of the flanges and the wheel. Some makers attach a ring of blotting paper to each side of their wheels for this purpose, but it is a good plan to use leather or rubber washers in addition.

The clamping nut should be tightened just enough to hold the wheel firmly in place, otherwise clamping strain may cause the wheel to crack.

BALANCE OF WHEELS. The balance of a wheel should be kept in mind when making a selection, as it is most essential that it run perfectly true without vibration. It will not run true if it is out of balance either from the lead core or from want of truing on the face. A wheel may also be out of balance from uneven density. In this case it cannot be corrected and a new wheel should be substituted.

TRUING AND DRESSING WHEELS. The terms truing and dressing are often incorrectly used with reference to the conditioning of grinding wheels. *Truing*, as the name implies, is the process of correcting any runout of the wheel surface that may exist when the wheel, mounted on a spindle, revolves about its axis. After truing, subsequent conditioning of the wheel surface is called *dressing*.

Great importance is attached by all makers to keeping grinding wheels true for the production and finish of work, for economy in wheel wear, and for safety to the operator. The diamond is always preferred for this purpose. It should always be mounted in the diamond holder and supported as close as possible to the wheel. The diamond should be inspected periodically to make sure that it is not loose or dull, and if dull it should be reset.

Dressing is the resurfacing of the wheel to bring forth new, clean abrasive cutting edges for improved and faster grinding. It is good practice to present a sharp corner of the diamond to the wheel. For *rough grinding*, the wheel should be dressed at rather coarse feed. For *fine finish grinding*, the wheel should be dressed at about 2 to 6 inches per minute. Wheel dressing is very important to secure fine finishes.

The grade of wheel and character of the work govern the frequency with which the wheel surface should be trued. Soft grade wheels are apt to become untrue more quickly than those of harder grades. On the other hand, there is a tendency to glaze on the part of hard grade wheels and this is corrected by dressing the surface.

A new wheel that runs out considerably first should be trued up at slow speed. Its speed can then be safely increased to that at which it is to be run. Then the face should be trued again, as it does not necessarily follow that the wheel will run true at high velocity even if it does at a slow one.

When truing grinding wheels of large diameter or wheels for cylindrical or surface grinding, the diamond must be held in a fixed tool post or bracket, never held in the hand. There should be a constant flow of water or coolant to keep the diamond cool and to avoid filling the air with dust. Wheels of smaller diameter, or those used for small tool or reamer grinding, may be trued by holding the diamond in the hand.

SAFETY PRECAUTIONS. There is always the likelihood of grinding wheels bursting because of flaws, too high speed, being thrust into the work too abruptly, or faulty mounting on the spindle. For this reason, standard grinding machines are fitted with a guard that covers the wheel to prevent injury to the operator and damage to the machine or surrounding objects in case of accident. When a wheel bursts beneath one of these guards there is comparatively little chance for it to do any damage. The pieces usually fall harmlessly to the machine or floor. Under no condition should the grinding wheel be operated without a guard. In case of accident where this has been done, there is absolutely no excuse. A complete coverage of safety precautions is given in "The American Standard Safety Code for Use, Care and Protection of Grinding Wheels."

USE OF COOLANT. Coolant is used in grinding principally to keep the work cool and prevent distortion which results if the temperature of a piece is allowed to change while it is being ground. It should be used wherever possible when grinding. When the machinist is finish grinding to precise limits, it would be well for him to keep in mind that steel expands .000006 in. per inch per degree F. In other words, if a 3 in. diameter shaft is measured while its temperature is 10°F. above room temperature, it will be smaller by $.000006 \times 3 \times 10 = .00018$ in. when it cools off. Considering the fact that today's production frequently calls for grinding small parts to limits of $\pm$ .000050 in. or less, he should never forget the importance of temperature.

Coolants also serve to wash the particles of metal and loose abrasive from the surface of the wheel, keeping it clean and free-cutting. A copious volume should be presented at the point of contact of the wheel and the work. In surface grinding, coolant should be used wherever there is much hardened work to be ground, although it can often be dispensed with in grinding cast iron. (*See* Chap. 23 for recommended coolants.)

Polishing Abrasives

When machining processes are completed and the workpiece is finished to size, there will always be grooves or irregularities, however small, on the surface of the metal, due to cutting or abrasion. The average depths of these scorings can be measured in microinches (millionths), and due to the advance of modern technology such degrees of finish are becoming more frequently specified. Polishing is the process of leveling off the microscopic *hills and valleys* on the surface of the metal, and as such is quite different from machine finishing or superfinishing in that dimensional accuracy is not sought.

For polishing metal, the most common abrasives are emery, corundum, alundum, carborundum, crocus, and rottenstone. Emery, rottenstone, and corundum are minerals. Alundum and carborundum are made in an electric furnace by subjecting certain mixtures to extremely high temperature. Crocus is an oxide of iron and is used in the form of bricks or glued to a cloth. It is a very mild abrasive but produces an extremely high polish.

Grading Polishing Abrasives. Whether in their natural state or from the electric furnace, polishing abrasives are first crushed and ground, then passed through sieves of varying fineness and graded accordingly. Abrasive grades are numbered according to the mesh per inch through which they pass, from coarse to fine: 10, 12, and so on up to 250 and flour.

Emery Cloth. The grades of emery cloth are indicated by the same numbers and letters that apply to loose abrasive. They range from coarse to fine: 40 to 120, F and FF. For work having a large roughly filed surface use 46 or 54; then finer grades until the desired finish is obtained. If the work has been filed smoothly use 60 and 90 and finish off with 120 and flour emery.

Grinding Machines

The process of grinding, to produce very accurate dimensions or fine finishes on precise work, can be generally separated into two types of operations—production of (1) curved or (2) flat surfaces.

Cylindrical grinding machines, including the many variations for specialized work—internal, disc, centerless, crankshaft, and the like—produce curved surfaces. *Surface* grinding machines are used for plane or flat surfaces.

Cylindrical Grinding Machines. Cylindrical grinding machines include the *universal* grinding machine and the *plain* grinding machine. The universal is for all-round external, internal, and conical work, whereas the plain grinder is used for production of straight and tapered cylindrical parts in quantities and is essentially a manufacturing machine.

Universal Grinding Machine

The original universal grinding machine was developed to meet the need for a machine to grind needle bars, foot bars, and shafts for sewing machines. Early machines for such work had been constructed by mounting an emery wheel on the carriage of a lathe.

However, the need of a machine designed particularly for grinding was apparent, and in 1876 the first universal grinding machine was developed by Brown & Sharpe Mfg. Co. and exhibited at the Philadelphia Centennial Exposition.

The universal grinding machine is now recognized as an indispensable tool in a well-equipped shop, and it has superseded the lathe to a great extent for finishing to exact measurements.

Like the lathe, it is provided with a headstock and footstock for rotating work between centers. The headstock and footstock are mounted on a reciprocating table which travels the work across the face of the grinding wheel. To permit grinding tapers, the upper half of the table swivels on a central pivot to the desired angle. Cross feed is obtained by forward movement of the slide on which the wheel is mounted.

The headstock and grinding wheel pivot may be clamped at various angles, thereby permitting the grinding of abrupt tapers, discs, and a great variety of toolroom and production work.

Universal grinding machines also incorporate a fixture carrying a small diameter high speed grinding wheel for internal grinding of work held on the headstock.

Where the volume of production grinding warrants, standard attachments such as wheel truing and balancing devices, back rests, collets and magnetic chucks, automatic cycles, spark timing, and sizing arrangements can materially reduce production costs.

The various universal grinding machine power movements and feeds are obtained by mechanical or hydraulic means and manual adjustments are indicated by accurately graduated dials.

Concentric and accurate grinding is greatly dependent on the preciseness of the headstock and grinding wheel bearings. These may be of plain, antifriction, or hydrostatic type.

LIVE CENTER GRINDING. While accurate, round work can be prepared with perfect centers and good work center holes, it takes a nearly perfect headstock to produce truly round, live center, or chuck held finished work. However, headstocks with hydrostatic bearings for their spindles have been found very successful in rotating work around a true axis without deviations which cause errors in roundness. Pockets of high pressure oil support the spindle and oppose any displacement of the spindle from its designed position. Work accuracy to .000010 in. limits is possible with a hydrostatic headstock.

SETTING THE TABLE. To set the table for grinding straight work, the zero lines must be set to coincide with the corresponding lines on both the headstock graduations and the table swivel graduations. Regardless of how carefully these adjustments are made, it will be necessary to put a piece of work between the centers, and after taking a light cut along its whole length, carefully measure the work at both ends with a micrometer caliper. If there is a difference in diameter, make a slight adjustment of the table by turning the adjusting screw at the end. Continue this correction until the work is of the same diameter at both ends.

For slight tapers, the table may be set by means of the swivel adjustment and the table graduations, but inasmuch as these graduations can only be approximate as to accuracy, a standard taper ring gage or similar device is necessary to test the taper for accuracy.

To eliminate the customary *repeated trial and correction* method for grinding exact tapers or straight shafts, the "Electralign" provides a straightforward means for electronically securing precise settings of the swivel table and greatly speeds production.

ABRUPT TAPERS. Where the work is held in a chuck on the headstock spindle, *abrupt tapers* can be ground by swiveling the headstock. When the work is between the centers, an abrupt taper can be obtained by setting the wheel slide at an angle. In the case of two abrupt tapers on a piece, both headstock and wheel slide should be swiveled, each serving to grind a taper. Work held in a chuck or on a face plate can be efficiently face ground by turning the headstock 90 degrees, or at right angles, to the bed ways. With such a setup, power cross feed and table travel can be employed.

SPEED OR TRAVEL OF TABLE. The width of the wheel face and the quality of the finish desired should determine the table speed. For roughing large work on a large machine, use a travel of one-half to three-fourths of the width of the wheel face for each revolution of the work. On less sturdy machines this may be modified to one-third of the width of the face of the wheel. A highly accurate finish may be obtained with a travel of one-fourth to one-third.

FEED OF WHEEL. For roughing, the depth of cut may be .001 in. to .004 in. at each table reversal; for finishing, from .0001 in. to .0005 in. at each reversal. From practice it will be possible to determine whether a cut is light or heavy from the volume of the stream of sparks that issues from the cut.

ALLOWANCE FOR CYLINDRICAL GRINDING. Work that is not to be hardened may be rough turned .006 in. to .010 in. large. Work that may be particularly large, or long and slender, or easily sprung, should have an allowance of from .020 in. to .030 in. When parts are being rough ground it is well to grind them to within .002 in. or .003 in. before finishing. Using this method the wheel has only to be dressed occasionally.

ALLOWANCES FOR FITS. The allowances given in Table 41 are recommended for use in the manufacture of machine parts, to produce satisfactory commercial work. These are for ordinary conditions; for special cases it may be necessary to increase or decrease the allowances given in the table.

CARE AND LUBRICATION OF GRINDING MACHINES. All wearing surfaces should be carefully guarded and kept well supplied with oil. Many units have sealed lubrication and need no attention, but automatic lubricating systems should be checked periodically and only proper high grade oil used. Center points should be kept well oiled and true and the whole machine kept as clean as possible.

The extremely close fitting of parts on many modern, superprecise machines requires lubricants which must meet exacting specifications. Be sure to follow the machine manufacturer's recommendations particularly on spindle and table way oils.

Plain Grinding Machine

The plain grinding machine is essentially a manufacturing machine tool, and as such is made very rigid to stand up under heavy cuts. As flexibility for

TABLE 41

ALLOWANCES FOR FITS

The allowances given in the table are recommended for use in the manufacture of machine parts, to produce satisfactory commercial work. For special cases, it may be necessary to increase or decrease the allowances given in the table.

Diameter, Inches	Allowances, Inches
Running Fits for Shafts — Speeds Under 600 R.P.M. — Ordinary Working Conditions	
Up to ½	−0.0005 to −0.001
½ to 1	−0.00075 to −0.0015
1 to 2	−0.0015 to −0.0025
2 to 3½	−0.002 to −0.003
3½ to 6	−0.0025 to −0.004
Running Fits for Shafts — Speeds Over 600 R.P.M. — Heavy Pressure — Working Conditions Severe	
Up to ½	−0.0005 to −0.001
½ to 1	−0.001 to −0.002
1 to 2	−0.002 to −0.003
2 to 3½	−0.003 to −0.004
3½ to 6	−0.004 to −0.005
Sliding Fits for Shafts with Gears, Clutches, or Similar Parts which must be Free to Slide	
Up to ½	−0.0005 to −0.001
½ to 1	−0.00075 to −0.0015
1 to 2	−0.0015 to −0.0025
2 to 3½	−0.002 to −0.003
3½ to 6	−0.0025 to −0.004
Standard Fits for Light Service where Part is Keyed to Shaft and Clamped Endwise — No Fitting	
Up to ½	Standard to −0.00025
½ to 3½	Standard to −0.0005
3½ to 6	Standard to −0.00075
Standard Fits with Play Eliminated — Parts Should Assemble Readily — Some Fitting and Selecting may be Required	
Up to ½	Standard to +0.00025
½ to 3½	Standard to +0.0005
3½ to 6	Standard to +0.00075
Driving Fits for Permanent Assembly of Parts so Located that Driving cannot be done readily	
Up to ½	Standard to +0.00025
½ to 1	+0.00025 to +0.0005
1 to 2	+0.0005 to +0.00075
2 to 6	+0.0005 to +0.001
Driving Fits for Permanent Assembly and Severe Duty and where there is Ample Room for Driving	
Up to 2	+0.0005 to +0.001
2 to 3½	+0.00075 to +0.00125
3½ to 6	+0.001 to +0.0015
Forced Fits for Permanent Assembly and Very Severe Service — Hydraulic Press Used for Larger Parts	
Up to ½	+0.00075 to +0.001
½ to 1	+0.001 to +0.002
1 to 2	+0.002 to +0.003
2 to 3½	+0.003 to +0.004
3½ to 6	+0.004 to +0.005

grinding a wide variety of work is not required, neither headstock nor wheel slide is designed to swivel, and only straight and outside taper work can be performed. Otherwise the principal parts are similar to the universal grinding machine.

Where the face of the grinding wheel is wider than the surface being ground, *plunge* or straight-in feed grinding, with the table stationary, is often used. A *reciprocating spindle* (incorrectly called oscillating) moves the wheel endwise back and forth a short distance as it advances into the work. This breaks up the wheel marks and permits better finish.

BACK RESTS. Back rests are necessary fixtures for supporting slender work so that vibration will be reduced and a greater depth of cut made possible.

THE PLAIN BACK REST. The plain back rest is used for short or small work and employs bronze shoes in contact with the rotating surface of the work.

THE UNIVERSAL BACK REST. Universal in all its movements, this back rest is capable of the most delicate adjustment to maintain contact with and support the work. Usually when grinding long slender pieces, one universal back rest is used for each six diameters of length.

THE CENTER REST. A center rest is an accessory to support small diameter work that is liable to spring under grinding pressure. It is used in the same way as a steady rest on an engine lathe.

INTERNAL GRINDING. As the name implies, *internal grinding* is the operation of grinding straight or tapered holes smooth and true, in work rotated on the headstock of a universal or universal and tool grinding machine (or specialized internal grinding machine). When this kind of work is done on a universal grinder, the attachment swings down and is bolted to the wheel platen. To obtain efficient surface speeds for the small diameter grinding wheels, the spindle speeds are necessarily high—100,000 r.p.m. or more where hydrostatic spindles are used.

WHEELS FOR INTERNAL GRINDING. Rigidity is difficult to obtain for the spindle in this operation and consequently there is necessity for reducing to a minimum the pressure of the grinding wheel on the work (using as large wheel diameter as possible with consequent maximum area of wheel contact). We must use softer wheels for internal grinding than for external work. Most commonly used are vitrified wheels 1/4 in. to 2 1/2 in. diameter, and 1/4 in. to 3/8 in. face; numbers 120, 90, 80, 70, and 60; grades J, K, 1/4, 1/2, and 1. Elastic wheels are recommended on brass.

MAGNETIC CHUCK. The *magnetic chuck* is frequently used to hold the work on surface or universal grinding machines. These rectangular or rotary magnetic chucks are of two types—electromagnetic and permanent magnet. Permanent magnet chucks have the advantages of electromagnetic chucks but do not require electric current, as they are constructed with permanent magnets. The magnets are of a special alloy, have a strong holding power, and last indefinitely. A simple 180 degree movement of a crank or turn of a key holds or releases the work.

UNIVERSAL AND TOOL GRINDING MACHINE. The universal and tool grinding machine may be regarded as the true toolroom or general purpose grinding machine. It can do external, internal, face, form, and surface grinding with standard equipment and its many adaptable attachments. For the shop with milling cutters to sharpen, but with insufficient volume to warrant a cutter sharpening machine, the universal and tool grinder can be used to sharpen all the regular types of milling cutters. Frequently this type of machine is used as a single-purpose form tool grinding machine by those who have batteries of automatic screw machines. When so arranged all parts not needed for form grinding are omitted.

The machine is very similar to a universal grinding machine with the addition of vertical adjustment of the grinding wheel. Accurate settings are easily obtained, facilitating a wide variety of set-ups.

This versatile machine is adaptable to practically any kind of grinding job that may arise.

Surface Grinding Machine

The grinding of flat surfaces was originally performed with a grinding wheel attached to a planer. Most modern surface grinders utilize the same principle of a reciprocating table traversing under the grinding wheel. There is also a rotary-type machine, known as the vertical spindle, which mounts the work on a rotating table and carries it under the vertically mounted wheel.

Fine surface finishes and high accuracy are obtainable on surface grinding machines. They have considerable stock removing ability, and the heavier machines can finish right from the rough casting.

Horizontal Spindle Surface Grinding Machine. A horizontal spindle surface grinding machine with magnetic chuck is usually found on both toolroom operations and production work. It is exceedingly accurate and easy to set up and operate.

The table reciprocates under the rotating grinding wheel, feeding a small amount transversely at the end of each stroke. The depth of cut is obtained by vertical adjustment or down feed of the grinding wheel.

A steady, continuous transverse feed provides for wheel truing and dressing.

Vertical Spindle Surface Grinding Machine. Work mounted on the rotating table of the vertical spindle surface grinder is carried under the end face of the grinding wheel. Several speeds are provided for rotating the table, which also has a crosswise feed. Depth of cut is controlled by the position of the wheel which can be raised or lowered.

The coolant flows from the center of the wheel and is distributed by centrifugal force between the wheel and the work.

Some vertical spindle surface grinders are made with a reciprocating table.

Speeds and Feeds. Wheels on planer-type surface grinders are usually operated at a surface speed of from 5000 to 6000 feet per minute; those on the rotary machines range from 4000 to 4500 r.p.m. The work speed may be up to 125 f.p.m. for the planer type and 90 f.p.m. for the rotary.

For rough grinding, fast work speeds and coarse feeds are used. For finish grinding, use slow work speeds and fine feeds.

Coarse, soft grinding wheels usually are most satisfactory, the degree of softness depending upon the work and type of machine.

Cutter Grinding. Milling cutters and other cutting tools are readily sharpened on a universal or universal and tool grinding machine. Where the amount of work warrants, a cutter grinding machine is an economical investment.

Grinding Cutter Tooth Relief. Both disc wheels and cup wheels are used for sharpening cutters. The disc wheel, which is perhaps used more commonly, leaves a slight concavity on the land, whereas the cup wheel produces a flat clearance or land. Generally, this slight difference is not important, although one advantage claimed for cup wheel sharpening is a better finish.

With a Disc Wheel. Sharpening a cutter mounted with teeth facing downward, relief is obtained back of the cutting edges by having the center of the cutter below the horizontal plane of the axis of the wheel, as shown in A, Fig. 6.

When the teeth face upward, as shown in B, Fig. 6, the center of the cutter should be slightly above the center of the wheel. The dotted center lines illustrate this. The tooth rest should be on the horizontal center of the cutter.

With a Cup Wheel. The amount of offset of the wheel depends upon the diameter of the cutter being ground. The tooth rest is set either above or below the horizontal center of the cutter, depending upon the direction the teeth face (C and D, Fig. 6).

A and C, Fig. 6 show that the generated heat would be going toward the cutting edge. B and D, Fig. 6 show the heat going toward the heel or heavy section of the tooth. B and D, Fig. 6 are preferred because there is much less danger of burning or softening the cutting teeth.

The Best Relief Angle. The recommended relief angle varies in accordance with the cutter diameter. The relief angle for a cutter of 1/16 in. diameter would be 22 degrees, whereas the relief angle for cutters 3 1/2 in. in diameter and over is 4 degrees. The width of land should not be allowed to get so wide that the heel rubs against the work. A new type of

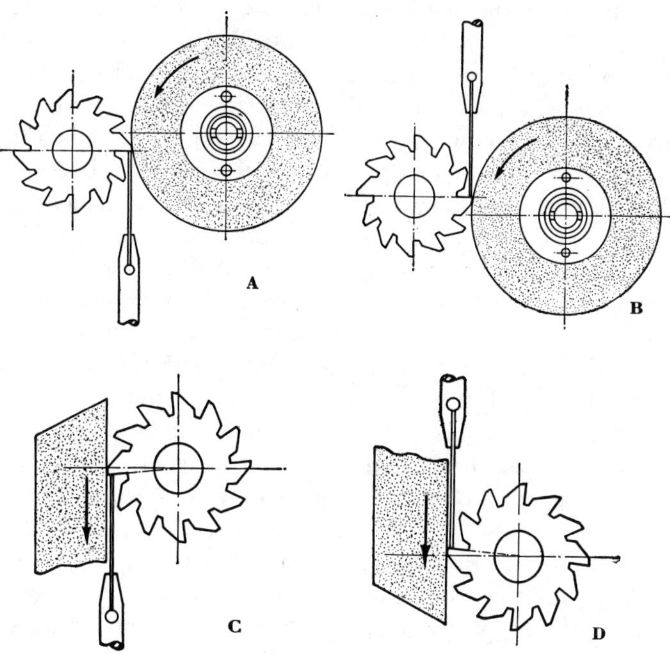

Figure 6. Position of the disc or cup wheel with relation to cutter when grinding reliefs.

tooth form having *eccentric relief* is common on end mills. By removing metal back of the land, it reduces interference problems at the heel. This style of relief can be applied only to cutters with helical flutes. A plain wheel either swung around or trued to an appropriate angle will generate eccentric relief lands. The end or side teeth should be ground slightly concave to prevent drag. Too much relief will increase chipping and chatter while cutting.

There are several ways to check the amount of relief. One simple method is to measure the drop in thousandths of an inch in the width of the land and, by reference to a table, determine the relief. This can be done by two dial indicators, one to measure rotation, the other to measure the drop or clearance (Fig. 7). The cutter should be mounted in bench centers to provide easy means of rotation under these indicators.

Figure 8 shows a "Tri-Mike" used to measure 3-flute cutter quickly and accurately when sharpening.

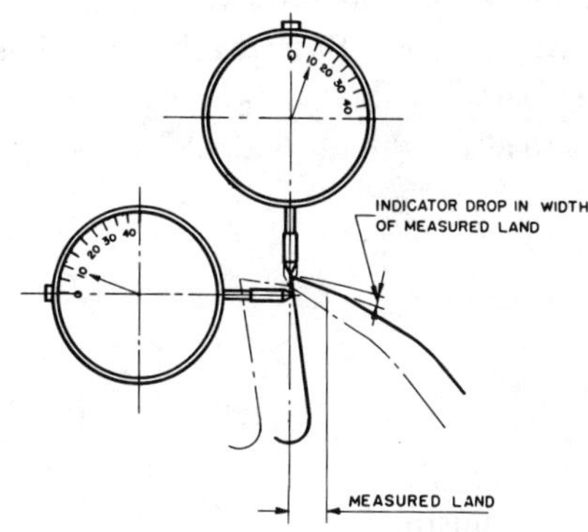

Figure 7. Checking amount of relief of a cutter.

Other Grinding Processes

Among many processes coming under the general field of grinding, the following are most frequently encountered.

CENTERLESS GRINDING. Many cylindrical parts, such as automobile pistons and shafts, either straight or tapered, can be effectively ground by the centerless

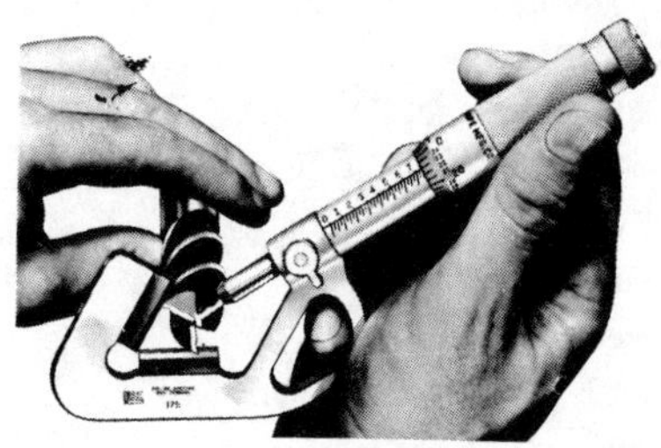

Figure 8. Tri-mike measures three-flute cutters quickly and accurately when sharpening.

method which does not require that the work be mounted on centers.

The work is supported on a work rest between the grinding wheel and a regulating wheel which can be inclined to feed the work longitudinally at the desired rate. The peripheral speed of the regulating wheel is adjustable to impart uniform rotation and proper peripheral speed to the work. Various adaptations permit centerless grinding of tapered parts, those having shoulders and even internal grinding of cylindrical parts having holes.

GRINDING GEAR TEETH. Grinding gear teeth is a generating process for finishing hardened gear teeth by grinding using the same generating principle as in gear cutting. As the gear is rolled past the face of the revolving grinding wheel, the entire working surface of a tooth is ground.

LAPPING. Lapping is a form of refined grinding. It is resorted to for final finishing of either hardened or unhardened cylindrical or flat surfaces, particularly where fine finish and extremely accurate size are desired. The lapping tool or lap, of suitable size and form, is made of some soft metal such as cast iron or copper; it must be softer than the metal it is finishing. Very fine abrasive flour is made into a paste by mixing with lard oil or vaseline. When the lap is coated with this compound and manually or mechanically rubbed against the work, the lap becomes *charged* with the abrasive which is imbedded into its surface and cuts the harder work material.

Lapping can produce exceptional quality of finish and an extreme degree of precision.

HONING. Honing is a process applied to the cylindrical surfaces of bores to generate a true cylindrical form to precise dimensional limits and to secure the desired surface finish. Abrasive stones spaced around the periphery of a circular head are expanded to bear evenly against the bore under adjustable pressure. A combined rotary and reciprocating motion of the hone generates a true cylindrical form.

SCREW THREAD GRINDING. Very precise screw threads are produced by thread grinding. The process corects any distortions which may occur in heat treating and grinds threads highly accurate in form and lead. The face of the grinding wheel is formed to the shape of the thread. As the screw is rotated and traversed by a lead screw past the grinding wheel, the screw thread is accurately formed.

Internal threads are ground by the same principle.

TUMBLING. Tumbling is the process whereby small parts are cleaned or given a desired surface finish. A *tumbling* barrel is used, which is rotated at an inclined angle to keep the parts *tumbling*. Sawdust, beach sand, soda water, or some other cleaning agent may be used, depending on what result is desired.

Chapter 21

Tool and Die Making

Many a worker nowadays is starting on his way to become a toolmaker—and possibly eventually a foreman, superintendent, or outstanding design engineer. This will not happen suddenly, overnight, for it takes years to acquire knowledge through experience, skill through practice, and engineering ingenuity through the solving of many problems. These qualifications the toolmaker must have, but with them he is a king among skilled workers—above all others in the metal-working field, in prestige as well as pay.

Qualifications of a Toolmaker

The first-class toolmaker must be so well qualified that he is capable of operating all the machine tools, not only in maintenance shops, but in experimental laboratories, toolrooms, and production departments as well. He will be called upon to build the necessary cutting tools, jigs, fixtures, and gages required for the production department, and to build special machinery parts and other complicated mechanisms necessary to construct, alter, or modify present-day high speed or automatic devices used in manufacturing.

The qualified toolmaker will be required to:

1. Effect temporary or permanent repairs to machinery and other devices which may be special and complicated, designed and built to do a specific production task. Such work is of utmost importance to the management of a production operation;

2. Work closely with the engineering department in the making of prototype mechanisms, their assembly, debugging, and initial operations to create specialized equipment needed in modern manufacturing plants. This is of prime importance in meeting the incessant demands of industry for greater production at lower cost.

Education

Other qualifications of the toolmaker are that he have an education equivalent to the completion of a first-rate high school. He must have a good basic knowledge of drafting and engineering drawing techniques and be able to understand clearly and completely the language of blueprints, sketches, and specifications defining the work he is to perform. A good working knowledge of geometry, trigonometry, and other mathematics is also necessary.

Skill

The ability to read and set fine measuring tools quickly and accurately is very important. Part of his work will be in the range of one-thousandth, often it will be in the realm of one ten-thousandth part of an inch and, at times his work will be measured to millionths. Needless to say, reliable accuracy can be obtained in this fine range only with considerable skill and meticulous care. These conditions constantly test the toolmaker's ingenuity, sense of accuracy, and infinite capacity for taking pains in his work.

Knowledge

It is easy to understand that the toolmaker must possess a thorough concept of the principles involved in all mechanical devices with which he is working. He must also possess the knowledge of the fundamentals of all machine tools and inspection devices so that he can apply himself resourcefully. These requirements are achieved only through rigid training, personal study, and experience.

After completing an apprenticeship in the general shops, the machinist desiring to become a toolmaker really starts another apprenticeship in the toolroom.

The novice toolmaker is first permitted to perform the simpler operations of toolmaking. As skill and experience are acquired he is entrusted with more intricate work, until such time as he is able to master any work which may come into his department. A good toolmaker is forever improving both his workmanship and his knowledge of tools and toolmaking. It is only after many years of such work and study that he may consider himself an accomplished *all-around* expert toolmaker.

The toolmaker has a responsibility to management, for without ingenious toolmaking no efficient production line would exist. He has responsibility to his fellow workers to be safety-conscious, not only to himself in his work, but to others when the results of his work are passed on for someone else to use.

Toolmaker's Kit

The toolmaker takes great pride in his kit of tools. Almost invariably he will have a neat wooden or metallic case, in which are fitted various drawers to keep a well balanced assortment of tools. In addition to the usual tools of the machinist, there will be found universal bevels, protractors, steel squares, toolmakers' knife-edge straight edges, vernier calipers, both micrometer and vernier height and depth gages, scribers, parallels, scales, and various other tools and gages adapted to any particular work upon which he may be employed. A test indicator, vee blocks and clamps, toolmaker's vise, angle plates, toolmaker's clamps, and locating buttons are some of the other more common tools usually found in the first-class toolmaker's kit. A good toolmaker gives his tools the best of care and is constantly upgrading them with new or improved tools.

Layout and Machining

A toolmaker must be extremely accurate in laying out his work prior to machining. The layout is the foundation and it is basic that the toolmaker's surface plate technique and handling of height gages and verniers permit him to determine and balance the excess stock on his workpiece. The layout for machining must be clear and precise, as it is used for constant reference. While the toolmaker proceeds with the layout of the workpiece, he mentally pictures the necessary operations to be performed through to its completion, including basic heat treating and welding, although they are usually handled by specialists in the field.

Jigs and Fixtures

Making jigs and fixtures is an important part of a toolmaker's duties. Generally the distinction between jigs and fixtures is that *jigs* are special devices for the purpose of supporting work and guiding tools, so that work done on numerous similar pieces will be uniform, independently of the skill of the operator. *Fixtures* are devices that support and hold work with no particular guidance of the cutting tools. The toolmaker has ample opportunity to display his ingenuity in devising various arrangements for clamping and holding work.

Small Cutting Tools

Because a toolmaker may be called upon to make a special reamer, drill, milling cutter, and the like, a thorough understanding of the design and use of these tools is of considerable aid in producing a good practical tool. A knowledge of cutting angles and clearances and their effects on various metals is most important. The various shapes and types will have become well known to a toolmaker due to his prior experience as an accomplished machinist.

Gage Making

An important specialty of toolmaking is gage making, which requires considerable experience in precision grinding and lapping. For production gaging, there are many standard commercial inspection gages available, such as indicators, ring gages, plug gages, and the like, but quite often a special gage will do the job much more effectively on the production line. The toolmaker engaged in gage making must be critically precise, as his results will control the accuracy of production. He is working to very fine tolerances, so he must be able to use all types of standard grinding machines together with specialized optical contour grinders and comparators. He must also be skilled in fine honing and lapping necessary to obtain the most critical precision.

Die Making

Die making is a branch of toolmaking dealing with the cutting, forming, and embossing of material through the use of stamping dies. The field is very broad, covering thin to thick metals, and from small intricate watch parts to large automotive bodies. Cutting, forming, embossing, piercing, notching, blanking, louvering, and coining are some of the operations performed with dies. Dies are made in many types for specific needs, from single operation dies through compound, progressive, and transfer dies, all of which may become so intricate they will tax the abilities of the finest of die makers. The die maker must be well versed in the actions of materials processed in dies, as well as being an experienced toolmaker. Comprehensive publications on die making may be found in most libraries.

The toolmaker is often an instructor and group leader. Because of his broad knowledge, the toolmaker is a likely candidate for promotion into the supervisory field. He is a master craftsman because he takes great pride in his work and results, and he merits all the admiration he invariably receives.

Chapter 22

Gears and Gear Cutting

If this entire book were devoted to the subject of gear design, it would be inadequate to cover the subject. Our purpose, therefore, is to acquaint you with the very simplest of theory as well as fundamentals of gears, their elements and manufacture, as a foundation upon which to build further knowledge of this important metalworking practice.

Kinds of Gears

There are four kinds of gears ordinarily cut in a machine shop: (1) spur gears (including racks and internal gears), (2) helical or spiral gears, (3) bevel gears, and (4) worm gears. (*See* Fig. 1.) Spur and straight-tooth bevel gears are the most common types made in the general machine shop, so we shall confine most of our reference to these two types.

Spiral bevel gears and hypoid gears (Fig. 1) are variations of bevel gears and are described later in this chapter. Special equipment is required to produce them.

Figure 1. Types of gears.

Gear Teeth

For many years there were two recognized forms of teeth in spur gearing—the involute (single curve form), and the cycloidal (double curve form). These forms permit gears to run together smoothly and with constant relative velocity. At the present time the involute form is used almost exclusively, and therefore a simplified explanation of the involute principle is given here. (*See* Fig. 2.)

The Involute Principle. The involute curve is simple, easy to construct, and has characteristics that are obvious. Unfortunately it is not equally obvious and simple just how these characteristics operate on a functioning gear train.

An *involute* is defined as a curve traced by any point of a perfectly flexible inextensible thread kept taut as it is unwound from another curve. In I, Fig. 3 we have such a figure abcdef traced by the end of a thread unwinding from a stationary circle ABCDEF. The important thing to note here is that Bb, Cc, Dd, Ee, and Ff are all tangent to the circle, and meet the involute abc def at right angles at points, b, c, d, e, f, respectively.

Now, considering II, Fig. 3, let the thread hang vertically while the circle unwinds it by advancing progressively from positions A, B, C, D, E, F. The points a, b, c, d, e, f on the thread will then generate a series of involutes, all of which meet their respective radii along line af at right angles.

Therefore, *the contact surface of gear teeth constructed to conform with these involute curves will meet the line of force af at right angles wherever they touch or intersect.*

The application of this principle is shown in the cross section of gear and rack, III, Fig. 3. Involute cut gear teeth always act at right angles to line of force af, even though for mechanical reasons in ac-

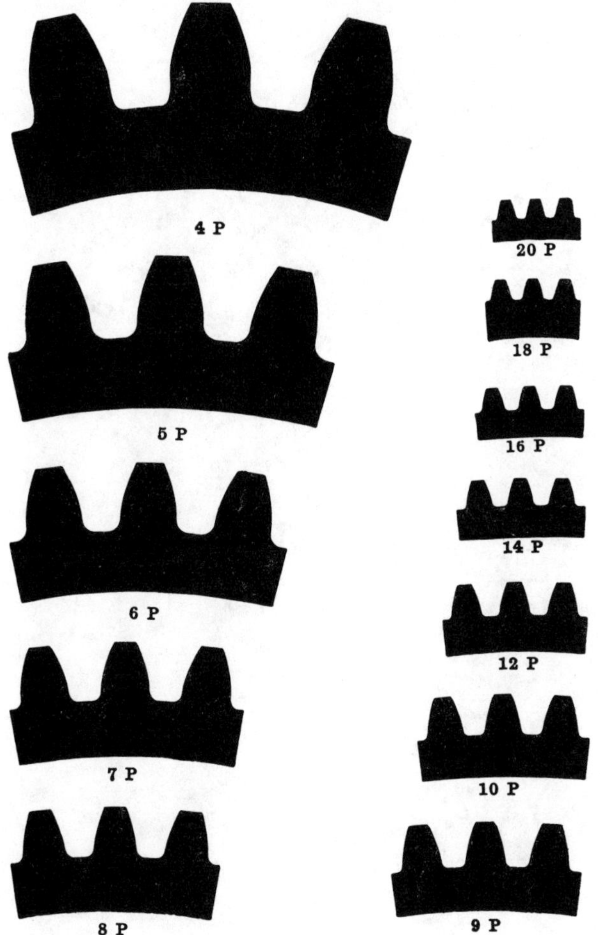

Figure 2. Comparative sizes of involute gear teeth.

tual practice they are modified by a pressure angle.

Advantages of the involute form are that it presents fewer difficulties when cutting; also that it is the only form of tooth which permits center distances to be varied slightly and still have the gears transmit uniform motion.

Pressure Angles and Undercutting. Most modern gears are produced by the hobbing or shaping method. In either case, these are processes of cutting as though the cutter and the gear teeth were in mesh. (*See* III, Fig. 3.) Consider the rack as a cutter with cutting action vertical to the plane of the printed page. After each shaving cut the gear cutter (rack) and the gear blank (gear) will progressively feed along the pitch line af, automatically forming an involute tooth.

If the number of teeth in the gear is very small and/or the circular pitch excessive, it is easy to see that the cutter will undercut the gear tooth too much. A natural undercut is shown at left in Fig. 4, occurring in the ranges of low numbers of teeth.

When one gear drives another, pressure is exerted at the point of tooth contact along a straight line which is tangent to the base circle of each gear. The angle between this line of action and a line perpendicular to the center line of the two gears is known as the pressure angle of the gearing.

The involute form is commonly made with its pressure angle varying from 14 1/2° to 20°. Figure 4 illustrates two involute forms with different pressure angles. With a 14 1/2° pressure angle, undercut will be present on all gears 31 teeth and under. As the pressure angle increases the undercut is less, so that with a 20° pressure angle the undercut starts at 17 teeth.

The involute form of gear is made to both standard and short depths. Teeth of short depths are made in several proportions and are called *stub teeth.* Whether gears are produced by hobbing or shaping, one tool, either a hob or a shaper, will cut all numbers of teeth. Because of the generating action, the shape of all teeth will be correct even though they vary widely in form from small pinions to large gears, and they will all run together in a gear train.

It is not possible to mill with a rotary cutter the gear tooth shapes in many gears with small numbers of teeth, due to the undercut form.

Terminology of Gear Tooth

Diameter, when applied to gears, is usually understood to mean the pitch diameter. However, outside diameter is quite frequently used and it is good practice to make certain which of the diameters is intended.

Diametral Pitch is the number of teeth to each inch of the pitch diameter.

Example—If a gear has 40 teeth and the pitch diameter is 4 in., there are 10 teeth to each inch of the pitch diameter, and the diametral pitch is 10.

Diametral Pitch Required, circular pitch given. Divide 3.1416 by the circular pitch.

Example—If the circular pitch is 2 in., divide 3.1416 by 2, and the quotient, 1.5708, is the diametrical pitch.

Diametral Pitch Required, number of teeth and outside diameter given. Add 2 to the number of teeth and divide by the outside diameter.

Example—If the number of teeth is 40, and diameter of blank is 10 1/2 in., add 2 to the number of teeth, making 42, and divide by 10 1/2. The quotient 4 is the diametral pitch.

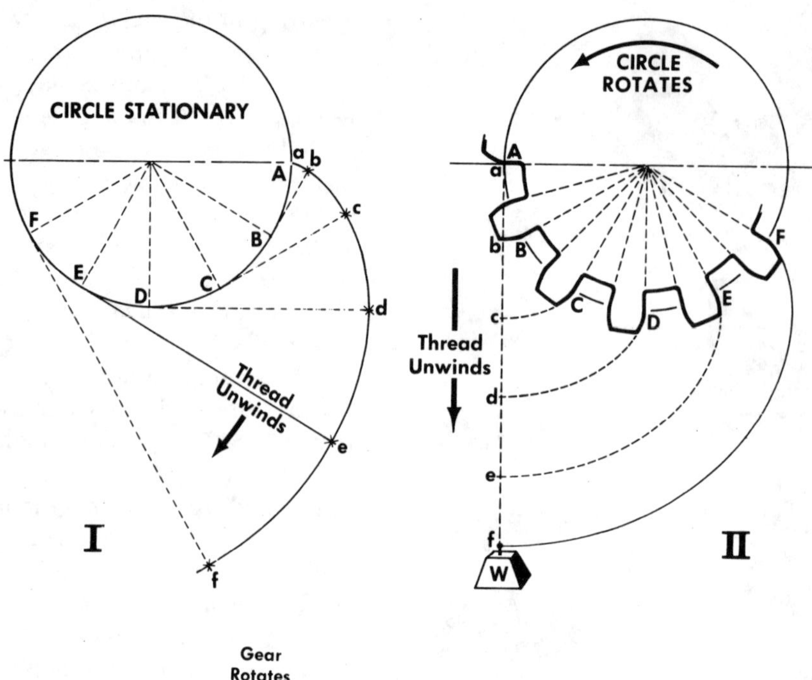

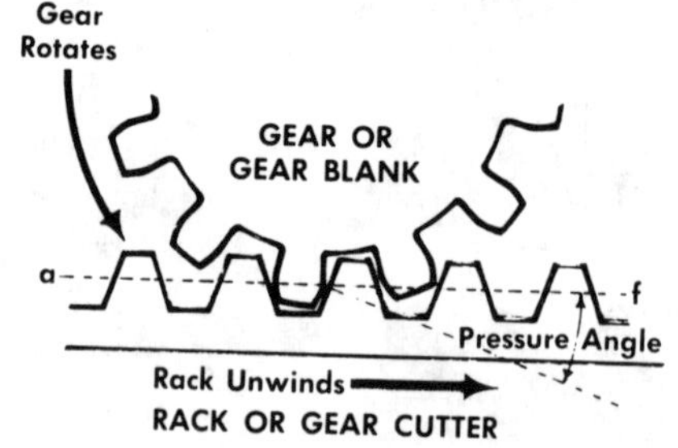

III

Figure 3. Involute principle in gearing.

Figure 4. Left, a 10-tooth pinion with undercut resulting from pressure angle of 14½°; right, without undercut because of a larger pressure angle.

Circular Pitch is the distance from the center of one tooth to the center of the next, measured along the pitch line.

Example—If the distance from the center of one tooth to the center of the next tooth, measured along the pitch line, is 1/2 in., the gear is 1/2 in. circular pitch.

Circular Pitch Required, diametral pitch given. Divide 3.1416 by the diametral pitch.

Example—If the diametral pitch is 4, divide 3.1416 by 4, and the quotient, .7854 in., is the circular pitch.

Number of Teeth Required, pitch diameter and diametral pitch given. Multiply the pitch diameter by the diametral pitch.

Example—If the diameter of the pitch circle is 10 in. and the diametral pitch is 4, multiply 10 by 4, and the product, 40, will be the number of teeth in the gear.

Number of Teeth Required, outside diameter and diametral pitch given. Multiply the outside diameter by the diametral pitch and subtract 2.

Example—If the outside diameter is 10 1/2 in. and the diametral pitch is 4, multiply 10 1/2 by 4, and the product, 42, less 2, or 40, is the number of teeth.

Pitch Diameter Required, number of teeth and diametral pitch given. Divide the number of teeth by the diametral pitch.

Example—If the number of teeth is 40 and the diametral pitch is 4, divide 40 by 4, and the quotient 10 in. is the pitch diameter.

Outside Diameter Required (size of gear blank), number of teeth and diametral pitch given. Add 2 to the number of teeth and divide by the diametral pitch.

Example—If the number of teeth is 40 and the diametral pitch is 4, add 2 to the 40, making 42, and divide by 4. The quotient, 10 1/2 in., is the outside diameter of the gear or blank.

Thickness of Tooth at Pitch Line Required. Divide the circular pitch by 2; or divide 1.57 by the diametral pitch.

Example—If the circular pitch is 1.047, and the diametral pitch is 3, divide 1.047 by 2, or 1.57 by 3, and the quotient, .523 in., is the thickness of the tooth.

Whole Depth of Tooth is equal to the product of .6866 multiplied by the circular pitch.

Example—If the circular pitch is 2 in., the whole depth of tooth is .6866 × 2 in., or 1.3732.

Whole Depth of Tooth Required. Divide 2.157 by the diametral pitch.

Example—If the diametral pitch of a gear is 6, the whole depth of tooth is 2.157 divided by 6, which equals .3595 in.

Distance Between Centers Required (between two meshed gears). Add the number of teeth together and divide one-half the sum by the diametral pitch.

Example—If two gears have 30 and 50 teeth, respectively, and are 5 pitch, add 50 and 30, making 80. Divide by 2, and then divide the quotient 40, by the diametral pitch 5, and the result, 8 in., is the distance between centers.

Speeds and Feeds

As in any milling operation, speeds and feeds are determined by the material being cut and the requirements of tool life and surface finishes. (*See* Chaps. 13 and 14.)

Gear Making Processes

The three common processes for producing gears are *milling, hobbing,* and *shaping,* although in some instances they are stamped, drawn, or cast. The machinist will probably encounter some milling of gears, although the greater preponderance of gears in the machines he uses will have been produced by hobbing or shaping. A quick glance at the three processes in their simplest form will help in later understanding of the limitations and advantages of each.

In the *milling process* (A, Fig. 5) the gear tooth is cut by a formed milling cutter revolving in a plane perpendicular to the gear blank as it advances into the cut. After each tooth space is form-cut, the work is indexed into position for the next cut. Undercut teeth cannot be formed, and, as the shape of the tooth is an exact reproduction of the cutter form, the proper one must be used according to the number of teeth in the gear.

Hobbing (B, Fig. 5) is a generating process. The hob is similar to an oversize screw whose thread has been gashed to produce a large number of cutting

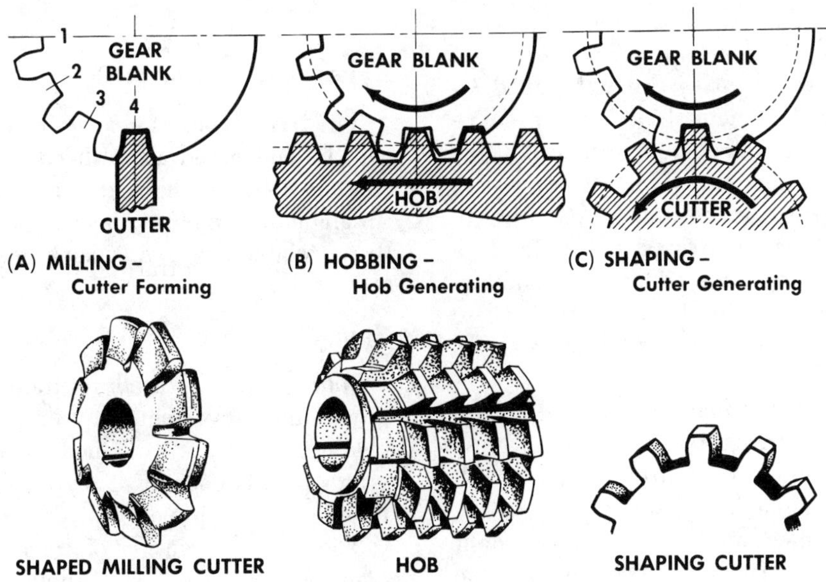

Figure 5. Gear making processes.

teeth. As the hob revolves on its own axis, the *screw* action advances its cutting teeth, keeping pace with the rotary feed of the gear blank and progressively generating a true involute.

Shaping (C, Fig. 5) is also a generating process. The cutter resembles a spur gear, cutting endwise by its reciprocating action perpendicular to the side of the gear blank. Work and cutter are fed by rotation after each pass, generating true involute teeth on the blank.

Upon comparison, it is clear that both hobbing and shaping processes will correctly vary the form of the gear tooth, regardless of the diameter of the blank or the number of teeth to be cut. The *milling process* will cut only one inflexible shape corresponding to the preformed cutter used.

As previously mentioned, the basic methods of producing gears are milling, hobbing, shaping, stamping, drawing, and casting. Work so produced may be finished to a finer degree of accuracy and surface finish by grinding, shaving, lapping, or burnishing, where such refinement is required.

The Milling Process

A *milling machine* can be used for cutting gears by using the proper accessories. This method is usually used where a few gears of a kind are required or where the volume of work does not justify the expenditure for a production gear hobbing or shaping machine.

GEAR MILLING CUTTERS. Many years ago a system of gear cutters was developed, capable of cutting gears from 12 teeth up to a rack. There are eight cutters in a set for each pitch. Although called *involute gear cutters* they actually do not produce true involute shapes. A rotary cutter cannot mill the correct shape of true involute form on gears with low numbers of teeth, for it cannot undercut. In order to approximate the correct shape of tooth, a composite form was developed. This is a combination of both involute and cycloidal curves. These cutters are called *gear milling cutters—range type.* (*See* Table 42.)

Gears milled with gear milling cutters will not interchange correctly with gears of a true involute shape as produced with a standard hob. There will be interferences in the flank or lower portion of the gear teeth. In the range system, each of the eight cutters is designed for the correct profile for the lowest number of teeth in each range. *For example,* the number 8 cutter has the form of a 12-tooth gear. The number 1 cutter has the form of a 135-tooth gear. The approximation on the other numbers of teeth does not cause too great an error in the result. If greater accuracy is wanted, there are available cutters with 1/2 numbers so that the error on form at the high end of the range is reduced.

If it is necessary to cut true involute gears with milling cutters, special cutters can be made for each number of teeth from the largest gear down to the point where undercut occurs. The low limit will depend on the pressure angle.

Gear milling cutters are usually made of high speed steel, form relieved, and their design is such that they can be sharpened by grinding the faces of the teeth without altering their form.

TABLE 42
RANGE OF TEETH PRODUCED BY STANDARD GEAR MILLING CUTTERS IN EACH PITCH

Cutter Form Number	*Range of Teeth*
1	135 thru a rack
2	55 " 134
3	35 " 54
4	26 " 34
5	21 " 25
6	17 " 20
7	14 " 16
8	12 and 13

Types and Cutting of Gears

The basic types of gears with which the machinist will be concerned are utilized to transmit power or motion between shafts that are parallel, intersect at an angle, or are offset. Several gear cutting processes are available to produce such gears.

Spur Gears

Spur gears are used to transmit or manipulate power and movement between parallel shafts. Their characteristics are explained in the elementary diagrams of this chapter. They may be cut by milling, hobbing, or shaping.

The basic dimension of a spur gear is the pitch diameter (Fig. 6). The diametral pitch indicates the size of the tooth. Other terminology employed in connection with spur gear teeth is given in Fig. 6.

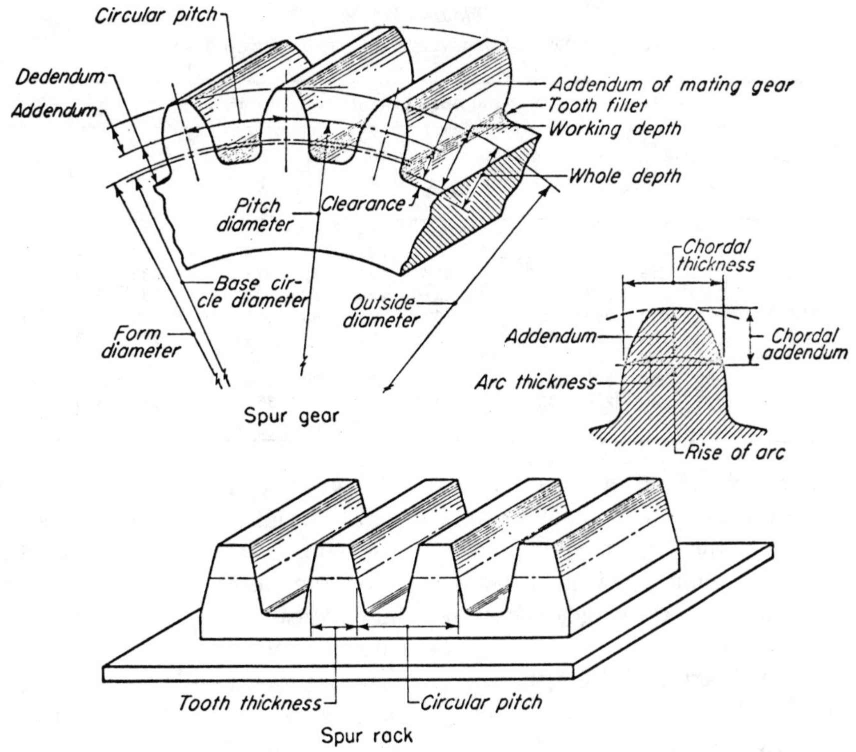

Figure 6. Spur gear terminology.

Bevel Gears

Bevel gears are used to transmit power or movement from shafts that intersect at an angle. A bevel gear may be milled or generated, although the milling process does not produce a theoretically perfect outline for a bevel gear tooth. The curve and dimensions of a bevel gear tooth, when correctly formed, change constantly from one end of the tooth to the other. Therefore, bevel gears whose teeth are produced with a cutter of fixed curvature are not theoretically correct. The cutter usually has a curve that will make the correct form at the outer part of the face of the gear, but it will naturally leave the spaces too large at the inside end.

Bevels of medium and small pitch are occasionally cut by the milling process, particularly when the requirements are not too exacting. Coarse pitch gears and gears that run at high speeds are sometimes roughed out by the milling process and finished by generating.

MILLING BEVEL GEARS. Although bevel gears are rarely milled in production shops, there are occasions when the knowledge of the principles to follow are useful.

On most bevel gears that are cut with a fixed curve cutter, it is necessary to cut through the blank twice, setting the cutter off-center, first to one side and then to the other. Thus the tooth can be tapered.

When milling cutters are used to cut bevel gears, the length of face of the gear should not be longer than one-third of the apex distance.

SETTING THE CUTTER OFF-CENTER. In milling bevel gears, especially steel or cast iron gears of coarse diametral pitch, it is good practice to take one roughing cut entirely around the blank with the cutter set at *central*. Then, to broaden the cut from the width at the small end of the teeth to the wider end, it is necessary to set the cutter off-center, index the blank slightly, and cut to the correct width at the larger end.

The amount to set the cutter off-center can be calculated by means of the following formula and Table 43:

$$\text{Set-over} = \frac{\text{Tc}}{2} - \frac{\text{(Factor from table)}}{\text{P}}$$

where P is the diametral pitch of the gear to be cut and Tc is the thickness of the cutter used, measured at the pitch line. Given as a rule, this would read as follows. In the vertical columns of Table 43, select the factor corresponding to the proper *ratio* and cutter number. Divide this factor by the diametral pitch, and subtract the quotient from one-half the cutter thickness at the pitch line.

TABLE 43
TABLE FOR OBTAINING SET-OVER FOR CUTTING BEVEL GEARS

No. of Cutter	Ratio of Apex Distance to Width of Face												
	$\frac{3}{1}$	$\frac{3\frac{1}{4}}{1}$	$\frac{3\frac{1}{2}}{1}$	$\frac{3\frac{3}{4}}{1}$	$\frac{4}{1}$	$\frac{4\frac{1}{4}}{1}$	$\frac{4\frac{1}{2}}{1}$	$\frac{4\frac{3}{4}}{1}$	$\frac{5}{1}$	$\frac{5\frac{1}{2}}{1}$	$\frac{6}{1}$	$\frac{7}{1}$	$\frac{8}{1}$
1	.254	.254	.255	.256	.257	.257	.257	.258	.258	.259	.260	.262	.264
2	.266	.268	.271	.272	.273	.274	.274	.275	.277	.279	.280	.283	.284
3	.266	.268	.271	.273	.275	.278	.280	.282	.283	.286	.287	.290	.292
4	.275	.280	.285	.287	.291	.293	.296	.298	.298	.302	.305	.308	.311
5	.280	.285	.290	.293	.295	.296	.298	.300	.302	.307	.309	.313	.315
6	.311	.318	.323	.328	.330	.334	.337	.340	.343	.348	.352	.356	.362
7	.289	.298	.308	.316	.324	.329	.334	.338	.343	.350	.360	.370	.376
8	.275	.286	.296	.309	.319	.331	.338	.344	.352	.361	.368	.380	.386

BEVEL GEAR CUTTERS. Special cutters are made for this purpose. They have the involute form of tooth but with thinner teeth than the regular spur gear cutters. *Bevel gear* cutters are numbered from 1 to 8. They provide for cutting all numbers of gears from 12 to a crown gear.

BEVEL GEAR GENERATING MACHINE. The generating motion for cutting bevel gears on a bevel gear generating machine is obtained by rolling the gear blank in relation to the cutting tool. In the case of the two-tool generative bevel gear planer the teeth of a gear are formed by two cutting tools working with a reciprocating planing motion on each side of the tooth. Each tool cuts alternately on its forward stroke, and as soon as a tooth is finished the machine automatically indexes so that the next one is brought into position.

In a process called *coniflex generating,* the tool holders give a crowning action to the tool blades. This produces a heavy bearing near the middle of each tooth to give smoother rolling action and allow for minor misalignments.

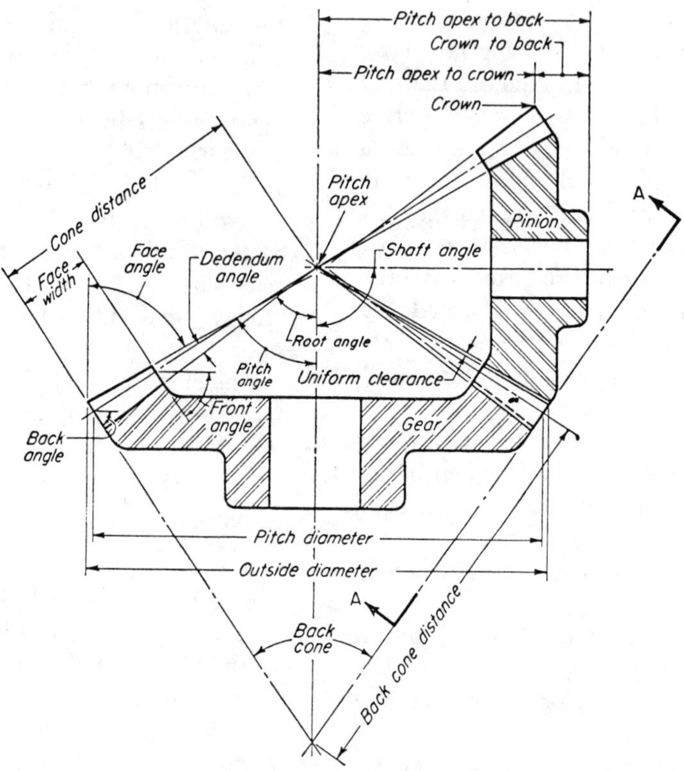

Figure 7. Bevel gear terminology.

There are coniflex generating machines which produce bevel gears with this center bearing by means of two rotary cutters that roll in mesh with the teeth.

Spiral Bevel Gears

Spiral bevel gears have teeth of spiral or curved form, with the curve of the teeth of one member being right-hand while those of the mating member are left-hand.

Spiral bevels may be used in place of straight bevels, the only necessary precaution being to provide suitable thrust bearings to take the increased thrust.

The teeth of spiral bevels come into contact gradually instead of touching all points simultaneously across the face. This increases the average number of teeth in contact, making the gears stronger and quieter.

METHOD OF CUTTING SPIRAL BEVEL GEARS. Spiral bevel gears, with their teeth curved on the arc of a circle, are machined by a circular cutter of the face mill type. The blades have straight-sided cutting edges to correspond to the tooth shape of a crown gear. The teeth are generated by rolling the revolving cutter with the gear blank in order to conform to the meshing action of the crown gear tooth to which the cutter corresponds. In other words, spiral bevel gear teeth are generated or shaped by making the gear blank and rotary cutter roll together in exactly the same manner as if the cutter were a crown gear.

Hypoid Gears

Hypoid gears are spiral bevel gears with offset axes. They have the advantage of permitting transmission of power between offset or nonintersecting shafts. Until the development of hypoid gears, no successful method had been evolved for cutting teeth in bevel gears that were to run on offset shafts.

The tooth action of hypoid gears combines the rolling action of spiral bevel gears with some additional sliding, giving quiet operation and permitting the use of a low number of teeth.

These gears, used principally for automobile rear axles, allow for lower drive shafts, resulting in many major changes in the design of the automobile body. They are finding uses also in many other places where the offset of shafts is advantageous.

Helical Gears

Helical gears may be used to transmit motion between shafts that are either parallel or not parallel. They may be cut on a milling machine, hobbing machine, or gear shaper.

Helical gears should *not* be substituted for spur gears without giving thought to the resultant axial thrust load on the shafts involved. If no provision can be made for the axial thrust, double helical or herringbone gears can be used, either of which cancels out the axial thrust load on the shaft bearings.

Herringbone gears are sometimes made by fastening a left- and right-hand helical gear together. They are also made from the solid with a groove to clear the cutter in the center. A gear shaper has been developed to cut a double helical gear from a solid blank.

The tooth action of helical gears in the plane of rotation is the same as spur gears with the added advantage that there is an overlap of teeth in the direction of the axis. A single helical gear has either a right- or left-hand helix, while a double helical gear has both right- and left-hand helices. The same applies to herringbone gears.

The Hobbing Process

Automatic gear hobbing machines are used to generate spur, helical, and worm gears, as well as shapes other than gear teeth (ratchet or saw teeth, straight sided splines, and the like). In hobbing gears, a hob is used instead of a formed cutter, and the gear blank and hob revolve together in a continuous cutting operation, progressively feeding through the blank. The hob teeth are arranged like cutting edges gashed in an oversize screw, and upon rotation of the hob these give the same action as the passing teeth of a rack. (*See* Gear Making Processes described previously.) Thus, the generating process is created by rotating hob and gear blank together in a definite velocity ratio, which is determined by the number of teeth in the gear and the number of threads in the hob.

In the case of the single-threaded hob, one revolution of the hob is accompanied by a movement of the gear blank through a distance equal to one tooth. The change gears are arranged to furnish this ratio between revolutions of the work spindle and the hob spindle. When the hob has completed a gear it has generated a series of correct involute teeth.

THE HOB. Hobs for spur or helical gears may have as many as three threads for roughing cuts; but for finishing, a single-thread hob is advisable. One single hob of a given pitch can cut all numbers of teeth of spur and helical gears within the capacity of the machine. When hobbing helical gears, it is advisable to use a right-hand hob to cut a right-hand gear, and a left-hand hob to cut a left-hand gear.

Hobs are usually made of high speed steel, and if they are to be used where a high degree of accuracy is required they should be ground on the form of the teeth. Such hobs are known as ground hobs.

To sharpen hobs, grind the face of the teeth through the gash. Care should be taken to observe whether the gash is straight, angular, or helical. If it is helical, the lead will be marked on the end of the hob, and the hob should be sharpened helically to maintain accurate tooth form.

FEED OF HOB. As noted, one revolution of the hob is accompanied by a movement of the gear blank through a distance equal to one tooth. Hence, if cutting a 60-tooth gear the hob would make 60 revolutions to 1 revolution of the gear blank. The feed would be the feed of the hob per revolution of the gear blank.

The Shaping Process

Internal gears, quill or cluster gears, helical gears, sprockets, ratchets, saw teeth, and cams may be cut satisfactorily by the shaping process. The cutter, of a special form, is carried on the end of a ram which reciprocates vertically and imparts a planing action to the cut.

The gear blank is put on a vertical spindle so that it lies in a horizontal plane. The reciprocating cutter is fed straight into the blank until it reaches the proper depth, whereupon the work and cutter are slowly rotated in unison, comparable in all respects to the meshing of two gears. The teeth of the reciprocating cutter, by this rotary movement, generate the required shape of the gear teeth. The chip is taken on the downward movement, although by an adjustment of the machine and the reversing of the cutter, the chip can be taken on the upward movement.

THE SHAPER CUTTER. One cutter only is required for each pitch to the full capacity of the machine. It is usually made of high speed steel and resembles a spur gear in the outline of its teeth. The cutter is sharpened by grinding the concave face without changing the tooth form.

Each tooth of a helical shaper cutter is sharpened individually at an angle to the axis, in a special indexing fixture.

Shaving of Gear Teeth

The *gear shaving principle* is a relatively new method of finishing gear teeth. A gear-type tool or cutter is employed which has serrations cut in the involute profiles of the teeth. This tool has very accurate tooth profiles and is brought in mesh against the mating gear under pressure rotation. The gear has been accurately pre-cut previously by hobbing or shaping, so the amount of stock removed by the shaving process is approximately .002 in. from each tooth surface.

The shaving cutter is usually in the form of a helical gear; and the axes of the cutter and the product gear are crossed. The crossed axes plus endwise motion in the machine cause the shaving action to follow up and down the tooth face, giving a very accurate and smooth finish.

A crowning action is available on some shaving machines to provide a thicker tooth in the center section. The crown varies from .002 in. to .0015 in. height in the middle, depending upon design. The result is a gear that runs quietly even under shaft deflection or misalignment.

Chapter 23

Lubrication and Coolants

Wherever motion is induced between two pieces of metal in contact there is friction, and the work performed to overcome friction generates heat. When this heat becomes excessive it must be controlled, and there are two means of doing this. We must either reduce the friction or remove the heat.

Lubrication is simply a method of reducing friction by separating the metals with a film of oil, substituting a fluid *floating* action for the friction of metal-to-metal contact. Thus, a shaft revolving in a lubricated bushing is actually resting on oil. There is still friction, of course, but of a molecular nature, and the heat generated is usually negligible.

Unfortunately, machine cutting procedures by their very nature depend upon forceful contact of metal to metal, so heat must be controlled by removal. Here we apply coolants which are usually a small part soluble oil for lubrication, combined with a large proportion of heat-conductive liquid, usually water, which carries off the heat.

Lubrication

There are still many older machine tools which employ sight-feed oilers which can be regulated to apply varying numbers of drops per minute, depending upon requirements. Such oilers permit the oil supply to be shut off when the machine is not operating, as an over-supply of oil under certain conditions can be harmful. If the supply is shut off, it should be started again when the machine is again in operation.

The common oil cup will probably always be the most prevalent and useful type of lubrication for simple machinery. When oiling, be sure that the oil level recedes, indicating that the lubricant is going to its intended place. And as in any other oiling device, before putting oil in, remove all foreign matter around the fitting to assure only clean oil entering the bearings.

Automatic Lubrication. Modern machine tools are usually designed with automatic means of lubrication. However, it is the responsibility of the operator to be certain that the oil reservoir contains an adequate supply. Usually there is a level indicator line which shows the oil level. Though it may indicate there is an adequate supply, if the level does not change over a reasonable period, suspicion should be aroused that the system may not be operating properly. If the oil level change indicates excessive oil consumption, a check should be made to determine the cause.

Machine tools designed with automatic lubrication, particularly high speed or precision machines, usually have a plate with visible instructions regarding the characteristics of the proper lubricant. To use the wrong lubricant can be as bad as none at all. Dangerous and costly fires have been caused by using an oil with a low flash point to lubricate a bearing designed to operate at a reasonably high temperature.

A *bearing lubricant* is expected to perform the following functions:

1. Maintain an unbroken film between metal surfaces to prevent excessive wear;
2. Prevent excessive friction and consequent heat; absorb and carry away heat normally generated between moving surfaces, thereby keeping operating temperatures as low as possible;
3. Maintain its properties within allowable limits under severe operating conditions; remain stable.

Viscosity

Viscosity is the resistance which a fluid offers to flow—a measure of fluid friction. Light loads require oils of lower viscosity than heavy loads.

TABLE 44
COMPARISON OF S.A.E. AND S.U.V. NUMBERS

S.A.E.	S.U.V. @ 100°F.
10	150-250
20	250-400
30	400-600
40	600-850
50	850-1500
60	1500-2000
70	2000-4000

STANDARDS OF VISCOSITY. Viscosity of machine tool oils is designated by Saybolt Universal Viscosity (S.U.V.) numbers, often referred to as Saybolt Universal Seconds (S.U.S.). These designations are derived from the instrument most often used by American engineers to measure viscosity—The Saybolt Universal Viscometer (or Viscosimeter) (Fig. 1). This instrument measures the number of seconds it takes for 60 cubic centimeters of liquid to flow through a standard orifice at a given temperature, usually 100°F. The body or fluidity of the oil determines the rate at which it passes through the orifice.

The viscometer consists of a reservoir for the oil, surrounded by a bath heated by heating coils to bring the oil to the temperature at which the viscosity is to be measured. The bottom of the reservoir discharges through the standard viscometer orifice, and the number of seconds it takes for the liquid to reach the 60 cc level in the lower container gives the S.U.V. rating.

A general purpose machine oil is 300 S.U.V. at 100°F. It will take 300 seconds for 60 cc of general purpose machine oil to pass through the orifice. As an example of the need for selectivity, this 300 S.U.V. oil would be satisfactory to lubricate an average size milling machine table, but too light to lubricate a large planer table. Again, suppose a precision grinding machine spindle 2 in. in diameter, operating at 2000 R.P.M., with .0008 in. clearance, is designed to use 60 S.U.V. lubricating oil. If by mistake 150 S.U.V. was used, the bearing would quickly overheat and seize, no doubt with resultant damage to the spindle assembly.

S.A.E. (Society of Automotive Engineers) numbers are arbitrarily set for different viscosities but their S.U.V. range is too wide for machine tool use. Table 44 shows the relative S.A.E. and S.U.V. ratings.

There are special characteristics incorporated in machine tool lubricants for particular purposes, a few of which are listed in Table 45.

Coolants and Cutting Fluids

Coolants and cutting fluids fall into two main groups, those based on water and those based on oil.

WATER-BASED COOLANTS. Where cooling is the principal factor, water-based cutting compounds are preferred. Therefore, grinding coolants are usually water-based with a rust preventive added in the form of soluble oil to protect the machine surfaces from corrosion. Emulsions of 30-to-1 up to 100-to-1

TABLE 45
CHARACTERISTICS OF MACHINE TOOL LUBRICANTS

Purpose	Special Characteristics	Usual Viscosity S.U.V. @ 100° F.
General Lubrication	Film strength Metal protection	150-250
Plain Bearing Spindles	Oxidation stability Anti-rust Anti-corrosion Film strength	30 (high speed) to 150 (low speed)
Hydraulics	Same as above, plus Water separation Anti-foam	150-300
Gear Cases	Oxidation stability Film strength Anti-rust Anti-corrosion Extreme pressure	300-900 (light duty) to 2500
Ways	Anti-rust Anti-corrosion Lubricity-oiliness Extreme pressure	300 (average load) to 1000 (heavy load)

are used, depending upon the grinding application. 30-to-1 means 30 parts water to 1 part soluble oil. Therefore, 30-to-1 will prevent rust better than 100-to-1, but will not have as good cooling qualities. When using emulsion, care must be taken not to just keep adding water when replenishing the coolant supply. Periodically, the coolant tank should be cleaned out and filled with new coolant of the recommended mix.

Oil-Based Coolants. Thread cutting and drilling operations involve considerable friction; therefore cutting oils which are usually mineral oil with additives to improve cutting qualities are preferred over water-base emulsions.

Special Caution. Special caution is recommended when machining magnesium. There is constant danger of fire if care is not exercised. Magnesium is usually machined dry. However, if a coolant is desired use a mineral oil or mineral-fatty oil blend, because water will intensify combustion of magnesium.

Some other unusual materials and applications require special cutting fluid compounds for best results. Many of the oil companies issue excellent booklets on this subject.

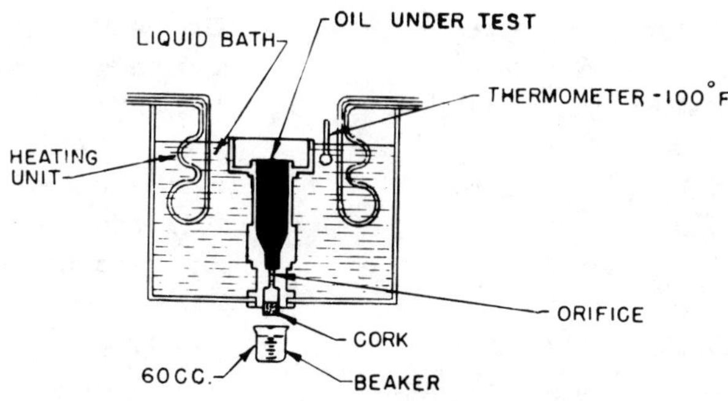

Figure 1. Saybolt universal viscometer setup for testing oil at 100°F.

Appendix

TABLE 1
MISCELLANEOUS METRIC CONVERSION FACTORS

Millimetres × .03937 = inches.
Millimetres ÷ 25.4 = inches.
Centimetres × .3937 = inches.
Centimetres ÷ 2.54 = inches.
Metres × 39.37 = inches. (Act Congress)
Metres × 3.281 = feet.
Metres × 1.094 = yards.
Kilometres × .621 = miles.
Kilometres ÷ 1.6093 = miles.
Kilometres × 3280.8693 = feet.
Square Millimetres × .00155 = sq. inches.
Square Millimetres ÷ 645.1 = sq. inches.
1 Square Millimetre = 1973.5 circular mills.
Square Centimetres × .155 = sq. inches.
Square Centimetres ÷ 6.451 = sq. inches.
Square Metres × 10.764 = sq. feet.
Square Kilometres × 247.1 = acres.
Hectary × 2.471 = acres.
Cubic Centimetres ÷ 16383 = cubic inches.
Cubic Centimetres ÷ 3.69 = fl. drams (U.S.P.).
Cubic Centimetres ÷ 29.57 = fluid oz. (U.S.P.).
Cubic Metres × 35.315 = cubic feet.
Cubic Metres × 1.308 = cubic yards.
Cubic Metres × 264.2 = gallons (231. cu. in.).
Litres × 61.022 = cubic in. (Act Congress).
Litres × 33.8 = fluid ounces (U.S. PHAR.)
Litres × .2642 = gallons (231. cu. in.).
Litres ÷ 3.78 = gallons (231. cu. in.).
Litres ÷ 28.316 = cubic feet.
Hectolitres × 3.531 = cubic feet.
Hectolitres × 2.84 = bushels (2150.42 cu. in.).
Hectolitres × .131 = cubic yards.
Hectolitres ÷ 26.42 = gallons (231. cu. in.).
Grammes × 15.432 = grains. (Act Congress).
Grammes ÷ 981. = dynes.
Grammes (Water) ÷ 29.57 = fluid ounces.
Grammes ÷ 28.35 = ounces avoirdupois.
Grammes per cu. cent. ÷ 27.7 = lbs. per cu. in.
1 Gram = .03216 ounce troy.
Joule × .7373 = foot pounds.
Kilo-grammes × 2.2046 = pounds.
Kilo-grammes × 35.3 = ounces avoirdupois.
Kilo-grammes ÷ 907.2 = tons (2,000 lbs.).
1 Metric ton = 2204.6 pounds.
Kilo-gr. per sq. cent. × 14.223 = lbs. per sq. in.
Kilo-gram-metres × 7.233 = foot lbs.
Kilo-gr. per Metre × .672 = lbs. per foot.
1 Kilogram per sq. millimeter = 1422.32 lbs. per sq. in.
1.0335 Kilo-gr. per sq. Cent. = 1 atmosphere
1.0335 Kilo-gr. per sq. Cent. = 14.7 lbs. per sq. in.
Kilo-gr. per Cu. Metre × .062 = lbs. per cu. ft.

TABLE 2
MEASURES OF PRESSURE AND WEIGHT

1 lb. per sq. in. = 2.0416 inches of mercury at 62° F.
1 lb. per sq. in. = 27.71 inches of water at 62° F.
1 atmosphere = 14.7 lbs. per sq. inch.
1 atmosphere = 33.947 feet of water at 62° F.
1 atmosphere = 30.011 inches of mercury at 62° F.
1 inch of water 62° F. = 62.355 lbs. per sq. foot.

TABLE 3
MISCELLANEOUS MEASURES

1 Gal. of water at 62° F. = 231 cu. inches.
1 Gal. of water at 62° F. = 8.335 lbs.
1 cu. ft. of water at 62° F. = 62.287 lbs.
1 cu. ft. air at 32° F. and atmosphere pressure = .080728 lbs.
1 lb. avoirdupois = 453.6 grams.
1 lb. avoirdupois = 7000 grains.
1 lb. apothecaries = 5760 grains.
1 lb. troy = 5760 grains.
1 Carat (Metric) = 3.0865 grains = .200 grams.
1 Cord of wood = 128 cu. feet.
1 Acre = 43,560 sq. feet.
1 Furlong = 220 yards.
1 Fathom = 6 feet.
1 Knot = 1.1516 Statute Mile.
1 span = 9 inches.
1 hand = 4 inches.

TABLE 4

TEMPERATURE CONVERSIONS

Albert Sauveur type of table. Look up reading in middle column; if in degrees Centigrade, read Fahrenheit equivalent in right hand column; if in degrees Fahrenheit, read Centigrade equivalent in left hand column.

-459.4 to 0			0 to 100						100 to 1000						1000 to 2000						2000 to 3000					
C		F	C		F	C		F	C		F	C		F	C		F	C		F	C		F	C		F
-273	*-459.4*		-17.8	*0*	32	10.0	*50*	122.0	38	*100*	212	260	*500*	932	538	*1000*	1832	816	*1500*	2732	1093	*2000*	3632	1371	*2500*	4532
-268	*-450*		-17.2	*1*	33.8	10.6	*51*	123.8	43	*110*	230	266	*510*	950	543	*1010*	1850	821	*1510*	2750	1099	*2010*	3650	1377	*2510*	4550
-262	*-440*		-16.7	*2*	35.6	11.1	*52*	125.6	49	*120*	248	271	*520*	968	549	*1020*	1868	827	*1520*	2768	1104	*2020*	3668	1382	*2520*	4568
-257	*-430*		-16.1	*3*	37.4	11.7	*53*	127.4	54	*130*	266	277	*530*	986	554	*1030*	1886	832	*1530*	2786	1110	*2030*	3686	1388	*2530*	4586
-251	*-420*		-15.6	*4*	39.2	12.2	*54*	129.2	60	*140*	284	282	*540*	1004	560	*1040*	1904	838	*1540*	2804	1116	*2040*	3704	1393	*2540*	4604
-246	*-410*		-15.0	*5*	41.0	12.8	*55*	131.0	66	*150*	302	288	*550*	1022	566	*1050*	1922	843	*1550*	2822	1121	*2050*	3722	1399	*2550*	4622
-240	*-400*		-14.4	*6*	42.8	13.3	*56*	132.8	71	*160*	320	293	*560*	1040	571	*1060*	1940	849	*1560*	2840	1127	*2060*	3740	1404	*2560*	4640
-234	*-390*		-13.9	*7*	44.6	13.9	*57*	134.6	77	*170*	338	299	*570*	1058	577	*1070*	1958	854	*1570*	2858	1132	*2070*	3758	1410	*2570*	4658
-229	*-380*		-13.3	*8*	46.4	14.4	*58*	136.4	82	*180*	356	304	*580*	1076	582	*1080*	1976	860	*1580*	2876	1138	*2080*	3776	1416	*2580*	4676
-223	*-370*		-12.8	*9*	48.2	15.0	*59*	138.2	88	*190*	374	310	*590*	1094	588	*1090*	1994	866	*1590*	2894	1143	*2090*	3794	1421	*2590*	4694
-218	*-360*		-12.2	*10*	50.0	15.6	*60*	140.0	93	*200*	392	316	*600*	1112	593	*1100*	2012	871	*1600*	2912	1149	*2100*	3812	1427	*2600*	4712
-212	*-350*		-11.7	*11*	51.8	16.1	*61*	141.8	99	*210*	410	321	*610*	1130	599	*1110*	2030	877	*1610*	2930	1154	*2110*	3830	1432	*2610*	4730
-207	*-340*		-11.1	*12*	53.6	16.7	*62*	143.6	100	*212*	413.6	327	*620*	1148	604	*1120*	2048	882	*1620*	2948	1160	*2120*	3848	1438	*2620*	4748
-201	*-330*		-10.6	*13*	55.4	17.2	*63*	145.4	104	*220*	428	332	*630*	1166	610	*1130*	2066	888	*1630*	2966	1166	*2130*	3866	1443	*2630*	4766
-196	*-320*		-10.0	*14*	57.2	17.8	*64*	147.2	110	*230*	446	338	*640*	1184	616	*1140*	2084	893	*1640*	2984	1171	*2140*	3884	1449	*2640*	4784
-190	*-310*		-9.4	*15*	59.0	18.3	*65*	149.0	116	*240*	464	343	*650*	1202	621	*1150*	2102	899	*1650*	3002	1177	*2150*	3902	1454	*2650*	4802
-184	*-300*		-8.9	*16*	60.8	18.9	*66*	150.8	121	*250*	482	349	*660*	1220	627	*1160*	2120	904	*1660*	3020	1182	*2160*	3920	1460	*2660*	4820
-179	*-290*		-8.3	*17*	62.6	19.4	*67*	152.6	127	*250*	500	354	*670*	1238	632	*1170*	2138	910	*1670*	3038	1188	*2170*	3938	1466	*2670*	4838
-173	-280		-7.8	*18*	64.4	20.0	*68*	154.4	132	*270*	518	360	*680*	1256	638	*1180*	2156	916	*1680*	3056	1193	*2180*	3956	1471	*2680*	4856
-169	*-273*	-459.4	-7.2	*19*	66.2	20.6	*69*	156.2	138	*280*	536	366	*690*	1274	643	*1190*	2174	921	*1690*	3074	1199	*2190*	3974	1477	*2690*	4874
-168	*-270*	-454	-6.7	*20*	68.0	21.1	*70*	158.0	143	*290*	554	371	*700*	1292	649	*1200*	2192	927	*1700*	3092	1204	*2200*	3992	1482	*2700*	4892
-162	*-260*	-436	-6.1	*21*	69.8	21.7	*71*	159.8	149	*300*	572	377	*710*	1310	654	*1210*	2210	932	*1710*	3110	1210	*2210*	4010	1488	*2710*	4910
-157	*-250*	-418	-5.6	*22*	71.6	22.2	*72*	161.6	154	*310*	590	382	*720*	1328	660	*1220*	2228	938	*1720*	3128	1216	*2220*	4028	1493	*2720*	4928
-151	*-240*	-400	-5.0	*23*	73.4	22.8	*73*	163.4	160	*320*	608	388	*730*	1346	666	*1230*	2246	943	*1730*	3146	1221	*2230*	4046	1499	*2730*	4946
-146	*-230*	-382	-4.4	*24*	75.2	23.3	*74*	165.2	166	*330*	626	393	*740*	1364	671	*1240*	2264	949	*1740*	3164	1227	*2240*	4064	1504	*2740*	4964
-140	*-220*	-364	-3.9	*25*	77.0	23.9	*75*	167.0	171	*340*	644	399	*750*	1382	677	*1250*	2282	954	*1750*	3182	1232	*2250*	4082	1510	*2750*	4982
-134	*-210*	-346	-3.3	*26*	78.8	24.4	*76*	168.8	177	*350*	662	404	*760*	1400	682	*1260*	2300	960	*1760*	3200	1238	*2260*	4100	1516	*2760*	5000
-129	*-200*	-328	-2.8	*27*	80.6	25.0	*77*	170.6	182	*360*	680	410	*770*	1418	688	*1270*	2318	966	*1770*	3218	1243	*2270*	4118	1521	*2770*	5018
-123	*-190*	-310	-2.2	*28*	82.4	25.6	*78*	172.4	188	*370*	698	416	*780*	1436	693	*1280*	2336	971	*1780*	3236	1249	*2280*	4136	1527	*2780*	5036
-118	*-180*	-292	-1.7	*29*	84.2	26.1	*79*	174.2	193	*380*	716	421	*790*	1454	699	*1290*	2354	977	*1790*	3254	1254	*2290*	4154	1532	*2790*	5054
-112	*-170*	-274	-1.1	*30*	86.0	26.7	*80*	176.0	199	*390*	734	427	*800*	1472	704	*1300*	2372	982	*1800*	3272	1260	*2300*	4172	1538	*2800*	5072
-107	*-160*	-256	-0.6	*31*	87.8	27.2	*81*	177.8	204	*400*	752	432	*810*	1490	710	*1310*	2390	988	*1810*	3290	1266	*2310*	4190	1543	*2810*	5090
-101	*-150*	-238	0.0	*32*	89.6	27.8	*82*	179.6	210	*410*	770	438	*820*	1508	716	*1320*	2408	993	*1820*	3308	1271	*2320*	4208	1549	*2820*	5108
-96	*-140*	-220	0.6	*33*	91.4	28.3	*83*	181.4	216	*420*	788	443	*830*	1526	721	*1330*	2426	999	*1830*	3326	1277	*2330*	4226	1554	*2830*	5126
-90	*-130*	-202	1.1	*34*	93.2	28.9	*84*	183.2	221	*430*	806	449	*840*	1544	727	*1340*	2444	1004	*1840*	3344	1282	*2340*	4244	1560	*2840*	5144
-84	*-120*	-184	1.7	*35*	95.0	29.4	*85*	185.0	227	*440*	824	454	*850*	1562	732	*1350*	2462	1010	*1850*	3362	1288	*2350*	4262	1566	*2850*	5162
-79	*-110*	-166	2.2	*36*	96.8	30.0	*86*	186.8	232	*450*	842	460	*860*	1580	738	*1360*	2480	1016	*1860*	3380	1293	*2360*	4280	1571	*2860*	5180
-73	*-100*	-148	2.8	*37*	98.6	30.6	*87*	188.6	238	*460*	860	466	*870*	1598	743	*1370*	2498	1021	*1870*	3398	1299	*2370*	4298	1577	*2870*	5198
-68	*-90*	-130	3.3	*38*	100.4	31.1	*88*	190.4	243	*470*	878	471	*880*	1616	749	*1380*	2516	1027	*1880*	3416	1304	*2380*	4316	1582	*2880*	5216
-62	*-80*	-112	3.9	*39*	102.2	31.7	*89*	192.2	249	*480*	896	477	*890*	1634	754	*1390*	2534	1032	*1890*	3434	1310	*2390*	4334	1588	*2890*	5234
-57	*-70*	-94	4.4	*40*	104.0	32.2	*90*	194.0	254	*490*	914	482	*900*	1652	760	*1400*	2552	1038	*1900*	3452	1316	*2400*	4352	1593	*2900*	5252
-51	*-60*	-76	5.0	*41*	105.8	32.8	*91*	195.8				488	*910*	1670	766	*1410*	2570	1043	*1910*	3470	1321	*2410*	4370	1599	*2910*	5270
-46	*-50*	-58	5.6	*42*	107.6	33.3	*92*	197.6				493	*920*	1688	771	*1420*	2588	1049	*1920*	3488	1327	*2420*	4388	1604	*2920*	5288
-40	*-40*	-40	6.1	*43*	109.4	33.9	*93*	199.4				499	*930*	1706	777	*1430*	2606	1054	*1930*	3506	1332	*2430*	4406	1610	*2930*	5306
-34	*-30*	-22	6.7	*44*	111.2	34.4	*94*	201.2				504	*940*	1724	782	*1440*	2624	1060	*1940*	3524	1338	*2440*	4424	1616	*2940*	5324

− 29	*− 20*	− 4	7.2	*45*	113.0	35.0	*95*	203.0	510	*950*	1742	788	*1450*	2642	1066	*1950*	3542	1343	*2450*	4442	1621	*2950*	5342
− 23	*− 10*	− 14	7.8	*46*	114.8	35.6	*96*	204.8	516	*960*	1760	793	*1460*	2660	1071	*1960*	3560	1349	*2460*	4460	1627	*2960*	5360
− 17.8	− 0	− 32	8.3	*47*	116.6	36.1	*97*	206.6	521	*970*	1778	799	*1470*	2678	1077	*1970*	3578	1354	*2470*	4478	1632	*2970*	5378
			8.9	*48*	118.4	36.7	*98*	208.4	527	*980*	1796	804	*1480*	2696	1082	*1980*	3596	1360	*2480*	4496	1638	*2980*	5396
			9.4	*49*	120.2	37.2	*99*	210.2	532	*990*	1814	810	*1490*	2714	1088	*1990*	3614	1366	*2490*	4514	1643	*2990*	5414
						37.8	*100*	212.0	538	*1000*	1832				1093	*2000*	3632				1649	*3000*	5432

TABLE 5

INTERCONVERSION TABLE FOR UNITS OF VOLUME AND WEIGHTS MULTIPLY BY

To Convert From	To Cu. In.	To Cu. Ft.	To Cu. Yd.	To Fl. Oz.	To Pt.	To Qt.	To Gal.	To Grain	To Oz. Troy	To Oz. Av.	To Lb. Troy	To Lab. Av.	To C.C. or G.	To L. or Kg.
Cu. in.	1.00000	$0.0_{3}5787$	$0.0_{4}2143$	0.554112	0.034632	0.017316	0.004329	252.891	0.526857	0.578037	0.043905	0.036127	16.3871	0.016387
Cu. ft.	1728.00	1.00000	0.037037	957.505	59.8442	29.9221	7.48052	436996	910.408	998.848	75.8674	62.4280	28316.9	28.3169
Cu. yd.	46656.0	27.0000	1.00000	25852.6	1615.79	807.896	201.974	117990_{3}	24581.0	26968.9	2048.42	1685.56	764556	764.556
Fl. oz.	1.80469	0.001044	$0.0_{4}3868$	1.00000	0.062500	0.031250	0.007813	456.390	0.950813	1.04318	0.079234	0.065199	29.5736	0.029573
Pt.	28.8750	0.016710	$0.0_{3}6189$	16.0000	1.00000	0.500000	0.125000	7302.23	15.2130	16.6908	1.26775	1.04318	473.177	0.473177
Qt.	57.7500	0.033420	0.001238	32.0000	2.00000	1.00000	0.250000	1460.45	30.4260	33.3816	2.53550	2.08635	946.354	0.946354
Gal.	231.000	0.133681	0.004951	128.000	8.00000	4.00000	1.00000	58417.9	121.704	133.527	10.1420	8.34541	3785.42	3.78542
Grain.	0.003954	$0.0_{5}2288$	$0.0_{7}8475$	0.002191	$0.0_{3}1369$	$0.0_{4}6850$	$0.0_{4}1712$	1.00000	0.002083	0.002286	$0.0_{3}1735$	$0.0_{3}1428$	0.054799	$0.0_{4}6479$
Oz. Troy. . .	1.89805	0.001098	$0.0_{4}4068$	1.05173	0.065733	0.032867	0.008217	480.000	1.00000	1.09714	0.083333	0.068571	31.1035	0.031104
Oz. Av.	1.72999	0.001001	$0.0_{4}3708$	0.958608	0.059913	0.029957	0.007489	437.500	0.911457	1.00000	0.075955	0.062500	28.3495	0.028350
Lb. Troy. . .	22.7766	0.013181	$0.0_{3}4882$	12.6208	0.788800	0.394400	0.098600	5760.00	12.0000	13.1657	1.00000	0.822857	373.242	0.373242
Lb. Av.	27.6799	0.016018	$0.0_{3}5933$	15.3378	0.958611	0.479306	0.119826	7000.00	14.5833	16.0000	1.21528	1.00000	453.593	0.453593
C.C. or G. . .	0.061024	$0.0_{4}3531$	$0.0_{5}1308$	0.033814	0.002113	0.001057	$0.0_{3}2642$	15.4323	0.032151	0.035274	0.002679	0.002205	1.00000	0.001000
L. or Kg. . . .	61.0237	0.035315	0.001308	33.8140	2.11337	1.05669	0.264172	15432.3	32.1507	35.2739	2.67923	2.20462	1000.00	1.00000

Note: The small subnumeral following a zero indicates that the zero is to be taken that number of times, thus, $0.0_{3}1428$ is equivalent to 0.0001428.

Values Used in Constructing Table: 1 in. = 2.540001 cm.; 1 cu. in. = 16.387083 g. H_2O at 4° C. (39° F.); 1 lb. av. = 453.5926 g.; 1 gal. = 8.34541 lb.; 1 lb. av. = 27.679886 cu. in. H_2O at 4° C.; 1 lb. av. = 7000 grains; 1 gal. = 58417.87 grains; 241 cu. in. = 1 gal. = 3785.4162 g.

Table 6
Interconversion Table for Units of Energy Multiply by

To Convert From	To B.t.u.	To Cal.	To Ft.-Lb.	To Ft. Tons	To Kg.-m.	To Hp.-Hr.	To Kw.-Hr.	To Joules (Abs.)	To Lb. C.	To Lb. H_2O
B.t.u. (mean)	1.00	0.252	778.000	0.389001	107.563	$0.0_{3}3929$	$0.0_{3}2931$	1054.8	0.046876	0.001031
Calories (mean)	3.968	1.000	3091.36	1.544	426.84	0.001559	0.001163	4185	$0.0_{3}2729$	0.004089
Ft.-lb.	0.001285	$0.0_{3}3239$	1.000	0.000500	0.1383	$0.0_{6}5050$	$0.0_{6}3767$	1.355	$0.0_{7}8840$	$0.0_{5}1325$
Ft. Tons	2.571	0.6478	2000.00	1.000	276.511	0.001010	$0.0_{3}7535$	2712.59	$0.0_{3}1768$	0.002649
Kg.-m.	0.009297	0.002343	7.23301	0.003617	1.000	$0.0_{5}3653$	$0.0_{5}2725$	9.806	$0.0_{6}6394$	$0.0_{5}9580$
Hp.-hr.	2544.99	641.327	1980000	990.004	273747	1.000	0.745000	2685600	0.1750	2.62261
Kw.-hr.	3411.57	859.702	2654200	1327.10	366959	1.34041	1.000	3600000	0.2346	3.51562
Joules (absolute)	$0.0_{3}9477$	$0.0_{3}2389$	0.737356	$0.0_{3}3637$	0.101937	$0.0_{6}3725$	$0.0_{6}2778$	1.000	$0.0_{7}6518$	$0.0_{6}9766$
Lbs. C.	14544	3665	113150_{3}	5658	1564396	5.714	4.263	153470_{3}	1.000	14.98
Lbs. H_2O	970.40	244.537	754971	377.487	104379	0.381270	0.284424	1023966	0.06674	1.000

Note: The small subnumeral following a zero indicates that the zero is to be taken that number of times, thus, $0.0_{3}1428$ is equivalent to 0.0001428.

The ton used is 2000 lb. "Lb. C" refers to pounds of carbon oxidized, 100% efficiency equivalent to the corresponding number of heat units. "Lb. H_2O refers to pounds of water evaporated at 100° C. (212° F.) at 100% efficiency.

TABLE 7

MENSURATION—LENGTH

Circumference of circle = diameter × 3.1416.
Diameter of circle = circumference × 0.3183.
Side of square of equal periphery as circle = diameter × 0.7854.
Diameter of circle of equal periphery as square = side × 1.2732.
Side of an inscribed square = diameter of circle × 0.7071, cr circumference × .2251.
Length of arc = number of degrees × diameter × 0.008727.
Circumference of an ellipse = half the sum of the two diameters × 3.1416.

TABLE 8

MENSURATION—AREA

Triangle = base × half perpendicular height.
Parallelogram = base × perpendicular height.
Trapezoid = half the sum of the parallel sides × perpendicular height.
Trapezium = found by dividing into two triangles.
Circle = diameter squared × 0.7854 or circumference squared × 0.07958, or circumference × ¼ diameter.
Sector of circle = length of arc × half radius.
Segment of circle = area of sector less triangle.
Side of square of equal area as circle = diameter × 0.8862, or circumference × 0.2821.
Diameter of circle of equal area as square = side × 1.1284.
Ellipse = long diameter × short diameter × 0.7854.
Regular polygon = sum of sides × half perpendicular height from center to sides.
Surface of cylinder = circumference × height + area of both ends.
Surface of sphere = diameter squared + 3.1416, circumference × diameter, or circumference squared × .3183.
Surface of a right pyramid or cone = periphery or circumference of base × half slant height + area of base.
Surface of a frustrum of a regular right pyramid or cone = sum of peripheries or circumferences of both ends × half slant height + area of both ends.
Hexagon = area of circle same as short diameter × 1.104.
Octagon = area of square same diameter × .84375.

TABLE 9

MENSURATION—SOLID CONTENTS

Prism, right or oblique = area of base × perpendicular height.
Cylinder, right or oblique = area of section at right angles to sides × length of side.
Sphere = diameter cubed × 0.5236, or surface × one-sixth diameter, or circumference cubed × .0169.
Pyramid or cone, right or oblique, regular or irregular = area of base × one-third perpendicular height.

TABLE 10

MENSURATION—MISCELLANEOUS

To find diagonal of any square, multiply the side by 1.414.
To find the long diameter of a hexagon multiply the short diameter by 1.155.
Doubling the diameter of a circle or square increases the area four times and the circumference twice.
Weight of hexagon = weight of round × 1.104.
Weight of octagon = weight of square × .84375.
Weight of square = weight of round × 1.273.
Weight of round = area of circle in inches × .283.

Table 11

Conversion of Millimeters into Inches

Millimeters	Inches	Millimeters	Inches	Millimeters	Inches	Millimeters	Inches	Millimeters	Inches
1	0.0394	51	2.0079	101	3.9764	151	5.9449	201	7.9134
2	0.0787	52	2.0472	102	4.0157	152	5.9842	202	7.9527
3	0.1181	53	2.0866	103	4.0551	153	6.0236	203	7.9921
4	0.1575	54	2.1260	104	4.0945	154	6.0630	204	8.0315
5	0.1968	55	2.1653	105	4.1338	155	6.1023	205	8.0708
6	0.2362	56	2.2047	106	4.1732	156	6.1417	206	8.1102
7	0.2756	57	2.2441	107	4.2126	157	6.1811	207	8.1496
8	0.3150	58	2.2835	108	4.2520	158	6.2205	208	8.1890
9	0.3543	59	2.3228	109	4.2913	159	6.2598	209	8.2283
10	0.3937	60	2.3622	110	4.3307	160	6.2992	210	8.2677
11	0.4331	61	2.4016	111	4.3701	161	6.3386	211	8.3071
12	0.4724	62	2.4409	112	4.4094	162	6.3779	212	8.3464
13	0.5118	63	2.4803	113	4.4488	163	6.4173	213	8.3858
14	0.5512	64	2.5197	114	4.4882	164	6.4567	214	8.4252
15	0.5905	65	2.5590	115	4.5275	165	6.4960	215	8.4645
16	0.6299	66	2.5984	116	4.5669	166	6.5354	216	8.5039
17	0.6693	67	2.6378	117	4.6063	167	6.5748	217	8.5433
18	0.7087	68	2.6772	118	4.6457	168	6.6142	218	8.5827
19	0.7480	69	2.7165	119	4.6850	169	6.6535	219	8.6220
20	0.7874	70	2.7559	120	4.7244	170	6.6929	220	8.6614
21	0.8268	71	2.7953	121	4.7638	171	6.7323	221	8.7008
22	0.8661	72	2.8346	122	4.8031	172	6.7716	222	8.7401
23	0.9055	73	2.8740	123	4.8425	173	6.8110	223	8.7795
24	0.9449	74	2.9134	124	4.8819	174	6.8504	224	8.8189
25	0.9842	75	2.9527	125	4.9212	175	6.8897	225	8.8582
26	1.0236	76	2.9921	126	4.9606	176	6.9291	226	8.8976
27	1.0630	77	3.0315	127	5.0000	177	6.9685	227	8.9370
28	1.1024	78	3.0709	128	5.0394	178	7.0079	228	8.9764
29	1.1417	79	3.1102	129	5.0787	179	7.0472	229	9.0157
30	1.1811	80	3.1496	130	5.1181	180	7.0866	230	9.0551
31	1.2205	81	3.1890	131	5.1575	181	7.1260	231	9.0945
32	1.2598	82	3.2283	132	5.1968	182	7.1653	232	9.1338
33	1.2992	83	3.2677	133	5.2362	183	7.2047	233	9.1732
34	1.3386	84	3.3071	134	5.2756	184	7.2441	234	9.2126
35	1.3779	85	3.3464	135	5.3149	185	7.2834	235	9.2519
36	1.4173	86	3.3858	136	5.3543	186	7.3228	236	9.2913
37	1.4567	87	3.4252	137	5.3937	187	7.3622	237	9.3307
38	1.4961	88	3.4646	138	5.4331	188	7.4016	238	9.3701
39	1.5354	89	3.5039	139	5.4724	189	7.4409	239	9.4094
40	1.5748	90	3.5433	140	5.5118	190	7.4803	240	9.4488
41	1.6142	91	3.5827	141	5.5512	191	7.5197	241	9.4882
42	1.6535	92	3.6220	142	5.5905	192	7.5590	242	9.5275
43	1.6929	93	3.6614	143	5.6299	193	7.5984	243	9.5669
44	1.7323	94	3.7008	144	5.6693	194	7.6378	244	9.6063
45	1.7716	95	3.7401	145	5.7086	195	7.6771	245	9.6456
46	1.8110	96	3.7795	146	5.7480	196	7.7165	246	9.6850
47	1.8504	97	3.8189	147	5.7874	197	7.7559	247	9.7244
48	1.8898	98	3.8583	148	5.8268	198	7.7953	248	9.7638
49	1.9291	99	3.8976	149	5.8661	199	7.8346	249	9.8031
50	1.9685	100	3.9370	150	5.9055	200	7.8740	250	9.8425

TABLE 11 (CONTINUED)

Millimeters	Inches	Millimeters	Inches	Millimeters	Inches	Millimeters	Inches	Millimeters	Inches
251	9.8819	301	11.8504	351	13.8189	401	15.7874	451	17.7559
252	9.9212	302	11.8897	352	13.8582	402	15.8267	452	17.7952
253	9.9606	303	11.9291	353	13.8976	403	15.8661	453	17.8346
254	10.0000	304	11.9685	354	13.9370	404	15.9055	454	17.8740
255	10.0393	305	12.0078	355	13.9763	405	15.9448	455	17.9133
256	10.0787	306	12.0472	356	14.0157	406	15.9842	456	17.9527
257	10.1181	307	12.0866	357	14.0551	407	16.0236	457	17.9921
258	10.1575	308	12.1260	358	14.0945	408	16.0630	458	18.0315
259	10.1968	309	12.1653	359	14.1338	409	16.1023	459	18.0738
260	10.2362	310	12.2047	360	14.1732	410	16.1417	460	18.1102
261	10.2756	311	12.2441	361	14.2126	411	16.1811	461	18.1496
262	10.3149	312	12.2834	362	14.2519	412	16.2204	462	18.1889
263	10.3543	313	12.3228	363	14.2913	413	16.2598	463	18.2283
264	10.3937	314	12.3622	364	14.3307	414	16.2992	464	18.2677
265	10.4330	315	12.4015	365	14.3700	415	16.3385	465	18.3070
266	10.4724	316	12.4409	366	14.4094	416	16.3779	466	18.3464
267	10.5118	317	12.4803	367	14.4488	417	16.4173	467	18.3858
268	10.5512	318	12.5197	368	14.4882	418	16.4567	468	18.4252
269	10.5905	319	12.5590	369	14.5275	419	16.4960	469	18.4645
270	10.6299	320	12.5984	370	14.5669	420	16.5354	470	18.5039
271	10.6693	321	12.6378	371	14.6063	421	16.5748	471	18.5433
272	10.7086	322	12.6771	372	14.6456	422	16.6141	472	18.5826
273	10.7480	323	12.7165	373	14.6850	423	16.6535	473	18.6220
274	10.7874	324	12.7559	374	14.7244	424	16.6929	474	18.6614
275	10.8267	325	12.7952	375	14.7637	425	16.7322	475	18.7007
276	10.8661	326	12.8346	376	14.8031	426	16.7716	476	18.7401
277	10.9055	327	12.8740	377	14.8425	427	16.8110	477	18.7795
278	10.9449	328	12.9134	378	14.8819	428	16.8504	478	18.8189
279	10.9842	329	12.9527	379	14.9212	429	16.8897	479	18.8582
280	11.0236	330	12.9921	380	14.9606	430	16.9291	480	18.8976
281	11.0630	331	13.0315	381	15.0000	431	16.9685	481	18.9370
282	11.1023	332	13.0708	382	15.0393	432	17.0078	482	18.9763
283	11.1417	333	13.1102	383	15.0787	433	17.0472	483	19.0157
284	11.1811	334	13.1496	384	15.1181	434	17.0866	484	19.0551
285	11.2204	335	13.1889	385	15.1574	435	17.1259	485	19.0944
286	11.2598	336	13.2283	386	15.1968	436	17.1653	486	19.1338
287	11.2992	337	13.2677	387	15.2362	437	17.2047	487	19.1732
288	11.3386	338	13.3071	388	15.2756	438	17.2441	488	19.2126
289	11.3779	339	13.3464	389	15.3149	439	17.2834	489	19.2519
290	11.4173	340	13.3858	390	15.3543	440	17.3228	490	19.2913
291	11.4567	341	13.4252	391	15.3937	441	17.3622	491	19.3307
292	11.4960	342	13.4645	392	15.4330	442	17.4015	492	19.3700
293	11.5354	343	13.5039	393	15.4724	443	17.4409	493	19.4094
294	11.5748	344	13.5433	394	15.5118	444	17.4803	494	19.4488
295	11.6141	345	13.5826	395	15.5511	445	17.5196	495	19.4881
296	11.6535	346	13.6220	396	15.5905	446	17.5590	496	19.5275
297	11.6929	347	13.6614	397	15.6299	447	17.5984	497	19.5669
298	11.7323	348	13.7008	398	15.6693	448	17.6378	498	19.6063
299	11.7716	349	13.7401	399	15.7086	449	17.6771	499	19.6456
300	11.8110	350	13.7795	400	15.7480	450	17.7165	500	19.6850

Table 12
Conversion of Inches into Millimeters

In.	Mm.	In.	Mm.	In.	Mm.	In.	Mm.	In.	Mm.	In.	Mm.	In.	Mm.	In.	Mm.
1/16	1.6	2 9/16	65.1	5 1/16	128.6	7 9/16	192.1	10 1/16	255.6	12 9/16	319.1	15 1/16	382.6	17 9/16	446.1
1/8	3.2	2 5/8	66.7	5 1/8	130.2	7 5/8	193.7	10 1/8	257.2	12 5/8	320.7	15 1/8	384.2	17 5/8	447.7
3/16	4.8	2 11/16	68.3	5 3/16	131.8	7 11/16	195.3	10 3/16	258.8	12 11/16	322.3	15 3/16	385.8	17 11/16	449.3
1/4	6.4	2 3/4	69.8	5 1/4	133.4	7 3/4	196.9	10 1/4	260.4	12 3/4	323.8	15 1/4	387.3	17 3/4	450.8
5/16	7.9	2 13/16	71.4	5 5/16	134.9	7 13/16	198.4	10 5/16	261.9	12 13/16	325.4	15 5/16	388.9	17 13/16	452.4
3/8	9.5	2 7/8	73.0	5 3/8	136.5	7 7/8	200.0	10 3/8	263.5	12 7/8	327.0	12 3/8	390.5	17 7/8	454.0
7/16	11.1	2 15/16	74.6	5 7/16	138.1	7 15/16	201.6	10 7/16	265.1	12 15/16	328.6	15 7/16	392.1	17 15/16	455.6
1/2	12.7	3	76.2	5 1/2	139.7	8	203.2	10 1/2	266.7	13	330.2	15 1/2	393.7	18	457.2
9/16	14.3	3 1/16	77.8	5 9/16	141.3	8 1/16	204.8	10 9/16	268.3	13 1/16	331.8	15 9/16	395.3	18 1/16	458.8
5/8	15.9	3 1/8	79.4	5 5/8	142.9	8 1/8	206.4	10 5/8	269.9	13 1/8	333.4	15 5/8	396.9	18 1/8	460.4
11/16	17.5	3 3/16	81.0	5 11/16	144.5	8 3/16	208.0	10 11/16	271.5	13 3/16	335.0	15 11/16	398.5	18 3/16	462.0
3/4	19.1	3 1/4	82.5	5 3/4	146.1	8 1/4	209.6	10 3/4	273.1	13 1/4	336.5	15 3/4	400.0	18 1/4	463.5
13/16	20.6	3 5/16	84.1	5 13/16	147.6	8 5/16	211.1	10 13/16	274.6	13 5/16	338.1	15 13/16	401.6	18 5/16	465.1
7/8	22.2	3 3/8	85.7	5 7/8	149.2	8 3/8	212.7	10 7/8	276.2	13 3/8	339.7	15 7/8	403.2	18 3/8	466.7
15/16	23.8	3 7/16	87.3	5 15/16	150.8	8 7/16	214.3	10 15/16	277.8	13 7/16	341.3	15 15/16	404.8	18 7/16	468.3
1	25.4	3 1/2	88.9	6	152.4	8 1/2	215.9	11	279.4	13 1/2	342.9	16	406.4	18 1/2	469.9
1 1/16	27.0	3 9/16	90.5	6 1/16	154.0	8 9/16	217.5	11 1/16	281.0	13 9/16	344.5	16 1/16	408.0	18 9/16	471.5
1 1/8	28.6	3 5/8	92.1	6 1/8	155.6	8 5/8	219.1	11 1/8	282.6	13 5/8	346.1	16 1/8	409.6	18 5/8	473.1
1 3/16	30.2	3 11/16	93.7	6 3/16	157.2	8 11/16	220.7	11 3/16	284.2	13 11/16	347.7	16 3/16	411.2	18 11/16	474.7
1 1/4	31.7	3 3/4	95.2	6 1/4	158.8	8 3/4	222.3	11 1/4	285.7	13 3/4	349.2	16 1/4	412.7	18 3/4	476.2
1 5/16	33.3	3 13/16	96.8	6 5/16	160.3	8 13/16	223.8	11 5/16	287.3	13 13/16	350.8	16 5/16	414.3	18 13/16	477.8
1 3/8	34.9	3 7/8	98.4	6 3/8	161.9	8 7/8	225.4	11 3/8	288.9	13 7/8	352.4	16 3/8	415.9	18 7/8	479.4
1 7/16	36.5	3 15/16	100.0	6 7/16	163.5	8 15/16	227.0	11 7/16	290.5	13 15/16	354.0	16 7/16	417.5	18 15/16	481.0
1 1/2	38.1	4	101.6	6 1/2	165.1	9	228.6	11 1/2	292.1	14	355.6	16 1/2	419.1	19	482.6
1 9/16	39.7	4 1/16	103.2	6 9/16	166.7	9 1/16	230.2	11 9/16	293.7	14 1/16	357.2	16 9/16	420.7	19 1/16	484.2
1 5/8	41.3	4 1/8	104.8	6 5/8	168.3	9 1/8	231.8	11 5/8	295.3	14 1/8	358.8	16 5/8	422.3	19 1/8	485.8
1 11/16	42.9	4 3/16	106.4	6 11/16	169.9	9 3/16	233.4	11 11/16	296.9	14 3/16	360.4	16 11/16	423.9	19 3/16	487.4
1 3/4	44.4	4 1/4	108.0	6 3/4	171.5	9 1/4	235.0	11 3/4	298.4	14 1/4	361.9	16 3/4	425.4	19 1/4	488.9
1 13/16	46.0	4 5/16	109.5	6 13/16	173.0	9 5/16	236.5	11 13/16	300.0	14 5/16	363.5	16 13/16	427.0	19 5/16	490.5
1 7/8	47.6	4 3/8	111.1	6 7/8	174.6	9 3/8	238.1	11 7/8	301.6	14 3/8	365.1	16 7/8	428.6	19 3/8	492.1
1 15/16	49.2	4 7/16	112.7	6 15/16	176.2	9 7/16	239.7	11 15/16	303.2	14 7/16	366.7	16 15/16	430.2	19 7/16	493.7
2	50.8	4 1/2	114.3	7	177.8	9 1/2	241.3	12	304.8	14 1/2	368.3	17	431.8	19 1/2	495.3
2 1/16	52.4	4 9/16	115.9	7 1/16	179.4	9 9/16	242.9	12 1/16	306.4	14 9/16	369.9	17 1/16	433.4	19 9/16	496.9
2 1/8	54.0	4 5/8	117.5	7 1/8	181.0	9 5/8	244.5	12 1/8	308.0	14 5/8	371.5	17 1/8	435.0	19 5/8	498.5
2 3/16	55.6	4 11/16	119.1	7 3/16	182.6	9 11/16	246.1	12 3/16	309.6	14 11/16	373.1	17 3/16	436.6	19 11/16	500.1
2 1/4	57.1	4 3/4	120.7	7 1/4	184.2	9 3/4	247.7	12 1/4	311.1	14 3/4	374.6	17 1/4	438.1	19 3/4	501.6
2 5/16	58.7	4 13/16	122.2	7 5/16	185.7	9 13/16	249.2	12 5/16	312.7	14 13/16	376.2	17 5/16	439.7	19 13/16	503.2
2 3/8	60.3	4 7/8	123.8	7 3/8	187.3	9 7/8	250.8	12 3/8	314.3	14 7/8	377.8	17 3/8	441.3	19 7/8	504.8
2 7/16	61.9	4 15/16	125.4	7 7/16	188.9	9 15/16	252.4	12 7/16	315.9	14 15/16	379.4	17 7/16	442.9	19 15/16	506.4
2 1/2	63.5	5	127.0	7 1/2	190.5	10	254.0	12 1/2	317.5	15	381.0	17 1/2	444.5	20	508.0

TABLE 13
DECIMAL EQUIVALENTS OF MILLIMETERS AND FRACTIONS OF MILLIMETERS

Advancing by 1/100 mm and 1 mm

1 mm = 0.03937 in. 1 cm = 0.3937 in.
1 dm = 3.937 in. 1 m = 39.37 in.

mm	Inches	mm	Inches	mm	Inches	mm	Inches	mm	Inches
1/100 =	.00039	41/100 =	.01614	81/100 =	.03189	21 =	.82677	61 =	2.40157
2/100 =	.00079	42/100 =	.01654	82/100 =	.03228	22 =	.86614	62 =	2.44094
3/100 =	.00118	43/100 =	.01693	83/100 =	.03268	23 =	.90551	63 =	2.48031
4/100 =	.00157	44/100 =	.01732	84/100 =	.03307	24 =	.94488	64 =	2.51968
5/100 =	.00197	45/100 =	.01772	85/100 =	.03346	25 =	.98425	65 =	2.55905
6/100 =	.00236	46/100 =	.01811	86/100 =	.03386	26 =	1.02362	66 =	2.59842
7/100 =	.00276	47/100 =	.01850	87/100 =	.03425	27 =	1.06299	67 =	2.63779
8/100 =	.00315	48/100 =	.01890	88/100 =	.03465	28 =	1.10236	68 =	2.67716
9/100 =	.00354	49/100 =	.01929	89/100 =	.03504	29 =	1.14173	69 =	2.71653
10/100 =	.00394	50/100 =	.01969	90/100 =	.03543	30 =	1.18110	70 =	2.75590
11/100 =	.00433	51/100 =	.02008	91/100 =	.03583	31 =	1.22047	71 =	2.79527
12/100 =	.00472	52/100 =	.02047	92/100 =	.03622	32 =	1.25984	72 =	2.83464
13/100 =	.00512	53/100 =	.02087	93/100 =	.03661	33 =	1.29921	73 =	2.87401
14/100 =	.00551	54/100 =	.02126	94/100 =	.03701	34 =	1.33858	74 =	2.91338
15/100 =	.00591	55/100 =	.02165	95/100 =	.03740	35 =	1.37795	75 =	2.95275
16/100 =	.00630	56/100 =	.02205	96/100 =	.03780	36 =	1.41732	76 =	2.99212
17/100 =	.00669	57/100 =	.02244	97/100 =	.03819	37 =	1.45669	77 =	3.03149
18/100 =	.00709	58/100 =	.02283	98/100 =	.03858	38 =	1.49606	78 =	3.07086
19/100 =	.00748	59/100 =	.02323	99/100 =	.03898	39 =	1.53543	79 =	3.11023
20/100 =	.00787	60/100 =	.02362			40 =	1.57480	80 =	3.14960
21/100 =	.00827	61/100 =	.02402	1 =	.03937	41 =	1.61417	81 =	3.18897
22/100 =	.00866	62/100 =	.02441	2 =	.07874	42 =	1.65354	82 =	3.22834
23/100 =	.00906	63/100 =	.02480	3 =	.11811	43 =	1.69291	83 =	3.26771
24/100 =	.00945	64/100 =	.02520	4 =	.15748	44 =	1.73228	84 =	3.30708
25/100 =	.00984	65/100 =	.02559	5 =	.19685	45 =	1.77165	85 =	3.34645
26/100 =	.01024	66/100 =	.02598	6 =	.23622	46 =	1.81102	86 =	3.38582
27/100 =	.01063	67/100 =	.02638	7 =	.27559	47 =	1.85039	87 =	3.42519
28/100 =	.01102	68/100 =	.02677	8 =	.31496	48 =	1.88976	88 =	3.46456
29/100 =	.01142	69/100 =	.02717	9 =	.35433	49 =	1.92913	89 =	3.50393
30/100 =	.01181	70/100 =	.02756	10 =	.39370	50 =	1.96850	90 =	3.54330
31/100 =	.01220	71/100 =	.02795	11 =	.43307	51 =	2.00787	91 =	3.58267
32/100 =	.01260	72/100 =	.02835	12 =	.47244	52 =	2.04724	92 =	3.62204
33/100 =	.01299	73/100 =	.02874	13 =	.51181	53 =	2.08661	93 =	3.66141
34/100 =	.01339	74/100 =	.02913	14 =	.55118	54 =	2.12598	94 =	3.70078
35/100 =	.01378	75/100 =	.02953	15 =	.59055	55 =	2.16535	95 =	3.74015
36/100 =	.01417	76/100 =	.02992	16 =	.62992	56 =	2.20472	96 =	3.77952
37/100 =	.01457	77/100 =	.03032	17 =	.66929	57 =	2.24409	97 =	3.81889
38/100 =	.01496	78/100 =	.03071	18 =	.70866	58 =	2.28346	98 =	3.85826
39/100 =	.01535	79/100 =	.03110	19 =	.74803	59 =	2.32283	99 =	3.89763
40/100 =	.01575	80/100 =	.03150	20 =	.78740	60 =	2.36220	100 =	3.93700

TABLE 14
DECIMAL EQUIVALENT PARTS OF ONE INCH

16	32	64	Decimal	16	32	64	Decimal	16	32	64	Decimal
		1/64	.015625		11/32	22/64	.343750			43/64	.671875
	1/32	2/64	.031250			23/64	.359375	11/16	22/32	44/64	.687500
		3/64	.046875	3/8	12/32	24/64	.375000			45/64	.703125
1/16	2/32	4/64	.062500			25/64	.390625		23/32	46/64	.718750
		5/64	.078125		13/32	26/64	.406250			47/64	.734375
	3/32	6/64	.093750			27/64	.421875	3/4	24/32	48/64	.750000
		7/64	.109375	7/16	14/32	28/64	.437500			49/64	.765625
1/8	4/32	8/64	.125000			29/64	.453125		25/32	50/64	.781250
		9/64	.140625		15/32	30/64	.468750			51/64	.796875
	5/32	10/64	.156250			31/64	.484375	13/16	26/32	52/64	.812500
		11/64	.171875	1/2	16/32	32/64	.500000			53/64	.828125
3/16	6/32	12/64	.187500			33/64	.515625		27/32	54/64	.843750
		13/64	.203125		17/32	34/64	.531250			55/64	.859375
	7/32	14/64	.218750			35/64	.546875	7/8	28/32	56/64	.875000
		15/64	.234375	9/16	18/32	36/64	.562500			57/64	.890625
1/4	8/32	16/64	.250000			37/64	.578125		29/32	58/64	.906250
		17/64	.265625		19/32	38/64	.593750			59/64	.921875
	9/32	18/64	.281250			39/64	.609375	15/16	30/32	60/64	.937500
		19/64	.296875	5/8	20/32	40/64	.625000			61/64	.953125
5/16	10/32	20/64	.312500			41/64	.640625		31/32	62/64	.968750
		21/64	.328125		21/32	42/64	.656250			63/64	.984375

TABLE 15
DIAGONALS OF HEXAGONS AND SQUARES

Across Flats	Across Corners		Across Flats	Across Corners		Across Flats	Across Corners	
	Hexagons	Squares		Hexagons	Squares		Hexagons	Squares
1/16	.072	.088	1 3/8	1.587	1.944	2 11/16	3.103	3.800
1/8	.144	.177	1 7/16	1.659	2.032	2 3/4	3.175	3.889
3/16	.216	.265	1 1/2	1.732	2.121	2 13/16	3.247	3.979
1/4	.288	.353	1 9/16	1.804	2.209	2 7/8	3.319	4.065
5/16	.360	.441	1 5/8	1.876	2.298	2 15/16	3.391	4.154
3/8	.432	.530	1 11/16	1.948	2.386	3	3.464	4.242
7/16	.505	.618	1 3/4	2.020	2.470	3 1/16	3.536	4.331
1/2	.577	.707	1 13/16	2.092	2.563	3 1/8	3.608	4.419
9/16	.649	.795	1 7/8	2.165	2.651	3 3/16	3.680	4.507
5/8	.721	.883	1 15/16	2.237	2.740	3 1/4	3.752	4.596
11/16	.793	.972	2	2.309	2.828	3 5/16	3.824	4.684
3/4	.865	1.060	2 1/16	2.381	2.916	3 3/8	3.897	4.772
13/16	.938	1.149	2 1/8	2.453	3.005	3 1/2	4.041	4.949
7/8	1.010	1.237	2 3/16	2.525	3.093	3 5/8	4.185	5.126
15/16	1.082	1.325	2 1/4	2.598	3.182	3 3/4	4.330	5.303
1	1.154	1.414	2 5/16	2.670	3.270	3 7/8	4.474	5.480
1 1/16	1.226	1.502	2 3/8	2.742	3.358	4	4.618	5.656
1 1/8	1.299	1.591	2 7/16	2.814	3.447	4 1/8	4.763	5.833
1 3/16	1.371	1.679	2 1/2	2.886	3.535	4 1/4	4.904	6.010
1 1/4	1.443	1.767	2 9/16	2.958	3.623	4 3/8	5.051	6.187
1 5/16	1.515	1.856	2 5/8	3.031	3.712	4 1/2	5.196	6.363

Diagonal of hexagon equals 1.155 times distance across flats.

Diagonal of square equals 1.414 times distance across flats.

TABLE 16

AMERICAN STANDARD THREAD DIMENSIONS AND TAP DRILL SIZES—FRACTIONAL SIZES

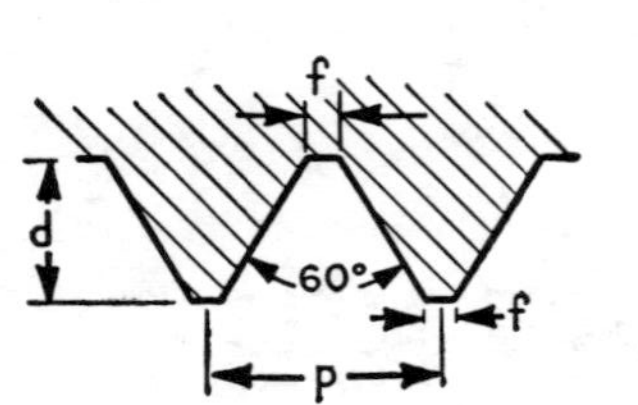

p = pitch = $\dfrac{1}{\text{no. of threads per inch}}$

n = number of threads per inch

d = depth = pitch × .649519 or $\dfrac{.649519}{n}$

f = flat = $\dfrac{\text{pitch}}{8}$

Nominal Size	Outside Diameter, Inches	Pitch Diameter, Inches	Root Diameter, Inches	Tap Drill	Decimal Equivalent of Tap Drill	Nominal Size	Outside Diameter, Inches	Pitch Diameter, Inches	Root Diameter, Inches	Tap Drill	Decimal Equivalent of Tap Drill
1/16–64	.0625	.0524	.0422	3-64	.0469	27	.5625	.5384	.5144	17-32	.5312
72	.0625	.0535	.0445	3-64	.0469	5/8–11	.6250	.5660	.5069	17-32	.5312
5/64–60	.0781	.0673	.0563	1-16	.0625	12	.6250	.5709	.5168	35-64	.5469
72	.0781	.0691	.0601	52	.0635	5/8–18	.6250	.5889	.5528	37-64	.5781
3/32–48	.0938	.0803	.0667	49	.0730	27	.6250	.6009	.5769	19-32	.5937
50	.0938	.0808	.0678	49	.0730	11/16–11	.6875	.6285	.5694	19-32	.5937
7/64–48	.1094	.0959	.0823	43	.0890	16	.6875	.6469	.6063	5-8	.6250
1/8–32	.1250	.1047	.0844	3-32	.0937	3/4–10	.7500	.6850	.6201	21-32	.6562
40	.1250	.1088	.0925	38	.1015	12	.7500	.6959	.6418	43-64	.6719
9/64–40	.1406	.1244	.1081	32	.1160	16	.7500	.7094	.6688	11-16	.6875
5/32–32	.1563	.1360	.1157	1-8	.1250	27	.7500	.7259	.7019	23-32	.7187
36	.1563	.1382	.1202	30	.1285	13/16–10	.8125	.7476	.6826	23-32	.7187
11/64–32	.1719	.1516	.1313	9-64	.1406	7/8– 9	.8750	.8028	.7307	49-64	.7656
3/16–24	.1875	.1604	.1334	26	.1470	12	.8750	.8209	.7668	51-64	.7969
32	.1875	.1672	.1469	22	.1570	14	.8750	.8286	.7822	13-16	.8125
13/64–24	.2031	.1760	.1490	20	.1610	18	.8750	.8389	.8028	53-64	.8281
7/32–24	.2188	.1917	.1646	16	.1770	27	.8750	.8509	.8269	27-32	.8437
32	.2188	.1985	.1782	12	.1890	15/16– 9	.9375	.8654	.7932	53-64	.8281
15/64–24	.2344	.2073	.1806	10	.1935	1 – 8	1.0000	.9188	.8376	7-8	.8750
1/4–20	.2500	.2175	.1850	7	.2010	12	1.0000	.9459	.8918	59-64	.9219
24	.2500	.2229	.1959	4	.2090	14	1.0000	.9536	.9072	15-16	.9375
27	.2500	.2260	.2019	3	.2130	27	1.0000	.9759	.9519	31-32	.9687
28	.2500	.2268	.2036	3	.2130	1 1/8– 7	1.1250	1.0322	.9394	63-64	.9844
32	.2500	.2297	.2094	7-32	.2188	12	1.1250	1.0709	1.0168	1 3-64	1.0469
5/16–18	.3125	.2764	.2403	F	.2570	1 1/4– 7	1.2500	1.1572	1.0644	1 7-64	1.1094
20	.3125	.2800	.2476	17-64	.2656	12	1.2500	1.1959	1.1418	1 11-64	1.1719
24	.3125	.2854	.2584	I	.2720	1 3/8– 6	1.3750	1.2667	1.1585	1 13-64	1.2187
27	.3125	.2884	.2644	J	.2770	12	1.3750	1.3209	1.2668	1 19-64	1.2969
32	.3125	.2922	.2719	9-32	.2812	1 1/2– 6	1.5000	1.3917	1.2835	1 11-32	1.3437
3/8–16	.3750	.3344	.2938	5-16	.3125	12	1.5000	1.4459	1.3918	1 27-64	1.4219
20	.3750	.3425	.3100	21-64	.3281	1 5/8– 5 1/2	1.6250	1.5069	1.3888	1 29-64	1.4531
24	.3750	.3479	.3209	Q	.3320	1 3/4– 5	1.7500	1.6201	1.4902	1 9-16	1.5625
27	.3750	.3509	.3269	R	.3390	1 7/8– 5	1.8750	1.7451	1.6152	1 11-16	1.6875
7/16–14	.4375	.3911	.3447	U	.3680	2 – 4 1/2	2.0000	1.8557	1.7113	1 25-32	1.7812
20	.4375	.4050	.3726	25-64	.3906	2 1/8– 4 1/2	2.1250	1.9807	1.8363	1 29-32	1.9062
24	.4375	.4104	.3834	X	.3970	2 1/4– 4 1/2	2.2500	2.1057	1.9613	2 1-32	2.0312
27	.4375	.4134	.3894	Y	.4040	2 3/8– 4	2.3750	2.2126	2.0502	2 1-8	2.1250
1/2–12	.5000	.4459	.3918	27-64	.4219	2 1/2– 4	2.5000	2.3376	2.1752	2 1-4	2.2500
13	.5000	.4500	.4001	27-64	.4219	2 3/4– 4	2.7500	2.5876	2.4252	2 1-2	2.5000
20	.5000	.4675	.4351	29-64	.4531	3 – 4	3.0000	2.8376	2.6752	2 3-4	2.7500
24	.5000	.4729	.4459	29-64	.4531	3 1/4– 4	3.2500	3.0876	2.9252	3	3.0000
27	.5000	.4759	.4519	15-32	.4687	3 1/2– 4	3.5000	3.3376	3.1752	3 1-4	3.2500
9/16–12	.5625	.5084	.4542	31-64	.4844	3 3/4– 4	3.7500	3.5876	3.4252	3 1-2	3.5000
18	.5625	.5264	.4903	33-64	.5156	4 – 4	4.0000	3.8376	3.6752	3 3-4	3.7500

TABLE 17

STANDARD FOR WIRE GAUGES (DIMENSIONS OF SIZES IN DECIMAL PARTS OF AN INCH)

Number of Wire Gauge	American or Brown & Sharpe	Birmingham or Stubs' Iron Wire	Washburn & Moen, Worcester, Mass.	W. & M. Steel Music Wire	American S. & W. Co.'s Music Wire Gauge	Imperial Wire Gauge	Stubs' Steel Wire	U. S. Standard Gauge for Sheet and Plate Iron and Steel	Number of Wire Gauge
00000000	...	...	...	.0083	...	...	...	...	00000000
0000000	...	...	...	.0087	...	...	...	...	0000000
000000	...	...	...	.0095	.004	.464	...	.46875	000000
00000	...	...	...	.010	.005	.432	...	.4375	00000
0000	.460	.454	.3938	.011	.006	.400	...	.40625	0000
000	.40964	.425	.3625	.012	.007	.372	...	.375	000
00	.3648	.380	.3310	.0133	.008	.348	...	.34375	00
0	.32486	.340	.3065	.0144	.009	.324	...	.3125	0
1	.2893	.300	.2830	.0156	.010	.300	.227	.28125	1
2	.25763	.284	.2625	.0166	.011	.276	.219	.265625	2
3	.22942	.259	.2437	.0178	.012	.252	.212	.250	3
4	.20431	.238	.2253	.0188	.013	.232	.207	.234375	4
5	.18194	.220	.2070	.0202	.014	.212	.204	.21875	5
6	.16202	.203	.1920	.0215	.016	.192	.201	.203125	6
7	.14428	.180	.1770	.023	.018	.176	.199	.1875	7
8	.12849	.165	.1620	.0243	.020	.160	.197	.171875	8
9	.11443	.148	.1483	.0256	.022	.144	.194	.15625	9
10	.10189	.134	.1350	.027	.024	.128	.191	.140625	10
11	.090742	.120	.1205	.0284	.026	.116	.188	.125	11
12	.080808	.109	.1055	.0296	.029	.104	.185	.109375	12
13	.071961	.095	.0915	.0314	.031	.092	.182	.09375	13
14	.064084	.083	.0800	.0326	.033	.080	.180	.078125	14
15	.057068	.072	.0720	.0345	.035	.072	.178	.0703125	15
16	.05082	.065	.0625	.036	.037	.064	.175	.0625	16
17	.045257	.058	.0540	.0377	.039	.056	.172	.05625	17
18	.040303	.049	.04575	.0395	.041	.048	.168	.050	18
19	.03589	.042	.0410	.0414	.043	.040	.164	.04375	19
20	.031961	.035	.0348	.0434	.045	.036	.161	.0375	20
21	.028462	.032	.03175	.046	.047	.032	.157	.034375	21
22	.025347	.028	.0286	.0483	.049	.028	.155	.03125	22
23	.022571	.025	.0258	.051	.051	.024	.153	.028125	23
24	.0201	.022	.0230	.055	.055	.022	.151	.025	24
25	.0179	.020	.0204	.0586	.059	.020	.148	.021875	25
26	.01594	.018	.0181	.0626	.063	.018	.146	.01875	26
27	.014195	.016	.0173	.0658	.067	.0164	.143	.0171875	27
28	.012641	.014	.0162	.072	.071	.0149	.139	.015625	28
29	.011257	.013	.0150	.076	.075	.0136	.134	.0140625	29
30	.010025	.012	.0140	.080	.080	.0124	.127	.0125	30
31	.008928	.010	.0132	...	.085	.0116	.120	.0109375	31
32	.00795	.009	.0128	...	.090	.0108	.115	.01015625	32
33	.00708	.008	.0118	...	.095	.0100	.112	.009375	33
34	.006304	.007	.0104	...	...	.0092	.110	.00859375	34
35	.005614	.005	.0095	...	...	.0084	.108	.0078125	35
36	.005	.004	.0090	...	...	.0076	.106	.00703125	36
37	.004453	...	...	...	...	.0068	.103	.006640625	37
38	.003965	...	...	...	...	.0060	.101	.00625	38
39	.003531	...	...	...	...	.0052	.099	...	39
40	.003144	...	...	...	...	.0048	.097	...	40

TABLE 18
UNITED STATES STANDARD GAUGE SIZES

No. of Gauge	Approximate Thickness, Inches, (Fractions)	Approximate Thickness, Inches, (Decimals)	Weight per Sq. Ft., Ounces, Avoirdupois	Weight per Sq. Ft. Pounds Avoirdupois	No. of Gauge	Approximate Thickness, Inches, (Fractions)	Approximate Thickness, Inches, (Decimals)	Weight per Sq. ft., Ounces, Avoirdupois	Weight per Sq. Ft., Pounds, Avoirdupois
0000000	1-2	.5	320	20.00	17	9-160	.0563	36	2.25
000000	15-32	.4688	300	18.75	18	1-20	.05	32	2.
00000	7-16	.4375	280	17.50	19	7-160	.0438	28	1.75
0000	13-32	.4063	260	16.25	20	3-80	.0375	24	1.50
000	3-8	.375	240	15.00	21	11-320	.0344	22	1.375
00	11-32	.3438	220	13.75	22	1-32	.0313	20	1.25
0	5-16	.3125	200	12.50	23	9-320	.0281	18	1.125
1	9-32	.2813	180	11.25	24	1-40	.025	16	1.
2	17-64	.2656	170	10.625	25	7-320	.0219	14	.875
3	1-4	.25	160	10.00	26	3-160	.0188	12	.75
4	15-64	.2344	150	9.375	27	11-640	.0172	11	.6875
5	7-32	.2188	140	8.75	28	1-64	.0156	10	.625
6	13-64	.2031	130	8.125	29	9-640	.0141	9	.5625
7	3-16	.1875	120	7.5	30	1-80	.0125	8	.5
8	11-64	.1719	110	6.875	31	7-640	.0109	7	.4375
9	5-32	.1563	100	6.25	32	13-1280	.0102	6 1-2	.4063
10	9-64	.1406	90	5.625	33	3-320	.0094	6	.375
11	1-8	.125	80	5.00	34	11-1280	.0086	5 1-2	.3438
12	7-64	.1094	70	4.375	35	5-640	.0078	5	.3125
13	3-32	.0938	60	3.75	36	9-1280	.0070	4 1-2	.2813
14	5-64	.0781	50	3.125	37	17-2560	.0066	4 1-4	.2656
15	9-128	.0703	45	2.8125	38	1-160	.0063	4	.25
16	1-16	.0625	40	2.5					

TABLE 19
HARDNESS CONVERSION

ROCKWELL HARDNESS TEST			BRINELL HARDNESS TEST			SCLERO-SCOPE HARDNESS TEST
Diamond Cone			Steel Ball 10 mm., Load 3000 Kg.			
150 Kg. C Scale	100 Kg. D Scale	60 Kg. A Scale	Diameter of Ball Impression, mm.	Hardness Number	Equivalent 1000 Lb. Sq. In.	
....	....	....	2.00	946	464	......
....	....	....	2.05	898	439	......
....	....	....	2.10	857	419	......
....	....	....	2.15	817	399	......
72	82	89	2.20	782	383	107
69	80	87	2.25	744	365	100
67	78	85	2.30	713	350	96
65	76	84	2.35	683	334	92
63	74	83	2.40	652	318	88
61	72	82	2.45	627	307	85
59	71	81	2.50	600	294	81
58	69	80	2.55	578	282	78
56	68	79	2.60	555	271	75
54	67	78	2.65	532	260	72
52	65	77	2.70	512	251	70
51	64	76	2.75	495	242	68
49	63	76	2.80	477	233	66
48	62	75	2.85	460	226	64
47	61	74	2.90	444	217	61
45	60	73	2.95	430	210	59
44	59	73	3.00	418	205	57
43	58	72	3.05	402	197	55
41	57	71	3.10	387	189	53
40	56	71	3.15	375	183	52
39	55	70	3.20	364	178	50
38	54	69	3.25	351	172	49
37	53	69	3.30	340	167	47
36	52	68	3.35	332	162	46
35	52	68	3.40	321	157	45
34	51	67	3.45	311	152	44
33	50	67	3.50	302	148	42
31	49	66	3.55	293	144	41
30	49	66	3.60	286	140	40
29	48	65	3.65	277	136	39
28	47	65	3.70	269	132	38
		64				
27	46	64	3.75	262	128	37
26	45	63	3.80	255	125	36
25	45	63	3.85	248	121	36
24	44	62	3.90	241	118	35
23	43		3.95	235	115	34

TABLE 20
MORSE TAPERS

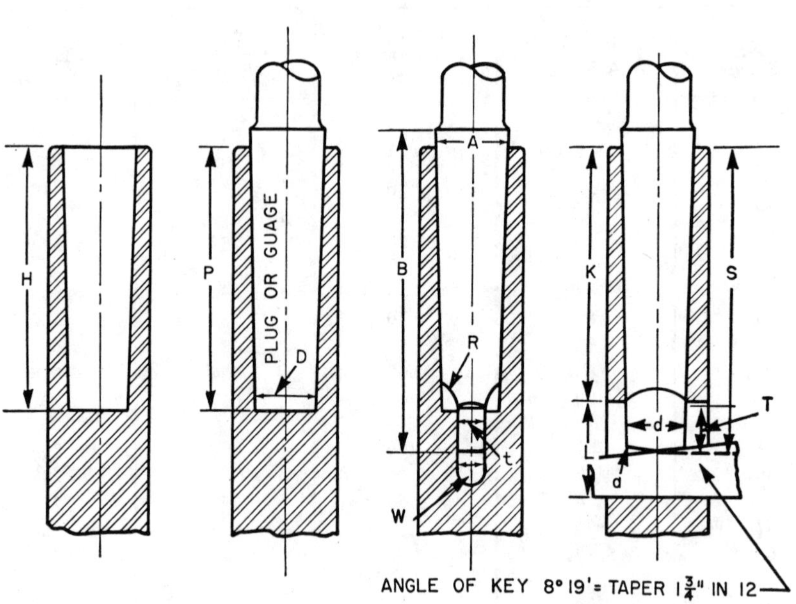

	Plug		Shank				Tongue					Keyway					
	D	A	B	S	H	P	t	T	d	R	a	W	L	K			
Number of Taper	Diameter Small End	Diameter at End of Socket	Whole Length	Depth	Depth of Hole	Standard Plug Depth	Thickness	Length	Diameter	Radius	Radius	Width	Length	End of Socket to Keyway	Amount of Taper per Inch of Length	Amount of Taper per Foot of Length	Number of Key
0	0.252	0.3561	2 11/32	2 11/32	2 1/32	2	0.1562	1/4	0.235	5/32	0.04	0.160	9/16	1 15/16	0.05205	0.62460	0
1	0.369	0.475	2 9/16	2 7/16	2 3/16	2 1/8	0.2031	3/8	0.343	3/16	0.05	0.213	3/4	2 1/16	0.04988	0.59858	1
2	0.572	0.700	3 1/8	2 15/16	2 5/8	2 9/16	0.250	7/16	17/32	1/4	0.06	0.260	7/8	2 1/2	0.04995	0.59941	2
3	0.778	0.938	3 7/8	3 11/16	3 1/4	3 3/16	0.3125	9/16	23/32	9/32	0.08	0.322	1 3/16	3 1/16	0.05020	0.60235	3
4	1.020	1.231	4 7/8	4 5/8	4 1/8	4 1/16	0.4687	5/8	31/32	5/16	0.10	0.478	1 1/4	3 7/8	0.05194	0.62326	4
5	1.475	1.748	6 1/8	5 7/8	5 1/4	5 3/16	0.6250	3/4	1 13/32	3/8	0.12	0.635	1 1/2	4 15/16	0.05263	0.63151	5
6	2.116	2.494	8 9/16	8 1/4	7 3/8	7 1/4	0.750	1 1/8	2	1/2	0.15	0.760	1 3/4	7	0.05214	0.62565	6
7	2.750	3.270	11 5/8	11 1/4	10 1/8	10	1.1250	1 3/8	2 5/8	3/4	1.18	1.135	2 5/8	9 1/2	0.05200	0.6240	7

TABLE 21
CONVERSION OF MINUTES OF ARC INTO DECIMALS OF A DEGREE

Min. of Arc	Decimal of a Degree	Min. of Arc	Decimal of a Degree	Min. of Arc	Decimal of a Degree	Min. of Arc	Decimal of a Degree	Min. of Arc	Decimal of a Degree	Min. of Arc	Decimal of a Degree
¼	0.00416	10¼	0.17083	20¼	0.33750	30¼	0.50416	40¼	0.67083	50¼	0.83750
½	0.00833	10½	0.17500	20½	0.34166	30½	0.50833	40½	0.67500	50½	0.84166
¾	0.01250	10¾	0.17916	20¾	0.34583	30¾	0.51250	40¾	0.67916	50¾	0.84583
1	0.01666	11	0.18333	21	0.35000	31	0.51666	41	0.68333	51	0.85000
1¼	0.02083	11¼	0.18750	21¼	0.35416	31¼	0.52083	41¼	0.68750	51¼	0.85416
1½	0.02500	11½	0.19166	21½	0.35833	31½	0.52500	41½	0.69166	51½	0.85833
1¾	0.02916	11¾	0.19583	21¾	0.36250	31¾	0.52916	41¾	0.69583	51¾	0.86250
2	0.03333	12	0.20000	22	0.36666	32	0.53333	42	0.70000	52	0.86666
2¼	0.03750	12¼	0.20416	22¼	0.37083	32¼	0.53750	42¼	0.70416	52¼	0.87083
2½	0.04166	12½	0.20833	22½	0.37500	32½	0.54166	42½	0.70833	52½	0.87500
2¾	0.04583	12¾	0.21250	22¾	0.37916	32¾	0.54583	42¾	0.71250	52¾	0.87916
3	0.05000	13	0.21666	23	0.38333	33	0.55000	43	0.71666	53	0.88333
3¼	0.05416	13¼	0.22083	23¼	0.38750	33¼	0.55416	43¼	0.72083	53¼	0.88750
3½	0.05833	13½	0.22500	23½	0.39166	33½	0.55833	43½	0.72500	53½	0.89166
3¾	0.06250	13¾	0.22916	23¾	0.39583	33¾	0.56250	43¾	0.72916	53¾	0.89583
4	0.06666	14	0.23333	24	0.40000	34	0.56666	44	0.73333	54	0.90000
4¼	0.07083	14¼	0.23750	24¼	0.40416	34¼	0.57083	44¼	0.73750	54¼	0.90416
4½	0.07500	14½	0.24166	24½	0.40833	34½	0.57500	44½	0.74166	54½	0.90833
4¾	0.07916	14¾	0.24583	24¾	0.41250	34¾	0.57916	44¾	0.74583	54¾	0.91250
5	0.08333	15	0.25000	25	0.41666	35	0.58333	45	0.75000	55	0.91666
5¼	0.08750	15¼	0.25416	25¼	0.42083	35¼	0.58750	45¼	0.75416	55¼	0.92083
5½	0.09166	15½	0.25833	25½	0.42500	35½	0.59166	45½	0.75833	55½	0.92500
5¾	0.09583	15¾	0.26250	25¾	0.42916	35¾	0.59583	45¾	0.76250	55¾	0.92916
6	0.10000	16	0.26666	26	0.43333	36	0.60000	46	0.76666	56	0.93333
6¼	0.10416	16¼	0.27083	26¼	0.43750	36¼	0.60416	46¼	0.77083	56¼	0.93750
6½	0.10833	16½	0.27500	26½	0.44166	36½	0.60833	46½	0.77500	56½	0.94166
6¾	0.11250	16¾	0.27916	26¾	0.44583	36¾	0.61250	46¾	0.77916	56¾	0.94583
7	0.11666	17	0.28333	27	0.45000	37	0.61666	47	0.78333	57	0.95000
7¼	0.12083	17¼	0.28750	27¼	0.45416	37¼	0.62083	47¼	0.78750	57¼	0.95416
7½	0.12500	17½	0.29166	27½	0.45833	37½	0.62500	47½	0.79166	57½	0.95833
7¾	0.12916	17¾	0.29583	27¾	0.46250	37¾	0.62916	47¾	0.79583	57¾	0.96250
8	0.13333	18	0.30000	28	0.46666	38	0.63333	48	0.80000	58	0.96666
8¼	0.13750	18¼	0.30416	28¼	0.47083	38¼	0.63750	48¼	0.80416	58¼	0.97083
8½	0.14166	18½	0.30833	28½	0.47500	38½	0.64166	48½	0.80833	58½	0.97500
8¾	0.14583	18¾	0.31250	28¾	0.47916	38¾	0.64583	48¾	0.81250	58¾	0.97916
9	0.15000	19	0.31666	29	0.48333	39	0.65000	49	0.81666	59	0.98333
9¼	0.15416	19¼	0.32083	29¼	0.48750	39¼	0.65416	49¼	0.82083	59¼	0.98750
9½	0.15833	19½	0.32500	29½	0.49166	39½	0.65833	49½	0.82500	59½	0.99166
9¾	0.16250	19¾	0.32916	29¾	0.49583	39¾	0.66250	49¾	0.82916	59¾	0.99583
10	0.16666	20	0.33333	30	0.50000	40	0.66666	50	0.83333	60	1.00000

TABLE 22
CIRCUMFERENCES AND AREAS OF CIRCLES

Diam. In.	Circum. In.	Area Sq. In.	Diam. In.	Circum. In.	Area Sq. In.	Diam. In.	Circum. In.	Area Sq. In.	Diam. In.	Circum. In.	Area Sq. In.
1/16	.1963	.00307	3 1/2	10.995	9.6211	31	97.389	754.769	66	207.345	3421.19
1/8	.3927	.01227	3 3/4	11.781	11.044	32	100.531	804.249	67	210.487	3525.66
3/16	.5890	.02761	4	12.566	12.566	33	103.672	855.30	68	213.628	3631.68
1/4	.7854	.04909	4 1/4	13.351	14.186	34	106.814	907.92	69	216.770	3739.28
5/16	.9817	.07670	4 1/2	14.137	15.904	35	109.956	962.11	70	219.912	3848.45
3/8	1.1781	.1104	4 3/4	14.922	17.720	36	113.097	1017.88	71	223.053	3959.19
7/16	1.3744	.1503	5	15.708	19.635	37	116.239	1075.21	72	226.195	4071.50
1/2	1.5708	.1963	5 1/4	16.493	21.647	38	119.380	1134.11	73	229.336	4185.39
9/16	1.7671	.2485	5 1/2	17.278	23.758	39	122.522	1194.59	74	232.478	4300.84
5/8	1.9635	.3068	5 3/4	18.064	25.967	40	125.664	1256.64	75	235.620	4417.86
11/16	2.1598	.3712	6	18.849	28.274	41	128.805	1320.25	76	238.761	4536.46
3/4	2.3562	.4418	7	21.991	38.484	42	131.947	1385.44	77	241.903	4656.63
13/16	2.5525	.5185	8	25.132	50.265	43	135.088	1452.20	78	245.044	4778.36
7/8	2.7489	.6013	9	28.274	63.617	44	138.230	1520.53	79	248.186	4901.68
15/16	2.9452	.6903	10	31.416	78.540	45	141.372	1590.43	80	251.328	5026.55
1	3.1416	.7854	11	34.558	95.033	46	144.513	1661.90	81	254.469	5153.00
1 1/16	3.3379	.8866	12	37.699	113.097	47	147.655	1734.94	82	257.611	5281.02
1 1/8	3.5343	.9940	13	40.840	132.732	48	150.796	1809.56	83	260.752	5410.61
1 3/16	3.7306	1.1075	14	43.982	153.938	49	153.938	1885.74	84	263.894	5541.77
1 1/4	3.9270	1.2271	15	47.124	176.715	50	157.080	1963.50	85	267.035	5674.51
1 5/16	4.1233	1.3530	16	50.265	201.062	51	160.221	2042.82	86	270.177	5808.80
1 3/8	4.3197	1.4848	17	53.407	226.980	52	163.363	2123.72	87	273.319	5944.68
1 7/16	4.5160	1.6229	18	56.548	254.469	53	166.504	2206.18	88	276.460	6082.12
1 1/2	4.7124	1.7671	19	59.690	283.529	54	169.646	2290.22	89	279.602	6221.14
1 5/8	5.1051	2.0739	20	62.832	314.160	55	172.788	2375.83	90	282.744	6361.73
1 3/4	5.4978	2.4052	21	65.973	346.361	56	175.929	2463.01	91	285.885	6503.88
1 7/8	5.8905	2.7611	22	69.115	380.133	57	179.071	2551.76	92	289.027	6647.61
2	6.2832	3.1416	23	72.256	415.476	58	182.212	2642.08	93	292.168	6792.91
2 1/8	6.6759	3.5465	24	75.398	452.390	59	185.354	2733.97	94	295.310	6939.78
2 1/4	7.0686	3.9760	25	78.540	490.875	60	188.496	2827.43	95	298.452	7088.22
2 3/8	7.4613	4.4302	26	81.681	530.930	61	191.637	2922.47	96	301.593	7238.23
2 1/2	7.8540	4.9087	27	84.823	572.556	62	194.779	3019.07	97	304.734	7389.81
2 3/4	8.6394	5.9395	28	87.964	615.753	63	197.920	3117.25	98	307.876	7542.96
3	9.4248	7.0686	29	91.106	660.521	64	210.062	3216.99	99	311.018	7697.69
3 1/4	10.210	8.2957	30	94.248	706.860	65	204.204	3318.31	100	314.159	7853.98

TABLE 23
CUTTING SPEEDS FOR TURNING—DRILLING—TAPPING WITH HIGH SPEED STEEL CUTTING TOOLS

Material	Turning Speeds		Drilling Speeds		Tapping Speeds	
	Ft. per Minute	Lubricant	Ft. per Minute	Lubricant	Ft. per Minute	Lubricant
Aluminum	300–400	Comp. or Kerosene	200–330	Comp. or Kerosene	90–110	Kerosene & Lard Oil
Brass, leaded	300–700	Dry or Comp.	200–500	Comp.	150–250	Comp. or Lt. Base Oil
Brass, red and yellow	150–300	Comp.	75–250	Comp.	60–150	Comp. or Lt. Base Oil
Bronze, leaded	300–700	Comp.	200–500	Comp.	150–250	Comp. or Lt. Base Oil
Bronze, phosphor	75–150	Comp.	50–125	Comp.	30– 60	Comp. or Lt. Base Oil
Cast Iron	50–110	Dry	100–165	Dry	70– 90	Dry or Comp.
Cast Steel	45– 90	Comp.	35– 45	Comp.	20– 35	Sul. Base Oil
Copper, leaded	300–700	Comp.	200–500	Comp.	150–250	Lt. Base Oil
Copper, electro.	75–150	Comp.	20–125	Comp.	30– 60	Lt. Base Oil
Chrome Steel	65–115	Comp.	50– 65	Comp.	20– 35	Sul. Base Oil
Die Castings	225–350	Compound	200–330	Compound	60– 80	Kerosene & Lard Oil
Duralumin	275–400	Compound	250–375	Compound	90–110	Comp. or Ker. and Lard Oil
Fiber	200–300	Dry	175–275	Dry	80–100	Dry
Machine Steel	115–225	Compound	80–120	Compound	40– 70	Comp., Sul. Base Oil or Ker. & Para
Malleable Iron	80–130	Dry or Comp.	80–100	Dry or Comp.	35– 70	Comp. or Sul. Base Oil
Mang. Bronze	150–300	Comp.	75–250	Comp.	60–150	Lt. Base Oil
Mang. Steel	20– 40	Comp.	15– 25	Comp.	10– 20	Comp. or Sul. Base Oil or Ker. & Para
Moly. Steel	100–120	Comp.	50– 65	Comp.	20– 35	Sul. Base Oil
Monel Metal	100–125	Comp. or Sul. Base	40– 55	Sul. Base	20– 30	Sul. Base or Kero. and Lard Oil
Nickel Silver 18%	75–150	Comp.	50–125	Comp.	30– 60	Sul. Base or Kero. and Lard Oil
Nickel Silver, leaded	150–300	Comp.	75–250	Comp.	60–150	Sul. Base or Kero. and Lard Oil
Nickel Steel	85–110	Comp. or Sul. Base	40– 65	Sul. Base Oil	25– 40	Sul. Base Oil
Plastics, hot-set molded	200–600	Dry	75–300	Dry	40– 54	Dry or Water
Rubber, Hard	200–300	Dry	175–275	Dry	80–100	Dry
Stainless Steel	100–150	Sul. Base	30– 45	Sul. Base	15– 30	Sul. Base
Tool Steel	70–130	Comp.	50– 65	Comp.	25– 40	Sul. Base or Kero. and Lard Oil
Tungsten Steel	70–130	Comp.	50– 65	Comp.	20– 35	Sul. Base
Vanadium Steel	85–120	Comp.	45– 65	Sul. Base	25– 40	Sul. Base

The above speeds have been collected from several sources and are suggested as practical for average work. Special conditions may necessitate the use of higher or lower speeds for maximum efficiency.

TABLE 24
MULTIPLE THREADS

"Pitch" is *not* the No. of Threads per inch.
"Pitch" is the distance from one thread to the next (measured parallel to axis of screw) regardless of the thread being single, double or any other multiple.
"Lead" is the distance the screw advances in one turn.
Lead and Pitch of a single thread are equal.
Lead of a double thread is twice the lead of a single thread.
Lead of a triple thread is three times the lead of a single thread, etc.

$$\text{Cotangent of Helix Angle of a screw} = \frac{\text{Circumference of Pitch Diameter}}{\text{Lead}}$$

Lead (given in inches)

T.P.I.	Single	Double	Triple	Quadruple	Quintuple	Sextuple	Septuple	Octuple	Nonuple	Decuple
3	1/3	2/3	1	1 1/3	1 2/3	2	2 1/3	2 2/3	3	3 1/3
4	1/4	1/2	3/4	1	1 1/4	1 1/2	1 3/4	2	2 1/4	2 1/2
4 1/2	2/9	4/9	2/3	8/9	1 1/9	1 1/3	1 5/9	1 7/9	2	2 2/9
5	1/5	2/5	3/5	4/5	1	1 1/5	1 2/5	1 3/5	1 4/5	2
6	1/6	1/3	1/2	2/3	5/6	1	1 1/6	1 1/3	1 1/2	1 2/3
7	1/7	2/7	3/7	4/7	5/7	6/7	1	1 1/7	1 2/7	1 3/7
8	1/8	1/4	3/8	1/2	5/8	3/4	7/8	1	1 1/8	1 1/4
9	1/9	2/9	1/3	4/9	5/9	2/3	7/9	8/9	1	1 1/9
10	1/10	1/5	3/10	2/5	1/2	3/5	7/10	4/5	9/10	1
11	1/11	2/11	3/11	4/11	5/11	6/11	7/11	8/11	9/11	10/11
12	1/12	1/6	1/4	1/3	5/12	1/2	7/12	2/3	3/4	5/6
13	1/13	2/13	3/13	4/13	5/13	6/13	7/13	8/13	9/13	10/13
14	1/14	1/7	3/14	2/7	5/14	3/7	1/2	4/7	9/14	5/7
15	1/15	2/15	1/5	4/15	1/3	2/5	7/15	8/15	3/5	2/3
16	1/16	1/8	3/16	1/4	5/16	3/8	7/16	1/2	9/16	5/8
18	1/18	1/9	1/6	2/9	5/18	1/3	7/18	4/9	1/2	5/9
20	1/20	1/10	3/20	1/5	1/4	3/10	7/20	2/5	9/20	1/2
22	1/22	1/11	3/22	2/11	5/22	3/11	7/22	4/11	9/22	5/11
24	1/24	1/12	1/8	1/6	5/24	1/4	7/24	1/3	3/8	5/12
28	1/28	1/14	3/28	1/7	5/28	3/14	1/4	2/7	9/28	5/14
32	1/32	1/16	3/32	1/8	5/32	3/16	7/32	1/4	9/32	5/16
36	1/36	1/18	1/12	1/9	5/36	1/6	7/36	2/9	1/4	5/18
40	1/40	1/20	3/40	1/10	1/8	3/20	7/40	1/5	9/40	1/4
44	1/44	1/22	3/44	1/11	5/44	3/22	7/44	2/11	9/44	5/22
48	1/48	1/24	1/16	1/12	5/48	1/8	7/48	1/6	3/16	5/24
56	1/56	1/28	3/56	1/14	5/56	3/28	1/8	1/7	9/56	5/28
60	1/60	1/30	1/20	1/15	1/12	1/10	7/60	2/15	3/20	1/6

Table 25
Table of Tangents

A table of tangents is essential in converting taper per foot into degrees and minutes when calculating the proper setting of the compound rest for taper cutting. In this table, tangents are listed for every 15 minutes of an angle. To obtain angles for intermediate tangents, use interpolation. For example: The tangent of the taper in the example in Chapter 18 is .024975, which is between the tangent readings of 1° 15′ and 1° 30′. The exact reading is obtained as follows:

$$.02618 - .02182 = .00436$$
$$.024975 - .02182 = .003155$$
$$\frac{.003155}{.00436} \times 15 \text{ min.} = 11 \text{ min.}$$

1 deg. 15 min. + 11 min. = 1 deg. 26 min.,*required angle.*

Degrees	Minutes	Tangent	Degrees	Minutes	Tangent	Degrees	Minutes	Tangent
0	0	.00000	12	0	.21256	24	0	.44523
	15	.00436		15	.21712		15	.45047
	30	.00873		30	.22169		30	.45573
	45	.01309		45	.22628		45	.46101
1	0	.01745	13	0	.23087	25	0	.46631
	15	.02182		15	.23547		15	.47163
	30	.02618		30	.24008		30	.47697
	45	.03055		45	.24470		45	.48234
2	0	.03492	14	0	.24933	26	0	.48773
	15	.03929		15	.25397		15	.49314
	30	.04366		30	.25862		30	.49858
	45	.04803		45	.26328		45	.50404
3	0	.05241	15	0	.26795	27	0	.50952
	15	.05678		15	.27263		15	.51503
	30	.06116		30	.27732		30	.52057
	45	.06554		45	.28203		45	.52612
4	0	.06993	16	0	.28674	28	0	.53171
	15	.07431		15	.29147		15	.53732
	30	.07870		30	.29621		30	.54295
	45	.08309		45	.30096		45	.54862
5	0	.08749	17	0	.30573	29	0	.55431
	15	.09189		15	.31051		15	.56003
	30	.09629		30	.31530		30	.56577
	45	.10069		45	.32010		45	.57155
6	0	.10510	18	0	.32492	30	0	.57735
	15	.10952		15	.32975		15	.58318
	30	.11393		30	.33459		30	.58904
	45	.11836		45	.33945		45	.59494
7	0	.12278	19	0	.34433	31	0	.60086
	15	.12722		15	.34921		15	.60681
	30	.13165		30	.35412		30	.61280
	45	.13609		45	.35904		45	.61882
8	0	.14054	20	0	.36397	32	0	.62487
	15	.14499		15	.36892		15	.63095
	30	.14945		30	.37388		30	.63707
	45	.15391		45	.37887		45	.64322
9	0	.15838	21	0	.38386	33	0	.64941
	15	.16286		15	.38888		15	.65563
	30	.16734		30	.39391		30	.66188
	45	.17183		45	.39896		45	.66818
10	0	.17633	22	0	.40403	34	0	.67451
	15	.18083		15	.40911		15	.68087
	30	.18534		30	.41421		30	.68728
	45	.18985		45	.41933		45	.69372
11	0	.19438	23	0	.42447	35	0	.70021
	15	.19891		15	.42963		15	.70673
	30	.20345		30	.43481		30	.71329
	45	.20800		45	.44001		45	.71990

TABLE 25 (CONTINUED)

Degrees	Minutes	Tangent	Degrees	Minutes	Tangent	Degrees	Minutes	Tangent
36	0	.72654	54	0	1.3764	72	0	3.0777
	15	.73323		15	1.3891		15	3.1240
	30	.73996		30	1.4019		30	3.1716
	45	.74673		45	1.4150		45	3.2205
37	0	.75355	55	0	1.4281	73	0	3.2708
	15	.76042		15	1.4415		15	3.3226
	30	.76733		30	1.4550		30	3.3759
	45	.77428		45	1.4687		45	3.4308
38	0	.78128	56	0	1.4826	74	0	3.4874
	15	.78834		15	1.4966		15	3.5457
	30	.79543		30	1.5108		30	3.6059
	45	.80258		45	1.5252		45	3.6679
39	0	.80978	57	0	1.5399	75	0	3.7320
	15	.81703		15	1.5547		15	3.7983
	30	.82434		30	1.5697		30	3.8667
	45	.83169		45	1.5849		45	3.9375
40	0	.83910	58	0	1.6003	76	0	4.0108
	15	.84656		15	1.6160		15	4.0867
	30	.85408		30	1.6318		30	4.1653
	45	.86165		45	1.6479		45	4.2468
41	0	.86929	59	0	1.6643	77	0	4.3315
	15	.87698		15	1.6808		15	4.4194
	30	.88472		30	1.6977		30	4.5107
	45	.89253		45	1.7147		45	4.6057
42	0	.90040	60	0	1.7320	78	0	4.7046
	15	.90834		15	1.7496		15	4.8077
	30	.91633		30	1.7675		30	4.9151
	45	.92439		45	1.7856		45	5.0273
43	0	.93251	61	0	1.8040	79	0	5.1445
	15	.94071		15	1.8227		15	5.2671
	30	.94896		30	1.8418		30	5.3955
	45	.95729		45	1.8611		45	5.5301
44	0	.96569	62	0	1.8807	80	0	5.6713
	15	.97416		15	1.9007		15	5.8196
	30	.98270		30	1.9210		30	5.9758
	45	.99131		45	1.9416		45	6.1402
45	0	1.0000	63	0	1.9626	81	0	6.3137
	15	1.0088		15	1.9840		15	6.4971
	30	1.0176		30	2.0057		30	6.6911
	45	1.0265		45	2.0278		45	6.8969
46	0	1.0355	64	0	2.0503	82	0	7.1154
	15	1.0446		15	2.0732		15	7.3479
	30	1.0538		30	2.0965		30	7.5957
	45	1.0630		45	2.1203		45	7.8606
47	0	1.0724	65	0	2.1445	83	0	8.1443
	15	1.0818		15	2.1692		15	8.4489
	30	1.0913		30	2.1943		30	8.7769
	45	1.1009		45	2.2199		45	9.1309
48	0	1.1106	66	0	2.2460	84	0	9.5144
	15	1.1204		15	2.2727		15	9.9310
	30	1.1303		30	2.2998		30	10.385
	45	1.1403		45	2.3276		45	10.883
49	0	1.1504	67	0	2.3558	85	0	11.430
	15	1.1605		15	2.3847		15	12.035
	30	1.1708		30	2.4142		30	12.706
	45	1.1812		45	2.4443		45	13.457
50	0	1.1917	68	0	2.4751	86	0	14.301
	15	1.2024		15	2.5065		15	15.257
	30	1.2131		30	2.5386		30	16.350
	45	1.2239		45	2.5715		45	17.610
51	0	1.2349	69	0	2.6051	87	0	19.081
	15	1.2460		15	2.6394		15	20.819
	30	1.2572		30	2.6746		30	22.904
	45	1.2685		45	2.7106		45	25.452
52	0	1.2799	70	0	2.7475	88	0	28.636
	15	1.2915		15	2.7852		15	32.730
	30	1.3032		30	2.8239		30	38.188
	45	1.3151		45	2.8636		45	45.829
53	0	1.3270	71	0	2.9042	89	0	57.290
	15	1.3392		15	2.9459		15	76.390
	30	1.3514		30	2.9887		30	114.59
	45	1.3638		45	3.0326		45	229.18

TABLE 26

SURFACE CUTTING SPEEDS (REVOLUTIONS PER MINUTE REQUIRED TO OBTAIN SURFACE CUTTING SPEEDS ON VARIOUS DIAMETERS)

Cutting Speed Ft. Per Min.	40	50	60	70	80	90	100	120	140	180	200	225	250	275	300
Diam. in In.	**Revolutions Per Minute Required**														
1	153	191	229	267	306	344	382	458	535	688	764	860	955	1050	1150
1⅛	136	170	204	238	272	306	340	408	476	612	680	765	850	935	1020
1¼	123	153	183	214	245	274	306	367	428	551	612	687	764	840	916
1⅜	111	139	167	195	222	250	278	334	389	500	556	625	694	764	834
1½	102	127	153	178	204	230	254	305	356	457	508	561	636	700	754
1¾	87	109	131	153	175	196	218	262	305	392	436	491	545	600	655
2	76	95	115	134	153	172	191	229	267	344	382	430	478	526	574
2¼	68	85	102	119	136	153	170	204	238	306	340	382	424	466	510
2½	61	76	91	107	122	138	153	184	213	275	306	349	382	420	459
2¾	55	69	83	97	111	125	139	167	195	250	278	313	348	382	417
3	51	63	76	89	102	114	127	153	178	228	254	287	318	350	382
3¼	46	58	70	81	93	105	117	140	164	211	234	265	294	323	353
3½	43	54	65	76	87	98	109	131	153	196	218	245	273	300	327
3¾	40	51	61	71	81	91	102	122	143	184	205	229	254	280	305
4	38	47	57	66	76	86	95	115	134	172	191	214	238	262	286
4½	34	42	51	59	67	76	84	102	119	153	170	191	213	232	255
5	30	38	45	53	61	68	76	91	107	138	153	172	191	210	229
5½	27	34	41	48	55	62	69	83	97	125	139	156	173	191	208
6	25	31	38	44	51	57	63	76	89	114	127	144	160	175	192
6½	23	29	35	41	47	52	58	70	82	106	117	132	147	162	177
7	21	27	32	38	43	49	54	65	76	98	109	123	136	150	164
7½	20	25	30	35	40	45	50	61	71	91	102	114	127	140	153
8	19	23	28	33	38	43	47	57	66	86	95	108	119	131	144
8½	18	22	26	31	36	40	45	53	62	81	90	101	112	124	135
9	16	21	25	29	33	38	42	50	59	76	84	95	106	117	127
9½	16	20	24	28	32	36	40	48	56	72	80	90	101	111	121
10	15	19	22	26	30	34	38	45	53	68	76	86	95	105	115
11	13	17	20	24	27	31	34	41	48	62	69	78	86	95	104
12	12	15	19	22	25	28	31	38	44	57	63	71	79	87	95
13	11	14	17	20	23	26	29	35	41	52	58	66	73	80	88
14	10	13	16	19	21	24	27	32	38	49	54	61	68	75	81
15	10	12	15	17	20	22	25	30	35	45	51	57	63	70	76
16	9	11	14	16	19	21	23	28	33	43	47	53	59	65	71
17	9	11	13	15	18	20	22	27	31	40	45	50	56	61	67
18	8	10	12	14	17	19	21	25	29	38	42	47	53	58	63
19	8	10	12	14	16	18	20	24	28	36	40	45	50	55	60
20	7	9	11	13	15	17	19	22	26	34	38	43	47	52	57
21	7	9	10	12	14	16	18	21	25	32	36	40	45	50	54
22	7	8	10	12	13	15	17	20	24	31	34	39	43	47	52
23	6	8	10	11	13	15	16	19	23	29	33	37	41	45	49
24	6	8	9	11	12	14	15	19	22	28	31	35	39	43	47

Table 27
Decimal Equivalents

FRACTIONS						DECIMALS	FRACTIONS						DECIMALS
½	4ths	8ths	16ths	32nds	64ths		1	4ths	8ths	16ths	32nds	64ths	
					1/64	.015625						33/64	.515625
				1/32		.03125					17/32		.53125
					3/64	.046875						35/64	.546875
			1/16			.0625				9/16			.5625
					5/64	.078125						37/64	.578125
				3/32		.09375					19/32		.59375
					7/64	.109375						39/64	.609375
		1/8				.125			5/8				.625
					9/64	.140625						41/64	.640625
				5/32		.15625					21/32		.65625
					11/64	.171875						43/64	.671875
			3/16			.1875				11/16			.6875
					13/64	.203125						45/64	.703125
				7/32		.21875					23/32		.71875
					15/64	.234375						47/64	.734375
	1/4					.25		3/4					.75
					17/64	.265625						49/64	.765625
				9/32		.28125					25/32		.78125
					19/64	.296875						51/64	.796875
			5/16			.3125				13/16			.8125
					21/64	.328125						53/64	.828125
				11/32		.34375					27/32		.84375
					23/64	.359375						55/64	.859375
		3/8				.375			7/8				.875
					25/64	.390625						57/64	.890625
				13/32		.40625					29/32		.90625
					27/64	.421875						59/64	.921875
			7/16			.4375				15/16			.9375
					29/64	.453125						61/64	.953125
				15/32		.46875					31/32		.96875
					31/64	.484375						63/64	.984375
½						.5	1						1.

TABLE 28

SUGGESTED FEED PER TOOTH FOR SINTERED CARBIDE TIPPED CUTTERS

Material	Face Mills	Helical Mills	Slotting and Side Mills	End Mills	Form Relieved Cutters	Circular Saws
Plastics	.015	.012	.009	.007	.005	.004
Magnesium and Alloys	.020	.016	.012	.010	.006	.005
Aluminum and Alloys	.020	.016	.012	.010	.006	.005
Free Cutting Brasses and Bronzes	.020	.016	.012	.010	.006	.005
Medium Brasses and Bronzes	.012	.010	.007	.006	.004	.003
Hard Brasses and Bronzes	.010	.008	.006	.005	.003	.003
Copper	.012	.009	.007	.006	.004	.003
Cast Iron, Soft (150–180 B.H.)	.020	.016	.012	.010	.006	.005
Cast Iron, Medium (180–220 B.H.)	.016	.013	.010	.008	.005	.004
Cast Iron, Hard (220–300 B.H.)	.012	.010	.007	.006	.004	.003
Malleable Iron	.014	.011	.008	.007	.004	.004
Cast Steel	.014	.011	.008	.007	.005	.004
Low Carbon Steel, Free Machining	.016	.013	.009	.008	.005	.004
Low Carbon Steel	.014	.011	.008	.007	.004	.004
Medium Carbon Steel	.014	.011	.008	.007	.004	.004
Alloy Steel, Annealed (180–220 B.H.)	.014	.011	.008	.007	.004	.004
Alloy Steel, Tough (220–300 B.H.)	.012	.010	.007	.006	.004	.003
Alloy Steel, Hard (300–400 B.H.)	.010	.008	.006	.005	.003	.003
Stainless Steels, Free Machining	.014	.011	.008	.007	.004	.004
Stainless Steels	.010	.008	.006	.005	.003	.003
Monel Metals	.010	.008	.006	.005	.003	.003

TABLE 29

MACHINABILITY RATINGS AND CUTTING SPEEDS FOR STEEL

AISI Number	Machinability Rating	Approximate Cutting Speed F.P.M.	AISI Number	Machinability Rating	Approximate Cutting Speed F.P.M.
B1111	94	155	3130*	72	120
B1112	100	165	3135*	70	115
B1113	136	225	3140*	66	110
C1117	91	150	4130*	72	120
C1118	91	150	4140*	66	110
C1119	100	165	4620	66	110
C1137	72	120	5120	76	125
C1141	70	115	5130	57	95
C1141*	81	135	5140*	70	115
C1144	76	125	6120	57	95
C1010†	...	120	8620	66	110
C1017	72	120	8630*	72	120
C1019	78	130	8640*	66	110
C1020	72	120	8650*	60	100
C1030	70	115	8720	66	110
C1035	70	115	8740*	66	110
C1040	64	105	E9310*	51	85
C1045	57	95	E9315*	49	80
2330*	70	115	E9317*	49	80
2340*	57	95	9763*	54	90

* Annealed. † Light Feeds.

TABLE 30

RANGE OF VALUES OF a OBTAINED IN VARIOUS MILLING OPERATIONS WITH HIGH SPEED STEEL AND SINTERED CARBIDE CUTTERS

Type of Milling Cutter	Cutting Material	Material Cut		Values of a		
		Kind	Brinell Hardness Number	Minimum	Maximum	Average
1. Face Mills; Shell End Mills Plain Mills; 50° and 70° Helical Mills	High Speed Steel	S.A.E. 4345 Steel	330	0.90	1.45	1.25
		S.A.E. 4150 Steel	190	2.00	2.50	2.25
		N.E. 8949 Steel	240			
		S.A.E. 3145 Steel	180			
2. Face Mills	High Speed Steel	Cast Iron	170	0.51	1.01	0.76
3. Plain Mills	High Speed Steel	Cast Iron	170	1.15	1.45	1.30
4. Form Relieved Cutters	High Speed Steel	S.A.E. 1020 Steel	160–170	1.48	2.45	1.96
5. Plain Mills	High Speed Steel	S.A.E. 1020 Steel	160–170	2.10	2.90	2.50
6. Face Mills	Sintered Carbide	N.E. 8630 Steel	200	1.50	2.50	2.00
7. Face Mills	Sintered Carbide	Cast Iron	190	0.50	1.00	0.75
8. Peripheral Mills	Sintered Carbide	14 S-T Aluminum Alloy	. . .	0.50	1.00	0.75

TABLE 31

SUGGESTED FEED PER TOOTH FOR HIGH SPEED STEEL MILLING CUTTERS

Material	Face Mills	Helical Mills	Slotting and Side Mills	End Mills	Form Relieved Cutters	Circular Saws
Plastics	.013	.010	.008	.007	.004	.003
Magnesium and Alloys	.022	.018	.013	.011	.007	.005
Aluminum and Alloys	.022	.018	.013	.011	.007	.005
Free Cutting Brasses and Bronzes	.022	.018	.013	.011	.007	.005
Medium Brasses and Bronzes	.014	.011	.008	.007	.004	.003
Hard Brasses and Bronzes	.009	.007	.006	.005	.003	.002
Copper	.012	.010	.007	.006	.004	.003
Cast Iron, Soft (150–180 B.H.)	.016	.013	.009	.008	.005	.004
Cast Iron, Medium (180–220 B.H.)	.013	.010	.007	.007	.004	.003
Cast Iron, Hard (220–300 B.H.)	.011	.008	.006	.006	.003	.003
Malleable Iron	.012	.010	.007	.006	.004	.003
Cast Steel	.012	.010	.007	.006	.004	.003
Low Carbon Steel, Free Machining	.012	.010	.007	.006	.004	.003
Low Carbon Steel	.010	.008	.006	.005	.003	.003
Medium Carbon Steel	.010	.008	.006	.005	.003	.003
Alloy Steel, Annealed (180–220 B.H.)	.008	.007	.005	.004	.003	.002
Alloy Steel, Tough (220–300 B.H.)	.006	.005	.004	.003	.002	.002
Alloy Steel, Hard (300–400 B.H.)	.004	.003	.003	.002	.002	.001
Stainless Steels, Free Machining	.010	.008	.006	.005	.003	.002
Stainless Steels	.006	.005	.004	.003	.002	.002
Monel Metals	.008	.007	.005	.004	.003	.002

TABLE 32

TABLE OF SQUARE, CUBE, AND FOURTH POWERS OF THE DIAMETERS FOR ROUND WIRES—ROUND WIRE TABLE—STEEL

American Steel & Wire Co.'s Steel Wire Gauge	Fraction of 1 Inch	Decimal Equivalent		Section Area in Square Inches	Pounds per Foot	Feet per Pound	Square of Diam. in Inches	Cubes of Diam. in Inches	Fourth of Diam. in Inches
		Inches	Millimeters						
....	2	2	50.8	3.1416	10.6719	.09370	4	8	16
....	1 15/16	1.9375	49.21	2.9483	10.015	.0998	3.75391	7.27319	14.09181
....	1 7/8	1.875	47.63	2.7612	9.379	.1066	3.51562	6.59179	12.35962
....	1 13/16	1.8125	46.04	2.5802	8.764	.1141	3.28516	5.95434	10.79225
....	1 3/4	1.75	44.45	2.4053	8.170	.1224	3.06250	5.35937	9.37891
....	1 11/16	1.6875	42.86	2.2365	7.597	.1316	2.84766	4.80542	8.10915
....	1 5/8	1.625	41.28	2.0739	7.047	.1419	2.64062	4.29101	6.97290
....	1 9/16	1.5625	39.69	1.9175	6.513	.1535	2.44141	3.814697	5.96046
....	1 1/2	1.50	38.10	1.7671	6.003	.1666	2.25000	3.37500	5.06250
....	1 7/16	1.4375	36.51	1.6230	5.513	.1814	2.06641	2.970458	4.270034
....	1 3/8	1.375	34.93	1.4849	5.044	.1982	1.89062	2.599609	3.57446
....	1 5/16	1.3125	33.34	1.3530	4.596	.2176	1.72266	2.26098	2.96754
....	1 1/4	1.25	31.75	1.2272	4.168	.2399	1.56250	1.95312	2.44141
....	1 3/16	1.1875	30.16	1.1075	3.762	.2658	1.41016	1.67456	1.98854
....	1 1/8	1.125	28.58	.9940	3.377	.2961	1.26562	1.42382	1.60181
....	1 1/16	1.0625	26.99	.8866	3.012	.3320	1.12891	1.19946	1.27443
....	1	1.00	25.4	.7854	2.667	.3748	1.0000	1.00000	1.00000
....	15/16	.9375	23.81	.6903	2.345	.4265	0.87891	0.82397	0.7724761
....	7/8	.875	22.23	.6013	2.043	.4896	0.76562	0.66992	0.586182
....	13/16	.8125	20.64	.5185	1.761	.5678	0.66016	0.53637	0.435806
....	3/4	.750	19.05	.4418	1.501	.6663	0.56250	0.42187	0.316406
....	11/16	.6875	17.46	.3712	1.261	.7930	0.47266	0.32495	0.223404
....	5/8	.625	15.88	.3068	1.042	.9595	0.39062	0.24414	0.152588
....	9/16	.5625	14.29	.2485	.844	1.185	0.31641	0.177978	0.100113
....	1/2	.50	12.7	.19635	.667	1.50	0.25000	0.125	0.062500
7.0	....	.4900	12.45	.1886	.640	1.561	0.24010	0.11765	0.05765
6.0	....	.4615	11.72	.1673	.5682	1.760	0.21298	0.09829	0.04536
....	7/16	.4375	11.11	.1503	.5107	1.958	0.19141	0.08374	0.036636
5.0	....	.4305	10.93	.1456	.4945	2.022	0.18533	0.079784	0.0343473
4.0	....	.3938	10.0	.1218	.4137	2.417	0.155078	0.06107	0.02405
....	3/8	.375	9.53	.1104	.3752	2.665	0.14062	0.05273	0.0197753
3.0	....	.3625	9.208	.1032	.3506	2.852	0.13141	0.047634	0.01727
2.0	....	.331	8.407	.0860	.2923	3.421	0.10956	0.03626	0.0120036
....	5/16	.3125	7.94	.0767	.2605	3.838	0.09766	0.030517	0.009537
1.0	....	.3065	7.785	.0738	.2506	3.990	0.09394	0.02879	0.008825

TABLE 32 (Continued)

TABLE OF SQUARE, CUBE, AND FOURTH POWERS OF THE DIAMETERS FOR ROUND WIRES—ROUND WIRE TABLE—STEEL

American Steel & Wire Co.'s Steel Wire Gauge	Fraction of 1 Inch	Decimal Equivalent		Section Area in Square Inches	Pounds per Foot	Feet per Pound	Square of Diam. in Inches	Cubes of Diam. in Inches	Fourth of Diam. in Inches
		Inches	Millimeters						
1	...	.283	7.188	.0629	.2137	4.680	0.08009	0.02267	0.006414
2	...	.2625	6.668	.0541	.1839	5.439	0.06891	0.01809	0.004748
...	1/4	.25	6.35	.0491	.1667	5.997	0.06250	0.01562	0.003906
3	...	.2437	6.19	.0466	.1584	6.311	0.05939	0.014473	0.003527
4	...	.2253	5.723	.0399	.1354	7.384	0.05063	0.011405	0.00256972
5	...	.207	5.258	.0337	.1143	8.747	0.04285	0.00887	0.001836
6	...	.192	4.877	.02895	.0984	10.17	0.03686	0.00708	0.00135895
...	3/16	.1875	4.76	.0276	.0938	10.66	0.03516	0.00659	0.00124
7	...	.177	4.496	.0246	.0836	11.96	0.03133	0.00555	0.000982
8	...	.162	4.115	.0206	.070	14.28	0.02624	0.00425	0.000689
9	...	.1483	3.767	.0173	.0568	17.04	0.02199	0.00326	0.000484
10	...	.135	3.429	.0143	.0486	20.57	0.01823	0.00246	0.000332
...	1/8	.125	3.18	.0123	.042	23.99	0.015625	0.00195	0.000244
11	...	.1205	3.061	.0114	.0387	25.81	0.01452	0.00175	0.000211
12	...	.1055	2.68	.0087	.0297	33.68	0.01113	0.001174	0.00012388
...	...	.095	2.413	.0071	.0241	41.53	0.00903	0.000857	0.00008145
13	...	.0915	2.324	.0066	.0223	44.77	0.00837	0.000766	0.0000701
...	...	.090	2.286	.0064	.0216	46.27	0.0081	0.000729	0.0000656
...	...	.085	2.159	.0057	.0193	51.88	0.00723	0.000614	0.0000522
14	...	.080	2.032	.0050	.0171	58.56	0.0064	0.000512	0.0000410
...	...	.075	1.905	.0044	.0150	66.63	0.0056	0.000422	0.0000316
15	...	.072	1.829	.0041	.0138	72.30	0.0052	0.000373	0.0000269
...	...	...	...	...	...	...	0.0050	0.000358	0.0000254
...	...	.067	1.702	.0035	.01197	83.50	0.0045	0.000301	0.0000202
...	...	.063	1.60	.00311	.01058	94.44	0.00397	0.000250	0.0000158
16	1/16	.0625	1.588	.0031	.0104	95.95	0.00391	0.00024	0.0000153
...	...	.059	1.499	.0027	.0092	107.7	0.00348	0.00021	0.0000121
...	...	.054	1.372	.0023	.0078	128.53	0.00292	0.000157	0.00000850
17	...	.053	1.346	.0022	.00749	133.43	0.00281	0.000149	0.00000789
...	...	.051	1.29	.0020	.0069	144.10	0.00260	0.000133	0.00000677
...	...	.049	1.245	.00188	.0064	156.11	0.00240	0.000118	0.0000057648
18	...	.0475	1.207	.001772	.006	166.12	0.00226	0.000107	0.00000509
...	...	.047	1.194	.00173	.0059	169.68	0.00221	0.000104	0.00000488
...	...	.045	1.143	.00159	.0054	185.09	0.00203	0.000091	0.00000410
...	...	.043	1.092	.00145	.0049	202.71	0.00185	0.0000795	0.00000342

TABLE 32 (Continued)

TABLE OF SQUARE, CUBE, AND FOURTH POWERS OF THE DIAMETERS FOR ROUND WIRES—ROUND WIRE TABLE—STEEL

American Steel & Wire Co.'s Steel Wire Gauge	Fraction of 1 Inch	Decimal Equivalent		Section Area in Square Inches	Pounds per Foot	Feet per Pound	Square of Diam. in Inches	Cubes of Diam. in Inches	Fourth of Diam. in Inches
		Inches	Millimeters						
19	....	.041	1.041	.00132	.0045	222.97	0.00168	0.0000689	0.00000283
....	....	.039	1.00	.00119	.00405	246.42	0.00152	0.0000593	0.00000231
....	....	.037	.9398	.001075	.00365	273.78	0.00137	0.0000507	0.0000018741
....	....	.035	.889	.00096	.0033	305.97	0.00123	0.0000429	0.00000150
20	....	.0348	.8839	.00095	.0032	309.50	0.00121	0.0000421	0.00000147
....	....	.033	.8382	.00085	.0029	344.18	0.00109	0.0000359	0.00000119
21	....	.03175	.8065	.00079	.0027	371.82	0.00101	0.0000320	0.00000102
....	....	.031	.7874	.00075	.00256	390.02	0.00096	0.0000298	0.000000924
....	....	.029	.7366	.00066	.00224	445.68	0.00084	0.0000244	0.000000707
22	....	.0286	.7264	.00064	.0022	458.38	0.00082	0.0000231	0.000000669
....	....	.026	.6604	.00053	.0018	554.46	0.00068	0.000023393	0.000000457
23	....	.0258	.6553	.00052	.0018	563.09	0.00067	0.0000172	0.000000443
....	....	.024	.6096	.00045	.0015	650.72	0.00058	0.0000138	0.000000332
24	....	.023	.5842	.00042	.0014	708.53	0.00053	0.0000122	0.000000280
....	....	.022	.5588	.00038	.00129	774.41	0.00048	0.0000106	0.000000234
25	....	.0204	.5182	.00033	.00110	900.65	0.00042	0.00000849	0.000000173
....	....	.020	.508	.00031	.0010	937.04	0.0004	0.000008	0.00000016
26	....	.0181	.4597	.00026	.00087	1144.08	0.000328	0.00000593	0.000000107
....	....	.018	.4572	.00025	.00086	1156.83	0.000324	0.00000583	0.000000105
27	....	.0173	.4394	.000235	.00079	1252.34	0.000299	0.00000518	0.0000000896
28	....	.0162	.4115	.000206	.00070	1428.19	0.000262	0.00000425	0.0000000689
....	....	.0160	.4064	.0002	.00068	1464.12	0.000256	0.00000410	0.0000000655
29	....	.015	.381	.000177	.0006	1666.58	0.000225	0.00000338	0.0000000506
30	....	.014	.3556	.00015	.00052	1912.31	0.000196	0.00000274	0.0000000384
....	....	.013	.3302	.00013	.00045	2217.83	0.000169	0.00000220	0.0000000286
....	....	.012	.3048	.00011	.00038	2602.87	0.000144	0.00000173	0.0000000207
....	....	.011	.2794	.000095	.00032	3097.64	0.000121	0.00000133	0.0000000146
....	....	.010	.2540	.00008	.00027	3748.14	0.000100	0.0000010	0.000000010
....	....	.009	.2286	.00006	.00022	4629.19	0.000081	0.000000729	0.00000000656
....	....	.008	.2032	.00005	.00017	5856.47	0.000064	0.000000512	0.00000000410
....	....	.007	.1778	.00004	.00013	7649.27	0.000049	0.000000343	0.000000002401
....	....	.006	.1524	.00003	.000096	10411.50	0.000036	0.000000216	0.00000000130
....	....	.005	.127	.00002	.000066	14992.56	0.000025	0.000000125	0.000000000625
....	....	.004	.1016	.00001	.000042	23425.87	0.000016	0.000000064	0.000000000256

Table 33

Relationship Between the Brinell Hardness of the Part to Be Milled and the Cutting Speed of the Milling Cutter for Different Cutting Tool and Work Materials

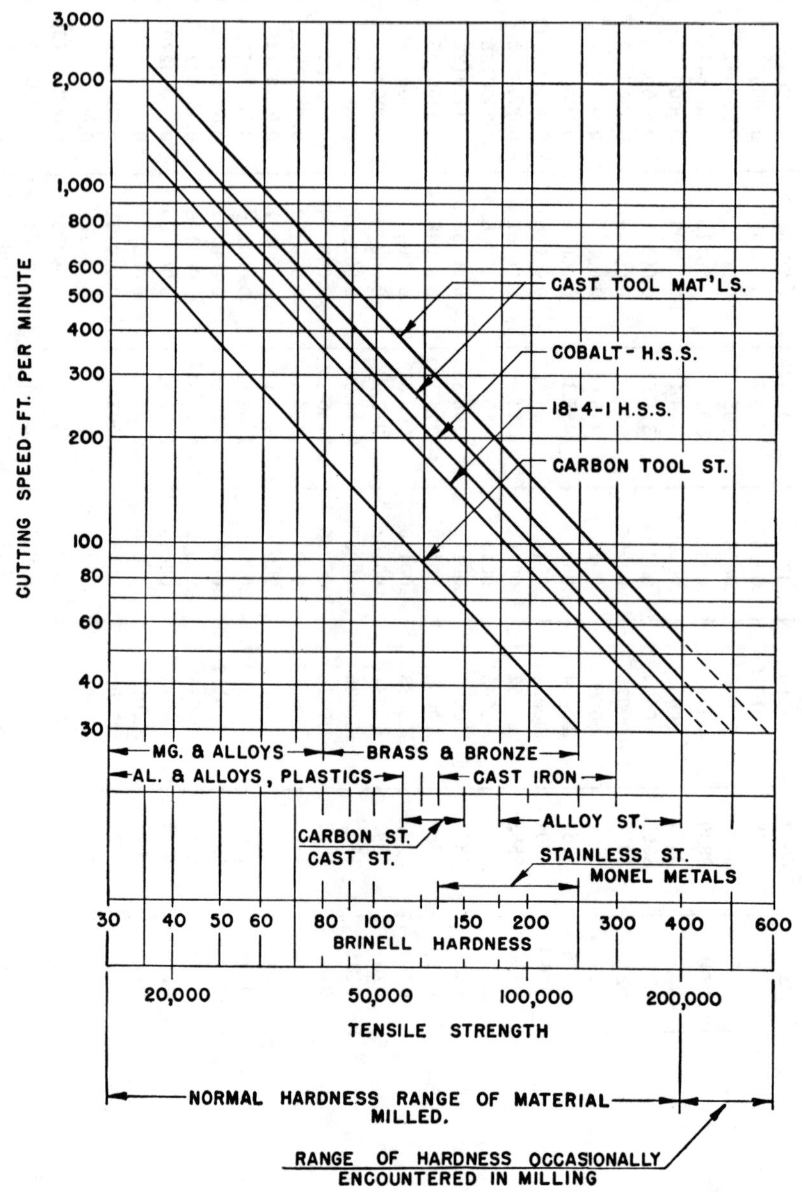

TABLE 34
CUTTING SPEEDS IN FEET PER MINUTE

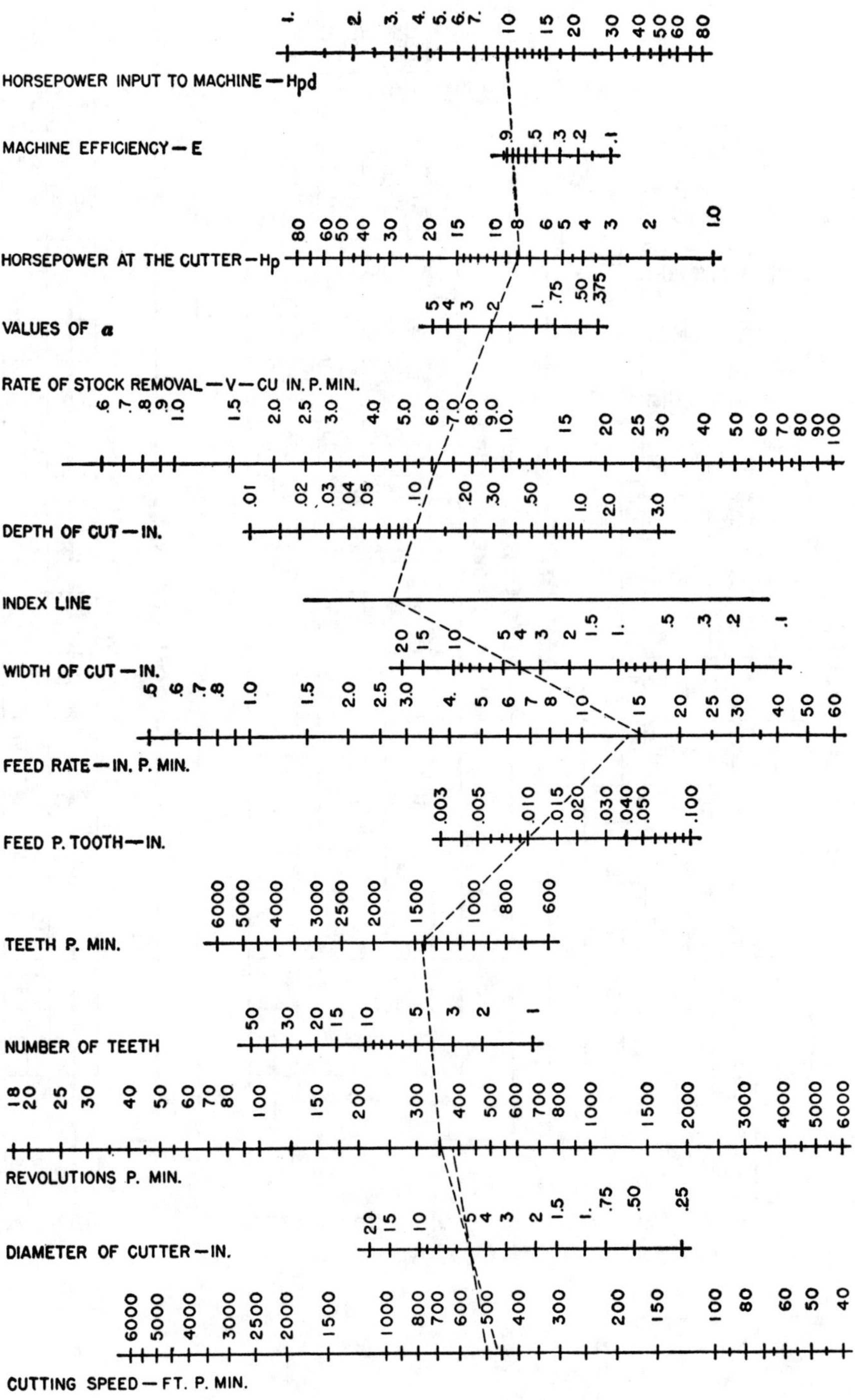

TABLE 35

CUTTING SPEEDS IN FEET PER MINUTE—HIGH UTILITY AND HEAVY DUTY

16″ HIGH SPEED

LENGTH OF STROKE IN INCHES

STROKES PER MIN.	1	2	3	4	5	6	7	8	9	10	11	12	13	14	15	16
15	4	6	7	10	13	16	19	20	23	25	28	29	30	33	35	36
22	6	9	12	15	17	20	23	26	29	32	35	38	41	43	46	49
33	7	12	17	22	28	32	38	42	46	51	55	59	64	67	71	75
45	9	16	22	29	36	42	49	55	61	67	74	80	84	90	96	101
68	12	23	35	44	54	64	74	84	94	103	112	120	129	136	145	154
99	16	33	48	64	78	93	107	120	135	146	159	172	185	197	208	220
145	25	48	71	93	114	136	158	178	198	218	236					
200	34	65	97	127	158	187	216	245								

16″ UTILITY (strokes 1–16)

20″ UTILITY (strokes 1–20)

LENGTH OF STROKE IN INCHES

STROKES PER MIN.	1	2	3	4	5	6	7	8	9	10	11	12	13	14	15	16	17	18	19	20
12	3	4	6	8	9	10	13	15	16	18	20	21	23	24	26	27	28	30	31	32
17	4	6	8	11	13	16	18	21	23	25	28	30	32	34	36	38	40	42	44	46
26	5	8	13	17	20	24	28	32	35	39	42	46	49	52	55	58	61	64	67	70
36	6	12	17	23	28	34	39	44	49	54	59	63	68	72	77	81	85	90	93	97
54	9	18	26	34	43	50	58	66	73	81	88	95	102	108	115	121	128	133	140	146
77	13	25	37	49	61	72	83	94	105	115	125	135	145	154	164	172				
115	19	37	56	73	91	108	124	140	156	172	188	202								
157	26	51	76	100	127	147	170	192	214											

16″ HEAVY DUTY (strokes 1–16)

20″ STANDARD (strokes 1–20)

LENGTH OF STROKE IN INCHES

STROKES PER MIN.	1	2	3	4	5	6	7	8	9	10	11	12	13	14	15	16	17	18	19	20
11	3	4	5	7	9	11	13	14	16	17	19	20	21	23	24	25	26	27	28	29
15	4	6	8	10	12	14	16	18	20	22	24	26	28	30	32	34	35	37	39	40
23	5	8	12	15	19	22	26	29	32	35	38	41	44	46	49	52	55	57	60	62
31	6	11	15	20	25	29	34	38	42	46	51	55	58	62	66	70	73	76	80	83
47	8	16	23	30	37	44	51	58	65	71	77	83	89	94	100	106	112	116	121	126
68	11	23	33	44	54	64	74	83	93	101	110	119	128	136	144	152	161	168		
100	17	33	49	64	79	94	109	123	137	150	163									
138	23	45	67	88	109	129	149	169												

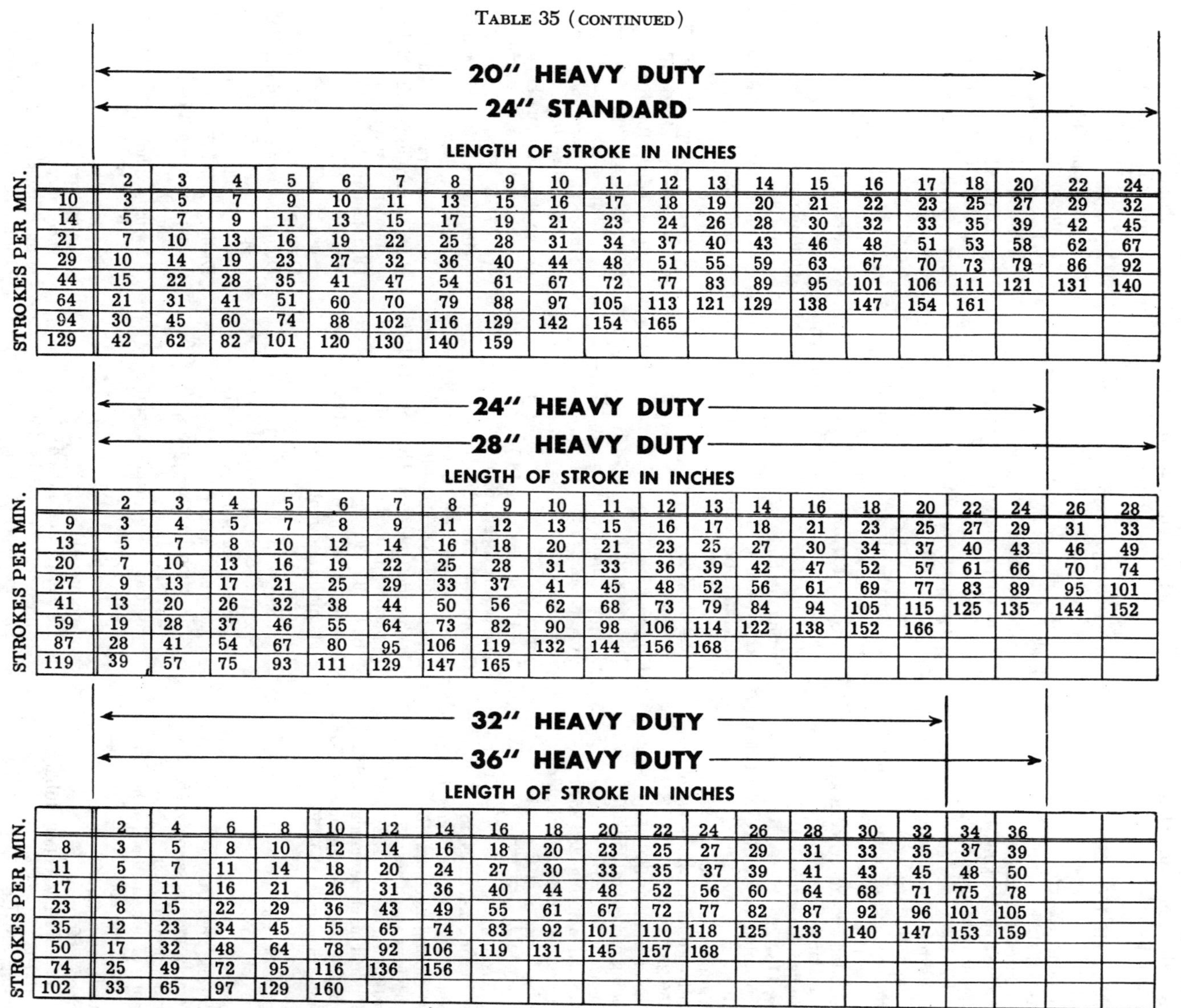

TABLE 35 (CONTINUED)

20" HEAVY DUTY (stroke lengths 2–20)
24" STANDARD (stroke lengths 2–24)

LENGTH OF STROKE IN INCHES

STROKES PER MIN.	2	3	4	5	6	7	8	9	10	11	12	13	14	15	16	17	18	20	22	24
10	3	5	7	9	10	11	13	15	16	17	18	19	20	21	22	23	25	27	29	32
14	5	7	9	11	13	15	17	19	21	23	24	26	28	30	32	33	35	39	42	45
21	7	10	13	16	19	22	25	28	31	34	37	40	43	46	48	51	53	58	62	67
29	10	14	19	23	27	32	36	40	44	48	51	55	59	63	67	70	73	79	86	92
44	15	22	28	35	41	47	54	61	67	72	77	83	89	95	101	106	111	121	131	140
64	21	31	41	51	60	70	79	88	97	105	113	121	129	138	147	154	161			
94	30	45	60	74	88	102	116	129	142	154	165									
129	42	62	82	101	120	130	140	159												

24" HEAVY DUTY (stroke lengths 2–24)
28" HEAVY DUTY (stroke lengths 2–28)

LENGTH OF STROKE IN INCHES

STROKES PER MIN.	2	3	4	5	6	7	8	9	10	11	12	13	14	16	18	20	22	24	26	28
9	3	4	5	7	8	9	11	12	13	15	16	17	18	21	23	25	27	29	31	33
13	5	7	8	10	12	14	16	18	20	21	23	25	27	30	34	37	40	43	46	49
20	7	10	13	16	19	22	25	28	31	33	36	39	42	47	52	57	61	66	70	74
27	9	13	17	21	25	29	33	37	41	45	48	52	56	61	69	77	83	89	95	101
41	13	20	26	32	38	44	50	56	62	68	73	79	84	94	105	115	125	135	144	152
59	19	28	37	46	55	64	73	82	90	98	106	114	122	138	152	166				
87	28	41	54	67	80	95	106	119	132	144	156	168								
119	39	57	75	93	111	129	147	165												

32" HEAVY DUTY (stroke lengths 2–32)
36" HEAVY DUTY (stroke lengths 2–36)

LENGTH OF STROKE IN INCHES

STROKES PER MIN.	2	4	6	8	10	12	14	16	18	20	22	24	26	28	30	32	34	36		
8	3	5	8	10	12	14	16	18	20	23	25	27	29	31	33	35	37	39		
11	5	7	11	14	18	20	24	27	30	33	35	37	39	41	43	45	48	50		
17	6	11	16	21	26	31	36	40	44	48	52	56	60	64	68	71	775	78		
23	8	15	22	29	36	43	49	55	61	67	72	77	82	87	92	96	101	105		
35	12	23	34	45	55	65	74	83	92	101	110	118	125	133	140	147	153	159		
50	17	32	48	64	78	92	106	119	131	145	157	168								
74	25	49	72	95	116	136	156													
102	33	65	97	129	160															

Index